The
INTERNATIONAL CRITICAL
COMMENTARY
on the Holy Scriptures of the Old and
New Testaments

GENERAL EDITORS

J. A. EMERTON, F.B.A.
Fellow of St. John's College
Emeritus Regius Professor of Hebrew in the University of Cambridge
Honorary Canon of St. George's Cathedral, Jerusalem

C. E. B. CRANFIELD, F.B.A.
Emeritus Professor of Theology in the University of Durham

AND

G. N. STANTON
Professor of New Testament Studies,
King's College, University of London

FORMERLY UNDER THE EDITORSHIP OF

S. R. DRIVER
A. PLUMMER
C. A. BRIGGS

D1086973

EPHESIANS

A CRITICAL AND EXEGETICAL COMMENTARY

ON

EPHESIANS

BY

ERNEST BEST

*Emeritus Professor of Divinity and Biblical
Criticism in the University of Glasgow*

T & T CLARK INTERNATIONAL
A Continuum imprint
LONDON • NEW YORK

T&T Clark LTD
A Continuum Imprint

The Tower Building
11 York Road
London. SE1 7NX

15 East 26th Street
New York, NY 10010
USA

www.tandtclark.com
Copyright © T&T Clark Ltd, 1998

First published 1998
Reprinted 2001
This edition 2004

ISBN 0 567 08445 0

British Library Cataloguing-in-Publication Data
A catalogue record for this book is available from the British Library

Typeset by Fakenham Photosetting Limited
Printed and bound by The Cromwell Press Ltd, Trowbridge

Dedicated
to
The University of Glasgow

CONTENTS

PREFACE

Ephesians is not an easy book on which to write a commentary. Goodspeed[1] describes it as 'the Waterloo of commentators. It baffles them.' The second of these sentences is undoubtedly true; how the first is to be understood depends whether one is British or French! It is unnecessary to list here the features which make the book so difficult to interpret; they will rapidly appear in the discussions of the Introduction. Protestant scholars on the whole prefer to write on Romans and Galatians and when, often reluctantly, they turn to Ephesians they regularly evaluate it in Pauline terms. It is however true that Protestants have given greater attention to Ephesians in recent years as a result of the ecumenical movement. If the nature of the church is to be discussed, then Ephesians can hardly be ignored. Catholic scholars have been much more happy with Ephesians for the church has been traditionally central to their theology, and it has been a Catholic scholar, H. Schlier, who has done most to direct and inspire modern discussion of Ephesians, even though his main positions have not always been acceptable. Today there are commentaries on Ephesians from every denominational angle. The existence of so many in itself creates a difficulty for those who would write on the letter.

John Eadie published the first edition of his commentary in 1854; it went through several editions both prior to and after his death in 1876. In the final edition, if not in the earlier, he quotes from about one hundred previous commentaries on Ephesians. A hundred and twenty years have passed since then; it is impossible to keep track of the number that now exist. It is often said that there are more scientists alive today than the total number of dead scientists; surely the same is true of NT scholars! I have only read a fraction of present printed commentaries and in this commentary I refer to fewer than I have read; many are written at a popular level; some of them may have exciting things to say which I have missed; but it is impossible to read them all if anything is ever to be written. In addition to the commentaries there is an ever-increasing flow of monographs and of articles in academic journals.

[1] E. J. Goodspeed, *The Meaning of Ephesians*, Chicago, 1933, 15.

xi

This raises the first serious problem for commentators:[2] how comprehensively should they list the names of scholars who adhere to some particular point of view? Eadie's lists sometimes run far beyond two lines, and that merely of names without references; if all the names of scholars were listed today and proper references given in the modern manner, many lines of type would be required and far too many trees would have to be cut down to provide the paper for them! I have therefore made no attempt to be exhaustive in listing names. Few actually produce new ideas. Is it sufficient then to list the first person to introduce a new angle? Very often this will be a Greek or Latin Father, and not some late-twentieth-century scholar who rediscovers the same angle (see footnote on Sampley re 5.33). The reasons for the points of view of the Fathers will almost certainly have been modified or altered in the course of study. I take it that it is more important to set out the arguments for and against any point of view than to list names. Sometimes lack of space has forced me to direct readers' attention to previous commentators who have dealt in detail with all the views prior to their own writing. Of course names can be a great help to research students who feel they ought to examine every book and article that has been written in the last ten years and comment on them rather than on the text. There are however better means for research students to find out what has been written than examining lists of references in commentaries. I have tried in the notes to cut down on references to other scholars but at least to list all the important relevant literature at the beginning of each section. But there are gaps in these lists; some articles are not listed because I have not heard of them, or having heard of them have not been able to get access to them, or having heard of them and read them have not thought them sufficiently illuminating. There is a considerable body of writing which mediates the ideas of scholars to preachers and teachers of religion; such writing serves a very useful purpose but is rarely significant for the present type of commentary. I have attempted to arrange the bibliographical lists in chronological, not alphabetical, order; the latter order is of no significance but the former allows the careful student to see how writers have been influenced, or not influenced, by their predecessors, and perhaps to construct a *Wirkungsgeschichte*.

Before leaving the subject of commentaries it is necessary to say that all commentators stand on the shoulders of those who have preceded them. I am grateful to the many who have previously written on Ephesians, most of all to Gnilka and Schnackenburg, though I have not always agreed with them. The number of times

---

[2] I have attempted to say a little about how commentaries should be written in 'The Reading and Writing of Commentaries', *ExpT* 107 (1995/6) 358–62.

their names appear in the index of authors bears no relation to the way their thought has penetrated and excited my own. Quotations from them or other commentators are few and far between because I have tended to read them, the relevant monographs and the learned articles, think about what I read and then formulate what I wanted to say in my own words. I have not attempted to offer a complete list of the commentaries on Ephesians; to compile such a list would use up too much space, and too much of my time! I have mainly listed only those to which I have referred.

All exegesis is controlled by the situation of those who write. They will necessarily view the text on which they work from the angle of the age in which they live and this may lead them to see new aspects of it and put fresh questions to it. They will also be affected by their church allegiance, if any, and, since Ephesians has much to say about the church, in its case this will be important. The coloured glasses we wear, usually without realising we do so, affect the way we read texts. I have not always agreed with the majority of commentators but when I have dared to disagree it has only been after long thought and with great hesitancy, though the latter may not always appear in the way I have expressed myself. A number of minor variations in an approach can in the end modify the total view and so if I have made some kind of contribution in respect of an overall view of Ephesians it is only because of a multitude of minor differences. Perhaps more than most commentators I have tried to observe what is not said in Ephesians for I believe that this can be a real help in putting what is said into its proper perspective.

Some other matters require mention here. Since I do not think Ephesians was written primarily to a congregation in the city of Ephesus I have not concentrated on detailing the religious, social, economic and political situation of that city; it does not go unmentioned for it is a city in the area where the recipients of Ephesians lived and life in it cannot have been greatly different from that in the remainder of Asia Minor.

In giving examples of grammatical and syntactical rules I have normally chosen these from the NT; the rules may well hold for all Greek or for Hellenistic Greek in particular, but since those studying Ephesians will have their New Testaments readily available, to ignore this and suggest parallels in other Greek authors is to give needless trouble. The use of examples drawn from the NT should not however be taken to suggest that there was a special canonical form of Greek or that an example drawn from the NT carries more weight than one from elsewhere.

I have employed a number of unusual abbreviations. In particular I have referred throughout to the writer of the letter as AE. There are two reasons for doing this. To write 'the author of the letter' each time would use up too much paper and too many trees. By using AE

I have left it to readers to expand it as they will, substituting, if they wish, Paul's name or that of some other of their choice. I have become increasingly convinced that Paul did not write Ephesians; on many occasions I have been compelled to say that Paul could have been the author if he had changed, developed, or otherwise modified what we know from his major letters; there is a limit to the number of times this can be done and it remain reasonable. Only in the third chapter does a decision about authorship affect in any major way what is deduced as the meaning of the text. For similar reasons to my use of AE for the author of the text I have used A/Col for the author of Colossians. There are naturally many reference to the *Haustafel* (5.22–6.9) and I have used for this the abbreviation HT. The abbreviations for biblical books are those of the series; I have also used Ψ and Kgdms where I have wished to draw special attention to the Greek text of the OT.

The text employed has been the 27th edition of Nestle–Aland and where textual matters have been concerned I have used their abbreviations of the names of the Fathers but have used the normal English names in the actual notes on verses.

Commentaries are denoted only by the name of the author and it is assumed, unless otherwise stated, that reference is being made to their comment on the relevant verse. Where a commentator is also responsible for another book and reference is being made to it and not the commentary, this is indicated by the use of a word from the title of that other book.

It finally remains for me to thank Professor Cranfield for the invitation to write this commentary. I have enjoyed writing it and even more the freedom he and Professor Stanton have given to contributors to this series to do it their own way and I have appreciated the lack of pressure he has put on me to complete the task. I am also grateful to the editors of the series for the helpful comments they have made to the first draft.

My thanks are also due to the Libraries and Librarians of the universities of Glasgow and St Andrews.

Finally my thanks are due above all to Emeritus Professor J. C. O'Neill, who when he knew that I had been ill offered to assist me in the correction of the proofs of this volume. No greater love has a scholar of a colleague than voluntarily to read his proofs. If any misprints or mistakes remain I must bear the blame.

I dedicate this commentary to the University of Glasgow where I first began to lecture on Ephesians and from whose Library staff I received much courteous and willing help, and in gratitude for the degree of D.D. conferred on me by the University at Commemoration, June 1997.

LITERATURE

Commentaries

(referred to only by the name of the author in what follows)

Origen: J. A. F. Gregg, 'The Commentary of Origen upon the Epistle to the Ephesians', *JTS* 3 (1901–2) 233–44, 398–420, 554–76

Marius Victorinus: MPL 8, 1235–94

Ephraem of Syria: *S. Ephraemi Syri commentarii in ep. D. Pauli*, Venice, 1893, 140–56

Ambrosiaster: CSEL 81, 71–126

Chrysostom: MPG 62, 9–176; and *Interpretatio Omnium Epistolarum Paulinarum*, IV, Oxford, 1852, 104–419

Jerome: MPL 26, 467–590

Theodore of Mopsuestia: MPG 66; and H. P. Swete, *Theodore of Mopsuestia on the Minor Epistles of S. Paul*, I, Cambridge, 1880, 112–96

Severian of Gabala: K. Staab, *Pauluskommentare aus der griechischen Kirche*, Münster, 1983, 304–13

Pelagius: *Texts and Studies* IX, Cambridge, 1922, 344–86 (ed. A. Souter)

Theodoret of Cyrrhus: MPG 82, 505–58

John of Damascus: MPG 92, 821–56

Oecumenius: MPG 118, 1169–256

Theophylact: MPG 124, 1031–138

Oecumenius of Tricca: Staab, op.cit., 448–52

Primasius: MPL 68, 607–26

Photius of Constantinople: Staab, op.cit., 611–21

Thomas Aquinas *Opera Omnia* (ed. S. E. Fretté et P. Maré), XXI, Paris, 1876, 260–343

Grotius, *Annotationeas Novi Testamenti*, 1624

Erasmus, D. *Opera*, VI, Leiden, 1705, 831–60

Calvin, J. CR 79, 141–240

Beza T. de *Annotationes majores in Novum Testamentum*, 1594

Zanchius, H. *Commentarius in Epistolam Sancti Pauli ad Ephesios*, c. 1605, (reprint) Amsterdam, 1888

xv

Locke, J. *A Paraphrase and Notes on the Epistles of St Paul to the Galatians, 1 and 2 Corinthians, Romans, Ephesians,* 1707 (reprinted, Oxford, 1987, II, 607–61)

Bengel, J. A. *Gnomon Novi Testamenti* (Tübingen, 1773): Textis recusa adjuvente J. Steudel, Tübingen, 1850, III, 256–84

Harless, G. C. A. *Commentar über den Brief Pauli an die Ephesier,* Erlangen, 1834

Meyer, H. A. W. *An die Epheser* (KEK), Göttingen, 1843

Eadie, J. *Commentary on the Epistle to the Ephesians,* 1854[1], 1883[3] (reprinted Minneapolis, 1977).

Hofmann, J. C. K. *Der Brief Pauli an die Epheser,* Nördlingen, 1870

Ellicott, C. J. *The Epistles of Saint Paul,* 1854[1], (reprinted Andover, 1884)

Barry, A. *Galatians, Ephesians, and Philippians,* London, n.d.

Hodge, C. *A Commentary of the Epistle to the Ephesians,* 1856 (reprinted Grand Rapids, 1980)

Alford, H. *The Greek Testament, Ephesians,* 1849–61, with revision by E. F. Harrison, Chicago, 1968, III, 6–26, 68–151

Beck, J. *Erklärung des Briefes an die Epheser,* Gütersloh, 1891

Macpherson, J. *Commentary on St. Paul's Epistle to the Ephesians,* Edinburgh, 1892

Findlay, G. G. *The Epistle to the Ephesians,* London, 1892

Soden, H. von *Die Briefe an die Kolosser, Epheser, Philemon; die Pastoralbriefe* (Hand-Commentar zum NT), Freiburg, 1893[2]

Wohlenberg, G. *Die Briefe an die Epheser, an die Colosser, an Philemon und die Philipper ausgelegt,* Munich, 1895

Abbott, T. K. *The Epistles to the Ephesians and to the Colossians* (ICC), Edinburgh, 1897, 1–191

Haupt, E. *Die Gefangenschaftsbriefe* (KEK), Göttingen, 1897

Dale, R. W. *The Epistle to the Ephesians,* London, 1901

Gore, C. *St. Paul's Epistle to the Ephesians,* London, 1902

Robinson, J. A. *St Paul's Epistle to the Ephesians,* 1903[1], 1904[2]

Westcott, B. F. *Saint Paul's Epistle to the Ephesians,* 1906 (reprinted Grand Rapids, 1979)

Belser, J. *Der Epheserbrief des Apostels Paulus,* Freiburg, 1908

Henle, F. A. von *Der Epheserbrief des hl. Apostels Paulus,* Augsburg, 1908

Ewald, P. *Die Briefe des Paulus an die Epheser, Kolosser und Philemon*[2], Leipzig, 1910, 1–262

Salmond, S. D. F. *The Epistle to the Ephesians* (Expositor's Greek Testament III), London, 1910, 201–395

Dibelius, M. *An die Kolosser, Epheser, an Philemon* (Handbuch zum NT 12), 1913[1], Revised edn of H. Greeven, Tübingen, 1953, 54–100

Murray, J. O. F. *The Epistle to the Ephesians,* Cambridge, 1914

Vosté, J.-M. *Commentarius in Epistolam ad Ephesios*, Rome and Paris, 1921

Lock, W. *The Epistle to the Ephesians*, London, 1929

Scott, E. F. *The Epistles of Paul to the Colossians, to Philemon and to the Ephesians*, London, 1930, 117–257

Erdman, C. R. *The Epistle of Paul to the Ephesians*, Philadelphia, 1931

Synge, F. C. *St. Paul's Epistle to the Ephesians*, London, 1941

Könn, J. *Die Idee der Kirche. Bibellesungen über den Epheserbrief*, Cologne, 1946

Huby, J. S. *Paul. Les Epîtres de la captivité*, Paris, 1947, 127–259

Asmussen, H. *Der Brief des Paulus an die Epheser*, Breklum, 1949

Masson, C. *L'Épître de saint Paul aux Éphésiens* (CNT IX), Neuchâtel, 1953, 133–228

Beare, F. W. *The Epistle to the Ephesians*, Interpreter's Bible, X, 1953, 595–749

Rendtorff, H. *Der Brief an die Epheser* (NTD 8), Göttingen, 1955, 56–85

Simpson, E. K. (with F. F. Bruce) *Commentary on the Epistles to the Ephesians and Colossians* (NICNT), Grand Rapids, 1957, 15–157

Allan, J. A. *The Epistle to the Ephesians*, London, 1959

Benoit, P. *Les Épîtres de Saint Paul aux Philippiens, à Philemon, aux Colossiens, aux Éphésiens*[4], Paris, 1959, 74–108

Grosheide, F. W. *De Brief van Paulus aan de Efeziers*, Kampen, 1960

Rienecker, F. *Der Brief des Paulus an die Epheser*, Wuppertal, 1961

Zerwick, M. *Der Brief an die Epheser*, Düsseldorf, 1962

Foulkes, F. *Ephesians*, Leicester, 1963

Schlatter, A. *Der Brief an die Epheser*, Stuttgart, 1963 (first edn 1909)

Staab, K. (with J. Freundorfer) *Die Thessalonicherbriefe, die Gefangenschaftsbriefe, die Pastoralbriefe* (RNT), Regensburg, 1965, 114–66

Dahl, N. A. et alii *Kurze Auslegung des Epheserbriefes*, Göttingen, 1965

Gaugler, E. *Der Epheserbrief*, Zürich, 1966

Hendriksen, W. *Ephesians*, Carlisle, Penn, 1967

Thompson, G. H. P. *The Letters of Paul to the Ephesians, to the Colossians and to Philemon*, Cambridge, 1967

Houlden, J. H. *Paul's Letters from Prison*, London, 1970, 233–341

Gnilka, J. *Der Epheserbrief* (HTK), Freiburg, Basel, Vienna, 1971

Schlier, H. *Der Brief an die Epheser*[7], Düsseldorf, 1971

Conzelmann, H. *Die kleineren Briefe des Apostels Paulus* (Das Neue Testament Deutsch 8), Göttingen, 1972, 56–91

Hugedé, N. *L'Épître aux Éphésiens*, Geneva, 1973
Καραβιδοπουλος, I. Δ. Ἑρμηνεία τῆς πρὸς Ἐφεσίους τοῦ Ἀποστόλου Παύλου, Thessalonica, 1973
Bouwman, G. *De Brief aan de Efesiërs*, Bussum, 1974
Ernst, J. *Die Briefe an die Philipper, an Philemon, an die Kolosser, an die Epheser* (RNT), Regensburg, 1974, 245–405
Barth, M. *Ephesians* (Anchor), 2 vols., New York, 1974
Taylor, W. F. (with J. Reumann) *Ephesians, Colossians*, Minneapolis, 1975
Roon, A. van *De Brief van Paulus aan de Epheziers*, Nijkerk, 1976
Caird, G. B. *Paul's Letters from Prison*, Oxford, 1976, 9–94
Mitton, C. L. *Ephesians* (NCB), London, 1976
Stott, J. R. W. *The Message of Ephesians*, Leicester, 1979
Bratcher, R. G. and Nida, E. A. *A Translator's Handbook on Paul's Letter to the Ephesians*, London, 1982
Mussner, F. *Der Brief an die Epheser*, Gütersloh, 1982
Schnackenburg, R. *Die Brief an die Epheser*, Neukirchen-Vluyn, 1982 (ET *The Epistle to the Ephesians*, Edinburgh, 1991)
Patzia, A. G. *Colossians, Philemon, Ephesians*, San Francisco, 1984, 102–276
Bruce, F. F. *The Epistles to the Colossians, to Philemon and to the Ephesians* (NICNT), Grand Rapids, 1984, 227–416
Lindemann, A. *Der Epheserbrief*, Zürich, 1985
Penna, R. *La Lettera agli Efesini*, Bologna, 1988
Lincoln, A. T. *Ephesians* (Word), Dallas, 1990
Roberts, J. H. *Die Brief aan die Efesiërs*, Kaapstad, RSA, 1990
Bouttier, M. *L'Épître de saint Paul aux Éphésiens* (CNT IX), Geneva, 1991
Martin, R. P. *Ephesians, Colossians and Philemon* (Interpretation), Louisville, 1992, 1–79
Pokorný, P. *Der Brief des Paulus an die Epheser*, Leipzig, 1992
Kitchen, M. *Ephesians*, London, 1994

Literature cited either by author's name or name plus short title

Adai, J., *Der Heilige Geist als Gegenwart Gottes in den einzelnen Christen in der Kirche und in der Welt*, Frankfurt am Main, 1985
Allan, J. A., 'The "In Christ" formula in Ephesians', *NTS* 5 (1958/9) 54–62
Allen, T. G., 'The Body of Christ Concept in Ephesians' (unpublished Ph.D. thesis, University of Glasgow, 1982)
Arnold, C. E., *Ephesians: Power and Magic* (SNTSMS 63), Cambridge, 1989

Bankhead, R. C., *Liturgical Formulas in the New Testament*, Clinton, S. Carolina, 1971

Barth, M., *The Broken Wall*, London, 1960

Barton, S. C. and Horsley, G. R. G., 'A Hellenistic Cult Group and the New Testament Churches', *JAC* 24 (1981) 3–41

Benoit, P. 'Rapports littéraires entre les épîtres aux Colossiens et aux Éphésiens', *Neutestamentliche Aufsätze* (FS J. Schmid, ed. J. Blinzler, O. Kuss and F. Mussner), Regensburg, 1963, 11–22

Berger, K., *Formgeschichte des Neuen Testaments*, Heidelberg, 1984
'Hellenistiche Gattungen im Neuen Testament', *ANRW* II 25.2, 1031–1432, 1831–85
Theologiegeschichte des Urchristentums, Tübingen and Basel, 1994

Best, E., *One Body in Christ*, London, 1955
1 Peter, London, 1971
1 & 2 Thessalonians, London, 1972
'Ephesians i.1', *Text and Interpretation* (FS M. Black, ed. E. Best and R. McL. Wilson), Cambridge, 1979, 29–41*
'Dead in Trespasses and Sins (Eph 2.1)', *JSNT* 13 (1981) 9–25*
'Ephesians 1.1 Again', *Paul and Paulinism* (FS C. K. Barrett, ed. M. D. Hooker and S. G. Wilson), London, 1982, 273–9*
'Paul's Apostolic Authority—?', *JSNT* 27 (1986) 3–25*
'Recipients and Title of the Letter to the Ephesians: Why and When the Designation "Ephesians"?', *ANRW* II 25.4, 3247–79
'The Revelation to Evangelize the Gentiles', *JTS* 35 (1984) 1–30*
Paul and His Converts, Edinburgh, 1988
The Temptation and the Passion (SNTSMS 2), 2nd edn, Cambridge, 1990
'Ephesians 2.11–22: A Christian View of Judaism', *Text as Pretext* (FS R. Davidson, ed. R. P. Carroll), Sheffield, 1992, 47–60*
'The Use of Credal and Liturgical Material in Ephesians', *Worship, Theology and Ministry in the Early Church* (FS R. P. Martin, ed. M. J. Wilkins and T. Paige), Sheffield, 1992, 53–69*
'Thieves in the Church', *IrishBS* 14 (1992) 2–9*
Interpreting Christ, Edinburgh, 1993
Ephesians (New Testament Guides), Sheffield, 1993
'Ephesians: Two Types of Existence', *Int* 47 (1993) 39–51*
'Ministry in Ephesians', *IrishBS* 15 (1993) 146–66*
'The Haustafel in Ephesians', *IrishBS* 16 (1994) 146–160*
'Who used Whom? The Relationship of Ephesians and Colossians', *NTS* 43 (1997) 72–96

Those marked * have been reprinted in *Essays on Ephesians*, Edinburgh, T. & T. Clark, 1997

Beyer, K., *Semitische Syntax im Neuen Testament* (SUNT 1), Göttingen, 1962

Bousset-Gressmann, Bousset, W., *Die Religion des Judentums im späthellinistischen Zeitalter*, 3rd edn, ed. H. Gressmann, Tübingen, 1926

Braun, H., *Qumran und das Neue Testament*, 2 vols., Tübingen, 1966

Bruce, F. F., *The Epistle to the Colossians, to Philemon and to the Ephesians*, Grand Rapids, 1984

Bultmann, R., *Theology of the New Testament*, London, 1952

Burger, C., *Schöpfung und Versöhnung. Studien zum liturgischen Gut im Kolosser- und Epheserbrief* (WMANT 46), Neukirchen-Vluyn, 1975

Caragounis, C. C., *The Ephesians Mysterion: Meaning and Content*, Lund, 1977

Carr, W., *Angels and Principalities* (SNTSMS 42), Cambridge, 1981

Cerfaux, L., *La Théologie de l'Église suivant saint Paul*, Paris, 1948

Coutts, J., 'The Relationship of Ephesians and Colossians', *NTS* 4 (1957/8) 201–7

Cross, F. L. (ed.), *Studies in Ephesians*, London, 1956

Deichgräber, R., *Gotteshymnus und Christushymnus in der frühen Christenheit*, Göttingen, 1967

Du Plessis, I. J., *Christus as Hoof van Kerk en Kosmos*, Groningen, 1962

Dupont, J., *Gnosis. La connaissance religieuse dans les épîtres de saint Paul*, Louvain, 1949

Ernst, J., *Pleroma und Pleroma Christi*, Regensburg, 1970
Die Briefe an die Philipper, an Philemon, an die Kolosser, an die Epheser (RNT), Regensburg, 1974, 245–405

Everling, O., *Die paulinische Angelologie und Dämonologie*, Göttingen, 1888

Fanning, B. M., *Verbal Aspects in New Testament Greek*, Oxford, 1990

Faust, E., *Pax Christi et Pax Caesaris*, Göttingen, 1993

Fee, G. D., *God's Empowering Presence: The Holy Spirit in the Letters of Paul*, Peabody, Mass., 1994

Fischer, K. M., *Tendenz und Absicht des Epheserbriefs* (FRLANT 111), Göttingen, 1973

Gabathuler, H. J., *Jesus Christus: Haupt der Kirche—Haupt der Welt*, Zürich, 1965

Gewiess, J., 'Die Begriffe πληροῦν und πλήρωμα im Kolosser-und Epheserbrief', *Vom Wort des Lebens* (FS M. Meinertz), Münster, 1951, 128–41

Gibbs, J. G., *Creation and Redemption: A Study in Pauline Theology* (SupNT 26), Leiden, 1971

Gielen, M., *Tradition und Theologie neutestamentlicher Haustafelethik* (BBB 75), Frankfurt am Main, 1990

Gnilka, J., *Der Kolosserbrief* (HTK X, 1), Freiburg, 1980 'Paränetische Traditionen im Epheserbrief', *Mélanges Bibliques en hommage au R. P. Béda Rigaux*, Gembloux, 1970, 397–410

Goodspeed, E. J., *The Meaning of Ephesians*, Chicago, 1933

Goppelt, L., *Der erste Petrusbrief* (KEK), Göttingen, 1978

Gundry, R. H., *Sōma in Biblical Theology* (SNTSMS 29), Cambridge, 1976

Guthrie, D., *New Testament Introduction*, 3rd edn, London, 1970

Hahn, F., *The Titles of Jesus in Christology*, London, 1969

Halter, H., *Taufe und Ethos: Paulinische Kriterien für das Proprium christlicher Moral*, Freiburg, 1977

Hanson, S., *The Unity of the Church in the New Testament: Colossians and Ephesians*, Uppsala, 1946

Holtzmann, H. J., *Kritik der Epheser- und Kolosserbriefe*, Leipzig, 1872

Jewett, R., *Paul's Anthropological Terms*, Leiden, 1971

Joüon, P., 'Notes philologiques sur quelques versets de l'Épître aux Éphésiens', *RSR* 26 (1936) 454–64

Kamlah, E., *Der Form der katalogischen Paränese im Neuen Testament*, Tübingen, 1964

Käsemann, E., *Leib und Leib Christi*, Tübingen, 1933

Kirby, J. C., *Ephesians, Baptism and Pentecost*, London, 1968

Knox, W. L., *St. Paul and the Church of the Gentiles*, Cambridge, 1939

Kramer, W., *Christ, Lord, Son of God* (SBT 50), London, 1966

Kuhn, K. G., 'Der Epheserbrief im Lichte der Qumrantexte', *NTS* 7 (1960/1) 334–45

Larsson, E., *Christus als Vorbild*, Uppsala, 1962

Lemmer, H. R., 'Pneumatology and Eschatology in Ephesians—The Role of the Eschatological Spirit in the Church' (D.Th. dissertation, University of South Africa, 1988)

Lincoln, A. T., *Paradise Now and Not Yet* (SNTSMS 43), Cambridge, 1981

Lindars, B., *New Testament Apologetic*, London, 1961

Lindemann, A., *Die Aufhebung der Zeit. Geschichtsverständnis und Eschatologie im Epheserbrief*, Gütersloh, 1975
Paulus im ältesten Christentum, Tübingen, 1979

Lohse, E., *Colossians and Philemon* (Hermeneia), Philadelphia, 1971

Lona, H. E., *Die Eschatologiie im Kolosser- und Epheserbrief*, Würzburg, 1984

Löwe, H., 'Christus und die Christen: Untersuchungen zum

Verständnis der Kirche in den grossen Paulusbriefen und im Kolosserund Epheserbrief' (Dissertation, University of Heidelberg, 1965)

MacDonald, M. Y., *The Pauline Churches* (SNTSMS 60), Cambridge, 1988

Mackay, J. A. *God's Order: The Ephesian Letter and the Present Time*, London, 1953

Martin, R. P., *Reconciliation: A Study of Paul's Theology*, London, 1981

Merkel, H., 'Der Epheserbrief in der neueren exegetisch Diskussion', *ANRW* II 25.4, 3156-246

Merklein, H., *Das kirchliche Amt nach dem Epheserbrief*, Munich, 1973

Christus und die Kirche, Stuttgart, 1973

Meuzelaar, J. J., *Der Leib des Messias*, Kampen, 1979

Meyer, R. P., *Kirche und Mission im Epheserbrief*, Stuttgart, 1977

Miletic, S. F., *'One Flesh': Eph 5.22–4, 5.31. Marriage and the New Creation* (AnBib 115), Rome, 1988

Mitton, C. L., *The Epistle to the Ephesians*, Oxford, 1951

Moore, G. F., *Judaism*, 3 vols., Cambridge, MA, 1927–32

Moule, C. F. D., *The Epistles to the Colossians and to Philemon*, Cambridge, 1957

Mussner, F., *Christus, das All und die Kirche*, Trier, 1955

'Beiträge aus Qumran zum Verständnis des Epheserbrief', *Neutestamentliche Aufsätze* (FS J. Schmid), Regensburg, 1963, 185–98

O'Brien, P. T., *Colossians, Philemon* (Word), Waco, 1982

Ochel, W., 'Die Annahme einer Bearbeitung des Kolosser-Briefes im Epheser-Brief in einer Analyse des Epheser-Briefes untersucht' (Dissertation, Marburg, 1934)

Odeberg, H., *The View of the Universe in the Epistle to the Ephesians* (Act. Univ. Lund), Lund, 1934

Overfield, P. D., 'The Ascension, Pleroma and Ecclesia Concepts in Ephesians' (Ph.D. thesis, St Andrews, 1976)

Penna, R., *Il 'Mysterion' Paolino*, Brescia, 1978

Percy, E., *Der Leib Christi: In den paulinischen Homologumena und Antilegoumena*, Lund, 1942

Die Probleme der Kolosser und Epheserbrief, Lund, 1946

Pfammatter, J., *Die Kirche als Bau. Eine exegetisch-theologische Studie zur Ekklesiologie der Paulusbriefe*, Rome, 1960

Pokorný, P., *Der Epheserbrief und die Gnosis*, Berlin, 1965

Der Brief des Paulus an die Kolosser, Berlin, 1987

Porter, S. E., *Verbal Aspect in the Greek of the New Testament with Reference to Tense and Mood*, New York, 1990

Preisendanz, K., *Papyri graecae magicae. Die griechischen Zauberpapyri*, Leipzig and Berlin, 1928–

Rader, W., *The Church and Racial Hostility. A History of Interpretation of Eph 2:11–22*, Tübingen, 1978

Reumann, J., *Righteousness in the New Testament*, Philadelphia, 1982

Reynier, C., *Évangile et Mystére. Les enjeux théologiques de l'Épître aux Éphésiens* (LD 149), Paris, 1992

Roberts, J. H. *Die Opbou van die Kerk volgens die Efese-brief*, Groningen, 1963

Roels, E. D., *God's Mission: The Epistle to the Ephesians in Mission Perspective*, Franckcr, 1962

Romaniuk, K., *L'Amour du Père et du Fils dans la sotèriologie de Saint Paul*, Rome, 1961

Sanders, J. T., 'Hymnic Elements in Ephesians 1–3', *ZNW* 56 (1965) 214–32

The New Testament Christological Hymns. Their Historical and Religious Background (SNTSMS 15), Cambridge, 1971

Schenke, L., *Die Urgemeinde. Geschichtliche und theologische Entwicklung*, Stuttgart, 1990

Schille, *Frühchristliche Hymnen*, Berlin, 1965

Schlier, H., *Christus und die Kirche im Epheserbrief*, Tübingen, 1930

Schlier, H. and Warnach, V., *Die Kirche im Epheserbrief*, Münster, Westfalen, 1949

Schmid, J., *Der Epheserbrief des Apostels Paulus. Seine Adresse, Sprache und literarischen Beziehungen*, Freiburg, 1928

Schmithals, W., *Theologiegeschichte des Urchristentums*, Stuttgart, 1994

Schubert, P., *Form and Function of the Pauline Thanksgivings* (BZNW 20), 1939

Schürer, E., *The History of the Jewish People in the Age of Jesus Christ*, 2nd edn, ed. G. Vermes, F. Millar, M. Black, 3 vols., Edinburgh, 1973ff

Schweizer, E., *Der Brief an die Kolosser* (EKK), Zürich, Cologne, 1976

Selwyn, E. G., *The First Epistle of St. Peter*, London, 1946

Spicq, C., *Notes de lexicographie néotestamentaire*, 3 vols., Fribourg, 1978, 1982

Stacey, W. D., *The Pauline View of Man*, London, 1956

Steinmetz, F. J., *Protologische Heils-Zuversicht. Die Strukturen des soteriologischen und christologischen Denkens im Kolosser und Epheserbrief*, Frankfurt am Main, 1969

Studies in Ephesians, see Cross, F. L.

Tachau, P., *'Einst' und 'Jetzt' im Neuen Testament* (FRLANT 105), Göttingen, 1972

Thornton, L. S., *The Common Life in the Body of Christ*, Westminster, 1942

Trebilco, P., *Jewish Communities in Asia Minor* (SNTSMS 69), Cambridge, 1991

Turner, M., 'Mission and Meaning in Terms of "Unity" in Ephesians', *Mission and Meaning* (FS P. Cotterell, ed. A. Billington, A. Lane and M. Turner), Exeter, 1995, 138–66

Usami, K., *Somatic Comprehension of Unity. The Church in Ephesus* (AnBib 101), Rome, 1983

Van Roon, A., *The Authenticity of Ephesians* (SupNT 39), Leiden, 1974

Vermes, G., *The Dead Sea Scrolls in English*[3], London, 1987

Vielhauer, P., *Oikodome. Das Bild vom Bau in der christlichen Literatur vom Neuen Testament bis Clemens Alexandrinus*, Karlsruhe, 1939, and Munich, 1979

Warnach: see Schlier and Warnach

Wengst, K., *Christologische Formeln und Lieder des Urchristentums*, Gütersloh, 1972

Wink, W., *Naming the Powers*, Philadelphia, 1984

Ziesler, J. A., *The Meaning of Righteousness in Paul* (SNTSMS 20), Cambridge, 1972

Zuntz, G., *The Text of the Epistles* (Schweich Lectures, 1946), London, 1952.

ABBREVIATIONS

Special Abbreviations

A/Col = Author of Colossians
AE = Author of Ephesians
DSS = Dead Sea Scrolls
FS = Festschrift (volume of essays dedicated to named persons)
HT = *Haustafel*

Abbreviations: Works of Reference

ABD = *Anchor Bible Dictionary*, ed. D. N. Freedman, New York, 1992
BAGD = *A Greek–English Lexicon of the New Testament and Other Early Christian Literature*, ed. W. Bauer (ET[2] W. F. Arndt, F. W. Gingrich, F. W. Danker), Chicago, 1979
BDR = F. Blass, A. Debrunner, F. Rehkopf, *Grammatik des neutestamentlichen Griechisch*[14], Göttingen, 1976
Biblia Patristica = *Biblia Patristica: Index des citations et allusions bibliques dans la littérature Patristique* (ed. J. Allenbach et alii), Paris, 1975ff
Burton = *Syntax of the Moods and Tenses in New Testament Greek*[3], Edinburgh, 1955
DPL = *Dictionary of Paul and His Letters*, ed. G. G. Hawthorne, R. P. Martin, D. G. Reid, Leicester, 1993
EDNT = *Exegetical Dictionary of the New Testament*, ed. H. Balz and G. Schneider, 3 vols., ET Edinburgh, 1990ff
Hennecke–Schneemelcher = *New Testament Apocrypha*, ed. E. Hennecke, W. Schneemelcher, ET[2] ed. by R. McL. Wilson, 2 vols., London, 1991, 1992
LSJ = *Greek–English Lexicon*, ed. H. G. Liddell, R. Scott, H. S. Jones, R. McKenzie, Oxford, 1951
MH = J. H. Moulton and W. F. Howard, *A Grammar of New Testament Greek*, vol. 2, Edinburgh, 1929
MHT = J. H. Moulton, W. F. Howard and N. Turner, *A Grammar of New Testament Greek*, vol. 3, Edinburgh, 1963
MM = J. H. Moulton and G. Milligan, *The Vocabulary of the Greek Testament*, London, 1914–29

Metzger = B. M. Metzger, *A Textual Commentary on the Greek New Testament*, London, 1971
Moule = C. F. D. Moule, *An Idiom Book of New Testament Greek*, Cambridge, 1953
Moulton–Turner = *A Grammar of New Testament Greek*, vol. IV, by J. H. Moulton and N. Turner, Edinburgh, 1976
NIDNTT = *The New International Dictionary of New Testament Theology*, ed. C. Brown, Exeter and Grand Rapids, 1975–8
Robertson = A. T. Robertson, *A Grammar of the Greek of the New Testament in the Light of Historical Research*[3], New York, 1919
SB = H. L. Strack and P. Billerbeck, *Kommentar zum Neuen Testament aus Talmud und Midrasch*, Munich, 1922–61
Thrall = M. E. Thrall, *Greek Particles in the New Testament*, Leiden, 1962
TWNT = *Theologisches Wörterbuch zum Neuen Testament*, ed. G. Kittel and G. Friedrich, Stuttgart, 1933ff
Zerwick = M. Zerwick, *Biblical Greek* (ET by J. Smith), Rome, 1963
The abbreviations for Greek and Latin authors are normally those used in LSJ and Lewis and Short

Abbreviations: General

AnBib   Analecta biblica
Ang   Angelus
ANRW   Aufstieg und Niedergang der römischen Welt (ed. H. Temporini and W. Haase), Berlin
ARW   Archiv für Religionswissenschaft
ASNU   Acta seminarii neotestamentici upsaliensis
ASSeign   Assemblées du Seigneur
ASTI   Annual of the Swedish Theological Institute
ATR   Anglican Theological Review
AusBR   Australian Biblical Review
BeO   Bibbia e oriente
BETL   Bibliotheca ephemeridum theologicarum lovaniensium
BETS   Bulletin of the Evangelical Theological Society
Bib   Biblica
BibLeb   Bibel und Leben
BJRL, BJRULM   Bulletin of the John Rylands University Library, Manchester
BSac   Bibliotheca Sacra
BT   The Bible Translator
BTB   Biblical Theology Bulletin
BZ   Biblische Zeitschrift
BZNW   Beihefte zur *ZNW*

CBQ   *Catholic Biblical Quarterly*
CNT   Commentaire du Nouveau Testament
Conc   *Concilium*
CQR   *Church Quarterly Review*
CR   Corpus Reformatorum
CRINT   *Compendium Rerum Iudaicarum ad Novum Testamentum*
   (ed. S. Safrai and M. Stern), Assen, 1974
CSEL   Corpus scriptorum ecclesiasticorum latinorum
CTM   *Concordia Theological Monthly*
DR   *Downside Review*
EKK   Evangelisch-Katholischer Kommentar zum Neuen
   Testament
EstBib   *Estudios biblicos*
EstT   *Estudios theologicos*
ETL   *Ephemerides theologicae lovanienses*
EvQ   *Evangelical Quarterly*
EvT   *Evangelische Theologie*
Exp   *Expositor*
ExpT   *Expository Times*
FRLANT   Forschungen zur Religion and Literatur des Alten und
   Neuen Testaments
GCS   Griechische christliche Schriftsteller
GraceTJ   *Grace Theological Journal*
Greg   *Gregorianum*
GuL   *Geist und Leben*
HR   *History of Religions*
HTK   Herders Theologischer Kommentar zum Neuen Testament
HTR   *Harvard Theological Review*
IKZ   *Internationale kirchliche Zeitschrift*
Int   *Interpretation*
IrishBS   *Irish Biblical Studies*
JAAR   *Journal of the American Academy of Religion*
JAC   *Jahrbuch für Antike und Christentum*
JBL   *Journal of Biblical Literature*
JSNT   *Journal for the Study of the New Testament*
JSNTSup   *JSNT Supplement Series*
JTS   *Journal of Theological Studies*
KEK   H. A. W. Meyer, Kritisch-exegetischer Kommentar über das
   Neue Testament
LCL   Loeb Classical Library
LD   Lectio Divina
LJ   *Liturgisches Jahrbuch*
LS   *Louvain Studies*
LTJ   *Lutheran Theological Journal*
LV   *Lumière et Vie*
MPG   J.-P. Migne, *Patrologia graeca*

MPL   J.-P. Migne, *Patrologia latina*
NedGTT   Neuerduitse Gereformeerd Teologiese Tydskrif
NICNT   The New International Commentary on the New
  Testament
NRT   La nouvelle revue théologique
NT   Novum Testamentum
NTOA   Novum Testamentum et Orbis Antiquus
NTS   New Testament Studies
OJRS   Ohio Journal of Religious Studies
PSV   Parola Spirito Vita
PGM   Papyri graecae magicae (ed. K. Preisendanz)
QD   Questiones Disputae
RAC   Reallexikòn für Antike und Christentum
RB   Revue biblique
RefR   Reformed Review
RefTR   Reformed Theological Review
RelSB   Religious Studies Bulletin
RestQ   Restoration Quarterly
RevExp   Review and Expositor
RGG   Religion in Geschichte und Gegenwart
RHR   Revue de l'histoire des religions
RivBibIt   Rivista Biblica
RNT   Regensburger Neues Testament
RSPT   Revue des sciences philosophiques et théologiques
RSR   Recherches de science religieuse
RThom   Revue Thomiste
SBE   Semana Biblica España
SBFLA   Studii biblici franciscani liber annuus
SBLDS   SBL Dissertation Series
SBLMS   SBL Monograph Series
SBS   Stuttgarter Bibelstudien
SBT   Studies in Biblical Theology
SC   Sources chrétiennes
ScEc   Sciences Ecclesiastiques
ScEs   Science et esprit
Scr   Scripture
SE   Studia Evangelica
SEÅ   Svensk exeegetisk årsbok
SHAW   Sitzungsberichte der Heidelberger Akademie der
  Wissenschaften
SJT   Scottish Journal of Theology
SNTSMS   Society for New Testament Studies Monograph Series
ST   Studia theologica
SUNT   Studien zur Umwelt des Neuen Testament
SupNT   NT Supplement Series
SymBU   Symbolae biblicae upsalienses

TBT   *The Bible Today*
ThBl   *Theologischer Blätter*
TGl   *Theologie und Glaube*
TJ   *Trinity Journal*
TQ   *Theologische Quartalschrift*
TSK   *Theologische Studien und Kritiken*
TTZ   *Trier theologische Zeitschrift*
TU   Texte und Untersuchungen
TynB   *Tyndale Bulletin*
TZ   *Theologische Zeitschrift*
UUÅ   Uppsala universiltetsårsskrift
VC   *Vigiliae christianae*
VCaro   *Verbum Caro*
VD   *Verbum domini*
VoxEv   *Vox Evangelica*
WD   *Wort und Dienst*
WMANT   Wissenschaftliche Monographien zum Alten und Neuen
   Testament
WTJ   *Westminster Theological Journal*
WUNT   Wissenschaftliche Untersuchungen zum Neuen Testament
ZNW   *Zeitschrift für die neutestamentliche Wissenschaft*
ZRGG   *Zeitschrift für Religions- und Geistesgeschichte*
ZTK   *Zeitschrift für Theologie und Kirche*

INTRODUCTION

R. D. Shaw, *The Pauline Epistles*, Edinburgh, 1903, 331–400; R. Scott, *The Pauline Epistles*, Edinburgh, 1909, 180–208; T. Zahn, *Introduction to the New Testament*, I, Edinburgh, 1909, 479–522; J. Moffatt, *Introduction to the Literature of the New Testament*[3], Edinburgh, 1918, 373–95; M. Goguel, *Introduction au Nouveau Testament*, IV.2, Paris, 1926, 431–73; H. J. Cadbury, 'The Dilemma of Ephesians', *NTS* 5 (1959–60), 91–102; E. Käsemann, *RG*[3], II, 517–19; W. G. Kümmel, *Introduction to the New Testament*, London, 1966, 247–58; P. Benoit, *Dictionaire de la Bible, Supplément*, VII, 1966, 195–211; W. Marxsen, *Introduction to the New Testament*, Oxford, 1968, 187–98; P. Vielhauer, *Geschichte der urchristlichen Literatur*, Berlin, 1975, 203–15; J. A. T. Robinson, *Redating the New Testament*, London, 1976, 61–7; R. P. Martin, *New Testament Foundations*, II, Exeter, 1978, 223–38; H.-M. Schenke and K. M. Fischer, *Einleitung in die Schriften des Neuen Testaments*, I, Berlin, 1978, 174–90; J. P. Sampley, 'The Epistle to the Ephesians', in J. P. Sampley, J. Burgess, G. Krodel, R. H. Fuller, *Ephesians, Colossians, 2 Thessalonians, The Pastoral Epistles*, Philadelphia, 1978, 9–39; D. Howard, 'An Introduction to Ephesians', *SWJT* 22 (1979) 7–23; H. Koester, *Introduction to the New Testament*, Philadelphia, 1982, 2, 267–72 (= §12.2b); J. Gnilka, *TRE* IX, 1982, 743–50; H. Merkel, *ANRW* II 25.4, 3156–246; R. F. Collins, *Letters That Paul Did Not Write*, Wilmington, Delaware, 1988, 132–70; J. Reumann, *Variety and Unity in New Testament Thought*, Oxford, 1991, 114–23; V. P. Furnish, *ABD*, II, 535–42; C. E. Arnold, 'Ephesians', *DPL*, 238–49; H. Hübner, *Biblische Theologie des Neuen Testaments, 2*. Göttingen, 1993, 363–75; U. Schnelle, *Einleitung in das Neue Testament*, Göttingen, 1994, 348–65.

Since most commentaries in their introductions cover to a greater or lesser degree the material which follows, they have been listed neither in the above bibliography nor in those preceding particular sections. Since Merkel has supplied a historical survey of discussion on Ephesians arising out of the rise of the historical–critical method, none will be given here.

1. RECIPIENTS

1. 1. It is only possible to deal at this point with those whom AE conceived of as reading his letter. Others may also have read it.

1

Ephesians was written to believers; these did not necessarily live in Ephesus (see on 1. 1f) but were either (a) members in a group of Christian communities which we cannot identify but which probably lay in Asia Minor (cf 1 Peter) and may possibly have included the community at Ephesus, or (b) Christians in general, though probably those in a restricted area like Asia Minor. The letter itself does not supply us with sufficient information to make a final decision between these possibilities, let alone to determine the exact geographical location of the readers. In favour of (a) is the implication that Tychicus was sent with the letter (6. 21f) and must have known where he was going; but the reference to Tychicus may only be part of AE's pseudonymous framework. In favour of (b) are the absence of any kind of greeting, the very general nature of both the address ('to the saints and faithful') and the conclusion ('peace be to the brothers'). Hypothesis (b) is probably, but by no means certainly, to be preferred. If however (a) is chosen then the communities AE has in mind were probably a number of churches in different cities rather than a number of house churches in one particular city; it is unlikely that the letter would have been carried round from house to house since there were times when the members of all the house churches in a city met together (cf 1 Cor 14.23) and these would have offered appropriate occasions for the letter to be read; house churches existed in Colossae (4.15) yet the letter to that church was to be read to the church as a whole. The letter contains nothing by way of an identifiable heresy or persecution which might supply some information about its addressees. The area where the readers lived may not have been large for although pieces of tradition are used (see §9.2) these pieces do not appear to have been widely known; there is no evidence for their existence in other contemporary Christian writing; this suggests a restricted area. Possibly however AE thought all Christians knew these traditions. AE wrote with believers in mind, but not all believers, for his stress lies on those of Gentile origin and he excludes those who have been converted through Paul's preaching (1.15).

1.1.1. AE may in fact not have known much about his readers. In the *Haustafel* of 5.22–6.9 he deals only with husbands and wives, parents and children, masters and slaves who live in wholly Christian households. It is extremely difficult to believe that there was then, or ever since, a Christian community in which every member of every household was a believer. Evidence for divided households is found in 1 Cor 7.12–16; 1 Pet 2.18–3.6. In view then of AE's failure to understand the true nature of the households in his communities, we have to look very carefully at any information he does supply about his readers. His failure to understand correctly life around him is seen also in the way in which he describes the secular world (4.17–19); non-Christians in the ancient world would not have accepted the high colouring of this description; in this case AE's failure may be more excusable (see on 4.17–19). Incidentally this description of 4.17–19 would exclude his non-Jewish readers from any previous attachment to a synagogue as 'God-fearers'. Although in almost all the other NT writings Christians are seen as subject to outside pressure, if not persecution, this is not reflected in any counsel AE gives his readers. This should lead us to look carefully at the purpose of the letter (§8).

1.2. Lacking detailed information on the situation of the readers we can learn little about their social composition. Some of his readers knew Greek, though not all may have used it as a first language (cf Acts 14.11); the letter would have been translated by those who knew Greek for the benefit of those who did not. That there were slaves among those he expected to read his letter, or hear it read, is confirmed by the fact that he addresses them (6.5–8), but this does not prove that there were also wealthy households for even relatively humble households had one or two slaves and every small business required them. The sins from which AE expects them to break free now that they believe are in no way exceptional: untruthfulness, bad temper, theft, bawdy and scandalous talk (4.25–31), fornication, adultery and greed (5.3–5).

1.3. We can assume his readers were baptised (4.5; 5.26). While in the later church candidates received catechetical instruction prior to baptism there is no reason to see this as the practice in AE's time; in none of the cases of recorded baptism in Acts is there any period of instruction between the request for baptism and the baptism itself. Catechetical instruction must have followed after baptism. The intended readers had probably been converts for varying lengths of time. 4.21 implies they have already received some instruction. It is impossible to say by whom or when they had been evangelised. It was certainly not by Paul, whether he is the author or not (1.15; 3.2). Usami, *passim*, argues that AE had two groups in mind, the 'we' and the 'you', which are to be distinguished through the length of time they had been Christians; the 'we' for a much longer time than the 'you', who are recent converts. The 'we' group would have included both Jewish and Gentile Christians of long standing. But there cannot have been a rigid gap between these two supposed groups for converts were regularly being made; there are other and much more probable explanations of the variation between first and second person plural.

1.4. The readers have been Christians long enough to be expected to accept the OT as an authoritative guide for conduct in at least some areas of life (5.31; 6.2f). As well as explicit quotations, the OT is also regularly alluded to and played on in the course of the argument (e.g. Isa 57.19 in 2.12–17), so AE must have believed some readers had a reasonably detailed knowledge of it (cf §9.1).

Christian tradition is also used (§9.2). Since they would have received some tradition in their post-baptismal instruction there is no reason to see all of them as Christians of long standing. AE's use of liturgical language (e.g. 1.3–14; 3.14–21) proves only that he liked to express himself in such language and says nothing about his readers. Equally his use of complex arguments (e.g. 1.9f) says nothing about their intellectual capabilities; preachers regularly talk far above the heads of their hearers. AE's use of the OT might imply his readers were Jewish Christians but since a large portion of the argument of the letter relates to the acceptance of Gentiles as believers and since the readers are addressed in the second plural as Gentiles who have forsaken pagan ways (2.1f; 3.1; 4.17), the majority of them must have been Gentiles. Were there however no Jewish believers among them (cf Barth, 10; id. *Israel und die Kirche*, Munich, 1959 7, 30)? Many of the terms used about the readers (e.g. 1.1, saints, faithful) had been first applied by Jewish Christians to themselves. Gentiles are sometimes referred to in the third person (3.6, 8) (cf Roels, 117–19). The author himself was a Jewish Christian (see §2.2.2). There was indeed a large Jewish population in Asia Minor, the probable area of destination of the epistle. It is difficult to believe that even by the end of the first century, if Ephesians is as late as that, there were churches in which there were no Jewish Christians.

1.5. Asia Minor is generally accepted as the geographical location of the readers. The letter itself, because of its very general nature, offers however no substantial clues to their location. There are no references to outside events like persecution or heresy which might enable us to tie it down, or at least to eliminate some possible areas. It was AE's intention to deal with the internal life of Christian communities. The tradition about Asia Minor as the location grew up during the long period when the reference to Ephesus in 1.1 was accepted without hesitation as the true text. Now that that reading is no longer acceptable (see on 1.1) is it possible to retain Asia Minor as the location of its intended readers? At some stage a name was inserted in 1.1 and the selection of Ephesus shows that those who chose it thought of Asia Minor as its area of circulation. Marcion's belief that 1.1 contained the name Laodicea could also be held to support Asia Minor as the intended area.

1.5.1. If AE used Colossians (but see §2.5) it could be assumed that he came on that letter in the area to which it was written and thus wrote his own to the same general area. The earliest evidence for knowledge of the letter is found in Ignatius and Polycarp; the latter was bishop of Smyrna in Asia Minor and Ignatius passed through the area on his way to Rome. Tychicus is the only Christian named in Ephesians; he is also named in Col 4.7f; if Colossians was written to Colossae then he was associated with the area during at least some part of his life. Acts 20.4 implies he was a native of the area and 2 Tim 4.12 also links him with it; however Tit 3.12 (cf 1.5) implies some of his life was spent in Cyprus.

1.5.2. If it could be shown that Ephesians has affinities with other writings belonging to Asia Minor this might help to pin it down.[1] Kirby, 166–8, has argued for a number of similarities with the Gospel of John, e.g. use of the light–darkness contrast, restriction of love to fellow community members, need for unity in the community, emphasis on the importance of knowledge. These ideas are certainly shared but they are shared also with a number of other NT writings which do not belong to the area of Asia Minor. Indeed, all NT writings have a considerable number of concepts in common. Therefore to prove that any two writings are closely associated it is necessary not only to point out their similarities but also show these similarities as unique to these two writings. It is true the final edition of John may have been written in Asia Minor but it probably passed through several stages in its composition and may have gathered the alleged similarities in other areas. A close resemblance between Ephesians and 1 Peter, which is addressed to a somewhat similar area, has also been seen; indeed, some scholars have seen one as depending on the other (see §2.4.5.6); dependence in either direction is however unlikely, and 1 Peter, though it may be addressed to the same area, was probably written in Rome. There are also important differences between the letters; in particular 1 Peter refers frequently to the persecution of believers, a subject absent from Ephesians. The HT of 1 Peter (2.13–3.7) is very different from that of Ephesians (5.22–6.9; cf Best, 'Haustafel') and it does not appear that either could have been derived from the other. Revelation is also a writing certainly associated with Asia Minor as seen in the names of the seven churches; like 1 Peter and unlike Ephesians it implies persecution was rife. Heresy was a feature of late first-century Christianity in Asia Minor as we see from 1 John, Rev 2, 3 and Ignatius, *Trall* 10; *Smyrn* 2; 5; 7; *Eph* 9.1; *Magn* 10; *Philad* 6. But not all the heresies are the same and if AE was planning to cover Christians in a wide area he may have deliberately avoided referring to both heresy and persecution because he was concerned with the inner condition of the communities which would receive his letter.

1.5.3. Arnold (*passim*, but especially 5–40) sees much in Ephesians which is easily explained on the supposition of a background in Asia Minor, instancing among other things magic and the 'powers'. What he says is true but is subject to the same criticism as Kirby; Asia Minor could provide a suitable background for Ephesians but

---

[1] On the development of similarities and dissimilarities between NT writings see Berger, *Theologiegeschichte*, especially 183f, 274–6, 425–7, 521–3, 543–7 in respect of Ephesians.

Arnold has not shown that there were not other suitable areas. Our knowledge of the details of magic is mainly derived from papyrus finds in Egypt and not Asia Minor. The 'powers' feature in Rom 8.38f and Paul would hardly have mentioned them unless he had been confident that Roman Christians would have understood the reference. Faust, 15 n. 43, assumes without arguing the case that the provenance of Ephesians was Asia Minor and uses that assumption to throw light on 2.11–22. His argument depends however in large parts on events in the wider Roman Empire and these would have had the same impact in many of its areas. The 'proof' is again not sufficiently rigorous.

1.5.4. In the end the features shared with Colossians are the strongest argument for Asia Minor but the argument needs careful formulation. If AE used Colossians it may be concluded that at some stage in his life he was a resident of Colossae or another city in that area, encountered that letter and wrote to the same area. However (see §2.5), AE may not have depended on Colossians in any direct literary sense. He and A/Col may have belonged to the same Pauline school (§3), which was perhaps centred on Ephesus. They share some of the same traditional material, e.g. the HT, the vice lists. Tradition is normally used in the hope that it will be recognised as tradition and so carry weight in an argument. One minor feature in Ephesians may support Asia Minor as its provenance; it is the only area where μεσότοιχον has been found as an architectural term (see on 2.14).

1.6. It would be wrong to conclude that it can be definitely established that AE wrote for readers in Asia Minor but a stronger case can be made out for this area than any other and it should probably be accepted as the area of the intended readers. Little difference in fact would be made to the interpretation if it had been written to some other area. Assuming Asia Minor as the provenance of the letter it is impossible to estimate the number of believers in the area at this time. Evangelism began in the time of Paul; Pliny, *Ep* 10.90, says that at the time when he wrote there were many Christians; our writing lies somewhere in between the time of Paul and that of Pliny. During this period the church will have been growing; Pliny says that in his time there were already those who were giving up belief; there is however no feeling in Ephesians that there is even the beginning of a drift away from Christianity which AE might wish to stem.

2. AUTHORSHIP

Percy, *passim*; J. N. Sanders, 'The Case for the Pauline Authorship', *Studies*, 9–20; D. E. Nineham, 'The Case against the Pauline Authorship', *Studies*, 21–35; H. J. Cadbury, 'The Dilemma of Ephesians', *NTS* 5

(1958/9) 91–102; L. Cerfaux. 'En faveur de l'authenticité des épîtres de la captivité', *Littérature et Théologie Pauliniennes*, Bruges, 1960, 59–71; R. Kasser, 'L'autore dell'Epistola agli Efesini', *Protestantesimo* 17 (1962) 74–84; J. Murphy-O'Connor, 'Who Wrote Ephesians?', *TBT* 18 (1965) 1201–9; J. I. Cook, 'The Origin and Purpose of Ephesians', *RefR* 18 (1965) 3–18; Van Roon, *passim*; Caragounis, 35–56; J. B. Polhill, 'An Introduction to Ephesians', *RevExp* 76 (1979) 465–80; G. A. M. Vleugels and J. C. Coetzee, 'Onderzoek naar de synoptische relatie van de brieven aan de Efeziërs en aan de Kolossenzers', *In die Skriflig* 22 (1988) 37–46; M. D. Goulder, 'The Visionaries of Laodicea', *JSNT* 43 (1991) 15–39; J. H. Roberts, 'The Enigma of Ephesians – Rethinking some positions on the basis of Schnackenburg and Arnold', *Neot* 27 (1993) 93–106.

2.1. In approaching this topic a number of areas must be covered: external evidence, relation to Colossians, relation to the Pauline letters, vocabulary, syntax, style, thought. Before turning to these areas it is important to set out the main possibilities:

i. Both Colossians and Ephesians were written by Paul.
ii. Both were written by the same person who was not Paul.
iii. Paul wrote Colossians; the author of Ephesians is unknown.
iv. Paul wrote Ephesians; the author of Colossians is unknown.
v. The two letters were written by two different unknown authors.

2.2. *Profile of the Author*
Demetrius says in respect of the letter:

The letter, like the dialogue, should abound in glimpses of character. It may be said that everybody reveals his own soul in his letters. In every other form of composition it is possible to discern the writer's character, but none so clearly as in the epistolary.[2]

If he is correct it should be possible before turning directly to the question of the identity of the author to give a brief sketch of the kind of person for whom we should be looking.
2.2.1. The author is almost certainly a man. 6.13ff depicts the struggle in which Christians are involved in male terms. In 4.13 the author uses ἀνήρ where ἄνθρωπος would have been more suitable. In 5.31 marriage is described in terms of the husband's action without reference to the wife's. Drunkenness (5.18) is more often a male than a female sin. In 5.5 the masculine πόρνος is used where there is a feminine πόρνη (cf 1 Cor 6.15). In 4.28 a male term in the singular (plurals often cover both sexes) is used to denote a thief; men wishing to obtain money illegally are more likely to turn to theft than women, who if they need money will seek it through prostitution rather than theft. In 6.4, after referring generally to parents, AE focuses attention on fathers. There is not sufficient extant contemporary literature written by women to know if they

---

[2] *On Style*, 227 (Loeb translation, W. Roberts).

would have used male terms in the same way as contemporary male writers did, for example in using the masculine to denote common gender. AE was then almost certainly male and masculine pronouns will therefore be used when referring to him. Even though he was a male and uses martial imagery in 6.13ff that gives no reason to suppose that he had served in the Roman army. Jews in Asia Minor were normally exempt from military service.[3] The details of Roman military equipment were probably as well known to everyone as are the latest military planes to youngsters today. Of course if Paul was the author there would have been no need to prove the author was male.

2.2.2. The author was a Jewish Christian.[4] He often uses the first plural to indicate that both he and his readers are Christians. Occasionally however his first plural contrasts him with Gentiles and he addresses them as Gentiles (2.1–3, 11–14, 19–22; 3.1ff). If however AE was not Paul and was deliberately attempting to imply Paul was the author he would almost certainly have made this distinction. His Jewishness is however corroborated in other ways. Kuhn, 334f, points to his language, idiom and type of exegesis (e.g. his use of Isa 57 in 2.11ff), to his knowledge of Qumranian ideas or ideas similar to them, to the way, apart from direct quotation, he works the OT and its concepts into his argument, to his emphasis on Israel as that to which the believers are joined. Though a Jew and acquainted with the ideas found in the Qumran writings there is no reason to suppose he ever belonged to that community (cf §10.5.2). His Jewishness is also seen in the use of Jewish liturgical forms, e.g. the eulogy (1.3ff), the doxology (3.20f), and would be reinforced if it were true that he drew 4.8 directly from a targum (but see notes on 4.8). If a Jew he was almost certainly a Hellenistic Jew as we see from his awareness of Stoic and related ideas and perhaps also from his knowledge of Hellenistic rhetoric (§2.2.3). Again his Jewishness would not require to be established if it was certain that Paul was the writer. If he was not Paul he stands in the Pauline tradition as the relation of his letter to the main Paulines and his use of Pauline ideas show (§2.6).

2.2.3. What does his writing reveal about the quality of his mind? He is at home in writing Greek but his style is complex rather than simple and direct. Many of his sentences are lengthy and overloaded with subordinate clauses whose precise relationship to one another and to the whole is often difficult to determine. He rarely uses one word when two will do, often linking synonyms with 'and' or placing them in a genitival relationship (e.g. 1.4, 8, 11, 19). It may

---

[3] Cf Trebilco, 16–19, 172.

[4] M. B. Pedersen, 'Jode eller Hedning?—Efeserbrevets forfatter', *Dansk Teologisk Tidsskrift* 51 (1988) 277–88, is exceptional in arguing that AE was a Gentile on the grounds of the change of person in 1.11–14 (but see notes there).

be that though he thinks profoundly he is unable to express himself easily (cf Kant), or it may be that his thinking is muddled. Which of these is true? A complete answer can only be reached once his letter has been worked through but provisionally we can say that the former is more likely.

Often when his language is complex it also sounds liturgical; he may have been accustomed to lead in worship and this may have influenced his style. His style is however not that of an uneducated person. He plays on the roots underlying εὐλογέω in 1.3, χάρις in 1.6f (cf 2.4; 4.1), ἀγάπη in 2.4, καλέω in 4.1 and βαίνω in 4.9f (cf 5.2, 15f). There is alliteration through π in 1.23 (cf 3.12; 6.12d), and through η in the endings of 4.9; κ sounds throughout 4.24, as in 4.28 (note also the χ sound in this verse) and 5.23f. 5.15 contains the contrast ἄσοφοι / σοφοί. σύν is used effectively in 2.6 and 3.6; the sound οικ runs right through 2.19–22 (cf the δυ sound in 6.10f). ου and ω echo through 3.9 as do υ and α in 4.2. πᾶς and εἰς dominate 4.6 and 4.12f respectively. 2.11–22 and 5.23f have chiastic structure, as may also 1.3–3.21 (so Roberts). There is a parallelism of clauses in 1.13; 1.18; 4.22–4. To appreciate this we need to remember that AE wrote so that what he wrote would be heard rather than silently read. De Zwaan[5] finds throughout the first part of the letter a rhythmical logic in the creation of clauses similar to the style of Hebrew poetry. Some of the infelicities of AE's style may arise from his joint Jewish and Greek inheritance. Despite signs of stylistic good sense he does not seem to have taken sufficient care over some of the larger matters of composition; the parenthesis of 3.2–13 appears from nowhere as if it were a last moment decision to include it.

Most of his ethical teaching is straightforward, dealing only with simple duties (see Essay: Moral Teaching). This may have been what he saw as necessary for his readers, and it is certainly true that at no stage do believers get beyond a need to take care over the simplest of duties. Doubts arise however when we come to the HT which gives advice only to those who live in entirely Christian households (see on 5.22–6.9). There is a similar HT in Colossians (3.18–4.1) and probably both letters use a pre-existing form.[6] AE apparently did not realise the inadequacy of its advice for many of his readers. It is hard to see Paul failing in this way. Yet AE shows sensitivity at times to his Greek readers; 2.8–9 expresses in language they would appreciate the kernel of Paul's teaching on righteousness; in 4.24 he uses a Hellenistic expression rather than a Jewish to summarise good conduct.

---

[5] J. de Zwaan, 'Le "Rhythme logique" dans l'épître aux Ephésiens', *RHPR* 6 (1927) 554–65; cf Van Roon, *Authenticity*, 121ff.

[6] See Best, 'Haustafel' and, within, Detached Note: The *Haustafel*.

In his first three chapters AE sustains an argument which is clear in its main outline even if difficult in its detail. He treats problems that have not previously been adequately developed in relation to the church and provides in 2.11–22 a new argument in answer to the old problem of the relationship of Jewish and Gentile believers. It is in the paraenesis of his last three chapters that his teaching at times appears to be tired and 'off the boil'. The injunctions though simple lack penetration. The one point where his argument comes alive is his development of the first section of the HT where he includes further teaching on the church. In his discussion of the struggle of believers with the powers he develops an accepted image of the Christian's armour. In doing so he reveals an unresolved tension in his thinking between what we might describe as the 'theological' position of believers (they sit in the heavenlies, 2.6; the powers have been conquered, 1.20f) and their position 'on the ground' (they are still subject to sinful failure, 4.25ff; they still need to fight the powers, 6.10ff); this tension appears at other places, for example in his teaching on the unity of the church (see §6.4).

2.3. There is a final initial problem: if AE is not Paul, why does he write in Paul's name? Is this not dishonest? It is impossible to enter fully into this question on which much has been written.[7] Pseudonymity undoubtedly existed in the ancient world; it needs to be distinguished from: (1) anonymous authorship (it should be recognised that books which we regard as anonymous may originally have had a name attached to them which has not survived); (2) the use of a

---

[7] We can only list a little of the relevant literature: J. A. Sint, *Pseudonymität im Altertum. Ihre Formen und ihre Grunde*, Innsbruck, 1960; K. Aland, 'The Problem of Anonymity and Pseudonymity in Christian Literature of the First Two Centuries', and D. Guthrie, 'The Development of the Idea of Canonical Pseudepigrapha in New Testament Criticism', both in *The Authorship and Integrity of the New Testament* (SPCK Theological Collections 4), London, 1965; D. Guthrie, *Introduction*, 671–84; H. R. Balz, 'Anonymität und Pseudepigraphie im Urchristentum', *ZTK* 66 (1969) 403–36; W. Speyer, *Die literarische Fälschung im heidnischen und christlichen Altertum* (HAW I, 2), Munich, 1971; K. von Fritz (ed.), *Pseudepigrapha I* (Fondation Hardt, Entretiens XVIII), Geneva, 1972; M. Rist, 'Pseudepigraphy and the Early Christians', *Studies in New Testament and Early Christian Literature* (FS A. P. Wikgren, ed. D. E. Aune, SupNT 33), Leiden, 1972, 75–91; B. M. Metzger, 'Literary Forgeries and Canonical Pseudepigrapha', *JBL* 91 (1972) 3–24; W. Trilling, *Untersuchungen zum Zweiten Thessalonicherbrief*, Leipzig, 1972, 133–58; N. Brox, *Falsche Verfasserangaben. Zur Erklärung der frühchristlichen Pseudepigraphie* (SBS 79), Stuttgart 1973; K. M. Fischer, 'Anmerkungen zur Pseudepigraphie im Neuen Testament', *NTS* 23 (1976/7) 76–81; N. Brox (ed.), *Pseudepigraphie in der heidnischen und jüdisch-christlichen Antike* (Wege der Forschung CDLXXXIV), Darmstadt, 1977; J. Zmijewski 'Apostolische Paradosis und Pseudepigraphie im Neuen Testament', *BZ* 23 (1979) 161–71; F. Laub, 'Falsche Verfasserangaben im neutestamentlichen Schriften', *TTZ* 89 (1980) 228–41; A. G. Patzia, 'The Deutero-Pauline Hypothesis: An attempt at Clarification', *EvQ* 52 (1980) 27–42; D. G. Meade, *Pseudonymity and Canon. An Investigation into the Relationship of Authorship and Authority in Jewish and Earliest Christian Tradition*, Grand Rapids, 1987; R. Bauckham, 'Pseudo-Apostolic Letters', *JBL* 107 (1988) 469–94.

pen-name, i.e. the adoption by authors of names other than their own under which to write; (3) plagiarism, where authors take something written by someone else and apply their own names to it. Pseudonymous writing takes place when authors choose to write under the names of people whom their readers already know and respect, and who, normally, are dead. The term 'forgery' is to be avoided in discussing pseudonymous authorship since the word carries an emotive and negative overtone though, once a writing has been examined, it may be correct to use the term. In so far as scripture is concerned we cannot avoid discussion by asserting that its writings are canonical, therefore inspired, therefore wholly accurate in all their statements, in particular statements relating to authorship. To do so would be simply to accept one possible conclusion before examining the evidence. Though for centuries Hebrews was assumed to be by Paul, the realisation that it was not did not lessen the respect for it; what is important is its content. Were Ephesians not by Paul its content might still be true and helpful to believers.

2.3.1. It cannot be denied that pseudonymous writing existed in the ancient world: the disciples of Pythagoras wrote much which they attributed to him; plays were written in the names of the earlier great Greek dramatists; it is widely held that Plato did not pen all the letters attributed to him, though it is not agreed which are genuine. It is however unlikely that the NT writers knew of such pseudonymous writing and deliberately imitated it. It is more important to inquire if pseudonymous writing existed as a first-century phenomenon lying within the Jewish inheritance of believers.

2.3.2. It is generally accepted that many OT books were not written in their entirety by their supposed authors; Isaiah may have written part of the prophecy attributed to him but others made additions. First-century Christians were hardly aware of this. However they were familiar with later Jewish pseudonymous writings which came into being in or around their period. Among them were apocalyptic writings like the Enochic literature and 4 Ezra and some writings in the wisdom tradition; though it is not explicitly said that Solomon composed the Wisdom of Solomon this can be deduced from its contents (it is written by a king who built a temple and describes events which happened in Solomon's lifetime); also pseudonymous are the Sentences of Pseudo-Phocylides written around the turn of the era in Ionic dialect. The process of creating pseudonymous literature was thus in being among Jews at or near the time Ephesians was being written and its author was a Jew.

2.3.3. In the century after Christ Christians created pseudonymous literature. The *Kerygma Petri*, of which only fragments remain, was intended to be an account of Peter's preaching and for a time some believers accepted it. The last few verses of the *Gospel of Peter* attribute that writing to him. Col 4.16 led to the composition of a letter allegedly by Paul to Laodicea. The *Protevangelium of James* is attributed to James. The *Gospel of Thomas* may in its present form be much later than these but it has clearly evolved from an earlier form. Apart from compiling writings of their own Christians sometimes interpolated Jewish books, e.g. the *Martyrdom and Ascension of Isaiah*, and they inserted at least some clauses into the *Testimonium Flavianum* in Josephus *Ant* 18.63f. Long after the second century Christians continued producing pseudonymous literature.

2.3.4. If Christians lived in the Jewish atmosphere which produced pseudonymous literature and in the second century themselves produced that kind of literature, we have to ask whether it is impossible that they should have done so in the first century. 2 Th 2.2, whether 2 Thessalonians is by Paul or not, proves the existence of such literature in the first century. 2 Peter would be accepted by most scholars as further evidence, but we cannot use it at this stage in the discussion since those who deny that Christians wrote pseudonymously would argue it was by Peter.

2.3.5. To return to our initial question: is a pseudonymous writing by a first-century Christian to be judged as dishonest? This question may be acute since AE stresses truthfulness (4.15, 25; 6.14). The need for truthfulness is absolute but the perception of what is truth varies from age to age and from culture to culture; it is wrong then to judge the first century by our standards of truth. Leaving aside the question of authorship it can quite easily be seen that deception is accepted as a proper activity in parts of the OT e.g. Gen 20.2; 27.1ff; Josh 2.1–7; 2 Kings 10.15–27. If these seem remote from the first century we find the same approval of deception in Philo, *Qu Gen* 4.67, 206, and Origen, *c. Cels* 4.19. If then pseudonymous writing was acceptable to contemporary Jews and AE was a Jew, and if it was also acceptable to second-century Christians, are we to expect a different standard of truth from authors of the first century whose writings have been accepted into the canon? We cannot expect a standard of honesty from NT writers other than what was normal in their Jewish Christian culture. If we accept what AE wrote in respect of slavery, in particular that he did not condemn it, and do not seek to eliminate it from Ephesians because it does not meet our ideas of freedom, must we not also accept the standards of honesty in respect of authorship of his time?

If AE, or other first-century Christian pseudonymous authors, had been asked to justify what they did, they might have replied that they were doing nothing other than what their contemporaries did and that they wrote to help other believers with no personal gain for themselves. AE in particular might also have defended himself on the grounds that at times when Paul was unable to visit his churches he sent someone from the circle of his assistants to represent him; AE might even have been at one time a member of that circle and gone on missions for Paul. Moreover AE does not write with the intention to deceive, but only to instruct Christians in the new situations in which they were finding themselves in the way Paul would have done had he still been alive. That AE's teaching diverges at times from Paul's does not invalidate such a conclusion, for all the writings of the NT differ in points from one another. Had Tertullian been told that Ephesians had been written by a disciple of Paul he would have had no difficulty in accepting it, for he accepted the Gospels of Mark and Luke because they were written by the disciples, respectively, of Peter and Paul, saying that the works which disciples publish belong to their masters (*adv Marc* II 5.3–4).

It is true that by the third century various pseudonymous writings are condemned because they were not written by those whose names they bore or because they were unorthodox in theology. Yet this was some time later. The author of Jude apparently accepted *1 Enoch* as written by Enoch; later Tertullian, *de cultu fem* 1.3, accepts it, though Origen, *c. Cels* 5.54, has his doubts. If for the moment we assume that AE was not Paul, why was it that the non-Pauline authorship of Ephesians was not detected and the letter rejected as 3 Corinthians and the Epistle to Laodicea were?

Setting aside Goodspeed's suggestion that Ephesians was written to head the first collection of Pauline letters as probably untrue (see §8.3.1.), we need to remember that there was no complete, or even partial, collection of Pauline letters when Ephesians came into circulation; it was just another letter, and therefore in the fluid state of the canon before the end of the first century, could be accepted as Pauline. Its teaching was generally compatible with that of other Pauline letters and there was nothing in it about Paul which ran contrary to what was known of his career.

Up to now we have only dealt in generalities and suggested that it was possible for first-century Christians to have written pseudonymously. This does not prove that any particular book was pseudonymous. But given that possibility the NT books have to be examined individually to see whether the external and internal evidence in respect of each does, or does not, imply that it was not written by the person who is named as author. We therefore turn now to Ephesians itself and see if support within it favours Pauline authorship or that of someone else.

2.4. *External Evidence*

T. Zahn, *Geschichte des neutestamentliche Kanons*, I, Erlangen, 1888, 816ff; Westcott, xxv–xxxii; Abbott, ix–xii; *The New Testament in the Apostolic Fathers*, Oxford, 1905; Schmid, 16–36; A. E. Barnett, *The Use of the Letters of Paul in pre-Catholic Literature*, Chicago, 1932; id. *Paul*

Becomes a Literary Influence, Chicago, 1941; Mitton, *Epistle*, 160–9; Hendriksen, 54–6; Gnilka, 15–20; Van Roon, *Authenticity*, 37–44; A. Lindemann, *Paulus im ältesten Christentum* (BHT 38), Tübingen, 1979, 174–232, 263–90; Best, *ANRW* II 25.4, 3257–63.

2.4.1. The discussion of the external evidence in relation to the time when Ephesians came to be known is in effect a discussion also of the upper date for its composition.

2.4.2. The earliest known attributions of the letter to Paul come from Irenaeus (1.8.5; 5.2.3; 8.1; 14.3; 24.4) and Marcion as testified by Tertullian, *adv Marc* 5.17 (Marcion of course regarded the letter as written to Laodicea). In the third century the letter was widely used by both the orthodox and their heretical opponents and it is regularly attributed to Paul. It should not be assumed that those who used Ephesians prior to Irenaeus did not believe it was by Paul; it was not customary in Christian literature of the period to identify sources. In the beginning Ephesians was a part of the developing tradition and set alongside surviving oral tradition.

2.4.3. Use of the letter can be traced back into the period prior to Irenaeus and Marcion, though not its attribution to Paul. Care is necessary here since a similarity between Ephesians and another writing may have come about because both writings are independently indebted to oral, credal, catechetical or liturgical tradition, or even other written material. It is also not sufficient to show in respect of a phrase from Ephesians that there are parallels to it; it needs also to be shown that other parallels to the phrase in a wider literature are rare. The computer now gives us a much greater knowledge of ancient literature. An example will illustrate what is meant. Mitton, *Epistle*, 201, in discussing the relation of Eph 4.24 and Lk 1.75, both of which combine δικαιοσύνη and ὁσιότης, says 'there is no evidence that this association was in any way customary'. However we now know that the two nouns occur in combination in Philo alone nine times and their cognate adjectives seven times; in all Greek literature there are over a hundred occurrences. We must then be cautious in assuming dependence when we encounter the same phrase in two different documents. Barnett's criteria leave him much too willing to accept the slightest resemblance in a later writing as indicating the influence of Ephesians. The Oxford study, *The New Testament in the Apostolic Fathers*, is stricter. Perhaps the most satisfactory set of criteria are those of Lindemann, *Paulus*, 17–19.

It is unnecessary to examine literature later than the Apostolic Fathers since if knowledge of Ephesians is found in them we can assume it existed prior to them and therefore to any later literature. Naturally during the study (speculation?) over almost two centuries a great many possible instances of the dependence of the Apostolic Fathers on Ephesians have been pointed out; closer examination has led to the rejection of most suggestions; we shall therefore only examine those supported by a reasonable number of modern scholars.

2.4.3.1. 1 Clement[8]

1 Clem 46.6 has been held to depend on Eph 4.4–6 but since there are verbal differences and AE employs traditional material in 4.4–6 (here and elsewhere for statements about passages in Ephesians see notes on the relevant passages) it is impossible to prove dependence. The same is true of 1 Clem 64.1 and Eph 1.3f where both use liturgical language. The phrase about the eyes of the heart in 1 Clem 36.2; 59.3 and 1.18 is found widely in contemporary and earlier literature and therefore again dependence cannot be proved. Similarly the references to light and darkness in both 1 Clem 59.3; 36.2 and Eph 1.18; 4.18 may be due to the influence of the Qumranic and apocalyptic writings. In 1 Clem 46.7 and Eph 4.25 the reference to members one of another could be independent; Clement may have drawn directly on the fable of Menenius Agrippa which would have been current in Rome from where he wrote. Subjection to others (1 Clem 38.1 and Eph 5.21) is a common Christian theme (see on Eph 5.21). There is then here nothing which compels the conclusion that Clement knew Ephesians.

2.4.3.2. Ignatius[9]

Eph 12.2 is a typical epistolary exaggeration ('Paul mentions you in all his letters') and is not to be translated as to suggest that Paul wrote about them all through his Ephesian letter (see Abbott, ix–x; Schmid, 28f). Ign *Eph* 9.1 resembles Eph 2.20–2 in using building imagery but that imagery was in wide use and there are no striking verbal similarities; indeed the resemblance to 1 Cor 3.9 is just as strong. *Eph* 4.2; *Trall* 11.2 both describe Christians as members of Christ but this could have been derived as easily from 1 Cor 6.15 and Rom 12.4f as from Eph 5.20. So far as Ign *Eph* 1.1 and Eph 5.1 go imitation was a widespread topos in the ancient world. Ign *Eph* 20.1 uses the phrase 'new person' and equates that person with Christ but this is not the usage in either Eph 2.15 or 4.24; Ignatius rather reflects the idea of Christ as the Second Adam. A number of similarities have been discerned between Ignatius' *Ephesians* and the eulogy of Eph 1.3–14 and it has been argued that Ignatius knew canonical Ephesians and drew on it to impress the Ephesians; this implies that Ignatius possessed a copy of canonical Ephesians in which Ephesus appeared in 1.1 and there is no certainty that any copy did so at this stage. The similarities, if they exist, are in highly liturgical language and do not necessarily imply Ignatius' knowledge of canonical Ephesians.[10] Ign *Polyc* 6.2 avers that believers should love their wives as the Lord loves the church and thus seems to depend on Eph 5.25 but there is no development of the marital metaphor as in Ephesians and a different word σύμβιος is used for 'wife'. Ign *Polyc* speaks of the Christian's armour as does Eph 6.14–17 except that the pieces of armour are not all the same and are not spiritualised in the same way (see also 1 Th 5.8). There are no other likely parallels but these taken together

---

[8] Cf D. A. Hagner, *The Use of the Old and New Testaments in Clement of Rome* (SupNT 34), Leiden, 1973; A. Lindemann, *Die Clemensbriefe* (HNT 17), Tübingen, 1992, and *Paulus*, 177–99.

[9] Cf Lindemann, *Paulus*, 199ff.

[10] See further, Best, *ANRW* II 25.4, 3259f.

create a fair possibility that Ignatius knew our Ephesians. If so, this brings extant evidence for its existence down to about AD 110.

2.4.3.3. Polycarp

One or two passages make possible Polycarp's knowledge of Ephesians. *Phil* 1.3 may recall Eph 2.5, 8, 9 (see on 2.9). Both however may have been using tradition; Polycarp's εἰδότες ὅτι suggests this was so in his case. His οὐκ ἐξ ἔργων may come from Eph 2.9, though for anyone who knew Paul's thought in a general kind of way it was a natural addition; Polycarp moreover fails to make use of other material in Eph 2.8–10 which would have been relevant to his purpose. More probably in his 12.1 Polycarp depends on Eph 4.26.[11] Both quote Ps 4.5 and add a reference to not permitting the sun to go down on anger although there is no necessary connection between this and the main exhortation. Harrison has argued that Polycarp's letter is a combination of two letters[12] and this enables him to place this possible quotation in the later letter which he dates around AD 133; this cannot be finally proved; yet there seems little doubt that Polycarp knew our Ephesians; this brings knowledge of it no earlier than the letters of Ignatius for 9.1 implies that Ignatius has already been martyred.

2.4.3.4. 2 Clement

2 Clem 14.2 refers to the church as the body of Christ and to Christ as the male and the church as the female (cf Eph 5.22ff). The words, ἄρσην, θῆλυς, for male and female are not the same as those of Eph 5.22 and there is no reference to a marital relationship. There is then no dependence here and none also of 2 Clem 19.2 on Eph 4.18, for the darkening of the understanding is a general idea and there is insufficient verbal similarity to suggest direct dependence.

2.4.3.5. *Did* 4.10f and *Barn* 19.7 refer to the attitudes of masters and slaves to one another but need not depend on Eph 6.5–9 since the *Haustafel* was well known in early Christianity and the master–slave relationship was one needing instruction. *Barn* 16.8–10 likens the church to a temple and so might depend on Eph 2.19–22 but the image is widely used and there are no real verbal similarities; κατοικητήριον though rare in the NT is frequent in the LXX. The mystic indwelling of Christ is a frequent NT conception.

2.4.3.6. Hermas, *Mand* 3.1–4, contains a set of ethical instructions some of which border on those in the collection of Eph 4.25–30, yet both are miscellaneous collections and an overlap is not surprising. *Mand* 10.2.1–6 in referring to the Holy Spirit offers no real parallel to Eph 4.30. *Sim* 9.13.5 and 9.18.4 refer to one Spirit and one body but the possible parallel in Eph 4.4–6 is traditional material and so no dependence can be proved.

2.4.3.7. The Nag Hammadi documents offer no clear occasions of dependence except in relation to 6.12: *Hyp Arch* II, 4 86.20–27; *Exeg Soul* II, 6 131.9–13; *Teach Silv* VII, 4 117.14f; *Testim Truth* IX, 3 32.28. *Gos Phil* II, 3 76.11 and *Treat Seth* VII, 2 59.4 could be vague reminiscences of 1.21 and 4.24 respectively. None of these writings can be dated earlier than the

---

[11] Cf C. M. Nielson, 'Polycarp, Paul and the Scriptures', *ATR* 47 (1965) 199–216.
[12] See P. N. Harrison, *Polycarp's Two Epistles to the Philippians*, Cambridge, 1936, 16, 268.

latter half of the second century and so bring us no earlier than the information already obtained in the Apostolic Fathers.

2.4.4. This examination of the Apostolic Fathers shows there is a fair possibility that either Ignatius or Polycarp or both knew Ephesians; it may then have been known by AD 110 and therefore must have been written some time prior to that. This would suggest a date prior to AD 90.

2.4.5. When we turn to the writings of the NT we enter a more difficult area, for a similarity between Ephesians and another writing could be explained by assuming that Ephesians used the other writing. Naturally those NT writings which were written prior to Ephesians, like the earlier letters of Paul, can be ignored. Moreover no one appears ever to have suggested a dependence either way between Ephesians and the Synoptic Gospels and so they need not be considered.

2.4.5.1. Since Revelation comes from the same area, Asia Minor, as Ephesians, it represents a writing in which we might expect to find parallels with Ephesians.[13] While there are similarities in the use of concepts, for example between Rev 3.21 and Eph 2.6, Rev 7.2–3 and Eph 4.30; 1.13 (use of σφραγίζω), verbal similarities are few. It is more likely that Rev 18.4 and Eph 5.11 both draw on Phil 4.14 than either on the other. The concluding greetings (Rev 22.21; Eph 6.23f) are similar but then they are similar to those in most NT letters. Both Revelation and Ephesians use marital imagery but Revelation uses it eschatologically and is thus nearer to 2 Cor 11.2 than to Ephesians. Thus similar concepts are to be found but no verbal similarities and therefore no dependence of Revelation on Ephesians, or vice versa (cf Gnilka, 19).

2.4.5.2. At first sight there appear to be a considerable number of parallels between the Pastorals and Ephesians, yet none is close. Mitton, *Epistle*, 173–5 (cf Hendriksen, 35–8) reduces considerably the lists given by earlier scholars but even those he retains do not stand up to examination. Both 2 Tim 2.15 and Eph 1.13 use the phrase 'the word of truth' but Mitton fails to show that it is not a phrase found elsewhere; it is brief; its two nouns were in regular Christian usage; the parallel could have arisen by chance or both authors used a familiar phrase (see notes on 1.13). Both 1 Tim 1.15 and Eph 3.8 depict Paul as a sinner but not in identical words; 1 Cor 15.8f is likely to have been the source of both. That Tit 2.5 and Eph 5.22–4 both refer to the obedience of wives merely reflects the contemporary patriarchal culture. The Pastorals and Ephesians then share a number of common ideas but there is no real evidence to suggest dependence either way.

2.4.5.3. Similarities exist between Ephesians and Luke-Acts;[14] both use ten words not otherwise found in the NT. As already noted, the combination of ὁσιότης and δικαιοσύνη (Lk 1.75; Eph 4.24) was common in Greek

---

[13] See Mitton, *Epistle*, 170–3.

[14] See Mitton, *Epistle*, 198–200; R. P. Martin, 'An Epistle in Search of a Life-Setting', *ExpT* 79 (1967/8) 296–302; Martin believes Luke was the author of Ephesians.

literature and cannot therefore suggest indebtedness on either side. Both refer to the ascension (Acts 1.9; Lk 24.51; Eph 1.20; 4.8–10) but there are many references to it in the NT and Luke describes the event whereas AE does not. Both contrast drunkenness and inspiration through the Spirit (Acts 2.15; Eph 5.18) but charismatic inspiration has regularly had to defend itself against the charge of drunkenness. Perhaps the major argument for the linking of the writings is the reappearance in Ephesians of terms found in Paul's address to the Ephesian elders (Acts 20.18–35), but these, scattered throughout Ephesians, provide no evidence to support a literary relationship.[15]

2.4.5.4. There are similarities of thought but not wording between Ephesians and the Johannine literature (Moffatt, 384f; Abbott, xxviii; Schmid, 370f; Murray, lxxxviii–xci; Kirby, 166–8): the eschatology is more realised than in the Synoptic Gospels and Paul, the unity of the church is stressed in a more abstract way than in Paul, the duty of love towards others is restricted to love to other church members, light and darkness are contrasted, the relation of Jews and Gentiles comes in for consideration. Lack of verbal similarity compels the rejection of literary dependence.

2.4.5.5. Conceptual but not verbal similarities are also found in Ephesians and Hebrews. After an exhaustive examination Vanhoye sees no literary dependence on either side but suggests they date from about the same period and were written for Christians of the same area.[16]

2.4.5.6. Outside the Pauline corpus the NT writing which has been viewed as closest to Ephesians is 1 Peter.[17] Moffatt has been one of the few to regard 1 Peter as a source for Ephesians; if so 1 Peter would provide no evidence for the existence of Ephesians. An examination of the HT in Ephesians leads clearly to the rejection of such a view; it is extremely unlikely that anyone taking over the form in 1 Pet 2.13–3.7 would eliminate its realism in which slaves have cruel masters and wives domineering husbands; the opposite process is however just conceivable (but see Best, 'Haustafel'), though there are extensive differences. The Petrine HT has a section on the attitude of believers towards the state, lacks the section treating parents and children and uses different words to describe masters (δεσπότης for κύριος) and slaves (οἰκέται for δοῦλοι). It is generally acknowledged that Ephesians and Colossians resemble one another; yet where Ephesians parallels 1 Peter it normally also parallels Colossians; this makes it difficult to identify 1 Peter as a

---

[15] E. Käsemann, 'Ephesians and Acts', *Studies in Luke–Acts* (FS P. Schubert, ed. L. E. Keck and J. L. Martyn), London, 1968, 288–97, does not deal with the literary relationship of Acts and Ephesians but with certain similarities in their theological approaches.

[16] A. Vanhoye, 'L'épître aux Éphésiens et l'épître aux Hébreux', *Bib* 59 (1978) 198–230; cf Penna, 41f.

[17] See Abbott, xxiv–xxvii; Moffatt, 337f, 381–3; Goguel, 447–50; Schmid 339–61; Mitton, *Epistle*, 176–97; id. 'The Relationship between 1 Peter and Ephesians', *JTS* 1 (1950) 67–73; Selwyn, *1 Peter*, 385–462; Percy, 436–40.

source for Ephesians. Do then the similarities between Ephesians and 1 Peter indicate the latter as knowing the former? (i) Both begin with an eulogy, but so also does 2 Cor 1.3; the form was almost certainly in use in early Christian worship. (ii) Both 1 Pet 1.10–12 and Eph 3.2–6 speak of revelation and prophets, but in 1 Peter the prophets are those of the OT and in Ephesians those of the early church. (iii) 1 Pet 2.2–6 and Eph 2.19–22 share: (a) the idea of the Christian community as a building, but the imagery appears in Jewish and early Christian thought (see on 2.19–22), (b) the concept of access to God, but this was also a common Christian idea, (c) Christ as the 'angle-stone', but they probably use the term in different ways and derive it independently from Isa 28.16. (iv) 1 Pet 3.22 and Eph 1.20f employ the same theological ideas, but the former is probably using a traditional hymn and the latter depends on a different tradition. (v) Both 1 Pet 2.1 and Eph 4.25 use ἀποτίθημι in relation to ethical behaviour, but the verb is regularly used in that way. (vi) Both 1 Pet 3.19f and Eph 4.8–10 refer to a descent of Christ; in 1 Pet 3.19f it is into Hades but in Eph 4.8–10 it is to earth. (vii) They have a number of similar words and phrases, e.g. πρὸ καταβολῆς κόσμου (1 Pet 1.20; Eph 1.4), but these similarities are by no means frequent and there are also instances where the same words are used with different meanings, e.g. πάροικοι (1 Pet 2.11; Eph 2.19). All in all it is therefore unlikely that 1 Peter knew and used Ephesians. How then do we account for the similarities between them? Since Selwyn's work (*1 Peter*, 385–462) most commentators[18] now accept the existence of much common thinking among the first Christians and therefore see no necessary dependence of 1 Peter on Ephesians.

2.4.6. Nothing in this examination of the NT material necessitates the lowering of the estimate previously reached as to the upper limit of around AD 90 for the writing of Ephesians. The lower limit would be of course Paul's lifetime and presumably fairly late within it, i.e. around AD 60 (see §5).

Is there anything within the content of the letter or the situation of its intended readers which would enable us to date it more precisely within the period AD 60–90? Those who argue that the middle wall of partition (2.14) refers to a balustrade in the Jerusalem temple have used this both to argue for a date prior to the fall of the city and a date after it; if however the middle wall is a metaphorical wall (see on 2.14) such arguments are irrelevant. Indeed so little is known about the situation to which the letter is directed that nothing can be learnt from it about its possible date. As for the content, the apostles and prophets (2.20; 3.5) appear to be a defined and recognisable

---

[18] See the commentaries on 1 Peter of Goppelt (KEK), 49; Schelkle (HTK) 7; Knoch (RNT) 16–18; Spicq (Sources Bibliques) 15f; cf Percy, 440.

group belonging to the past, and already in a position of reverence so that they can be termed 'holy' (3.5); this, if true, would imply that the Twelve and Paul were dead. Although AE begins in 4.7 by implying that every believer has a charismatic gift, when he comes to details he lists only those who could be described as holding official positions within the church (4.11), as if the ministry was now becoming a more fixed element in the church than in Paul's lifetime. AE uses tradition freely, e.g. the HT, 4.4–6; 5.2, 25; 2.5 (see §9.2); tradition takes some time to be formulated and its use would fit better with a date later rather than earlier in the possible period. The imminence of the parousia has disappeared; it is difficult to assess the significance of this since belief in its imminence continually reappears and Paul in Phil 1.21–5 may be said to be less certain of a speedy return of Christ than in his earlier letters. The balance of this information favours a date late in the possible period (AD 60–90) but there is much else to be considered.

Naturally if the letter was written by Paul then it was written while he was in prison; we know of three possible places of imprisonment where he might have had time to write and therefore three possible times; the places are Caesarea, Ephesus and Rome (see §5.4); of these the last is the most likely and would imply that the letter was written late in Paul's lifetime.

2.5. *Ephesians and Colossians*[19]
2.5.1. The close similarity between Colossians and Ephesians has long been recognised and explained in various ways but mainly through the theory that AE knew and used Colossians. H. J. Holtzmann, *Kritik der Epheser- und Kolosserbriefe* (Leipzig, 1872), was the first to explore the problem in depth.[20] Today most commentators simply assume after a brief examination of the evidence that Colossians was written prior to Ephesians and the latter composed in its light. There have been occasional attempts to reverse the order and argue the priority of Ephesians but none has gained widespread acceptance. The priority of Colossians is then the accepted position for commentators who reject the Pauline authorship of Ephesians; when they come to passages where the letters appear similar they do not stop to argue grounds for Colossian priority but simply explain how and why AE modified Colossians in using it. The possibility that A/Col used Ephesians is not even considered. The problem of priority is of course settled quite simply for those who with Marcion assume that Ephesians is the letter to Laodicea referred to in Col 4.16; such a letter, if it ever existed,

---

[19] See Mitton, *Epistle, passim*; Schmid, 384–455; Goodspeed, 79–165; Ochel, *passim*; Percy, 362–419; Van Roon, *Authenticity*, 413–37; J. B. Polhill, art.cit.
[20] For a brief history of attempted solutions to the problem see Best, 'Who Used Whom?'

must have pre-existed Colossians since it is referred to in that letter.

2.5.2. There are three possible solutions to the literary relationship of the two letters:

(i) The author of Ephesians used Colossians.

(ii) The author of Colossians used Ephesians.

(iii) Neither author used the other's letter.

These possibilities do not exclude Pauline authorship.

2.5.3 The concept of 'use' requires examination. Did AE (A/Col) have a copy of Colossians (Ephesians) in front of him as he wrote, or, having once read and studied it, did he carry its wording in his mind?

2.5.3.1. Some care also needs to be exercised in respect of the extent of influence. If one letter has incorporated a piece of tradition and there is a parallel to it in the other, has the author of the second been influenced directly by the tradition or by the letter containing it? If Ephesians shows similarities to Col 1.15–20, has this come about because he knew the traditional hymn behind Col 1.15–20 and used it, and not because he was using Colossians?[21]

2.5.3.2. When also we examine parallels between the letters and attempt to deduce influence we need to take care that we are not dealing with phrases and ideas common to all early Christianity, e.g. 'The God and Father of our Lord Jesus Christ' belonged to the liturgy of the early church and so cannot be used to prove the influence of either Eph 1.17 or Col 1.3 on the other.

2.5.3.3. Mitton, *Epistle*, continually points to places where he holds that AE in using Colossians has conflated two Colossian passages which are not close together in Colossians, e.g. in 1.7 AE is supposed to have conflated Col 1.14 and Col 1.20. Similar cases of conflation however can be pointed to on the part of A/Col if he used Ephesians. But this is not the way authors use documents. Normally when one author draws on a document it is to borrow its ideas. Authors normally do not search the documents of other writers to find suitable words with which to express their own ideas. They may however remember phrases and words in the other document and use them again combining them in new ways. The random nature of the way AE is supposed to have drawn on references from Colossians, and vice versa, suggests neither had a copy of the other's writing in front of him as he wrote but may have had its words in his mind.

---

[21] On the manner in which in the ancient world authors used written material see F. G. Downing, 'Redaction Criticism: Josephus' *Antiquities* and the Synoptic Gospels', *JSNT* 8 (1980) 29–48; id. 'Compositional Conventions and the Synoptic Problem', *JBL* 107 (1988) 69–85; S. L. Mattila, 'A Question Too Often Neglected', *NTS* 41 (1995) 199–217.

2.5.4. But is the view that AE had Colossians in mind as he wrote or that A/Col had Ephesians in mind not contradicted by the great verbal similarity of Eph 6.21f and Col 4.7f? These passages form a major factor in any resolution of the problem of dependence. It is sufficient now to point out that a good case can be made for the priority of either passage and its use by the author of the other (see notes on 6.21f; see also these notes for possible ways of dealing with their great verbal similarity).

2.5.5. It would appear proper now to examine all the possible parallels between Ephesians and Colossians and ask which seem to underlie the other. The passages are however best considered in their context; we therefore indicate here the relevant passages; the discussion will be found in the notes. The passages are mainly those identified by Mitton by his double underlining in his setting out of the text (*Epistle*, 279ff). They are 1.1f; 1.4; 1.7; 1.8b, 9a; 1.10; 1.15–17; 1.18; 1.20; 1.21; 1.22f; 2.1f, 5; 2.15b; 2.16; 2.20; 3.2–5; 3.6f; 3.1–13 (at 3.13); 3.15; 3.16; 3.17; 4.2; 4.14; 4.16; 4.18; 4.22–4; 4.31f; 5.5; 5.19f; 5.22–6.9 (see in particular on 6.1 and 6.5–9); 6.18; 6.21f; 6.23f.[22] Some readers may think the discussion stresses too much the dependence of A/Col on Ephesians and that a neutral picture has not been offered; yet so many commentaries and introductions ignore the possibility of the dependence of Colossians on Ephesians that those who have been brought up in this tradition, as the present writer was, tend to give too high a value to the passages indicating dependence on the part of Ephesians.

2.5.6. Drawing together now the results of the examination of the above list of passages, we see that in some the relationship is most easily explained on the assumption that AE knew Colossians and in others on the assumption that A/Col knew Ephesians; there are also a considerable number of passages about whose dependence it is impossible to make any definite judgement. How are these seemingly contradictory findings to be reconciled? It should be noted that the number of passages where there appears to be similarity is much less than is normally thought once the passages where both letters may depend on tradition have been excluded. There are also passages which look alike in translation but are much less alike in Greek because in the Greek synonyms have been used which are translated into English with the same English word. The Greek words for vigilance are different in the apparently similar passages of Col 4.2 and Eph 6.18, for the provocation of children in Col 3.21 and Eph 6.4, for revelation in Col 1.26 and Eph 3.5; why should one author if dependent on the other have made these arbitrary substitutions? Finally there are the two passages Col 4.8f; Eph 6.21f where

---

[22] The passages have been gathered together and discussed in greater detail in Best, 'Who Used Whom?'

the verbal similarities are so great that the only explanation seems to be the use of one document by the author of the other (see notes on 6.21f for discussion).

2.5.7. As well as passages with verbal similarities there are those containing similar ideas but lacking verbal resemblance (see above on synonyms used to express the same idea). In the absence of verbal similarity it is exceedingly difficult to prove that either author is dependent on the thought of the other since many common beliefs were shared in the early church. Yet it is perhaps right to note dissimilarities in thought. If AE used Colossians he will have read in Col 3.11 that in Christ all differences are abolished, and not only those between Jew and Gentile; why then does he limit himself to the reconciliation of the Jewish–Gentile division in humanity and not refer to the abolition of the slave–free distinction as in Col 3.11? This is significant since he discusses the relation of slaves and masters and in a sense treats them as equals in that both can respond to his teaching. A main theme in Colossians is the defence of the community against heresy; the communities to which AE writes may have faced different heresies from the Colossian community but AE is not unaware of disturbing trends in his communities (4.14); why then since he does refer to Christ as head does he not adopt the safeguard suggested in Colossians against heresy, holding on to Christ the head (2.19)? Equally if A/Col knew Ephesians why is his teaching on husband–wife relations so brief and why does he not sustain his exhortation about the need for obedience from children with the commandment from the Decalogue which is used in Ephesians?

2.5.8. Apart from Eph 6.21f and Col 4.7f there is nothing to suggest that either author had the document of the other before him as he wrote. If he did, did he have before him the original letter or a copy? If the former the two letters must have been despatched at the same time. If the latter it is necessary to ask if copies of letters were retained in those days. These two passages aside, any use throughout the remainder of the two letters by one author of the other appears to be a general use; each author has a good knowledge of what the other has written, carries it in his mind and expresses his own ideas through the words of the other. But since the evidence suggests that it is sometimes AE who has Colossians in mind and sometimes A/Col who has Ephesians in mind, the simple theory that one letter was known by the author of the other fails to account for the facts.

2.5.8.1. It should be noted that these facts do not fit easily with the view that Paul was the author of the letter which depended on the other of which he was not the author, for it is unlikely that he would have been influenced so extensively by a letter he had not written. On the other hand these facts do not conflict with the theory that he wrote both for he could easily have used the same words in the two letters. This would be equally true if the letters had a common author who was not Paul. If there was a common author, whether Paul or another, then their similarities suggest that they were written at almost the same time.[23] Yet their dissimilarities in the use of terms (see below) would suggest that some time had passed during which the common author had gained new insights and used his words in new ways. The facts also do not foreclose the possibility of different authors. Further light will be thrown on the problem of authorship when we investigate whether the letters are sufficiently similar in their thought, vocabulary and style to Paul's thought, vocabulary and style for him to have written them, and, a more difficult question, whether they are similar enough in thought, vocabulary and style to one another for both to have been written by the same author, a person other than Paul.

   2.5.8.2. If the same author wrote both letters it is possible to see him rewriting Eph 6.21f or Col 4.7f to fit into his second letter. If he dictated to a secretary he might well have instructed the secretary, 'conclude this letter as you did the other'. But it is not quite as simple as that. Supposing Ephesians was the earlier letter, it concludes with Eph 6.21–4, but Col 4.7f does not conclude Colossians; there follows a series of personal greetings. So the instruction would have been complex. If Colossians had been the earlier letter then the secretary would have to have been told, 'Repeat what I said about Tychicus as messenger in my letter to Colossae but modify the reference to him and, since this is a general letter, leave out the personal greetings and the reference to Onesimus'. Yet the additions and variations between the two passages still remain a problem. Would the secretary have altered these on his own? Would he not have required detailed instructions on how to modify the one he had already written? This suggests that it is easier to assume that there was no secretary. A common author, however, could have carried in his mind what he wrote in one letter and used it in the other, provided the letters were written in quick succession. If this is so, it is more likely that Ephesians was written first and that when the author came to write Colossians he clarified the clumsy nature of Eph 6.21 and increased the praise reference to Tychicus. It should be noted that the supposition of the use of secretaries in relation to authorship is always difficult (on the use of secretaries see §2.7.6).

   2.5.8.3. There are other possibilities. Van Roon, *Authenticity* 426ff, argues that Paul wrote an original draft letter which was later worked over by secretaries who produced our Ephesians and

---

[23] We must reject the suggestion of M. Kiley, *Colossians as Pseudepigraphy*, Sheffield, 1986, 41, that Ephesians shows greater divergence from the normal pattern of the Pauline letter and therefore must be later than Colossians; the divergence arises simply because Ephesians is a general letter.

Colossians; these secretaries also used additional material belonging to the Pauline circle, a circle consisting of Paul, Timothy, and the two secretaries; it was not then a post-Pauline circle. This solution certainly accounts for the similarity of Eph 6.21f and Col 4.7f but seems to leave a lot of other matters unexplained. Klijn,[24] who accepts that when we look at parallel passages we cannot argue that the dependence is all on one side, offers a similar solution in supposing the existence of a third document on which both A/Col and AE depended. The supposition of unknown documents however is always hazardous.

2.5.9. This section of our investigation thus leaves us with the three possible solutions with which we began (§2.5.3); other areas must be examined before it is possible to decide between them. However, it removes one main argument from those who believe the non-Pauline authorship of Ephesians can be firmly asserted on the basis of the use of Colossians by Ephesians. If the author is not Paul, it is almost impossible to identify him. Goodspeed suggested Onesimus; Mitton, Tychicus, *Epistle* 27, 268; R. P. Martin (in various writings) Luke (but according to D. J. Rowston, 'Changes in Biblical Interpretation: the Example of Ephesians', *BTB* 9 (1979) 121–5, this was suggested earlier by P. Jones); R. Scott, 23f, Silas.

2.6. *Ephesians and the remaining Paulines (apart from Colossians)*[25]
Did AE know or use any of the other and earlier Pauline letters? A mere glance at them shows that the parallels between them and Ephesians are much less frequent and definite than those between Ephesians and Colossians. Our question naturally does not arise if AE was Paul; the fewer parallels would then be explained by the longer time interval between the writing of Ephesians and the earlier letters than that between Ephesians and Colossians. If AE was not Paul what signs are there of Pauline influence on him? Assuming Paul is dead, and this is a reasonable assumption to make if AE is not Paul, then any influence of Paul on him must have come through oral memory of Paul, or actual knowledge gained from some of his letters.

It is fairly easy to see that AE is aware of and accepts major Pauline ideas not found in Colossians nor common in the non-Pauline parts of the NT; 2.8–10 reveals a knowledge of Paul's teachings on salvation by faith and not works; 4.17–19 reflects Paul's view of the unredeemed Gentile world as seen in Rom 1.21–4. The question of AE's knowledge of particular Pauline letters as distinct from his general knowledge of Pauline ideas is

---

[24] A. J. F. Klijn, *An Introduction to the New Testament*, Leiden, 1967, 102.
[25] Cf Mitton, *Epistle*, 98–158. Goodspeed, *Meaning*, 77ff.

however much more difficult to resolve. Here verbal similarities are important. However, it is not necessary to ask on which side dependence lies since Ephesians is later than the main Paulines; Rom 16.25-7 may be a possible exception as a non-Pauline addition to Paul's Romans. As in the discussion of Ephesians and Colossians, some similarities can be safely ignored; the Pauline epistolary formulae vary among themselves and AE's use of a similar formula does not prove dependence on any particular Pauline letter. The same is true in respect of liturgical forms (e.g. doxologies, 6.24 and 3.20f, Berakoth, 1.3ff; see notes on the passages). The mode of transition from the theological argument to the paraenesis (4.1) is also Pauline, though not framed in precisely the same way as in any Pauline letter. Credal formulae may also predate Paul though appearing in his letters (5.2, 25 and Gal 2.20; possibly 2.5); their appearance in Ephesians does not then prove dependence. 4.4–6 includes sections of tradition, if it is not itself a creed. The one passage in this area which may reveal knowledge of an actual letter is 1.15–17 which has strong verbal similarities with Philem 4–6; it would not be surprising if AE had known this letter in view of his association with A/Col who almost certainly did know it.

In some places the similarity of language may be purely coincidental because the words are normal (in each case see the notes on the relevant passages), e.g. 'I, Paul' (3.1 and 2 Cor 10.1; Gal 5.2), οἱ λοιποί (2.3 and 1 Th 4.13), or where the same words appear with a completely different reference ('every name' 1.21 and Phil 2.9, 'not having hope' 2.12 and 1 Th 4.13). Quite a number of other cases of verbal similarity must be excluded because, though the Ephesian phrases correspond to those in the Paulines, they are known and used more widely (e.g. 6.5, 'fear and trembling', 5.17, 'the will of the Lord/God') or are so widespread in Paul that AE cannot be tied down in using them to a particular letter (5.1, the idea of imitation, 6.6, 'slaves of Christ', 'the powers'). Some phrases may have been derived directly from the OT rather than indirectly through Paul (e.g. 5.2, the fragrant offering, 5.31 and the use of Gen 2.24). There are also similarities which can be disregarded because they derive from Jewish or Hellenistic culture (5.23, husband as head of, or superior to wife). Common Greek words used in their normal Greek manner can also be ignored: in 2.3 ἀναστρέφω is not dependent on 2 Cor 1.12, nor are παρρησία and its cognate verb (3.12; 6.19f) dependent on 1 Th 2.2.

2.6.1. More positively there seems no reason to deny AE knew: (a) Romans: the words Paul uses to describe the pagan world in Rom 1.21, 24 and the thought are very similar to Eph 4.17–19; the teaching on faith and works in 2.8–10, while it could derive from Galatians, lies in language closer to Romans, and it is difficult to find other places where there may be indebtedness to Galatians; the teaching on the members and body of Christ is close to that of Romans; Luz[26] lists a number of places where AE may depend on Romans 12. (b) 1 Corinthians: the teaching in Ephesians about the body and its members (4.11; 5.30) reflects even more closely what we find in 1 Corinthians (12.12, 28) than Romans; the concept of the church as a building, and in particular as a holy temple (2.20–2), is close to 1 Cor 3.9–17; the use of the metaphor of building to indicate spiritual growth in 4.12, 16 is similar to its use in 1 Cor 14.3, 5, 12, 26; the origin of the vice list reflected in Eph 5.3, 5 may lie in 1 Cor 5.11; 6.9; underlying both 1 Cor 15.27 and Eph 1.22 is the same non-septuagintal form of Ps 8.6 and the idea of the subjection of the powers; yet Eph 2.6 clashes with 1 Cor 4.8 suggesting that if AE had read 1 Corinthians he had not fully understood it. (c) 2 Corinthians: the close association of sealing and ἀρραβών in 2 Cor 1.22 and Eph 1.13f does not appear to be a matter of chance; granted contact here, it is possible to see other points of possible contact (e.g. Eph 6.20 and 2 Cor 5.20) yet none is as close; it is interesting to note that all the more likely passages in 2 Corinthians which may have affected Ephesians come from its first nine chapters; AE may not have possessed the letter in the form we have it. (d) Philemon: the language of vv. 4–6 is close enough to that of Eph 1.15–17 to suggest influence, but Philemon is so short that it is difficult to draw any certain conclusion. (e) In respect of Galatians, Philippians, 1, 2 Thessalonians it is impossible to trace clear dependence of Ephesians on them; the equipment of the soldier is different in Eph 6.14–17 and 1 Th 4.8; to walk worthily (Eph 4.1; 1 Th 2.12) is a natural combination of ideas; Eph 3.8 may resemble Gal 1.15f, but for any Pauline disciple Paul's preaching to the Gentiles was a significant part of his life; Gal 2.9 is similar to Eph 3.2 but 1 Cor 3.10 might equally have been the influence.

It is then reasonably certain that AE knew Romans and 1 Corinthians, that he probably knew Philemon and some parts of 2 Corinthians, but we cannot be sure that he knew Galatians, Philippians, 1, 2 Thessalonians. In each case his knowledge is much less detailed than his knowledge of the content of Colossians. Ephesians, though, is brief and AE may not have revealed all his knowledge of Paul's letters within it. There is however enough to conclude that AE stood in the Pauline tradition. It is important also to remember that while he knew Paul's teaching he adapted and developed it.

2.7. *Vocabulary, Syntax and Style*
Moffatt, 385–9; Schmid, 131ff; Percy, 179–252; Merklein, 19–25; Moulton–Turner, 84f; Van Roon, *Authenticity*, 100ff.

Already long before the rise of the historical–critical method, Erasmus in the brief introductory sentences to his commentary remarked on the difference in style between Ephesians and the other Paulines; it is not then surprising that attention is now regularly given to this feature. Though language and style are at times difficult to disentangle we commence by looking at features which relate primarily to language. We exclude comparison with Colossians and

---

[26] U. Luz, 'Rechtfertigung bei den Paulusschülern', *Rechtfertigung* (FS E. Käsemann, ed. J. Friedrich, W. Pohlmann, P. Stuhlmacher), Tübingen, 1976, 365–83.

the Pastorals. Interestingly Ephesians and Colossians share some twenty-one words not in the remainder of the NT (cf Van Roon, *Authenticity*, 173 n. 1); this is an unusually high proportion and confirms their close association. Similarly they lack a number of words which are frequent in the other Paulines.[27]

2.7.1. *Hapax legomena* are often counted as a help in determining authorship; they are in fact rarely a good guide since subject-matter affects the choice of words. Thus a considerable number of the *hapax legomena* in Ephesians are found in 6.14–17, a passage relating to military equipment, a subject to which Paul does not refer elsewhere in such detail. In fact the number of *hapax legomena* in Ephesians is not exceptional and therefore tells us nothing in respect of its authorship 'in relation to Paul. The presence of words shared with Paul is to be expected on the supposition of either Pauline authorship or AE's membership of a Pauline school.

2.7.2. The existence of different authors is sometimes betrayed through their use of synonyms. Paul uses σατανᾶς but διάβολος is found in Ephesians; Paul however uses a variety of words to indicate the devil: ὁ πειράζων (1Th 3.5), ὁ πονηρός (2 Th 3.3; cf Eph 6.14), βελιάρ (2 Cor 6.15, if written by Paul); so this particular variation may not be significant. AE uses ἐν τοῖς ἐπουρανίοις five times (1.3, 20; 2.6; 3.10; 6.12); the phrase is not in Paul; he uses ἐν τοῖς οὐρανοῖς (2 Cor 5.1; Phil 1.20; cf Col 1.5, 16, 20; we should note the difference here also with Colossians); Paul however does use the adjective ἐπουράνιος five times in 1 Cor 15.40–9 and once in Phil 2.10. Where AE uses οὐρανός he uses it in the plural (1.10; 3.15; 4.10; 6.9) while Paul normally uses it in the singular. σωτήριον (Eph 6.17) is not used by Paul who uses σωτηρία, but AE's use should be discounted for it comes when he is quoting from Isa 59.17. Although Paul uses a number of words to describe the powers and the idea is common to him and AE, he never uses κοσμοκράτωρ (Eph 6.12), nor does he use πνευματικός for the same purpose, though employing it regularly in other connections as an adjective. Paul never uses χαριτόω to indicate bestowal (Eph 1.6) but χάρις with a verb, nor does 'he use δῶρον (Eph 2.8) though he uses a number of cognate nouns. Paul may use λέγει to introduce quotations but when he does so he always names the subject, whereas when AE uses it in 4.8 and 5.14 he does not (see notes on 4.8). While Paul uses ἅγιος as an adjective (e.g. Rom 1.2; 7.12; the better reading lacks it in 1 Th 5.27) he applies it only to concepts, objects and places and never to people as does AE in 3.5. The sequence αἷμα καὶ σάρξ (Eph 6.12) is unusual; where Paul uses the phrase (1 Cor 15.50; Gal 1.16) the words are in the reverse and more normal

---

[27] Cf R. Morgenthaler, *Statistik des neutestamentlichen Wortschatzes*, Zürich, 1958, 184.

order. Kuhn, 334f, argues that semitisms are many times more frequent in Ephesians than in Paul. Bujard[28] has shown that when the comparative length of the letters is taken into account there is in both Colossians and Ephesians an infrequent use of many connecting particles (δέ, ἀλλά, γάρ, οὖν) compared with Paul, and an excessive use of καί. Colossians and Ephesians also use the infinitive in different ways from the other Paulines (Bujard, op.cit., 53–8). Ephesians uses the article with χριστός much more frequently than Paul. ἀδελφός referring to believers and not to a biological relationship is found only twice in Ephesians (6.21, 23) but approximately 120 times in the remaining Paulines (plus 5 times in Colossians and 4 times in the Pastorals).

2.7.3. More directly in the area of style are the large number of long sentences: Moffatt lists 1.3–14; 1.15–22; 2.1–7; 2.11–13; 2.14–16; 2.19–22; 3.1–7; 3.8–12; 3.14–19; 4.1–6; 4.11–16; 4.17–19; 4.22–4; 5.3–5; 5.18–23; 5.25–7; 6.1–3; 6.5–8; 6.14–20. Many of these are difficult to disentangle because of the multitude of clauses within them. Noticeable also are the number of sequences of genitives: Percy, 188f, lists 1.9; 1.13; 1.17; 1.18; 2.2; 2.3; 2.12; 2.15; 3.2; 3.7; 3.9; 3.11; 3.21; 4.3; 4.4; 4.12; 4.13; 4.14; 4.22; 4.24; 4.29; 4.30; 5.6; 5.8; 5.9; 5.11; 5.26; 6.12; 6.15; 6.19. There is only one question in Ephesians (4.9), though questions are frequent in Paul.

2.7.4. Sanday and Headlam (*Romans* ICC, 1v), who accept the authenticity of Ephesians, summarise well the difference between Ephesians and Romans:

The difference is not so much a difference of ideas and of vocabulary as a difference of structure and composition... The sense of dissimilarity reaches its height when we turn from the materials (if we may so speak) of the style to the way in which they are put together. [In contrast to the vivacity of Romans] we have a slowly-moving onwards-advancing mass, like a glacier working its way inch by inch down the valley. The periods are of unwieldy length; the writer seem   · stagger under his load.

2.7.5. In response to these st   tic attacks on the Pauline authorship of Ephesians, it is poin   · out that the genuine Paulines contain long sentences (e.g. 2 Th !   12; 1 Cor 1.4–8; Rom 3.21 6; 4.16 ':· 9.22–4; 16.25–7; Phil 1.3–7; Philem 8–14), but thes   io not (· with anything like the same freq'   :y as in Ephesians.   in Roon ,   ies that passages can be selected   ·m the genuine Paulines which offer stylist. features similar to those of Ephesians. Rom 1.11–5.21 has no   ·stions and ἀδελφός does not appear in it; yet it has no very long sentences, uses πᾶς only 6 times against fifty times (double the expected number in proportion to length) in Ephesians,

---

[28] W. Bujard, *Stilanalytische Untersuchungen zum Kolosserbrief als Beitrag zur Methodik von Sprachvergleichen* (SUNT 11), Göttingen, 1975, 24–53.

and γάϱ twelve times against eleven times in the whole of Ephesians. While then it is certainly possible to select passages in the genuine Paulines each of which has some of the stylistic features of Ephesians, it is not possible to pick one which has even half the features of Ephesians, let alone all of them. Other suggestions have been made to account for the admitted stylistic differences: by the time Paul wrote Ephesians he was an old man and had lost his earlier vigour; prolonged inactivity in gaol had slowed him down; there is no involvement with controversy in Ephesians. While the point about controversy must be conceded, there is no way of checking that he had lost his vigour and become inactive because of old age or prison life apart from assuming he wrote Ephesians. Neither Bunyan nor Bonhoeffer lost writing vigour when in prison. As far as age goes, if this is a factor, it should be possible to produce evidence that style varies with age and it would not be necessary to produce it from the first century for aging is something that happens in every generation and would presumably have the same effect; unfortunately those who use this argument never offer the evidence.

2.7.6. Sometimes the hypothesis of a secretary is suggested to account for the differences of style and thought between Ephesians and the other letters. Richards[29] has investigated the use of secretaries in the ancient world and applied the results to the Pauline corpus. That Paul used secretaries can be seen from Rom 16.22 where he names one and Gal 6.11 where he takes the pen from the secretary's hand to write the letter's last few verses. Those Paul associates with himself in the addresses of his letters may also have been secretaries. Richards, 190, lists the explicit and implicit evidence for the use of secretaries in respect of each letter; the only letters for which he finds no evidence are Ephesians and the Pastorals; despite this he asserts that Ephesians was 'written with secretarial assistance' because it was written from prison where Paul might not have had freedom to write; this, however, assumes Paul's authorship of the letter which is what needs to be proved. There are also factors which suggest no secretary was used for Ephesians: there is no co-sender and no sign of a change in the handwriting as in Gal 6.11. The use of the first person singular in the letter in respect of Paul (1.15; 3.1; 4.1) suggests he had no associate in its writing. If a secretary was used, and necessarily not just one who took down the letter in shorthand otherwise there would be no stylistic differences, the secretary must have had some part in formulating the language; but language and thought are so intimately related that the secretary's influence on the thought cannot be eliminated; Ephesians could not

---

[29] E. R. Richards, *The Secretary in the Letters of Paul* (WUNT 2.Reihe 42), Tübingen, 1991; cf R. N. Longenecker, 'Ancient Amanuenses and the Pauline Epistles', *New Dimensions in New Testament Study* (ed. R. Longenecker and M. C. Tenney), Grand Rapids, 1974, 281–97.

then be claimed to be wholly Pauline. That Richards has not examined this is all the more surprising since he notes, 53, that Philostratus 'could differentiate between the letters of Marcus written by Marcus and those written by a secretary' (he quotes Philostratus of Lemnos, 2.28, ed. Kayser; cf Cicero, *Ep Att* 7.17). A secretary does not then account for the differences between Ephesians and the undoubted Paulines.

2.7.7. It must be allowed that what is said about style, whether in defence of Pauline authorship or against it, is always very much a subjective judgement, and this holds true for the opinion of Sanday and Headlam quoted in §2.7.4. Can objective tests be devised? Those who counted the proportion of *hapax legomena* in the Pauline letters believed this was an objective test but this test is of no help in relation to Ephesians (see §2.7.1). The objectivity of this test derives from the element of counting. Are there other factors in writing which can be measured in a similar objective manner and are not dependent on content or the age of the author?[30] It has long been recognised that such factors probably exist, e.g. sentence length, but in the past they were too difficult to calculate because of the immense labour in counting every item individually. The use of the computer has changed this. The first to realise this and to employ the computer was A. Q. Morton; in a series of books and articles, many in conjunction with S. Michaelson, he has discussed among other ancient writings the Pauline letters. As he and others pursued this line of examination two questions quickly became apparent: What were the best statistical methods to use? What features in writing would best serve to identify authorship? About the first there is less disagreement than about the second. As for the second many suggestions have been explored, the use of seemingly unimportant words like ἐν, ὅς etc., the length of sentence, the number of words beginning with τ, the number of letters in each word. It is now generally agreed that no one of these is sufficient but that a number must be used together. Yet even allowing for this researchers still reach different results. Morton has widened the type of tests he has used but has seen no reason to alter his original position that the only genuine Paulines are Romans, 1, 2 Corinthians, Galatians, with

---

[30] M. D. Goulder, 'The visionaries of Laodicea', *JSNT* 43 (1991) 14–39, scornfully rejects all such ideas, saying 'The denial of Pauline authorship is the consequence of the widespread temptation to substitute counting for thinking' (21). Yet in this very article there are occasions when he counts, though he may not realise he is doing it. How can he know that 'turgid appended phrases and clauses' are a feature of Paul's style (p. 38) if he has not counted them and contrasted his counting with that in respect of other writings? Part of his argument involves him listing *measurement* expressions (pp. 33f) and saying they are more numerous than in Paul generally; how can he know this if he has not counted the number of such expressions, and the number in Paul generally? Clearly his initial statement invalidates what he says here and therefore reduces his argument to nonsense.

the possible addition of Philemon (its brevity makes a definite decision impossible).[31] A. Kenny concludes that 'twelve of the Pauline Epistles are the work of a single, unusually versatile author'.[32] This seems a very indefinite conclusion; perhaps Paul was not an 'unusually versatile author'; surely the point of Kenny's examination was to determine whether Paul was an unusually versatile author or not. Kenny makes no allowance for the number of quotations in Ephesians, arguing that they would have no effect since they total only fifty-nine words (p. 121); the preformed material is however much more extensive than this, especially if Ephesians depends on other Pauline letters. In fairness to Kenny it must be said that he finds 1 Corinthians to be further away from the Pauline centre than Ephesians (p. 98). K. J. Neumann, who does allow for some quotations but by no means for all (he gives a list on p. 230f), while less certain about the Pastorals, concludes that 'Ephesians is more Pauline than any other known style [he is comparing it with other Christian writings, Hebrews, 1 Clement, Ignatius], but there are still differences'.[33] D. L. Mealand argues that 'The distinctiveness of Colossians and Ephesians emerged more clearly as the tests proceeded', confirming 'the views of those who have argued that these letters are deutero-Pauline'.[34] The variety of conclusions arises from both the choice of statistical method and the literary factors highlighted, and means that the certainty for which those who have used this method hoped has not yet been fully attained. While then we must take into account these statistical methods it is not yet the time to write off the traditional and apparently more subjective methods.

2.8. Thought[35]

It is not necessary to repeat here what will be discussed in the exegetical notes on the various passages to which we refer; conclusions reached there are assumed here (see also §6). It is important to point out that though we shall be examining possible differences between Ephesians and the generally accepted Paulines this should not be taken to imply that there are not also great similarities. Since most, if not all, of the writers of the NT held to a set of central beliefs there is bound to be very much which will be

[31] See in particular his *Literary Detection*, Bath, 1978.

[32] Anthony Kenny, *A Stylometric Study of the New Testament*, Oxford, 1986, 100 (Ephesians is included in the twelve).

[33] *The Authenticity of the Pauline Epistles in the Light of Stylostatistical Analysis* (SBLDS 120), Atlanta, GA, 1990, 225.

[34] 'The Extent of the Pauline Corpus: A Multivariate Approach', *JSNT* 59 (1995) 61–92 at 86. See also H. H. Greenwood, 'St Paul Revisited', *Literary and Linguistic Computing* 7 (1992) 43–7 and 8 (1993) 211–19, who reaches a similar result and also suggests a difference between Ephesians and Colossians.

[35] Cf M. Bouttier, 'L'horizon catholique de l'épître aux Éphésiens', *Mélanges F. -J. Leenhardt*, Geneva, 1968, 25–33.

common between Paul and any NT writing; thus to prove a similarity of thought on some particular point between Ephesians and Paul tells us very little.

2.8.1. The church forms one of the main themes of Ephesians and it is appropriate to begin with it (for full details see Essay: The Church). While AE's teaching on it can be said to be in line with Paul's and not to depart from his major emphases but only to represent a development, yet there are considerable differences. There is a change of emphasis because Ephesians writes about the universal church rather than individual congregations and the head is no longer one member among others but is Christ. The latter difference is shared with Colossians; as for the former, Colossians is interested both in the local church and the universal. Significant also is the way in which the church rather than Christ occupies the centre of attention. Whereas Paul relates the eucharist to the unity of believers (1 Cor 10.16f; 11.17ff) and Ephesians stresses unity, especially in 4.4–6, AE does not mention the eucharist. While Paul's genuine letters show him as the historical founder of particular churches, in Ephesians apostles and prophets are depicted theologically as the foundation of the universal church (2.20); in Paul the foundation was Christ (1 Cor 3.11) and the prophets function as guides to the existing church (1 Cor 14.3, 5, 6, etc.) and not as part of its foundation. This is a variation which Ephesians does not share with Colossians. Ephesians differs significantly from the earlier Paulines in the place given to the continuance of Israel in which unlike Paul AE has no interest (see Detached Note: Israel and the Church); yet it must be acknowledged that Paul had once before changed his position, as a comparison of 1 Th 2.14–16 and Rom 9–11 shows.

2.8.2. If it is true that Christ is not to the same degree the central theme of Ephesians as in the other Paulines, that is not to say that he is ignored. Without him there would have been salvation for neither Jew nor Gentile. The church is not some undefined body but always his body. Yet in comparison to the amount of space given in the other Paulines to the discussion of the main events of Christ's life, incarnation, death, resurrection and ascension, his incarnation is only hinted at in passing at 4.9 and his cross receives relatively little attention; the ascension however is brought much more to the fore (1.20f; 2.6; 4.8–10). Paul speaks of believers being crucified or dying with Christ; this idea is still present in Colossians but is not found in Ephesians; here being raised with Christ is taken as already accomplished (2.6, so also in Col 3.1) rather than as an event of the future as in Paul. The soteriology of Ephesians is thus more realised than Paul's. In Galatians Paul appears to set himself up as the sole recipient of the revelation that God intends Gentiles as well as Jews to be redeemed; this stress on his position is continued in Ephesians but the apostles and prophets are introduced as apparently equal recipients of that revelation; in Colossians the revelation is made to the saints, i.e. all Christians (Col 1.26). The stress on the reconciliation which Christ's death effected lies in Ephesians on the reconciliation at the horizontal level of people with people, and not exclusively on the reconciliation of people with God as in Paul and Colossians (see on 2.16). Ephesians and Colossians use in this connection the double compound ἀποκαταλλάσσω whereas Paul used καταλλάσσω; but though Ephesians and Colossians use the same word they employ it differently.

Already in Paul there are signs that he saw the whole cosmos as the object of God's redeeming love (Rom 8.19–21; Phil 2.9–11); this becomes much clearer in Colossians and Ephesians (see on 1.10). In line with this Christ is given a greater cosmic role, again in both Ephesians and Colossians, than in the earlier Paulines (see on 1.10, 22f; 3.10; 4.10). This cosmic interest may account for the proportionally greater prominence given to the powers than in the earlier Paulines. Interestingly Ephesians and Colossians present a cosmos without an underworld whereas one is customary in Paul (e.g. Phil 2.10). The essence of Paul's teaching on salvation through God's grace and not through works is seen in 2.8–10, but the terms in which it is expressed are recast and at one point 'works' is used with a good sense. This is a theme, however, which is hardly mentioned in Colossians.

2.8.3. In Ephesians salvation as present fact is stressed much more strongly than in Paul in that believers are viewed as already raised from death and seated in the heavenlies (2.6). Future expectation accordingly receives much less attention though it does not disappear (1.18; 4.4; the reference to hope in 1.12; 2.12 do not relate to a final future hope but to the expectation of Gentile Christians that they have the same position in God's plan as Jewish Christians); the parousia is not mentioned. Ephesians does not echo Paul's sense of the transitoriness of the world (1 Cor 7.31). In other letters Paul shows himself, and by inference all believers, as weak and in continual need of the grace and strength of God (2 Cor 4.7ff; 6.3ff; 12.9); AE never mentions this element in his depiction of the Christian life. Equally missing is any trace of an internal struggle in believers which is set out so eloquently in Rom 7.7ff; AE does not feel obliged to grapple with the place of the Law in God's plan of salvation or with the continuance of Israel (see on 2.15). *Heilsgeschichte* is not prominent in Ephesians. Finally there are a number of major terms which Ephesians employs in a different way from Paul, and sometimes also from their use in Colossians: οἰκονομία (see on 1.10; 3.2, 9), μυστήριον (see on 1.9), πλήρωμα (see on 1.23).

2.8.4. Perhaps the most significant variation from the earlier

Paulines lies in the ethical area (see Essay: Moral Teaching §6.3.2). In the light of the restriction in Ephesians of the HT to households consisting entirely of believers it is very difficult to see Paul as either compiling such a code or, if he received it in the tradition, embodying it in what he writes (see Best, 'Haustafel'). It would be equally difficult to see him ignoring the relation of believers to the world in which they live; Ephesians however shows them neither as under pressure from it nor as affecting it in any way; in particular Ephesians lacks a missionary impulse; in this it also contrasts with Colossians (see Col 4.5f). While Paul sees all sections of humanity as standing in an equal relation to God (1 Cor 12.13; Gal 3.28) AE is only concerned about the reconciling of Jews and Gentiles. For Paul, to marry is not wrong but inadvisable because the future is uncertain in view of the impending parousia; marriage may at times be necessary to control sexual passion but the state of celibacy is superior to it. In the Ephesian HT marriage is assumed as normal and no objections are offered to believers marrying; the celibate is not seen as superior to the married person; Ephesians does not even discuss how the celibate should behave. When we turn to the actual details of behaviour there is a lack of penetration on the part of AE when compared with the way Paul goes to the heart of conduct and relates it to the centre of the Gospel; for example, he bases an appeal for more money in a collection on Christ's incarnation (2 Cor 8.9). Both Paul and AE conceive of the Christian life as a struggle and use martial terms to describe it; Paul however gives the struggle an eschatological context (1 Th 5.8; Rom 12.11–14) which is missing in AE's picture of the struggle with the powers.

In many cases the thought of AE could be a development of that of Paul; if this is so his mind must have retained all its vigour and this would invalidate the view that the differences between Ephesians and Paul are due to his increasing age. Yet his vigour and sharpness are not seen in the moral teaching of Ephesians which is prosaic and lacks his sparkle. If AE can be seen as the author of the theological thought of Ephesians he cannot then be seen as the author of its moral teaching, and vice versa.

2.9 Conclusion

The external data suggest a date between AD 60 and AD 90. The lack of evidence for knowledge of Ephesians until Ignatius and Polycarp and certain internal data would suggest a date towards the end of that period. There is a relationship with Colossians but it cannot be proved that AE used that letter; the customary argument that his use of it would imply he was not Paul cannot then be sustained. The vocabulary and style vary slightly from Paul's in such a way as to suggest, but not compel, rejection of Pauline authorship. The thought of the letter, in particular in relation to its moral teaching, shows variation at times from Paul's and there are no outside circumstances to which this can be attributed. While AE's teaching on the church could be a legitimate development of Paul's, this cannot be said of the HT which does not display Paul's awareness of the real situation of believers. Many of the objections to Pauline authorship are not individually capable of disproving it but it is their cumulative effect which suggests another author. In assessing the evidence it is not a case of saying with Guthrie (p 504) that 'a chain is as strong as its weakest link' for the evidence is not presented as a chain; the arguments are independent of one another and not linked together. If an analogy has to be chosen the argument resembles much more the successive blows of a forester felling a tree; the first few blows of his axe appear to make no impression but as he continues striking, the tree weakens and eventually falls. If non-Pauline authorship is accepted it should also be noted that there are sufficient indications to imply that the authors of Colossians and Ephesians were different people.

3. A PAULINE SCHOOL[36]

3.1. In the evidence presented above we have noted places where AE and A/Col agree and disagree with one another. Usually A/Col appears to come nearer to Paul than AE. There are however areas where this is not true. Colossians is not as Jewish as Ephesians; unlike the latter and unlike Paul it makes little use of the OT; there are few signs of Semitic influence. Colossians rarely refers to the Spirit and differs in that from both Ephesians and Paul. The mystery which is Christ in Colossians is in Ephesians the mystery of the uniting of Jew and Gentile. All this, and much besides, would imply that AE and A/Col were different people.

3.1.1. If neither Ephesians nor Colossians is dependent on the other, how then are their similarities and dissimilarities to be accounted for? There are two possibilities: the same person wrote both or their authors were closely associated through belonging to the same Pauline school. The use of the term school to describe the association of disciples should not be taken to suggest that Paul deliberately set up a group of disciples to continue his work. History shows that all innovative thinkers have produced followers who after their death pursue and develop their thought. There is every likelihood that this would have happened in the case of Paul. During

---

[36] On Pauline schools in relation to Ephesians and Colossians see H.-M. Schenke, 'Das Weiterwirken des Paulus und die Pflege seines Erbes durch die Paulus-Schule', *NTS* 21 (1974/5) 505–18; H.-M. Schenke and K. M. Fischer, 233–47; H. Conzelmann, 'Die Schule des Paulus', *Theologia Crucis—Signum Crucis* (FS E. Dinkler, ed. C. Andresen and G. Klein), Tübingen, 1979, 85–96; M. Kiley, op.cit., 90–107; Lindemann, *Paulus*, 36–8; Schnelle, 45–50.

his education in Jerusalem he would have attached himself as a pupil to a group learning from some prominent teacher of the Law; the group of pupils would in fact have formed a school. Later during his missionary work he associated younger Christians with himself.[37] While at times he sent them to churches which he had founded he also will have had them with him during long periods and it would have been only natural if he and they had discussed his theology. He may in fact have been involved with fellow workers from quite an early stage (Acts 13.1). It would not have been surprising if after his death some of his young associates had stayed together and drawn others, for example, the leaders of the churches he had founded, to form with them one or more groups. 1 Cor 1.12 implies the existence even during his lifetime of a group of disciples. At least in some of the churches he founded there would have been those eager to follow his teaching, think through its continuing relevance and apply it to situations which Paul himself had not encountered. 'School' may be too formal a term with which to describe such people; the same objection applies also to 'circle' which is sometimes used. It is probably better to speak more vaguely of a group, though since school is in regular use we do not reject its use. There would probably have been a number of groups of Pauline followers; one produced our letters, another the Pastorals, another 2 Thessalonians if it is not Pauline, perhaps another Acts.[38] One or more of these schools may also have been responsible for editing Paul's letters, in particular 2 Corinthians, and probably also for their initial collection. To say that AE and A/Col were members of such a school does not imply they had worked with Paul himself, or that they had known him, but it does not exclude these possibilities. We are not of course suggesting that either Colossians or Ephesians was a corporate product of the group but that the authors of each were members. The group would naturally have consisted of more than the two authors. Its members probably lived somewhere in Asia Minor in the light of the geographical references in Col 4.13 to Laodicea and Hieropolis.

3.2. What should we expect to find in a group of people dependent on an initial figure and attempting to follow up and adapt his thinking? In exploring this we need to proceed carefully for what is common to Ephesians and Colossians and different from Paul, e.g. less expectancy of an immediate parousia, may also be found in other contemporary Christian writings and would not therefore prove the association of AE and A/Col. Any group would certainly have talked among themselves and begun to think in similar ways.

---

[37] W.-H. Ollrog, *Paulus und seiner Mitarbeiter* (WMANT 50), Neukirchen-Vluyn, 1979.
[38] K. Backhaus, 'Der Hebräerbrief und die Paulus-Schule', *BZ* 37 (1993) 193–208, argues for the existence of a school in Rome which produced Hebrews.

As we look for evidence we assume that neither author as he wrote had a copy of what the other wrote in front of him. There are a number of elements we should expect to find:

3.2.1. A similar development of the thought of the initial figure which is not found elsewhere: (i) Both AE (2.6) and A/Col (2.12; 3.1) view the resurrection and ascension of believers as having already taken place in distinction from Paul who viewed them as future; Paul himself condemns their view in 1 Cor 4.8 and it is also condemned in 2 Tim 2.18 and is not a belief common to the late first century. (ii) Paul described the church as the body of Christ but left Christ's precise position within it undefined; both our authors identify him as head of the body (Eph 4.16; 5.23; Col 2.19). (iii) Both authors accept Paul's idea that believers on conversion become new people and in describing this they use the same image of a change from an old being to a new (Eph 4.22–4; Col 3.9–11). (iv) Paul gave a cosmic setting to Christianity; both AE (1.20, 22; 3.10) and A/Col (1.15–20; 2.8) bring this out more clearly. (v) While the relation of the forgiveness of sin to the death of Christ is implicit in Paul it is brought out explicitly by both AE (1.7) and A/Col (1.14; 2.13). (vi) Neither AE nor A/Col employ ἀδελφός as regularly as Paul and when they do (Eph 6.21, 23; Col 1.1, 2; 4.7, 9, 15) they do not use it as he does as a term of address. (vii) Like Paul both authors know there is a future but whereas he tends to express this in temporal terms they are beginning to think spatially and to set the future 'above' rather than 'ahead' (Eph 2.6; Col 3.1–3). (viii) Paul used ἐκκλησία generally of local congregations though the universal sense is not absent; A/Col uses it twice of the local (4.15f) but the universal seems more important for him; AE uses it exclusively of the universal. (ix) Naturally both authors refer to their master and in doing so give him a unique position (he may already have given himself one, 1 Cor 15.8–10) yet they do it in different ways; in Col 1.24 he is given a soteriological role; in Eph 3.3 he is the sole recipient of the revelation that the Gospel is intended for the Gentiles, though this is qualified in 3.5. Interesting in all this is the way in which in several cases when a Pauline idea is being extended or developed the two authors do this slightly differently, presumably because their minds work differently and they are facing different problems. Thus in (i) they express its implication differently: AE goes on to say that believers have ascended with Christ, but A/Col speaks of a life above. In respect of (ii), A/Col sees believers as able to resist false ideas if they adhere to the head but AE stresses the need to obey the head. In the case of (iii) they use different terms (see on 4.22–4) and AE is more aware of the change as a process. As for the cosmic nature of Christianity (iv) they not only express its nature differently but relate it differently to their main themes.

3.2.2. They take up terms Paul has used, e.g. πλήρωμα,

μυστήριον, οἰκονομία, and extend them in new, but not always in the same directions (see on 1.23; 1.9; 1.10 respectively).

3.2.3. Groups tend to evolve and employ common phrases though not always with the same connotation. A group worshipping together would create a common stock of terms to characterise their worship and we find this in Eph 5.19 and Col 3.16. Other phrases used in common are ἅγιος καὶ ἄμωμος (Eph 1.4; 5.27; Col 1.22) and ἔχομεν τὴν ἀπολύτρωσιν, τὴν ἄφεσιν (Eph 1.7; Col 1.14); in the latter case different words are used to denote sin. ἐξαγοραζόμενοι τὸν καιρόν (Eph 5.16; Col 4.5) is a striking phrase whose meaning is not easy to tie down (see on 5.16) but which once in the vocabulary of the group would be used by more than one member. Groups also introduce new words, again not always applying them in the same way; so we find the double compound ἀποκαταλλάσσω (Eph 2.16; Col 1.20, 22; Paul uses the single compound καταλλάσσω); the group may have found the word in the preformed tradition of the Colossian hymn; another instance of this phenomenon is ἀπαλλοτριόομαι (Eph 2.12; 4.18; Col 1.21). A related phenomenon comes with AE's use of ἀφή (4.16) which is difficult to explain in Ephesians; once however we realise it was a term in use in the group its meaning becomes evident from Col 2.19; the group has been accustomed to use the word and AE has simply not realised that his readers would not have known the discussions of the group.

3.2.4. While groups will share ideas they will express them with different words; so AE and A/Col use synonyms to denote 'vigilance' (Eph 6.18; Col 4.20), 'new' (Eph 4.24; Col 3.10), 'revelation' (Eph 3.3; Col 1.26).

3.2.5. Groups receive traditional formulae and use them as required; it is not then surprising that our authors use the same form of the HT though another exists (1 Pet 2.13–3.7). AE expands the first and second sections but A/Col does not; both expand the final and in doing so (see on 6.5–9) use similar language but apply it differently. Both letters are dependent on the same vice catalogues (see on 5.3–5) and a common preformed tradition underlies Eph 2.1, 5 and Col 2.13 (see on 2.1). However, if the OT is regarded as tradition this provides a striking difference, for AE uses it much more regularly than A/Col; this is not surprising since a main theme of AE is the church which stands in continuity with Israel; A/Col's neglect is however unexpected if the opponents he attacks had a strong Jewish element in their theology; perhaps his readers require a 'Christian' refutation; had he been directly addressing his opponents he might have used the OT. Like AE, A/Col approaches, but to a lesser degree, the thought and expression of the Qumran literature (see references to Qumran indexed in Lohse, *Colossians*, 222). Both use ἅγιοι in the sense of heavenly inhabitants (Col 1.12; Eph 1.18;

2.19). We should expect all the members of the group to know the same Pauline letters; AE probably knew Romans, 1, 2 Corinthians, Philemon (see §2.6.6); A/Col appears to have known Romans, 1, 2 Corinthians, Galatians, Philippians, Philemon (see Lohse, *Colossians*, 182); since both letters are short, it is not surprising that one or other should not show acquaintance with some of Paul's short letters; they both know the same longer letters.

3.2.6. There is a certain similarity of style between the two letters as Percy has demonstrated, e.g. in the use of dependent genitives and of unnecessary synonyms. Both have a sonorous and liturgical tone which might come from working together.

3.3. All this is not to say that there are no real differences between the letters, but many of these result from the different objectives of their authors. A major obstacle however in accepting AE and A/Col as members of the same group may appear to be the verbal similarity of Eph 6.21f and Col 4.7f, but we have seen that this similarity is a difficulty for all theories of the authorship of Ephesians; it is no greater for the view that both authors belonged to the same group than for other theories of their relationship. The two authors may have discussed together how they should finish off their letters with the result that they express themselves with almost but not quite identical words. Another obstacle to common membership in a school is the absence in Colossians of references to the Spirit; it may be that A/Col avoided such references since his opponents made much of the Spirit.

3.4. Instead of supposing a Pauline school should we accept the similarities between the letters as arising from common authorship, whether that of Paul or someone else? If we re-read the evidence it will be seen that many of the similarities to which we have pointed are related to differences which are not likely to have come from the same author. For that reason common authorship of the two letters, other than that of Paul, has rarely been espoused. If however Pauline authorship is not acceptable, we should note that those who have approached authorship statistically and have rejected Paul's authorship of Ephesians have also rejected common authorship for the two letters.

4. PICTURE OF PAUL

Percy, 342–53; Fischer, 95–108; Merklein, *Amt*, 335–45; C. K. Barrett, 'Pauline Controversies in the Post-Pauline Period', *NTS* 20 (1973–4) 229–45; H.-M. Schenke, 'Das Weiterwirken des Paulus und die Pflege seines Erbes durch die Paulus-Schule', *NTS* 21 (1974–5) 505–18; M. de Boer, 'Images of Paul in the Post-Apostolic Period', *CBQ* 42 (1980) 359–80; H. Merklein, 'Paulinische Theologie in der Rezeption des Kolosser– und Epheserbriefes', *Paulus in den neutestamentlichen Spät-*

schriften (ed. K. Kertelge, QD 89), Freiburg, Basel, Vienna, 1981, 25–69, esp. 29–37; J. Gnilka, 'Das Paulusbild im Kolosser– und Epheserbrief', *Kontinuität und Einheit* (FS F. Mussner, ed. P.–G. Müller und W. Stenger), Freiburg, Basel, Vienna, 1981, 179–93; MacDonald, 123–36; F. Montagnini, 'La figura di Paolo nelle Lettere ai Colossei e agli Efesini', *RivBiblt* 34 (1986) 429–49; U. Luz, 'Überlegungen zum Epheserbrief und seiner Paränese', *Neues Testament und Ethik* (FS R. Schnackenburg, ed. H. Merklein), Freiburg im Breisgau, 1989, 376–96.

If Paul did not write Ephesians he is certainly its implied author. What picture of him then does the real author paint? Is it the same as the picture derived from the certainly genuine letters?

4.1. In 1.1 Paul is described as an apostle of Jesus Christ. He himself uses this term, apostle, to introduce himself in the two Corinthian letters, Romans and Galatians, but not in 1 Thessalonians, Philippians, Philemon, and 2 Thessalonians if it is not pseudonymous. It is not then a term on which he placed a high personal evaluation. An examination of the places in his letters where, apart from the addresses, he describes himself as an apostle shows that it is mainly in restricted contexts. At no point do we find him issuing instructions to others on the basis of his apostleship (cf Best, 'Authority'). When he exercises authority over his converts he does not begin from the position of an apostle but of a father (cf Best, *Converts*, 73–96). When he presents himself as an apostle there are always special circumstances. In 1, 2 Corinthians and Galatians there were those who denied he was an apostle, by which they meant someone of equal status with Peter. Romans is a letter written to a church which he has never visited and since attacks on him have spread through the churches he finds it necessary to emphasise from the beginning his equality with Peter. When AE terms him an apostle in the address of his letter he thus gives Paul status equal to that of any of the Twelve and so lends authority to what is presented as his teaching. It was of course impossible to present him as 'father' since the readers were not his converts; for a similar reason Paul refrained from calling himself 'father' when writing to the Roman Christians.

4.2. That AE chooses to write in Paul's name implies that he and those to whom he writes revered him. The survival of respect and reverence for Paul in the final part of the first century can be seen in the way various writings were ascribed to him, Colossians, the Pastorals, and 2 Thessalonians if he did not write it. That these writings appeared as letters implies also that his reputation as a letter writer also survived. This is particularly so in the case of Ephesians for it is not really a letter in the ordinary sense (see below §7). It would be wrong however to assume that Paul was held in universally high esteem in all circles of the church. The author of Revelation denigrates him when he allows for only twelve gates into heaven corresponding to the twelve apostles (21.12–14). Luke hesitates to call him an apostle, and when he does so places him on a level with Barnabas (14.4, 14), and this may be a sign of some turmoil about his position.

4.3. In 3.1 and 4.1 AE describes Paul as a prisoner; this tells us nothing that we do not know from the genuine letters and Acts. 3.1 leads into an important passage, 3.2–13, where Paul is a central figure and we shall return to this. The final reference to Paul comes at the close of the letter (6.19f) where prayer is to be offered for him as a missionary proclaiming the gospel. That Paul is set out as missionary, though not stressed in Ephesians, again accords with what we learn elsewhere. That Paul asks for prayer for himself brings out another facet of the picture, Paul the man of prayer. All his letters contain passages in which he prays for their recipients but the element of prayer is more extensive in Ephesians (1.3–14, 15–23; 3.14–21) than in any of the others. Finally we should note negatively that though Paul is presented as prisoner and missionary nothing is done to stress him as a hero of the faith. Doubtless this did not need to be done.

4.4. 3.2–13 is the most important passage about Paul. He is a prisoner and consequently suffers (3.1, 13), which corresponds with what we learn elsewhere (see on 3.1). People do not suffer without a cause, be it to preserve their high opinion of themselves or through an obstinate refusal to be beaten into submission. Paul is said however to suffer for others (cf 2 Cor 1.6; 4.12). The 'others' of 3.13 are not a limited group belonging to a single congregation but the Gentiles. Sometimes his sufferings are described as apostolic; this is incorrect for suffering belongs to the lot of all Christians and not of apostles alone, and the historical Paul linked his Christian existence, and not just his apostolic existence, to the cause of taking the gospel to the Gentiles (Gal 1.16; 2.7–10; Rom 11.13) and the εἰ γε of 3.2 shows readers were already aware of this. 3.3 traces back his mission to the Gentiles to a revelation he received. It is not possible to determine from that brief reference whether AE believed this revelation was given to Paul directly in the Damascus Road experience, or was a deduction from it, or was given at some other time, for AE emphasises Paul here as the recipient of revelation rather than the active missionary. The reception of the revelation means that God has allotted a place to Paul in the accomplishment of his plan (3.2). This idea is found in earlier letters (Gal 1.11f, 15f; Rom 1.5f; 11.13). Yet AE is aware that tradition holds Paul was not the sole person to receive a revelation about the Gentiles and so adds a reference to the apostles and prophets (3.5; see Best, 'Revelation'); presumably he realises at least some of his readers may know about this second tradition. Yet he omits any mention of those like Barnabas and the believers in Antioch (Acts 11.19ff) who probably preceded Paul in preaching to the Gentiles; perhaps he did not know of them (he had not read Acts!). His information will almost certainly have come directly or indirectly from Paul himself who in his genuine letters does give himself a special position in relation to the Gentiles.

4.5. AE describes Paul in 3.1–13 as διάκονος (3.7). This need not necessarily carry the sense of humble service though it does carry that of service (see on 3.7), in this case the service of bringing the gospel to the Gentiles. AE thus again stresses that Paul did not just drop into his work for the Gentiles or think it out as a grand scheme for himself, but was specially appointed to it by God, probably in a way others were not; as the one appointed by God he was given the power to carry it out. Perhaps it is this term, διάκονος, with its association with humble service that leads AE to introduce another facet of his picture of Paul, a facet, as it were, at the other extreme from that of apostle: he is the very least (comparative of a superlative) of all believers (3.8). In this 'belit-tling' of Paul AE follows a lead found in Paul himself (1 Cor 15.9), though he makes it more extreme (see on 3.8). Paul apparently regarded his lowly position in comparison with the Twelve as due to his pre-conversion persecution of believers; AE does not indicate in what Paul's inferiority lay.

4.6. The plan of God involves preaching salvation not only to the Gentiles but also to the powers (3.10). Does AE envisage a special role for Paul in this? He certainly cannot be omitted from the process for he is a member of the church which fulfils God's plan. Yet in the context he is more than just a member for he has been responsible for the shape of the church which does the preaching in that it comprises both Gentiles and Jews, and it is this unified church which is part of, if not all of, the message to the powers.

4.7. There are more general ways in which AE, whether consciously or unconsciously, presents Paul: (i) As a teacher, in that the content of the letter, which is teaching, is ascribed to Paul; this accords fully with the picture of Paul in his genuine letters. (ii) As capable of much more meditative, reflective and liturgical writing than we find in his genuine letters; some (see §2.7.5) attribute this characteristic of Ephesians to Paul's old age or the length of time he spent in prison when he could carry out no active mission work. (iii) As out of touch with the life of believers in that he thinks (see the HT) all Christians live in households which are entirely Christian; this does not accord with what we learn in other letters of Paul's knowledge of the struggle that could exist within households where not all were Christians. (iv) Negatively, AE does not present Paul as (a) a role model for believers in the way Paul offers himself as someone to be imitated (1 Cor 4.16; 11.1; Phil 3.17) nor (b) a hero of the faith.

4.8. We can now return to our initial question: Is the picture of

Paul presented in Ephesians in harmony with that which he gives of himself in the certainly genuine letters? The answer must be in large part 'Yes'. Certain characteristics are, we might say, stretched a little further, e.g. his belief that he had a unique place in God's plan, or his picturing himself as inferior to all believers and not to the apostles alone; yet it is easily conceivable that Paul could have developed his thinking in these ways. As for Paul believing himself to have a unique place in God's plan, this appears in other ways in the genuine Paulines: he avers that he was the last to whom the risen Jesus appeared and expresses himself in such a way as to imply that to no one else after him would the risen Jesus appear (1 Cor 15.8); he summons his converts to imitate him (Phil 3.17; 1 Cor 4.16; 11.1; in this last passage he parallels himself with Christ); he affirms his version of the gospel as the only correct version (Rom 2.16; Gal 1.7–9); he is the only one entrusted with the gospel to the Gentiles (Gal 2.7). Yet the uniqueness which Paul claims for himself is balanced in other letters in ways missing in Ephesians, for in those letters he puts himself on the same plane as other Christians in repeatedly calling them 'brothers' and, if Rom 7.7ff is in any way autobiographical, he is aware of his own sin. The only area where there is a definite difference concerns his view in Ephesians of churches as consisting only of purely Christian households. It is natural that there should be some differences in the picture of Paul in Ephesians and in the other letters simply because it is a short letter and cannot present as rounded a picture as the longer letters, and of course also the picture in any single letter is always less than the total picture.

5. WHERE AND WHEN WRITTEN

Haupt, 70ff; Ewald, 1–7; Abbott, xxix–xxxi; G. S. Duncan, *St Paul's Ephesian Ministry*, London, 1929; id. 'Were Paul's Imprisonment Epistles written from Ephesus'?, *ExpT* 67 (1955/6) 163–6; Percy, 467–74; Bo Reicke, 'Caesarea, Rome and the Captivity Epistles', *Apostolic History and the Gospel* (FS F. F. Bruce, ed. W. W. Gasque and R. P. Martin), Exeter, 1970, 277–86.

It is proper to consider these questions on the supposition of both non-Pauline and Pauline authorship. We have already in part discussed the date in §2.4 where it was argued that it was probably written prior to AD 90. Can we give more precision to that in the light of the content of the letter and on the supposition first of non-Pauline authorship?

5.1. Both Revelation and 1 Peter, which were written to approximately the same area of Asia Minor as Ephesians, record the existence of persecution. Ephesians says nothing about persecution.

Does this imply Ephesians was written prior to persecution breaking out? Acts however implies that there was persecution and harassment from the first days of the church and the exact dating of the persecutions referred to in Revelation and 1 Peter is very difficult; at least in the latter case they were probably not state persecutions but were due rather to mobs or civic action and limited to local areas. It may also be that since AE is so much concerned with the inner life of the communities to which he writes and the effect of the actions of members on one another that he does not have space or time to consider outside factors which might disturb them. Paul experienced various kinds of mob violence as well as civic harassment all through his mission activity. But what about imprisonment? AE depicts Paul as a prisoner. If Acts is to be believed Paul was in prison on many occasions; AE, however, gives no clue as to the place of imprisonment. A writing featuring the universal church rather than individual congregations suits the period leading up to the end of the first century.[39] On the whole there is nothing here to alter our earlier verdict on the date of the letter and it should be placed in the period AD 80–90.

5.2. When however we turn from the imprisonment of the implied author to that of the real author on the supposition that he was Paul it may be possible to obtain a clearer picture of where the letter was written from and when; the two issues are related. Acts records several imprisonments of Paul, in Philippi, 16.23–40, in Caesarea, 21.33ff, and in Rome, 28.16. It is not only in Ephesians that Paul says he was a prisoner but also in Colossians, Philippians and Philemon. In addition he affirms in 2 Cor 11.23 that he suffered many imprisonments. Some of these were probably of brief duration like that in Philippi and would have given him neither time nor opportunity to write letters. Unfortunately it is not known where or when all his imprisonments took place or how long they lasted. Those in Caesarea and Rome were of sufficient duration for the composition of one or all of the so-called prison letters. It has been argued that Paul was also a prisoner during the long time he spent in Ephesus.[40] There is no need to discuss the likelihood of such an imprisonment; since we cannot prove it did not take place it is necessary to take it into account.

5.3. Ephesians is so devoid of personal detail that by itself it provides no clue as to the place or time of imprisonment. However, as we have seen, it is closely associated with Colossians and that letter provides much more information. Colossians is also associated with

---

[39] Cf C. R. Bowen, 'The Place of "Ephesians" in the Letters of Paul', *ATR* 15 (1933) 279–99.

[40] This has been advocated in great detail by Duncan, op.cit., who provides a history of the idea prior to his own time.

Philemon which again contains relevant personal information.[41] Philippians is not linked in any way to these three and it is impossible to prove that the imprisonment referred to in it was the same as that of the other three, though traditionally all four have been linked together as the captivity epistles. We therefore ignore Philippians in our discussion of where Paul was imprisoned, and also assume that he wrote Colossians and Philemon as well as Ephesians. Colossians and Philemon imply that communication between Paul and Colossae and its area was not difficult; in Philem 22 Paul asks for a guest room to be made ready for him on his release and this suggests a short interval between release and his arrival with Philemon, which would hardly be likely if he was writing from Caesarea or Rome. These and other factors favour Ephesus. However, one serious factor counting against Ephesus is the argument used by many in sustaining Pauline authorship of Ephesians, that its difference in style from the vigour of the earlier letters comes because Paul was an old man and could be expected to write in a more placid manner. If the imprisonment had been in Ephesus he would not have been old enough for this. Also an imprisonment there does not allow sufficient time for the development of his theology, especially in respect of the church, in Ephesians and Colossians beyond what is found in the earlier letters. We turn then to the factors favouring imprisonment in Rome or Caesarea. When we put together the personal information of the three letters it would appear that at the time of their writing Paul was accompanied by, or was in regular touch with, a large entourage. This is more likely to have been true of Rome than Caesarea. Again an escaping slave like Onesimus was most likely to flee to Rome where he could remain anonymous among the great city crowds. In Rome Paul also seems to have had much greater freedom, at least for part of the time of his imprisonment, than would normally be expected for a prisoner (Acts 28.30). That Paul perhaps suffered two imprisonments in Rome is irrelevant to our discussion. Yet the distance between either Rome or Caesarea and Colossae is greater than that between the latter and Ephesus. The matter of the place of imprisonment cannot be said to be firmly resolved but the traditional siting in Rome is probably to be preferred. Naturally when we determine the place of imprisonment the date is also determined. If Rome or Caesarea it is late in Paul's life and Ephesians would then have been written in the early sixties.

6. THOUGHT

Of the literature listed below, some books and articles assume Paul did not

---

[41] The place of imprisonment is treated in much greater detail in commentaries on Colossians which assume Pauline authorship and these should be consulted. Here we can only point to a few of the more important arguments.

write Ephesians and these are the most helpful; some assume he did and,
though not separating out the material in Ephesians from that in the other
letters, have often valuable things to say, yet because they do not separate
out the material it may be difficult to discern this. The relevant sections in
the commentaries are not listed.

F. C. Baur, *Paul: His Life and Work*, II, London, 1875, 1–44; O. Pfleiderer,
Paulinism. A Contribution to the History of Primitive Christian Theology,
II, London, 1877, 162–93; B. Weiss, *Biblical Theology of the New
Testament*, II, Edinburgh, 1885, 75–124; H. J. Holtzmann, *Lehrbuch der
neutestamentlichen Theologie*, Freiburg im Breisgau and Leipzig, II, 1897,
225–58; F. Mussner, 'Die Geschichtstheologie des Epheserbriefes', *BibLeb*
5 (1964) 8–12; F. F. Bruce, 'Paul in Rome 4. The Epistle to the Ephesians',
BJRL 49 (1966/7) 303–22; R. Baulès, *L'insondable richesse du Christ* (LD
66), Paris, 1971; H. Ridderbos, *Paul. An Outline of His Theology*, Grand
Rapids, 1975; B. Corley, 'The Theology of Ephesians', *SWJT* 22 (1979)
24–38; H. Merklein, 'Paulinische Theologie in der Rezeption des Kolosser-
und Epheserbriefes', *Paulus in den neutestamentlichen Spätschriften* (ed. K.
Kertelge), Freiburg im Breisgau, 1981, 25–69; R. E. Brown, *The Churches
the Apostles Left Behind*, London, 1984, 47–60; Collins, op.cit.; A. T.
Lincoln in A. T. Lincoln and A. J. M. Wedderburn, *The Theology of the
Later Pauline Letters*, Cambridge, 1993, 75–166; K. Berger, *Theologiegeschichte des Urchristentums*, Tübingen and Basel, 1994, 543–7.

If Paul did not write Ephesians its thought deserves to be considered
in its own right and not merely in the light of the way it may agree
with or differ from Paul. In what follows many passages in the letter
are referred to briefly without detailed exegesis; justification for the
points of view adopted will be found in the exegetical notes. AE's
chief contribution to theology is his outline of the nature of the
church and the conduct which its members should show to one
another. These two aspects of his theology require detailed treatment
and are not discussed here but separately in two Essays: The
Church, Moral Teaching.

6.1. *Cosmic Setting*
The mood in which the theology of Ephesians is presented is that of
devotion and prayer (1.3–14, 15–23; 3.14–21) rather than that of
logical development or polemic and confrontation with the opinions
of others. Since part of the teaching on the nature of the church
concerns the union of Jewish and Gentile believers we might have
expected the theology to be set in a framework of *Heilsgeschichte* as
in Galatians where Gentile believers become the children of
Abraham (3.29). The framework of Ephesians is, however, cosmic
(B. Corley, art.cit.), extending from prior to the foundation of the
world (1.4) to its consummation (1.10). God has created the
framework and his primary position in relation to it is set out at the
beginning (1.3). The framework contains a plan of redemption
which is now being revealed through Christ (1.3–14) and which
includes Gentiles as well as Jews (2.11–22; 3.1–13).

6.2. If the framework is cosmic then AE will be concerned not only with the relation of believers to God but also with that of the cosmos itself. The cosmos is God's creation (3.9), and he prepared for it before it existed (1.4f); its consummation lies also in his hands (1.10). The cosmos consists not only of the material universe, but of human beings and supernatural powers (1.21; 2.2; 3.10; 6.12). Some of these powers may be wholly opposed to God, unlike humans who are sometimes opposed and sometimes not. From a physical angle the cosmos consists of two parts, earth and heaven, which interact while being distinct. We would expect humanity to be confined to earth but believers while still living physically on earth already sit in the heavenlies (2.6). Unbelievers, confined to earth, are under the control of supernatural powers (2.2); believers struggle with these same powers (6.10ff).

6.2.1. Believers are believers not because they have chosen to believe but because God selected them before the world came into being (1.4). This does not however imply they existed prior to their birth; God knows they will be born and determines what thereafter their lives will be. In a somewhat similar way the church did not pre-exist the incarnation, except in so far as it is identifiable with Israel (see Essay: The Church). Most of the terms AE uses in referring to election and predestination are found elsewhere in the NT, principally in (other parts of?) Paul: ἐκλέγομαι (1.4; 1 Cor 1.27, 28), θέλημα (1.1, 5, 9, 11; 1 Cor 1.1; 2 Cor 8.5; Gal 1.4), προορίζω (1.5, 11; Rom 8.29f); εὐδοκία (1.5, 9; Phil 2.13), προτίθεμαι, πρόθεσις (1.9; Rom 3.25; 8.28), βουλή (1.11; Acts 2.23; 20.27), κλῆσις (1.18; 1 Cor 1.26; Phil 3.14), προετοιμάζω (2.10; Rom 9.23).

6.2.2. Gentiles entering the church would not have been surprised to learn that their lives were governed by external non-human forces for almost everyone in the ancient world believed that the way they lived was controlled by the stars, various deities and sub-deities and by magic exercised by other people. Fate, ἡ εἱμαρμένη, determined what should happen. The supernatural powers of which AE writes fit into this pattern of non-human control. Later in much gnostic thinking the nature of each human life was predetermined so that people fell into one or other of two categories, those who would be saved and those who would not; there was also sometimes a third category whose end was indeterminate. Belief in fate has always been a strong element in popular piety: 'his name was on that bullet'. AE seeks to release his readers from fate in a number of ways. He argues that Christ has brought to an end the domination of the powers (1.19–23), that the election of believers is determined by God in Christ (1.4f), that God is not a remote stern figure acting arbitrarily but a father (1.2, 3; 3.14; 4.6; 5.20; 6.23) to whom they have access (2.18; 3.12); God above all is rich in mercy, loves them (2.4; 4.32; 6.23) and acts graciously towards them (1.2; 2.8; 3.2, 7).

6.2.3. That God elects shows he does not act haphazardly but in accordance with a plan (1.10). The plan is one which though once hidden has now been revealed (1.9) and relates to redemption. Believers, as individuals and together as the church, are part of this plan and were given their place in it before God created the world (1.4) and they have been elected to be his children (1.5). Even their good deeds have been predetermined (2.10). Every plan has a beginning; God's began prior to the foundation of the world (1.4f) but remained hidden until he made it known to Paul and the apostles and prophets (3.3, 5). Part of the plan was the acceptance of Gentile believers on a par with Jewish believers (2.11–22); this acceptance was no afterthought designed to correct a flaw in the carrying out of the plan. If plans have starting points they also do not meander on aimlessly but have definite endings; their conclusions are inbuilt. AE indicates the conclusion of God's plan in 1.10 (cf 3.21). God's plan moreover relates to the whole universe and not to believers alone and does not consist only in the redemption of a select few with the rest of the cosmos abandoned. AE's awareness of the cosmic width of God's plan is seen in his continual interest in the powers, even though these appear to be hostile. Christ has his place within the plan as its primary element. AE makes no explicit statement about his pre-existence but if believers were elected in him before the foundation of the world this implies he existed prior to God's thinking about believers, and was therefore pre-existent.[42] 4.9 confirms this. Christ was both in the plan from the beginning and will be there at its conclusion since all things are to be brought to a head in him (1.10). God's plan might well be described as 'in Christ'.

6.3. *Christ*
The framework is cosmic; the plan is directed by God; the central character is Christ. Even if Christ pre-existed the cosmos he is given no role in its creation as in John 1.1–4; Col 1.15–17, but is allotted a place in its consummation (1.10; cf 1 Cor 15.20–8; Phil 2.9–11); more normally in the NT he is related to the end as its returning saviour.

6.3.1. In common with other Pauline letters Christ is accorded his customary NT titles: son of God, Lord, Messiah (Christ), but again in common with Paul he is not termed son of man. In contra-distinction from Paul and many other parts of the NT, AE makes nothing of the concept of Christ as servant (Phil 2.7; Mk 10.45; Jn 13.1–20; cf 2 Cor 8.9) and while the incarnation is implied in 4.9, it is only in passing as AE treats another subject. AE differs from Paul in more frequently prefixing the article to the noun 'Christ', indicating that he does not always regard this as a name but also as a

---

[42] Contra J. D. G. Dunn, *Christology in the Making*, London, 1980, 235.

title (see notes at 1.10); he thereby reminds his Gentile readers that they now belong to a community whose origin lies in Judaism. The concept of Christ as the Second Adam may underlie some passages, e.g. 1.22 where Ps 8 is used, and possibly also 5.22–33, if that passage reflects Adam and Eve (but see notes there); yet the idea is not featured as much as in the genuine Pauline letters. AE also differs from Paul in linking Christ more clearly to God's election of believers (1.4f). He resembles Paul in not stressing any events in the earthly life of Jesus other than his incarnation (4.8), death and resurrection (1.20; 2.16; 5.2). 4.21 probably indicates that he was aware Jesus was a teacher though he gives none of his teaching. He mentions and stresses proportionately much more than Paul his ascension (1.20; 4.8). This stress is related to his central theme of the church for it is the ascended Christ who gives the church gifts of ministry (4.8); in Paul (1 Cor 12.28; Rom 12.3ff) it is God who does so through the Spirit. Believers have ascended with Christ to be with him in the heavenlies (2.6).

6.3.2. It is through the way he associates Christ with the church that AE makes his main christological contribution, though some of what he says was latent in Paul. In the depiction of the church as a building, Christ, in 1 Cor 3.11 its foundation, is now identified more precisely in 2.20 as its angle-stone, which whatever its meaning (see on 2.20) certainly indicates a unique position in relation to the church. In the OT the marital image was applied to Yahweh and Israel; in Ephesians Christ becomes the groom or husband of the church which is his bride or wife; Paul had already moved in this direction (2 Cor 11.2). As the husband both loves and rules over his wife, so Christ as head both loves and rules over the church (5.22f); this produces a clear distinction between Christ and the church. Christ is head not only of the church but also of the cosmos (1.22), indicating again a cosmic christology. Christ as head of the body which is the church is involved more closely with believers than he is as head of the universe. In the genuine Paulines Christ is linked to believers in many different ways: they are baptised into him, are in him, die with him and will rise with him; he is the Second Adam whose destiny affects theirs. This makes it possible to speak of a corporate Christ;[43] this is true also for Ephesians, though less emphatically since believers are not said to die with him; however they do rise and ascend with him (2.6), and are in him (4.17; 6.1, 21); yet the corporate aspect of 'in Christ' is less frequent than in the genuine Paulines (see Detached Note: In Christ). The playing down of the corporateness is in line with the presentation of Christ as groom or husband of the church for this image draws a line between Christ and believers. The closeness of Christ to the church is seen

[43] Cf C. F. D. Moule, *The Origin of Christology*, Cambridge, 1977, 47–96.

also in that he fills the church (1.23; cf 3.17–19), though there is no reason to see the church as completing him (see on 1.22f) or of him as growing when the church grows or matures (4.12–16); these ideas would accord ill with the distinction AE draws between him and the church.

6.3.3. In conclusion it can be said that the thrust of the christology of Ephesians, while not out of line with that of other Pauline letters, or indeed the vaster part of the NT, is ecclesiological, just as its teaching on the church may be described as christological. Yet the link between the theological earlier part of the letter and the paraenetic later part is not christological (cf Collins, 159) but ecclesiological.

6.4. *Salvation*
L. Morris, *The Apostolic Preaching of the Cross*, London, 1955; id., *The Cross in the New Testament*, Exeter, 1967, 180–259; V. Taylor, *The Atonement in New Testament Teaching*, London, 1940, 55–101.

Ephesians is at one with the remainder of the NT in seeing human salvation as achieved by God through Christ; yet in common with the other NT authors AE expresses this in his own way.

6.4.1. For AE salvation is not an afterthought but part of the divine plan from the beginning (3.9), yet within that plan it represents a new stage (1.9f; 3.5) in making known the extent of God's salvation as including Gentiles. As elsewhere in the NT Jesus' death is central to the understanding of salvation (1.7; 2.13, 16). In the way he presents that death AE does not however develop a theology of the atonement, be it one of substitution, expiation, propitiation, or vicarious satisfaction, other than to say it is one for others (5.2); his words are general enough to fit any theory. The references to blood (1.7; 2.13) and sacrifice (5.2) may imply that his understanding was basically Jewish, not surprising if he was a Jewish Christian; yet Gentiles would have had no difficulty in accepting such a view.

6.4.2. One principal way in which Paul expresses redemption is by using the root δικαιο-, understood in a Jewish way rather than with its normal Greek secular understanding; AE only once uses the root with redemptive significance (6.14; in 4.24; 5.9 he uses it to describe good behaviour). However, he uses σώζω (2.8) to convey teaching similar to Paul, probably because he reckons this would be more easily understood by his Gentile readers. Salvation means that believers; (a) are forgiven their sins (1.7); this is a more Lukan (Acts 2.38; 5.31; 10.43) than Pauline way of expressing salvation, though the Paul of Acts does express it in this way (13.38; 26.18); (b) are delivered from the grip of the evil supernatural powers which controlled them before conversion (2.2; 6.11, 12) so that they are brought from pagan darkness into the light of God (4.18f, 5.8, 11;

6.12); (c) if Gentiles, are reconciled to Jewish believers; Paul had of course emphasised this through his teaching on justification; AE writes more directly of Jews and Gentiles being reconciled to one another (2.16); (d) receive spiritual gifts to be used in the service of the church (4.7). Salvation is always deliverance from something; in Paul it is from sin and the curse cf the Law; AE says much less about sin and the Law than Paul and much more about deliverance from the powers, though he does not ignore salvation from sin (1.7). More important for AE is the victory Christ has won (1.20) over the powers and the contest which Christians have with them (6.12–17). Interestingly AE does not refer to the need to fight temptation.

6.4.3. While for Paul salvation is corporate in that believers become members of the church, he never actually says, as AE does, that God redeems the church as a whole (5.25); it is no surprise when AE says this since he lays so much emphasis on the church. But AE does not ignore the salvation of the individual for 5.25 is balanced with 5.2 and it is individuals who are elected (1.4f). For AE the scope of redemption embraces more than the church, for all creation comes within his view; in 3.10 the gospel is made known to the powers, and this would hardly be done if they were incapable of redemption; in 1.10 Christ is set out as the summation of all that exists, implying its ultimate reconciliation to God (see on 1.10). However if AE has all creation in view this does mean that he saw this as the re-creation of an original unity (see on 1.10) for he never refers to an original unity, stressing instead that something new happened through Christ (cf 4.24). What comes into existence through redemption is something which never previously existed.

6.4.4. When AE says that believers have been saved (2.8, note the perfect tense) he places their salvation more firmly in the past than does Paul who sees salvation as either in process or as future; only at Rom 8.24 does Paul use a past tense of it and there he qualifies it with a reference to hope. In general AE stresses more insistently than Paul the present nature of the new life of believers; they already enjoy forgiveness (1.7) and access to God (2.18; 3.12). This reaches its climax in 2.6 where they are described as having been raised with Christ and sitting with him in the heavenlies. The result is a fully realised soteriology. This is a better term with which to describe what we find in Ephesians than the more normal 'realised eschatology'[44] since AE evinces little interest in eschatology, using few of its traditional terms (an exception is his reference

---

[44] On the possible realised eschatology of Ephesians see Steinmetz, *passim*, Lindemann, *Aufhebung, passim*; Lona, 241ff; Arnold, 145ff; Lemmer, *passim*; P. Benoit, 'L'Évolution du langage apocalyptique dans le corpus paulinien', *Apocalypses et théologie de l'espérance* (LD 95), Paris, 1977, 299–335; H. R. Lemmer, 'A multifarious understanding of eschatology in Ephesians: A possible solution to a vexing issue', *Hervormde Teologiese Studies* 46 (1990) 102–19.

to the two ages in 2.21), but much in soteriology. Sometimes stress is laid on the then/now contrast in the position of believers, but for AE the real contrast is outside/inside; once believers had been outside the church but now they are within it. Paul normally presents the resurrection of believers as future but in Colossians it is already regarded as accomplished fact (2.12; 3.1). AE goes one step further when he makes the ascension as well as the resurrection accomplished fact (2.6; the qualification 'in Christ Jesus' hardly alters this, *pace* Arnold, 148). For the reasons leading AE to take this further step see on 2.6. For Paul, dwelling with the Lord, which is presumably implied in ascension, is future (1 Cor 15.49; 2 Cor 5.6–8); Paul's own rapture to heaven (2 Cor 12.2f) was only temporary and Phil 3.20 refers to a future parousia. In Ephesians believers are already fellow-citizens with the saints who are either angels or glorified believers (see on 1.18 and 2.19). AE does not mention the parousia, and Christ's victory over the powers which in Paul is future (1 Cor 15.24) he views as already accomplished (1.20–23). 1.10 also seems to imply the present fulfilment of God's plan. 2.20 suggests a completed building since God dwells in it, a conclusion which is reinforced if the angle-stone is the locking stone. The need for alertness (6.18) is no longer tied to the expectation of the parousia (Mk 13.33; 1 Th 5.6f). There is here an important variation from Paul who went out of his way to reject the view that believers had already reached their goal of reigning in heaven (1 Cor 4.8; cf 2 Tim 2.18). For Paul full salvation might be said to be 'ahead', at the end of time; for AE it already exists 'above', in heaven.

6.4.5. Yet much of what AE says does not sit easily with this. If believers are already in the heavenlies, and presumably therefore perfect, why should they need moral teaching to which AE devotes half of his writing? Why warn readers against falling back into their pagan past (2.1ff; 2.11ff)? If the powers are already subject to Christ, why advise readers how to struggle with them (6.10ff)? The last point may not be so important for the powers are in the heavenlies and believers, if in the heavenlies, would necessarily encounter them; the difficulty here is how to understand the heavenlies (see Detached Note: The Heavenlies), which are certainly not identical with the heaven of much modern piety. There are also more positive indications that AE has not surrendered belief in the future and its importance. Believers await an inheritance (1.14, 18; 5.5), and inheritances are always future. They have already received a down payment (1.14), implying there is something more to come. The church to which they belong has not yet attained maturity and needs to grow (2.21; 4.16; cf 3.19), as do its individual members (4.13). Believers are told they have a hope (1.18; 4.4), again implying there is something better in the future. Their new being is

in process of formation (4.23f; contrast Col 3.10). In 4.30, unlike
1.7, the day of redemption seems to be future. If the reference to the
evil day in 6.13 is to the last day, then believers are already in the
period leading up to that day and there is a future day of salvation.
6.8f implies a reckoning with God and while God's wrath (5.6)
could be a present reality, the reckoning must be future.

6.4.6. Ephesians then contains two tendencies difficult to reconcile with one another. On the one hand AE continues the traditional
early view that there is a future goal to be attained. On the other he
stresses that what tradition expected is already present reality. It is
impossible to eliminate from his letter the evidence supporting either
view. AE received the former as a part of his Christian inheritance;
it was widely held; if he had wished to repudiate it he would have
needed to have made this much clearer; writing in Paul's name he
would have known that Paul held this view; writing to a wide
constituency he must have realised that most of his readers would
also have accepted the traditional position for it is found in almost
all the NT writings both prior to and after Ephesians; it can only be
eliminated from John's Gospel by assuming within it layers of
development. If AE did not believe in the parousia why did he not
directly repudiate it?

As for the alternative view, there were others who held it, as
Paul's repudiation of it in 1 Cor 4.8 demonstrates. It possibly
originated in a misunderstanding of what Paul said about the
resurrection of believers. Christ died; they died with him. Christ
rose; they must have risen with him; so Col 2.12f; 3.1. Christ
ascended; they must have ascended with him (Eph 2.6). There is
here a kind of logical progression from what Paul taught to what we
find in Ephesians. Everything stressing the reality of the present
existence of believers would assist this progression, and there was
much which did: believers were new creations (2 Cor 5.17; Gal
6.15), born again and enjoying the present reality of eternal life (see
Gospel of John). The delay in the parousia moreover would shift
interest from thinking in terms of a new age lying ahead in time to
thinking of a heaven above, a move from using temporal categories
to express belief, to using spatial (cf Lindemann, *Aufhebung*,
49–66). 1 Th 4.13ff shows there were believers who were worried
about what happened to them after death; a heaven above to which
they went would offer a solution. When we take such views into
account it is possible, without resort to the introduction of gnostic
influence, to explain the realised soteriology of Ephesians.

6.4.7. Given that the existence of these two apparently differing
views in Ephesians can be explained, the problem remains why its
author did not see their incompatibility. Perhaps all that can be said
is that the presence of incompatible ideas is a common phenomenon
in growing organisations as they adapt to new situations. AE may

simply never have noticed the clash. Indeed the clash may be more deeply entrenched in Christian faith than is often realised: God's kingdom is here and it is yet to come; believers are God's children and yet they sin.

6.5. *The Holy Spirit*
H. B. Swete, *The Holy Spirit in the New Testament*, London, 1909, 231–42; P.-A. Harlé, 'Le Saint-Esprit et l'Eglise chez saint Paul', *VCaro* 19 (74, 1965) 13–29; Adai, *passim*; Lemmer, *passim*. G. D. Fee, *God's Empowering Presence: The Holy Spirit in the Letters of Paul*, Grand Rapids, 1994, 658–733.

6.5.1. Jewish belief, generally though not universally, regarded the Holy Spirit as an eschatological gift of God. Christians believed the Spirit was already working in them. It is appropriate then to discuss the role of the Holy Spirit in Ephesians directly following on that of a realised soteriology. πνεῦμα is an ambiguous term and we exclude from consideration places where it refers to evil supernatural forces (2.2; 6.12) or is used anthropologically (4.23). It is difficult to know whether to refer to the Spirit with a neuter, masculine or feminine pronoun; since Ephesians does not appear to attribute personality to the Spirit (the nearest it comes to this is in 4.30), we shall use sometimes a personal pronoun and sometimes a neuter. Traces of the Spirit's eschatological orientation remain in 1.13f where it is an 'earnest' or 'down payment' of what is later to be received. It is not that believers have received a first instalment of the Spirit and will receive him in full later but he is the first instalment of what is to be received later. They received the Spirit when they became believers and were sealed with him (1.13; 4.30). This sealing took place when they were converted and moved from paganism to Christianity, but does not necessarily refer to the actual rite of baptism (see on 1.13). Just as God foreordained that they should believe (1.4f) so he has sealed them with the Spirit and their position is thus, as it were, doubly secure. Sealed with the Spirit they are now in receipt of numerous blessings related to the Spirit (1.3). AE does not list these; they have to be deduced from the rest of his letter and naturally more blessings exist than are explicitly mentioned.

6.5.2. Among the blessings are wisdom and revelation (1.17); the revelation relates to the equality of Jewish and Gentile believers in the church; the wisdom includes an understanding of salvation in all its width and depth (1.17–19). The Spirit strengthens believers in their Christian existence (3.16) and is therefore closely related to Christ since he dwells in those who have been strengthened (3.17). As worshippers believers use forms which either appear spontaneously among them through the Spirit or, having been part of the previously inspired worship of others, became part of tradition

(5.19). The Spirit, not wine, should enthuse worship (5.18). He is active not only in believers as individuals but also as members of the church; they form a temple for God in him (2.22) and he mediates the access of both Jews and Gentiles to God (2.18). The close relation of the Spirit to their corporate existence is seen most clearly in 4.3f where 4.4 belongs to a piece of tradition which sets body (= the church) and Spirit alongside one another, an association going back at least to 1 Cor 12.13. The unity believers enjoy within the community is then a unity created and preserved by the Spirit (4.3).

6.5.3. There are variations in the ways AE regards the Spirit as acting from what we find elsewhere in the NT; since these are mainly omissions they are probably due either to the brevity of the letter or to its naturally restricted area of interest. Despite 4.30 the Spirit is not depicted as influencing the moral life of believers. The gifts of ministry they enjoy are connected to Christ (4.7, 11) and not to the Spirit as in 1 Cor 12.4ff; 14.2, 12ff. The Spirit is not, as in Acts, a guide in travel and mission work, but then Ephesians is not narrative and has no interest in mission activity. Yet the connection Acts makes between the conscious movement of the church as directed by the Spirit to include the Gentiles (13.1–3) is reflected in 3.5. Since Ephesians does not refer to persecution there was no need for AE to say, as in the Gospels (Mk 13.11), that the Spirit would sustain believers when attacked.

6.5.4. That AE finds it necessary in order to express himself fully to refer to each member of the Trinity should not lead to the view that he was consciously aware of God's Trinitarian nature or to claiming that Ephesians alone in the Pauline corpus 'represents a primitive endeavour to relate the trinitarian nature of God to the Christian gospel'.[45]

6.6. *Christian Existence*
As AE depicts the life of Christians it is as always in relationship to God or Christ, the powers, or other Christians, but, curiously, never in relation to unbelievers.

6.6.1. AE viewed believers as living their lives in a world subject to the control of supernatural beings in a way difficult for modern Western readers to appreciate. For Gentiles the stars laid out what would happen; magic was used to affect their own lives and the lives of others; natural disasters, famine, plague, flood were the result, not of natural causes, but of supernatural; fate was dominant. When they became Christians the supernatural did not cease to control them but it emanated from God. This suggests a comparison between their pre-Christian existence and their Christian, and it is a comparison which AE makes. In 4.17–19 pagan life is seen as one lived in darkness without reference to God and as lacking a true

[45] J. W. Bowman, 'The Epistle to the Ephesians', *Int* 8 (1954) 188–205.

understanding of life; it was wholly given over to the basest forms of sexual and other sins and under the control of the devil (2.2). The old person who lived in that way has now been replaced with a new person (4.22, 24). Christian life is a new life (cf 2.15). Gentiles previously lacked the 'comforts' which Jews had enjoyed, for the latter had never been wholly without God, always had hope and were within his care (2.12). Gentile Christians have now been brought within the same care and given the same hope as Jews; Jewish and Gentile believers together are the recipients of the only true salvation, worshipping the same God and participating in the same hope.

6.6.2. AE's explanation of Christian existence is made with reference not to the world but to the church. Before conversion believers will have been members of many corporate associations, the family, their business, civil authorities, their religion. Of these AE displays interest only in the family and the church. The new lives of believers are then to be understood in relation to the lives of other believers. AE does not work this out theologically after the manner of Paul in 1 Cor 12.12ff and Rom 12.3–8 (see Essay: The Church) but practically in the way they should treat one another (see Essay: Moral Teaching). Believers became Christians through faith and baptism (4.5; 5.26), faith featuring not only in their initial response but throughout their whole Christian existence (1.19; 2.8; 3.12, 17). As members of the church they are related not only to other believers but also to God who has elected them (1.4). They are his children (1.5; 5.1; cf 5.8), are accepted by him as saints (1.1, 18, etc.), and as holy and blameless (1.4); their sins are forgiven (1.7; 2.5); they are 'light' (5.8) and wise (5.15); they receive insight into what God does (1.18; 3.18f; 5.8–10). They are joined in fellowship with Christ (2.13; 2.5, 6; 3.17; cf the formula 'in Christ'), have been raised with him and have ascended with him into the heavenlies. Strengthened by the Spirit (3.16) they are being renewed into a fresh existence (4.23f). Their daily life is described principally in two ways, as 'walking' (περιπατέω; 2.10; 4.1, 17; 5.2, 8, 15), suggestive of a slow but steady progress, and as struggle (6.10ff), for they have to fight to hold their position against supernatural attack. It is not however described as humble service as in much of the remainder of the NT (e.g. Mk 9.35; 10.43f; Lk 22.26f; Jn 13.12–16; Phil 2.5); this lack of emphasis is in keeping with AE's christology where (see §6.3.1) Christ is not presented as servant; the disciple's life should follow the pattern of his Lord's; this provides another example of AE's consistency. Believers stand within a tradition (note the use in the letter of traditional forms and concepts) which they must uphold. Moral standards are set for them (see Essay: Moral Teaching §4), though their salvation is not the result of living by these standards; they should keep them because they are Christians.

6.6.3. As believers they sing (5.19) and pray (6.18f). At the beginning they were baptised, though references to this are few;[46] only 4.5 is certain; 5.26 is highly probable; baptismal allusions may underlie other passages (1.13; 2.4–7; 4.22–4; 4.30; 5.14) though the letter is not a baptismal tract or liturgy (see §8.3.7). There is no reference, however, to participation in the eucharist.

6.7.1. Finally something should be said about the place of Ephesians in the developing theology of the church. Do we find in it the beginning of its catholicisation? The answer depends on how we define catholic.[47] The letter certainly makes it clear that its writer and readers do not belong to the first stage of the church, for apostles and prophets are figures of the past (2.20; 3.5). There is the beginning of the growth of a theology of 'glory', for the ascension receives as much attention as the cross and while believers are associated with Christ in his rising and ascension they are not associated with his suffering and death (cf Rom 6.3–11; Gal 2.19f; 6.14). There is little stress on Christian existence as one of suffering (cf 1 Cor 15.31; 2 Cor 4.10–12). Greater attention is given to moral teaching in line with later writings and out of accord with Paul. Yet, though it is assumed that the church will continue to exist for the parousia is not regarded as near, no preparation is laid out for its future such as we find in the Pastorals with their instructions on the choice of bishops and deacons, nor are detailed warnings given against heretical teaching. The letter does not emphasise its own teaching as orthodox. While the existence of ministry is envisaged the ministry still remains within the charismatic orbit rather than being institutionalised. The universal church is stressed but not in such a way as to imply it is an institution. The sacraments are not emphasised as essential elements in the polity of the church; the eucharist is not even mentioned. No clear boundaries are drawn defining those who belong to the church and distinguishing them from those who do not. Thus though Ephesians contains some elements which would be regarded as characteristic of the later 'catholic' church, they are few. It might be said that Ephesians is on the way to presenting a 'catholic' church but it is by no means there.

6.7.2. The various writings of the NT show that early Christian thinking developed along diverging, though not necessarily contradictory, lines. Ephesians lies on the line of development which passed through Paul, a line which began prior to him (he uses tradition, e.g. 1 Cor 15.3–5) and laid its stress on the benefits for believers of God's action in Christ. Paul concentrated on drawing

---

[46] See V. Warnach, 'Taufwirklichkeit und Taufbewusstein nach den Epheserbrief', *Liturgie und Mönchtum* 33/4 (1963/4) 36–51.

[47] Cf U. Luz, 'Erwägungen zur Entstehung des "Frühkatholizismus". Eine Skizze', *ZNW* 65 (1974) 88–111.

out the meaning of the cross and resurrection of Christ; AE to some extent reduced this emphasis and instead, or in addition, increased attention on the ascension. This Pauline line of tradition is different from that lying in the Synoptic Gospels with their stress on the Kingdom of God, the following of Jesus and obedience to his teaching. At times the different lines of tradition say the same thing using different words: for example, περιπατεῖν and ἀκολουθεῖν in the moral area, new birth and new creation of the nature of Christian existence, the vine and the body in relation to corporateness. The lines of development of course overlap and intertwine (cf Berger, *Theologiegeschichte, passim*).

7. LITERARY CHARACTER

7.1. In recent years much attention has been paid to the literary genre of the NT writings without any definite conclusions being reached in respect of Ephesians. Indeed some scholars (e.g. Kennedy,[48] Blomberg[49]) who attempt to place the writings of the NT into known literary categories and explain them in terms of ancient rhetoric simply avoid discussing Ephesians. Stowers in his study of ancient epistolography,[50] while not attempting to categorise the NT writings, succeeds in mentioning all the other NT letters apart from Ephesians. Aune, though categorising most NT letters, makes no attempt to do this in the case of Ephesians.[51] Typical again is a collection of essays on rhetoric and the NT[52] which barely mentions Ephesians. The treatment given by others (e.g. Strecker[53]) is often all too brief. This failure to classify Ephesians is not surprising when we read and analyse the letter.

7.1.1. An additional problem arises from the need to provide actual definitions of particular genres, as an example from modern literature shows. We know what we mean by a detective story, a thriller and a romance, but when we pick up a book in the library which professes to be either the first or second we can never be sure that it will not also contain important elements of the other two. Many writings are in fact of mixed genre. Additional difficulties are

[48] G. A. Kennedy, *New Testament Interpretation through Rhetorical Criticism*, Chapel Hill, NC, 1984. He briefly mentions Ephesians on p. 156 but only to say its author must have been 'someone of considerable rhetorical skill'.
[49] C. L. Blomberg, 'New Testament genre criticism for the 1990s', *Themelios* 15 (1990) 40–9.
[50] S. K. Stowers, *Letter Writing in Greco-Roman Antiquity*, Philadelphia, 1986.
[51] D. E. Aune, *The New Testament in its Literary Environment*, Philadelphia, 1987.
[52] *Rhetoric and the New Testament: Essays from the 1992 Heidelberg Conference* (JSNTSup 90), ed. S. E. Porter and T. H. Olbricht, Sheffield, 1993.
[53] G. Strecker, *Literaturgeschichte des Neuen Testaments* (UTB 1682) Göttingen, 1992, 71f.

created because, first, writers are individuals and do not necessarily commence, consciously or unconsciously, with a precise form in mind, and, secondly, they may not have had any detailed training in rhetoric; many lay preachers pick up how to preach from listening to other preachers rather than through formal training. AE however was not uneducated and may have received some formal instruction in rhetoric; apart from that he will have heard speeches and sermons and read letters and so have gathered some idea of the way to approach what he wished to write. Authors moreover write as individuals and not necessarily in accordance with set plans. While the structure of the formal speech received considerable attention in the ancient world that of the letter did not. There were textbook ·n letters but they confined themselves to discussing the different ·s of letters, public and private, congratulatory, commendatory, au is- ory, etc., and the purpose and style appropriate to each but not their detailed structure.[54]

7.2.1. Ephesians has the normal Pauline epistolary address and closing greetings, but as with each of Paul's letters there is some variation.[55] In Ephesians the address is in general terms rather than directed to a defined constituency; it is not followed directly by a prayer but a eulogy. The author associates no fellow Christians with him as co-authors and he names none as recipients of his greetings at the end. The letter does not reveal the character of its author as Demetrius, *On Style*, 227, says letters should (see §2.2). It lacks Paul's normal warmth. Is it then a genuine letter or a writing of another type dressed up as a letter? Aune, op.cit., 170, comments in respect of letters generally:

> Epistolary prescripts and postscripts could be used to frame almost any kind of composition. The epistolary conventions of many letter-essays, philosophical letters, and novelistic and fictional letters functioned frequently in this way. In fictional and pseudepigraphical letters the epistolary conventions often function as a legitimating device setting the composition back to an earlier period or attributing it obviously to a famous person of the past.

7.2.2. As well as the address and final greetings Ephesians contains sections of well-known minor genres: prayers, theological

---

[54] A. J. Malherbe, 'Ancient Epistolary Theorists', *OJRS* 5 (1977) 3–77; id: *Ancient Epistolary Theorists* (SBLSBS 19), Atlanta, 1988.

[55] More attention has been given to the letter genre than any other in the NT and we can only list here a fraction of the relevant literature. In addition to what has already been mentioned see H. Koskenniemi, *Studien zur Idee und Phraseologie des griechischen Briefes bis 400 n. Chr.*, Helsinki, 1956; K. Thraede, *Grundzüge griechisch-römischer Brieftopik*, Munich, 1970; W. G. Doty, *Letters in Primitive Christianity*, Philadelphia, 1973; A. J. Malherbe, op.cit.; K. Berger. 'Hellenistische Gattungen im Neuen Testament', *ANRW* II 25.2, 1326ff; J. L. White, 'New Testament Epistolary Literature in the Framework of Ancient Epistolography', *ANRW* II 25.2, 1730–56; id. *Light from Ancient Letters*, Philadelphia, 1986; D. E. Aune, op.cit.

discussions, semi-narratives and paraenesis; all these are found in other Pauline letters and also in writings of other genres. Ephesians contains nothing about Paul's movements, but this is not surprising since he is depicted as in prison. Its general nature makes it impossible to deduce from it any precise situation (e.g. heresy, persecution) to which it may have been addressed.

7.3. But is Ephesians a genuine letter? Many alternative suggestions have been made. Roughly speaking the views of those who do not regard Ephesians as a genuine letter may be classified as follows: (a) a tractate, with which should be associated a theological essay as being similar (Schlier spells this out as a *Weisheitsrede*), (b) a liturgical writing (e.g. Kirby), (c) a meditation (Conzelmann, 87), (d) a speech, (e) a homily, with which should be included the possibility that it is a sermon. In each case it is assumed that for some reason it has been turned into a letter.

7.3.1. (a) is justified because of the detailed theological discussions of the nature of the church and the reconciliation of Jewish and Gentile believers, yet it fails to account for the presence of extensive passages of devotional and paraenetic material. Advocates of (b) stress the extensive devotional material. Too little is known of the liturgies of the period for a firm conclusion to be drawn here, and a distinction has to be made between the use of liturgical language and a liturgy itself; the references to baptism are too few for it to have been a baptismal liturgy; since baptism would have been seen as a significant event in their lives by Christians who had been converted from paganism, it would not be surprising to find some references to it in any Christian writing. The presence of only one direct baptismal reference (4.5) also renders it unlikely that it represents a sermon preached at the baptism of new converts (cf Caragounis, 46 n. 83). Had it been a eucharistic sermon there would have been some reference to the eucharist, yet there is none. (c) fails for the same reason as (a), the amount of paraenetic material. (d) is supported by the final main section, 6.10–17, which resembles a peroration and by the material in the main body of the letter which instructs and persuades to action; yet the prayer in the middle (3.14–21) and the opening eulogy would have been inappropriate to a speech; praise of the addressees at the start would be, but not praise of God.

7.3.2. This leaves (e) as the most probable, for a homily could contain devotional material, theological discussion, narrative and moral counselling. A homily would also normally lack precise reference to the circumstances of the recipients for they would never be the same. A homily could of course have originated as a sermon from which for purposes of wider circulation passages relevant to the original delivery would have been removed. The NT contains other homilies: Hebrews, James, Jude, though in some way they are made to appear as letters. It should be remembered that NT letters, with the possible exception of Philemon, were never intended for private reading; they would be read aloud at gatherings for worship and so the characteristics of 'letter' would be forgotten, especially if, as in the case of Ephesians, these characteristics were not emphasised. But is it possible to regard Ephesians as a homily which has later been turned into a sermon by the addition of epistolary openings and conclusions? Certainly the introductory address (1.1f) bears little relation to the content of the letter, and could have been added later but the conclusion, 6.18–24, flows easily from what precedes and thus does not appear to be a later addition. It seems best then to think of AE as intending to write a homily but, realising that Paul normally wrote letters, deliberately disguising his homily as a letter. It is consequently of mixed genre.

7.3.3. In passing we should note two recent suggestions. Hendrix,[56] following up some work of Danker,[57] has put forward the view that Ephesians is modelled on the honorific decrees engraved on Greco-Roman monuments. While such decrees may have been the model for 1.3–14 it is much more difficult to accept them as models for the remainder of the letter, for the duties of those helped by benefactors are put in much more general terms than in the paraenesis of Ephesians. In any case the presence of moral instruction in Ephesians does not require a model from the Greco-Roman world; it formed a regular part of all earlier Jewish and Christian teaching. If we were to look for a contemporary model that of the inscription found at Philadelphia (see Barton and Horsley, §10.2.3) might be more suitable for in it there is praise of the gods followed by moral exhortation. But does everything that is written have to have one precise, identifiable model? Authors when writing draw simultaneously on many models and mix them in such a way that their compositions are always in some particulars different from other writings. A different type of suggestion has been made by Cameron[58] who sees the letter as so constructed that it is possible to deduce its structure without recourse to an examination of its content; yet the divisions in the letter which Cameron discovers are, almost without exception, the same as those commentators working from content have regularly discerned.

7.3.4. Imprecision about the literary character of Ephesians as a whole does not imply that its individual sections cannot be categorised in respect of genre and we shall be content with an analysis and identification of these based on their content. Reid remarks in respect of Paul, but what he writes is also true of Ephesians,

The greatest danger when categorizing Paul's writings is the propensity to prescribe a single typology to an entire letter. ... [Paul] enmeshed various forms of epistolary and rhetorical traditions into his letters. To describe,

[56] H. Hendrix, 'On the Form and Ethos of Ephesians', *USQR* 42/4 (1988) 3–15.

[57] F. W. Danker, *Benefactor: Epigraphic Study of a Graeco-Roman and New Testament Semantic Field*, St Louis, 1982.

[58] P. S. Cameron, 'The Structure of Ephesians', *Filologia Neotestamentaria* 3 (1990) 3–17.

not prescribe (according to ancient rhetorical theory), Paul's argumentative strategy seems to be the safest methodological approach when classifying his letters.[59]

Rhetorical analysis in any case depends on prior determination of content and content is more important than form. It is not because Eph. 1.1f appears at the beginning of Ephesians that it is termed the address but because of its content. Heb 1.1–4 begins that writing but its content shows it is not an address. Uncertainty with regard to genre means that, for instance, it is wrong to describe 1.3–3.21 as the prayer section because there are prayers in it and because prayers come at the beginning of letters. 2.1–3.13 is not prayer and should not be forced into that category to accord with a doubtful classification of genre. If Ephesians is not primarily a letter there is no need to labour to determine precisely which section of it should correspond to the so-called body of the letter. The argument starts out from 1.3 with its stress on what God has done for readers and ends at 6.18–20 after exhorting them to stand firm in the faith. Indeed the exhortation of 6.10–18 comes much closer to the peroration of a speech than anything normally found in a letter. Even if we say that Ephesians resembles in some way a speech and if, as was customary in the ancient world, it was not read privately but read aloud to the addressees, there is one distinct difference from a speech, the absence of the living presence of the writer. Sermons and lectures delivered with passion and impressing their hearers at the time may not be so impressive when read afterwards in print. The original hearers of Ephesians, if it was primarily a speech, may not have been aware of its muted character; this may only belong to our written form. It is also important when considering the effect of a writing or homily on its addressees to remember the emotion that particular words can arouse in them. To those converted from paganism to Christianity and baptised in the name of Christ the word baptism does not just recall a rite but also their past pagan life and their new Christian life. The emotive effect of words is often more persuasive than logical argument.

However in view of the difficulty of determining with any certainty the genre of Ephesians and because it is generally referred to as a letter we shall continue to apply that term to it while recognising that it is more probably a homily.

8. PURPOSE AND OCCASION

When we approach these issues we need to rid our minds of any idea that Ephesians was written to provide material for modern ecumenical

[59] J. T. Reid, 'Using Ancient Rhetorical Categories to Interpret Paul's Letters: A Question of Genre' in Porter and Olbricht, op.cit., 292–324.

discussions. It may further the understanding of the churches today as to their mutual relationship, but the church of its day was not worried by such issues. All else apart, to take the letter in this way concentrates attention entirely on some areas of its theology while ignoring others as well as ignoring its paraenetic material, which is quite as extensive as its theological.

8.1. Because of the letter's general nature and our consequent inability to tie it to any particular situation, the answers to the question of purpose have been many and diverse but to that of occasion few. Occasion and purpose are normally related though there are exceptions. Sunday requires a sermon from a minister; that is its occasion and the occasion remains the same throughout the year, yet the purpose of the sermon will vary from Sunday to Sunday, though at times its content and purpose will be determined by the Christian year. Content and purpose are necessarily related. In respect of Ephesians, lacking clues to its occasion, we have only its content from which to work; as different elements in the content are emphasised so different purposes may emerge. As far as content goes Ephesians contains two main elements: the first three chapters have a high theological content; the second three are largely paraenetic. 4.1 connects the two; there is a change here from a prevailing indicative to a prevailing imperative with the implication, 'God has been good to you, therefore be good to him and your neighbour.' The vast majority of commentators in determining the purpose have emphasised the first, or theological part, perhaps because their training makes them think theology is more important than conduct. Exegesis however shows that the relation between the two parts is not simply one of indicative and imperative; there is a clear relation between the content of the indicative and the content of the imperative. The paraenesis centres on the behaviour of believers towards one another (see exegesis of 4.1ff and Essay: Moral Teaching §3) and the theology on the internal life of the church and its relation to Christ. Thus the letter's two parts are intimately connected. This is the most important factor to be borne in mind in considering the purpose.

8.2. There are also other factors, and we now list them with that factor as the factors requiring attention in any discussion of occasion and purpose, pointing out that it is as important to note also those factors which we would expect but which are missing:

1. The unity of the two parts of the letter and their concentration on life within the church.

2. The amount of material about the church and yet the absence of discussion about its place and that of its members in the external world.

3. The concentration on the church universal rather than on the life of particular congregations.

4. The obvious interest in the relation of Gentile and Jewish Christians, though this does not seem to be an issue worrying writer or readers.

5. The generalised nature of the letter and the absence of personal references.

6. The absence of polemic against any group aberrant in belief or conduct, especially since Colossians, the Johannine literature and Revelation, all from approximately the same area and period, reveal the existence of heretical tendencies.

7. The absence of any reference to persecution, though 1 Peter and Revelation show Christians as subject to it in the same area and period and though Paul is depicted in it as a prisoner.

8. The very high proportion of paraenetic material in comparison with other letters.

9. The absence of eschatological expectancy, though present in 1 Peter and Revelation from the same area; the same absence is found also in the Gospel and letters of John.

10. The bearing of authorship on purpose; many of the alleged purposes are independent of a decision about Pauline authorship.

11. The assumption arising from the HT that all the households are wholly Christian.

8.2.1. There are other issues to keep in mind in considering purpose: (a) Authors when they write may have both a main purpose and also subsidiary purposes; for that reason it may not be possible to unify all the features of a writing under one purpose. (b) The situations determining writing need not be local but may be wide cultural situations; this would accord with the general nature of Ephesians. (c) Authors do not necessarily state their purposes openly and it may not be possible to deduce their purposes from the surface content of the text, as an illustration will show: in gatherings of official church bodies a young cleric may suggest a revolutionary advance; it will be discussed for a while and then an elderly cleric will commend it and propose the setting up of a committee to think it through; his surface purpose seems to be to advance the idea but the underlying purpose is to get it away from the public eye into a small group where it can either be killed directly or discussed for so long that it is forgotten. (d) Few authors write for their own satisfaction (cf E. F. Scott, 123) but have some purpose in mind, even if it be only the making of money.

8.3.1. Goodspeed[60] has been probably the only scholar to offer a theory connecting purpose and occasion. He argues that after Paul's

---

[60] E. J. Goodspeed, *The Meaning of Ephesians*, Chicago, 1933. This is his principal writing on the subject though he has treated it in many other books and articles, e.g. 'The Place of Ephesians in the First Pauline Collection', *ATR* 12 (1929/30) 189–212.

death interest in him declined rapidly; then Acts appeared and was read by a Gentile Christian who probably lived in Colossae for he had a thorough knowledge of Paul's Colossians; deducing that if Paul had written one letter to one church and if he had founded a number of churches as Acts showed then there ought to be other letters to other churches, he set about finding them, and when he had obtained a number he issued them as a collection. In doing this he realised that some kind of introduction to, or commentary on, them would be needed to make Paul's message relevant to his (that is, the collector's) own time, He therefore composed Ephesians, placing it at the head of the collection.[61] This theory, though widely accepted for a time, is today almost universally rejected because of its inherent difficulties: (1) Ephesians is not found at the head of any extant list of the Pauline letters despite the considerable variation among them.[62] To overcome this it has been suggested that when Marcion compiled his list with Galatians at the head he simply switched the places of Ephesians and Galatians.[63] It can be no more than a guess that Ephesians headed the original collection of Paul's letters and an even greater one that Marcion put Galatians in its place. (2) There is little to suggest that Paul was neglected after his death: the authors of Ephesians, Colossians, 2 Thessalonians, the Pastorals, would never have used Paul's name unless their readers had been acquainted with him and respected him.[64] (3) There is no certainty that Acts preceded and did not follow the initial collection of Paul's letters. (4) Ephesians would not have been a suitable introduction to, or updating of, Pauline thought; while it contains many Pauline ideas (see §§2.6, 7) the balance is not correct; there is too much on the nature of the church and too little on the place of the cross and the righteousness of God. (5) There is no certainty that there was ever an original and unique collection of Paul's letters; it is more likely that a number of small collections were made locally and later joined together.[65]

8.3.2. Although Ephesians contains only one verse (4.14) which sounds polemical this has not prevented suggestions as to false positions against which AE may have directed his letter. Following on the work of the *Religionsgeschichtliche Schule*, many have seen Ephesians as intended to refute a growing gnosticism. Evidence of this was seen in gnostic belief in a wall dividing heaven and earth; if

[61] This point had already been made by J. Weiss, *Earliest Christianity*, II, New York, 1959 (the German original, *Urchristentum*, dates from 1917).

[62] See Best, 'Recipients', 3270–5, and references there.

[63] Cf C. L. Mitton, *The Formation of the Pauline Corpus of Letters*, London, 1955, 65–74.

[64] On the continuing influence of Paul after his death see, for example, A. Lindemann, *Paulus im ältesten Christentum*, Tübingen, 1979.

[65] See K. Aland, 'Die Entstehung des Corpus Paulinum', in his *Neutestamentliche Entwürfe*, Munich, 1979, 302–50; Best, 'Recipients'.

however AE found and changed a reference to such a wall in the supposed hymn underlying 2.14–18 he was not supporting gnosticism but eliminating it (see on 2.14–18). Gnostic tones have been detected in other passages and are discussed in the relevant notes (see on 2.19–22; Detached Note: Body of Christ; on 5.22–33; and below §10.5). If there appear to be gnostic elements in Ephesians it is much more likely that AE has used some terms which, if not then, later became current in gnostic thought in order to express his own ideas, because these terms were known to his readers and their use would enable them to understand his message.[66]

D. C. Smith developed a complex and far-fetched theory in which AE is regarded as opposing a group of Gentile Christians who before they became Christians had been converted to a Judaism which valued spiritual circumcision above physical.[67] Consequently they saw themselves as superior to Jews by birth and despised them. When they became Christians they continued to despise Jews by birth who had become Christians, arguing that the blood of 2.13 was that of circumcision (this is unlikely; see on 2.13). Believing as 'spiritual' Jews that the wall between heaven and earth had been broken, as Christians they regarded themselves as already raised into heaven (2.6). However AE shares with Colossians the realised resurrection of believers (Col 3.1) and this belief cannot therefore have entered Ephesians from a supposed group of 'spiritual' Jews. Moreover for AE the wall (2.14) lies between Jew and Gentile and not between heaven and earth. Even more improbable is the view of Cornelius[68] that the letter was written to circulate in Rome in order to support Paul against those who argued for Peter's superiority. Lindemann sees the conflict imagery of 6.10–17 as indicating the church was being persecuted and the letter as written to sustain believers under pressure;[69] 6.10–17 is however only a small element in the letter and it is difficult to relate the remainder of the letter to persecution. Beatrice[70] views 6.10–17 as directed against satanic Jewish opponents but it is difficult to discern any anti-Judaism in that passage. Goulder, art.cit., 21, argues that the letter was directed against Jewish-Christian visionaries; in the course of making this argument he assumes positions which are normally rejected: that ἅγιοι denotes an elite group, that in 2 Cor 12.1ff Paul is not referring to himself, that Ephesians was written specifically to Laodicea and no other church. Each of these is less than probable and their combined probability is very low. Also Goulder in

[66] For a survey of the discussion of gnostic influence in Ephesians see Merkel, 3176–95.

[67] D. C. Smith, 'The Ephesian Heresy', SBL papers, 1974, 45–54; id. 'The Ephesian Heresy and the Origin of the Epistle to the Ephesians', OJRS 5 (1977) 78–103.

[68] F. Cornelius, 'Die geschichtliche Stellung des Epheserbriefes', ZRGG 7 (1955) 74–6.

[69] A. Lindemann, 'Bemerkungen zu den Adressaten und zum Anlass des Epheserbriefes', ZNW 67 (1976) 235–51.

[70] F. Beatrice, 'Il combattimento spirituale secondo san Paulo. Interpretazione di Ef 6, 10–17', Studia Patavina 19 (1972) 359–422.

sketching out the background of Jewish speculation draws on material which must be dated later than the letter. Finally, and perhaps most importantly, he fails to account for the large element of paraenesis in the letter.

8.3.3. Fischer sees in the letter a twofold polemical thrust. (1) (pp. 21–39) The titles of ministers in 4.11 do not reflect those to be expected in the post-Pauline period. From approximately the same period come the Pastorals, Acts 20.18–35 and 1 Clem 42.4 and these reveal the emergence of a non-charismatic ministry of bishop, elder and deacon. AE's naming of evangelists, teachers and pastors is an attempt to oppose this new type of ministry and to continue that of Paul. But: (a) AE does not particularly stress the charismatic nature of the list in 4.11 (see on 4.7–11) but rather that of all believers. (b) 'Evangelist' is not one of the titles found in the genuine Paulines for ministers, so in advocating this name AE would not have been faithful to the Pauline tradition. (c) The ministry is still fluid at the time of Ephesians; for example, 1 Peter 5.1–5 refers to elders but not to bishops; there is no reference to ministry in Colossians where the author had ample opportunity to make such a reference in his final greetings (3.7ff); titles cannot then have been all-important. (d) The passage in which 4.11 occurs is not sufficiently polemical to suggest AE was excluding a new type of ministry. (2) (pp. 79–94) While a polemical thrust is often seen in the discussion of Jewish and Gentile Christians, Fischer views this not as an attempt to persuade Jewish Christians to accept Gentiles but the reverse. AE, suspecting that Gentile Christians have been boasting of their position within the church, writes to remind them that Jewish Christians have also a right to be there. The evidence for such a view is simply not present in Ephesians (see on 2.15b). Pokorný, 41ff, sees those whom AE addresses as people who have lost their first enthusiasm and are in danger of deserting their Pauline inheritance; some believers in Asia Minor placed John above Paul to the extent of excluding Paul from the apostles (Rev 21); the Pauline tradition as taught in Ephesians is seen as indispensable for the unity of the church and as based on its historical foundation and not on spiritualist or syncretistic ideas. If AE had intended to stress the position of Paul he would have been better not to have written 3.5 which allows John a position at least level with that of Paul.

8.3.4. Because the letter pays so much attention to the relationship of Jewish and Gentile Christians, many view it as intended to deal with that relationship. At the time of its composition there was a considerable Jewish population in Asia Minor, some of whom naturally became Christians. All the first believers also had been Jews and many of them had opposed the acceptance of Gentiles as their equals in the church. Arguments about this may not have wholly died down by AE's time and so he writes both to reassure his Gentile readers that they have a full and legitimate place in the church[71] and to justify Paul's work in arguing for their admission. It cannot be denied that AE may have been thinking of Jewish–Gentile relationships as he wrote and this may have been a subsidiary purpose, yet it occupies too small a proportion of the letter to be its main purpose. In particular nothing in the large paraenetic section connects, even remotely, with the Jewish–Gentile issue. Paul certainly receives considerable attention but there is no emphasis suggesting that the communities which he had not founded personally should learn to look on him as their founder (cf Kümmel). Chadwick[72] sees quite another purpose in the extensive references to the Jews. In the ancient world new ideas were suspect; a long history gave importance to peoples and concepts; we see this idea exemplified in Josephus' *Contra Apionem* where he argues for apologetic reasons that Jews are an ancient race. In Greek eyes then there was a danger that the church could be disregarded because it was new. Over against this AE argues that the church is continuous with Israel and therefore could claim Israel's history as behind it; its members moreover were elect from even before the foundation of the world. The church then is not to be despised but given an honourable place. Yet Jews were not popular in the ancient world, and it may not have been any advantage to Christians to be associated with them. Again, while the interest in Judaism and the Jews cannot be gainsaid as a subsidiary reason for the writing of the letter, it is not its main purpose since it makes so much of the letter's content irrelevant. Schmithals[73] regards the occasion of the letter as that of the expulsion of Jewish Christians from the synagogue and its 'chief purpose ... was to secure the acceptance by the gentile Christians from the Pauline communities of their Christian brothers who came from the synagogue and at the same time to acquaint the latter with the Pauline tradition'. It is however difficult to detect anything in the letter specifically directed to this purpose; many important Pauline ideas are absent and on this hypothesis the paraenesis becomes irrelevant.

8.3.5. Chadwick saw outer cultural considerations as the main factor leading to the writing of Ephesians. However even if his

[71] E.g. J. B. Polhill, 'An Introduction to Ephesians', *RevExp* 76 (1979) 465–80. W. Grundmann, 'Die νήπιοι in der Urchristlichen Paränese', *NTS* 5 (1958/9) 188–215, suggests (p. 194 n. 1) that there may have been an influx of Jews into Asia Minor after the uprising in Palestine of AD 66–70 which renewed speculation on Jewish–Gentile relationships. That this influx may have taken place does nothing to meet the general objections to this view.

[72] H. Chadwick, 'Die Absicht des Epheserbriefes', *ZNW* 51 (1960) 145–53.

[73] W. Schmithals, 'The *Corpus Paulinum* and Gnosis', *The New Testament and Gnosis* (FS R. McL. Wilson, ed. A. H. B. Logan and A. J. M. Wedderburn), Edinburgh, 1983, 107–24, at 122.

particular view is rejected there may have been other outward circumstances which it was written to counter (cf Gnilka, 47; Schnackenburg, 35; Lona, 435f). It was a cosmopolitan period in Asia Minor with a rapidly changing economic and political situation; cities were being constantly reminded that they could not settle their own destinies but belonged to the larger unit of the Empire. Religious syncretism prevailed. In all this flux believers needed to see in their faith a stabilising influence. AE however pays no attention to what was happening outside the church and is apparently indifferent to this external flux. If an external crisis existed and was worrying believers, then we should expect signs of it also in other Christian writings from the same period, but apart from the threat of persecution such signs are absent. If believers are summoned to stand firm (6.10ff), it is not in the light of the political and economic situation or of various new religions but in the context of heavenly forces seeking to draw them away from their faith. The outward circumstances however may not have been those of the economic and political sphere but those of the general church situation (cf Houlden, 253; Martin, *Foundations*, 233). The theological thought of the Gospel and epistles of John and of Revelation, all of which were current in approximately the same area as Ephesians, find no place for Paul; Revelation with its stress on 'twelve' (twelve gates and twelve apostles, 21.12–14) explicitly excludes a thirteenth apostle, that is, Paul. Ephesians may then be countering an anti-Pauline sentiment. Yet 1 Peter which belongs to the same area has a very close association with Pauline thought and anti-Paulinism may not then have been so widespread. Paul's position indeed is only emphasised in a small portion of the letter and its reinforcement cannot be regarded as a main purpose.

8.3.6. One popular explanation of the purpose of Ephesians sees it against the background of Colossians. Eadie, p. li, thought of Paul, dispirited after what was happening in Colossae, pouring out in Ephesians his inmost thoughts on the transcendental doctrines of the Gospel. Bruce, 241, expresses the same idea describing Ephesians as the 'logical sequel' to Colossians in 'expounding the cosmic role of the church' as Colossians had that of Christ. These and similar views of the purpose have usually been advanced by those adhering to Pauline authorship, yet those who have rejected that authorship have also expressed the purpose in similar ways. Moffatt, 393, spoke of it as 'a catholicised version of Colossians', a phrase which many have picked up and used. Such a solution to the purpose is impossible if either the two letters do not have a common author or AE did not use Colossians. Although this explanation is popular it is not without major difficulties. Similarities in thought exist between the two letters (see §2.5 and §3) but there are also differences which cannot be easily explained on the assumption of generalisation.

Colossians is directed against a specific heresy; Ephesians is not; yet heresies of various kinds were rampant in the contemporary church; we might therefore have expected AE to make some general statement about how heresy might be defeated, for example, by holding fast to Christ (cf Col 2.19). Colossians has a quite general view of all humanity as equal in God's eyes (3.11); AE argues only for the equality of Jews and Gentiles (2.11ff) even though he sees some equality between masters and slaves (6.5–9). The recognition in Col 4.5 that believers need to consider their relationship to the outside world is dropped by AE. The extent of attention paid in Ephesians to the church is hardly an extension, development or catholicisation of what is in Colossians; it moves off in another direction. The introduction of references to salvation through grace in Eph 2.8–10 picks up nothing in Colossians. It does however suggest that Ephesians itself, like Colossians, is another development or adaptation of Paul. Yet here caution is necessary. Ephesians may be a development or adaptation of Paul, but adaptation or development by themselves will not be the purpose of Ephesians but the result of the purpose. The purpose has been to meet a new situation and in meeting it the author who is a Paulinist will draw on his master. AE did not begin by saying to himself, 'I must extend Paul's thought'; he began with a situation he saw needed addressing and because he was a Paulinist he dealt with it in Pauline terms and so extended Paul's theology. Of course if Paul is the author he will naturally be adapting and developing himself.

8.3.7. Interest in liturgy and the recognition that Ephesians contains liturgical fragments has led some scholars to regard the letter from that angle. In particular Dahl has stressed the connection of the letter with baptism.[74] Addressed to Gentiles who had been fairly recently baptised, its purpose is to remind them of the significance and importance of their baptism. Luz describes it as *Tauferinnerungsgottesdienst*.[75] It is true the letter contains a number of possible references to baptism, 4.5; 5.26; 1.13; 4.30; 4.22–4; but only the first of these is certain and 5.26 highly probable; 5.14 may also be part of a baptismal hymn; 1.13; 4.30; 4.22–4 are not references (see notes on the passages).[76] The move from paganism to Christianity of believers was centred on a ceremony, and that

[74] N. A. Dahl, 'Adresse und Proëmium des Epheserbriefes', *TZ* 7 (1951) 241–64; id. 'Das Gehemnis der Kirche nach Eph. 3, 8–10', *Zur Auferbauung des Leibes Christi* (FS P. Brunner, ed. E. Schlink and A. Peters), Kassel, 1965, 63–75; id. 'Interpreting Ephesians: Then and Now', *Currents in Theology and Mission*, 5 (1978) 133–43.

[75] U. Luz, 'Überlegungen zum Epheserbrief und seiner Paränese', *Neues Testament und Ethik* (FS R. Schnackenburg, ed. H. Merklein), Freiburg, Basel, Vienna, 1989, 376–96.

[76] Cf Warnach, art.cit.; R. Fung, 'The Doctrine of Baptism in Ephesians', *Studiae Biblicae et Theologicae* 1 (1971) 6–14.

ceremony will have remained a significant event throughout their lives. It would not be unnatural for a preacher or writer making points about how his readers should live to remind them of its beginning. That AE refers to baptism directly or obliquely does not then make his letter a baptismal address. Dahl's theory however has one advantage over many others in that it makes the paraenetic section credible, for when Gentiles became Christians they took on a new ethic. However, Dahl's view does not explain why the ethic should be one relating only to the internal life of the church (see Essay: Moral Teaching §3). If believers were being reminded they had entered a new world it would have been natural to say something about their relation to the one they had left. Kirby also seeks to understand the letter liturgically, and does so by relating it to the Jewish festival of Pentecost, a festival which through the coming of the Holy Spirit became important also for Christians. After explaining the significance of Pentecost for contemporary Judaism and the OT passages used in connection with it, he turns to the letter and argues its relation to the festival. He notes that Ephesians contains comparatively more references to the Spirit than any other Pauline letter apart from Romans, but in Romans they tend to be grouped together whereas in Ephesians they are spread throughout. The most important OT link between the letter and Pentecost is Ps 68 which may be referred to at 4.8. Yet it is not clear that Ps 68 is being used consciously at 4.8 (see on 4.8) and the references to the other OT passages associated with Pentecost are even less certain. Because of the vagueness of the allusions and the inaccurate way Ps 68.18 is quoted it is very doubtful if AE's readers would have realised they were reading a Pentecostal address. There is also much less confidence today in the existence of Jewish lectionaries and a Jewish liturgical canon in the first century than when Kirby wrote.[77]

8.3.8. Occasionally it is suggested that the readers of the letter were in a state of spiritual crisis which the letter was written to meet (e.g. Schnackenburg, 34; Lincoln, 440[78]). Crisis is a strong word; all congregations are always in some kind of crisis, though mostly these are minor. The crisis may come from outside occasioned by a cultural, economic, political or syncretistic situation; such pressures have been discussed above (§8.3.5) and dismissed. If there was a crisis it more probably lay within the community, or communities, and in the areas of heretical thought, moral conduct, worship, or

---

[77] Cf P. Bradshaw, *The Search for the Origins of Christian Worship*, London, 1992, 1ff; J. Heinemann, *Prayer in the Talmud: Forms and Patterns*, Berlin/New York, 1977; id. 'The Triennial Lectionary Cycle', *JJS* 19 (1968) 41–8.

[78] Lincoln is not consistent for he supplies another and more reasonable purpose in his introduction; see §8.4 below; AE may of course have written with more than one purpose in mind.

leadership. None of these possible areas of dispute, however, looms large in Ephesians. There is no summons to worship more regularly, or attend the eucharist, or pray more often; leaders are mentioned but thei is no sign that their authority is being disregarded; though the dis͟ between Jewish and Gentile believers is recognised it does not appear to be an active factor; the extent of the paraenetic section and its content might suggest that believers were not always on good terms with each other, yet there are no signs of deep division. Finally the idea that the letter is written to deal with a serious crisis has to face the difficulty that it is a general letter and not one written to a particular situation. The same major crisis would hardly be affecting several congregations simultaneously. In any case to say that the letter was written because of a spiritual or other crisis does not of itself tell us what the purpose was; the nature of the crisis has to be identified and then the letter is a response to that particular crisis and not simply to crisis itself. In a variation of this view it is sometimes said that AE recognised the immaturity of his potential readers and set out to do something about it; this is true, but is it really saying anything? What preacher addressing believers would deny that his or her sermon was not designed to help them mature in their faith and life?

8.3.8.1. Arnold, 165–71, provides a variation of the idea of a spiritual crisis by suggesting that the readers feared the supernatural forces associated with the powers and manifesting themselves in magic and witchcraft. It is certainly true that the powers feature more prominently in Ephesians than in other letters and that the final section (6.10–20) centres on their activity and how believers can be freed from them. Yet the major part of the letter has nothing to do with the powers but is concerned with the nature of the church and the kind of behaviour to be expected from believers. In this the letter coheres. There is nothing in the letter which directly connects the powers to the church. They are, rather, an important factor in the milieu of the readers, a milieu which is cosmic and supernatural and not just economic, political, scientific, artistic, and cannot therefore be ignored. Yet the moral teaching about how believers should live within the church is not directly related to supernatural evil apart from the general exhortation of 4.27. Sin has a human aspect as well as a supernatural and needs to be fought on the human level; hence the exhortations which do not mention supernatural powers and the lack of a summons to believers to pray for help against the temptation to untruthfulness, theft, lust, etc. That AE discusses the fight against the powers is a subsidiary but not a main purpose.

8.3.8.2. Penna, 58, writes of a lack of grasp on the part of the readers of the new nature of the church in bringing together Jews and Gentiles and of the new moral teaching of their faith; he sees the two halves of the letter as held together by the idea of the 'new person' (2.15; 4.24; cf 3.16; 4.13); this link however only explains the connection formally but not substantially.

8.4. To establish the purpose of the letter it must be looked at as a whole and minor interests and sections must not be elevated to a primary position. It is necessary also to take account of what from our knowledge of early Christianity we might expect to find but is missing: believers are not summoned to a life of suffering in the following of Christ, a steadfast witness about their faith to a pagan world, or perseverance until the end comes. Yet what is there holds together; the first half sets out teaching on the unity of the church and its relation to Christ; the second half instructs believers how they are to live with one another within their Christian communities. Lincoln, lxxviiif, is on the way to accepting this when he says AE writes both to intensify his readers' adherence to Christian convictions and to encourage them to live in accordance with Christian values.[79] But he has not adequately grasped the coherent nature of the letter. If this is taken into account we can say that AE writes to ensure the corporate maturity of believers and does so by driving home the nature of the body they joined when they left the pagan world, and the type of behaviour which would produce true growth in their communities; since they are Gentiles he has necessarily to touch on the Jewish–Gentile question. There has never been a Christian group which has not required reminding of its need to mature and this need is the contingent factor which has led to the letter and the presentation of a Pauline-type theology to meet it. All this is set within a supernatural or cosmic framework from which through recollection of their election and baptism and through prayer and worship believers receive the love and strength to grow. That the content of the moral teaching may appear in our eyes at times to fall below that of Jesus and Paul is irrelevant; AE obviously considered it met his purpose. That AE concentrates on the interior life of the Christian community does not mean he could not have written another piece on behaviour in respect of the outside world. He has not done so but chosen to concentrate on another area of Christian living. The purpose which inspired his letter does not require a special situation, for at all times and in all places Christian communities need to be reminded that they should act as unified wholes and not as groups of individuals and should stand firm against supernatural forces. Beker's view,[80] that it is difficult to discern a contingency factor in respect of Ephesians, should be

---

[79] M. Breeze, 'Hortatory Discourse in Ephesians', *Journal of Translation and Text Linguistics* 5 (1992) 313, sees the connection between the two parts of the letter but regards the first part as motivational of the second; the first, theological, part has however a value of its own; if nothing more, it forms the logical base for the second half.

[80] J. C. Beker, *Heirs of Paul*, Minneapolis, 1991, 68–71.

mentioned here. His understanding of what constitutes a contingency factor is too narrow; contingencies range from an author's inner need to a general cultural situation and do not necessarily centre on the particular problems of a particular congregation. The sermons most ministers preach Sunday by Sunday are not tied to specific flaws in their congregations but are of a general nature intended to help their people mature.

8.4.1. So far we have identified a number of possible subsidiary purposes but not the main purpose. Was there a general situation which provoked the letter? We can only hazard a guess. All those entering the church from paganism came from membership in various groups, either from groups related to their work such as trade guilds or groups concerned in different ways with the ongoing life of the community or cult groups (see §10.3). They would have participated in at least some of these. Now as Christians they have entered a new group and it is important that they should realise its nature and the conduct required of them in it. The new group has both an eternal setting and, since they are Gentiles, a setting in relation to Israel. Paul's position also needs stressing, for it is because of his missionary work that they owe their relation to Israel, even though they may not have been converted by him. The relation to Israel and the reference to Paul then represent subsidiary purposes.

8.4.2. It can be seen that this conclusion meets most of the desiderata set out in §8.2. Given this purpose there was no need to mention the End; since persecution did not necessarily affect the inner life of congregations it could be ignored; a summons to proclaim the Gospel to outsiders might relate to the size of a congregation but not its nature. The one important element in the list of §8.2 which has not been explained is the restriction of the HT to wholly Christian households though the presence of the HT is certainly fitting since it deals with the conduct of believers to one another. Both its presence and its narrowness may perhaps be due to its use within the Pauline school to which AE and A/Col belonged; neither author may have realised its limitations. Its narrowness certainly suited AE's general purpose since to have dealt with the relation of Christian and pagan spouses would have been to bring in the relation of the church and the outside world, a subject AE has decided to ignore.

9. PREFORMED MATERIAL

Schmid, 313–31; C. H. Dodd, *According to the Scriptures*, London, 1952; E. E. Ellis, *Paul's Use of the Old Testament*, Edinburgh, 1957; H. Löe, 'Christus und die Christen: Untersuchungen zum Verständnis der Kirche in

76 COMMENTARY ON EPHESIANS

den grossen Paulusbriefen und im Kolosser–und Epheserbrief' (unpublished dissertation, Heidelberg, 1965); A. T. Hanson, *The New Testament Interpretation of Scripture*, London, 1980; id. *The Living Utterances of God*, London, 1983; A. T. Lincoln, 'The Use of the OT in Ephesians', *JSNT* 14 (1982) 16–57; D.-A. Koch, *Die Schrift als Zeuge des Evangeliums*, Tübingen, 1986; T. Moritz, 'The Use of Israel's Scriptures in Ephesians' (Ph.D. thesis, King's College, University of London 1994), a summary in *TynB* 46 (1995) 393–6.

A. C. King, 'Ephesians in the Light of Form Criticism', *ExpT* 63 (1951/2) 143–6; G. Schille, 'Liturgisches Gut im Epheserbrief' (unpublished dissertation, Göttingen, 1952); id. *Frühchristliche Hymnen*, Berlin, 1965; K. Wegenast, *Das Verständnis der Tradition bei Paulus und in den Deuteropaulinen* (WMANT 8), Neukirchen, 1962; J. T. Sanders, 'Hymnic Elements in Ephesians 1–3', *ZNW* 56 (1965) 214–32; Fischer, 136–78; M. Barth, 'Traditions in Ephesians', *NTS* 30 (1984) 3–27; Merkel, 3222–38; S. E. Fowl, *The Story of Christ in the Ethics of Paul* (JSNTSup 36), Sheffield, 1990; Best, 'Use'.

All writers are indebted to their predecessors who have discussed their subject in that they pick up their ideas and develop them. Writers also regularly quote or allude to material already in existence, i.e. preformed material.

9.1. The first obvious source of preformed material for the writers of the NT is the OT. 'Old Testament' is used here in a general kind of way, for it is not strictly the correct title under which to classify the material in mind. When AE wrote the term was not in use to refer to what we call the OT, for there was no NT from which it needed to be distinguished. It is also not correct to speak in this connection of the OT canon, for 'canon' was not a term in use to describe an authoritative set of writings. Certainly all the writings in what we call the Hebrew canon were accepted as authoritative by both the Jews and Christians of our period. But were there other writings which Christians regarded as authoritative? Jude apparently accepts *1 Enoch*, or some parts of it, as such (vv. 14f). Paul uses expansions of the OT story current in Jewish circles but not in the OT itself as if they were as authoritative for him as the OT text (1 Cor 10.4; Gal 4.29). He introduces 1 Cor 2.9 in the same way as he introduces the OT, but it does not correspond exactly to any passage in the OT. Mt 27.9 is not in our Jeremiah though it apparently was in the Evangelist's. Different NT authors may then have operated with different OT 'canons', or sets of authoritative writings, both from one another and from what we accept. When then we discuss AE's use of the OT do we mean what we designate as the OT or what he would have designated as authoritative Jewish writings? Variations also exist between the MT and the LXX, but these variations cause no problem for AE always uses the LXX and never refers to passages where the difference between the MT and the LXX is significant. Since his references to the LXX are few we cannot be sure what manuscript tradition he followed. In the manner of its divergence from the MT the LXX sometimes resembles a targum. Did the targums carry the same authority for AE as the MT or the LXX? This is an important issue, for the quotation in 4.8 is much closer to what is found in one targum than to either MT or LXX (see on 4.8). It is important also to inquire where a suspected OT text is used whether readers would have recognised its source and would have granted authority to that source.

9.1.1. What degree of variation is acceptable in a citation from the OT if it is still to be regarded as from the OT? Paul regularly varies the tense and mood of verbs, changes the person or modifies singular into plural (see Koch, 110–15) and normally does so to accommodate his citations to their place in his argument. Sometimes the modification affects the actual meaning as when he adds πᾶς to his quotation of Isa 28.16 in Rom 10.11 (he does not add it when quoting the same passage in Rom 9.33). However, Eph 4.8 contains a massive alteration from both LXX and MT in the citation of Ps 68.18, for in 4.8 Christ is said to give gifts instead of God receiving them as in the MT and LXX. While the variation from God to Christ is not out of accord with similar variations when OT passages are being quoted, that from receiving to giving is. What would children say if told on their birthdays that they were not going to receive gifts from their uncles and aunts but must instead give gifts? It is better then not to regard this quotation as drawn from the OT. A. T. Hanson wisely says that if someone has 'altered the text of Scripture in order to adapt it for a proof, it fails altogether as a proof' (*Interpretation*, 7). Despite this, when he comes to write about Eph 4.8 he says 'Here is an absolutely explicit citation of Psalm 68.18 ... The point that strikes us at once is that the author has apparently altered the psalm in order to accommodate it to the meaning he wished to extract from it' (*Utterances*, 98f). We accept the first quotation from Hanson and therefore do not regard the use of Ps 68.18 in 4.8 as a quotation of scripture.

9.1.2. AE does not alert us with an introductory formula when citing the OT in 5.31 and 6.2f. There must be many Jewish texts which are no longer extant or of which the form in which we have them is not the same as their first-century form. Could it be that AE quotes from such writings at other places and we recognise neither what he quotes nor even that he is quoting? This is a question which by its very nature it is impossible to answer.

9.1.3. We are accustomed to draw a distinction between early church credal or liturgical material and OT material; did such a distinction exist for AE? Were they equally authoritative in his eyes? When Paul quoted the creed of 1 Cor 15.3–5, did it carry for him the same authority as an OT passage? When in 1 Cor 7.10 he instructs married people as 'from the Lord' and not himself the

instruction must have come from the Lord through Paul; would AE
have put an instruction coming from God through Paul on the same
level as an OT instruction? The distinction we draw in respect of
preformed material as deriving from the OT, and possibly other
Jewish writings, or as deriving from the early church, may not
represent a distinction AE would have recognised. To put this
another way: when AE quotes what we regard as OT scripture was
he aware he was quoting the OT, or did he think he was using
preformed Christian material? This is a difficult question to resolve
for much OT material had become so absorbed into Christian speech
that at times the Christians who used it may not have been aware of
its ultimate source. We cannot then always distinguish between an
author's direct use of the OT and an indirect, for the relevant OT
words may have become part of Christian language.

9.1.4. 5.31 and 6.2f are two clear instances where AE knowingly
cites the OT. Neither is formally introduced as a citation but both
would have been familiar to readers (see on the passages) and
therefore not require an introductory formula. 6.2f is made relevant
to the argument through the omission of a phrase from the original
(Exod 20.12). 5.31 applies Gen 2.24 to human marriage in accordance with its original sense, but it is also used in a way unforeseen in
the OT in relation to Christ and the church in that it supplies the
scriptural basis for AE's association of human marriage with the
marriage of Christ and the church; it might be said to be the text
governing 5.22–33. A combination of Isa 57.19 and 52.7 underlies
2.17 and probably 2.13; the Isaianic passages are given a new
meaning in providing an argument for the admission of Gentiles into
the church and AE is probably aware that he is both quoting and at
the same time adapting the meaning. In 4.25 AE cites Zech 8.16
without an introductory phrase; the final chapters of Zechariah were,
however, widely used in the NT and since the actual passage is also
quoted in *T Dan* 5.2 AE was probably aware he was quoting and his
readers may have been also. The same is true of his use of Ps 4.5 at
4.26 for this Psalm probably lay in the Jewish ethical tradition much
of which was taken over by the first Christians. Ps 110.1 and Ps 8.6
underlie 1.20, 22; the reference, particularly in the case of Ps 110.1,
is brief; the two Psalms were already joined in Christian thought (1
Cor 15.25, 27); Ps 110.1 is quoted in accordance with what appears
to have been Christian usage rather than in the precise terms of the
LXX; it may then well be that AE is here picking up Christian
language rather than consciously quoting the OT. AE thus perceives
in the Psalms a christological sense. Some of the final words of 5.2
recall Exod 29.18 and Ezek 20.41 but the total phrase is liturgical
and AE probably drew it from its use in Christian worship and not
directly from the OT. In his description of the Christian's armour
(6.14–17) AE probably depends on Isaiah at a number of points;

like Zechariah, Isaiah was one of the best-known OT books in the early church. The spiritualisation of the various pieces of armour was already present in it and some of the relevant passages already in use among Christians (1 Th 5.8). It is possible AE, given the clue from 1 Th 5.8 (cf Wisd 5.18), searched out in Isaiah the other passages. In all of this there is nothing in which he departs from the ways in which other NT writers use the OT except that he never employs an introductory phrase to show he is quoting.

9.2. There is also preformed material of Christian origin. Paul, who was in effect a second-generation Christian, employed this type of material (e.g. 1 Cor 15.3–5; Phil 2.6–11) and AE would have done the same. What is not in mind here is AE's general dependence on the Pauline letters, his use of Pauline metaphors and concepts, or his special dependence on Colossians, if this existed (6.21f is a special case; see notes on it); equally to be excluded is any use of liturgical phrases like 'the God and Father of our Lord Jesus Christ' or 'amen', and of epistolary (1.1f) and liturgical forms like the doxology (3.20f), the benediction (6.23f) and the eulogy (1.3ff).

9.2.1. Authors use preformed material for a number of purposes: (i) they hope it will adorn what they write, e.g. a verse of poetry; (ii) they believe the preformed material expresses what they wish to say better than anything they themselves could write; (iii) they quote the statement of an opponent in order to refute it; (iv) the preformed material acts as a kind of text from which they can develop their own ideas; (v) it sums up what they have been attempting to say; (vi) they believe its quotation would carry some authority with their readers; (vii) it provides a standard way for expressing what they wish to say, as in the case of the address of a letter. In respect of AE we can almost certainly say there are no clear instances of (i) and (ii) unless the quotation in 4.8 was regarded as poetry; (iii) is absent since Ephesians is not a polemical writing; (vii), the use of standard forms, reveals little about the author or what he is writing; there do not appear to be any instances of (v). This leaves (iv) and (vi). Quotations as such do not need to be pointed out when they can be presumed to be known to readers; thus AE did not acknowledge his quotations in 5.31 and 6.2f. In considering whether preformed material would be known to readers we have to remember that AE was not writing to a single community which he had founded and which would accordingly know his teaching, but to a much wider circle. If it was certain, which it is not, that all converts received precisely the same instruction when they first became Christians this difficulty would be eliminated.

9.2.2. In the case of AE's use of the OT we possess his source and therefore can be sure he is quoting; this is not so for the Christian material preceding AE, apart from Paul's letters. It is therefore much more difficult to detect such material. Tests exist which can help in discerning it: a break in subject-matter before and after it or the use in it of a vocabulary foreign to the author. It is unnecessary to list these tests since this has been done many times.[81] We shall discuss only those passages where exegetes, using these tests, have suggested a strong possibility that preformed material exists. Accordingly we do not discuss 1.3–14; 1.20–3; 2.4–10; 2.14–18; 2.19–22; 3.5; 5.25–7; for their exclusion see notes on them and Best, 'Use'. Discussion of the origin and earlier context of the preformed material will also be found in the notes and is therefore omitted here.

9.2.3. At only two points, 4.8; 5.14, does AE indicate he is using preformed material. He did not take 4.8 directly from Ps 68 but probably knew it as a piece of floating tradition (it does ultimately depend on Ps 68.18; see notes); yet if his readers had looked up either MT or LXX they would certainly not have found it. Since he introduces it with διὸ λέγει but does not use this or any other formula to introduce the OT at 5.31 and 6.2f, it is probable his readers, or some of them (he is writing to a wide circle), would not have known it. 5.14 is probably a passage from a baptismal hymn (see notes). The introductory formula in each case serves to give authority to the passages whether his readers knew them or not. 4.8 is employed to confirm 4.7 rather than to serve as a basis for what follows. 5.14 sums up the preceding argument. 4.4–6, with the omission of some words from v. 4 which link it to what precedes (see notes and Best, 'Use'), is preformed hymnic or credal material and as such probably known to AE's readers; the added words in v. 4 serve to connect it to vv. 1–3 and drive home what is touched on there, the unity of believers; the quotation is also a base for what follows in the remainder of the letter relating to unity. Probably a couplet underlies both 2.1, 5 and Col 2.13 (see on 2.1):

καὶ ὑμᾶς ὄντας νεκροὺς τοῖς παραπτώμασιν
συνεζωοποίησεν [σὺν] τῷ Χριστῷ.

This is the underlying basis for the argument of 2.1–10 for it stresses both the human condition prior to Christ and salvation through him. 5.2b may well incorporate two pieces of tradition, the first that Christ gave himself for believers and the second comparing what he did to the sweet smell of sacrifice, the latter deriving ultimately from the OT but probably already in use in Christian circles.

9.2.4. The *Haustafel* was a piece of tradition (cf Best, 'Haustafel'). Originally non-Christian it had been adapted for Christian use prior to its appearance in Ephesians and Colossians. It is the most extensive piece of tradition used by AE and he expands each of its three sections. In the first he introduces a new facet of his

---

[81] See, for example, Barth, *NTS* 30 (1984) 3–25; Schille, 15–20; Fischer, 110–11.

teaching on the church, in the second he drives home its point by adding an OT quotation, and in the third he makes clear to Christian slaves their responsibilities to their masters. In view of the way he modified the traditional form it is surprising that he did not remove from it the impression that it relates only to wholly Christian households; yet had he done so he would not then have been able to make the link in the first section to Christ and the church. Catalogues of virtues and vices were well known in the ancient world and used by Christians; A/Col used one at 3.5 and AE may be drawing on the same catalogue at 5.3, 5. If there was a recognised form of post-baptismal catechetical instruction in the early church, and we cannot be sure there was, it is difficult to determine what it was and even more difficult to decide where AE has used it and where he has ignored it. If AE used it the parts he employed would be highlighted for his readers and the parts he omitted would make them wonder why they were omitted. In the same way when his readers saw his enlargement of the HT, which presumably they knew, they would pay special heed to his variations, as they would also to his reproduction of the formula of 5.2 at 5.25 where he applies the underlying tradition to the church instead of the individual.

9.2.5. We should note: (i) The absence of quotations from the teaching of Jesus, or at least from those parts of it known to us, yet 4.20f suggests that his readers were not unacquainted with some of it. (ii) There is nothing which tells us that the preformed tradition used by AE originated with Paul or in the Pauline school; certainly the HT did not. By the time AE wrote there were several strands of tradition developing in the church resulting in the Synoptic Gospels, the Johannine literature, the Pastoral Epistles, Hebrews, Revelation, and he could have drawn on one or other of these strands as well as on the Pauline. (iii) There is no call by AE to his readers to hold on to the tradition they have received from him or from Paul; presumably he assumes they will.

9.2.6. Finally it should be remember that AE was a child of his time and in common with other believers and with non-Christians he accepted the preformed ideas of his culture, e.g. the necessity of slave labour, the superiority of husbands. Of course neither he nor his readers would probably have recognised such ideas as tradition for they were too much part and parcel of their culture; they would have assumed their universal truth.

9.3. There is one last relevant question: If AE used pre-existing material did he or someone else later add to what he wrote? This is the question of the integrity of the letter. It can be seen to arise in different ways.

9.3.1. In attempting to solve the problem of the relation of Ephesians to

Colossians, Holtzmann raised the possibility that Colossians passed through more than one edition. An alternative approach would be to argue that an original Ephesians was revised with additions. It contains stretches where it is close in thought and wording to Colossians and stretches where there is little relation between the two. Were the latter portions added later? Ochel argued that AE wrote a brief letter in which he depended on Colossians and then later supplemented this with some already existing liturgical (e.g. the eulogy, 1.3–14) and paraenetic material (e.g. the HT). If, as some say (see on 1.3–14), the eulogy provides a clue to the content of the whole letter it must have been integral to the letter, and, even if it does not set the subject-matter of the whole, it is in no way out of accord with it; it is also by no means certain that the eulogy was a pre-existing liturgical unit. Kirby has an almost opposite point of view to Ochel in seeing the origin of the letter in a liturgy which was later supplemented with epistolary material; yet he hardly regards the original liturgy as a letter, so that he does not envisage two editions of the letter as such. Goguel, IV.2, 473f, says the original Ephesians lacked the references to Paul (3.1–13; 4.1; 6.20) and that their omission leaves a coherent account. 3.2–13 is certainly parenthetical. Yet if someone wished to add a reference to Paul why should he do so by introducing a parenthesis within what he added? Moreover a parenthesis is not out of accord with AE's style (cf 2.2–4). If the desire was to lend Paul's authority to what already existed, 3.1 would have been enough. Moreover 3.1 which carries the explicit reference to Paul does not belong to the parenthesis. Munro's theory (see Detached Note: The *Haustafel*, for discussion) is more complex than those of Ochel and Goguel in that it involves two editions of both Ephesians and Colossians. She views 4.28f, 32c; 5.1, 2a; 5.14b–18a; 5.21–6.9 as added in the second edition of Ephesians. If, as we argue, the addition of the HT is unlikely then the probability that the other passages were added is even less. Carr, with little justification, views 6.12 as a later addition (see Detached Note: The Powers, and notes on 6.12).

9.3.2. Morton has disputed the integrity of the letter on statistical grounds.[82] On the basis of a cusum chart analysis he believes 5.25–6.4 is an insertion, perhaps added when the letter was incorporated into a collection of Pauline letters in a codex rather than a scroll. Cusum analysis works with units of sentence length. 5.25–6.4 contains seven sentences and is just statistically long enough to enable a conclusion to be drawn; it also satisfies the criterion that any insertion must begin with the beginning of a sentence and end with the completion of another. Unfortunately for the theory two (5.31; 6.2f) of the seven sentences of 5.25–6.4 were certainly not written by AE since they are OT citations. It is not then surprising that Morton discovers an irregularity in respect of authorship in this section. In addition 5.25–6.4 contains a section, 6.1–4, which Col 3.20, 21 shows belonged to the HT. There is no obvious reason why AE should have left out this part of the HT on the relation of parents and children.[83]

---

[82] A. Q. Morton, *The Authorship and Integrity of the New Testament Epistles, University of Glasgow, Department of Computing Science, Research Report*, Glasgow, 1993; 4 Upper Adelaide St, Helensburgh, G84 7HT, 151–7, 164f.
[83] The detection by Morton of 5.25–6.4 as not by AE may confirm his method of analysis for in addition to the OT questions 6.1 comes from the tradition; of the seven sentences four are not then by AE.

9.4. On the whole Ephesians reads smoothly, though this can only be justified from the commentary itself. There are admittedly two major parentheses, 2.2–4 and 3.2–13, which could be detached, for in each case the argument is carefully renewed at the end of the parenthesis; yet the material within the parentheses does not contradict anything in other parts of the letter and indeed helps to advance the argument.

10. BACKGROUND

Gnilka, 32ff; Fischer, 173–200; Koester, II, 271f; Merkel, 3176ff; Lona, 41–65.

10.1. In discussing this it is first necessary to identify those whose background concerns us. At least four possible people or groups of people come into consideration: (1) the contemporary inhabitants of Asia Minor, assuming that this is the area to which the letter is addressed; (2) the readers whom AE had in mind as he wrote; (3) AE; (4) Paul, if he is AE and therefore the author. As far as Paul is concerned we probably do not need to discuss his background for in seeking the author's background it is the background which is relevant to Ephesians which has to be considered. If Paul wrote Colossians then he may have been aware of gnosis but that does not prove he allowed gnosis to determine his thought in Ephesians; Ephesians must be examined separately to determine the level of gnostic thought within it. As well as the contemporary readers there are all who have read the letter since then, including today's readers. Their backgrounds differ greatly from readers in the ancient world and for that reason they have read, or will read, the text differently. Insight into how the letter has been read between the time it was written and now can be gained from earlier commentaries. As for readers today, it is impossible to take them into account in this type of commentary. Occasionally reference is made to the difference between the total background of the ancient world and that of modern western culture but this cannot be treated in detail. An understanding of what Ephesians means today requires too much knowledge, sympathy and understanding of individual readers' needs for it to be considered; it also requires too much from the commentator for him to feel fit to undertake the task.

If we leave Paul aside and look at the first three groups it can be quickly seen that the answers in respect of them may not be the same. If AE (this is still true if he was Paul) was a Jew and his actual and implied readers were not, then his background would differ from theirs. So far as the first two groups are concerned AE views his implied readers as having passed their pre-Christian lives in an atmosphere of almost total moral and religious darkness (4.17–19); his actual readers, in particular any non-Christian readers into whose hands the letter might fall, would have strenuously disputed this. AE also views his actual readers as living in households in which all the members were believers, and in many cases this would not have been true. These distinctions necessitate our looking separately from time to time at the backgrounds of the three groups. Naturally there are many areas of life where the groups shared the same background.

Assuming Asia Minor as the area in which the letter was written and to which it was directed it is impossible in our limited space to take up the general background of life there;[84] we can only pick out the factors that appear important relative to the content of the letter. More detailed discussion of these factors will be found at the points where they relate to the content.

10.2.1. Leaving aside the use of a common language, Greek, which would apply to other NT writings from the area, the first special factor relates to peace; Faust, *passim*, implies that the restoration of peace to the Empire after the Jewish insurrection of AD 70 affected life in Asia Minor and led to AE's emphasis on peace in 2.11–22; for discussion see notes on 2.11–22.

10.2.2. A second important consideration is the presence of Jews in Asia Minor where they were a not inconsiderable minority. Van der Horst, op.cit., 160, estimates that there were approximately a million. Their presence may have been a factor in the formation of 2.11–22 and other passages, for the church saw itself both in continuity and discontinuity with Judaism. Moreover AE uses the Jewish Bible in some of his discussion.

10.2.3. A third factor relates to the wider content of the letter in which the nature of the church and the behaviour expected from its members towards one another is presented. Those who became Christians came from a society containing many small groups based on common interests, e.g. burial clubs, trade associations, minor

---

[84] Much has been written on the Asia Minor of our period; for some insight into aspects of its culture relevant to Ephesians see S. Applebaum, 'The Legal Status of Jewish Communities in the Diaspora' and 'The Organisation of the Jewish Communities in the Diaspora', *CRINT The Jewish People in the First Century*, I (ed. S. Safrai and M. Stern), Assen, 1974, 420–63, 464–503; A. S. Di Marco, 'The cities of Asia Minor under the Roman Imperium', *ANRW* II 7.12, 658–97; R. E. Oster, 'Ephesus as a Religious Center under the Principat, I Paganism before Constantine', *ANRW* II 18.3m, 1661–728; P. W. van der Horst, *Essays on the Jewish World of Early Christianity* (NTOA 14), Freiburg, 1990; Schürer, III.1, 17–36. Although the letter may not have been written in or to Ephesus itself yet as by far the largest city in the area the culture of the surrounding towns and cities will have been affected by its life; on this see G. H. R. Horsley, 'The Inscriptions of Ephesos and the New Testament', *NT* 34 (1992) 105–68.

religious cults.[85] Trade associations were not like modern trade unions in being organisations of employees; instead they contained both employers and employees, all workers at the same trade. Whether believers belonged or not to any of these groups they will certainly have known about them since they were widespread in Asia Minor. Those in the groups will have shared some kind of communal activity. Nothing in Ephesians allows us to conclude that all believers belonged to these groups or the kind of groups to which they belonged. Yet these groups, though their interests were different, had many common features. Details of the internal organisation and operation of particular groups is not always known to us but certain general statements can be made. They were not residential communities; there was no communal living as at Qumran or later Christian communities of nuns or monks, though there would be occasional shared meals. They had at least a rudimentary form of organisation with office-bearers. Religious cults would have had a priest or priests who guided and controlled their religious activities. Burial clubs had treasurers who collected dues and paid out money when a member died or had later to be remembered, and members paid regular contributions. Those wishing to belong to any of these groups had to apply for membership and be approved. Quite often slaves were members and sometimes, though less often, women; the latter usually gained their membership through that of their husbands. Groups held regular meetings which members were expected to attend and their behaviour when they met for either business or social pleasure was controlled; disruptive conduct was not permitted; those who offended might be fined or in some cases expelled. Those wishing to speak had to have the permission of the presiding officials. Even though the main purpose of the group might not be religious, sacrifices were often offered. While groups might have ostensible public purposes, feasting was often one of their more important actual activities. In some groups stress was laid on the duty of members to keep internal peace and help one another.[86]

An inscription from Philadelphia dating from the first or second

---

[85] For a comprehensive outline of these groups see F. Poland, *Geschichte des griechischen Vereinwesens*, Leipzig, 1909; also, S. Dill, *Roman Society from Nero to Marcus Aurelius*, London, 1904, 251–86; A. H. M. Jones, *The Roman Economy* (ed. P. A. Grunt), London, 1974, 35–60; N. M. Tod, *Sidelights on Greek History*, Oxford, 1932, 69–96; H. Lietzmann, *An die Korinther I/II*, Tübingen, 1949, 91ff; G. La Piana, 'Foreign Groups in Rome during the First Centuries of the Empire', *HTR* 20 (1927) 183–403 at 330–48, 265–76; E. A. Judge, *The Social Pattern of Christian Groups in the First Century*, London, 1960, 40–8; P. Herrmann, J. H. Waszink, C. Colpe, R. Kotting, 'Genossenschaft', *RAC* X, 81–135.

[86] On the application of modern sociological theory to small groups see D. C. Duling, 'Small Groups: Social Science Research Applied to Second Testament Society', *BTB* 25 (1995) 179–93.

century BC gives an insight into one group (see Barton and Horsley);[87] this group referred to itself as an οἶκος. Anyone, male or female, slave or free, could be a member. Members were sworn never to deceive anyone, use magic or spells, practise contraception or abortion, or use love potions. They are always to act favourably towards their own group and if they find others offending against its rules they are to expose them, for the gods will not bear with those who break the rules. Men are not to have sexual relations with boys, virgin girls or married women other than their wives; this apparently does not exclude the keeping of a mistress or resort to prostitutes. Freeborn women are more strictly controlled for they are not permitted sexual relations with any men other than their husbands; failure to observe this could lead to exclusion from the group. The god (singular) wishes obedience and the gods (plural) will be gracious (ἵλεως) to those who obey and give them the good things which the gods give to those they love; the disobedient will be punished. One goddess, that of the οἶκος, is asked to create good thoughts in members. We note that the picture of life within the group conflicts with what AE implies about Gentile behaviour in 4.17–19 and, more importantly, if what is true of this group can be generalised, then those who became Christians were already used to membership in small groups with strict rules about conduct. To encounter similar, if not the same, regulations on becoming Christians would not then have surprised them. But they might have been surprised by the exclusive nature of their new group. This would have entailed them dropping out of some of these groups, particularly those of a religious nature and those concerned with members' burials since believers now had an altered attitude to death. It would have been easier for them to have continued membership in trade associations though difficulties would arise when sacrifices were offered; probably some of the troubles Paul discusses in 1 Corinthians 8–10 arose out of such membership.

10.2.4. The fourth area of background picks up and generalises what we have just seen in relation to the Philadelphian group. AE and his readers, actual and implied, both before and after conversion, shared a belief in the existence and importance of religion. They would all have accepted the supernatural as affecting their lives, manifesting itself in different ways and in different areas of

---

[87] I am indebted to Dr Richard Oster for drawing my attention to this inscription. Apart from the edited text and commentary in Barton and Horsley, a translation of the inscription will also be found in A. D. Nock, 'Early Gentile Christianity and its Hellenistic Background', *Essays on Religion and the Ancient World* (ed. Z. Stewart), Oxford, 1972, 49–133 at pp. 65f. Another group is described in C. Roberts, T. C. Skeat, A. D. Nock, 'The Gild of Zeus Hypsistos', *HTR* 29 (1936) 39–87. See more recently and more generally, J. S. Kloppenberg and S. G. Wilson, *Voluntary Associations in the Graeco-Roman World*, London and New York, 1996.

life. While there were some atheistic or agnostic philosophers in the ancient world, they were not among the implied readers and would have been few among the actual readers. The supernatural element in first-century Christianity would not have repelled possible believers. The existence of such a shared belief in the supernatural meant there was no need for AE to explain or defend its existence, though necessarily he would have to redefine its nature.

10.3. Were there however more restricted strands of thought within the culture of AE and his implied and actual readers which would have determined what he wrote? If there were, how would these strands have affected the way in which they understood what he wrote? For scholarly purposes it is necessary to distinguish these strands and the groups holding them but it is important to realise that in actual practice they merged into one another and cannot be rigidly distinguished. Different groups moreover might use the same imagery yet read different content into it. If we say AE was a Jew that does not mean he would not have employed gnostic ideas or that they would not have affected his thinking. If we allow that gnostic attitudes and concepts already existed in first-century Asia Minor, it has to be asked if AE was aware that they may have affected the presentation of what he wished to say and the way his readers may have heard what he wrote. If there was a danger of them reading him in a gnostic tone does he do anything to support or counter this?

10.3.1. It is important then to identify possible gnostic concepts and attitudes, remembering that what holds for the developed gnostic systems of the second century may not necessarily be extrapolated back into the first century. Foerster[88] and Wilson[89] are largely in agreement in defining what constitutes gnosis: the true God and the cosmos which has been created by another divinity are opposed to one another; human beings are essentially divine or have a divine spark within them but have 'fallen' and are entrapped in a hostile world which is subject to hostile supernatural beings; from these they need to be freed so that the divine spark may return to its true home in heaven; they can achieve this only through knowledge of their condition brought to them by a divine redeemer. Though present in the gnosis of the second century not all of this may have been clearly thought out in the first; in particular there are doubts about the existence in that period of a redeemer myth.

10.3.1.1. Given the widespread acceptance of gnostic ideas in the first century, there is considerably less enthusiasm now than in the heyday of the *Religionsgeschichtliche* movement to discern their influence on Ephesians. It seems AE was neither motivated by gnosis nor did he set out to counteract its influence among his

---

[88] W. Foerster, *Gnosis*, (ET) Oxford, 1972, vol. I, 9.
[89] R. McL. Wilson, *TRE* XIII, 536f.

readers. If he and A/Col belonged to the same Pauline school, or if he used Colossians, it is of course impossible to deny his awareness of gnostic ideas and of the need to oppose them. Yet while these may have been current in the culture of Asia Minor, the Colossian church may have been the only one where believers had to face gnostic teaching in even a crudely developed scheme. AE's purpose however was different from that of A/Col in that he was not seeking to oppose false ideas but to build up the internal life of the communities to which he was writing. Moreover he had to give advice which would fit the situation of a majority rather than a minority of communities and he knew A/Col had dealt with the situation in Colossae.

10.3.1.2. An examination of Ephesians does not reveal any positive evidence that AE was consciously opposing gnosticism. If 2.14–18 contains a gnostic hymn in which a wall between heaven and earth is destroyed and if this hymn was known to his readers and if he transformed the wall into one between Jew and Gentile then his readers would have seen him, not as accepting gnostic ideas, but as contesting them; however it is doubtful if a hymn ever underlay 2.14–18 and even if it did that it was originally gnostic (see on 2.14–18). The phrase τῷ τὰ πάντα κτίσαντι (3.9) may contradict the gnostic idea of a demiurge creating the world, yet AE does not appear to be using it to deny such a view but only in accordance with the normal way it was employed in Judaism and Christianity. AE is not attacking gnosis in 3.19 (see notes) nor an excessive individualism deriving from an incipient gnosticism in 4.15f. Later gnosticism contained two strains of ethical thinking, one leading to asceticism and the other to a lax attitude to morality; AE neither opposes asceticism nor does his setting out of guidelines for behaviour suggest he is dealing with a disregard of morality. Marriage for him is not a way of controlling lust but part of the normal life of believers. Human beings are certainly at odds with the Divine Being but this is not because they are 'material' and he 'spiritual' but because they sin. AE does not stress their fallen nature. The world contains evil, i.e. sinful, people (4.17–19), but is not itself evil.

10.3.1.3. Yet AE certainly uses terms and ideas which appear in the second-century gnostic systems: pleroma (see on 1.23), a descending and ascending redeemer (see on 2.17; 4.9f), 'building' used of a group of people (see on 2.20), 'mystery' (see on 1.9). These terms and ideas however did not have an exclusively gnostic reference in the first century. The ascension of the believer with Christ (2.6) may resemble the gnostic ascent of the soul to heaven but other explanations are more likely for its origin (see on 2.6). AE may use a number of images which the later gnostics employed but these also appear more widely: 'enlightenment of the eyes of the heart' (1.18), 'body' to denote a collection of people (see Detached Note: The Body of Christ), αἰών to denote an evil supernatural personal power (2.2; cf 3.9), believers as already raised and exalted (2.6); AE refers also to the great range of God's love (3.18), the 'inner person' (3.10), the 'perfect man' (4.13), and uses the metaphors of clothing (4.22–4), spiritual marriage (5.22–33), light/darkness (5.8; for a discussion of all these see exegetical notes). The hymn of 5.14 can be understood gnostically but it does not need to be so understood; in any case it was not written by AE. Although the evidence for the use of these terms and ideas comes from the later gnostic systems, it cannot be denied that they may have been in use in the first century among the proto-gnostic groups who later developed the second-century systems. Finally the employment by AE of ideas of understanding and knowledge proves nothing; it is very difficult to explain anything without using such concepts and AE does not use them excessively. It is possible that when he did use them he did so deliberately, knowing their background and believing that with them he could explain his own thinking or, perhaps more probably, he used them without realising their possible gnostic background. He certainly could not have foreseen their later second-century gnostic usage. What cannot be denied is the presence in Ephesians of ideas and terms with which those who were gnostically inclined would have been happy. Later gnostics made much use of 6.12 (so Arnold, 12) but so also did the orthodox as a glance at *Biblia Patristica* will show. If we say that AE did not view his implied readers as influenced by gnostic ideas we cannot deny that some of his actual readers may have had gnostic inclinations; it would appear though that AE did not recognise this and did nothing to counter his readers in this respect.

10.3.2. Turning now to two related but subsidiary areas it is very difficult to see AE as writing with the Mystery Religions in mind. His use of the term 'mystery' comes from Judaism rather than paganism (see on 1.9). The Mystery Religions are not reflected in the references to works of darkness and things done in secret (5.11f) and to drunkenness (5.18). The cry to wake up in 5.14 may be similar to cries in the Mysteries but it need not be. If AE had been attacking these religions he would have needed to be much clearer. The second subsidiary area is that of magic. Recourse to magical practices to bend supernatural powers to one's purposes was found everywhere in the ancient world and at all levels of society (see Arnold, *passim*[90]). Though most extant spells come to us from Egypt magic was in use in Asia Minor as the Ephesian *grammata*, Acts 19.19 and the Philadelphian inscription (see Barton and Horsley) show. For other references to magic in the NT see Acts 8.19–24;

[90] Cf H. C. Kee, *Medicine, Miracles and Magic in New Testament Times* (SNTSMS 55), Cambridge, 1986, 95–121.

13.4–12; Gal 5.20; 2 Tim 3.8, 13; Rev 9.21; 18.23. Arnold suggests that the abundance of words denoting 'power' in Ephesians arises from the need of believers to defend themselves against magic, but there were many other supernatural influences from which they would have needed to defend themselves. The 'powers' are not connected solely to magic. If AE had magic in mind as a major influence on his readers it is surprising that he does not refer to it explicitly. It is repudiated in many of the NT references (see above) to it and even in the pagan Philadelphian inscription (see Barton and Horsley). Perhaps AE did not explicitly repudiate magic as he did not explicitly repudiate idolatry because he does not expect his readers would practise either within their communities.

10.4. While standards between one society and another may vary, every society has a code of conduct, and the Gentile believers to whom AE writes will have known such codes in their pre-Christian life. Because codes varied it is impossible to draw up a precise list of what was regarded as good and bad behaviour in contemporary popular estimation in Asia Minor, yet probably any list would not have differed greatly from Stoic moral teaching. This itself had much in common with other moral teaching. People have always reflected on the way they should behave and, since the problems facing them are always much the same, they are bound at times to reach similar conclusions as to what constitutes good and bad behaviour. The HT illustrates this for almost everyone in the ancient world would have accepted its teaching. The similarities between AE's and Stoic teaching appear at various points in the paraenesis; see for example 4.14, 18, 19, 31; 5.10, 12; 6.10ff (life seen as warfare) and the notes on them; vices that AE rejects (5.3, 5) would also have been rejected by the Stoics. We may note that AE deals with many of the same areas of conduct with which members of the Philadelphian cult were concerned (see Barton and Horsley). Those converted to Christianity would not then have been entering a world with entirely new values. Yet they would have found differences; though AE does not go out of his way to point these out, they emerge as he writes. Most ancient moralists would have accepted two of the three virtues set out in 4.2 but they would have been surprised by the third, ταπεινοφροσύνη, which they would have regarded as a vice. Stoics would not have taken such a harsh view of non-Stoics as AE does of non-Christians (4.17–19). At times AE seems to be saying the same thing as Stoics but a closer look shows differences. For both AE and Stoics conduct should be fitting, but for Stoics what is fitting is what accords with nature, while for AE it is what is appropriate to a member of the body of Christ. Both would agree in looking on God as father (4.6) but their understanding of what this meant would differ since at least part of AE's understanding had its origin in the teaching of Jesus. Both would agree that there was some kind of equality between master and slave, but while for Stoics this lay in their common humanity for AE it existed because both worshipped the same God. These examples show that the overall approach to behaviour on the part of AE and Stoics was crucially different, AE's being based on his faith in Christ while that of the Stoics on their profound sense of cosmic unity. AE assumes his readers have adopted his overall approach for generally when he gives reasons for how they should behave it is based on that overall approach. A possible area where he may have been mistaken about his actual readers lies in his use of the OT; his use suggests he believed his readers would pick up his quotations and allusions for he never points them out; converts of long standing would have done so but not those recently converted.

10.5. Probably AE lived in the same area as those to whom he wrote and therefore shared with them the same wide cultural background, but just as everyone has a personal slant in their attitude to their background so AE will have had; in his case it was not however the normal slight variation arising out of the different trade he pursued or the size of his household; it came from his religious and racial background, for he was a Jew by race if no longer Jewish in faith. His upbringing will have led him to look with suspicion on those with a purely pagan background (cf 4.17–19). To say that he was Jewish does not however completely define his background, for contemporary Judaism, though depending on the OT, was not uniform but contained many strands which were mingled in varying proportions in any particular Jew. That the OT itself was important to AE can be seen from his use of it (see §9.1). Its influence on him can also be observed in his use of Jewish phrases and concepts, ταπεινοφροσύνη (4.2), fear and trembling (6.5), blood and flesh (6.12), children of wrath (2.3), sons of disobedience (5.6), the community as wife or bride (5.22–33), and in a more general way in his anthropology.

10.5.1. AE would not have been affected to the same degree by all strands of Judaism. Apocalypticism was not a strong influence, though this may have been due to his realised eschatology and concentration on the present existence of the church. Yet he employs concepts (e.g. mystery) whose immediate background was apocalyptic and a glance at his paraenesis shows many parallels with the ethical teachings of Jewish apocalyptic writings (e.g. *The Testaments of the Twelve Patriarchs*), though this may only be because these writings do not provide a substantially different ethic from general Jewish moral teaching.

10.5.2. He shows a greater degree of dependence on, or influence from, the teaching of the DSS.[91] The group or groups which

---

[91] Cf Kuhn; Mussner, 'Beiträge'.

produced these writings are probably the ultimate, though not the direct, source of his use of the temple to denote a community (2.21), 'saints' to include heavenly inhabitants (1.18; 2.19; 3.18), 'lot' or inheritance (1.14, 18), and mystery (1.9; 3.3f, 9). At the same time his style and language, especially in the eulogy (1.3–14), resemble passages in the DSS. None of this is however strong enough evidence to suggest he was ever a member of the community, or communities, which produced these writings.[92] Even though his main emphasis lies on the nature of Christian community he does nothing to make it resemble what we find in them; the communities they depict were hierarchically arranged (1QS 6.8f, 22; CD 13.1ff; 14.7–12), and exercised discipline over their members (1QS 5.23f; 6.13–7.2; CD 16.7f; 9.17ff) whom they selected carefully (1QS 5.10f; 6.13–15); all these features serve to weld communities together and are normal to them as they develop, and all appeared quickly in the later church, yet they are not so clearly present in Ephesians; in particular AE does not refer to discipline. Also some members at least, if not all, of the community at Qumran itself appear to have been celibate, but for AE marriage was normal.

10.5.3. AE does not exhibit much of the type of thinking which we associate with the rabbis. The alteration to Ps 68.18 at 4.8 would accord with rabbinic exegesis but AE probably received it in the tradition and was not himself responsible for it. The union of Ps 8.6 and Ps 110.1 in 1.20, 22 again resembles rabbinic exegesis but the linkage was already present in Christian tradition (see on 1.22) and therefore he did not make it. The combination of Isa 57.19 and 52.7 in 2.17 is again rabbinic in type but Isa 57.19 was widely used in Judaism (see on 2.17) and one instance of the combination of texts does not by itself imply direct contact with rabbinic thinking. The lack of influence on AE of rabbinic-type thinking is confirmed by the small number of references to rabbinic literature compared to the multiplicity of references found in commentaries on the major Pauline letters.

10.5.4. Moving to the more hellenised strands of Judaism we find that much of AE's ethic is similar to that in Philo, the later Wisdom literature, Pseudo-Phocylides (see exegetical notes). His general picture of the universe also accords with or is similar to what is found in these writings. This supports the view that AE was a Hellenistic Jew. Probably some of his cosmological and anthropological ideas, e.g. that God fills the universe or his use of the term

---

[92] Contrast J. Murphy-O'Connor, 'Who Wrote Ephesians?', *TBT* 1 (1965) 1201–9. E. Testa, 'Gli errori combattuti da S. Paolo nelle cattivita e Qumran', *S. Paolo da Cesarea a Roma* (ed. B. Mariani), Torino, 1963, 229–42, argues that after one of the attacks on the Qumran community in the first century BC some of its members may have emigrated to Asia Minor; the evidence is not strong but it is impossible to prove the emigration did not take place.

'inner man' (the more Semitic term would have been 'heart'), probably also reached him through Hellenistic Judaism (see on 1.23). The formulation of behaviour in terms of righteousness and holiness (4.24), while again Hellenistic, was derived from Hellenistic Judaism where it is frequent in Philo and Josephus. Another Hellenistic term he employs is ἀφθαρσία (6.24). The use of σωτήρ (5.23) could have been drawn either directly from Hellenism or mediated through Hellenistic Judaism. The idea of the imitation of God (5.2) lies nearer to Hellenism than Judaism.

10.6. Finally we should note: (1) The absence of direct quotations from the Jesus tradition; considering their relative length, AE does not differ here from Paul, though 4.20f may imply a recognition that his readers have some acquaintance with Gospel material. (2) AE's background includes the Christian tradition into which he came when he was converted. His readers, implied and actual, will also have participated in this part of his background in a way they did not in his Jewish; admittedly their participation was probably less than his, for he had probably been a believer for a much longer period than most of them.

11. TEXT

Zuntz, *passim*; P. Benoit, 'Le codex paulien Chester Beatty', *RB* 46 (1937) 58–82; W. H. P. Hatch and C. B. Welles, 'A Hitherto Unpublished Fragment of the Epistle to the Ephesians', *HTR* 51 (1958) 33–5; H. J. Frede, *Epistula ad Ephesios* (Vetus Latina 24/1), Freiburg, 1962–4; I. A. Moir, 'The Text of Ephesians Exhibited by Minuscule Manuscripts based in Great Britain—Some Preliminary Comments', *Studies in New Testament Language and Text* (SupNT 44; FS G. D. Kilpatrick, ed. J. K. Elliott), Leiden, 1976.

It is impossible today to work from the original text in the form in which it left AE's hand; instead a reconstructed text must be used and that chosen for this series and therefore this volume is that of NA^{27} = UBSGNT^9. It is mainly the variants offered by NA^{27} which are considered in the exegetical notes. The greater number of these are the result of scribes attempting to clarify apparent or actual difficulties in the text they were copying by altering the syntax or style. Rarely do these variants affect meaning. Sometimes to improve clarity words are changed (4.18), added (2.4) or omitted (3.1). In a number of places a usage which is seemingly non-normal is replaced by a more normal, e.g. the change from ἐπί to ἐν in 1.10. Some variations appear to be attempts to bring the text into line with that of the LXX where an OT passage is being either quoted or alluded to (see 2.17; 4.8; 5.30, 31) or into line with other NT texts (e.g. the addition of ἀμήν at 6.24; the change from φωτός to πνεύματος at 5.9; the variant at 6.20 is probably due to the influence of Col 4.4). There are a small number of places where alterations have apparently been made to improve pastoral intensity by changing the first plural to the second (1.16, 19; 4.32; 5.2; 6.12) or by the insertion of 'brothers' (5.15; 6.10; in both instances at the beginning of sections which were probably used in lectionaries); in each case a more direct approach is created and the general meditative nature of Ephesians lessened.

There are a number of places where variant readings alter, if only slightly, the sense of passages; some of these alterations may be deliberate and some accidental, e.g. the omission or addition of τὴν ἀγάπην at 1.15, of τοῦ Χριστοῦ at 3.13, of πάντας at 3.9, of ἡμῖν at 4.6, of τοῦ διαβόλου at 4.14, of ἡ in 2.21, the change from καινόν to κοινόν in 2.15. There are a few instances of variation which can be ascribed to nothing other than scribal error, e.g. the omission of μή by 𝔓⁴⁶ at 4.30. 𝔓⁴⁶ has also singular readings at 6.12, 23, though it is not so certain whether they are deliberate alterations or errors. The readings of οὐρανίοις at 1.20 and ἐπιθυμίαις at 2.1 may also be simple errors. Theological opinion probably led to the omission of καὶ πατήρ in 1.3, ἀποστόλοις in 3.5, καί in 3.21, and either to the omission or addition of ἐν κυρίῳ at 6.1 and of πρῶτον at 4.9.

The greatest number of variants in respect of either addition or omission is found in D F G but these are mainly due to attempts to improve the grammar or style. Abbott, xl–xliv, lists the readings peculiar to ℵ, A, B, D, G; the variants in 𝔓⁴⁶ are listed and discussed in Benoit, art.cit. B has a large number of variants some of which relate to theological terms: omission of τοῦ Χριστοῦ (with 𝔓⁴⁶) at 2.13, of ἀποστόλοις at 3.5, of πνευματικαῖς at 5.19 (again with 𝔓⁴⁶), of ἐν κυρίῳ at 6.1 of τοῦ εὐαγγελίου at 6.19. There is however no consistent pattern. A discussion of each of these variants will be found at the appropriate place in the exegetical notes.

I

SALUTATION
(1.1–2)

O. Roller, *Das Formular der paulinischen Briefe* (BWANT IV 6), Stuttgart, 1933; Schmid, 37–129; K. Berger, 'Apostelbrief und apostolische Rede/ Zum Formulae frühchristlicher Briefe', *ZNW* 65 (1975) 190–231; W. G. Doty, *Letters in Primitive Christianity*, Philadelphia, 1977, 29–31; D. A. Black, 'The Peculiarities of Ephesians and the Ephesian Address', *GraceTJ* 2 (1981) 59–73; K. Berger, *ANRW* II 25.2, 1289–91, 1326–63, esp. 1330–40; J. L. White, 'New Testament Epistolary Literature in the Framework of Ancient Epistolography' *ANRW* II 25.2, 1751f; F. Schnider and W. Stenger, *Studien zum neutestamentlichen Briefformular* (New Testament Tools and Studies), Leiden, 1987, 3–41; D. E. Aune, *The New Testament in its Literary Environment*, Philadelphia, 1987, 183–6.

1 Paul, apostle of Christ Jesus by the will of God
    to saints and believers in Christ Jesus,
2   grace to you and peace
        from God our Father and the Lord Jesus Christ.

Paul, at least from the time of his earliest extant letter, used with modifications the ancient letter form, approximating more closely to Near Eastern than to Hellenistic usage. Later Christian letter writers followed him in this (1.1f; Col 1.1f; 1 Pet 1.1f; 2 Pet 1.1f; Jude 1f; cf 1 Clem 1.1; the letters of Ignatius). The genuine Paulines differ in minor ways from each other. That Eph 1.1f differs slightly from the others thus gives no clue as to whether Paul wrote it or not. If it is not Pauline its author certainly knew Colossians and some of the other letters, e.g. Romans, 1 Corinthians, Philemon (Introduction §2.6), and would have picked up the form from them. Similarity to Colossians is most noticeable through the use of πιστοῖς, yet Ephesians differs from that letter in (i) using it substantivally and not adjectivally, (ii) the non-use of 'brothers' and (iii) the absence of a co-author. The address is less extensive than in some of Paul's other letters (Rom 1.1–7; Gal 1.1–5; 1 Cor 1.1–3). AE must have deliberately chosen the epistolary form to introduce what he writes even though it is probably not a genuine letter and certainly not a personal letter addressed to a single person or group of people and dealing with their problems (Introduction §7). It is equally not a letter addressed to people in general, for it is assumed that all its readers are Christians, and probably that they are of Gentile and not Jewish origin. AE could have in mind all believers or all believers in a particular area. It has a certain air of impersonality as can be seen in the concluding benediction where the recipients are addressed in the third person and not the second as elsewhere in Paul. It is doubtful if AE was thinking of a precise group of people, other than Gentile Christians.

1. If Paul did not write the letter then its author has given it at the outset his authority, and in particular his authority as apostle. The use of a title lends a kind of official nature to the letter (Schlier), though of course only to those who acknowledge the title. This 'official' nature goes well with the unique position accorded Paul in 3.3, 7ff. 'Apostle' has a considerable range of meaning.[1] At one extreme it indicates a member of the Twelve, among whom there was no place for Paul; Rev 21.12–14 with its twelve gates also understands it in this way. In Luke and Acts 'apostle' generally designates one of the Twelve, though in Acts 14.4, 14 Paul is termed an apostle, but Barnabas is described as an apostle at the same time. At the other extreme the word simply means 'messenger' (Jn 13.16; Phil 2.25; 2 Cor 8.23). Between these extremes Andronicus and Junia are counted as apostles (Rom 16.7) and Paul describes himself as an apostle but places alongside himself in the same category Silvanus and Timothy (1 Th 2.6). In Rom 1.1 and Gal 1.1 he terms himself an apostle and also in 1 Cor 1.1; 2 Cor 1.1 where, though associating others with himself, he does not apply the word to them. In Phil 1.1; 1 Th 1.1; 2 Th 1.1 (if genuine); Philem 1 he does not use the term at all. In what circumstances does he then use it?[2] He may have used it in the first instance in 1 Th 2.6 because it indicated he had been sent by Christ; elsewhere he seems to use it whenever he feels his position is challenged by those who say he is inferior to other leaders, in particular inferior to the Twelve (1, 2 Corinthians, Galatians). He makes the same claim in Romans, but by the time he wrote this letter to people he had never visited he was aware that there were those who challenged his position and he therefore needed to tell them that he was in no way inferior to those who

---

[1] Out of the vast literature on this word it is sufficient to point to H. Mosbech, 'Apostolos in the New Testament', *ST* 2 (1945) 165–200; P.-A. Harlé, 'La notion biblique d'apostolicité', *ETR* 40 (1965) 133–48; W. Schmithals, *The Office of Apostle in the Early Church*, London, 1969; C. K. Barrett, *The Signs of an Apostle*, London 1970; R. Schnackenburg, 'Apostles Before and During Paul's Time', *Apostolic History and the Gospel* (FS F. F. Bruce, ed. W. W. Gasque and R. P. Martin), Exeter, 1970, 287–303; Merklein, *Amt*, 288–306; J. A. Kirk, 'Apostleship since Rengstorf: Towards a Synthesis', *NTS* 21 (1974/5) 249–65; J. H. Schütz, *Paul and the Anatomy of Apostolic Authority* (SNTSMS 26), Cambridge, 1975; J. D. Bühner, *EDNT* I, 142–6; W. A. Bienert, 'The Picture of the Apostle in Early Christian Tradition', in Hennecke–Schneemelcher, I, 5ff.

[2] For a full discussion see Best, 'Authority'.

regularly used the term of themselves. It appears that he found it more and more necessary to apply the term to himself, yet at no point where he does so does he issue commands or directions to those he addresses. It is arguable that if he had been asked to choose a word to describe himself he would have preferred 'father' or 'parent' (1 Cor 4.14ff; Gal 4.19; 1 Th 2.7, 11; 2 Cor 6.13; 12.14; Phil 2.22; Philem 10) or a term from the word group διαχον—(cf Rom 15.25; 1 Cor 3.5; 2 Cor 3.6ff; 4.1; 5.18; 6.3f; 11.8, 23). AE has probably used 'apostle' in Eph 1.1 because he knows Paul used it in the addresses of some of his letters, and because by the time AE wrote the word signified someone of importance and authority in the church. Yet AE's use of the terms is inconsistent, for in 3.5 (see notes there) he names a group, the apostles and prophets, of which Paul (see 3.3) is clearly not a member and where the apostles are the Twelve. The same is probably true of 2.20 (see notes there); Paul was not a part of the foundation of the church as were the Twelve who had been selected by the incarnate Christ. All this makes it difficult to know what AE means when in 1.1 he calls Paul an apostle. He certainly regards his apostleship as derived from Christ Jesus; Paul is not someone who stands alone and whose authority lies within himself. He also appears to assume that an apostle is someone with authority so that he becomes a guarantor of the tradition (Merklein, *Amt* 342).

Throughout the NT the order of the words Jesus and Christ varies; here Christ precedes Jesus in $\mathfrak{P}^{46}$ B D P 33 *pc* lat sy[h]; Ambst but the reverse order is found in $\aleph$ A F G Ψ $\mathfrak{M}$ it vg[cl] sy[p]. Barth believes that when either Christ comes first or when it is preceded by the definite article AE is referring to Christ as the Jewish Messiah. In view of the regular variation of order and the actual variation between the order here and in v. 2 it is impossible to sustain such an understanding; see also on 1.10.

Whether or not the Christian use of apostle derives from Hebrew *shaliach*, Paul viewed himself as the representative or ambassador of Christ; it was not a position to which he had appointed himself; God chose him (Gal 1.1, 12f; cf Eph 4.11). He represents Christ because it is God's will. His authority does not rest on his claim to be equal with Peter, John and James but on God's appointment (Rienecker). διὰ θελήματος θεοῦ is applied to Paul's apostleship also in 1 Cor 1.1; 2 Cor 1.1; Col 1.1. It probably became an accepted expression in respect of Paul's position in the Pauline schools (cf 1 Tim 1.1; 2 Tim 1.1); Gal 1.1 expresses the same idea but differently. God has not only appointed Paul but has ordained all that has or is to happen (1.5, 9, 11), including what is to happen to Paul; Paul is thus a part of God's total scheme and his particular place in it is at least partially revealed in 3.2f, 7ff.

We need not suppose AE has copied the address from Col 1.1f, for if he had there is no reason why he should have omitted the reference to Timothy; he retains that to Tychicus in 6.21. In all of Paul's other letters except Romans he associates someone else with him in the address. If it is deemed that one of AE and A/Col copied the other it would seem more reasonable then to assume that A/Col spotted that Ephesians did not resemble the other Paulines in respect of an additional name in the address and added one.

According to ancient epistolography once a writer has identified himself he also identifies those to whom he is writing and AE does this here, yet the identification is uncertain for the textual tradition varies.[3] The vast majority of MSS and Fathers read τοῖς ἁγίοις τοῖς (om D) οὖσιν ἐν Ἐφέσῳ καὶ πιστοῖς (the A text) but ℵ* B* 6, 424ᶜ 1739; Orig (Marcion?) read τοῖς ἁγίοις τοῖς οὖσιν καὶ πιστοῖς (the B text); differing from both these 𝔓⁴⁶ reads τοῖς ἁγίοις οὖσιν καὶ πιστοῖς (the P text). In addition it should be noted that all the textual traditions give the superscription as 'To the Ephesians'.[4] As we begin to assess this evidence it is important to realise that AE was someone who was able to write intelligibly and therefore must have written something sensible which people could easily understand; also whatever he wrote must accord with the general non-specific nature of the content of the letter.

Although the A text can be translated it is very difficult to find a satisfactory meaning for it. It relates the place name only to 'saints' (contrast Col 1.2) and so creates two groups, the saints who are in Ephesus and the believers who are in Christ Jesus. There are no traces elsewhere in the letter of two groups apart from Jews and Gentiles, or Jewish Christians and Gentile Christians. It is however impossible to equate these with the two nouns, for when AE uses ἅγιοι elsewhere it includes both Jewish and Gentile Christians (1.18; 3.8; 4.12; 5.3); there is also no reason why one group should be given a geographical location and the other a theological. It is even more difficult to accept this reading with its reference to Ephesus if we assume Paul is the author, for he was largely responsible for the existence of the church in Ephesus, yet the author of this letter neither knows his readers nor do they know him (1.15; 3.2; 4.20f). The limitation of the readers to one church also runs into difficulty with the non-specific nature of the letter's content. Almost all this applies equally even if with Marcion we assume the letter was written to Laodicea. To overcome these problems it has been suggested that the letter was a circular letter[5] and that there was a

---

[3] For a full discussion of how this evidence has been assessed see Best, 'Ephesians i.1' and 'Ephesians i.1 Again'.

[4] Since we do not have the manuscript used by Marcion we do not know what its superscription was, though it was probably 'To the Laodiceans'.

[5] For an interesting discussion and refutation of this possibility see C. R. Bowen, 'The Place of "Ephesians" among the Letters of Paul', *ATR* 15 (1933) 279–99.

gap where 'in Ephesus' appears; when Tychicus carried the letter from one church to another he filled in the gap with the appropriate name, which would have been Laodicea in the copy Marcion possessed. Most of the difficulties listed above still apply. In addition, no examples can be found from the ancient world containing such a gap[6] and in any case the ἐν ought to have remained to show Tychicus where he should insert the name. If the reference to Ephesus, or some other city, was originally present and was eliminated we would have expected τοῖς οὖσιν also to have been eliminated, for if it is difficult to translate the A text it is almost impossible to translate the B text, as Origen's discussion of it shows. Despite vigorous searches and many suggestions no satisfactory solution has been advanced.[7] Had it been possible to translate the B text there would have been no need to add a place name; the reason for the appearance of the A text out of the B is therefore obvious. It is also difficult to see if Ephesus was originally present why it was eliminated; Black, art. cit., suggests it was to universalise the letter; but the content shows AE already intended it to be a general letter and if he could endure the place name being associated with a general letter there is no reason to suppose others could not. The manuscript evidence suggests the B text must be accepted as earlier than the A. The P text may be said to be supported by D in lacking τοῖς and it is possible to translate it (cf MHT, 152) by taking οὖσιν either as redundant 'officialese' which need not be translated, or as 'local', i.e. 'to the local saints and believers'. Either of these would fit in with the general nature of the letter. Yet if the P text were original it is very difficult to see how the B text ever arose from it.

Because of these difficulties a number of ingenious guesses have been made as to the original text. Limitations of space make it impossible to list, let alone consider, all of them. We comment only on that of Van Roon, *Authenticity*, 80ff, accepted in modified form by Lincoln, 3f. They suppose that there were originally two place names τοῖς ἁγίοις τοῖς οὖσιν ἐν ... καὶ ἐν ... πιστοῖς ἐν Χριστῷ Ἰησοῦ. For some reason the place names were omitted but the καί was inadvertently left thus creating the B text. This theory requires not one but two scribal blunders, for, as we have seen, it is the τοῖς οὖσιν which creates the real difficulty in translation when it is not followed by a geographical place name. To assert that the original reading had two place names does nothing to assist in dealing with the non-specific nature of the letter; nothing in the letter suggests its author had two identifiable communities in mind.

The non-specific nature of the letter and the absence of identifiable communities suggest the original address was general: τοῖς

---

[6] Roller, 199–212, 520–5.
[7] Cf Zuntz, p. 228, n. 1 and BDR §413.4.

ἁγίοις καὶ πιστοῖς ἐν Χριστῷ 'Ιησοῦ;[8] this would fulfil the requirement that AE wrote intelligibly. With this in mind an approach from the angle of the collection of the Pauline letters becomes possible.[9] These were probably first gathered in small groups which were later united. As soon as any letters were linked, even in small groups, they required to be distinguished from one another. With letters entrusted to personal couriers, as Paul's were, no identification was needed on their outside (cf White, art.cit., 1751). When Philippians needed identification in its collection, 'to Philippi' or something similar would have been written on the outside of its roll, and so with other letters. If 'Ephesus' had been originally present in our letter it would have been written on the outside, but, since it was not, it could not have been written there. Lacking a place name it was probably identified with its first significant words indicating the addressees, τοῖς ἁγίοις. At some later stage when the collection had grown and it was seen that all the other Pauline letters had a geographical or personal identification, 'who are in Ephesus' was inserted. It was quickly realised that the reference to 'the saints' was now unnecessary and these words were dropped, but at the same time 'who are in Ephesus' was carried in some manuscripts into the body of the letter and made to follow 'to the saints', thus producing the A text. However, some scribes knowing the letter had originally no geographical identification omitted the name, thus creating the B text. The P text probably arose from a careless scribe faced with three words all ending in οις.

Another problem however still remains in relation to the word Ephesus in the address. If the letter had no original geographical identification, why was Ephesus chosen when it was decided that a name was necessary? There is no reason to assume that the scribe who inserted the name did not believe that Paul wrote the letter. Did he not realise that the author is supposed to have no knowledge of the community, or communities, to which it was written, and Paul had a close association with the Ephesian church? Other scribes may have inserted the names of other cities. Marcion either inserted Laodicea or found it in the manuscript he used. It is possible other manuscripts contained other names. Why was Ephesus inserted in some manuscripts and why has it survived as the most common identification? A number of suggestions have been made, none very satisfactory (see Best, 'Recipients'). Presumably when the Pauline letters were first brought together as a whole, Ephesus was already

[8] Support for this conjecture can be found in Schmid, 125ff; cf M. Goguel, 'Esquisse d'une solution nouvelle du problème de l'épître aux Ephésiens', *RHR* 111 (1935) 254ff and 112 (1936) 73ff, at p. 254 n. 1; P. Dacquino, 'I destinatari della letters agli Efesini', *RivBibl* 6 (1955) 102–10; Kirby, 170.

[9] On their collection see most recently, D. Trobisch, *Die Entstehung der Paulus-briefsammlung*, Göttingen, 1989.

present in the manuscript in use, but how did it get there? (1) When
the letter had been written it was sent to Ephesus for copying and
distribution and the name then became associated with it. (2)
Ephesus was the most important city in Asia but no letter had been
written to it, so it was picked for the nameless letter. (3) The letter
was written in Ephesus and distributed from there and so the name
of that city was applied to it. (4) Ignatius wrote a letter to Ephesus
which has some similarities with our letter (see Introduction
§2.4.3.2); in writing his letter he must have used ours and therefore
our letter must have been sent to Ephesus. (5) Paul had written a
letter to Ephesus but it was lost; our letter without a geographical
identification was known and it was assumed it must have been the
lost letter.

Returning now to the proposed original address 'to the saints and
believers in Christ Jesus', we can see that there is no suggestion of
two groups but of one described with two words (they have a common article). ἅγιοι is a term frequently used of all Christians (for
other possible meanings see on 1.18; 2.19), especially in the addresses of letters (Rom 1.7; 1 Cor 1.2; 2 Cor 1.1; Phil 1.1; Col 1.2). It
derives from the OT where God is often termed the Holy One; his
people are then also holy or saints. πιστοί is much less frequent as a
description of Christians, appearing mainly in the later NT writings
(Acts 10.45; 2 Cor 6.15; Col 1.2; 1 Tim 4.3, 10, 12; 5.16; 6.2; Tit
1.6). Since the words saints and believers are linked in Col 1.2,
though πιστοί is there used adjectivally, they may have been an
accepted description of Christians in the Pauline school. When used
adjectivally as in Col 1.2 πιστοί probably means 'faithful'. Used as a
noun in Eph 1.1 it will belong to the same semantic field as 'saints'
and should be translated as 'believers'. In Col 1.2 the phrase 'faithful
brothers' taken as a whole belongs also to the same semantic field.
'In Christ Jesus' applies to both nouns and not to 'believers' only
(Bouttier); the use of ἐν with a personal reference following on a
form of the root πιστ is unusual in the NT (only Jn 3.15 v.l.; in Mk
1.15 the object is not a person but the gospel; see also on 1.13).
Referring to both nouns 'in Christ Jesus' must be given one of its
normal meanings (see Detached Note: In Christ). Its use here is
similar to that in Phil 1.1; 2 Cor 12.2; Rom 8.1 implying a personal
relationship to Christ, if not necessarily a relationship of believers as
a whole, though the plural may suggest the latter.

2. AE uses here a stereotyped wish that God should bless his
addressees.[10] Χάρις and εἰρήνη, two basic concepts of Pauline

---

[10] See in addition to the literature listed at the head of this paragraph J. M. Lieu,
'"Grace to You and Peace": The Apostolic Greeting', *BJRULM* 68 (1985/6)
161–78; G. Friedrich, 'Lohmeyers These über das paulinische Briefspraeskript
kritisch beleuchtet', *ZNW* 46 (1955) 272–4; T. Y. Mullins, 'Benediction as a New
Testament Form', *Andrews University Seminary Studies* 18 (1977) 59–64.

theology, had been united in the earliest of Paul's epistles (1 Th 1.1). Whether he or someone else (the origin of the formula does not concern us) had brought them together, he continued to use them as his standard form (2 Th 1.2; 1 Cor 1.3; 2 Cor 1.2; Gal 1.3; Phil 1.2; Philem 3; Rom 1.7; Col 1.2) and AE, if he is not Paul, has simply taken over the form. Its stereotyped nature is seen in the absence of articles. If then this is a formula, it is vain to seek a connection between grace and peace and the content of what follows, though it is true that both terms feature in the letter ('grace', 1.6, 7; 2.5, 7, 8; 3.2, 7, 8; 4.7, 29; 6.24; 'peace' 2.14, 15, 17; 4.3; 6.15, 23; see these passages for the meaning of the words); grace is in any case an important concept in every Pauline letter and peace appears in all except 2 Corinthians (even there it is in the initial and final blessings). No emphasis is then to be placed on the use of either word in the present greeting. Whether AE, if he is not Paul, understood precisely the same by these words as Paul cannot be proved, but his later use of them suggests his understanding differed little. AE is not the source of the grace and peace he desires for his readers; these come from God and Christ (no attempt should be made with Jerome to relate grace to God and peace to Christ) and a similar double expression is found in all the letters apart from 1 Th 1.2; in Col 1.2 there is no reference to Christ. There are equivalent greetings in Jewish writings (*2 Bar* 78.2; *Jub* 12.29; 22.8f) but of course they lack the mention of Christ; the presence of his name makes clear that our greeting is Christian. In secular letters the opening wish might have no reference to God at all and the sender is then the source of the greeting. Christ and God the Father are here apparently put on a level (cf 6.23); normally in the NT God's gifts come through Christ rather than directly from God. God is defined here as the Father (see on 1.3) of believers; this term became for Christians their most characteristic description of him; Jews and some pagans also described him in the same way but with varying understanding. That the whole of v. 2 appears so regularly in early Christian letters suggests it may have been used in worship.

II

GOD, THE BLESSED, BLESSES
(1.3–14)

T. Innitzer, 'Der Hymnus in Eph 1,3–14', *ZTK* 28 (1904) 612–21; E. Lohmeyer, 'Das Proömium des Epheserbriefes', *ThBl* 5 (1926) 120–5; A. Debrunner, 'Grundsätzliches über Kolometrie im Neuen Testament', *ThBl* 5 (1926) 131–4; E. Gaugler, 'Heilsplan und Heilswirklichung nach Epheser, 1,3–2,10', *IKZ* 20 (1930) 201–16; Ochel, 18–32; G. Castellino, 'La dossologia della lettera agli Efesini (1,3–14)', *Salesianum* 8 (1946) 147–67; N. A. Dahl, 'Addresse und Proömium des Epheserbriefes', *TZ* 7 (1951) 241–64; C. Maurer, 'Der Hymnus von Epheser 1 als Schlüssel zum ganzen Briefe', *EvT* 11 (1951/2) 151–72; J. Coutts, 'Ephesians i.3–14 and I Peter i.3–12', *NTS* 3 (1956/7) 115–27; S. Lyonnet, 'La Bénédiction de Eph., 1,3–14 et son arrière-plan Judaïque', *A la rencontre de Dieu* (FS A. Gelin), Le Puy, 1961, 341–52; Roels, 40ff; Du Plessis, 57–69; J. Cambier, 'La bénédiction d'Eph 1,3–14', *ZNW* 54 (1963) 58–104; J. Schattenham, *Studien zum neutestamentlichen Prosahymnus*, Munich (1965), 1–10; J. T. Sanders, 'Hymnic Elements in Ephesians 1–3', *ZNW* 56 (1965) 214–32; Schille, 65–73; R. Deichgräber, 40–3, 65–76; P. Dacquino, 'La "Benedizione" di Ef 1,3–14', *Divus Thomas* 70 (1967) 475–82; H. Krämer, 'Zur sprachlichen Form der Eulogie Eph 1,3–3', *WD* 9 (1967) 34–46; Kirby 84–9, 103–10, 126–38; F. Lang, 'Die Eulogie in Epheser 1,1–3', *Studien zur Geschichte und Theologie des Reformation* (FS E. Bizer, ed. L. Abramowski and J. F. F. Goeters) Neukirchen, 1969, 7–20; R. Trevijano Etcheverria, 'Estudio sobre la eulogia Paulina (2 Cor. 1,3 y Ef. 1,3)', *Burgense* 10 (1969) 35–61; Bankhead, *Liturgical Formulas*, 91–101; Gibbs, *Creation*, 114–34; Fischer, 111–18; M. Coune, 'A la louange de sa gloire', *AsSeign* 46 (1974) 37–42; Romaniuk, 153–83, 244–7; Lindemann, *Aufhebung*, 89–106; R. Schnackenburg, 'Die grosse Eulogie Eph 1,3–14', *BZ* 21 (1977) 67–87; Caragounis, 36–96, 113f; B. Villegas, 'La christologia de la gran benedicion de Efesios', *Teologia y Vida* 19 (1978) 279–97; P. T. O'Brien, 'Ephesians 1: An Unusual Introduction to a New Testament Letter', *NTS* 25 (1978–9) 504–16; N. H. Keathley, 'To the Praise of His Glory: Ephesians 1', *RevExp* 76 (1979) 485–94; Usami, 71–124; P. Iovino, 'La "conoscenza del mistero"', *RivBibl* 34 (1986) 327–67; J. H. Barkhuzen, 'The strophic structure of the eulogy of Ephesians 1:3–14', *Hervormde Teologiese Studies* 46 (1990) 390–413.

3 Blessed is the God and Father of our Lord Jesus Christ
    who has blessed us with every spiritual blessing
        in the heavenlies
        in Christ:

4   according as he chose us in him
                before the foundation of the world
                to be holy and blameless before him,
            in love (5) foreordaining us
                as his adopted children [sons] through Jesus Christ
                according to the good pleasure of his will,
6   to the praise of the glory of his grace,
                with which he graced us in the beloved;
7   in him we have deliverance through his blood,
                the forgiveness of trespasses,
                according to the riches of his grace
8   which he made to abound to us;
            in all wisdom and understanding (9) making known to us
            the mystery of his will,
                according to his good pleasure
                which he purposed in him
10   for the administration of the fullness of times,
            to sum up all things in Christ,
                the things in heaven and on earth;
            in him (11) in whom also we were given a lot,
                being foreordained according to the intention
                of him who works everything
                according to the desire of his will,
12   that we might be to the praise of his glory,
                we who had [previously] hoped and continue to
                                                            hope
                because of Christ;
13   in whom also when you had heard the word of
                                                            truth,
                    the gospel of your salvation,
                in whom also when you had believed
            you were sealed with the Holy Spirit of promise,
                who is the earnest of our inheritance,
14   for the deliverance,
                the acquiring of the inheritance,
                for the praise of his glory.

(i) The cry 'Blessed (εὐλογητός) is (are you) God' is found in
isolated form in the OT, and is a response to something in the
context (cf Ps 41.14; 68.36; 89.53;106.48; 119.12; Neh 9.5; 1 Chron
16.36; Tob 3.11). It is also found in the OT and in other Jewish
writings[1] in more structured form where it is followed by a clause,
or clauses, giving the ground for the cry. There are brief cries of

---

[1] J. Heinemann, *Prayer in the Talmud: Forms and Patterns*, Berlin, 1977,
77–103.

thanksgiving to God for deliverance from enemies (Exod 18.10; 1 Sam 25.39; 2 Sam 18.28; Ps 31.21f; 124.6; Jth 13.17; 1QM 14.4). Deliverance however is not only from physical enemies (1QM 18.6ff). Other circumstances can lead to a Berakah ('blessing', 'eulogy'): the gift of a son as successor to David on the throne of Israel (1 Kgs 1.48; 5.21(7); 2 Chron 2.11, 12; cf 1 Kgs 10.9; 2 Chron 9.8), the gift of wisdom, revelation and understanding (1 Esdr 4.40, 60; 1 QS 11.15; 1 QH 10.14; 11.27, 29; cf Ezra 7.27), help in time of need (Ps 28.6; 1 QH 5.20; Tob 11.13), unspecified blessings (Ps 66.20; 72.19f; 144.1f; Ps Sol 6.6; 1QH 16.8). As responses to the activity of God eulogies are phrased in both the second and third persons. There are a number of extended Berakoth ('blessings') in which several areas of response to God are covered and more than one reason supplied (1 Kgs 8.15ff, 56ff; 1 Chron 29.10ff; 2 Chron 6.4ff; Tob 8.5ff, 15ff; 13.1ff; Dan 3.26ff (LXX), 52ff (LXX); 1 Macc 4.30ff; Lk 1.68ff; 1QApocGen 20.12ff; 1QM 18.6ff). In extended Berakoth the 'blessing nuance' may be lost as the passage continues and passes into other areas of prayer; this is so in the case of the two other epistolary Berakoth in the NT (2 Cor 1.3ff; 1 Pet 1.3ff). Eph 1.3–14, though straying towards the end, keeps more consistently within the area of blessing.

Berakoth were regularly used in Jewish worship[2] (e.g. Shemoneh Esreh), above all at meals. Jesus would have used one when he fed the multitudes or ate with his disciples, in particular at the Last Supper (Mk 14.22; Mt 26.26). In this way they passed into Christian worship including that of the eucharist. εὐλογεῖν is used in 1 Cor 10.16 in a eucharistic connection and in the feeding narratives which were regularly understood eucharistically (Mk 6.41; 8.7; Mt 14.19; Lk 9.16). It is not however used in the Pauline account of the Last Supper (1 Cor 11.22ff) and was gradually replaced by εὐχαριστεῖν in eucharistic contexts.[3]

Berakoth may have been employed eucharistically in AE's community and this may have prompted him to use one here or he may have imitated 2 Cor 1.3ff. The latter is less probable because even if he knew 2 Corinthians (see Introduction §2.6.3) Eph 1.3ff is developed differently from 2 Cor 1.3ff and unlike the latter is followed by a normal thanksgiving section. If there is any relationship with 1 Pet 1.3ff, dependence lies on the part of 1 Peter (Introduction §2.4.5.6). Elsewhere AE displays knowledge of Jewish ways and a Jewish form would have come naturally to him. There are a number of Jewish letters outside the NT which begin with a Berakah (1 Kgs 5.21f; 2 Chron 2.10f; Euseb Praep Ev 9.34;

[2] Cf S. Lyonnet, art.cit.
[3] Cf J. M. Robinson, 'Die Hodajot-Formel in Gebet und Hymnus des Frühchristentums', Apophoreta (FS Ernst Haenchen ed. W. Eltester and F. H. Kettler), Berlin, 1964, 194–235.

Josephus *Ant* 8.53; cf Dahl, art.cit., pp. 250f). Although these all derive from 1 Kgs 5.21f, this does not mean that they would have appeared, as Gnilka suggests, as a single example to an ancient reader. Gnilka is however correct in saying that they do not indicate a fixed epistolary form, yet their existence shows that the Berakah was an accepted way of beginning a letter (Dahl, 251; they are however too few in number to be categorised as a form 'Brief-eingangs-Eulogie', Dahl, 250). If, as is probable, 1 Pet 1.3ff is dependent on neither 2 Cor 1.3ff nor Eph 1.3ff,[4] this increases the probability that the form was in use among Christians. Although the form is mostly found in the third person in the OT, the majority of contemporary occurrences were in the second.[5] The NT usage, apart from the epistolary introductions, is also in the third person (Lk 1.68ff; Rom 1.25; 9.5; 2 Cor 11.31). While this may tend to lessen the argument for derivation from current Jewish liturgical usage, it is difficult to see how anything other than the third person could be used in a letter; in any case it does not lessen the argument for derivation from Jewish usage. In this connection we should note also, as the exegesis will show, the great number of Jewish concepts in the eulogy.

When Berakoth are followed by clauses giving the grounds for blessing these grounds are expressed through participles, relative clauses or clauses introduced by causal conjunctions. The ground can be extended beyond the simple initial reason, as it is in Eph 1.3ff, and may either be linked directly to a concrete situation or be more general as in Eph 1.3ff. What is said in Eph 1.3ff may arise out of the situation of the death, resurrection and ascension of Christ but it is not tied to an actual situation in the life of a particular group of Christians (e.g. deliverance from some particular persecution); it applies to all Christians for all their lives.

How far does the eulogy extend? While most Berakoth pass almost imperceptibly into other areas, 1.3–14 continues to supply grounds for the original benediction. Although the tenor changes after v. 10 and even more in vv. 13f where the liturgical style is less evident, vv. 11–14 continue to contain reasons for blessing God. The whole passage holds together so well that it is probably better to regard all of it as eulogy, as against Caragounis, 47ff, who, restricting the eulogy to vv. 3–10, insists on a strict and narrow definition of eulogy. Kirby, 129ff, regards the eulogy as extending beyond v. 14; he adds 2.1–10; 2.11–22; 3.14–21 to it, adopting the view that 2.4–10; 2.14–18; 2.19–22 were originally hymnic in character. 1.15–23 cannot belong however because no Pauline letter

[4] See L. Goppelt, *Der erste Petrusbrief*, Göttingen, 1978, 48–51.
[5] Cf W. S. Towner, '"Blessed be Yahweh" and "Blessed art thou, Yahweh"': The modulation of a Biblical Formula', *CBQ* 30 (1968) 386–99.

contains both a Berakah and a thanksgiving; 3.2–13 for its part is clearly parenthetical. This extended Berakah was intended 'for use in public worship, possibly at the Eucharist' (138). As far as 1.15–23 is concerned, it is true that no Pauline letter contains both a Berakah and a thanksgiving, but Ephesians is not a Pauline letter, the number of Pauline letters is too few to draw firm conclusions as to a universal practice, the inclusion of a Berakah is itself unusual, and letter writers are free to vary patterns. It is unlikely that 2.4–10; 2.14–18; 2.19–22 were originally hymns (see notes on the passages and Best, 'Use'). There is no particular reason for linking 2.1–22 to 1.3–14. It cannot be denied that Berakoth were suitable for public worship but there is nothing in the greatly extended Berakah to suggest a connection with the eucharist.

Most Pauline letters begin with a thanksgiving; why then does AE use a eulogy? It cannot be, as Schubert[6] suggests, that eulogies are appropriate to an occasion where a hostile audience has to be faced (this is not even true of 2 Corinthians) or when a general letter is being written (while 1 Peter may be a general letter, 2 Corinthians is not). It may be true that a eulogy is used where God's acts are to be celebrated rather than the experiences of the writer and readers (cf Dahl, 251f), but this does not answer the question why AE chooses to celebrate God's acts in his letter. O'Brien,[7] following up a hint of Schenk,[8] suggests that Berakoth are used when thanks are being returned to God for blessings in which both writer and readers participate, while thanksgivings are used when thanks are being returned for mercies shown to the readers. Most of the Jewish Berakoth certainly include the speaker among those who have been blessed. Again this does not wholly answer the question why AE chose a eulogy to begin his letter since he also includes a thanksgiving (1.15ff). Perhaps all we can say is that the number of letters containing eulogies is too small for any general rule to be deduced and that the answer may lie in the personal psychology of AE; he likes liturgical language and a eulogy lends itself to this better than a straightforward prayer.

(ii) 1.3–14 is one long sentence with a complex array of subordinate clauses and phrases whose exact relation to one another is often difficult to determine. Many have spoken harshly of it, e.g. E. Norden '... das monströseste Satzkonglomerat ... das mir in griechischer Sprache begegnet ist ...'.[9] There have also been more appreciative verdicts, e.g. 'Kunstwerk von höher Schönheit'

---

[6] P. Schubert, *Form and Function of the Pauline Thanksgivings*, Berlin, 1939, 183f.

[7] P. T. O'Brien, *Introductory Thanksgivings in the Letters of Paul* (SupNT 49), Leiden, 1977, 239.

[8] W. Schenk, *Der Segen im Neuen Testament*, Berlin, 1967, 99f.

[9] *Agnostos Theos*, Leipzig, Berlin, 1913, 253.

(Rendtorff, p. 61). Robbins[10] argues that in terms of ancient rhetoric it is 'a genuinely artistic creation'; he divides it into eight periods (not sentences), each long enough to be spoken without the need to draw breath and notes that it includes two well-designed couplets in vv. 10 and 13. Hendrix[11] correctly criticises Robbins because his eight periods are uneven in length. The intricate relationship of clauses and phrases connected in a variety of ways is un-Semitic, though there are many phrases and concepts which in themselves appear Semitic rather than Hellenistic. Un-Semitic is the lack of parataxis, asyndeta and *parallelismus membrorum*. The eulogy also contains Hellenistic concepts and expressions. Danker[12] suggests that the style resembles what is found in inscriptions to benefactors which regularly have long intricate sentences; since these inscriptions were erected in public places AE would certainly have seen them and their style may have influenced him. Yet those to which Danker points do not reveal the presence of repeated phrases as in the eulogy, so their influence can only have been slight. Danker is on even more doubtful ground when he suggests that the concepts used in these inscriptions may also have exercised an influence. All documents which thank people for their good deeds will contain the same kind of concepts and language. The concepts and language of Ephesians, however, resemble so much of what is found in other NT writings that it is unnatural to go beyond the NT to seek their source. It is much more probable that the overall form of the eulogy is a combination of normal Greek and Semitic hymnic style, the latter being seen in the words indicating that we have a Berakah (v. 3a). The manner in which de Zwaan[13] was able to set out the passage displays connections with Hebraic style, even if his particular layout is unacceptable. Ideas are piled together in Semitic manner as in the Qumran hymns[14] even though the actual way in which they are related to one another is Greek. The repetition of similar concepts is Semitic rather than Greek (van Roon, 135ff), as is also the use of prepositions (van Roon, 121–8).

That the eulogy is carefully constructed can be seen from v. 3 where εὐλογέω appears three times though after the first appearance synonyms could have been used; there are recurring phrases, κατὰ

[10] C. J. Robbins, 'The Composition of Eph 1:3–14', *JBL* 105 (1986) 677–87.

[11] H. Hendrix, 'On the Form and Ethos of Ephesians', *USQR* 42 (1988) 3–15.

[12] F. W. Danker, 'Sacral-Bureaucratic Factors: A Key to Ephesians'. A working draft of this paper was read at a seminar group of the SNTS general meeting in Cambridge 1988; I have not been able to trace its further publication. Without being directly related to Ephesians, many of the ideas of the paper appear also in Danker's *Benefactor: Epigraphic Study of a Graeco-Roman and New Testament Semantic Field*, St Louis, Missouri, 1982.

[13] J. de Zwaan, 'Le "Rhythme logique" dans l'épître aux Ephésiens', *RHPR* 6 (1927) 554–65.

[14] Cf Kuhn; Mussner, 'Beiträge'.

τὴν εὐδοκίαν (βουλὴν) τοῦ θελήματος αὐτοῦ (vv. 5, 9, 11), εἰς ἔπαινον δόξης (vv. 6, 12); ἐν and κατά are used frequently, the former in particular in the phrase ἐν Χριστῷ with its variants; ἁγίους and ἀμώμους sound well together. Three significant participles (εὐλογήσας, προορίσας, γνωρίσας, vv. 3, 5, 9) represent steps in the argument of vv. 3–10; from v. 11 onwards the verbs are in the first plural. With these as clues many attempts have been made to discern within vv. 3–14 a strophic structure. No general agreement has been reached and Sanders' verdict, '... every attempt to provide a strophic structure for Eph 1.3–14 fails',[15] still stands even over attempts made since he wrote (e.g. Fischer, 111–18). Given this failure and the repetition of phrases, did AE adapt to his own purpose a hymn[16] containing them? Reconstructions of such a hymn have been so diverse and so subject to individual opinion that none has proved generally acceptable. Material employed by an author is normally detected through deviation from the author's normal style, language and theology, and by observing some kind of clear division at its start and finish. Admittedly there are clear breaks before and after the eulogy but the other tests cannot be met. Ochel, 19–32, made one of the earliest attempts to discern an underlying 'hymn'; he eliminated from 1.3–14 those passages which might be held to depend on Colossians either in wording or thought, a process which would be impossible if Ephesians is not held to depend on Colossians; his result destroys the play on εὐλογέω in v. 3 and on the root χαρ- in vv. 6f. In its language and style the eulogy is not dissimilar to the remainder of the letter which has other lengthy and complex sentences (1.15–23; 2.14–18; 3.2–7; 3.8–12; 3.14–19; 4.11–16). The theology of 1.3–14 is not out of accord with what follows; indeed many writers believe the eulogy is used to introduce the main topics of the letter (see (iv) below). If AE did not adopt and modify an existing hymn then it is unlikely that he has employed a Berakah extracted from a baptismal or eucharistic liturgy.[17] The eulogy may be suitable for either purpose, and AE may have presided in the worship of his own community and been influenced by what he did there, but that is not the same as asserting that the eulogy belongs to a liturgy. Sonorous and dignified language may be spontaneous, produced by the occasion, rather than deliberately drawn from a source.

[15] J. T. Sanders, 'Hymnic Elements in Ephesians 1–3', ZNW 56 (1965) 214–32.

[16] On the 'hymn' form see K. Berger, ANRW II 25.2, 1149ff and the literature he cites on p. 1149. See also S. E. Fowl, The Story of Christ in the Ethics of Paul (JSNTSup 36), Sheffield, 1990, 31ff.

[17] K. Gamber, 'Anklänge an das Eucharistlichgebet bei Paulus und das jüdische Kiddush', Oestkirkliche Studien 9 (1960) 254–64, sees parts of the eulogy as drawn from a much larger Christian compilation which had been influenced by Jewish prayers.

(iii) If then AE neither adapted an existing hymn nor created one, we must seek the structure of the eulogy in its content rather than in a formal pattern. There are a number of leading ideas and these provide the most satisfactory basis for an analysis, though we should avoid the over isolation of leading ideas from one another. The eulogy hangs together as a whole, beginning and ending with praise of God. The note of praise sounds throughout as the reasons for it, in the final issue lying in God's loving purpose, are introduced from different angles. Ideas pile up on top of one another; part of the difficulty of dismemberment lies in the flow of almost synonymous words.

Verse 3 introduces the theme of God's blessing; the way he blesses is detailed in what follows. This verse also shows that he is the real subject of all that is subsequently said. His will is repeatedly stressed, a will governed not by arbitrariness but by love and grace. God then has a plan[18] for the cosmos, which has been hidden but is now revealed through his son (Acts 22.14f; Mt 11.25–7; cf Wisd 9.13–18; 2 Esdr 6.20); his plan refers not only to history but includes the cosmos and its redemption. One aspect of the plan, the acceptance of the Gentiles, is not mentioned in the eulogy but appears in 2.11–22; 3.1–13. V. 3 also indicates that it is the members of the church who are the recipients of his blessing activity. Christ for his part mediates God's blessings to us as is emphasised by the repeated references to him, mainly through personal and relative pronouns, and Christ is depicted both in his redemptive and cosmic roles: God's eternal will is executed through Christ and the cosmos summed up in him; salvation comes through his death.

(a) God's blessings began prior to history (vv. 4f), for in his love, and his will is governed by his love, he chose and foreordained us that we should have a position before him as his children. (b) In order to have such a position our sins must be forgiven (vv. 7, 8a); this is again an act of God's grace. (c) But God's blessings include more than a position before him as his redeemed; he imparts to us an understanding (vv. 8b–10) of his total purpose for the cosmos, previously a secret hidden from all. Here the eulogy reaches a kind of summit and this once achieved the climb begins again, as it were from half-way up the hill (vv. 11–14). (d) While everything may be summed up in Christ, believers need reminding that they have been given a place in all that God does (vv. 11f) so that their hope may be reinforced. (e) Finally AE applies all he has said to his readers by changing from the first person to the second (vv. 13f), at the same

[18] Cf G. Lohfink, 'Der präexistente Heilsplan und Hintergrund des dritten Vaterunserbitte', *Neues Testament und Ethik* (FS R. Schnackenburg, ed. H. Merklein), Freiburg, 1989, 110–33.

time bringing out further aspects of God's blessing. As believers his readers have received the Spirit which is a first instalment of yet greater gifts to come. So we move from the blessings of God initiated before time, through the present, to those which are yet to come in their fullness.

(iv) If AE did not adopt preformed material it is possible he wrote the eulogy to introduce the remainder of the letter. Some scholars (e.g. Dahl, art.cit.; Schlier, 72; O'Brien; Maurer; Castellino; Caragounis, 45ff) see a close relation between the eulogy and what follows, arguing that the themes of the letter are already suggested in it. Care is important here. A lecturer introducing his subject may indicate briefly and explicitly the points he will later develop. AE has certainly not done that. It is also possible that a writer having decided what he is going to say in the main part of his writing may consciously or unconsciously allow this to colour his introduction through the use of leading ideas or words. The use of words in this connection is not as important as that of ideas; that AE chooses an unusual word for the heavens (v. 3) and uses it again later does not mean that there is a connection between the eulogy and the remainder of the letter, but only that he likes this word when talking about heaven. On the other hand, if he develops in the later part of the letter ideas which he has formally introduced in the eulogy, then the eulogy could be regarded as introducing the thought of what follows. The leading ideas of the eulogy are God's choice of believers, his purpose in all that he does, his adoption of them and deliverance from sin, his revelation of a mystery which includes the summing up of all in Christ, his giving believers an inheritance and an earnest in the Holy Spirit of their later reception of that inheritance.

It cannot be said that God's choice or election of believers and his adoption of them, or the stress on his will, or that of which the Holy Spirit is the earnest are further developed, though deliverance from sin and the place of the believer in God's present plan are. The unveiling of the mystery of the summing up of all in Christ may be said to presage the bringing together of Jew and Gentile (3.1–13), and mystery reappears at 6.19. But before we accept too easily AE's intention to prepare in the eulogy for what follows, we should remember that much of what is common to the eulogy and the body of the letter was part of the common stock of NT ideas, e.g. deliverance from sin, the adoption of believers, grace, the headship of Christ if this is present in 1.10. Bengel described vv. 3–14 as *compendium evangelicum*. It is not surprising that words and phrases like 'in Christ', 'mystery', reappear later if they are the ways in which AE expresses himself. 'In Christ' is a phrase belonging to the Pauline school, as is the term 'mystery' in the light of its use in Colossians; the use of ἐπουράνιος instead of οὐράνιος merely shows AE's preference for the former; none of these demonstrates that he is making a deep connection between the eulogy and what follows. Finally we note that there are major themes in the body of the letter which are not mentioned in the eulogy. The church is a major theme and the group of believers is variously described as church, body, building, bride. Yet the eulogy lacks all these words. Instead the first and second persons plural are used and opinions differ whether a corporate significance should be read into 'in Christ', and if it can this can only be justified in the light of the later teaching on the church. There are good grounds for regarding the eulogy as christologically based rather than controlled by the ecclesiology of the remainder of the letter.[19] Finally it should be noted that the eulogy makes no reference to the paraenesis which occupies half the letter. The eulogy is not then a thematic introduction to the letter.

3. As we have seen, AE has taken over and re-shaped a Jewish liturgical formula. Jewish Berakoth may speak of God *simpliciter*. 'Blessed[20] is (be) the Lord' (e.g. Exod 18.10; 1 Sam 25.39), or may identify him more precisely, 'Blessed is (be) the Lord, the God of Israel' (e.g. 1 Sam 25.32; 1 Kgs 1.48); 1 Chron 29.10 introduces God as father into a eulogy. In Eph 1.3 he is identified as 'the God and Father of our Lord Jesus Christ', i.e. in Christian terms. The Christians worship the same God as the Jews but view him in a new way. There is thus both continuity and discontinuity between the faith of the Old and New Testaments.

τοῦ κυρίου ἡμῶν Ἰησοῦ Χριστοῦ probably goes with θεός as well as with πατήρ. Many early commentators (e.g. Theod Mops), concerned how this might affect Trinitarian doctrine, associated the phrase only with πατήρ and, taking καί as epexegetical, translated 'God who is the Father of our Lord Jesus Christ'.[21] AE can have had no such worries for at 1.17 he speaks of the God of Jesus Christ. The total phrase appears also at 2 Cor 1.3; 11.31; Rom 15.6; 1 Pet 1.3 (the text is uncertain at Col 1.3), suggesting it was a liturgical unit. 'God' and 'Father' are also closely linked in Jn 20.17; 1 Cor 15.24; Gal 1.4; Eph 5.20; Phil 4.20; 1 Th 3.11; Rev 1.6. Since God initiates the plan of salvation described in the eulogy he may rightly be termed the God of our Lord Jesus Christ. The initial phrase lacks a verb and can be translated either as 'Blessed is God' or 'May God be blessed'. In the only two NT places (Rom 1.25; 2 Cor 11.31) where the verb is spelt out with a part of εἶναι the correct rendering is 'is'. This suits the context of 1.3–14 making it begin with a statement of fact rather than a wish, for all that follows depends on the initial statement of God's 'value'. Prayer follows later in the letter; 1.3–14 though using prayer language tells us rather what

[19] So F. Montagnini, 'Christological Features in Ep 1:3–14', *Paul de Tarse: Apôtre du notre temps* (ed. Lorenzo De Lorenzi), Rome, 1979, 529–39.
[20] On the form of εὐλογητός see Caragounis, 79 n. 3.
[21] Cf Best, 'Fashions in Exegesis: Ephesians 1.3', *Interpreting Christ*, Edinburgh, 1993, 160–77.

God has done for believers. B uniquely omits καὶ πατήρ; this is unacceptable as is the longer omission in 𝔓⁴⁶ where the eye of its scribe must have slipped from the final Χριστοῦ of v. 2 to the same word in v. 3.

The grounds for the Berakah are introduced by ὁ εὐλογήσας ... and explicated in what follows; v. 3b is too general to permit their identification. The change in meaning of εὐλογεῖν would have puzzled readers unacquainted with Jewish Greek. Whereas εὐλογεῖν in the sense 'praise, speak well of' (v. 3a) is standard Greek, the sense 'bestow a gift' appearing in v. 3b is not. It derives from Hebrew *brk* which has both senses; this led to εὐλογεῖν being used throughout the LXX with both meanings and to a similar usage in early Christianity (cf Lk 2.34; Act 3.26; Rom 15.29; Gal 3.9, 14; Heb 7.1, 6; 12.17; 1 Pet 3.9). Mature Christians would have easily picked up the play on the word. The triple use of the root in v. 3 incorporating both senses is an example of AE's skill as a writer.

The triple use of the root εὐλογεῖν in v. 3 may however be a 'secondary Hebraism' (MH, 485) which anyone familiar with Jewish Greek might employ (cf. Gen 27.41; 49.25; *Jub* 22.30). Since εὐλογία is anarthrous πάσῃ should mean 'every' rather than 'the whole' but this rule was not rigid in Hellenistic Greek (Moule, 93ff; MHT, 199ff; BDR, §275; Robertson, 771ff) and there are a number of instances in Eph where decision is difficult: 2.21; 3.15; 6.18 (3.8?).[22] 'Whole' is clearly the correct understanding in 1.8; 4.2, 31; 5.9 where the nouns are anarthrous and abstract. In v. 3b εὐλογία is probably abstract (so usually in the NT but not at 2 Cor 9.6). If χάρισμα or δῶρον had been used instead, neither would have been abstract. If 'every' gives the correct sense then the phrase may indicate 'every charismatic blessing'; such blessings would not be limited to glossolalia, healing and prophecy but include love, joy, peace, etc. 'Every' should not however be taken too literally for it and its compounds are regularly used in the Pauline letters in the transition from the address to the body of the letter in a non-literal manner. Yet the sense 'the whole' is more appropriate to the context since the passage goes on to cover the entire sweep of the divine economy rather than to individualise particular blessings (cf Rom 15.29, 'fullness of blessing').

πνευματικῇ has been interpreted in a variety of ways. From the beginning, as noted by Origen, it was wrongly used to differentiate between the gifts of the two Testaments, then to differentiate non-material gifts from material or from what 'is earthly and sensuous' (Westcott). It does not mean 'misteriosa, transcendente, non dell'ordine umano' (Dacquino, 476). More correctly Alford (cf Cambier, 64): 'in the N.T. [it] always implies the working of the Holy Spirit, never bearing merely our modern inaccurate sense of spiritual as

---

[22] On the Pauline use of πᾶς see Hyon Suk Hwang, 'Die Verwendung des Wortes πᾶς in den paulinischen Briefen' (Erlangen dissertation, 1985).

opposed to bodily'. The whole blessing is said to be spiritual because it belongs to the sphere of the Spirit, who has worked, is working and will continue to work until God's plan is complete and who himself belongs to that plan's eschatological fulfilment. It is not spiritual in the popular charismatic sense but in the sense in which the gifts of Gal 5.22 are ultimately from the Spirit. The blessing is enjoyed now and does not belong only to the future for (1.13) every Christian is sealed with the Spirit (cf Adai, 50–60)

To what moment does the aorist participle εὐλογήσας refer? The description which follows ranges from election by God prior to baptism and conversion (v. 4), through redemption (v. 7), to future consummation in Christ (v. 10), and the participle cannot be restricted to refer only to Christ's incarnation (Abbott, Harless), or to the moment of conversion (Westcott) or baptism (Gnilka, Schlier). The aorist probably indicates the completed action of God lying in the past of both writer and readers, an action on which conversion and baptism depend. God's blessings belong to the economy of salvation which he has already set in motion and which continues in the present activity of the Spirit. From God's point of view his blessings are already complete. Because this is so the eulogy can begin 'Blessed is God'. That Christians became aware of the blessings at conversion/baptism does not mean that that was the moment they came into existence.

ἡμᾶς means the writer and readers as in 1 Pet 1.3ff (unlike 2 Cor 1.4 where it signifies either Paul or Paul and Timothy). Houlden (preceded according to Meyer by Koppe) refers it to Paul alone arguing that AE presents Paul here as he does in 3.1ff as part of God's plan. However, AE uses the first singular of Paul in 3.1ff and if he had been thinking only of Paul in 1.3ff he would have done the same. We note his change to the singular at 1.15 when referring to Paul alone.

ἐν τοῖς ἐπουρανίοις is a further qualification. The sense is local, but the phrase serves also to reinforce the divine origin of the blessings. Christ sits in the heavenlies (1.20) and believers sit with him because they have been made to live with him (2.6). What belongs to the heavenlies is therefore already ours (for fuller discussion see Detached Note: The Heavenlies).

ἐν Χριστῷ (see Detached Note: In Christ), the third phrase in the verse beginning with ἐν, is the final qualification. With what is it to be construed and how is it to be understood? ἐν is AE's favourite preposition; he often uses it twice or more within a few words (1.20; 2.2, 3, 4, 5, 6, 13, 15, 21, 22; 4.14; 6.18). Both 'in Christ' and 'in the heavenlies' are repeated in 2.6 suggesting their close association. This does not mean that the heavenlies are in Christ for at 1.20 he is said to be in them; nor can 'in Christ' be regarded as a redefinition of 'the heavenlies' (so apparently Schlier); this would be unnecessary. 'In Christ' could also be taken instrumentally with εὐλογία (Dibelius; cf

Allan, 'In Christ'): the spiritual blessing which believers receive is effected by God through Christ. It is not clear what this would add to what has already been said, though this may not be a fundamental objection in view of AE's redundant style. Christ has already been mentioned in relation to God and Christians would not have thought of the πνεῦμα apart from him. 'In Christ' could also be construed with εὐλογήσας (Gaugler, Barth) though distance is an obstacle. Barth argues that the verb followed by the preposition governing a name is found also in Gen 18.18 (cf 12.3) in respect of Abraham and he ascribes to Christ 'a similar passive and active, parabolic and dynamic function' (p. 78) as to Abraham. In both Genesis passages, unlike ours, the pronoun referring to Abraham is not separated from but follows directly on the verb. The addition of 'in Christ' may however have been influenced by the Genesis passages where blessing is said to be in Abraham (cf Gal 3.14). However, the local significance of ἐv in the preceding phrase 'in the heavenlies' does suggest that ἐv should be taken similarly in 'in Christ' (so Schlier). Such a significance would be in line with the Pauline use of the phrase in which believers are seen as 'in Christ', as members of his body (Belser; Dahl, *Auslegung*, 18; Bouwman). Christians are blessed because they are united to Christ.

Verse 3 is a very general statement setting the tone for what follows but leaving the nature of the spiritual blessing unidentified. This is filled out in vv. 4ff: God's past eternal election (vv. 4–5a) realised in present existence (5b–8, 11–14) is to be consummated in the future (9–10). Although God, Christ and the Spirit all feature in v. 3 it would be wrong to think that AE deliberately created a Trinitarian formulation. He cannot however adequately describe God's blessing without introducing all three persons of the Trinity.

DETACHED NOTE I
THE HEAVENLIES[23]

The NT contains no unified concept of heaven. It cannot be defined as the place where God dwells or where the righteous dead live. It is understood differently in different NT books and sometimes differently within the same book. In Heb 8.1 (cf 9.24) Christ is said to sit at the right hand of God in the heavens, but in 4.14 he passes through the heavens to God and in 7.26 he is above the heavens.

[23] See R. M. Pope, 'Studies in Pauline Vocabulary: of the Heavenly Places', *ExpT* 33 (1912) 365ff; H. Odeberg, *The View of the Universe in the Epistle to the Ephesians*, Lund, 1934; Mussner, *Christus*, 11ff; Percy, 180–3; Van Roon, Authenticity, 213–15; Gibbs, 128–32; H. Traub and G. von Rad, *TWNT*, V, 495–543; Lindemann, *Aufhebung*, 49–56; A. T. Lincoln, 'A Re-examination of "the Heavenlies" in Ephesians', *NTS* 19 (1972/3) 468–83; Caragounis, 146–52; W. H. Harris, '"The Heavenlies" Reconsidered: Οὐρανός and Ἐπουράνιος in Ephesians', *BSac* 148 (1991) 72–89. For the wider aspects see H. Bietenhard, *Die himmlische Welt im Urchristentum und Spätjudentum* (WUNT 2, Tübingen, 1951) and M. P. Nilsson, *Geschichte der griechischen Religion*, Munich, 1961, II, 702–11.

Both plural and singular are used to say apparently the same thing (Heb 9.1 and 9.24). In accordance with Jewish thought in which there can be many heavens, the plural can also be signified (2 Cor 12.2). Since, again according to Jewish thought, there is to be a new heaven and a new earth (Isa 66.22), heaven need not be regarded as perfect.

To denote heaven the NT uses two words or groups of words distinguished in their adjectival forms as ἐπουράνιος and οὐράνιος. The latter is by far the more frequent; the former is found only twenty times, mainly grouped in particular writings or passages: five occurrences in 1 Cor 15.40–9, five in Ephesians and six in Hebrews. In Ephesians it is found only in the phrase ἐν τοῖς ἐπουρανίοις (this could be either masculine or neuter) which therefore appears to be a fixed formula, though not found elsewhere in the NT. ἐν would seem to indicate a local reference and 1.20; 2.6; 3.10; 6.12 easily conform with this. 1.3 is more difficult and it has been variously interpreted. Chrysostom, rejecting the local reference, took it of the heavenly things which are beyond change. However, the vast majority of commentators attempt in some way to preserve the local reference. Lightfoot wrote of 'the heaven which lies within and about the true Christian', Caird says it stands 'for man's invisible, spiritual environment', Scott thinks the best English equivalent would be 'in the invisible world'. All such interpretations have been influenced by Greek spiritualising conceptions. The explanation of Gibbs that the phrase 'does not refer to a specific, literal locale but, rather, to the realm of God's sovereignty' though expressed differently seems to interpret it similarly. Such interpretations are really attempts to demythologise heaven, though of course into a non-existentialist framework. Schlier (45–8 and *Kirche*, 1–18) more deliberately attempts to demythologise, believing that AE's use of the phrase is derived from gnostic ideas and accords with a gnostic world picture. There is a plurality of heavens in the uppermost of which is Christ; below him is the church; opposed to the church but still within the heavenlies are the powers. The heavenlies represent the dimension of the transcendant in human life through which possibilities of existence open up, possibilities typified by Christ and the powers and in respect of which a decision must be made. If Christ is chosen believers find themselves both in the heavens and above them since they are in Christ's body and under his headship.

Odeberg (cf Lona, 297–301) rejects the identification of the two Greek words for heaven and sees τὰ ἐπουράνια as incorporating that which is ἐπὶ τῆς γῆς. It then becomes 'a term designating the whole of the Spiritual Reality' (p. 12); in consequence 'in the heavenlies' loses any spatial significance. But Odeberg's basic view of the heavenlies cannot be sustained. Five instances of one Greek word and four of the other are statistically too few to enforce a major distinction between them if their normal meaning is the same, unless a clear and undisputed difference can be discerned in their use; this is not so in Ephesians. Odeberg is concerned, as it were, to keep believers on earth but 2.6 reflects 1.20 and Christ is in heaven in 1.20. Caragounis and Lincoln, both rejecting Odeberg's view, come independently to somewhat similar opinions. For Caragounis believers exist simultaneously on two planes, the earthly and the heavenly (p. 150). The heavenly blessings of 1.3 'have heaven as their source and as their goal, since the blessings, as later named, are to the intent and effect that man should attain his alloted position in heaven' (p. 150). Lincoln writes (p. 481), 'the believer is regarded as involved in two spheres of existence simultaneously'; cf Alford, 'Materially, we are yet in the body; but in the Spirit, we are in heaven'. Lincoln sees 'spiritual' and 'heavenly' in 1.3 as almost synonymous (cf 1 Cor 15.40–9) and relates his conclusion to a realised eschatology. The Spirit belongs to the New Age as does the new heaven. The spiritual blessings in the heavenlies are 'benefits which belong to believers now because God in Christ has blessed them and sealed them with the Spirit' (p. 471). It cannot be denied that a reference to spiritual blessings implies some form of realised eschatology but does this necessarily apply to 'in the heavenlies'? If it does, why does AE need to add 'now' in 3.10? The warfare described at 6.12 was never believed to exist in the eschatological period alone. 'In the heavenlies' does not then by itself provide a realised eschatological slant.

Whatever our modern views of heaven, no believers in the ancient world would have doubted the statement of 1.20 that Christ sits at God's right hand in heaven for the heavenly session was part of accepted belief. Those believers would also not have been surprised to learn that the cosmic powers were active in heaven and that there was warfare between them and humanity (6.12). Such warfare would make it necessary for the wisdom of God to be made known to the powers in heaven (3.10). What is surprising is that this should be taking place now (see on 3.6). However, this is not out of accord with the consummation of all in heaven and earth in Christ (1.10). The reference to the heavenlies in 2.6 may most easily be understood along the lines: believers died with Christ (a common Pauline idea), they have been made alive with him (either a Pauline idea or a development of it, see on 2.6), they sit with him in the heavenlies. If this final statement is true then since they sit in heaven they must enjoy the blessings of heaven. This brings us back to 1.3 where the reference to Christ can be seen to be appropriate: we sit with him in heaven as members of his body.

Verse 3 therefore assumes that the readers already accept what is found later in the letter in respect of the heavenlies. AE is not giving new teaching but using acknowledged teaching and adapting it to his

own ends. There is similar teaching in Col 3.1–4 where believers are
bidden to set their minds on τὰ ἄνω, a phrase whose meaning is
defined only by its opposite τὰ ἐπὶ τῆς γῆς. The things that are
above must bear some relation to the blessing in the heavenlies of
1.3. That blessing is itself undefined except by the adjective
πνευματικός. The remainder of the eulogy spells it out. Perhaps AE
would have been puzzled to say precisely what believers receive and
used a vague but comprehensive phrase which implies that whatever
blessings God has in mind for them when they are in heaven they
enjoy now on earth.

Since in Greek there is no significant difference in meaning
between ἐπουράνιος and οὐράνιος nor in AE's use of them, it is not
clear why he should have chosen the former here. He may have been
attracted to it as the longer and more sonorous. More probably he
chose it because it was already part of a fixed liturgical form, 'in the
heavenlies'. He may possibly have created the form himself, liked it
and continued using it; all writers have 'pet' phrases (cf Percy,
182f). This however does not account for his first use of the word
(v. 3) which, as we have seen, seems to assume its existing use.
More probably then in the light of its usage in Colossians it was a
phrase of AE's Pauline school.

Granted that AE's use of the phrase is consistent, how does it fit
with the other passages in the letter which relate to heaven and
earth? Mussner, *Christus*, 11ff, has shown in great detail that there
were a number of cosmologies current in the ancient world.
Generally speaking in the contemporary Greek picture there was
'keiner Platz für das Reich der Toten unter der Erde'. AE's use of
'the heavenlies' accords with this. The cosmic powers belong to
heaven and not to an underworld hell (3.10; 6.12). At 2.2 Satan is
the ruler of the forces 'of the air', i.e. the sub-lunar region above the
earth (cf Foerster, *TWNT*, I, 165). Nothing in AE's use of οὐρανός
conflicts with this two-decker picture of the cosmos. 6.9 places God
in the heavens; 4.10 sees Christ ascending above the heavens. At
1.10 all that is in heaven and earth is brought together in Christ; that
this should be necessary with respect to what is in heaven accords
with the evil cosmic powers as present there. At 3.15 every πατριά
(this could include evil powers) in heaven and earth is named. At
1.10 and 3.15 only two spheres of existence are named, i.e. a two-
decker universe. The only possible reference to an underworld is in
4.9 but see discussion there. Apart from this we always have a two-
decker cosmos. This is true also of Colossians (cf 1.16, 20). To be
contrasted is Phil 2.10. The absence of any mention of an underworld in Ephesians and Colossians may follow simply because
neither letter refers to the destiny of the unbelieving dead. Its
absence may however also be seen to conform to the acceptance in
both letters of an ultimate reconciliation of all to God. Dead

believers and those reconciled to Christ are with him and therefore in heaven.

4. AE now begins to spell out the spiritual blessings and supply the reasons why God can be called blessed, and commences, not from a call to believers to remember their conversion experience, but from the position that God has given believers in that he has chosen them. This is the firm foundation on which all the blessings such as adoption and forgiveness are erected, and from which they flow.

Although καθώς (cf Percy, 243–5) may be used to introduce quotations (so Barth) when it does so it is regularly followed by a word like γέγραπται. There is no such word here; what follows is not then a quotation but AE's own composition. καθώς may have either a causal or comparative sense (BDR §453.2, n. 4). It may also carry both senses with one or other predominating. The causal probably predominates here.

God is called blessed, not because we decide to turn to him nor because he foresaw that we would be deserving of salvation, but because he chose us and his choice preceded creation.[24] Although ἐκλέγομαι is rarely used in the NT of God's eternal choice the concept is present (Rom 8.28f; 2 Tim 1.9; Tit 1.2; Jn 15.16; 17.24; 1 Pet 1.1f). It, of course, goes back into the OT (Deut 7.6f; 14.2) and was continued in Judaism (*Jub* 18.30; 22.9; *1 En* 93.2; 2 Esdr 3.13; *2 Bar* 48.19f; 1QS 11.7; 1QSb 1.2; 1QM 10.9).[25] The ἐκ of ἐκλέγομαι should not be taken (*pace* Salmond) as if it emphasised the selection of a small group out of a larger; it does not have this sense in Lk 9.35; 23.35. Election and predestination in our passages are not related primarily to individual salvation but to God's purpose.[26] AE displays no interest in those who are not chosen, though as the remainder of the letter shows he is clearly aware that there is a difference between those in and those not in the church. A eulogy of praise and context of love is not the place in which to refer to the damnation of unbelievers. The seemingly logical deduction that when some are chosen others are rejected is not worked out in the NT, though later it came to be discussed widely in the church. (On the whole question see M. Barth 104–9 and K. Barth, op.cit.) Depending on how 1.10 is understood, it may be that AE does not believe that there will be any who will be ultimately rejected; all

[24] Cf C. R. Smith, *The Bible Doctrine of Grace*, London, 1956, 141–86; H.-M. Dion, 'La prédestination chez saint Paul', *RSR* 53 (1965) 5–43; O Hofius, ' "Erwählt vor Grundlegung der Welt" (Eph 1.4)', *ZNW* 62 (1971) 123–8; J. Calvin, *Institutes*, IV 1.2.

[25] See H. H. Rowley, *The Biblical Doctrine of Election*, London, 1950; T. C. Vriezen, *Die Erwählung Israels nach dem Alten Testament* (ATANT 24), Zurich, 1963; G. Quell, *TWNT*, IV, 148ff; K. Barth, *Church Dogmatics*, Edinburgh, 1957, II.2, 3–506.

[26] Cf D. E. H. Whiteley, *The Theology of St Paul*, Oxford, 1964, 94f.

will be brought together in Christ. There is no clear statement here as to the purpose of God's election of believers; no immediate task ('saved to serve') is laid before them. Their election however gives them a new status; they are holy and blameless and have become God's children (v. 5).

ἡμᾶς identifies those whom God elects but probably is not used in order to individualise them for AE places emphasis throughout on the unity of Christians as members of the church. It is not said that Christ is elect; a distinction is thus made between him and believers. Whereas in Judaism it was the nation, or the faithful remnant, which was the primary subject of election, for AE the elect group consists of all, both Jews and Gentiles, who in being reconciled to God have been reconciled to one another (cf 2.14–17) and who form the body of Christ. The church is elect. We tend in thought to distinguish the church from those who from time to time are added individually to it; this is a distinction which cannot be made in a pre-temporal situation. All the elect were elected pre-temporally and the church is comprised of all the elect. The stress on election should reassure Gentile believers that they are in no inferior position to Jewish believers.

God elected the church πρὸ καταβολῆς κοσμοῦ. While καταβολή may suggest a throwing down from a height (cf Chrysostom, Jerome) the word was used regularly in Greek to denote a beginning or foundation; there is then no need to see in it any idea of being thrown down, least of all a gnostic allusion to the fall of the cosmos (Schille 70); the simple βάλλω at times means little more than 'put' (Jn 5.7). The phrase καταβολῆς κοσμοῦ is used in the NT with two prepositions, ἀπό (e.g. Mt 25.34; Lk 11.50) suggesting something taking place at the time of creation and πρό (Jn 17.24; 1 Pet 1.20; cf 1 Cor 2.7) suggesting a pre-creation event.

'Before' is a familiar concept since events are regularly apprehended in temporal sequence, but it is difficult to give a precise meaning to 'before creation'. AE uses it to emphasise God's sovereignty, an idea appearing again in the stress on his will in vv. 5, 9, 11. Nothing that has happened since creation led God to elect his people; his election was not a response to human sin (first mentioned in v. 7) or the failure of Israel, but was intended from the time he intended the universe. God is not a chess player who makes his next move only after he has seen the last move of his opponent. He works to a plan (cf 1QH 13.10; CD 2.7; Philo, Opif Mundi 16ff) and that plan always included the church. The church is not then simply a sociological phenomenon appearing under appropriate conditions. Yet if we say God works to a plan we must allow that for AE God is not primarily a great architect but a loving Father. The pre-temporal election of his people is only one side of a complex picture of God.

The election is said to be 'in Christ', a connection not made in Rom 8.28–30. What does it signify? In relation to Christ it implies he had a role wider than that of redeeming humanity through his incarnation, death and resurrection. As in Col 1.15ff he has a role in creation (cf 3.9; Roels, 25f); v. 4 thus prepares the way for v. 10. Christ's pre-existence is found in many parts of the NT, in particular in the hymn of Col 1.15ff which AE probably knew as tradition (cf Jn 17.5; 1 Pet 1.20). If then the church is chosen in Christ and he existed prior to creation, does this imply the church's pre-temporal existence? Behind this could lie the idea of Christ as a representative or inclusive figure (see Detached Note: In Christ) and this may supply the reason why AE thought of 'election in Christ'. However, an instrumental interpretation of 'in Christ' would also be possible.[27] Whatever interpretation is chosen, the conclusion that the church pre-existed does not necessarily follow (Essay: The Church §5). It is in any case improbable that 'in Christ' is meant by way of contrast with the choice of Israel in Abraham (*Gen R.* 44 (27a), see SB III, 579); that choice was not pre-temporal but took place in history and Jews come within it because of their physical descent from Abraham.

The introduction of the reference to Christ has further significance. Election is related to the one who died, rose and ascended. This makes his love known and God's action seen as one made in love (cf Rom 9.18, 25). The introduction of Christ thus brings together what may seem two incompatible ideas: God elects us before we exist and without our consent; we respond freely to his activity in Christ. Christ is the unifying factor in this.

God does not act aimlessly and his choice must have a purpose or result (ἵνα may be final or consecutive; there is little distinction here) and in v. 4 this is that believers are holy and without fault and become his children. Though 2.10 suggests that 'good works' have been prepared in advance for Christians there is no suggestion that God saw that particular people would be good and so chose them. Both ἅγιος and ἄμωμος are terms drawn from the cultus (for the second see Num 6.14; 19.2; Exod 29.37f; Heb 9.14); in time both were used more generally of moral behaviour (again for the second see Ψ 14.2; 17.24; Sir. 31.8; 40.19; Eph 5.27; Phil 2.15; Jude 24; Rev 14.5).[28] Yet their cultic origin is not totally lost here, for the holiness and faultlessness is a holiness and faultlessness before God (for κατενώπιον see BDR §214 n. 8; Robertson, 644).

It is regularly assumed AE depends here on Col 1.22, παραστῆσαι ὑμᾶς

---

[27] The reading ἑαυτῷ of F G is clearly wrong; it would presumably mean that God chose us for himself, thereby eliminating Christ.

[28] On changing ideas in relation to purity see M. Newton, *The Concept of Purity at Qumran and in the Letters of Paul* (SNTSMS 53), Cambridge, 1985, *passim*.

ἁγίους καὶ ἀμώμους καὶ ἀνεγκλήτους κατενώπιον αὐτοῦ, and conjectured that he dropped the final adjective as lacking a cultic background; in the LXX the work appears only at 3 Macc 5.31; it has a moral sense in 1 Tim 3.10; Tit 1.6f and an eschatological in 1 Cor 1.8; AE is also supposed to have substituted εἶναι for παραστῆσαι. But it is *a priori* equally possible that A/Col added the extra adjective to what he found in Ephesians and changed the verb because he wished to stress the juridical nuance (cf the commentaries of Lohse, Martin, O'Brien). A more probable solution than either of these lies in the recognition that ἁγίους καὶ ἀμώμους was an existing liturgical phrase of the Pauline school of AE and A/Col; it reappears at 5.27, and a similar phrase at 1 Pet 1.19. A liturgical use of the phrase would accord with its cultic origin and it would be quite natural to add a reference to God, κατενώπιον αὐτοῦ, to a liturgical phrase (cf Holtzmann, 47f, and Best, 'Who used Whom?'). The phrase does not then have a primarily moral flavour; this is again true at 5.27.

What does AE mean by his use of the adjectives? Are they to be understood in a realised sense—believers are already holy and faultless even as they are already justified—or do we have an implied exhortation—believers have been elected so that they may strive to be holy and faultless? A statement counselling moral behaviour would not be appropriate in a eulogy though one affirming the status and position before God of those who are elect would be. The general drift of the passage suggests AE in using the phrase wished to emphasise the present position of Christians. Believers are already holy and without fault before God, as is the church (5.27). This accords with the cultic sense of the words and follows on their election by God.

If God has elected believers this should give them confidence in the face of opposing cosmic powers (6.12ff) and should free them from any idea that they are at the mercy of a faceless fate. Often when people who appear inadequate for an important position are elevated to it they suddenly reveal new capabilities; they respond to their new position and gain confidence from it. So AE's Gentile believers are given a new confidence as God's elect to meet whatever comes to them. As the following reference to love shows, God's election, or his foreordination, is linked to his love (5.2). Realising God loves them and has chosen them makes them new people (4.24) fit for new tasks.

5. This and the following verse extend the thought of v. 4 and election is seen to be a foreordination to adoption.

It is disputed whether ἐν ἀγάπῃ[29] goes with what precedes or what follows. It has been taken with v. 4 because: (a) it is associated with what

---

[29] On the use of ἀγάπη in Ephesians see J. Plo Bonafont, 'Teologia del Sagrado Corazon en la Epistola a los Efesios (I–III)', *Miscelana Comillas* 53 (1970) 75–126; V. Estalayo-Alonso, 'Agape en la carta a los Efesios', *Estudios Teologicos* 1 (1974) 79–127.

precedes in 4.2, 15, 16; 5.2; (b) ἀγάπη normally refers in Ephesians to human love (1.15; 3.18; 4.2, 15, 16; 5.2; 6.23); (c) Paul rarely speaks of God's love; (d) even if we reject the human reference the phrase might still be taken with v. 4 and associated with either ἐξελέξατο (God elects because of his love) or προορίσας. It has been taken with v. 5 because: (a) the verbal form regularly refers to the love of God and of Christ (2.4; 5.2, 25) and the noun is so used in 2.4 and 3.19; in fact there are too few instances to permit the drawing of firm statistical conclusions in relation to whether it refers in Ephesians to human or divine love; (b) Paul is probably not the author of Ephesians and so we can draw no conclusions from his general practice; (c) the general course of the argument in the eulogy relates to what God has done for people rather than to their attitude to him, even less their attitude to one another; (d) if it refers to human love it must be linked with the two adjectives signifying sanctity in v. 4, but these are primarily religious or cultic rather than moral terms (see above); in their context they denote a position before God; (e) ἐξελέξατο is too distant for a satisfactory connection; (f) to take it with προορίσας would overload the latter with adverbial qualifications; (g) in 3.17, where ἐν ἀγάπῃ refers to divine love, it is best taken with what follows. The arguments for the connection with what follows appear the stronger and we (cf Caragounis, 84–6) therefore join the phrase to v. 5 noting that this is the solution adopted by most of the Greek Fathers (e.g. Chrysostom; Origen allows both possibilities). If it refers to God's love its theological significance is unchanged no matter with which participle it is associated.

Believers have not only been chosen before the foundation of the world, they have also been foreordained (προορίσας)[30] to be adopted. Because foreordination as AE uses the concept applies here to people it is to be distinguished from a general predestination of all that happens. The members of the group who are foreordained are identical to those who are chosen and presumably their election and foreordination are to be thought of as simultaneous, though it is doubtful if simultaneity is a concept relevant to a pre-temporal period. Neither participle thus precedes the other in time, the aorist of the second being that of 'identical action' (Burton, 64f). Its προ relates it to the foundation of the world. The two participles are differing ways of expressing the sovereign purpose of God. The expression of the same thought in more ways than one is not unnatural in a eulogy. The reference to love implies that God's purpose originates in and is controlled by his love; it is not an arbitrary exercise of power. Nothing is said here about the perseverance to final salvation of those who are foreordained and their relation to what happens in 1.10 is left unexamined. Neither election nor foreordination in AE's eyes cuts out the need for moral effort.

[30] See Dion, art.cit., 25ff; K. L. Schmidt, *TWNT*, V, 453f; L. C. Allen, 'The Old Testament Background of (προ)ὁρίζειν in the New Testament', *NTS* 17 (1970/1) 104–8.

Had they done so he would never have gone on to lay down in 4.1ff guiding lines for conduct and encouraged his readers to live by them, nor would he have threatened them with the judgement of God (5.5f).

Foreordination though not mentioned explicitly in the OT is found in the Qumran writings (1QH 4.31; 15.13–22) and in Paul (using the same verb as here) at Rom 8.29f; 1 Cor 2.7; the idea is probably also present in 1 Th 5.9; Rom 9–11; it is found again in 1 Pet 1.1f; 2.8; Ign *Eph* (address). Jeremiah (1.5) was called before his birth and was therefore predestined to fulfil his mission. Foreordination and election are to be distinguished from the impersonality of Greek concepts of fate (e.g. it is all written in the stars) because a personal and loving God operates them. Without the knowledge that fore-ordination is the result of God's love foreordination would be wholly inexplicable. As in v. 4 the ἡμᾶς should not be taken as individualising believers, as affirming anything about their ultimate salvation, or as implying a fearful fate for unbelievers (the latter is depicted in 1 Pet 2.8; Jude 4). Like v. 4, v. 5 exists to say something positive about believers. AE in referring to their election and foreordination, and in common with most Jewish references to them, does not enter into the philosophical and religious issue of the relation of the human will to the divine plan; Stoicism was already alert to this problem but it was some time before it attracted the detailed attention of Christians (cf Schnackenburg, 312ff). AE is clearly not aware of it for he counsels believers to pray for others (6.18f) and their prayer could have no effect if everything is already arranged. AE's paraenetic section shows he does not ignore the place of the human will; probably those to whom he wrote were not worried by the problem in the way the later church became. Again AE does not discuss election as implying an intervention of God into the historical process; his readers in common with almost all in the ancient world would not have been worried by such a question.

Believers have been adopted by God and have not made them-selves his children;[31] God has foreordained them to this. It was a common theme of primitive Christianity that God was the Father of believers and they his children. From this the concept of adoption developed and apparently was first employed by Paul (Rom 8.15; 9.4; Gal 4.5; in Rom 8.23 the text is uncertain). Adoption is a legal rather than a religious term and Paul probably derived it from Roman rather than Jewish or Near Eastern law; in the latter it was

---

[31] Epictetus, i.3.2, says it is a great honour to be a son of God but for him all are God's sons (cf Acts 17.28), and not merely the limited group of believers.

much less clearly developed.[32] AE took it over as an idea which his readers knew and, whatever its origin, which they would probably have understood in the light of Roman law. It may have been a pre-Pauline idea for Gal 3.26 treats it as if it was known. In Rom 9.4 Paul applies it to Israel but not all Israelites were sons (Rom 9.6). In Roman law 'the adoptee was taken out of his previous state and was placed in a new relationship of son to his new father, his new paterfamilias. All his old debts were cancelled, and in effect the adoptee started a new life as part of his new family' (Lyall, op. cit., 83). He was now under the control of his new father and responsible to him alone. But he could, and usually did, also become his new father's heir (1.11). It is, of course, a male-oriented term for which there were alternatives (e.g. παῖδα ποιεῖσθαι) which did not have this orientation. However, AE would not be responsible for this orientation if the term had been chosen previously by Paul.

Since AE uses adoption metaphorically we must be careful not to press the idea too far. It is not set in opposition to 'children of wrath' (2.3) and we cannot deduce from it anything about the 'previous' family of believers ('Satan's slave-camp', Simpson) nor that Paul has only male believers in mind because normally only males were adopted among the Romans. There are also clear differences between human and divine adoption. The father who adopted a son did so out of his own need, wishing either to continue his family or to provide himself with an heir; he is concerned with his own interests. God however does not adopt in that way for he already has a son and heir; he adopts because he loves those he adopts. The contemporary human father usually adopted someone from a social status similar to his own; God adopts believers to lift them up into a new status, similar to that of his own son. The adoption indeed takes place through (διά) that son (in Rom 8.15 through the Spirit) and the adoptee is chosen so that he may become like that son and bear his image (Rom 8.29; 1 Cor 15.49; 2 Cor 3.18). This is another point where the metaphor breaks down for no one mediated the adoption in Roman law. Since adoption takes place through Christ this implies that the sonship of believers is different from his, though AE

---

[32] See W. H. Rossell, 'New Testament Adoption—Graeco-Roman or Semitic?', *JBL* 71 (1952) 233–4; M. W. Schoenberg, 'St Paul's notion of the adoptive sonship of Christians', *Thomist* 28 (1964) 51–75; S. Drago, 'La nostra adozione a figli di Dio in Ef. 1,5', *RivB* 19 (1971) 203–19; J. I. Cook, 'The Concept of Adoption in the Theology of Paul', *Saved by Hope* (FS Richard C. Oudersluys; ed. J. I. Cook) Grand Rapids, 1978, 133–44; F. Lyall, *Slaves, Citizens, Sons: Legal Metaphors in the Epistles*, Grand Rapids, 1984, 67–99; B. Byrne, *Sons of God—Seed of Abraham* (AnBib 83), Rome, 1979; J. M. Scott, *Adoption as Sons of God* (WUNT 2.Reihe 48), Tübingen, 1992; T. J. Burke, 'The Characteristics of Paul's Adoptive Sonship (HUIOTHESIA) Motif', *IrishBS* 17 (1995) 62–74.

would not have disagreed with Paul in describing Christ as firstborn among his brothers (Rom 8.29).

It is not easy to decide whether in the final clause εἰς αὐτόν refers to God or Christ. Both interpretations make good sense. In favour of the latter is: (i) the frequency in the eulogy with which the pronoun refers to Christ; (ii) in 4.13–16 the same phrase envisages a movement towards Christ (those who behave like sons become like Christ); (iii) adoption contains within itself the reference to God (yet if αὐτόν refers to Christ it goes too far to identify believers with Christ's members as does Pelagius). On the other hand: (i) an explicit reference to God would round off the metaphor (we are adopted into God's family), (ii) would parallel the 'before him' of v. 4, (iii) would lead more easily to v. 5b where the pronoun does refer to God; also (iv) God is the subject of the clause and the meaning of the reference to Christ is unclear. If then we accept the reference to God it suggests the sense of goal; the final purpose of election is to bring believers to God who has taken the initiative in Christ to draw them to himself.

Two adverbial phrases (v. 5b, v. 6a) round off the first section of the eulogy; these are almost independent subordinate clauses and qualify what has preceded. Such phrases are frequent throughout Ephesians, not only in the eulogy; they are also found in the genuine Paulines in liturgical and confessional passages (Schlier indicates Rom 1.2ff; 3.25f; 15.13; 2 Cor 1.11; 7.12; 9.14; 1 Th 3.13) yet by no means as regularly as in Ephesians.

Verse '5b is solemn and Hebraic in tone;[33] similar phrases are found in CD 3.15; 1QH 4.32f; 5.4; 11.9 and the genitival linkage of synonyms is a characteristic of AE (Percy, 186). The phrase emphasises both God's freedom in foreordination and that he is the source of foreordination. εὐδοκία is rarely found outside the LXX, the NT and literature influenced by them (Spicq, III, 307–15; Schrenk, *TWNT*, II, 740–8; Romaniuk, 153–83); Origen says the word was coined by the LXX translators. In addition to it our passage contains a number of other words denoting God's will. In the LXX εὐδοκία renders a range of Hebrew words and has two basic meanings: favour (this is the more frequent in the NT) and purpose. The reference to love suggests the former here and would reinforce the graciousness of God's will; it also appears to be the most satisfactory meaning in v. 9; so, despite the association of βουλή with θέλημα in an apparently parallel phrase in v. 11 and AE's love of successive genitives with similar meaning, the sense 'favour' should probably be accepted here. Whichever the meaning,

---

[33] On the Jewish background of this and similar phrases in vv. 12, 14 see Fr. Dreyfus, 'Pour la louange de sa gloire (Ep 1, 12.14). L'origine vétéro-testamentaire de la formule', *Paul de Tarse. Apôtre du notre temps* (ed. L. De Lorenzo), Rome, 1979, 233–48.

the totality of God's will is to be seen in this passage, moving from a pre-temporal determination to a post-temporal consummation (1.10). Behind all that happens is a personal God, not just arbitrary fate.

6. V. 6a like v. 5b qualifies προορίσας: God foreordains so that the glory (for δόξα see 1.17) of his grace should be praised.

Strings of genitives are frequent in Ephesians (Percy, 26f, 90); on the anarthrous δόξης see Moule, 115; MHT, 179f. Are the genitives to be taken separately here or is one to be understood adjectivally (NRSV 'his glorious grace', Bruce 'the glorious praise')? In the latter case since 'grace' is qualified by 'his' it is probably the main term. The taking of one of the words adjectivally is sometimes justified on the grounds that we have a basically Hebrew liturgical phrase and since Hebrew lacks adjectives it employs instead the construct state (the use of the genitive as an adjective is not in fact unGreek). Even if AE intended it in this way could his Greek readers have been expected mentally to translate nouns into adjectives? If then we translate with an adjective we may lose the effect of the words on their original readers and lessen their 'weight'; Alford comments 'beware of the miserable hendiadys *"his glorious grace"*, by which all the richness and depth of meaning are lost'. If however one substantive is to be rendered as an adjective there is much to be said for choosing the second (cf BDR §168.2, n. 2), since in vv. 12, 14 the first two appear without the third.

God's foreordination began in his love; it results in the praise of his grace (AE stresses God's grace, 1.7; 2.5, 8). The initiating love is now depicted as undeserved; this naturally follows from foreordination; the idea of an undeserved gift moreover is basic to 'grace' in 1.7; 2.5, 8 (though not in 3.2, 7, 8; 4.7). God's foreordination has not been forced on him by anything in those whom he elects. Realising this they will praise him. Blessed by him, they bless him (v. 3). God has acted so that he may be praised. AE wishes to show here the proper response to God's foreordaining love and is as little concerned to deal with the moral question of reconciling God's love with its purpose in leading to his praise as he was in squaring foreordination with human freewill. The praise which is the desired outcome of God's goodness is stressed again in vv. 12, 14, though there without the mention of grace. At first sight the praise may appear only to be offered by 'us', i.e. the believing community, but 3.10 may suggest it is also offered by the 'powers'. That all creation worships God has been a constant theme of Christian hymnody and earlier of the Psalms.

The repetition of v. 6a in vv. 12, 14 would suggest that we have now completed a stage in the argument; we are however immediately driven on by the relative clause; v. 6b is a transition clause following a kind of chorus line at the end of a stanza; it continues the theme of God's all-embracing grace but also prepares us for its manifestation in history (vv. 7ff). In the relative clause of v. 6b two key terms reappear in different guises: χάρις as ἐχαρίτωσεν and ἀγάπη as ἠγαπημένῳ. How we understand the first of these is related to the form of the relative pronoun which is read.

If we choose the inferior reading ἐν ᾗ of ℵ² D (f) G Ψ 𝔐 we are predisposed to see ἐχαρίτωσεν as indicating a change in believers who are made gracious by God's grace. Unlike most of the Fathers, Chrysostom reads ἧς but when he comes to comment he writes as if he had the other reading, says God made us ἐπεράστους and goes on with an imaginative illustration in which a hideous leper is changed into a lovely youth. The ancient commentators follow Chrysostom in this understanding of the word, an understanding and reading which prevailed until after the Reformation (e.g. Thomas Aquinas, Calvin, AV) but which since then has gradually been superseded, at first by Protestants and then by Catholics, by the sense of the bestowal of grace; this interpretation was a result of the adoption of the superior reading ἧς 𝔓⁴⁶ ℵ* A B P 6 33 etc.); the genitive is an attraction from the accusative.

We take ἐχαρίτωσεν then with the same sense as χάρις and as indicating God's graciousness towards those whom he has fore-ordained, noting that the union of two forms of the same root is not uncommon in Ephesians (cf 1.3; 2.4 and Percy, 32f). It is difficult to find a precise one-word English equivalent to the verb which conveys the same sense as the noun. The double use of the root reinforces the idea of the free abundance of God's grace. It is grace which controls his ordaining power and it is this grace which is displayed to us 'in the loved one'.[34]

The perfect participle ἠγαπημένος is applied in the LXX to Israel (Deut 32.15; 33.5, 26; Isa 44.2) and to particular Israelites (e.g. Abraham, 2 Chr 20.7), none of whom are obvious messianic types; in the NT it is applied to the church (Col 3.12; 1 Th 1.4; cf Ign *Eph* preface, *Rom* preface). In each case it is God who loves; this is also true of v. 6 (*pace* Origen, Pelagius, Ewald). The verbal adjective ἀγαπητός is used of Christ in Mk 1.11 (*par*); 9.7 (*par*); 12.6 (*par*); 2 Pet 1.17, again indicating God's love. When however it is used of believers, it normally implies that they are loved by other believers (Acts 15.25; Rom 12.19; 16.5, 8, 9, 12, etc.) though occasionally it refers to God's love (Rom 1.7; 11.28). AE's phrase here is a more Greek expression than that in Col 1.13 where we have 'son of his love'.

Through its use in the baptismal and transfiguration narratives the verbal adjective[35] ἀγαπητός became a technical title for the Lord which continued to be used in early Christian literature, e.g. 1 Clem 59.2f; Ign *Smyrn* preface (for details see Schlier, 57, n. 1). Its particular significance in the Gospel stories is debated, being seen as derived from either Isa 42.1 and so connected to the Isaianic servant

[34] The *v.l.* υἱῷ αὐτοῦ of D* F G 629 it vg^cl sy^h** sa; Ambst is an explanatory addition probably occasioned by the accounts of Jesus' baptism which drew together his sonship and his being the beloved of God (Mk 1.11).
[35] See E. P. Groenewald, 'Jesus – Jeshurun', *NedGTT* 2 (1961) 197–204.

or Gen 22.2 and linked to Isaac as type of Christ in his sacrifice.[36] The titular use of the verbal adjective has in Eph 1.6 apparently passed over to the perfect participle but that gives no reason for supposing that it carried over with it the reference to baptism; had AE had baptism in mind he would surely have used the verbal adjective, though as later usage (2 Pet 1.17) shows, even it did not always carry this reference. Since many other titles for Christ were available why did AE select such an unusual one at this point? 'In his son' would have seemed appropriate after the reference to adoption. Sonship and deliverance may have been associated in the Pauline school of which AE and A/Col were members for the concepts appear together also in Col 1.13f. AE's choice of the term may also have been influenced by the ἐν ἀγάπῃ of v. 4; that and the cognate participle form an *inclusio* indicating a unit of thought. In v. 7 we move on to a fresh unit. Penna suggests that AE's preference for the perfect participle over the verbal adjective may come from the greater intimacy of the latter, instancing Deut 32.15; 33.5, 26; Isa 44.2.

7. From the pre-temporal election of believers AE moves to its historical realisation through the redemption which God has effected for them 'in Christ'. This might indicate Christ as the means of redemption, but since this is expressed through the reference to blood it more probably implies inclusion in him: believers have their redemption in living fellowship with Christ. There is a temporary change here in the verb to the first plural; elsewhere God is the subject of the verbs in vv. 3–10. The verb moreover is in the present tense[37] contrasting with the prevailing aorists. The present tense implies redemption and forgiveness are present possessions and this is in keeping with AE's stress on the present nature of salvation (see Introduction §6.4.4).

Verse 7a is similar to Col 1.14 but with two differences: the addition of the reference to blood, which Mitton, *Epistle*, 281, suggests AE may have drawn from Col 1.20, and the substitution of παραπτωμάτων for ἁμαρτιῶν. There are common references to redemption and forgiveness and also to Christ, though the latter is expressed in slightly different terms ('son of his love' in Col 1.13b, 'in the beloved' in Eph v.6). The connection of 'blood' with salvation was made early in Christian tradition (Mt 26.28; Rom 3.25; 5.9; 1 Cor 10.16; 11.25, 27); AE makes it also at 2.13; there is no need then to see here the influence of Col 1.20, which in any case is part of a traditional hymn AE may have known independently of Colossians. The essential common element with Col 1.14 is ἐν ᾧ ἔχομεν τὴν ἀπολύτρωσιν, τὴν ἄφεσιν. ἀπολύτρωσις and ἄφεσις were common words in early Christianity; ἐν ᾧ was a necessary link in both Ephesians and Colossians

[36] Cf G. Vermes, *Scripture and Tradition in Judaism*, Leiden, 1961, 194ff.
[37] The ἔσχομεν of ℵ* D* Ψ 104 1505 *pc* co; Ir^lat^ is the weaker reading; it sets redemption and the forgiveness of sin in the past, presumably at conversion/baptism.

because the context was christological; since AE uses ἁμαρτία elsewhere (2.1) it is difficult to see why he should have made the change here to παραπτωμάτων. The death of Christ was related to sin from a very early period in the church, being found in pre-Pauline material (e.g. 1 Cor 15.3; Rom 3.24f; in the latter both 'blood' and 'redemption' are found). It is easier then to see AE constructing his phrase out of common words with which both he and A/Col were acquainted than as copying it from Colossians.

ἀπολύτρωσις is used in two ways:[38] (a) of release, e.g. of a prisoner, where a price is paid, (b) of deliverance in a general way. Though infrequent in non-biblical Greek it normally has meaning (a) which it obtains from the basic root. When we turn to biblical Greek the picture changes. Due to the influence of context and the underlying Hebrew, λυτροῦν and its cognates regularly have meaning (b), though there are possible exceptions, e.g. Mk 10.45; 1 Pet 1.18. The compound with ἀπό, including cognates, appears only three times in the OT, twice (Zeph 3.1; Dan 4.34 LXX) with meaning (b) and once (Exod 21.8) with meaning (a). Given this usage NT writers were free to pick either meaning. Apart from Ephesians and Colossians they appear to have chosen (b), though Rom 3.24 may be an exception. General usage, when it is infrequent, cannot however by itself determine the meaning in particular instances. Each case must be individually examined. There is nothing in Col 1.14 or the two other Ephesian references (1.14; 4.20) to indicate the payment of a price. Yet may this not be indicated by 'blood' in 1.7 (so many commentators from Origen onwards)? When AE referred to blood (it is not in Col 1.14) was he not intending to suggest Christ's death as the price paid for the redemption of believers? If so, it would have been normal to use a genitive of price and omit διά. His failure to do so justifies our rejection of this interpretation and acceptance of meaning (b). This is not of course to say that the idea of a price does not appear elsewhere in the NT (e.g. 1 Pet 1.18).

If AE used ἀπολύτρωσις here without envisaging the payment of a price that does not mean that his readers would have understood it in that way. If they normally thought of the word in relation to a price to be paid and if they have only been Christians for a short period and have not picked up the special Jewish understanding of the term, they may have thought of 'blood' as the price to be paid for their redemption. Those who had been Christians for a longer period and had come to know more of the OT would gradually have moved from this interpretation to that which sees it as a term signifying deliverance without thought of payment.

The second phrase of v. 7, which refers to the forgiveness[39] of sins, is parallel with the first and may serve to explain it as in Col

---

[38] Cf L. Morris, *The Apostolic Preaching of the Cross*, London, 1955, 9ff; D. Hill, *Greek Words and Hebrew Meanings* (SNTSMS 5), Cambridge, 1967, 49ff; K. Kertelge, *EDNT* I, 138–40; G. Friedrich, *Die Verkündigung des Todes Jesu im Neuen Testament*, Neukirchen-Vluyn, 1982, 82–6.

[39] Cf V. Taylor, *Forgiveness and Reconciliation*, London, 1941, 1ff; R. Bultmann, *TWNT*, I, 506ff.

1.14 'the forgiveness of sins' explicates the meaning of 'deliverance'. The Colossian heretics may have had their own conception of deliverance regarding it primarily as from the powers (Abbott, Gnilka, ad Col 1.14) which A/Col disputes with his reference to forgiveness, but there is no reason to suppose that AE in using the same phrase was contending against a similar false view. Before their conversion believers had been dead in trespasses and sins (2.1); now they are delivered. AE's use of 'trespasses' and not 'sins' is not significant (cf Best, 'Dead'); he appears to like the latter word (cf 2.1, 5); for the meaning of both words see on 2.1. The content of 'deliverance' however is not completely defined by 'forgiveness', as can be seen from 1.14; 4.30. Paul rarely uses ἄφεσις but Luke likes it (Acts 2.38; 5.31; 10.43; 13.38; 26.18; Lk 1.77; 17.3f; 24.47) and connects it with repentance and the beginning of the Christian life (cf Mk 1.4). The connection with repentance is not made here and would be inappropriate in a section concentrating on God's initiatory action. Forgiveness may appear to deal only with the past through the removal of guilt but such a removal enables the one who is freed to live a new life set free from the burden of the past. AE may have chosen 'forgiveness' rather than the justification language of Paul as being more easily appreciated by Greek readers.

If 'blood' does not indicate the price paid, what does it signify?[40] As a term it entered Christian usage prior to Paul (Rom 3.25), and though he did not use it regularly (Rom 5.9) apart from his references to the eucharist (there is no need to see such a reference here) it gradually came to be employed more widely (Col 1.20; Eph 1.7; 2.13; 1 Pet 1.2; 1 Jn 1.7; 5.6–8), above all in Hebrews. It always carries some reference to the death of Christ but it is unlikely that it simply indicates that death as bloody and violent. In most cultures it carries overtones of power, defilement, cleansing, etc. (e.g. 1 Kgs 22.38, the taurobolium, the drinking of blood, menstrual blood) and in particular is linked to sacrifice. Meuzelaar, 100, indeed suggests that its introduction here may have been influenced by the earlier ἁγίους καὶ ἀμώμους (v. 4). It was the sacrificial association which led Christians to use it of Christ's death. Its overtones would have helped Gentiles to see it as possessing effective power to deliver and forgive sins. Unlike the death of Christ the deaths of the two who were crucified with him were bloody and violent but were not sacrificial. The thought of 1.7 is thus not far different from that of Rom 3.24f, though expressed in much less 'Jewish' terms. The deliverance AE has in mind is possessed now (in 4.30 it has a future aspect) and this is not out of accord with the general realised

[40] Cf H. W. Robinson, *ERE* II, 714–19; W. D. Davies, *Paul and Rabbinic Judaism*, London, 1948, 232ff; J. Behm, *TWNT*, I, 171–5; J. H. Waszink, *RAC* II, 459–73; H. Weissemann and O. Böcher, *TRE*, 6, 727–36; O. Böcher, *EDNT* I, 37–9; F. Laubach, *NIDNTT*, I, 220–4.

eschatological position of the letter (Introduction §6.4). AE makes
no attempt to explain how Jesus' death and sin are related; he simply
accepts this as true; it had been a part of Christian thinking from the
beginning (1 Cor 15.3).

The foreordination of believers was to the praise of the glory of
God's grace; it is God's grace and not 'Christ's', for in v. 6 the
grace was certainly God's and v. 8 continues with God as subject.
God's grace is also the cause of the deliverance of believers. Of that
grace[41] there are inexhaustible and boundless 'riches'. 'Riches'[42] is
one of AE's favourite terms (1.18; 2.7; 3.8, 16; on the gender of
πλοῦτος see §BDR 51.2; Robertson, 261f). It may have been in use
in the Pauline school for A/Col also uses it (1.27; 2.2); it is not
frequent in Paul (only six times). The Qumran writings emphasise
the wealth of God's mercy and grace (1QS 4.3–5; 1QH 4.32; 7.27;
11.28; 12.14; 18.14; frag 2.5; cf Deichgräber, 74). Not only does
God deliver through his grace but those delivered are able to praise
him for that grace and for the depths of his compassion; their
deliverance is not the result of their own activity but of God's; all
Christian existence begins and ends in grace.

8. God being rich in grace has bestowed it (ἧς, a genitive by
attraction is the object of the verb) in abundance on all believers;
περισσεύειν though only here in Ephesians is a Pauline favourite; in
v. 8 as in 2 Cor 9.8 and 1 Th 3.12 it is used transitively. Paul affirms
the abundance of grace in Rom 5.20.

1.8b–10 is a difficult section of the eulogy to construe. To what is
v. 8b to be attached? Is the reference to divine (Origen, Theod
Mops, Eadie, Alford, Gnilka) or human wisdom (Ambrosiaster,
Pelagius and the majority of modern commentators)? Those choos-
ing the latter interpretation connect v. 8b to v. 8a; Chrysostom,
Cambier, 83f, Percy, 309 n. 66, exceptionally connect it to v. 9.

φρόνησις is regularly distinguished from σοφία as relating to the
more practical aspects of wisdom rather than the theoretical (e.g.
Aristotle, *Nic Eth*, 1141a; Philo, *Praem Poen* 81) and it is argued
that it would therefore be inappropriate to apply the word to God. It
is however so applied in Jer 10.12; Prov 3.19 where the two nouns
are used together of his creative activity. What God finally does in
summing up all things (v. 10) cannot be unlike his activity in
creation. The words are found together also in Prov 1.2; 8.1; 10.23;
3 Kgdms 5.9; Dan 1.4 (Theod); 2.23 (LXX); Josephus *Ant* 8.171.
AE is fond of setting together words of almost similar meaning (1.4;
2.1, 4, 19; 3.17; 4.14, 16, 17, 24; 5.2, 27; 6.5, 18; cf Percy, 20) and
he may not have distinguished them in his mind. Can however the

---

[41] The *v.l.* χρηστοτητός is poorly attested (A 365 *pc* bo) and is probably due to the
influence of Rom 2.4.

[42] Cf H.-M. Dion, 'La notion paulinienne de "Richesse de Dieu" et ses sources',
ScEc 18 (1966) 139–48.

epithet 'all' be properly applied to God's wisdom? In particular, anarthrous πᾶς would normally mean 'every, all kinds of' and this again may make its use in relation to God even more unlikely. But the rule in relation to the article is not strict (cf Mt 3.19; cf MHT, 199f, and see on 1.3). Moreover 'all' is regularly applied to God ('almighty, omniscient'; cf 1 Clem 35.3, 'all holy'; 55.6, 'all seeing'). Strict logic may not be the best guide here. If 8b is attached to 8a it is difficult to follow the flow of thought. What abounds in grace? It must mean that grace abounds in the form of wisdom and prudence; but this reads more into the words than is actually present and suddenly changes the activity of grace from deliverance to the impartation of wisdom. ἧς is the object of the verb and nothing more is needed to complete it (Gnilka). Finally words dealing with wisdom go fittingly with a word indicating the making known of a mystery (v. 9). 'The revealer of (a mystery) wisely selects his audience, and prudently chooses the proper time, place, and method for his disclosures' (Eadie). If this is so it seems wiser to associate the reference to wisdom with v. 9 and regard it as God's wisdom. Whatever God does he does with wisdom and insight. Although there was much speculation on wisdom in Judaism and it was at times regarded as a pre-existent hypostasis, this is absent here (see further on 1.17 and 3.10).

9. Mitton suggests that in vv. 8b, 9a AE has conflated Col 3.16; 1.9, 28, all of which have ἐν πάσῃ σοφίᾳ with the reference to making wisdom known in Col 1.27. ἐν πάσῃ σοφίᾳ is however a frequent phrase in the LXX (Job 26.3; Ψ 106.27; Ecclus 1.1; 37.21; Dan 1.4, 17) and appears in the NT at Acts 7.22. AE could have picked it up independently. It is true that in Col 1.27 we find similar words to Eph 1.9a but in Col 1.27 they do not occur together as in Eph 1.9a. AE repeats his phrase in 3.3, 5 indicating that for him it is a natural and not a borrowed phrase.

γνωρίζω[43] is regularly used in connection with revelation (Rom 16.26; Eph 3.3, 5, 10; Col 1.27) and associated with the disclosure of mysteries. While it may be gracious of God to disclose his mysteries, the participle here does not depend on ἐχαρίτωσεν or ἐπερίσσευσεν and indicate a second element in God's grace, but represents a new step in the eulogy. Believers, foreordained and already possessing their deliverance, are now told about the secret of the ultimate destiny of the cosmos. This knowledge is made known to all believers and is not restricted to Paul or the apostles (so Thomas!) whatever may be true of the revelations of 3.3, 5. Even in 3.3, 5 it is implied that the apostles and prophets did not keep to themselves the understanding of the mystery they had received but made it known to all believers.

[43] The reading γνωρίσαι is weakly attested, F G (latt), and can be ignored.

The use in the NT of the term 'mystery' has been traced[44] to the Mystery Religions or, more generally, to gnosticism; yet even if it first came into use in those areas it had been widely extended long before our period as a metaphor into other areas, e.g. philosophy. However, the parallels in non-biblical thought to its NT use are by no means as precise as those provided by the OT and Judaism. μυστήριον appears in the Greek translations of Daniel as a rendering of Aramaic rz referring to secrets once hidden and then disclosed. The Qumran documents provide further evidence supporting the view that the term entered Christianity directly from its Jewish background. Caragounis exceptionally maintains a Jewish background yet finds little in Qumran to support the way AE uses it. However, we do not need to evaluate the rival claims of Qumran and apocalytic Judaism as the source of the term since AE's use depends on earlier Christian use in Paul and simultaneous use in Colossians. In addition there is the existence in Judaism and Christianity, but also in many religions, of the idea of a God whose ways are past finding out. If he is to be known and his world fully understood, then he must disclose himself; so the term is often associated with verbs denoting revelation (1.9; 3.3–5, 9f; 6.19; 1 Cor 2.6–10; Rom 16.25–7; Col 1.26f; 4.3f). Believers have not solved the 'mystery' on their own nor have they worked out its content through rational reflection. Inaccessible to human reason the 'secret' is made known through divine action, of which it is occasionally said the Spirit is the agent (1 Cor 2.6–10). There is normally also a human agent (e.g. Daniel, Enoch, Paul, prophets, apostles). The 'mystery' has lain long hidden in God prior to its revelation (1 Cor 2.7; Eph 3.9; Rom 16.25).

What is made known in the mystery may be the understanding of a dream or vision (e.g. Daniel 2.19), a description of how and when the end will come (Dan 2.27–9; 2 Bar 85.8ff; 1QpHab 7.1–5), an unveiling of the divine structure of the cosmos (1 En 71.4; 2 Bar 48.2f), an explanation of God's activity in human affairs (1 En 63.3; 1 QM 14.14; 1QH 9.23f), or, outside Judaism in the Mystery Religions, knowledge of ceremonies and ritual that lead to salvation (cf also 1QS 9.18f). The word can also of course be used in a non-

---

[44] See G. Bornkamm, *TWNT*, IV, 809–34; A. Böhlig, 'Mysterion und Wahrheit', *Wissenschaftliche Zeitschrift der Universität Halle*, 4 (1955) 361–74; K. Prumm, 'Zur Phänomenologie des paulinischen Mysterion und dessen seelischer Aufnahme. Eine Übersicht', *Bib* 37 (1956) 135–61; K. G. Kuhn, 336; R. Rigaux, 'Révélation des Mystères et Perfection à Qumrân et dans le N.T.', *NTS* 4 (1957/8) 237–62; J. Coppens, 'Le "mystère" dans la théologie paulinienne et ses parallèles qumraniens', *Littérature et théologie pauliniennes* (ed. A. Descamps), Bruges, 1960, 142–65; L. Cerfaux, *Le Chrétien dans la théologie Paulinienne* (LD 33), Paris, 1961, 433–91; id. 'L'influence des "mystères" sur les épîtres de S. Paul aux Colossiens et aux Éphésiens', *Recueil Cerfaux*, III (BETL 18), Gembloux, 1962, 279–85; R. E. Brown, *The Semitic Background of the Term Mystery in the New Testament*, Philadelphia, 1968; Barth, 123–7; Caragounis, *passim*; R. Penna, *Il "Mysterion" Paolino* (Brescia, 1978); A. E. Harvey, 'The use of Mystery Language in the Bible', *JTS* 31 (1980) 320–36; Bouttier, 288–93; K. J. Carl, 'Mysterion in the New Testament', *Bangolore Theological Forum* 16 (1984) 119–39; Reynier, *passim*; M. N. A. Bockmuehl, *Revelation and Mystery* (WUNT 2.Reihe 56), Tübingen, 1990.

religious way (Tob 12.7, 11; Jth 2.2). It is impossible to say much about the Mystery Religions since their beliefs and practices were effectively kept secret, but on the whole within Judaism and early Christianity the content of the revelation did not centre on God's nature (e.g. that he was loving or jealous) or ontological christology ('Jesus is God') or statements of the nature of the gospel (the content of 1 Cor 15.3–5 is not termed a mystery); in any case from the time of their conversion Christians had some appreciation of what the gospel was; it was open to them and not hidden. Instead what were revealed were particular truths relating to the way God acts or has acted, e.g. in comprehending all things, in accepting Gentiles—Locke says the acceptance of Gentiles was called a mystery against Jews who might argue that their religion contained nothing about their admission. Whatever the meaning of mystery in the church, it was a word with which readers were acquainted and therefore a bridge to what AE wished to say. The mystery may be the gospel (6.19) or Christ (Col 2.2) but without any indication how they were such. Sometimes the content of the mystery is not made clear (Mk 4.11). Although the word is frequently used in the singular this does not imply that there is only one mystery; yet it is likely that a particular writer when using the term would have only one mystery in mind, revealing its different aspects through his various references. Lindemann, *Aufhebung*, 93f, errs when he says the mystery has no historical context for when it is used again in 3.3ff it stands in the historical context of Paul, the apostles and the prophets.

When mysteries are made known they are made known not to humanity as a whole but to privileged sections within it; in the Mystery Religions, the initiates; in Judaism and Christianity, the people of God. The promise is not that at some future time, e.g. after death, a disclosure will be made to believers but that they are put in possession of the secret now, although they may not fully understand it now (cf Col 1.26–8; 1 Cor 2.6–10). The mystery may also be disclosed beyond humanity to the 'powers' (3.10) and (potentially) to all people (Rom 16.25–7) though they may only come to understand it when they become Christians.

Mystery in the NT often relates in some way or other to membership in the people of God (Rom 11.25; 16.25–7; Col 1.26f; 1 Tim 3.16; Eph 3.3, 4, 9), and this may colour other passages where the content is not made clear (Col 2.2; 4.3). This is not surprising for Paul asserts (Gal 1.11f) that it was as a result of divine revelation that he evangelised the Gentiles. Indeed, generally speaking, the early church believed its mission to the Gentiles was not the result of reflection on the OT (Rom 16.25f may be an exception) or on the inner significance of the life of Jesus, but came through a direct command or revelation of God (e.g. Mt 28.16–20; Lk 24.47–9; Acts

1.8; 9.15; 10.1ff; cf Best 'Revelation') and was thus a disclosure of something previously hidden. The explicit linking of 'mystery' to the Gentile mission as in 3.3ff (see notes there) is mainly post-Pauline. Paul uses the word with other connections (1 Cor 2.7; 4.1; 13.2; 14.2; 15.51; 2 Th 2.7). It was the fact that he used the word when joined to his belief that he occupied a special place in God's plan for the admission of Gentiles that led his disciples to employ it to connect him with that admission. Mystery is also linked with Christ, more in Colossians (1.27; 2.2; 4.3) than in Ephesians (3.4); the two ideas however fit easily together since it is the new fact of Christ which permits Gentiles to be members of the church.

As the 'all' of v. 10 shows, the 'mystery' of v. 9 relates to something more ·comprehensive than the salvation of individual believers or the acceptance of Gentiles, though their acceptance was itself a first step towards an even greater comprehensiveness. The use of the word 'mystery' in v. 9 may also have been influenced by its eschatological associations in Judaism for v. 10 has an eschatological flavour. But why has AE used the word at all? The thought would run just as easily without it, 'God had made known to us his will ... ' (the same is true in 6.19 where all that would be strictly required would be '... to make known the gospel'). Its employment reinforces the idea of revelation—what God had intended for the eventual fate of the universe lay hidden and unknown, a mystery, until revealed to Paul or other followers of Christ. The redemption which it involves was not then some afterthought but part of God's plan from the beginning (Bouttier). So in 6.19 it emphasises that what Paul proclaims is not something he has himself devised but a revelation of God to him.

It is common to speak with Robinson, 240, of a mystery as 'a secret which God wills to make known and has charged his Apostles to declare to those who have ears to hear it'. This needs to be given more precision. When initiates joined a Mystery Religion they came to know certain secrets which were never made public. Because the NT has been widely published it appears as if the mysteries of which it speaks were intended to be open to all who could read or listen; there is nothing hidden about them. The message of the original preachers of the gospel was not 'We have mysteries to reveal' but 'there is salvation in Christ'. Once those who responded to this message had been baptised, they learned, perhaps only after a lengthy period, that God had revealed new aspects of salvation (e.g. the admission of Gentiles to the church). They were still however only a tiny group in possession of precious knowledge otherwise not widely known; as an elite they may have thought themselves important. The mystery was not deliberately kept secret but it was not made widely known. In contrast from initiates into the Mystery Religions, no oaths bound Christians to keep secret what they knew, though Paul is not permitted to reveal what he learnt in his rapture (2 Cor 12.1ff). If their friends in other religions boasted of their secret knowledge the Christians could boast of theirs, yet unlike their friends they could reveal what they knew; but since there were few believers there was no widespread proclamation of the secrets.

Martin suggests that a group of gnostically inclined believers within the churches thought they themselves were the only ones who had penetrated the secret of the universe and were not prepared to let others into their 'secret', and so in contrast AE argues that God's secrets have already been made accessible to all in the church. If Martin is correct it is difficult to see why AE did not counter this erroneous view directly by saying that none of God's secrets remained hidden or were the possession only of some believers.

What AE affirms has been made known is the mystery of God's will in relation to the summing up of the All in Christ (v. 10b). Before reaching that climax, however, an intervening clause (vv. 9b, 10a) has to be fitted into the argument. This could be taken as two clauses (v. 9b and v. 10a) but is better viewed as one and regarded as a parenthetical qualification of γνωρίσας (all the possibilities are discussed in detail by Haupt). If taken as two clauses, v. 9b would go with v. 9a, but with what would v. 10a be connected? Since it does not reveal the content of what God makes known it cannot depend on v. 9a. If it goes with v. 10b it is difficult to find a meaning for εἰς; it would probably have to indicate purpose—the final end of the summing up of the All would be the administration of the fullness of the times. This would make 10a the climax. Yet v. 10b is more obviously the climax. Vv. 9b and 10a are therefore to be treated as a unit. While this unit could be taken with v. 10b (so Haupt) it would be clumsy. It goes better with v. 9a (so Schlier, Gnilka, Schnackenburg) just as in v. 5 the κατά clause qualifies προορίσας.[45] It functions like a refrain, though not appearing at the end of a stanza. The seeming equivalence of θέλημα and εὐδοκία[46] is not out of keeping with AE's style and is avoided if we take the latter as meaning 'goodwill, pleasure' (see on v. 5). God has acted not with dictatorial freedom (so Masson, Hugedé) but with a freedom conditioned by goodwill.

God's goodwill is further defined through the relative clause ἣν κτλ. The verb here would normally mean 'to plan, purpose', and in view of AE's love of the heaping up of synonyms there is no need to

---

[45] For the word see Dion, art.cit., 19–23. ἐν αὐτῷ probably refers to Christ though some take it of God (ἑαυτῷ is read by P). God's will is linked to Christ and is not independent of him; apart from Christ God's will would not be known.

[46] Some texts, D F G b vf^mss; MVict omit αὐτοῦ probably regarding it as pleonastic in view of the following ἐν αὐτῷ (so Bruce).

render it with the NRSV as 'set forth'. Because of the number of times in the eulogy πρό prefixes words some commentators (Schlier, Gnilka, Barth) give προέθετο a pre-temporal meaning— God's goodwill which he purposed before time began. There is little evidence that the word ever had this nuance and the fact that a word can be split into its constituent parts does not mean it ought to be. It would seem to require a special effort on the part of the reader to take the verb in this way and if AE has intended a pre-temporal meaning there were other ways to achieve this. Yet when we think of hearers or of people reading the letter aloud (documents were never read silently in the ancient world) the πρό would have been continually echoing in their ears from the beginning of the eulogy with pre-temporal sense and they could easily have drawn this sense from it within the present context. Even if this suggestion is rejected there is, however, no idea that God makes known the mystery of his will as an afterthought following on human sin.

10. As we have seen v. 10a goes with v. 9b.

οἰκονομία[47] can have an active or a passive sense. The term originated in relation to the administration of households: the administrator was the οἰκονόμος and his activity οἰκονομία (cf Lk 16.1–8). The root was gradually widened to take in the administration of cities and states. Paul used it of his work of advancing the Gospel, not inappropriately since the church is the household of God (1 Cor 4.1; 9.17), and it was employed to cover God's government of the universe.[48] In this light there is no need to suppose that pagan religion was the source of Christian usage.[49] The noun, though at first used actively, came to take on a passive sense indicating an arrangement or plan, naturally of course that to which the οἰκονόμος worked. The active and passive senses are difficult to distinguish since administrators normally work to a plan, whether their own or another's. In the Pauline corpus the root is regularly linked with 'mystery' (1.10; 3.2, 9; Col 1.25–7; 1 Cor 4.1). In Col 1.25 the sense of the word is active:[50] God has given Paul a commission to evangelise the Gentiles; the underlying thought here is closer to Eph 3.2 than to 1.10 or 3.9.

In 1.10 the activity or plan, whichever sense is ascribed to

---

[47] On the root see J. Reumann, '"Stewards of God"—Pre-Christian Religious Application of OIKONOMOS in Greek', *JBL* 77 (1958) 339–49; id. 'OIKONOMIA-Terms in Paul in Comparison with Lucan Heilsgeschichte', *NTS* 13 (1966/7) 147–67; id. 'Oikonomia = "Covenant". Terms for Heilsgeschichte in Early Christian Usage', *NT* 3 (1959) 282–92; id. '"Jesus the Steward". An Overlooked Theme in Christology', *SE* V (= TU, 103, Berlin, 1968) 21–9; W. Tooley, 'Stewards of God', *SJT* 19 (1966) 74–86; Spicq, 2.606–13; Mitton, *Epistle*, 91–4; O. Michel, *TWNT*, V, 151–5.
[48] Cf Reumann, *NTS* 13 (1966/7) 147–67.
[49] Cf Reumann, *JBL* 77 (1958) 339–49.
[50] So the commentaries of Lohse, Schweizer, Gnilka, Moule, Bruce; otherwise O'Brien.

οἰκονομία, is not Paul's but God's. If the main emphasis lay on 'plan'[51] we should expect κατά rather than εἰς to introduce the word; that κατά would not sound well after its use in v. 9 is hardly a sufficient objection. Moreover if 'plan' were the sense, the plan would be the summing up of all 'in Christ' but AE has already dealt with this in his use of μυστήριον. We then accept the active sense and take εἰς as telic 'with a view to the carrying through of the fullness of the times'. We may also assume that if God administers he does so in accordance with his own inner plan, a plan which incorporates the choice and redemption of believers (vv. 4–7) as well as the summing up of the All.

τοῦ πληρώματος (for the word see on 1.23; it is not used here with its technical theological sense) τῶν καιρῶν is not the same phrase as that of Gal 4.4 and carries no reference here to the incarnation. 'The times' can be either the events which occur in time (Schlier) or the periods of time which together comprise time (so almost all other commentators). These periods may themselves be either the days, months and years into which time is divided (Haupt) or, more probably, the periods mentioned in the apocalyptic writings (Gnilka, Schnackenburg; cf Tob 14.5; 2 Esdr 4.37; *2 Bar* 14.1; 20.6; 40.3; 81.4; 1QpHab 7.2, 13f). The 'times' in this sense cannot properly be distinguished from the events which must take place before the end. Ephesians, unlike the apocalyptic writings, says nothing about these events. Their fullness denotes a completion (cf Lindemann, *Aufhebung*, 95), or an end-point to time which will be identical with the summing up of all things in Christ. It is in the fullness of the times that time attains its meaning (Asmussen).

Verse 10b picks up and discloses the content of the mystery which has been known (9a); this disclosure forms the peak to which the eulogy has been building up.[52] There is no reason with Barth to suspect that AE employs a quotation here; the stylistic grounds he offers are insufficient; v. 10b fits the current of the argument so well at this point which requires an identification of the mystery that, even if AE is supposed to be quoting, what he quotes cannot be out of accord with what he wants to say.

Whom or what does τὰ πάντα comprise? In 3.9 the term indicates the whole creation (see 3.9 and Detached Note: The Heavenlies) and we should not reject that meaning here (cf 1.22; 4.10; Rom 11.36; 1 Cor 8.6; 15.27; Phil 3.21; Heb 1.3; 2.10; Rev 4.11). Neither should we restrict it to sentient beings, least of all to the 'good'; the things in heaven include not only the angels but also the evil powers and the things on earth include unbelievers.

---

[51] So Cullmann, *Christ and Time*, London, 1951, 33; Michel, 155.
[52] Findlay is exceptional in regarding vv. 9f as parenthetical and thus in not viewing v. 10 as the intellectual summit of the eulogy.

ἀνακεφαλαιοῦσθαι[53] has been understood in a number of different ways depending on the sense given to ἀνά and whether it is regarded as a compound of κεφάλαιον or of κεφαλή. Little evidence exists for its use independently of our verse. What there is suggests it could be used in relation to the totalling up of a sum of numbers and, more importantly, of the bringing of an argument to a conclusion through the summary repetition of its main points or headings (the κεφάλαια). The whole argument is not repeated so the word does not properly carry the sense of a complete repetition or recapitulation, though this may enter if ἀνά is given the sense 'again'; a summary to some extent always entails some repetition. However, prepositions in compounds in Hellenistic Greek do not always carry their full weight but often only indicate an intensification of the thought of the root. The summarising sense is clearly the meaning in Rom 13.9; the sense of repetition comes in *Protevangelium of James*, 13.1; that of recapitulation is a key thought in Irenaeus (see Lawson, Dufort, McHugh). In the Latin Fathers the sense of restoration or renewal predominates. Later thought however only tells us which among a number of possible meanings particular patristic writers decided was the meaning in v. 10 and does little to indicate AE's meaning. Whatever meaning we adopt for it in 1.10 must fit in with AE's general teaching.

The phrases τὰ πάντα and τὰ ἐπὶ τοῖς οὐρανοῖς καὶ ἐπὶ τῆς γῆς have suggested to some that AE depends here on Col 1.16, 20 but the Colossian passages appear in a hymn which may have been independently known to AE and was perhaps a hymn of the Pauline school. In any case both phrases are regular expressions for the cosmos. It is not surprising that they should have been brought together (cf 1 Chron 29.11; Esther 4.17c). The variant in Eph 1.10 of ἐν for ἐπὶ brings Ephesians closer to Colossians; the support for it is relatively strong (A F G K P Ψ 33 81 104 365 1175 1739 1881 2464 *pm* sy[h]; τε ἐν is read by ℵ 323 945 *pc*; Ambst); however it probably appeared as the regular preposition with 'heavens' (e.g. 1.3, 20) or was influenced by the Colossians text.

How does AE understand ἀνακεφαλαιοῦσθαι?[54] The idea of reconciliation must be excluded if by that it is intended to suggest that things on earth are reconciled to things in heaven but not if the reconciliation of the All to God is intended. In that case the thought resembles Col 1.20, but, if this is what AE wished to say, it is hard

---

[53] On the word see J. Lawson, *The Biblical Theology of Saint Irenaeus*, London, 1948, 140–98; Hanson, 123–6; Schlier, *TWNT*, III, 681f; W. Staerck, *RAC* I, 411–14; Roels, 60–76; Du Plessis, 63–9; Usami, 112–24; J.-M. Dufort, 'Le récapitulation paulinienne dans l'exégèse des Pères', *Sciences Ecclesiastiques* 12 (1960) 21–38; J. McHugh, 'A Reconsideration of Ephesians 1.10b in the Light of Irenaeus', *Paul and Paulinism: Essays in honour of C. K. Barrett* (ed. M. D. Hooker and S. G. Wilson), London, 1982, 302–9; Schnackenburg, 315–18; P. J. Hartin, '*ΑΝΑΚΕΦΑΛΑΙΩΣΑΣΘΑΙ ΤΑ ΠΑΝΤΑ ΕΝ ΤΩ ΧΡΙΣΤΩ*', A South African Perspective on the New Testament (ed. J. H. Pitzer and P. J. Hartin), Leiden, 1986, 228–37; W. V. Crockett, 'Universalism and the Theology of Paul' (Ph.D. thesis, University of Glasgow, 1986), 269ff; M. Kitchen, 'The ἀνακεφαλαίωσις of All Things in Christ: Theology and Purpose in the Epistle to the Ephesians' (Ph.D. thesis, University of Manchester, 1988), 69–101.
[54] For a *Wirkungsgeschichte* see Schnackenburg, 315–18.

to see why he chose this unusual word and did not say 'reconcile' as
in Col 1.20.[55] If the word is taken to suggest renewal or restoration[56]
then this presupposes that some original situation was being
recreated or renewed; in turn this implies that an original situation
(of perfection?) must have been destroyed. Such ideas are found in
Paul (Christ as the Second Adam, the new creation in Christ) and
therefore must be regarded as possible for AE, though he does not
elsewhere explicitly refer to them. While the gnostic emphasis on a
fallen material world is not found in Ephesians there is much which
shows a lack of harmony in the existing world: Jews and Gentiles
need to be reconciled to one another; human sin requires forgiveness; the powers are actively hostile towards humanity. Yet there is
little in the contemporary use of the word to suggest it implied
renewal or restoration, both of which involve considerably more
than repetition. If repetition is present it is most likely to be derived
from the rhetorical significance of the word as indicating a final
résumé which repeats the main ideas of an argument.

McHugh, art. cit., offers here a complex and ingenious solution derived
from Irenaeus, in which Christ 'resumes' in himself the history of salvation.
Christ does this through (i) his incarnation where there is a fresh beginning
with the new Adam, (ii) his earthly life which is a new beginning for
humanity, (iii) his resurrection, restoring to humanity its lost immortality,
and (iv) his (future) inauguration of the new world in which he will reign
over heaven and earth. In this God has recapitulated all that he has done in
Christ. There are major difficulties to this, difficulties which do not apply to
Irenaeus. AE has no interest in the incarnation or earthly life of Jesus; when
the new humanity appears in 4.24 it is not specifically tied to Christ; AE's
main interest lies in the resurrection and ascension of Christ. In addition this
scheme has no place for the death of Christ which is the source of human
unity (2.14–18). Finally it appears to make Christ, and not God, the subject
of the infinitive. Bouttier offers an alternative to this in which he sees the
remainder of what follows in the letter as spelling out what Christ sums
up.

If the idea of repetition is present this would come at the end and
this fits the idea of the completion or fulfilment of the times. Christ
as the résumé of the All at the end would naturally also involve a
reconciliation of the All to God with a consequent unity among
whatever comprises the All. Yet the emphasis of
ἀνακεφαλαιοῦσθαι lies more on the idea of 'summing up' than on
reconciliation. But what does summing up in Christ mean? It might
be regarded as implying that Christ is the 'head' of the All, and
undoubtedly this is true. Yet when we recall the sense of résumé we

[55] For Greek ideas on the the unity of the cosmos, see Hanson, 46–57.
[56] M. Turner, 'Mission and Meaning in Terms of "Unity" in Ephesians', *Mission
and Meaning: Essays presented to Peter Cotterell* (ed. A. Billington, A. Lane and M.
Turner), Exeter, 1995, 138–66.

might do better (to play on words) to describe him as 'the heading'. This retains the rhetorical sense of the verb, except that a heading is normally found at the beginning of an argument rather than the end. Hanson, 127f (cf Gibbs, 120), speaks of Christ as the 'representative' of the world; but this is a hazy term. Representatives are normally appointed by those they represent and the cosmos has not appointed Christ to any position; the concept also lacks any idea of a summing up. The concept of 'summing up' for its part, though it includes the idea of the creation of unity (Salmond; Steinmetz, 79), also goes beyond it. In what way would Christ be the 'summing up' of the universe? Perhaps in the way an architect's plan sums up what is built; the shape of what comes into existence is both summarised in the plan and determined by it.

Christ's relation to the cosmos gradually came to concern the early Christians and they saw his importance as lying in areas beyond the simple forgiveness of sin. The cosmic nature of OT thought began to appear in passages like Isa 11.6–9 and Ezek 34.25–7 and became more explicit in the concept of a new heaven and a new earth (Isa 65.17; 66.22). In the light of this Christians began to connect Christ both to creation (Jn 1.3; 1 Cor 8.6; Col 1.15–17; Heb 1.2) and to the end. Rom 8.19–23 does not make the latter connection explicit but it lies in its context; it becomes explicit in 1 Cor 15.20–8; Phil 2.9–11; Col 1.20; Eph 1.10, though in each case in different ways. In v. 10 the sense of 'in Christ' (see Detached Note: In Christ) may be that Christ carries out the summing up but more probably that everything comes together in him; what is divided is unified in him. The significance of the cosmos is made known in him. The cosmic nature of their faith might have been appreciated by Gentiles as echoing the thought of a future Golden Age (Virgil, *Eclogues* iv 11.4–11, 21.9; Ovid, *Metamorph* 1.84ff; Horace, *Epode* 16). As far as early Christianity is concerned it must be allowed that there is also a strain, a more widely found strain, in scripture which sees part of creation as finally remaining outside the love and care of God and Christ, perhaps acknowledging his sovereignty but not willingly offering any allegiance; where this holds, the stress lies on the defeat of evil and not on its summing up in Christ. The existence of both strains must be accepted, yet we need to ask which represents more closely the central drive of the NT. Eph 1.10 seems to do so.

Is it however correct to speak of a future in which the world is summed up in Christ? The verb is an aorist infinitive. This is properly timeless and there is no need to see it (cf Roels, 70) as referring to the past event of Christ's death as if it was carrying on v. 7. As an aorist infinitive it could have a future reference but there is much in Ephesians which envisages what we would term the future as already present. In 1.20–3 Christ already holds the powers in subjection; in 2.6 believers already sit with him in the heavenlies. It is not out of keeping with these passages if then we say that the universe is (cf Lindemann, 96–9), and not will be, summed up in Christ. The consummation of the All is as much an event outside the normal parameters of time as are the choice and foreordination of believers (vv. 4f).

The cosmos is summed up 'in *the* Christ'. What is the significance of the article?[57] AE prefaces Christ with it more frequently than any other writing of the Pauline school. He uses it in the phrase 'in the Christ' in 1.10, 12, 20 and apart from this at 2.5, 13; 3.4, 8, 17, 19; 4.7, 12, 13, 20; 5.2, 5, 14, 23, 24, 25, 29; 6.5. Many of these are normal, being instances of the article used with a genitive because the governing noun has the article. Even with these eliminated there are still significant variations from normal Pauline usage. In the genuine Paulines the article is only used four times with the simple dative, four times with the simple accusative, seven times with the nominative, yet three, two, five times respectively in Ephesians. The phrase 'in Christ Jesus' appears regularly in Paul but AE on occasion drops 'Jesus' and employs the article. There is clearly a problem here. It is normally held that in the early church 'Christ' quickly ceased to be a title and became a name. AE's use of the article suggests that he is aware of the titular nature of 'Christ'. But why should he revive this sense? At no point where he uses it does it appear to add anything to his meaning. 1.10 gains nothing by recalling readers to Christ's messiahship, for there is little in Jewish messianic speculation to connect the Messiah to the consummation of the cosmos, as distinct from his position in respect of Israel's salvation. It may be that AE has simply decided to emphasise the Jewish side of Jesus. In 2.11ff in showing his concern for the relation of Jews and Gentiles he implies the prior superior position of Jews in the work of God. Perhaps Gentile Christians might too easily forget this priority. The subtle reminder that Christ is a title will recall to them the Jewish origin of their faith. Yet when we would expect the use of the article because AE is writing about Jewish beliefs it is missing (2.11), though present in 2.12. 4.15; 5.32 are other places where the article might have been expected since it appears with κεφαλή and ἐκκλησία. AE's use of the article with Christ seems quite haphazard and no significance should be attached to it.

---

[57] See Kramer, *Christ, Lord, Son of God*, London, 1966, 203ff; Overfield, 289ff; M. Hengel, *Between Jesus and Paul*, London, 1983, 65–77; N. A. Dahl, 'The Messiahship of Jesus in Paul' in his *Jesus the Christ*, Minneapolis, 1991, 15–25. For the background to the term messiah see M. Karrer, *Der Gesalbte* (FRLANT 151), Göttingen, 1990; A. Chester, 'Jewish Messianic Expectations and Mediatorial Figures in Pauline Christology', *Paulus und das antike Judentum* (WUNT 58; ed. M. Hengel and U. Heckel), Tübingen, 1991, 17–89.

11. ἐν αὐτῷ at the end of v. 10, though appearing redundant, creates the bridge to the next stage of the eulogy in which attention returns from the cosmic to blessings granted more directly to believers; the two are related through the entrance of a more eschatological strand in relation to believers. If v. 10 was the peak to which we climbed through vv. 3–10, we now appear to descend from it, yet this is not so, for a climb begins now to a new peak.

But does the change here to the first person plural indicate attention as focussed now on some believers only and no longer on all?[58] A first plural can be understood in various ways: 'we and you', 'we in contrast to you', 'we, my own special group' (e.g. if a plurality of authors had been named in 1.1f), or the authorial 'we'. The context must determine its precise meaning on each occasion. καί qualifies the verb and does not affect the identification of its subject: in addition to other gifts we receive an inheritance.

The vast majority of commentators see the alternatives as lying only between Jewish believers and all believers. Many from Pelagius onwards (e.g. Abbott, Beare, Barth, Hugedé) consider that the first person plural which has obtained from v. 3 and meant all believers now changes its reference and applies only to Jewish Christians. They do so because: (i) the change from 'we' to 'you' in vv. 13f suggests that in the latter the recipients alone are in mind; since these are Gentile Christians the preceding 'we' must refer to Jewish believers; (ii) the article with 'Christ' (v. 12) is an explicit reference to the Jewish Messiah (Barth, Beare); (iii) the change makes it easier to understand προηλπικότας in v. 12, for in 2.12 Gentiles are said to have had no hope prior to becoming Christians; (iv) 'to the praise of his glory' (v. 12) is an etymological substitution for 'Jew' (Barth); (v) the theme of the letter is the unity of Jewish and Gentile Christians and so the division is natural at this point (Ernst). In response to this we would argue that if a change of referent were intended at v. 11 AE would have brought this out more clearly as he does at 2.11; there is nothing in 1.11 to suggest the 'we' has any other reference than in 1.3–10; it is true that one of the themes of the letter is the unity of Jewish and Gentile Christians but this is a deduction we draw after we have read it; scholars may have it in mind as they read v. 11; AE however wrote Ephesians expecting it to be listened to, not worked over in the study! Only at the end of v. 12 would hearers have a clue that Jewish Christians were intended; they would then have to go back in their minds and rethink what they had heard and would wonder if they should read

---

[58] R. A. Wilson, '"We" and "You" in the Epistle to the Ephesians', SE II (= TU 87) (1964) 675–80; D. Jayne, '"We" and "You" in the Epistle to the Ephesians 1.3–14', ExpT 85 (1973/4) 151f; M. Carrez, 'Le "Nous" en 2 Corinthiens', NTS 26 (1980) 474–86; Bouttier, 291f; Usami, 104–8.

the new significance back to vv. 3–10.[59] For the same reason any attempt to limit the 'we' of vv. 11f to Paul and his associates fails. As we have seen in discussing v. 10, (ii) is a non-argument; the article with Christ has no particular messianic significance at 1.10, 20; 2.5; 3.17; 4.20; 5.2, 14, 24; 6.5. The best that can be said for (iv) is that it is fanciful. We must leave (iii) until we come to v. 12, noting that there, unlike here, the reference is clearly to Gentiles. It is not inappropriate that at the end of the eulogy AE should turn his attention more specifically to his readers and tie in what he says to them; the same variation between 'we' and 'you' occurs in the eulogies of 2 Cor 1.3ff and 1 Pet 1.3ff.[60] Finally it is important to note that there is nothing in vv. 13f which is specifically oriented towards the way in which Gentiles rather than Jews become Christians. So we conclude that there is no change of the referent of 'we' in v. 11 (e.g. Haupt, Ewald, Dibelius, Dahl, Cambier).

Other suggestions have been made. Faust, 212–17, argues that the first plural throughout 1.3–14 signifies Jewish Christians because the eulogy is a Jewish form of prayer and the verb εὐλογεῖν and its cognates are found regularly in inscriptions in synagogues in Asia Minor. But: (i) eulogies are also found in 2 Cor 1.3ff and 1 Pet 1.3ff and the root came to be associated with the eucharist (1 Cor 10.16; Mk 14.22); there is then no need to see the eulogy as a specifically Jewish prayer. (ii) If the first plural denotes Jewish believers throughout 1.3–14, does it do so also in 4.7, 13, 15, 25; 5.2; 6.12? We should expect some consistency in usage unless a distinction is being drawn between 'you' and 'us'. M. B. Pedersen, 'Jøde eller hedning?—Efeserbrevets forfgatter', *Dansk Teologisk tidsskrift* 51 (1988) 277–88, argues that AE has in mind first- and second-generation Christians; the first generation had 'hoped' (v. 12) before the second had done so. This view is somewhat similar to that of Usami. Both depend on an unlikely meaning of the reference to hope in v. 12. See also Introduction §1.3.

ἐκληρώθημεν[61] signals the new area into which the eulogy has turned. The verb, applied originally to the casting of lots, obtained the more general sense of allotting or assigning and came to be used in an allied way in its two (three) appearances in the LXX, 1 Kgdms 14.41; Isa 17.11; Esth 4.11(A). The Israelite tribes were allotted portions of land which became their inheritance (Num 26.52ff; 36.1ff; Josh 12.7); thus the word is linked to the idea of inheritance. This has led to it being understood in our passage as indicating either that we have been given a 'lot' (inheritance) by God or that we have been allotted to God as his inheritance. The concept of Israel as the

---

[59] E. Käsemann, 'Ephesians and Acts', *Studies in Luke–Acts* (ed. L. E. Keck and J. L. Martyn), London, 1976, 288–97 is apparently forced into this position. Bouttier makes the change one of genre; the first plural appears in confessional statements.

[60] Cf Dahl, 'Adresse … ', 256.

[61] Dacquino, 479 n. 11, puts in a lengthy defence of the variant ἐκλήθημεν, A D F(*) G; it was probably caused though the substitution of a familiar word for an unusual and difficult one, perhaps under the influence of Rom 8.30.

'lot' or chosen portion of God among the nations is found regularly in the OT (Deut 9.29; 32.8–10; Zech 2.12 [LXX v. 16]) and is emphasised in Qumran (1QS 2.2; 1QM 1.5; 13.5) where opponents of the community are known as the lot of Belial (1QM 1.5; 4.2; 1QS 2.4f) or of darkness (1QM 1.11; 13.5). So the church might be described as the 'lot' of God. Yet since the concept of inheritance is explicitly present later in vv. 14, 18 it may seem better to see it already in v. 11. 'Adoption' (v. 5) also harmonises with the reception of an inheritance. Acts 20.32 and 26.18 suggest the equivalence of κληρονομία and κλῆρος (cf Deut 9.29 and 3 Kgdms 8.15). Already in Col 1.12 κλῆρος was applied to the inheritance of Christians.

What then is the nature of the inheritance which Christians receive? If that of Israel was physical Palestine that of the Christians might well be 'heaven' (cf Col 1.12), but it is more probably their adoption, forgiveness, sealing with the Spirit, that is to say all the blessings intended in v. 3. In the NT it has eschatological associations (Mt 5.5; 1 Cor 6.9f; 15.50). In Ψ 15.7 (cf Dan 12.13) it is God himself. Thus it may be equated with salvation (Pokorný). Whatever its nature they have not obtained it through their own efforts; they were foreordained to receive it. προορίζειν, in view of its use in v. 5, probably has the same pre-temporal meaning here and does not refer to 'ordination' within the time between creation and prior to the coming of Christ, though such an interpretation would be possible if the first plural referred only to Jewish Christians. Christians receive their inheritance in accordance with God's intention, and they receive it in union with Christ (ἐν ᾧ) who as his son is God's heir. Verse 11b, with its varying, almost synonymous word (cf Percy, 186) expressing God's[62] active[63] purpose and will (βουλή though frequent in the LXX is not a Pauline term), emphasises that what the church has and is, all (τὰ πάντα is not of course 'creation' as in 1.10) comes from God.

12. εἰς τὸ εἶναι depends on ἐκληρώθημεν which is the main thought of vv. 11f, and may be either consecutive (in consequence of receiving the inheritance Christians are to the praise of God's glory) or final (they have been given the inheritance so that they may be to his praise). At times the distinction between consecutive and final is slight; in Paul εἰς τό is usually final (MHT, 143; Burton, §409). εἰς ἔπαινον ... though repeated from v. 6 (see notes there) and appearing again in v. 14 is not a chorus defining stanzas; if it were it would be succeeded on each occasion by the same phrase (none follows it in v. 14), and the stanzas would be of at least

---

[62] The insertion of θεοῦ by D F G 81 104 365 1175 pc a vg^mss sa bo^ms; Ambst spells out what is intended.

[63] ἐνεργέω is restricted in the NT to supernatural energy; cf Robinson, 241–7; K. W. Clark, 'The Meaning of ἐνεργέω and κατεργέω in the N. T.', JBL 54 (1935) 93–101.

approximately the same length; in any case there are more than three stanzas, or, rather, divisions of thought.

The 'we' who are to be to the praise of God's glory are now further defined as those who had previously hoped and still continue to hope (this appears to be the significance of the perfect participle) in Christ. The article prevents us taking the participle predicatively, 'that we are to be ... those who hoped'; if this were so v. 12a would be parenthetical and come more appropriately at the conclusion of the verse (Schnackenburg). Those who interpret vv. 11f of Jewish Christians and vv. 13f of Gentile Christians assume that the προ of προηλπικότας refers either to the hope that Jews had of a Messiah (Rom 1.2; 3.21; 16.26) which Gentiles did not have (e.g. Westcott, Ernst) or else to the belief of Jewish Christians which preceded in time that of Gentile Christians (Bruce, Scott).[64] The article with Χριστῷ does not necessarily indicate that AE is thinking of the Messiah (see on 1.10). Abbott argues that if AE had intended to refer to all believers and say they had hoped in Christ from the time of their conversion the perfect participle of the simple verb without προ would have sufficed. But προελπίζειν may mean the same as the simple verb for the element conveyed by the preposition is already contained within the simple verb; this is true of the use of this preposition with other roots (cf Rom 1.2 and Col 1.5). In Hellenistic Greek prepositions often do little more than stress the main thought of their verb. The word itself is rare and the few known instances lie in line with this interpretation.[65] The preposition can on occasion indicate 'previousness' rather than 'priority' (cf 3.2; 2 Cor 12.21; 13.2). If then we do not give to it the strong meaning 'before others', there is no reason to modify our conclusion that vv. 11f are not to be restricted to Jewish Christians.[66] This conclusion, which goes back as far as Theod Mops, also avoids the need to make 'in Christ' the object of 'hoped'. The object of hope is normally expressed with either the dative or a preposition (1 Cor 15.19 is probably not an exception). 'In Christ' thus retains here its formulaic significance and relates either to the togetherness of Christians in Christ (Gnilka) or gives the reason for hope (Masson; cf Phil 2.19).

[64] Cf. Joüon; A. Jankowski, 'L'espérance messianique d'Israël selon la pensée paulinienne en partant de *Proelpizein* (Ep 1,12)', *De la Torah au Messie* (FS H. Cazelles, ed. M. Carrez, J. Doré, P. Grelot), Paris, 1981, 475–81, gives a full discussion of the possibilities and concludes in favour of a reference to Jewish Christians.

[65] K. M. Woschitz, *Elpis, Hoffnung*, Vienna, 1979, 590–4, quotes the few places where it occurs other than in our verse.

[66] There does not seem to be any particular merit in the views of either Jayne, art. cit., that the 'we' refers to an earlier generation of believers than that of the readers, or of Wilson, art. cit., that the 'you' of v. 12 refers to newly baptised Christians; on general grounds we have rejected the view that Eph is written to newly baptised converts (see Introduction §1.3).

Since conversion all Christians have hope (see further on 1.18 and 4.4 for its nature). It is not simply a hope in the parousia or a hope that all humanity may have in a future Golden Age; that all Christians continue having a hope is seen in passages like 1 Cor 15.19; 2 Cor 1.10; 1 Tim 4.10.

13. While the main line of thought of this verse is clear the repeated ἐν ᾧ causes considerable difficulty in working out the details. Its first occurrence picks up the same phrase in v. 11 with the same antecedent, Christ: the Christ in whom we are sealed is the one in whom we received our lot. The second occurrence can be taken as resuming the first, the intervening words being parenthetical and/or parallel, or as a fresh step in the argument with Christ still the antecedent, or as with some word (e.g. 'gospel' or 'word') in 13a as antecedent. In view of the continual use throughout the eulogy of phrases with ἐν referring to Christ, the last possibility is unlikely. Only an examination of the content will indicate which of the others is to be preferred. Whatever the conclusion the principal verb is ἐσφραγίσθητε (Beare's suggestion of carrying on the verb of v. 11 into the relative clause is highly improbable) and the first words of v. 13 are not to be understood as 'in whom also you are' (Alford, Meyer, Barth); if so εἶναι would need to be expressed (Abbott) and the following πιστεύσαντες would be unnecessary (Haupt).

If, as we have already argued (see v. 11), the change to 'you'[67] in vv. 13f does not indicate that AE now specifically addresses only Gentile Christians, why did he make the change? Has he in mind the newly baptised among his readers (Wilson, art.cit.)? Even if we reject the general thesis that the letter is a baptismal tract it is true that v. 13 uses evangelistic language and may be directed at new converts, but almost all Christians at that time were new converts. Some, believing AE used an existing hymn as the basis for his eulogy, account for the change of person by supposing that vv. 13f are his addition to it (e.g. Schille, 68f), an impossible solution if all the eulogy is attributed to AE. More probably AE wishes to bring home to his readers that he is not simply describing God's activity as in a vacuum but wishes them to see their own place in it. The change between first and second persons recurs repeatedly in the letter and probably represents the kind of change which every preacher makes in the course of a sermon.

The terms of v. 13, 'hear, believe, word, truth, gospel, salvation', are those of Christian mission. The gospel is preached, people hear, respond and are sealed with the Spirit. 'The word of truth' means the

---

[67] There are variant readings which change the two second person pronouns in this verse into the first. The evidence for the first variant is the stronger: ℵ² A K L Y 326 629 630 1241 2464 *al*. It is surprising that many of the scribes who altered the first did not also alter the second. Pressure for the change probably came from the many first plurals in the earlier verses.

word whose content is truth and not 'the truthful word'; the phrase is found also in other post-Pauline literature (Col 1.5; 2 Tim 2.15; Jas 1.18) and implies an objectification of the gospel. Sometimes it is argued that AE is indebted at this point to Colossians but the phrase as we have seen appears elsewhere, both nouns are very common in the NT and there is nothing in the context which would imply AE used Colossians and not that A/Col used Ephesians; the phrase may have belonged to the Pauline school. The two nouns are used extensively, though separately, in relation to the spread of the gospel. When truth is emphasised it suggests a possible attack on untruth in the background; since Ephesians, unlike Colossians, is not polemical no need exists to see here a latent attack on heresy. Converts lived in an overwhelmingly pagan environment and the use of the word will have continually reminded them of the 'untruth' from which they had escaped (4.17–19). Unlike pagan philosophy or religion, Christianity is true and its 'truth' in the final issue is Christ himself (Jn 14.6; cf Gal 5.7; 2 Th 2.12). In Christ is found salvation and so 'the word of truth' is redefined as 'the gospel of your salvation', i.e. the gospel which brings or reveals salvation, not the gospel which is salvation, for gospel and salvation are not terms of the same type. The concept of salvation would have been known to AE's readers before they began to believe; as believers they now see salvation in a new light.

There are two ways of hearing: some hear and pay no heed; others hear and are saved (Mk 4.9; Acts 3.22ff; 4.19; Gal 3.2, 5; Rom 10.14–18; 1 Jn 4.6; Rev 2.7).[68] It is the latter hearing of which AE writes; he does not think of a chance physical hearing in the market-place which is quickly forgotten, but of the hearing which becomes belief. Because believing hearing is implied throughout v. 13a, little new is said in the description of readers as πιστεύσαντες; this summarises and repeats v. 13a. Those who believe have heard the word of truth, the gospel of salvation. The second ἐν ᾧ thus resumes the first and is not the object of the participle; πιστεύειν + ἐν is unusual both in the LXX and the NT; in the NT only in Mk 1.15 and Jn 3.15 v.l.; in the former case the object of belief is not Christ but the gospel. Each ἐν ᾧ then refers to the principal verb; believers are sealed either in participation with Christ or through Christ. The verb and the two participles are aorists, but we do not need to envisage three successive steps: hearing, believing, being sealed. As we have seen, the hearing is believing hearing and participles can indicate an event contemporaneous with the main verb (cf Mt 19.27; 27.4; Acts 10.33; 27.3). This holds even if sealing is understood as a metaphor for baptism for since there was no

---

[68] Cf A. von Dobbeler, *Glaube als Teilhabe* (WUNT 2.Reihe 22) Tübingen, 1987, 18–25.

period of catechetical instruction in the early church (cf Acts 8.36–8; 16.31–3) baptism could be said to coincide with belief.

Is however sealing a reference to baptism or some element within it like the laying on of hands? The image of sealing[69] has little in itself which would lead us to accept or reject either idea. Seals are used to indicate ownership (Rev 7.3–8; 9.4), to authenticate (Jn 3.33; 6.27; 1 Cor 9.2) and to protect what is sealed (Mt 27.66; Rev 20.3). Hellenistic religion has little to teach about the Christian usage of the image, though, whatever AE may have had in mind, the possibility cannot be ignored that his readers may have understood the seal as some form of magical protection (cf *Pistis Sophia* 195–7). The image was used in Christianity prior to Ephesians; in 2 Cor 1.22 it is connected as here with the ἀρραβών of the Spirit. The argument supporting the view that sealing means baptism in 1.13 is complex and depends more on allusion than direct evidence; explicit evidence is not found until after the time of Ephesians (2 Clem 7.6; 8.6; Hermas, *Sim* 8.2.3f; 6.3; 9.16.3–7; 17.4; *Acts of Paul and Thecla* 25; *Testim Truth* IX, 3 69.7–11). However: (i) in Rom 4.11 (cf *Barnabas* 9.6) circumcision is termed a seal[70] and though the Jewish evidence comes from much later, it is not unreasonable to suppose that Paul employs an idea to which he had been accustomed in his Jewish days (the description of circumcision as a 'sign' goes back as far as Gen 17.11–13). (ii) In Col 2.11f baptism and circumcision are drawn closely together but commentators are by no means agreed on their equivalence (*pro* Gnilka, Lohse, Pokorný; *contra* O'Brien, Schweizer, Martin); even if they are not equivalent in Col 2.11f AE might have assumed they were. (iii) The giving of the Spirit is regularly associated with baptism (Acts 2.38; 1 Cor 12.13) but is also associated with the laying on of hands in an action distinct from baptism (Acts 8.16; 19.6). In the case of Cornelius the coming of the Spirit, revealed in glossolalia, was the sign for him to be baptised (Acts 10.44–8). In missionary activity this was probably the normal pattern; people who showed signs of the Spirit were baptised. Such people, as Cornelius, might well have been described as 'sealed' with the Spirit prior to baptism.

None of this compels, acceptance of sealing as a metaphor for baptism in v. 13. If the letter were a baptismal tract there would be stronger grounds for making the equation; failing this the issue must remain in doubt. If AE intended us to understand that he had baptism in mind why did he not simply use the word? In the absence of the

[69] See G. W. H. Lampe, *The Seal of the Spirit*, London, 1951, 3ff; P. W. Evans, 'Sealing as a Term for Baptism', *Baptist Quarterly* 16 (1955) 171–5; D. Mollatt, 'Symbolismes baptismaux chez saint Paul', *Lumière et Vie* 26 (1956) 205–28; G. Fitzer, *TWNT*, VII, 939–54; Lyall, op. cit., 148–52; Adai, 61–78; A. Lindemann, *Die Clemensbriefe* (HNT 17), Tübingen, 1992, 220f; Fee, 668–72.
[70] See SB III, 495, re 2 Cor 1.22.

actual word we are left with the impression that for AE the divine aspect of becoming a Christian lies not in the act of baptism but in the coming of the Spirit to believers (cf Adai, 68). From the first moment of faith Christians believed the Spirit was with them. If the direct connection of sealing with baptism is in doubt there is less reason to connect it (with Schlier) with the laying on of hands, for the supporting allusions to circumcision are now irrelevant and there is no certainty that the laying on of hands accompanied baptism in this period.

The Spirit can be regarded as either the tool which leaves the mark of the seal on the object being sealed or the mark which is left. It is here almost certainly the latter. The activity of the Spirit should not be limited to charismatic gifts in the narrow sense but seen in the fruit of the Spirit (Gal 5.22f). Their sealing indicates to believers (cf 2 Cor 1.22) that they belong to God and are under his protection. A promise is related to the Spirit; this may be either that of the OT and Judaism (cf Acts 2.17; Gal 3.14; Lk 24.49 for this idea) which is now fulfilled ('the promised Spirit'; cf Sellin for further evidence supporting this understanding) or, slightly more probably, the promise of a future fullness of God's blessings to be given in eschatological times (cf 3.6).

14. ἀρραβών[71] (also at 2 Cor 1.22; 5.5; cf Rom 8.23), 'earnest', is a legal and commercial term of Semitic origin adopted into Greek (for its history see Abbott, MM, and the articles in *RAC* and *TWNT*)[72] which commits both giver and recipient to the completion of a deal under penalty. Yet the earnest is not just a pledge or guarantee that something will be given later; it is itself a partial gift, and is perhaps better translated as 'first instalment'. It is improbable that we have here a rejection of gnostic claims to full salvation (so Conzelmann) for if the word was intended polemically we should expect it to be qualified as 'only an earnest'.

Lindemann, *Aufhebung*, 104, wrongly equates this earnest with the inheritance and so eliminates any element of futurity[73] (cf Lona, 421, n. 239). The first instalment is the Spirit, not a portion of the Spirit

---

[71] If ὅς is read here as in ℵ D Ψ 𝔐 the reference is to the preceding πνεῦμα with the relative being attracted into the masculine through ἀρραβών. It may well have been the original reading and have been amended to the neuter (𝔓[46] A B F G L P 6 81 etc.) to make its reference clear. If the neuter was original then the masculine is an idiomatic or stylistic improvement, or an attempt to treat the Spirit as personal (cf Metzger).

[72] Lyall, op. cit., 145-8. Cf N. Schultz, 'St Paul Describes the Spirit as Arrabon. Would St Luke and St John have agreed?' *LTJ* 11 (1977) 112-21; F. W. Horn, *Das Angeld des Geistes* (FRLANT 154), Göttingen, 1992, 389ff; A. J. Kerr, "Αρραβών', *JTS* 39 (1988) 92-7.

[73] R. Stober, 'A Possible Link between the Epistle to the Ephesians and the Book of Ruth', *SE* IV (= TU 102), 343-6, sees a possible connection through this and other words with Ruth; his theory is over-ingenious.

of which the remainder will be given later, but the whole Spirit. Sealed with the Spirit, Christians have begun to participate in their inheritance of salvation and have a legal claim to inherit it fully; the metaphor perhaps breaks down at this point for heirs do not receive part of their inheritance in advance but all when the testator dies. The life of the church in which Jew and Gentile are now reconciled is an earnest of life in the world to come when all will be summed up in Christ. The concept of inheritance[74] has already been introduced through ἐκληρώθημεν (v. 11) and is implicit in sonship (v. 5). In Paul the idea is used in connection with the relationship of Jewish and Gentile believers (Rom 4.13f; 8.17; Gal 3.18, 29; 4.1, 7, 30) and, in a more normal and less theological way, of the inheritance of future salvation (1 Cor 6.9, 10; 15.50; Gal 5.21). These two aspects reappear in Ephesians: Gentile Christians are fellow-heirs with Jewish (3.5); all Christians (v. 14) have yet to enter on their full inheritance of salvation. We can observe here the tension that runs throughout the epistle, for Christians already sit with Christ in the heavenlies (2.6) and therefore appear to enjoy full salvation.

The purpose of the sealing with the Holy Spirit is now brought out in two parallel phrases introduced by εἰς; the first εἰς might be temporal, 'up to the time of' (cf Schlier, Masson), but it is easier to give it the same meaning as the second. The second phrase repeats one already used (vv. 6, 12) and is a fitting conclusion to the whole eulogy: it is God's final purpose that the church should be to his glory. If 1.10 was the intellectual peak this is the liturgical.

The earlier phrase is much more difficult to construe because περιποίησις[75] can be understood either (a)[76] with Schnackenburg, Masson, Abbott as *nomen actionis* (cf 1 Th 5.9; 2 Th 2.14; Heb 10.39), 'the acquiring of the inheritance', or with Dibelius, Cambier, Schlier, Gnilka as *res acquisita*, 'God's redeeming of his inheritance' (cf 1 Pet 2.9; the verbal form appears with this sense in Lk 17.33; Acts 20.28; 1 Tim 3.13). If (a) is chosen the genitive is probably epexegetical re-expressing ἀπολύτρωσις (for this see on 1.7; here as in 4.30 final salvation is in view and we have another instance of the inversion of genitives, so Sellin); if (b) is chosen it will be a genitive of the object. If the meaning is (b) then it is not

---

[74] On the use in Paul and Ephesians of the concept of inheritance see Herrmann and Foerster, *TWNT*, III, 757ff; P. L. Hammer, 'A comparison of *kleronomia* in Paul and Ephesians', *JBL* 79 (1960) 267–72; D. R. Denton, 'Inheritance in Paul and Ephesians', *EvQ* 54 (1982) 157–62; and, more generally, J. D. Hester, *Paul's Concept of Inheritance*, Edinburgh, 1968.

[75] See S. Lyonnet in Lyonnet and L. Sabourin, *Sin, Redemption and Sacrifice* (AnBib 48), Rome, 1970, 112–18.

[76] Almost all the Fathers choose (a); see D. A. Conchas, 'Redemptio acquisitionis', *VD* 30 (1952) 14–19, 81–91, 154–69. For a wider study of the interpretation of the word cf C. Kruse, 'Il significato de ΠΕΡΙΠΟΙΗΣΙΣ in Eph 1,14', *RivBiblt* 16 (1968) 465–93; he supports (a).

said to whom the possession belongs (in 1 Pet 2.9 and Mal 3.7 the context makes this clear) and we must assume that the theological theme of God's people as his possession was well enough known for there to be no need to express it; the idea of Israel as God's possession is expressed in other ways (cf Isa 43.21; Deut 4.20; 7.6); there is however no trace elsewhere in Ephesians of this idea and there is little evidence for it in contemporary Jewish literature. On the other hand it may be said to cohere with the earlier part of the eulogy in that his people became God's possession because he elected and foreordained them. If we select the meaning (a) we have to understand 'inheritance' a second time ('for the deliverance, that is the obtaining possession of the inheritance'). This is not an insurmountable obstacle and it is the meaning adopted unanimously by the Latin Fathers and by almost all the Greek and is probably preferable.

DETACHED NOTE II
IN CHRIST

Best, *One Body*, 1ff (and references there to earlier studies); Percy, 288ff; Maurer, 'Der Hymnus von Epheser I als Schlüssel zum ganzen Briefe', *EvT* 11 (1951/2) 151–72; Allan, 'In Christ'; F. Neugebauer, *In Christus*, Göttingen, 1961, 175–81; M. Bouttier, *En Christ*, Paris 1962; Roels, 44–7, 92–6; Gnilka, 66–9; Barth 69–71, 107–8; C. F. D. Moule, *The Origin of Christology*, Cambridge, 1977; Adai, 63–5; Ernst, 281ff; Usami, 91–112; A. J. M. Wedderburn, 'Some observations on Paul's use of the phrases "In Christ" and "With Christ" ', *JSNT* 25 (1985) 83–97.

Throughout the eulogy the phrase 'in Christ' has recurred repeatedly, eleven times in the twelve verses, though it has been in variant forms; while this high rate is not maintained throughout the remainder of the letter the phrase appears twice as frequently (in all thirty-three times, Schmid, 196) as in the genuine Paulines. Does AE employ it in the same way as Paul? We note first the appearance of new forms: ἐν τῷ Χριστῷ (3.11), ἐν τῷ Ἰησοῦ (4.21), ἐν τῷ κυρίῳ Ἰησοῦ (1.15), ἐν τῷ ἠγαπημένῳ (1.6). The article appears in the phrase several times though only twice in Paul (1 Cor 15.22; 2 Cor 2.14). Neugebauer, 131–49, has argued that the phrase 'in the Lord' tends to be limited to imperatival constructions by Paul but allows (pp. 180f) this may not be true of Ephesians; its use in 1.15; 2.21; 5.8; 6.21 confirms this. This suggests that some of the precision with which Paul used the phrase may have been lost or modified. Whether Paul inherited the phrase from earlier Christians or created it is irrelevant for Ephesians; AE, if he is not Paul, knew it as a Pauline phrase.

For Paul the phrase may be said to have two main thrusts, the instrumental and the local, each predominating from time to time but neither ever totally absent. These two thrusts still appear in Ephesians but with variations. In the instrumental usage God is now much more often introduced explicitly as the subject of action in Christ which benefits believers; this is found in Paul only at 2 Cor 2.15; 5.19 (but see also Col 1.19; 2.9, 15) but in Ephesians at 1.3, 4, 6, 9, 10, 20; 2.6, 7; 3.11; 4.32. Often also in Ephesians God is the real subject where the verb is passive (Maurer, 189); this is found four times in Paul, four times in Colossians, and there are also a number of passages in Paul where God is clearly the subject (Rom 6.23; 8.2; Gal 3.14); this variation must not then be over-exaggerated. The frequent use of God as subject produces a triangular relationship (God—Christ—the church) and here the usage is clearly instrumental. This sense is not only very frequent in Ephesians but also goes beyond Pauline usage in that it may refer to God's pre-temporal activity in Christ (1.4, 11) and to his cosmic activity (1.9, 10). The number of instances in which the local sense predominates are fewer than with Paul; this is at least partly accounted for by the absence from Ephesians of a section of personal greetings and because there are no passages in which Paul is under pressure to defend himself (4.1 is the closest). Yet the local sense does occur and mostly in corporate form. When, 6.1, children are told to obey their parents 'in the Lord' (for the reading see on 6.1) only an obstinate insistence that 'in the Lord' must be taken imperatively with the verb, and we have seen that not all instances in Ephesians are imperatival, forbids us seeing the phrase as connecting parents and children; children are addressed as members of the Christian community and as such should obey their parents (cf 1 Cor 7.39). When in 4.17 AE testifies 'in the Lord' he does so because he and his readers are members of the church; he would not have used the phrase if addressing non-Christians. When in 6.21 it is said that Tychicus, the beloved brother and servant in the Lord, will give the readers information, 'in the Lord' goes more easily with servant and brother than with the verb; Tychicus will tell them because he is a brother to them and serves them in the church. For the local sense see also the notes on 2.13, 15, 21 (cf Bouttier, op. cit., 57f). The local significance, and in particular the corporate, has not then disappeared from Ephesians and there is no reason to suppose it may not lie in the background in many cases where the instrumental sense predominates; only the interpretation of individual texts can show if it is present.

III

A PRAYER FOR KNOWLEDGE
(1.15–23)

J. Flowers, 'Paul's Prayer for the Ephesians. A Study of Eph. i.15–23', *ExpT* 38 (1926/7) 227–33; Ochel, 32–42; P. Schubert, *Form and Function of the Pauline Thanksgivings* (BZNW 20), Berlin, 1939; G. T. Montague, *Growth in Christ: A Study in Saint Paul's Theology of Progress*, Fribourg, Switzerland, 1961; W. G. Doty, *Letters in Primitive Christianity*, Philadelphia, 1977; L. Ramaroson, 'Une Lecture de Éphésiens 1,15–2,10', *Bib* 58 (1977) 388–410; P. T. O'Brien, 'Ephesians I: An Unusual Introduction to a New Testament Letter', *NTS* 25 (1978/9) 504–16; Lindemann, *Aufhebung*, 204–17; Fischer, 118–20; Overfield, 1–88; T. G. Allen, 17–115; Usami, 154–66; Arnold, 51–6.

15 So I for my part when I heard of your loyalty
  to the Lord Jesus and to all the saints
16 do not cease returning thanks for you
  mentioning you in my prayers,
17 that the God of our Lord Jesus Christ,
   the Father of glory,
  should give you the Spirit of wisdom and revelation,
  in knowledge of him,
18 the eyes of your heart having been enlightened
  to know him so that you may understand
  what is the hope of God's calling,
  what are the riches of the glory of the inheritance
   he provides among the holy ones,
19 and what is the exceeding greatness of his might
   towards us who believe,
  in accordance with the power of the vigour of his
   strength
20 with which he empowered Christ,
  in that he raised him from the dead
  and seated him at his right hand in the
   heavenlies
21   above every rule and authority and power
   and dominion or whatever they are termed,
  and that not only in this age
  but also in the coming age;

22   and has set in subjectidn all under his feet
                      and given him who is head over all to the
23   church, which is his body,
                      the fullness of him who is being totally filled.

This paragraph is again one long sentence. NA[27] unlike UBS[3]
divides it into two making a division after v. 19 but v. 20 begins a
relative sentence depending on what precedes. A better case might
be made for a division after v. 21 for at that point we change from
participles to finite verbs; yet the thought is continuous and v. 22
provides two clauses parallel to those of v. 20. To take vv. 15–23 as
one sentence is not out of keeping with AE's style. Whatever the
decision vv. 15–23 comprise thanksgiving (vv. 15f), intercession
(17–19), and lead to theological statement (20–3).

In most Pauline letters a thanksgiving report and intercession
follow the address; Ephesians instead begins with a eulogy (1.3–14).
A eulogy, unlike a thanksgiving, is praise of God without direct
reference to those before, or on behalf of whom, it is offered; initial
intercessions in letters relate directly to the condition of the
recipients. Because of its nature intercession would not then flow
naturally out of eulogy; hence the brief thanksgiving report creating a suitable transition.[1] Eulogy moves also into thanksgiving in
Dan 2.20–3 (cf 1 Esdr 4.60). In providing thanksgiving and intercession AE conforms to the general Pauline pattern, though 2
Corinthians differs in moving directly from a much briefer eulogy to
the body of the letter without thanksgiving or intercession. Though
AE conforms to the general Pauline pattern it is wrong, with Penna,
to describe 1.15–22 as the letter's epistolary opening. For it is not an
opening and it is not even certain that Ephesians is a letter (see
Introduction §6). The prayer is important and needs a suitable
introduction. Sometimes the whole of 1.15–3.21 is taken as the
prayer because 3.14–21 is again explicit prayer. This forces on
Ephesians a pattern which is not even true of all the genuine Pauline
letters; neither 2 Corinthians nor Galatians has thanksgiving and
intercession. In Ephesians itself 2.1–22 and 3.1–13 are better
described as doctrine or narrative. AE's eulogy has already broken
the 'normal' pattern and he must be allowed some of the freedom
which is characteristic of letters. 3.14–21 should therefore be taken
as a separate prayer section; as Paul in Rom 11.33–6 adds a
doxology to his doctrinal section so AE adds a prayer and doxology
to his. The brief thanksgiving contains most of the elements usually
found in a Pauline thanksgiving and the movement of thought in vv.
15–23 is somewhat similar to that in Col 1.9–20. Is there a literary

_____
[1] See G. P. Wiles, *Paul's Intercessory Prayers* (SNTSMS 24), Cambridge, 1974,
156ff.

relation between the two and if so what is it? This will be examined at the places in the text which appear to offer the closest parallels (see also Introduction §2.5). Vv. 15f set out the relation between AE, or Paul if the first person is understood as Paul and not someone else, and the readers. In vv. 17–19 interest centres on the readers and the benefits the prayer will bring them. In vv. 20–3 attention centres on Christ.

1.20–3 have sometimes been regarded as a hymn or as based on one.[2] Certainly the verses contain a number of phrases drawn from the catechetical and/or liturgical traditions which with some careful editing could be made to resemble a hymn or credal statement. That however is very far from saying they are a hymn or formal statement of belief or even are adapted from either. Themes, like the death of Christ and its significance, which we might have expected in a hymn of formal statement, are missing. Rather then than using a preformed piece of tradition AE has simply drawn from the tradition those elements which suit his particular purpose (cf Gnilka; for a detailed examination see T. G. Allen, 28–35). Similar sets of traditional theological statements appear in 1 Pet 3.18–22; Polyc *Phil* 2.1f; Ignatius, *Trall* 9.1f and, more diffusely, in 1 Cor 15.20, 24.8. Each of these has its own peculiarities: 1 Pet 3.19 brings in the preaching to the spirits in prison; our passage has no reference to the death of Christ (present in the context of 1 Cor 15); it also ends (v. 23) with a statement about the church, a statement which has been regarded as either the climax of the passage or, much less probably, as an afterthought (so Barth, 154; Ernst, *Pleroma*, 106f). If vv. 20–3 are not drawn as a unit from the tradition, even less reason exists for regarding 15–23 as an insertion based on verses in Colossians into a liturgical passage consisting of 1.3–14; 2.1–10 (so Kirby, 131–3), for 1.15–23 already contains liturgical material and the relationship to Colossians is not one of literary dependence but similar to what is found elsewhere in the letter. There is also an important connection in thought between 1.20–3 and 2.1–6.[3]

AE, realising he must attract readers' attention after the eulogy's stiff theological thought and impersonal nature, now refers directly to them with a brief thanksgiving for their Christian existence (vv. 15f) and a longer intercession for their deeper insight into God's ways (vv. 17–19). God's ways are ways of power and might so his intercession leads him on to say something about what God did in raising Christ and taking him into heaven; the result was a triumph over the supernatural hostile powers which readers believe control

---

[2] See Deichgräber, 161–5; J. T. Sanders, 'Hymnic Elements in Ephesians 1–3', *ZNW* 56 (1965) 241–32; Dibelius, 64; Schille, 103, n. 4; Ernst, *Pleroma*, 105–8; Fischer, 118–20; Best, 'Use'.

[3] Cf T. G. Allen, 'Exaltation and Solidarity with Christ: Ephesians 1.20 and 2.6', *JSNT* 28 (1986) 103–20.

them (vv. 20–2). This in turn leads AE finally to introduce one of the most important themes in the letter, namely the church (vv. 22f), and at the same time to return to the letter's cosmic setting.

15, 16. διὰ τοῦτο forms the transition from the eulogy. It could point forward but more probably refers back to the eulogy as a whole or to some part of it. The recipients of the letter have heard the Gospel and responded (vv. 13f) and so there is reason to give thanks for their response, yet vv. 13f relate to all Christians and cannot therefore be the basis for the particular thanksgiving of vv. 15f (Percy, 386–9). The precise nature of the connection between the eulogy and vv. 15ff is not clear, but the eulogy certainly supplies grounds for the thanksgiving. διὰ τοῦτο is probably little more than an indication of a new paragraph with new subject-matter; it is used elsewhere as a transition to a new paragraph: Mt 6.25; Rom 5.12; 2 Cor 4.1; Col 1.9; 1 Th 2.13; the final two of these are in prayer contexts; Col 1.9 in particular is very similar to Eph 1.15. AE uses connecting phrases and participles without much significance also at 2.11; 3.1, 14.

Paul now speaks, or is made to speak, in the first person, as κἀγώ emphasises; the singular is correct since no one else was mentioned in 1.1. What is the significance of καί (on its use see BDR §442.8b)? It cannot mean 'I Paul as well as others' since there are no others in the context, nor can it be related to 'heard' for there is nothing to which the 'hearing' would be additional. Despite its distance from the participles of v. 16 it should probably be taken with one of them, 'I also give thanks, make mention', 'I who have uttered the eulogy have more to say'.

In contrast to Col 1.8 and 1 Cor 1.11, AE's (Paul's) informants are not identified; the absence of a reference accords with the general nature of the letter; since it was directed to more than one church it would have been necessary to name several informants. καθ᾽ ὑμᾶς is a circumlocution for ὑμῶν (BDR §224.1, n. 3; Zerwick §130). The aorist participle (contrast the present participle in Philem 5) taken in conjunction with 3.2 and 4.20–1 indicates that Paul, or AE, had never visited the readers. According to Acts 19.1ff Paul spent a considerable time in Ephesus on his main visit, though there had been a brief initial visit, 18.19–21. The inference from our verse that the author had never visited the recipients cannot be countered by arguing that AE only refers here to the faith of those who have been converted since he left Ephesus (so Hodge) or that a long period had elapsed since his final visit and that therefore he needs to be updated;[4] nothing in the text implies he had fresh converts in mind and, though in every church Paul had founded new converts

---

[4] So D. A. Black, 'The Peculiarities of Ephesians and the Ephesian Address', *GraceTJ* 2 (1981) 59–73.

would have appeared after he left, in no letter does he address himself to them; moreover nothing in the text implies the lapse of a long period of time. Theodoret appears to have been the only Father aware of this problem but he does not offer a reasoned solution; the ancient commentators were much more concerned to understand the use of God and Father in v. 17! AE's phrases are stereotyped and sufficiently general to fit a circular or general letter. If AE implies Paul has not heard of their faith, does he really mean that he himself has not had that information or is it just a part of the framework of pseudonymity?

Mitton, *Epistle*, 65, 283, 285, views vv. 15–17 as derived from Colossians; parallels certainly exist.[5] The clause beginning with ἀκούσας is similar to that of Col 1.4, but it is also similar to clauses in Phil 1.27; 2 Th 3.11 and is a perfectly normal clause if reference needs to be made to information received. Its similarity with Col 1.4 would be increased if the reference to love in v. 15 is taken as original and not as the result of the influence of Col 1.4; yet in any case the linking of faith and love is natural (cf Gal 5.6; 1 Th 3.6; 5.8; 1 Tim 1.14; 2.15; 4.12; 2 Tim 1.13; 2.22; Tit 2.2; Philem 5). If a reference needs to be made to the spiritual condition of the recipients then one to their faith would be customary (Rom 1.8; 1 Th 1.2f; 2 Th 1.3). In Col 1.4 the object of faith is Christ Jesus yet in Eph 1.15 it is the Lord Jesus; why should AE have changed what is his normal phrase for describing Christ to an unusual one if he was dependent on Col 1.4 where his normal phrase appears? 'All the saints' which AE shares here with Col 1.4 is used again by AE at 3.8, 18, passages which have not been influenced by Colossians; it is a frequent phrase in the Pauline letters (e.g. Rom 16.15; 2 Cor 1.1; 13.12) yet is not found elsewhere in Colossians. If then there is literary dependence of one letter on the other, this would suggest A/Col is indebted to Ephesians. εὐχαριστεῖν (v. 16) is the natural verb to use in a thanksgiving and therefore cannot indicate dependence. παύομαι is the only word which both letters have in common and which is not found in a similar context elsewhere, but that does not prove AE depends on Colossians; it could as easily be the other way round. In v. 17 'the God of our Lord Jesus Christ, the Father of glory', while similar to a phrase in Col 1.13, is also similar to many other phrases (Rom 15.6; 2 Cor 1.3; 11.31; 1 Pet 1.3) and is more probably derived from liturgical use than from Colossians; there are in fact verbal differences with Col 1.3. Also in v. 17 we find ἐπίγνωσις and this, though appearing only four times in Paul, is a favourite phrase of A/Col (1.9, 10; 2.2; 3.10); AE however uses it again at 4.13 in a context independent of Colossians. The noun then probably belonged to the pool of words in the Pauline school to which AE and A/Col belonged. In the πνεῦμα σοφίας of v. 17 the nouns are related differently from Col 1.9 and are in fact a normal formulation (see on v. 17). Apart from the similarities of Ephesians here with Colossians it also has similarities with Philem 4–6 (cf Rom 1.8–10; 1 Th 1.2). Finally it needs to be pointed out that whereas the expressions we have been discussing in Ephesians occur together, this is not so of their alleged parallels in Colossians where they are found in 1.4f and

[5] Cf Best, 'Who used Whom?'.

1.9f. The indications then are that if there is dependence of one letter on the other it is more probably that of Colossians on Ephesians; if there is any dependence on the part of AE it is not on a document but through remembering what is in Colossians so that different parts of that letter are brought together. But more probable than the dependence of one author on the other is the dependence of both on a pool of words and phrases belonging to their Pauline school.

Before turning to the content of vv. 15f we need, as already indicated, to examine whether τὴν ἀγάπην should be read. Its omission is strongly supported by the textual evidence: 𝔓⁴⁶ ℵ* A B P 33 1739 1881 2464 *pc* boᵖᵗ; Hier. If then it was omitted, that omission was early. Col 1.4, on which it is possible our passage may be modelled if AE used Colossians, contains it as does Philem 5; it could easily have been omitted by homoeoarcton (cf Metzger); it is difficult to find a meaning for 'faith towards all the saints'. That love if included would create the frequent triad, faith, hope (v. 18), love, may help to explain why it was included but gives no reason for reading it. Col 1.4; Philem 5 could also have influenced its introduction; moreover its precise position varies; it comes at the end of the verse without τήν in 81 104 326 365 1175 *pc*; with the article it precedes the reference to the saints in ℵ² D¹ Ψ 𝔐 latt syʰ sa boᵖᵗ; it occupies the same place but the article connecting saints to it is missing in D* F G. This suggests that if we can find a satisfactory meaning for the phrase without the reference to love we should accept it as the harder reading. We note first that faith is related to 'the Lord Jesus' whereas the normal relation is to Christ (cf Kramer, 199f); 'Lord' is rather the title of confession. πίστις can be given the sense of 'loyalty, faithfulness'; it does not refer to an initial act of faith but to a continuous activity. Loyalty or faithfulness towards fellow Christians could be important in many difficult situations; fellow members must be upheld. Somewhat hesitantly we suggest what is meant is that the recipients should have loyalty based in the Lord Jesus and directed towards all the saints (cf Barth, Scott, Ewald, etc.) and that therefore the reference to love should not be read.

Whether we accept or reject the reading which includes love, a dual reference is present: to be a Christian involved being related both to Christ and to fellow Christians; whatever ἅγιοι may mean elsewhere (see on v. 18) it refers to human believers here. If we accept the inclusion of the reference to love there is a problem in that AE then thinks only of love towards fellow believers and not, as Jesus taught, towards all human beings; this however would not be out of line with his ethical teaching (see on 4.25 and Essay: Moral Teaching §3); indeed it might be said to set the tone for it. For the growth of this modification of Jesus' teaching see also on 4.25. Calvin in his note on our verse subtly alters Jesus' teaching when he writes 'love, properly ordered, begins with' the saints, 'and then flows to all others'. If πίστιν is understood as loyalty to other Christians it looks inwards and not outwards.

AE says that he does not cease (not to be taken literally) some activity; is it giving thanks (the thanks would be directed to God and not to the readers) or interceding? Elsewhere Paul in his opening sections, expressing himself in a variety of ways, continually prays for his readers (Rom 1.9; Phil 1.3f) or gives thanks for them (1 Cor 1.4; 1 Th 1.2; 2 Th 1.3; Philem 4); either alternative would then accord with his practice. Col 1.9 suggests the connection with praying but if AE did not copy Colossians this is irrelevant. Since 'giving thanks' is nearer the verb it is probably better to associate the 'not ceasing' with it. For AE to say Paul does not cease praying is a typical exaggeration, and should not be taken literally as if Paul were never off his knees! ὑπὲρ ὑμῶν goes more appropriately with the first participle (cf 5.20); a simple genitive would have sufficed with the second.[6] μνείαν ποιεῖσθαι (ὑμῶν is to be understood) is an epistolary expression (see MM, 414) used in connection with prayer and should therefore be understood here as 'mentioning' rather than 'remembering', though clearly if AE mentions his readers when he prays (ἐπί is temporal) he does so because he remembers them. Schlier wrongly says that it is an apostolic prerogative to given thanks and intercede for the church; any Christian may do this.

17. ἵνα is neither telic nor imperatival here but indicates the content of the intercession; (cf 3.16; Col 1.9; see Moule, 145; Robertson, 994). This commences with two solemn descriptions of God, both probably derived from liturgical usage. There are no similar solemn descriptions elsewhere in the genuine Paulines in the movement from thanksgiving to intercession, but what is found here fits the style of Ephesians (the nearest parallel is Col 1.3). At first sight we would have expected 'Father' and 'God' to be interchanged (cf 1.3) and this led some older commentators to interchange them, or to regard 'of our Lord Jesus Christ the Father' as parenthetical, or invert 'Father' and 'glory' (see Henle for references and a full discussion). The phrase was also used in the early christological disputes; God is the God whom Jesus worshipped. The first phrase identifies the God who is addressed as the Christian God but not however in deliberate contrast to the OT's 'the God of Abraham, Isaac and Jacob'. This kind of evocation of God when pleading with him became normal in Christian prayer from 1 Clem 64 onwards. The second phrase, 'the Father of glory' picks up δόξα from v. 14 and attributes a quality to God which we should expect to bear some relation to the content of the prayer. Normally 'father of' would be followed by the name of a person, however a metaphorical use of father is found in Jas 1.17; 2 Cor 1.3 (cf Heb 12.9) with the sense 'source of'; thus here he is the source of glory to those who are his children. The phrase may be derived from liturgical usage (cf Ψ 23.7; 28.3; Acts 7.2; 1 Cor 2.8) and is not then an indirect reference

---

[6] The variant ὑμῶν for which the evidence is weak, D² (ᶜF G) Ψ 𝔐 lat sy, added in some texts to the second participle reinforces this conclusion.

to Christ, he being equated with δόξα since God is his father. 'Of glory' could be taken as adjectival, signifying 'the glorious father'; but this is weak. Sellin, returning to an older interpretation, argues that we have an inversion of the genitive and it should be understood as 'the glory of God' and compares 2 Cor 4.6; the glory of God is Jesus Christ and so God is the father of glory; it seems easier to understand 'father' as meaning 'source of'. δόξα itself is a complex term;[7] two meanings seem possible here: (i) 'might, power' (as in 3.16; Rom 6.4); God's might is emphasised in v. 20 and linked as in Rom 6.4 with his might in the resurrection; (ii) 'splendour', since 'glory' is taken up in v. 18 where the connotation is 'splendour'; v. 18 is closer than v. 20 and so (ii) is probably its significance here. 'Splendour' with its implication of 'sight' is appropriate to the impartation of knowledge and the enlightenment of the eyes. It is difficult to find an English word which carries these two senses of δόξα but perhaps 'majesty' may do so, as an old term for royal beings who have, or had, both power and splendour.

Two parallel requests (17b and 18a), both concerned with knowledge, give the content of the prayer. The readers' loyalty (faith) and love (if ἀγάπην is read) are not in question; what they need is more knowledge (contrast Phil 1.9). Knowledge, a theme already present in vv. 8f, is of great importance to AE; what follows indicates the areas where he believes his readers' knowledge should grow. God is requested to give them 'the spirit of wisdom and revelation ... '. This is not simply a prayer that they should be more intellectually alive, though they should be, but goes much deeper for the biblical concept of wisdom does not relate to intellectual processes alone: the fear of the Lord is the beginning of wisdom. The revelations AE prays for his readers are not insights into scientific or artistic truth, but relate to the way they are to live their lives.

The reading δῷ (B 1739 1881 pc) is poorly supported but it is difficult to know how to understand the alternative δώῃ. The former is a subjunctive. The latter could be either a subjunctive or, read as δῴη, an optative. Both the subjunctive and the optative forms are unusual though possible. The optative may carry a sense of uncertainty yet is often found in prayers (e.g. Rom 15.5, 13; 1 Th 3.11, 12). Paul uses δῷ elsewhere as a subjunctive but this is irrelevant if AE is not Paul; AE uses it in Eph 3.16; 4.29. Burton, §§200, 225; BDR §§95.1 n. 2; 369.1 n. 4; 386.4 n. 5; MHT, 100, 128; MH, 210, all prefer the subjunctive δώῃ; Robertson, 309, 326f, 940, 983, 994, prefers the optative.

Does πνεῦμα refer to God's Spirit or the human spirit? For those

---

[7] See A. M. Ramsay, *The Glory of God and the Transfiguration of Christ*, London, 1949; G. von Rad, *TWNT*, II, 235–58; H. Hegermann, *EWNT* I, 832–41; S. Aalen, *NIDNTT*, II, 44–52.

who use language which capitalise all nouns this is an unimportant question when translating, but for those using languages which do not it is essential to make a decision. Of course if it refers to the human spirit, then for believers it is the human spirit as inspired by the divine Spirit. Since the readers have already been sealed with God's Spirit (v. 13) and may be presumed to possess it, many commentators take the human reference pointing out that πνεῦμα lacks the article and that there are many parallel phrases to a spirit of wisdom (= a wise spirit), e.g. Exod 28.3; Num 5.14; Deut 34.9; Zech 12.10; Lk 13.11; 1 Cor 4.21; Gal 6.1. The absence of the article cannot however be a valid objection to a reference to the divine Spirit for it is often anarthrous (Mt 12.28; Mk 1.8; Lk 1.15, 35, 41, 67; Rom 1.4; 1 Pet 1.2). Moreover while a spirit of wisdom can mean a wise spirit, a spirit of revelation can hardly mean a revelatory spirit (a spirit open to revelation?). That the Spirit is said to be given is more appropriate to something handed over from outside and is in accord with contemporary Jewish usage (e.g. Wisd 7.7).[8] Believers are not immediately made completely wise when converted and sealed with the Spirit; an area exists then where enrichment is necessary and it can only come from the Spirit (Gaugler; cf 1 Cor 2.12, 14; 12.8). We note that in this verse all three persons of the Trinity are mentioned though AE has no developed Trinitarian theology. If the Spirit of wisdom stood alone here it would suggest direct dependence on Isa 11.2, but because of the addition of 'revelation' any dependence is probably indirect; Isa 11.2 affected later Jewish thought extensively and wisdom and the Spirit are regularly related (see Schlier, 78, n. 1). When the Spirit is absent there is no true wisdom (for the meaning of wisdom see on 3.10); human speculation cannot bring knowledge of God; wisdom is hidden in God (Col 2.3) and he alone can make it known (1 Cor 2.10–11); although there is considerable agreement here with 1 Corinthians, Ephesians lacks the idea of wisdom as the foolishness of God (cf Steinmetz, 111).

What is the Spirit of revelation? It is certainly not here the mode of the bestowal of wisdom as Eadie suggests. If the Spirit of wisdom imparts wisdom presumably the Spirit of revelation imparts revelations; the origin of true knowledge in God is thus again stressed. Ephesians differs here from Colossians which, while it has much to say about wisdom, has nothing to say about revelation. The charismatic discussion of 1 Cor 14 refers to 'revelations' (vv. 6, 26, 30); these are revelations or disclosures of some particular matter. In 3.3 AE speaks of a revelation given to Paul relating to the admission of the Gentiles and though this is much more general it is still the

---

[8] Cf S. D. Macarthur, 'Human Spirit in Pauline Usage' (Ph.D. thesis, University of Glasgow, 1980), 166; Fee, 675–9.

disclosure of a particular truth. There is nothing in our context which enables us to tie down how particular the revelations will be nor to elucidate their content. There is no reason to suspect that AE is thinking exclusively of apocalyptic revelations. If AE has been influenced by Col 1.9 the revelations will probably be practical in nature rather than insights into the divine being (Gnilka).

The final phrase of v. 17 is normally attached to what precedes and regarded as supplying God's purpose in giving the Spirit. However, from the beginning some (e.g. Origen, Chrysostom) have construed the phrase with v. 18; in 1.4f, 8f AE connected adverbial clauses beginning with ἐν to following participles and may have done the same here; it would mean that believers would have their spiritual eyes enlightened through the knowledge of God. This interpretation provides a point of departure for further insights (Gnilka). Whichever way we take the phrase, αὐτοῦ is the object of ἐπίγνωσις and refers to God and not to Christ or the Spirit. What AE prays for his readers is not understanding of human nature but an understanding of God; he is not setting out an anthropology but a theology. A/Col uses ἐπίγνωσις four times, equalling the number of times it is used in all the genuine Paulines; AE uses it here and at 4.13 in a passage influenced by Colossians. It may then have been a word current in the Pauline school which, since Paul did not make frequent use of the actual term though he has much to say about knowledge, may have derived it from Hellenistic thought where it was an important concept. It was important also at Qumran (1QS 4.2ff; 1QH 12.11f). The word as used in Ephesians and Colossians does not appear to have a meaning different from the simple γνῶσις.[9] What is given is not knowledge of the nature of the world or of human nature; it does not refer primarily to theoretical knowledge or its accumulation; it is not the disclosure of the mystery of 3.3, 5 since this has already been made known to apostles and prophets; it is practical and experiential knowledge and should lead to obedience to and love for God and to the care of the oppressed and downtrodden. In the light of what follows it probably also relates to knowledge of God's calling, the believer's inheritance and God's might. If this is so, in what way does an understanding of God differ from an understanding of music or art? Neither Paul nor AE ever discusses the existence of the arts and so it is vain to seek in them an answer to a question like this.

18. As so often in AE's long and complex sentences the meaning is clear though the construction is not. πεφωτισμένους τοὺς ὀφθαλμούς is probably a second object dependent on δῴη (Gnilka,

[9] See Robinson, 248–54; H. Clavier, 'Recherche exégétique et théologique sur la notion paulinienne d'epignosis', SE VI (= TU 122); R. Bultmann, TWNT, I, 688–715; C. Noyen, 'Foi, charité, espérance et "connaissance" dans les Épîtres de la captivité', NRT 94 (1972) 892–911, 1031–52.

Abbott, Schnackenburg, Hugedé) but it could depend on ὑμῖν with
the dative changed into the accusative under the influence of εἰς τὸ
εἰδέναι (Schlier, Lincoln). There is little reason for taking it as
parenthetical (Barth) or as an accusative absolute (Bengel) for such
accusatives are infrequent except with impersonal verbs. The phrase
may be tautological following on v. 17 (Percy, 187), but it again
stresses in AE's manner that true understanding comes from God
alone and is the Spirit's work (Adai).

καρδία is here as often the centre of personality.[10] It should
neither be contrasted with the mind, as if mental processes are to be
suppressed, nor equated with it, as if a mere intellectual grasp of the
issues is all that is needed. The metaphor of the eyes of the heart
appears elsewhere (CH 4.11; 7.1; 1 Clem 36.2; 59.3; since Clement
probably did not know Ephesians his use of it indicated the
metaphor was generally known; see also 1QS 2.3). There are similar
phrases relating to the mind or soul (Plato, Rep 519B, 533D, 540A;
Aristotle, Nic Eth VI 12.10; Philo, Spec Leg 3.2). Consequently
there is no need to envisage gnostic influence (pace Pokorný,
Gnosis, 112). The enlightening[11] of the eyes was also widely used
metaphorically (Ps 19.8; Ezra, 9.8; Bar 1.12; Odes Sol 11.14; 1QS
2.3; 4.2). Despite his impressive intellectual ability Paul would have
remained a Pharisee had his Damascus Road experience not opened
his eyes (Könn). Certainly AE, if he is not Paul, would have thought
of Paul as having an enlightened heart but what he prays for here is
the enlightenment of the hearts of his readers. The hearers of a
sermon need enlightenment as much as its preacher; if they do not
have it, or do not obtain it during the sermon, they will not be able to
appropriate what is being said.

By the second century enlightenment had become a technical term
for baptism (Justin, Apol I, 61.12; 65.1; Sib Or 8.247, 271). This
meaning may already be present in Heb 6.4, but is it in our verse?
Though there is no necessary affinity between baptism and enlightenment, it was natural that in the course of time they should come to
be associated, for new Christians came to see the truth (the minds of
unbelievers are in darkness 4.18; 5.8; Rom 1.21) around the same
time as they were baptised. Yet it was through the hearing of the
gospel that they saw the truth and this came prior to baptism (cf
Noyen, art.cit.). Since there is no obvious link in the context to

[10] Cf W. Gutbrod, Die paulinische Anthropologie (BWANT 67), Stuttgart, 1934,
65–75, 167–70, 241–4; Stacey, 194–7; Jewett, 305–33; F. Baumgärtel, J. Behm,
TWNT, II, 609–17; T. Sorg, NIDNTT, II, 180–4; G. Dautzenberg, EDNT II, 114–23. AE
uses the singular and the plural rather inconsistently (MHT 23). The reading διανοίας is
ill supported and was probably caused by 4.18; it is also found at 1 Cor 14.25. The
omission of ὑμῶν (𝔓46 B 6 33 1175 1739 1881 pc) would not affect the sense; the textual
evidence is fairly evenly divided; it should however probably be read.

[11] On the whole area of 'light' and 'enlightenment' see H. Conzelmann, TWNT, IX,
302–49.

baptism, there is no need to see v. 17 as alluding to it. The insight believers gained when they heard the gospel continued with them (this is the significance of the perfect participle); they became children of light (1 Th 5.5) and shone as lights in the world (Phil 2.15). The metaphor of enlightenment was so frequent in the ancient world that there is no need to suppose AE derived it from the Mysteries or gnosis; his readers, however, may have seen a connection, yet they will also have been aware of the differences between Christian enlightenment and any other. For AE salvation includes knowledge as well as those elements like adoption and the forgiveness of sin which we normally associate with it (Pokorný).

The purpose (εἰς + infin. could also indicate result) of the enlightenment of the heart is now presented in three parallel clauses introduced by τίς, τίς, τί and further aspects of the salvation of which AE spoke in the eulogy are brought forward. The three clauses are best understood as parallel (Ewald, Gnilka) and inter-related rather than the first as clarified and expanded by the second and third (Schlier, Haupt), or the third as the climax of the sequence, for it is difficult to see the third as in any way expanding or clarifying the first.[12] Three of the leading ideas (hope, inheritance, power), one from each clause, are also found together in 1 Pet 1.3–5.

Mitton, *Epistle*, 285, sees dependence here on Col 1.27 through the phrase ὁ πλοῦτος τῆς δόξης and the word ἐλπίς; but the latter is a frequent term in Ephesians and is linked as here with κλῆσις at 4.4. As for the former, AE unlike A/Col has used the masculine form of the word for riches; there is no obvious reason for the change; 'riches of glory' may have been a phrase in the Pauline school. If there is literary dependence A/Col is as likely to have depended on Ephesians here as AE on Colossians.

(a) The first of the parallel clauses speaks of the hope[13] which is brought to light through God's calling of believers; 4.4 again associated hope and call, an association found only in Ephesians. Because their call was pre-temporal (see on 1.4f) and not simply the result of subjective experience, the hope of believers is soundly based. It is brought about by enlightened knowledge (Usami, 158). Hope is an important theme in Paul (Gal 5.5; Rom 5.2–5; 8.24f; 15.4; 2 Cor 3.12) and this provides the background for AE's use of the concept. In v. 18 the emphasis does not lie primarily on the expectant hoping of believers for, as Eadie comments, it would not require enlightened eyes to produce the emotion of hoping. Instead the emphasis lies on the content of what is hoped for (*res sperata*); if

---

[12] This conclusion is unaffected by the omission or insertion of καί between the first and second clauses; the omission has by far the stronger support: 𝔓⁴⁶ ℵ* A B D* F G 0278 33 81 104 1175 1739 1881 *pc* it vg^(st. ww); Ambst Pel.

[13] Woschitz, op.cit., 954–6.

this is the sense of hope here, it is not seen as one member of the triad, faith, hope, love, and so provides no reason for reading 'love' in v. 15. The actual content of the hope is not spelt out but has to be gleaned from the rest of the letter. Gentile, though not Jewish, believers were without hope before they believed (2.12); now they possess hope. It is not then the hope of redemption, even if redemption is understood as being with God or Christ in heaven, for they have already been raised and sit with Christ in the heavenlies (2.6). If this appears to eliminate any future sense from hope, believers should remember that they are summoned to live worthily (4.1), are instructed in the nature of worthy living (4.2ff) and still require defensive armour against the assaults of the devil (6.10ff). A tension then exists between the certainty of attained salvation and the need to live as those who have not fully attained it; already heirs of salvation, having received the first-fruits of the Spirit (1.14), they have not yet fully entered into their inheritance. Even if the content of their hope is not spelt out it needs to be distinguished from the hope of better conditions on earth, of a new social order, of attaining great wealth, or of a contented mind.

(b) The second parallel clause explains the knowledge God has given us into the riches (see on 1.7) of the glory of the inheritance (see 1.14 for the word); as in 1.14 the church is not God's inheritance but the inheritance is what the church receives; the former interpretation would rob the final reference to the saints of meaning. Even though the phrase is wordy it is better as in v. 17 not to treat δόξης (for the word see on v. 17) as if it were an adjective and render 'glorious riches' or 'glorious inheritance'. The phrase 'riches of glory', also in Col 1.27, probably belongs to the Pauline school. In Col 1.27 it relates to the universality of salvation as including Gentiles but here to the inheritance of believers in heaven. Believers do not just look forward to this inheritance; they already partake of it since even now they sit with Christ in the heavenlies (2.6).

Who are oἱ ἅγιοι?[14] Normally the word means Christian believers (cf 1.1 and the frequent Pauline use of the word in this sense). If this is its sense here nothing is added to the meaning of the verse. If we take the implied second plural as indicating Gentile believers then the 'saints' might be Jewish Christians, Gentile believers being viewed as given a place within the OT people of God (cf Acts 26.18). However AE is concerned here with heaven and not conditions on earth, and nothing suggests that he has the division of

---

[14] Cf P. Benoit, "Ἅγιοι en Colossiens 1.12: Hommes ou Anges?', in *Paul and Paulinism. Essays in honour of C. K. Barrett* (ed. M. D. Hooker and S. G. Wilson), London, 1982, 83–101; Löwe, 162–5; D. W. B. Robinson, 'Who were "The Saints"?', *RefTR* 22 (1963) 45–53; H. Balz, *EDNT* I, 16–20; C. Brown and H. Seebass, *NIDNTT*, II, 223–32.

Gentiles and Jews in mind. Even if he᾽ was thinking of Jewish believers he was certainly not thinking exclusively of those in Jerusalem (1 Cor 16.1; Rom 15.31; 2 Cor 8.4; 9.1). An increasing number of commentators, especially since the discoveries at Qumran, understand the saints here to refer to the 'heavenly ones' or 'angels' (e.g. Pokorný). Extensive evidence exists for this sense of the word, stretching back into the OT (e.g. Job 15.15; Ψ 88.6, 8; Isa 57.15; Amos 4.2; Ecclus 45.2; Dan 8.13) and appearing more regularly in the inter-testamental literature (e.g. 1 En 1.9; 12.2; 39.1; Jub 31.14; 1QM 12.1; 1QH 3.22f; 11.11f). 1QS 11.7f, 'God has given them [various spiritual blessings] to His chosen ones as an everlasting possession, and has caused them to inherit the lot of the Holy Ones' (ET from Vermes) moves in the same area as Eph 1.18 in linking the members of the earthly community with the holy ones in heaven in relation to spiritual blessings (cf Wisd 5.5; 1QH 3.21f). According to 2.6 believers already sit in the heavenlies. There is then no reason to reject the interpretation of the saints as the heavenly ones in 1.18; it is also the probable meaning in 2.19 and is possible in 3.18; it was already present in Paul (1 Th 3.13); the saints on earth share their inheritance with the angels. This sharing exists now and does not belong to the future. The ἐστίν of the first clause must be carried into this clause as into the third. As the church is already blessed in the heavenly places (1.3) so it already partakes of its inheritance.

19. (c) The third clause relates to God's power and, though not a climax, is probably put last as supplying a link from v. 18 to vv. 20–3. Without God's power we would not have any certain hope, resurrection or inheritance. In typical manner AE stresses with a favourite word, τὸ ὑπερβάλλον (2.7; 3.19; in Paul at 2 Cor 3.10; 9.14; cf 4.7), the exceeding greatness (μέγεθος is *hapax legomenon* in the NT) of his power. A reference to God's grace rather than his power might have been expected, but the two are not far apart; God's grace is not his amiability but his power to save. His power operates on us; the first person is surprising in an intercession and probably led to the variant second.[15] AE sees himself as much in need of help as other believers; there is a similar change at 2 Cor 13.3f, though AE does not depend on that passage; God's power works in him as in other Christians. AE is not however suggesting that 'we who believe' consists of himself and a few others (the apostles, so Aquinas) and excluding his readers. The first person also leads appropriately into vv. 20–3 which contain credal-type statements. God's power operates on (εἰς) believers. It is God who is

---

[15] D* F G P 33 104 629 1175 *al* it; Ambst. The variant separates writer and hearers and serves to intensify the form of direct address; the first plural suits the idea of a meditation much better. On the Pauline use of εἰς ὑμᾶς see Percy, 205–8.

great and not those who 'know' as some gnostics supposed (Iren 1.13.3; cf 1.21.4). While it is true that God's power operates within believers, it also operates on them as it were from outside. Its external nature is confirmed here by the reference in v. 20 to God raising Christ. It is not however introduced here as a power which will eventually raise believers for they have already been raised with Christ (2.5f). The power is active now just as the hope and the inheritance exist now. When the readers appreciate the meaning of these three prayer clauses (18, 19a) they will 'be better equipped to fulfil their responsibilities and tasks in living and being to the praise of God's glory' (Roels, 173).

Verse 19b with its multiple words for power begins the movement from intercession to theological statement. The concept of power is picked up, developed and made the basis for what God has done in Christ (20–3). The precise relation of v. 19b to what precedes is not however clear. (a) It has been attached to δώῃ (v. 17) but this is remote and it is not obvious how the Spirit of wisdom and revelation and the enlightenment of the eyes are explained by the multiple reference to power. (b) The connection with εἰς τὸ εἰδέναι is less remote but again it is difficult to see how knowing comes through power. (c) Direct dependence on τοὺς πιστεύοντας eliminates any accusation of remoteness (Ochel, 37) but the participle is not a significant word in the sentence and vv. 20–3, which are important, cannot be made subservient to it (Abbott); vv. 20–3 are not introduced as an explication of faith. (d) It could depend on all three clauses of vv. 18, 19a (Gnilka, Haupt) as giving the ground for their claim; yet v. 19b only takes up the theme of the third clause. (e) It could depend on v. 19a alone; this has the advantage that v. 19b then continues the theme of v. 19a, God's power (Abbott, Schlier). This does not imply that v. 19a is made the most important of the three clauses; it is merely the nearest. We may dismiss (a), (b), (c); (e) is preferable to (d).

Three words for power, typical of AE's redundant style, now emphasise God's might.[16] Words denoting power are frequent in Ephesians (see Arnold, *passim*) and it is not always easy to distinguish between them. δύναμις and ἐνέργεια are usually differentiated as potential and realised power;[17] the power which is potential in v. 19a is realised in the resurrection of Christ (see v. 20).

---

[16] κατά + acc + gen is not infrequent in Ephesians (1.5, 7, 11; 2.2; 3.7, 16). In the present instance we have a string of dependent and almost synonymous genitives, again a characteristic of the letter (cf Percy, 27, 193f; Kuhn, *NTS* 7 (1960–1) 334–46 at 335f).

[17] W. Grundmann, *Der Begriff der Kraft in der neutestamentlichen Gedankenwelt* (BWANT 8), Stuttgart, 1932; K. W. Clark, 'The Meaning of Ἐνεργέω and Καταργέω in the New Testament', *JBL* 54 (1935) 93–101; G. Bertram, *TWNT*, II, 649–51; Arnold, 72–5.

The other two terms, κράτος, ἰσχύς (found together also in Job 2.16 LXX), are approximately synonymous and lie in the area of potentiality rather than realisation (attempts, such as those of Abbott, Westcott, Barth, to differentiate between all the words, are not wholly successful).[18] While many religions stress the power of the deity, what is more important is the nature of that power and the way it is exercised. For AE the power of God is closely related to his grace and love (love was related to his electing power in 1.4f), and in our present passage God's power is exercised in the raising and exalting of Christ and in the raising, exalting and delivering from sin of believers (2.1–10). V. 19b then both picks up what has been said and throws us forward to what will be said. Missing from AE's discussion of God's power is the way Paul relates it to the weakness of Christ in the cross (1 Cor 1.17ff) and his abandonment of power in his incarnation (Phil 2.6ff). AE only alludes to the incarnation in 4.9f and does so there only as a foil to the ascension on which his stress lies. Our present passage emphasises the majesty of Christ and not his humiliation. It needs also to be said that the power of God is not seen in 'miracle'; despite God's power, Paul remains a prisoner.

It is probable that the prayer ends here, to be briefly resumed at 3.1 and then, at length, in 3.14–19. Scholars enjoy defining passages as eulogies, thanksgivings or intercessions and then drawing precise boundaries for what they have identified; it is by no means certain that NT authors kept in mind the desire of scholars for clear boundaries. One theme or form often drifts unconsciously into another.

20.[19] Apart from its nature as a relative clause dependent on ἐνέργειαν, this verse is linked to v. 19b through the cognate verb ἐνήργησεν and the continuation of the theme of power (it is difficult to reproduce in English the play on words). God, not believers, is the subject of what follows. The main verb[20] of the clause governs both the following participles and the two finite verbs in v. 22 as the content of their clauses shows. God's power is exercised in four specific acts: he (i) raises Christ, (ii) seats him at his right hand, (iii) subjects all things to him, (iv) makes him head of the church. The article is again found with Christ.[21] It may serve here to prepare

[18] Double expressions are common in later Judaism; e.g. Tg Isa 40.10; 51.5; Deut 9.26, 29 LXX; 26.8; 1QH 4.32; 1QS 11.20; 1QM 11.5.

[19] On 1.20–3 see Overfield, 1–88.

[20] The perfect is read here by A B 81 *pc* which is largely Egyptian though lacking some important witnesses; if read it would express the action and its continuing results in that Christ still rules over the powers. The aorist, which has a much wider range of support, expresses the once-for-allness of God's enabling power. Whichever is read the essential meaning is unaffected.

[21] On the very early association of the name 'Christ' with the resurrection, see Kramer, 19–26.

readers for the OT allusion and is more appropriate than 'the Lord'; the latter is the christological term usually associated with Ps 110.1, but it would be improper to speak of the empowerment of the Lord. We probably do not have here another instance of the 'in Christ' formula; 'in' denotes the place of God's activity.

Mitton, *Epistle*, 285, views AE as dependent here on Col 2.12; 3.1 where we also find the resurrection of Christ and a reference to the right hand expressed in very similar words. The resurrection of Christ is a common credal theme in the NT expressed usually as here with ἐγείρειν and ἐκ νεκρῶν (e.g. Rom 4.24; 6.4; 10.9; 1 Cor 15.12; Gal 1.1; 1 Th 1.10). The ascension to God's right hand is also a credal theme. There was no need for AE to go to Colossians to get either idea or wording for them.

The aor. indic. ἐκάθισεν is read by D F G Ψ 𝔐 b r; Ambst but the evidence, 𝔓92vid ℵ A B Ψ 0278 33 81 etc., favours the participle. Either could easily have been changed into the other through the influence of the associated participle or indicative. Much of the evidence supporting the participle inserts αὐτόν after it. This is probably a clarificatory scribal addition since Christ is usually described as himself taking his seat at God's right hand. The variant using the simpler οὐρανοῖς (B 365 629 *pc* syᵖ; MVict) is almost certainly a scribal error.

(i) That God raised Christ from the dead was a basic belief of the first Christians; it is found in early confessional statements (e.g. 1 Cor 15.4; 1 Th 1.10; Rom 10.9) and in all strata of the NT. The particular phrase 'raised from the dead' is also widespread (e.g. Rom 4.24; 6.4; 8.11; 10.9; Gal 1.1; 1 Pet 1.21) with God as explicit or implicit subject (where Christ is subject the verb is usually ἀνίστημι and not ἐγείρω). The resurrection of Christians is also regularly related to that of Christ. The connection is not explicit here but 2.6 refers to both the resurrection of believers and their heavenly session and is to be linked in thought to 1.20.[22]

(ii) God has seated the one whom he raised at his right hand in the heavenlies. Whether or not Christ's ascension and resurrection were originally distinguished (cf Rom 8.34; Phil 2.9; Col 3.1; 1 Tim 3.16), by the time of Ephesians they are envisaged as distinct events. Once it was accepted that Christ appeared in physical form after his resurrection it was necessary to devise some means to move him to heaven where it was believed he now dwelt. This led to the separation of resurrection and ascension. The ascension (and/or the heavenly session) is sometimes simply stated as a fact; sometimes, as here, attention is drawn to the activity of the Exalted One as ruling (cf 1 Pet 3.22) or interceding (Rom 8.34); it is only in Acts 1.9–11 that the ascension is described physically. At times Christ is said to sit down at God's right hand (Heb 1.3; 10.12) and at other times God is said to seat him (Acts 2.33–5; 5.31); the latter accords better

---

[22] On the connection see T. G. Allen, 'Exaltation and Solidarity with Christ: Ephesians 1.20 and 2.6', *JSNT* 28 (1986) 103–20; Ramaroson, art.cit.

with Ps 110.1 and fits the flow of the present passage. While Psalm 110[23] was probably not taken as messianic prior to Christianity, believers rapidly gave it this sense. It is the Psalm most frequently quoted or alluded to in the NT, especially in relation to the heavenly session, and was early associated with Ps 8 (see on v. 22). Whether Ps 110 originally created, shaped or was simply used to express belief in the heavenly session, by AE's time it was accepted as prophesying it and used to express it. Probably AE simply accepted from the tradition both the heavenly session and its connection with Ps 110, for he expresses the reference to the right hand of God through ἐν δεξιᾷ which is the normal phrase in the early Christian tradition though the LXX of the Psalm has ἐκ δεξιῶν.

The session at God's right hand is made more precise in two ways: (a) it is in the heavenlies (see Detached Note: The Heavenlies); (b) in the heavenlies Christ is above[24] the 'powers' (v. 21). 'Above' is a spatial term like 'in the heavenlies', 'right hand', and 'under' (v. 22). It is difficult to know whether AE took these spatial terms literally or metaphorically. Origen, probably influenced by Philo, is certainly aware of the problem. The association of 'aboveness' with a position of power is natural; a royal throne is set on a dais. So if Christ is set above some other beings he may be assumed to have power over them. His power and authority are also implied in the reference to the right hand. In the ancient world to be seated at the right hand was to be given the position of honour and the one who occupied it was the one closest in power to the one beside whom he sat, here God. The imagery involved, if it be imagery, is spatial rather than temporal. Since Christ already sits in the heavenlies he already has authority and power. The setting of the powers above the earth accords with AE's general view of the cosmos. In 4.10 Christ is above the heavens rather than in the heavenlies; the difference may be accounted for since 'heaven' was not a precisely defined term in the ancient world (see Detached Note: The Heavenlies); there is then no major inconsistency between 4.10 and 1.21.

21. The superiority[25] of Christ to the powers is depicted here in a

---

[23] On the use of the Psalm see SB IV, 452–60; Lindars, *Apologetic*, 45–51; Hahn, 101ff; D. M. Hay, *Glory at the Right Hand: Psalm 110 in Early Christianity* (SBLMS 18), Nashville and New York, 1973; M. Gourgues, *A la droite du Dieu. Résurrection de Jésus et actualisation du Psaume 110, 1 dans le Nouveau Testament*, Paris, 1978; W. R. G. Loader, 'Christ at the Right Hand—Ps CX.1 in the New Testament', *NTS* 24 (1978) 199–217.

[24] ὑπεράνω does not necessarily mean 'far above', since in Hellenistic Greek the addition of prepositions need not affect the meaning of the basic root, cf Heb 9.5; see BDR 215.2 n. 3.

[25] On ὑπεράνω see Carr, 98. The word shows that the area in which the powers exist is not Hades, underneath the earth; if that were their area there would have been no need to affirm that Christ was above them.

different manner from Phil 2.9–11; there those below Christ hail him as Lord. Only those whose subjection is willing and not the result of a forced defeat can offer a genuine and acceptable 'hailing' of Christ. However, in Eph 1.21 defeat is probably envisaged for there would be no point in referring to Christ's ascension as one indicating superiority to good angels; that would be obvious. The powers are then to be regarded as hostile; only in overcoming hostile powers would Christ's might be displayed (Mussner, *Christus*, 21). This conclusion is confirmed by the language of v. 22. But does that not create a conflict with 1.10? The summing up of all things in Christ suggests a willing submission rather than the subjection of hostile elements. The NT in fact contains two strains of thought (see on 1.10): a belief that Christ conquered the powers; a belief that all who oppose him will eventually be won over. That the latter view only emerges briefly at various points in church history and is always speedily overcome by the former in ecclesiastical thought is not surprising, but does nothing to invalidate its truth.

Four 'titles'[26] are applied here to the powers but there is no need in view of the following phrase to see in that an attempt at their exhaustive enumeration (four winds, four points of the compass, etc.; compare the use of 'four' in Revelation). Equally we should not suppose that they are set in either a descending or ascending order of importance. In 1 Cor 15.24ff the subjection of the powers is in process and not yet complete but has a purpose, that God may be all in all; in vv. 21f the subjection is already complete and is an end in itself (Lindemann). Since AE is not sure he has named all the powers or classes of powers (the names he gives are not standard definitions) he adds a clause to ensure none has been excluded. Had he not done so, some of his readers who knew them by other names might have worried if the powers they knew had in fact been overcome; we may compare the way in which in some magical spells a whole series of gods or demons is invoked by name in case the omission of one name should cause the spell to fail. The clause is not a scornful rejection of the powers as if they had no real existence nor does it indicate their worth or value. In the ancient world a name was more than a verbal symbol; it was believed to have a genuine relation to the reality to which it was attached;[27] to know the name of a demon gave power over it (Gen 2.19f; Mk 5.9). In the Philippian hymn God gives Christ a new name, Lord, indicating a new position of superiority. By listing names and

---

[26] That three of the 'titles' are the same as those of Col 1.16 does not indicate dependence on Colossians since the titles were in general use and Col 1.16 is a part of the Colossian hymn to which AE might have had direct access apart from Colossians.

[27] See H. Bietenhard, *TWNT* V, 242–83; C. A. Schmitz, K. Baltzer, B. Reicke, *RGG* IV, 1301–6; H. Bietenhard and F. F. Bruce, *NIDNTT*, II, 648–56.

implying there are other names for the powers, AE is not however claiming that knowledge of names gives Christians superiority to the powers but saving his readers from possible doubts. It is Christ alone who has superiority. In this it has been assumed that 'naming' a power is the same as invoking that power but from where did the powers originally get their names? Allen[28] suggests the powers were given their names by God, indicating their inferiority to him. If God gave the powers their names and if he sent Christ, then Christ's superiority to them is the more certain. If God, not Christ, gave the powers their names then this makes it unlikely that Christ is here regarded as the Second Adam giving names as did the first Adam.

The final clause of the verse does not qualify παντός as if suggesting where the unnamed powers may be found, but qualifies all that precedes it in the verse. Christ is above the four named powers and any others that may exist, whether belonging to this age or the age to come. αἰών (see on 2.2) can be taken either spatially (= world) or temporally (= age); even though most of the imagery in vv. 20f is spatial, because of the associated τῷ μέλλοντι it almost certainly has temporal significance here (*pace* Haupt, Scott). The first Christians derived the doctrine of the two ages from Jewish apocalyptic but modified it since the Messiah with whom the coming age was associated had already come. The reference to the coming age is a little strange here since Ephesians has on the whole a realised eschatology (cf Introduction §6.4) and since Christ is already above all the powers; the phrase, though not in Paul, is found in Mt 12.32 (cf Heb 6.5) and has probably been drawn from the liturgical or catechetical tradition (cf Lindemann, *Aufhebung*, 210). Such tradition tends to be conservative and to continue to employ phrases after their original significance has been abandoned. AE probably therefore uses a well-known phrase without seeking to align it with his general eschatological position. Whether this is so or not, he is certainly asserting that Christ rules the powers now and will continue to do so; there are no limits to his rule (Steinmetz, 60f). Believers need not fear the powers since they are already delivered, at least potentially, from them, though they still need to wage war against them (6.12), a war for which they are divinely equipped.

DETACHED NOTE III
THE POWERS

O. Everling, *Die paulinische Angelologie und Dämonologie*, Göttingen, 1888; M. Dibelius, *Die Geisterwelt im Glauben des Paulus*, Göttingen,

[28] T. G. Allen, 'God the Namer: A Note on Ephesians 1.21b', *NTS* 32 (1986) 470–5.

1909; Mussner, *Christus*, 18–27; G. H. C. MacGregor, 'Principalities and Powers: The Cosmic Background of Paul's Thought', *NTS* 1 (1954/5) 17–28; G. B. Caird, *Principalities and Powers*, Oxford, 1956; C. D. Morrison, *The Powers That Be*, London, 1960; H. Schlier, *Principalities and Powers in the New Testament*, Freiburg, 1961; U. Bianchi, 'Cristo e le "potenze" (archai ed exousia)', *Asprenas* 16 (1969) 315–21; M. H. Scharlemann, 'The Secret of God's Plan: Studies in Ephesians—Study Three', *CTM* 41 (1970) 338–46; J. Michl, *RAC* V, 53ff; P. Schäfer, *Rivalität zwischen Engeln und Menschen*, Berlin, 1975; J. Y. Lee, 'Interpreting the demonic powers in Pauline thought', *NT* 12 (1979) 54–69; Stott, 267–75; Carr, *passim*; R. Yates, 'The Powers of Evil in the New Testament', *EvQ* 52 (1980) 97–111; P. T. O'Brien, 'Principalities and Powers and their Relationship to Structures', *RefTR* 40 (1981) 1–10; P. Benoit, 'Pauline Angelology and Demonology', *RelSB* 3 (1983) 1–18; Wink, *passim*; P. T. O'Brien, 'Principalities and Powers: Opponents of the Church', *Biblical Interpretation and the Church* (ed. D. A. Carson), Exeter, 1984; Arnold, 41–69, 103–22, 129–34; id. 'The "Exorcism" of Ephesians 6.12 in Recent Research: A Critique of Wesley Carr's View of the Role of Evil Powers in First-Century AD Belief', *JSNT* 30 (1987) 71–87; Faust, 459ff; G. Van Rheenen, 'Cultural Conceptions of Power in Biblical Perspective', *Missiology* 21 (1933) 41–53.

Prior to Ephesians Paul had employed terms similar to those of 1.21 (Rom 8.38f; 1 Cor 2.6–8; 15.24–8; and perhaps Gal 4.9); these had been taken up in Colossians (1.16; 2.9f, 13–15). AE did not then invent the terms of 1.21 and we do not need to trace their origin. It is in fact obscure. The names suggest beings with authority. It is probable that Paul derived both the terms and the ideas which they represent from Judaism, although similar ideas, if designated with different terms, existed in the Hellenistic world as the many references to them in the Fathers and in gnostic writings show (*Hyp Arch* II, 4 86.21–5; 92.22ff; *Exeg Soul* II, 6 131.9–13; *Apoc Paul* V, 2 19.3f; 23.20–2; *Auth Teach* V, 3 28.32–4; *Teach Silv* VII, 4 114.1–10; 117.14–16; *Ep Pet Phil* VIII, 2 135.2; 137.10–17, 22–9; *Melch* IX, 1 20.22–3; *Testim Truth* IX, 3 32.27f; 59.9f). It came naturally to both Fathers and gnostics to use them. There were of course other names for supernatural beings in Judaism in addition to those in Ephesians (cf *1 En* 61.10f; *2 En* 20–2). Given AE's adoption of the terms the number of times he refers to them suggests that they were important for him or that he believed them important to his readers. Satan was originally an angel in the heavenly court and these supernatural powers were believed, at least by some, to inhabit the air or heaven (2.2; *1 En* 61.10).

To what then did AE take them to refer and to what did his readers? In considering this we have to realise that while a word or title may be used throughout a period the understanding of its referent may alter. 'Satan' remained a name in Judaism but though originally referring to an angel at the court of Yahweh (Job 1.6ff) it came to designate the supernatural opponent of God. The referents of AE's terms were in Judaism: (a) political, in the widest sense, persons or bodies, those people or bodies who control other people and bodies; (b) supernatural beings who exercise or attempt to exercise control over one another and over the created world including humanity. 'Supernatural' is used here for lack of a better word; in the ancient world the natural and supernatural were not clearly distinguished as with us but closely interwoven. In the messages to the seven churches (Rev 2.1–3.22) the angel of each church is addressed, yet it is the church itself which hears the message and is summoned to take action. Folk angels and the nations to which they were attached were similarly capable of being confused. In this way basically political terms can be applied to spiritual powers. In their earliest use the terms of 1.21 appear to have referred to good supernatural beings, in so far as they referred to such beings at all; however as in the case of Satan they came in time to denote evil supernatural beings, and this change took place prior to Paul (cf Wink, 151ff). The myth of the fallen angels probably contributed to this change. Within Judaism we encounter demons who require to be exorcised (cf 1 Sam 16.14; 18.10–12; 19.8–10 and the Gospel exorcism stories) and spirits associated with Satan (e.g. 1QM). That these two aspects cannot be considered separately is seen in the phrase 'unclean spirits' which can denote both demons and associates of Satan.

The Jews and the first Jewish Christians saw their lives as affected by, if not under the control of, both hostile supernatural beings and earthly rulers and governments. It is this which may have led them to apply terms like ἀρχαί and ἄρχοντες to the evil supernatural powers. Assisting this identification would have been Jewish belief in folk angels. The latter might be regarded as friendly or hostile as the nations over which they were placed were friendly or hostile to Israel. Such a view is supported by the ambiguity of 1 Cor 2.6–8. If the terms came into use in some such way this would account for their application to both friendly and hostile powers. Carr, 45ff, has disputed this, arguing that in the NT they always refer to friendly powers, being the angels that surround God's throne and worship him. In arguing for this he is forced to deny that Eph 6.12 belongs to the original text of Ephesians (there is no textual evidence to support his claim) and is involved in some most contorted analysis of particular texts (e.g. Col 2.15) so as to remove from them any reference to hostile beings. Carr's methodology is incorrect; had he begun with Eph 6.12 he could easily have accommodated the other passages to it with much simpler exegesis.[29] We shall simply assume that hostile powers are referred to in

[29] For criticism of Carr see Arnold, *JSNT* 30 (1987) 71–87; R. A. Wild, 'The Warrior and the Prisoner: Some Reflections on Ephesians 6:10–20', *CBQ* 46 (1984) 284–98; Wink, 23–6.

Eph 1.21f; 2.2; 3.10; 6.12 and probably also in 4.8 (see notes on these passages); Col 2.15, 18; 1 Cor 15.24–8. We leave aside the στοιχεῖα of Gal 4.3, 9; Col 2.8, 20 because it is by no means certain that these refer to spiritual powers; we also assume that only 'earthly' rulers are intended in Rom 13.1–3. In Col 1.16 Christ is said to create the powers; this does not entail their friendliness; in Judaism, and Christianity, there is no ultimate dualism; Satan did not come into existence apart from God; hostile angelic powers must have also had their origin in him. Like Satan they may have been originally thought of as non-evil. The hymn of Col 1.15–20 ends with a reconciliation of all to Christ; there is no reason to conclude the 'all' of v. 20 excludes the powers of 1.16; if they require to be reconciled they must have been to some extent hostile. In the Philippian hymn, 2.6–11, the final result of Christ's work is that everything in heaven, on earth and under the earth bows down to him; if so, there must have been a time when they did not bow, a time when some of them must have been hostile.

When the Hellenistic readers of Ephesians heard the terms of 1.21 what came into their minds? Clearly they may have thought of political and social power in its many forms. That can hardly have been all, though some older exegetes did attempt to sustain this position. The terms do not normally have a supernatural reference in Greek and this must therefore have been carried over from Jewish Christianity. Of what then did Jewish Christians, and later Gentile Christians, think when they heard the words? It is impossible to be precise. There is no doubt they believed in all kinds of supernatural evil. Paul views the opponents who seek to undo his work in Corinth as controlled by Satan (2 Cor 11.13–15); so also Luke (22.3) and John (13.2) regard Judas as controlled by him. There were demons who made people sick and needed to be exorcised; the exorcism accounts would not have been so carefully preserved if this had not been a problem as much in the Hellenistic world as in the Jewish; Mark indeed added 9.28f to the account of an exorcism in order to teach his readers how to deal with the supernatural; the demon of the storm (Mk 4.39) requires to be rebuked. Paul personalises law, sin, death, the flesh and so turns them into supernatural forces, but this does not mean that we should 'internalise' the powers and transform them into psychological forces. The power of the state is regarded as friendly in Rom 13.1–7 but not in Rev 13 where its hostility is traced to supernatural forces. In addition to this, magic with its dependence on supernatural force was an ever-present reality in the Hellenistic world (e.g. Acts 19.19). It was easy to explain the forces operating in it as demonic (Justin, *Apol* I 56). Christians had to account for idolatry and they claimed the gods whom others worshipped were demons (1 Cor 11.20). In so far as the emperors became the objects of a cult, they will have been seen as an evil supernatural influence with the double understanding of 'ruler' as heavenly and earthly. The pagan gods were related to the stars as were the powers (Rom 8.38f), and astrology was an ever-present and potent factor in directing behaviour. Fate, in so far as the Greek world saw it as controlling life, was supernatural and so could be taken to be a power. Many of these ideas came to be more clearly stated in the second century, in particular the astrological connections of the powers and the demonic understanding of pagan worship. That does not mean that these connections were not being made at the time of Ephesians. Any or all of the forces which perverted the good and even course of the universe and, in particular, made life difficult for Christians could be seen as supernatural. These did not need to be identified with specific names, as AE indicates when he adds to his list in 1.21 the reference to other 'names'.

There are inconsistencies between the various references to the powers in the NT. We have already dealt with one apparent inconsistency (creation by God) in relation to Col 1.16. A more significant inconsistency exists in relation to the time when the powers are overcome. In 1 Cor 15.24–8 they become subject to Christ at the parousia while in Rom 8.38f Christians are assured they need not fear them now. In Col 2.14f they are already defeated because they have been nailed to the cross (cf Col 1.20; Jn 12.31; 16.11) but in Eph 1.21f their defeat follows on the ascension of Christ. Christian thought was in process of formation at this period and consistency should not be expected. All the passages agree in seeing the defeat of the powers as related to the Christ-event. Though the powers have been defeated (Eph 1.20f) their influence has still to be fought (Eph 6.10ff). This apparent contradiction within Ephesians is part both of the inconsistency in relation to the time of their defeat and of a general biblical tension and similar to that of the indicative–imperative contrast. Christians are sons and daughters of God, therefore they should behave as such. The power of death has been destroyed, yet Christians still die. Granted Christ's victory over the powers Christians are not subject to them in the same way as they were prior to conversion for they are now equipped with spiritual weapons (Eph 6.10ff) with which to fight them. Just as those who are called to be children receive the Spirit so those who know of the defeat of Satan and his powers receive the means to fight him.

It is not part of the purpose of this commentary to explain the powers in twentieth-century terms either as political, social and economic forces, or as the power of tradition, ethical custom, race, or as psychological psychoses or forces like sex within us which we cannot control. Even if we were able to explain the powers in this kind of way in respect of some NT passages, it is not possible to do so for Ephesians for in it the powers are related to heaven (1.20f; 3.10; 6.12; cf Stott, 272f). For AE's readers the powers are supernatural and cannot be reduced to, and explained in, natural terms. Yet even if some in the West today do not believe in such supernatural powers it is necessary to remember that there remain those in the West and in other parts of the world who do. Though the powers may be connected to the heavenlies and thus to the stars and can therefore be regarded as controlling the lives of people, there is however an important difference between those who believed in them in the first century and those who read astrological columns in newspapers and magazines today; in the ancient world a real relationship was believed to exist between the stars and the gods; astrology was then a part of religion in a way it is not for the normal Westerner interested in astrology today.

This is not to deny that people today do not at times feel themselves frustrated by forces over which they have no control; these forces may be political or economic; they may be part of the culture and ethos in which they live. People may believe themselves under the uncontrollable power of a lust for food or sex, or the desire to have more and more possessions or power over others. They may see their jobs as controlled by remote financial forces or their lives as unfulfilled because of a faulty gene. They may be ambitious to perform tasks for which their physique renders them incapable; a five-foot, seven-stone young man will never be an international rugby-football forward; a woman lacking imaginative power will never be a successful novelist. People are affected by events that without their consent intrude into their lives. They may be destroyed by an accidental infusion of blood from someone who was HIV positive. They may die young without realising their full potential. In other words the same kind of tragedies happen to us as happened in the ancient world, but we attribute them to natural and not supernatural causes; we seek rational, not magical, explanations for them and, in so far as it is possible, scientific means for their cure.

This in an odd way shows up the difficulty of understanding 1.20–3. While AE and his readers might in some way accept the concept that supernatural beings are already subject to Christ their conqueror, we cannot understand, to take an example, the car accident in which some innocent person dies as an event subject to Christ; it is a stubborn fact and it and others like it will go on recurring while the world lasts. Once we have transformed spiritual beings into facts and observable forces we cannot see them as already overcome by Christ. Again it is difficult for us to take seriously the idea that the church proclaims the wisdom of God (3.10) to facts and observable forces. On the other hand when we encounter unpleasant facts and forces we may be able to face them

better if we equip ourselves with the spiritual armour offered in
6.14–17. It is probably therefore wrong to attempt to transform the
powers into anything which we can observe and measure, though
many of the things we can observe and measure affect us in
unexpected ways.

22. Roberts[30] regards vv. 22f as a transition section between the prayer
and the body of the letter alleging that there are similar transition passages
in the other Pauline letters at this point and that the transitional passages are
credal statements using language familiar to the readers. Whatever may be
true of the other Pauline letters it is difficult to compare Ephesians with
them if Ephesians is not by Paul and, more importantly, even if it is, it may
not be a letter (cf Introduction §7). It is true that v. 22 contains credal-type
statements and the change from participles to finite verbs in it may suggest
the use of preformed material, but v. 23 does not appear to be credal
and there is no reason to suppose that vv. 22f ever existed as an independent
unit (see Introduction to this section). It cannot be both transitional and
credal for it makes no reference to one central credal feature, the death of
Jesus, a feature which is found both in what precedes and what follows it.
As for its transitional nature, this may be true but in a continuous argument
any section forms a transition between the preceding paragraph and the
next.

(iii) The remaining two main statements of vv. 20–3 are
expressed with finite verbs and not participles as in v. 20, the change
being occasioned perhaps by the lengthy intervention of v. 21 or by
dependence on credal material which was expressed with finite
verbs. The central thought continues to be God's action in relation to
Christ. If Christ sits at God's right hand (v. 20), a position of
authority, then the universe has been made subject to him and this is
now expressed with a vivid metaphor drawn from Ps 8.6[31] which
continues the spatial imagery (Lindemann, *Aufhebung*, 211). What
applied originally to 'man' is especially applicable to the Son of
man (cf Heb 2.6f); it is very questionable if AE is attempting to say,
as Robinson suggests, that Christ fulfils human destiny, though of
course this may be true. Christ has, as it were, his foot placed
triumphantly not only on the necks of the powers but on everything
within the universe. It is not sufficient to say (v. 21) that Christ is
superior to the powers in the same way as a duke is to an earl, for
the earl may not be subject to the duke though the latter ranks
higher. The powers are not merely inferior to Christ, they are subject
to him. Ps 8.6 is used also at 1 Cor 15.27; Heb 2.6–8. Ps 110.1 is
also quoted in 1 Cor 15.25 and the Psalm is cited regularly in

[30] J. H. Roberts, 'Belydenisuitsprake as Pauliniese briefoorgange', *Hervormde
Teologiese Studies* 44 (1988) 81–97.
[31] On Ps 8 see F. J. Moloney, 'The Targum on Ps. 8 and the New Testament',
Salesianum 37 (1976) 326–36.

Hebrews; Ps 110 and Ps 8 were then probably linked early in Christian thought, even prior to Paul, and given messianic significance (it is thus unnecessary for us to ask whether either possessed this in Jewish thought).[32] Although Ps 110.1 also refers to 'feet' it is likely that their mention here comes from Ps 8.6 rather than Ps 110.1 because Ps 8.6 refers to 'all' but Ps 110.1 only to 'enemies'. Ps 110.1 might also suggest a subjection lying in the future while Ps 8.6 (aorist tense) places it firmly in the past. 1 Cor 15.24–7 and Eph 1.20–3 have a number of common features (use of Ps 110, the 'powers', quotation of Ps 8.6 in a form differing from that of the LXX), but these similarities are insufficient to imply dependence of Ephesians on 1 Corinthians (cf Gnilka, etc.) for there are also important differences; 1 Cor 15.23ff concentrates on the sequence of events within the End, Eph 1.22 on the totality of Christ's lordship; unlike 1 Cor 15, Eph 1.22 represents a realised eschatology in keeping with other parts of the letter (see on 1.10); in Eph 1.22f God is the subject while in 1 Cor 15.20–8 it is Christ. If direct dependence is excluded, it can be said that AE is indebted to the same tradition as Paul, a tradition also reflected in 1 Pet 3.22; Phil 2.5–11. Miletic, 79ff, argues for the actual dependence of Eph 1.19–23 on 1 Cor 15.20–8 and goes on to deduce that since the latter features the first and second Adam the former should also. If however there is no direct dependence, but both passages use the same tradition, there is no need to deduce the presence of the first and second Adam in the background of Ephesians at this point. AE does not identify the nature of the subjection; the Psalm quotation implies its present existence as fact and that it is both total and absolute (Belser); yet as we go on through the letter we find that all is not subject to Christ for evil still exists to perplex believers.

(iv) The fourth (καί is probably not to be taken epexegetically with Lindemann, *Aufhebung*, 212, 'in that') and final action of God (v. 22b) introduces the church and relates Christ to it; with this half verse we begin one of the most difficult sections (vv. 22b–3) of the letter. God has given Christ (αὐτόν is emphatic by position) as, or 'to be', head of the church; 'head' may be taken as in apposition or predicatively; there is little difference in meaning. There are two difficulties: (1) In biblical Greek δίδωμι can mean not only 'give' but also 'appoint, instal' (cf Barth, Bouwman, etc.). If given the latter sense here we should expect the genitive ἐκκλησίας; moreover the translation 'gave' contrasts well with v. 22a (Du Plessis, 71). Irrespective of the meaning of δίδωμι nothing suggests AE thought

---

[32] Cf W. Schmithals, *Theologiegeschichte*, 52–69; J. Lambrecht, 'Paul's Christological Use of Scripture in 1 Corinthians 15, 20–28', in his *Pauline Studies* (BETL 115), Leuven, 1994, 125–49.

of the church as a pre-existing entity to which at some point Christ was given or appointed (see Essay: The Church §5). The four actions of God in vv. 20, 22 are not temporally successive but simultaneous. Christ's body could not exist before he did. (2) How is ὑπὲρ πάντα related to its clause? Without it 'head' could not be taken straightforwardly in relation to 'body (v. 23) as in Col 1.18. In order to preserve this meaning some (e.g. Barth, 157f) give the phrase a basically adjectival significance, 'supreme head', instancing the absence of the article; but the word was anarthrous in the quotation in v. 22a and so πάντα here may well refer back to πάντα there and the article be unnecessary (cf Gnilka, Schlier, Masson). In addition if AE is saying Christ is 'supreme head' this implies a comparison with some other head; but what other head could be in mind? πάντα is therefore to be given the same reference in both v. 22a and v. 22b. This means that despite the absence of the article with κεφαλήν the headship of 22a is that over the cosmos[33] and Christ has a cosmic position.

Why has 'head' been introduced here? (On 'head' see Detached Note: The Body of Christ). It is unlikely to be a recollection of 1.10 where it was not the main element in ἀνακεφαλαιόω. It has a natural association with 'body' (v. 23). Head, body and church already form a group; all three appear in Col 1.18 and two of them in Col 1.24; 2.19. Was then 'head' introduced to prepare for the reference to 'body' in v. 23? This would be a satisfactory solution if the headship intended was that over the church and not that over the cosmos. 'Head' might derive from what has preceded; Christ has been set out as Lord of all; it is a short step from this to view him as head of all with the reference to 'feet' influencing the choice of 'head' rather than 'Lord' to express this.[34] It is possible Christ's headship over both cosmos and church is in mind.[35] God in his graciousness has given the Christ, the cosmic head, to the church and he is then naturally its head; the nature of that headship is not worked out here but comes later in 4.15f; 5.22f. It is certainly not simply one of overlordship as with the cosmos, for that would not entail the church being his body. The church, however, for its part might be said to come under Christ's cosmic headship in view of its organic union with him (cf Caird). Yet the headship of Christ over it would be different. See Detached Note: The Body of Christ, and Essay: The Church.

1.22f might be thought to be derived from Col 1.17–19, 24; 2.9f since there are a number of words in common, yet words that come close together

[33] Cf R. Penna, 'La proiezione dell'esperienza communitaria sul plano storico (Ef. 2,11–22) e cosmico (Ef. 1,20–23)', *RivBiblt* 26 (1978) 163–86.
[34] So G. Howard, 'The Head/Body Metaphors of Ephesians', *NTS* 20 (1973/4) 350–6.
[35] Cf Warnach, in Schlier–Warnach, 12; Pokorný, *Gnosis*, 70–6.

in 1.22f are not close together in Colossians; κεφαλή in Col 1.17–19 is a part of a pre-Colossian tradition and therefore may have been accessible to AE apart from Colossians. πλήρωμα while found in Col 2.9 is used differently from Eph 1.23; Col 1.24 speaks of the body which is the church but Eph 1.22f of the church which is the body. There is no need then to see AE's dependence here on Colossians.

23. The difficulties of this verse have long been recognised.[36] There are three basic interrelated problems: (i) How does the pleroma clause relate to the rest of vv. 22, 23? (ii) What is the meaning of pleroma? (iii) How are we to take the participle πληρουμένου? However, before we turn to these questions we must look at the brief introductory clause. Paul had already identified the church with the body of Christ in Romans and Corinthians and while in those epistles it is not entirely clear if the body of Christ denotes the whole church or individual congregations, this ambiguity has disappeared in Ephesians where it is applied to the whole church; in Colossians it is applied to both local congregation and the whole church (see Essay: The Church). Is however v. 23a parenthetical or part of the main argument?[37] This brings us to question (i).

Does the pleroma clause relate directly to v. 23a and be in apposition to σῶμα (the majority of modern commentators) or does it refer back to v. 22, in which case it might be in apposition to either ἐκκλησία (this would be very little different in meaning from the former suggestion) or αὐτόν?[38] The last is rendered

[36] On v. 23 and πλήρωμα see Robinson, 255–9; A. E. N. Hitchcock, 'Ephesians i.23', *ExpT* 22 (1910/11) 91; F. R. Montgomery-Hitchcock, 'The Pleroma as the Medium of the Self-Realisation of Christ', *Expositor*, Ser 8, XIV, 1932, 135–50; id. 'The Pleroma of Christ', *CQR* 125 (1937) 1–18; Schmid, 182–93; C. F. D. Moule, 'A Note on Ephesians i.22, 23', *ExpT* 60 (1948/9) 53; id. '"Fullness" and "Fill" in the New Testament', *SJT* 4 (1951) 79–86; Gewiess; S. Aalen, 'Begrepet πλήρωμα i Kolosser- of Efeserbrevet', *Saertrykk an Tidsskrift for Teologi og Kirke* (1952) 49–67; Mussner, *Christus*, 45–61; Best, *One Body*, 139–44; A. Feuillet, 'L'Église plérôme du Christ d'après Éphés., 1,23', *NRT* 78 (1956) 449–72, 593–610; P. Benoit, 'Corps, tête et plérôme dans les épîtres de la captivité', *RB* 63 (1956) 5–44; id. 'The "pleroma" in the Epistles to the Colossians and the Ephesians', *SEA* 49 (1984) 136–58; Du Plessis, 71–8; Roels, 229–48; A. R. McGlashan, 'Ephesians i.23', *ExpT* 76 (1964/5) 132f; R. Fowler, 'Ephesians i.23', *ExpT* 76 (1964/5) 294; M. Bogdasavich, 'The idea of the Pleroma in the Epistles to the Colossians and the Ephesians', *DR* (1965) 119–30; R. Hermans and L. Geysels, 'Efesiers 1,23: Het pleroma van Gods Heilswerk', *Bijdragen* 28 (1967) 279–93; J. Ernst, 'Das Wachstum des Leibes Christi zur eschatologischen Erfüllung im Pleroma', *TGl* 53 (1967) 164–87; id. *Pleroma und Pleroma Christi*, Regensburg, 1970, 105–20; R. Yates, 'A Re-examination of Ephesians 1.23', *ExpT* 83 (1971/2) 146–51; Merklein, *Amt*, 70–3; Lindemann, *Aufhebung*, 204–17; R. P. Meyer, 26–48; 60–3; P. D. Overfield, 'Pleroma: A Study in Content and Context', *NTS* 25 (1978/9) 384–96; Meuzelaar, 121–46; I. de la Potterie, 'Le Christ, Plérôme de l'Église (Ep 1,22–23)', *RB* 58 (1977) 500–24.
[37] Synge takes the clause to be a gloss without supporting manuscript evidence; this appears to be no more than an attempt to avoid the problems of the verse.
[38] So Moule, art.cit. *SJT*; Hitchcock, art.cit.; de la Potterie, art.cit.; Caird.

difficult by the remoteness of the clause from αὐτόν and is clumsy since κεφαλήν is already in apposition to the pronoun; it would also imply that what is being explained is the nature of Christ but, unlike Colossians, our letter is much more concerned with ecclesiology than christology.

Questions (ii) and (iii) are closely linked and we turn to (iii) first. πληρουμένου (note the number of words in v. 23b whose first letter is π) can be either middle or passive; if middle it might have an active meaning; the use of the middle for the active is not unusual in Greek (e.g. Col 4.1, παρέχεσθε, 2.15, ἀπεκδυσάμενος; cf MHT, 54–6; BDR §316; Moule, 24–6). We might then conclude that AE has used the middle for the active (so Schnackenburg, Gnilka and many others), were it not that when he needs to use the active of this verb in 4.10 he does so and that the middle never appears in the NT or the LXX.[39] If it has an active sense τὰ πάντα would naturally be its direct object in view of its previous use. It then becomes difficult to find a meaning for ἐν πᾶσιν other than one of intensification (Van Roon, *Authenticity*, 236). Many therefore take τὰ πάντα as an accusative of respect, yet even among those who do so there is little agreement as to the interpretation of πᾶσιν. Attempts to give the participle a true middle significance have not been successful. It is then wiser to accept it as a passive.

The Versions, except Peshitta, and the Fathers, apart from Theodoret and Oecumenius (cf more recently de la Potterie, art. cit., Benoit, art. cit., *SEA*), take it as a passive; that it rarely appears in the NT as a present passive (Roels, 246) hardly seems relevant if the form exists. As a passive it means someone or something (it can be either masc. or neut.) is being filled with someone or something. De la Potterie argues that when the verb is used passively elsewhere in the Pauline corpus it always refers to the filling of human beings (Rom 1.29; 15.14; 2 Cor 7.4; Phil 1.11; 4.18; Eph 3.19; 5.18; Col 1.9; 2.10) and never to the filling of Christ or God. The final part of that statement is true, but in Rom 8.4; 2 Cor 10.6; Gal 5.14 things and not humans are being filled so that the first part is not true. No reason exists then to create an absolute rule about the object of the filling. There is however nothing to exclude Jesus being regarded here as a human subject, for in 1.20–3 and 2.1–6 a parallel is drawn between what God has done in Christ and what he has done in human beings. We cannot then exclude the use of the passive with reference to Christ. Moreover elsewhere in the NT Christ is spoken of as 'full of grace and truth' (Jn 1.14) and of the Holy Spirit (Lk 4.1); in Col 2.3, though the verb is not used, it is said that all the treasures of wisdom and knowledge are hidden in him and this idea is very much the same; in 1 Cor 1.24 he is said to be the wisdom of

---

[39] So Hermans and Geysels, art.cit.; de la Potterie, art.cit.

God which must mean that God's wisdom fills him. In Col 1.19; 2.9
all the fullness of God dwells in Christ and this is again very much
the same idea. There is then no reason why we should not
understand the participle as meaning Christ is being filled. In that
case τὰ πάντα ἐν πᾶσιν must be taken adverbially, 'totally', without
any exception (Moule, 160). God cannot be taken as the object of
the filling for he fills and is not filled.

If then Christ is being filled, with what or whom is he being
filled? This is not stated. In Col 1.19; 2.9 it is God who is said to
dwell in him. Given this, it is not difficult[40] to see AE conceiving of
Christ as being totally filled with God (the 'totally' representing the
πᾶν of Col 1.19; 2.9), though it would also be possible to view him
as filled with every grace and blessing. The present participle would
indicate a constant filling, and thus a dynamic rather than a static
relation between Christ and God, and the adverbial phrase would
obviate any idea that Christ was inadequately related to God.

Before leaving consideration of the participle we note that de la Potterie
has used his rejection of a 'human' reference to argue for the participle as a
neuter substantive referring to σῶμα[41] with τὸ πλήρωμα as in apposition to
αὐτόν and v. 23a as parenthetical. Christ then becomes both the fullness of
the church and its head. He supports this theory with three further
arguments: (a) Elsewhere in Ephesians and Colossians pleroma relates not
to the church but to Christ. Yet all that is said in Col 1.19; 2.9; Eph 3.19 is
that 'all the pleroma' dwells in Christ; this is not to equate the pleroma with
Christ; if pleroma is to be equated with anyone here it is surely with God
rather than Christ; Moreover there is no proper relation of pleroma to Christ
in 1.10. The only clear example of this is in 4.13. In 1.23 however, Christ
fills the cosmos and not the church, and his relation to the church differs
from that to the cosmos; this is an insufficient basis for identifying Christ
and the pleroma. (b) He detects a balanced literary structure. V. 22a divides
into two phrases; he subjected all things/under his feet; so also does v. 22b:
and gave him as head/over all to the church; v. 23a is parenthetical but
balanced clauses are found again in v. 23b: the fullness/of that which is
continually filled in it and in each of its members. However, these final two
balancing clauses lose the rhythm because of their great disparity in length
and the balance of the second pair of phrases in v. 22b does not exist if
'head over all' is a unit. The structure does not then possess the balance
suggested. (c) His third argument derives from the general style of
Ephesians and it must be allowed that there is nothing in that style which
would necessitate the rejection of v. 23a as parenthetical and the assumption
that τὸ πλήρωμα stands in apposition to αὐτόν, though as we have argued it
may not be the easiest way of taking it. Finally if this theory is true we
would expect the participle to be feminine, for ἐκκλησία and not σῶμα is
the leading concept, the latter being found only in a parenthesis (cf
Schnackenburg).

[40] Cf Feuillet, art.cit., 458.
[41] Hermans and Geysels, art.cit., also take it as neuter but refer it to the work of
salvation.

Lightfoot[42] and others have argued that πλήρωμα must be taken passively because of the nature of its formation, but such a rule cannot be strictly enforced; only the context can determine in any instance whether such a formation is to be taken passively or actively. The word is found in the NT with a number of meanings. Appearing twice in Colossians (1.19; 2.19) and four times in Ephesians (1.10; 23; 3.19; 4.13) it is sometimes argued that in these epistles it has a technical meaning (Schlier, 97; contrast Roels, 234f) and this is often related to its origin. A number of sources have been suggested in respect of its origin:

(a) Gnosticism (so Schlier). The word is found as a technical term in some of the gnostic systems of the second century, in particular in Valentinianism. These references are too late to impart any certainty to the supposition that AE and A/Col borrowed the term from them; the reverse process is more likely and it would have been aided by the concept of God as filling the universe which is found in Greek philosophy, for gnosticism was syncretistic.

(b) A/Col may have found his opponents, who may or may not have been gnostics, using the term and turned it against them (so Lightfoot).[43] Mirror reading is always hazardous; because the *Haustafel* sets out behaviour for wholly Christian households, we cannot deduce that only such households existed in the communities to which AE wrote; the assumption that A/Col's opponents used the term is therefore gratuitous. What can be said is that assuming Col 1.15–20 was a hymn adopted by the author of Colossians then the word possessed a theological use prior to Colossians. If it has the same meaning in Ephesians, and this is not certain, and if Ephesians was in some way a general letter, then since AE does not define it, there is a good chance its theological usage would have been understood without explanation by a fairly wide circle of believers in Asia Minor who would have known the Colossian hymn. It was then already an accepted term before AE came to write, but that does not settle the question of its origin.

(c) Stoicism (so Benoit[44]). Here it is important to distinguish between the word and the concept. The word is not found in early or middle Stoicism[45] but appears in *CH* 16.3; 12.15; 6.4. However, the idea that 'God' fills all things with his presence so that the cosmos is completely full with no vacuum in it is a basic doctrine of Stoicism. Such an explanation of the term's origin is more appropriate to Colossians where the interest is cosmic than to Ephesians where it is ecclesiological, and Benoit devotes much more of his attention to Colossians. However, Stoic influence cannot be ignored, even if terms do not exactly correspond; if a concept is in wide use it can affect those thinking under its cultural influence with the result they may be the more ready to pick it up and use it even if not precisely in the way it has been previously used; 4.10 may show more Stoic influence than 1.23 where the filling of the cosmos is not in question. Stoics see a different

---

[42] J. B. Lightfoot, *Colossians*, 255–71.
[43] Cf Lightfoot, op.cit., 255–71.
[44] *SEA* 49 (1984) 136–58; cf J. Dupont, *Gnosis*, 453–71.
[45] Cf Ernst, *Pleroma*, 11; Overfield, art.cit., 309; van Roon, *Authenticity*, 229.

identification between 'God' and the universe than AE does between Christ and the church because for him Christ is both its head and source.

(d) Jewish Hellenism (Feuillet, Gnilka). The word is found in the LXX (e.g. Jer 8.16; Ezek 19.7) and in Philo (e.g. *Praem et Poen* 65, *Spec Leg* 2.200, 213), and the idea of God as filling the universe would be pre-Stoic in Jer 23.24 (LXX). Jewish Hellenism, in keeping with Judaism, however, clearly distinguished between God and the universe. Moreover since the term is used with both passive and active significance in Jewish Hellenism there is nothing here to assist us to settle this issue in respect of Ephesians.

From this it results that when we come to examine the meaning of pleroma in 1.23 we have to accept it as a term which was already in theological use but was also widely used without such significance. It is associated with its cognate verb at 1.23; 3.19; Col 2.9f and this suggests its meaning must be closely related to that of the verb. At 3.19; Col 1.19; 2.9 we have πᾶν τὸ πλήρωμα; since this phrase first appears in the Colossian hymn (1.19) and since it is partially redundant, for pleroma itself can carry the sense of totality, the phrase in distinction from the word may well be 'technical'. Conversely the absence of πᾶν τὸ at Eph 1.23; 4.13 may suggest non-technical usage. We cannot then begin from the assumption of a unitary meaning for the word in Ephesians (cf 1.10), let alone Ephesians and Colossians. In 4.13 the pleroma is that of Christ but in 3.19 that of God (cf Col 2.9; in Col 1.19 it is undefined). This suggests that the defining agent in 1.23 might be either Christ or God; it is in fact determined by the cognate participle whose subject (see above) is probably Christ.

One solution to the whole phrase of v. 23 sees Christ as completed by the church. The noun is given an active sense as 'completion' and viewed as in apposition to σῶμα; the participle is taken as passive and the final phrase is adverbial. This understanding was popular with the Fathers (e.g. Chrysostom, Oecumenius, Ambrosiaster), with some of the Reformers (Calvin, Beza) and more recently with many English-speaking scholars under the influence of Robinson. Head and body are a unit; a head is incomplete without a body; the church completes Christ. This interpretation does not transgress in any way the grammar of the verse. Objections to it are based on: (i) The lack of support for it elsewhere in Ephesians and in the NT; it is not possible to support it from Col 1.24 for its meaning (the church, or Paul, completes Christ's sufferings?) is too uncertain (see the commentaries) for the basing of any argument on it. (ii) The immediate context of Eph 1.23 does not favour the idea of the completion of Christ since the stress has been on Christ's greatness and it would be surprising if it was now said that he needed completion (Grosheide). (iii) Though head and body may form a whole, v. 22 did not refer to Christ's headship of the body but to his headship of the cosmos and it would be inappropriate to introduce the church as a completion of that headship. (iv) More generally in the biblical pattern it is people who are filled by God or Christ (e.g. Eph 3.19); they are never depicted as filling him. (v) If the church completes Christ it is difficult to see how he can be its head and the source of its life (4.16), and also love it and give himself for it (5.25). Some of the theological difficulty of the theory might seem to be taken away if 'complement' were substituted for 'completion'; head and body complement one another; the body is the instrument for the execution of the head's will. This again is not the way in which AE views the relation of head and body,[46] especially in this passage where we are not concerned with the activity of believers, either individually or as a whole, in the world.

Attempts have been made to overcome the objection to any idea of the church as the completion or complement of Christ by viewing Christ as an inclusive personality. According to Yates[47] Christ is being totally filled, i.e. made complete, as reconciled believers are incorporated into him. They are then his filling out or completion (pleroma) in the world as they represent him through his body the church. This is an ingenious solution but the introduction of believers as those who fill Christ comes from nowhere. When Christ and believers are brought together in relation to filling it is he who fills them (Col 2.10) and not they who fill him. More importantly there is no other place where the concept of inclusive or corporate personality is explained through the idea of 'filling'. The concept itself underlies a considerable area of biblical and primitive thought but those for whom it is a part of their culture never need to explain it with words; it is modern Westerners with their much more individualistic approach to personality who require words like 'fill' to envisage what the concept means. An inclusive personality is not 'filled' with others; he is others.

There is no easy solution to the exegesis of v. 23. All that can be said is that it is probably best to take both the participle and pleroma as passive and the clause as in apposition to σῶμα; then the pleroma is filled by the subject of the participle who is Christ and who is himself being filled by God. Christ is both head to the church and fills it as his pleroma. As we go on to examine other passages in which AE explains his concept of the church as Christ's body, we shall see that this interpretation is not inconsistent with them. Presumably AE has introduced pleroma as a further explanation of the relation of Christ and the church to obviate any idea of the body being interpreted primarily in a 'political' sense, as a collection of members working together for a common purpose, and to root his

[46] Cf Roels, 242; Percy, *Leib*, 50, n. 93.
[47] Art.cit.; cf Overfield, *Ascension*, 189–203.

concept of Christian community firmly in christology. The fullness
is an accomplished fact, as is the existence of the church. Yet in 3.19
AE prays for the fullness. He is moving towards a realised
eschatology but has not completely departed from the more traditional eschatology (cf his attitude to the powers in v. 21 and 6.10ff).
Finally we note that the implicit question of v. 19 as to the greatness
of God's power has now been answered and the 'hope of your
calling' explained.

DETACHED NOTE IV
THE BODY OF CHRIST

Schlier, *Christus*, 37–48; id. *TWNT*, III, 672–82; Käsemann, 137ff; Percy,
Leib; Hanson, 113–16; Mussner, *Christus*, 118–74; S. Bedale, 'The
Meaning of κεφαλή in the Pauline Epistles', *JTS* 5 (1954) 211–15; P.
Benoit, 'Corps, tête et plérôme dans les épîtres de la captivité', *RB* 63
(1956) 5–44; J. Reuss, 'Die Kirche als "Leib Christi" und die Herkunft
dieser Vorstellung bei dem Apostel Paulus', *BZ* 2 (1958) 103–27; P.
Pokorný, 'Σῶμα Χριστοῦ im Epheserbrief', *EvT* 20 (1960) 456–64; H.
Hegermann, 'Zur Ableitung der Leib-Christi-Vorstellung', *TLZ* 85 (1960)
839–42; C. Colpe, 'Zur Leib-Christi-Vorstellung im Epheserbrief', *Juden-
tum, Urchristentum, Kirche* (FS J. Jeremias, ed. W. Eltester, BZNW 26),
Berlin, 1960, 172–87; B. A. Ahern, 'The Christian's Union with the Body
of Christ in Cor, Gal, and Rom', *CBQ* 23 (1961) 199–209; I. J. du Plessis,
Christus as Hoof; E. Schweizer, *TWNT*, VII, 1064–79; id. 'Die Kirche als
Leib Christi in den paulinischen Homologumena' and 'Die Kirche als Leib
Christi in den paulinischen Antilogemena' in his *Neotestamentica*, Zürich,
1963, 272–92; M. Adinolfi, 'Le metafore greco-romane della testa e del
corpo et il corpo mistico di Christo', AnBib 18, Rome, 1963, 333–42; J. H.
Roberts, *Opbou*, 60–108; H. J. Gabathuler, *Jesus Christus: Haupt der
Kirche—Haupt der Welt*, Zürich, 1965; I. J. du Plessis, 'Die Agtergroond
van die Hoof-Liggaam-Beeldspraak by Paulus', *NedGTT* 8 (1967) 116–22
and 9 (1968) 41–8; E. Käsemann, 'The theological problem presented by
the Motif of the Body of Christ' in his *Perspectives on Paul*, London, 1971
(German 1969), 102–21; J. Ernst, *Pleroma*, 157–74; A. J. M. Wedderburn,
'The Body of Christ and related concepts in 1 Corinthians', *SJT* 24 (1971)
74–96; Jewett, 201–87; Merklein, *Amt*, 83–97; Fischer, 48–78; Van Roon,
Authenticity, 266–319; W. A. Meeks, 'In one Body: The Unity of
Humankind in Colossians and Ephesians', *God's Christ and His People* (FS
N. A. Dahl, ed. J. Jervell and W. A. Meeks), Oslo, 1977, 209–22;
Meuzelaar, *passim*; T. G. Allen, Appendices B and C, 340ff; J. D. G. Dunn,
'The Body of Christ in Paul', *Worship, Theology and Ministry in the Early
Church* (FS R. P. Martin, ed. M. J. Wilkins and T. Paige), Sheffield, 1992,
146–62.

When AE wrote he was aware already of the use of the term 'body
of Christ' as a designation for the church, since he probably knew 1
Corinthians, even if he did not know Romans. In any case the image
was in use in the Pauline school of which he was a member as

Colossians shows. We can assume that the phrase had been much talked over within that school. There are however differences between the way it is used in Ephesians and its earlier usage in 1 Corinthians and Romans; most of these differences Ephesians shares with Colossians. Before discussing them it should be noted that the differences do not of themselves prove non-Pauline authorship; authors regularly adapt their imagery to suit new situations and contexts. The main differences are:

a. A special position in the body is given to the head and it is equated with Christ.

b. The body is envisaged as growing (4.15f).

c. The body has cosmic connections (3.9f; 1.22f).

d. Stress on diversity among members is missing, though Christians are still regarded as related to one another in the body (4.25; 5.30).

e. Jewish and Gentile Christians are united in the body (2.16); this aspect is absent from Colossians and only vaguely present in 1 Cor 12.13 where the Jew/Gentile contrast is only one among a number of contrasting alternatives.

f. The relation between the church as body and the eucharist which is found in 1 Cor 10.16f does not appear in Ephesians.

Apart from the first in this list most of these variations are unimportant.

The concept of the growth of the church, or of Christians, is found in 1 Cor 3.6f; 2 Cor 9.10; 10.15. In the second and third of these passages, and probably also in the first, it refers to a maturing, that is a growth in quality rather than quantity. This is true also of its use in Eph 2.21; 4.15f where it relates to both the building imagery and that of the body (4.16). Being a general concept (Christians mature) which has come to be associated with the body image it has no special significance in respect of the body. So far as a cosmic dimension goes, it is not the body as such which has this dimension but the church (1.10; 3.21) and this aspect is not then a true development of the body image. The absence of stress in Ephesians on the use of the image to display diversity among members may simply be due to the lack of need to bring out this aspect; it was emphasised in 1 Cor 12.12ff because of division in the Corinthian church over charismatic gifts; if no clear divisions needing correction exist within a community there is no need to draw out this aspect; it was of course already present in the widespread secular use of the image. Apart from the Jewish–Gentile division, and it is related to the body in 2.16, no important divisions may have existed within the communities to which AE was writing. As for his reference to the Jew–Gentile division, AE may be following up and developing the vague connection in 1 Cor 12.13 to it.

Another possible variation is frequently suggested: in 1 Corinthians and Romans the body of Christ is the individual congregation while in Ephesians and Colossians it is the whole church. The origin of the use of the phrase body of Christ[48] as denoting the church does not lie in the fable of Menenius Agrippa (see below); if it did it would apply only to single congregations.[49] Paul knew that the church was the continuation of the people of God, for since there was only one people of God there could be only one church; he must then have conceived of the church as neither a group of individuals sharing a common interest nor a collection of congregations. That instead he saw the church as a whole emerges from time to time: for example in Gal 1.13; 1 Cor 15.9; in some of the descriptions of it in the addresses of his letters where he writes 'to the church which is in ... ' and not 'to the church of ... ' (1 Cor 1.2; 2 Cor 1.1). In 1 Cor 12.13 the body as church is related to baptism and in 10.16f to the eucharist, thus suggesting a universal concept rather than one confined to a local congregation. If 1 Cor 12.28 refers to the local church then it must have had within it a number of apostles; this is unlikely; it would not be if it refers to the whole church. If a contrast then exists between the earlier epistles and Ephesians and Colossians in respect of emphasis it is not an absolute one.

The most prominent feature of the image in the earlier epistles is its use when Paul is arguing, as in the fable, for the necessary diversity of function of members within a group (1 Cor 12.12ff; Rom 12.3ff), and this might suggest it was derived directly from the fable. Yet when Paul introduces the theme to his converts in 1 Cor 12.12, the earlier of the two passages, it is significant that he does not do so with a phrase like 'I recall to you (what I taught you when I was with you)' or 'Do you not know (because I taught you)' or 'As you know'. Instead he brings it in as if the Corinthians did not already know the use of the fable in relation to the church, though of course they would have known the fable itself in one of its many forms for Corinth was a Roman colony. If he had been interested

---

[48] For surveys see Best, *One Body*, 83–95; Jewett, 227–50; Du Plessis, art.cit., etc. Käsemann sought to explain its appearance in 1 Corinthians through the myth of a descending and ascending redeemer; Schlier restricted such gnostic influence to Ephesians and Colossians (Schlier, 90–9, and *Christus* 37–48; Käsemann, 56ff; this view received some support from Pokorný, *Gnosis*, 49). The existence of the myth of the descending and ascending redeemer as early as Pauline times has been heavily criticised by C. Colpe, 'Zum Leib-Christi-Vorstellung im Epheserbrief'; id. *Die religionsgeschichtliche Schule*, FRLANT 78, Göttingen, 1961; H.-M. Schenke, *Der Gott 'Mensch' in der Gnosis*, Göttingen, 1962; C. H. Talbert, 'The Myth of a Descending-Ascending Redeemer in Mediterranean Antiquity', *NTS* 22 (1975/6) 418–40. Fischer, 59–62, has argued that some of the examples provided by Käsemann and Schlier are in fact pre-gnostic. In the light of this more recent discussion, few today see the myth as the source either of the body image or of the head–body relationship in Colossians and Ephesians.

[49] The metaphor is found widely in ancient literature, e.g. Livy ii 32; Dion. Halic. vi 86.2; Dio Chrys. 36.16 §398d; it may go back to Aesop.

only in the theme of unity and diversity as given in the fable, he would have ended his discussion at 12.27 with 'now you are a body and individually members of it'. Instead he continues: 'now you the body of Christ . . . ', thus connecting the body to Christ. As Paul uses the phrase it cannot be thought of apart from Christ. The church is never any body nor the rump of a body but always the body *of Christ*. What Paul has done in 12.12ff is to apply the fable's concept of diversity within unity to an accepted togetherness of believers. It is this which enables him to end 12.12 with the enigmatic 'so it is with Christ'. When we look a little more closely into 1 Corinthians we discover, as we have already noted, that he has used the term 'body' in relation to the togetherness of believers prior to the discussion of 12.12ff.

The origin of Paul's conception of the church as the body of Christ then lies deep in his theology and is to be connected among other things to his view of the relation of believers to Christ beginning in conversion/baptism and continuing through participation in the eucharist. Though the phrase 'body of Christ' is not used, the idea is present in 6.15 and 10.17. Whether in the latter passage body has the same connotation as in 10.16 or not, it indicates that believers form a body (Best, *One Body*, 88ff). In 6.15 the bodies of believers, which in Paul's terminology simply means 'believers', are members of Christ (*ibid*. 74ff). It is possible also that 'the body' in 11.29 refers to the church (*ibid*. 107ff). It is however unlikely that there is any allusion to it in 1 Cor 1.12f and Gal 3.16, 28f, though these relate to the togetherness of believers. This togetherness also underlies Paul's thinking when he uses phrases like 'in Christ', 'with Christ', and those which depict him as our representative and when he thinks of Christ as the Second Adam. We note also that in 1 Cor 12.13 believers are said to have been baptised into one body and in Gal 3.27 baptism is into Christ. In the light of all this it is not surprising to find the reference to Christ in 1 Cor 12.12 and to discover the first explicit occurrence of the phrase 'body of Christ' in 1 Cor 12.27. The most significant factor in its use is not then that of a unity embodying diversity, but the relation of the church to Christ. Believers are together with one another and with Christ. Paul can use the phrase because for him 'body' is not a simple physical concept; it is often equivalent to the personal pronoun.[50] This argument from the use of the phrase in 1 Corinthians may be supported from its use regarding unity and diversity in Rom 12.4ff. Paul has not taught the Roman Christians and so he cannot know if they would understand the body-of-Christ imagery by itself. Since they would understand the idea in the fable he can introduce that

---

[50] On 'body' see Käsemann, *Leib*, 1–50; Best, *One Body*, 215ff; Stacey, 181ff; Jewett, 201ff; Gundry, *passim*.

aspect of the concept; their own experience would also have given them some idea of togetherness with Christ; so he writes of 'one body in Christ' for togetherness is related to being in Christ; 'one body in Christ' involves both diversity in unity and togetherness with Christ. In conclusion we can say that the phrase 'body of Christ' existed prior to its expansion through the fable (cf Benoit 'Corps ... ', 118). Given then that the phrase did not originate with the fable, that the fable does not convey its original significance and that the theme of diversity within unity is not its basic significance, we can see that when the fable's theme is not prominent in Ephesians (the 'member' element still survives in 4.25; 5.30) its author is not departing from the original Pauline drive. The diversity aspect is not prominent because AE had no occasion to use it in his argument; the divisions that rent the Corinthian church, even if present in some of the communities AE had in mind, were not present in all. AE is not arguing for unity in the way this is done in Corinthians but accepting it as something given to the church by God.

As indicated earlier, the major variation in the presentation of the body imagery in Ephesians compared with that of the earlier epistles lies in the identification of Christ as head. Since this variation is also found in Colossians we may assume that it appeared in the Pauline school to which the authors of Ephesians and Colossians belonged rather than being thought up individually by the authors of the two letters. κεφαλή[51] is used physically of the uppermost part of the body and then in a similar way applied to such things as the tops of mountains. How is it used metaphorically? Here it ranges in meaning from overlordship to source or origin. Of these meanings in Greek and Roman literature the latter is rare in respect of people though occurring more regularly in relation to rivers; Grudem gives only four instances (Philo, *Congressu* 61; Artemidorus Daldianus, *Onirocriticus* 1.2, 35; 3.66). In relation to people the two meanings are not unrelated. In a patriarchal society the husband in a family functions as both its biological source and its ruler. If Christ is understood as the Second Adam he might then be regarded as both origin and ruler of believers. In discussing Christ as head of the church two questions then face us: What led to the identification of Christ as head? What is the significance of the identification?

[51] See J. M. Gonzalez Ruiz, 'Sentido soteriológico de ΚΕΦΑΛΉ en la christologí de San Pablo', *Anthologia Annua*, 1 (1953) 185–224; S. Bedale, art.cit.; Van Roon, 275ff; Usami, 117–24; Miletic, 74–87; W. Grudem, 'Does *kephale* ("Head") Mean "Source" or "Authority Over" in Greek Literature? A Survey of 2,336 Examples', *TJ* 6 (1985) 38–59; id. 'The Meaning of *kephale* ("Head"): A Response to Recent Studies', *TJ* 11 (1990) 3–72; R. E. Cervin, 'Does κεφαλή Mean "Source" or "Authority Over" in Greek Literature? A Rebuttal', *TJ* 10 (1989) 85–112; J. A. Fitzmyer, 'Another Look at *Kephale* in 1 Corinthians', *NTS* 35 (1989) 503–11; id. '*Kephale* in 1 Corinthians 11.3', *Int* 47 (1993) 52–9.

It is easiest to assume that the idea of Christ as head arose out of a discussion among believers on his relation to the church as his body. Greek converts would have had no difficulty in linking the fable to the variety within unity of a group of people. To go on and relate this to the members of the group as members of a particular person conceived in terms of his body was quite another matter. For Greek thought the body is not the person, as it could be for Jews (cf Rom 12.12; 1 Cor 13.3; Phil 1.20, etc.), but a less important part of the person. Body and soul make up the whole, but of the two the body, being physical matter, is inferior. To prevent this inherent inferiority of body being carried over into the representation of the church as the body of Christ, it was necessary to define Christ's position in relation to his body. But even if we accept this as the origin of the discussion which eventually led to Christ being regarded as head, it does not of itself explain why he came to be depicted as head and not some other part of the body. The use of head might seem to be excluded since in the expanded image of 1 Cor 12.12ff ordinary members of the church had already been identified with the head of the body (12.21), as had the eyes and ears which are parts of the head (12.16). Greek thought would indeed have been happier with the idea of Christ as, say, soul and not as head.

The cosmos was regularly pictured as a body in Greco-Roman literature and as such viewed as an 'ensouled body': Aristotle, *Anima* 411a; Diogenes Laertes, 1.27; Plato, *Tim* 30A–4C, 36E, *Phileb* 29E–30C; Sextus Emp *Math* IX 85; Seneca, *Ep* 65.24; Philo, *Migr Abr* 219f; *Rer Div* 155; *Abr* 74, 272; *Fuga* 110; *Ebr* 30. If the cosmos is a macroanthropos, it is so as an ensouled 'anthropos'. The state, city or empire is also envisaged as a 'being': Isocrates, *Or* 7.14; cf 12.138; Plato, *Gorg* 464B; Philo, *Spec Leg* 3.131; Seneca, *Clem* I 5.1. Occasionally even the household is depicted as a 'being': Aristotle, *Pol* 1255B; Plutarch, *Praec Coniug* 33–4 (II 142Ef). But if Christians were to describe Christ as the soul of his body which is the church, this might have implied a dualism with a consequent belittling of the body. Assuming the identification of Christ as head in relation to the church took place in Pauline communities, it needs to be recognised that the soul was not an important anthropological concept in Pauline thought (ψυχή, only thirteen times in the Pauline corpus) and is not used of the higher part of a human being.[52] It is directly linked to 'body' in 1 Th 5.23 in the phrase 'spirit, soul and body', where the terms together indicate the whole life of the human being without suggesting that any one of them is superior to the others. It comes nearest to expressing the whole person in Eph 6.6 and Col 3.23. At 1 Cor 15.44 the adjective ψυχικός is used to qualify σῶμα and describe the earthly or physical

[52] Cf Stacey, 121–7; Jewett, 334–57.

existence of human beings. In Phil 2.2, 19, 20 compounds of the noun express the togetherness of believers (Jewett, 349f), but even allowing for this it would not be a suitable term to express the difference between Christ and believers. It carries neither the idea of origin, nor of overlordship, both of which can be associated with head. However, to explain why AE did not use soul to spell out Christ's relationship to the church does nothing to explain why head was chosen, except to eliminate one of the possibilities. There were several others: the eyes, Dio Chrys *Or* 33.16, the tongue, Midr Ps 39 §2, the heart, Midr Ps 14 §1 (see SB III, 447f), the brain, ἐγλκέφαλος, Hipp *Phil* 5.7.35, but this last is associated with the head and head is more common and more easily applicable; the inner person (3.16, see notes there) was also a possibility, but this would not be sufficiently distinct from body for both of these represent the whole person. Moreover none of these terms is frequent and AE may not have been aware of them as possibilities.

In beginning our answer as to the reason for the choice of head, we need to observe how κεφαλή is used in Ephesians and Colossians other than in relation to the body. In Eph 5.23 it relates husband and wife but we can safely ignore this as the origin of its use, since in the discussion at this point it is linked to the Christ–church relationship. In 4.15 and Col 2.19 it is again the Christ–church relationship which is at issue. But in 1.22 Christ's headship relates to the cosmos and not directly to the church and the same seems true of Col 2.10. In Col 1.18 the reference is to a headship over the church but most commentators argue that in the hymn underlying Col 1.15–20 the headship was one over the cosmos. It may signify origin here since it is to some extent set in parallel to ἀρχή and πρωτότοκος; its significance would thus differ here from Eph 1.22. Since it is in the hymn its usage must predate both Ephesians and Colossians. If the origin of the Colossian hymn lay in a heretical group, and it may not have, this group may have been the first to use it and so introduced it into the theological discussion from where it was picked up by A/Col and AE (cf Gabathuler, 60). Since in 1 Cor 8.6 Christ had already been set in relation to the cosmos, the ground was prepared for the acceptance of the idea. This would suggest that within the Pauline school Christ was first described as head in relation to the cosmos and the idea then transferred to the church.

As well as the cosmos being regarded as an ensouled human being there is also evidence for it as a person with a head: Orphic Frag. 168, lines 2, 9, 12 (Kern, 201f); Chrysippus, see *Stoic vet frag* (ed. Von Arnim) III 4; Posidonius, see Sextus Emp *Adv Mathem* IX 78f; Philo, *Qu Exod* 2.117. In Diod Sic I 11.5f and P. Leid (see Preisendanz, *PMag* XII 243) the head is mentioned but has no special position. While there is not much evidence here, it does indicate that the leading or ruling member of a community, e.g. the state, might be termed its head. This evidence is reinforced from other sources without any suggestion of the whole being regarded as an ensouled body: Plato, *Leg* 12.964DE; Plutarch, *Pompey* 51.1, 646B; Seneca, *Clem* I 4.3; II 2.1; Cicero, *Mur* 51; *Flacc* 42; Q. Curtius Rufus X 9.4; Deut 28.13; Judg 10.18; 11.8f, 11; 2 Kgdms 22.44; 3 Kgdms 20.12 (cf A and B texts); Isa 7.8f; 9.13f; *Jub* 1.16; *1 En* 103.11; *T Zeb* 9.4; Philo, *Praem Poen* 114, 125; *Vit Mos* 2.30; *Spec Leg* 3.184. Once 'head' had been introduced into the discussion it would have been possible for Christians to choose this as the word to describe Christ's own position in relation to the church, his body. An additional factor assisting the identification of Christ as head might have been the idea of *Stammvater*, for the latter would both be the source of his descendants and their ruler (cf Philo, *Praem Poen* 125; *Vita Mos* 2.60, 65; *Qu Gen* 2.9).

Of the occasions when Christ is described as head in Ephesians he is clearly depicted as overlord in 5.23 and 1.22. Probably this holds also for 4.15 (see notes) even if Christ, and not the head, is to be viewed as the source of the body's growth and development.

IV

FROM DEATH TO LIFE
(2.1–10)

R. Schnackenburg, 'Er hat uns mitauferweckt', *Liturgisches Jahrbuch* 2 (1952) 159–83; Mussner, *Christus*, 18–20, 24–7, 91–4; P. Benoit, 'Rapports Littéraire'; Schille, 53–60; M. Legido Lopez, 'La Iglesia entre la communion y la tentacion', *Salmanticensis* 15 (1971) 205–32; Fischer, 121–31; Lindemann, *Aufhebung*, 106–44; U. Luz, 'Rechtfertigung bei den Paulusschülern', *Rechtfertigung* (FS Ernst Käsemann, ed. J. Friedrich, W. Pöhlmann, P. Stuhlmacher), Tübingen, 1976, 365–83; L. Ramaroson, 'Une lecture de Éphésiens 1,15–2,10', *Bib* 58 (1977) 388–410; Halter, 233–42; Best, 'Dead'; G. Barbaglio, 'Siamo risorto con Cristo!', *PSV* 5 (1982) 224–33; J. Reumann, *Righteousness* §§ 166ff, pp. 92ff; A. T. Lincoln, 'Ephesians 2:8–10: A Summary of Paul's Gospel?', *CBQ* 45 (1983) 617–30; Lona, 245–56, 360–405; Adai, 245–60; T. G. Allen, 'Exaltation and Solidarity with Christ: Ephesians 1.20 and 2.6', *JSNT* 28 (1986) 103–20; A. J. M. Wedderburn, *Baptism and Resurrection* (WUNT 44), Tübingen, 1987.

1 And you [he made alive] who were dead
   in your trespasses and sins
2   in which you used to walk
      according to the aeon of the world
      according to the ruler of the kingdom of the air
         the spirit who is active now in the sons of disobedience
3 among whom we also all once spent our lives
   in the desires of the flesh
      doing the wills of the flesh and of the intentions
      and were by nature children of wrath like everyone
                                                                    else—
4 But God who is rich in mercy
      because of his great love with which he loved us
5 [and] we who were dead in trespasses he made alive with
                                                                    Christ,
      —by grace you have been saved—
6   in that with Christ he has raised us
      and made us to sit in the heavenlies in Christ Jesus
7   so that he might exhibit in the coming aeons
      the overflowing riches of his grace
      by means of his kindness in Christ Jesus.

197

8 For you have been saved by this grace through faith;
 this has not come from yourselves;
 it is the gift of God—
9   not from what you have done
  so that no one should boast—
10 we are his making, created in Christ Jesus
 with a view to good works prepared by God beforehand
 so that we should walk in them.

Three sections of 'narrative' now follow: 2.1–10 tells the story of the move of Gentile believers from paganism to Christianity, 2.11–22 that of their move into the people of God, 3.2–13 that of Paul's special position in respect of their move.

AE commences 2.1–10 with a reference to the condition of his readers before they believed (v. 1) and seems to have intended to go on at once to speak of God's remedy for their condition when he realises he has not described that condition adequately; a simple reference to sin is insufficient. So he breaks off from what he was about to say, causing an anacoluthon; syntactical irregularities like this are not unusual in Paul but he is by no means unique in this and the appearance of one here cannot be used either to support or deny his authorship. AE describes the pre-Christian condition of his readers, not only as one of sin (v. 1), but also (v. 2) as one of control by supernatural evil forces; in sinning they were not their own masters but were under external control. The digression continues in v. 3 stressing that actual wrong desires governed them in acting sinfully, and pointing out that in so acting they had made themselves subject to God's judgement. With v. 4 AE begins to pick up again one of his main themes, salvation, which, had he not made his diversion, would have been the main clause of the sentence which began in v. 1. With the theme of salvation expressed, he repeats in v. 5 the thought of v. 1, adding the essential statement that those who were dead have received new life in Christ. That new life is defined in v. 6 in terms which link it to what was said in 1.20 about Christ's resurrection and heavenly session. Believers have been brought to life in that with Christ they have been raised and like him given seats within the heavenlies. The dead condition of unbelievers differs, however, from that of Christ; his death had been physical, theirs spiritual. It is this difference which occasioned v. 1 and its expansion in vv. 2f. But there is a similarity between the risen condition of believers and Christ for they were raised with him when they believed or were baptised. This similarity extends further in that they have been seated with him in the heavenlies, though not like him at God's right hand; they do not then reign as he reigns. Yet their new position serves to exhibit the grace of God to the approaching 'aeons' and thus they have a role in making salvation

known on a cosmic scale. The theme of their salvation, enunciated
first in v. 5b, is (vv. 8–10) expanded and explained in a way that
both generalises what Paul had taught and yet retains essential
contact with it. Their salvation is not the result of their own efforts
but is God's gracious gift; none of them can boast of what they
contributed to their present position as believers. They are God's
creation and even the good works they perform as Christians were
prepared for them by him beforehand.

The argument thus flows from a negative description of the earlier
position of the readers as held by sin and the powers of evil to a
positive description of their present position as saved. It is a kind of
narrative of the life of a typical believer (Penna). This change in
their position results from their being caught up in what happened to
Christ. In a sense AE leaves here his major theme of the togetherness of Christians to take it up again in 2.11–22, but he does so
because it is essential to explain before going further how his
readers have become Christians; togetherness in the church is only
possible for Christians. This passage is thus a necessary preparation
for what is to follow.

Attempts have been made to discover liturgical and credal
material within 2.1–10 and we shall examine these attempts as we
come to them in the exegesis (see on v. 1 and before v. 4). A gloss,
consisting of vv. 5b, 8f is also possible (see on vv. 8f). The passage
as a whole may be an *inclusio* since we have περιπατεῖν both in v.
2 and at the end of v. 10; this would be easier to accept if the first
occurrence of the verb had been at the beginning of the passage.
Apart from this it is held together internally by the repetition in v. 5
of phrases from v. 1 and by the repetition in v. 8 of the final clause
of v. 5, 'saved by grace'. Its unity is however marred by the lengthy
anacoluthon of vv. 2f.

1.[1] ὑμᾶς being accusative requires a verb to govern it but this
does not appear until v. 5 where part of v. 1 is repeated. The initial
καί of both verses creates a problem. In v. 1 it might suggest a close
connection with what precedes, 'you also being dead as Christ was
dead', but our death in no way resembles his death; as the first word
in the sentence it is moreover difficult to give it the sense 'also,
especially' (so Barth) and relate it to Gentiles alone. 'You' here
denotes the readers, mainly Gentiles but also including Jews.
Alternatively καί might be taken as continuative indicating a new
stage in the argument (cf Acts 1.15; 2.1; Rom 13.11; 1 Cor 2.1; 3.1).
There is a connection between Christ's new life and ours and this
will be drawn out later in the passage. Much more probably the use
of καί should be related to its use in Col 2.13a; does our verse then
depend on Col 2.13? But the initial καί there is also difficult (cf

[1] I have treated this verse more fully in 'Dead'.

Haupt, 91 n. 2). Wengst has therefore suggested that AE used a traditional couplet:

καὶ ὄντας ἡμᾶς νεκροὺς τοῖς παραπτώμασιν
συνεζωοποίησεν (ὁ θεὸς) σὺν Χριστῷ.[2]

When AE used the first line of the couplet at v. 1 he added ἁμαρτίαις and varied the first plural to the second to suit his context. Having repeated the first line of the couplet in v. 5 he then used the second. The couplet was one current in the Pauline school and part of a larger passage to which it was linked through the καί. The supposition of such a couplet accounts satisfactorily for its appearance in vv. 1, 5 and Col 2.13a.

In Col 2.13 circumcision is mentioned, probably implying a baptismal reference. By omitting the reference to circumcision AE has reduced the baptismal colouring here, if not removed it altogether, though he does refer explicitly to baptism in 4.5; and probably in 5.26. His addition of a second word for 'sins' is in keeping with his normal love of synonyms. There is no reason to doubt that the words are synonyms though the plural of ἁμαρτία is unusual in the Pauline corpus;[3] that of 'trespasses' is not. In each case the plural indicates actual sins as distinct from a sinful condition. While it is true that neither word implies a breaking of the Law, this is no reason to see v. 1 as referring only to Gentiles (so Barth) for 'trespasses' recurs in v. 5 which must include Jews since it is cast in the first person plural.[4] For the same reason there can be no suggestion that before conversion Gentiles were dead while Jews were not.

This brings us to the crux of the verse: What does it mean to be dead in sins? It is the pre-Christian condition in which both Jews and Gentiles exist. Though v. 6 introduces the idea of a resurrection with Christ there is no idea in v. 1 of a 'death with Christ' as in Rom 6.3ff. A connection between death[5] and sin gradually appeared in

---

[2] K. Wengst, *Christologische Formeln und Lieder des UrChristentums* (SNT 7), Gütersloh, 1971, 186ff; cf C. Burger, *Schöpfung und Versöhnung* (WMANT 46), Neukirchen-Vluyn, 1975, 84. It will be realised that I have changed my view as expressed in 'Dead'; this came about as a result of a changed view on the relationship of Ephesians and Colossians.

[3] Best, 'Dead', 12f. The unusual plural may have caused the variant ἐπιθυμίαι in B or it may result from the influence of v. 3.

[4] For fuller discussion see Best, 'Dead', 13f, and notes on 1.11–13 for discussion of 'we' and 'you'.

[5] Cf R. Bultmann, *TWNT*, III, 7–25; IV, 896–9; G. F. Moore, *Judaism*, I, 474ff; A. Feuillet, 'Mort du Christ et mort du chrétien d'après les épîtres pauliniennes,' *RB* 66 (1959) 481–513; H. Schlier, 'Tod und Auferstehung' and 'Der Tod im urchristlichen Denken' in his *Der Geist und die Kirche*, Freiburg, Basel, Vienna, 1980, 33–53, 101–16; J. Nélis, 'L'antithese littéraire ΖΩΗ-ΘΑΝΑΤΟΣ dans les épîtres pauliniennes,' *ETL* 19 (1943) 18–53; G. Schunack, *Das hermeneutische Problem des Todes*, Tübingen, 1967.

Jewish theology through reflection on Gen 3 (cf Ezra 3.7; Wisd 2.24; Ecclus 25.24; etc.) and on the idea that the soul that sins dies (Ezek 18.20; cf 4 Ezra 3.25f; 8.59f; Baruch 54.15, 19; etc.). While this speculation may have originally related to biological death this is not the connection here; instead we have to envisage a realised eschatological conception of death, an idea present also in 5.14; Col 2.13; Jn 5.24; 1 Jn 3.14 (cf *Sentences of Sextus* 7); Luke also may be indebted to it in the parable of the prodigal son (15.24, 32). It is consistent with the idea of 'new birth'; if at some stage believers come to life they must have been previously dead. In Eph 2.5 Christians are said to be made alive with Christ; before this they were dead. The nearest equivalent to the idea is probably that of 1QH 11.10–14, 'For the sake of Thy glory Thou has purified man of sin ... that bodies gnawed by worms may be raised from the dust ... that he may stand before Thee ... to be renewed together with all the living ...'.[6] 'The author of this hymn understands his entrance into the community as an eschatological event. He has been brought from the realm of death and alienation, from God to life.'[7] The idea of a pre-conversion death continued among the early Christians (Ign *Philad* 6.1) and was developed in gnosticism (e.g. Hipp *Ref.* 6.35.6; *CH* I 19; VII 2; Clem Alex, *Exc Theod* 58.1; 80.1).

The sins which produce death are not those of Adam nor are they particularly heinous sins. They are those words, deeds and thoughts which separate from God (cf 2.12; 4.18). The idea is not that people are born alive and slowly die through sinning and are then made alive again at conversion. Still less is there any suggestion that people begin by being spiritually alive and then die because of sin. AE does not have in mind a process of slow dying or moral degeneration. In using his phrase he is not passing a moral judgement on society (contrast 4.17–19; Rom 1.18ff) but a theological judgement on the pre-conversion existence of all. He is not indicating that there is a certain point in the development of human life at which 'death' takes place (e.g. when sin comes to be recognised as sin). The lifestyle of the non-Christian is one which may be described as death or as one of sins and trespasses. People are born dead and remain so until they come to believe (Calvin). Those who are dead in this way cannot come to life of their own accord; only God can make them live; so the passage goes on to speak of the way God gives life (vv. 5, 6). But before it does this it approaches the life of the unbeliever from another angle, as one under the control of alien supernatural forces.

2. The relative clause (the pronoun is feminine because ἁμαρτίαι

---

[6] ET by Vermes, 195.

[7] G. W. E. Nickelsburg, *Resurrection, Immortality and Eternal Life in Inter-testamental Judaism* (Harvard Theological Studies XXVI), Cambridge, MA, 1972, 156. For fuller references see Best, 'Dead', n. 54.

is the nearer of the two nouns to which it refers) with which AE introduces this new step in his argument mangles the grammar. This would not have happened had he continued after v. 1 with words similar to those of vv. 4f '... God, who is rich in mercy because of his great love for us, made us alive with Christ ...'. Verse 1 has not however described fully the pre-Christian life of believers and so AE qualifies it with vv. 2f, breaking the thread of his thought yet at the same time indicating that what is said in vv. 2f is important. He had already argued (1.21) that people are subject to the control of the powers and now he takes up this aspect of pre-Christian life.

The Christians took over from their Jewish background the metaphor of movement along a road or path to describe behaviour.[8] The particular word, περιπατεῖν, AE uses is a feature of the Pauline paraenesis and is not therefore a direct Semitism. In proportion to their length both AE and A/Col use it more regularly than Paul and it was therefore probably a word of their Pauline school. It is unusual to find two prepositional phrases associated with it (two phrases are found in Rom 13.13), though it is followed by phrases introduced by both ἐν (Rom 6.4; 2 Cor 4.2) and κατά (Rom 8.4; 14.15; 1 Cor 3.3; 2 Cor 10.2); their equivalence is seen in 2 Cor 10.2, 3. Here in 2.2 the ἐν and αἷς clearly indicates the manner of their life as sinful. What then does κατά indicate? It might be taken simply as 'after the manner of, conforming to', yet AE is hardly saying that unbelievers lived 'after the manner of the ruler of the power of the air', i.e. in the same way as the devil lives. The preposition rather implies that in some way they have come under the control of the devil. In Rom 8.4 to walk κατὰ πνεῦμα must mean under the control of the Spirit as κατὰ σάρκα (cf also 2 Cor 10.2) means to walk controlled by the flesh; the preposition probably also offers more than a simple description of 'manner' in 2 Cor 11.17; Rom 8.27; 15.5. The closest parallel to 2.2 is Col 2.8 where we appear to move beyond the simple description of manner into something deeper in the final κατὰ Χριστόν. Believers do not now walk under the control of the devil though they once did (cf Steinmetz, 52f). In the Pauline corpus Christians are regularly reminded of their pre-Christian condition (cf Rom 5.8–11; 6.19–21; 7.5; 11.30; 1 Cor 6.9–11; Gal 4.3, 8; Eph 5.8; Col 1.21; 2.13; 3.7; Tit 3.3).[9] 'Once' they lived in such and such a way; 'now' they live differently. The verb is aorist here rather than imperfect, presumably

---

[8] Cf W. Michaelis, *TWNT*, V, 42ff; S. V. McCasland, 'The Way', *JBL* 77 (1958) 222–30; J. A. Fitzmyer, 'Jewish Christianity in Acts in the Light of the Qumran Scrolls'; id. *Essays on the Semitic Background of the New Testament*, London, 1971, 271–303; E. Repo, *Der 'Weg' als Selbstbezeichnung des Urchristentums*, Helsinki, 1964; Usami, 23–9.

[9] See P. Tachau, *'Einst' und 'Jetzt' im Neuen Testament* (FRLANT 105), Göttingen, 1972; cf Lindemann, *Aufhebung*, 67–73.

because the past life of believers is regarded as a unified whole which is over and done with.

αἰών[10] is a complex term normally indicating a period of time whether brief or lengthy (the two ages) but occasionally the universe (Heb 1.2; 11.3). However both prior to and after the beginning of the Christian movement it was used of deities. In the singular, and especially in Egypt, it denoted the 'second' God, associated with the cosmos as a 'time'-God. The usage in the singular is continued in some gnostic systems (cf Epip *Pan* 45.1.3; Iren *adv Haer* 1.1.1; 30.2, 11; Hipp *Ref* 6.14.6) and in the magical papyri (e.g. Preisendanz, IV 1169, 2198, 2314), but it is also used even more extensively of a multiplicity of aeons belonging to the spiritual sphere (Iren *adv Haer* 1.1.2; Clem Alex, *Exc Theod* 47.3; 64.1; Hipp *Ref* 6.29.6; *Ap John* II, 1 8.1–9.26; *Ap Adam* V, 5 64.11–66.4; *Val Exp* XI, 2 27.38; 40.27–41.38; *Trim Prot* XIII, 1 37.1–39.14).

How then is αἰών used in 2.2? If ἄρχων in the next phrase indicates a personal being, would not the parallelism require the identification of ὁ αἰών with this being? In Col 2.8 there are three parallel clauses introduced by κατά; in the third the word it governs is personal, in the first it is not, and it is not clear whether it is or is not in the second. It is not possible then to argue for an exact parallelism within 2.2 on formal grounds. Here the Fathers took only the second and third of the phrases as referring to the devil as they show when they regularly quote the verse but omit the first phrase (e.g. Origen, *c. Cels* 7.52; Clem Alex, *Protrep* I.8.1). Origen, ad loc, however allows the two possible meanings (temporal and personal). If αἰών is not taken here to refer to a deity, how is it to be understood in relation to κόσμος? The two nouns are comparable entities. The former is primarily temporal in significance and the latter spatial, but since the content of what fills time and what fills space is the same the two words came to be used with similar meaning (cf 1 Cor 2.6, 8 with 3.19 and Jn 16.11). The pleonastic nature of the whole phrase would not be out of accord with AE's style and would denote the totality of existence regarded from the angles of both time and space (so the majority of commentators). οὗτος then imparts to the phrase the separation of that totality from God rather than suggesting a contrast with a perfect future world; both 'this world' (1 Cor 3.19; 5.10; 7.31; Jn 8.12, 23; 18.36) and 'this aeon' (Rom 12.2; 1 Cor 1.20; 2.6) can carry an evil connotation. Unbelievers live as those who have an existence separated from

[10] On the word see R. Reitzenstein, *Das iranische Erlösungsmysterium*, Bonn a. Rh., 1921, 151ff; E. Norden, *Die Geburt des Kindes*, Leipzig, 1924, 24–50; M. Zepf, *ARW* 25 (1927) 225–44; A. D. Nock, 'A Vision of Mandulis Aion', *Essays on Religion and the Ancient World* (ed. Z. Stewart), Oxford, 1972, 375–400; H. Sasse, *TWNT*, I, 197–209; id. *RAC* I, 193–204; M. P. Nilsson, *Geschichte der Griechischen Religion*, II, Munich 1961,[2] 488ff; C. Colpe, *Die religionsgeschichtliche Schule* (FRLANT 78), Göttingen, 1961, 209–16; Lindemann, *Aufhebung*, 56–9; Adai, 249f; Wink, 82–4; Carr, 100–4.

God and therefore an evil existence characterised by sins and trespasses. Yet when all that has been said it is simpler to take αἰών as designating an evil personal power (so Schnackenburg; Lindemann; Schlier; Gnilka; Conzelmann; Adai, 251) and thus preserve the parallelism with the next phrase; such a meaning would easily have been picked up towards the end of the first century.[11] The essential meaning of the two interpretations hardly differs. The devil[12] had many names in contemporary Judaism and early Christianity and the adoption of the name of a pagan god or evil power would not be unexpected, especially since 'this aeon' already possessed an evil connotation.

While it is clear that the second κατά phrase refers to the devil, it is not obvious why AE chose this particular phrase or what is its peculiar flavour. ὁ ἄρχων is used elsewhere in the NT and early Christianity of a personal power of evil (Jn 12.31; 14.30; 16.11; Ign *Eph* 17.1; 19.1; *Magn* 1.2; *Trall* 4.2; *Rom* 7.1; *Philad* 6.2); the plural is also used widely of supernatural evil powers. It was thus perfectly natural for AE to choose the word to designate the devil rather than a Jewish name like Satan; he knows it will be understood in the Greek world. The 'air' is the region, or part of the region, between heaven where God dwells and the earth (see Detached Note: The Heavenlies) and is peopled with evil beings; alternatively it is the sphere in which the evil powers are active *T Levi* 3.1–3; *T Benj* 3.4; *2 En* 7.1–5; 18.3–6; 29.5; *Asc Isa* 7.9–12; 10.29f; 11.23; Iren *adv Haer* 1.29.4; *Hyp Arch* II 4, 95.19–23; 96.10–12; Diog. Laertes 8.32; Plut *Mor* 274B; Orig *c. Cels* 8.35; *Asclepius* VI 8, 76.21–8; *Teach Silv* VII, 4 117.14–16; (in Philo it is normally good beings who inhabit this area; cf *Conf Ling* 174–7; *Plant* 14; *Gig* 6; *Somn* 1.134ff; *Spec Leg* 2.45).[13]

The most difficult word in the second phrase is ἐξουσία. It could be taken adjectivally, 'the powerful ruler of the air' or 'air' could be adjectival, 'the ruler of the airy power', or all three nouns could be given their full value as nouns: 'the ruler with authority over the air' or 'the ruler of the power which the air exercises'; of these the first two have little to commend them and the second two require us to

---

[11] Lincoln objects that αἰών has a temporal meaning in 1.21 and 2.7 and can hardly therefore have a different meaning here. But its temporal meaning in 2.7 is by no means certain. Apart from that if a word has a number of meanings its sense in any particular place must be determined from its context. Within 2.3 σάρξ is used with two different senses, and with yet another in 2.11!

[12] On the devil cf T. Ling, *The Significance of Satan*, London, 1961; E. Langton, *Essentials of Demonology*, London, 1949; W. Foerster, *TWNT*, II, 69–80; VII, 151–64; J. Kallas, *The Satanward View*, Philadelphia, 1965; W. Wink, *Unmasking the Powers*, Philadelphia, 1986, 1–40.

[13] Cf Bousset-Gressmann, 338; Schlier, 103 n. 1; SB IV, 515–19; O. Everling, *Die paulinische Angelologie und Dämonologie*, Göttingen, 1888, 105–9; Langton, op.cit., 99ff, 186ff; Mussner, *Christus*, 16ff; Knox, *Gentiles*, 187 n. 2.

read too much into the genitives. There is no evidence for giving ἐξουσία a collective sense as do many earlier commentators (Meyer, Belser, Henle, Alford, etc.). The whole phrase is most easily understood if the word has the sense of the sphere or area in which authority is exercised (cf Gnilka, Schlier, Ewald, Schnackenburg, Lincoln), a meaning which it probably gathered from its use as a translation of *mmślh*[14] in 4 Kgdms 20.13 (Isa 39.2 *v.l.*); Ψ 113.2; cf Ecclus. 24.11; 1 Macc 6.11; it has this sense in Lk 6.4; 22.53; 23.7; Col 1.13 (cf *Act Thom* 10; Orig *c. Cels* 6.31). Before their conversion believers therefore lived lives controlled by the ruler of the demonic spirits or evil angelic beings who inhabit or control the space above the earth and below heaven. As spirits 'of the air'[15] they are near to man and can easily lead him into evil.

In relating the third phrase to what precedes it, it might appear easy to take τοῦ πνεύματος as a genitive in apposition to τοῦ ἀέρος (so Schlier, Hugedé) but 'air' is used here with a spatial connotation not possessed by πνεῦμα. Nor is it easy to take the phrase as dependent on τὸν ἄρχοντα; 'the ruler of the spirits', i.e. the evil spirits, would be a possible phrase but not the singular, 'the ruler of the spirit'. If 'spirit' denotes the human spirit (so Haupt) it is tautologous to speak of it as energising the disobedient; in any case ἐνεργεῖν is normally used of supernatural and not human energy (see on 1.19f). It is better then to take πνεῦμα as in apposition to τὸν ἄρχοντα (cf Ewald, Grosheide, Masson, Abbott, Gnilka), the genitive being occasioned by the preceding genitives (for appositions which transgress strict grammatical correctness see BDR §137.3; cf §167.2). The spirit is then an (the) evil spirit, a regular meaning of the word in Jewish Greek derived from its Hebrew significance.[16] It is much more appropriate to the context to take it in this way with many of the early Fathers than as 'spiritual influence', though this is a possible meaning at 1 Cor 2.12.[17] ἐνεργεῖν goes naturally with this understanding of 'spirit'. This evil spirit is active 'now'. With what does this 'now' contrast? There is nothing in the passage which suggests a past free from the activity of this spirit; it was the spirit in which believers once walked; now at least they are partly set free from it, and in their future when Christ is all in all it

[14] Cf W. Foerster, *TWNT*, II, 562–75; Mussner, *Christus*, 19, takes it as an 'Abstraktum' signifying the demons who are under the rule of the archon.
[15] For such spirits 'in the air' see *Asclepius* VI, 8 76.21–8; *Teach Silv* VII, 4 117.14–16.
[16] E. Schweizer, *TWNT*, VI, 443, says its use in Ephesians comes closer to gnostic or pre-gnostic Judaism than in Paul. C. Bussmann, *Themen der paulinischen Missionspredigt auf dem Hintergrund der spätjudisch-hellenistischen Missionsliteratur*, Bern and Frankfurt/M, 1975,[2] 130, says it is not frequent in Jewish mission literature. See also M. Isaacs, *The Concept of Spirit*, London, 1976.
[17] Cf Isaacs, op.cit., 97f, 105f; while she contests the meaning 'spiritual being' at 1 Cor 2.12 she accepts it in 2.2.

will have lost all its power. While this understanding is possible, it is more likely that AE is reflecting on the present condition of the world outside the Christian community rather than contrasting past and future (for the usage cf 1 Tim 6.17; 2 Tim 4.10; Tit 2.12).

The evil powers exercise their present activity in 'the sons of ἀπειθείας' (cf 5.6[18]); the form of the phrase is Semitic, though also occasionally occurring in Greek uninfluenced by the OT,[19] and is found regularly in the NT (Mk 3.17; Lk 10.6; 16.8; 20.34; Acts 4.36; Eph 5.8; 1 Pet 1.14). It is equivalent here to 'disobedient sons'. The Spirit of God now works in believers but the evil spirit among all others. ἀπείθειας can refer either to unbelief (cf the contrast in Jn 3.36; Acts 14.1, 2) or disobedience (cf Rom 10.21; 2 Tim 3.2). It is often difficult to determine which meaning is primary in the NT for the two senses are closely related; disobedience is not just disobedience to a set of moral rules, but disobedience to God in the rejection of the salvation offered in Christ and is therefore unbelief. Since those in whom the evil spirit is active are also those who are dead in trespasses and sins (v. 1) it is preferable here to use the rendering 'disobedience'. This disobedience produces unbelief as obedience would produce life and so obedience cannot be far from faith and disobedience from unbelief.[20]

In breaking the structure of his sentence at 2.2 AE must have felt that to characterise the past life of his readers and the present life of unbelievers solely in terms of a death in sins and trespasses was not sufficient. Although AE says 'once' he may not be thinking primarily in terms of time but rather in terms of area or sphere. His readers were under the control of external forces when they were outside the church; now within it they are under other influences. AE does not refer to forces acting on people to excuse them (so Chrysostom). Those who, like AE, accept a dualistic view of existence in which God is opposed by a personal evil spiritual power, even if that power is ultimately subject to God, must characterise life apart from God as in the control of that power. There may be more than one aspect to the control exercised by that power if, for instance, we take the 'aeon of this world' as indicating the totality of existence and not referring directly to the evil power.

[18] The phrase appears as a variant reading at Col 3.6 probably under the influence of Eph 5.6.

[19] See MH, 441; MHT, 208; BDR §62.6; Moule, 174f; A. Deissmann, *Bible Studies*, Edinburgh, 1901, 163–6; F. W. Danker, 'The υἱός phrases in the New Testament', *NTS* 7 (1960/1) 94; W. Klassen, '"A Child of Peace" (Luke 10.6) in First Century Context', *NTS* 27 (1980/1) 488–507.

[20] W. D. Davies, 'Paul and the Dead Sea Scrolls', *The Scrolls and the New Testament* (ed. K. Stendahl), London, 1958, 157–82 at 147f, parallels our phrase with 'the sons of evil' (1QS 3.13ff) but this is correctly disputed by Braun, *Qumran*, I, 216f, as an exact parallel. There is no need to go to Qumran for a parallel; the idiom was frequent and would naturally throw up the present phrase.

This would suggest pressure from both natural and supernatural forces. Even if we accept this understanding of 'aeon' and do not view it as a 'god', it is difficult to see any early Christian making such a clear distinction between natural and supernatural; supposing those elements can be distinguished, they are both active in the compulsion towards evil. Over and above the separation from God caused by sins and trespasses another factor exists: the power evil beings exercise on human life. AE does not picture this power as coming from the 'material' nature of existence as with some gnostics; nor is it present because of creation by an evil god.

How should those who no longer accept the idea of supernatural evil powers as affecting human life understand what AE is saying? Ought they to speak of the *Zeitgeist* or the spiritual and moral atmosphere of society? Such a simple substitution cannot be made, not only because the *Zeitgeist*, since it is the product of human thinking and action, is not a personal being, but because the atmosphere of society is not wholly evil, as by definition spiritual forces opposed to God are. In Christian or post-Christian society Christianity has affected society and encouraged factors operating for good within it; only if we deny the existence of goodness apart from Christianity can we assert the wholly evil atmosphere of paganism. Such negative judgements may be implied in what AE says (cf 4.17–19), but if so we should regard him as making a theological and not a sociological judgement on society. How then are we to understand what AE is saying in respect of control by external evil powers? He appears to be claiming that the life of pagan society is dominated not only by a personal will towards sin but also by supernatural forces driving it to evil. Such forces still exist, though we may not term them supernatural. They are the pressures of society, which if not wholly evil are not wholly good: poverty, upbringing and environment, genetic constitution, physical disability, economic decisions taken at a distance. These are wider than the spiritual atmosphere of a culture and they exercise a compulsion on those who are subject to them so that the end result may seem the same as for those who believe they are trapped by supernatural forces. Only those who wear the armour of God (6.12ff) can resist them.

3. The digression is continued but with a return to the human aspect of sin and a sudden change from the second person plural to the first; thus questions are raised about who is intended by the first plural and how the verse relates to what precedes. The introductory relative οἷς could be taken to refer back to παραπτώμασιν in v. 1 (so Joüon), but since this is remote and the feminine relative in v. 2 refers to both sins and trespasses it is easier to refer it to the immediately preceding υἱοῖς. The combination 'we all' renders difficult the interpretation of the first person plural. Stress on the 'we'[21] implies a contrast with the 'you' of v. 2 suggesting that Jewish Christians may now be in mind (so Abbott, Barth, Schlier, Ernst, Bruce, etc.); stress on the 'all' suggests it is to be understood of both Jews and Gentiles ('you Gentile Christians once lived in sin ... in fact we all, Jews and Gentile Christians, did so; so Gaugler, Grosheide, Ewald, Schnackenburg, Lindemann, etc.). This is preferable, and it is this understanding of the first plural which is continued from here through the remainder of 2.1–10.

The former solution could be supported if: (i) the change of person in 1.13 came from the Jewish–Gentile contrast, and we have rejected this; (ii) οἱ λοιποί means 'the remaining Christians', i.e. Gentile Christians, but this seems hardly necessary after vv. 1f; it is more natural to take it of non-Christians as giving a better transition to v. 4 through contrast; (iii) though our section is introductory to vv. 11–21 where the unity of Jewish and Gentile Christians is the theme, it has its own purpose and is not merely introductory. There is nothing moreover in v. 3 which is particularly relevant to Jews; it cannot be said that Jews unlike Gentiles are subject only to the desires of the flesh and not to the devil. ἀναστρέφεσθαι (see Spicq, I, 85–8) and περιπατεῖν have a similar meaning in vv. 2, 3 (Gnilka's attempt to suggest that the former carries a community nuance missing in the latter is ill-founded as 5.2 shows) and the former is not particularly Jewish, indeed it is the latter which derives its meaning from its use in Jewish Greek (see on v. 2); if v. 3 referred only to Jews, we might then have expected the verbs to have been reversed in position. ἀναστρέφεσθαι is used in 4.22 of all people. Finally it should be noted that in vv. 4f the first person plural must mean 'all Christians'; a sudden change in reference between v. 3 and v. 4, though possible, would be difficult. There is however a third way of understanding the first plural where the contrast is drawn between readers (vv. 1f) and writer (v. 3); AE's tact leads him in v. 3 to associate himself with his readers in sin (so Mitton, Simpson, Masson); this way of taking it however removes the writer from ever having been under the control of the devil.

All were among the sons of disobedience because all once lived in conformity with the desires of the flesh. It is wrong to regard v. 3 as an unmythological interpretation of v. 2 (so Lindemann, *Aufhebung*, 113). Such a change from v. 2 may accord with modern ideas of the causes of sin but AE would have accepted the descriptions of both v. 2 and v. 3 as valid. ἐπιθυμία, strictly a morally neutral word (e.g. 1 Th 2.17; Phil 1.23), regularly carries an evil connotation in the NT, probably under Jewish influence.[22] Greek readers would however have easily picked this up since, though for a different reason, the word also has a bad sense in Stoic philosophy being one of the passions which reason ought to control, if not eliminate. The desires

---

[21] The variant ὑμεῖς, A* D* 81 326 365 *pc*, is insufficiently supported and is an obvious attempt to solve the difficulty. F G L omit the pronoun but leave the verb as a first person plural.
[22] For the word see F. Büchsel, *TWNT*, III, 162–72.

of Jews and Christians however are evil because they are opposed to God's will, not because they disturb 'calm reason'. The evil sense of ἐπιθυμία in v. 3 is made clear through its connection with 'flesh' (cf Gal 5.16; 1 Jn 2.16; 2 Pet 2.18). While evil desires are often used to describe non-Christian existence (1 Pet 1.14; Tit 3.3; 1 Th 4.5) they are also present in Christians (Rom 13.14; Gal 5.16; Eph 4.22). It is not indicated here what they are, but AE would probably have included those he lists in 5.3–5.

'The desires of our flesh' sounds a characteristically Pauline phrase but Paul rarely uses a personal pronoun with 'flesh'.[23] The noun appears eighty-nine times in the Pauline literature but is accompanied by the pronoun on only fourteen occasions, seven of which are found in Ephesians and Colossians. Of the others (Rom 6.19; 7.18; 11.14; 2 Cor 4.11; 7.5; Gal 4.14; 6.13) only Rom 7.18 could be said to carry a connection with sin, but in fact 'my flesh' is there equivalent to the personal pronoun. When the pronoun is present, 'flesh' cannot be understood as a power from outside affecting human existence. Before we determine more exactly its meaning in v. 3a, we must examine v. 3b where it is again found.

The latter is apparently parallel to the former and explanatory of it (ποιοῦντες replaces ἀνεστράφημεν etc.). ἐπιθυμίαι and θελήματα differ little in meaning; the plural of the latter is unusual in biblical Greek (Isa 44.28; 58.13; Jer 23.26; Acts 13.22) and probably due here to the influence of the other plural. σάρξ is replaced by the double phrase σάρξ καὶ διάνοιαι. The plural of the latter[24] is again unusual in biblical Greek (Num 15.39; 32.7; Josh 5.1; Esdr 4.26; Dan 11.14) and usually has a bad connotation; this adheres to it in v. 3. While the singular has a wide range of meanings the sense of the plural must lie in the area of 'thoughts, ideas, intentions, decisions'. Since AE does not use the singular here he cannot be intending any dualistic division or opposition between flesh (material existence) and mind (intellectual, spiritual existence) as might be expected in a wholly Greek context.[25] AE may have used the plural both to eliminate this possibility and to create a feeling of comprehensiveness: all our intentions are evil. Sin belongs not only to the human body but also to the mind and the will. The two words together also serve to prevent an easy equation in v. 3a of the desires of the flesh with the *yetzer hara'* of rabbinic thought. In the latter the 'evil

[23] For the discussion of the history of the way the word has been understood in Paul see Jewett, 49ff. Adequate references will be found there and in Schweizer, Baumgärtel and Meyer, *TWNT*, VII, 98–151 (137f for treatment of Ephesians); cf also W. Gutbrod, *Die paulinische Anthropologie* (BWANT 67), Stuttgart, 1934, 92–9, 145–60; Käsemann, *Leib*, 4–23, 100–18; A. Sand, *Der Begriff 'Fleisch' in den paulinischen Hauptbriefen*, Regensburg, 1967.

[24] On the word see Behm, *TWNT*, IV, 961–5.

[25] Cf Gutbrod, op.cit., 155f; E. Schweizer, 'Die hellenistischen Komponente im neutestamentlichen σάρξ-Begriff', *ZNW* 48 (1957) 237–53, at 253.

impulse' is rooted in the heart (διάνοια often translates the Hebrew words for heart).[26] Returning now to the meaning of 'flesh' in v. 3a, the parallelism between v. 3a and v. 3b suggests that in v. 3a 'flesh' must apply to the whole of human existence, indicating a life lived apart from God, or, in less religious terms, a life governed by human (cf 2.11; 6.5 for this translation of σάρξ) desires whose main aim is self-expression. That between v. 3a and v. 3b 'flesh' should to some extent have changed its sense is not surprising for this regularly happens when writers use a word with a wide range of meaning. In neither case has the word its characteristic Pauline sense; this is true also of the use of sin and death in v. 1; thus we have Pauline language in these verses without Pauline thought.

The third clause of the verse[27] is neither a further explanation of v. 3a nor a consequence of either it or v. 3b but is coordinate with both. It was not that Christians became children of wrath because they sinned. V. 3c provides a parallel or alternative description of non-Christian existence. V. 3a and v. 3b together describe the activity of non-Christians and therefore of the readers before they became Christians; v. 3c is a statement of status. At first sight (cf MHT, 208) 'children of wrath' appears to employ a similar idiom to 'sons of disobedience' (2.2) but the genitive functions differently; sons of disobedience are disobedient people; children of wrath are not angry people but people subject to the wrath of God; for this form of the idiom see Jn 17.12; Lk 20.36; 2 Th 2.3; 2 Pet 2.14; the two forms are not always easy to distinguish since the quality of life relates to ultimate destiny, cf Mt 13.38; 23.15; Jn 12.36; Rom 9.8; Gal 4.28; 1 Th 5.5. The idiom of v. 3c is probably Semitic in origin (cf 1 Kgdms 20.31; 2 Kgdms 12.5; Ψ 78.11; 101.21; Isa 57.4) but is not unknown in non-biblically oriented Greek. Almost exact parallels to our expression appear in *Apoc Mos* (see *Life of Adam and Eve*) 3.2 where Cain is described as a 'son of wrath' and in *Sib Or* 2.309, 'children of anger'; those so termed end in eternal perdition. These parallels suggest that in 2.3 the wrath[28] in mind is the eschatological wrath of God, though as such this wrath is not necessarily future and may be experienced now (cf Rom 1.18ff; 13.4f and see on 5.6), for AE has a realised eschatology. It should be understood as personal

---

[26] Cf W. D. Davies, *Paul and Rabbinic Judaism*, London, 1948, 21.

[27] On the history of the Catholic (he has little to say about Protestant) interpretation of v. 3c see J. Mehlmann, *Natura Filii Irae* (AnBib 6), Rome, 1957; for Protestant interpretation see D. L. Turner, 'Ephesians 2:2c and *Peccatum originale*', *GraceTJ* 1 (1980) 195–219.

[28] On the wrath of God see A. T. Hanson, *The Wrath of the Lamb*, London, 1957; L. Morris, *The Apostolic Preaching of the Cross*, London, 1955, 161ff; id. *The Cross in the New Testament*, Exeter, 1976, 189–92; Kleinknecht *et alii*, *TWNT*, V, 382–448; G. H. C. MacGregor, 'The Concept of the Wrath of God in the New Testament', *NTS* 7 (1960/1) 101–9; G. Bornkamm, 'The Revelation of God's Wrath (Romans 1–3)' in his *Early Christian Experience*, London, 1969, 47–70.

wrath rather than impersonal, though the parallel with human wrath should not be drawn too closely for unlike human anger God's anger is neither malicious nor spiteful. The absence here of an explicit reference to God (it is present in the parallel of Col 3.6) is no more surprising than the similar absence in the references to grace in vv. 5, 8.[29] That believers were once, and unbelievers are now, subject to the eschatological wrath of God coheres with their being once dead in trespasses and sin.

How does the qualification φύσει[30] affect the phrase? The word has no equivalent in biblical Hebrew and is found only in later Jewish Greek. Within our context it could mean either 'character' or 'constitution': children of wrath because of behaviour or children of wrath as human beings. If the former we would expect an ethical quality to be stated (cf Josephus *Ant* 14.13, 44; *BJ* 1.204, 255) and ἐγινόμεθα would be more appropriate than ἦμεθα (Ewald). The understanding of the whole phrase as 'subject to wrath as human beings' accords better with v. 1. Unbelievers are 'dead', not because of a succession of sins which brought death, but because they have never come alive as believers. As dead they are subject to judgement (cf Jn 3.36) and so may properly be described as 'subject to wrath'. 'Children of wrath by nature' thus describes 'a permanent condition'[31] in the relation of unbelievers to God. It is not a judgement on the factual degree of their sin. If any parallel or contrast is intended with the actual world, it may be with Stoic teaching where living according to nature is true living; such living for AE would be subject to the judgement of God. Granted that what we have here is not Stoic teaching, the theological distinction between nature and grace should not be read into the phrase; if there is a contrast it lies between what men are left to themselves and what they become when God makes them to live, that is, the contrast is between 'then' and 'now' or between those outside the church and those within it and not between the ways in which each state is attained.

Has that 'outside' state been created by 'original sin' as the use of 'children' might suggest? In the idiom however 'children' is not used literally. There are a number of possibilities: (i) original sin in the traditional hereditary sense; (ii) an involvement in sin through 'constitution' or 'nature', regarded either as providing an innate capacity for sin or as belonging to human nature as such, whether considered individually or socially; (iii) the person who lives without God is subject to God's wrath; (iv) an involvement with sin through actual sins so that 'character' becomes sinful. (iii) and (iv) seem excluded as referring to actual behaviour and not taking φύσει

---

[29] See my discussion in *Thessalonians*, 84–7.
[30] On φύσις see Koester, *TWNT*, IX, 246–71; R. M. Grant, *Miracle and Natural Law in Greco-Roman and Early Christian Thought*, Amsterdam, 1952, 3–18.
[31] A. T. Hanson, op.cit., 103.

sufficiently seriously; (ii) is probably what is being said but there is nothing which would render (i) untenable and equally nothing demanding its acceptance. In either case the use of 'nature' implies that unbelievers left to their own devices cannot escape God's judgement. Moule's rendering (p. 174), 'left to ourselves we are destined to suffer the consequences of sin', is satisfactory if the consequence of sin is God's judgement and not merely 'the retribution that overtakes wrong-doing, whether it takes the form of judicial sentence in a law court (Rom 13.4), of national disaster (1 Th 2.16), or of a progressive moral degradation (Rom 1.19–32)' (Caird, ad loc). Rejecting this latter view it must be asked when God's judgement takes place. If for AE it is possible to envisage believers as already sitting in heavenly places (v. 6) it seems possible to conceive of unbelievers as already under the judgement of God and sentenced.

2.1–3 explain non-Christian human existence in two ways: as governed internally by sin and externally by evil supernatural powers. Can these two approaches be reconciled? While economic pressures on people may come from outside as a result of the human greed of others, a person's genetic constitution cannot be blamed on the sin of others. AE had probably not thought much about economic pressures as such; their results on individuals he would probably have put down to evil supernatural forces; as for sins, he would also probably have put these down both to human nature and, with much traditional theology, to outside powers like the devil.

Does a hymn or credal fragment underlie vv. 4–10? Schille, 53–60, sees a hymn commencing with δέ at the beginning of v. 4 and ending with the break before v. 11. To this AE added v. 5c and vv. 8f. There is no dependence on Colossians; similarities are to be explained because both employed a common *Vorlage*. However, it is very difficult to work out any proper strophic structure for this supposed hymn. The idea of being made alive (v. 5) picks up that of being dead in v. 1 and the idea of being raised and given a seat in the heavenlies with Christ follows on the resurrection and ascension of Christ in 1.20. Thus the passage fits easily into its context, suggesting it was written for it. Finally the content of vv. 5c, 8f is too important to be a side thought. There is no reason then to see here the use of pre-existing material with which all the readers would be acquainted, though it is impossible to deny that AE may have made use of liturgical material to which he was accustomed. In particular this means we cannot argue that we have here a portion of a baptismal liturgy. Many words appear which could have a baptismal connection but they do not necesarily have this connection. See on v. 5 and Best, 'Use', for fuller discussion.

4. If unbelievers were once dead in sin, under the power of evil supernatural beings, controlled by their own wicked desires and subject to God's wrath, they could expect no mercy from God, yet (δέ) surprisingly, that is not so for God is rich in mercy. Thus the anacoluthon of vv. 2, 3 not only elaborates v. 1 but also sets off more strongly the contrast appearing with v. 4. The new position of believers is a result only of the nature and activity of God. As in chap. 1 so here again the initiative in salvation lies with God and we have a *theo*logy rather than a *christo*logy. It is probably wrong to overstress here the contrast between the 'wrath of God' (v. 3) and his 'mercy'. When AE began v. 1 he had v. 4 in mind; v. 3c is not then a climax carefully built up through vv. 1–3b to be contrasted with v. 4. The real contrast lies between 'death' (vv. 1, 5) and 'life' (συνεζωοποίησεν, v. 5). It is introduced with a general statement of God's nature: πλούσιος (a favourite term of AE, see on 1.7, though he normally prefers the neuter) ὢν ἐν (for the construction instead of the more usual genitive see Jas 2.5; 1 Tim 6.18; 1 Kgdms 2.10) ἐλέει; since the latter is not a passive concept it leads on naturally to a succession of active verbs.

Some commentators (e.g. Schlier, Conzelmann, Gnilka; see Gnilka, 117, n. 5, for further references) have seen a connection between the use of ἔλεος and baptism and instance 1 Pet 1.3 and Tit 3.5 as parallels. This connection may also appear in vv. 5f where the themes of being dead and being raised with Christ may be related to baptism through Rom 6.1ff and Col 2.12; in Col 2.12 baptism is clearly in mind. The connection of ἔλεος with baptism is certainly present in Tit 3.5, but it is not immediately so in 1 Pet 1.3 unless that letter is taken to be a baptismal sermon or liturgy; this is unlikely.[32] ἔλεος is also used in 'election' contexts (Rom 9.23; 11.30–2; 1 Pet 1.3) and since this is a theme prominent in 1.3–14 it may have determined its choice here. It is more probable, however, that AE chose the word because it is one occurring frequently in the OT, and is a synonym for ἀγάπη which he is just about to use. (For the possible relation of vv. 5f to baptism see discussion there.) Noting the paronomasia in v. 4b (cf 1.3) we need to ask whether the clause is to be connected backwards to v. 4a or forwards to v. 5. If it is connected backwards, then to write of God's love is another way of saying that he is merciful, and the aorist tense[33] of ἠγάπησεν would not be restricted to the event of the cross. If it is connected forwards, the aorist would have a once-for-all significance relating to the essence of God's action in the death of his son. Perhaps it is wrong to select one of these alternatives. Rather v. 4b is a connecting link

[32] See Best, *1 Peter* (NCB), London, 1971, 20–7; L. Goppelt, *Der erste Petrusbrief* (KEK), Göttingen, 1978, 37–40; C. F. D. Moule, 'The Nature and Purpose of 1 Peter', *NTS* 3 (1956) 1–11.

[33] An aorist of an extended act, Burton, §39, or a timeless aorist, Porter, 237.

between v. 4a and v. 5. God's love in the death of his son is a part of his merciful attitude towards people which reaches its climax in that death, so that through that death those who are dead in sin are made to live. The new life of Christians is then related directly to God's action in Christ rather than to his nature as merciful.

αὐτοῦ is omitted by 𝔓⁴⁶ D* F G b; Ambr Aug; the meaning is not affected. The variant ἠλέησεν 𝔓⁴⁶ b d; Ambst which also omits ἦν is probably due to the desire to give a main verb to v. 4 and so remove the difficulty caused by the καί at the beginning of v. 5; its substitution weakens the sentence and though creating another paronomasia it would not be as easily grasped as that in the text which plays on the root ἀγαπα. ἀγάπην is a cognate accusative (Moule, 32; MHT, 245). For contrasting views and arguments on this second variant see Ramaroson, art.cit., and Romaniuk, 212f.

5. Here as at v. 1 the initial καί is difficult and probably due to the use of preformed material (see on v. 1). This assumption is better than taking it to mean 'also' or giving it concessive value. As we have seen, scribes modified v. 4 so that καί could have its normal meaning 'and'. It is probably best left untranslated and the words following it taken as the object of συνεζωοποίησεν (for detailed studies of attempts to find a meaning for καί when no allowance is made for the use of preformed material, see Ewald and Haupt). Our verse repeats the essential content of v. 1 with the omission of 'sins',[34] which was an addition in v. 1 to the preformed material; it also alters the second person to the first. The verb provides the new element in what AE is saying.

συζωοποιεῖν is not found in non-Christian Greek and only here, in Col 2.13 and in later Christian writing dependent on these two verses. The simpler ζωοποιεῖν is however used regularly by Paul (cf Jn 5.21; 6.63; 1 Pet 3.18) and almost always in a resurrection context (Rom 4.17; 8.11; 1 Cor 15.22, 36, 45). He uses it twice in the future tense of the resurrection of believers (Rom 8.11; 1 Cor 15.22) and twice as a present participle describing the activity of God or Christ (Rom 4.17; 1 Cor 15.45). All his references may be understood as relating to the future final resurrection, whereas here and in Col 2.13 the act of making alive lies in the past. This distinction is not sufficient to compel a reference here to Christ as the Second Adam.[35] It is also not clear that the word necessarily carries a resurrection connotation, for this does not appear to be the case in *Jos As* 8.10f where it seems to apply rather to conversion.[36]

---

[34] There are quite a number of variants here. 𝔓⁴⁶ reads σώμασιν, D*, partially supported by F G, substitutes ἁμαρτίαις. Ψ Orˡᵃᵗ read the phrase of v. 1, as does B, but with ἐπιθυμίαις for ἁμαρτίαις. The variety of alteration suggests the difficulty of the phrase, a difficulty probably caused by the initial καί.
[35] So Macpherson, 162f; Coutts.
[36] Cf A. J. M. Wedderburn, op.cit., 218f.

This would appear to be its primary significance here where the verb's reference to 'life' contrasts vividly with the concept that those outside the Christian community were previously dead. When it is said that the Spirit gives life (1 Cor 15.45; 2 Cor 3.6; Jn 6.63) there is no explicit connection with resurrection. In v. 5 we have in fact the first of three steps, the verbs of v. 6 denoting the second and third: made alive, raised, seated in the heavenlies. Dead people cannot bring themselves back to life (Könn) and so the first step here, and the following two, come from God. We can arrange neither to be born nor to be reborn.

The antithesis between death and life in v. 5 is not however the same as that in Romans 6 where a past dying with Christ is usually understood as contrasting with a future rising with him, and of course it is not the same as in those passages where 'with Christ' refers to a final future existence. What we have here must have arisen independently,[37] for the death is one existing from the time of birth, is one in sin (see v. 1) not one with Christ. There is much in the NT, e.g. the new creation in Christ (2 Cor 5.17) or the concept of the new birth, testifying to the present new life of believers (see Best, 'Dead', for parallels). Those born anew commence, as it were, a new life just as dead unbelievers begin to live when they are made alive by God. The new life must have begun at some point, as is indicated here (cf Col 2.13) by the use of the aorist. Paul, of course, uses the aorist in respect of justification (Rom 5.1, 9; 8.30; 1 Cor 6.11).

When do believers begin to enjoy this new life? (a) at the resurrection of Christ? (b) at the moment when faith began? (c) at their baptism? (d), and very much a counsel of despair, after death, the verb being taken as an unfulfilled aorist (so Meyer, Salmond)? (a) is a possibility (cf Caird, Lock) in the sense that when Christ who was a representative or inclusive figure was raised all were potentially raised with him; the aorist ἠγάπησεν in v. 4, which can be referred to the Christ-event, gives some support to this view. Yet believers were dead in an entirely different way from Christ and therefore can hardly have been 'included' in him when he was made alive. The choice must then lie between (b) and (c). The readers, once dead, have been made alive and this would have taken place at the moment they became Christians. But is this the moment when faith began or the moment when they were baptised? The reference to 'faith' (v. 8) would support (b); the reference to baptism is clear in the similar passage of Col 2.13.[38] But the distinction later theologians have drawn between the moments of faith and baptism,

[37] Cf P. Siber, *Mit Christus leben: eine Studie zur paulinischen Auferstehungshoffnung*, Zürich, 1971, 202ff.
[38] E. Larsson, *Christus als Vorbild* (ASNU 23), Uppsala, 1962, 105–8.

derived from the post-New Testament practice of enforcing a lengthy catechumenate, would have been unreal to the primitive church. Acts shows that once belief had been affirmed baptism followed directly as the first act of obedient faith (cf 2.41; 8.36; 10.47f; 16.31–3); Acts probably represents in this respect both what originally happened and the practice of its own period which was more or less contemporary with that of Ephesians. It is probably then incorrect to ask whether AE had faith or baptism in mind; for him they would have been an indissoluble unity.

We have assumed here that the σύν of the verb related believers to Christ. However, if ἐν is read before τῷ Χριστῷ this will not be so. This reading has good support: 𝔓⁴⁶ B 33 a (g) vgᶜˡ; MVict Ambst Chr. If ἐν was not originally present it may have appeared either through duplication of the final syllable of the verb or under the influence of the familiar formula 'in Christ' which is found in vv. 6, 7; however, had the formula been already present it would surely not have been altered. Commentators who accept it understand the σύν to refer to the drawing together of Jewish and Gentile Christians. If v. 5 had lain in 2.14–22, or even in a passage about the unity of the church, this might have been a possible understanding but, since it does not, it is not. As for the togetherness of Jewish and Gentile Christians, this is related neither to the ultimate purpose (v. 7) of being made alive nor to the main drive of the passage on the saving mercy of God; to accept it would destroy the strong link between v. 6, where the σύν would have to continue to carry this meaning, and 1.20, where the simple forms of the same basic verbs are used of Christ. Generally in the Pauline corpus where verbs are compounded with σύν the reference is to a linking with Christ. Where the verb is used in Col 2.13 there is no idea of a relationship of Jewish and Gentile Christians. The view of Lindemann (ad loc and *Aufhebung*, 118ff) that it simply means 'we together' is more than a little weak. We therefore reject the reading ἐν. In Col 2.13 the reference to Christ is made clear with an additional σὺν αὐτῷ; Paul does not usually spell out the reference in this way; AE is therefore more Pauline than A/Col and so he will hardly have been copying from him. For the article with Christ see on 1.10.

οὗ, with or without τῇ, is read before χάριτι by D* F G a b vgᶜˡ syᵖ; MVict Ambst Aug and is almost certainly an attempt to iron out the sudden break before v. 5a. χάριτι is anarthrous indicating that emphasis rests on the contrast with other possible means of salvation rather than on the nature of the actual action as gracious (cf MHT, 176; Zerwick, §76).

A brief parenthesis now breaks the sequence of thought: χάριτί ἐστε σεσῳσμένοι. (For a discussion whether this and vv. 8f may be a gloss or glosses see on vv. 8f.) If AE's readers have been made alive this is not through any effort or goodness on their part but only because of the grace of God. AE develops this thought in vv. 8–10 but he cannot wait until then to express his wonder at what God has done. The parenthesis as such stands out from the ongoing argument through the sudden change from the first person to the second; there are changes in person again at v. 8 and v. 10. It is unlikely that AE wishes to distinguish in v. 5b between himself and his readers or between Jewish and Gentile Christians as if either he or Jewish Christians were not saved in the same way as others. Barth, 221, suggests the second person represents the antiphonal response of the leader of worship to the hymn of the people which he assumes is found in vv. 4–7 (elsewhere, 217f, Barth appears to doubt whether a hymn underlies our passage). But why should the leader isolate himself in this way from his congregation, implying that they need grace whereas he does not? Moreover if the readers of the letter are to be able to recognise an antiphonal response they must be assumed to know the liturgy in question and, while this might be possible in a letter addressed to one congregation which the author knew well, it is hardly likely in the case of a general letter where the writer may not know all the communities he is addressing. It is then better to take the parenthesis as an interjection of the author in which by a change of person he drives home his point more forcefully (so Henle, Macpherson), recognising at the same time that it could indeed be a quotation of a phrase regularly used in worship (cf Lindemann, *Aufhebung*, 173).

The perfect tense σεσωσμένοι is unusual in the Pauline corpus. Paul normally uses the verb in the future (e.g. Rom 5.8, 9; 9.27; 1 Cor 3.13) or with a future reference (e.g. Rom 11.14; 1 Cor 5.5), though he also speaks of salvation as an ongoing process (1 Cor 1.18; 15.2; 2 Cor 2.15) and uses the cognate noun to describe that process (Rom 10.10; 2 Cor 6.2). Only once (Rom 8.24) does he set salvation in the past and there it is qualified by a reference to hope. Moreover he does not elsewhere connect χάρις with σώζειν relating it instead to δικαιοῦν. In view of these differences from Paul's normal usage, it is surprising to find Foulkes describing the present clause as Paul's 'favourite summing up of the gospel'. Bruce is surely more correct when he says the clause 'departs from *distinctively* Pauline usage' (italics as in Bruce). We must leave a discussion of the significance of the changes until vv. 8–10. For the moment we note that the perfect tense, and a periphrastic perfect at that (cf Moule, 18f; Burton §84), suggests that the 'state of salvation' is in mind; 'life' will now be continuous since death is past.

6. In Col 2.13 being made alive with Christ is explained as the forgiveness of sin and the cancellation of the legal bond; Eph 2.6 explains it through a change of imagery which relates it to the resurrection and ascension. This appears to create a temporal sequence with ascension with Christ following on resurrection with him, but this is an illusion so far as AE is concerned; believers once raised are in heaven and are there immediately seated. So the two verbs of v. 6 do not follow chronologically on the being made alive of v. 5. It is better to regard all three verbs as aspects of the same act of God, made alive, raised, seated. 'Made alive' comes first because nothing can happen without the dead being made alive. Being made alive with Christ is not Paul's normal expression for entrance into the Christian life, though as a word which he related to resurrection (Rom 4.17; 8.11; 1 Cor 15.22, 36) it could suggest the present change of imagery. Paul usually describes the passage from pagan to Christian life by means of σύν compounded with verbs of dying and rising. AE follows the same way of thinking, perhaps suggested to him by his own use of σύν in v. 5; v. 6 thus offers an alternative explanation of what it means to be a Christian. AE chooses the same verbs as those of 1.20, verbs drawn from the Christian credo, but now compounded with σύν. It is interesting that at this point his sequence of events differs from that of Col 2.12f where burial and resurrection with Christ precede being made alive from the death of sin and the latter is apparently the explanation of the former. AE can have a different order because his primary focus is not on baptism, a conclusion all the stronger if he did not use Colossians here; lacking the interest in baptism he is able to drop the idea of dying or being buried with Christ. For AE rising with Christ and sitting with him in heaven explain the significance of being made alive.

It is unnecessary to explore the origin of the formula uniting σύν with various verbs of dying and rising;[39] by the time of Ephesians it was part and parcel of Pauline imagery; in Paul the verbs relating to resurrection are normally in the future. However, in our verse resurrection with Christ is set in the past and with it is linked the heavenly session with Christ, both seen as accomplished facts. The change to the past tense in respect of resurrection with Christ had already been made in Col 2.12; 3.1. It is not unnatural. The present nature of new life with Christ following on a past death with him is certainly indicated in the genuine Pauline letters (Rom 6.4, 10, 11,

---

[39] For discussions of the formula see E. Lohmeyer, 'Σὺν Χριστῷ' in *Festgabe für A. Deissmann* (ed. K. L. Schmidt), Tübingen, 1927, 218–57; W. T. Hahn, *Das Mitsterben und Mitauferstehen mit Christus bei Paulus*, Gütersloh, 1937; J. Dupont, ΣΥΝ ΧΡΙΣΤΩΙ. *L'union avec le Christ suivant saint Paul*, Bruges, 1952; Best, *One Body*, 44–64; O. Küss, *Der Römerbrief*, Regensburg, 1963, 319–81; R. C. Tannehill, *Dying and Rising with Christ* (BZNW 32), Berlin, 1966; E. Schweizer, 'Die "Mystik" des Sterbens und Auferstehens mit Christus bei Paulus', *EvT* 26 (1966) 239–57; id. 'Dying and Rising with Christ', *NTS* 14 (1967/8) 1–14; G. Wagner, *Pauline Baptism and the Pagan Mysteries*, Edinburgh and London, 1967; R. Schnackenburg, 'Todes- und Lebensgemeinschaft mit Christus' in his *Schriften zum Neuen Testament*, Munich, 1971, 361–91; H. Frankemölle, *Das Taufverständnis des Paulus: Taufe, Tod und Auferstehung nach Röm 6* (SBS 47), Stuttgart, 1970; Siber, op.cit., 191ff; A. J. M. Wedderburn, 'Paul and the Hellenistic Mystery-Cults: On Posing the Right Questions' in *La Soteriologia dei culti orientali nell'impero Romano* (ed. U. Bianchi and M. J. Vermaseren), Leiden, 1982, 817–33; id. 'Hellenistic Christian Traditions in Romans 6?', *NTS* 29 (1983) 337–55; id. *Baptism and Resurrection, passim*.

13, 7.4; Gal 2.20; 2 Cor 4.10, 12; 5.17); there is no point in exhorting believers to live a new life if that life belongs only to the future. In Rom 6.1ff dying and rising with Christ is associated with baptism; baptism was a past fact for believers; it was inevitable that some who had been baptised should eventually come to think of their resurrection as past fact since they were already enjoying the new life that resurrection would bring; indeed we find that when the pastness of resurrection with Christ is first positively stated in Col 2.12 it is linked to baptism; A/Col may however have had some hesitation about this, since in 3.5 he writes of the new risen life as hidden with God. In Eph 2.6 there is no explicit reference to baptism and it is difficult to argue for an implicit one, since AE does not use the verbs denoting dying and being buried with Christ which are particularly linked with it in Rom 6; the absence of a reference to baptism is not unreasonable, since from the beginning expressions relating to new life with Christ were not exclusively associated with the rite (cf Gal 2.19f; 6.14; 2 Cor 4.10; 5.14; Phil 3.10[40]); Christians of that period did not distinguish so clearly between the moment when faith began and baptism took place as we do (see on v. 5). The past nature of Christ's own resurrection would also lend momentum to the acceptance of the past nature of that of believers. The idea may also be implicit in the pre-Ephesian and probably non-Pauline hymn of 5.14.[41]

The transfer of believers from the death of sin and the realm of the devil is expressed more strongly in v. 6 than elsewhere in the NT when it is said that believers have sat down with Christ in the heavenlies. In other places their reign is set in the future (2 Tim 2.12; Rev 3.21; 5.10; 20.4; 22.5; cf 1 Cor 6.2f; 1 Pet 2.9;[42] Mt 13.43; Rom 8.17, 30). Believers are distinguished from Christ in that they are not said to sit at God's right hand.

A number of factors contributed to the NT teaching on the heavenly session of the saints: (i) apocalyptic sayings, e.g. Dan 7.18, 22, 27; *I En* 108.12; (ii) the saying of Jesus underlying Mt 19.28; Lk 22.30 (the idea is present in Mk 10.37); (iii) the targumic development of Exod 19.6;[43] (iv) the angels, or holy ones, and the members of the Qumran community are sometimes grouped together (1QS 11.7f; 1QH 3.21–3; 11.10–12[44]) thus implying the presence of the members of the community in heaven; (v) the unity of believers with Christ who has already taken his seat in heaven (1.20). It is this last factor which was the most important for Christians. All this makes it unnecessary to suppose with Reitzenstein the influence of the

[40] Cf Best, *One Body*, 46; Tannehill, op.cit., 41–3.
[41] Cf Siber, op.cit., 200–2.
[42] Cf Best, 'I Peter II 4–10—A Reconsideration', *NT* 11 (1969) 270–93.
[43] See J. H. Elliott, *The Elect and the Holy* (SupNT 12), Leiden, 1966, 50ff.
[44] Cf Mussner, 'Beiträge', 200–3.

concept of baptism as a heavenly journey[45] the evidence for which is relatively late (e.g. the Mandean literature); Schlier points to the *Odes of Solomon* but these may have been affected by Christianity.

Colossians and Ephesians share the idea of a past resurrection of believers with Christ, and in Ephesians it is impossible to decide whether AE thought the moment when this took place was that of faith or baptism (see v. 5). In accepting a past ascension of believers, AE goes beyond Colossians which in 3.3 says only that believers are now hidden with God. It is however logical to accept ascension with Christ once a past resurrection with him has been accepted. In this AE may have advanced beyond Colossians through his greater interest in the ascension of Christ (1.20–3; 4.8) and a desire to preserve a parallel with 1.20; it is moreover not out of keeping with his belief that the church is active in the heavenlies (3.10), where it has access to God (2.18), and with 2.19, if the 'saints' there are the inhabitants of heaven. However, in 1 Cor 4.8 Paul spoke scornfully of some who believed that they were already reigning as kings; the claim of some Corinthian believers to speak with the tongues of angels may also indicate a belief that they were already in heaven. It is improbable that what Paul attacks here represents a pre-Pauline belief against which he contends in Rom 6.1ff by arguing for a future resurrection with Christ.[46] In 2 Tim 2.18 the belief that resurrection is already past is condemned as heretical.[47] Was there then a division among disciples of Paul in that some moved towards a more realised soteriology than others?[48] If so, were there those, including Paul if he had still been alive, who would have condemned what AE writes as heretical since he affirms a past resurrection and present session in the heavenlies? Before we turn to consider this we should realise that this is no one-off statement by AE for, as we have seen, it accords with 3.10 and 2.19. Believers live simultaneously in two spheres, earth and heaven. (On the soteriology of Ephesians, see Introduction §6.4.)

What is missing from the use of the σύν formula in Ephesians is any connection with verbs of suffering (Rom 8.17) and dying (Rom 3.4, 6) with Christ. This leaves the impression that AE is concerned too much with seeing Christians as in a position of glory without first passing through suffering (Rom 8.17), an impression reinforced by his failure when he later discusses the behaviour of believers to say anything about what they may have to endure.

[45] R. Reitzenstein, *Die Vorgeschichte des christlichen Taufe*, Leipzig, 1929, 104f, 167ff; Wagner, op.cit., 21ff, gives a full literary documentation.

[46] Cf Wedderburn, 'Paul and the Hellenistic Mystery-Cults'.

[47] On the acceptance and development of the idea see Lona, 374–418.

[48] The realised nature of the heavenly session of believers goes so much against what we would expect and so differs from Paul that it is not surprising that Bratcher and Nida suggest that translators should insert a phrase like 'as it were'.

Did AE go too far here in speaking of a heavenly session for Christians? In considering this it is wise to remember the particular flavour AE gives to 'in the heavenlies' (see Detached Note: The Heavenlies). These are not the perfect heaven of later Christian thought, but a place where evil powers still fight to maintain their position (6.10ff). AE does not then see believers who sit in the heavenlies as freed from the struggle with evil and sin, and in the second part of his letter he has much advice and exhortation to give to them for this struggle. His teaching on the heavenlies is then at least consistent. The background to Paul's attack in 1 Cor 4.8 on those who claim to reign already is their spiritual enthusiasm. This does not appear to be a danger for AE's recipients; when he comes to spell out charismatic gifts in 4.7, 11 he has difficulty in moving beyond the official ministry! The background to 2 Tim 2.18 is not so clear; the belief of those accused there of heresy may have been generated by the Greek separation of body and soul so that though the body still remains on earth, the soul as perfect rises to immortality. Within the course of church history groups have appeared from time to time claiming to be perfect, an assertion which amounts to much the same as the claim to be already in heaven. It cannot then be surprising to find the idea present at an early stage of the church. It is noticeable that the writer of 2 Timothy moves directly in 2.19 to a demand for moral behaviour. Whatever defence however is put up to explain the meaning of AE's words within his context, it cannot be denied that they are open to wrong deductions; our verse is quoted in gnostic contexts in support of a present spiritual resurrection (*Treat Res* I, 4 45.27; cf 49.16–28). Ephesians may thus be on the way to what ended as gnosticism.

What does AE mean by sitting in the heavenlies? In 1.20 Christ's seat in the heavenlies implies his superiority to the powers; in the heavenlies he occupies a position of authority, he reigns. We should expect the same to be intended of Christians; they reign,[49] or rather, to be more precise in view of the use of σύν, they participate in

[49] 2.6 implies all Christians will sit with Christ in the heavenlies yet Mt 19.28 suggests that only the Twelve will reign there. Has a function originally restricted to them been widened here or has one intended for all been narrowed in Matthew? Mt 19.28 may not be the form of Jesus' original logion; in the parallel of Lk 22.30 the number of thrones is undetermined; the saying may then have been spoken originally to all followers of Jesus (cf G. Schmahl, *Die Zwölf im Markusevangelium*, Trier, 1974, 29–36). Once the 'overlordship' of the Twelve was stressed, the saying was restricted to them; prior to that it had penetrated the Christian tradition in the wider sense as we see from 1 Cor 6.2f; Rom 5.17; 2 Tim 2.12 (if this is an early fragment), and even into heretical Christianity as shown by 1 Cor 4.8. If Mt 19.28 correctly reproduces the original logion then we must see both the wider (the disciples) and the narrower (the Twelve) concepts as present from almost the beginning. A certain incompatibility has continued to exist between them.

Christ's reign. Yet it is not said that believers are exalted to the right hand of God as was Christ. Their position in the heavenlies is not then identical with his.[50] Perhaps a little more can be learned from 3.10 (see there) where a cosmic role is given to the church (see also 2.7). In 6.10ff believers are offered equipment for exercising authority over evil spiritual powers, for, unlike Christ, Christians so long as they live are still threatened by these powers. It would seem that AE in following through the apparent parallel of rising with Christ and sitting with him has not been able to express adequately what he wished to say and has left himself open to misunderstanding, and that not only in a too realistic sense by gnostics.[51] More usually the realism has been undervalued; Origen appears to regard what is said as signifying no more than an attitude of mind (*c. Cels* 8.22; *Comm Mt* 10.14); Thomas Aquinas, recognising the past tenses, speaks of the certitude of hope; Chrysostom (ad loc) writes round the problem by speaking of the body of Christ which goes to heaven with Christ its head, and modern attempts to explain it in terms of the anthropos myth in effect do the same. The problem is not new to Christianity for no one supposes that when in Ps 110.1 the king is said to be at God's right hand he was actually sitting there, yet it is basic to the description of the Christian life; on the one hand believers are still plagued by sin; on the other they already reign (Rom 5.17) in a new type of existence. AE is faithful to both sides of this paradox but throughout the letter he tends to stress its second element and 2.6 taken out of the context of the letter is open to serious misunderstanding. Those who stress the first element also look forward more consistently to a future eschatological realisation of the second. The future is not stressed by AE but it has not fully disappeared (e.g. 1.14, 18; 2.21; 4.4, 15f, 30; 5.5, 16, 21).

AE qualifies the verbs in two ways: the first qualification, 'in the heavenlies', applies only to the second verb and is necessitated by the parallelism with 1.20. The second, 'in Christ Jesus', qualifies both and may have been drawn in through its association with 'in the heavenlies' in 1.3. It does not imply that σύν has changed its meaning in v. 6 from v. 5, as if Jewish Christians and Gentile Christians rise together with one another in Christ Jesus.[52] The existence of the σύν formula in many compounds in the earlier Paulines excludes such a change in meaning; it would also be strange to find the preposition varying in meaning between v. 5 and v. 6 since there is no more here than in v. 5 to suggest AE has the

---

[50] Mk 10.35–9 implies all who reach heaven will have seats.

[51] Some church Fathers also spoke over-realistically of the newly baptised as transferred to paradise but they balanced this with an emphasis on the progress the baptised needed to make; cf J. H. Bernard, 'The Odes of Solomon', *JTS* 12 (1910/11) 1–31.

[52] Cf Von Soden and Ramaroson, art.cit.

unification of Jewish and Gentile Christians in mind. The linking of the σύν and the 'in Christ' formulae is unusual.[53] The latter formula sets out Christ as the 'place' where God acts for us whereas the former supplies the sense of fellowship with Christ. Such an interpretation accords with 1.3. It is only because of what God has done in Christ that believers have risen and are seated with him in the heavenlies.

7. God does not raise believers to the heavenlies merely for their own good but that he might exhibit, or prove,[54] the wealth of his grace. But to whom, or what, or when, does God exhibit or prove his grace? As we saw on 1.21; 2.2, αἰών is a word with a number of meanings. Here the plural is used. This makes it unlikely that τοῖς αἰῶσιν τοῖς ἐπερχομένοις means 'the coming age' (Mk 10.30, which has a similar phrase, uses the singular as does 1.21); it is just possible, but unlikely, that the plural has been derived from the liturgical phrase ὁ αἰών τῶν αἰώνων. Why should God wish to make his grace known in the age to come, when almost by definition that is the age when no one will doubt it? If the plural is to be taken as a genuine plural, then it is better to understand it as suggesting that the future consists of a number of periods of time (so Origen, de Princip. II 3.5). The aeons would be the future history of this age and of the age to come; ἐπερχόμενοι would indicate these ages as they approach from the future (so Gnilka, Gaugler, Ernst, Bruce). It would however be wrong to attempt to identify the aeons as particular periods of history or as implying the rise and decay of civilisations. God, by what he has done for the writer and readers of the letter, is able to exhibit or prove his grace to future ages; the aorist subjunctive ἐνδείξηται is a little difficult but can be understood in that the past resurrection and sitting in heaven, though taking place once for all, can be a display of God's grace for ever and so regarded as one act. Lindemann's (Aufhebung, 129f) rejection of the future reference seems to be based more on his theory that Ephesians contains only a fully realised eschatology than on an actual reading of the text.

The main difficulties in referring αἰῶσιν to the 'coming ages' lie elsewhere: (i) It gives a unique position to the writer and readers. It is easy to see how God's grace towards them could be displayed to those among whom they live but an approaching aeon will shortly be an aeon which is past and it will have within it believers, as well as those in AE's aeon, in whom God's grace will be seen and it would have been better to refer to these. (ii) Human beings will not be aware that writer and readers have sat down in the heavenlies unless they have spiritual perception; in that case they will be

[53] On the relation of the two formulae see Frankemölle, op.cit., 116–20; Best, One Body, 59–63.
[54] On the meaning 'prove' for ἐνδείκνυμαι see MM s.v.

believers and will not require God's grace to be exhibited to them in this way; this conclusion might be avoided if those who are intended in the approaching ages are beings with spiritual sight, i.e. supernatural beings. Since good angels will already know God's goodness they would not need such a testimony; presumably then the aeons are evil supernatural beings.

To avoid these difficulties the aeons have been understood as supernatural personal beings (Lindemann, *Aufhebung*, 129f; Schlier, Pokorný, *Gnosis*, 114; Dibelius). The evidence for this use of the word is widespread in second-century gnosticism (see on 2.2) and the aeons could be viewed either as friendly (Schlier) or hostile (Lindemann, R. Reitzenstein, *Das iranische Erlösungsmysterium*, Bonn, 1921, 235f). In either case such an understanding follows on well from v. 6: the aeons inhabit the heavenlies in which the believers sit. If the aeons are assumed to be hostile then we would understand ἐπερχόμενοι as meaning 'come against, attack' (cf Lk 11.22; Josephus *Ant* 5.195; 6.23, and see LSJ *s.v.* for this meaning). It is more natural to regard the aeons as hostile since if they were friendly they would not require God's grace to be shown to them. It cannot be objected to this view that the αἰῶνες are not listed in 1.21 for that list is not exhaustive. 3.11 may be said to present a similar idea for there the divine mystery is made known through the church to the supernatural powers. However, this whole view runs into several difficulties: (i) ἐνδείκνυσθαι ἐν never means 'to show, or prove, to'; at best it could mean 'among' (cf Schnackenburg). (ii) In 3.21 the aeons are related to the γενεαί, a temporal term, though one often also used to denote actual people who naturally live in time (cf 3.5 and 3.9).

There is no easy solution. Col 1.26 contains the same problem of interpretation (see the differing views of commentators). It may be that AE plays on the ambiguity of αἰῶνες and wishes to say that the exaltation of reader and writers to their position in the heavenlies will indicate the grace of God to the future ages which contain personal supernatural beings. This makes the primary significance of the word temporal. Whatever meaning is chosen for 'aeons' the verse again suggests that AE sees a cosmic significance in Christian salvation; God is concerned with more than the salvation of individuals or even of the church as a whole.

What God exhibits or proves is τὸ ὑπερβάλλον πλοῦτος[55] τῆς χάριτος. AE uses again the phrase of 1.7 (see there) with the addition of ὑπερβάλλον; this root, a favourite of Paul and AE (Eph 1.19; 2.7; 3.19), is not found elsewhere in the NT. 'Grace' picks up v. 5 and prepares for v. 8. To have been made to live and been raised

---

[55] For the gender see on 1.18; the variant of D¹ Ψ 0278 𝔐 giving the masculine is an attempt to harmonise with 1.18.

to sit with Christ in the heavenlies is the result of God's grace and of that alone (v. 8b). It might seem that AE had said all that needed to be said but he goes on to add in his customary style a seemingly superfluous ἐν χρηστότητι.[56] With what should it be connected? Its position excludes it being taken with the subject of the sentence, 'God being good has exhibited ...', or with the verb, 'God has exhibited in his goodness the overflowing riches ...' (in this case it would require the addition of αὐτοῦ), or as adverbial, 'God has compassionately exhibited the overflowing riches ...' (this leaves ἐφ' ἡμᾶς hanging). It is probably best then to take it as dependent on χάριτος[57] and understand it either causally, 'God exhibits the ... of his grace because of his goodness', or instrumentally, '... by means of his goodness'. If the former, God's goodness is the cause of his grace; this is unlikely since grace is the more fundamental term for Paul and his school. Since God's action and purpose are never unrelated to Christ the sentence is rounded off by referring to him. While this might be taken as a reference to the corporate Christ (God exhibits his grace towards those who are in Christ) it is much easier to see Christ as the place where, or means whereby, God's grace is exhibited. There is nothing vague about God's grace; it is anchored in Christ.

We have now come to the end of the flow of argument which began at 2.1, was interrupted by vv. 2f, but picked up again by v. 4. With v. 8 a fresh sentence begins.

8. Resurrection and heavenly session are essential parts of salvation for AE and so, γάρ, he now states this explicitly by picking up the phrase he had already used in v. 5c, developing it, returning as he does so to the second plural, and supplementing it in two ways: (i) he adds the article to 'grace', implying that it is the grace already referred to in vv. 5, 7, i.e. the grace which operates 'in Christ Jesus' and is exhibited in the aeons; (ii) he introduces the reference to 'faith'. Vv. 8f have a high concentration of Pauline concepts. Paul developed the themes of grace, faith, salvation, boasting and works during his struggle on behalf of Gentile Christians; if however Rom 3.24 is a pre-Pauline fragment he may not have been the first to use them;[58] yet even if that is so, AE has derived them directly from Paul, as the inclusion of 'works' and 'boasting' shows.

[56] On the word see M. A. Siotis, 'La "ΧΡΗΣΤΟΤΗΣ" de Dieu selon l'Apôtre Paul', *Paul de Tarse: Apôtre du notre temps* (ed. L. De Lorenzi), Rome, 1979, 201–32. The root varies a little between 'kindness' and the more general sense of moral goodness; yet 'kindness' with which we have translated it here seems a little weak to indicate the greatness of God's mercy.

[57] Lindemann, *Aufhebung*, 132, says that χρηστότης explains χάρις.

[58] Commentators on Romans differ; Käsemann regards it as pre-Pauline; Cranfield does not; for fuller references to the discussion see U. Wilckens, *Der Brief an die Römer*, 1978, I, 183 n. 490.

Paul employs both διά and ἐκ with πίστεως, sometimes using the article and sometimes not; this probably occasioned its insertion in some manuscripts.[59] To whose faith does AE refer? That of Christ or that of believers? It can be argued, though probably incorrectly, that when Paul uses the phrase he intends the former. Whether that is so or not, it does not appear to be the case here (*pace* Barth, 224f); AE introduces and stresses references to Christ so regularly that if he had Christ in mind we should have expected a following genitive 'of Christ'. In 3.12, 17 the phrase refers to the faith of believers. Since in vv. 8b–10 the place of believers is stressed, v. 8 probably also refers to their faith. If καὶ τοῦτο referred directly to πίστεως, and it probably does not (see below), this would put the matter beyond doubt. 'Faith' is always faith in someone or something; its object is not here defined but in 1.13, 15; 3.12 it is Christ and we may assume it is the same here. AE uses the genitive and not the accusative in the phrase διὰ πίστεως for believers are saved not because of their faith but through it; it is their response to what God has done; it represents their openness to his activity; it is not something which combined with that activity produces salvation. God's activity and human receptiveness are two sides of one coin. Paul regularly employed 'faith' language in arguing the case for the admission of Gentiles, but it is unlikely that AE is thinking of their admission here, even though in 2.11–22 his theme is the unity of Gentiles and Jews in Christ. Paul never thought, nor does AE, that Gentiles alone and not Jews needed to respond to God in faith.

In v. 8b AE picks up and develops v. 8a. What is the connection? Since Chrysostom καὶ τοῦτο has often been referred to 'faith', thus defining it as God's gift. While this may be theologically true, it is not what v. 8 signifies, even though examples exist of neuter pronouns taking up feminine nouns. If faith is defined here as God's gift, οὐκ ἐξ ὑμῶν would be parenthetical, yet it belongs to the main theme and in what follows the idea pursued is not that of faith but the antithesis of grace and human activity. τοῦτο must therefore be given a more general reference and, with the great majority of modern commentators, taken to refer to the whole of v. 8a (for the usage see Rom 13.11; 1 Cor 6.6, 8; Phil 1.28; cf BDR §290 n. 7). It indicates a new step in the argument: believers are not the source of their own salvation; it is not ἐξ ὑμῶν, but is God's gift. This emphasis is already present in the OT (e.g. Isa 31.1; 42.5f; 43.3, 11; Hos 1.7; Ps 33). Locke comments that since unbelievers have been described as dead there is nothing they can do to save themselves. A new aspect of the meaning of grace is also drawn out here (cf Haupt); in v. 7 it was related to χρηστότης; now it is seen as God's

---

[59] A D² Ψ 1881 𝔐. For the phrase διὰ πίστεως in Paul see Rom 3.25, 31; 2 Cor 5.7; Gal 3.14, 26; Phil 3.9; cf Col 2.12. AE uses it again at 3.17.

gift, freely given and not called forth in any way by what the recipients have said or done, or by any quality or talent that lies within them, or by anything which results from their natural powers (AE would have in mind human effort towards salvation in Stoicism and in contemporary religion and magic). God alone is the cause of salvation and it is a gift. δῶϱον is found only here in the Pauline corpus though related terms appear; however none is used sufficiently regularly for it to be argued that AE has changed the Pauline terminology. Indeed by his use of the present word and not χάϱισμα he may be indicating that faith is not one among a number of gifts which believers may receive but is a basic gift underlying all others.

9. Both v. 8b and v. 9 are comments on v. 8a (cf Lincoln, art.cit.) and are similarly structured: a negative statement followed by another which either adds more information to it (v. 8b) or qualifies it (v. 9). V. 9 uses terms, 'works', 'boasting', drawn from the Pauline polemic. In that polemic the 'works'[60] are those of the Law (e.g. Rom 3.20, 28; Gal 2.16; 3.2, 5, 10); they are not so defined or restricted here; indeed there is little to suggest that the Jewish Law is in mind; it is indeed only mentioned once in Ephesians (2.15). Paul refers often to boasting.[61] There is a legitimate boasting in God and what he has done (e.g. Rom 5.2, 11; 1 Cor 1.31) and in the Christian success of one's converts (e.g. 2 Cor 7.14; 9.2), but there is also an illegitimate boasting in works and activity (e.g. Rom 4.2; 2 Cor 11.16; Gal 6.13) and in the Law (Rom 2.23); the Law itself may be the content of such boasting (Rom 3.27; 4.2, 4; 1 Cor 1.28–31). In v. 9 boasting is clearly wrong. It is not however easy to decide how to understand ἵνα. It could be final ('and that means incidentally that no one should boast'), or consecutive ('the result of all this is that no one should boast'), or imperative ('let therefore no one boast', cf Moule, 144–6). Boasting about themselves and their religious activities is excluded for those who depend on grace for their salvation. There is a change in v. 9 from the second plural of v. 8 to the third singular, due either to a desire to drive home the point by individualising it or because a well-known Pauline 'tag' has been employed. If the latter were the case it might also account for the difficulty in construing ἵνα.

It would appear as if AE having stated his position in v. 8 now restates it in v. 9 in more Pauline terms or, if Paul is the author, that he drops back in v. 9 into his traditional terms. These terms, with

---

[60] For the Pauline use of 'work' and 'works' see C. Crowther, 'Works, Work and Good Works', *ExpT* 81 (1969–70) 66–71.

[61] J. Sanchez Bosch, *'Gloriarse' segun San Pablo* (AnBib 40), Rome, 1970; cf C. K. Barrett, 'Boasting (καυχᾶσθαι, κτλ.) in the Pauline Epistles', *L'Apôtre Paul: Personnalité, style et conception du ministère* (BETL LXXIII, ed. A. Vanhoye), Leuven, 1986, 363–8.

others (justification, faith, grace, works of the law), were originally derived from the Jewish perspective of Paul's polemic. Underneath that perspective is a much wider issue of the relation of humanity to God, of which the judaising problem is only one aspect. Does salvation come from moral living, intellectual appreciation of the truth as in philosophy or gnosticism, or from passing through certain rites? AE's changes have put the question in universal terms which would be more quickly appreciated in the Hellenistic world: 'grace' and 'faith' cannot easily be changed but they ought to be understood by everyone, and in case 'grace' is not it is interpreted as 'gift of God'; 'justification', the Jewish legal word, is replaced with the non-specific 'salvation';[62] the idea that obedience to the Law is not a factor in gaining salvation or justification is replaced by the all-embracing οὐκ ἐξ ὑμῶν: there is nothing people can do for themselves which can be a factor in their salvation. Then having universalised the problem of the Law as a way to God, AE falls back in v. 9b into the traditional language in order to show the continuity of his thought with that of Paul, though even here by not defining 'works' as those of the Law he lets us see that he is widening the original issue. It cannot be denied that Paul himself may have seen the need to widen the issue as he continued to be rejected by synagogues and increasingly turned to evangelising only Gentiles. Yet that he continues to use the traditional terms in Philippians (see 3.2–11) which cannot be dated much earlier than Ephesians (if he is the author) suggests he may never have seen the need to widen the issue. Whether Paul wrote Ephesians or not, vv. 8f represent a transplanting of the Pauline doctrine of justification into Hellenistic soil;[63] it is in this sense that we should understand the many statements of commentators that in vv. 8f we find the heart of Paul's Gospel. With the widening of the issue the original tie to the Jewish Law has been lost and a more basic and profound issue brought to the fore. In consequence there is no reason to suggest (*pace* Barth) that either v. 9 or its immediate context is polemically oriented. It also follows that we should be cautious in saying that AE like Paul uses σῴζειν with a different meaning from δικαιοῦν. He may indeed use it to convey what is intended with the latter but as including an extension into future salvation. Eventually the salvation

---

[62] It is true that for Paul 'salvation' and 'justification' can at times be equivalent (Rom 10.10) but the normal relation is expressed better in Rom 5.9 where justification is past and salvation is future.

[63] Lincoln, art.cit., writes of the 'generalisation' of the Pauline position. This is a better explanation than simply to think of it as the loss of the apocalyptic dimension with Luz, art.cit., 382, and J. C. Beker, *Paul the Apostle*, Edinburgh, 1980, 214.

vocabulary took over in the later parts of the NT (Acts 2.47; 4.12; 15.1, 11; 2 Tim 1.9; Tit 3.5; Heb 7.25).[64]

Hübner[65] suspects that v. 5b and vv. 8f are not original but glosses or interpolations. V. 5b interrupts the argument and there are clear breaks before v. 8 and after v. 9; in v. 5b and at v. 8 there is a change from the first plural to the second, yet the first plural returns in v. 10; the style of the interpolation is closer to Pauline diatribe than AE's normal plerophoric style; although we have 'works' in both v. 9 and v. 10, the word has a different reference in the two verses; vv. 8f appear to represent a more Pauline theology. On the other hand there is no textual evidence for any insertion or modification; elsewhere in the letter there are sudden changes between first and second persons (e.g. 1.13; 2.14); it is by no means certain that vv. 8f contain a more Pauline style and vocabulary; that in v. 8 AE should use a terminology more acceptable to his Hellenistic readers is not out of accord with what he does elsewhere ('forgiveness', 1.7); only v. 9 could be said to be Pauline in style and language; while it is possible to see v. 8f being inserted, it is difficult to see why v. 5b, which says much the same as v. 8a, should also have been inserted; it is also difficult to envisage a situation which would have led to the insertions. Hübner's suggestion must therefore be rejected.

10. If v. 9 is parenthetical because it adds nothing to the argument but only recalls Pauline terminology, then we must see the introductory γάρ of v. 10 as going back beyond it to pick up v. 8, or rather as picking up both v. 9 and v. 8. The return in v. 10 from the second person of v. 8 to the first person of vv. 3–7 is made easier through the indefinite third person singular of v. 9. αὐτοῦ is emphatic by position and stresses God's initiative in salvation (cf MHT, 190; Robertson, 681); the salvation itself is described as his 'making', ποίημα. The translation of this as 'workmanship' in many EVV is unfortunate since it suggests a play on ἔργα; there is no facile connection between our works and God's work. The English 'making' is a good rendering since it is as colourless as the Greek ποίημα, a word applied to a wide range of action stretching from work on physical material to the composing of poetry; nothing here however suggests AE regards believers as God's 'poem'! The word appears in only one other place in the Pauline tradition (Rom 1.20) where it is applied to the original creation of the universe. According to the biblical tradition God's creative activity did not cease with creation but continued in history (e.g. Ps 64.9; 92.4; Isa

---

[64] Does Polycarp, *Phil* 1.3, εἰδότες, ὅτι χάριτί ἐστε σεσωσμένοι, οὐκ ἐξ ἔργων, quote from Eph 2.8f? The latter probably contains a known tag and by itself would not suggest quotation. What however of the additional οὐκ ἐξ ἔργων? If this is a quotation from 2.9 then the 'wider' οὐκ ἐξ ὑμῶν has been passed over. That means Polycarp chose the former because it was more Pauline; in that case he might just as easily be regarded as quoting from Paul himself rather than Ephesians in his utilisation of the tag. There is nothing in his letter requiring the narrower term.
[65] H. Hübner, 'Glossen in Epheser 2', *Vom Urchristentum zu Jesus* (FS J. Gnilka, ed. H. Frankemölle and K. Kertelge), Freiburg, Basel, Vienna, 1989, 392–406.

29.16; the root is used in all of these). God is always 'making' and his 'saving' is just an aspect of his 'making' (cf Isa 41.11–20; 45.7f; 51.9–11 in each of which the thought moves easily between the two aspects). Thus what this word brings out here is not that salvation is a second creation but that it is God who creates it and not we ourselves; this is another way of expressing the same truth as v. 8b where salvation is God's gift.

If salvation is to be regarded as a second creation it is κτισθέντες which suggests it. Although the LXX of Genesis 1 and 2 does not use this root in relation to creation it is the main NT word for it (Mt 19.4; Mk 13.19; Col 1.16; 1 Tim 4.3; Rev 10.6). With this background it is taken up and used of those who become Christians, first in Paul (Gal 6.15; 2 Cor 5.17) and then, and proportionately more often, in Ephesians (2.10, 15; 4.24) and Colossians (3.10). To be saved is to be created anew by God; those who were dead in sins have been brought to life (2.1, 5). This gives salvation a wider significance than merely a forgiveness of sin; believers are created anew (cf 4.24 and 2 Cor 5.17). The first creation contained distinctions; one was that between Jews and Gentiles, and since God called Abraham he can be said to have created that distinction. If the distinction is to be abolished then God must create again and this idea is developed in 2.14ff with the root being used at 2.15 (cf Gal 6.15). It may however be wrong to envisage a second creation in Ephesians; for AE the creation of believers is the only genuine creation, just as in John's Gospel the only genuine life is eternal life; 2.1–10 draws no contrast between the first creation and the creation of believers. Perhaps Findlay, 117, is correct in stressing that there are not two creations, only one; salvation is creation reaffirmed; there has been no change in God's original plan; rather it is now carried fully into effect; we have here the completion of God's creative activity (cf Caird). 'In Christ Jesus' can hardly mean here 'in fellowship with Christ', or 'by incorporation into the Body of Christ' (so Belser, Salmond); it must be taken in the same way as in 2.6 and 1.7; Christ is thus brought into the process of creation.

Since God never acts purposelessly, he creates believers 'with a view to'[66] the good works which they will perform, not that his original creation did not have this end in view. In so far as people exist they exist to carry out God's will, and though they may be dead in sins (v. 1) it cannot be said that God created them to be dead in this way; he created them, whether as believers or unbelievers, to 'walk' in good works. The same word is used here as in v. 2, perhaps deliberately, to bring out the contrast. The lifestyle of the

---

[66] For ἐπί as indicating purpose see MHT, 272; BDR §235; Zerwick, §129; Moule, 50; Robertson, 605. Abbott gives it a conditional sense but it is difficult to see how good works can be so regarded if they have been prepared in advance.

believer has changed from one of sins under the power of Satan to one of good works. The plural 'good works' corresponds to the plural 'trespasses and sins'. Paul normally uses the plural ἔργα pejoratively,[67] e.g. as part of the phrase 'the works of the law' (Rom 3.20, 27f; Gal 2.16, etc.); but even where there is no explicit reference to the Law it still carries a bad connotation (Rom 13.12; Gal 5.19). While the singular may be similarly used (1 Cor 5.2), it more often has a good sense (Rom 2.7; 1 Cor 9.1; 15.58, etc.). The plural is used once neutrally (Rom 2.6) and in 2 Cor 9.8 we have a virtual plural with a good sense.[68] In the later NT writings the plural is used regularly with a good sense (e.g. Mt 5.16; Jn 3.21; Acts 9.36; Heb 10.24; 1 Pet 2.12; Rev 2.19) and is very frequent in the Pastorals. Jewish usage can teach us little; good works would include almsgiving and hospitality; works of the Law could not be evil.[69] No Greek reader encountering the phrase would have been put off by it. All in all, while Paul might have used the phrase, especially in a new context, it is easier to understand its use here if Paul is not the author. The concept of the life of believers as new and good is not however un-Pauline. 'Good works' represents a reinterpretation for Gentile Christians of phrases such as 'newness of life' (Rom 6.4), 'sanctification' (Rom 6.19, 22; 1 Th 4.3), 'the fruit of the Spirit' (Gal 5.22). Good works are never the cause of salvation but ought to be its fruit.

All this is straightforward, but the same cannot be said of προητοίμασεν in the relative clause (οἷς is a dative of attraction referring to ἔργοις). It would not be surprising to find a reference to the 'preparation' or 'election' of believers (Rom 9.23), or to their being prepared for good works (2 Tim 2.21; 3.17; Tit 3.1), and this is the way in which some commentators (e.g. Masson, Abbott) and translations (REB 'the life of good deeds which God has designed for us') have understood it. However, such a rendering would require an explicit ἡμᾶς in the clause and render meaningless the προ of the verb and so must be rejected. The need for the present clause is caused perhaps by the very vagueness of 'good works' and is intended to indicate that there is something new in the Christian life. Had AE written 'created in Christ Jesus for sanctification' or some similar clearly Christian expression he would not have required the clause.[70]

---

[67] On 'good works' see Crowther, art.cit.

[68] There is a virtual plural in Col 1.10 associated also with περιπατέω. AE can hardly have borrowed from Col 1.10 since he uses a normal plural and the association with a verb of behaviour is natural in both contexts.

[69] Cf SB III, 160–2, 585; IV, 536f, 559f.

[70] R. Scott, *The Pauline Epistles*, Edinburgh, 1909, 188, believes the idea of the predetermination of good works solves the problem of the difference between Paul and James!

It is the prefix προ which causes the problem. It can be taken either narrowly within the verse in relation to περιπατήσωμεν, i.e. as indicating preparation before the conversion of believers, or widely from the letter as a whole as indicating preparation before the foundation of the world. In favour of the narrower interpretation it can be said that ἑτοιμάζειν may mean no more than 'appoint, ordain' (cf Gen 24.14; Mt 25.34; 1 Cor 2.9) and pre-preparation might not then carry the same significance as προ-ορίζειν; the moment of the creation of the good works would then be either when believers were converted or just before they performed them; the idea would be similar to the description of their lives as the fruit of the Spirit. Yet in view of the regularity with which the prefix is used in Ephesians (1.4, 5, 9, 11) with the pre-creation connotation (cf Rom 9.23) the wider understanding is preferable, though clearly the more difficult to understand. Whichever solution is chosen the clause stresses that good works do not derive from believers themselves and are therefore not meritorious. God is the sole cause of the good deeds of believers. This is an idea which is often found elsewhere, e.g. Gal 5.22; it is the present form of its expression which is strange. Yet when the idea of human activity as coming from God is combined with that of believers as chosen beforehand to be holy (1.4f), it seems a natural consequence. When however we move into the area of election and predestination, natural consequences of previous statements often appear difficult, if not illogical.

If the good works of believers have been created in advance, have believers become automatons? Do they just slip into, or put on like a coat, a set of good works which lie in advance along the sequence of their lives? Believers were once dead in sins and trespasses and under the control of Satan (vv. 1f) and might equally then have been considered to be automatons. So v. 10 corresponds in a way to vv. 1, 2. It may be that by using the plural 'works' instead of a unified concept like 'sanctification' AE indicates the possibility of the freedom of believers to accept or reject any one particular good work which has been prepared beforehand. Since AE goes on in chaps. 4–6 to urge his readers to good works he cannot, if he is consistent, be imagining here that they will always perform them, yet if they do fulfil the prepared good works they have no cause to boast and v. 10 thus picks up v. 9.

V

JEW AND GENTILE: ONE IN CHRIST
(2.11–22)

P. Feine, 'Eph 2,14–16', *TSK* 72 (1899) 540–74; J. Bover, ' "In aedificatio-nem corporis Christi". Eph. 4.12', *EstBib* 3 (1944) 313–42, at 321–33; Percy, 278–88; Hanson, 141–8; H. Sahlin, ' "Die Beschneidung Christi". Eine Interpretation von Eph. 2:11–22', *SymBU* 12 (1950) 5–22; E. K. Lee, 'Unity in Israel and Unity in Christ' in Cross, 36–50; Mussner, *Christus*, 76–118; Roels, 125–32; Roberts, *Opbou*, 60–75, 105–22; Löwe, 176ff; P. Richardson, *Israel in the Apostolic Church* (SNTSMS 10), Cambridge, 1969, 147–58; A. Gonzalez Lamadrid, '*Ipse est pax nostra* (Estudio exegetico-teologico de Ef 2,14–18)', *EstBib* 28 (1969) 209–61, 29 (1970) 101–36, 227–66; M. H. Scharlemann, 'The Secret of God's Plan. Studies in Ephesians, Study Four', *CTM* 41 (1970) 410–20; G. Klinzling, *Die Umdeutung des Kultus in der Qumrangemeinde und im Neuen Testament* (SUNT 7), Göttingen, 1971, 184–92; 'The Two Made One. Some Observations on Eph. 2:14–16', *OJRS* 1 (1973) 34–54; Merklein, *Christus*, 16–61; id. 'Zur Tradition und Komposition von Eph 2,14–18', *BZ* 17 (1973) 79–102; Fischer, 132–7; Van Roon, *Authenticity*, 370–6; P. Stuhlmacher, ' "Er ist unser Friede" (Eph 2,14). Zur Exegese und Bedeutung von Eph 2,14–18', *Neues Testament und Kirche* (FS R. Schnackenburg, ed. J. Gnilka), Freiburg, 1974, 337–58; M. Zerwick, 'He is our Peace (Eph 2:11–18)', *Biblebashyam* 1 (1975) 302–11; Lindemann, *Aufhebung*, 145–92; D. C. Smith, 'The Ephesian Heresy and the Origin of the Epistle to the Ephesians', *OJRS* 5 (1977) 78–103; M. Wolter, *Rechtferti-gung und zukünftiges Heil* (BZNW 43), Berlin, 1978, 62–73; W. Rader, *The Church and Racial Hostility. A History of the Interpretation of Ephesians 2:11–22*, Tübingen, 1978; R. Penna, 'La proiezione dell'esperienza communi-taria sul piano storico (Ef. 2,11–22) e cosmico (Ef. 1,20–23)', *RivBiblt* 26 (1978) 163–186; id. 'L'évangile de la Paix', *Paul de Tarse, Apôtre du notre temps* (ed. L. De Lorenzi), Rome, 1979, 175–99; L. Ramaroson, ' "Le Christ, notre paix" (Ep 2,14–18)', *ScEs* 31 (1979), 373–82; R. P. Martin, *Reconciliation: A Study of Paul's Theology*, London, 1981, 157–98; A. D. Edwards, 'An exegesis of Ephesians 2:14–17' (Ph.D. thesis, University of Glasgow, 1982); Usami, 45–70; R. Schnackenburg, 'Zur Exegese von Eph 2,11–22; Im Hinblick auf das Verhältnis von Kirche und Israel', *The New Testament Age* (ed. W. C. Weinrich), Macon, GA, 1984, 467–91; E. Grässer, *Der Alte Bund im Neuen*, Tübingen, 1985; F.-J. Steinmetz, 'Jenseits der Mauern und Zäune', *GuL* 59 (1986) 202–14; A. T. Lincoln, 'The Church and Israel in Ephesians 2', *CBQ* 49 (1987) 605–24; D. A. Smith, 'Cultic Language in Ephesians 2:19–22. A Test Case', *RestQ* 31 (1989) 201–17; W. Schweitzer, 'Überlegungen zum Verhältnis von Christen und Juden nach Epheser 2,11–22', *WD* 20 (1989) 237–64; Best, 'A Christian View'; Faust, *passim*.

11 You should remember then
       that you were once Gentiles by birth
       belonging to those who are called 'uncircumcision'
         by those called 'circumcision'
         which is a physical matter,
12   that you were at that time
       apart from Christ,
       separated from the community of Israel,
       and strangers in respect of the covenants of promise,
       with no hope,
       and without God in the world.
13   But now in Christ Jesus you who were once afar
       have become near through the blood of Christ.
14 For Christ is our peace,
       he who made the two one
       and destroyed the middle wall of the fence which
                             separates,
       that is, the hostility (in his flesh),
15   inasmuch as he made of no effect the law
       consisting of commandments
       and expressed in regulations,
       so that he might create out of the two in himself
       one new (human) being,
       thus making peace,
16   and that he might reconcile
       both to God through the cross in one body
       after killing enmity by it.
17   And when he came
       he proclaimed the good news
       of peace to those far off
       and of peace to those near at hand;
18   for this reason
       we both have through him access
       in one Spirit to the Father.
19 For you are no longer foreigners and strangers
       but are fellow citizens with the holy ones
       and belong to God's household,
20   since you have been built on the foundation
       consisting of the apostles and prophets
       with Jesus Christ himself being the angle-stone,
21   in whom (Christ) all the building
       being neatly fitted together
       grows into a holy sanctuary in the Lord,

22   in whom also you have been built together
               into a place which God indwells in Spirit.

The dispute in the early church about the admission of Gentile
Christians as full and equal members with Jewish Christians had lost
its virulence by the time of Ephesians; though the case no longer
needed to be argued, it still continued to echo, brought to the fore
from time to time by the vast numerical superiority of Gentiles in an
area such as Asia Minor and the smaller numerical superiority of
Jews to Christians. If Jews were God's chosen people and Gentiles
were not, and if Gentile Christians were not Jews and yet the elect of
God (1.4f), what were they? Did they form a new group distinct
from Gentiles and also from both Jews and Jewish Christians and, if
so, how should that group be characterised? If Jews and Gentiles are
equal in Christ, do Gentile Christians take over some or all of the
privileges and responsibilities of Jews? These are the kind of
questions which lie behind 2.11–22; yet because we know so little
of the churches to which AE wrote it is difficult to point to any
actual situation in them which may have led to the raising of these
questions. The letter is of course too general for us to be able to tie
down the Jewish–Gentile discussion to any one city or area and this
discussion can hardly be used in the argument as to its purpose (see
Introduction §8.3.4). Faust sees vv. 14–18 as reflecting the re-
establishment of the Pax Romana after the Jewish War. This may
explain AE's use of the term peace in his discussion but reveals
nothing about the letter's ultimate purpose.

The discussion unveils a new aspect of the work of Christ: the
reconciliation of people not only to God but also to one another.
Salvation is more than believers receiving forgiveness of their sins,
deliverance from the grip of the powers, adoption as children of
God, and union with Christ in resurrection and exaltation. Salvation
means union with one another. 1.10 implied something of this but on
a grander and less precise scale; in 2.11–22 the cosmic framework
sinks into the background and the idea is expounded exclusively in
terms of the Jew–Gentile distinction, though it clearly has a much
wider reference in relation to division between groups of people all
of whom are Christian. As presented here the framework is
historical, the relation of Jews and Gentiles. Relations between them
were never easy; Jews were proud to be God's people; Gentiles
looked askance at their curious ways. From another angle we may
say that while 2.1–10 was narrative in dealing with the redemption
of the individual, 2.11–22 might be categorised as narrative recount-
ing what happened to a group, the Gentiles. This naturally launches
us into a discussion of the nature of the church. Since so many of the
themes of the letter surface in 2.11–22 it has been termed its
theological centre (cf Conzelmann, 67; Merklein, *Christus*, 12;

Barth, 275), but this can only be true if we ignore the large final paraenetic section where Jewish–Gentile relations never surface. Indeed this and other passages might be regarded as preparation for the paraenesis. The whole letter in fact holds together in such a way that it is impossible to speak of a centre or a key passage (see Introduction §8).

2.11–22 consists of three sections, vv. 11–13, 14–18, 19–22; the first and third are marked off from the second in being couched in the second person plural whereas the third is largely in the third person with God or Christ as subject. 2.11–13 describes the position of Gentile Christians before and after they became Christians. The contrast again uses the once–now (or inside–outside, now expressed as near–far) schema to make its point and is expressed in Jewish terms. General theological terms (sin, faith, resurrection, ascension) were used in 2.1–10; the choice of explicit Jewish terms is now forced on AE because he wishes to deal with the relation of Jewish and Gentile Christians within the church. In vv. 11–13 the contrast may appear to lie between Gentiles and Jews but in vv. 14–18 it is between non-membership of the Jewish people and membership of the church. The church is then more than a reformed Judaism. As well as the temporal contrast there is also a spatial (v. 13). The middle section, vv. 14–18, looks like an excursus; unlike the surrounding material it is either in the third person singular with God as subject or, when it becomes plural, largely in the first plural.

The present position of Gentile Christians in contrast with their original place outside Israel is developed positively in the third section, vv. 19–22, through a description of the church with ever-changing imagery, though with only vague reference to the once–now schema. Verses 14–18 thus form the bridge between the original position of Gentile Christians and their present position and do so through the discussion of their reconciliation with Jewish Christians (vv. 14–18). In this way the connection between soteriology and ecclesiology is brought out.

On the large scale there is then a certain similarity between the first and third sections and attempts have been made to see a circular or chiastic pattern in vv. 11–22.[1] These have not been successful since they involve too much being forced to fit into a preordained scheme. Yet there are clear parallels between the first and third large sections. Gentile believers were once alienated from God, in the flesh, without a Messiah, excluded from citizenship in Israel, now they are near God, in the Spirit, built together with a Messiah, fellow

[1] E.g. Kirby, 156f; J. Giavini, 'La Structure Littéraire d'Eph. 2.11–22', *NTS* 16 (1969/70) 209–11; I. H. Thomson, *Chiasmus in the Pauline Letters* (JSNTSup 111), Sheffield, 1995, 84–115. For detailed criticism of these and similar proposals see Lincoln, 126.

citizens within Israel. There is then a balance between the first and third sections; this has been brought about through Christ who has made peace and brought Jewish and Gentiles believers together in himself.

In addition to this careful structuring of the whole passage, attempts have been made to uncover within it pieces of preformed material, a gnostic or other hymn in 2.14–18 and a baptismal hymn in 2.19–22. These will be considered when we come to the second and third sections. The whole passage has also been taken to be a midrash on Exod 21.1–22.2 3 and its Haftorah, Isa 56.1–9; 57.19,[2] but the connection between the OT basis and the NT passage is too fragile to sustain the argument.

11.[3] The once–now contrast (cf. Lona, 256–67) is not concerned with the length of the period between conversion and the present and so tells us nothing about how long the readers have been Christian. There is also a change in the way the contrast is presented from that of 2.1–3; it is no longer stressed as that between once a sinner and now saved, but between once a Gentile outside God's people and now a Christian within that people. If in the communities to which AE writes there are still some Jewish Christians aware of their Jewish heritage and if there are Jews in the area whom the Christians may encounter, and there were a large number of Jews in Asia Minor, second- and third-generation Gentile Christians might still be forced through their contact with Jews to think about their origin. Few Christians today think of themselves as Gentiles but that should not lead us to think that those of AE's day were similarly unaware of their Gentile origin. It would also be wrong to suppose that all the readers were direct converts from paganism and first-generation Christians. Even if they were, this would give no indication of the date of the letter since most Christians in this period were such converts.

Whether they are recent converts or those of long standing, they are told to keep on remembering (the verb is in the present tense) the change in their position. Since what has happened in the past (the exodus, the cross) creates the present, remembering has always been important to both Jews and Christians; here however believers are not summoned to recollect the great things God has done externally in the past but what he has done in their own lives: once they were outside his people, now they are within.

Διό bases vv. 11–13 on the general sense of vv. 1–10 rather than on v. 10 alone (Chrysostom) or on any other particular statement in

---

[2] C. Perrot, 'La lecture synagogale d'Exode XXI,1—XXII,23 et son influence sur la littérature Néo-Testamentaire' (FS Gelin), *A la rencontre de Dieu*, Le Puy, 1961, 223–39. Other scholars have followed Perrot's lead in this, e.g. Stuhlmacher, art.cit.; for criticism see Lincoln, 126f.

[3] I have treated vv. 11, 12 in more detail in 'Christian View'.

vv. 1–10. As with some other connections between major passages (cf 1.15; 3.1; 3.14) the sequence of thought is not entirely clear,[4] yet this gives no excuse for reconstructing the text with Ewald who on the basis of Marcion's supposed text reads μνημονεύοντες ὑμεῖς ποτὲ τὰ ἔθνη (the participle is also read by F G Victor). Part of the connection between 2.11–13 and 2.1–10 may lie in the resumption of the once–now schema (for the schema see Tachau, op.cit., 134ff). Both Jewish and Gentile Christians were once dead in sin, but Gentile Christians lacked in addition the physical sign, circumcision, which the Jews had as God's people. In v. 12 AE details what else he thought they lacked. The once–now schema is thus developed here in respect only of Gentile Christians.

The addressees are first identified physically as of Gentile birth, τὰ ἔθνη ἐν σαρκί (on the absence of the article see BDR §272.2 n. 4; MHT, 221f; Percy, 54f); 'flesh' is not used here with its Pauline theological sense and so no contrast is intended with spiritual regeneration (Jerome). Left to themselves Gentiles would never have classified themselves as Gentiles, though they might have distinguished between themselves and barbarians or between nationalities. In their eyes Jews were simply one more race or nation. Only encounter with Jews would have made them aware of Jewish feeling on Gentile identity. Gentile Christians, even if they had met no Jews, would of course have become aware of the distinction through their use of the OT which would not have been so easily assumed then to be a Christian book as it is today. AE may have recalled his readers to the distinction here because of a possible tendency on their part to forget or ignore, as Marcion did later, their Jewish heritage. Apart from that, people always belong to large groups and AE reminds them of the two major human groups as seen by a Jew. The emotional involvement found in the case of Paul (cf. Rom 3.1f; 9.4f) is lacking here.

AE has no intention of emphasising circumcision as a main factor in the Jewish–Gentile contrast, yet it cannot be ignored. Its presence reminds us that what he is discussing is the pre-Christian existence of Gentiles and not of all people (*pace* Lindemann, *Aufhebung*, 146). As a physical distinction made in the flesh by human hands it no longer possesses for Christians any religious significance (cf Gal 5.6; 6.15; 1 Cor 7.19). The contrast is not then between a physical circumcision and one of the heart (Rom 2.28f). Probably neither of the references to flesh should be given the derogatory sense the word often has in Paul (Percy, 262), though that sense is just possible in the second reference since circumcision belongs to the sphere of unredeemed humanity (Caird). For a detailed discussion of

---

[4] This led to the text being emended; a few mss omit διό; F G substitute διὰ τοῦτο and K *pc* lat δι’ ὅ.

earlier views see Harless. Underlying what AE writes is the mistaken, but widely held, assumption in the ancient world, that only Jews were circumcised. If Paul wrote our letter he would probably have been aware that it was also a custom among other Semitic peoples because of his sojourn in Arabia; his discussion of Ishmael in Gal 4.21–31 confirms that awareness.[5]

The adjective χειροποιήτου (on the absence of the article see Robertson, 774, 777) is used in the LXX of idols (Lev 26.1, 30; Isa 2.18; Dan 5.4, 23; cf Acts 17.24) and in the NT of the Jewish temple (Mk 14.58; Acts 7.48; Heb 9.11, 24), always with the intention of stressing the inadequacy of its referent.[6] Jews would never have applied it to their God-ordained circumcision, though like Paul they could (Rom 2.29) spiritualise it into a circumcision of the heart (Deut 10.16; Jer 4.4; Ezek 44.7, 9; Lev 26.41; 1QS 5.5; 1QH 18.20; 1QpHab 11.13; Philo, De Spec Leg 1.305); Paul indeed speaks of Christians as the true circumcision (Phil 3.3).[7] The adjective is used in Col 2.11 and AE probably derived it from the Pauline school to which he and A/Col belonged. Col 2.11 relates it to baptism but there is no such reference in Eph 2.11. What AE says here about circumcision is similar to Paul's idea that neither circumcision nor uncircumcision is of value (Gal 5.6; 6.15); AE however does not go as far in devaluing it as does Paul in Phil 3.2. Though λεγομένης is correctly rendered 'so-called' it does not necessarily carry the derogatory flavour of the English word. AE neither positively attacks circumcision, nor suggests baptism as a substitute (cf Percy, 391), nor spiritualises it. Either of the last two positions would probably have taken him a step further than he would have wished in lining up Christians more directly as the successors of Jews.

Περιτομή, originally signifying the rite, came to mean, as here, the group of people, i.e. the Jews, who are circumcised (cf. Acts 10.45; Rom 3.30; Col 4.11; etc.). The Jews made no allowance for the existence of other circumcised peoples. They used ἀκροβυστία (probably a corruption of ἀκροπροσθία, cf BAGD s.v.; BDR §120.4, n. 5; MH, 277; K. L. Schmidt, TWNT, I, 226f), originally meaning foreskin, to signify the group of uncircumcised people, i.e. the Gentiles (cf. Rom 2.26; Col. 3.11). On circumcision see R. Meyer, TWNT, VI, 72–83; H. C. Hahn, NIDNTT, I, 307–12; Barth, 279–82; R. Stummer, RAC II, 159–69; N. J. McEleney, 'Conversion, Circumcision and the Law', NTS 20 (1973–4) 319–41; Meuzelaar, 75–87; H. Wissmann and O. Betz, TRE V, 714–22.

The summons to the readers to remember (μνημονεύετε) resembles

[5] Cf Lloyd Gaston, 'Israel's Enemies in Pauline Theology', NTS 28 (1982) 400–23 at 406f.
[6] For the word see E. Lohse, TWNT, IX, 425f; D. Juel, Messiah and Temple (SBLDS 31), Missoula, Montana, 1977, 143–58.
[7] On the spiritualisation of circumcision in the early church see E. Ferguson, 'Spiritual Circumcision in Early Christianity', SJT 41 (1988) 485–97.

the Deuteronomic appeal to the Israelites to recall their former slavery in Egypt (Deut 5.15; 15.15; 16.12; 24.18, 22); it is more than an instruction to recollect particular facts or situations; once recollected they should be evaluated and the evaluation acted on, cf. Lk 17.32; Jn 15.20; Acts 20.35; Col 4.18; 2 Tim 2.8; Heb 13.7. Recollecting their past should then lead readers to consider the great change that has come over their position; v. 12 makes clear that this is much more than ignoring the absence of circumcision. Even when believers are not told to remember their past, it is often thrust on their attention (Rom 9–11; Gal 4.8–11, 21–31; 1 Pet 2.10).

12. Circumcision may be the obvious place to begin a discussion of the distinction between Jew and Gentile and it may be tactful to get it out of the way at the beginning as repulsive to Gentiles (Roels 120f)[8] but there are more important things to remember, and so AE now expresses the distinction in new ways.[9] Verse 12 is parallel to v. 11 as the ὅτι and the ποτέ and τῷ καιρῷ ἐκείνῳ indicate (on the latter phrase see BDR §292.2, n. 3; §200.2, n. 9 and MHT, 243). The ὅτι is not causal but serves to introduce five descriptions of the Gentile condition. 4.17–19 throws a different light on that condition. For the present AE writes a description of the disadvantages which Gentiles suffered as seen, not by a Jew, but by a Jewish Christian. Paul's list in Rom 9.4f is in contrast a list of the advantages of being a Jew. Some commentators (e.g. Robinson, Masson) take the first phrase as qualifying what follows, 'You (when you were in the period) without Christ had no share in ...', but it is more natural to take it predicatively. Standing by itself it is the basis for the other phrases; in Rom 9.4f it is the climax of the list; the present list has no climax. The two lists are complementary: Rom 9.4f states the privileges of Israel and Eph 2.12 the disadvantages of the Gentiles. They also serve different purposes.[10] AE as a member of the Pauline school may have known that Paul drew up lists and he selected the qualities he wished from among them. The list in v. 12, compiled by a Christian, would not necessarily be the same as one drawn up by a Jew. The second and third phrases are coupled by καί as are the fourth and fifth; there is no reason with Merklein (*Christus*, 18) to take either καί as epexegetical or consecutive.

The first phrase refers to Christ (χωρίς, 'without, apart from'; see BAGD, LSJ for meaning and use as a preposition). Before becoming Christians Gentiles would probably not have known the term 'Christ', and a Jew would probably not have put it first in a list of

---

[8] Philo does the same in *Spec Leg* before turning to discuss the Law.

[9] Much has been written on the way Jews and Gentiles thought of one another; for a summary see Best, 'Christian View'.

[10] Cf M. Rese, 'Die Vorzüge Israels in Rom 9,4f und Eph 2,12', *TZ* 31 (1975) 211–22; id. 'Church and Israel in the Deuteropauline Letters', *SJT* 43 (1990) 19–32; G. Sass, *Leben aus den Verheissungen* (FRLANT 164), Göttingen, 1995, 408–33.

privileges. Gentile Christians are now 'in Christ'. What would it mean to be without him? Christ can be conceived as present with Israel: (i) in his pre-incarnate state (e.g. 1 Cor 10.4; 1 Pet 1.11; Jn 12.41 (von Soden, Barth);[11] (ii) as living and dying in historical Israel (Haupt; Merklein, *Christus*, 18); (iii) as the Messiah for whom Israel hoped (Schlier; Gnilka; Mussner, *Christus*, 77). Nothing elsewhere suggests AE believed in a pre-incarnate presence of Christ with Israel. Limiting the reference to the historical Christ makes only a trivial point and would have been true merely for a brief period. (iii) is to be preferred in the light of 1.12 which, whether its subject is Jewish Christians or all Christians, indicates that AE believed Jewish Christians had the hope of a Messiah. But once Jesus had come and been accepted as Messiah believers would not have been able to separate (iii) from (ii). Note the absence of the article with Christ, surprising in view of the number of times AE uses it since in this case there is a clear messianic reference (see on 1.10).

In the second phrase πολιτεία has a wide range of meaning.[12] The term refers here neither to the 'way of life' of Israel (cf 2 Macc 8.17; 4 Macc 8.7) which would render 2.19 difficult, nor to the constitution of Israel (Josephus *Ant* 4.45; 13.245), but to membership in Israel, or, more exactly, to possessing the rights, privileges and duties which go with belonging to Israel as a defined political and religious community, though not in the modern sense a nation (2 Macc 13.14; 4 Macc 17.9); our rigid separation between politics and religion was unknown in the ancient world. From this community the Gentiles were excluded; the perfect participle ἀπηλλοτριωμένοι (for the following genitive cf BDR §180.1, n. 2; MHT, 235) recalls Col 1.21. If Gentiles are in a state of exclusion from Israel (AE, like Paul, uses the title preferred by Jews) this does not imply that they were once included and then expelled or that they separated themselves; it was God who separated Jews and Gentiles through his choice of Abraham; neither 2.14ff nor 3.6 indicates the restoration of an original unity. 'Israel' does not designate the church[13] here (Hanson, 142) but empirical Israel; when it denotes anything other than the Jewish people, or a part of it, this is made clear, e.g. Gal 6.16 (even there, it is doubtful if the church is intended).

Like the second phrase the third continues to express the

[11] For the idea see A. T. Hanson, *Jesus Christ in the Old Testament*, London, 1965.
[12] Cf LSJ, BAGD, Spicq, II, 710–20; Strathmann, *TWNT*, VI, 516–35; K. L. Schmidt, *Die Polis im Kirche und Welt*, Zürich, 1940, 1–40; R. Schnackenburg, 'Die Politeia Israels in Eph 2,12', *De la Torah au Messie: études d'exégèse et d'herméneutique bibliques offertes à Henri Cazelles*, Paris, 1981, 467–74; Faust, 89–111.
[13] Israel can denote the church; see P. Richardson, op.cit., 70ff.

condition of the Gentiles in Jewish terms: they are strangers (ξένοι, for the word see v. 19) in respect of the covenants of promise (on the genitive see BDR 180.3, n. 4; Moule, 41f; MHT, 215; Robertson, 398, 516, 658).[14] There is no implication that they once belonged. The plural 'covenants'[15] is unusual, appearing in the NT only at Rom 9.4, where the singular is a variant, and Gal 4.24, which mentions two covenants of which only one refers to Israel. Normally God is regarded as having a covenantal relationship with Israel which was renewed or reaffirmed on a number of occasions. In Jewish literature the plural regularly means 'promises, decrees, oaths'.[16] The sense 'promises' is impossible in 2.12 because of the following ἐπαγγελίας and while 'oaths' is possible both here and in Rom 9.4, there seems little reason to prefer it to the normal 'covenant'. It would be possible to understand the renewal of the covenant as indicating several covenants (cf 2 Macc 8.15; Sir 44.17–45.26) but it is more likely that Christians would have viewed the new covenant of Jer 31.31–4 in the light of its fulfilment in Christ and connection with the eucharist as a second covenant, different from that made with Abraham. The covenant made with Noah is irrelevant as predating that made with Abraham and in any case it is not a covenant made with Israel. AE speaks of a promise (singular) as associated with the covenants and though the term promise is not frequent in the OT, appearing almost as often in Ephesians as in the whole of the OT (cf Sass, op.cit., 13ff), there is a forward look in the covenants relating to the continuance of Israel which could be seen as indicating a promise. Gentiles are strangers in respect of that forward look and so to that promise. It is possible that AE has also in mind OT passages which imply that Gentiles will share in the future messianic period (Isa 42.6; 49.6) but unlikely since, if this were so, he would not have gone on to write of the Gentiles as being once without hope.

The final two phrases are couched in terms which appear to lack any reference to Israel (so Schnackenburg, 'Zur Exegese') yet to a Jew they would have been natural consequences of the preceding three in representing the 'spiritual' condition of Gentiles. But the latter, who would not have been troubled by the first three accusations, would have rejected these two as false because, with few exceptions, they did not regard themselves as atheists or without hope; it is wrong with Robinson to view non-Jewish hope as already

---

[14] The difficulties of the whole phrase led to textual emendation; F G read 'promises of the covenant'.

[15] On the concept see G. Quell and J. Behm, *TWNT*, II, 105–37; G. E. Mendenhall, *IDB* I, 714–23; J. Guhrt, *NIDNTT*, I, 365–72; D. J. McCarthy, *Old Testament Covenant: A Survey of Current Opinion*, Oxford, 1972.

[16] For the plural 'covenants' see C. Roetzel, 'Διαθῆκαι in Romans 9,4', *Bib* 51 (1970) 377–90.

fulfilled in a past Golden Age or, because some pessimistic epitaphs exist, to deny it altogether.[17] AE's dismissal of Gentile hope springs from his different perspective.[18] The reference to hope follows naturally on that to the promise, for hope arises out of promises. Jewish hope was wider than the expectation of a Messiah or an afterlife; it was essentially the hope that the Jewish people should continue to be God's people and he their God, though the hope might be expressed with varying emphasis in different periods and by different people. AE may have thought of it in terms of inheritance which has a future aspect (1.14) and is a privilege of the Jew in which the Gentile Christian will share (3.6; remember that AE is detailing Jewish privilege as seen from a Christian perspective). 'In the world' probably relates to both the final two phrases but not as suggesting the world as the content of hope; while they lived in the world apart from Christ there was no real hope for Gentiles.

ἄθεοι can mean:[19] (i) those who do not believe in God; the word was used in this way against both Jews (Josephus, *c. Ap.* 2.148) and Christians (*Mart Polyc* 3.2; 9.2) since they did not worship any of the gods recognised among the Gentiles; (ii) godless, impious; a moral rebuke which would hardly be in place here; (iii) abandoned by God or the gods. In using the word AE will have intended some combination of (i) and (iii). Neither charge could have been made to stick absolutely. Paul is not going against his Jewish upbringing when he allows that Gentiles have some knowledge of the true God (Rom 1.18ff; cf Acts 17.16ff), nor as a Christian had he completely abandoned them for he planned their ultimate redemption (Rom 9–11). Pagans might have laughed scornfully at AE's charges, but his Gentile-Christian recipients would have agreed with them. While AE associates hopelessness and godlessness many today who do not believe in God would deny that they were without hope, though their hope might lack a transcendental dimension.[20]

The five phrases of v. 12 might be taken to represent what, from a Christian point of view, is good in Judaism, and good rhetorical practice would have amplified them in the following discussion. Yet AE has not done this. Vv. 14–18 could be regarded as an expansion

[17] For contemporary views on death see A.-J. Festugière, *La vie spirituelle en Grèce à l'époque hellénistique*, Paris, n.d., 163–80.
[18] On hope see K. M. Woschitz, *Elpis: Hoffnung. Geschichte, Philosophie, Exegese, Theologie eines Schlüsselbegriffes*, Vienna, 1979.
[19] Cf LSJ; E. Stauffer, *TWNT*, III, 120–2. For 'atheism' in the ancient world see J. Thrower, *A Short History of Western Atheism*, London, 1971, 37–48; J. N. Sevenster (SupNT 41), Leiden, 91–102; E. M. Smallwood, *The Jews under Roman Rule*, Leiden, 1976, 378ff; H. Conzelmann, *Heiden-Juden-Christen*, Tübingen, 1981, 43–6, 130f, 231f.
[20] For a sketch of some modern views on and forms of hope see Woschitz, op.cit., 10ff.

of the first and v. 19 of the second, but nothing picks up the other three. We should note also the list's failure to mention either the temple or the Law; the absence of a reference to the former is surprising since in v. 21 the Christians are described as the new temple, but perhaps less surprising if it had been already destroyed.

Another way to understand vv. 11f has been suggested by Lindemann, *Aufhebung*, 140–3 (cf Steinmetz, 54–7; Tachau, 142f). If in 2.1–10 the once–now contrast was that between non-Christians and Christians should not (2.11f) continue this? τὰ ἔθνη would not then mean actual Gentiles but all people before they became Christians and ἐν σαρκί would refer to the area outside redemption and not be understood physically. If so, v. 12 would describe how both Jews and Gentiles are viewed by Christians: all were once without the Messiah (before Jesus came), without hope and godless. If Israel is understood as the community of salvation all were once outside it and strangers to the covenants of promise. In Christ (v. 13), their present position, they are near to God. This makes the contrast existential rather than temporal or spatial, making v. 12 simpler to understand. However, it creates greater difficulties than it solves. τὰ ἔθνη means Gentiles at 3.1, 6, 8; why should the meaning be different here? Indeed on this view it is hard to see why the reference to Gentiles was introduced at all; the argument could have moved directly from 'remember' to v. 12. In view of the reference in v. 11 to physical circumcision it is easier to take the first ἐν σαρκί physically. It would also have been easier to omit the 'political' term πολιτεία and simply said 'outside Israel', i.e. the church. Here we should recall that Ephesians is a general letter and therefore words like Israel and Gentiles cannot be given 'private' meanings, as would be possible with a narrower audience which the writer had visited and instructed, but must be given their normal significance. Lindemann also fails to explain how Christians would have understood 'covenants of promise' in respect of their own faith and it is difficult to see how they could do this; it is even more difficult to see how Christians could include Jews under the term 'godless' unless they adopted the position of Marcion, but since AE quotes the OT approvingly this was not his position. Finally the Jewish–Gentile contrast is certainly present in 2.14–18 and 3.1–13 and it is simpler to see it as beginning in our passage than at v. 14.

If it is difficult to accept Lindemann's argument it is even more difficult to accept that of Usami, 45ff, who argues that the contrast is between new converts and those of longer standing.

13. νυνί[21] (emphatic by position) picks up the 'once' of v. 11 and the 'at that time' of v. 12. Verse 13 is no longer subordinate to

---

[21] In using the phrase νυνὶ δέ AE does not depend on Col 1.22 as Mitton, 289, suggests; the phrase is frequent in Paul (fifteen times).

μνημονεύετε, since no act of remembering is now required, but is a fresh sentence indicating the great transformation which God has made in the position of the readers. Once they were 'afar' but now they are 'near'. While the implications of this change begin to be worked out here they are brought out more fully in vv. 14–18. Temporal terms have now been changed to spatial. The terms 'near', 'afar',[22] are probably drawn from Isa 57.19, a text used more directly in v. 17. Ps 148.14 says Israel is near to God. In Isa 57.19 however a contrast is drawn between Jews in exile and those in the homeland (cf 43.6; 60.4; Ezek 11.16; etc.); this is probably also the meaning in Acts 2.39, though not in Acts 22.21. In later Judaism Isa 57.19, or at least its terms, are applied to proselytes who became Jews.[23] Lincoln, 'The Church', rejects the reference here to Isa 57.19 and assumes AE is using proselyte terminology independently. While it is true Jewish proselyte terminology used the terms it is difficult to believe in the light of v. 17 that AE had not the Isaiah passage in mind. Gentiles were also at times regarded as 'afar' (*Num R* 8 [149d]). Those joining the Qumran community are said to draw near (*qrb* 1QS 6.16, 19, 22; 7.21; 8.18).

'Afar' and 'near' are relative terms requiring a fixed point from which to be measured. This could be Judaism, the church, or God. It can hardly be the church even though the characteristics of Judaism which the Gentiles lack have been described in v. 12, since those described as 'near' are actually in the church and not just 'near' to it. The choice is then between Judaism and God; since 'the blood of Christ' is normally used in relation to redemption it may seem better to understand the nearness as that to God; yet the mention of nearness after v. 12 and the use of the terms in v. 17 leave us also with the thought of Gentiles as near to Israel.[24] There is then a certain degree of ambiguity or ambivalence, and this runs right through vv. 14–18 in that it is difficult to separate the 'horizontal' relation of Gentiles to Jews from their, and also Jews', 'vertical' relation to God. For their part the Gentiles, once far off (Deut 29.22; 1 Kgs 8.41; cf Deut 4.7; Ps 148.14) and without God (v. 12), are now near to him. Echoes of this idea of nearness may lie in Acts 22.21; Lk 15.20 (Mk 12.34 suggests there can be a relative nearness but the terms in Ephesians are used absolutely). Gentiles became (aor., ἐγενήθητε, a divine passive, Bouttier) near when they believed or were baptised. The phrase contains no clue as to when this

---

[22] Cf Meuzelaar, 60ff; J. A. Loader, 'An Explanation of the Term *prosēlutos*', *NT* 15 (1973) 270–7; W. C. van Unnik, 'The Redemption in I Peter i 18–19 and the Problem of the First Epistle of Peter' in his *Sparsa Collecta* II, 3–82, Leiden, 1980; Derwood C. Smith, 'The Ephesian Heresy', *ProcSBL* 1974, 45–54.

[23] On the use of proselyte terminology see Faust, 111–14, who refers to Philo, e.g. *Qu Gen* 2.29 and relates it to becoming wise. See also Edwards, op.cit., 177ff.

[24] Lindemann, *Aufhebung*, 155, sees here a reference only to God.

happened nor does it imply that the writer has always been 'near', or 'nearer' for a longer period than his readers have. It is only a reminder of their change in position. It goes too far to say that the Gentiles have now gained what v. 12 implied they lacked. They have not become members of the community of historical Israel though they have of the new Israel; they are under a new covenant, not that made with Abraham. This verse contains a mixture of temporal and spatial terms; neither is fully adequate to express AE's meaning.

There are two qualifying phrases; the second, ἐν τῷ αἵματι τοῦ Χριστοῦ, clearly goes with the verb and is to be understood instrumentally. The NT normally relates 'blood' (see on 1.7 for the concept) to the death of Christ and AE is indebted to tradition for this connection. It has however been argued that the present reference is not to the death but to the circumcision blood of Christ.[25] There appears no reason to doubt that in the first century of our era in some circles of Judaism circumcision had been given sacrificial significance, though there is no reference to this in the Mishnaic passage celebrating circumcision (m Ned. 3.11). The sacrificial connection could have come from the exegesis of Exod 4.24–6 where the circumcision blood of Moses' son may be seen as saving Moses' life. But if Moses is an antitype of Christ then this would imply that it was the blood of Christians which saved Christ and not the reverse. If, however, as in some Jewish tradition, it is the life of the son which is saved then it is not the blood of Moses (= Christ) which saves. The argument for the allusion to circumcision blood in v. 13 is perhaps strengthened by the reference to circumcision in v. 11 and because in the possible parallel of Col 2.11 to Eph 2.11 circumcision is explicitly mentioned. However, there is no unanimity in the understanding of Col 2.11; it may refer to: (a) Christ's death (so Moule, Martin, O'Brien); (b) baptism (Gnilka, Lohse, Pokorný); our discussion of v. 11 showed that there was a strand in the OT, in the Judaism of Qumran and in early Christianity which spoke of a non-physical circumcision and it is easier to link the reference of circumcision in 2.11 to this than to baptism; (c) the forgiveness of sins which makes the new life possible (Schweizer). Thus Col 2.11 has no certain reference to the physical circumcision of Christ. No reason exists then either in 2.13 or in 2.11 to depart from the normal understanding relating blood to Christ's death, a conclusion supported by the semi-parallel of Col 1.20. So understood 2.13 gives the first indication of a theme which is followed up

[25] Cf H. Sahlin, art.cit.; G. Vermes, 'Baptism and Jewish Exegesis', NTS 4 (1958) 308–19; id. Scripture and Tradition, Leiden, 1961, 178–92; Kirby, 157f; Barth, ad loc.; Derwood C. Smith, 'The Ephesian Heresy'. 𝔓⁴⁶ B omit the article with Christ; this is not significant for the discussion about circumcision, or indeed at all, since the article appears to be used haphazardly with Christ in Ephesians.

in vv. 14–18, that Jews and Gentiles are reconciled to one another through the cross. In keeping with v. 8 AE does not say that the Gentiles have brought themselves near to God or Israel; it is God who has brought them near. It should be noted finally that no statement is made about when this took place; it may have been at baptism or at the moment of initial faith; but it is of God.

The second qualifying phrase, 'in Christ Jesus', might also be taken instrumentally (so Allan, 'In Christ'; Büchsel, 145) but two instrumental phrases both introduced by ἐν would be clumsy and, if instrumental, 'in Christ Jesus' ought to have been more closely linked to ἐγενήθετε ἐγγύς (perhaps following it, so Harless); there is also some contrast between νυνὶ δὲ ἐν Χριστῷ 'Ιησοῦ and τῷ καιρῷ ἐκείνῳ χωρὶς Χριστοῦ in v. 12 suggesting that our phrase refers to no longer being apart from Christ but to being with him. Mussner (*Christus* 87, n. 13) suggests a mystical-modal meaning and this is re-explained by Merklein (*Christus*, 24) as 'in einem Zustand, der durch Christus eindeutig bestimmt ist'; this is ambiguous since it can be taken as indicating either the inclusive sense or the instrumental depending on which part of the explanation is emphasised. The inclusive sense is the simpler and fits in with the spatial manner of AE's thought.

As we have already noted, vv. 14–18 stand by themselves because we change at v. 14 from the second plural to the first and return to the former at v. 19 and because Christ becomes the subject of the verbs of vv. 14–18. Verses 14–18 are thus a unit within vv. 11–22 and many, following Schlier, have argued that this unit is based on an existing piece of tradition, probably, as Schille suggested, a hymn, which AE adapted.[26]

In support of this it is argued: (i) The passage contains a number of *hapax legomena*: ten in respect of the remainder of Ephesians, three in respect of a

[26] Schille, 24–31; Sanders, *Hymns*, 14f, 88–92; id. 'Elements'; E. Testa, 'Gesù pacificatore universale. Inno liturgico della Chiesa Madre (Col. 1.1,15–20 + Ef. 2,14–16)', *SBFLA* 19 (1969) 5–64; J. Gnilka, 'Christus unser Friede—ein Friedens-Erlöserlied in Eph 2.14–27', *Die Zeit Jesu* (FS H. Schlier), Freiburg i. Br., 1970, 190–207; K. Wengst, *Formeln und Lieder des Urchristentums*, Gütersloh, 1972, 181–6; H.-M. Schenke, 'Die neutestamentliche Christologie und der gnostische Erlöser', *Gnosis und Neues Testament* (ed. K.-W. Tröger), Berlin, 1973, 205–29; Fischer, 131–7; P. Stuhlmacher, ' "Er ist unser Friede" (Eph 2.14). Zur Exegese und Bedeutung von Eph 2,14–18', *Neues Testament und Kirche* (FS R. Schnackenburg), Freiburg i. Br., 1974, 337–58; C. Burger, *Schöpfung und Versöhnung: Studien zum liturgischen Gut im Kolosser- und Epheserbrief*, Neukirchen-Vluyn, 1975, 117–39, 144–57; Lindemann, *Aufhebung*, 156–8, and ad loc.; Rader, 196–201; R. P. Martin, *Reconciliation*, 167–76; G. Wilhelmi, 'Der Versöhner-Hymnus in Eph 2.14ff', *ZNW* 78 (1987) 145–52. See also the commentaries ad loc. For criticism of the idea that vv. 14–18 include a section of preformed tradition see Deichgräber, 165–7; Merklein, *BZ* 17 (1973) 79–102; Edwards, 21ff; Schnackenburg; Ernst; M. S. Moore, 'Ephesians 2:14–16: A History of Recent Interpretation', *EvQ* 54 (1982) 163–8; Merkel, 3230–5; Best, 'Use'.

ten-letter Pauline corpus. (ii) The passage contains conflicting concepts, dealing sometimes with the reconciliation of humanity to God and at others with the reconciliation of Jews and Gentiles. (iii) The passage contains concepts unique to Ephesians and out of context here. (i) and (ii) suggest that there are words and phrases to be eliminated to recover the tradition, and (iii) those to be retained to make the passage theologically consistent. This done, it may be possible to construct the underlying tradition, usually taken to be a hymn, but possibly a creed. Attempts to do this have been based on different sections of the passage: vv. 14–18 (Schille); vv. 14–17 (Gnilka, Burger, Fischer, Pokorný); vv. 14–16 (Wengst, Sanders, Wilhelmi, Lindemann, Testa, Lincoln). Martin, *Reconciliation*, is unique in choosing as his base vv. 13–19. Since the total context shows AE's primary interest as lying in the reconciliation of Jews and Gentiles it is to be assumed that he added the references to this, and that the original tradition treated only reconciliation with God. But what would have been the nature of the latter reconciliation? Here attention focuses on the unusual phrase μεσότοιχον τοῦ φραγμοῦ which is taken to indicate a gnostic background (see later discussion of the phrase). In the alleged hymn the barrier between heaven and earth is broken by the descent of the heavenly redeemer; Schlier originally found evidence for this only in gnosticism (*Christus*, 18–26) but later in his commentary added evidence from Jewish Apocalyptic. Once, using (i) and (ii), what does not refer to reconciliation with God has been eliminated, it should be possible to detect normal hymnic characteristics, e.g. participial clauses, parallelism, good line structure.[27] Schille's own attempt failed since the lines he produced were of unequal length, some of them much too long. Succeeding attempts have been more successful in this respect.

It is impossible to outline and assess here each of these attempts in detail.[28] We can only offer some general criticisms in respect of the alleged hymn while in no way wishing to deny that hymns were in use in the early church as 5.14 shows:

(a) Once the hymn has been isolated it should be possible either to see it as capable of independent existence or to suggest a context into which it once fitted. Almost all attempts retain τὰ ἀμφότερα; this would require a prior reference; an original independent existence is therefore improbable. Most reconstructions of the hymn take the neuter to refer to the spheres of heaven and earth rather than to two groups of people, so permitting the hymn a gnostic context, though not a particular context; only Testa, art.cit., succeeds in giving a particular context by regarding 2.14–16 as the third strophe in a hymn of which the first two were Col 1.15–17 and Col 1.18–20; however since he treats the text more or less as it stands and does nothing to remove the ambiguity of concepts which created the suspicion of an underlying hymn, he leaves unsolved the problems which originally led to the search for tradition; moreover though he produces lines of equal length these bear no relation to content.

[27] Cf E. Stauffer, *New Testament Theology*, London, 1955, 338f; Schille, 16–20, 47–50; Barth, 6ff.
[28] For a detailed examination of the reconstructions of Gnilka and Wilhelmi see Best, 'Use'.

(b) Vv. 14–18 contain ten *hapax legomena*. Ephesians contains 2,411 words of which more than two hundred are *hapax legomena* (it is difficult to count the exact number; if cognates of words which occur once are to be counted then this number is greatly increased). Vv. 14–18 has eighty-four words and we should expect seven *hapax legomena*, yet ten is not statistically significant. It is interesting that scholars who use *hapax legomena* as a clue never retain them all, but only those that suit their theory; Martin, *Reconciliation*, does not use them as a clue for his reconstruction.

(c) We turn now to examine the words, phrases or concepts thought to be unique to our passage: (i) 'The middle wall'; nothing else in the letter suggests AE thought of a middle wall separating heaven and earth, and other solutions in respect of this wall are possible (see below). (ii) 'One new (human) being', v. 15, is said to be uniquely conceived as corporate whereas in 4.24 it denotes an individual; the 'being' of 2.15 is not however necessarily corporate (see below), and in any case the 'being' of 4.13 is. (iii) 'Flesh'; the use of the term in vv. 14–18 is said to depart from AE's customary usage and is applied to Christ; the latter is true but does not seem exceptional; more generally flesh is used here as an alternative to blood and the cross (see notes), and such a usage would not be out of line with AE's normal practice. (iv) In 2.16 Christ is the creator of reconciliation but elsewhere its mediator, and in 2.14–18 he, not God, is the principal actor; but he is also the principal actor in 4.7–16; 5.22–33; granted then that AE can see him as principal actor there is no reason why he should not have presented him as creator of reconciliation. (v) ἐλθών (v. 17) is a particularly difficult word and commentators differ on how to understand it (see notes); in some alleged hymns it can be relatively easily explained as relating to the descent of the heavenly redeemer when he broke through the wall separating heaven and earth (for other possible solutions see notes). (vi) The main conceptual confusion in the passage is its double approach in presenting two issues: the relationship of Gentile to Jew; the relationship of both to God. Yet this double approach, as we saw, began to appear in v. 13 and therefore has not been produced by AE's tampering with an underlying hymn. The double aspect is inevitable once the question of inter-human reconciliation is raised. How is this to be related to the reconciliation of humanity to God? We cannot enter here into the general problem which theologians have answered very differently as they have regarded one or other reconciliation as prior and basic to the other.

Taken all in all then, the great majority of the points raised by those who see an underlying hymn are explicable on the basis of AE's authorship. A number of general points, however, work against the idea of the use of a section of preformed tradition:

(i) If AE used an existing piece of tradition and not just individual phrases from the tradition, why did he take a hymn relating to the separation of heaven and earth and reapply it to the separation of Jews and Gentiles? It would have been so much easier for him to have written directly about the latter. If his readers knew the alleged hymn, what did he gain by confusing them by altering what they knew? It is true that Paul altered traditional material; he inserted into the hymn of Phil 2.6–11 the words 'even the death of the cross', but did so to bring home to his readers an essential point which, assuming they knew the hymn, would not confuse them but enable them to grasp the main issue. AE's alleged alterations are far too extensive for this to provide a satisfactory model or parallel. If however his readers did not know the hymn what was his purpose in using it at all? He makes no attempt here or elsewhere in the letter to correct its 'gnostic' views and so lead his readers away from gnosticism, incipient or otherwise. It would have been so much easier for him if he wished to correct what he took to be erroneous gnostic views to have done so by directly identifying and refuting them. Interestingly when at 5.14 he does quote a hymn he explicitly says so.

(ii) It is not an unfair criticism of the many reconstructions of the underlying tradition to point out that no two attempts agree. Agreement is lacking even in respect of the verses chosen to form the base for any reconstructions.

(iii) Since we do not accept the hymn there is no need to provide a separate exegesis of it or examine AE's alleged redaction for clues to his own meaning.

(iv) Other solutions to the difficulties of the passage have been offered: (a) It contains a complicated chiastic structure involving all vv. 11–22 (Giavini, art.cit.; Kirby, 156f); to reject this is not to deny that vv. 11–13 balance vv. 19–22. (b) It is a midrash woven around the three Isaianic texts (see above). (c) It is a rewriting of Col 1.21–3;[29] certainly there are common words but they are used differently (cf Lincoln, 130). None of these suggestions is very satisfactory.

14. Verse 14a provides the theme or text for vv. 14–18, peace. The word itself appears three times and the theme is also expressed through the ideas of 'reconciliation', 'oneness' and their opposite 'enmity'.[30] Although these emphases also appear in Colossians (1.20–3) and may belong to the Pauline school they are much more prominent in Ephesians. AE and A/Col probably derived them from their master (cf Rom 5.1; 15.33; 16.20; Gal 5.22), and behind him from the OT, and not from the *Pax Romana* in which they lived and from which in various ways they may have benefited nor from Jesus

---

[29] Cf Merklein, art.cit.; id. 'Paulinische Theologie in der Rezeption des Kolosser- und Epheserbriefes', *Paulus in den neutestamentlichen Spätschriften* (ed. K. Kertelge), Freiburg, 1981, 25–69.
[30] On peace see G. von Rad and W. Foerster, *TWNT*, II, 398–418; E. Brandenburger, *Friede im Neuen Testament*, Gütersloh, 1973; G. Baumbach, 'Das Verständnis von eirēnē im Neuen Testament', *Theologische Versuche* 5 (1975) 32–52; M. Klemm, *EIPHNH im neutestamentlichen Sprachsystem*, Bonn, 1977; R. Penna, 'L'évangile de la paix', *Paul de Tarse: Apôtre du notre temps* (ed. L. De Lorenzi), Rome, 1979, 175–99; H. Beck and C. Brown, *NIDNTT*, II, 776–83; W. Klassen, *ABD* V, 207–12; K. Wengst, *Pax Romana and the Peace of Jesus Christ*, London, 1987.

who had said that he had not come to earth to bring peace but a
sword (Mt 10.34). Is AE then unfaithful to Jesus? We shall return to
this after v. 18 when we have explored what he has to say about
peace. Gentiles who were afar (v. 11) have now been brought near
(v. 13) through the blood of Christ for, γάρ, he is our peace; αὐτός
is emphatic without implying a contrast with another source of
peace. The change here from the second person plural to the first
means vv. 14–18 apply to Jews and Gentiles without distinction.
2.14a does nothing to resolve the ambiguity already observed in v.
13: Christ may be the creator of peace between Jew and Gentile, the
horizontal relationship, or between God and both Jew and Gentile,
the vertical relationship, or the creator of peace for both relationships. In stressing Christ as peace AE prepares for an important
element in his later paraenesis, the need for unity within the
community (4.3).

The identification of Christ with peace is at first sight surprising;
we more naturally think of him as making peace (v. 15) or
proclaiming it (v. 17) than being it; the identification parallels that in
which he proclaims the word and is the Word, is life and gives life
(Col 3.4; cf 1 Cor 1.30), or where believers are light and impart light
(5.8). While peace may have been personified in the Greco-Roman
world in relation to the *Pax Romana*,[31] the ultimate origin of AE's
description of Christ as peace probably lies in Isa 9.6 which he
would have understood as a messianic passage (cf Mic 5.4; AE also
plays in our passage on Isa 57.19; 52.7)[32] and in Jewish expectations
of eschatological peace. In v. 12 AE said Gentiles were without the
Messiah, in v. 13 he viewed them as near and now (v. 14) as sharing
with Jews in the one Messiah. But this does not explain how he
understood Christ as peace.

Jewish and Greek thinking on peace differed. It was at this time
an important concept in the Greco-Roman world following on the
re-establishment of the *Pax Romana* after the quelling of the Jewish
rebellion and the destruction of Jerusalem (Faust, 226ff), for
Vespasian had revived the ideas of Augustus on peace. This might
have suggested a link with Gentile–Jewish relations, and perhaps an
implicit comparison of Christ to the emperor who was regarded as
the creator and maintainer of peace (Faust, 324, 378ff). Yet this
cannot have been the sole factor, nor even the most important, for
the word peace had been widely used from much earlier in Christian
worship, e.g. 'the kiss of peace', and in Christian letters where it
supplemented the Greek greeting (see on 1.2). We can assume AE's

[31] E. Dinkler, *Eirene: Der urchristliche Friedensgedanke, SHAW.PH* 1973, 20f; W.
S. van Leuwen, *Eirene in het Niewe Testament*, Wageningen, 1940, esp. 207–11.
[32] For the association of the Messiah with peace see SB III, 587; IV, 910f. There is
no reason to see here a reference to the peace offering, cf F. D. Coggan, 'A Note on
Ephesians 2.14', *ExpT* 53 (1941/2) 242.

readers once they had been converted would quickly become alert to the cluster of new ideas which came with the word from Judaism. They would of course also have brought with them into their Christianity ideas of peace which belonged to the Greco-Roman world in which they lived; there peace signified a condition of non-war in which stability and good order flourished. While for a Jew it could signify the absence of conflict (6.15), it also meant much more. Since the theme of conflict between Jew and Gentile or between either and God is at best only implicit in 2.11–13, it is proper to understand peace here in its wider Jewish sense where it refers to both physical and spiritual well-being, comes close to meaning salvation and attains eschatological significance. Peace is the end of alienation; people can be alienated from God, from one another or internally alienated; the first two aspects are present here, the third is not. Peace as salvation is God's gift. After referring to blood in v. 13 AE might have gone on to say that Christ is our salvation but instead he says he is our peace; this provides him with an easy transition to the discussion of Jewish and Gentile relationships. He will also have been influenced by Isa 57.19 to which he alluded in v. 13 and will use again in v. 17 for it contains the word 'peace'.

Vv. 14b–15a consist of three participial clauses whose subject is Christ; of these clauses the first two are parallel, but it is not clear where the second ends and the third begins. The aorist participles follow appropriately on the reference to the blood of Christ for the action they denote is related to his death. The existence of the two groups, Jews and Gentiles, was already introduced in vv. 11–13. While the neuter, τὰ ἀμφότερα, can be used to describe groups of people (cf Gal 3.22; 1 Cor 1.27f; Heb 7.7 and see BDR §§138.1; 263.4; MHT, 21[33]) it is surprising to find it here because AE uses the masculine in what follows. Its presence was one factor leading to the supposition that AE employed pre-existing tradition here (see below) which contained it but where the reference was not to people but to the heavenly and earthly spheres. The later masculine references are supposed to have come when AE introduced the reference to Jews and Gentiles. But if AE brought in the later references and considerably altered the original hymn, why did he not correct the neuter into a masculine to suit what followed? If he was writing freely it may be that he envisaged the neuter as completed by a neuter noun, e.g. γένη or, more probably, since in the next clause he uses the spatial image of a wall, χωρία. It is also possible that he used the neuter as bringing out more clearly the two

---

[33] On the use of the neuter where we might expect the masculine see E. Pax, 'Stilistische Beobachtungen an neutralen Redewendungen im Neuen Testament', *SBFLA* 17 (1967) 335–47. Faust, 137, sees the use of ἀμφότερα as derived from the political sphere.

totalities of Jews and Gentiles (Feine). He then either sees two peoples made into one people or two areas made into one area. The two groups are not strictly Jews and Gentiles; it is Christians from both these groups who are made into the new group. Jews and Gentiles as such still exist as independent groups.

We have taken the second participial clause as parallel to the first and continuing it but some (Schlier; Masson; Hugedé; Merklein, *Christus*, 31; Salmond) regard it as explaining it; this is unlikely since this sense could have been easily expressed without ambiguity. λύειν is regularly used of the destruction of physical objects (Jn 2.19; Acts 27.41) and whatever the meaning of 'middle wall' it is suggestive of a real or metaphorical building.

To what does τὸ μεσότοιχον τοῦ φραγμοῦ (v. 14) refer? Walls serve different purposes; they can be used to separate one group of people from another, sometimes erected for this purpose by a third group; they can be erected by one group to protect themselves from another group with emphasis either on excluding the other group or on preserving the identity of the erecting group, or erected in order to keep others out or to keep themselves in. Their existence can cause enmity when they exclude a group from what they regard as their legitimate position or prevent a group from being released from a position in which they are oppressed. Walls can be metaphorical or physical. It has been normal to understand the wall of v. 14 as non-material and referring to something else. With these possibilities in mind it is necessary to ask what the wall was which AE envisages Jesus as breaking down.

(i) An answer which became popular early this century suggests AE had in mind the stone balustrade which separated the area in the Jerusalem temple into which Gentiles were allowed to enter from the areas into which their entrance was prohibited. This balustrade was a 1.5m-high wall (cf Josephus *Ant* 15.417; *BJ* 5.193–4; cf *m Mid* 2.3) carrying inscriptions threatening death to Gentiles who crossed it. They were allowed into the outer court but no further. Two stones bearing the inscription in whole or in part have been discovered (*OGI* V 598 = *CIG* 2.1400);[34] their discovery led to the popularity of this solution. The balustrade represented in Jewish eyes a distinction between themselves and Gentiles, a distinction which in Christian eyes had been destroyed through Christ's death. This understanding of the wall fits the present context of the Jewish–Gentile distinction and prepares for the mention of the temple at vv. 21f. Paul, if the author of Ephesians, would have been aware of this wall since he had lived in Jerusalem and had been accused of bringing a Gentile, Trophimus, across it (Acts 21.29). It is said the animosity between Jews and Gentiles was very bad

---

[34] See Robinson, 160, for the text and, 60, for a translation.

during the time of his imprisonment in Caesarea and if he wrote Ephesians from there then this would have been at the front of his mind.[35] This solution is more likely to be true if Ephesians is Pauline. Whether it is or not, it encounters serious objections: (a) Would readers in Asia Minor have been aware of the balustrade and its significance? The temples of Asia Minor had no similar walls. (b) Neither in Josephus nor in the inscriptions is this wall termed a μεσότοιχον, (c) If Ephesians is not Pauline then by the time it was written the temple had been destroyed by the Romans and not by Christ; this would make the reference meaningless. (d) The destruction of the balustrade would only be relevant if the argument of 2.14–18 had been about the admission of Gentiles to ordinary Jewish privileges and this is not AE's argument; when elsewhere in the NT Christians are seen as enjoying Jewish privileges these are not ordinary privileges but those of the priesthood (e.g. Rom 12.1f; 1 Pet 2.5, 9). (e) While 2.11–22 looks forward to the building of a temple in v. 21, it is not a physical temple but a spiritual. An unimportant variation to this solution sees the middle wall as the curtain of the temple which was torn in two at the time of the death of Jesus (Mk 15.38); AE however refers to a wall and not a curtain. Finally we should note that if the wall is not the balustrade there is nothing to be learnt from it about the date of Ephesians.

(ii) The area in mind may be the whole cosmos and the wall one dividing the supernatural realm from the earthly. This solution was first advocated in detail by Schlier, *Christus*, 18–26, though the idea goes back to F. C. Baur, *Paulus: der Apostel Jesu Christi*, 1845, 436; it has since been accepted by many others (Dibelius, 69; Pokorný; Fischer, 133); Lindemann, *Aufhebung*, 161–6, goes further than most in that he appears to see AE as retaining, not merely correcting, gnostic thought; this, as in v. 12, leads him to an existentialist understanding of the passage and to playing down the Jew–Gentile contrast. Schlier started his discussion from the unusual neuter τὰ ἀμφότερα which he took to be non-personal and to indicate the heavenly and earthly spheres; a wall or barrier separates these; he found evidence for this at first in gnosticism and then (in his commentary) in Jewish apocalyptic. Noting that the Law which is a fence protecting Judaism from Gentile ideas also has a cosmic position,[36] he went on to argue that the gnostic Redeemer descends through the heavenly wall, encounters enmity from the

[35] Cf Bo Reicke, 'Caesarea, Rome and the Captivity Epistles', *Apostolic History and the Gospel* (FS F. F. Bruce, ed. W. W. Gasque and R. P. Martin), Exeter, 1970, 277–86, at 282.

[36] Rabbinic expansions of Ezek 4.3 which relate it to prayer as a way to God after the destruction of the temple sometimes refer to a wall but shed no light on our passage; cf B. M. Bokser, 'The Wall Separating God and Israel', *JQR* 73 (1983) 349–74.

heavenly powers and the Jewish folk angels (the heavenly powers and the Law are connected in Gal 3.19; Col 2.8, 10), destroys the wall and the enmity, and thus creates peace. This solution accounts for the ambiguity in relation to the nature of reconciliation; AE has used gnostic terms to which his readers are accustomed and which relate to God–human reconciliation and has superimposed on them a Christian interpretation dealing with the division between Jews and Gentiles. Schlier also drew in many of the other ideas of 2.14–22 arguing that they were gnostic.

Schlier's solution however encounters considerable difficulties: (a) The evidence offered is often late (e.g. the Mandean literature, the long recension of Ignatius) and when early is not exact, e.g. *1 En* 14.9 and parallel passages speak of a wall but never of its destruction; in *3 Bar* 2.1ff the wall has gates through which Baruch and the angels pass and thus does not need to be destroyed. (b) The crucial word μεσότοιχον is missing from all the literature, except where there has been Christian influence as in the long recension of Ignatius. (c) There is little certainty as to which gnostic concepts were current in the area to which Ephesians was addressed. (d) The connecting links in the various steps in the formulation of Schlier's argument are both complex and tenuous; if it was AE's intention to explain the relationship of Jews and Gentiles through the use of gnostic terminology he cannot be said to have done it very successfully. (e) As Schnackenburg notes, AE does not elsewhere separate heaven and earth in a way similar to that required by this theory (see also Detached Note: The Heavenlies). (f) The wall of the Law does not possess the alleged cosmic significance (Merklein, *Christus*, 39f). (g) Schlier's solution may explain the wall in an alleged underlying gnostic piece of tradition, but leaves too much unexplained in relation to the actual text and thus his interpretation provides no explanation for the latter.

(iii) If the 'area' which the wall divides is taken as the world of people then the Jews often regarded the Law as a wall which separated them from the Gentiles and protected them from Gentile impurities (*Ep Aristeas* 139, 142; *1 En* 93.6; 89.2; Prov (LXX) 28.4; Philo, *Virt* 186; *m Abot* 3.18[37]). The origin of this idea may lie in Exod 19.12, 21–4 and a metaphorical use of 'wall' in relation to division can be seen in CD 4.12; 8.12, 18 where some, probably the Pharisees, are accused of building a wall. Like the first solution this again fits easily into the context of a division between Jews and Gentiles; moreover v. 15 goes on immediately to refer to the Law as being rendered ineffective. Unlike the temple balustrade it is easier to assume that there would be Gentiles in Asia Minor who would

---

[37] See SB I, 693f., III, 588. In *m Abot* 1.1 the Law is not the fence but there is a fence around the Law (the oral law?) to protect it from its teachers.

have some notion of the Law as that which separated them from Jews, produced the impression that Jews were arrogant and exclusive, and caused Jews to despise Gentiles; Jewish adherence to the Law was then responsible for creating the barrier between them and Gentiles. Unfortunately, as with the other solutions, the key words are never found in connection with this supposed wall. The passages from *Ep Aristeas* come closest in using περιφράζω, a word derived from the same root as φραγμός. This solution also seems to imply that the wall which represents the Law, or the Law itself, must be described as 'enmity' (which is chosen depends on the way the later part of v. 14 is construed; see below) and it is not easy to see a follower of Paul and one who quotes the Pentateuch approvingly (5.31; 6.2f) as accepting it. Lindemann objects also that this understanding would set on its head the Jewish view of the Law as a protecting agency by making it into something which separates, and this would be very anti-Jewish; arguments are however often turned on their heads in discussion. While it is true that some Gentiles who were well acquainted with Judaism might have accepted that the Law separated them from the Jews, by no means all Gentiles would necessarily have thought in that way. Strictly the wall only existed from the Jewish point of view.

(iv) None of these solutions is completely satisfactory. Each takes the wall to represent something; in (i) a physical wall in the temple at Jerusalem, in (ii) a 'spiritual' or non-material wall between heaven and earth, and in (iii) a spiritual concept, the Jewish Law. It may however simply be that we have an ordinary metaphor of a separating wall and are wrong to look for recondite meanings in it.[38] It is not unnatural for people when they disagree, or when they see others disagreeing, to speak as if there was a separating factor ('I can't get through to them; it's as if there was a wall between us'). The wall could then be regarded as purely metaphorical and not indicative of some theological idea. Jews and Gentiles are distinct groups; there was much keeping them apart. Greco-Roman literature shows that Jews were despised for their peculiar ways and their high opinion of themselves as the unique people of God. Their belief that they were God's people led them to look down on those who were not; they refused to assimilate themselves to the prevailing culture; they regarded the Romans who oppressed them as arrogant (cf *Ps Sol* 17 for the mutual attitude of Jews and Romans). On both sides there were inhibiting factors which led each to look down on and

---

[38] Cf Robert Frost's 'Mending Walls' (*Selected Poems*, New York, 1963, 23f),
Before I built a wall, I'd ask to know
What I was walling in or walling out.
And to whom I was like to give offense.
Something there is that doesn't love a wall.
That wants it down.

despise the other. In such circumstances it becomes perfectly natural for both sides, and not Jews only, to think of a wall dividing them. The walls of Mic 7.11; CD 4.12; 8.12, 18 are not the Law but metaphorical walls. But why is μεσότοιχον used? It is an ordinary architectural term without any necessary religious reference, except in so far as it may be used in describing religious buildings; as an architectural term it was well known in Asia Minor, being found seven times in the instructions for the erection of the temple at Didyma.[39] It is used metaphorically in a non-Christian context in Athenaeus, *Deipn.* 7.14. 281D (ed. G. Klaiber). Some of the Fathers seem also to regard it as metaphorical, though they are not unanimous about its reference (Origen, Theophylact, John of Damascus). The second word φραγμοῦ is a genitive of apposition and such a use of a synonym is fully in line with AE's normal plerophoric style. AE therefore uses both words to describe a real division between Jews and Gentiles, which both would have agreed existed, but which had no specific theological significance, though if Jews had been forced to think the matter through they would have agreed that their distinction from Gentiles rested on their being a holy people who had special rules of their own. Gentiles would have viewed the separation in quite a different way.

We have not yet considered where to place the division between the second and third participial clauses, and the relation of the third to the preceding two. If the third clause simply paralleled the first two, then we would expect some connecting particle, probably another καί; if it was intended to represent a climax we should similarly expect something to indicate this; it is best then to take the third clause as explanatory of either the second or, better still because of their association, of the first and second. Von Soden's proposal that a parenthesis begins after ἔχθραν and ends with the same word in v. 16 has little to commend it; admittedly AE is not averse to parentheses but if one was here we should expect ἀπέκτεινεν rather than the participle (cf Abbott).

There are three units to be attached to either the second or third participle: (a) ἔχθραν (to take this with Haupt as a gloss is a counsel of despair); (b) ἐν τῇ σαρκὶ αὐτοῦ; (c) τὸν νόμον ... δόγμασιν (since AE likes runs of seemingly synonymous nouns this phrase may be treated as a unit; for the pattern see 1.17; 2.7). If

---

[39] I am grateful to Professor Peter Richardson for this information. The word occurs in temple inscriptions at 25A 13; 26B 21; 27A 88, 120; 27B 68, 75, 77 and relates to a dividing wall in a set of stairs; see T. Wiegand, *Didyma, II, Die Inschriften*, Berlin, 1958. For the importance of Didyma see J. Fontenrose, *Didyma. Apollo's Oracle, Cult and Companions*, Los Angeles, London, 1958. For the architectural use of similar terms see also Pausanius, *Testimonium*, 1.15, 1.10; 2.1; 8.9, 1.1f, and Josephus *Ant* 8.67.3–68.1; 8.71.2–72.1; Josephus applies it to a wall in the temple but not to the balustrade.

καταργήσας is not to be left high and dry then (c) must be linked to it. This leaves the following possibilities: (i) (a) and (b) may belong to the second clause; (ii) (a) may belong to the second and (b) to the third; (iii) (a) and (b) may belong to the third; (iv) (b) may be parenthetical. (i) (see Warnach, n. 49; Käsemann, *Leib*, 140f; Conzelmann) provides an answer as to when or how the middle wall was broken down (Salmond, 'he who in his crucified flesh broke down the wall ...'); if it is adopted (a) and (b) cannot however be taken as one phrase: 'the enmity in his flesh' is impossible. (a) will be in apposition to 'the middle wall ...' and suggest that the wall was the enmity. However if (a) is in apposition to the middle wall and (b) has also to be attached to the participle, it would have been easier if (a) had preceded the participle so that the linkage could be more clearly seen (the association of λύω with ἔχθραν is not unknown, Euripedes *Troades*, 50). (ii) (see Gnilka; Schlier; Masson; Schnackenburg; Merklein, *Christus*, 32): (a) goes as in (i) and ensures that the middle wall is understood metaphorically and not as an actual wall; it is hard to see how a physical dividing wall could be described as hostile. (b) defines the moment of καταργήσας as the event of Christ concentrated in his death. (iii) (see Ewald, Robinson, Beare, Bruce, Lindemann): (a) is now the direct object of καταργήσας; though it is often said that this noun could not be the direct object of the verb, 1 Cor 15.26 shows this is possible;[40] (c) will then be in apposition to it; but while the Law may be said to have caused enmity between Jew and Gentile it is hardly itself the enmity; the apposition would also be easier if (b) did not come between (a) and (c). (b) is indeed peculiarly placed; it would be better before (a) or, preferably, next to the participle. As in (i) (a) and (b) cannot be taken as one phrase. In favour of this solution is the chiastic structure which then appears in the first two participial clauses. (iv) It may be that we should take (b) out of the construction; at this point in his argument AE realises that he has not made it clear where Christ comes into the action and so inserts a phrase to tie down all three participles to the Christ-event; if this is so, and this is often how people write letters, then he would probably insert the phrase at a break in his thought; such a break would exist if (a) goes with what precedes and (c) with what follows.

We now turn to the individual phrases. A reference to enmity is not unnatural after one to peace. Where enmity exists much more is needed than the cessation of hostility; healing is also needed; the Semitic concept 'peace' contains both ideas. As we have seen, an ambiguity exists in the passage in relation to the horizontal and vertical components of reconciliation and we therefore need to ask

[40] Cf A. T. Hanson, *The Wrath of the Lamb*, London, 1957, 106.

whether the enmity is that between humanity and God (cf Rom 5.10) or between Gentile and Jew; the flow of thought suggests the latter as the more important at this point; in addition the reference to the middle wall implies that the hostility is two-sided, lying on both its sides, and God cannot be the party on one side for he is not hostile to humanity. Yet is 'enmity' not too strong a term to designate the difference between Gentile and Jew? It would be quite wrong to suppose that every Jew regarded every Gentile as an enemy, and vice versa, but the Jewish nation kindled hatred and scorn in many people[41] and many Jews from their privileged position as God's people came to regard as enemies those who belittled God's Law. Moreover the statement about hostility is that of an outside observer, neither Jew nor Gentile (whatever he previously was AE is now a Christian), and the views of outside observers often differ from and are more harsh than those of participants. With the destruction of the middle wall the enmity disappears; the two belong together and it is impossible to say, especially if the wall is 'metaphorical', which precedes the other.

We have taken 'in his flesh' as parenthetical, indicating where and how the action of the participles is achieved. It thus carries the same significance as blood in v. 13 and cross in v. 16. But why has AE used 'flesh' and not a word like 'death' (cf Col 1.22)? Since there is no underlying hymn it cannot be the source of 'flesh' and flesh is not a reference to the incarnation as such,[42] though it could be to Christ's human life taken as including his death (cf Thomas Aquinas; Robinson, 63; Mitton; Beare) since only those 'in the flesh' are able to die. Perhaps AE chose 'flesh' in preference to 'body' in view of his other use of body in this passage and the letter as a whole; his choice could also have been anti-docetic.

15. The phrase (v. 15a) about the rendering ineffective of the Law again evinces AE's love of a succession of similar words (Percy, 189). ὁ νόμος is not law in general but, as the context indicates, the Jewish Torah; AE only uses the word here but since he shows indebtedness to Paul's teaching on justification (2.8–10) we can assume that he rejects any idea of salvation through the Law. ἐντολή is used again in 6.2 of one of the ten commandments, implying that these continue to have value for AE. In contrast to ὁ νόμος the plural refers to the individual prescriptions of the Law (cf

---

[41] Cf M. Whittaker, *Jews and Christians: Greco-Roman Views*, Cambridge, 1984, 14–130; M. Stern, 'The Jews in Greek and Latin Literature', *CRINT* II, 1101–59; id. *Greek and Latin Authors on Jews and Judaism*, 3 vols., Jerusalem, 1984; V. Tcherikover, *Hellenistic Civilisation and the Jews*, New York, 1979, 344–77; E. M. Smallwood, *The Jews under Roman Rule* (SJLA 20), Leiden, 1976; L. H. Feldman, *Jew and Gentile in the Ancient World*, Princeton, 1993, 84–176.

[42] Cf Pokorný, 'Epheserbrief und gnostische Mysterien', *ZNW* 53 (1962) 160–94 at 153.

Sellin⁴³). ἐν δόγμασιν, though omitted by 𝔓⁴⁶ vgᵐˢ, fits AE's style too well for it to be a gloss; it could easily have been dropped as apparently redundant.⁴⁴ Col 2.14, a passage not unrelated to ours, also uses the noun, and both there and here it probably means 'legal decrees or regulations' (possibly a usage of the Pauline school for it is not used by Paul) and its meaning is then similar to ἐντολή. As often in Ephesians it is impossible to differentiate fully between almost synonymous words coming in sequence. There is no reason to see a reference either to a new law given by Christ or to Christian doctrine (cf Chrysostom;⁴⁵ Harless has a long discussion of all the possibilities) as rendering the Jewish Law ineffective. Nothing AE writes suggests that he would differ from Paul in seeing the Law as abrogated by anything other than the cross; the whole context of 2.14–18 has that death in view. The two nouns AE has put in the plural suggest that he envisages here the actual regulations of the Law which showed up the differences between Jews and Gentiles and created hostility. There is nothing in the context to suggest AE is thinking only of circumcision and regulations about purity and food (so many commentators).⁴⁶ It can be argued that Col 2.14–22 relates to ritual laws (cf Faust, 117) but if so that limitation arises out of the context of Colossians and cannot determine the meaning here. The distinction between moral and ritual laws is by no means hard and fast and is not one which the Law itself drew; the law of retaliation is not ritual yet it is abrogated (Matt 5.38–42). It is therefore better to regard the whole law as at issue here.

As for καταργήσας the verb appears only here in Ephesians but is found regularly in the genuine Paulines, sometimes in relation to law (Rom 3.31; 7.2, 6). Presumably AE and his readers were aware of this usage. If in 6.2 AE quotes approvingly from the Decalogue and if he himself sets down moral rules in 4.1ff, it is unlikely that he

---

⁴³ Joüon takes ἐντολή to refer to the major commandments and δόγμασιν to refer to prescriptions.

⁴⁴ C. J. Roetzel, 'Jewish Christian–Gentile Christian Relations. A Discussion of Eph. 2,15a', ZNW 74 (1983) 81–9, takes the phrase as a later addition to the text; AE himself had already added v. 15a without it to an original hymn; the phrase was added to counter the idea that the coming of Christ had made the principle of the commandments obsolete for 'perfect' or 'spiritual' Christians. It is however doubtful if there ever was an original hymn. For criticism of Roetzel see M. Kitchen, 'The status of law in the Letter to the Ephesians', Law and Religion (ed. B. Lindars), Cambridge, 1988, 141–7.

⁴⁵ The meaning probably goes back beyond Chrysostom; see Ptolomaeus, Epistle to Flora 6.6, with G. Quispel's note in his edition, SC 24, 95–6.

⁴⁶ N. J. McEleney NTS 20 (1973/4) 33; there were great disputes among the Reformers about how much of the Law AE had in mind; cf Rader, 78–96. Philo distinguished between the Law of God and the actual laws of Moses; the latter, are mainly ritual, are inferior to God's Law and require to be understood allegorically if they are to be accepted (cf Faust, 138–50). This kind of approach would probably not have been understood by AE's readers though they might have distinguished between the ὀρθὸς λόγος of the Stoics and the actual laws of society.

would regard law as such as abolished or destroyed; yet it can no longer be a means of salvation (see 2.8–10) and used to enforce the separation of Jew and Gentile. AE thus expresses in his own way what Paul says about the ending of the Law through Christ (Rom 7.4; 10.4; Gal 3.13), but unlike Paul he makes no attempt to defend the Law or claim that it is good (cf Rom 3.31; 7.12, 14; 13.8–10). Has the Law then no continuing function? The Law as the duty of love remains and binds both Jews and Gentiles. Lastly in view of the horizontal–vertical ambivalence of the passage it may be that AE thinks at this point of the Law as separating Jew from Gentile and also both from God.

The three participial clauses are now succeeded by two final clauses (vv. 15b, 16) giving the purpose for the removal of the wall and the making of Law of no effect. To what are they to be attached? For their basis they require something more important than v. 15a which is itself either subordinate to v. 14bc or in apposition to it (Mussner notes the absence of any introductory particle). They cannot depend directly on v. 14b since v. 15b expresses the same basic thought as v. 14b. The intervention of v. 15a makes direct dependence on v. 14c improbable and in any case v. 14b and v. 14c are tied together. Probably then vv. 15b, 16 relate to the whole of vv. 14–15a since the same concepts, peace, enmity, two, one, making (creating), he (in his flesh, in himself), run through both sets of clauses; vv. 15b, 16 give them a new context. In scripture creation is normally the prerogative of God (so in 2.10) but here Christ creates, as also in Col 1.16; Jn 1.3.

What Christ creates is 'the one new (human) being' and he creates this person out of the two, i.e. Jews and Gentiles; we note the change from the neuter (v. 14) to the masculine; whatever the significance of the earlier neuter, people are now in mind. But as individuals or groups? Are Jews and Gentiles made (i) as individuals into a new type of humanity, or (ii) as groups into a new corporate person? Either is grammatically possible and in both cases a new[47] being comes into existence which did not exist prior to the death of Christ. The earliest support for (i) is found in Clem Alex *Stromata* 3.70.2, GCS 228.1 (cf Mussner, *Christus*, 87; Henle; Grosheide; Masson; Meyer; Macpherson; Salmond). Those favouring it have argued: (a) If Jews and Gentiles were being made as groups into a new corporate whole there would have been no need to change from the neuter. (b) ἕνα picks up ἕν from v. 14 as δύο picks up ἀμφότερα emphasising that in the Christian community there is only one type

---

[47] On καινός see W. Barclay, 'The One, New man', *Unity and Diversity in New Testament Theology* (FS G. E. Ladd, ed. R. A. Guelich), Grand Rapids, 1978, 73–81. That Barclay overplays the distinction between καινός and νέος in respect of Hellenistic Greek does not affect the significance of the evidence provided for the former term.

of humanity. (c) In 4.24 (cf Col 3.10) the new being is not a corporate being but a transformed individual; the addition of ἕνα in v. 15 is necessary since in 4.24 the contrast is between the same person before and after conversion whereas in v. 15 a new type of person is being made out of two former types. (d) If a new corporate being were intended there was no need to speak of *one* new person. (e) AE may be playing on the concept of the new creation which would have been a part of the theology of the Pauline school (2 Cor 5.17; Gal 6.15)[48] and it is not out of keeping with his method of working that he should adapt it to his own purposes; Gal 6.15 had already related the new creation to the Jewish–Gentile conflict. (f) The variant κοινόν $\mathfrak{P}^{46}$ F G, while unlikely (even less likely is the καὶ μόνον of K), shows that some early scribes accepted the individualistic meaning and removed all doubt with their variant. (g) The argument that proselyte baptism has affected AE's theology here (Lincoln, art.cit.) may be true but is not necessarily so since proselytes do not become 'new people' but are only likened to 'new people' (Bouttier; Lindemann, *Aufhebung*, 170). (h) Faust, 125–9, draws attention to Philo's 'two' men which he derives from Gen 2.7 (cf *Leg Alleg* 1.31f, 53–5; 3.104); renewal, ἀνακαινίζειν, is also related to conversion in *Jos As* 8.9; 15.5. Faust, 129–37, links the theme of two who are 'opposites' becoming one to Philo (e.g. *Qu Gen* 2.35f) and to neo-Pythagoreanism and sees the idea in 2 Clem 12.2; *Gos Thom* 22. It cannot be denied that the reconciliation of opposites was a common theme and therefore may have influenced AE but nowhere else does it refer to Jews and Gentiles. The one new person is of course neither superman nor sexless, and the idea is not derived from democratic idealism but from the cross.

Supporters of (ii) (e.g. Schlier; Gnilka; Schnackenburg; Barth; Roels, 127–32; Lindemann, *Aufhebung*, 167f) argue: (a) In 5.22–33 the new Christian group of former Jews and Gentiles is pictured as a single individual, the bride, and in 4.13 as a mature person, though ἀνήρ is used there and not ἄνθρωπος. (b) AE is following up here the Pauline idea of Gal 3.28. (c) V. 15 and v. 16 are parallel and in v. 16 the new group is depicted as 'one body' and this one body is not an individual but the church (cf 4.4). (d) The corporate concept could have been derived from a number of possible backgrounds: the new Adam (Houlden; Ernst; Warnach, 16f; Hanson, 144f) who may be understood corporately (Rom 5.15–21; 1 Cor 15.22) or the myths of the *Urmensch* redeemer or the *anthropos* (Mussner, *Christus*, 88–91, dispute the validity of the last two ideas). While it

---

[48] For the background to 'new creation' see G. Lindeskog, *Studien zum neutestamentlichen Schöpfungsgedanke*, Uppsala, 1952; E. Sjöberg, 'Widergeburt und Neuschöpfung im palästinischen Judentum', *ST* 4 (1950) 44–85; id. 'Neuschöpfung in den Toten-Meer-Rollen', *ST* 9 (1955) 131–6; U. Mehl, *Neue Schöpfung* (BZNW 56), Berlin, 1989.

would be wrong to depend too closely on particular texts which are
often late, the general idea of corporateness was current and could
easily have crystallised into what we have. On balance (i) is to be
preferred; (ii) in any case appears in v. 16. Whichever view is
chosen there is again a realised eschatology since the new creation
in Jewish thought belonged to the end time.

Christ has created the one new man ἐν αὐτῷ. To what does the
pronoun refer? αἷμα is too remote; σάρξ is feminine and σῶμα is
not mentioned until v. 16; there is no reason however why the
pronoun, even if given a smooth breathing, should not be taken
reflexively (see Metzger's note on Phil 3.21).[49] What then would the
phrase mean? (i) It may be instrumental[50] but it is difficult to see
what this adds to the original 'he created ...'. If people do
something it is always by or through themselves. The instrumental
interpretation certainly implies a clear distinction between Christ
and the one new man, which accords with what AE writes elsewhere
on the church—it is the body, Christ is the head; he is the saviour,
the church is the saved. (ii) It is better to give the phrase its
customary sense in which believers are 'in Christ'—that he might
create in himself, that is, in his corporate existence. Those who are
'in him' are new beings, or if the one new human being is
understood corporately Christ is seen as identifying himself with this
new being. In either case Gal 3.28 probably foreshadows what we
have, and it accords with the intimate relation between Christ and
the church which runs through the whole of Ephesians.

The final ποιῶν εἰρήνην returns us to the opening words of v. 14
and the theme of peace. The creation of the new person takes place
simultaneously with the making of peace (pres. part., not necessarily
signifying a continuous activity as if Christ keeps on making peace,
though this indeed may be true). The peace is clearly that between
Jew and Gentile. The good ruler in the ancient world created peace,
e.g. *pax Augusta* (see Faust, *passim*) and so a recognisable virtue is
transferred to Jesus though set in an entirely new context. Faust,
412ff, indeed sees a soteriological connection with events in the
Roman world in that Vespasian and Titus are made world rulers by
Jupiter and overcome the division of the world which had come
through the Jewish rebellion. The Romans were involved in the
crucifixion of Jesus; in contrast it is his shameful crucifixion which
actually brings peace.

16. This verse is not a consequence of v. 15b but parallel to it;
terms are balanced (two–both, create–reconcile, in him–in one
body, making peace–killing; cf Bouttier); like v. 15b it depends on

---

[49] ἑαυτῷ is found as a variant in ℵ² D G Ψ 𝔐 latt; Mcion^T Epiph.
[50] F. Büchsel, ' "In Christus" bei Paulus', *ZNW* 42 (1949) 141–58 at 145; Allan,
'In Christ'.

ἵνα and provides a second purpose relating to the whole of vv. 14b-15a. Unlike v. 15b which spoke of the bringing together of Jews and Gentiles, v. 16 treats the relationship of both to God; thus the ambiguity of horizontal and vertical which commenced in v. 13 is continued and at the same time resolved. Not only do Jew and Gentile (the use of οἱ ἀμφότεροι suggests AE thinks of the two groups rather than of the individuals comprising them, cf BDR §274.3) move towards one another; both move towards God. Neither movement may be said to be prior to the other or regarded as its basis, unlike Mt 5.23f (cf *m Joma* 8.9) where the horizontal precedes the vertical. Here the reconciliations are as inseparable as the two great commandments of love. The two groups are reconciled to God by Christ;[51] it is not God who is reconciled to them. The double compound ἀποκαταλλάσσειν is found only elsewhere in the NT in Col 1.20, 22; the Colossian hymn, which AE probably knew apart from its existence in Colossians, may have been AE's source or the word may have been in use in the Pauline school. AE's usage differs from A/Col's in that he introduces the aspect of reconciliation between humans, making Christ, not God, its subject. Paul uses the simpler καταλλάσσειν. The double compound is probably only an intensification of the Pauline word and carries no idea of a restoration of a once-lost unity (as supposed by Chrysostom, Theophylact, Calvin, Harless); this would have been possible if God had been the subject since all were once in unity with him prior to Adam's fall. Paul presents God as the initiator of reconciliation (2 Cor 5.18–20; Rom 5.10f; 11.15; in 1 Cor 7.11 reconciliation is a purely human activity relating to a divided marriage). AE agrees with Paul and A/Col in relating reconciliation to the death of Christ; while 'body' and 'flesh' are linked to the idea in Col 1.22 they are used differently here and in v. 14.

Mitton parallels v. 16 with Col 1.20-2 noting the use of common words,

---

[51] On reconciliation see V. Taylor, *Forgiveness and Reconciliation*, London, 1941, 83–129; D. E. H. Whiteley, *The Theology of St Paul*, Oxford, 1964, 130–54; D. Lührmann, 'Rechtfertigung und Versöhnung', *ZTK* 67 (1970) 437–52; E. Käsemann, 'Some Thoughts on the Theme "The Doctrine of Reconciliation in the New Testament"', *The Future of our Religious Past* (FS R. Bultmann, ed. J. M. Robinson), New York, 1971, 49–64; P. van den Bergh, 'Verzoening in de Bijbel', *Collationes* 21 (1975) 22–41; J. A. Fitzmyer, 'Reconciliation in Pauline Theology', *No Famine in the Land* (FS J. L. McKenzie, ed. J. W. Flanagan and A. W. Robinson), Missoula, Montana, 1975, 155–77; I. H. Marshall, 'The Meaning of "Reconciliation"', *Unity and Diversity in New Testament Theology* (FS G. E. Ladd, ed. R. A Guelich), Grand Rapids, 1978, 117–32; O. Hofius, 'Erwägungen zur Gestalt und Herkunft des paulinischen Versöhnungsgedankens', *ZTK* 77 (1980) 186–99; Martin, *Reconciliation*; G. Friedrich, *Die Verkündigung des Todes Jesu im Neuen Testament*, Neukirchen-Vluyn, 1982, 95–118; C. Breytenbach, *Versöhnung: Eine Studie zur paulinischen Soteriologie* (WMANT 60), Neukirchen-Vluyn, 1989; S. E. Porter, *DPL* 695–9; id. καταλλάσσω *in Ancient Greek Literature with Reference to the Pauline Writings*, Cordoba, 1994.

ἀποκαταλλάσσω, ἐν σώματι, διὰ τοῦ σταυροῦ; the words may be the same but the thought is different. In Colossians reconciliation is between God and earth, in Ephesians between Jew and Gentile; the body in Colossians is that of the incarnate Jesus, in Ephesians the church; though both refer to the cross A/Col spells it out by referring to blood; there is no reason why AE should have deleted this for he uses it in 1.7; 2.13. People do not go to documents to pillage words and ignore their thought.

The reconciliation of human beings to God is not expressed elsewhere in the NT so clearly as by Paul and his school (the LXX uses the verb for it in 2 Macc 1.5; 5.20; 7.33 where God, not humanity, is the object of reconciliation; in 2 Macc 8.29; Isa 9.4; Jer 31.39 the reconciliation is entirely on the human level); the idea may indeed have been introduced into Christian thought by Paul. The metaphor is derived from the social and political sphere where it is used of the bringing together of those who for some reason are apart and is used in this way in Mt 5.23f; Acts 7.26; 1 Cor 7.10f. AE was the first to use it to describe the new relationship of Jews and Gentiles, and it is a not inappropriate metaphor in the context of peace, but he does not use it directly of their being brought together; that was expressed in a different way in v. 15b; yet since he speaks of groups and not individuals as reconciled this cannot be far from his thoughts. Whatever advantages Jews may once have had (v. 12) no distinction is now made between the ways in which they and Gentiles are reconciled to God. In Col 1.20 the cosmos is said to be reconciled to God; AE is closer to Paul in restricting reconciliation to humans (in 2 Cor 5.18 the cosmos is the world of humanity), yet unlike Paul he speaks of the reconciliation of groups, though this will of course imply the reconciliation of the individuals within the groups who respond to the divine activity.

Christ reconciles the two groups 'in one body' (cf the same phrase in Col 3.15 where already body is linked to peace). If we associate the reference to the body closely with that to the cross, the body in v. 16 might be the physical body of Christ which hung on the cross (so Chrysostom; Theodoret; Percy, 281–6; id. *Leib Christi*, 29; Bengel; Harless; etc.). If this were so, we should expect 'in his body' or possibly 'in a (the) body' and ἐπί with the dative rather than διά with the genitive; ἑνί which Mussner regards as stressed would also be superfluous. Since AE uses 'body' in the singular elsewhere of the church he would probably have used 'flesh' here if he had meant Christ's physical body. The vast majority of commentators[52] accept the reference here as to the church, and this is true even if the 'one new man' in v. 15b is understood individualistically.

---

[52] Asmussen is unique in seeing a triple reference to the crucified body, the eucharistic body and the church body; Penna sees a double reference to the first and third of these.

Accepting that the reference is to the church, we see that both vertical and horizontal relationships are fully present, Jews and Greeks being simultaneously reconciled to God and to one another. The former is the primary reference; if it were the latter εἰς would have been used instead of ἐν. The absence of the personal pronoun 'his' with body does not imply that AE is thinking only in terms of the social and political metaphor of the body and its members, as if all that was being said was that two groups have been formed into one group. There is too much background to the corporate use of 'body' in the Pauline corpus for it to slip back into its original (if that was its original) simple metaphorical meaning here.

With the reference to the cross Christ's death, which has been underlying all that preceded, is now made explicit. Redemption is connected here to the cross and not to the resurrection, not that AE ignores the latter. The body which is the church came into existence through Christ's death. It would be possible to take διὰ τοῦ σταυροῦ with what follows (von Soden), but this would overload the participle and ἐν αὐτῷ could not then refer to the cross but would refer to σώματι or be taken reflexively (neither of these possibilities is eliminated if 'through the cross' belongs to what precedes). This is AE's only reference to the way Christ died (cf Col 1.20; 2.14), though Paul regularly uses the cognate verb in referring to it and assumes that reconciliation takes place through Christ's death (Rom 15.10f; 2 Cor 5.18–20; cf Col 1.20, 22).

ἐν αὐτῷ could refer to (i) the body, but this is relatively distant, or (ii) the cross, and killing and cross are terms belonging to the same word field, or (iii) it could be taken reflexively, 'in himself' (Schnackenburg), as in some manuscripts (F G *pc* lat) and as we saw was possible in v. 15a. If (iii), it cannot be linked too closely to 'enmity' as if Christ destroyed some enmity internal to himself, perhaps referring to the temptations (so Barth); such an interpretation would require a clear reference since neither Paul nor AE shows much interest in the historical Jesus. The enmity also cannot be that of those who crucified Christ (von Soden). If (iii) is correct, what is the meaning? The corporate sense which is probable in v. 15b would not be applicable here since any enmity between Jew and Gentile did not exist in Christ; it would have to mean something like 'killing the enmity by his own action' and διά would have been the more appropriate preposition. It is easier to accept (ii) with Gnilka (there is a similar difficult decision to make in Col 1.20; 1 Jn 5.10; Jas 5.20; see Zerwick §211). The enmity which is killed is that between Jew and Gentile (Eadie) as in v. 14 and not that between humanity and God (Haupt, Abbott) or both (Scott). It received its death blow in the cross; ἀποκτείνας may be an aorist participle of action identical with that of the main verb (Burton, §139) indicating one particular event, Christ's death. Christ is killed and he kills!

DETACHED NOTE V
ISRAEL AND THE CHURCH

The church is new for it did not exist prior to Christ, but how new is new? Do we have a third group, consisting of neither Jews nor Gentiles, standing alongside both and yet different from both? Has a new people of God, contrasting with Israel the old people, come into existence? Have Gentile Christians been absorbed into Israel so that they continue it? What, in short, is the relation of the church to Israel?[53]

The NT writings provide varying answers to our questions. In Rom 9–11 Paul argued at length that Israel had not dropped out of God's sight and that the evangelisation of the Gentiles was a step on the way to its rehabilitation. This may represent a change in his original thinking for in 1 Th 2.14–16 he appears to see Israel as subject for ever to the wrath of God.[54] Other parts of the NT reflect in greater or lesser degree his earlier position. Mark sees the cross as God's judgement on Israel, presumably because though the Jews had the Law and the prophets they had not recognised their Messiah.[55] Matthew's form of the parable of the vineyard suggests that Israel loses its heritage and that it is given to another, the church (21.33–43). Acts 28.28 has often been read in the sense that God has turned away from Israel and in future salvation is to be offered to the Gentiles alone. Jn 8.44 sees Judaism as satanic in outlook. In Hebrews Judaism has had and perhaps still has its place, but it is an inferior place to Christianity. It is not easy to harmonise these

[53] The discussion of the relation of Christians and Jews has been expanding rapidly in recent years as a result of the Holocaust; it is impossible to list all the literature; we name only some which has a bearing on Paul and Ephesians rather than on the general problem: J. N. Sevenster, *The Roots of Antisemitism in the Ancient World* (SupNT 42), Leiden, 1975; P. Sigal, 'Aspects of Dual Covenant Theology', *Horizons in Biblical Theology*, 5 (1983) 1–48, at 24–8; F. Mussner, *Tractate on the Jews*, London and Philadelphia, 1984, 1–51, 133–53; R. Penna, 'L'évolution de l'attitude de Paul envers les Juifs', *L'Apôtre Paul* (BETL 73, ed. A. Vanhoye), Leuven, 1986, 390–421; *Anti-Judaism in the Early Church*, vol. I, ed. P. Richardson with D. Granskow, vol. 2, ed. S. G. Wilson, Waterloo, Ontario, 1986; A. T. Lincoln, 'The Church and Israel in Ephesians 2', *CBQ* 49 (1987) 605–24; Schweitzer, art.cit.; M. Rese, 'Church and Israel in the Deuteropauline Letters', *SJT* 45 (1990) 19–32; *Jews and Christians* (ed. J. H. Charlesworth), New York, 1990; D. D. Sutherland, 'Gen. 15.6 and Early Christian Struggles over Election', *SJT* 44 (1991) 443–51; G. Theissen, 'Judentum und Christentum bei Paulus. Sozialgeschichtliche Überlegungen zu einem beginnenden Schisma', *Paulus und das antike Judentum* (WUNT 58, ed. M. Hengel), Tübingen, 1991, 331–59; for the views of M. Barth see below. Schnackenburg, 321–5 provides a *Wirkungsgeschichte* of the discussion of the relationship.

[54] Though much ingenuity has been spent on arguing that these verses are non-Pauline I see no reason to deny his authorship other than their lack of harmony with Romans; like many people Paul continued to think through his original ideas and reach better conclusions.

[55] Cf Best, *The Temptation and the Passion* (SNTSMS 2), 2nd edn Cambridge, 1990, xlii, 83f, 98–100.

statements with one another. It is not always easy to harmonise any one particular writer's statements. Paul's position changed between 1 Thessalonians and Romans. Within John, 4.22 sheds quite a different light on Jewish–Gentile relations from 8.44. The NT does not offer then a uniform picture in respect of the future position of Israel over against Christianity and at times there is also a lack of uniformity in particular writers.[56]

Markus Barth has argued in a number of publications as well as in his commentary that the church has been incorporated into historical Israel.[57] He affirms that there can only be one Israel and if the church is Israel it must include all Jews, whether believing or not (*Broken Wall*, 122, 8), for AE never draws the distinction of Rom 9.6 that not all Israel is Israel. Over against Barth we would argue: (i) His view robs the newness (v. 15) of its newness and gravely diminishes the discontinuity before and after Christ if all that has happened is in effect a widening of the boundaries of Israel by the addition of Gentile believers. (ii) Both Jews and Gentiles are in need of saving grace (2.1–10); Gentiles who do not accept this remain outside the one new being or are not made into new people. What then of Jews who do not accept God's saving grace? Do they have access to God (2.18) other than through Christ? (iii) Had AE wished to suggest that Gentile believers became a part of historic Israel he would have made 'nearness' in 2.13 mean nearness to Israel. (iv) In the terms of 2.1–4 both Jews and Gentiles before they believed stood on the same level as transgressors of God's will; both must be changed if both are to be redeemed. (v) AE must have known there were unbelieving Jews yet says nothing about them; this then means he saw them as a group distinct from both Christians and Gentiles. (vi) If Gentile Christians were absorbed into Israel they would come under the Torah, yet the Law has been abrogated for the church.

Looking more generally at the problem it is clear that: (i) AE evaluates Israel positively in a way he does not evaluate Gentiles, as both 2.12 and his use of the OT and non-use of secular writings show; he implicitly agrees with Paul in that the Gospel is given first to the Jew and then to the Gentile. (ii) He can also be critical of Israel in so far as he downgrades circumcision (2.11) and speaks of the abrogation of the Law (2.15a), a criticism which remains even if his reference is only to the ceremonial law. His criticism of Israel does not extend to blaming her for the death of Jesus (contrast 1 Th 2.14–16). There is no polemic against the Jews in Ephesians; 2.11f implies God favoured them more than Gentiles. Since his interests

---

[56] On the variety of view cf W. Schmithals, *Theologiegeschichte*, 225ff.
[57] *Israel und die Kirche im Brief des Paulus an die Epheser* (Theologische Existenz Heute 75), Munich, 1959; 'Conversion and Conversation. Israel and the Church in Paul's Epistle to the Ephesians', *Int* 17 (1963) 3–24; *The People of God* (JSNTSup 5), Sheffield, 1983; *Broken Wall*, 105ff.

lies elsewhere there was no point in him making a statement about their ultimate fate. (iii) While he associates Gentile Christians and Jewish Christians (3.6) there is no evidence that he associates Gentile Christians and non-Christian Jews. This means that at least for AE the church is continuous with Israel in a way in which it is not continuous with the Gentile world; 'die Kirche ohne Israel ein geschichtsloses Abstraktum wäre' (Mussner, 74). (iv) There is also discontinuity between Israel and the church for the church has an access to God through Christ which Israel did not have. (v) If the church is the continuation of Israel we might have expected AE to identify Israel as the church's foundation but instead he identifies this as the apostles and prophets (2.20). (vi) At no point does he make a direct comparison between Israel and the church and suggest the latter's superiority.

In comparison with Paul who argued in Rom 11 that God has not rejected unbelieving Jews, AE appears to ignore them. It cannot be argued that he was unaware of their continued existence for there were far too many Jews in Asia Minor for that to be possible. His different approach from Paul may perhaps have arisen because he was less personally involved with the Jews than Paul. It is however more probably a part of his general lack of interest in the world outside the church; equally he displays no interest in the survival of unbelieving Gentiles, not even suggesting that church members should seek to convert them. Since his main purpose is to build up the church and maintain its unity, he has no need to refer to the continuance of Israel; since also the Jews are not apparently disturbing the harmony of his communities he has no need to be anti-Jewish. In ignoring the future position of unbelieving Jews AE certainly does not go so far as *Barn* 13.1ff which explicitly excludes them from the covenant,[58] and certainly not as far as the hostility expressed towards them in Melito, *On the Pascha* 42–3, 99. He can therefore be acquitted of any charge of anti-Semitism and also of one of anti-Judaism. It may be that our worries in respect of AE's position come from our realisation that the Jews have continued to exist through two millennia and therefore some explanation is necessary. For AE there are three groups of people, the Jews, the Gentiles and the church. AE would not then have rejected the traditional term for the church: the third race. The term goes back at least as far as *Kerygma Petri* (= Clem Alex *Strom* 6.5.39–41; cf *Diognetus* 1; in Aristides, *Apology* 2, the Syriac version adds a fourth group, the Barbarians).

17. AE now returns to the theme of peace first announced in v. 14a. Our verse might be construed as parallel to vv. 15b, 16 or some part of them, or as dependent on them, or, more probably, as an

---

[58] Cf D. D. Sutherland, art.cit.

independent sentence. If the last, καί connects back to v. 14a, 'He is our peace ... and he has proclaimed peace.' In vv. 14b-16 he is said to have made peace, but being peace and making peace do not avail or benefit unless the peace is made known: AE brings this out by using Isa 57.19, to which he had already alluded in v. 13 (see there for the background to its use). In saying that Christ proclaimed peace AE goes beyond the choice of a simple word, such as κηρύσσω, which would merely mean that Christ announced it, and chooses instead εὐαγγελίζομαι which in itself contains a valuation of the proclaimed message as good news; he probably drew the verb from Isa 52.7[59] where it is connected to the concept of peace. Christians have traditionally drawn the association of peace with the Gospel also from other OT passages, e.g. Nah 1.15; Isa 9.5f; 11.6–9; 54.10 (so Roberts). There are allusions to Isa 52.7 in Acts 10.36; Rom 10.12, 15 (cf Faust, 152–62), in both cases in the context of the place of Gentiles in the church; Faust therefore suggests that Isa 52.7 may have been already in use prior to AE in respect of Jewish–Gentile relations. AE might have been aware of this use as a member of a Pauline school. Faust, 164–77, notes also that in Acts 10.36 and Rom 10.12, 15 it is apostles who proclaim God as the God of all and not of Jews only; he also links the Pauline announcement of peace to the activity of the Philonic logos as maker of peace (e.g. *Quis Dives* 205f); the Philonic peace is that between heaven and earth.

Peace is again understood with its Jewish significance (see on v. 14) in going beyond the cessation of hostility to the total well-being of those to whom it is offered. It is not merely, 'I am no longer angry with you', but more positively, 'I seek your well-being.' In quoting Isa 57.19 AE follows neither LXX nor MT. (i) He adds ὑμῖν to adapt the text to his needs and thus implies that he is not interested here in the fulfilment of OT promises (cf Lincoln). (ii) He splits the double reference in the OT, 'peace, peace', and applies 'peace' separately to the two categories, 'far off', 'near at hand',[60] so that he sees peace as affecting both groups in the same way. 'You, the far off' are the Gentiles, to whom he is principally writing; interestingly he has not added an 'us' to 'near at hand' and has consequently not associated himself with this group, the Jews. As we saw in v. 13 'far off' and 'near at hand' refer respectively to Gentiles and Jews (AE preserves the Isaianic order and this probably accounts for his placing Gentiles first). In v. 17 AE deals with the

---

[59] Isa 52.7 contains a number of concepts important in early Christian thought, cf Lamadrid, art.cit., 114–16.

[60] The omission of the second reference to peace in Ψ 𝔐 sy^h Mcion^T, Tyc, probably reflects knowledge that the LXX did not have εἰρήνην before ἐγγύς and is not therefore significant.

vertical aspect of the ambiguity running through our passage: the peace that is proclaimed is that between God and Gentile and between God and Jew and not that between Gentile and Jew. There is no distinction in the way God offers peace to Jew and Gentile or in the nature of the peace as it is described in v. 18.

The understanding of ἐλθών, an aorist participle, forms the main problem in v. 17: when did Christ preach peace? The participle could denote an action simultaneous with the main verb or one prior to it; the main verb has been understood in many different ways, resulting in a number of different solutions: (i) A preaching prior to the incarnation; although A. T. Hanson[61] does not list our passage among those where a pre-incarnate activity of Christ might be detected (cf 1 Cor 10.1–11; Heb 3.1–6; Jn 8.56), this is a possibility. However AE nowhere else shows himself aware of such an activity on the part of Christ and, more importantly, it is impossible to find a point in pre-incarnational Israelite history to which our text could refer. (ii) The incarnation itself as a proclamation of peace (Harless, Hofmann); but AE shows little interest in the incarnation; for him the centre of Christ's earthly life is his death. (ii) Christ's earthly life as itself his preaching (Chrysostom; Mussner, *Christus*, 101; Masson; Haupt; Rendtorff; Macpherson); those who adhere to (ii) usually (with Chrysostom) combine this view with it; the Gospels present Jesus as saying of himself that he has 'come' (Mt 5.17; 9.13; 10.34; Lk 19.10; etc.); yet Jesus' activity as reflected in the Gospels appears to have been directed towards Jews alone (Mt 10.5, 23; 15.24), though there were occasions when he dealt with Gentiles (Mk 7.24–30); the sermon in the synagogue at Nazareth (Lk 4.16–30) could also be interpreted as relating to all people (cf also Mt 8.11; Mk 14.9); this however may be to lay too much stress on the way a modern critical historian would read the Gospels. Yet even allowing for that, AE would surely have seen that Christ preached first to Jews, those near at hand, and only secondly to Gentiles, thus reversing the order of 'far off', 'near at hand' in v. 17. Moreover AE, in common with his master, reveals little interest in the earthly activity of Jesus; also the aorist participle should represent an action following on that of vv. 14–16, the cross, or at least one simultaneous with it. This objection could be evaded if v. 17 is regarded as picking up v. 14a with vv. 14b-16 and their references to Christ's death as parenthetical. (iv) The resurrection as Christ's preaching (Ambrosiaster, Aquinas, Bengel, Murray, Van Roon, Caird); the 'coming' is then an event after the death. In 3.5f AE says that a revelation was given to the apostles and prophets about the inclusion of the Gentiles in God's people which is in line with the tradition enshrined in Mt 28.16–20; Lk 24.47–9; Acts 1.8;

---

[61] See his *Jesus Christ in the Old Testament*, London, 1965.

Jn 20.21b[62] and he may have thought of that command as given by Jesus when he came to the disciples in his resurrection. Jn 20.21–3 indeed describes a post-resurrection message relating to peace. However, 'coming' is hardly the word to describe the resurrection, the giving of a command to preach is not itself preaching, and the command was given only to the apostles (and prophets), that is only to a few people, none of whom could be described as 'far off'.[63] (v) A preaching of Christ in the coming of the Spirit; this would post-date his death (Meyer, Westcott, Hodge, Salmond, Alford). While John shows Jesus as speaking regularly of the coming of the Spirit to teach the disciples (Jn 14.25f; 15.26; 16.14f) and while AE believes in the active presence of the Spirit, there is nothing to suggest he thinks of an actual coming in which there is a proclamation of peace to Jews and Gentiles. (vi) Christ preaches in that he instructs and inspires those who then proclaim the Gospel to Jew and Gentile; since he is the content of what they preach he may be regarded as himself the proclaimer (Abbott, Gnilka, Schnackenburg). Such preaching post-dates his death and by AE's time was addressed to Gentiles as well as Jews; moreover a part of the task of missionaries will be the bringing of peace (Mt 10.13) and when missionaries are received it is as if Christ were received (Mt 10.40f; Lk 10.16). This however requires us to read too much into the participle. If AE had intended this meaning he could have said it much more simply: 'sending disciples, he proclaimed ...' Moreover the aorist participle and main verb suggest a completed action but this preaching is one that is still continuing.[64] This solution may lie closest to the political parallel in that the enemy, the Jewish nation, was first conquered and then in the triumph in Rome peace was proclaimed (cf Faust, 403–7). (vii) The ascent of the crucified saviour through the cosmic barrier represents his preaching and revelation (Schlier). If this were so ἀναβάς would have been the proper word, and there would need to have been an earlier reference to a descent. 1 Pet 3.19 is not a parallel for it relates to a preaching to the 'spirits' and not to those near and far. The gnostic and other evidence which Schlier offers in support of his view is also relatively late. His interpretation might possibly have been present in the supposed hymn underlying the passage (see above) with the coming relating to the descent of the saviour through the cosmic

[62] 3.3 represents a different tradition of the origin of the command to take the Gospel to the Gentiles; see Best, 'Revelation'.

[63] Houlden provides a variation of this view by regarding it as referring to a preaching by Christ at his ascension to the heavenly powers (cf 1 Pet 3.19). But the acceptance of the ascending Christ as preaching was not widespread; cf Best, *1 Peter*, 141–6; 155–7.

[64] Bouwman regards ἐλθών as in fact meaningless (cf Lk 15.18; Acts 5.17; 8.27), but while AE is often over-wordy with synonymous nouns he does not appear to be one who uses unnecessary participles.

middle wall. In 2.14–18 however the wall is destroyed in the event of the cross, and not in either a descent or ascent. (viii) The cross itself may be the proclamation (Merklein, *Christus*, 58f). This would accord with the aorist of the main verb but render the participle unnecessary. Alternatively the whole life of Jesus from incarnation to death might be regarded as a unit, which as a unit proclaims peace.

None of these solutions is wholly satisfactory and perhaps Barth, 285, is correct when he says that it is impossible to tie the reference down to any one solution. Attempts to combine more than one (Mussner,[65] Vosté) do not appear to be any more successful; they simply open the door to even more negative arguments. If we have to choose, (iii) and (vi) are probably least objectionable. Whatever the meaning it is the same Gospel which is preached to those near, the Jews, and those afar, the Gentiles. Even if Jews are not within the church, they are not outside the range of the Gospel; in this respect Jews and Gentiles are equal.

18.[66] While ὅτι could be given a causal significance (Ewald, Schnackenburg, Salmond) it is difficult to see v. 18 as providing the reason for something in the preceding verses; rather it summarises and explains what has gone before (Gnilka, Haupt): the Gospel of peace is the joint access of Jew and Gentile (note the first person plural as in v. 14a) to the Father. Such access is only possible once enmity has been removed, both have been made into a new type of being and form one body, and peace exists. We find in Rom 5.1 the same close association of peace with access and there as here a present tense indicates a continuing experience on the part of believers (contrast the perfect tense of Rom 5.2). What continues depends on what once happened in the death of Christ and so δι᾽ αὐτοῦ is placed emphatically at the beginning, for here, as throughout vv. 14–17, Christ is the active agent of redemption.

προσαγωγή can be taken either transitively (= introduction, so Barth) or intransitively (= access, so Gnilka, Schnackenburg, Schlier, Abbott, Robinson). The noun appears three times in the NT, here, 3.12 and Rom 5.2, with the cognate verb at 1 Pet 3.18 where it is transitive; at Rom 5.2 the noun could be either transitive, or intransitive; at Eph 3.12 the latter alone is possible because of the parallel with παρρησία and the qualifying phrase. Either sense is grammatically possible in 2.18. If it is intransitive, then Christ is the one who acts to create access; if transitive, then he (through him) is the one who introduces believers to God. The former is preferable because of the use in 3.12 and because it is more difficult to fit the reference to the Spirit to the meaning 'introduction'. There is

---

[65] In his commentary he changed his position from that in *Christus*.
[66] On this verse see Adai, 161–78; Lemmer, 275–9; Fee, 682–5.

however very little difference in essential meaning: believers come to God only through what Christ has done for them or as he introduces them. The root was used in the contemporary world to describe the approach of people to a ruler (see LSJ) and, more importantly, for the offering of sacrificial gifts (Lev 1.2, 3, 10, etc.). AE has then selected a word common in the cultus rather than drawn one from Rom 5.1f to use for his own purposes (Gnilka); Christ presents believers to his Father. If God is to be encountered the way must be opened, not from our end but from his (cf Pokorný). Despite the cultic background however, Christ is not depicted here as in Hebrews as High Priest, though as in Hebrews (9.12; 10.19–22) access is a consequence of the cross. The religious and philosophical systems of the ancient world offered different and unsatisfactory ways to God. Access is not conceived here individualistically, every man his own priest, but is an access of the whole church comprising both Jews and Gentiles, an access experienced in worship. Through their cultus Jews already had access, though of a limited nature; Gentiles had none; now both have the same free access. We come here to the climax of AE's argument. Though not explicitly mentioned, 2.6 already implied access for believers.

This access is said to be 'in one Spirit'. Is this (a) the divine Spirit (Chrysostom, Gnilka, Schlier, Schnackenburg, Adai, Lemmer), or (b) the human spirit (Jerome, Scott, Haupt), or (c) the human spirit as affected by the divine Spirit? Those who hold to (b) probably mean (c) since the human spirit of believers is always one in which the divine Spirit dwells. If (c) is accepted (cf Phil 1.27) then we deal with the attitude in worship of those who are given access, or with their consciousness of being redeemed, or it is being suggested that Jews and Gentiles are engulfed in the same spirit, a kind of *esprit de corps*. There is a certain parallelism between v. 16 and v. 18 for both speak of a relation to God; in v. 16 it takes place 'in one body', here 'in one Spirit'. Where in 4.4 body and Spirit are again linked it is certainly the divine Spirit which is in mind, and we may therefore assume the same here. If then (a) is intended and a relation exists between the body of Christ and the Spirit it would be too simple to envisage it as similar to that of the human spirit in the human body. The relation of the body (= the church) to Christ is complex, so also is that of the Spirit to him. The introduction of the Spirit at this point is not inappropriate for a writer of the Pauline school since Paul related the Spirit and adoption (Rom 8.14–16; Gal 4.6). Children have access to their fathers. Access to God the Father may be opened through the Christ-event but it is mediated through the Spirit. Believers enjoy the blessings of the Spirit (1.3), are sealed by the Spirit who is the initial instalment of full redemption (1.13f; 4.30), the Spirit works in them (3.16), and they are built into a dwelling-place of God in the Spirit (2.22). ἐνί is important because as Jews and Gentiles receive redemption through the one Lord so they have the same access in the Spirit to the one Father in worship and service. AE does not say that Gentiles have gained an access that earlier belonged to Jews alone, but that both Jews and Gentiles have a new access; there is an unresolved tension then here with v. 12 where AE set out Jewish privileges. The Spirit is a unifying power which gives here an upward movement to God in contrast to the downward of 1.3 (Adai, 174). We note finally that many of the words here like 'access' have spatial connotations. There is also here a triadic reference, Father, Christ, Spirit, which emerges naturally from AE's theology. God is described here as Father which, though Jews applied it to him, has a special ring for Christians because of the prominence given it by Jesus.

We can see then that AE has taken up Paul's use of the concept of reconciliation between God and man, aware of its employment in the Colossian hymn in relation to the reconciliation of the all to God, and seeing the need to explain the relationship of Jews and Gentiles, he has applied it to this and in so doing has created the confusion between the vertical and horizontal ideas of reconciliation. At the same time in taking this step he has realised that these two aspects of reconciliation go together and that each is meaningless without the other. Though AE was not directly considering the general problem of racial or social reconciliation, he shows that its horizontal and vertical aspects cannot be separated. Such a twofold reconciliation moreover is achieved, not through education, social reform, military might, or revolution, but through the death of Christ.

At the beginning of the discussion of v. 14 the question was raised whether AE was faithful to Jesus in saying that Jesus was peace since Jesus had said he had not come to bring peace. The saying of Jesus relates to the calling of disciples; when someone heeds the call of Jesus the probable result will be the breakup of the family to which he or she belongs, so the peace to be expected within families will be destroyed; in that sense Jesus is a disturber of the peace. However, AE is not writing about the call of disciples but about what should happen within an existing Christian community. In saying that Jesus is peace he is not thinking of peace in general, or referring to peace between nations or tribes, between social classes or between races. In our passage as it developed we saw that the result of God's action in Christ was both the reconciliation of humankind to himself and that of Jewish and Gentile Christians to one another. This fits in with the general tenor of his writing. His paraenesis (4.1–6.20) treats the behaviour of believers towards one another, not their behaviour towards the world outside the church (see Essay: Moral Teaching). All that we know of the early church implies that there was no peace between it and the world; persecution, whether official or casual, affected believers. AE does not refer to the relationship of believers with the world outside the church. If peace and reconciliation go together there could not be reconciliation between the church and the world for the world would not permit it. What Jesus had said about himself and peace is not contradicted therefore by what AE writes. When then he says Jesus is peace he means loyalty to Jesus should result in peace within Christian communities. AE is not interested in peace or oneness between the nations; he has no passage equivalent to Col 3.11. The peace he espouses is not established by force of arms nor maintained by careful diplomacy as was the *Pax Romana*; it comes from the weakness of a crucifixion carried out perhaps to maintain the *Pax Romana*.

Before examining vv. 19–22 in detail we must enquire if AE depends here on a section of underlying tradition as W. Nauck suggests.[67] He argues that the verses are based on a baptismal hymn similar in content to the alleged baptismal hymn of 1 Pet 2.4ff; for the existence of the latter he accepts Selwyn's arguments (*1 Peter*, 268–81). He also regards Col 1.(12)13–15, which contains many similar words and concepts to our passage, as based on a baptismal hymn. Selwyn's arguments for 1 Pet 2.4ff as a baptismal hymn have not however been generally accepted.[68] While Col 1.15–20 can be accepted as based on a hymn, there is no certainty that it was a baptismal hymn, and its similarity in words and content to Eph 2.19–22 is slight. When we examine[69] the three strophes into which Nauck divides his hymn the lines are of varying length and the great majority of criteria which normally indicate the presence of a hymn are missing. The separation of πᾶσα οἰκοδομὴ συναρμολογουμένη ... in strophe 2 from αὔξει in strophe 3 destroys the relation of the strophic structure to the thought structure.[70] There is also little in 2.19–22 which relates directly to baptism. The style of the verses is not dissimilar from that of other portions of the letter. It is much more probable that the resemblance of 2.19–22 to 1 Pet 2.4ff arises from the use of images and concepts common to early Christianity and that to Col 1.12–20 from AE's independent use of the hymn used by A/Col. It is also too simple to see vv. 19–22 as a development of Col 1.22b, 23 (so Merklein, *Amt*, 121). The image of the building and its foundation and the description of Christians as ἅγιοι were already part of Christian thought.

19. ἄρα οὖν, a combination frequently used by Paul (Rom 5.18; 7.3, 25; 8.12; 9.16, 18; 14.12, 19; Gal 6.10; 1 Th 5.6; 2 Th 2.15),[71] is an 'emphatically inferential connective' (Thrall, 10f) indicating that a conclusion is now drawn from what preceded. The discussion of the Jewish–Gentile relationship reaches it climax in vv. 19–22

[67] 'Eph. 2.19–22—ein Tauflied?', *EuTh* 13 (1953) 362–71.
[68] Cf L. Goppelt, *Der erste Petrusbrief* (KEK), Göttingen, 1978, 139f.
[69] Cf Bankhead, *Liturgical Formulae*, 107f; Merkel, 3235–7; Merklein, *Amt*, 119f.
[70] The revised structure suggested by G. Klinzing, *Die Umdeutung des Kultus in der Qumrangemeinde und im Neuen Testament*, Göttingen, 1971, 190, n. 61, fails to overcome most of these difficulties.
[71] οὖν is omitted by 𝔓⁴⁶ᵛⁱᵈ F G Ψ 1739 1881 *pc* sy^p but should probably be read in view of the general infrequency of the double particle.

(Penna) and the syllable οἰκ echoes throughout the verses. Jewish Christians and Gentile Christians are equally members of the church and in that light AE expounds a part of his understanding of the church. In doing this he returns to v. 12 for some of its words (πολιτεία, ξένοι) and ideas; they were used there to stress the superiority of the Jews and AE now modifies them for his present purpose. The Gentiles were once ξένοι and πάροικοι.[72] It is difficult to distinguish between and define precisely the meaning of these two words because their significance varied in different communities.[73] By and large they indicated those who living in a community did not possess full citizenship and AE is probably only seeking to say that Gentiles do not belong to a defined community. But to what community? The use of ξένοι might suggest Israel was in mind but the community of which they are now members is the church, so AE is probably thinking of their previous non-membership of that body. But is it the church on earth or that in heaven?

The answer comes in v. 19b. Whereas v. 19a was negative, v. 19b is positive. The Gentiles are citizens together with others (all citizens are full citizens), but with which others?[74] What is the reference of the σύν of συμπολῖται (for the basic word see on v. 12)? Who are οἱ ἅγιοι? A number of suggestions have been made: (i) The Jewish patriarchs and other celebrated Jews (Chrysostom, Theophylact); since this entails a most unusual meaning of the word it may be dismissed. (ii) The Jews (Barth, Bengel, Meuzelaar, 63f); this would imply that Christians are joined to Israel which retains its position as the people of God, a view previously rejected (cf Detached Note: Israel and the Church); ἅγιοι does not normally mean the Jews in the NT. Support might come from 2.12 where Gentiles were not πολῖται of Israel, but AE's use of imagery keeps constantly shifting and this view would have been more easily expressed with πολῖται σύν τοῖς ἁγίοις. (iii) Jewish Christians (Vielhauer, 116; Dibelius; Grosheide; Caird; von Soden; Roels, 150f; Faust, 184–8). While there are occasions when οἱ ἅγιοι may mean Jewish Christians, especially the original Jewish-Christian community (Rom 15.26), the link to v. 12 is not as strong as in (ii) for in v. 12 πολιτεία denoted Israel and not the Jewish-Christian community. Faust argues that the root ἁγι-is used in relation to Jewish synagogues in Asia Minor and supports his argument from

---

[72] On the words see G. Stählin, *TWNT*, V, 1ff; K. L. and M. A. Schmidt, *TWNT*, V, 840ff; Spicq II, 592–6; F. Lyall, 'Roman Law in the Writings of Paul—Aliens and Citizens', *EvQ* 48 (1976) 3–14; J. H. Elliott, *A Home for the Homeless*, London, 1981, 24–37, 185f.

[73] In relation to Asia Minor see M. Rostovtzeff, *The Social and Economic History of the Roman Empire*, Oxford, 1926, 236ff. The second word is found in the NT also at Acts 7.6, 29; 1 Pet 2.11.

[74] 1739 1881 substitute καί for ἐστέ and D¹ Ψ 𝔐; Hier omit the word altogether; there is no reason to reject the text.

3.5 where he takes 'holy apostles and prophets' to mean Jewish apostles and prophets. This is most unlikely, for the use of the root ἁλι- is so widespread that its appearance in synagogues has little significance. Again while it might be argued that the apostles and prophets (v. 20) were the foundation of the original Jerusalem community, it is hardly with them that AE's readers are made fellow citizens. Finally 'saints' normally means Christians (1.1; 4.12; 5.3; 6.18). (iv) Christians (Mussner, *Christus*, 105f; Pfammater, 76f; Haupt; Abbott; Ernst; Masson; Merklein, *Amt* 137f; Gaugler). This is the word's usual meaning in the NT though at 1.18 we saw reason to believe AE was aware of another meaning, that of (v) below. It is difficult to see why AE should have used such a complex expression to say that Gentiles now belong to the church (ἐστὲ ἅγιοι would have sufficed) though it must be allowed that he likes rotund phraseology. There has been no previous stress on the 'saints' as a separate group except where, as in 1.1, the readers are clearly accepted as part of the group. This interpretation does make a proper contrast with v. 12. (v) Angels, heavenly beings (Lindemann, *Aufhebung*, 183 and commentary; Bouwman; Gnilka; Mussner who changed his view in his commentary from that in *Christus*; Schlier; Van Roon, 355; Schnackenburg allows this as a possibility). We have already argued that this is the probable meaning in 1.18. 2.6 supports it in that believers are already raised with Christ and sit with him in the heavenlies. The citizenship of members of the Qumran community was in the heavens with the sons of heaven (1QS 11.7f). In Judaism (*2 Bar* 4.2ff; *Ps Sol* 17.30; Philo *Conf Ling* 78) and early Christianity (Gal 4.26; Phil 3.20; Heb 11.9f; 12.22) the concept of the heavenly city appears regularly. This view is, however, difficult if it is held that συμπολῖται echoes the πολιτεία of v. 12, but such an echo is not necessary. (vi) Glorified believers; Schlier and some others rightly combine this view with the previous since believers raised to heaven cohabit with heavenly beings. This combination of (v) and (vi) seems the most satisfactory.

The image now changes to the warmer metaphor of the readers as members of a household, almost implying kinship: οἰκεῖοι τοῦ θεοῦ. The house and the city were very similar concepts in the ancient world. In Philo οἰκείωσις is used to indicate nearness to God (*Cherub* 18; *Post Cain* 12, 135; cf *Qu Exod* II 29). This phrase then, unlike the first which referred to a relationship among believers, relates believers to God. Christians form a community related to Christ (Mk 3.33–5; 10.29f) or God (Heb 3.1–6; 1 Pet 5.17) behind which lies the concept of Israel as God's house (Exod 16.31; 2 Sam 1.12; Num 12.7; Ps 127; 1QS 8.5; CD 3.19; *1 En* 89.29ff). Believers are children of God (2 Cor 6.18), adopted as such (1.5) and given access to him (2.18), the head of the household. All this implies intimacy. The οἰκεῖοι (for the word see Gal 6.10; 1 Tim 5.8 and

O. Michel, *TWNT*, V, 136f) are members of the house, not necessarily kinsfolk but certainly not slaves; nor are they 'guests— here to-day and away to-morrow' (Eadie)—well treated when present but forgotten when gone. The extended family was an important unit in contemporary society and Cynic-Stoic preaching made use of the image of the family (see Hugedé p. 91, n. 87); AE's Gentile readers would then easily grasp his idea even if they were not aware of its OT background.

But where is God's household and who is in it? Does it consist only of living Christians and confined to this world or does it also exist in the heavenlies and contain angels and dead believers? We have already seen that the latter is the more probable; that it is the correct interpretation is supported here by the absence of a reference to Christ. In the letter elsewhere the relationship of Christians and Christ is stressed (e.g. they are in him, are raised with him, are members of his body), and that relationship to him is linked to his earthly existence, be it only his death and resurrection. The earthly link cannot predominate when we think of a relationship to God; this makes it fitting to take God's household as being in the heavenlies and including heavenly beings. AE has thus passed in this verse beyond the consideration of the place of Gentiles in the church and is working out the place of all, Gentile and Jewish, who form the one church of God. Gentile Christians, once refugees, are now neither homeless nor stateless (cf Stott). Those who were once outsiders are now insiders.

20. The imagery, having changed from membership of a city to that of a household, now changes to the building which contains the household, and those who dwell in the household (v. 19) are pictured as the bricks with which it is built. The use of building imagery was foreshadowed with the architectural term 'middle wall' (v. 14). The building has a foundation, the apostles and prophets, on which believers are built. The aorist participle, ἐποικοδομηθέντες, implies a past act, presumably that of their conversion/baptism, and the passive voice God as the builder (Christ was the subject in vv. 14–18); the participle should also probably be understood causally. The past tense signifies the existence of the building (= the church) prior to the addition to it of the readers, but does not indicate anything about when the church first came into being.

The imagery of building in relation to communities is widespread: cf J. Bover, ' "In aedificationem corporis Christi". Eph. 4,12', *EstBib* 3 (1944) 313–42; Vielhauer; Pfammater, *Bau*; Roberts, *Opbou*; O. Michel, *TWNT*, V, 122–61; T. Schneider, *RAC* I, 1265–78; F. Schnider and W. Stenger, 'The Church as a Building and the Building up of the Church', *Conc* 10 (1972) 21–34; J. Renard, 'Temple and Building in Pauline Images of Church and Community', *Review of Religions* 41 (1982) 419–31; I. Kitzberger, *Bau der Gemeinde*, Würzburg, 1986; M. Barker, *The Gate of Heaven*, London, 1991.

It is found in the OT with the house indicating a group of people (Gen 7.1; 1 Sam 20.16; Ruth 4.11; Num 12.7; Jer 31.4), in Qumran with the city indicating a group (1QH 6.25–7; 7.8f; see O. Betz, 'Felsenmann und Felsengemeinde' *ZNW* 48 (1957) 49–77 at 50–4, 59–61), and in Hellenistic Judaism (Philo, *Sobr* 66; *Abr* 56). In secular Greek the city rather than the house is used metaphorically of the community (see LSJ). The image of building is also used extensively of the building up or edifying of believers (Rom 15.2, 20; 2 Cor 10.8; 12.19; 13.10; Gal 2.18; Col 3.16; 1 Th 5.11) and this aspect appears in 4.12, 16. Gnostic influence is held to govern AE's use of the metaphor (Dibelius, Schlier), but there is no certainty that the evidence is pre-Christian. It is probably a 'natural' metaphor appearing independently in a number of areas. In any case it had already been adopted into Christian thought prior to the writing of Ephesians, being derived probably from the OT and Judaism.

The metaphor of building is used in two distinct ways, statically, in depicting a group of people as an edifice, and dynamically, of the maturing of people in their faith. In the first case the implied subject of the erection of the edifice is God or Christ; in the second it may be either God or Christ, but is more usually believers who build up themselves or one another in conduct and faith. The image is used in 2.20–2 in the first way (cf 1 Cor 3.9, 16) and in the second in 4.12, 16, 29 (cf 1 Cor 10.23; 14.4–20; 2 Cor 10.8; 12.19; 13.10; 1 Th 5.11). In the second also there is normally no reference to the type of edifice which is being erected; it is either the church viewed as a community of believers (not a structure of wood and stone) or individual believers. This second dynamic usage is by far the more frequent in the Pauline corpus and probably derives directly from the OT and not from the static.

There is no reason to see AE's use of ἐποιχοδομέω as dependent on Col 2.7. The verb could equally be derived from 1 Cor 3.10ff. A/Col combines it with ῥιζοομαι and if AE was using Col 2.7 it would have been natural for him to take over this verb as well; he has no objection to it since he uses it at 3.17. The way the verb is used in the two letters also differs; AE's use here is the 'static'; A/Col's in 2.7 the 'dynamic'. In Eph 2.20 believers are built on the foundation of apostles and prophets but in Col 2.7 on Christ.

Like all buildings the edifice of v. 20 has a foundation. In 1 Cor 3.10 it is Jesus Christ and it is laid by Paul, not God. It is possible to take a similar meaning here and see the apostles and prophets as those who lay the foundation, so NEB 'built upon the foundation laid by the apostles and prophets'; this is changed in REB to the more correct 'the foundation of the apostles and prophets'. In v. 20 Christ, a person, is one stone in the building and it is difficult to see the apostles and prophets as those who built him in; only the desire to harmonise v. 20 with 1 Cor 3.10 could have led to the NEB translation. The genitive is one of apposition (cf Robertson, 498; Pfammater, *Bau*, 80–4; there are few grounds for taking with Alford the genitive as possessive). Even if Paul is the author of Ephesians there is no reason why he should not have modified his use of the building metaphor from 1 Cor 3.10; authors regularly vary their use of metaphors.[75] The foundation is not of course the rock or ground on which the lowest stones or bricks are laid but the lowest level of the building on which the remainder rests. We might have expected AE to say that the foundation of the church was Israel rather than the apostles and prophets; in not doing so he indicates that the church is not just a simple continuation of Israel.

But who are the apostles and prophets and why are they introduced? They are certainly not introduced as great figures of the past who might act as role models for conscientious Christians (cf Ign *Eph* 11.2; 12.2; Polyc *Phil* 3.2; 11.3). Apostles and prophets are different groups and not, as the non-repetition of the article might suggest, the same group, defined by two different titles, apostles who are also prophets[76] (in Rev 21.14 the apostles alone are the foundation). A single article may govern two distinct groups (cf Mt 3.7; Lk 22.4; Acts 15.2) and here its use may suggest a formulaic expression, an explanation reinforced by the coupling together of the two groups again at 3.5 (see notes there). There is no apparent reason why apostles should be termed prophets at 2.20; they are clearly not so in the list of 4.11. On the other hand there is no reason to see in v. 20 an abbreviation of the list of 4.11, as if the foundation included others than these two groups.[77] The two groups however are so tied together by the one article that those who wish to deduce from the reference to the apostles as foundation that the church is apostolic must equally be ready to accept that the church is prophetic.

Neither apostles nor prophets are precisely identified by their titles for both terms are used loosely. Apostle (see on 1.1) can have a wide sense with undefined edges and be somewhat equivalent to 'missionary' (Rom 16.7; 1 Th 2.6) and a restricted sense as indicating the Twelve or the Twelve plus Paul; it can denote missionary figures of the first generation and include Paul and Barnabas (cf Acts 14.4, 14). There is little in our context to indicate which sense is intended, but in 3.5 where there is a parallel usage it probably means the Twelve without Paul since he appears separately at 3.3. This sense would be supported if our understanding of prophets is correct (see below). It is sometimes argued that Paul

[75] Cf P. L. Hammer, 'Canon and Theological Variety: A Study in the Pauline Tradition', *ZNW* 67 (1976) 83–9.

[76] So Harless, Pfammater, 93–7, L. Cerfaux, 'Pour l'histoire du titre *Apostolos* dans le Nouveau Testament', *RSR* 48 (1960) 73–92.

[77] For an exhaustive examination and refutation of the view that apostles and prophets are the same people see R. F. White, 'Gaffin and Grudem on Eph 2:20: In defense of Gaffin's Cessationist Exegesis', *WTJ* 54 (1992) 303–20.

could never have spoken of himself as a foundation and that therefore we can deduce non-Pauline authorship, yet in the light of the unique position he sometimes gives to himself (see Best, *Converts, passim*) it is not impossible that he should have described himself as part of the foundation. Moreover to speak of people as foundation does not imply that they are a past group and dead; 'he founded our society' may be said of someone who is still alive. 'A modern missionary might speak of himself and his colleagues as the pioneering workers, and no one would accuse him of self-exaltation' (Scott, 178). It is relatively easy to see how the Twelve (= the apostles) could have been regarded as the foundation of the church; they are figures of the past;[78] it was not simply that they were the first members of the church but it was from their preaching after the resurrection that the church grew; their preaching may also be said to have given the church its shape, though Paul and Barnabas did the same in accepting Gentiles as full members. Their (the Twelve, or the Twelve plus Paul and Barnabas) position would thus be analogous to some interpretations of Peter as the rock on which the church is built (Mt 16.18).[79]

The prophets were taken to be those of the OT by Origen, *Cant* II 1, 11, GCS 8, 157, Chrysostom, Theodoret, Ambrosiaster, Calvin, Beza, Roberts, *Opbou*, 122–9; Marcion presumably understood them in this way for Tertullian, *adv Marc* V, 17, 6, says he omitted the reference to them. More generally, from Pelagius onwards, they have been assumed to be those of the early church who either foresaw the future (Acts 11.28; 21.10f) and/or proclaimed the truth of God in particular situations.[80] Had the OT prophets been intended the order would have been 'the prophets and the apostles' (neither Polyc *Phil* 6.3 nor Ign *Philad* 5.1f are true exceptions to this since in both cases it is clear from the context that OT prophets are in mind). If AE had been wishing to refer to the OT since the foundation of

---

[78] G. Klein, *Die Zwölf Apostel* (FRLANT 77), Göttingen, 1961, 66–75, argues that the apostles and prophets are not a group of the past here or in 3.5 or 4.11 but a continuing group (cf. Fischer, 33–9). Since Christ as the angle-stone continues to have a relation to the church, so also should the apostles and prophets. There are however important distinctions. The apostles and prophets are no longer alive and so their relation to the church belongs to the past; Christ is alive. If they are a continuing group they have successors; Church has no successor.

[79] This represents an important modification of my position in *One Body*, 162.

[80] On prophets see e.g. E. Fascher, ΠΡΟΦΗΤΗΣ. *Eine sprach- und religionsgeschichtliche Untersuchung*, Giessen, 1927; Best, 'Prophets and Preachers', *SJT* 12 (1959) 129–50; G. Dautzenberg, *Urchristliche Prophetie. Ihre Erforschung, ihre Voraussetzungen im Judentum und ihre Struktur im ersten Korintherbrief*, Stuttgart, 1975; D. Hill, *New Testament Prophecy*, London, 1979; D. E. Aune, *Prophecy in Early Christianity and the Ancient Mediterranean World*, Grand Rapids, 1983; U. B. Müller, *Prophetie und Predigt im Neuen Testament, Formgeschichtliche Untersuchungen zur urchristlichen Prophetie*, Gütersloh, 1975; Merklein, *Amt*, 306ff.

the church is being considered, a better phrase would have been 'the law, the prophets and the apostles'. In 3.5 where we again have the double phrase it is early church prophets who are intended (see notes on 3.5) for OT prophets are hardly responsible for the command to evangelise the Gentiles. In 4.11 the prophets are charismatic figures who are listed among the ministers of the church and therefore must be NT prophets.[81]

How however could NT prophets, who were certainly honoured in the early church (1 Cor 12.28; Rev 18.20) and were probably still a living force at the time of Ephesians (*Did* 10.7; 11.7ff), be regarded as the foundation of the church or as bearers of revelation? 3.5 provides a clue for it associates prophets with apostles in the transmission of the divine command to evangelise the Gentiles. This command is given in variant forms and to groups whose membership is defined in different ways in Mt 28.16–20; Lk 24.47–9; Acts 1.8; Jn 20.21b (cf Best, 'Revelation'). Since contemporary prophets gave directions about the future activity of the church it is not difficult to see how some might have thought of them as involved in the original command to evangelise, and if they were, they were involved in the admission of the Gentiles and thus in a decision about the shape of the church; they could then be considered alongside the apostles as its foundation. In Acts 13.1–3 prophets were involved in moving the church into a new venture; in doing so they were shaping its nature; this was necessarily something belonging to the past of AE.[82] It is also always difficult to dissociate activity from the people exercising it and so, though strictly it is the revelation which permits the admission of Gentiles, those who mediated the revelation could be taken to be its foundation. Another approach reinforcing this conclusion is possible (see Best, 'Ministry'). The book of Revelation describes itself as a prophecy (1.3; 22.7, 10, 18, 19); prophets predict the End in Mk 13.22; if 1 Th 4.15f, or some part of it, was a revelation to the church through a prophet, prophets again have an eschatological connection. May it not be that a part of the foundation of the church is the security of its end in God? If so, prophets have a role in its foundation.

Apostles and prophets are seen here, because of the single article, as one group, containing both apostles and prophets; whether AE has created this group for his own purposes or taken it from the tradition (Merklein, *Amt*, 141f) is difficult to say. Here and in 3.5 the group's function belongs to the past, not simply as first believers, which might be the case if apostles alone were mentioned, but as the basis for what follows in that its members were the channels of

---

[81] There is no reason to accept the view of F. C. Baur, *Paul: His Life and Works*, Vol. II, London, 1875, 24ff, that they are referred to because of Montanism.
[82] Cf Best, 'Acts xiii.1–3', *JTS* 11 (1960) 344–8.

revelation. They are temporally prior to others and prior also in the reception of revelation (3.5) and therefore capable of sustaining the building, but not by themselves, as the final clause shows.

Verse 20b, while certainly implying that Christ has a special position within the building, does not, in terms of our present knowledge, make clear what that position is, for it is impossible to determine with any certainty the precise meaning of ἀκρογωνιαῖος;[83] because of this we use the neutral translation 'angle-stone'.[84] Before examining the word we note that grammatically αὐτοῦ can refer either to θεμελίῳ (Christ being the angle-stone of the foundation) or Χριστοῦ (the angle-stone being Christ himself); the first requires understanding the angle-stone as a part of the foundation and lessens the distinction between Christ and the group of apostles and prophets; the second imposes no restriction on the placement, or meaning, of the angle-stone, stresses the significance of Christ in himself and creates a degree of distinction between him and the apostles and prophets; it is therefore preferable.

Two main interpretations have been offered of ἀκρογωνιαῖος: cornerstone,[85] capstone.[86] Luke may have been aware of the word's ambiguity for in 20.18 people can both fall over the stone and it fall on them! It is generally assumed that the word is used under the influence of Isa 28.16 where it relates to, or is a part of, the foundation; this is the meaning in 1 Pet 2.6–8 where Ψ 117.22 explains it as κεφαλὴ γωνίας and it is a stone at ground level over which people can trip. This has led some to regard it as a stone at a corner which is used in squaring off the building. This would imply a unique position for Christ. But it cannot be proved that such stones existed for none has ever been discovered in ancient buildings of the Greco-Roman world. All that has been found are long stones which run along the foundation, one end of which may be at a corner, but these do not jut out for people to stumble over and in any building

---

[83] D* F G 629 latt; Or^pt add λίθου; it serves to clarify, what is not really in doubt, that the building metaphor is in mind.

[84] The translation 'keystone' which I adopted in *One Body*, 165f, goes too far in implying a stone in a particular position other than in the foundation; at best the evidence only suggests a stone in the upper part of a building, not a locking stone; arches with keystones existed in this period but domes did not.

[85] Schnackenburg; Pfammater; R. J. McKelvey, 'Christ the Cornerstone', *NTS* 8 (1961/2) 352–9; id. *The New Temple*, Oxford, 1969, 195–204; Lindemann; Percy, 330–2, 485–8; Bouwman; Roberts, *Opbou* 60–6; Masson; Hugedé; Merklein, *Amt*, 144–52; K. T. Schäfer, 'Zur Deutung von ἀκρογωνιαῖος Eph 2,20', *Neutestamentliche Aufsätze* (FS J. Schmid; ed. J. Blinzler, O. Kuss, F. Mussner), Regensburg, 1963, 218–24; S. Lyonnet, 'De Christo summo angulari lapide secundum Eph 2,20', *VD* 27 (1949) 74–83.

[86] J. Jeremias, 'Der Eckstein', *Ang*, 1 (1925) 65–70; id. 'Κεφαλὴ γωνίας— Ἀκρογωνιαῖος', *ZNW* 29 (1930) 264–80; id. 'Eckstein—Schlusstein', *ZNW* 36

there are a number of them so that no one can be regarded as unique. The further suggestion that Christ as the cornerstone unites the two walls of Jewish and Gentile Christians (Theod Mops, Chrysostom, Jerome, Thomas Aquinas, Calvin) is fanciful. If Christ is a stone in the foundation, even at the corner, does that distinguish him sufficiently from the apostles and prophets who also belong to the foundation? 1 Cor 3.10 makes clear Christ's unique position for he alone is the foundation. If the apostles and prophets are regarded as laying the foundation some of the difficulties are avoided but we have seen that this is not what is meant. In Mk 12.10f; 1 Pet 2.6–8 it is easy to take Christ as cornerstone because neither passage refers to the foundation.

It is these difficulties that have led to the acceptance of the alternative view of Christ as the capstone, the stone which locks an arch, not a dome, together. There are a number of instances of the use of the word where it implies a stone which is high above the ground: Isa 28.16 (Peshitta); 4 Kgdms 25.17 (Symmachus); *Test Sol* 22.7–23.3; the background to these references is the Jerusalem temple. If the readers would not have known enough about the temple in Jerusalem to pick up a reference to the 'middle wall' as the balustrade, would they have picked up this as a 'high' stone in it? Tertullian, *adv Marc* 3.7, appears to think of a stone high in the building. Richardson[87] suggests two possibilities from the temple at Didyma, and we can assume that if the readers did not know much about the architecture of the Jerusalem temple they would know something about that at Didyma which was renowned in contemporary Asia Minor: (i) the massive lintel over the great doorway between the πρόναος and the room with the two columns; since a reference to 'access' has just been made in v. 18 this would be an appropriate meaning; the word is also used of a stone above the doorway of the Jerusalem temple in *Test Sol* 22.7–23.3. (ii) A cornerstone above the level of the pilasters which surround the inner courtyard. It must be said that Richardson does not suggest that these stones actually bore the name 'cornerstone'. A stone high in a building also accords with the idea of Christ as the head of his body, the church. However, this solution to the meaning of the angle-stone is difficult in that it implies that the building is well on to completion for in the next verse the growth of the church is stressed; buildings do not grow up to stones above them. Has Christ moreover no place in the church until it is partly complete? Yet there must be

(1937) 154–7; id. *TWNT*, I, 792–3; IV, 277–83; L. Gaston, *No Stone on Another* (SupNT 23), Leiden, 1970, 190–4; Gnilka; Barth; Vielhauer; Hanson, 131; Dibelius; Conzelmann; Bruce; Beare; K. H. Schelkle, *RAC* I, 233f; Lampe, *Lexicon, s.v.*; Cerfaux, *L'église*, 260.
    [87] In a paper read at a seminar of SNTS in Dublin, 1989; see on 2.14.

a sense in which the church is already complete, for v. 22 says it is God's dwelling-place; can he be envisaged as dwelling in an incomplete building? There is a high degree of eschatological realisation in the letter (cf Introduction §6.4) and this may be yet another instance.

Both understandings of angle-stone can then be sustained with contemporary, but slender, evidence and both run into theological difficulties. Perhaps in the present state of our knowledge the problem is insoluble. However, the context shows clearly that AE wishes to allot to Christ a place in the building different from that of the apostles and prophets and more important than that of either of them.

21. The imagery again changes; the building is said to grow and is identified as a temple. Both this verse and v. 22 are introduced by ἐν ᾧ and are parallel; for this reason the relative in both cases probably refers to Christ rather than to the foundation or the angle-stone, though of course the latter is Christ. Moreover AE likes the phrase 'in Christ' or one of its parallels.

But what is it that grows 'in Christ'? οἰκοδομή can be used of either an actual structure or the process of building. At first sight the qualifying πᾶσα seems to imply the former with the meaning 'each building, every building'. Haupt, Mitton, Percy, 463, give it this sense. ℵ[1] A C P 6 81 326 1739[c] 1881 pc; Or[com 1739mg] insert ἡ, giving the meaning 'all building, all that is being built'. This renders the best sense but support is not strong and it is difficult to see how the other arose if it was original. Good Greek would require for this meaning the insertion of the article but Koine Greek does not always follow the classical rule (cf BDR §275.2, n. 4; Zerwick, §190; Moule, 94f; MHT, 199f; Robertson, 772); there are other instances in the NT of the absence of the article: Mt 28.18; Acts 1.21; 2.36; 7.22; 23.1; Col 1.15, 23; 4.12; 1 Pet 1.15 (Eadie lists examples from Classical Greek). Nowhere else does AE, unlike Paul, have individual communities (every building) in mind, least of all individual believers, but always the whole church. It is not possible to get round this by suggesting that he is thinking of a temple complex in which there would be several structures for he goes on to define the structure as the ναός, or sanctuary, which would be a single building. AE is not then thinking here of the growth of each separate congregation which receives his letter, still less of Jews and Gentiles being built together (Jerome, Aquinas), but of the one church of God. It would in any case be a little absurd to think of apostles and prophets as foundations of individual communities (Gaugler).

In important ancient buildings the stones were carefully fitted together, συναρμολογουμένη[88] (only elsewhere at 4.16), being

---

[88] Cf G. H. Whitaker, 'Studies in Texts', *Theology* 13 (1926) 335f.

smoothed where their surfaces met, dowel holes drilled and dowels inserted. The stones which are here being fitted together (present tense) are not the two groups, Jewish and Gentile Christians, but individual believers. Thus the argument which moved in v. 20 from believers as members of a household into the material with which the house was built and indicated the positions of apostles, prophets and Christ now depicts believers as harmoniously related to the believers beside, above and below them. No stone should be out of place (Origen, *Cor Cat, JTS* 9 (1907–8) 246). Since in fact believers do not always fit harmoniously together, as 4.25ff shows, the church is pictured as it ought to be rather than as it is.

The building is said to grow, αὔξει (for the form see BDR §101 n. 11). While growth is something more normally associated with organic life it is not difficult to see it being transferred metaphorically to buildings in the course of erection and 1 Cor 3.6–17 (cf Jer 31.28) shows how easy it is to move from the organic to the building metaphor.[89] 1 Pet 2.5 refers to 'living stones'. Growth (note the present tense of verb and participle) suggests that not all the stones have yet been built in; believers are added daily to the church and the growth is extensive in numbers rather than intensive in love as at 4.16. Growth implies incompleteness which conflicts with any idea of Christ as the final stone and with an over-realised eschatology. The builder is not identified; in 1 Cor 3.10 Paul as builder lays the foundation on which others build, though immediately prior to this God is described as the source of growth (1 Cor 3.6). We may assume then that in v. 21 God is the ultimate builder. However, both the fitting together and growth are 'in Christ', the angle-stone. The ἐν of ἐν ᾧ might be taken instrumentally but in view of the corporate nature of the whole image it is better given a corporate or local sense. It is difficult to see how stones are smoothly joined together by their relation to the angle-stone and we must assume a mingling of metaphors. Perhaps it is that believers are shaped, smoothed and joined together by their relation to Christ whom they are to resemble (2 Cor 3.18; Phil 3.21).

The imagery changes again and the building is viewed as a temple or sanctuary (there is no idea of a slow change into a temple); ναός is the actual sanctuary where the god may be supposed to dwell as distinct from the whole temple complex, τὸ ἱερόν (cf 1 Cor 3.16). The movement in metaphor from house to temple is made easier since the Jerusalem temple was sometimes termed the house of God

[89] For the mingling of building and body metaphors see Philo, *Leg Alleg* 2.6; *Acts Thomas* 6f (Lipsius Bonnet, 109f); Hermas, *Vis* 9; 1QS 8.5; 11.8; *Odes Sol* 38.17. See also D. C. Smith, 'Cultic Language in Ephesians 2:19–22. A Test Case', *RestQ* 31 (1989) 201–17. Schlier, 143–5, sees gnosticism as a factor in AE's mingling of the metaphors but it is not certain that the gnostic evidence can be dated prior to Ephesians.

and the idea of the temple had already been spiritualised in both Greco-Roman and Jewish thought,[90] so that the world or man or a part of man (his mind or heart) could be termed 'temple'. Paul had already applied the image of the temple to the community (1 Cor 3.16f; 2 Cor 6.16; cf 1 Pet 2.4f); he had taught this during his first stay in Corinth (note the 'do you not know' of 1 Cor 3.16), and his disciples would know it; the idea probably also underlies Jn 2.13–22 and the Markan use of the logion of 14.58; 15.29. It can be traced to the Qumran Community (1QS 5.5f; 8.4–10; 11.8).[91] Believers appear here as the material out of which the community is built. Gentiles who were once not allowed to enter the Jerusalem temple have become a part of this temple. As the material of the temple the position of believers contrasts here with 1 Per 2.4f where they serve within the temple as a spiritual priesthood (e.g. Rom 12.1f; 1 Pet 2.5; Heb 13.15f). If Christians are already regarded by AE as inhabitants of heaven (see on v. 19) then he may also have the heavenly temple[92] in mind. The Christians, Jews and Gentiles, as temple replace every earthly temple as the dwelling-place for God and at the same time are the realisation of the expected heavenly temple.

Finally the holy temple is said to be ἐν κυρίῳ; here as elsewhere in Ephesians the Lord is Christ and not God (as Mussner, *Christus*, 110, and Ewald). The existence of the church is centred on Christ. Since ἐν ᾧ goes with the verb and/or participle it is easier to take ἐν κυρίῳ with 'holy sanctuary'. It can relate either to the sanctuary (Christ determines its existence and nature, Gnilka) or, more probably, to ἅγιον (the sanctuary is holy because of its connection with Christ).

22. This verse is in part parallel to the preceding (ἐν ᾧ refers back to Christ and not to ναός, and as in v. 21 is to be given a corporate sense; note also the two compounds with σύν) and in part develops it so that the temple is expressly identified as the place of God's dwelling. The verse with its sudden renewed direct address to the readers forms a suitable climax to the whole section, 2.11–22. What was theory in vv. 20f is now made relevant to the readers; they have not been left out, but have been built together with those

---

[90] Cf H. Wenschkewitz, 'Die Spiritualisierung der Kultusbegriffe Tempel, Priester und Opfer im Neuen Testament', *Ang* 4 (1932) 77–230; J. C. Coppens, 'The Spiritual Temple in the Pauline Letters and its Background', *SE* VI (= TU 112), 53–66; McKelvey, op.cit., 42ff; Klinzling, op.cit., 50ff; D. C. Smith, art.cit.; E. Schüssler Fiorenza, 'Cultic Language in Qumran and in the New Testament', *CBQ* 38 (1976) 159–77.

[91] Cf McKelvey, 46–53; Best, *Following*, 213–25; B. Gärtner, *The Temple and the Community in Qumran and the New Testament* (SNTSMS 1), Cambridge, 1965, 47ff; Gaston, op.cit., 163ff; I. H. Marshall, 'Church and Temple in the New Testament', *TynB* 40 (1989) 203–22.

[92] Cf McKelvey, op.cit., 25ff.

already in the church on a foundation of the apostles and prophets and with Christ as the angle-stone.

The temple already exists and the readers are built (the verb is a *hapax legomenon* in the NT, in LXX only at 1 Esdr 5.65 where it has an active sense) into it, presumably by God. But if they are built into something already in existence, what is that something (the σύν relates to this)? (a) The Jewish people. We have already dismissed the idea that Gentile believers are added to the Jewish people to create the church (see Detached Note: Israel and the Church); nothing here suggests a change in this view. (b) The first Jewish Christians (Gnilka). In vv. 14–18 stress lay on the making one of the two groups of Jewish and Gentile Christians and so it might not be inappropriate here to regard Gentile Christians as built into the new Jewish-Christian people of God and this may be the significance of the σύν in 3.6. Against the acceptance of this view is the present tense of the verb; when vv. 14–17 discussed the unity of Jewish and Gentile Christians aorist tenses were used with the unification envisaged as accomplished in the cross; the present tense here implies that Gentiles are built into a church already containing some Gentiles. (c) Apostles, prophets and Christ. It is improbable that AE thinks of his readers being added only to the foundation and angle-stone. (d) The existing church which consists already of Jewish and Gentile believers (cf Schnackenburg); the present tense of the verb suggests a process, believers are being built together with those who are already parts of the building, the existing Jewish and Christian believers; the σύν of this verb then corresponds to the σύν of συναρμολογουμένη. If the church is regarded as containing both heavenly and earthly members (see on v. 19) this interpretation is not affected. It is the most probable. (e) It is however just possible that the reference of the σύν may be to Christ alone as in 2.5f.

The temple is now identified as the place of God's dwelling.[93] Believers are built together for the purpose of (εἰς) being a place where God would dwell. That the gods inhabit earthly buildings is an idea found widely in the contemporary religions and is also present in the OT (Exod 15.17; 3 Kgdms 8.13; in both of these κατοικητήριον is used; see also Mal 3.1)[94] and elsewhere in the NT (1 Cor 3.16). The OT also has passages where God is said to be in his people (Exod 25.8; 29.45; Lev 26.11; Ezek 37.27). Once people and temple are identified the objection that God cannot dwell in a physical building is removed. If unbelievers point to their temples as the places where their gods live and ask Christians where theirs are to be found they can respond by saying that God dwells in their

[93] B reads χριστοῦ which would make the temple Christ's dwelling, theologically possible but unlikely in the present context.
[94] On the place and the manner of God's presence in Israel see R. E. Clements, *God and Temple*, Oxford, 1965.

community. It is true he may also dwell in individuals and local house churches but the emphasis here is on his dwelling in the community as a whole. But can God live in what is incomplete? Presumably if the angle-stone, as a high-up stone, is in position there is a sense in which the building is complete.

God's dwelling is ἐν πνεύματι (for the word see Adai, 178–93; Lemmer 150–4, 254–65). The parallelism of our verse with v. 21 together with this being its final phrase will imply that it is the Holy Spirit which is referred to here (cf Ps 18.6; 27.4f; 46.5, 7; 68.36). It does not suggest that the dwelling is simply metaphorical or non-material; such an understanding of πνεῦμα would add nothing to an already metaphorical context. It is in any case clear that the temple of v. 21, unlike those of the OT and of the cities where AE's readers live, is non-material. πνεῦμα does not indicate the builder but denotes the mode of God's activity or the way in which his dwelling is made possible. The Spirit is the Spirit of power and this lends a dynamic aspect to God's presence in the temple.[95]

---

[95] For a *Wirkungsgeschichte* in respect of the church as building see Schnackenburg, 325–8.

VI

PAUL AND THE GENTILES
(3.1–13)

K. Sullivan, 'The Mystery Revealed to Paul—Eph.3:1–13', *Bible Today* 1 (1963), 246–54; Merklein, *Amt*, 159–231; Caragounis, 96–112; Lona, 277–308; Reynier, *passim*.

1 Because of this I, Paul, Christ's prisoner
    on behalf of you Gentiles—
2 Surely you have heard of God's plan
    in respect of the grace given me for you,
3   namely that by revelation God made known
      the mystery to me,
        just as I wrote in brief above,
4   which when you read
      you are able to understand
    my insight into the mystery of Christ,
5   (a mystery) not made known
      in other periods to humanity
    as it has been revealed
      now to his holy apostles and prophets
      through the Spirit,
6   that the Gentiles are heirs together,
          members of the same body,
          sharers in the promise,
          through the gospel
7   of which I became a minister
      in accordance with the gift of the grace of God
      given me,
        in appropriate proportion
        by the working of his power.
8 To me this grace was given,
    me, lower than the least of all the saints,
  to proclaim to the Gentiles
    the unimaginable riches of Christ,
9   and to enlighten all
      as to the plan of the mystery,
      hidden throughout the ages
      in God who made everything,

10   so that the much variegated wisdom of God
        might be made known now through the church
        to the rulers and authorities in the heavenlies,
11   according to his intention from before the ages,
        which he resolved in the Messiah Jesus our Lord,
12   in whom we have boldness and access in confidence
        through his faithfulness.
13 Therefore I beg you not to lose heart
     at my tribulations on your behalf
     seeing that they are for your glory.

With his theological argument concerning the basis for the redemption of Gentile alongside Jewish Christians complete, AE moves on to intercede for the former (vv. 1, 14ff); prayer follows naturally after the reference to the temple (2.22). In approaching the prayer AE introduces the name of Paul. This leads him to break off the movement towards intercession in order to discuss how Paul had himself been instrumental in making known God's plan for the Gentiles. If Paul is himself the author then his emphasis on himself, 'I, Paul', reminds readers of his part in evangelising the Gentiles. 2.11–22 may have laid the theological basis for this, but there is also need to explain the historical process and so he (AE or Paul) breaks off to do this and inserts vv. 2–13, returning to the intercession at v. 14. Vv. 2–13 are thus a lengthy parenthesis; the style and language are sufficiently similar to that in the remainder of the letter to raise no suspicion that they are a later gloss. That vv. 2–13 are parenthetical does not mean they are unimportant. They give, in fact, the grounds for Paul's right to address the readers.

Paul was an apostle and his personal position has already been referred to: he was part of the foundation (2.20). This however only made him one among a number of apostles and prophets. Yet he was not just one among a number but had a unique position in relation to the Gentiles: he is *the* apostle to the Gentiles. What are the grounds for describing him in this way? It was neither insight into the OT nor a brainwave on his part which led him to see that the Gospel must include Gentiles. God had given him a revelation to that effect. The inclusion of the Gentiles had been part of God's plan from the beginning, but had previously been kept secret; it has now been made known to Paul (v. 3) and others (v. 5). Paul also had been empowered to be the primary instrument for its accomplishment (vv. 7–8). Vv. 7, 8 hold together, though v. 7 is the conclusion of the first main sentence (vv. 2–7) and v. 8 the beginning of the second (vv. 8–12). They form the transition from the statement of Paul's place in God's plan to the outline of his fulfilment of his role. A revelation has been made whose content was the acceptance of the Gentiles into God's people (v. 6). God's plan has however an even wider cosmic ambit (v. 10), and this was his intention from the beginning through Christ (vv. 11–12). That Paul suffered was therefore of little importance and should not discourage the readers; in fact it was for their good (v. 13). The 'once–now' schema appears here again, though not now relating to a personal change in believers as in 2.1ff, but to God's action in withholding knowledge and then disclosing it.

This is the most personal section of Ephesians; if written by Paul it allows us to view Ephesians as a letter and not a homily or theological tractate. If it is post-Pauline, then the section must be seen as part of the theological argument in indicating how God chose one particular human being to work out his purpose. Whether Pauline or not, it contains some extreme statements in respect of Paul which accord him a very high, if not unique, place; these statements are matched only by his claim to have been the last person to see Christ (1 Cor. 15.8) and the possible claim in Col 1.24 that his sufferings are in some way related to those of Christ in benefiting the church. AE may have had in his mind a thought similar to Col 1.24 as he composed our section. Both AE and A/Col hold Paul in equal veneration and their school will have mulled over his significance. Merklein, *Amt*, 161, regards 3.1–7 as an interpretation of Col 1.24–8 while Bouwman argues that 2.11–22 takes up Col 1.21–3 and 3.2–13 plays on the idea of Paul as 'minister' and on the concept of mystery derived from Colossians. However, the idea that Paul's trials would benefit his converts is found more widely in his letters (1 Cor 1.3–7; 2 Cor 4.12) and so would have influenced his followers. The presence of the Gentiles in the church is indissolubly linked to Paul's position in God's economy.

It is not easy to tie down the genre of the passage (cf Reynier, 15–28). Though v. 1 heads what looks like being a liturgical section that section does not in fact commence until v. 14. Our paragraph is narrative, in so far as any part of Ephesians can be so described, for it recounts an action of the past, a revelation, and a continuing activity, a making known of the revelation. As narrative it is in part autobiographical (note the extensive use of the first person singular), though if Paul is not the author it might be better to describe it as pseudo-autobiographical. It is not, however, a 'testament' for there is no sign that Paul's death is near and no play on the idea that this might be his final writing to the readers. One of the main themes is 'revelation' but the revelation has already been disclosed and action in relation to it has already taken place. The genre is not then purely apocalyptic. It is perhaps a mixture of apocalyptic and pseudo-autobiography; genres do not need to be 'pure'. Although it may be correct to describe vv. 2–12(13) as a digression, it is not a carefully planned digression and cannot therefore be a *digressio* in the sense of ancient rhetorical criticism. As a digression in the ordinary sense of the word it fills an essential gap in the argument and it would be wrong therefore to look on it as a gloss (cf Kirby, 129–32). That AE breaks into his argument here suggests that he had not cleverly planned what he was going to write.

Attempts have been made to discover a structure within the passage. Lona, 277ff, sees a chiasmus in vv. 2–7 and another in vv. 8–10, but the sections which are supposed to balance one another are so different in length as to render this highly unlikely. Reynier, 43ff, attempts to correct Lona's deficiencies with an even more elaborate scheme which is so involved that it becomes unbelievable that it could have been deliberately intended. It is true that v. 5 contains two parallel but opposing clauses, but who has not written sentences of this type without consciously intending to display literary skill?

1. There are two preliminary questions of construction. (i) There is no predicate; sections of the textual tradition attempt to correct this with words which might supply one (πρεσβεύω in D 104* pc, κεκαύχημαι in 2464 pc; none has sufficient support; the possibilities are discussed in great detail and dismissed by some of the earlier modern commentators (Alford, Eadie, etc.). Vv. 2–13 are best regarded as parenthetical with an anacoluthon at v. 1. That verse is hardly a 'chapter heading' as Usami, 152f, seems to imply. AE broke off from the intercession he was about to make because the simultaneous mention of Paul and the Gentiles suggested a gap in his argument. Certainly Paul himself could have broken off in this way, for regularly in his certainly genuine letters we find anacolutha; there is also one at 2.1; the present break can therefore be regarded as neither favouring nor militating against Pauline authorship. Would a pseudonymist however have created anacolutha? Perhaps since AE is a good writer he did so in conscious imitation of Paul (Bouwman), being influenced by the words and ideas of the Pauline school as reflected also in Col 1.21ff. More probably it came about through the realisation that something important for the argument had been omitted. The presence of ancolutha in the letter probably indicates that it was dictated. (ii) What is the referent of τούτου χάριν (the phrase is repeated at v. 14)? It may refer (a) backwards or (b) forwards or (c) be a transitional phrase without precise reference. (b) is difficult for there is little to which it could be linked in vv. 2ff (for discussion see Henle). While (c) is possible, the repetition of the phrase at 3.14 renders it unlikely. If then we choose (a) there remain a number of possibilities; it can hardly refer back to all of chap. 2 because 2.1–10 is not relevant. 2.11–22 and 2.19–22 are more probable; it is best to take it as referring to 2.11–22 with special emphasis on 2.19–22.

It is not clear if 'Ιησοῦ should be read after Χριστοῦ with 𝔓⁴⁶ ℵ¹ A B (C) D¹ Ψ 33 1739 (⁵630 1881 al) 𝔐 lat sy saᵐˢˢ bo; Orˡᵃᵗ, or omitted with ℵ* D* F G (365) pc saᵐˢˢ bo; MVict. Both the single word and the double phrase appear regularly throughout the NT; it is perhaps easier to imagine a copyist adding the extra word than omitting it. Philem 1, 9 could also have influenced the addition. 'Christ' by itself is more frequent in Ephesians than in association with 'Jesus'. On balance it seems better to omit 'Jesus'.

The double ἐγὼ Παῦλος stresses the identity of Paul. Paul uses it
when he wishes to emphasise either an argument or his own position
(2 Cor 10.1; Gal 5.2; 1 Th 2.18; Philem 19; cf Col 1.23). Only here
and in Col 1.23 is it tied to his mission to the Gentiles. While the
greater part of the letter will yield the same theological meaning
whether Paul is regarded as author or not, that cannot be said of
3.2–13. If AE specifically mentions Paul as author he will be
reminding his readers that Paul sealed his mission with a martyr's
death in prison; in this way he will deepen the appeal of what he
writes in setting out Paul as the architect of the church of Jews and
Gentiles (cf Gnilka). When he wrote in Paul's name, AE played on
his readers' knowledge that Paul wrote letters; now he plays on their
knowledge that he was a prisoner; the very introduction of his name
reminds them of everything they know about him. AE makes use of
Paul's name in this way because his readers venerate Paul. The real
emphasis of 3.2–13 however does not rest on Paul as prisoner but on
him as God's instrument in bringing the gospel to Gentiles, yet his
position as prisoner contrasts strongly with the position he is given
later in the passage as the unique recipient of revelation. If it is Paul
himself who writes, then he also draws attention to himself by using
his name and referring to himself as prisoner; this would impress his
readers with the importance of what he is about to say. If Paul wrote
this, it is interesting that he does not say, 'I, Paul, the apostle and
prisoner ...'. Whatever authority he may claim here he lets it rest on
himself as one called by God, and not on some special position he
may have been accorded in the church.

On other occasions when Paul introduces his own name he does
so usually because he, his position as apostle, or his teaching have
been attacked. Ephesians however contains no trace of any attack on
him or his teaching; he is never on the defensive. He is introduced,
or introduces himself, with the intention of being shown as the one
who prays for the Gentiles; 3.14ff gives the prayer. Paul's name is
introduced then with pastoral intent, but once introduced the
discussion is given a new direction beginning from the reference to
him as a prisoner on behalf of others.

Paul endured several imprisonments (2 Cor 11.23). On a number
of occasions he refers to himself as in prison or in bonds (Phil 1.7,
13f, 17; Philem 1, 9, 10, 13) and these imprisonments become a
standard theme of the post-Paulines (Col 4.10; 2 Tim 1.8; 2.9); AE
reverts to the theme again at 4.1 and 6.20. But what does 'Paul, the
[the article has no special significance; he is not the prisoner *par
excellence*] prisoner of Christ' mean? If AE is indebted to Col
1.21ff, why did he not write of Paul the διάκονος of Christ? In the
light of Paul's actual imprisonments the reference cannot be taken as
purely metaphorical as if Paul were simply Christ's captive, held by
his love (cf Hodge). This may be true but would not entail the

elimination of the idea of a physical imprisonment. In the literal sense he is a prisoner of Caesar, or of someone holding authority under Caesar. Yet he is kept a prisoner, not by physical restraint, but by his relation to Christ and his love for the Gentiles, on whose behalf he is a prisoner. He is Caesar's prisoner because he is first of all Christ's prisoner, not just a Christian who through some misfortune happens to find himself in prison; neither is he simply a prisoner of conscience, as are many because of their unwillingness to give up a cause to which their lives have been dedicated. His life is dedicated to a person. What in fact we have here is a christological use of 'prisoner', an idea already present in Phil 1.12–14; Philem 9. Paul's imprisonment is not then a sign of God's displeasure; whatever happens to him will be for the good of the gospel (Phil 1.12–26). His imprisonment contrasts strongly with his previous activity as a missionary (cf vv. 8ff).

If the historical Paul wrote these words, to which of his many imprisonments does he refer? Apart from those of which we are ignorant there are three possibilities, Caesarea, Ephesus, Rome. It will almost certainly be the latter, since if we credit Paul with the letter we will place it near the end of his life (see Introduction §5.3, 4). A decision about the place of Paul's imprisonment does not affect the theological thought of the letter. Whether Paul wrote the letter or not, the reference to him as prisoner is much more vivid in recalling his life to others than would have been 'minister' (Col 1.25) or slave (Phil 1.1).

Paul is a prisoner on behalf of others, the Gentiles. It is historically true that he was frequently imprisoned because of his mission to the Gentiles, though he himself never expressly elsewhere connects the two. Acts recounts how when in his preaching in synagogues he spoke of God's interest in the Gentiles there were sometimes disturbances which led to imprisonment. His final imprisonments in Caesarea and Rome were basically the result of his mission to the Gentiles. It is however just possible that the phrase ὑπὲρ ὑμῶν τῶν ἐθνῶν could be taken differently and regarded as a link to v. 14, as if the sentence was intended to run 'I pray on behalf of you Gentiles'; this however would leave the phrase hanging at its present point without any connection; it is therefore better to relate it to what preceded, 'Paul, Christ's prisoner on behalf of you Gentiles'. Since the passage ends (v. 13) by speaking of his sufferings for the glory of the Gentiles (so Salmond) ὑπέρ can probably be given the more precise meaning 'to benefit you Gentiles' (cf Robertson, 630; for the meaning see Mk 9.40; Col 1.24; Rom 8.32; Heb 5.1; cf Salmond). On the significance of Paul's suffering for others see on v. 13. Paul played an essential role in the spread of the gospel and it is this, with other matters, which AE breaks off to bring out in vv. 2ff.

Before we leave v. 1 we should note that the reference to 'you Gentiles' neither implies that this is a catholic letter to all Gentiles (Beare) nor indicates that it is addressed to individual believers (Hofmann) rather than a church or churches. What is written is intended for Gentiles in a number of churches, identifiable only in so far as Paul was not their founder.

2. The parenthesis, or digression, begins here. AE has already argued (1.3–14; 2.11–22) that the Gentiles are within the church because this was and is the way in which God has arranged his plan of salvation. Now he turns his attention to the human agent, Paul, through whom God carried out his plan and expands the phrase 'on behalf of you Gentiles' (v. 1). Paul first needed to receive the revelation of God's plan (vv. 2–7) before he could act on it (vv. 8–12). AE does not discuss whether there were Gentiles in the church prior to Paul's mission or, if so, its significance for the claim made about him here. Unlike statements Paul makes in other letters about his position in relation to the Gentiles, vv. 2–13 have no polemical edge.

It may be assumed (this is the implication of εἴ γε; see BDR §439.3; Moule, 164; Abbott, iv, v, 78; Robertson, 1147–9; Thrall, 88) that the readers already know something about Paul as apostle to the Gentiles (cf Percy, 343, n. 6); there would have been no point in AE writing in Paul's name if they had not heard of him, and knowledge about his activity among the Gentiles was the most likely item of information that everyone would have known. The readers' knowledge would have been indirect and not through personal acquaintance or AE would have said, 'if you remember'. Paul had neither evangelised them nor visited them in person; it is very difficult to believe that if he had ever been with them he would not have told them of his special mission to Gentiles; it is possible, though highly unlikely, that in the time since he had been with them all to whom he had preached had died and that entirely new congregations had come into existence! AE does not explain how the letter's recipients come to know about Paul. He uses the same introductory particle εἴ γε in relation to catechetical instruction at 4.21 and perhaps this was how they learned (Gnilka), but there is little evidence that the command to Paul to evangelise the Gentiles ever formed part of catechetical instruction; had it been then, as v. 5 shows, it must have existed in two forms for Mt 28.16–20 and Acts 1.8 view the command as given not to Paul but to the apostles (cf Best, 'Revelation'). AE does not then probably intend to suggest deliberate instruction (ἠκούσατε is a very general term); there may have been a brief previous communication (cf v. 3). Whatever way the readers were informed, the subject is now to be developed and they are to learn more about the connection between Paul and their own presence in the church.

οἰκονομία is the difficult word in the verse and it is best approached through the phrase accompanying it, ἡ χάρις τοῦ θεοῦ ἡ δοθείσης μοι, a phrase which reappears in v. 7, suggesting v. 2 and v. 7 may form an *inclusio* (Reynier, 61–8). Grace in Pauline writing normally denotes the amazing, redeeming love of God, manifest above all in the inclusion of the Gentiles in the church (cf Barth, 358f). It is by God's grace that people become Christians. But it is not the conversion of Paul which is related to grace here; instead the idea is that God gave Paul grace in relation to the Gentiles; they are the ultimate beneficiaries of the grace as εἰς ὑμᾶς indicates. Apart from its sense in relation to God's redeeming love, χάρις is sometimes used more concretely (cf BAGD *s.v.*) with a meaning similar to χάρισμα (cf 4.7; 1 Pet 4.10). God has given Paul a gift to be used for the benefit of the Gentiles, though of course charismatic gifts are not restricted to work among them for at 4.7 there is no special reference to the Gentiles. The phrase about the gift of grace is Pauline (1 Cor 3.10; cf Rom 12.3, 6; Gal 2.9). In 1 Cor 15.10 and Gal 1.15f Paul connects the grace of God to his commission and work in respect of the Gentiles (cf Rom 1.5). AE was aware of the way Paul would use the phrase and therefore, not inappropriately, employs it here with reference to God's mercy towards the Gentiles. It is because Paul is the recipient of God's gift for the Gentiles that he dares evangelise them and speak with authority not only to the churches he has founded but also to those he has never known or visited.

What now is the relation of the phrase to οἰκονομία[1] and what is the meaning of the latter in our context (see on 1.10 for the word)? A similar phrase and use of οἰκονομία appear in Col 1.25 but it has a more Pauline appearance here (Conzelmann). The noun can be taken either passively or actively; and either God or Paul can be its implied subject. If Paul is the implied subject it is improbable that the word can have a passive sense for God makes plans and not Paul; if it is taken passively in Col 1.25 then God is the subject there. It is easier to see Paul as the implied subject if the word is given an active sense, 'my stewardship of the charisma given to me from God for you' (cf Barth; so also Grosheide, Houlden, Van Roon, Lincoln), it being implied that the stewardship was given to Paul by God (χάριτος would then be a genitive of the object or possibly epexegetical); the word is used in a similar way in 1 Cor 9.17 and in 1 Cor 4.1 Paul describes himself as an οἰκονόμος. Yet in both Eph 1.10 and 3.9 God is the subject and, since the word is used consciously, there is much to be said for a consistent usage (cf Merklein, *Amt*, 174). Moreover this section of the passage stresses

---

[1] χάρις should probably not be given an adjectival sense (with Percy, 342–4) because of the dependent participle.

God's use of Paul in the conversion of the Gentiles rather than his mission as his own activity. Paul's place is conveyed through χάριτος. If Paul were the subject of οἰκονομία we should expect this to be made clear and we should also expect δοθείσην because it is really the 'administration' which is given to Paul rather than the grace (cf Mitton, *Epistle*, 94). It is better then to take God as the subject of οἰκονομία with either passive or active meaning.[2] The two meanings are not so far apart as the difference between active (Schlier, Scott, Masson, Schnackenburg) and passive (Gnilka, Haupt, Gaugler) might suggest. If God administers or arranges to do something he can be expected to do it according to a plan. That God works to a plan is closely linked to the idea of foreordination (cf 1.4, 5, 9). Whether we accept the passive or active sense, χάριτος is epexegetical, 'God's arranging (arrangement) which consists in the (divine) charisma given (by him) to me for you' (τοῦ θεοῦ can be linked with either χάριτος or δοθείσης). The place of Paul in God's activity is of course guaranteed by the reference to the charismatic gift he has received and it is probably unnecessary to see[3] a double reference to God's plan and Paul's role in οἰκονομία. The initiative lies with God who gives Paul his position *vis-à-vis* the Gentiles. The salvation of the Gentiles (εἰς ὑμᾶς picks up ὑπὲρ ὑμῶν from v. 1) cannot be understood apart from Paul, and that does not mean apart from what he tells us about it but apart from his place within God's plan of salvation. This also means that the Gentiles, and in particular the readers (εἰς ὑμᾶς), have their place within God's plan.

3. ὅτι is read by ℵ A C D Ψ 33 1739 1881 𝔐 a cg sy sa^mss bo but omitted by 𝔓46 B F G b d sa^ms; Ambst. If it is omitted (so Zuntz, 196) then v. 3 begins a new sentence which runs on at least to v. 7 and is explanatory of v. 2. However, the resulting short sentence (v. 2) would be unlike AE's normal style (Gnilka). It is then better to read ὅτι, view it as dependent on ἠκούσατε and translate it as 'namely that'. What follows is still explanatory of v. 2. The meaning is unaffected whether the word is read or not.

A mystery has been made known to Paul κατὰ ἀποκάλυψιν. The anarthrous noun does not necessarily mean 'one particular revelation' as in Gal 2.2; Rom 16.25, but serves to identify the means through which Paul came to his knowledge (cf the phrase of Gal

---

[2] Caird's attempt at a compromise in rejecting both Paul and God as subjects, and rendering 'the outcome of my special commission from God' (Robinson had suggested this meaning at 1.10 but does not himself accept it at 3.2) fails because the parenthesis does not deal with the outcome of Paul's activity among the Gentiles but with his theological position in respect of them.

[3] So Reumann, 'OIKONOMIA Terms in Paul in Connection with Lucan *Heilsgeschichte*', *NTS* 13 (1966/7) 165; Michel, *TWNT*, V, 154; Van Roon, *Authenticity*, 175.

1.12) or the basis for that knowledge (Lincoln). He had not been driven to the conclusion that Jews and Gentiles were in the same position before God either as a result of interpreting the OT or as a deduction from a democratic philosophy, or indeed any philosophy. It was not something he had been taught by other Christians, nor was it the product of his research for his Ph.D. at the University of Antioch! He had come to this knowledge through a direct and personal communication from God. This remains true even if with Houlden κατὰ ἀποκάλυψιν is taken to refer to a particular revelation; the distinction Houlden draws between revelations of Christ in the genuine Paulines and a revelation here about the Gentiles is not however valid; see Rom 2.5; 8.19; 1 Cor 14.6, 26; Gal 2.2. Already in Galatians (1.11f, 15f) Paul linked his preaching to the Gentiles to an act of revelation on God's part. It is assumed here (see v. 2) that AE's readers know of this revelation.[4]

Revelation is mediated in different ways, sometimes through dreams and vision, sometimes through a new understanding of scripture as when it is allegorised (so Philo) or made to apply to a new situation as in the Qumran writings. Scripture itself is of course revelation. Revelation is not necessarily given in some outward experience, oral or visual, as in Mt 28.16–20 by the risen Christ or as in the apocalypses through angels. 3.3 does not say when or how Paul received his revelation about the Gentiles.[5]

It is generally held that Paul received the revelation about the acceptance of the Gentiles when he was converted. Caird disputes this, arguing that ἀποκάλυψις is in Paul's eyes one among many gifts of the Spirit (1 Cor 14.6; 2 Cor 12.1, 7). As a prophet he could be inspired to receive new interpretations of the OT (cf v. 5), the veil of incomprehension covering it having been removed (2 Cor 3.12ff). However, v. 5 does not say that in other generations the sons of men did not look deeply enough into the OT to discern the revelation but that it had been withheld from them, though they had the OT. The knowledge given to Paul was then something new. Although it can be argued that Paul received divine revelations throughout his life (cf 2 Cor 12.1–10) the accounts in Acts of his conversion link that conversion, though in different ways, to his commission to take the Gospel to the Gentiles. In Acts 9.15; 22.15 the commission is mediated through Ananias rather than given to Paul directly; in 26.12ff where Ananias is not mentioned Paul receives it directly at the time of his conversion; in Acts 22.21 it comes when he is praying in the temple. Moreover it is not always a commission to go only to Gentiles (Acts 9.15f) and Acts normally depicts his

---

[4] We may compare what the righteous teacher says of himself, 1QpHab 7.4f; 1QH 2.13; 1QS 9.18–20; cf 4 Ezra 14.26, 45f (cf Mussner).

[5] Cf M. N. A. Bockmuehl, *Revelation and Mystery* (WUNT 2.Reihe 56), Tübingen, 1990, 7–128.

missionary activity in each city as commencing with the Jews. The implication of Gal 1.12ff is that the revelation was associated with Paul becoming a Christian.[6] Yet this does not imply that Paul became aware of his special missionary task precisely at the moment of conversion. It may have taken time for the implications of his Damascus Road experience to come home to him; perhaps he only realised its full meaning while he was meditating on the experience during his time in Arabia (Gal 1.17). Though ἐγνωρίσθη is an aorist this does not mean that the revelation was instantaneous, taking place at the moment of conversion, but that it began and ended prior to the time of the writing of Ephesians; the aorist could cover the period of time in which Paul thought out the full significance of his conversion. The verb is passive[7] implying that God had given Paul his revelation. Whatever we conclude about the time when the revelation was given, it is important to note that AE accords Paul a special position in respect of it, for it was given to him alone; this is the implication of the use of μοι here and in v. 3. The emphasis on the first person continues in the passage, though the third appears temporarily in v. 5.

AE may be indebted for his knowledge of Paul's conversion to Galatians, or the tradition which it created; Col 1.24–8 reflects the same tradition (see below for possible dependence on Colossians). Colossians stresses Paul as the proclaimer of the Gospel, but Ephesians stresses him as the recipient of revelation (Merklein, *Amt*, 175f). Naturally his activity is not excluded (it becomes explicit in v. 8); he never became a prisoner because he received a revelation but because he preached.

What God revealed to Paul was 'the mystery' (for the word see on 1.9). The use of mystery in connection with both οἰκονομία and the Gentiles may go back to Paul (1 Cor 4.1; Rom 11.25). AE uses three words here, ἀποκάλυψις, γνωρίζω, μυστήριον; all relate to 'revelation' and often appear together in revelatory contexts; all three in Rom 16.25f, the first two in Gal 1.11f; the first and third in 1 Cor 2.7–10; 2 Th 2.6f; the second and third in Eph 1.9; 6.19. An associated set of ideas which are found together is hidden, revealed, proclaimed (1 Cor 2.6–8, 10–12, 13–16; Col 1.26–8; Tit 1.2f), and of course AE goes on to speak of proclamation in vv. 9f. In 1.9 the mystery is that of God's will which (1.10) in some way implies a comprehensiveness in God's intention. This comprehensiveness is also present here though cut down to the inclusion of the Gentiles in God's plan. The mystery is now described as 'of Christ' (v. 4), though too much should not be made of this since Christ is

---

[6] On all this see Best, 'Revelation', 13ff.
[7] The reading ἐγνώρισε, D² 𝔐, is an obvious correction, and the addition of γάρ in F G an attempt to improve the flow of the argument.

mentioned in 1.9f. In Colossians the mystery is also related to Christ (4.3; 2.2) who, as content of the word of God, is preached to the Gentiles so that he is in them (1.25–7). It is not easy in Ephesians to equate (with Pokorný) mystery and Gospel, for this might imply that the Gospel was unknown prior to Paul's conversion. Both in Colossians and in Ephesians the mystery is something previously unknown but now known (Col 1.26; Eph 3.4, 5); in Col 2.2 it is not yet fully appreciated by believers but appears to be in Ephesians, certainly at least by Paul. In Ephesians also the mystery is tied more closely than in Colossians to the personal position of Paul (3.3ff).[8] There are consequently differences and similarities in the use of 'mystery' in the two letters (Mitton, *Epistle*, 86–91, over emphasises these); it is not beyond the bounds of possibility that one person could have used the word with these varying nuances, but it is more probable that the members of a Pauline school would have done so.

The present passage expands what AE had earlier sketched more briefly (προγράφω can refer to something previously touched on in the same writing, cf. MM, BAGD) about 'mystery' and the admission of Gentiles (1.9f; 2.11ff). In the earlier passages he had written of their admission but not of Paul's role in it (cf Percy, 350). Some who equate AE with Paul believe that he refers here to his earlier letters. This would imply the availability in all the communities to which Ephesians was sent of at least one of these letters, probably Galatians or Colossians. But could Paul have been sure that every community would know the content of at least one or other of these letters? If Galatians is supposed to have been known could it be described as 'brief'? If Colossians (so Bouwman), then its readers were told to get hold of the letter to Laodicea but the readers of Ephesians are not told to get hold of that to Colossae; Colossians moreover was not a circular letter; the very instruction of Col 4.16 to exchange letters with Laodicea indicates that letters were not automatically circulated. It is then best to assume that, whether Paul was the author or not, v. 3 refers to the earlier parts of the present letter. AE is consistent here in that he does not make Paul say 'Remember what I told you when I was with you' since elsewhere he does not present Paul as ever having been with them. Those, like Goodspeed (*Meaning*, 42f) and Mitton (*Epistle*, 233–6), who argue that Ephesians was written as an introduction to the first collection of Paul's letters, suppose that the reference is to that collection. On general grounds we have rejected their theory (see Introduction §8.3.1). More particularly with regard to 3.3 it is difficult to see how AE, writing in Paul's name and obviously venerating him, could refer to his letters as written ἐν ὀλίγῳ (similar

---

[8] On the use gnostics made of Paul's special position see E. H. Pagels, *The Gnostic Paul. Gnostic Exegesis of the Pauline Letters*, Philadelphia, 1975, 121f.

phrases in Heb 13.22; 1 Pet 5.12 refer to the letters in which they appear); even the sections about the admission of Gentiles in the various letters are all in all much larger than our section in Ephesians.[9]

4. This verse is linked to v. 3 by πρὸς ὅ, a rare usage of the preposition in the NT (Lk 12.47; 2 Cor 5.10; Gal 2.14; also Hermas, *Mand* 11.3) but classical (see BDR §239.8). The connection is to v. 3b (cf Gnilka, Schlier, Haupt, etc.) rather than v. 3a for there has been no previous reference to a special revelation to Paul. If AE's readers peruse carefully what he has written (v. 5 excludes any idea that AE has in mind the reading of the OT[10]) they will know the content of the mystery, if not how it was revealed to Paul. ἀναγινώσκοντες (the participle has almost an imperatival tone) simply means 'read' and not 'read again', as if implying that they should go back and read again the first part of the letter. The reading would be aloud, as was normal in the ancient world, and would probably have been in the course of worship (Col 4.16; 1 Th 5.27; Rev 1.3), and this may have occasioned the choice of a present participle. Westcott and Beare are wrong to think of private study of the letter. The reading of the letter in worship imparts to it a certain finality; it is not ephemeral (cf Ernst).

Since the letter contained no previous reference, apart from v. 3, to a special revelation to Paul it is appropriate here to speak of his insight (σύνεσις) in respect of what he has already written. μου is not intended to suggest a contrast between Paul and someone else and it does not imply an unworthy boasting on his part, which might be the case if the insight were purely human. σύνεσις (συνίημι) ἐν is non-classical and MM do not list it as present in the papyri. It is probably drawn from the Greek OT where, particularly in Daniel (1.4, 17; 9.13, 23; 10.1, 11; see both LXX and Theod) it is explicitly used of the understanding of dreams and visions and implicitly associated with revelations. Since the context here is one of revelation it should not be taken as referring to human insight but to an understanding given by God into his mystery (see also *T Reub* 6.4; *T Levi* 2.3; 18.7; Col 1.9; 2.2;[11] 2 Tim 2.7; Ignatius, *Polyc* 1.3; 1QH 2.13; 12.13; cf Kuhn). Christian insight is of course never

[9] L. Davies, "'I wrote afore in few words'' (Eph. iii.3)', *ExpT* 46 (1934/5) 568, suggests Rom 16.25-7 was written to Ephesus and is the relevant passage. We cannot be sure Rom 16.25-7 was written to Ephesus or even that Ephesians was written to the church there.

[10] As suggested by F. J. A. Hort, *The Romans and the Ephesians: Prolegomena*, London, 1895, 150f.

[11] In the Colossian passages insight is not restricted as in Ephesians to Paul but is something all Christians possess. When Merklein, *Amt*, 163, attempts to distinguish between these two uses by suggesting that AE is deliberately making a distinction he goes beyond what the statistical evidence will bear.

simple human insight for it takes place in a mind responsive to God and enlightened by his Spirit. σύνεσις thus continues the claim of v. 3. The revelation Paul received has worked itself into his mind and become a part of him (cf Bouttier); 'insight' is a suitable word to describe this process; in 2.11–22 it was expressed, not in the terms of a special revelation, but of what was believed in the church. It should also be noted, and this is important if Paul himself is the author, that the appeal is not to Paul as person or apostle but to divine revelation; there is no self-glorification on Paul's part.

Merklein, *Amt*, 216–18, on the assumption that AE knew Colossians, regards 3.3b, 4 as his insertion into the Colossian *Vorlage*; from that he argues that the μου refers not to Paul but to AE who thereby presents his own extension of Paul's thought to his contemporary situation; otherwise, he holds, v. 4 would be redundant. Any redundancy here however would not be surprising since it is a common feature of the epistle. Leaving aside the general issue of AE's contribution to Pauline thought, and it is surely present throughout the letter, it is necessary to ask if it is especially present in v. 4. Would AE have used an apocalyptically nuanced phrase like σύνεσις ἐν of himself? Would this not imply that he was placing himself among the apostles and prophets? If so, one of the reasons, that the apostles and prophets are a group of the past, used in arguing that the author is not Paul but a later writer, would not be applicable. If vv. 3b, 4 are parenthetical would it not be advisable to add v. 5 to them? V. 3a would link well to v. 6 (cf Bratcher and Nida) and v. 5 could be regarded as an afterthought of AE when he remembered that another tradition existed (see on v. 5) relating the mission to the Gentiles to a revelation to the apostles rather than to Paul.

What mystery (for the word see on 1.9) is referred to here? Col 4.3 (cf 2.2) uses the same phrase, 'the mystery of Christ', yet if the mystery there is Christ that is not so here. Here it must be the same as that of v. 3, the uniting of Gentile and Jewish Christians; as such it is a subsection of the greater mystery of the unification of all things in Christ (1.10). The uniting of Jew and Gentile can be described as the mystery of Christ because it is through him that it is attained, for both Jew and Gentile are now in the one body of Christ. Yet it is God who planned and accomplished the mystery. The mystery of Christ, while not identical with the mystery of God's will, is contained within it.

5. ὅ refers back to μυστήριον in either v. 3a or v. 4. If the former then vv. 3b, 4 must be treated as parenthetical (Bouwman) and v. 5 probably joined with them in the parenthesis. It is however easier to choose the connection to v. 4, even though ἀπεκαλύφθη recalls ἀποκάλυψιν in v. 3a. This choice does not necessarily eliminate the parenthesis. The meaning in unaffected whichever linkage is chosen. It is not until v. 6 that the content of the mystery is stated. Structurally v. 5 consists of two balancing statements, a negative and a positive, each possessing three items: a temporal datum, a verb denoting revelation, and the mention of recipients, or non-recipients, of the revelation.

Barth believes that v. 5 is a quotation from an early hymn or confession because of the balancing of the two clauses and the use of non-Pauline expressions, e.g. 'sons of men', 'holy apostles and prophets'. The presence of non-Pauline expressions is irrelevant if the letter is not by Paul. Nothing in the phraseology is out of accord with AE's normal liturgical style. It is true that the recipients of the revelation of the mystery are not the same as in v. 3, but two strands of tradition about this existed in the church and AE is using the tradition of the second strand though not quoting it in any of its known variants, of which no two agree (cf Best, 'Revelation').

The two halves of the verse are related by ὡς; they indicate an absolute contrast between a past period of ignorance and a present one of knowledge, the past period being in effect that of the OT and the present that of the NT. But was there complete ignorance in the OT concerning God's plans for the Gentiles? It is not difficult to find passages which allow a place for them (Gen 12.1–3; 18.18; Isa 2.2–4; 11.10; 34.22; 49.6; 60.3; Jer 3.17; Jon 4; Zech 9.9f). Mare[12] points out that some of these texts are understood in this way in the NT (Isa 42.6; 49.6 in Lk 2.32; Gen 12.3; 17.5; 28.14 in Gal 3.7f, 29). The NT also contains places where it is implied that the writers of the OT were not entirely ignorant in respect of God's intentions towards the Gentiles (Rom 1.2; 9.25f; 13.9ff; Gal 3.8; Acts 15.15ff; 17.11f; 1 Pet 1.10–12). In the light of this ὡς could be given a comparative meaning, 'as clearly as'; God's purpose for the Gentiles was not understood as clearly in the OT as now after the death and resurrection of Christ (so Abbott, Beck, Foulkes, Macpherson). How does such an understanding accord with the concept of revelation to Paul in v. 3? It suggested something new, not that Paul came to appreciate a truth which had lain hidden from the Jews though written in their scriptures. Were the latter the case, then v. 3 ought to have run 'the understanding of the mystery was made known to me by revelation' and something similar would be expected here and in 3.9f. Since it is almost impossible to find OT passages to parallel 3.9f, those verses cannot refer to the imparting of a true understanding of already known passages. Those who take ὡς as 'as clearly as' sometimes argue that the new revelation means that the Gentiles are now incorporated into the same body as the Jews (Mussner, cf Bruce); this is to split hairs. There are moreover no good grammatical or stylistic reasons for modifying the absolute nature of the contrast implied by ὡς. This absolute nature is supported by 1.9 and is found in, or can be read into, other parts of the NT (Rom 16.25–7; Col 1.26; Gal 4.21–31; 1 Cor 2.7ff; Tit 1.2f;

[12] W. H. Mare, 'Paul's Mystery in Ephesians 3', *BETS* 8 (1965) 77–84.

2 Tim 1.9f). In the commission to the Twelve (Mt 28.16–20; Acts 1.8) to go into all the world the command is presented as something new and not as the unfolding of an existing though partly veiled secret. Eph 3.2ff stands under the general schema in relation to revelation of 'once hidden—now revealed'[13] which appears to exclude OT revelation. There is both continuity and discontinuity between the testaments; our passage stresses the discontinuity, perhaps over-stresses it, but it is corrected elsewhere by the importance given to the OT by AE when he quotes it. The non-recipients of the revelation were 'the sons of men', a frequent biblical idiom for humanity in general, or all Israel (Gen 11.5; Ψ 11.2; Joel 1.12; Jer 38.19; Dan 3.82; Mk 3.28); occasionally it can refer to particular people (Ψ 79.18; Ezek 2.1, 3, and often in Ezekiel to Ezekiel); in this case the singular is used. Its OT usage however gives no reason for seeing it in v. 5 as including the prophets and patriarchs (so Jerome, Ellicott in attempts to avoid the implication of an absolute ignorance on the part of the OT). If it refers to all humanity then that includes all Israel. The passive ἐγνωρίσθη (implicit subject God) implies that human ignorance in this connection came from God and was not simply the result of human weakness. The time of their ignorance is expressed by ἑτέραις[14] γενεαῖς (a temporal dative; cf Moule, 43; MHT, 243; BDR §200.4; the noun is used with temporal sense at 3.21; Acts 14.16; 15.21; Col 1.26; Ψ 48.12; 88.2; Lk 1.50; Exod 17.16). Though γενεαί can be used of the spiritual powers,[15] this cannot be the meaning here for it would destroy the carefully balanced contrast within v. 5 and the powers are not introduced until v. 10. Steinmetz, 51–67, arguing from 5.8; 2.2f; 2.11ff; 3.9f, believes that the contrast between v. 5a and v. 5b is not basically temporal but theological and refers to forms of existence (without salvation—in salvation). While this explanation may be true of 2.2f and 5.8, it is difficult to sustain at 3.5 (cf Merklein, 182–7) where the contrast is not between those outside the church and those inside but between those outside and a limited inside group (apostles and prophets) through whom knowledge is now mediated to the church.

Turning now to v. 5b the revelation is said to be made τοῖς ἁγίοις ἀποστόλοις αὐτοῦ καὶ προφήταις ἐν πνεύματι. ἅγιοι, strictly an adjective, is normally used substantively in the NT. This might

---

[13] Cf D. Lührmann, *Das Offenbarungsverständnis bei Paulus und in den paulinischen Gemeinden* (WMANT 16), Neukirchen-Vluyn, 1965, 117–22.

[14] Some gnostic groups apparently depended on a manuscript tradition containing the variant ταῖς προτέραις; see Hippolytus, *Ref* 5.8.5 (89.27–90.1); 6.35.1 (164.7ff); 7.26.7 (205.6ff), apparently an attempt to avoid any reference to the OT; cf A. Orbe, 'Una variante heterodoxa de Eph. 3, 5a', *Greg* 37 (1956) 201–19; Steinmetz, 57f.

[15] Cf Jonas, *The Gnostic Religion*, 51ff. There may be more justification for this meaning at Col 1.26.

suggest placing a comma after it (cf Cerfaux, *L'église*, 104–6) and translating 'the saints, i.e. his apostles and prophets'. This interpretation must be rejected as implying that only apostles and prophets are saints. Were it intended there would need to have been some word like μάλιστα qualifying apostles and prophets (so Haupt). Some manuscripts (B b; Ambst) avoid any possible difficulty by omitting the reference to the apostles so that we only have 'holy prophets'; this brings v. 5 closer to Col 1.26, but manuscript support is weak. 'Holy prophets' is of course a known phrase (Lk 1.70; Acts 3.21; 2 Pet 3.2) in which 'holy' is adjectival. This idiom suggests that 'holy' is probably also adjectival in v. 5 and refers to both apostles and prophets, which as in 2.20 (see there for the two words), is a fixed phrase denoting one group in AE's mind. That the group is *now* the recipient of revelation implies that the prophets belong to the same period as the apostles, i.e. they are Christian prophets.[16] Merklein, 188–9 (cf Adai, 154), links 'holy' to apostles alone and is then forced to associate 'in the Spirit' with 'prophets'. His attempt to justify 'holy' as qualifying only apostles because they are the bearers of revelation and norms of the tradition is much too involved and never gets off the ground. Also suppositions of derivation from Col 1.26 are more than a little hypothetical once we observe that the verbs used for revelation in Col 1.26 and Eph 3.5b are not the same; the verses have indeed only two words in common: νῦν and ἁγίοις. The phrase of Col 1.26 implies a revelation to all the people of God, AE's formulation one to the principal leaders of the church (cf Mitton, *Epistle*, 85f). A revelation restricted to the apostles and not to all believers does not indicate a later stage in church development; the revelation to a limited group was part of the tradition from the beginning (cf Mt 28.16–20, etc.); it is the revelation to all believers which is the new element. There is no need to restrict αὐτοῦ to apostles; ἐν πνεύματι has forced it into its present position (Schlier).

If then no valid grounds exist for taking ἅγιοι as other than an adjective, what does it mean? In view of the widespread use of the root in the NT in relation to God's activity in salvation it can hardly refer simply to the moral piety of the apostles and prophets. Probably its frequent association with 'prophets' led to its use here so that it also applies to apostles. Applied to both apostles and prophets it may indicate they have a special position in God's plan of salvation, and this would be in line with 2.20 (Van Roon,

[16] Faust, 195f, takes the adjective to mean 'Jewish' and 'Jewish apostles and prophets' would be a true statement, but it is a forced interpretation granted even that there are places where ἅγιοι indicates Jewish believers (1 Cor 16.1; 2 Cor 8.4; 9.1, 12; Rom 15.26f, 31). Since the word does not have this meaning throughout Ephesians (cf 1.1, 15; 3.18; 4.12; 6.18), it would not have been easy for readers to see that a special meaning was intended here.

Authenticity, 389, takes it as the equivalent of 'called'). Yet if the phrase is derived from 'holy prophets' the adjective was already losing much of its 'theological' meaning in that phrase. Nowhere in the NT is it used to distinguish Jewish or Christian prophets from those of other religions; it was tending rather to imply a position of dignity and importance (cf Ignatius, *Magn* 3.1, 'holy' presbyters). While therefore its *heilsgeschichtliche* meaning remains in the background, for it is from that meaning that the nuance of dignity and importance is derived, it is probably the latter which is to the fore here. It would certainly be wrong to see the adjective as suggesting that some apostles and prophets were 'holy' while others were not (cf Van Roon, *Authenticity*, 390). While for Paul the existence of false apostles (2 Cor 11.5, 13) was a problem, nothing in Ephesians suggests AE was thinking at all of such apostles; neither 2.20 nor 4.11 lends any support to the idea. The description of the apostles as 'holy' has often been used in the argument against Pauline authorship. Would Paul have given such a position of dignity to himself? To avoid this the adjective would then have to be given its full *heilsgeschichtliche* nuance. Also if Paul were the author he may have limited the term apostles (see on 1.1 and 2.20 for the term) to the Twelve, of which of course he was not a member, and so the adjective would not have applied to him. The phrase then need not be an insurmountable obstacle to his authorship. Yet it is more easily understood if he is not the author. In v. 3 he emphasised his own position as recipient of revelation; in line with this we might have expected him, if he were the author, to write here 'to us apostles and prophets'.

The final phrase ἐν πνεύματι has been related in different ways to the other words (cf the same phrase at 2.22); it refers of course to the Holy Spirit and has been linked to (i) the verb, (ii) 'his holy apostles and prophets', (iii) 'prophets' alone. If (iii) is chosen it would be natural to restrict αὐτοῦ to the apostles alone (Schnackenburg) yet the prophets belong to God as much as the apostles and since all prophecy is 'in the Spirit' their connection to the Spirit hardly needed to be stressed. Moreover in 2.20 the apostles and prophets together form a distinct group. There appears then no need to distinguish between them here by applying different phrases to them. (ii) would imply the existence of apostles and prophets who had no connection with the Spirit if those mentioned here need to be identified as recipients of the Spirit; nothing else in the letter suggests the existence of unspiritual apostles and prophets. (i) is probably then the best solution; in 5.18; 6.18 the phrase is also linked to the verb (Reynier, 149). The revelation is through the Spirit (Adai, 152f).

νῦν must refer to a period in which apostles and prophets existed, but is this a period in the past or the one in which AE lives? In 4.11

apostles and prophets begin a list which goes on to include evangelists, pastors, teachers, who are clearly still active in the community and nothing is said to distinguish the period of their ministry from that of the apostles and prophets. 4.11 would then be an explication of 4.7.[17] In 4.7 all Christians are said to have charismatic gifts yet if 4.11 explains 4.7, it lists only a few gifts of the prominent kind (contrast Rom 12.6–8; 1 Cor 12.4ff), and strictly speaking in 4.11 it is not gifts which are given to the apostles, etc., but the apostles, etc., who are gifts to the church (see on 4.11 and Best, 'Ministry'). 4.11 is not then a spelling out of 4.7. In 2.20 the apostles and prophets are the foundation of the church and this suggests a group belonging to the past, or at least a group which would cease to exist once its original members were dead (see on 2.20). There seems no reason to draw any other conclusion here. In defending his position in respect of our verse Klein (op.cit., 69–72) wrongly suggests that the true contrast in v. 5 is not between past and present but between a whole (the sons of men) and a part (apostles and prophets); if AE had intended this emphasis he would have needed to have made it more clearly. Indeed if a continuing group of apostles and prophets were in mind in v. 5b, then we would have expected its verb to be in the present tense and not in the aorist. When we look elsewhere in the NT[18] we find a strong tradition that a revelation of the universal nature of the gospel was made to a group approximately equivalent to the apostles (cf Mt 28.16–20; Lk 24.47; Acts 1.8; Jn 20.21). This revelation belonged to the past in the period immediately after the resurrection. It is not possible to recover from the varying statements about it a form of words which may have been original. Indeed if there had been any clear form of words it is difficult to see why the church was at first so slow to respond to it and admit Gentile believers. Probably the suggestion that there was a revelation preceded its exact formulation so that it came to be expressed in different ways and slightly different groups were regarded as its recipients. The one significant variation in Eph 3.5 is the introduction of the prophets among the recipients. However, within the early church these were recipients of revelations (1 Cor 14.29–31) and this may account for their presence in v. 5; apostles when receiving revelations were in fact acting in the role of prophets (see also on 2.20 for the linking of prophets with apostles).

Finally we should note that 3.1–13 contains two traditions about

---

[17] So G. Klein, *Die zwölf Apostel* (FRLANT 77), Göttingen, 1961, 66–9. Fischer, 37–9, argues for a similar understanding of apostles and prophets from quite another standpoint: AE is writing at a time when a new episcopal order is appearing and is opposing the emergence of episcopacy.

[18] See Best, 'Revelation', where I have worked this out in detail.

the revelation to evangelise the Gentiles. In 3.3 AE retains that belonging to the Pauline school in which Paul is portrayed as its recipient; in 3.5 he has added another strand from the tradition of the wider church. Paul was apparently not aware of this wider strand when he wrote Gal 2.1–10; if he wrote Ephesians, when did he become aware of it? The traditions of 3.3 and 3.5 may not have been the only two traditions current, for in Acts 10.9ff Peter received a revelation to take the gospel to Cornelius, and in Antioch the step to go to the Gentiles seems to have been taken almost spontaneously (Acts 11.20f) and prior to Paul's arrival in that city. Theologically all AE needed to say was that some person or group had received a revelation about the admission of Gentile believers into the church to justify their presence there. This purpose was fulfilled once he had mentioned Paul in v. 3; however, having done this he must have realised that his readers, or at least some of them, would have known of the tradition of a revelation to the Twelve and so he is forced to refer to it. Was it an afterthought? If so this would justify regarding vv. 3b–5 as parenthetical.

A number of commentators have seen AE as dependent in vv. 1–8 on Col 1.23–9 (see especially Lincoln, 169). There are several similarities (in each case the Ephesian reference is given first and the Colossian second): (a) Paul appears as writing in the first person (3.1; 1.23), (b) ὑπὲρ ὑμῶν (3.1; 1.24), (c) οἰκονομία ... τοῦ θεοῦ ... τῆς δοθείσης μοι εἰς ὑμᾶς (3.2; 1.25), (d) μυστηρίῳ ... γενεαῖς (3.4, 5; 1.26), (e) μυστηρίου τοῦ ἀποκεκρυμμένου ἀπὸ τῶν αἰώνων (3.9; 1.26), (f) τοῖς ἁγίοις ... (3.5; 1.26), (g) τοῖς ἔθνεσιν (3.8; 1.27), (h) κατὰ τὴν ἐνέργειαν ... δυνάμεως (3.7; 1.29). (a) is not significant in writings supposed to have been written by Paul. (b) comes naturally from those who venerate Paul and see him as conducting his ministry for others. In (c) the greater part of the phrase comes from the genuine Paulines (see above); AE is more faithful in this respect than A/Col for he retains the Pauline reference to grace. In (d) the mystery is hidden from the generations in Ephesians but made known to them in Colossians. In (e) the Ephesian passage is not closely tied in with the other passages at issue and AE, if he used Colossians here, dropped the reference to generations while retaining that to the ages, yet he likes synonymous expressions; if a literary solution is demanded it is more probable then that A/Col added 'generations' to Ephesians (cf Holtzmann, 49f). As for (f), in Ephesians ἅγιοι is an adjective but in Colossians a noun. As for (g), the reference to the Gentiles appears naturally in Ephesians, where it is a main subject, but only occurs here in Colossians; this would suggest it is more likely that A/Col has picked up a theme from Ephesians than the other way round. The phrases in (h) are very different; AE likes using roots twice in the same breath yet he has failed to follow Colossians here in this respect. Also to be noted is AE's non-use of his favourite πληρόω which appears in Col 1.27. More generally for AE the mystery is that of the admission of the Gentiles but for A/Col it relates to Christ. AE and A/Col use different verbs in relation to the ignorance which preceded the unveiling of the secret (3.5; 1.26); it is hard to see why the change was made. There is then no reason for assuming AE used Colossians in 3.1–8; indeed a good case could be made out for A/Col's use of Ephesians (see below re v. 6 and Best, 'Who used Whom'). If AE does not depend here on Col 1.23–9, it is also unlikely that Eph 3.1–13 is an expanded form of Col 1.23–9; the Ephesian passage contains too many ideas not present in the Colossian, e.g. the preaching to the powers, the revelation of the mystery to either Paul or the apostles and prophets, a different understanding of mystery, Paul as prisoner. On the other hand Col 1.23–9 could well be an abbreviation of Eph 3.1–13. The most probable solution in respect of the relation of the two letters here is that AE and A/Col belonged to the same Pauline school.

6. The content of the mystery is now disclosed.

εἶναι is epexegetical despite the absence of a demonstrative pronoun (cf 3.17; 4.22f; Rom 1.28; Acts 3.18; 20.24; see BDR §394.2). If AE was using Col 1.26f then he was forced into a change of construction since the clause in Col 1.27 beginning with τί depends on γνωρίσαι, for which there is no real equivalent in Eph 3.5 (Merklein). The liturgical language present in Col 1.27 is also surprisingly missing in Eph 3.6 if AE was using Colossians. The changes from Col 1.27 are so great that it is difficult to see Eph 3.6 as an 'editing' of the latter. It is rather a substitution or an entirely fresh composition.

Jews and Gentiles meet in the church on equal terms. Since an understanding of this mystery was already assumed in 2.11ff, it is surprising that its formal disclosure only comes now (Ernst); the emphasis may then lie here not so much on its content as on the fact of its disclosure and on those to whom the disclosure was made. The content of the mystery is expressed through three terms which echo ideas found elsewhere in the letter; of them the first and third also echo Jewish ideas: for συγκληρονόμα see 1.12, the Jewish Christians being the heirs with whom the Gentiles share; for συμμέτοχα τῆς ἐπαγγελίας[19] see 2.12 and its reversal in 2.13–17 (Mussner); the adjective is compounded with two prepositions both meaning 'with'; its genitive qualification applies to it alone since it has no relevance to the second description (Reynier, 106). In contrast to the other terms σύσσωμα introduces a clear Christian theme picking up the widespread use in the letter of σῶμα for the community; though there is a little evidence in Philo for regarding Israel as a living organism (*Spec Leg* 3.131; *de Virt* 103; *de Praem et Poen* 114, 125), there is nothing of the emphasis or interest that we find in the Pauline corpus; the word by its formation could be either an adjective or a noun, almost certainly the former to fit with the other two adjectives; of the three adjectives it is the one most characteristic of the ideas in the letter. This is its first known appearance in

---

[19] The addition of αὐτοῦ here with D¹ F G Ψ 𝔐 a vg^{cl} sy^h; Ambst does not have strong enough support and does not alter the meaning.

Greek literature[20] (since we do not know all Greek literature it is wrong to speak of it as a neologism) but this provides no justification for regarding it with Schlier as the most important in the series. There is no need either to see with Barth and Hendriksen a progression of importance through the three terms; they are simply different ways of expressing the same thought. In each case σύν refers to the unification of Jews and Gentiles rather than to the relation of either to Christ, though the latter is the normal way in which Paul uses compounds with σύν (Rom 6.4–8; 8.17; cf Eph 2.6f). The presence of these three compounds with σύν, though it is one of Paul's favourite prepositions, offers then no reason for seeing here (with Caird) a sign of his hand, for AE also uses the preposition frequently. That believers are fellow heirs with one another derives ultimately from the fact that they are fellow heirs with Christ (Rom 8.17); that they belong to the same body follows from their being members of the body of Christ. In Christ too the 'promise' of God is fulfilled (2 Cor 1.20); the noun compounded with the preposition again brings out the common participatory element.

AE has Gentile believers in mind here and not, as Barth argues, Gentiles as such, for there is no reason to suppose he is making a universalist statement, or, what would necessarily follow, that all Jews would be saved. These Gentile believers are fellow heirs with Jewish believers, not with all Jews, of the promised inheritance (see 1.14, 18 for its nature), fellow members of the body of Christ and fellow recipients of the promise of God. Together they form the new people of God, the 'third race' (cf Penna, *Mysterion*, 72–5). 'Promise' in the singular may refer either to the total of what is promised in the OT in relation to salvation or to the particular promise made to Abraham on which the whole position of Jews rested and which is seen in some parts of the NT to apply to Gentile Christians (Gal 3.29). There is no reason to restrict the promise to that of the Spirit and so find a Trinitarian reference: heirs of the Father, members of the body of Christ, sharers in the Spirit (so Lock).

Behind the togetherness of Gentile and Jewish believers in the one people of God lies God's activity in Christ; this is brought out in the final two phrases of the verse which relate to all that preceded in the verse. ἐν Χριστῷ Ἰησοῦ applies to all three adjectives and serves either to stress the idea of the fellowship of Jewish and Gentile believers as taking place in Christ or indicates the sphere of God's activity, Christ's death and resurrection by which they were brought together (2.14–17). τὸ εὐαγγέλιον can refer to either the content of what is preached or the act of preaching. The latter interpretation is

---

[20] Working from the known meaning of σῶμα as 'slave', E. Preuschen, 'CYNCΩMOC', *ZNW* 1 (1900) 85–6, argued that the translation should be 'fellow slave'.

to be preferred, since the unification of Jew and Gentile is not automatic but takes place as a response to preaching and vv. 7f goes on to stress the actual ministry of Paul (cf 1 Cor 4.15). If 'the gospel' is taken to indicate its content we should have to take 'in Christ Jesus' as denoting the spiritual sphere within which Jews and Gentiles are fellow heirs (cf Ernst).

If v. 6 supplies the content of the mystery of vv. 3f how does this mystery relate to that of 1.9f? Both refer to a unification or bringing together; 3.3–6 restricts this to human beings, Jewish and Gentile believers comprising its totality; in 1.9f all creation is gathered together to Christ. 3.3–6 therefore represents a partial fulfilment of 1.9f. Dibelius may be correct in viewing the two mysteries as identical, for that of 3.3–6 attains a cosmic dimension in 3.10. Unresolved is the identity of those to whom the revelation of 1.9f was made known, and when it was made known and how it was made known. AE tells us nothing about these matters. He clearly knows the mystery and we assume that he believes Paul knew it and perhaps also that the apostles and prophets knew it.

7. 3.2–6 treated the place of Paul, and others, in God's plan and the nature of the mystery which was disclosed. In v. 7 we begin to be told how Paul communicated what he had learnt to others. Vv. 8–12 continue the account of the communication of the revealed mystery; v. 7 is in effect a transition verse between the disclosure and the action taken in response to that disclosure. At this point it becomes difficult to distinguish between the gospel and the mystery, yet there must be a distinction for the gospel was proclaimed prior to Paul's conversion and the disclosure to him of the mystery. Was the earlier proclamation not that of the true and full gospel? The apostles and prophets now drop from view and Paul alone occupies the centre stage; if he has a ministry to fulfil it is necessary both to say what it is and to describe how he accomplished it. The move from the content of the mystery to its proclamation is made through the reference to the gospel which in v. 6 probably referred to the activity of preaching rather than its content (cf Rom 10.14f). In fact, in so far as we know the story, Paul was the leading exponent of the gospel to the Gentiles, though the evidence of Acts (e.g. 10.44–8; 11.20f) suggests he was neither the first to preach it nor the only one to do so. If Acts is correct, Peter had evangelised Cornelius before Paul was brought to Antioch, and it cannot be assumed Barnabas ceased his missionary work with Gentiles after his split with Paul. The speedy growth of the early church shows that there must have been many Gentile areas which were evangelised by people whose names remain unknown. AE may not then know the whole story of the evangelisation of the Gentiles, but he is not so much concerned with Paul's historical place in it as with his theological position as the recipient of God's grace. In this he follows a line which Paul had

originally put forward (e.g. Rom 1.1, 5; 1 Cor 1.1; Gal 1.1, 15f) and
which was continued later by the Pastorals alongside their veneration for him (2 Tim 1.11; Tit 1.3).

διάκονος,[21] used here to describe Paul's function, is not a word
which would stress either his importance or personal renown. The
root originally ranged widely in meaning from waiting at table to the
action of communicating, including that of the impartation of
heavenly knowledge, and this range of meaning would have been
known to Greek readers. Because it does not refer narrowly only to
humble service, like 'slave', it is seen by AE as a suitable term to
describe Paul's ministry. The sense of the impartation of heavenly
knowledge would be appropriate in v. 7 (Collins, op.cit., 233; see 2
Cor 3.7–9; 4.1, 5, 18 for a similar use in relation to Paul's ministry).
Whether it would also have carried for Greek readers the sense of
humble service (cf Mk 10.42–5; Lk 22.25–7) in its present context
is debatable. It was brought into Christian thought to denote both
Jesus' service to others (e.g. Mk 10.45) and their service to him (Mk
1.31; 15.41; Lk 8.3). Eventually among Christians it came to
designate a particular group of people exercising a special function
in the church. Before attaining this technical sense it was used, as
here, of various people in the church and their different activities
(Rom 16.1; 1 Cor 3.5; 12.5; 16.15; 2 Cor 8.4; 9.1, 12, 13; Phil 1.1;
Col 1.7; 1 Th 3.2). Paul used the root to describe his own ministry
(Rom 11.13; 15.25, 31; 2 Cor 3.3, 6; 4.1; 5.18; 6.3, 4; 8.19f; 11.8,
23; cf Col 1.23, 25) but in a general kind of way and not in relation
to his ministry to the Gentiles alone; Rom 11.13 refers to that
ministry and where Paul uses the root in connection with the
collection for the church at Jerusalem he may also have it in mind.
In Col 1.23, 25 it is attached specifically to the Gentile ministry and
its use in relation to that ministry may have been common in the
Pauline school of AE and A/Col. AE probably derived his usage
from there rather than directly from Romans or 2 Corinthians (in
Eph 4.12; 6.21 it does not relate to Paul). It continued in use in the
Pauline schools to describe his activity (1 Tim 1.12–16). How much
the flavour of humble service clung to it by this time is difficult to
answer, but Gentiles coming freshly to it would hear it with such
overtones. It is interesting that Paul does not say, or is not made to
say, 'of which I am an apostle'; apart from 1.1 AE makes no

---

[21] Cf H. W. Beyer, *TWNT*, II, 81ff; W. Brandt, *Dienst und Dienen im Neuen
Testament*, Gütersloh, 1931; D. Georgi, *Die Gegner des Paulus im 2. Korintherbrief*
(WMANT 11), Neukirchen-Vluyn, 1964, 31–8; H. J. B. Combrink, *Die Diens van
Jesus. 'N Eksegetiese Beskouing oor Markus 10: 45*, Groningen, 1968, 39ff; K. Hess,
NIDNTT, III, 544–8; L. De Lorenzi, 'Paul "diákonos" du Christ et des Chrétiens',
Paul de Tarse, Apôtre du notre temps (ed. L. De Lorenzi), Rome, 1979, 399–454; J.
N. Collins, *DIAKONIA: Re-interpreting the Ancient Sources*, Oxford, 1990; R.
Bieringer, 'Paul's Understanding of Diakonia in 2 Corinthians 5, 18' in R. Bieringer
and J. Lambrecht, *Studies on 2 Corinthians* (BETL 112), Leuven, 1994, 413–28.

reference to Paul as apostle and in this he may be following Paul's own lead (see Best 'Authority').

The subject of the first aorist passive ἐγενήθην (a Doric and Hellenistic form; see BAGD s.v.; BDR §78 n. 2) is probably God implying that Paul did not appoint himself to his ministry. διάκονος is anarthrous and could be rendered *a* minister or *the* minister; the article can be omitted when a noun is followed by a genitive (οὗ functions as such here) without implying indefiniteness (cf 1.14; Rom 3.25, etc.; interestingly the usage occurs again at Mk 9.35 in relation to διάκονος; see MHT, 179); its occurrence in v. 7 may be due to Semitic influence (cf Moule, 117; E. C. Colwell, 'A Definite Rule for the Use of the Article in the Greek New Testament', *JBL* 52 (1933) 12–21, who suggests without giving examples that the usage is common in relative clauses).

Whether we translate *a* or *the* minister, the context does nothing to suggest that AE regards Paul as one among a number who have been given the ministry to the Gentiles. Yet it goes too far if, with Merklein, *Amt*, 222f, we understand 'minister of the gospel' as implying that Paul is not only its proclaimer but also its norm. If there is any suggesting here of Paul as more than the proclaimer of the Gospel it lies in his subordination to the Gospel; the latter is the norm and Paul must adhere to it.

κατὰ τὴν δωρεὰν[22] ... μοι (the string of genitives is typical of Ephesians) qualifies διάκονος making absolutely clear that whatever Paul is in relation to the Gentiles he is by the gift of God's grace (either noun would seem sufficient; the doubling up is typical of Ephesians; on the use of μοι for the reflexive pronoun see BDR §283.3). Most of v. 2 is repeated here. When God gives he is not simply conferring a benefit; the gift entails also a particular duty. τῆς χάριτος (see on v. 2 for the word) can be a genitive either of apposition or of object; the former is more appropriate if grace means 'saving grace'; the latter if it is viewed as denoting the equipment for a particular task. Here as in v. 2 it means the latter: the grace which calls to and empowers the recipient for a duty. Paul (cf 1 Cor 15.10), or AE, does not clearly distinguish, as systematic theologians do, between saving grace and the grace which equips for a special function. Paul's conversion (saving grace) and his call to minister to Gentiles (the 'grace' of our verse and of 3.2; Rom 1.5; 15.15f; 1 Cor 3.10; Gal 1.15f) were not two distinct events in either his eyes or those of his school, for it was on the Damascus Road that he was saved through grace and received grace to be the minister to the Gentiles (cf v. 8). The inseparability of 'saving grace' and missionary activity should be true not only for Paul but for all Christians.

[22] The gift is probably to be understood as a gift of the Spirit (cf 4.7) because it appears here in the context of ministry (cf J. D. G. Dunn, *ExpT* 81 (1969/70) 249–51, yet hardly to be made as precise as Grotius who explains it as the gift of tongues!).

The second κατά phrase does not parallel the first (*pace* Westcott, Beare) but depends on δοθείσης (the accusative, supported only by D² Ψ 1739 1881 𝔐, is the inferior reading but, if accepted, does not affect the meaning). The power is that of God. AE uses two nouns, ἐνέργεια, δύναμις; the same two appear in Col 1.29, but there is no need to see the influence of Colossians for AE had already used both nouns in 1.19 (for their meaning see notes there); the preposition probably denotes that Paul received the power appropriate to the ministry to which he was appointed. It is this power and not some inborn ability or talent which enables him to be the servant of the Gospel. Whether such a clear distinction can be made in actual practice is another matter; it was Paul's nature to be zealous, whether prior to his conversion in respect of the Law or the persecution of Christians, or after in respect of the Gentiles. God uses people with different talents, if not characters, in different ways. It is difficult then to say that the 'energy' with which Paul pursued his mission was simply and solely a matter of grace. Within Ephesians God's energy and power operate in relation to the resurrection and ascension of Christ (1.19f), the building up and sustenance of the church as his body (4.16), the prearrangement of affairs by his will (1.11), the transformation of believers (3.20). God's power is thus related to many issues and it would be wrong to restrict it here to one particular facet, e.g. the power of resurrection (so L. De Lorenzi, art.cit.). In so far as power is stressed it serves to lead into v. 8 and Paul's proclamation to the Gentiles.

8. A new sentence begins here and continues to the end of v. 12. In v. 8b the grace given to Paul is defined as that for preaching Christ to the Gentiles and that might suggest that v. 8a was parenthetical (so Westcott), but αὕτη by position points forward linking the two halves of the verse and the thought moves forward to the process of the proclaiming of the Gospel. This has three steps distinguished from one another in stating those to whom it is offered: the Gentiles (v. 8), all people (v. 9), the powers (vv. 9f).

In v. 8a AE stresses the great contrast between Paul missioner to the Gentiles and Paul prior to his conversion: 'it was precisely to me [μοι emphatic by position] *though* [Caragounis, 101] I was less than the least ...'.[23] While ἐλαχιστότερος, a comparative of a superlative, is logically impossible, it is, though unusual, a known grammatical formation (BDR §61.2; MHT, 31). Paul places himself below any (this is the significance of the omission of the article; MHT, 199f; BDR §275) Christian whom any reader may care to name. Is Paul then excluded from the number of the saints? The statement differs

---

[23] It is true that *paulus* in Latin means 'little' but it is unlikely that AE plays here (so Stott) on Paul's name; by no means all readers would know Latin and even for those who did a considerable imaginative jump would have been necessary to make the connection.

here from the apparently similar 1 Cor 15.9, 'I am the least of the apostles', in that: (i) We have the comparative of the superlative and not just a superlative. (ii) The comparison is made with all the saints and not with the apostles alone; there is no justification for taking ἁγίων with Gaugler and Conzelmann to refer to the apostles and prophets because it was applied to them as an adjective in v. 6, nor for omitting it with $\mathfrak{P}^{46}$; in the latter case 'all' would be undefined. (iii) 1 Cor 15.9 does not exclude Paul from the number of the apostles as v. 8 excludes him from the number of the saints. (iv) The 'grace' of 1 Cor 15.9f was the grace which saved Paul; that of v. 8 is the grace equipping him for his mission. If we can accept the illogical adjective there is no reason to see the phrase as excluding Paul from the saints. Since AE has spoken of the apostles in v. 5 and his point could have been made as easily by comparing Paul to them, we may assume that he is not indebted here to 1 Cor 15.9 but is using a tradition current in the Pauline school deriving from Paul himself which contrasted his pre-Christian and Christian existence; 1 Cor 15.9 is one expression of this; 1 Tim 1.15 confirms that the tradition existed. The Pauline school did not soften but intensified the tradition. The tradition may also have influenced Ignatius, *Trall* 13.1. However, the contrast between pre-conversion failure and post-conversion success is a familiar feature of Christian hagiography (Bouwman). Our discussion has assumed Paul was not the author of Ephesians, but in the light of 1 Cor 15.9 there can be no possible psychological objection to his penning Eph 3.8. Whether Paul is the author or not, the phrase serves to emphasise his humility.

AE does not specify in what way Paul regarded himself as 'less than the least', perhaps he assumed his readers knew. Despite 1 Tim 1.15 there is no hint in the major Pauline letters of an excessive consciousness on his part of sin. He does not hesitate to put himself forward as someone to be imitated (1 Th 1.6; 1 Cor 4.16; 11.1; 2 Th 3.7), he never seems to allow that his advice to his readers might be prejudiced, and he never exercises any self-criticism.[24] Probably AE assumes the same reason for what he writes about Paul as that underlying 1 Cor 15.9, Paul's pre-conversion persecution of Christians. The undisputed letters contain several references to this suggesting that sorrow at it was never far from his mind (1 Cor 15.9; Gal 1.13, 23; Phil 3.6; cf Acts 7.58; 9.1, 2). The total context of Ephesians may have strengthened the contrast between before and after conversion in that it relates to the Saul who persecuted *Jewish* Christians and the Paul who forced Jewish Christians to accept *Gentile* Christians as equals.

If v. 8a repeated briefly the thought of v. 7 in saying that Paul was

[24] For further detail see Best, *Converts*, 156–8.

given a gift in relation to the Gentiles, v. 8b goes further in referring to Paul's actual preaching to them (for the use of the infinitive after αὕτη cf Acts 15.28f; 1 Cor 7.37; 1 Th 4.3; Jas 1.27; and see BDR §394.1; MHT, 139). Preaching to the Gentiles (emphatic by position; ἐν, if read with D F G Ψ 33 1739 1881 𝔐 latt, will mean 'among') is not of course the only 'grace'; Paul would presumably have allowed that James, Peter and John had a 'grace' to preach to the Jews (Gal 2.7–9). Again AE fails to recognise that there were others prior to Paul, alongside Paul and since Paul who had or have a 'grace' to preach to the Gentiles; such was the tremendous impression Paul made on the early church (or on his own school?) that there was no place left for others, and AE did not expect the church to last for ever, leaving plenty of time for others.

When Paul uses εὐαγγελίζεσθαι he does not normally give it a direct object for in Christian parlance its object lies within itself. Where Paul does express a direct object it is the cognate noun (1 Cor 15.1; 2 Cor 11.7; Gal 1.11), Christ (Gal 1.16), the faith (Gal 1.23), the faith and love of others (1 Th 3.6), peace (Eph 2.17), and in an OT quotation 'good news' (Rom 10.15 = Isa 52.7). In most of these cases the context necessitates the expression of the object. Here in 3.8, in accordance with AE's verbose style, the object is expressed through a noun, πλοῦτος, a favourite of AE (1.7, 18; 2.7; 3.8, 16; see on 1.7), and a less usual adjective ἀνεξιχνίαστον.[25] The adjective is used of God's activity in the world (Job 5.9; 9.10; 34.24; Rom 11.33; cf 1 Clem 20.5); it is an extension of this usage that we find in Eph 3.8 (cf *Odes Sol* 12.6; *Prayer of Manasseh* 6; *Diog* 9.5) in that what is praised is God's mercy rather than his activity in creation. Although the word is known outside the Bible (BAGD *s.v.*) it is controlled here by its biblical usage (*pace* Peterson who sees it as partly derived from gnosticism). Implied in it are both the wonder of God's activity and the inability of the human mind, even after revelation, to deduce and plumb the depths of God. This accords with the earlier stress on revelation as leading to the admission of the Gentiles (vv. 2–6). The total phrase draws out the wonder of the good news. The riches are those of Christ, which are either those which he supplies, if so they would be those detailed elsewhere in the letter, or those which consist in Christ himself (so 1.7, 18; 2.7; 3.16); in view of usage elsewhere in the epistle the second alternative is preferable. AE uses the article here with Christ and may be deliberately emphasising Jesus as the Jewish Messiah in whose riches the Gentiles participate.

9. Grace has been given Paul not only for preaching the riches of

---

[25] On the word see E. Peterson, *TWNT*, I, 359f; R. E. Thomas. 'Ephesians iii.8', *ExpT* 39 (1927/8) 283; I. Mehlmann, "Ανεξιχνίαστος—investigabilis (Rom 11,-33; Eph 3, 8)', *Bib* 40 (1959) 902–14.

Christ (v. 8) but, καί, also (perhaps 'and so' or 'that means') 'to bring to light...' or 'to enlighten all ...'. Which translation is selected depends on the text read.

The alternative renderings correspond to the omission of πάντας with ℵ* A 6 1739 1881 *pc*; Ambst Aug, or its reading with 𝔓⁴⁶ ℵ² B C D F G Ψ 33 𝔐 latt sy co; Tert. In the NT φωτίζειν normally takes an object (1 Cor 4.5; 2 Tim 1.10 are exceptions) and since the context does not provide any obvious candidate and if none was originally present scribes may have inserted πάντας; if that had happened we would have expected to find a number of different insertions (cf Metzger, ad loc); αὐτούς would have been a suitable candidate referring back to 'Gentiles' in v. 8. If an object is read the connection with v. 10 becomes more difficult and so this is the *lectio difficilior*.

The translation 'bring to light' emphasises the revelation itself, though naturally there will be people, and possibly also the heavenly powers (v. 10), who are enlightened; the translation 'enlighten all' stresses those who are enlightened, though not excluding the content of the enlightenment. 'All' should probably be read (see above), though there can be little certainty about this and we shall also glance at the consequences if it is not read. If 'all' is read who are meant? Had AE been thinking only of the Gentiles he would have used the pronoun 'them'. Since the content of the mystery is the co-membership of Jews and Gentiles and these together form all humanity, it is better to give 'all' its widest sense, 'all people'. If enlightenment is taken to include redemption (cf 2 Cor 4.6) is this then a universalist statement? It appears like one, but since the reading is uncertain it would be wrong to press it. Moreover 'all' is not emphatic by position. In 1.18 where the same verb is used God was its subject; here it is Paul. In each case darkness symbolises the past state of unbelief, and light that of redemption. Those who have been enlightened are those who have been evangelised (v. 8; cf Heb 6.4; 10.32). Here however enlightenment lies closer to the imparting of knowledge, knowledge of God's plan. Gentile Christians needed to be evangelised and brought into the church; Jewish Christians were already in the church but needed enlightenment about God's plan just as much as Gentile Christians; this may be the reason for the change from the idea of evangelisation to that of enlightenment.

The content of what is brought to light or of the instruction given to all is ἡ οἰκονομία²⁶ τοῦ μυστηρίου. οἰκονομία (for the word see 1.9; 3.2) cannot refer here to Paul's stewardship, even if it does so in 3.2, but to the plan of God or the working out of that plan. It is the plan, of course, and not the mystery itself, in which all are

²⁶ The rendering 'fellowship' in the KJV comes from the Textus Receptus and lacks good support (see Metzger, ad loc).

instructed or on which light is thrown. That of course does not
mean that the mystery is not revealed (cf v. 3). The mystery (for the
word see on 1.9) is the same mystery as that of vv. 3f; v. 6 gives its
content, viz., the co-membership of Jews and Gentiles in the body
of Christ; it is not the mystery of 1.10, as Lindemann, *Aufhebung*,
222, supposes, though the latter may include the former. The
mystery is of course also related to Christ (v. 4). The arrangement
relating to the mystery, or its working out, is not discussed here in
detail, though Paul's part in it is brought out. The plan's accomplishment does not necessarily entail a long process beginning with
Abraham and running through Jewish history, a detailed *Heilsgeschichte*. The οἰκονομία may indeed only cover what has
happened in Christ but will include the place of Paul in its
accomplishment; this would make it accord more closely with 3.2.
Cosmic implications appear in v. 10.

The mystery has been hidden (ἀποκεκρυμμένου, perfect participle), up to the 'now' of v. 10, ἀπὸ τῶν αἰώνων. ἀπό could be taken
either temporally (hidden during periods of time; so Gnilka; Barth;
Mussner, *Christus*, 25f; Gaugler; Schnackenburg; Lincoln) or
spatially (hidden away from personal beings; so Schlier; Dibelius;
Steinmetz, 63; Lindemann, *Aufhebung*, 223). The latter sense,
though less usual, is found in the LXX (4 Kgdms 4.27; Ψ 118.19;
Isa 40.27; Jer 39(32).17) and in the NT (Lk 10.21; cf Hermas, *Sim*
9.11.7; see BDR §155.3, n. 3; MH, 460ff). The 'now' of v. 10
suggests a temporal contrast, implying a temporal understanding of
the preposition. Linked to the understanding of ἀπό is that of
αἰώνων, a word also having temporal and personal significance (see
on vv. 2, 7). The plural provides no reason for rejecting the
temporal meaning as we see from Lk 1.33; Rom 9.5; 11.36; Gal
1.5; Phil 4.20. Since, however, v. 10 refers to the heavenly powers
perhaps the personal meaning should be adopted, the personal
beings would then be the powers mentioned there; yet why are
similar words not used in the two verses or v. 10 run 'be made
known to *them*'? The two meanings are in fact not unrelated, for if
the aeons are personal beings we must ask when was the plan
hidden from them and if they are periods of time we must ask from
whom the plan was hidden.[27]

Though v. 9 has seven words in common with Col 1.26, an
unusually high number (cf Mitton, *Epistle*, 56), there is no reason to
see dependence on AE's part (see above).

Marcion (Tertullian, *adv Marc* 5.18) gave a very different answer to the

---

[27] R. McL. Wilson, 'The *Trimorphic Protennoia*', *Gnosis and Gnosticism* (ed. M.
Krause), Leiden, 1977, 50–4, points out, p. 54, n. 2, that at XIII' 1 44.31–3 Eph 3.9
appears to have been given a temporal sense by the gnostic writers of the treatise.

question about those from whom the plan of the mystery was hidden; omitting ἐν (as also in ℵ* 614) before τῷ θεῷ he said the secret was hidden from the God of the OT. If ἐν is read, 'in God' indicates where the plan of the mystery was hidden, suggesting that God was the one who did the hiding. Support for the addition at the end of the verse of διὰ Ἰησοῦ Χριστοῦ in D² (⁵0278) 1881 𝔐 syʰ** is weak (see Metzger, ad loc).

The God who has hidden within himself (ἐν τῷ θεῷ), or possibly, 'hidden by him', the plan of the mystery is finally defined as τῷ τὰ πάντα κτίσαντι. This is a little surprising since AE's interest, unlike that of Colossians, lies in the second creation rather than the first. How is the phrase to be accounted for? (a) It could be the use of a familiar liturgical phrase. The praise of God as the creator of all things was widespread in contemporary Judaism (e.g. Wisd 1.14; Ecclus 24.8; *3 Macc* 2.3; Esth 4.17c: Jth 13.18; 1QH 1.13f; 16.8; 1QM 10.8f; *1 En* 9.5; 81.3; *Jub* 7.36) and was accepted into Christianity (Acts 14.15; Col 1.16; Rev 4.11; *Did* 10.3; 1 Clem 33.2–6; Hermas, *Mand* 1.1; *Sim* 5.5.2);[28] AE would hardly have used this liturgical phrase without thought, for it is not the way he writes; he may add synonym to synonym but here we have the introduction of a fresh idea. (b) The divorce between creation and redemption became a common theme in some gnostic circles in the second century; Schlier therefore argues that AE introduced the reference to creation to ensure its link with redemption. Schlier's references are drawn from the second century and we cannot be certain that this tendency existed in the first (Barth, Bruce). But even granted it did, the phrase in v. 9 would be a roundabout way of countering it, and if AE had been concerned about such a possible divorce we should expect more evidence elsewhere in the letter. (c) The view of Beare that the plan of the mystery is inherent in creation must be dismissed as fanciful; nothing else in the letter supports it and much attaches 'mystery' to Christ rather than to creation. For AE creation is not perfect; otherwise it would not require reconciliation as 1.9f indicates (cf Gnilka); if it is not perfect any inbuilt secret plan would be imperfect. (d) More probable than any of these is the view that the phrase is intended to place the time when the plan was hidden as prior to creation; it was no afterthought but part of God's intention from the beginning. In that way it accords with AE's emphasis on God's foresight and predestination (1.4, 5, 12). Creation and redemption are in the final issue the result of the work of the one God; the presence of this idea does not necessarily imply a polemic against a proto-gnosticism or proto-Marcionism. The plan of God built into the first creation is now realised in the church, the second creation (Ernst). (e) It is

---

[28] Cf Bousset-Gressman, 358–60.

possible there may also be a forward reference: God as creator is sovereign over all including the powers (v. 10).

10. God's final purpose (it is unlikely that ἵνα indicates consequence) in endowing Paul with grace is that the manifold wisdom of God may now[29] be made known to the heavenly powers. This brings us back to the cosmic scope of 1.10. Our verse partially parallels v. 7, but now it is not Paul who is the proclaimer of the Gospel but the church. Nothing in the preceding discussion from as far back as 2.11 has prepared us for this reference (cf Wink, *Naming*, 93) or indeed for that to wisdom (Schnackenburg). But there is much to suggest that Paul and his school knew Jewish wisdom speculation and were aware of the opposition to humanity of the heavenly powers. Verse 10 is not dependent on κτίσαντι, since this is only a subordinate participle and such dependence would suggest that God created the powers in order to make his wisdom known to them; neither is v. 10 dependent on ἀποκεκρυμμένου (Belser), for this would imply that God hid the plan of his mystery so that his wisdom should be made known to the powers. The contrast is between 'hidden and then revealed' and not between 'hidden so as to be revealed'. Verse 10 depends on ἐδόθη: the proclamation to the Gentiles (v. 8) and the instruction of all in the plan of the mystery leads to the wisdom of God being made known through the church to the powers. It is God's plan to reconcile Jews and Gentiles in one body, the church, and so provide the powers with knowledge of his desire to win them (cf Lincoln, *Paradise*, 187).

The powers (for these see on 1.21) are those 'in the heavenlies' (see Detached Notes: The Heavenlies, The Powers);[30] ἐν τοῖς ἐπουρανίοις qualifies them and not γνωρισθῇ; although the article might have been expected ταῖς ἐν τοῖς ..., the verb is relatively remote and the article is not necessary (Abbott gives examples). As we saw earlier, the reference is to 'hostile' powers or angelic beings. Were friendly supernatural beings intended, as Carr, *Paradise*, 98ff, suggests, it is not clear why God required to make his wisdom known to them; 1 Pet 1.12 (cf 1 Tim 3.16; *1 En* 16.3; *2 En* 24.3) has been adduced to support such a view and Mk 13.32 may suggest that angels do not possess all knowledge. However in Lk 15.7 angels are said to rejoice when sinners repent, thereby indicating another stream of tradition in which they understand God's way of salvation (cf 1 Cor 4.9; *Jub* 4.15, 21, 22). If God

---

[29] F G 629 lat sy^P; Tert MVict omit νῦν which would remove the historical reference; support for the omission is weak.

[30] The phrase can hardly mean 'among the heavenly beings' (M. Goguel, *Introduction du nouveau Testament*, IV, 2, Paris, 1920, 441, n. 1), for then we should expect ἐν ταῖς ...

makes his wisdom known to hostile angels, it can be assumed he
makes it known to good angels, but do the latter need to wait for
that knowledge until the church has come into existence?
It is God's wisdom[31] which is made known to the heavenly
powers. We might have expected his grace, or the lordship of Christ
as in Phil 2.9–11 (cf v. 11 here), or salvation to be revealed, but it
is wisdom; this follows appropriately after the many terms denoting
revelation in 3.2–13. In 1 Cor 1.18ff God's wisdom is related to the
cross, and this relationship lies in the background here for the
revelation which is disclosed is that of the reconciliation of Jews
and Gentiles and the basis for this is the cross (2.14–22). Wisdom
is not a simple concept capable of being expressed in a brief
statement, but a complex idea with many aspects. AE will have
been influenced in his understanding of it chiefly by the existing
Jewish Wisdom literature reaching him, if he was not born a Jew,
by way of early Christianity. Jewish thinking on wisdom had of
course been affected by non-Jewish ideas and AE's understanding
may also have been affected by contemporary non-Jewish, non-
Christian ideas, for example those of gnosis. AE however says so
little about wisdom (1.8, 17; 3.10) that it is difficult to discern
outside influences. At 1.8, 17 wisdom is set in parallel with other
terms and is not personified or made into a hypostasis as sometimes
in Judaism; nothing then leads us in 1.8, 17 to discern the presence
of a wisdom myth, and the same is true of 5.15. That the myth has
not affected the use of wisdom in those places cannot be taken as an
argument that this has not happened in 3.10 provided other good
grounds exist for suspecting such an influence. But the evidence
offered by Schlier (159–66) is remote and late. When wisdom is
personified in the Wisdom literature it is presented as active; in
3.10 it is conceived as passive, for it does not make itself known to
the heavenly powers but is made known (cf Gnilka); it is not the
revealer but the revealed. As such it is described by the infrequent
adjective πολυποίκιλος; ποικίλος already expresses the idea of

[31] On the use of the term wisdom in this passage see Schlier, *Christus*, 60–5; N. A.
Dahl, 'Das Geheimnis der Kirche nach Eph. 3, 8–10', *Zur Auferbauung des Leibes
Christi* (FS P. Brunner, ed. E. Schlink and A. Peters), Kassel, 1965, 63–75; Barth,
355f; S. Cipriani, '"Sapienza" e "Legge" in Colossesi ed Efesini', *RivBiblt* 35
(1987) 283–98. More generally on wisdom see U. Wilckens and G. Fohrer, *TWNT*,
VII, 465ff; G. von Rad, *Wisdom in Israel*, London, 1972; G. C. Stead, 'The
Valentinian Myth of Sophia', *JTS* 20 (1969) 75–104; G. W. MacRae, 'The Jewish
Background of the Gnostic Sophia Myth', *NT* 12 (1970) 86–101; *Israelite Wisdom*
(FS Samuel Terrien, ed. J. G. Gammie, W. A. Brueggemann, W. L. Humphreys, J. M.
Ward), Missoula, Montana, 1978; *Studies in Ancient Israelite Wisdom* (ed. J. L.
Crenshaw), New York, 1976; *Aspects of Wisdom in Judaism and Early Christianity*
(ed. R. L. Wilken), Notre Dame and London, 1975; J. D. G. Dunn, *Christology in the
Making*, London, 1980, 163–212; R. E. Murphy, *The Tree of Life: An Exploration of
Biblical Wisdom Literature*, New York, 1990.

variety and the addition of πολύς simply serves to emphasise this and is in line with the richness of AE's language (cf Percy, 187; Van Roon, 164, 185).[32]

3.9f connect mystery and wisdom,[33] a connection already made in 1 Cor 2.6–8 (cf 1QS 4.18) where there are also references to 'hiddenness' and the 'powers', if οἱ ἄρχοντες refers to the latter. In Eph 3.9 the mystery is hidden; in 1 Cor 2.7 it is the wisdom of God; yet since in 3.10 the wisdom is to be made known to the powers it can be assumed that it was previously hidden from them, and, in the light of 1.17, probably also from the readers. A similar connection of ideas exists in Col 1.27f; 2.2f, where the mystery is related both to the Gentiles and Christ. In 1 Cor 1.24 wisdom and Christ are equated. Since then the Gentiles are acceptable because of what Christ has done, we may suspect that the mystery in 3.9 also relates to him, but neither it nor wisdom is explicitly identified with him; indeed the adjective πολυποίκιλος would be odd as applied to Christ. V. 10 does not then directly equate Christ and wisdom. The 'hiddenness' of wisdom is a theme in Jewish wisdom teaching (e.g. Job 28.12–28; Bar 3.14ff; 2 Bar 14.9; 48.36). Yet wisdom is not necessarily hidden, for she is known to those who love God (Ecclus 1.10) and is found in Israel (Ecclus 24.8–23; Bar 3.9–4.4) dwelling with the righteous (Ecclus 4.18; 14.20–15.8; 51.13–30; Wisd 7.27f). People do not discover wisdom; it is beyond their understanding (Job 28.12ff; Ecclus 1.1–6; Wisd 9.13ff) and must be disclosed to them; so here wisdom is made known to the powers. It is normally God who discloses wisdom; in 3.10 he is said to do this through the church. In the immediate context wisdom is related to the co-membership of Gentiles with Jews in the church, but in itself wisdom cannot be restricted in this way. Yet v. 10 does not permit the view that a wider revelation of wisdom is disclosed to the powers; that it is made known to them through the church appears to restrict their knowledge to this one aspect.

God's wisdom has now been made known, γνωρισθῇ; the aorist suggests a single action rather than a continuous process of slow revelation. When was wisdom made known? Because this is related to the church it must be since the church came into existence, and, since the church is the church of Jewish and Gentile Christians, it must be since the cross and resurrection of Christ. Yet there is nothing to suggest that the making known belongs to the future, a disclosure at the end of time. The νῦν is the 'now' of the church, and the moment of making known belongs to the past of AE. It would be wrong to imagine a three-stage process in which Paul

---

[32] On the adjective see H. Seesemann, TWNT, VI, 483f; Reynier, 158–60. The Vulgate rendering multiformis misunderstands the word.
[33] Gos Truth, 1, 3 18.11–19 appears to reflect knowledge of 3.9f.

preaches, Jews and Gentiles come together to form the church and, after it has grown to a certain size, God's wisdom is revealed to the powers. There is a time of hiddenness, the period prior to Christ or to his ascension, and then, 'now', a period of disclosure, the period of the apostles, prophets and Paul.[34]

But how is God's wisdom made known to the powers through the church? Did Christ make it known when he ascended into the heavenlies, or, possibly, when he descended into Hades, as some interpretations of 1 Pet 3.19; 4.6 might suggest? Since believers are already in the heavenlies (2.6) the church must also be there; the church can thus be an appropriate vehicle for the disclosure of God's wisdom to the powers since they also are in the heavenlies. In addition the church has some continuity with Israel and wisdom has a special relationship with Israel (Ecclus 24.8, 23; Bar 3.22f). Finally wisdom has already been disclosed to the church (1.8, 17; 3.2ff; cf Roels, 169). That good angels know what happens on earth is seen in passages like 1 Pet 1.12; Lk 15.7; it is then possible to conceive of the evil powers as also aware of the church; if they are involved in the warfare of 6.10ff this must be so.

In 1 Cor 2.8 Paul says the powers would not have crucified Christ if they had known who he was; that ignorance belonged to the period prior to his death, prior then also to the period of the church; so there is no inconsistency if they have now come to spiritual knowledge. The church is of course not here a particular local community, which might have been so if Ephesians had been written to a single congregation; it is the whole church, the body of Christ. Whereas vv. 8f spoke of Paul's missionary activity, v. 10 does not suggest any activity on the part of the church, for example, that it taught the powers. It is the very existence of the church, the church of Jews and Gentiles in which there is no division, that discloses the wisdom of God to them. This idea is close to that of Jn 17.21 where the world is saved when it sees believers are one. If the division between Jews and Gentiles was due to the activity of the powers its removal would speak to them.[35] Descriptions of the church as God's theatre (Bengel), or attempts to say how the church proclaims the wisdom of God (Barth), or depict the church as preaching to the angels of the Gentile nations (Wink, *Naming*, 89–96) are thus beside the point. The church has a heavenly and an

---

[34] Lindemann, *Aufhebung*, 221ff, sees both parallelism and difference between 3.9f and 3.2ff, the former being cosmologically and mythologically determined, the latter ecclesially and historically. He is only able to make this distinction because he omits 'all' in v. 9, takes the aeons there to refer to the powers and dissociates vv. 9f from v. 8. While there may be cosmological and mythological elements in vv. 9f, if 'all' is read and v. 8 is taken into account, the historical cannot be eliminated.

[35] See P. S. Minear, 'The Vocation to Invisible Powers: Ephesians 3:8–10' in his *To Die and to Live*, New York, 1977, 89–100.

earthly dimension; the former is indicated when it is termed the body of Christ or his bride and he its angle-stone.

While AE may stress that wisdom is made known to the powers because some may have thought, as the Colossian heretics may have, that the powers mediated wisdom to the church,[36] this does not fully explain the significance of wisdom being made known to them. The significance will in part depend on how the powers are understood. If these in their control of the universe represent its 'meaninglessness' (Gnilka), then wisdom reveals to them, and of course to the universe, the divine meaning of the universe. If the powers are the influences which lie behind and order world history (Schlier), then wisdom reveals the divine purpose of history. If the powers represent the social, cultural and religious forces, the earthly institutions which control human lives, then these 'are given a unique chance by God: they are entitled to see in their midst the beginning of a new heaven and a new earth' (Barth, 365). If the powers are the 'spiritual environment' in which people live and in which forces compete to control them, then we are assured that 'even such structures of power and authority as the secular state are capable of being brought into harmony with the love of God' (Caird). If the powers are primarily responsible for human religious errors, wisdom needs to be revealed to them so that their erroneous teaching may no longer affect people (Hugedé, 112, n. 56). If the powers are taken to be the rulers of 1 Cor 2.8 who crucified the Lord of glory, their great error is now brought home to them (Scott), but whether this results in their reconciliation or destruction is not made clear. If the powers are those which control the Gentiles, then by the formation of a church containing both Jews and Gentiles their stranglehold is broken; the existence of the church reveals to them their failure (Mussner, *Christus*, 21f). There is a reversal then of what would have been expected: it is not the stars or the heavenly powers which control human life but human life, represented as the church, which controls or will control the powers.

None of this makes clear whether, when the powers come to know the wisdom of God, this means they have been or will be saved. Will they have lost their ability to harm humanity? Within Jewish Wisdom literature those who know wisdom are those who are faithful to God. To learn wisdom is not to be supplied with a selection of interesting information; the powers do not then learn a little more about how the world works but are given a way of life; to know wisdom is to live in that way. The reconciliation of Jews and Gentiles in the church is a kind of pilot scheme for a much greater reconciliation in which the powers will in turn be embraced

---

[36] Cf M. Turner, 'Mission', 147.

(cf Bruce). This suggests that when the wisdom of God, and note it is not human wisdom, is made known to the powers their response will be positive. Yet in 6.12 they are still hostile to the members of the church; in 1.22 Christ is their head to whom they are made subject, not someone with whom they are reconciled. On the other hand in 1.10 there is a summing up of all things in Christ, and the powers must be included among 'all things'. There are two inconsistencies here: (i) Can the powers still be active if they have been defeated in Christ's death, resurrection and ascension? This is an inconsistency which seems to belong to the fabric of NT Christianity, paralleling the idea of the Kingdom of God as both realised and yet to come. (ii) The second inconsistency arises out of the way God is conceived: does he overcome cosmic evil by destroying it or by winning it to himself in love (Col 1.20)?

We have seen above how various scholars have reinterpreted the powers and so understood v. 10. If the powers do not exist, they cannot be demythologised and to speak of the disclosure to them of God's wisdom is meaningless. Our passage began with the disclosure to Paul of the mystery; it ends with the winning of the cosmos, and so his mission is given a cosmic dimension (Sullivan, art.cit.). His position, which at the start seemed to be unique as the one who first brought salvation to the Gentiles, is now seen as unique because it relates to the salvation, or destruction, of the cosmos.

11. God is the subject of ἐποίησεν and also the real subject of κατὰ πρόθεσιν.[37] τῶν αἰώνων could be the subject of the latter if the aeons are personal beings (so Schlier; Lindemann, *Aufhebung*, 228; Steinmetz, 64f) but this would imply that they themselves determined that at some date the mystery should be disclosed to them! We have already rejected a personal meaning for the aeons in v. 9, and it is highly probable that the words have the same sense here as there. Had personal beings been intended a pronoun would probably have been used 'according to their intention' (referring back to v. 10), or one or both of the words for the powers in v. 10 would have been repeated here. The aeons are then periods of time inhabited by personal beings. This leaves a wide range of possible meanings. The genitive might be adjectival (a Semitism? cf BDR §165.1) and equivalent to 'eternal' (Bouttier) and governed by a continued προ from the noun (Sellin, who sees the influence of 1.9, 11), or, disregarding the influence of the preposition, 'for the ages' (Ewald, Barth), 'belonging to the ages' (Haupt) or 'continuing through the ages' (Robinson, Gnilka, Scott). The third and fourth of these are purely temporal; the second is not out of accord with the

---

[37] Clem Alex reads πρόγνωσιν. Chrysostom has the normal reading but understands it in the sense 'foreknowledge'; this provides no reason for the acceptance of Clement's reading.

meaning we have given to the aeons, and the reference is then to God's purpose for the ages and what fills them. Yet probably the first, eternal, is most suitable.

How is ἐποίησεν to be understood? (a) 'according to the purpose ... which he made, resolved' (Ewald, Conzelmann, Barth, Schnackenburg); (b) 'according to the purpose ... which he accomplished' (Haupt, Abbott, Schlier, Gnilka, Lincoln). If (b) is intended ποιεῖν is a rather colourless word; ἐπιτελεῖν or a compound of πληροῦν would have been more suitable. The phrase ποιεῖν τὸ θέλημα, often adduced as a parallel, is not a true parallel since in it the 'will' to be accomplished is that of someone else. Accepting then (a) it is necessary to ask how much of what is referred to earlier in the passage is to be regarded as lying within God's purpose. Certainly v. 10. Yet is the grace given to Paul for his ministry not also to be included? What also about the period during which the plan or mystery was hidden? The structure of the sentence suggests we do not go back beyond v. 8 but also suggests that there is no need to limit God's intention to v. 10. If it was his purpose to make his wisdom known to the powers, he achieved this through the church and vv. 8, 9 show how his grace (how does this differ from his intention?) brought the church into being through Paul. It is impossible then to limit God's intention to v. 10; vv. 8, 9 must also be brought in. It is then easier to say that what they describe lay always in God's plan. This fits with the way we have taken the initial phrase of the verse. That in much Jewish teaching wisdom was regarded as eternal makes it easier to accept this, and perhaps to see here another factor which led AE to introduce wisdom. We should note the unique position that all this gives to Paul whom, unlike the apostles and prophets, AE brings into the centre of God's intention.

God made his purpose known 'in Christ Jesus our Lord', thus giving his purpose a christological orientation. The threefold title, Christ, Jesus, Lord, is found elsewhere in varying forms in the address (1.2) and final greetings (6.23f), at the beginning of the eulogy (1.3) and the renewal of prayer (1.17), and in the thanksgiving of 5.20. It is thus used at solemn and liturgical moments. Its use here is then deliberate and emphatic and not simply evidence of AE's prolixity. This probably implies also that we should not seek a particular reference in each of the titles to what preceded or will follow, in particular that the name 'Jesus' implies an allusion to the incarnation. Significance may however lie in the one point at which the use of the three titles differs from the other instances in that Christ is placed first with the definite article. This could be a deliberate messianic reference, for the divine intention included the history of the people from whom the Messiah came. It is through the Messiah that Jew and Gentile are united in one body and that wisdom is proclaimed even to the powers. Apart from this a strong strand of early christological thought connected Christ with wisdom and understood him in its terms.

12. The Christ in whom God made his purpose known is *our* Lord and AE now returns from cosmic speculation to his readers (cf v. 1), using the first plural as at the end of v. 11, and not the second, because he and his readers, or Jews and Gentiles if that is the distinction, stand in the same relation to God's grace. The redemption and reconciliation of believers takes place through the same Christ as the one through whom God's purpose was made known to the aeons. The significance of redemption (ἔχομεν, present tense) for believers is now spelt out.

παρρησία,[38] originally relating to behaviour towards others and indicating the democratic freedom to speak out an opinion, came in Jewish Greek to be used also of freedom to speak to God. While people may have an inherent or democratic right to address others and express their opinion, it is only through Christ (note the emphatic double reference, ἐν ᾧ, αὐτοῦ) that they gain the right to speak without fear to God. Without Christ they may shout rashly at him and go unheard but with Christ believers may speak boldly knowing that they will be heard. We cannot accept van Unnik's argument (art.cit., 277) that the reference here is to the preaching of the Gospel, though this may be the meaning in 6.19f. Believers have access, προσαγωγή (see on 2.18 for the word), to God; the two nouns παρρησία and προσαγωγή have a single article and probably form a hendiadys, 'boldness to enter' (Bratcher and Nida). The idea comes in appropriately here because in v.14 the thought moves on to access to God in prayer. Believers may enter the door of prayer with confidence, ἐν πεποιθήσει[39] (only elsewhere in the NT in Paul, 2 Cor 1.15; 3.4; 8.22; 10.2; Phil 3.4), sure that they will receive an audience. Their confidence is increased because they are already in the heavenlies (2.6) and together form the temple in which God dwells (2.19–22). AE had previously used προσαγωγή in 2.18 (see there for its meaning) and we need not see dependence here on Rom 5.2; in Rom 5.2 the access is to grace and not God and it is not certain whether πίστις should be read. ἐν πεποιθήσει qualifies only προσαγωγή for παρρησία contains within itself the element of confidence. The positive reference to confidence is necessary since access of itself does not give confidence; the guilty prisoner is given

---

[38] For the word see H. Schlier, *TWNT*, V, 869–84; W. C. van Unnik, 'The Christian's Freedom of Speech in the New Testament' and 'The Semitic Background of παρρησία in the New Testament', in his *Sparsa Collecta*, II (SupNT 30), Leiden, 1980, 269–89, 290–306; S. B. Marrow, 'Parrhēsia and the New Testament', *CBQ* 44 (1982) 431–46.

[39] The variant τῷ ἐλευθερωθῆναι of D* may, as Barth says, be a good interpretation but it is not original.

access to the judge when brought before ·him but he wishes he was not there for he lacks confidence in the procedure. Christians however approach God without anxiety, not because of clear consciences or past good behaviour, but because of Christ. The three nouns afford another example of AE's love of approximate synonyms (Percy, 186); note also the play on the initial π. The theme of confident access to God appears regularly towards the end of the first century (Heb 4.16; 1 Pet 3.18; 1 Clem 2.3; 35.2). Within the Pauline writings access to God depends on faith, but faith is not however mentioned so regularly in the later writings. In Ephesians, in line with the undoubted Paulines, salvation comes through faith (2.8) resulting not only in an objective status giving access to God but also in an inner attitude, a bold and free approach.

It is possible that in v. 12 the faith is not that of believers but of Christ,[40] αὐτοῦ being taken as a possessive and not an objective genitive. Both usages appear in Paul, the latter being the more frequent. In Eph 1.15; Col 1.4 the object of faith is expressed by ἐν and at Col 2.5 by εἰς; other instances relating to the personal faith of believers may have no object stated (Eph 2.8; 3.17; 6.16, 23; Col 1.23). If in 3.12 αὐτοῦ is an objective genitive it is strictly unnecessary, since in the light of the ἐν ᾧ an undefined faith would be taken as having Christ as object. In defence of the objective meaning it is sometimes argued that αὐτοῦ may be a redundant pronoun in Semitic fashion, but can we be so sure of Semitic influence? Unfortunately we do not have enough evidence elsewhere in the letter to enable us to reach a firm decision on usage, and any conclusion can at best be only probable.

13. αἰτοῦμαι lacks an object and ἐγκακεῖν[41] a subject; both must be supplied from the context. The three most probable solutions, all grammatically possible, would result in the following renderings: (i) I pray God that I may not lose heart in my trials (thus many of the Fathers, but not many modern commentators apart from Grosheide and Dibelius); (ii) I pray God that you may not lose heart because of my trials; (iii) I beg you not to lose heart because of my trials. (i) Since in v. 13 AE has spoken of access to God and in vv. 14ff offers a prayer it is natural to take v. 13 as a prayer with διό referring back to v. 12. The infinitive has then the same subject as the main verb. If this is the correct rendering, μου is not strictly necessary, and if v. 13 is a prayer and is followed by another in vv. 14ff, we should expect v. 14 to begin with καί. When elsewhere Paul speaks of his

---

[40] For discussion of the significance of the genitive 'of Christ' in the Pauline corpus see G. Howard, 'The Faith of Christ', *ExpT* 85 (1973/4) 212–15; M. D. Hooker, ΠΙΣΤΙΣ ΧΡΙΣΤΟΥ, *NTS* 35 (1989) 321–42; R. B. Hays, *The Faith of Jesus Christ* (SBLDS 56), Chico, CA, 1987.

[41] The variant spelling ἐκκακεῖν is not strongly supported (C D² F G Ψ 0278 1739 1881 𝔐); its acceptance would not change the meaning (see LSJ).

sufferings he does not envisage the possibility of despair but rejoices in them (Rom 5.3; 2 Cor 12.10; Col 1.14); if Paul is not the author but someone is writing in his name that person would hardly present his hero as subject to despondency. The final clause of the verse is strongly positive in tone and would be considerably weakened if Paul is supposed to be in danger of despair. Paul's personal feelings do not surface elsewhere in the letter in distinction from most of his others; 6.21f is a possible exception but in it there is no suggestion of his losing heart. (ii) Because this solution would entail the introduction of a different object for the main verb from that of the subject of the infinitive, it is grammatically the most complex and therefore the least likely; it also remains subject to many of the difficulties of the first solution. (iii) This is the most satisfactory and provides the smoothest transition to the final clause.[42] The readers are in greater danger of losing heart than Paul. αἰτοῦμαι (the middle need not have a reflexive significance but can mean the same as the active, see LSJ) is a general word and not confined to religious usage. AE's readers know of Paul's imprisonment and they might be afraid that they would also be imprisoned or might believe that God was no longer using Paul as his minister (in 2 Corinthians Paul defends himself against such ideas). If this is the true solution διό links back not only to v. 12 but to the whole preceding argument about Paul's place in God's economy of salvation, at the same time picking up the reference in v. 1 to his imprisonment. The readers are encouraged to believe that whatever befalls them should not lead to despair.

θλίψεις refers to Paul's imprisonment; for the word see H. Schlier, TWNT, III, 139–48; the ἐν is that of attendant circumstances, Robertson, 588f. If in 1 Th 3.3, 4, 7 the word carries strong eschatological overtones relating to the messianic woes, these are absent here even though Paul's tribulations have a wider context than his own life; they are on behalf of his readers, ὑπὲρ ὑμῶν (cf v. 1). His imprisonment is neither personal tragedy nor personal victory; it is the result of what he had done in making known the salvation of God for the Gentiles. The connection with his readers is made more precise in the final clause of the verse, although it was already present in the use of ὑπέρ with its soteriological connections (cf Mk 14.24; Rom 5.8; 8.32). ἥτις[43] (assimilated to δόξα; cf BDR §132 n. 1; Robertson, 729) refers back to θλίψεσιν and not to the verb and may be given a slightly stronger sense, 'seeing that', than ἥ and so in effect supply a further reason for not losing heart. Several places in the Pauline corpus relate his sufferings to the good of his

---

[42] Robinson supports it by supposing that an original ὑμᾶς was lost through homoioteleuton with the last letters of the verb.

[43] The variant ἥ τίς is poorly supported (1175 1881) and may be ignored.

converts; in these he depicts himself, or is depicted, as suffering representatively (2 Cor 1.6; 4.12; 12.15; Col 1.24; 2 Tim 2.10). Representative suffering and suffering for the benefit of others are familiar phenomena, for example, a parent for a child; both ideas were known and accepted in the ancient world.[44] Col 1.24 might be thought to be the source for our verse[45] were not its language so different: there is no apparent reason for the change from πάθημα to θλῖψις and v. 13b has certainly not been derived from Col 1.24. A more probable source is the type of thinking found in the Corinthian letters. Paul and his fellow Christians belong together in the body of Christ; what affects one affects all; if one suffers all suffer (1 Cor 12.26); but also if one suffers others are strengthened in their faith (cf Best, *Converts*, 125–37), and some may indeed be converted (the blood of the martyrs is the seed of the church).

In 2 Cor 1.6 Paul's sufferings are for the encouragement and salvation of his readers, in 4.12 they bring life to them, and in 12.15 his life is spent on behalf of their lives. We might then have expected AE to write here 'which are for your strengthening' or even 'for your salvation'. Instead he refers to glory. This is a variant of the theme, for the 'life' in question is not physical or psychic life but eternal life, the life which is associated with glory (1.18; Col 1.27). In Rom 8.17f; 2 Cor 4.17 Paul connects his suffering to his own glory. All this suggests that the connection of his suffering with the glory of others is within the range of his thought, and does not require the supposition that AE is not Paul, though it naturally does not imply he is; if AE is not Paul all he has done is to take up a Pauline theme and develop it. The clause does not mean that the readers are to give glory to Paul or to boast about him, and AE is not setting Paul in the place of Christ as redeemer, for too much in the letter indicates the unique position he gives to Christ (1.3–11; 2.5f, 12–16; 5.2, 25f) for that to be true. We have now come full circle back to 3.1 (a kind of *inclusio*); we are therefore ready to move on to the next stage, the prayer of 3.14ff.

Throughout 3.1–13 Paul is given a unique position, for a mystery once revealed never needs to be revealed again. Can however the suffering of any Christian bring glory to other Christians? While Paul at times gives himself a position different from that of others in the church, he also recognises his equality with them; he terms them

---

[44] See M. Hengel, *The Atonement. The Origin of the Doctrine in the New Testament*, London, 1981, 9ff; S. K. Williams, *Jesus' Death as Saving Event. The Background and Origin of a Concept*, Missoula, MT, 1975, 153–61. 𝔓⁴⁶ 0278* 81* *pc* bo^{ms} avoid all seeming theological difficulty by reading ἡμῶν for ὑμῶν.

[45] Cf G. H. P. Thompson, 'Ephesians iii.13 and 2 Timothy ii.10 in the light of Colossians i.24', *ExpT* 71 (1960) 187–9; J. P. Bonafont, 'Teologia del Sagrado Corazon en la Epistola a los Efesios (I–III)', *Miscalana Comillas* 53 (1970), 75–126, at 96–108.

his brothers and with them is a member of the one body of Christ. Just as he refreshes them so they refresh him (Philem 20); in 1 Th 3.8 he says that he will live if they stand firm, and living does not mean merely going on existing but living in Christ. When the Philippians support him with money, it is their love flowing to him (Phil 4.15–17) and their prayers help in respect of his salvation (1.19). If this reciprocity is present in Paul's own writings it is not clear that AE takes the same view. We cannot really know how AE would answer our initial question, but we may be reasonably sure that Paul would have said that when any Christian suffers in the ministry of Christ he may bring glory to others.

VII

INTERCESSION AND DOXOLOGY
(3.14–21)

Percy, 302–12; Dupont, *Gnosis*, 471–528; Mitton, *Epistle*, 236–9; Mussner, *Christus*, 71–4; G. T. Montague, *Growth in Christ*, Kirkwood, MO, 1961, 96–112; P. Dacquino, 'Preghiera di S. Paolo per la perseveranza dei suoi cristiani', *BeO* 5 (1963) 41–6; C. Spicq, *Agape in the New Testament*, St Louis, MO, 1968, II, 258–68; Roels, 173–9; A. Feuillet, *Le Christ, Sagesse de Dieu*, Paris, 1966, 292–317; Ernst, *Pleroma*, 120–35; J. Plo Bonafont, 'Teologia del sagrado corazon en la Epistola a los Efesios (I–III)', *Miscelana Comillas* 53 (1970) 75–126 at 81–92; Caragounis, 74–7; P. D. Overfield, *Ascension*, 203–12; Usami, 166–80; Adai, 86–103; Lemmer, 158–63, 304–24; Arnold, 85–102.

14 For this reason I bow my knees to the Father,
15   from whom is named every (social) grouping
            in heaven and on earth,
16   that he may give you
            in accordance with the riches of his glory
         to be strengthened mightily by means of the Spirit,
            directed towards the inner person,
17   (and) Christ to dwell in your hearts through faith
            —you are rooted and grounded in love—
18   that you may have the ability with all the saints to grasp
            what is the breadth and length and height and depth
19   and to know the love of Christ
            which surpasses knowledge,
      that you may be filled
         to attain to the total fullness of God.
20 Now to the one able to do infinitely beyond anything
            which we ask or think
            in accordance with the power working in us,
21   to him is the glory
            in the church and in Christ Jesus
            unto all generations for ever and ever.
      Amen.

AE began 3.1 as if intending to launch into a prayer related to what he had just been writing, and prayer would have followed appropriately after the reference to the temple (2.21f, Eadie). For some

reason he drew back; more needed to be said before he could move
on from his discussion of the admission of Gentiles to God's grace
to offer his prayer; and so we had the parenthesis of vv. 2–13. The
reference in 3.1 is to Paul's sufferings on behalf of the Gentiles and
3.13 links back to this. The parenthesis explained his personal
involvement as the one who had both received the revelation of the
admission of the Gentiles (v. 3) and had been foremost in evangelising them. That gave him more than anyone else the right and the
duty to pray for the Gentiles. In the parenthesis the cosmic nuance of
salvation again came to the fore (vv. 9f) and this prepares for v. 15.
Macpherson, rejecting the view that vv. 2–13 form a parenthesis, is
forced to connect the prayer more directly to those verses but fails to
do so successfully.

The prayer, addressed like most of those in the NT to God rather
than Christ, provides a transition from the 'theology' of the first half
of the letter to the 'paraenesis' of the second. After a solemn
opening (vv. 14f) it becomes an intercession.[1] In his earlier
intercession (1.17ff) AE prayed that the readers should understand
their salvation; now he concentrates rather on their personal experience so that they may be spiritually deepened and adequately
prepared for the moral exhortations which are to follow. Above all,
if they are to be truly God's temple, they need to be strengthened in
love, and this is the main burden of the prayer. For AE merely to tell
them what good behaviour is would not of itself ensure that they
would follow his counsel and behave well.

Verses 14–19 form one long unwieldy sentence reminiscent of
the language and style of the initial eulogy (1.3–14), yet that gives
no reason to suppose that AE is employing a piece of preformed
tradition. Vv. 14f tell us to whom the prayer is addressed. The
content of the prayer follows in three successive clauses (vv. 16f;
18–19a; 19b), each beginning with ἵνα and each to some extent
dependent on the preceding; the first two have several qualifications;
the third is brief and forms the climax. The burden of the prayer is
that God's strength should become that of the readers, mediated
through the love of Christ in which they are already grounded. A
doxology rounds off the prayer and it is terminated with a solemn
'Amen' (vv. 20f). The doxology consists of one sentence, and
though comparatively brief it is stylistically similar to the eulogy;
unlike the intercession it is in the first plural, tying together writer
and readers. Its position makes it the conclusion to the doctrinal and
devotional first half of the letter and it prepares for the change of
tone in what is to follow.

An intercessionary prayer at this point in a Pauline letter is

---

[1] On the form of such interoessory prayers see G. P. Wiles, *Paul's Intercessory
Prayers* (SNTSMS 24), Cambridge, 1974, 146–258.

surprising; normally they follow the initial. address, and they occupy the same position in most of the NT letters. However, letter writing by its nature does not follow strict rules. In 1 Th 3.11–13 Paul introduced a prayer into the middle of his letter, and doxologies appear in different parts of other letters. The present unusual position should not however lead us with Haupt to assert that it forms the high point of the letter. All that can be said is that it is a turning-point.

The prayer contains several similarities to the language of Col 1.29–2.10 but there is no sequence of words directly dependent on Colossians. On the other hand there are phrases in Col 1.29–2.10 resembling what AE might have written, and yet they do not appear in Ephesians, e.g. κατὰ τὴν ἐνέργειαν αὐτοῦ τὴν ἐνεργουμένην ἐν ἡμῖν (Col 1.29). Since πλοῦτος is a favourite word of AE (5×) which he had already united with δόξα in 1.18, there is no need to suppose his use of it here derives from Col 2.2. ἐρριζωμένοι καὶ τεθεμελιωμένοι represents the combination of two well-known metaphors and there is no need to see dependence on Col 2.7 + 1.23; indeed if there is literary dependence it is more probable that A/Col took the words from Eph 3.17, split them up and united them with other metaphors (cf Holtzmann, 50f). The reference to hearts and love (Col 2.2; Eph 3.17) is as likely to have been borrowed from Ephesians by A/Col as the reverse. The double reference to being full (Col 2.9f) appears quite differently in Eph 3.19, and Eph 3.17 expresses the idea in a wholly other manner. ἐν οὐρανοῖς καὶ ἐπὶ γῆς cannot be derived from Col 1.16, 20 where in each case both nouns have the article; the phrase appears in varying forms in the NT (Mt 5.34f; 11.25; 28.18; 1 Cor 8.5; Eph 1.10) and must have been in common Christian usage. It is only when the two epistles are approached with the fixed idea in mind that Ephesians depends on Colossians that dependence can be detected here (cf Best, 'Who used Whom?').

14.[2] After the link back to v. 1 with τούτου χάριν the move to prayer is expressed, not with a simple 'I pray', but with a more complex phrase in the Pauline manner (cf Rom 1.9; Phil 1.4; 1 Th 1.2), yet, unlike 1.16, it does not resemble any that Paul employs.

Jews normally stood when praying[3] (Mt 6.5; Mk 11.25; Lk 18.11, 13; 1 Sam 1.26; 1 Kgs 8.14, 22; Josephus *Ant* 10.255; 12.98; *Tos Berak* 3.20; *m Ber* 5.1; *m Taan* 2.2) but kneeling and prostration (it is not always clear to which the words and phrases refer) were also known (1 Chron 29.20 LXX; Isa 45.23; Ps 95.6; Dan 6.11 Theod LXX, 'fell on his face'; *Prayer of Manasseh* 11); in 1 Kgs 8.54; 1 Esdras 8.73; 3 Macc 2.1 prostration where the forehead touches the ground is impossible because of the position of the hands. Kneeling is the approach to Baal in 1 Kgs 19.18 and may have been the regular posture in pagan worship, as in approaches to important people (2 Kgs 1.13; 1 Chron 29.20), perhaps implying submission including an

---

[2] On vv. 14f see J. Heriban, 'Da dio ogni paternità prende nome (Ef 3,14–15)', *PSV* 14 (1986) 143–60.
[3] SB I, 401f; Schürer[2] II, 448–50; E. van Severus, *RAC* VIII, 1160f.

appeal for help. Apart from Eph 3.14 it is only in OT quotations that kneeling is mentioned in the NT (Rom 11.4; 14.11; Phil 2.10). It is not known what the normal posture of worshippers in the early church was when praying. Mk 14.35; Lk 5.8; 22.41; Acts 7.60; 9.40; 20.36; 21.5 yield no certain answer but do not exclude the possibility of kneeling; Mt 26.39 implies prostration; the soldiers kneel in Mk 15.19 before Jesus but this is in mockery and not prayer. By the time of Origen there are references to the suitability of kneeling (*Hom Judges*, GCS 30, 475.16).

Whatever the contemporary normal posture in prayer, v. 14 refers to mental, not physical, kneeling; this is not to dispute those prayer manuals which say that posture is important. Since there is no word for prayer in v. 14, kneeling must have been instantly recognisable as indicating that a prayer was about to commence; had AE spoken of Paul as standing in the Jewish manner, his Gentile readers might have needed an explicit reference to prayer. Probably kneeling conveyed to them a greater sense of humbleness than would standing.

The prayer is addressed to (πρός) 'the Father'; only here and in 2.18 do we have the undefined 'Father'.

The variant reading which defines Father by adding 'of our Lord Jesus Christ' though having some good support (ℵ² D F G Ψ 0278 1881 𝔐 lat sy) is not as widely supported as its omission ($\mathfrak{P}^{46}$ ℵ* A B C P 6 33 81 365 1175 1739 *pc* vg^{ms} co; Or BasA Hier). Its insertion would serve to draw attention away from the word play πατέρα–πατριά, limit the reference to God as Father to his fatherhood of Jesus whereas v. 15 implies a wider reference, and destroy the coherence of the argument (Grotius). It is hard to see why it should have been omitted if originally present; its addition could easily have been made by a careless scribe accustomed to its association with 'Father' or by one deliberately attempting to exclude any idea of a universal Fatherhood of God.

The Fatherhood of God has been variously understood here: (i) The scribes who added 'of our Lord Jesus Christ' clearly thought that the reference was to Christ alone; the rejection of the variant entails the rejection of this view. (ii) The reference may be to God as Father of believers; this is the most common understanding in the NT of God as Father, but the word play with v. 15 implies that God's Fatherhood here embraces some who are in heaven. (iii) Most probably the Fatherhood is conceived cosmically involving all sentient beings in heaven and on earth (v. 15; cf 4.6). This view (see notes on 4.6) was well known in the ancient world, God being often regarded as the progenitor of all living beings; when however the Bible wishes to express the idea of God as universal Father it speaks of him as creator and not progenitor. The description here of God as Father saves him from being seen as a remote deity to whom it would be impossible to pray.

15. As Father God is the one who gives names (see on 1.21). In biblical thought this does not imply that those he names take on his name. A name is a means of identification, but it is much more. In the creation story Adam is given a responsibility for what God has created and gives names to the animals. Name-giving is thus associated with creation and to possess a name implies existence (cf Ps 147.4; Isa 40.26; Eccles 6.10); the name is also associated with redemption for believers are baptised into the name of Christ and so come under his authority. V. 15 is then saying something more than that God puts names on people and things; if that were all ὑπό would have been used instead of ἐκ. It is the source of the naming that is stressed rather than action of naming.

What is named is *every* πατριά,[4] not the *whole* πατριά; the latter would be πᾶσα ἡ πατριά (cf BDR §275.2; Robertson, 772; Moule, 94f). In any case such an understanding would not suit the context which with its reference to heaven and earth implies πατριά indicates a multiplicity. But a multiplicity of what? The Vulgate and Syriac translate the word as if it were an abstract noun meaning 'fatherhood' and those interpreters who follow them (e.g. Percy, 277 n. 30; Bruce) justify this on the grounds of the word play πατήρ–πατριά. We do not however need to see such a direct play on words; having used πατήρ, πατριά may have come naturally into AE's mind when thinking of a word for a social grouping (cf the change in meaning of εὐλογεῖν in 1.3 and the word play in v. 20). More importantly 'fatherhood' is not a recognised meaning of πατριά. In the LXX it always indicates a group of people with a common ancestor such as a family or tribe (Exod 12.3; Num 32.28; Jth 8.2; T Dan 1.2), but it is also often used in a wider way to denote a group linked by consanguinity with no implication of a common father, and even more widely of a social unit distinguishable from other social units (Ψ 21.28; 95.7; Ezek 20.32; Jth 8.18; Acts 3.25 in quoting Gen 22.18 substitutes it for τὰ ἔθνη). English translations frequently use 'family' but this is too limiting; '(social) grouping' is to be preferred as less exact. It should not be taken as if it indicated local congregations (Mitton, *Epistle*, 237f; Goodspeed, *Meaning*, 48f). The use of πᾶς implies more than two groupings are in view, and so excludes a reference merely to Jews and Gentiles or to one group on earth and one in heaven (cf the Jewish 'upper' and 'lower' families, Israel and the angels; b Berak 17a; b Sanh 38b, 98b, 99b; cf SB I, 743f; III, 594; J. Michl, *RAC* V, 89ff).

While it is easy to imagine different groupings on earth whether defined as nations, tribes, peoples which use a common language or inhabit an area with boundaries, it is more difficult to think of such groupings in heaven where there is neither physical consanguinity

---

[4] For the word see G. Schrenk, *TWNT*, V, 1017–21. Theod Mops read φρατρία here and understood by it a social grouping.

(cf Mk 12.25) nor limited geographical area (the variant οὐρανῷ, P 0278 81 104 365 945 1175 *al* a vg^mss sy^hmg; Hil, Epiph^pt is an obvious correction of the Semitic plural). Yet in heaven there are rulers, powers, principalities, seraphim, cherubim, ophanim (*1 En* 71.6ff; 61.10) and the angels are arranged in groups with leaders (*1 En* 69.3), though this should not suggest the archangels as fathers (cf Jerome).[5] There is no need to resort to thinking of the groups in heaven as those of dead believers or the church triumphant (so Hodge, Eadie quoting Bodius, i.e. Robert Boyd). Since no distinction is made in the earthly groupings between good and bad, it may be assumed none should be made in respect of those in heaven (*pace* Schnackenburg). Believers would be reassured when they realised that the powers were dependent on God (Houlden), and this may be why AE has not simply described God as the Father of every family in heaven and earth but has said that God named them, so setting him in a closer and authoritative relation to them.

Verse 15 builds up an impressive picture of the extent of God's authority and therefore of his power and so leads to, and fits with, the intercession which follows with its stress on his might and love.

16. AE now enters on the content of his intercession (ἵνα depends on κάμπτω) reusing many of the words and ideas of his earlier intercession, 1.17–19, with a similar tautological style as there and as in the Qumran writings (1QH 7.17, 19; 12.35; 1QM 10.5; cf Kuhn). God is the source of any strengthening in love that the readers are to receive and this because of his inexhaustible riches. πλοῦτος is a favourite term (see on 1.7) with AE which he connected with δόξα also in 1.18. The wealth of God's resources is there to sustain the readers in their daily lives.

δόξα (for the word see on 1.6) in its biblical usage carries two flavours: radiance, power. The former predominated in the refrain of the eulogy (1.6, 12, 14), the latter is more appropriate here and was prepared for in 3.13. τῆς δόξης should not be taken adjectivally ('glorious power'), for the genitive following πλοῦτος is not elsewhere adjectival (1.7, 18; 2.7; 3.8). δύναμις and the somewhat rare verb κραταιόομαι (Lk 1.80; 2.40; 1 Cor 16.13) introduce again the theme of power. The aorist infinitive (see on 4.22) of the verb cannot be taken to suggest that only now does the strengthening through the Spirit begin; believers will have experienced it from the moment they began to believe. In Lk 1.80; 2.40 the verb is associated with growth; growth is a process, not an instantaneous event; probably AE has growth in mind here; it is an idea not so easily fitted into the parallel of v. 17; Christ either dwells in the heart or he does not (but see on v. 17). It is God who strengthens (cf

---

[5] Cf Everling, op.cit., 104f.

Phil 4.13) just as it was he who was powerful to raise Christ from the dead (1.19f). Believers are not left to whistle up strength from within themselves in order to be able to do God's will (cf 6.10). The reason for their strengthening is not defined here but emerges in vv. 17b–19. It is necessary if the injunctions of the following paraenetic section of the letter are to be observed. AE's rather loose style makes it difficult to determine the exact significance of δυνάμει (Harless has an extensive note on the possibilities); it is associated with the same verb also in 2 Kgdms 22.33; an instrumental sense seems incorrect alongside διὰ τοῦ πνεύματος; it cannot suggest the area in which strengthening is to take place, for that is covered by the 'inner man'; it is probably not contrasted with love or knowledge as to the nature of the strengthening; it is best therefore taken adverbially, 'mightily'. The agency of strengthening is God's Spirit; the Spirit is regularly associated with power (1 Cor 2.4; 2 Cor 6.6f; Rom 1.4), an association deriving from OT ruaḥ.

It is the inner person, ἔσω ἄνθρωπος (on the adjectival use of the adverb see Robertson, 766) which is to be strengthened. εἰς may be equivalent here to ἐν (cf BDR §205, 207.4; MHT 255f; Zerwick §110; Robertson, 593) but this is unlikely. Even less likely is Barth's supposition (pp. 390ff) that we should assume a reference to growth, the growth of the inner person, and that the inner person is to be equated with Christ, for the parallel clause, v. 17a, employs another anthropological term, heart, implying an anthropological understanding of 'inner person' (cf Lincoln). The term 'inner person'[6] appears also in 2 Cor 4.16; Rom 7.22. The concept, though not always expressed with ἔσω, appears to have been current in Hellenistic thought; it is difficult to see how any reflection on the nature of the person could avoid the concept, if not the precise phrase; in fact it goes back at least to Plato, Rep 9.589A, appears in Hellenistic Judaism (Philo, Det Pot 23; Plant 42; Congressu 97), in gnosis (CH 1.15; 9.5; 13.7; Irenaeus, 1.21.4f; Hippolytus, 5.7.35f; Ep Pet Phil, NHC VIII, 2 137.20–2),[7] and then very frequently in the Fathers.[8] The term by its nature suggests some form of dualism which in Greek thought would be basically that of spiritual/material, but there is no uniform presentation of it.[9] As a current and indeed natural term to express the moral and spiritual side in people it was picked up by Paul who used it first in 2 Cor 4.16 (it is irrelevant whether he derived it from his Corinthian opponents or not) and then

[6] Cf Stacey, op.cit., 211–14; Jewett, op.cit., 391–401; Ernst, Pleroma, 126ff; T. K. Heckel, Der Innere Mensch (WUNT 2.Reihe 53), Tübingen, 1993.
[7] Schlier, Christus, 27ff, sees its origin in gnosis.
[8] See Biblia Patristica re 3.16, Rom 7.22 and 2 Cor 4.16.
[9] Cf R. Reitzenstein, Die hellenistischen Mysterienreligionen, 3.Aufl., Leipzig, 1927, 354f. According to gnostics it is the inner person who is redeemed, Irenaeus, 1.21.5 (cf 3.20.7); Hippolytus, 5.35; Tertullian, Resurrectione Carnis 40.4.

in Rom 7.22. In 2 Cor 4.16 it is contrasted with the outer being, though the outer being is not there devalued as 'material', but is that part of Paul which suffers in his missionary labours; the inner person is apparently set in parallel with the heart as that which God renews daily. In Rom 7.22, where the antithetical 'outer person' is not mentioned, the inner person is paralleled with the νοῦς and is almost equivalent to the personal pronoun. It is then the whole person viewed from one aspect, the aspect on which the Spirit may act. It is what people are 'deep down' within themselves (Houlden), yet it is not a purely psychological term for it involves the whole person. The inner person did not come into existence with baptism/ conversion, but in Ephesians it finds its purpose and fulfilment in those who are redeemed (Rienecker). It is not the old person (4.22) but when worked on by the Spirit it approximates to the new person (4.24; cf 1 Pet 3.4). AE does not use it with precisely the same significance as Paul; having found it in the Pauline vocabulary he was able to adapt it to his own purposes since it lacked fixed technical meaning; equally if AE is Paul he was free to adapt its usage. That it is paralleled with 'heart' in v. 17 and that love, power and understanding feature in the intercession show that not much adaptation was necessary.

17. Since no particle links this verse to the preceding it is probably parallel to it, yet also clarifies it. The parallelism is seen in the two διά clauses (faith and the Spirit are also linked in 1.13) and in 'inner person' and 'heart'. The two verses also express the same idea; v. 16 would have been more easily understood in the Hellenistic world; v. 17 is more Semitic (Hugedé). There is no temporal distinction between the two verses as if v. 16 were a necessary pre-condition of v. 17.

κατοικεῖν normally indicates a settling in or colonising tenancy which has a beginning and continues without interruption; in this it differs from παροικεῖν (see 2.19) which implies something less permanent. While this is the idea, the choice of the particular word may have been influenced by the use of the cognate noun in 2.22; it appears also in Col 1.19; 2.9, though in those verses the context is different; it may have been a word, not of Paul, for he does not use the compound verb but the simple οἰκεῖν, but of the Pauline school. The moment of settling in or colonising will have been that of conversion/baptism. Since then Christ has been the permanent tenant. In comparison to the corporate tenancy of 2.22 the tenancy is now individualised (Eadie). Corporate and individual aspects of the Christian life balance one another throughout the letter, the corporate reappearing in v. 18.

Paul had already argued that the Spirit of God dwelt in believers (Rom 8.9, 11; 1 Cor 3.16; cf 1 Cor 6.19); in the OT God's law is said to be written in the hearts of people (Jer 31.31–4) and his Spirit to be in them (Ezek 36.27). God also lives and walks among them (Exod 29.45; Lev 26.12). Wisd 1.4 implies the dwelling of wisdom in the wise. The Johannine literature expresses a thought parallel to Eph 2.17 with μενεῖν (Jn 14.17; 15.4–6; 1 Jn 2.14; 3.17, 24; 4.12, 15f), though often there it is believers who dwell in God or Christ; in Paul of course believers are regularly said to be 'in Christ'. He does however sometimes speak of Christ as in believers (Rom 8.10; 2 Cor 4.10f; 13.3, 5; Gal 2.20; 4.19; cf Col 1.27). In Paul the experience of believers in respect of the Spirit and of Christ is very similar. It is not then surprising to find AE writing of Christ in the hearts of believers. God does not force the indwelling of Christ on believers; it takes place διὰ τῆς πίστεως. AE has already used this phrase at 2.8 (see there for the meaning) and 3.12. Faith which began at conversion/baptism continues throughout the whole of the Christian life. It denotes a relationship between people. Believers have faith in Christ; this relationship eliminates any idea of a Christ-mysticism where the personality of believers would be absorbed into that of Christ. Instead obedience always remains an essential part of the relationship; the Christ who enters does so, not merely as guest, but as Lord (Rienecker). Vv. 16f again contain the raw bricks which eventually led to Trinitarian doctrine. God gives through the Spirit and Christ indwells.

Verse 17b centres on two perfect participles both in the nominative where the genitive or dative would have been expected (on the grammar of the clause see BDR §468 n. 3; Moulton, 182; MHT 230; Moule, 105, 179f; Moulton–Turner, 89); ἐν ἀγάπῃ qualifies both participles.[10] In 1.4f it was difficult to decide where to place this phrase; there we took it with what followed and this seems also the best solution here (*pace* Robinson; Tertullian, *Resurrectione Carnis* 40.4), for even if it is associated with what precedes we have two successive ἐν phrases and the participles are left high and dry, whereas in the light of their case they require some qualification. If, however, we take the participles as qualifying what follows then ἵνα ought to have preceded them and, though it is possible to find parallels where this does not happen, it would be clumsy (*pace* Origen). The clause then should be taken as independent (Eadie) or parenthetical (Ewald). The perfect tense of the participles implies a condition which came into existence in the past and still continues; the participles are not then part of the prayer, i.e. AE is not praying that the readers should be well founded in love, nor are they imperatival, 'be well founded in love'. Instead they state that believers have been and continue to be well founded in love. As empowered by the Spirit and indwelt by Christ they have been

[10] On the use of ἀγάπη in vv. 17–19 see V. Estalayo-Alonso, 'Agape in la carta a los Efesios', *EstT* 1 (1974) 79–127 at 111–21.

rooted and founded in love and therefore are able to grasp the nature of love, and so will be in a position to keep the injunctions of the later part of the letter.

The participles, which as we have seen there is no reason to think of as derived from Col 2.7 and Col 1.23, present two distinct but allied images; one botanical, the other architectural; it is imprecise to refer to them as a mixed metaphor, as Ellicott points out. The first, rare in the NT (Col 2.7), is found in Jewish writing (Jer 12.2; Ecclus 24.12; 1QS 8.5; 11.8; 1QH 6.15f; 8.4–11) and is related to the image of planting (1 Cor 3.5–9). The second (see on 2.20) is found much more widely in the NT (Mt 7.25; Lk 6.48f; 1 Cor 3.10–12; Eph 2.20; Col 1.23; Heb 6.1; 1 Pet 5.10; 1QS 5.5) and is related to the image of building or edification (1 Cor 14.3–5; Eph 2.20–2; 4.12, 16, 29). Both images appear together in 1 Cor 3.9. AE has already told his readers that they form part of a building whose foundation is the apostles and prophets (2.20); here the foundation is love. But is it divine or human love? In favour of the former is the lack of reassurance which human love would provide; in v. 19 Christ's love is clearly in view; the salvation of believers issues from God's love and not human love; if human love is meant it might imply that love was a pre-condition of salvation; if a human quality was to be expressed 'faith', following on from the earlier part of the verse, would have been more appropriate. On the other hand if the reference is to God's love why do we not have an αὐτοῦ as in 2.4 (Haupt)? ἀγάπη is used more often of human (1.15; 4.2, 15, 16; 5.2) than of divine (1.4; 2.4; 3.19) love in Ephesians; statistics however prove nothing when the two possibilities exist; context must decide the meaning. Perhaps at times little distinguishes human from divine love if the former is the result of the presence of the latter in the believer (Rom 5.5). Yet if our analysis of the construction of the passage is correct it seems necessary to decide in favour of divine love.

18. After the brief parenthesis of v. 17b the intercession is resumed. Though empowered by the Spirit and indwelt by Christ the readers still lack something (Ewald) and, as we shall ultimately see, this is not gnosis but love. The ἵνα clause here assumes that of v. 16 and takes it further; though underpinned by love believers need a fuller understanding of that love. The initial ἐξισχύειν appears elsewhere in scripture only at Ecclus 7.6 but is not infrequent in other Greek (LSJ, BAGD). It carries the nuance of the ability to attain an objective, here that of comprehending something or grasping it for oneself (this may be the implication of the middle καταλαβέσθαι; the word has a wide meaning which is played on in Jn 1.5[11]). On the basis of Phil 3.12f καταλαβέσθαι is sometimes

---

[11] For a detailed discussion of the word's meaning see Dupont, *Gnosis*, 501–21.

given a mystical flavour (Dibelius), but that sense is not necessary here (Dupont, *Gnosis*, 501f). It is also often used to denote the drawing of a conclusion on the basis of evidence (Acts 4.13; 10.34; 25.25); no evidence, however, is presented here and we must give it the wider sense of understanding; it then differs little from γνῶναι (v. 19). The object of knowing is love. If this is its ultimate objective the verb cannot denote a purely intellectual process and, since it is not love itself which is to be grasped but its extent, it cannot be taken existentially with Schlier. It is the same kind of knowledge as in 1.18; Col 1.27, a knowledge possible only because the Spirit has strengthened the readers and Christ indwells them (Lemmer). It is also a communal knowledge shared σὺν πᾶσιν τοῖς ἁγίοις, and this whether ἅγιοι means only believers[12] or includes also heavenly beings (Dahl, Houlden). Since we learn from other people, knowledge is generally communal; this is especially true of love whose nature can only be grasped through interaction with others. The true understanding of Christ's love is not then an individual experience but takes place in the community.

The final fourfold phrase is difficult; it is wrong to speak, as many commentators do, of four dimensions; there are only three spatial dimensions;[13] here width and length are two measurements at right angles in the same plane, height and depth two measurements at right angles to that plane but in the same vertical dimension and therefore indicate only one dimension. The phrase is then geometrically incorrect, a mistake which no educated Greek would have made. It may have been this difficulty which led to the inversion of the two final nouns in א A Ψ (1505) 1739 1881 𝔐 sy^h; (Or) Hier^pt (cf Zuntz, 153, n. 5). A single article governs the four nouns implying that they are to be taken as a unit and not interpreted separately; AE may be using a pre-existing formula. Since actual physical measurements cannot be in mind the phrase must be interpreted metaphorically. But what metaphor is involved? Eadie supplies a list and a brief discussion of the interpretations suggested prior to his time; most can be dismissed out of hand.

(a) In view of the dependence of the NT on the OT the latter seems the obvious place to begin the search (cf Feuillet, *Le Christ*, 292–319, and 'L'Eglise plérôme du Christ d'après Ephés., I,23', *NRT* 78 (1956) 449–72, 593–610). Ψ 138.8–10 though using spatial imagery to express God's omnipresence employs none of the actual words; Amos 9.2f uses only βάθος; Job 11.7–9 uses one of the words, a cognate of another and also μακρός; Ecclus 1.3 has two of the words. In each case the words are not set alongside one another

---

[12] L. Cerfaux, *Le Chrétien dans la théologie paulinienne* (LD 33), Paris, 1961, 447, thinks here of the first Jerusalem believers.
[13] Three was normal in Greek thought, cf Knox, *Gentiles*, 192.

as in v. 18 but appear in separate phrases or clauses. Where we find
four items in OT passages they relate to four areas, heaven, earth,
sea, sheol, and not to four measurements. Outside scripture but still
within Palestinian Judaism we find the idea of measurement in
different directions (*1 En* 60.11; 93.11–14; *2 Bar* 54.1–4) but the
use is non-metaphorical.

(b) Since there is no suitable Jewish parallel it is necessary to turn
to the Hellenistic world where several possibilities have been
suggested. In some philosophical thought, in particular that of
Stoicism (cf Dupont, op.cit., 481–9), the soul is thought to walk
(metaphorically) in heaven and, by seeing and understanding its
dimensions, to understand the greatness of God (Cicero, *Nat
Deorum* I 53f; *Tusc* I 64, 69f; V 69; Plutarch, *Mor* 939A; Seneca,
Nat Quaest 1.12f; *CH* 10.25; 11.20; *Asclep* 6; *Pistis Sophia* 133).
Yet we never encounter the fourfold formula and classical writers
would probably never have thought of four spatial dimensions.
Apart from the references in *CH* which are very slight, all relate to
human ability to know and not to revealed knowledge (cf Schnackenburg; for fuller discussion and rejection see Feuillet, op.cit.,
295ff). Dahl[14] argues that the fourfold formula is to be traced back
to discussions in various sources of the magnitude of the cosmos and
it refers 'to revealed knowledge of the immeasurable dimensions of
the universe'. He does not however find the precise fourfold formula
anywhere and, more importantly, fails to show how his interpretation fits into the present immediate context. If AE had intended
this, v. 18 would have ended with τοῦ κοσμοῦ. The closest verbal
parallel is found in a fourth-century magical papyrus, *PGM* IV
964–74, 979–85. Although this parallel has been noted by many
recent commentators it has been most strongly advocated by Arnold,
91f. The papyrus contains the fourfold formula but links with the
fourfold series two other nouns, φῶς, αὐγή, which are not spatial, so
that there is actually a sixfold formula and therefore no proper
parallel. Arnold attempts to overcome its late date by supposing that
texts existed prior to Ephesians which used the phrase, but he
provides no evidence to support this supposition. He justifies the
similarity to Ephesians by arguing that both in the letter at this point
and in the papyrus the main theme is power; the power in Ephesians
is however only given so that love may be understood; love is the
main theme. Dibelius uses this 'magical' parallel with other possible
parallels in gnostic writings and, noting the gnostic use of
καταλαμβάνεσθαι and γινώσκειν, argues for a gnostic origin for the
formula, but the evidence is insufficient. There is even less reason

[14] N. A. Dahl, 'Cosmic Dimensions and Religious Knowledge (Eph 3:18)', *Jesus
und Paulus* (FS W. G. Kümmel, ed. E. E. Ellis and E. Grässer), Göttingen, 1975,
57–75.

for accepting the hypothesis of Dacquino, art.cit., that AE is picking up a formula which the Colossian heretics had used; if Dacquino is right he would have needed to prove it was a formula of the Colossian heretics and then to prove AE had some contact with them. Since the terms of the formula could be applied to the measurements of a building it has been thought to refer to the heavenly city (Rev 21.16; cf Hermas, *Vis* 3.2.5; *b B. Bat* 75b; *Pesiq R* 143); this gives the formula too physical a sense and nothing in the context suggests a building is in mind. Schlier, working from the shape of the cross, argues for a reference to the cross as a world body, an idea taken up by later Christians (*Act Andr* 14, pp. 54f; *Act Petri* 38, pp. 95f; *Act Philip* 140, pp. 74f; cf Irenaeus, 5.17.4).[15] The references are late and no support for Schlier's proposal can be drawn from the supposed hymn underlying 2.14–16, since there is no certainty such a hymn ever existed. None of the solutions we have outlined is more than vaguely possible. Lacking then an indication of the contemporary use of the fourfold formula, it is better to see it as a typical piece of AE's hyperbole; physical measurements as we have seen were used metaphorically to express the extent of various subjects but were not tied to any one subject; AE uses four measurements to drive home the greatness of whatever the formula refers to.

To what then do the measurements refer? We might have expected a genitive to follow giving the answer. Various suggestions have been made as to what the genitive might have been. In line with the attempts to explain the formula it has been supposed it refers to wisdom (Van Roon, Feuillet), to the new Jerusalem and/or the heavenly inheritance (Dibelius, Conzelmann), the power of God (Arnold, 90ff), the cross (Schlier), the body of Christ (Usami, 178), God's plan of salvation or the mystery of salvation (Mussner, Percy, Schnackenburg), the redemptive activity of God (Beare). To be entirely rejected are the allegorical explanations of some of the Fathers (e.g. Athanasius, *De Incarnatione* 16; Augustine, *Doct Christ* 2.41; *In Joh* 118). It is difficult to argue for any of these from the immediate context which is that of love (v. 19), and with the majority of commentators we take this to be the reference. Paul had already moved in the direction of relating love to height and depth (Rom 8.39). The love will be that of Christ or of God. This love is without limits and ultimately immeasurable.

19. This verse is coordinate with v. 18 and to some extent parallel to it; both verses begin with verbs of 'knowing'; τέ which links them implies a somewhat closer connection than καί (Robertson, 1178f; cf BDR §443; MHT, 338f). There are two main concepts, knowledge

---

[15] On the cosmic cross see J. Daniélou, *The Theology of Jewish Christianity*, London, 1964, 279–92.

and love, either of which might have been the subject of the measurements in v. 18b. However, if it had been knowledge, we would have expected v. 19 to have begun (τῆς) γνώσεως and τέ to have been omitted; γνώσεως moreover occupies a subordinate position in the clause. γνῶναι has much the same sense as καταλαβέσθαι in v. 18. ὑπερβάλλειν can be used absolutely, as in 1.19; 2.7; 2 Cor 3.10, or comparatively as here. Believers need to grasp the intensity with which Christ loves them ('the love of Christ' is not their love for him but his love for them as in 5.2, 25; cf Romaniuk, 25–7). This love goes so far beyond any ordinary scheme of measurement that it cannot be fully understood; it surpasses knowledge. AE neither depreciates knowledge here as if he were attacking an early form of gnosis nor compares love and knowledge; if he were doing the latter, knowledge would come off as badly as every other virtue with which love might be compared (cf 1 Cor 13); in a sense love and knowledge are incomparable since the knowledge is human and the love divine. Knowledge is of course necessary, otherwise revelation could not be appropriated (1.9; 3.3ff) nor love understood. Yet Christ's love can never be fully grasped either intellectually or existentially. Elsewhere and with various images Paul attempts to explain the extent of Christ's love and of God's: that love extends to sinners (Rom 5.6), overcomes all obstacles (Rom 8.35ff), constrains believers (2 Cor 5.14). AE has in mind here its effects on believers; when love rules their lives they are able to face up to the moral duties which AE is about to lay on them in the remainder of the letter.

AE's prayer has been steadily building up to the final intercession of v. 19b. Believers can only grasp the extent of Christ's love when they have been strengthened through the Spirit in their inner being, Christ has come to dwell in their hearts and they are underpinned by love. The interpretation of v. 19b is disputed (for a summary of possible solutions see Ernst, *Pleroma*, 121–5) and its difficulty has led to one major textual variation.

πληρωθῇ πᾶν τὸ πλήρωμα is read by 𝔓⁴⁶ B 0278 33 (which adds εἰς ὑμᾶς) 1175 pc sa; this omits the difficult εἰς (33 changes its position) but the support for the text is widespread and includes many important witnesses, ℵ A C D F G Ψ (81) 1739 1881 𝔐 sy bo. The variant would translate as 'that all the fullness of God may be filled'. There is no sufficient reason to adopt it (cf Metzger). There are several other minor variants of which 1881, which reads χριστοῦ instead of θεοῦ, almost certainly under the influence of 4.13, is the most important.

The ultimate purpose of the prayer is the filling of believers; since there is no explicit statement saying with what they are to be filled this must be deduced from the context. The answer would be simple if we could give εἰς the meaning 'with' as do AV, RSV, REB and many other translations, but this would rob the preposition of its true value; believers are not directly filled with all the fullness of God. Elsewhere they are described as filled with the Spirit (5.18), joy and peace (Rom 15.13), all knowledge (Rom 15.14), the fruits of righteousness (Phil 1.11). Our context contains a play on words between the verb and its cognate noun πλήρωμα (see on 1.23 for the noun). What fills believers will be the same as that which fills God or that with which God fills; the distinction between the active and passive meanings of *pleroma* may be unimportant in this respect, for God will fill with that with which he is full. πᾶν is strictly unnecessary, for fullness implies totality; AE may then be using a fixed phrase which first appeared in the Colossian hymn (Col 1.19) and then entered the Pauline school; its presence eliminates any understanding of *pleroma* here as meaning the church, a possible meaning in 1.23. Col 2.9 provides the closest parallel to our passage but differs in that it is not said here as there that 'all the fullness of God' dwells in believers. Instead εἰς (cf 1.10, 14; 3.16; 4.12) suggests a movement towards all the fullness of God. There is a goal which has not yet been attained (this is a prayer) and the goal is to be filled with what distinguishes God. This taken abstractly and apart from the context might be the full total of either his attributes or the spiritual gifts which he imparts to believers. The context from v. 17 has however been that of love. The nature of God is love; his greatest spiritual gift is love. Probably then we should understand God as able to fill with that love (cf Belser; Spicq, op.cit.) which summarises his own being and to whose fullness AE's readers have not yet attained, but which in itself enables them to move towards their goal. This interpretation accords with 5.1 where believers are summoned to imitate God, again in a context of love. Their nature and God's should coincide but this can only happen when God fills them with his love.

20. The first and 'theological' section of the letter concludes, as Romans, with a doxology (cf Rom 11.26). The only possible response in the light of what has been said about God in 1.3–3.19 is to voice his praise. The doxology is probably not a separate item tacked on at the end of the intercession but should be regarded as a part of the prayer (Pokorný). This makes it significant then not so much for its content as for its ability to inspire praise (Penna).

The doxology[16] is a form appearing regularly in the NT but of uncertain origin. This probably lay outside Christianity since in many NT instances there is no specific Christian element; yet Palestinian Judaism contains no clear examples; there may however be some in Hellenistic Judaism. We have however no need to trace its origin since it was already in Pauline usage prior to Ephesians (Gal 1.5; Rom 11.36; Phil 4.20. Rom 16.25–7 may

---

[16] For the form see A. Stuiber, *RAC* IV, 210ff; G. Delling, *Worship in the New Testament*, London, 1962, 62–6; Deichgräber, 25–40; Berger, *Formgeschichte*, 236f.

however be post-Pauline); its widespread use is seen in later parts of the NT (1 Tim 1.17; 2 Tim 4.18; Heb 13.21; Jude 24f; Rev 1.6; cf 1 Clem 20.12; 32.4; etc.). It consists of three elements: the name or title of the addressee, a statement of praise, a period of time. Its simplest form (Rom 11.36; *Did* 9.2, 3) is 'to God is (be) the glory for ever'. It is not clear if the accompanying 'amen' belongs to the form or represents an expected response from hearers. Each basic element may be extended; the addressee may be unnamed but can be inferred from the context (e.g. Rom 16.25–7; Gal 1.5); normally it is God, but may be Christ, though the language can be ambiguous (Heb 13.21; 1 Pet 4.11). 1 Tim 1.17; Phil 4.20 are examples of extended references to the addressee. The element of praise may be limited to the single word δόξα (e.g. Gal 1.5; Phil 4.20; Rom 16.27) but is often more extensive (1 Pet 4.11; Rev 1.6). The normal temporal reference is not the simplest form but εἰς τὰς αἰῶνας τῶν αἰώνων (Rom 16.27; Gal 1.5; Phil 4.20). Doxologies normally appear towards the end of documents but they can come at important breaks in the argument (Rom 11.36; Gal 1.5; 1 Pet 4.11; 1 Clem 20.12; 38.4; 58.2); they also form a suitable ending to a hymn or prayer (Rom 11.33–6; 1 Tim 6.16).

The position of 3.20f as a doxology is unexceptional in coming at the end of the first half of the letter and at the end of the prayer. Each of its units has been extended beyond the basic form. These extensions because of their language, style and content mark it as AE's own construction (Masson): he has introduced into the form his main theme of the church and one of his favourite phrases 'in Christ'. V. 20 identifies the addressee, and this identification, perhaps because of its length, is renewed in v. 21. The 'praise' element uses the normal δόξα and is qualified with references to the church and Christ. The temporal element uses both γενεά and the more normal αἰών. At the beginning δέ makes the break with the preceding prayer but has no element of contrast.

The addressee is unnamed but God is the nearest referent (v. 19) and so the doxology is offered to him; it cannot be Christ since he is referred to in v. 21. AE describes the addressee with his normal exuberance of language. There is a play on words (δυναμένῳ–δύναμιν) which it is impossible to reproduce in English because the participle offers a shade of meaning which is absent from the English 'power, might'; God's power is the central element of the praise (Arnold, 100–2).

ποιῆσαι is qualified by both ὑπὲρ πάντα and ὑπερεκπερισσοῦ (only elsewhere in the NT at 1 Th 3.10; 5.13); ὧν is short for τούτων ἅ. It is possible AE altered the construction as he wrote (Haupt, Bouwman). The variant omitting ὑπέρ, 𝔓⁴⁶ D F G lat, was probably an attempt to simplify the syntax; the text has wide support, א A B C Iᵛⁱᵈ Ψ 0278 0285 33 1739 1881 𝔐 a sy co; Hier.

αἰτούμεθα moves us to the plural from the first singular which has governed the passage since v. 14; intercession by its nature cannot be offered by those for whom it is made, but they can be embraced in praise; hence the plural here' and in νοοῦμεν. Humans can neither encompass and contain God by their thinking (cf Isa 55.8f) nor even imagine how all-embracing his care for them is. The greatness of his care is linked to his power, a theme which came to prominence in the first intercession (1.19), was renewed in the second (vv. 16–18), and occurs repeatedly throughout the letter. This power is already at work; ἐνεργουμένην (for the word see on 1.11) may be (see Moule, 26) either middle, middle with an active sense, 'working', or passive, 'which is energising you', with God as the real subject; the last is preferable in view of AE's continuous emphasis on God's might (Barth).

21. The length of the first element of the doxology forces AE into resuming the address with αὐτῷ, a common word in the introductions of doxologies. The missing copula, as in 1.3, is indicative and not optative, for we have a statement of fact, rather than a wish or prayer (BDR §128.5; MHT, 296f; Robertson, 395f). God already has glory and there is no need to pray for him to receive it. δόξα (see on 1.6) belongs to God (3.16); it is because he has made his glory known, just as he made known his power and love, that humans can affirm his glory and praise him for it (cf the refrain in the eulogy, 1.6, 12, 14).

The second element of the doxology is extended. Christ, when not the one to whom the doxology is addressed, often appears as the one through whom God is approached (Rom 16.27; 1 Pet 4.11; cf *Mart Polc* 14.3), but here however glory is said to be 'in him' and then, surprisingly, the church is set in parallel with him.

The parallelism of church and Christ has led to variant readings: D² Ψ 𝔐 vg^ms sy sa^mss bo^ms; Cass omit καί, probably to avoid any suggestion of equality or identity between Christ and the church; D* F G Ambr Vic reverse the order of the nouns, probably to maintain the primacy of Christ. Neither variant is as strongly supported as the text which should be read as *lectio difficilior*.

In the phrase 'in the church and in Christ Jesus', ἐν must be given the same meaning on each occasion. Since it can hardly have any other than a local significance with reference to the church, it must mean the same when applied to Christ. Such a local significance is found elsewhere with the phrase 'in Christ' (see Detached Note: In Christ). AE appears to have come close here to equating Christ and the church, yet elsewhere he clearly distinguishes between them: Christ is head and bridegroom; the church is his body and wife or bride. As for the positioning of the church before Christ, the same order appears in 4.4f. In v. 21 AE may be seeking a climactic effect. καί does not necessarily imply equality. God's glory is both to be praised in the church and can be seen in the church, for the church is related to the fullness of Christ (1.23), and is his body and bride. In so far as the church is worthy, pure and immaculate, and this she is (5.27), she exhibits God's glory, and the powers learn from her. She is his dwelling-place in the Spirit (2.22; 1 Cor 3.16) and where he dwells, his glory dwells, as it did in the temple in Jerusalem. The church however has no human glory for, of and in herself, she is weak and sinful. God's glory is certainly to be found in Christ and may be ascribed to him (1 Cor 2.8; 2 Cor 3.18; 4.4; 8.23; Phil 4.19). It is neither the statement that God's glory is to be seen in the church nor that it is to be seen in Christ that is then exceptional, only their collocation. As for their collocation, Christ and the church are regularly related in the letter: 1.23, the church is the fullness of Christ; 2.21, Christ is its angle-stone; 4.15f, he is the head of his body which is the church; 5.22ff, he is the bridegroom (husband) of the church which is his bride (wife). It is their close relation which has led them to be put in parallel: 'The glory that belongs to the Head fills the Body; the glory that belongs to the Husband shines in his Wife, whose status is determined by his. Thus the glory that is seen in the Church is not its own glory but derives from Christ' (Best, *One Body*, 176). Perhaps AE has been carried away by his own enthusiastic use of words beyond what is strictly logical.

The third element of the doxology is again unusually lengthy, thereby emphasising the everlasting significance of God's glory. One generation, γενεά, is a limited period; many generations are an indefinitely long period and the plural is used in this sense in the OT (Exod 40.15; Ψ 105.31; Dan 6.27 LXX; Isa 51.8; Joel 2.2) and, though not so regularly, in the NT (Lk 1.50). In it the plural of αἰών is more usual (Mt 21.19; Mk 3.29; Rom 1.25; 11.36; 1 Cor 8.13) or the extended phrase οἱ αἰῶνες τῶν αἰώνων (Rom 16.27; Gal 1.5; Phil 4.20; 1 Tim 1.17; 2 Tim 4.18). The singular of the noun followed by the plural, as here, appears in Ψ 9.6. γενεά and αἰών are often associated in phrases denoting an unlimited period (Exod 40.15; Ψ 105.31; Isa 51.8; Joel 2.2; 4.20; Dan 6.27 LXX). The precise phrase in v. 21 is not found elsewhere but a considerable number of variant phrases use its two nouns; probably AE has composed the phrase in his typical plerophoric manner. No recondite meanings should be read into any one of the words but the phrase should be taken as a whole.

ἀμήν[17] appears regularly in the NT as the final word in doxologies and prayers (e.g. Mt 6.13; Rom 1.25; 9.5; 11.36; 15.33; 16.27). While it can also denote the response of a congregation affirming agreement with a prayer which has just been uttered, this is hardly its function here or indeed in many other NT passages. When a letter

---

[17] Cf P. Glaue, *RAC* I, 378ff; H. Bietenhard, *NIDNTT*, I, 97–9; J. Jeremias, *TRE* II, 389–91; Delling, op.cit., 71f; R. P. Martin, *Worship in the Early Church*, Grand Rapids, 1974, 36f.

was read aloud in a Christian gathering, unless believers knew it well, they would not have known where to respond with their 'Amen'. It is the author's way of affirming the importance of what he has just said, 'This is true', and so adding emphasis. Yet it may be that a skilful reader, realising the change of subject-matter which is just about to take place, would see it as an appropriate place to halt for a moment and draw breath, and in the brief interval the congregation would respond with their 'Amen' to his.

VIII

PARAENESIS
(4.1–6.20)

At 4.1 the tenor of the letter changes; up to now it has been basically doctrinal though including extensive liturgical passages, but teaching about God and praise of him are now replaced with concern for behaviour, though since the type of behaviour required is closely related to the previous teaching that aspect continues to appear. There is also a significant change of style in that, 4.11–16 apart, the long convoluted sentences of the earlier chapters disappear and are replaced by a crisper approach consisting mainly of brief sentences. 4.2f is the hinge on which the change swings, for it introduces the need for the kind of conduct which would enhance the unity of a group. The changes at 4.1 are apparently similar to those at Rom 12.1; in both the summons to behaviour is followed first by a general but brief exhortation (Eph 4.2f; Rom 12.1f) and then by a reference to the church (Eph 4.4–16; Rom 12.3–8) before the detailed ethical instruction is given. Yet the balance is different, for the exhortation in Romans is relatively much briefer in respect of the length of the letter than that in Ephesians where it occupies half the letter. Romans is the only Pauline letter in which this clear-cut division is obvious. Though there is a change in Galatians, its ethical teaching is more generalised than that of Ephesians. In 1 Thessalonians much of the doctrine follows the change at 4.1, the earlier sections being personal rather than doctrinal. In the other letters doctrine, personal detail and exhortation intermingle. AE may have known Romans and sought to imitate it; alternatively, as a member of a Pauline school he may have known that Paul based instruction for behaviour on doctrine and developed a trend in his master's work which had become clearest in his last writing. If Paul is himself the writer he may simply be following a pattern which as time went by he found more and more useful. If Berger, *ANRW* II 25.2, 1331, is correct in saying that secular letters did not contain paraenesis, Paul may have been responsible for introducing this type of discourse into the letter form; it is of course widely present in philosophical writings.

Behaviour is thus seen in Ephesians as both response to what God has done in Christ, and as the proper accompaniment to the praise of God, the two themes present in chaps. 1–3. Gentile Christians ought to be especially responsive since, as was argued in chaps. 2, 3, God has done so much for them. Yet doctrine to which behaviour is the response is not missing from the final three chapters (see 4.4–16; 4.32; 5.23–32) just as it is not wholly absent from chaps. 12–15 of Romans (see 12.3–8; 13.1–6; 14.9, 14, 17).

But why does AE after commencing his paraenesis (vv. 2f) break off from it with a discussion of the church (vv. 4–16)? Perhaps he realises he has not said enough about the nature of the church to provide a proper basis for the instruction of how Christians should live together; for the nature of the church is the theme of 4.4–16, even though the word church is not used. The virtues mentioned in vv. 2f are those appropriate to this theme and the need for 'one-ness' which they suggest is carried on in the repeated use of 'one' of vv. 4–6. Vv. 7–16 continue the theme in showing how diversity may be combined with unity, though unity precedes diversity. Discussion of unity had been already present in 2.11–22, but there it was the unity of Jewish and Gentile Christians; now it is the unity of all believers irrespective of racial or religious origin (cf Percy, 284). Thus the inner condition of the church is discussed in relation to individuals as individuals within it; only after this is it proper to discuss in detail the behaviour of Christians towards one another (4.17–5.14). The inner unity and strength of the community enable believers to live with one another. 4.2–16 thus sets all that follows within a corporate frame of reference. Did AE see the danger of an excessive individualism, arising perhaps from an incipient gnosticism? Individualism however always characterises behaviour; it manifests itself in Romans in differing attitudes to food and days. Ephesians however is too general to enable us to tie down the danger of individualism to particular influences.

The paraenetic motif of 4.2f seems to disappear in 4.4–16, though as we shall see it does not do so entirely; it becomes explicit again from 4.17 onwards. In 4.17–24 AE contrasts the present life of Gentile believers with their past pagan life. In 4.25–5.2 he picks on certain sins into which believers may fall and which would destroy community life, while avoiding them would build up that life. This is largely also the theme of 5.3–14 where the sins are set in the light of God's judgement (vv. 3–7), and the need of the community is brought out to confront those who sin so that they may reform themselves. In 5.15–21 warnings on conduct are again set together, now with a reminder of the help that may come from common worship. 5.21–6.9 discusses certain specific areas of behaviour pertaining to individual households rather than to the community as a whole. 6.10–20 indicates the personal devotional equipment that believers need if they are to live as AE sets out.[1]

---

[1] On the forms and topoi of paraenesis see J. I. H. McDonald, *Kerygma and Didache* (SNTSMS 37), Cambridge, 1980, 69–100.

Throughout 4.1–6.20 a number of terms appear which are also found in the paraenetic sections of the later NT letters (1 Peter, Colossians, James), e.g. putting off/on, resisting, being subject to. Many, in particular Carrington and Selwyn,[2] have attempted to argue from this to the existence of a primitive Christian catechism and to see it as related to baptism. Common topics are certainly present; in different areas the early Christian communities must have encountered the same general questions relating to behaviour, for example, the need to resist temptation and give up various sins. It is not then surprising that there should be common teaching, though it is not necessary that it should have been coordinated, or have existed in a common oral or written form, nor is it necessary to suppose that it preceded baptism; in the accounts of conversion in Acts baptism follows immediately on belief and there is no period of instruction. The paraenetic material in Ephesians is so general in nature and shared with so many other NT writings that it is difficult to discern any precise situation into which it might fit; it offers no help then in determining the date or destination of the letter. The material moreover betrays no interest in Christian behaviour in relation to the world outside the church nor of the effect of what was happening outside on the church; it is wholly concerned with what happens within the church; this is probably why AE chose to begin these chapters with a discussion of the nature of the church where the behaviour will take place.

[2] P. Carrington, *A Primitive Christian Catechism*, Cambridge, 1940; E. G. Selwyn, *First Peter*, 363ff.

IX

UNITY AND DIVERSITY
(4.1–16)

T. Soiron, *Die Kirche als der Leib Christi*, Düsseldorf, 1951, 150–67; Hanson, 148–55; J. M. Gonzalez Ruiz, ' "Los logos" de unidad en Ef 4.1–16', *XV SBE*, Madrid, 1955, 1–17; R. Schnackenburg, 'Christus, Geist und Gemeinde (Eph 4:1–16)', *Christ and Spirit in the New Testament* (FS C. F. D. Moule, ed. B. Lindars and S. S. Smalley), Cambridge, 1973, 279–96; H.-J. Klauck, 'Das Amt in der Kirche nach Eph 4,1–16', *Wissenschaft und Weisheit* 36 (1973) 81–110; Halter, 242–8; T. G. Allen, chap. III, pp. 178ff; H. P. Hamann 'Church and Ministry: An Exegesis of Ephesians 4:1–16', *LTJ* 16 (1982) 121–8; S. Basevi, 'La missione di Cristo e dei cristiani nella lettera agli Efesini. Una lettura di Ef 4.1–25', *RivBiblt* 38 (1990) 27–55; Lemmer, 166–73.

AE sets out here to treat the unity of the church and the manner in which it is both built up and preserved through the activity of its office-bearers and members. 4.4–6 shows unity as already existing and perfect, and 4.7–16 shows how it is to be continued and matured. 4.1–16 begins (4.2f) and ends (4.4–16) with explicit exhortation (Lemmer, 167). More than once AE begins a subject, drops it and then picks it up again. Thus intercession begun at 1.16f is resumed at 3.14 and 3.13f picks up 3.1; 2.5 resumes 2.1. Here 4.2f is picked up again at 4.17ff though there is no anacoluthon as at 3.1. In view of the attention given to the final few verses of this section in today's church in relation to unity, it is surprising to find how rarely the earlier Fathers quote the passage. Vv. 4, 5 with their reference to one baptism were important in the discussions whether heretics should be rebaptised (see Synod of Carthage, September 256) and vv. 9, 10 in christology because of their references to what happened to Jesus after his death.

A

UNITY
(4.1-6)

E. Käsemann, 'Epheser 4,1–6' *Exegetische Versuche und Besinnungen*, I, Göttingen, 1964, 284–7; Roels, 179–84. ·

1 I, the Lord's prisoner, exhort you therefore
    to live worthy of the calling with which you were called,
2   with all humility and gentleness,
        with patience,
        paying attention to one another in love,
      working zealously to preserve the unity of the Spirit
        by means of the peace that binds.
4 One body and
  one Spirit
    just as you were also called in one hope of your calling,
5 one Lord
  one faith
  one baptism
6 one God and Father of all
    who is over all
        and through all
        and in all.

4.1–6 contains three brief sections: v. 1 reminds us again that Paul is a prisoner and employs one of his favourite phrases for introducing ethical instruction; vv. 2, 3 set out in a general way how readers are to respond if the unity of the church is to be preserved; vv. 4–6 pick up the theme of unity, providing a series of declarations in each of which unity is stressed through the use of the word 'one' and God's total government through the use of 'all'.

Verses 4–6 are so tightly structured that they raise the question whether they, or some part of them, were pre-existing material (see Best, 'Use'). To point out as Mitton does, *Epistle*, 156f, that the verses are 'built up almost entirely of words and phrases derived from 1 Corinthians, and mainly from chapters viii and xii' does not imply that AE compiled them;[1] anyone who knew Paul or his

---

[1] On the passage see M. Dibelius, 'Die Christianisierung einer hellenistischen Formel', *Botschaft und Geschichte*, II, Tübingen, 1956, 14–29; Wengst, 141f.

Corinthian correspondence could have done this. There can be little doubt that v. 6 could have existed as a liturgical unit (see on v. 6) since similar units are found elsewhere in early Christianity, in pre-Pauline Judaism and in the Gentile world. The similarities between vv. 4–6 and Col 3.15 are then no more than broadly significant. Most modern commentators accept v. 5 as tradition though not necessarily previously linked with v. 6; they hesitate however over v. 4: (i) v. 4b is very similar to what AE would write; he likes καθώς clauses (1.4; 3.3; 4.4, 17, 21, 32; 5.2, 3, 25, 29) and repetition of word stems; (ii) v. 4b breaks the uniformity of rhythm in the expression; (iii) while v. 6 can easily be taken as liturgical or credal it is difficult to see how 'one body and one Spirit' could be taken in either of those ways; (iv) v. 4a would also be a vague beginning to a formula; (v) it would be unusual for a formula to commence with a reference to the church and not to God or Christ (v. 5 if originally detached began with the latter and v. 6 with the former); (vi) Lincoln, 228f, says that in vv. 2f AE has been using Col 3.12–15; he derived σῶμα from that passage and then himself wrote the remainder of v. 4; it is however perfectly natural to introduce σῶμα here for it is a key term of the letter and what follows is an exposition of it; (vii) the order of the first words, body, Lord, God, in each of the three verses is unexpected; the reverse order would be more normal; yet the present order represents the amount of attention, and therefore of importance, AE gives to these three themes (cf Wengst, 141f). While these arguments may seem conclusive in dismissing v. 4 as part of any formula it is difficult to see why AE should bring together two or more existing units. If v. 5 suggests a baptismal confession, v. 6 is not very appropriate for that purpose since many non-Christians would not have disagreed with it; it would not therefore have been useful as an initial Christian confession indicating a break with a past pagan life. Supposing there was a formula involving all vv. 4–6, it would have run:

one body, one Spirit, one hope,
one Lord, one faith, one baptism,
one God and Father of all,
  who is over all and through all and in all.

Such a formulation has a clear structure containing seven (a favourite number in religion and magic) units with the final unit containing three (again another favourite number) units. AE requires to tie this formula into his argument; he has already associated hope and calling in 1.18 and so he writes v. 4b in order to create a link with v. 1, and, since the balance of the structure has now been disturbed, he adds 'and' between body and Spirit. It might be thought that it would have been better to have linked the formula through the use of Spirit in v. 3, but Spirit is too important a concept for it to be obscured by the addition of other material. The formula as set out above has 'body' as its initial element and this suits AE's context, for in vv. 7–16 he proceeds to expound body. It is however possible that in the original formula lines one and two were interchanged. It would then have begun with a reference to Christ. AE however, wishing to concentrate on 'body', brought that concept and the line containing it to the beginning. If so his readers will have seen the alteration and realised that 'body' is the term which is important in what is to follow. It is indeed the only word in the whole formula which is important for him at this point in his argument. Vv. 5, 6 are not strictly relevant to what he is about to say, and it is difficult to see why they should have been introduced unless they already formed part of a statement known to his readers and therefore could not easily have been omitted. Our discussion of the individual verses will support this view.[2]

It is impossible to determine the role such a formula would have played in the early church for very little is known about its life and worship, and the distinctions which for analytical purpose we draw between liturgical, credal and catechetical material may not have been so apparent to the early Christians who would have used the same material for very different purposes. Baptism is too minor an element in the formula for us to be sure it was a baptismal hymn or confession or that it was used in catechetical instruction, and, as already suggested, v. 6 would not be appropriate to this end.

The statement is designed for internal Christian usage rather than to help non-believers to clarify the distinction between Christianity and their religions. In the light of its employment of body as indicating the body of Christ, the origin of the statement probably lay in the Pauline school. Though it contains the terms Lord, Spirit, God the Father it is not however to be taken as a deliberate Trinitarian formulation;[3] this would be more likely if both Spirit and Lord had headed their triads and the order had been Father, Lord, Spirit; Trinitarian order was however probably not yet fixed; 1 Cor 12.4–6 offers the order: Spirit, Lord, God. The existence of other elements between the terms also spoils any idea of a Trinitarian formulation. Yet even if our formula was not deliberately Trinitarian, it strongly influenced the language of later creeds, particularly those of the Eastern church.

1. A strong connection is made through οὖν (cf Rom 12.1; 1 Th 4.1; Col 3.1) with the preceding three chapters, and not just with 3.14–21 as Ellicott suggests. Barth regards all of chaps. 1–3 as doxological and the argument would then run 'you praise God and

---

[2] Vv. 4–6 is also taken as a unit of tradition by Hanson, 149ff, and Bruce. Bouttier suggests vv. 4–6 recall Phil 2.1–4 which also has a movement towards unity.
[3] Cf F. Martin, 'Pauline Trinitàrian Formulas and Church Unity', *CBQ* 30 (1968) 191–219.

therefore you should behave correctly': Roels, 179, allows the possibility of a connection with 3.20f alone if these verses are regarded as the climax of chaps. 1–3. AE has told his readers of their redemption in Christ with whom they have been raised and sit in the heavenlies so that although once Gentiles they now have equal place with Jews in the Church, the body of Christ. Their behaviour, to which the remainder of the letter will be devoted, should correspond with their position. 4.1 thus governs all that follows; the 'good works' of 2.10 are now to be detailed.

παρακαλεῖν[4] has a range of meanings; in the present context we can exclude those relating to comforting and consoling. παρακαλῶ ὑμᾶς was an epistolary formula sometimes used by those in authority writing to others whom for diplomatic reasons they did not wish to order. It is thus weaker and more friendly than 'command', 'instruct' (cf Philem 8ff). Paul uses it regularly writing, for example, from the position of a parent (1 Th 2.7) and AE has adopted it from him. Prisoners can hardly order others. The meaning here lies in the area, 'beseech, exhort', yet also carrying latent or implicit authority which ἐγώ serves to stress. Normally Paul associates 'brother' with the phrase (Rom 12.1; 15.32; 16.17; 1 Cor 16.15; 1 Th 4.10; 5.14) but this is a word which is lacking as an address in Ephesians. Its absence enhances the authority and diminishes the friendliness of the phrase. This lessening of intimacy also appears in the simple ἐν κυρίῳ instead of the more usual and extensive prepositional additions to the phrase. These changes are in keeping with the general nature of the letter.

Unlike most instances of the formula, its subject is here emphatically identified (only elsewhere at 2 Cor 10.1; Philem 9), 'I, the prisoner of the Lord'. Prisoners do not normally exercise authority; but Paul had authority within the church, because of his connection with the Lord, and he was suffering for his readers' Lord (cf Hugedé); but AE is not attempting to win their sympathy by recalling his imprisonment (contrast Ign Trall 12.2). ἐν κυρίῳ (see Detached Note: In Christ) because of its position goes with 'prisoner' and not with the verb (cf BDR §272.3, n. 4). It may possibly carry here the sense of fellowship (so Eadie, Beare). For the significance of the description of Paul as prisoner see 3.1.

The readers are summoned to live (περιπατεῖν, see on 2.2, 10) in a manner appropriate to their calling, as Paul himself does as a

---

[4] Cf H. Schlier, 'Die Eigenart der christlichen Mahnung nach dem Apostel Paulus', in his Besinnung auf das Neue Testament, Freiburg, 1964, 340–57; C. J. Bjerkelund, PARAKALO, Oslo, 1967; R. Hasenstab, Modelle paulinischer Ethik, Grünewald, 1977, 67–94; for other references see Klauck, art.cit., 86; Paraenesis: Art and Form Semeia 50 (ed. L. G. Perdue and J. G. Gammie, 1990; G. Sellin 'Die Paränese des Ephesen briefes', from Gemeinschaft am Evangelium (Fs W. Popkes, ed. E. Brant, P. S. Fiddes and J. Moltagen, Leipzig, 1996, pp. 281–98.

prisoner. περιπατεῖν dominates much of what follows (cf 4.17; 5.2, 8, 15) and is normally in the present tense though in 2.2, 10 and here it appears as an aorist; this is natural in 2.2 for the reference there was to the past life of the readers and 2.10 has an aorist subjunctive which is really timeless. The present aorist infinitive should be compared to those of 4.22, 24. In the Pauline corpus ἀξίως is variously linked to God (1 Th 2.12; cf 3 Jn 6; 1 Clem 21.1), Christ (Col 1.10, where it is also combined with περιπατεῖν, cf Polyc *Phil* 5.2), the gospel (Phil 1.27), the saints (Rom 16.2). The closest parallel to 4.1 is probably 1 Th 2.12 where καλεῖν is also used. Believers have not been called because they have lived worthily, but now that they have been called, worthy living should be their appropriate response. To live worthily is not just to live morally; there are two great commandments and worthy living relates as much to the first as to the second. The nature of worthy living is outlined first in 4.2f and then throughout the remaining paraenesis.

AE uses here both the verb καλέω and its cognate noun as in 1.6, 19, 20; 2.4 (cf Percy, 32); παρακαλέω is also a compound from the same root (for the attraction of the relative see BDR §294.2; Robertson, 716); all this helps to emphasise the fact of their calling by God who is the unspoken subject (cf 1 Th 2.12; Gal 1.6; 1 Cor 1.9; Rom 11.29). The Gentile readers are only where they are as believers and members of the people of God because God has acted. Their calling[5] is not to a special position or function within the church (Rom 1.1; 1 Cor 1.1) but to being Christians (Rom 8.28, 30; 9.11, 24; 1 Cor 1.9; 1 Th 4.7; Eph 1.18) and is closely related to their election (1.4). They are reminded here of their entry into the Christian life through their conversion/baptism. Since Christians are not isolated, their calling is a calling to be with other Christians (Col 3.15; cf 1 Cor 1.2; Rom 1.7) and so it is again referred to when the discussion of the church is taken up in 4.4. AE does not enter into the philosophical question of the relation of calling to the freedom of those who are called, but his later stress on conduct shows that he does not regard the call as affecting freedom of action.

2. In vv. 2, 3 AE outlines in general terms, using two prepositional phrases and two participial clauses, the nature of worthy living in relation to life within the Christian community rather than within society as a whole. Grammatically it would be possible to make the two prepositional phrases, or the second alone, depend on ἀνεχόμενοι (cf Bengel), yet if the former of these was true it would have been unnecessary to repeat the preposition and if the latter the first prepositional phrase would have been left hanging by itself; in

[5] On 'calling' see L. Coenen, *NIDNTT*, I, 271–6; H. H. Rowley, *The Biblical Doctrine of Election*, London, 1950; K. L. Schmidt, *TWNT*, III, 488–97; K. Barth, *Church Dogmatics*, II 2, Edinburgh, 1957; W. Bieder, *Die Berufung im Neuen Testament*, Zürich, 1961; R. Hasenstab, op.cit., 151–83.

either case the parallelism of the two participial clauses would have been destroyed (Haupt; for detailed discussion of the possibilities see Salmond). The three qualities or virtues highlighted by AE in the prepositional phrases are the final three in a sequence of five in Col 3.12 (see also Mt 11.29 for two of them); they are probably therefore a part of the paraenetic tradition (cf Halter, 244); the way in which AE has split them up suggests he has not derived them directly from Col 3.12. Vv. 2f assume unity exists and exhort those who enjoy it to maintain it.

ἀνεχόμενοι ἀλλήλων is found also in Col 3.13a and there are echoes in v. 3 of Col 3.14. Col 3.13b is wholly in line with AE's point here and he would probably have used it if he had known it; the echoes of Col 3.14 are only echoes (see on v. 3) and do not suggest AE was aware of it as he wrote. It could be argued as strongly, if not more so, that A/Col created his list in 3.12 by using Eph 4.2 and, dropping unnecessary words, that he expanded ἀνεχόμενοι ἀλλήλων in 3.13. More probable than the dependence of either writer on the other is the dependence of both on tradition.

The qualities which AE has selected in v. 2 lead appropriately into a discussion of unity. ἀλλήλων (also at 4.25, 32; 5.21) indicates that it is the relationship of members to one another that is above all important in what is to follow. AE emphasises his first two qualities through the use of πᾶς ('every kind of ... '), a favourite of his for this purpose (cf 1.8; 3.19; 4.19, 31; 5.3; 6.18).

The first virtue in the list would probably have surprised Gentile readers when as Christians they first encountered it. Normally the root ταπειν...[6] carries in Greek the derogatory sense of servility; for example, in Epictetus 3.24.56 ταπεινοφροσύνη, our present form of the root, heads a list of qualities which cannot be commended; this meaning of the root is found in the NT (Rom 12.16; 2 Cor 7.6; 12.21; Phil 3.21; Jas 1.9, 10); however the root, through its use in the LXX and Jewish Greek (Ψ 17.28; 33.19; 101.18; Prov 3.34), took on the meaning of non-assertiveness, and this is the more normal sense in the NT (Mt 11.29; Rom 12.16; 2 Cor 7.6; Phil 2.8; 1 Pet 5.5; in Mt 23.12; Lk 14.11; 18.14 it has both senses) and is the meaning in our verse. The customary English translation 'humble' indeed carries both senses. Though often used to describe a proper relationship to God, in v. 2 the root is used of the relationship of Christians to one another. Nothing is more destructive of group unity than that some should assert either themselves or their particular point of view. The same concern for unity governs the use of ταπεινοφροσύνη in Phil 2.3 (see also 1QS 2.24f; 4.3; 5.3 though

[6] On the root see A. Dihle, *RAC* III, 735–78; W. Grundmann, *TWNT*, VIII, 1–27; H.-H. Esser, *NIDNTT*, II, 259–64; K. Wengst, '... einander durch Demut für vorzüglicher halten ...'. Zum Begriff 'Demut' bei Paulus und in paulinischer Tradition', *Studien zum Text und zur Ethik des Neuen Testaments* (FS H. Greeven; BZNW 47; ed. W. Schrage), Berlin, 1986, 428–39.

of course the Greek word is not used in these cases) and is continued in 1 Clem 16.1, 17; 30.3, 8. True humility ensures the absence of the envy which can corrupt corporate activity and Jesus is its prime example (Mk 10.45), though it would be wrong to imagine that AE is actually thinking here of Jesus' earthly example; when his humility is stressed in the Pauline corpus, it relates to his descent from heaven (2 Cor 8.9; Phil 2.5, 8). The belief that they are among the saved and elect has sometimes made some Christians arrogant in relation to those they consider not to be saved. Humility is not self-depreciation, nor the suppression of the feeling, 'I'm important'; it is regarding oneself as unimportant because in the end one is so in relation to the group; it leads to recognising the genuine Christian existence of others and their importance.

The second term, πραΰτης,[7] in v. 2a is also joined with the first in Mt 11.29; Col 3.12. Like the first it was used in biblical Greek but, unlike it, had a good sense in non-biblical Greek and is commended by secular authors (e.g. Aristotle, Nic Eth 1125B, IV 5; M. Aurelius, 9.42). In the NT it is often depicted as the virtue with which to approach opponents and those who have strayed from the faith (1 Cor 4.21; 2 Cor 10.1; Gal 6.1; 2 Tim 2.25) and also the quality with which to treat those outside the church (Tit 3.2; 1 Pet 3.15). Though often rendered 'meekness' this is too passive a rendering for the present context; 'gentleness' suggests more adequately the manner with which other members of the church should be treated. A fruit of the Spirit (Gal 5.23) it is active in promoting unity and does not just seek to avoid trouble by ignoring what is wrong or taking things lying down. Such a gentleness towards others comes in part from an awareness of one's own sin.

The second prepositional phrase, v. 2b, contains only one quality, μακροθυμία.[8] The word was used in the LXX to describe God's merciful way with sinful humanity; he is patient and not easily angered (Exod 34.6; Num 14.18; Ψ 85.15; 102.8). This use reappears in the NT (Lk 15.7; Rom 2.4; 9.22; 1 Pet 3.20). Such a quality is necessary also within a community (cf 1 Th 5.14; 2 Tim 4.2); those who display it do not increase bitterness and its exercise should lead to the dissolution of existing tensions. It is an aspect of love (1 Cor 13.4) and a fruit of the Spirit (Gal 5.22), and God strengthens believers to practise it (Col 1.11).

Of the three virtues expressed here none is peculiarly Christian; the second and third are found in the contemporary secular society, and the first in Judaism.

[7] See F. Hauck and S. Schulz, TWNT, VI, 645–51; W. Bauder, NIDNTT, II, 256–9.
[8] See J. Horst, TWNT, IV, 377–90; U. Falkenroth and C. Brown, NIDNTT, II, 768–72. On all three virtues see also E. Larsson, Christus als Vorbild: Eine Untersuchung zu den paulinischen Tauf-und Eikontexten, Uppsala, 1962, 213–19.

In vv. 2b, 3 there is a change to participial clauses. The participles are in the nominative (*constructio ad sensum*, MHT, 230) agreeing with the subject of ἐκλήθητε and/or the understood subject of περιπατῆσαι. The use of participles instead of imperatives is found in a number of ethical contexts in the NT (Rom 12.9ff; Col 3.9, 10, 13, 16f; Heb 12.15; 13.5; 1 Pet 3.1, 7, 9; 4.8, 10) and in other contexts (2 Cor 8.24; Eph 3.17; Phil 1.29). The usage may have entered Christianity from Judaism (so D. Daube in E. G. Selwyn, *First Peter*, 467–88) but it is also occasionally found in Hellenistic Greek.[9] Its origin prior to its appearance in the NT does not concern us since by the time of Ephesians its use was already accepted practice.

Verse 2b with its implication of reciprocity, 'one another', makes it clear that AE is thinking primarily of behaviour within the community and not of that directed at those outside it. While ἀνεχέσθαι could suggest an attitude of endurance, a resignation to suffering, or a willingness to tolerate what others are doing in order to avoid trouble, it indicates here the more dynamic attitude of love (it reappears in v. 16). Love is never passive but always active, looking to see where others may be helped. It is the primary virtue in relationships (1 Cor 13) and the basis of all behaviour (Rom 13.9, 10; Gal 5.14). No one ever finds it easy to see and allow for the point of view and the actions of others; within the community Christians do not escape this but have regularly to deal with what they regard as the faults of their fellow-Christians and for this love is essential.

3.[10] The second participial clause, the fourth member of the general introductory exhortation, moves from the qualities of character which work for unity to a plea for its preservation; if unity needs to be preserved it must already exist; it does so in respect of Jewish and Gentile Christians (2.11–22) but the outlook here is wider and refers as much to Jewish–Jewish and Gentile–Gentile relations as to Jewish–Gentile relations. While parallel to the participial clause of v. 2b, v. 3 is also to some extent its result and a suitable climax to the phrases of v. 2 (Schlier, Schnackenburg). Those who pay attention to one another in love will work zealously to preserve unity. Unity, ἑνότης (only here in the NT and in 4.13; the word is found regularly in Ignatius, e.g. *Eph* 4.2; 5.1; 14.1; *Philad* 2.2; 3.2; 5.2), is something which Christians already possess; they are one body (4.4). They did not create their unity, though they can destroy it; the later parts of the paraenesis show how this can happen. Effort is necessary to maintain unity and believers must strive to this end with all zeal. σπουδάζοντες, a present participle, implies an active and vigorous effort (cf Gal 2.10; 2 Tim 2.15). There is something of an ambiguity here. If vigorous effort is

---

[9] Cf BDR §468.2; Moule, 179f; Moulton–Turner, 89; Porter, 370ff; A. P. Salom, 'The Imperatival Use of the Participle in the New Testament', *AusBR* 11 (1963) 41–9.

[10] On this verse see Adai, 207–14; Lemmer, 326–9.

needed to preserve an already given unity the possibility must exist of losing it; if it is lost, does the church no longer exist? How essential a mark of the church is unity and what is the nature of that unity? AE does not attempt to answer these questions. It may be this underlying ambiguity which led some commentators (Ambrosiaster, Thomas Aquinas, Calvin, and many moderns) to understand πνεῦμα here as the corporate spiritual feeling of the community, something created by the community and therefore able to be lost by it. However, the 'one Spirit' of v. 4 (cf 2.18, 22) is surely the Holy Spirit and if community spirit had been intended here we should have expected 'the spirit of unity' in parallel with similar expressions where spirit is followed by a noun indicating some quality, e.g. Isa 61.3; 1 Cor 4.21; Gal 6.1. The unity mentioned is not then the spiritual unity of those who think and act in the same way, or of those who elevate the spiritual above the material and believe forms and rites do not matter. It is the unity which the Spirit creates and preserves. Perhaps the ambiguity which lies here in the discussion of unity is in the final issue the same as that which underlies a realised soteriology (see Introduction §6.4) while sin still exists.

The final phrase of the verse is best taken as parallel to ἐν ἀγάπῃ in the preceding participial clause and thus as qualifying the participle, or possibly τηρεῖν (so Lemmer, 328), rather than the phrase about unity. In v. 2 love gave believers the means of living harmoniously with one another; here unity is preserved by the bond of peace, peace between members. σύνδεσμος was used primarily of ties joining things physically and then metaphorically with the same implication. It is used in this way of light as the tie that binds the cosmos (Plato, *Rep* 616BC; cf Philo, *Fuga* 112, who also uses it metaphorically but in a different way). Although it has cosmic and gnostic connections it goes too far with Gnilka to see these operative here; such connections have already been rejected in 2.14–16 and there is even less reason to accept them here. σύνδεσμος reappears in Col 3.14 where it is the 'bond of maturity' (or perfection) and 2.19 where it is what holds the members of the body together. The resemblances between Col 3.14f and our passage are too slender to imply AE's use of Colossians; had he been doing so there is no reason why he should have altered love to peace. σύνδεσμος may have been a term of the Pauline school. AE sees peace (epexegetical genitive) as the bond which ties together those who are united. Love (v. 2) may be the assumption for unity; peace is the cement of its working out in the church. Christ became the peace of the church in his death (2.14–18) and only because he is peace can there be peace between members and unity within the church. 2.14–18 revealed the two aspects of peace, between God and humanity and between one human being and another. It is the latter aspect which enters here but it is in tandem with the former and depends on it. In Col 1.20 peace is conceived cosmologically, here ecclesiologically. Peace is related to reconciliation (2.14–18) and reconciliation is necessary where there is division or the threat of it.

Does AE's stress on the unity of the church mean that he has some actual situation of disunity in mind? Certainly he knew of the earlier division between Jewish and Gentile believers (see 2.11–22) which may still have existed in some quarters, but is that all? It is difficult to tie down what he writes to any particular situation because of the letter's general nature, yet AE must have known of other previous divisions in the church and sensed the possibility of future divisions. Even if he is not Paul he cannot have been unaware of the way in which some questioned Paul's position and of the type of disputes dividing Christians in Corinth. Other writings in the NT (1, 2 Timothy, Titus, 1, 2, 3 John, Revelation) show how easily division could appear. Those who became Christians moreover brought into the church the divisions of society arising from sex, race, wealth, education, slavery, and they were not immediately overcome. Quite apart from all this, people in groups inevitably get on one another's nerves as anyone who has been a member of a group knows. There were thus many possible causes of strain, and the virtues listed in vv. 2, 3 would be necessary if the unity of the church was to be maintained. As a wise pastor AE knew that unity was always at risk unless zealous care was taken to preserve it.

4. The style now changes abruptly. While a few commentators (Dibelius, Gaugler) have understood vv. 4–6 as imperatival ('you ought to be the body') and thus as continuing the exhortation, this cannot be true for all the items in the list ('you ought to be the Lord'!), and it is important to retain the same sense throughout. Is then the link between vv. 4–6 and vv. 2, 3 causal (Abbott)? If so only the first item (one body) in the list would be relevant and an initial γάρ would be expected. It is better to take vv. 4–6 as preparation for what is to follow in vv. 7–16 and as continuing the theme of unity which is already present. Before AE begins to discuss diversity within the church, he stresses its unity. Again 'one body' might seem the only relevant item but the continued use of 'one' drives home the theme of unity. AE probably uses, as we have argued, an existing section of tradition and by using all of it, though it may not all be strictly relevant, he awakens echoes in the minds of his readers, echoes centring on 'one' and therefore on unity. Since AE is using preformed material there is no need to see him as influenced by Col 3.14f. In style vv. 4–6 are an acclamation or declaration.

The first phrase 'one body' recalls 2.16; Col 3.15; Rom 12.5, and there can be no doubt that AE understands it to refer to the church and not to the eucharistic or physical body of Christ. It suitably heads the list since what follows relates to the church and life within it. Normally when AE speaks of the body he makes a close reference, if not a direct one, to Christ, so that the body is identifiable as his (cf 1.23; 2.16; 4.12, 16; 5.23, 30); the absence of such a reference here probably arises from the use of tradition (Schnackenburg). But why one ('one' implies 'one only', cf Klauck, art.cit.) body? Ephesians is not a polemical writing contrasting the body of genuine believers with another of heretics claiming to be the only true body. Perhaps the emphasis on 'one' is in contrast with the variety within the body to which AE will go on (vv. 7–16; cf Rom 12.5; 1 Cor 12.12ff). The body is one over against this variety, yet this would be an unusual use of 'one'.

The body and (the 'and' as we have seen is caused by the elaboration of the third member of the triad) the Spirit[11] had been already connected in 1 Cor 12.13 and lie closely together in Eph 2.16, 18 (cf 2.22); the variety of gifts which exist in the body come from the Spirit (1 Cor 12–14). It is not then surprising to find here the Spirit associated with the body, though we should not think in anthropological terms of a spirit within a body, for the existence of charismatic gifts, though not expressly ascribed to the Spirit, appears in vv. 7–13.

V. 4b is introduced with καθώς which can be either causal or comparative; the latter is to be preferred for if the former is chosen (so Gnilka) this makes καί awkward and it is difficult to see what 'cause' comes into play. In v. 4b AE has rewritten the original 'one hope' in such a way as to connect the tradition contained in vv. 4–6 to what preceded.[12] This means that the important word here is ἐλπίς and not, as Lindemann, Aufhebung, 195, argues κλῆσις, for that would break the symmetry since 'one' is attached to ἐλπίς and not to κλῆσις (for further criticism see Adai, 198). AE had already related hope and calling in 1.18; both contain the element of expectancy. There is a connection with vv. 1–3 not only through 'calling' but also through Spirit, and the tradition is tied in again to its context through the discussion of the body of Christ in vv. 11–16. AE's readers received their hope[13] simultaneously with their call. They are not called to hope but as those who have been called given hope. Previously as Gentiles they had been without hope (2.12); now hope is a part of their inheritance (1.18). 'Hope' is not the feeling of hopefulness but is the content of their hope (res sperata). That

[11] See Adai 193–207; Lemmer 329–33. If spirit is not the feeling of corporate unity in v. 3 it is still less here (pace Haupt). The attempt of J. D. G. Dunn, Baptism in the Holy Spirit (SBT 2nd series, 15), London, 1970, 161f, to make the second member of each triad the most important might be sustained in respect of 'Spirit', but clearly fails in v. 5 where the most important is 'Lord'; the attempt is meaningless in respect of the third triad.

[12] The evidence, B 323 326 pc lat^pt sy^p sa bo^pt, is not sufficiently strong to lead to the omission of καί.

[13] For the word see Woschitż, op.cit., 598–601, and R. Penna '"La speranza alle quale siete stati chiamati" (Ef 4, 4)', PSV 9 (1984), 190–206.

content is not explicitly stated here though the connection to Spirit might suggest that the hope consisted in the full reception of the Spirit whose first-fruits they have already received (1.14). The absence of an explicit statement should not however lead us with Lindemann, *Aufhebung*, 195, to conclude that hope has no future reference; readers know the concept and would naturally fill it in from their normal usage which would have a future reference. It is true that their hope has been already partially fulfilled since they are members of the one body, yet there is a fuller hope (1.10, 13f). But what is the significance of the 'one'? In modern terms we might speak of secular and humanist hopes as if there were several; AE would not have regarded these as hopes since non-Christians are without hope (2.12). 'One' is part of the formula and is not used to contrast a Christian hope with a Jewish or secular.

5. In the triad of this verse we find successively the masculine, feminine and neuter forms of εἷς but we cannot be sure that this is a deliberate artistic device and not simply a matter of chance brought about by the gender of the nouns.

The title 'Lord' was applied to Jesus prior to Paul as its use in pre-Pauline material shows (Rom 10.9; Phil 2.11; 1 Cor 8.6; 12.3); granted this, we have no need in order to understand it here to trace the origins of its use to either Palestinian or early Hellenistic Christianity. Some of the statements where the term is used may have been confessional formulae associated with baptism. The title may then have been the one Christians learnt to use in indicating their new allegiance; this would require some identification of their new Lord over against the many non-Christian lords (cf Rom 10.9; 1 Cor 12.3); there is no identification of 'Lord' here. The origin of our triad probably does not then lie in a confessional statement intended for use by those becoming Christians, despite its reference to baptism. It is a statement for internal church use. What significance has 'one' here? Attempts (Schlier, Gnilka) to see it as expressing the one headship of Christ over either the cosmos (1.10, 22) or the church (4.15), while appropriate to the total context of Ephesians, do not obtain any support from the passage itself, especially when we remember that it occurs in preformed material. It may be that we should see in it the church's acknowledgement that it has only one Lord over against other religions which may have many.

πίστις has been understood here as the trust which believers have in Christ or as their personal faithfulness (e.g. Alford, Macpherson, Salmond, Hendriksen) but much more probably it denotes the content of their faith.[14] It is true this is not the normal Pauline sense

---

[14] On its possible meanings see Serafin de Ausejo, 'La "unidad de fe" en Eph. 4, 5–13', in *XIII SBE*, Madrid, 1953, 2–40. There is no reason to see it with Hanson, 153f, as the most important item in the list; its position militates against such a conclusion.

but he does give it this significance in Rom 1.5; 10.8; Gal 1.23; 3.23ff, and it becomes increasingly frequent in the later NT writings (Col 1.23; 2.7; 1 Tim 3.9; 4.1, 6). The content of the faith while in a sense invariant has always to be expressed in words and in relation to a particular context. Thus the NT contains a number of brief statements of its content (e.g. Rom 1.3, 4; 4.24, 25; 1 Cor 15.3–5; 1 Th 1.9, 10; Jas 1.27), which at first sight do not always agree; there is however a centre which they reflect in varying ways; any attempt to express that centre in words is itself subject to its context (see Best, *Interpreting Christ*, 86–113). Ephesians itself is an expression of the faith set in the context of ecclesiology. There is *one* faith, yet it has many verbal expressions. It would be hazardous to say that AE was unaware of the different ways in which the faith might be expressed and equally hazardous to suggest that he would claim that his own expression of it was not merely unique but wholly correct.

The 'one baptism' is obviously the Christian initiatory rite of water baptism and not Spirit baptism, though of course the two cannot be dissociated. The first two terms of v. 5 are linked to the third in so far as believers are baptised in, or into (the name of Christ) the Lord (Acts 8.16; 19.5) and confess their faith in him through a form of words containing the term 'Lord' (e.g. Rom 10.9, 10). Baptism is also linked to the Spirit and the body (1 Cor 12.13), for believers become members of the body on being baptised and thereafter the Spirit dwells in them (1 Cor 3.16; Rom 8.9) and they participate in the gifts of the Spirit (1 Cor 12.7). As baptised they are now united with one another (1 Cor 12.12f; Gal 3.26ff). They now also have a hope which was not theirs as unconverted Gentiles. Why should the baptism be described as *one*? It can hardly be one in contrast with the washings of Qumran (cf Heb 6.2), the Mystery Religions, or gnosticism (Iren *adv Haer* 1.21.2); nor does 'one' mean 'once for all', i.e. that it is unrepeatable, a position occasionally adopted by paedo-baptists against anabaptists, for as an initiatory rite that is implicit; 'one' is not also an attempt to assert that believers are all baptised with the same baptism (Van Roon, Grosheide), and it does not refer to some all-inclusive act of Christ in his baptism and death.[15] Probably AE uses it because it was already present in the formula; it may have served there to preserve the formula's symmetry. This is the only place in Ephesians where baptism is directly mentioned and it does not provide a sufficient basis for regarding the letter as, or as embodying, a baptismal tract, let alone for regarding vv. 4–6 as a baptismal confession.

Surprisingly the eucharist is omitted from the list of vv. 4, 5. In

[15] So J. A. T. Robinson, 'The One Baptism', *SJT* 6 (1953) 257–74; he is justly criticised by W. E. Moore, 'One Baptism', *NTS* 10 (1963/4) 504–16.

1 Cor 10.17 (cf *Did* 9.4) it is connected to the thought of unity. 'One bread' would have fitted well with our formula. If baptism may be described as the sacrament of unity because Christians are brought together through it, the eucharist is the sacrament which maintains unity. It is as easy to discover connections between it and the other items of vv. 4–6 as it is with baptism. It can hardly have been omitted on the grounds that since it is regularly repeated we could not say 'one eucharist' for this would be to take 'one' in the sense 'once for all', a sense which is elsewhere impossible in the list; in any case 'one bread' would have covered it. The original situation which called forth vv. 4–6 is now lost to us and it is probably impossible to answer the question. Had the formula been compiled today it would almost certainly have contained a reference to the eucharist.

6.[16] This is the climax of the sequence, the one God and[17] Father, who is the one God of one people (cf Josephus *Ant* 4.201). There can be little doubt that 'one' is here intended to make a monotheistic assertion and such an assertion would have been important for Gentile Christians (cf Rom 3.30; 1 Cor 8.4–6; Gal 3.20; 1 Tim 2.5; Jas 2.19), though unnecessary for Jewish Christians whose basic text was Dt 6.4. It also came naturally to Jews to think of God as Father, though this received a new emphasis and direction in the teaching of Jesus. Gentile Christians thus encountered God as Father from the beginning, yet since the idea was not entirely missing from Greek, in particular Stoic, thought, they were conditioned to accept it, even though they had previously understood it in a more pantheistic way. The association of God and Father is found regularly in the Pauline corpus (Rom 1.7; 15.6; 1 Cor 1.3; 2 Cor 1.2, 3; 11.31; Gal 1.3; Eph 1.3), with the words often linked by καί.

In the teaching of Jesus God's Fatherhood sets him in relation to all humanity. Is that the meaning here? In the Pauline corpus God's Fatherhood is generally seen as relating Christ to believers. Normally this limitation arises from the context and we cannot conclude that for Paul God's Fatherhood does not extend to non-believers, if only in a potential manner. In the confessional formulae of 1 Cor 8.6 God is presented as Father in relation to all things. To what then does πάντων refer here? It can be either neuter or masculine. Whatever is decided it is probably correct to see a consistent gender throughout v. 6 (*pace* Iren *adv Haer* 2.2.6; 4.20.2). Favouring the masculine (Haupt, Dibelius, Gaugler, Schlier, Schnackenburg) is the

[16] On the verse see Dibelius, op.cit., 14–29; Knox, *Gentiles*, 194 n. 1; K. Wengst, op.cit., 131–45; W. Pöhlmann, 'Die hymnischen All-Prädikationen in Kol. 1. 15–20', *ZNW* 64 (1973) 53–74 (at 66–74); J. Dupont, *Gnosis*, 329ff; M. Hengel, *Judaism and Hellenism*, London, 1974, I, 261–7.

[17] There are no good grounds for omitting καί with 51 pc vg[mss] sy[p] sa bo[pt]; Ir[arm]. εἰς probably goes with both God and Father.

general context relating to the unity of believers in the church and the immediately following ἑνὶ δὲ ἑκάστῳ ἡμῶν (v. 7) which can be regarded as individualising the preceding 'all'. The problem is of course solved in those manuscripts, D F G Ψ 0278 (1793ᶜ) 𝔐 lat sy Ir, which insert ἡμῖν before πᾶσιν but this is clearly the weaker reading and is explained by the desire to provide a solution. Favouring the neuter understanding (Robinson, Houlden, Gnilka, Barth, Lincoln, Lindemann, *Aufhebung*, 52–4) are: (i) the parallel Greek formulae which certainly relate to the cosmos and not to humanity (e.g. M. Aurelius 7.9); (ii) the relation in Jewish Hellenism of a cosmic fatherhood to God's role in creation (Philo, *Post Cain* 6; *Rer Div* 62; *Det Pot* 147; *Ebr* 147), though this is not viewed pantheistically as in Hellenism (cf Conzelmann); (iii) NT passages such as 1 Cor 8.6; Rom 11.36; Col 1.16; (iv) the cosmic use of 'all' at other places in Ephesians (1.10, 22, 23; 3.9; 4.10); (v) the cosmic role of the church in Ephesians (cf 3.10). The problem is made even more difficult to resolve because v. 6 was probably traditional and may not have been originally united with vv. 4, 5; separated from them and its present context there is little in it to support a masculine understanding. Yet in taking over the preformed material with v. 6 already a part of it, AE may have ignored its original reference and regarded the terms as masculine, since that would be more fitting to the context in which he uses it. If AE took up v. 6 as a separate piece of tradition and added it to a block consisting of vv. 4f he would probably have seen it as referring to all things. If AE knew the block as a whole and used it because he was interested only in the second triad, or the first and second, he may not have thought about the meaning of v. 6 in relation to his context. His readers knew the whole block of tradition and it was appropriate to quote it as a whole and his readers from their Gentile background would probably have understood 'all' as neuter. If AE intended a masculine understanding he has done nothing to preserve his readers from a neuter. In the end it is probably better to give 'all' a neuter meaning throughout with the sense, 'one creator God and Father who governs the cosmos, works through it and is present in it', but the sense might be 'one God and Father of humanity (or all Christians) who governs all, works through them all and is in them all' (presumably by means of his Spirit, Rom 8.9, 11; 1 Cor 3.15; 6.19; 2 Cor 6.16; Gal 3.5).

When we look back over vv. 4–6 we can see that there was a constant difficulty in determining the precise significance of the 'one' attached to each noun. Only in v. 6 can we be sure why it is used, as a rejection of multiplicity, yet it is hardly possible to see this meaning as intended throughout. In v. 6 the one God is defined so that there can be no confusion with other gods. The one Lord is

372 COMMENTARY ON EPHESIANS

not so defined; 'one Lord (who is) Jesus' would have sufficed for
this (cf 1 Cor 8.6). There are evil spirits as well as the Holy Spirit;
'one Spirit of God' or 'one Holy Spirit' would have given a precise
significance to the 'one'. There is no evidence that AE was
attempting to correct a heretical position held by his readers in
respect of a number of 'bodies' or 'baptisms' through his use of
'one'. It may then be better to see the use of 'one' as no more than a
rhetorical device to hold the sequence together.[18] Examples of its use
in this way can be found in ancient literature, e.g. Orphic Frag 168
lines 6f (see O. Kern *Orphicorum Fragmenta*, Berlin, 1922); Plut,
Mor 329AB; 983C; *Thes* 24.1; M. Aurelius 7.9; *CH* 11.11; Epictetus, 3.24.10. Brief lists appear in Jewish literature, *2 Bar* 48.24;
Josephus, *c. Ap.* 2.193; *Ant* 4.200f. The use also appears in early
Christian literature: 1 *Clem* 46.6; Ign. *Magn* 7.1, 2; *Philad* 4;
Hermas, *Sim* 9.17.4; 18.4. In none of these cases, apart from 1 Clem
46.6, does the list overlap that of Eph 4.4–6 to any great degree so
that there is no need to suppose the influence of Eph 4.4–6. As for 1
Clem 46.6 where we have successively God, Christ, Spirit, calling,
we may suspect rather than dependence on Ephesians the existence
of the list of Eph 4.4–6 in a variant form, thus confirming that it pre-
existed Ephesians. The absence from the list of either μία γνῶσις or
μία σοφία suggests it had a non-gnostic origin. Remoteness from the
gospel tradition is suggested by the absence of any reference to the
Kingdom of God; 'Father' as we have seen was not necessarily
derived from that tradition. Everything then goes to support the view
that 4.4–6 is a carefully designed list and, since only parts of it are
appropriate to the context of Ephesians, it was a list which AE
inserted because part of it was useful to him. In addition the effect of
the repeated use of 'one' is to drive home his central theme, unity.
Finally it is interesting to see how the passage comes to a climax in
God. Throughout Ephesians God is the principal actor; here his
supremacy is made clear.

[18] So Hanson, 149f; Dupont, op.cit., 344 n. 2, quotes H. Almquist, *Plutarch und das
Neue Testament*, 1946, 113, to the same effect, suggesting a rhetorical device which
was seized on by popular propaganda. See also E. Peterson, ΕΙΣ ΘΕΟΣ (FRLANT
24), Göttingen, 1926.

B

UNITY AND GROWTH OF THE CHURCH
(4.7–16)

(See also list re 4.1–16)

J. Bover, ' "In aedificationem corporis Christi" ': Eph 4,12' *EstBib* 3 (1944) 313–42 at 333–42; Vielhauer, 122–35; Hanson, 135–7, 155–61; Best, *One Body*, 148–54; Roberts, *Opbou*, 75–108, 129–61, 177–88; Ernst, *Pleroma*, 135–49; id. 'Das Wachstum des Leibes Christi zur eschatologischen Erfüllung in Pleroma', *TGl* 53 (1967) 164–87; Merklein, *Amt*, 57–118; P. Bony, 'L'Épître aux Éphésiens', *Le ministère et les ministères selon le Nouveau Testament* (ed. J. Delorme), Paris, 1974, 74–92; R. Schnackenburg, 'Das kirchliche Amt nach Eph 4,7–16', *Acta Congressus Biblici Cracaoviae* (ed. St. Grzybek and J. Chmiel), Cracow, 1974, 210–33; *Kirche im Werden* (ed. J. Hainz), Paderborn, 1976; *Das kirchliche Amt im Neuen Testament* (Wege der Forschung CDXXXIX, ed. K. Kertelge), Darmstadt, 1977; R. P. Meyer, *Kirche*, 65–77; Meuzelaar, 121–44; S. D. Clark, 'La enseñanza paulina sobre los dones y los ministerios. Un estudio exegético de Efesios 4,7–16', *RivB* 41 (1979) 141–53; H. P. Hamann, 'Church and Ministry: An Exegesis of Ephesians 4:1–16', *LTJ* 16 (1982) 121–8; T. G. Allen, *Body*, 178ff; R. Y. K. Fung, 'The Nature of the Ministry according to Paul', *EvQ* 54 (1982) 129–46; Lemmer, 333–72; S. Basevi, 'La missione di Cristo e dei Cristiani nella lettera agli Efesini', *RevBiblt* 38 (1990) 27–55.

On 4.7–10
Schlier, *Christus*, 2–4; Schlier–Warnach, 89f; Mussner, *Christus*, 41–4; R. Leivestad, *Christ the Conqueror*, London, 1954, 156–60; Roels, 161–3; Roberts, *Opbou*, 75–90; J. Cambier, 'La Signification Christologique d'Eph. iv. 7–10', *NTS* 9 (1962–3) 262–75; G. B. Caird, 'The Descent of Christ in Ephesians 4:7–11', *SE* 2 (= TU 87), Berlin, 1964, 535–45; C. H. Porter, 'The Descent of Christ: An Exegetical Study of Ephesians 4:7–10', *One Faith* (ed. R. L. Simpson), Enid, OK, 1966, 45–55; H. Schürmann, 'Die geistlichen Gnadengaben in den paulinischen Gemeinden', in his *Ursprung und Gestalt*, Düsseldorf, 1970, 236–67; P. F. Theron, 'Christus, die Gees, Kerk en Kosmos volgens Efesiërs 4:7–10', *NedGTT* 14 (1973) 214–23; Lindemann, *Aufhebung*, 218–21; Meuzelaar, 133–7; Overfield, 89–172.

7 Grace has been given to each one of us
    in accordance with the measure of the gift of Christ;
8 therefore it says:
    Ascending on high he led captives captive;
    he gave gifts to men.

373

9   And what significance has 'He ascended'
       unless he also descended into the lower regions,
           that is, the earth?
10   He who descended is himself also the one who ascended
               above all the heavens,
           so that he might fill all things.
11 And he gave some as apostles, others as prophets, others as
           evangelists, others as shepherds and teachers,
12   for the equipment of the saints,
       for their ministering activity,
       for the building up of the body of Christ,
13   until we all attain
           to the unity of faith and knowledge of the son of
               God,
           to a mature male,
           to the measure of the size of fullness of Christ,
14   that you may no longer be children,
           tossed by the waves,
           and blown about by every wind of teaching,
           by human trickery cunningly pointed towards the
               planning of error,
15   rather speaking truth in love
           let us grow in every respect unto him.
           who is the head, Christ,
16   from whom the whole body.
           fitted and held together
               through every ligament of supply,
                   in a powerful manner,
               in the proportion of each individual member,
           makes its increase
               unto its own upbuilding in love.

At v.7 AE changes from the second plural to the first, returning to
the latter at v. 17. Vv. 7–16 are consequently a distinct unit and this
is emphasised by the use of εἰς ἕκαστος in both v. 7 and v. 16 (an
inclusio). The movement from the second to the first person is
similar to that in 2.14–18; in each case AE wishes to identify Paul,
or himself, with his readers (cf 2.3). In 2.14–18 AE may have made
the change to drive home the point that there should be no Jewish
and Gentile controversy within the church; here he changes because,
intending to show the variety of gifts within the church, he does not
wish to leave himself (or Paul) in a superior position as though not
possessing or needing any of the gifts. With the use of the first
plural the direct paraenetic element appears to disappear, but it is
implied throughout since the duties laid down for 'us' are obviously
duties laid on the readers.

δέ signifies the beginning of a new section, a turn in the argument, but is not necessarily strongly adversative (cf 3.20; 5.3; 6.21); it provides a 'transitional contrast' (Eadie). We move from the stress on unity (vv. 4–6) to diversity in vv. 7–10, but unity returns as the prevailing theme in vv. 11–16. A true unity will not be monolithic (Bouwman) but will contain variety within itself, as Paul had already stressed in 1 Cor 12.12–31; Rom 12.3–8. The unity in question is of course that of the church, though strangely the word church is not itself used in this paragraph. Underlying it is the image of the body of Christ, though this concept is not made explicit until v. 12. AE does not need to explain it, for he can presume the familiarity of his readers with it through its use by Paul. There are however differences, or developments, compared with its earlier use by Paul and variations also from its use in Colossians, though the image is the only important point of contact vv. 7–16 have with that letter in respect of the church. AE has a view of his own to express and he expresses it, yet in so doing he shows himself Paul's pupil.

'One' was the term echoing through vv. 4–6; v. 7 continues it with 'each one' (cf v. 16) and in this way links together unity and diversity. But the 'one' of v. 7 also introduces a new turn of thought in setting out the diversity as deriving from the variety of gifts among the members of the church. This variety is not that of natural talent, educational attainment or cultural variation, but has its source in Christ the giver of the gifts of vv. 7, 8, 11. Members do not bring with them the gifts which AE has in mind when they enter the church, but on entering receive them. These gifts are not given for self-promotion, but for the building up the church in unity. The giving of the gifts is supported in v. 8 with a quotation seemingly drawn from Ps 68.18 to which is added a midrashic-type inter-pretation (vv. 9f); as an exegetical excursus it enables the quotation to be applied to Christ. It might seem that vv. 8–10 could be omitted without disturbing the flow of the argument, but if they were v. 11 would jar with v. 7 in that, unlike the latter, it offers a limited range of gifts to a minority of believers. The gifts went unidentified in v. 7; v. 11 specifies them, not as functions to be exercised, but as 'officials' who are given to the church. This variation causes some problems. The function of these officials towards other believers is then expressed (v. 12) and also the goal for all to aim at, first positively (v.13) and then negatively (v. 14). All of vv. 12–16 depend on v. 11. The naming of the office-bearers indicates a distinction between them and ordinary members of the church, a distinction which later developed into that between clergy and laity, though in no way does AE demean or devalue the ordinary or lay members of the church. In a sense vv. 7–14 are descriptive; the direct paraenetic element reappears in vv. 15, 16 though it was latent throughout. Vv. 11–16 are one sentence and provide another example of AE's complex and unwieldy style in which prepositional phrases intermingle with subordinate clauses and participles.

The unity which belongs to the church has not come because it has harmonised itself to the norms of society, or subjected itself to the powers, or accepted false teaching, or undervalued its own diversity, but arises out of its position in relation to God and Christ (vv. 4–6); the church may have an organisation but it is not simply a social organisation; it is the body of Christ.

7. δέ signals a change of subject and ἑνί picks up the use of 'one' in vv. 4–6, perhaps making the appeal to individual believers a little more emphatic, since ἑκάστῳ by itself would have conveyed what is needed. The move to the first person plural shows that Paul himself, or AE, is to be included within the process by which the whole church is built up into a unity. But is Paul included as Christian or apostle, AE as Christian or teacher?

Does the introduction of the first person plural mean that all believers are included or only those listed in v. 11 (ἐδόθη is a gnomic aorist emphasising the actual bestowal of the gift rather than its continual provision which would require the present tense, Beare)? The main argument (cf Schlier; Mussner; Merklein, Amt, 59ff) in favour of the restriction of v. 7 to specified leaders is the direct move from v. 7 to v. 11 with nothing intervening to suggest a change in respect of those in mind.

Merklein also argues: (a) There must be something new here beyond the charismatic discussions in 1 Corinthians and Romans where all receive charismata; yet there is no inherent reason why Ephesians should differ from the genuine Paulines. (b) There is a distinction between the 'all' of v. 6 and the 'each' of v. 7; yet this is only true if the 'all' of v. 6 relates to all humans and not all things. (c) The movement back to all believers only comes with v. 13; yet that is no reason for assuming v. 7 does not refer to all. (d) The change from the second plural of 4.1–6 to the first of v. 7 indicates a change of subject; yet AE may only have made this change because he wished to include Paul among the number of those who received gifts. (e) Verse 11 picks up the ἐδόθη of v. 7; yet it could be picking up the ἔδωκεν of v. 8. (f) If v. 7 and v. 11 do not refer to the same group of people then the unity of vv. 7–16 is destroyed; yet vv. 13–16 refer to a different group from that of v. 11 and would not this destroy the unity of the paragraph?

However, there are positive arguments in favour of taking v. 7 to refer to all believers with the vast majority of commentators. (i) Elsewhere charismatic gifts are given to all Christians and not office-bearers alone (Rom 12.6–8; 1 Cor 12.28–30; 1 Pet 4.10f). (ii) V. 7 differs strikingly from v. 11 in that in the former gifts are given to people, in the latter the gifts are the people. (iii) The paraenesis of the letter is addressed elsewhere to all believers except where it is made clear that limited groups are in mind (e.g. in 5.22–6.9); in particular 4.2, 3 apply to all believers. (iv) Vv. 13ff refer to all believers and this is a return to vv. 7–10. (v) ἑκάστῳ without ἑνί would have sufficed if only the list of v. 11 had been intended; the addition of ἑνί emphasises that no one is excluded from those who receive gifts. (vi) The existence of ministry is not a major theme in Ephesians; for example, the readers are never instructed to obey ministers. Perhaps AE inserted v. 7 so that no one should be envious either of those named in v. 11 or of their roles.

χάρις[1] is used here in relation not to redemptive grace as in 2.5, 8 but to special graces, an extension of its use in 3.2, 7, 8 of Paul's ministry; Paul had already used this sense (Rom 12.6); in v. 7 as in 3.2, 7, 8 it is associated with δίδωμι (cf Merklein, Amt, 63). Only those receiving redemptive grace receive charismatic graces. Within our context χάρις is the equivalent of χάρισμα (Rom 12.6; 1 Cor 12.4, 9, 28, 30, 31; cf 1 Cor 3.10; Gal 2.9; Rom 1.5; 12.3). It is not clear why AE did not use the latter; perhaps having already used the former in respect of Paul's ministry he wished to suggest that while others were not endowed with the same gifts as Paul they were endowed in the same way as Paul. It is not sufficient to say with Masson that God gives grace to each in accordance with the needs of his/her spiritual pilgrimage, for the grace is given not for the person but for the building up of the community. χάρις by its nature is a gift and its given nature is stressed through the verb whose subject is probably Christ since he is the giver in v. 8; in Rom 12.3ff and 1 Cor 12.28ff God is the giver; in 1 Cor 12.4–11 the Spirit is the giver; the position of Christ is thus emphasised here. The grace is given according to the μέτρον.[2] The word appears twice more in our passage (vv. 13, 16) but only twice elsewhere in Paul (Rom 12.3; 2 Cor 10.13), and has probably the sense 'full measure'. The giving is not random but in accordance with Christ's plan; he apportions gifts to believers.[3] Graces are not given because of an existing degree of faith in believers; they are gifts, not the result of works (cf Origen, Chrysostom). Are they however given to supplement the natural talents which believers already possess? AE does not enter into such questions, but the stress he lays on the givenness of the gifts suggests he would have had no place for any idea of inborn talent or educational achievement as predetermining who should have each particular gift. Graces however never destroy individuality and the

[1] The article should be read; it was probably omitted by some predecessor or predecessors of B D* F G L P* 082 6 326 1739 1881 al co because they suspected dittography with the preceding η in ἐδόθη.
[2] On the word see C. E. B. Cranfield, 'Μέτρον πίστεως in Romans xii.3', NTS 8 (1961/2) 345–51.
[3] Some gnostics influenced by Christianity also made use of the concept of gifts of grace, e.g. Interp Know XI, 1 15.23–16.19; 16.28–31; 17.36–18.11.

fact that they are given according to measure should preserve believers from envying the gifts bestowed on others.

8. Though AE often quotes without giving any indication that he is doing so (e.g. 4.25; 5.31; 6.2f), his διὸ λέγει here makes it clear that he is consciously citing. A number of questions at once raise themselves: From where does he cite? Why does he do so? What is the subject of λέγει?

We commence with the last question. Paul uses this verb, or an equivalent, to introduce OT quotations; he normally specifies the subject: scripture in Rom 4.3; 9.17; 10.11; Gal 4.30; God in Rom 9.15; 2 Cor 6.16; David in Rom 4.6f; 11.9; Isaiah in Rom 10.16; 15.12; Hosea in Rom 11.25. Only 2 Cor 6.2 (cf Jas 4.6) has a simple λέγει; though there is no stated subject at Gal 3.16, the quotation is identified as from the OT through the reference to Abraham and at Rom 15.10 by the preceding γέγραπται. AE uses the simple λέγει again at 5.14 which is not a quotation from scripture but probably part of a Christian hymn (see notes there). At first sight 4.8 appears to be a quotation from Ps 68.18; this we have seen not to be so (Introduction §9.1.1; 9.2.3); there is not only the major variation from 'receiving' to 'giving'[4] but also minor variations; these are either what we might expect in accommodating a quotation to its context (third person for second person, initial participle for finite verb[5]), or were made necessary by the change of verb ('to men' for 'among men'). Such changes take place regularly when the NT quotes the OT; and passages originally referring to Yahweh are regularly applied as here to Christ. Some translations clearly regard v. 8 as an OT quotation for they insert 'scripture' as the subject of λέγει, e.g. NEB, REB, GNB, Phillips. Most of those who write on AE's use of the OT never discuss whether what is here is a scriptural quotation. If someone quoted the Sabbath commandment (Exod 20.8–10; Deut 5.12–14) replacing 'six' with 'five' and 'seventh' with 'sixth' it would not be accepted as scripture even though it would appear to be in the spirit of the original commandment, but the variation in v. 8 does not preserve the original sense. This problem about the quotation of Ps 68.18 is not unique. When James cites Amos 9.11f in Acts 15.15ff, he is presented as quoting it in its LXX form because only the LXX version supports his argument; the LXX form probably arose out of a mistranslation of the Hebrew; but which is scripture, MT or LXX? James, or the author of Acts, certainly regards what he cites as scripture as the introductory formula ('as it is written') shows.

---

[4] Origen appears to have been aware of both verbs: in *Luc Hom*, GCS 49.2; 159.23f and *Comm Jn*, GCS 10; 165.27 he favours 'giving', but in *Matt Comm A* §132, GCS 38; 270.2 and *Ezek Hom* I.6, GCS 33; 351.8, 'receiving'.

[5] Codex Vaticanus does have the participle in the Psalm but it may have been influenced here by the Christian tradition of Eph 4.8.

Older commentators who spotted the difficulty about the nature of the quotation in v. 8 resorted to various explanations,[6] attributing the variation to a lapse in memory, to an inspired alteration (since it appears in the NT and the NT is scripture, it must be scripture!), to the belief that giving is more Christian than receiving (Calvin), that the altered text provides a deeper or more mystical meaning (Ellicott, Grotius), or explaining it as 'Christ received faith and gave gifts' (Theodoret, Oecumenius); Lock regarded it as part of a Christian hymn;[7] H. St. J. Thackeray suggested that the change lay in line with Jewish exegesis which permitted the interchange of the order of letters in a word (such a solution would imply AE had been rabbinically trained which would be true if AE was Paul but not necessarily if he was one of his disciples; the change would hardly have been appreciated by his readers).[8] However, recent commentators, having discovered that the same change of meaning in the verb is present in the Targum of Ps 68, have concluded that AE is not quoting the OT directly but the targum.[9] This assumes AE knew the targum and, since quotations introduced to confirm arguments, as here, are only effective if they are known not only to the writer but also to those who hear or read them, it must be assumed AE expected his readers to know the targum version of the Psalm. But were targums, renderings into Aramaic enabling those who spoke Aramaic but not Hebrew to understand Synagogue readings, in use in Asia Minor? Would not the Septuagint have fulfilled this function there where Jews normally spoke Greek? There were a considerable number of Jews in this area and, even though some of them continued to use Aramaic in their homes, would they not have been satisfied with a Greek translation for public worship? Almost all the extant Jewish inscriptions in Asia Minor are in Greek and use the LXX; occasionally Hebrew appears but never Aramaic (see Trebilco, *passim*). If it is difficult to think of AE's Jewish readers being familiar with the targum, it is almost impossible to conceive of his Gentile readers as familiar with it. It must of course be granted that AE, who was probably a Jew, may have been aware of the targum since we can detect quite a number of Semitic influences in his writing. But even if he had known it

---

[6] A full discussion of possible explanations will be found in R. A. Taylor, 'The Use of Psalm 68:18 in Ephesians 4:8 in Light of the Ancient Versions', *BSac* 148 (1991) 319–36; he settles for the use by AE of a variant text form.

[7] A suggestion which according to Meyer had been made earlier by Storr and Flatt.

[8] *The Relation of St Paul to Contemporary Jewish Thought*, London, 1900, 182.

[9] A. M. Harmon, 'Aspects of Paul's Use of the Psalms', *WTJ* 32 (1969) 1–23, at p. 6, denies that the targum is used here: 'It is best to regard this as an instance of deliberate alteration by Paul in order to bring out the full meaning of the passage'!

would he have regarded it as scripture? For Jews the targums were inferior to the MT.[10]

The targum version of Ps 68.18 runs as follows,

You ascended the firmament, Prophet Moses; you took captivity captive;
you learned the words of the Law; you gave them as gifts to the sons of man.[11]

Here Moses receives the Law and gives it to Israel; while 'sons of man' might indicate humanity as a whole it should probably be understood as referring to the Jews. It is clear v. 8 is no more a quotation of the targum than it is of the MT or the LXX; it differs from the targum in rejecting the references to Moses and the Law and in its second line it has only one action on the part of Christ ('giving') unlike the two of Moses. AE could easily have presented Christ as receiving from God the gifts he gives to believers. The targum, as we have it, is late yet it may preserve earlier tradition from our period. There is some evidence supporting the targumic understanding of the Psalm in other Jewish sources (*Midr Ps* 68 §11, 160a; *Exod R* 28.1; *Ab R Nathan* 2 (2a); cf SB III, 596–8)[12]. Philo in featuring Moses gives him almost mystical significance and his writings might have been known to Greek Jews in Asia Minor. R. Rubinkiewicz argues that the reading of the targum lies behind *T Dan* 5.10f[13] and there are many parallels between Ephesians and the XII Testaments. Justin Martyr, *Trypho* 39.4; 87.6, knows the form of Ps 68.18 as found in Ephesians but shows no sign of knowing Ephesians. The targumic tradition may thus have been early and fairly widespread.

There seem to be two possibilities: AE, or a predecessor, either replaced Yahweh with Christ in the MT or LXX of the Psalm and at the same time altered the verb, or replaced Moses with Christ in the thought of the targum, and at the same time removed the mention of Moses, the Law and the reception of the Law. The second seems

---

[10] Cf M. McNamara, *The New Testament and the Palestinian Targum to the Pentateuch* (AnBib 27), Rome, 1966, 38ff; Moore, *Judaism*, I, 302ff; Schürer, I, 99ff; P. S. Alexander, 'Jewish Aramaic Translations of the Hebrew Scriptures', *Mikra* (ed. M. J. Mulder), Assen, 1988, 217–53; R. le Déaut, 'The Targumim', *Cambridge History of Judaism* (ed. W. D. Davies and L., Finkelstein), Cambridge, 1989, 563–90.

[11] Translation as in M. McNamara, op.cit., 79. I have added punctuation and rearranged the layout to correspond to the two lines of Ps 69.18 as normally given in Greek texts.

[12] On the question whether Syriac texts were similar to the targum see E. Nestle, 'Zum Zitat in Eph 4,8', *ZNW* 4 (1903) 344f; cf Lindars, 52, n. 2, who thinks there was a variant Hebrew text behind the targum and 4.8 but admits this cannot be proved.

[13] 'PS LXVIII 19 (= EPH IV 8): Another textual tradition or Targum?', *NT* 17 (1975) 219–24.

more probable, since to suppose that two independent thinkers altered the verb in the Psalm in the same way at or about the same time and one replaced Yahweh with Christ and the other introduced Moses is hard to credit. The targumic tradition may have been known among some Jews in Asia Minor from which it was picked up either by Gentile Christians or, much more probably, by Jewish Christians, and adapted to suit their purposes. The early Christians were much freer in quoting the OT than modern scholars. The personal pronoun of Hab 2.4 is omitted by Paul (Rom 1.17; Gal 3.11) thus allowing the text to refer to a believer's faith; in quoting Deut 30.12–14 at Rom 10.6–8 he eliminates all the original reference to a commandment of the Law.[14] This freedom with the text exists in the OT itself: the Chronicler modified the material of 1, 2 Samuel and 1, 2 Kings (or vice versa if the latter books used 1, 2 Chronicles). If readers are to be convinced that an altered text still carries authority, it is necessary to suppose they knew it in its altered form, and in our case this would have to be true not just for a limited group in one church but in the churches over a relatively wide area to which the letter was addressed. It is possible that the altered form of Ps 68.18 would sound like biblical language to Gentile readers and so be acceptable to them; they could not be expected to know the LXX in any detail. All this suggests it is better to conjecture that AE himself did not alter the text but used a tradition known to him and his readers, though possibly it did not relate to Christ and the giving of gifts.[15]

AE's introductory formula is imprecise and does no more than inform readers that what follows is a quotation. If a Jew or a Jewish Christian had pointed out that the quotation differed from the original Psalm, AE could have defended himself by saying that he had made no claim to be quoting scripture. The quotation which follows the same introductory formula at 5.14 is not scripture but probably part of a Christian hymn (see on 5.14). Yet we need to be careful here. We would certainly not regard 5.14 as scripture, but did AE? We do not know. Jude quotes *1 Enoch* as though it were scripture; the author of 2 Timothy draws from Jewish tradition the names Jambres and Jannes as opponents of Moses and appears to regard the names as if they were mentioned in the OT (3.8). If AE uses the same imprecise formula at 5.14 and here and if 5.14 is not scripture are we to assume that AE did not regard 4.8 as a quotation from scripture? Yet it is a quotation from somewhere. But from where? Was it part of a Christian hymn as McNamara suggests

[14] On the ways in which Paul modifies quotations from the OT see D.-A Koch, *Die Schrift als Zeuge des Evangeliums* (BHT 69), Tübingen, 1986, 102–98.

[15] Cf T. Moritz, 'The Use of Išrael's Scriptures in Ephesians' (Ph.D. thesis, King's College, University of London, 1994).

(op.cit., 81 n. 28; there is no reason to accept his further suggestion that it belonged to the same hymn as 5.14)?[16] We cannot say. Certainly the change from the finite verb to the participle ἀναβάς and from the second person to the third would favour this. What is clear is that from wherever AE took it he saw that it was just what he needed to confirm his statement of v. 7 that Christ gives gifts to believers.

We have now answered the first and third of our initial questions. The second remains. From what we have said, AE at any rate uses the citation (did he realise it derived from Ps 68?) in order to confirm his statement of v. 7 and not in anticipation of v. 11, for in the latter verse God (Christ) does not give gifts to people but gives people to the church. It is also possible AE used it because he could develop it in relation to Christ's ascension, which he does in vv. 9f. It may have had an existing interpretation which he feels he ought to correct and therefore writes vv. 9f.

The citation itself requires little comment.[17] The double use of the root αἰχμαλ- is Semitic; the transference of the text to Christ fits in with much NT theology. Who however are the captives whom Christ leads captive? Since AE probably did not derive v. 8 directly from Ps 68, the Psalm can provide no answer. AE himself provides no explicit clues and perhaps it is wrong even to pose the question. Leivestad (cf Mitton) suggests AE had never even thought about the matter. Yet since most commentators make some attempt to answer the question, we probably ought to do the same. Any answer is inevitably linked to the understanding of vv. 9f. The introductory participle is almost certainly to be taken to denote an action simultaneous with the main verb so that the captives are brought up with Christ as he ascends and are not found at the completion of the ascent. If his descent involves his journey to Hades, then he will have brought the captives from there and they may well be the souls of the dead, or, more generally, Satan's captives; this is the opinion of most of the Fathers. If the ascent is taken to be that to the cross (so Oecumenius, Ambrosiaster) in the light of Col 2.14f the captives would be the powers. If the descent of v. 9 is to earth in the incarnation and the ascent that of the ascension, then in the light of 1.21f the captives will again be the powers. This solution goes back as far as Irenaeus who calls them the rebellious angels (*Epid* 83). Against this it may be said that the powers dwell in the heavenlies

---

[16] Fischer, 139, thinks it may have belonged to a collection of Testimonies; cf E. E. Ellis, *Paul's Use of the Old Testament*, Edinburgh, 1957, 16.

[17] The addition of καί by ℵ² B C*.³ D² Ψ 1739 1881 𝔐 sy; MVict at the beginning of the second line of the quotation does not affect the meaning but makes the syntax a little simpler for those unacquainted with the way Hebrew poetry connects lines without conjunctions. The addition of ἐν before τοῖς by F G 614 630 2464 *pc* vg^ms; Hier^pt may be a recollection of ἐν in the LXX.

yet the sphere of their activity where they interfere with believers is earth. Even if AE does not identify the captives he does identify in vv. 7, 11 the booty, i.e. what the captor in accordance with ancient custom distributes to his accompanying army. The booty is either charismatic gifts (v. 7) or church leaders (v. 11), or more probably both.

9. The ἀναβάς of the quotation is now picked up and developed and we appear to be led away from the main theme of Christ's gifts to the church; we return to it in v. 11. It may be that if AE and his readers associated Moses with Ps 68 they need to be shown that it could be more appropriately interpreted of Christ.[18]

The only question in the letter is in this verse, though Paul uses questions frequently. The article τό (cf Gal 5.14; Rom 13.9; BDR §267.1; MHT, 152; Robertson, 766) is used to reintroduce a part of the quotation. τί ἐστι has the sense 'what does this imply?' (Salmond). πρῶτον appears in ℵ² B C³ Ψ 𝔐 f vg sy sa^mss; Eus; it is probably an interpretative addition to clarify that the descent preceded the ascent and, possibly, to indicate that Christ's descent was into Hades; it is unlikely to have been omitted if originally present. μέρη is omitted by 𝔓⁴⁶ D* F G it; Ir^lat Clem^ex Thd Ambst; its presence or absence, the latter is probably the better reading, hardly affects the meaning.

Christ is the subject of ἀνέβη (note the return to the finite form of the verb as in the Psalm, though in the third person unlike the Psalm) and therefore also of κατέβη: the same person ascends and descends. The idea of Christ's ascension (see on 1.20 for references) is common in the NT. It completes his incarnation in a victorious manner. If he ascended into heaven to where did he descend and when did he do so?

The almost unanimous answer of the Fathers was that Christ descended into Hades after his death, e.g. Irenaeus, *Epid* 83; Origen, *Exod Hom*, GCS 29, 198.2; Tertullian, *adv Praxean* 30; Chrysostom, Jerome (Theod Mops and Ambrose *Ep* 76.10 appear to be the only exceptions). They take κατώτερα τῆς γῆς (a partitive genitive) as indicating a place lower than the earth and as in contrast to ὑπεράνω. In his ascent from Hades Christ brought with him the souls of the dead or the devil, death, sin, the curse. This view has also the support of some modern interpreters, e.g. Selwyn, *1 Peter*, 314–62; Beare; Robinson; Arnold, 57; A. T. Hanson.[19] Though none of the latter would probably have thought the evidence relevant, this view received a fresh impetus from the *religionsgeschichtliche Schule* at the turn of the century in its theory of the descent and

---

[18] Strangely the idea of descent and the bringing up of captives is transferred to Paul in *Apoc Paul* V, 2 23.13–16.

[19] *The New Testament Understanding of Scripture*, London, 1980, 126–41.

ascent of a heavenly saviour (see the work of W. Bousset and others).[20] While direct influence cannot be proved it is difficult to deny the existence of contemporary stories of descending and ascending redeemers; these would predispose Gentile believers to accept the idea in respect of Christ. It had already appeared, whether independently or under similar influence, in passages in John (e.g. 3.13; 6.35ff) and in Phil 2.6–11. The Fathers found support for their idea that Christ after his death and prior to his resurrection made a journey to the place of the dead in 1 Pet 3.19 (they also often took Rom 10.6–8 in this way). The idea eventually became embedded in the Apostles' Creed, though actual evidence for its acceptance only begins to appear in the middle of the second century (Justin, *Trypho* 72; *Gospel of Peter* 10 (41f)). It may have been to support this theory that πρῶτον was inserted in some texts (see above). A. T. Hanson says that Paul never uses καταβαίνω to refer to the incarnation; this is true, but Paul does not refer to the incarnation very often and could have varied his terms; the argument is in any case irrelevant if Paul did not write Ephesians. In this theory κατώτερα and ὑπεράνω are taken as contrasting terms, below the earth and above heaven. This implies a three-layer picture of the cosmos (heaven, earth, Hades) as in Phil 2.10; this is at variance with the picture elsewhere in Ephesians of two layers (heaven, earth) with the evil powers not below the earth but above it; they are subdued in heaven and not in Hades (cf 1.10, 20f; 2.2; 6.10 and see Detached Note: The Heavenlies). There may of course be more than one layer in heaven and it is to this that ὑπεράνω refers; this eliminates the contrast with κατώτερα. Although the total evidence is slight it is the resurrection and not the ascension which is normally associated with Hades; the ascension takes place from earth. In accounts of journeys to Hades the return is normally made to earth and not heaven (Schlier, *Christus*, 3f).

If the lower parts of the earth are not the underworld they must be earth itself (γῆς would then be either an epexegetical genitive or one of apposition) and the contrast would be with heaven, earth being below heaven.[21] (One must regret that AE did not make himself clear by writing either εἰς τὴν γῆν or ἕως ᾅδου.) At this point those who adhere to the theory of an ascent from earth diverge over the time and nature of the descent. Is the reference to the incarnation or to Pentecost?

The case for the latter has been argued vigorously and clearly by

---

[20] C. Colpe, *Die religionsgeschichtliche Schule*, Göttingen, 203–8, 161ff; Gnilka, 33–45; H.-M. Schenke, *Der Gott 'Mensch' in der Gnosis*, Göttingen, 1962, 155f.

[21] Cf Aelius Aristides 46.5 (3, p. 31) quoted in P. W. van der Horst, *Aelius Aristides and the New Testament*, Leiden, 1980, 61. Locke takes the unusual view that the descent was to the cross and the tomb.

G. B. Caird and more recently by W. H. Harris,[22] though of course Caird was neither its earliest nor at the time he wrote its sole supporter (cf Theron, Clark, Porter). Abbott had earlier advanced the view that the descent was that of Christ to dwell in the souls of believers (cf 2.17; 3.17; Jn 14.23), but the aorist κατέβη suggests a once-for-all descent and not an ever-renewed descent into a succession of believers (cf Gaugler); this objection cannot be raised against the view that it refers to Pentecost. The Spirit was given at Pentecost and the charismata are linked to the Spirit (1 Cor 12.8ff); Eph 4.7 refers to charismatic gifts from Christ and his gifts cannot be distinguished from those of the Spirit (1 Cor 12.4f); Acts 2.33 may indeed represent another tradition which sees Christ as the giver of the Pentecostal gift. Support for this view is drawn also from later Jewish tradition which placed the giving of the Law to Moses at Pentecost (Moore, *Judaism*, II, 48; *b Pes* 68b). Ps 68 was also an appointed reading for Pentecost. According to this theory Christ is viewed as ascending to heaven after the resurrection, descending at Pentecost with his gifts, and then ascending once again to heaven. Finally, as Harris points out, this view succeeds in incorporating vv. 9,10 into the argument of the letter and does not leave them as a parenthesis. The theory is attractive but has its weaknesses. It is clearly excluded if πρῶτον is read, for this places the descent prior to the ascent. Leaving this variant aside, v. 8 implies that Christ's gifts were associated with his ascension and not with his descent. It is difficult to see Christians interpreting Ps 68 in relation to Pentecost since it has no reference to the Spirit (cf Merklein, *Amt*, 68, n. 49), and nowhere suggests a descent of Christ. Moses and Christ appear to be equated; there is nothing elsewhere in Ephesians to support this (*pace* A. T. Hanson, op.cit., 137); if Ephesians suggests any OT figure as prefiguring Christ it is Adam rather than Moses (see on 5.22–33). Caird, art.cit., 542f, argues that Jewish tradition unearthed in Num 21.17f a reference to the Torah and Christians turned it into one to Christ; this however would imply that if Christ represents Torah and if, in the developed tradition of Ps 68, Moses was given the Torah, then Christian interpretation would see Moses as being given Christ; for AE Christ is not the given but the giver. It is certainly true that Ps 68 came to be associated in Jewish tradition with Moses and the Law but we cannot be sure that this view had appeared as early as our period[23] nor can we be sure,

---

[22] 'The Ascent and Descent of Christ in Ephesians 4:9–10', *BSac* 151 (1994) 198–214.
[23] There is much less certainty today about what was read and when in the synagogue in the first century; cf P. Bradshaw, *The Search for the Origin of Christian Worship*, London, 1992, 21–4; J. Heinemann, 'The Triennial Lectionary Cycle', *JJS* 19 (1968) 41–8; M. J. Moulder, 'The Reading of the Bible in the Ancient Synagogue', *Mikra*, Assen, 1988, 137–59.

as we have seen, that AE realised that the piece of tradition he was quoting derived ultimately from Ps 68. There is also no reason for holding with Kirby that Ephesians was related as a whole to Pentecost (see Introduction §8.3.7). As for the difficulty of vv. 9f being parenthetical it needs to be pointed out that AE is not averse to parentheses (2.2–4; 3.2–13). Perhaps the greatest difficulty for this theory, apart from its complexity (would Gentile Christians have been able to appreciate it without further explanation?), is the normal Christian association of the Spirit with a descent at Pentecost; it is true that Christ and the Spirit are often identified, or almost identified, but nothing suggests their equivalence in this passage; there are indeed many points in the letter where they are kept apart (1.3, 13; 2.20–2; 3.16f; 4.4f).[24] Christ moreover would not need to descend at Pentecost to give gifts to believers, for in the picture of Ephesians they are already in heaven with him (2.6).

If Christ's descent is not then to the underworld and is not linked to Pentecost, it must be the descent of the incarnation. It is true that καταβαίνω is an unusual word to denote this (it is applied to the parousia in 1 Th 4.16; cf Jas 1.17; Rev 3.12; 21.2, 10), but the incarnation as event is not often described in Paul. Even if this is the obvious solution it is still puzzling why the descent should be mentioned at all; perhaps it is because the descent of Christ preceded his ascent whereas we have the reverse in the case of Moses; it serves then to distinguish him from Moses. But the descent may be mentioned in preparation for v. 11 since it was the earthly Jesus who gave the apostles to the church. Whatever the meaning of the descent and ascent, the Fathers used this text christologically against Nestorius and Paul of Samosata. The ascension is of course presented as one of victory through the taking of captives and the distribution of gifts (the booty of the victory?).

10. We continue with the idea of the ascent and descent of Christ (αὐτός lacking the article is emphatic rather than meaning 'the same one') though these are now mentioned in reverse order (a chiastic arrangement, Lemmer, 346f).

That God sent Christ into the world or gave him to it was already accepted Pauline doctrine (Gal 4.4; Rom 8.3, 32; cf Jn 3.16f; 1 Jn 4.9f), but God is not depicted here as initiating the coming of Christ; Christ himself is responsible for his descent (cf Phil 2.6–8) just as he is for his ascent; normally in the NT the ascension is not directly referred to as an event but as the sitting of Christ at God's right hand; this he may have achieved either through his own effort or God's; in 1.20 God lifted Christ into heaven (cf Acts 1.9). If Christ descended this necessarily implies his pre-existence. Christ's ascent

---

[24] It should be noted that neither Adai nor Lemmer, who discuss the references to the Spirit in Ephesians, accept Caird's theory.

is said here to be 'above' the heavens (cf Heb 7.26) and not into the heavens (Acts 1.10), leaving the impression that AE conceived of him as passing through the heavens to something above and beyond them (see Detached Note: The Heavenlies for the varying ideas about heaven in the NT). Yet it may be wrong to give 'above' a physical sense; it may instead indicate superiority; in 1.20f Christ's ascent brings about his rule over the powers (ὑπεράνω is also used there) and Ps 68.18 contains the idea of victory. The 'superior' traditionally occupies a 'higher' position than the 'inferior'. In fact both senses, the physical and the metaphorical, may be intended. In any case the word probably indicates that Christ occupies the same position as in his sitting at God's right hand (1.20; cf Roels, 161). The Hebrew word for heaven is a plural, šmyn, and this leads sometimes to the use of the plural in the NT where we would expect the singular; this cannot be the case here for the qualification πάντων implies a multiplicity of heavenly regions.[25] This multiplicity was already a part of Pauline thought (cf 2 Cor 12.2). It is however impossible to say whether AE believed in three, seven or ten heavens. There is no reason to follow Schlier here and understand 'heaven' existentially rather than spatially.

The chiastic arrangement of ascent and descent in v. 9, 10ab sets off 10c by itself. It supplies either the purpose of the ascent or, possibly, its consequence (cf Lindemann, *Aufhebung*, 220 n. 88; the result of Christ's ascension is that he fills all things). As with ὑπεράνω we are led back to 1.20–3, and in particular to 1.23 where Christ was seen to fill the church and to be himself filled by God. Here Christ fills τὰ πάντα (cf 1.22) which can only mean the cosmos and not the church (*pace* Grotius; Beza; Belser; Meuzelaar, 135). Where τὰ πάντα is nominal and not adverbial it means the universe (cf 1.23; Col 1.16–20; 1 Cor 3.21f; 8.6) unless an alternative sense is signified (Hodge). God's filling the universe (see on 1.23) was a concept acceptable to Jewish Hellenism (Jer 23.24; Wisd 1.7; Philo, *Leg Alleg* 3.4; *Post Cain* 30; *Somn* 2.220–1; *Conf Ling* 136). In addition Gewiess argues that God's transcendence, power and rule are also found associated with his filling all things in Philo, *Post Cain* 14; *Gigant* 47; *Mos* 2.238. Jer 23.24 speaks of God filling heaven and earth and Jer 23.25ff goes on to speak of his power. Power is also naturally associated with exaltation to a high position. The concept of Christ's presence in every part of the universe was developed in *Gos Thom* §77 = II, 2 46.23–8 and Pap Oxyr 1. AE differs here both from Judaism in that Christ and not God fills the universe and from his own statement in 1.23 where Christ fills the church. The former alteration is acceptable in the light of the way

[25] See H. Traub and G. von Rad, *TWNT*, V, 501ff; SB III, 532ff; Lincoln, *Paradise*, 75–80.

the NT transfers functions ascribed to God in the OT to Christ. The latter accords with the cosmic position AE attributes to Christ in 1.10 and with his rule over the hostile powers. Granted this understanding of v. 10c, how does it fit into the argument? It does not lead on naturally to v. 11, for Christ fills the universe with his presence and not his gifts or blessings. It may not be intended to fit in with the argument but be an aside by AE to provide a fitting conclusion to vv. 9f; it thus leaves him free to return to his main theme; people sometimes write in this kind of way.

11.[26] Another of AE's long intricate sentences begins here and runs through to the end of v. 16. AE has rounded off the digression of vv. 9f with v. 10c which has probably no specific connection with v.11, unless Christ is regarded as filling the cosmos with his gifts; he now returns to the theme of the gifts. Vv. 9f were in effect a commentary on the first line of the quotation in v. 8 and vv. 11–16 are a commentary on its second. αὐτός picks up the same word in v. 10a: the giver is the one of whom we have just been speaking. ἔδωκεν picks up the use of the same verb in vv. 7f,[27] retaining its normal sense of 'give' and not 'appoint' (*pace* Van Roon, Roberts; see on 1.22). The church does not create its own leaders; Christ, not God as in 1 Cor 12.28, does so (Schlatter). Some of the Fathers used this affirmation about Christ to contest what they regarded as false doctrines of the Trinity (e.g. Jerome against Sabellius).

The gifts are not gifts made to people but gifts of people, people who have a particular role to play in the church; it may be assumed however that the charisma appropriate to the role which each is to play will have been bestowed (Calvin). It is not suggested that every believer will be one of these people, a change of emphasis from v. 7, and a change already foreshadowed in 1 Cor 12.4–30; that passage began by enumerating the various charismata with which different members of the community might be endowed, but ended by enumerating identifiable leaders, apostles, prophets, teachers; Paul apparently then ran out of 'titles' and continued by listing functions. Since none of the 'titles' is explained in 1 Corinthians, we may assume that Paul's readers were familiar with them. The same must be true of the titles mentioned in our verse in respect of AE and his readers. To ask (cf Merklein, *Amt*, 80) whether AE saw these identifiable leaders as present in the church from the beginning is to ask the kind of question in which AE was not interested, though historians may be; he deals with his current situation; we do not need then to trace out the origin of each title; it is sufficient to realise they were titles known to AE and his readers. There is also no need to

---

[26] For a detailed discussion of this verse see Best, 'Ministry'.

[27] The perfect tense δέδωκεν in $\mathfrak{P}^{46}$; Cl[pt] probably represents an attempt at clarification: the gifts, once given, still remain.

cross-identify his titles with those in other parts of the NT (e.g. the bishops and deacons of Phil 1.1) or with those which the later church came to use. In the first century the situation in respect of ministry was fluid; it was only after AE's time that titles and the functions attached to them began to harden. This fluidity of ministry makes it impossible to use AE's titles to date his letter. The titles are not mutually exclusive; Paul is termed both apostle and teacher in 1 Tim 2.7 (cf Acts 15.35). Indeed AE does nothing to differentiate from one another the functions of those he lists; they are considered as a group and not in respect of their individual contributions (Roels, 185). AE limits his list to five names, three of which were mentioned in 1 Cor 12.28, though there is no reason to suppose that he was directly dependent thereon; they appear in other parts of the NT. We note the absence from the list of titles drawn from other religions (e.g. ἱερεύς) or civil society (e.g. βουλευτής, δημιουργός, γυμνασίαρχος).

AE enumerates and distinguishes his list through μέν ... δέ ... δέ ... δέ ... (cf BDR §250; MHT, 36f; Robertson, 1152f). The article is probably not to be taken in the sense 'he gave some to be ...' but rather 'he gave those who are ...'. The initial μέν does not set the apostles in contrast to those who follow in the list (*pace* Schnackenburg; cf the enumerations of Mt 13.4–7; 13.8; 16.14; 21.35). If a contrast were intended here, a stronger particle would have been used to distinguish the first name from the rest or a fresh μέν with following δέ ... δέ ... to differentiate the other names from one another. Moreover in 2.20; 3.5 apostles and prophets are held together as a group.

If AE is Paul he would have classed himself among the apostles (cf 1.1) even though in 3.3 he sees some distinction between himself and the other apostles; he differed from them in that he had been called by the exalted Lord and not by the earthly Jesus as they were. If AE is not Paul doubtless he would have placed Paul in the same category; but where would he have placed himself? As evangelist, shepherd, teacher? It is impossible to say for, as we shall see, the roles are not clearly distinguishable. Apostles and prophets in 2.20 and 3.5 were figures of the past though the aorist of ἔδωκεν cannot be used here to support this, for then the evangelists, shepherds and teachers would also have to be confined to the past. The term apostle was not limited to the Twelve; there were still people so named at the beginning of the second century (see on 1.1; cf *Did* 11.3–12); prophets appear regularly as active during the NT period. Do the apostles and prophets of v. 11 then occupy a continuing role in the church? May not missionaries who take the gospel to fresh areas be regarded as initiating or founding apostles? We cannot draw this conclusion. If Paul wrote the letter he is still alive and if AE wrote in Paul's name he has to sustain the view that he is still alive. So in fact within the internal time frame of the letter all five 'ministers' still exist, though 2.20 and 3.5 suggest a past role for apostles and prophets.

In 1 Cor 12.28 as here the list is extended beyond apostles and prophets. Here the first additional category is that of the evangelist.[28] We need to be careful not to read modern usages of this term back into Ephesians. It does not refer to: (i) the authors of the Gospels; it only obtained that sense later; the first evidence is found in Hippolytus, *De Antichristo* 56 and Tertullian, *Adv Praxean* 23; (ii) those who conduct missions in existing Christian countries; (iii) those who travel as missionaries taking the gospel into fresh areas, though Eusebius applies it to them (*HE* 1.13.4; 3.37.2; 5.10.2; etc.); in this sense evangelists have been regarded as successors to the apostles; even if this understanding were acceptable there is no reason to go further with Klauck and suppose that shepherds and teachers have taken over the work of prophets. In keeping with his view that apostles and prophets occupy a founding position in the church, AE leaves no place for continuing prophetic activity in congregations, though all the rest of the NT suggests that this existed.

The NT mentions evangelists only twice elsewhere. In Acts 21.8 Philip whose work as a travelling missionary is recorded in Acts 8.4ff is described as one, yet in Acts 21.8 he is not a traveller but has an established home where his family live with him. In 2 Tim 4.5 Timothy is told to do the work of an evangelist and this appears to be equated with fulfilling his ministry and not be the title of an office (cf Merklein, *Amt*, 346). 1, 2 Timothy show what Timothy was expected to do; he is to remain at Ephesus (1 Tim 1.3) and exercise a ministry among established Christians; 2 Tim 4.2 sums up his ministry and confines it to one within the church. This is in line with the use of the word in Eph 4.11, for 4.12 shows that the ministry of those listed in 4.11 is directed towards believers. The NT use of the word then provides no evidence that it relates to a ministry outside the church. There is some confirmatory evidence that for a while the word continued to be applied to 'ministers' working within the church; 'readers' who did much more than read scripture aloud in services of worship were sometimes termed 'evangelists'.[29] The noun εὐαγγέλιον from which our word is derived throws further light on its meaning. While it regularly denotes the content of what is proclaimed to unbelievers, it is also used in relation to what goes on within the believing community (Rom 1.15; 1 Cor 9.14; 2 Cor 11.7; Gal 2.14; Phil 1.27); Mark uses the word to describe what he wrote (1.1) and he was addressing believers; he uses it also in his appeal for more dedicated lives from believers (8.35, 10.29). Indeed as if to mock our careful differentiation between ministers, Paul's

---

[28] For the word see G. Friedrich, *TWNT*, II, 734f.
[29] See A. Harnack, 'Die Quellen der sogennanten apostolischen Kirchenordnung', *TU* II.2 (1886).

evangelising of Sergius Paulus is described as teaching (Acts 13.12). The gospel in fact speaks as much to believers as to unbelievers; they continually need to be brought back to what in the first place led them to become Christians. There is no point in their lives at which they can move beyond the fundamentals of the gospel; AE indeed brings his readers back to the gospel in 5.2 in setting before them God's claims on their lives. This conclusion that part of the ministry of evangelists concerns life inside the community as well as, possibly, recruitment to it accords with what follows in v. 12 where the ministry of all five named officials is directed towards the community. Of course it would also be wrong to exclude evangelists from work directed towards unbelievers; as preachers they go both to the unconverted and the converted (Belser). Paul the apostle exercised that same dual role and in that sense evangelists might be regarded as successors to the apostles.

καί and the use of a single article link the final two names in the list, shepherds and teachers. Are there here two groups of people each fulfilling a separate and distinct role, or one group of people exercising two roles? This question can only be answered after the two roles have been identified.

Teachers[30] are listed after apostles and prophets in 1 Cor 12.28 (cf 14.26) and their work appears among the charismata of Rom 12.7. Not everyone would possess the charisma of teaching; the existence of 'specialist' teachers is confirmed by Gal 6.6; Jas 3.1; *Barn* 1.8; 4.9; Hermas, *Sim* 9.15.4. Teaching is set out as an important part of the work of Timothy and Titus (e.g. 1 Tim 4.6, 11, 13, 16; Tit 2.1, 7). AE himself was fulfilling the role of a teacher when he wrote his letter (cf Merklein, *Amt*, 350). Teachers will have both transmitted and interpreted tradition from the OT and earlier Christians (cf Rom 6.17; 1 Cor 4.17; Col 2.7; 2 Th 2.15) and drawn new lessons from it for fresh situations. Their task however will have gone beyond the imparting of information and the opening up of new ways of thought and have included exhortation to live by what they taught. In that sense they will have been leaders in their congregations. Interestingly none of those listed in v. 11 is specifically described as a leader, though in other letters words are used describing leadership (1 Th 5.12; 1 Cor 12.28; Rom 12.8). Leadership in the narrow sense of what is required to hold a community together and direct it may then have belonged in different ways to evangelists, teachers and shepherds; apostles and prophets must be excluded as no longer active but if they were then they too would have shared in leadership. Returning more specifically to the role of the teachers, Gentiles will have had

---

[30] See A. F. Zimmermann, *Die urchristlichen Lehrer* (WUNT 2.Reihe 12), Tübingen, 1984, especially 92–118; H. Schürmann, ' "... und Lehrer" ', in his *Orientierungen am Neuen Testament*, Düsseldorf, 1978, 116–56.

much to learn when they became Christians; in 4.20 AE writes of 'learning' Christ. Apart from designated teachers all Christians were also expected to be active in teaching (Heb 5.12; Col 3.16).

This seems relatively clear but the same cannot be said of ποιμένες. It is best to translate this as 'shepherds', so retaining the original underlying image and avoiding all the overtones in the modern use of 'pastor'. The shepherd image probably entered Jewish thought from its use in the Near East of rulers who led their people,[31] and then was adopted by Christians. It was an obvious metaphor easily understood by AE's Gentile readers. In the OT it was applied to God (Gen 49.24; Ps 23.1; 80.1; Isa 40.11) denoting his care and protection of his people (cf 1 Sam 17.34ff) and in the NT transferred to Christ (1 Pet 2.25; Heb 13.20; Jn 10.1–10; Mk 6.34; 14.27: Mt 25.32). It was applied in the OT to the leaders of Israel (2 Sam 5.2; Ps 78.71; Jer 2.8; 3.15; Ezek 34.2), and in the NT to the leaders of the church (Jn 21.16; Acts 20.28; 1 Pet 5.2), with the church itself being described as a flock of sheep (Jn 10.2ff; 21.16; Acts 20.28; 1 Pet 5.2; cf Jer 23.2f; 50.6, 17). Eph 4.11 is the only NT passage where the noun is used of leaders. The image is vague; its OT and pre-OT usage would suggest that primary emphasis would lie on shepherds as those who led (the shepherd in the East did not drive his flock but led it), provided for and protected those in their care. Yet to carry out these duties would not shepherds in the church have had to preach and teach, i.e. to act similarly to evangelists and teachers? If it is necessary to differentiate between these groups, it is probably right to stress in the case of shepherds either their leadership or general oversight (Acts 20.28; 1 Pet 5.2; yet Jn 21.16 hardly relates to leadership or oversight). But it may be wrong to attempt to draw rigid distinctions between evangelists, shepherds and teachers; in the modern church every priest or minister exercises all three roles. Rather we should see evangelising, shepherding and teaching as three essential ministerial functions. Some distinction exists between evangelising on the one hand and shepherding and teaching on the other in that the latter two functions are exercised entirely within the community, but the other both inside and outside it.

This approach perhaps provides a clue to the question whether shepherds and teachers form one group or two (the former explanation goes back as far as Jerome). Shepherding and teaching are different functions yet could be exercised from time to time by the

---

[31] On the image see J. Jeremias, *TWNT*, VI, 484–501; J. G. S. S. Thomson, 'The Shepherd-Ruler Concept in the OT and its application in the NT', *SJT* 8 (1955) 406–18; R. Schnackenburg, 'Episcopos und Hirtenamt: Zu Apg 20.28', in his *Schriften zum Neuen Testament*, Munich, 1971, 147–267; K. Kertelge, 'Offene Fragen zum Thema "Geistliches Amt" und das neutestamentliche Verständnis von der "Repraesentatio Christi"', *Die Kirche des Anfangs* (FS H. Schürmann, ed. R. Schnackenburg, J. Ernest, J. Wanke), Freiburg, Basel, Vienna, 1978, 583–605.

same people. Leadership involves truthful teaching for leaders have to say what is the correct direction to go, and teaching involves leadership for the teacher must be seen to be going the way he or she advocates. This explanation is preferable to that which regards pastors and teachers as local officials whereas evangelists operate in a wider area, an explanation going back to Chrysostom and Theodoret. That one article governs both teachers and shepherds does not identify them as one group, for the same is true of apostles and prophets in 2.20 and they form two groups. Yet if we accept the existence of two groups we should not think of a rigid separation between them. In new movements leadership in its various aspects, and teaching and exhortation must be included among these, is flexible and only hardens into fixed categories with the passage of time; the later church certainly shows the development of much more specialised categories but we do not need to follow out their appearance; it is sufficient to say that AE offers no template for the church's future ministry.

Does AE offer here an exclusive list of officials and functions? He does not mention presbyters, deacons and bishops. When he wishes to, he can make clear that his lists are non-exclusive (see 1.21; 6.12). He probably then intends this list to be exclusive. Yet it would be wrong to follow Fischer (see Introduction §8.3.3) in concluding that his omission of bishops was an attempt to preserve the Pauline conception of ministry. If the list is exclusive were then preaching, ruling and teaching the only ministries within the church of that time and area? Certainly they appear to be ministries, or functions, whatever they are called, which the church has always retained; their nature is permanent if their titles are not. All three might be regarded as primarily ministries with a verbal orientation yet surely there are non-verbal areas of ministry? 1 Pet 4.11 distinguishes between the areas of speech and practical service. Practical service appears as a form of ministry in Rom 12.7f; 1 Cor 12.9f, 28. διακονία as loving service sums up this type of ministry. It is advocated for all believers in the later paraenesis (4.28, 32; 6.18) but is apparently not seen as belonging to the duty of particular officials as in Acts 6.1–6. Grotius, noting the omission of workers of miracles, justified this on the grounds that their work did nothing to equip or prepare the saints. Yet even if this is true of those who heal or speak in tongues (and not all would allow this) it cannot be extended to cover all forms of loving care. Schnackenburg, 190f, suggests that the teaching and shepherding ministries are mentioned because of the danger of false belief (cf v.14) but 'caring' ministries by their love also preserve others from straying into false ways, especially if those false ways relate to matters of conduct rather than doctrine (see on v. 14); the problem of false doctrine never looms large in this letter. According to 4.12 ministers exist to build up the community and keep the members united, yet loving service will do this as much as teaching and shepherding. Worship does the same and in 5.19 it appears to be something for all believers. Prayer is a ministry open to all (6.18f). There is no mention of the eucharist which features so regularly in modern discussions of the church and no suggestion is made as to whether evangelists, teachers or shepherds should preside at it; equally AE says nothing about who should baptise. This means Ephesians does not supply guide-lines for the modern ministry. In keeping with this is the absence of any instruction how shepherds, evangelists and teachers should be chosen and appointed; there is no reason to suppose that there were not some method or methods (cf Acts 13.1–3; 1 Tim 4.14), but AE's failure to mention these suggests he did not think them important. Since AR has used plurals throughout it is impossible to decide whether he is thinking only of men holding these offices. Had he in mind both men and women he would still have used the masculine plural and it should be noted that Junia, a woman, is termed an apostle in Rom 16.7. The NT also records women as prophesying (Acts 21.9) and teaching (Acts 18.26).[32]

Those holding office as evangelists, teachers and shepherds are clearly distinct from believers in general and are therefore in the nature of permanent 'officials'. By introducing 'officials' AE may be said to have hastened the division between clergy and laity, have begun the sacralisation of the ministry and have suggested that ministry of a permanent and non-spontaneous nature was necessary. We should note finally that AE offers no argument for the existence of ministry, implying that this was not an issue within the communities to which he was writing. As for the purpose of the ministry, he treats this in the next verse.

It was important for their encouragement that those who were evangelists, shepherds and teachers should know that they had been selected and given to the church by Christ. The Twelve would certainly have realised this. It is difficult to say how others would have come to the same knowledge. Nothing AE writes suggests they had selected themselves nor does he imply that their position ultimately depended on the selection or goodwill of their communities. Dependence on Christ would enable them to hold steady when things were difficult and eliminate any reason for boasting of their position; no opening is left for them to claim any prerogative (Salmond). Their selection by Christ would also help their communities to accept and respect them even if their words and actions were at times disliked.

---

[32] E. Schüssler Fiorenza, 'Women in the Pre-Pauline Churches', *USQR* 33 (1975) 153–65, argues that the later church deliberately suppressed the part played by women in first-century Christianity.

If AE had been asked to describe his own ministry which term would he have chosen? If he was Paul he could have applied to himself all the functions or ministries listed. He was an apostle (1.1); he prophesied (1 Cor 14); he was an evangelist, preaching the gospel as a missionary to unbelievers (see Acts) and to believers (in all his letters he bases what he has to say on the essentials of the gospel); he wrote letters and visited the communities which he had founded to shepherd and teach their members. If AE was not Paul he would probably not have described himself as an apostle, if that is taken to imply a rank equal to that of the Twelve, though he might have thought of himself as an apostle on a lower scale. There is nothing 'prophetic' about his writing in the sense of the way he uses the term in 2.20. But he does proclaim the essentials of the gospel to his readers, teaches them about the OT and expounds and applies earlier tradition. We do not know enough about what he meant by shepherd to decide whether he thought he was shepherding them, but probably he did.[33]

12.[34] The purpose of Christ's gift of office-bearers to the church is now expressed through three prepositional phrases whose surface meanings are on the whole clear but whose interrelationship is difficult. There is no reason to regard them with Barth as part of a pre-Ephesian hymn; he provides no evidence and the setting of the three phrases alongside one another is wholly in AE's style. We examine first the surface meanings of each phrase.

In v. 12 we have the only NT use of the noun καταρτισμός, though the cognate verb appears regularly. LSJ offers four meanings for the noun: (i) restoration, reconciliation; (ii) the resetting of broken bones; (iii) furnishing, preparation; (iv) training, discipline. (i), if understood in the sense 'repair', is found in relation to the verb in Mt 4.21; Mk 1.19; 2 Cor 13.11; Gal 6.1; 1 Pet 5.10, but this meaning hardly fits the context of v. 12. (ii) is irrelevant. (iii) and (iv) would both fit the context. LSJ offers no evidence for (iv) but does for its cognates (cf Lk 6.40). This meaning if accepted would relate the noun only to the last 'official' listed in v. 11 and not the others. (iii) is therefore preferable but it requires an object; people are furnished or prepared for some purpose; this purpose could be found in v. 12b if it relates to an activity of the saints[35] for which church leaders are to prepare or equip them.

[33] Schnackenburg, 328–31, provides a *Wirkungsgeschichte* for the way the church interpreted this verse.
[34] On the verse see T. G. Gordon, ' "Equipping" Ministry in Ephesians 4?', *JETS* 37 (1994) 69–78.
[35] There is no reason to deviate here from the normal meaning of 'saints' as believers and view them as Jewish believers as does J. R. McRay, '*To Teleion* in 1 Corinthians 13.10', *RestQ* 14 (1971) 168–83; he sees the maturity of the church as evidenced in the Jewish acceptance of Gentiles.

In v. 12b ἔργον needs to be taken actively as in 1 Cor 15.58; Phil 2.30; 1 Th 1.3; 2 Tim 4.5, or given the related sense of 'what has been done' as in 1 Cor 3.13–15; 9.1 (cf Rom 14.20); it is not used in v. 12 as a moral term, but describes an ongoing activity seen in service. διακονία (see on 3.7 for the term) normally has some word or phrase qualifying it and indicating the nature of the service or else this can be determined from the context (e.g. Acts 6.1, 4; Rom 11.13; 15.31; 1 Cor 4.1). The qualification may be found here in v. 12c (a ministry which works towards the building up of the church). Only at Rom 12.7; 1 Cor 12.5 does διακονία lack a defining qualification and in both those passages, as here, the context is charismatic (v. 7). The root is often used by Paul of his preaching ministry (cf Schnackenburg) both within and outwith the church (e.g. 2 Cor 3.6–8; 4.1; 5.18) and this would correspond to the work of the evangelist (v. 11); yet there is no reason to restrict preaching to church officials. Collins, op.cit., 233f, taking the root to relate to communication, links it to the work of the teachers; but there seems no reason why 'lay' Christians should not communicate with one another; 5.19 indicates they do. More generally it is wrong to tie the meaning down to only one of the ministries of v. 11. The term certainly does not have here the 'official' sense which 'deacon' had later in the church. It can have a quite general sense (Heb 1.14; 2 Tim 4.11; Mk 10.43; cf Mk 10.45 for the verb). The absence of the article suggests the noun here is to be understood as equivalent to a verb (Haupt), i.e. as referring to the activity of ministering. Whether the word is applied here to the work of the office-bearers or to that of believers as a whole, in the light of its use by Jesus (Mk 9.33–6; 10.42–5) and the early church, it gives no support to a claim to self-importance.

The two concepts of v. 12c have already appeared in the letter: (i) 'building' in 2.20–2; the word is used here again in the sense of the process of constructing and not of a finished construction, but the metaphor has another connotation, educational rather than physical;[36] (ii) 'body of Christ' in 1.23; 3.6; 4.4 (on the use of the article with Christ see on 1.10; it is unexceptional here since it follows another genitive with the article). If 'building' is given its more physical sense it might imply the addition of new members to the community, though this does not necessarily follow as 2.20–2 shows, but if it has its more educational sense it would refer to the maturing of the community as in 2 Cor 10.8; 1 Cor 14.3, 12, 26. That the latter conclusion is correct is seen by the reference in 4.16 to growth in love. The metaphor is then used here with an ethical or educational sense. The mixing of the building and growth metaphors (the latter implicit in 'body') was already present in 2.21 and

[36] Cf Kitzberger, op.cit. p. 279 above, 322–6.

reappears in v. 16. But if the inspiration for the introduction of the building metaphor in 2.20–2 came from 1 Cor 3.9, which itself had as its background the Jewish use of 'building' to denote a community, the inspiration for 4.12, 16 lay in passages like 1 Cor 14.1–19, 26 (cf Rom 14.19; 15.2; 1 Cor 8.1; 10.23) where believers use their different charismata to build up other believers. The background to this is again Jewish (cf Isa 49.17; Jer 1.10; 18.9; 24.6; 31(38).28; 42(49).10; 45.4(51.34); Ψ 27.5; Ecclus 49.7), though in this case it would be a use which would be more easily appreciated by Greeks who did not think so readily of a community as a building. If many of the OT passages envisage God as the builder, it is again he who builds in 1 Cor 14.1ff, but through the charismatic gifts he has given to church members. The appropriation here of the idea of 1 Cor 14 was made easier because sometimes in the former the object of the building is expressly identified as the church (1 Cor 14.4, 5, 12), that is the body of Christ. The context of 4.12, 16 is again the giving of charismata to believers; thus the usage here is not directly related to 2.20–2 though still having its source in Pauline language. If the process of upbuilding is described here then v. 13 gives its result. AE says nothing directly about how the building up of the community is to be carried out; 1 Corinthians implied that it was through the charismatic gifts of all the community. Here it must be through the variety of gifts of administration, healing, prophecy which ordinary members possess. It is certainly not a purely instructional building up in the details of the true faith, for love is involved (v. 16). It will be a mutual building up (5.19; cf 1 Th 5.11).

If the three phrases can be explained in these ways how are they to be related to one another within the total paraenetic context? The punctuation in Greek printed texts is of little help since it reflects only the opinion of editors. 4.11 refers to the limited group of officials; v. 13 with its first plural draws in all believers; v. 12a refers to the officials of v. 11; at the beginning or end of v. 12bc or within it we must then move from the limited group to all believers; but where? If we take the three phrases as parallel then the change comes at the beginning of v. 13, a view held at least as early as Chrysostom. In its support Hamann[37] argues that the reference of 12bc to all believers is a modern view going back only to 1940 (it is in fact found in Erasmus!) and that καταρτισμός and its cognate verb cannot be followed by a further verbal qualification; yet in Rom 9.22; 2 Tim 3.17 we have prepositional phrases incorporating a verbal idea and in this they do not differ grammatically from our verse. If 12a, 12b, 12c are parallel then it is surprising that v. 12b,

---

[37] H. P. Hamann, 'The Translation of Ephesians 4:12—A Necessary Revision', *Concordia Journal* 14 (1988) 42–9.

the most general of the phrases, does not come first with 12a and 12c developing it; Grotius, recognising this, transposed their order! If the three phrases are parallel, the second and third should be preceded like the first with the article (Percy, 318f; Hofmann). Meyer, noting the variation from πρός to εἰς, sees the former as denoting the primary purpose and the latter secondary purposes (he gave leaders for the work of ministry and for building up the body of Christ; his main object being to perfect the saints); if this were so the ultimate purpose should be put last; Meyer's solution also makes difficult the transition to the first plural of v. 13. If all three phrases of v. 12 refer to the activity of the ministers then, as we have seen, it might be possible to relate 12a to the teachers and 12b to the evangelists, yet there is no apparent justification for relating 12c to the shepherds; in fact the activity of 12c is an activity of the whole church in v. 16 (apostles and prophets may be ignored in this connection as their ministry belongs to the past). No reason exists then to associate the phrases of v. 12 with different ministries (for other ways in which the ministries of v. 11 have been attached to the various phrases of v. 12 see Masson and Dibelius). This apart, the most probable meaning of 12a did not relate it to teaching but to preparing and equipping the saints. But preparation and equipment are always for some purpose; 12bc can give this. 12b itself (see above) requires something to explain it, otherwise διακονία is left vague; 12c fulfils this function; 12c is then not strictly parallel to 12b but amplifies it. The change in preposition between 12a and 12bc confirms that the movement from the discussion of the work of the ministers (v. 11) to that of the whole church takes place between 12a and 12bc. The change in preposition also militates against taking 12a and 12b together (so Beare following Goodspeed, 'in order to fit his people for the work of service'). The change and its position are in fact confirmed by the mention of the saints in 12a; were the change to come after 12c we would have expected that word in the phrase of 12c. Office-bearers then exist to prepare other believers for their service to the whole community; they have an enabling function; the clergy exist to serve the laity (cf Haupt).

This view is contested by Gordon, art.cit., who takes all of v. 12 to be the duty of the officials. He argues in support that a clear distinction is drawn between the ministry and the laity not only in 4.11f but throughout the NT and has no difficulty in pointing to a number of places where the ministry has a special position, e.g. Acts 6.4; 13.2–5; 1 Tim 3.2; 2 Tim 4.1–5; 1 Tim 5.17; Jas 3.1. This is not in dispute. What he fails to do is to consider whether there are passages showing non-ministers fulfilling what he would term ministerial functions; there are many, e.g. Eph 5.19; Rom 15.14; 1 Cor 14.26; Phil 1.15 (were those who preached so as to cause trouble for Paul officially 'ordained' ministers?); Col 3.16; 1 Th 5.11; in every case the church is being built up. Gordon lays too much emphasis on verbal communication as the primary function in service to the church; loving care is equally important. Since Gordon derides the understanding of v. 12 given here as too 'democratic', it is not unfair to say that his view is typical of those who would elevate the ministry into a privileged position.

The building up of the body of Christ is not then to be left to the ministry but is the responsibility of all believers. Yet the beginning of the clerical–lay division may be said to appear here. It is absent from v. 7 and 1 Cor 12.4ff; Rom 12.4ff, and essentially it conflicts with the image of the body of Christ where all members have their special functions. The clerical–lay division is of course found in other parts of the NT, e.g. Heb 13.24, even if at the same time the NT lays strong emphasis on all believers as possessing a ministerial function. The NT in fact lacks any general word for the clerical side of this division showing its relative unimportance within the NT period. All organisations as they develop spontaneously throw up leaders or have within them strong-minded people who take over leadership; division of labour between leaders and led is a perfectly natural development and should not be taken as a sign of a deteriorating theology (early catholicity?). AE's approach is not however made on the basis of conscious sociological insight but is justified on theological grounds, whether that theology be good or bad.

13. The purpose of Christ's gift of ministers to the church (v. 11) to prepare all its members (v. 12a) to serve (v. 12bc) is now made clear in three prepositional phrases which together with v. 14 probably depend on ἔδωκεν (cf Lemmer, 358f); the argument flows evenly and there is no reason to suppose with Barth either a pre-Pauline fragment or a later insertion; he regards the language as unPauline, though it would be hard to prove this; but unless we can be certain that Paul is the author of the letter there is no reason to point out unPauline language. The three prepositional phrases do not depend on one another but are in parallel; mutually reflecting on one another, together they serve to build up the total picture; no one of them is more important than any other, and there is no reason with Hofmann to insert a major break among them.

The goal is presented as the end of a journey; it has not yet been attained (for μέχρι see BDR §383.2; 485 n. 6; MHT, 110f; Robertson, 974f). Barth, 485f, rather fancifully envisages the journey as that of the bride to meet the ἀνήρ, Christ the bridegroom; if so ἀνήρ should have had the article; what the procession, if that is the idea, would initially meet would not be the groom but the unity in the faith. καταντάω[38] with εἰς points to a goal; the journey can be

---

[38] For the word see O. Michel, *TWNT*, III, 625–8; I. Peri, 'Gelangen zur Vollkommenheit. Zur lateinischen Interpretation von καταντάω in Eph 4.13', *BZ* 23 (1979) 269–78.

either geographical (Acts 16.1; 18.19; 21.7) or spiritual as here (cf Acts 26.7; Phil 3.11; 1 Clem 23.4; 63.1; 2 Kgdms 3.29; 2 Macc 6.14). Towards this goal we all should strive, and AE obviously includes in the 'all' Paul, and/or himself; 'all' also means all believers, and not all people as Jerome suggests; the idea of striving is in keeping with the hortatory sense of 4.1–6.20. οἱ πάντες may seem unnecessary, yet on the one hand it prevents the striving being over-individualised as if it said 'each of us', and on the other depersonalised as if it said 'let our communities ...'; the latter danger is perhaps the greater in a context which emphasises the unity of the church. Believers require to strive, not each individually, but together, cooperating with and helping one another; no one is exempt from this striving (cf Ewald).

The goal is first defined as unity.[39] Is the unity one created by faith and the knowledge of the son of God (it was created by the Spirit in v. 3), or one which a common faith and knowledge give or one that lies in faith and knowledge? How are faith and knowledge to be understood in the present context? Faith ranges in meaning between expressing the existential response to what God has done and the objective content of what is believed; the latter of course arises out of the former. AE is clearly not thinking of Christ's faithfulness (pace Barth) for the knowledge of the son of God can hardly be the knowledge which the son of God possesses (as Meuzelaar, 130–3, supposes), still less the knowledge which Christ the bridegroom has of the bride (Barth, 488f). The association of faith with knowledge, ἐπίγνωσις (see on 1.17 for the word), suggests that AE has in mind the objective sense of faith, as in v. 5. 'Knowledge' might also refer to the content of the faith (cf Calvin) but it is questionable if that content is to be thought of as just knowledge about the son[40] of God, for, if it were, the article would not be repeated before ἐπίγνωσις; its repetition distinguishes the two (καί is not explicative). The content of the faith is thus left undefined as in v. 5. AE would not of course have equated it with the content of his letter because his letter is directed to a particular situation and is not a full discussion of the nature of Christian belief. There can indeed be no absolute or invariable verbal expression of the faith (cf Best, *Interpreting Christ*, 50–64). However, since it is the Christian faith which is at issue the son of God will be a principal element in its expression. As a title of Jesus, son of God is found in varying proportions in almost all strands of NT thought,

[39] On this phrase see C. Noyen, 'Foi, charité, espérance et "connaissance" dans les Epîtres de la Captivité', *NRT* 94 (1972) 897–911.
[40] The variant reading of F G b; Cl[pt] Lcf which omits τοῦ υἱοῦ has little support and may be an accommodation to 1.17; the copyist's eye perhaps moved from one τοῦ to the next. If it was not present the parallelism of the three phrases would be broken since both the other phrases appear to refer to Christ.

though only here in Ephesians. Whether Jesus applied the term to himself or not, it certainly belongs to early formulations of the faith (cf 1 Th 1.10). Nothing suggests that AE is here making an attack on those who have a wrong knowledge of Christ for he says nothing about the nature of a true knowledge. In the light of all this the unity is probably that which belongs to, or comes from, a common faith and knowledge.

The very brevity of the second phrase makes it difficult to understand despite its use of two common words. ἀνήρ is the adult male (cf BAGD), normally in the fullness of his powers, as the adjective confirms. It is the word AE uses for the husband in 5.22–33, except at 5.31 where he is quoting the OT. When Paul refers to Adam he uses ἄνθρωπος, i.e. the human being without sexual orientation; this was the word AE used in 2.15 (cf 4.22–4); AE was thus aware of the distinction between the two words. τέλειος has a wide range of meanings.[41] Its cultic connections which appear in Hebrews can be safely ignored here where the context is ethical and the sense lies in the area of maturity, completeness and perfection; the seeming contrast with νήπιοι (v. 14) suggests we should prefer the sense 'maturity'. But is AE referring to the manhood of individual believers, of Christ or of the church? The implied contrast with v. 14 suggests that AE has the first of these in mind and is referring to individual believers (so Mussner, *Christus*, 62f; Percy, 321, etc.; this understanding appears at least as early as Clem Alex, e.g., *Stromata* 4.132.1). It cannot be denied that individual believers require to grow and mature in their faith; Col 1.28 uses τέλειος in this way but there it is associated with ἄνθρωπος; however the main drive in our context is corporate, relating to the building up of the church (vv. 12, 16). But if the individualistic interpretation is preferred, the implication of AE's use of ἀνήρ would then be that he was thinking only of male[42] believers and 4.22–4 shows he is not. More importantly, if a contrast is being drawn with νήπιοι in v. 14, we ought to have the plural here. The individualistic interpretation is then unsatisfactory; any other must lie in the area of corporate understanding. Could the 'man' be Christ? Schlier, *Christus*, 27–37, provides a considerable number of references to the use of the term 'man' for the heavenly saviour and in some of these we actually have the phrase, 'perfect (mature) man' (to those Schlier gives, add *Gos Phil* II, 3; 55.12; 75.20–4; 80.4; *Gos Mary* BG 8502.1; 18.16). Unfortunately most of

[41] Cf G. Delling, *TWNT*, VIII, 50–88; McRay, art.cit.; P. C. du Plessis, *Teleios: The Idea of Perfection in the New Testament*, Kampen, 1959.
[42] Origen, who on the whole gives an individualistic interpretation, is aware of the male nature of the image and suggests 'virgin' as the equivalent of the perfect man, *Matt Comm* 15.25, GCS 40; 424.22f.

the references are late and while the general idea may be early the
actual occurrences of the phrase may be derived from Christian
usage. Yet it cannot be denied that the heavenly saviour is often seen
as corporate; this also seems to be true of Christ in the Pauline
literature; as the first Adam in a sense contains all humanity within
himself so the second Adam contains all believers; it may not then
be necessary to depend here on later texts. While ἄνθρωπος would
have been normal in the corporate sense, ἀνήρ can also carry this
sense (cf 2 Esdras 3.1; 18.1). However, a corporate solution like this
has its own difficulties for it would have been normal for the phrase
to have been introduced with the definite article. This also militates
against a simple equation of the phrase with the church through the
parallel of 2.15, 'one new human being'; it is not in any case certain
that the phrase of 2.15 refers to the church (see notes on 2.15);
moreover 2.15 uses ἄνθρωπος and not ἀνήρ, and in 5.22f the
church is γυνή. There is no easy solution to these difficulties and
commentators offer both individualistic, referring to Christ, and
corporate, referring to the church, solutions. Even if no easy solution
is possible a corporate accords better with the context, and with very
great hesitation we must accept this and view the 'man' as the
corporate Christ (he is thus referred to in all three phrases) who is
the church.

The third phrase (cf Sellin, 100f), while introducing Christ, does
not make him the explicit goal to be attained. The *pleroma* (see on
1.23 for the word) of Christ can either be that which fills him or that
which he fills. In 1.23 he was seen as filled by God and as filling the
church; since here we have no suggestion of what might fill him the
phrase is better taken as denoting what he fills, and, as in 1.23, what
he fills will be the church, and not 'all things' as in 4.10. 3.19 also
spoke of believers being filled. There is tension between 1.23 and
our verse (and 3.19) in that in the former the filling is already a fact
whereas here it is still future; 'what in 1.23 was a statement of fact is
now a standard of attainment' (Best, *One Body*, 141); this however
is a tension normal to the letter. The goal to be attained is then the
measure, probably as in v. 7 the full measure, of the maturity or
stature of what Christ fills. ἡλικία when used of persons can refer
either to age or body size, and its meaning must be determined from
the context; the meaning is in fact often ambiguous (e.g. Mt 6.27; Lk
2.52; 12.25) since age (e.g. Jn 9.21, 23; Heb 11.11) and body size
(e.g. Lk 19.3; Ezek 13.18) are related. 'Age' is favoured by the
general context with its emphasis on maturity; adults are more
mature than children; νήπιοι (v. 14) would also contrast suitably
with the idea of maturity; yet that noun is plural. The content of v.
13 however is not necessarily to be determined by v. 14; it is
possible that when AE looked for a word to describe in v. 14 those
with erroneous views, his choice of νήπιοι would suggest that the

idea of 'age' lay in his mind. On the other hand filling and building are spatial metaphors and the idea of size goes more appropriately after μέτρον. If the body size is large then that indicates a mature adult. It is difficult to decide between the two interpretations and perhaps both should be seen as present.

The three prepositional phrases may appear to provide three distinct goals but there can only be one goal; they must therefore be seen as drawing out different aspects of that one goal (cf Roels, 199f). How then do they relate to one another? What is the one goal? Since the sentence continues to v. 16 we are not yet at a stage where we can answer the second of these questions; v. 16 suggests that the goal is the complete growth of the body of Christ; this would not be out of accord with what we have learnt from the three phrases. As for the first question, each phrase in v. 13 incorporates a reference to Christ involving an understanding of him and a relation to him. The church also is involved as the body of which he is head and as that which understands him and is to attain maturity through its relation to him. It is towards this goal that the ministry is to work by drawing in all members of the church so that they also take their place in working towards the goal. Since nothing is said about the missionary activity of ministers or believers in general, the goal must be an inward maturity and not an outward growth in numbers (Gnilka). This does not mean that AE was not interested in numerical growth; that is not his subject here; had there been no growth in numbers the churches to which he is writing would never have come into existence. Once in existence they cannot stand still but must mature or drop back. The goal, like all goals, would appear to be future, yet there is also a sense in which it has already been attained. The church is one, the body of Christ exists and cannot exist in any other than mature and perfect form. This is another aspect of the tension that runs all through the letter. When the goal is given a future reference the question arises as to the time of its attainment (μέχρι implies this question exists). AE throws no light on the answer, though answers have been given; Chrysostom saw it as attained in this life; Theod Mops in the future life. AE certainly does not say, 'It will be attained when Christ returns'; that might cut the nerve of effort by implying that we cannot bring it nearer because it depends on a supernatural and outside factor.

14. This is the third successive verse depending on v. 11 (Gnilka, Schlier and most commentators). Unlike v. 13 it is cast negatively. The ministry was given not only to enable the church to grow but also so that it would be able to resist any forces that might corrupt or destroy it. Ministers themselves are not the direct agents in this resistance; all believers are summoned to the task; should any fail, unity may become chaos. The structure of v. 14 is by no means simple and there are many ways of relating the various phrases to one another (Haupt gives a thorough discussion of the various possibilities), but the main thought is clear; that however is not to say that whatever AE is attacking can be identified with any certainty. The language is imprecise and, in keeping with AE's normal style, plerophoric (Schlier), with AE using a series of images: children, a storm at sea, dice playing. μηκέτι does not refer to the readers' pre-conversion period (as Theodoret supposes; cf Lindemann, who then views this verse as 'missionary' in that it depicts pre-Christian life) but to the period after conversion and prior to this letter, for prior to conversion believers had not been immature children, νήπιοι,[43] but dead in sin and under the power of Satan (2.1–3). Their pre-Christian condition is described also in 4.17–19 where sin is again to the forefront.

Correspondingly AE describes their Christian condition as immature rather than sinful (Grosheide); it may be for this reason that he uses the first plural and includes himself! The image of the child is used in various ways in the NT to describe recent converts or converts who have not progressed in their faith as they should (1 Cor 3.1f; 13.11; 14.20; Heb 5.13; it is used very differently in Mt 11.25; 18.3; Mk 10.13; Lk 10.21). Children tend to be volatile in their beliefs, and the readers might turn out to be unstable, foolish and incapable of understanding the truth, in contrast with the reference to knowledge in v. 13. The plural 'children' is probably individualistic in orientation contrasting with the togetherness that ought to exist among believers. Childish individualism drives people apart and shatters unity. Possibly behind the image of immature children lies that of rebirth; the readers have been born anew but have yet to grow up into adulthood.

AE now changes his metaphor, introducing the sea and its storms. The dangers of sea travel were sometimes used in the OT to depict life apart from God (Ps 107.23–7; Isa 57.20f), and sea travel was widely recognised in the ancient world as dangerous. Paul himself found this to be true; he was shipwrecked at least three times in his travels (2 Cor 11.25) and Acts describes yet another shipwreck when he was on his way as a prisoner to Rome (27.1ff). Despite his vivid acquaintance with the dangers of the sea this is the only occasion (assuming he wrote Ephesians) that he used the idea metaphorically (for the widespread contemporary use of storm imagery see Hugedé, 170, nn. 106–8). The verb κλυδωνίζω is used metaphorically in Isa 57.20 and by Josephus, Ant 9.239; the cognate noun is used in Jas 1.6 of the storm affecting believers (cf Jude 12f); for περιφέρω see Simpson, 97, n. 27. It is not however clear whether AE is depicting

---

[43] The word is regularly used metaphorically; see W. Grundmann, 'Die νήπιοι in der urchristlichen Paränese', *NTS* 5 (1958/9) 188–205; S. Légasse, 'La Révélation aux NHPIOI', *RB* 67 (1960) 321–48.

storm-tossed waves or storm-tossed ships; the effect is the same. The winds are those of false teaching. The singular διδασκαλία with the article might appear to suggest a reference to Christian teaching (Merklein, 107; Schnackenburg) but the qualification παντί with ἀνέμῳ indicates a variety of winds and therefore probably a variety of teaching. That should not however be taken to suggest that the winds of false teaching are blowing from outside into the church; the NT shows that believers were under continual pressure from other, at least seemingly so, Christians in respect of what was true teaching; each teacher would claim what he said was true. What later came to be accepted as true teaching had not been fully and clearly formulated by the time of Ephesians. Paul of course was always sure in his own mind what was true. Variety of teaching formed a continuing threat to unity. Doctrinal novelty (cf Macpherson) was normal in this initial period of the church. AE probably refers then here to the variety of teaching within the church rather than false philosophies and theologies entering it from outside. The remainder of the letter is devoted to ethical instruction; this suggests that the false teaching may be about behaviour. More churches have been broken up or debilitated through the lack of loving and honest conduct than by heretical teaching in the strict sense of doctrinal teaching. The failure of the church of Pergamum came through the eating of food sacrificed to idols and sexual indulgence (Rev 2.14; cf 3.20 in respect of the church at Thyatira). The errors of the Roman church (Rom 14.1–15.6) were partly ethical relating to food. When things go wrong theologians tend to look for a failure in orthodoxy rather than orthopraxis. It is true that not eating particular foods may appear a doctrinal problem but its ethical side was important. Those who belonged to trade guilds would often have been put in the position of deciding whether to eat or not; had they the moral courage to stand out from others in the guild? Some new Christians may have carried into their communities too much of their previous pagan environment and its culture. AE simply warns against the continual danger of the perversion of true Christian action and teaching. The vagueness of his reference means that we have no idea what he had in mind, even if he was thinking of one particular perversion; the one further reference to deceptive teaching (5.6) provides no more information to assist in its identification. The plural 'every wind' suggests he did not have one particular false teaching or vice in mind. Writing to a number of churches he might not be sure what were the perversions in each.

AE's third metaphor is drawn from dice playing. Though games with dice may not of themselves be dishonest, in the ancient world they were often associated with dishonesty and deception (cf SB III, 599; m Sanh 3.3; Epict 2.19.28; Vett.Val. 202, 6 [Kroll]) and dice playing became a synonym for trickery. Thus κυβεία, πανουργία, μεθοδεία, πλάνη carry much the same meaning in accordance with AE's typical style and are difficult to distinguish from one another. πανουργία is strictly neutral in sense (cf Prov 1.4; 9.5; 13.1,16) but had begun to carry, at least in Christian circles, a bad connotation (1 Cor 3.19; 2 Cor 4.2; 11.3; 12.16; cf Plut. *Mor.* 91B; Philo, *Sacrif* 32), describing people cunningly scheming to have their views adopted. μεθοδεία (cf Schmid, 146; Spicq, II, 548) is again neutral in sense; it implies a deliberate and planned procedure and takes its colour from its context which is here evil (the cognate verb can mean to devise or scheme evil, e.g. 2 Kgdms 19.28; Polyc *Phil* 7.1; Philo, *Mos* 2.212); there may be some who are deliberately misrepresenting the truth and seeking by skilful manipulation to lead believers astray (cf Mitton). πλάνη (cf H. Braun, *TWNT*, VI, 230ff; it is probably an objective genitive here) when it is not used literally of movement always carries a bad sense (2 Th 2.11; 1 Jn 4.6; Jude 11; 2 Pet 2.18; 3.17; similarly the adjective, 1 Tim 4.1; 2 Jn 7). Because of its meaning it can be set in contrast with what is true (2 Th 2.11; 1 Jn 4.6; *T Jud* 20.1); it forms then a suitable lead in to v. 15, and is to be understood generally and not as identifying a particular heresy (Merklein, *Amt*, 110). The total effect of these nouns is to stress the unscrupulous nature of certain undefined people who may be leading believers astray. The deceptive trickery is not attributed here to the devil[44] but is regarded as human; ἄνθρωπος is used derogatively (cf Mk 7.7; Mt 15.9; Col 2.8, 20–2); the plural is vague and again gives the impression with much else in the verse that the readers are assailed by a variety of false teachings. True teaching, especially that of Paul, is not of human but divine origin. Similarities with Col 2.8, 20–2 have led some to conjecture that the christological heresy denounced in that letter was also a problem for AE's church; the resemblances are however slight; it is less likely that AE has abbreviated Col 2.22 by omitting ἐντάλματα and added the reference to dice playing than that he depends directly on Isa 29.13 (LXX) as does Col 2.22.

15. This verse contrasts with (δέ) and is parallel to v. 14; its main verb is subjunctive being controlled by the ἵνα of v. 14; that verse was negative in tone; this is positive. It makes explicit the idea of growth which was already implicit in passages like 2.20–2 and present in the καταντήσωμεν of v. 13 with its implication of movement towards maturity.

The precise meaning of ἀληθεύοντες is disputed and doubt as to its meaning probably led to the reading of F G, ἀλήθειαν δὲ ποιοῦντες;

---

[44] τοῦ διαβόλου is added by A and probably represents an attempt to attribute a supernatural source to the evil; the devil only began to be related to temptation around this period; cf Best, *Temptation*, 28ff.

support for this is weak and it should be rejected.[45] The form of the verb suggests a sense other than that of simple speech (cf Abbott), yet there are good grounds for the rendering 'speaking truth'; it is usage and context rather than form which in the end must determine meaning, and v. 14 dealt with erroneous and deceitful opinions whose utterance might mislead believers (for this sense see Gal 4.16; Gen 20.16; 42.16; Isa 44.26; Ecclus 34.4; Philo, *Abr* 107; *Joseph* 95; *Mos* 2.177; Josephus, *BJ* 3.322; *Vita* 132).

If ἀληθεύοντες refers to speech, the meaning is not simply that believers are never to tell lies but always speak the truth, though this is what is said in 4.25. In the context of v. 14, where believers are warned against those who would lead them astray in respect of doctrine or ethics or both, truth should be understood as the truth of the gospel. The truth is the gospel (see on 1.13; 4.21; 6.14; cf Gal 2.5, 14; 5.7; Rom 1.18; Col 1.5; 2 Tim 2.15). The sense is then almost that they should speak or proclaim the gospel and stand firm against the corruptions tempting them to deviate from it (v. 14). That believers can and should proclaim the gospel to one another is obvious once we reject the idea that 'gospel' is only that which is addressed to unbelievers (see the discussion of 'evangelist' in v. 11 and also 5.19f). The true speaking of the gospel corrects error. ἐν ἀγάπῃ could be linked to either the preceding participle or the following verb; the former is to be preferred since the verb has already two qualifying phrases and the participle would otherwise lack any qualification, and this would contrast with the way error is richly qualified in v. 14. Salmond chooses the other option because the association of the same phrase with the main thought of v. 16 is weak; were it strong, one occurrence of the phrase would be sufficient. The object of the love is not stated; it could be directed towards God or Christ (Harless; this hardly seems warranted by the context of truthful speech or action), towards the world (Ernst; but the predominant orientation of the paraenesis relates to the internal life of the community), or towards other believers (the vast majority of commentators). Believers console, strengthen and correct one another through the gospel and so build up their communities. They can do this in love because their lives are founded on and built up by love (3.17). Our understanding of the participle avoids any clash between the two virtues of truth and love and any implication here that we must decide when truth needs to be forsworn for the sake of love; this is of course a genuine problem though not present here. If believers are to sustain one another through the gospel then 'love' eliminates certain ways they may do this; the gospel should not be

[45] On the reading cf J.-D. Dubois, 'Ephesians IV 15: "aletheuontes de" or "aletheian de poiountes". On the Use of Coptic Versions for New Testament Textual Criticism', *NT* 16 (1974) 30–4.

used to manipulate or scold them; they should not be hectored or patronised ('I know the truth, you do not').

When believers speak the gospel to one another the body is built up, or grows. αὐξάνω (cf BDR §160 n. 11; Robertson, 799) can be either transitive (1 Cor 3.6f; 2 Cor 9.10) or intransitive (Eph 2.21; Col 2.19; Mt 6.28; Lk 1.80; 2.40). In the former case τὰ πάντα will be its object, in the latter it will be an adverbial accusative or an accusative of definition ('in every respect'; cf BDR §160). In Ephesians and Colossians τὰ πάντα (cf Van Roon, 216–19) refers normally to the cosmos (1.11, 22; 3.9, 20; 4.6, 10; Col 1.16, 17, 20) but not always (cf 1.23; 5.13, 20; Col 3.8). Schlier, followed by Ernst; Steinmetz, 120; R. P. Meyer, 72–6; Howard,[46] accept the cosmic reference since τὰ πάντα in 1.10; 3.9; 4.10 links the cosmos to Christ and brings it within the area of redemption (cf Col 1.15–20), and such a reference would not be alien to contemporary philosophical (principally Stoic) and gnostic ideas (cf Bouttier). Yet to accept this implies a change in the meaning of σῶμα between v. 15 and v. 16 (see Merklein, *Amt*, 111, and below) and is out of line with the course of the argument throughout vv. 11–16 which relates to the church. That AE is interested in the cosmos elsewhere does not mean he must be interested in it here where his present concern is the church's growth (does the cosmos grow?). Growth is into Christ, basically the same idea as v. 13c, and is of the church as a whole and not primarily of its members as individuals. The metaphor of growth suggests that here the head (see on 1.22) is regarded as the source of growth in so far as it is identified with Christ and not as overlord or ruler of either the church or the cosmos, as suggested by Howard, art.cit., who dissociates the head from the body. Christ, v. 16, supplies the body with what it requires to grow. But how can the body grow into Christ who is its head? The thought is probably parallel to that of 2.20–2; there the building grows into a temple even though the final coping-stone is regarded as already in position. Here the church both grows into Christ, which means more than that it becomes like Christ, and grows from what he supplies to it; it is true that the picture may not accord with either contemporary or modern physiological theories, but have we any right to expect it to do so (see on v. 16)?.

A number of variants affect the last few words. ἡ before κεφαλή is omitted by D* F G 6 1739 1881 *pc*; Cl but read by 𝔓⁴⁶ ℵ A B C D² Ψ 33 𝔐; the latter evidence is clearly stronger; the meaning is not affected. ℵ² D F G Ψ 𝔐 add the article before χριστός; 𝔓⁴⁶ also reads the article though with it and the noun in the genitive, thus adding strength to the presence of the article and at the same time simplifying the syntax. The article is omitted by ℵ* A B C 6 33 81 1175 1241⁵ 1739 1881 2464 *pc*. There is thus strong

---

[46] G. Howard, 'The Head/Body Metaphor in Ephesians', *NTS* 20 (1974) 350–6.

evidence for both reading and omitting the article; probably the unusual frequency with which the article precedes Christ in Ephesians led to its insertion. If the article is read it would set ὁ χριστός alongside ἡ κεφαλή as a second predicate.

16. This verse concludes the long sentence which began at v. 11. The general sense is clear[47] though many details are not (Chrysostom describes it as obscure). The church is to grow from Christ its head and will grow in love. Growth has been the hidden agenda from v. 11. Much of the verse's obscurity arises out of its use of medical words. Modern physiology and anatomy have a different view of the human body and use terms differently from the ancient world;[48] ancient ideas have to be translated into modern terms and none may correspond exactly. Even if it was possible to find the proper corresponding terms we do not know whether AE was using his terms in accordance with correct contemporary usage. Scientific terms often pass into ordinary speech and are used loosely. Even if Paul is the author and Luke the doctor was with him when he wrote, that gives no guarantee of accuracy for Ephesians is written not for medical experts but for ordinary people. Our verse picks up terms from earlier verses: ἕκαστος and μέτρον from v. 7, οἰκοδομή and σῶμα from v. 12, ἀγάπη from vv. 2, 15. There is also a similarity in terminology, though less in thought, with Col 2.19 (cf Percy, 413–16, and Best, 'Who used Whom?')

Granted some similarity with Col 2.19, there is little to suggest AE had it in front of him as he wrote for there are many dissimilarities: the change in one participle, the omission of συνδέσμον without which it is difficult to understand the meaning of ἁφή, the noun ἐπιχορηγία replacing the cognate verb, the relationship of growth to Christ and not to God, the emphasis on the role of individual members in the growth of the body. Genuine similarity relates only to the general sense. Some words are repeated though not reproduced exactly (Mitton, *Epistle*, 61). The meaning of Col 2.19 is clear, that of Eph 4.16 is not; if AE has used Colossians he failed to understand what he was doing. Better than assuming direct dependence is to suppose that, as members of the Pauline school meditated on the image of the body of Christ and thought it through, a need was seen to identify more precisely the relation of Christ to the body (he becomes its head) and the way in which a living body could be understood as growing and maturing. As this was discussed certain words would be used to explain the image and eventually two authors facing different situations (AE that of the unity of the church, A/Col that of heresy) would write the matter up in slightly different ways, but using much of the same common language. Finally we should note that the thought of the head has not been prepared for in

---

[47] On its interpretation by the Fathers see S. Tromp, '"Caput influit sensum et motum". Col. 2,19 et Eph. 4,16 in luce traditionis', *Greg* 39 (1958) 353– 66.
[48] See F. W. Bayer, *RAC* I, 430–7.

Ephesians as it has in Colossians where holding fast to the head is part of the argument. If it is thought essential to argue for a strong literary relationship between the letters, it seems more probable that A/Col has clarified the obscurities of Eph 4.16 and has adopted its ἐξ οὗ, where the masculine is correct, without realising that in his context it should be feminine (cf Holtzmann, 51f).

ἐξ οὗ refers back to Christ (v. 15); whatever is described in v. 16 connects with Christ, but in what way? If Christ as head is the primary reference, we would have had ἐξ ἧς but, though the head may be a source of growth, the growth mentioned here is from Christ as person rather than as head (cf Roels, 107–9). Physiologically growth does not come from the head; head and trunk grow together (occasionally commentators have suggested that since babies have large heads in proportion to body size the body has to grow to match the size of the head!). Whether or not the ideas of Christ as head and as body had been originally distinct (e.g. Roberts, Lincoln; cf 1 Cor 11.3) AE is not responsible for bringing them together; this had already taken place in the Pauline school (cf Col 2.19); it is a natural association since human bodies always have heads.

σῶμα appears twice in the verse and this seems otiose. Schlier employs the double use to sustain his cosmic explanation of v. 15, seeing in its second occurrence a reference to the cosmos; it is repeated because its meaning has changed. It cannot be denied that the cosmos is sometimes described as a body (cf Detached Note: The Body of Christ), but we have seen no reason to accept Schlier's cosmic interpretation of v. 15. The second occurrence of 'body' probably arises out of the need to make the central theme explicit in the light of its distance from its first mention. Had AE instead used αὐτοῦ the pronoun would have been ambiguous. Moroever if its second appearance referred to the cosmos it is difficult to see what would be meant by the increase (growth) of the cosmos. It therefore refers to the church each time.

Our verse stresses the togetherness of those in the body, but it is not stressing the growth together of laity and ministers guided by the latter. The church is more than the passive object of ministerial activity (Dahl). Each individual has an important contribution to make if unity is to be maintained and growth to take place. The phrase συναρμολούμενον καί συμβιβαζόμενον which qualifies σῶμα brings out the way in which the togetherness of the body is sustained. The present participles indicate that the togetherness requires continual achievement. AE had already used the first participle in 2.21 (see there) and the second appears again in participial form in Col 2.19. Like our verse, Col 2.19 has also two participles of which the other reappears in a different guise here as ἐπιχορηγίας. Many attempts have been made to distinguish the two participles in meaning;[49] such attempts approach dangerously into the area of allegorisation. It is better with most modern commentators to view them in the light of AE's regular practice of using approximate synonyms to enforce his message; they do not therefore have essentially distinctive meanings. There is no reason to suppose that AE introduced the second participle because it would apply more easily to people; it is doubtful if this is so. Taken together the participles indicate the need for the community to remain united if it is to grow. They form a substitute, though a pale one, for the way members with their varying functions are told to act together in 1 Cor 12.12ff and Rom 12.3ff. It is true AE stresses here corporate growth more than the togetherness of members (Lincoln) yet the latter is not absent (both participles are compounds of σύν, Haupt). the following ἀφῆς relates members to one another. Thus the 'horizontal' relationship of members and, as we shall see, the 'vertical' relationship with Christ are both present.

ἀφή (cf Sellin, 101f) is probably a medical term whose exact significance is unclear (for discussions of possible meanings and its various interpretations by ancient commentators see Robinson, 186; Lincoln, 262f; Lightfoot, *Colossians*, 196f); the accompanying πάσης makes it in effect a plural. It represents whatever (i) holds the body together (in Col 2.19 it is parallel to σύνδεσμος), (ii) enables nourishment to pass from one part to another, (iii) the whole to be controlled by the head. The translation 'joints' is inadequate since joints exist to make articulation possible. In a sense Abbott's rendering 'contacts' is both in keeping with the basic meaning of the root and conveys some of its present connotation, but in the light of the way the word has changed its meaning since Abbott's time 'contact' itself would now require explanation. It is better to think in terms of ligaments, arteries and nerves, though no one of these by itself is correct since ligaments enable the body to act as a unit but do not convey nourishment and energy from one part to another, nerves convey not nourishment but information and arteries have no function in holding the body together. Even if we knew what part of the body AE had in mind, there may be no exact modern equivalent and efforts to determine this are probably wasted. 'Ligaments' has been chosen in the translation for lack of a better word. A more important discussion concerns the way some commentators seek to identify the ἀφαί with the ministers of v. 11 (a view going back at least to Erasmus) so that it is implied that it is through them that the body is held together and supplied with loving care. Such an interpretation differs little from the enabling role allotted to ministers in v. 12. If then the suggested identification is accepted nothing

[49] See G. H. Whitaker, 'συναρμολογούμενον καὶ συμβιβαζόμενον', *JTS* 31 (1930) 48f.

much is added to the content of what has 'already been said. But is such an interpretation exegetically correct? It verges on allegorisation and would be inappropriate in Col 2.19 where there is no discussion of the ministry. 4.16 may not depend on Col 2.19, but both authors come from the same Pauline school and may be supposed to use physical terms in much the same way unless there is positive evidence to the contrary. We have noted that v. 16 picks up terms from vv. 7, 12; v. 7 dealt with all members of the church and it is v. 12c which is picked up in v. 16 and v. 12c also refers to all members. Probably then v. 16 treats the contribution of all members of the church to its upbuilding and we should not see the clerical–lay division as present. ἐπιχορηγία is found in Phil 1.19 and its cognate verb in 2 Cor 9.10; Gal 3.5; Col 2.19; 2 Pet 1.5, 11; its meaning lies in the area 'help, supply, nourish, provide'. In our context it means that something is supplied to the body, or that the body is helped or nourished by Christ the head. Whatever it is, the ἁφαί transmit it; the final words of the verse suggest that it is love. The ἁφαί have a double function and syntactically they are connected both to the preceding participles and to ἐπιχορηγίας, though it would also be possible to take τῆς ἐπιχορηγίας in a passive sense indicating that the 'ligaments' have been supplied to the body; this seems pointless since the ligaments are in the body whether it is fitted and held together or not.

τῆς ἐπιχορηγίας is qualified by κατ᾽ ἐνέργειαν; this phrase is difficult to fit into the structure of the verse and this probably caused its omission in F G it; Ir^lat Lcf Ambst and its modification to καὶ ἐνεργείας in 𝔓^46 (though the latter may be due to scribal error). In 1.19 and 3.7 the preposition and the noun are combined but on each occasion the noun, unlike here, has the article (cf Phil 3.21; Col 1.19); in 2 Th 2.9 it lacks the article. The absence of the article suggests that the noun accompanying κατά should be taken adverbially. If so it would not qualify the participles, from which it is too distant, but τῆς ἐπιχορηγίας; whatever is supplied, is supplied in a powerful manner. The variant μέλους in the next phrase, read by A C Ψ 365 pc a vg sy^p bo, has probably been occasioned by the use of this word in 4.25; 1 Cor 12.22f; Rom 12.4f where in each case it is connected with 'body' used of the church. The meaning 'bodily part' for μέρος is found in the papyri; see MM, Preisigke-Kiessling, s.v. ποιεῖται, whose subject is πᾶν τὸ σῶμα and predicate τὴν αὔξησιν, could be either middle or passive or middle with an active meaning; the last is preferable. τοῦ σώματος is used here rather than a pronoun for clarity's sake. The final variant of αὐτοῦ or αὑτοῦ, ℵ D* F G 1505 pc for ἑαυτοῦ, does not affect the meaning.

There seems to be a break in the verse at this point as the emphasis on individual contributions is picked up in a new way with wording recalling v. 7. Each member has a proportional contribution to offer and makes it towards the growth of the body as a whole and not specifically towards the individuals within it. Least of all is it suggested that the office-bearers alone grow, or alone contribute to or create the growth of the body, though of course they have their role in equipping members to work towards growth. In the light of the final and emphatic reference to love, this growth should be understood as one of quality and not quantity. This accords with the stress in the earlier parts of vv. 11–16 on maturity rather than numbers. It is not that growth comes from within the body through some inner power, but it comes from Christ its head (ἐξ οὗ) *via* (in part) ministers (v. 11). The physiology may be incorrect, but AE has been forced into it by his choice of metaphor. In the final phrase the metaphor in fact changes to that of upbuilding and AE employs again the language he had used in v. 12 with the same meaning of ὁικοδομή as there (cf Kitzberger, 325f); it comes appropriately here after the mention of νήπιοι (v. 14) who necessarily require building up in the faith. Though it is not the body's own power which creates growth but Christ, the body through its members has a part to play in that growth; at least if it does not assist but remains quiescent, it will prevent it. Growth is not in knowledge, still less in numbers, but in love. The association of love with charismatic gifts goes back to 1 Cor 12–14. The final position of ἐν ἀγάπῃ in this long sentence makes it emphatic (for a similar connection of upbuilding and love see 1 Cor 8.1). In the light of the sentence's content the object of believers' love will not be Christ or God but one another; such a love of course has its source in Christ; 5.2 (cf 5.25) makes the same movement from Christ's love for believers to their love for one another. Love coming from Christ is the cement fitting and holding together the members, and all members without exception have their part to play in this. AE has provided here the picture not of a static church, but of one which is growing and maturing (an organism either grows or dies away, Gnilka). It is moving towards its goal (v. 13) and is enabled to do so through the love and power of its saviour and head, Christ.

X

OLD INTO NEW
(4.17–24)

J. Jervell, *Imago Dei*, Göttingen, 1960, 236–56; Roels, 128–32, 207–19; E. F. Klug, 'The Will of God in the Life of a Christian,' *CTM* 33 (1962) 453–68; J. Gnilka, 'Paränetische Traditionen im Epheserbrief', *Mélanges Bibliques* (FS B. Rigaux, ed. A. Deschamps and A. de Halleux), Gembloux, 1970, 397–410; C. Bussmann, *Themen der paulinischen Missionspredigt*, 1972, 137–41; Fischer, 148–50; 152–61; Halter, 248–56; H. Merklein, 'Eph 4,1–5,20 als Rezeption von Kol 3,1–17 (zugleich ein Beitrag zur Problematik des Epheserbriefes)', *Kontinuität und Einheit* (FS F. Mussner, ed. P. G. Müller and W. Stenger), Freiburg, 1981, 194–210; Usami, 30–6; E. Best, 'Two Types'.

17 This I go on to say and insist in the Lord
    that you live no longer as the pagans live
      in the worthlessness of your minds,
18   as those
      blind in understanding
      excluded from the life of God
        because of their inherent ignorance,
        because of the hardness of their hearts,
19   who being insensitive
      gave themselves over to undisciplined behaviour,
        working itself out in every kind of impurity,
        with covetousness.
20 But you have not learned Christ to that effect,
21   assuming [as we can] that you heard him
      and were taught in him,
    because the truth is in Jesus,
22   that you were to put off the old person
    of your earlier way of life,
    which was being corrupted through deceitful desires,
23   but to be renewed in the spirit of your minds,
24   and to put on the new person
    which has been created in God's likeness
    in true righteousness and holiness.

The paraenetic half of the letter, which appeared to commence with 4.1–3 but turned into a discussion of the unity and diversity of

believers, is now resumed and continued without interruption to the
end. What was said about behaviour in 4.2f related to conduct within
the community, but now when AE returns to the paraenesis this
element temporarily disappears to reappear at 4.25; this renders
difficult the connection with vv. 7–16; it may lie in the movement of
thought from believers as no longer babes but as growing up and so
requiring more instruction in behaviour (vv. 20f; cf Jerome), or,
more probably, 4.17–24 may be a necessary preparation for the
detailing of instruction about conduct which follows in 4.25ff. The
paraenesis implicit in 4.17–24 is not unrelated to the first half of the
letter since it focusses on the former Gentile attitudes of believers
whose new (theological) position in the people of God had been
explored in 2.11–22; 3.2–13. Merklein, art.cit., compares the basis
of this approach to ethical instruction, which derives from the
Christian–pagan contrast, to that in Col 3.1–4, where the similar
approach is based on an earthly–heavenly contrast. 4.17–24 is
verbally connected to what follows through the later repeated use of
περιπατεῖν (5.2, 8, 15).

As AE sees it, the peril facing Gentile believers is neither
persecution brought on by their new attitude to paganism nor the
influence of heretical intellectual ideas but a relapse into their
former pre-Christian ways, which are the ways of the world around
them. This could happen if believers forsook their faith or introduced their pre-Christian attitudes into the church. Although Ephesians may be described as a writing of the second or third Christian
generation, and a small minority of those to whom AE writes may
have been brought up in Christian homes, the majority will have
been first-generation Christians, some indeed may have only
recently been converted. This may be part of the reason for AE's
apparent diversion into the nature of the church in 4.4–16. One
important defence against non-Christian ways is for believers to
understand the nature of the new group they have joined and their
place in it. Small groups facing a hostile, or even a mainly neutral,
culture find it important to define the type of conduct their members
should display. Since it is usually easier to do this negatively by
stating what the group rejects in the world around it, small groups
normally stress the negative aspects. This was the position of the
Jews in the ancient world where their Law and customs held them
together; so the Pharisees regarded the Law as a fence protecting
their way of life. It should be no surprise then to find strong negative
features in AE's paraenesis. But the negative by itself is inadequate;
there is a distinctive and positive Christian way of life and AE sets
this out. In expressing both the negative and positive aspects he uses
traditional paraenetical material, mostly drawn from Judaism, but
material which was not out of accord with the teaching of many
pagan moral philosophers. From the beginning the church had

instructed its members in how to live and, since Christianity came out of a Jewish cradle, much of what was taught was similar to Jewish instruction; this may not have been needed for the first converts from Judaism but was very necessary when the majority of those entering the church came from the Gentile world.

One way of describing the new Christian life contrasts it with pagan ways, and this is how AE begins (vv. 17–19) before turning in later sections to more direct and detailed instruction. In 4.17–24 the thought moves twice from the negative to the positive. In vv. 17–19, after the general introduction of v. 17a, AE draws a picture of the heathen world which depends in part on previous Jewish thinking (e.g. Wisd 14.22–31; *Ep Arist* 152; Philo, *Vita Cont* 40–7). He then identifies the new element that has entered the lives of his readers (vv. 20–1) and concludes in vv. 22–4, where there is an antithetical *parallelismus membrorum* (Roberts), by contrasting their previous nature with their present; a new way of behaviour necessitates a new being from which it may proceed. Membership of the community involves a personal reorientation. In 4.2f AE set the Christian life in the context of the community; he later returns to this but for the moment he contrasts it with non-Christian living.

17. τοῦτο points forward and not backward (cf 3.8; 5.5; 1 Cor 7.29; 1 Th 4.15) and οὖν does not draw a conclusion from what precedes; it is difficult to see to what it could relate; instead it is resumptive, indicating a new stage in the argument (Robertson, 1191f; LSJ *s.v.* II, 1).

The double phrase λέγω καὶ μαρτύρομαι is impressive, solemn and wholly in AE's manner, though there are parallels in Paul (1 Th 2.12) and in secular Greek (Percy, 20, 240f); the first verb is weak but the second is not (cf Josephus *Ant* 10.104; see H. Strathmann, *TWNT*, IV, 517–19). The second should not be joined too closely to 'in the Lord' (see 1 Th 4.1; 2 Th 3.12 for their combination) as if AE were affirming on oath the truth of what he is saying. 'In the Lord' appears more regularly in the second half of the letter (4.1, 17; 5.8; 6.1, 10, 21) than the first (2.21); in the latter 'in Christ' (1.3, 10, 12, 20; 4.32), or combinations as 'in Christ Jesus' (1.1; 2.6, 7, 10, 13; 3.6; 4.21), 'in Christ Jesus our Lord' (3.11) are more common (for the phrase see Detached Note: In Christ). While the 'fellowship' aspect appears more often in the use of 'in Christ' it is not wholly lacking when the present phrase is used (cf Rom 16.2; 1 Cor 7.39). 'In the Lord' qualifies the verbs because AE is writing to fellow-Christians; it reminds them of the bond between Paul and their Lord and therefore of that between their Lord and themselves; both AE and his readers are members of the body of Christ and he is seeking to build them up in the faith (4.12f). The phrase may also serve to remind them of the authority of their Lord over them.

Their behaviour (for περιπατεῖν see on 2.2) is no longer to be as it once was. The precise significance of μηχέτι is not clear: it could mean that they should not fall back into pre-conversion ways but, more probably, means that they should not continue in ways which they will not have wholly abandoned when converted, for this appears to be the word's significance in v. 14. This understanding recognises that they will not have become perfect immediately they became Christian. They are no longer to live as (καί strengthens καθώς and is best omitted in translation, cf MHT, 335) pagans do (the verb is singular in accordance with classical standards though the noun often has a plural predicate, cf BDR §133, n. 3). The reading of א² D¹ Ψ 𝔐 vgᵐˢ sy which adds λοιπά is poorly supported and has probably been inserted under the influence of Rom 1.13. It emphasises the relationship of the converts to their previous culture.

The manner of their new life, expressed positively in 4.2f, is now put negatively: they are no longer to live as τὰ ἔθνη, a word whose meaning always needs to be determined from its context. It was used by the Jews to distinguish themselves from non-Jews in terms of religion, race and culture, with those elements variously stressed. This usage passed into early Christianity and is found in 3.1, 6, 8. These, not Jews by race or religious conversion, have been able to become members of the church on equal terms with Jewish Christians. Jews regarded the moral standards of Gentiles in general as debased and the first Christians, all Jews by birth, continued to think in this way and so applied the word to those who were neither Christians nor Jews, even though within the church the Jewish–non-Jewish distinction was disappearing. Consequently there is no single English word which can be used on every occasion to translate the term; the context must determine the rendering. In v. 17 the sense will be 'pagan' or 'heathen' since stress is being laid on the non-Jewish nature of the culture from which the readers have been converted. AE now briefly describes that culture; the sins with which he categorises it are largely the same as those Jews used of Gentile culture (Wisd 12–15; 18.10–19; *Ep Arist* 132–8, 140, 277; *Sib Or* 3.8–45, 220–35; *Jub* 22.16–18; *T Naph* 3.3). Jewish writers regularly summoned their fellow Jews not to live like Gentiles (Lev 20.23; Dt 18.9).

The first characteristic of the culture which the readers had left is expressed as an attitude of mind.[1] 'Mind' does not denote 'the mind or the intellect as a special faculty, but the knowing, understanding and judging which belong to man as man and determine what attitude he adopts'.[2] AE is not then describing a defect in the ability of his readers to reason but their 'mind-set', the total person viewed under the aspect of thinking. The mind, as AE views it, can be renewed (Rom 12.2) so that the old mind of unbelievers becomes a

[1] On 'mind' see Stacey, 198–215; Jewett, 358–90; J. Behm, *TWNT*, IV, 950–8; G. Harder, *NIDNTT*, III, 122–30.
[2] Bultmann, I, 211.

new mind in believers (cf 4.22, 24). A close connection exists then between mind and activity. The pre-Christian pagan mind is characterised here by ματαιότης.[3] The Christian understanding and use of this word is determined by the LXX. Idols are μάταιοι (Acts 14.15) and therefore all non-Jewish and non-Christian worship is worthless as unable to bring its worshippers to God. Non-Christian Gentiles have already been described as not knowing God (2.12). 'Worthlessness' is not however applied to idolatry alone but to the whole of pagan life (1 Pet 1.18; cf Jas 1.26; Rom 8.20), since for Jews and Christians an attitude to religion will ultimately work itself out in depraved behaviour (Jer 2.5; Isa 28.29; 30.15; 33.11; Rom 1.21ff; cf 1QS 5.19). Even the ways of those who are accounted learned in pagan society may be described with this word (1 Cor 3.20, quoting Ψ 93.11; the reference to the wise or learned comes from Paul; the original is not so restricted). Heathen culture being then devoid of real value, its religions will be also. This of course would not have been the verdict of those in it. The worthlessness does not lie in the world as such, for all that God made is good (Theophylact), but in the minds of those who live in it. The accusation of worthlessness was widely used in Jewish and Christian apologetic, even beyond the NT period, e.g. *Barn* 4.10; 20.2; 1 Clem 7.2; 9.1; in *Did* 5.2 it is one among a list of vices; in Ephesians and mostly elsewhere it describes a total attitude; for this reason it is probably wrong to see v. 17 as directly dependent on Rom 1.21ff. The next two verses spell out more fully where the worthlessness of the mind may lead.

18. AE now gives his picture of heathen life; in doing so he employs many of the words and ideas of Rom 1.18ff, though with such variations as to suggest that that passage is not being used directly; doubtless its theme remained a part of the Pauline tradition. It is a bleak picture and accords with a great part of Judaism's view of non-Judaism, though Judaism could also see non-Judaism in a softer light.[4] It is natural for AE to draw attention to the darker aspect since he wishes to warn his readers against relapsing into it.

Verse 18 consists of two participial clauses and two phrases introduced by prepositions and is followed in v. 19 by a relative clause; all are set together in a manner typical of AE (Percy 21f, 186f). The two participial clauses are best taken as parallel. With which is ὄντες to be associated? The rhythm of the sentence suggests with the first (Westcott); if taken with the second alone, in accordance with Col 1.21, it would make the second give the reason for the first (Abbott); it is however probably better to take it with both. Periphrastic tenses incorporating perfect participles serve to emphasise an existing state (MHT, 89; Burton §155; BDR §352, n. 4; Porter, 475; Fanning, 416–18) though providing no clue as to when the state began. The

[3] See O. Bauernfeind, *TWNT*, IV, 525–30.
[4] See Best, 'Christian View', for evidence for both aspects.

nom. pl. of the participles is a *constructio ad sensum*. The two prepositional phrases should not be distributed individually to the participial clauses whether sequentially or chiastically but related to both; the second prepositional phrase is probably parallel to the first rather than subordinate to it. ἐσκοτωμένοι is from σκοτοῦν; the more common verb σκοτίζεσθαι appears as a variant (D F G 082 1739 1881 𝔐; Cl) and is almost certainly a correction of the less frequent word which is found only elsewhere in the NT at Rev 9.2; 16.10, where in each case the other appears as a variant.

The Gentile world out of which the readers were converted remained in a state of blindness. Earlier AE had described believers as those who saw (1.18). The metaphor of sight, or lack of it, was used regularly by Jews of the spiritual as well as the mental condition of Gentiles: Jews see, others are blind; Jews are a light to blind Gentiles (Ps 135.16; Isa 42.6f; 49.6; 1QSb 4.27; Wisd 18.4); the non-Jewish world is one of darkness. In fairness it must be said that Jews also described fellow Jews as blind (*T Reub* 3.8; *T Dan* 2.4; *T Gad* 6.2; *T Levi* 14.11; 1QS 3.3; cf Mt 15.14; 23.16, 24; Rom 2.19). Christians took over the metaphor from Jews (Acts 26.18; Col 1.13; 1 Pet 2.9; Jn 8.12; Eph 5.11; 1 Th 5.4). It was also used widely in the ancient world, though generally in respect of mental rather than spiritual blindness; AE's readers would therefore have easily have grasped its significance. διάνοια[5] might seem to suggest only mental blindness. The word originally indicated the ability to think, then the organ through which understanding took place and finally the understanding itself. In the LXX and in the NT (where it is often equivalent to καρδία, Heb 8.10; 10.16 = Jer 31.33 LXX; cf 1 Pet 1.13; 2 Pet 3.1) it came to represent the whole person viewed as one who can experience knowledge, and understand and accept salvation. Those lacking this experience are blind, just as in 2.1 they were described as dead. Unlike the physically blind however they would be unaware of their condition. The perfect participle, while suggesting something which began in the past and still continues, does not imply a time when Gentiles once saw; AE is not interested at this point in such a question, and in 4.24 where he might have addressed it he writes not of a reconditioned person but of a new person. The idea of heathen blindness offers another similarity to Rom 1.21, though there the more normal verb σκοτίζειν is used and we have καρδία instead of διάνοια. The supposition of dependence on Rom 1.21 becomes less probable once we realise that the idea of worthlessness and blindness lay first in Jewish and then in early Christian teaching; Rom 1.21 itself probably depends on Wisd 13.1ff. The theology of Rom 1.18ff and some of its terms may well have been handed down within the Pauline community.

In the second participial clause AE employs ἀπαλλοτριόομαι

[5] See J. Behm, *TWNT*, IV, 961–5; G. Harder, *NIDNTT*, III, 123, 127f.

which he had previously used in 2.12 (see notes there) but gives a
new twist to its meaning in making it refer to exclusion from the life
of God (cf Col 1.21 for the sense[6]). The reference to the life of God
is strange; we would expect something like 'alienated from God' or
'excluded from salvation'. The life of God is presumably not God's
own life but the life he gives, and since God gives physical life to
both pagans and believers AE will be thinking of eternal life. Life
and light are associated in biblical thought; the Gospel of John
exploits their connection (e.g. 1.4; 8.12) but it runs back into the OT
(e.g. Ps 36.9). The two are also linked in gnostic thought (e.g. *CH*
1.9, 12). There is thus a natural movement, easily grasped by Gentile
readers, from the blindness of the first clause to the loss of life
implied in the second; the heathen are of course 'dead' in sin (2.1);
life and death are opposites. In writing of exclusion from the life of
God AE is not thinking of some kind of alienation which psychia-
trists could cure. What is required is not psychological treatment but
something wholly new, a new being (v. 24).

If the two passive participles allowed pagans to think their
condition was not their own fault, being the result of the action of
God or an evil power, the two prepositional phrases bring out their
responsibility. They are blind and excluded because of their ignorance and the hardness of their hearts (cf Percy, 266). Their
ignorance[7] cannot be offered as an excuse (as it may be in Lk 23.34;
Acts 3.17; 17.30; *T Zeb* 1.5; Epictetus, 1.26.5–7) for it does not
arise out of a lack of information about the world or morality. It is
an ignorance both about God, though not an intellectual deficiency
since the devils can believe God exists but do not come to true
enlightenment (Jas 2.19), and about their own true nature as people.
This ignorance has no higher and lower levels; all have it to the
same degree; neither learning nor experience can modify or remove
it (Rom 1.21f; Wisd 13.1, 7–9); it is not a passing or temporary
ignorance, nor is it one among a list of possible vices (contrast *CH*
13.7; in 13.8 ignorance seems to have a unique place over against
knowledge of God; cf 7.2). In Jewish thought, which again has
modelled what AE writes, ignorance, sin and unbelief are closely
linked (*T Gad* 5.7; 1QH 1.22f; 4.7; Wisd 14.22; 1 Th 4.5) and
ignorance is also linked to idolatry (Philo, *Decal* 8; *Spec Leg* 1.15).

The second prepositional phrase, parallel to the first and not (as
Schlier) its interpretation, expresses the same thought in another
way as a hardening of the heart.

It has however been argued, principally by Robinson, 263–74 (cf

---

[6] There is no need to see AE as depending here on Colossians; he had already used
διάνοια at 2.2 and he associates it here with a different word than in Col 1.21.
[7] On ἀγνωσία see L. Cerfaux, *RAC* I, 186–8; Dupont, 3–8; J. Gnilka, 'Paraenetische Traditionen', 401–3.

Lindars, 159–67), that πώρωσις should be translated as 'blindness' and not 'hardness'. He points out that (1) many of the ancient versions render the word and its cognates in that way both here and in other parts of the NT (as if they read πήρωσις), (2) the latter appears as a variant in some places, (3) in many of its NT occurrences 'blindness' fits the context, and (4) this is the way some of the Fathers understood πώρωσις. However, since there is no unanimity in the NT over the meaning of the word and 'blindness' is only a probable meaning in other places, the context should be left to determine the meaning on each occasion; in our case since 'blindness' is probably only an attempt to explain a difficult metaphor (hardening of the heart) and since there is already one reference to blindness in the verse it is better to remain with the meaning 'hardness'.

The metaphor of 'the hardening of the heart'[8] (the heart is the centre of personality, see on 1.18) is found elsewhere in the NT (Mk 3.5; 6.52; 8.17; Jn 12.40) where, unlike here, it is used to describe the condition of Jews (cf Rom 9.18; 11.7, 25). Jews used the image of hardness or stubbornness, often with the verb σκληροῦν and usually in relation to the heart, to describe the condition both of non-Jews (Exod 4.21; 7.3; 9.12; Jer 19.15) and of themselves (Isa 6.10; 63.17; Jer 7.26; 17.23; Ψ 94.8; 1QS 1.6; 2.14, 26; 3.3; 5.4; CD 2.17f; 3.5, 11f; 8.8). Sometimes the hardening is attributed to God (Exod 4.21; 10.20, 27; Dt 2.30) and sometimes it is regarded as self-inflicted (Exod 9.34f; 7.22; 8.15). AE thus accuses pagans of the same hardness of which scripture often accuses the Jews. It is a quality which belongs to unbelieving people as people whether they are Jews or Gentiles. Gnostics also used the image (*Ap John* II, 1 30.7–11; *Testim Truth* IX, 3 32.5–8). Hardness and blindness, or darkness, are sometimes associated elsewhere (2 Cor 4.3f; Jn 12.40 quoting Isa 6.10).

19. AE now spells out the nature of the pagan world in a new way.

Verse 19 is neither simply an interpretation of the 'hardening' of v. 18 nor does it supply a reason for what precedes; in Koine Greek ὅστις lost its distinction from ὅς and functioned regularly as a simple relative (BDR §293; MHT, 47f). ἀπαλγεῖν is used in various ways (see LSJ and the references there); Moule, 89, suggests the meaning 'cease to feel' as appropriate here. The variant ἀπηλπικότες of D F G P 1241ˢ *pc* latt syᵖ probably arose from simple scribal error or under the influence of 2.12.

The consciences of Gentiles do not stab them when they do wrong for they are insensitive in distinguishing what is morally good from what is evil. The thought is similar to that of 2.1 where Gentiles were regarded as dead. As with the perfect participles of v. 18 a continuing state is implied. No outside power (God or Satan?) has

---

[8] See L. Cerfaux, '"L'aveuglement d'esprit" dans l'évangile de saint Marc', *Recueil Lucien Cerfaux*, II, Gembloux, 1954, 1–10; Braun, *Qumran*, 218f; H. Räisänen, *The Idea of Divine Hardening*, Helsinki, 1976, 45ff.

inflicted their condition on them; they gàve themselves up to it; the subject of παρέδωκαν is here the Gentiles, unlike Rom 1.24, 26, 28 where it is God. This variation yet again renders unlikely the direct use of Romans by AE, as supposed by Mitton, *Epistle*, 120, 148, though it shows AE's awareness of Pauline thought. Bouwman suggests that he is demythologising the idea of Romans and Lindemann that he is rejecting it. The latter seems improbable since the participles of the context are probably divine passives. Perhaps AE simply wishes to bring out more clearly the responsibility of unbelievers for their own condition.[9] The variation between viewing the state of the Gentiles as their own fault or as inflicted on them from outside (2.2; 4.18) is similar to that in which believers at times see themselves as believing because of God's action (1.4; 2.1a, 5, 13, etc.) and at other times as making their own decision (1.13). This, the interrelation of divine election and human choice, is a continuing theological problem; AE tends to emphasise the former aspect though the change here from Rom 1.24 shows he realises it can be over-stressed.

Insensitive to the distinctions required by true morality, unbelievers gave themselves up to sin; this is now described with three nouns whose precise meaning is difficult to tie down because each is used both in a wide sense, embracing a range of sins, and in a more restricted way of particular sins. The relation of the final noun to the preceding two is also difficult. ἀσέλγεια appears regularly in vice catalogues (Mk 7.22; Rom 13.13; 2 Cor 12.21; Gal 5.19; 1 Pet 4.3; Wisd 14.26; *T Jud* 23.1; *T Levi* 17.11; Hermas, *Sim* 9.15.3) but it is also used with a more general significance (2 Pet 2.2, 18; Jude 4; Hermas, *Vis* 2.2.2; 3.7.2; *Mand* 12.4.6; Philo, *Vita Mos* 1.305; 3 Macc 2.26). In the catalogues it is normally found in the area where sexual sins are listed (Mk 7.22 is an exception; in *T Jud* 23.1 it is linked with idolatry) and this may still be its import when used more generally (e.g. Josephus *Ant* 8.318; 20.112) with it indicating sexual sin of many kinds; since however there are also clear instances where undisciplined behaviour without an explicit sexual connection is indicated (Jos *Ant* 4.151; 8.252), it is probably best understood as undisciplined behaviour especially, though not exclusively, of a sexual nature.

ἀκαθαρσία also appears in vice catalogues (2 Cor 12.21; Gal 5.19; Col 3.5; Prov 6.16; Eph 5.3), sometimes in proximity to ἀσέλγεια (2 Cor 12.21; Gal 5.19); it is rare in classical Greek; in Leviticus (see especially ch. 15) it refers regularly to ritual uncleanness. Apart from this restricted use, in some of its scriptural occurrences its connotation appears to be sexual (especially Gal

---

[9] It is very unlikely that in his use of παραδίδωμι AE is playing on its christological significance and preparing for 5.2, as suggested by Romaniuk, 36f.

5.19; Col 3.5) and this is also true when it appears by itself (1 Th 4.7; *T Jud* 14.5; *Barn* 10.8,18), though the reference may be more general (1 Th 2.3; Prov 6.16; Wisd 2.16; 3 Macc 2.17; *T Levi* 15.1). The phenomenon in which general moral terms are given a sexual orientation ('she is an immoral woman') appears in many cultures. There is nothing in the use of our two nouns to indicate a sexual orientation here. πάσης suggests a general meaning in respect of the second, 'every kind of impurity', though it could be 'every kind of sexual deviation'.

Like the two other terms, πλεονεξία[10] appears in vice lists (Mk 7.22; Rom 1.29; 1 Clem 35.5; *Barn* 20.1; *Did* 5.1; Polyc *Phil* 2.2; Hermas, *Mand* 6.2.5; 8.5; *CH* 13.7) and is found separately (Lk 12.15; 2 Cor 9.5; Eph 5.3; Col 3.5; 1 Th 2.5; 2 Pet 2.3, 14; cf 1 Cor 5.10f; 6.10; Eph 5.5). It is never a general term like the others but may indeed be given a wider reference ('a morbid lust of acquisition', Eadie on 5.3), indicating a desire for more than a fair share of whatever is at issue, e.g. wealth, possessions. Its rejection runs back to the Decalogue and it continued to be rebuked not only in Judaism (e.g. Philo, *Spec Leg* 4.5; *Vita Mos* 2.186; CD 4.17; 1QS 4.9ff) but equally, if not more so, in the Hellenistic world (e.g. Dio Chrys *Or* 17) where sexual sin was by no means so widely condemned. 1 Tim 6.10 was probably formulated under Hellenistic influence. Jewish and Christian thought often linked sexual sin with greed (CD 8.5; *T Levi* 14.5f; *T Jud* 17.1f; 18.2; *T Dan* 5.5–7) and also greed with idolatry (*T Jud* 19.1; Col 3.5; Eph 5.3; Polyc *Phil* 11.2); the latter connection underlies the words of Jesus about God and mammon (Mt 6.24; Lk 16.13) but is probably not present in v. 19; AE's readers would take πλεονεξία in the simple sense of greed. There is no reason to accept Chrysostom's understanding of it as 'immoderation' in sexual sin; this cannot be the meaning at 5.3 where it is distinguished from sexual sin (cf 5.5; 1 Cor 5.10; the two come closest at 1 Th 4.6). It is of course true that the wealthy may use their wealth for sexual indulgence but this is not the point. How does greed relate to what precedes? It is too distant from the verb to be directly linked to it (as BDR §187.2 suggests); the verb in any case is already linked to τῇ ἀσελγείᾳ. It is probably better to join it to ἀκαθαρσία through 'and'[11] (a Semitic usage, Kuhn, *NTS* 7 (1960/1) at p. 337) or 'with' (cf Phil 1.9; Col 4.2; MHT, 252; Van Roon, 114f).

AE paints here a very dark picture of the Gentile world. Questions immediately arise: From where did he derive his material? Why did he draw so dark a picture? Was he fair to the Gentile world? As to the

---

[10] For the word and concept see G. Delling, *TWNT*, VI, 266–74; Spicq, II, 704–6; id, *Les Épîtres Pastorales*, Paris, 1969, at 1 Tim 6.10.
[11] καὶ πλεονεξίας appears as a variant in D F G (1241ˢ) *pc* it vgᵐˢˢ; Cl MVict Ambst indicating the solution adopted by many in the ancient church.

first question almost all he says can' be traced back through Christianity to Judaism; it is found also in all strands of early Christianity (cf Mk 8.38; Acts 2.40; Rom 1.18–32; 1 Th 4.3–7; Tit 3.3; 1 Pet 4.3–4; *Did* 3.1–6; *Barn* 20). It must be allowed however that Judaism has kinder things to say; Josephus, *Vita* 12, for example, compares Pharisees and Stoics with no intention of denigrating either. That AE has taken over a traditional view suggests that his picture of the secular world was not derived from actual observation, and as we go on we shall find much to confirm this.

The answer to the second question is more complex. Moralists tend to overstress the dark side of any society they attack. Small groups seeking to distinguish themselves from their prevailing culture do the same; this has been particularly true of small religious groups. AE, needing to draw a sharp line between how his readers once lived and how they ought to live in order to encourage them to live in the new way, overemphasises their past behaviour. Since converts regularly overplay the distinction between their past and new life his readers might not have noticed a discrepancy between what he says and what they know of the outside world.

As for the third question, it is possible to find non-Jewish and non-Christian pessimistic descriptions of contemporary culture (e.g. Heraclitus, *Epistula* 7[12]). The satirists (e.g. Juvenal) concentrate on and pick out incidents from the dark side of society; they would not have been read if what they said was wholly untrue; like tabloid newspapers they highlighted what was obviously false in society and ignored what was good. On the other hand the fact that attention was paid to them implies that there were those who rejected the moral positions they satirised and accepted a different view. Thus AE's absolute picture of total darkness cannot be true. There is much else which shows that in fact it was prejudiced. When discussing 4.2 we saw that gentleness and patience were highly regarded by Greek and other thinkers. In 4.24 AE uses a word pair, δικαιοσύνη and ὁσιότης, to characterise Christian behaviour which pagan moralists and philosophers also used. The Stoics commended prudence, justice, courage and temperance as virtues and attacked immoderate desire for pleasure, including sexual indulgence (e.g. Plutarch, *Mor* 441A; Seneca, *Ep* 9.3ff; 75.7ff; Epictetus, 2.18.15, 19; 3.7.21; 4.1.122; M. Aurelius 9.42) and anger (see on 4.26f, 31). Virgil's *Fourth Eclogue* indicates an aspiration for better things. The existence of catalogues of vices and virtues shows condemnation of various sins and approval of various virtues. The qualities demanded of Christian leaders in the Pastorals are little different from those for good leaders in society as a whole.[13] Musonius Rufus writes of

[12] Gore, 255, gives a summary.
[13] See J. Roloff, *Der erste Brief an Timotheus* (EKK XV), 1988, 150.

people having an innate inclination towards virtue (Frag 2, Hense, 7.7f). In Frag 8 (Hense 34.16–35.6) he provides a not unfavourable picture of society. This is not simply a philosopher trying to put a good gloss on his world; the same is found or implied in inscriptions which represent popular non-philosophical belief, e.g. Barton and Horsley, CIL 8.11824.[14] Part of the problem arises from the concentration by early, and later, Christian moralists on sexual sin and other undisciplined behaviour. There were however areas where there was much to commend in the ancient world. Paul writes highly of Roman justice (Rom 13.1–7) from which he himself on a number of occasions benefited (e.g. Acts 16.35ff; 18.12ff; 21.31ff; 25.8ff). The sins of the nations criticised by Amos are what we would describe as social or political sins. What AE writes then represents a limited and unbalanced view of the nature of Gentile culture. Surprisingly he does not mention idolatry (contrast 1 Th 1.9f). The sins of society as a whole do not come into view; thus slavery is not condemned in the NT, nor the degradation of women. When we turn away from the restricted area of the Mediterranean we find societies in other areas, e.g. China, India, who venerate the golden rule and place a high value on honesty and truthfulness; not all are hotbeds of sexual immorality; monogamy is revered in many cultures. Finally, should it be said that while these cultures and societies may have high ideals they were not lived up to, no one who has read the history of Christianity would dare to suggest that Christians have lived up to their ideals. To sum up, AE's description of the pagan world must be classified as governed more by theology than by observation. It would presumably have prevented him entering into inter-faith dialogue with any other group than Jews.

What did AE's converts from the pagan world think of his description of it? Did they nod their heads in agreement or did they mutter 'He's got it all wrong'? If the latter, did it shake their confidence in the other things he wrote?

20. The basis of the readers' lives has been changed; ὑμεῖς is emphatic; it is not the basis of everyone's life that has been changed, only that of believers. They are then no longer to live as they once did as pagans. The abrupt beginning of v. 20 serves to stress the contrast between Christian and non-Christian existence (cf Macpherson). AE does not detail now the new Christian way of living (this begins at v. 25) but supplies the reason for the change.

οὐχ οὕτως picks up vv. 17–19; the καθώς of v. 21 does not depend on it. Various attempts have been made to amend the structure of v. 20. Beza suggested placing a period after οὕτως but this makes 20b begin too abruptly; we should expect some adversative particle 'But you have not

---

[14] A translation of the latter will be found in R. MacMullen, *Roman Social Relations*, New Haven and London, 1974, 44.

426   COMMENTARY ON EPHESIANS

learned ...', and perhaps the repetition of ὑμεῖς; the εἴ γε clause then also becomes superfluous ('You learned Christ if indeed you heard (of) him'; cf Ewald). V. 20 might be read as a question (Wohlenberg) with 21a as parenthetical and 21b picking up the οὕτως; if that were so 21a would surely have followed 21b; there is moreover no question that the readers are Christian and have heard Christ and been taught in him (cf Haupt).

ἐμάθετε τὸν Χριστόν is an unusual phrase though not because of the presence of the article (see on 1.10); AE is not stressing that they have learnt a special Jewish Messiah; 'Christ' in itself already contains a Jewish reference. It is unusual because a person is said to be learnt; normally subjects are learnt ('You have not learnt the Torah'[15]). The unexpected use of the accusative would surely have shocked readers into looking for a deeper meaning than simply understanding Christ as the subject of instruction, though certainly since their conversion they will have learnt about him and his teaching. So far as his teaching goes, while detailed instruction in morals follows from 4.25ff, it is difficult to associate much of it with the teaching of the historical Jesus in so far as we know it; none of the instruction of 4.25ff is introduced or enforced with a reference to him; the Jesus tradition moreover was not stressed in the churches adhering to Paul's ways. Learning Christ must also mean more than being taught about christology, though naturally since becoming Christians readers will have learnt about this. If 'learning Christ' meant learning about his teaching or person, v. 21a would have been differently expressed. More information about him would never have changed their way of life. Dibelius has attributed a 'mystical' significance to the phrase (to learn Christ is to grow in fellowship with him), pointing to *Odes Sol* 7.3ff, but this is by no means a clear parallel.[16] The phrase is probably best understood with the help of Colossians where in 2.6f the readers are said to have received Christ and to live in him and to have been taught, and in 1.6f to have heard and recognised the grace of God in truth as they were taught by Epaphras; in 4.20f AE uses many of these words and ideas but puts them to a different use; they were probably words and ideas of the Pauline school. AE may also have been influenced by phrases like 'to know Christ' (Phil 3.10), 'to proclaim Christ' (Gal 1.16; Phil 1.17f; Col 1.28), 'to preach Christ' (1 Cor 1.23; 15.12; 2 Cor 4.5), where in every case something more than the passing on of information about Christ is intended. Successful preaching brings its hearers into a relation with the living Christ; to respond to it is to

---

[15] While the tradition about Christ may be passed on, learning him is not the same as accepting tradition was among the Jews; cf K. Wegenast, *Das Verständnis der Tradition bei Paulus und in den Deuteropaulinen* (WMANT 8), Neukirchen, 1962, 131f.

[16] Wegenast, op.cit., 131f, sees the influence of initiatory experiences into the Mysteries, but again sufficient evidence is lacking to support this view.

learn Christ. It is this Christ into whom the readers have already
been said to be growing (4.15). The aorist tense of the verb probably
indicates the moment or period when they became Christians. As
Zerwick comments, to learn Christ is a good summary of what it
means to be a Christian.

21. As at 3.2 εἴ γε does not indicate doubt and may be
paraphrased, 'At any rate if you have heard ... as I know you have'
(Thrall, 88). If Paul is the author of the letter he would be assuming
that the readers were led into the Christian faith in the same way as
in the churches he himself evangelised. If he is not the author AE
will be making almost the same assumption. What learning Christ
(v. 20) entails is now further explained with two verbs. The first,
because of the way it is used, would have been almost equally as
startling as v. 20, for the accusative after ἀκούειν would normally in
good Greek indicate only the hearing of a sound and the readers
have certainly never heard Jesus physically; in later Greek however
it could occasionally indicate the hearing which includes understanding (BDR §173 n. 4; Robertson, 506f); hearing about Christ
cannot be the meaning since it would not be expressed by the
accusative; the hearing of Mk 9.7, though there the genitive is used,
is an example of the same type of hearing as here. The readers learnt
Christ (v. 20); they heard Christ (v. 21). The present phrase may
represent the idea that Christ himself is heard in those who proclaim
him (2 Cor 13.3; Lk 10.16a; cf Barth, 530). This becomes more
likely if we take into account the Christian belief that Christ is risen
and alive (Lindemann). The aorist tense suggests the hearing is that
of the time of conversion.

The second verb ἐδιδάχθητε is also troublesome because of its
tense and the way the pronoun is associated with it. The aorist
suggests it refers to a past period of teaching, often understood as a
time of initial catechetical instruction. A period of catechesis preceding baptism became the norm in the later church yet it is questionable
if it existed at the time of Ephesians. None of the conversions
recorded in Acts leaves time for instruction between the moment of
confession of faith and baptism (2.41; 8.12f, 36, 38; 9.18f; 10.47f;
16.15, 31–3; 19.1–6). However, for the faith of converts to be
deepened there must have been instruction after conversion/baptism
(1 Cor 4.17; Col 2.7; 2 Th 2.15, if neither 2 Thessalonians nor
Ephesians is by Paul they are of approximately the same period and 2
Thessalonians would be evidence as to current practice). The length
of time Paul stayed in any community varied; it was often brief
because either he felt the need to move on or was driven out by the
authorities. Instruction was continued through his letters and the
visits of his assistants (Timothy, Titus, Silas, etc.). Yet the deepening
of faith never ends, as AE recognised by writing Ephesians and
emphasising the need to mature (4.13ff). The aorist tense with its

suggestion of a fixed period is inappropriate to such ongoing teaching. If, as must have been the case, some readers had been Christians for only a brief period, and there had been post-baptismal catechetical instruction, they would still have been in its period; the aorist would again be inappropriate to this. Why then has it been used? The two verbs of hearing and being taught may refer to the same event of becoming a Christian looked at from distinct angles. Acceptance of Christ implies not only some relation to him but also acceptance of some understanding of who he is and what he has done, i.e. the acceptance of some body, however slender, of doctrine. The difference between hearing and being taught may also be implicit in the different use of the pronouns in each case.

If the accusative is unusual after ἀκούειν, ἐν αὐτῷ is even more so after διδάσκειν for it takes an accusative of what is taught. Larsson, 225, n. 2, followed by several commentators, regards the formation as Semitic where to be instructed in the Law may be expressed by בּ; for Christians 'tradition' replaces the Law and Christ is 'tradition'. This argument has too many steps in it to convince; while AE's readers would have accepted many OT and Jewish terms and ideas, it is highly improbable that they would have grasped the sense of this one. Barth regards the phrase as depicting Christ as the foundation of all Christian teaching, but AE would then have used ἐπί. The great majority of commentators take the phrase as an instance of the 'in Christ' formula and explain it in various ways, e.g. Christ as the atmosphere in which the teaching was given, those who are in Christ are taught (would this not require [ὑμεῖς] οἱ ἐν αὐτῷ ἐδιδάχθητε?); Zerwick carries the 'in Christ' interpretation too far when he equates it with 'in the church'. The clue to a more adequate interpretation lies in following the sense of 'in the Lord' in v. 17. AE speaks with authority to his readers because both he and they are linked in the Lord. The readers and those who taught them were also linked in the Lord and so their teaching was 'in Christ' and as with the previous two verbs the reference to Christ may be taken pregnantly in the sense of being taught Christ in such a way that their relationship to him was deepened. This interpretation would be strengthened if the verb is taken as a divine passive, 'you were taught by God in Christ'; the teaching would then be a part of the way in which God acts graciously towards them (e.g. 1.4, 6; 4.32).

The relationship of the final clause of the verse to what precedes and follows has been much discussed.[17] καθώς often carries a comparative sense (see BAGD) but it is difficult to see with what the comparison is made here; if it related back to v. 20 that would surely have been formulated in positive

---

[17] See in particular C. A. Scott, 'Ephesians IV.21: 'As the truth is in Jesus'', *Expositor*, 8th Series, III (1912) 178–85; I. de la Potterie, 'Jésus et la vérité d'après Eph 4,21', AnBib 17–18, Rome, 1963, 45–57. Harless reports at great length on all the options suggested up to his time.

and not negative terms (cf C. A. Scott, art.cit.); such an interpretation also makes v. 21a parenthetical, yet it is of heavier weight than v. 21b. Much less likely is Barth's suggestion that the conjunction should be taken as introducing a quotation (a regular usage, cf Mk 1.2; Rom 1.17) beginning with 'Truth in Jesus' and continuing through vv. 22–4; elsewhere when the conjunction is used in this way it is followed by a verb indicating that a quotation is being made. καθώς sometimes introduces the content of speech after a verb of saying (Acts 15.14; 3 Jn 3) and διδάσκειν might be thought to carry this meaning; the clause would then give the content of what was taught; however this sense of the conjunction is rare and the meaning of the verb would be strained. Not far distant from this interpretation, and much more probable, is to attribute a causal sense to the preposition as in 1.4; 4.32. So understood the clause could depend on ἐμάθετε, with v. 21a as possibly parenthetical, but more probably dependent on ἐδιδάχθητε.

The final clause raises two problems: (a) What is the subject of ἔστιν? (b) What is the significance of the use of the name Jesus?[18] (a) Normally the absence of the article with ἀλήθεια would imply it is a predicate but this rule is not strictly adhered to in the case of abstract nouns (BDR §258; MHT, 116ff, 177f). It is then preferable to translate 'the truth is in Jesus' rather than 'there is truth in Jesus' or 'he (Christ) is truth in Jesus'. The second of these is rather banal and leaves open the possibility of other places or people where truth may be found; AE always deals in absolutes in relation to Jesus. The third only has meaning if we imagine it as a defence against an attack which differentiated between Jesus and Christ, a position held by some with gnostic tendencies and attacked in 1 John; unlike 1 John however Ephesians is not a polemical letter and nowhere else does AE appear to be alert to the danger of separating Christ and Jesus. Truth, which must always be truth about something, is here almost equivalent to the gospel (see on 1.13; cf Rom 2.8; 2 Cor 13.8; Col 1.5).

(b)'Jesus' cannot be passed over as a stylistic variation (Lincoln); for this a pronoun would have sufficed. AE has then gone out of his way to introduce the name (the use of the article is probably not significant, cf BDR §260 n. 7; MHT, 106f). The name Jesus appears rarely in the Pauline corpus (Rom 3.26; 8.11; 1 Cor 12.3; 2 Cor 4.5, 10, 11, 14; 11.4; Gal 6.17; Phil 2.10; 1 Th 1.10; 4.14). Its presence here excludes any idea that the instruction is solely about the exalted Christ (e.g. that he intercedes in heaven for believers). At the other extreme, as it were, it is probably not intended to indicate that the instruction is based on the life and teaching of the historical Jesus; when the letter moves on to detailed moral instruction there is, in accordance with the normal trend in the Pauline corpus, no attempt to relate this to the earthly Jesus. Yet the use of 'Jesus' suggests the

---

[18] On the proposal to place a comma after ἀλήθεια see the discussion between Westcott and Hort as reported in Westcott, 70f.

historical person. By the time of the writing of Ephesians, assuming
Paul is not the author, both the Gospel of Mark and the double
tradition existed; there must by this time then have been some
instruction about Jesus' life and teaching (cf Schnackenburg). In v.
24 believers are told to put on the new person; some concreteness to
what this means may be supplied here by the reference to Jesus, just
as appears to take place through the use of the name in 2 Cor 4.10,
11; Gal 6.17. It is not some ideal Christ who is the pattern but the
incarnate Jesus; the name may then imply that the tradition which
is taught stretches back to the earthly figure and is founded on
him (Larsson, op.cit.). The name Jesus may be more appropriate to
ethical instruction than Christ with its christological implications
(Halter, 252).

22.[19] The verse begins with what is apparently an acc. + infin.
construction yet if vv. 22–4 depend on ἐδιδάχθητε (v. 21) ὑμᾶς should be
nominative, if it should be there at all. For this reason some commentators
(e.g. Gnilka, Abbott) make vv. 22–4 depend on v. 21b. This would be easier
if 'in Jesus' went with v. 22 'that in Jesus you put off ...' (Ewald; Barth
also, as we have seen and rejected, makes a break in the middle of v. 21b);
the significance however of 'putting off in Jesus' is not clear. 'In Jesus'
would be exceptional as an instance of the 'in Christ' formula and in any
case when people do something 'in Christ' they do it to others and not to
themselves (cf 1 Cor 7.39; Rom 16.8); it is also difficult to find a connection
in thought between Jesus and the putting off of the old person and the
putting on of the new; Jesus cannot function as a model in these respects
since the early Christians viewed him as sinless; he had then nothing to put
off. The difficulty caused by the ὑμᾶς is not solved by seeing it as
contrasting either with an understood τὰ ἔθνη, for then it would have
preceded the verb, or with Jesus, since he did not put off his old person. The
verbs of v. 17 are too distant to make vv. 22–4 depend on them (so Bengel),
and in any case a new sentence began with v. 20. Despite its difficulties the
easiest solution is still to take the three infinitives as dependent on
ἐδιδάχθητε with ὑμᾶς as resuming the subject after the parenthesis of v.
21b (for the grammatical 'irregularity' cf Lk 20.7 v.l.; Acts 25.21; Col 1.9f
v.l.; Hermas, Mand 12.6.4; 1 Clem 62.3; BDR §406, n. 1; MHT, 147f;
Robertson, 1038). If then the infinitives depend on the verb, do they indicate
purpose or consequence, or are they epexegetical? The last is the simplest
and most probable (Robertson, 1089; Moule, 127, 139). If that is the case
should they be given an imperatival sense? This usage is found in non-
Semitic Greek as well as Semitic; cf Moule, 126f; BDR §389; Robertson,
943f. Yet if AE intended this sense why did he not use imperatives? Roels,
210, points out that the use of the infinitive for the imperative is infrequent
in Paul, but if the letter is not by Paul this is irrelevant. Imperatives follow

---

[19] On vv. 22–4 see Tertullian, *Resurrectione Carnis* 45; M. Coune, 'L'épître (Ep
4,23–38). Revêtir l'homme nouveau', *AsSeign* 74 (1963) 16–22; P. W. van der Horst,
'Observations on a Pauline Expression', *NTS* 19 (1972/3) 181–7; Roels, 210–15;
Fischer, 153–61; Van Roon, *Authenticity*, 328ff; E. Stegemann, 'Alt und Neu bei
Paulus und in den Deuteropaulinen (Kol-Eph)', *EvT* 37 (1977) 508–36.

in vv. 25ff and are introduced with the same verb as begins v. 22; this is no reason for objecting (so Stott) to them here; vv. 22–4 give the major instruction which 4.25ff spell out in detail. ὑμᾶς appears to be even more difficult if the infinitives are understood as imperatives. Yet an imperatival sense is to be favoured (cf Salmond, Schnackenburg, Lincoln) because of the continuing context of ethical instruction and the nature of what is being taught. Teaching may consist in the simple giving of information or it may imply that action based on the information should follow (contrast the statements 'You were taught that Greek changed during the centuries' and 'You were taught to wear clean clothes'). AE is quite clearly not just giving information.

If then the infinitives are given an imperatival sense it follows necessarily that they refer to the future and not the past; the putting off/on of the old/new person cannot refer simply to baptism, though from early times this connection has been made (Chrysostom, Theod Mops, *Gos Phil* II, 3 75.22–4); whatever the action is, it lies in the future. The metaphor of the putting on and off of clothing is central to vv. 22–4; it is an obvious metaphor for people manifest their character by the way they dress.

The metaphor was well known in the ancient world (e.g. Plato, *Rep* 457A; Euripides, *Iph Taur* 602; Dion Hal, *Ant Rom* ix 5; Libanius, *Ep* 968), in particular in religious writing (Apuleius, *Metamorphoses*, xi. 24; *Acts Thomas* 36, 66, *CH* 7.2), in the OT (e.g. Job 29.14; 35.26; Ps 132.9; Isa 59.17; 61.10) and in Judaism (e.g. Ecclus 45.8; Philo, *Fuga* 110; *Ebr* 86; *T Levi* 8.2; *Asc Isa* 7.22; 9.1; *1 En* 62.14–16; 1QS 4.8). In view of this widespread usage there is no need to resort[20] to gnosis or the Mysteries to find the source of AE's use of the metaphor. Gnosis and the Mysteries indeed contain no proper parallel to his use. In the NT, apart from our present passage and Col 3.8–12, the metaphor is used, probably in catechesis,[21] of the putting on and off of various vices and virtues (Rom 13.12; 1 Pet 2.1; Heb 12.1; Jas 1.21; 1 Th 5.5; Eph 6.11; cf 1 Clem 13.1; 57.2) and of the nature of existence after death (1 Cor 15.53f; 2 Cor 5.2–4), but it is not used of the body as the garment of the soul.[22] In Rom 13.14; Gal 3.27; Eph 4.22–4; Col 3.9f what is put on and off is described in personal terms. Parallels to this usage are difficult to discover; the closest are those indicated above in Dionysius Halicarnassus and Libanius and in a fragment of Aristocles preserved in Eusebius, *Praep Ev* 14.18, 26 (see Van der Horst, art.cit.).

By the time AE came to write, the metaphor was well established in Christian circles and had already been applied to the putting on and off of 'persons'; this appears first in Paul in respect of the putting on of Christ (Rom 13.14; Gal 3.27; cf *Gos Mary* BG 8502.1

[20] See Schlier, *Christus*, 59; P. Pokorný, 'Epheserbrief und gnostische Mysterien', *ZNW* 53 (1962) 186f.
[21] Cf Selwyn, *1 Peter*, 393–400; P. Carrington, *A Primitive Christian Catechism*, Cambridge, 1940, 32–7.
[22] For this usage see Käsemann, *Leib*, 87–94. For a rejection of his view see Fischer, 153.

18.16) prior to being used of the old and new persons in Col 3.9f; Eph 4.22, 24 (cf 'the body of flesh', Col 2.11). There is then no need to look for parallels in the non-Christian world which might have influenced AE. In Gal 3.27; Col 2.11f the metaphor is connected to baptism;[23] is this relation present here?[24] Certainly that relation is absent from its secular and OT usage and on those occasions in the NT when it refers to the afterlife; it is difficult also to find that relation when it is used of the putting on and off of virtues and vices and of armour. The metaphor has then no automatic connection to baptism and each occurrence must be examined individually to see if it is present. In 4.22-4 the connection may be supported by 'old person' which recalls Rom 6.6 where the context is baptismal and by the parallel passage Col 3.8-12. There are however some significant differences between Colossians and Ephesians and it is impossible to call in Col 3.8-12 to determine the meaning of Eph 4.22-4.

In Col 2.11 what is put off is not the old person but the body of flesh, in 3.10 νέος is used of the new person whereas Eph 4.24 uses καινός, and in 3.9f we have aorist participles in relation to a past happening, presumably baptism, and aorist imperatives in 3.8, 12 in relation to something which has yet to be done; in Ephesians there are no participles or imperatives but aorist infinitives which carry no necessary reference to a past event. AE also uses ἀποτίθημι of the putting off of the old person in contrast to the ἀπεκδύομαι of Colossians, a variation perhaps caused by the use of the former verb in catechetical instruction. Again between the reference to putting off and putting on AE inserts v. 23 with a reference to a process of renewal to which there is no parallel in Col 3.8-12. Mitton, *Epistle*, 61, writes of 'a very close interdependence, and yet the freest development and rearrangement of the borrowed ideas'. This verdict harmonises with the theory that AE and A/Col belonged to the same Pauline school and used its imagery in varying ways. Holtzmann, 52-4, took Colossians to depend on Ephesians at this point.

If the putting on and off in Eph 4.22-4 referred to something that had happened in baptism, v. 24 would have followed directly on v. 22 (Haupt). It may of course be true that there had been teaching (v. 21) in the past about putting off and on, given probably at the time of baptism and conversion.[25] There are also difficulties in the

---

[23] P. Bradshaw, *The Search for the Origins of Christian Worship*, London, 1992, 41, in dependence on R. Scroggs and K. L. Groff, 'The Flight of the Naked Young Man (Mark 14:51-2)', *CBQ* 41 (1979) 412-18, finds support for a baptismal reference in the stories of Mk 14.51f and 16.5. These Markan passages are notoriously difficult to interpret. M. D. Hooker, *The Gospel according to St Mark*, London, 1991, 552, says of 14.51f that the verses are 'a total enigma'; cf Best, *Mark: The Gospel as Story*, Edinburgh, 1983, 26f.

[24] So Jervell, 236ff.

[25] Bruce indeed gets round the apparent difficulty here by assuming that AE writes to new Christians at the time of their baptism; however there is not sufficient evidence that Ephesians is addressed to Christians who have just been baptised.

presentation of Colossians where in 3.8 believers are told to put off various vices and in 3.12 to put on various virtues; in 3.9 they are told they have put off the old person and in 3.10 have put on the new. But it is the vices which make the old person old and the virtues which make the new new. The putting off of the old and the putting on of the new must then be a gradual process which takes place by a renewal; v. 23 enables AE to avoid the ontological difficulties of Colossians and concentrate his attention on the actual ethical procedure. He did however come close to an ontological statement in 2.15 where each believer is said to be a 'new person'; the relation between 2.15 and our passage lies in that the believer can only put off the old person because in a sense he has already been made a new person.

The aorist infinitives do not conflict with this by implying a past momentary action. The infinitive, imperative and subjunctive of the aorist do not carry the same implications in regard to time as the indicative and participle.[26] Non-finite forms of the aorist are found at Rom 13.12, 14; Eph 3.16, 17; 6.11 carrying a direct reference neither to the past[27] nor to baptism; thus the aorists in Eph 4.22, 24 need not imply baptism. Yet Eph 4.23 has a present infinitive; is not some deliberate distinction being made? Similar variations of tense between aorist and present appear in the other verbal sequences (cf Mk 8.34; Mt 16.24; 6.25–34; Lk 9.23; 2 Tim 4.5; 1 Pet 2.17) where we should expect internal consistency.

Occasionally the origin of the use of the clothing metaphor is traced to the way believers disrobe before baptism and after baptism put on new clothes.[28] This custom, the change from old to new clothes, not the stripping off of clothes and the putting on of the same clothes again, cannot be detected earlier than well into the second century. There is in any case no need to resort to such a theory since the metaphor was well known in the ancient world.

In view of the way AE has coupled the old and new persons, we must leave the discussion of the nature of the old person until we can consider the two together at v. 24. Here in v. 22 we have two qualifying phrases. Even if the metaphor has been drawn from the catechetical tradition it may not be fully understood by all AE's

[26] On the aorist see Burton §§35ff, 98; Robertson, 821–910; BDR §§332, 335–7; F. Stagg, 'The Absurd Aorist', *JBL* 91 (1972) 222–31; K. L. McKay, 'On the Perfect and Other Aspects in New Testament Greek', *NT* 23 (1981) 289–329; id. 'Time and Aspect in New Testament Greek', *NT* 34 (1992) 209–28; Fanning, 359–64; Porter, 321–401.

[27] Fanning, 361, terms these 'ingressive' aorists as indicating a practical break with the past and the beginning of a new life. Such beginnings need to be repeated for the Christian 'must be progressively leaving behind aspects of the "old life" and reaching out anew for the things which alone are worthy of the new life in Christ'; this is more a description than an explanation why aorists have been used.

[28] Cf W. A. Meeks, 'The Image of the Androgyne: Some Uses of a Symbol in Early Christianity', *HR* 13 (1974) 165–208, at 183–9.

readers and requires some amplification. ,The first phrase connects the old person to his or her pre-Christian way of life: κατά (almost equivalent to the genitive here, Zerwick §130) τὴν προτέραν ('earlier'; no longer first of two, though in fact only two are in view here; BDR §62 n. 1; Robertson, 280, 662) ἀναστροφήν (see on 2.3 for the root). The former way of life has already been described in vv. 17–19 (cf 2.1f) and much more about it can be inferred from the remainder of the letter in so far as certain behaviour is no longer regarded as appropriate for believers. The second phrase depicts the old person as in a process of corruption, φθειρόμενον (present participle), through the desires[29] of the flesh. The present tense implies a continuing process and therefore 'oldness' is not an inherited defect but something believers create for themselves. Since in 2.1 believers in their pre-Christian state were regarded as dead in sin there may be an inconsistency here, perhaps arising through AE's use of diverse strands of tradition; at this stage of Christianity not everything had been fully thought through. If 2.1 presented a realised eschatological death, 4.22 presents an eschatological death realising itself. The corruption spoken of here is not of course a destroying of the old person but indicates instead the old person's increasing reality. This inevitably leads to complete corruption in death, not merely physical but eternal death. The corruption takes place through deceitful desires. ἀπάτης (see Spicq, I, 116–18) is a genitive of definition or an adjectival genitive, possibly a Semitism (cf MH, 485; Moule, 174–6); this is preferable to taking it as one of subject which would 'personalise' deceit; deceit does not produce desires but desires may deceive. Wrong ἐπιθυμίαι (for the word see on 2.3) are seductive (cf Rom 7.11), but in the end they only deceive and fail to provide what they promise as Adam and Eve found in Eden (Gen 3.1ff; cf Van Roon). In 2.3 desires were seen as sinful and connected to the flesh; as such they cannot do other than bring corruption and ultimate destruction.

23. We now move from the negative to the positive (logically, of course, putting off precedes putting on) and the clothing metaphor is temporarily dropped to be taken up again in v. 24. Although v. 23 intervenes between the putting off of the old person (v. 22) and the putting on of the new (v. 24), it is not to be taken as suggesting a time interval between the two as if the old was put off, renewal took place and then the new was put on.

𝔓46 D1 K 33 323 1241ˢ pc latt; Cyp read the imperative of ἀνανεόω, probably due to a desire to make clear an imperatival sense. The infinitive can be either a middle with an active significance (see LSJ) when what is renewed is normally stated, or a passive (cf BAGD) where as here it is the

---

[29] The singular, ἐπιθυμίαν, is found as a variant in D boᵖᵗ; Lcf; this support is weak and the plural suits the context much better; evil is manifold; cf Gal 5.19.

subject which is being renewed. Like the infinitives in v. 22 it should be given an imperatival sense. The change from the aorist (v. 22) to the present may be to emphasise that renewal is not instantaneous but gradual. The change from the old person to the new must have a beginning and a conclusion, even if that conclusion lies beyond this life. It may be that the aorists of vv. 22, 24 represent what in God's eyes has happened (the old person has been put off and the new put on) while v. 23 represents its realisation in practice.

AE, unlike A/Col, has inserted v. 23 into his use of the old/new contrast. The verb he has used is based on νέος where A/Col has used a verb based on καινός; while for all practical purposes the two are synonyms,[30] the change again suggests that AE is not copying Colossians. In v. 24 AE uses καινός, which forms the root of the word used by Paul in speaking in Rom 12.2 of the renewal of the mind. Despite the verbal variation AE remains within the circle of Pauline ideas. Renewal is an ambiguous term; if the ἀνά is stressed it may refer to the restoration of a previous condition (cf Esth 3.13b; 1 Macc 12.10; 14.18, 22), but in Hellenistic Greek prepositions added to verbs often served only to intensify the meaning of the verbal stem. It is unlikely that restoration is intended here, for nowhere else does AE depict the restoration of the Gentiles to a condition they once enjoyed and lost; the new being of v. 24 is not equated with either the first or second Adam. Gentiles were never in the condition of paradise but always outside the covenanting mercies of God. Equally renewal does not mean rejuvenation (through monkey glands or hormone treatment?) as suggested by Barry and Foulkes, as though youthful energy can now be brought to the task of putting on the new being.

What is the role of the πνεῦμα in renewal? It has been interpreted as either the Holy Spirit, and taken as an instrumental dative (Origen, Theophylact, Oecumenius), or the human spirit[31] as the sphere in which renewal takes place. Since the word can have either meaning it is not sufficient to count instances and say that elsewhere in Ephesians or in the Pauline corpus one meaning appears more regularly than the other; a coin may be tossed six times and come down heads each time; the chance of it coming down heads on the seventh is still one in two, the same as at the beginning of the sequence; context must decide meaning, not the number of occurrences. Favouring a reference to the Holy Spirit are: (a) A power to bring about renewal is required and this would be the Holy Spirit (cf Tit 3.5); but the infinitive could be a divine passive and God be the

---

[30] While earlier Greek distinguished between καινός and νέος, the distinction had vanished by the time of Ephesians; see R. A. Harrisville, 'The Concept of Newness in the New Testament', *JBL* 91 (1972) 222–31.

[31] The variant which reads ἐν before the word though well supported ($\mathfrak{P}^{49}$ B 33 1175 1739 1881 *pc*) probably represents an attempt to resolve the problem.

one who renews. (b) Since the background to the metaphor of putting off and on may be baptism and the Spirit is given to believers at baptism (e.g. 1 Cor 12.13; Acts 2.38) a reference to the Holy Spirit is appropriate; yet it is by no means certain that AE sees baptism as the background to the metaphor in 4.22–4. (c) Masson suggests AE started to write 'renewed by the Spirit' and then remembering Rom 12.2 added 'of your mind' and so caused the confusion; it is difficult to estimate the validity of such an argument. Favouring a reference to the human spirit are: (a) 'The spirit of your mind' is wholly in keeping with AE's style of using approximate synonyms with one in the genitive (cf Percy, 186, 196). (b) If the divine Spirit were intended the genitive νοός is surprising. Probably then the reference is to the human spirit.[32] It is questionable if AE would have drawn a rigorous distinction between that spirit and νοῦς; both refer to the inner rather than the outer person. In the Pauline letters unregenerate people can be regarded as having a 'spirit', a spirit unable to understand the things of God (1 Cor 2.10–16). This spirit is not necessarily evil though it may act in an evil manner (2 Cor 7.1), as may the spirit of believers (1 Cor 7.34). These are regularly held to possess a πνεῦμα (Rom 8.16; Gal 6.18; 1 Th 5.23) through which they respond to God; they are renewed in it (in Col 3.10 it is the new person which is renewed) as they are in their mind (see on 4.17 for 'mind') by God acting through his Spirit. In a sense the spirit and the mind represent what continues from the old person to the new, though they are changed in their continuation.

24. Just as the putting off of the old person was qualified with two phrases, so also is the putting on[33] of the new (for the metaphor see on v. 22). The first of these indicates that the new person has been created, κτισθέντα (cf 2.10 for the idea in relation to people); God is the real subject of this participle; the aorist denotes the moment of baptism/conversion. God who once created in Eden (Gen 1.27) creates again what has been spoiled by sin (4.17–19). Several of the words used here are the same as those in Col 3.10 but are employed differently, and one word, εἰκών,[34] important there, is missing here so that there is no direct reference to anything which the new person may resemble. κατά could indicate (cf 2 Cor

---

[32] See E. Schweizer, *TWNT*, VI, 394–449; J. D. G. Dunn, *NIDNTT*, III, 693–707; Stacey, 128–45; Jewett, 167–200.

[33] The imperative again appears as a variant for the infinitive and is better supported than the imperative in v. 23: ἐνδύσασθε is read by 𝔓[46] ℵ B D¹ K 104 323 1241ˢ 1881 *al* latt; Clᵖᵗ; however almost no support exists for the imperative in v. 22 and since consistency is to be expected in the three verses it is better to read the infinitive here, giving it as in the other verses an imperatival sense. In regard to the aorist see on v. 22.

[34] On the word see F.-W. Eltester, *Eikon im Neuen Testament* (BZNW 23), Berlin, 1958, 156–64.

7.9–11) the manner of creation, 'created in the way God creates' (cf Ewald), but this does not say anything of significance; God can hardly create in any other than in a Godlike manner. More probably the idea here is similar to that of Col 3.10 (and of Gen 1.26f) with the preposition signifying 'in the likeness of God' (cf 1 Pet 1.15; Heb 8.5; see Moule, 59; MHT, 268). We shall return to this after discussing the second qualifying phrase. This may be attached either directly to the infinitive or indirectly through the participle; whichever is chosen the meaning is hardly affected. The phrase describes the result, or intended result, of God's creating and not its manner.

δικαιοσύνη and ὁσιότης and their cognate adjectives and adverbs are used together as a comprehensive phrase for virtuous living[35] in both secular and Jewish Greek (cf Introduction §2.4.3). Sometimes they are distinguished so that the first relates to behaviour towards other human beings and the second to behaviour towards the gods (Plato, *Gorgias* 507AB; *Rep* 10.615B; *Laws* 2.663B; Josephus, *Ant* 8.245) but normally this is not so (Plato, *Thaetetus* 176B). Even if this distinction could be maintained it should not lead us to see (with Calvin) the two words as exemplifying the two tables of the Decalogue. ὁσιότης came much more into use in the later sections of the OT as a glance at Hatch and Redpath will show. Philo found them as a pair in secular Greek (e.g. in Plato) and in the LXX (Deut 9.5; 32.4; Ψ 144.17 where the parallelism implies the Psalmist regarded them as almost synonyms; Wisd 9.3) and used them regularly (*Sacrif* 57; *Spec Leg* 1.304; *Virt* 47, 50; *Sobr* 10; *Fuga* 63); cf Josephus (*Ant* 8.245, 295; 9.35; 15.138).

In the light of the frequent usage of δικαιοσύνη and ὁσιότης as a word pair it is not surprising to find them associated in the NT (Lk 1.75; 2 Th 2.10; Tit 1.8; Rev 16.5) and in early Christianity (1 Clem 14.1; 45.3; 2 Clem 6.9; 15.3). Their significance would have been easily grasped by Gentile Christians. AE will have known them as a word pair describing personal piety in accordance with God's will. Because they formed an ethical word pair it is pointless to enquire whether Paul could have used δικαιοσύνη of human behaviour (2 Cor 6.7; 9.10; Phil 1.7; 4.8 imply he could); AE also gives the root an ethical connotation in Eph 5.9; 6.14.[36] Their existence as a word pair also means AE neither selected them from a list of possible virtues in order to highlight them, nor attempted to distinguish between them as specifying conduct towards God and towards other human beings. Yet it is legitimate to ask why AE chose this word pair and neither the list of virtues of Col 3.12, which are apparently more Christian, nor 'love', which would sum up Christian conduct

---

[35] See R. A. Wild, ' "Be imitators of God' ': Discipleship in the Letter to the Ephesians' in *Discipleship in the New Testament* (ed. F. F. Segovia), Philadelphia, 1985, 127–43.

[36] On the use of the root in Ephesians see Spicq, III, 120–51; Reumann, *Righteousness*, 92 (§167); Ziesler, *Righteousness*, 153f.

more adequately. The use of love in the two great commandments (Mk 12.29–31) shows that it covers all human activity and in Paul it is the supreme virtue (1 Cor 13.13). AE himself employs it frequently. Perhaps it was the secular usage of the word pair which led AE to prefer it here; if so it gives an interesting insight into his approach to his readers; he will use terms they already know so that they can grasp his meaning. The words moreover are sufficiently general for his audience to read into them their own Christian ideal of behaviour. By connecting the word pair directly to the new Christian existence, AE has given a more ethical slant to the new person than does A/Col (cf Wild, art.cit.) and this enables him to move directly into his detailed paraenesis (4.25–6.20). The final word of the phrase, ἀληθείας, parallels the ἀπάτης at the end of v. 22 and qualifies both preceding nouns.[37] It is possible to read deep meaning into the word for the gospel is truth (cf 1.13; 4.21; Col 1.5), and righteousness and holiness are founded on the gospel, but it is easier to take it as an adjectival qualification of the other two nouns (cf Moule, 174–6). The contrast 'deceit/truth' may reflect the same contrast as found in Qumran (e.g. 1QS 4.2–11);[38] 'truth' would then be a genitive of the subject: the righteousness and holiness which truth produces (see on ἀπάτης v. 22); this however gives too much prominence to truth as an agency and it is doubtful if the contrast would have been easily appreciated in this way by Greek readers.

Translations of ἄνθρωπος vary. 'Man' is no longer possible in English. 'Being' and 'nature' are too abstract and cover a wider range of existence than the merely human; 'human being' and 'human nature' are too long; 'humanity' is not individually oriented; 'self' is better but still loses something of the flavour of the original; we have therefore chosen 'person' as best representing the non-male use of ἄνθρωπος. Yet the real problem does not lie in the choice of a suitable English word but in understanding how a 'person' can be put off or put on. There will always be a something which puts off and puts on the old and new persons. But what is the 'something'? 'Person' is inadequate, for old person and new person as put off and put on are not the complete person. The difficulty here has long been recognised; e.g. *Acts Philip* 8 speaks of ἀπορρῖψαι ... τὸν νοῦν τοῦ παλαιοῦ ἀνθρώπου. When the old person is put off the person does not go out of existence and come back into existence when the new person is put on. What does not go out of existence in the putting off of the old person is what maintains the continuity between the old and new persons; it is idle to ask how AE would

---

[37] The variant καὶ ἀληθείᾳ, D* F G it vg^mss; Cyp Lcf, destroys the parallelism and weakens the meaning.

[38] Cf J. Murphy-O'Connor, 'Truth: Paul and Qumran' in *Paul and Qumran* (ed. J. Murphy-O'Connor), London, 1968, 206–13.

have defined this continuous element, perhaps by 'the spirit of your mind' (v. 23). This is a philosophical and psychological problem in which he was not interested. The underlying continuity appears once we observe how the new person retains much of the existence of the old. Leaving aside the gradual disappearance of sin, if the old person had artistic skill the new will have it also; the ability to reason and to understand a foreign language will continue; skilled technicians do not lose their skill on becoming Christians; the person with enthusiasm remains enthusiastic, though where the enthusiasm is applied may differ (Paul was as enthusiastic about persecuting Christians prior to his conversion as about evangelising Gentiles after it). Memory is continuous through the experience of conversion and baptism. This means it is both difficult to define the continuity between the old and the new persons, and also what precisely is put off and put on. The problem does not disappear if it is supposed that the change from old to new person is instantaneous, something in any case which we cannot assume for AE in the light of v. 23.

Leaving aside this philosophical and psychological issue we need to approach the matter exegetically. Paul, assuming he did not write Ephesians and Colossians, never used the phrase 'new person', but he does speak of the crucifixion of the old person with Christ (Rom 6.6) in a context of baptism and of the dissociation of Christian existence from sin. Gal 5.24 suggests a relation between the old person and the flesh (cf 1 Cor 3.3). If the putting off of the old person is not a single instantaneous action it resembles daily dying (1 Cor 15.31; 2 Cor 4.10–12) and repentance (Rom 2.4; 2 Cor 7.9f; 12.21; for Paul repentance is part of Christian living and not simply a prerequisite for conversion). Paul may have envisaged a similar contrast to that of old and new persons when he wrote of an outer and inner being (2 Cor 4.16; Rom 7.22; cf Eph 3.16; 1 Pet 3.4). If however Paul does not speak directly of the new person nor apply the clothing metaphor to the putting off of the old, he does write of the putting on of Christ; in Gal 3.27 this is related to baptism; in Rom 13.14 this relation cannot be present because we have an imperative addressed to those who are already Christians. Paul also writes of Christians as those made anew (2 Cor 5.17; Gal 6.15[39]) and in this way introduces both the concept of newness and, through the idea of creation, the original Adam; this raises the possibility of either the identification of the old person with Adam and the new with Christ or their paralleling with Adam and Christ, an interpretation which may gain support from Paul's contrast of the first and second Adam in 1 Cor 15.45ff, where he indeed introduces the

[39] On these passages and their background in Isa 43.16–21; 65.16–23 see U. Mehl, *Neue Schöpfung* (BZNW 56), Berlin, 1989, *passim*.

idea of the putting off of mortality and the putting on of immortality (15.53f).

The concept of the new person appears first in Col 3.10 and in contrast to that of the old person (3.9), though of course the concept of newness in relation to God's activity is found in the OT (e.g. Isa 43.19; Jer 31.21, 31–4; Ezek 11.19; 18.31). In Col 3.10 the putting off and on are related to baptism though the aorist participles but there is no idea of a period of renewal as in Eph 4.22–4. The concept of old and new persons will thus have belonged to the Pauline school; in taking it over AE and A/Col have used it differently; if it had no explicit baptismal connection A/Col introduced one; if it had, AE dropped it. Of course, if AE's readers had heard these terms when they were baptised, their present use would recall their baptism to them. AE has also used the 'new person' concept independently at 2.15 where it probably refers neither to the church nor to the corporate Christ but to the individual Christian who is not a Jew or a Gentile but a new person. At 4.24 the new person cannot be identified with Christ, as Gal 3.27 and Rom 13.14 might suggest, for the new person is said to have been created. In Ephesians also Christ and the new person are kept distinct in so far as Christ is the head of the church and therefore of each new person who, as new, will be obedient to him (Houlden). The κατὰ θέον of 4.24 in any case suggests a resemblance of the new person to God rather than Christ (cf 5.1). That itself however might suggest a resemblance of the new person to the pre-fall Adam created in the image of God. But likeness to God (contrast εἰκών in Col 3.10) is not explicitly mentioned in Eph 4.24. Eden was not, then, a foreshadowing of the new person (Scott, Dahl). If there is no reason to see the new person as Christ, it follows that there is no reason to see the old person as the fallen Adam.[40] Yet the new person cannot be cut off entirely from Christ; he is its pattern and as the new person is continually renewed it is renewed into his likeness (2 Cor 3.18). In 1 Cor 15.49 resurrected Christians are said to bear the image of the heavenly man, Christ, and this in the context of the putting on of immortality (15.53f). It is in this context of a realised eschatology that the new person fully resembles Christ. In Eph 4.22–4 the context however is one of ethical behaviour and not ontology (Macpherson; Roels, 212). If we now return to the discussion of the continuity between the old person and the new, we might say that the old person is the person of sin (cf Gundry, 134–6), the new that of righteousness and holiness, always remembering that an 'essential' person cannot be isolated in any way which

---

[40] J. R. Díaz, 'Palestinian Targum and New Testament', *NT* 6 (1963) 75–80, suggests a parallel to the putting off and on in God's stripping Adam of his pre-fall glorious clothing, but this seems too far-fetched for AE's readers to have grasped.

would isolate him or her from the words, deeds and thoughts of the actual person. But in thinking of the old person as the sinful person and the new person as the righteous person we must be careful not to suggest that the old person is totally sinful and the new totally righteous. Yet we should not push this too far, for in 4.17–19 AE has painted such a dark picture of the non-Christian Gentile world and in 2.1 he has described non-believers as dead, so that he might have regarded the old person as the person of sin and the new as the person of righteousness. Yet in so far as the latter is concerned AE goes on to detail the conduct he wishes from his readers in such a way as to suggest he did not think of them as totally righteous. If we move to a more modern idiom and try to express what the old and new persons mean we might speak of an old mind-set and a new mind-set or an old lifestyle and a new lifestyle.

AE has now set out the basis of his ethical position; believers are new people called to live in righteousness and holiness. In 4.25ff he spells this out in practical terms in respect of their relation to one another.

XI

BEHAVE SO AS TO PRESERVE UNITY
(4.25–5.2)

E. F. Klug (*as previous section*); M. Coune, 'L'Épître (Ep 4.23–28). Revêtir l'homme nouveau', *AsSeign* 74 (1963) 16–32; J. Gnilka, 'Paraenetische Traditionen', 403–5; Halter, 256–69; G. Agnell, *Work, Toil and Sustenance*, Lund, 1976, 126–32; F. Montagnini, 'Echi di parenesi cultuale in Ef 4,25–32', *RivBiblt* 37 (1989) 257–82.

25 Putting off lying
everyone should speak the truth to neighbours
for we are members one of another.
26 If angry do not sin,
do not let the sun go down while you are still irritated
27 nor give an opening to the devil.
28 Let the thief thieve no longer
but rather labour working honestly with his own hands
for the (common) good
so that he may have (something) to share with the needy.
29 Do not allow evil speech to emerge from your mouth
but only whatever is good
so as to build up where there is need
in order to bring a blessing to those who hear.
30 And do not pain the Holy Spirit of God
in whom you were sealed for the day of deliverance.
31 Let all bitterness and wrath and anger and shouting and
denunciation be put away from you
with all malice.
32 But be good to one another, compassionate, forgiving each
other
even as God has forgiven you in Christ.
5.1 Be then imitators of God as (his) beloved children
2   and behave lovingly,
even as Christ loved us
and gave himself on our behalf
a sweet-smelling offering and sacrifice to God.

AE now begins to describe how the old person ought to differ from the new and what being a new person entails, and does this in the context of the need to maintain the unity of the community. He has

442

explained the theology of unity; now he comes to its practice. The major imperatives were given in 4.2f, 22–4; now minor imperatival statements fill in the detail. AE's admonitions and exhortations are so general that it is impossible to build up from them a picture of the situation of his readers. Yet though general they are not vague but down to earth and in this respect differ from the more theological approach of 4.17–24. Here and in succeeding paragraphs AE has taken over ethical material originating in Judaism, if not in the secular world, and christianised it, usually through the motivation he offers. His exhortations relate to life within the community (cf 4.2), as is immediately made explicit in 4.25b, and not to the behaviour of Christians towards non-Christians. It might be said that if the community is to make an evangelical impact on those around it, its members ought to pull together, but AE is not interested in this aspect of their life.

S. Basevi, art.cit. (see on 4.1–16), takes v. 25 with 4.1–24 making a major division after rather than before v. 25 on the grounds that v. 25 continues the theme of truth from 4.15, 21, 24. However, v. 25 sets out clearly the underlying position of what follows in that it refers to conduct among believers and as an injunction provides the pattern for those in 4.26ff.

Accepting v. 25 as the beginning of the pericope it should probably be seen as continuing to 5.2 (cf Schnackenburg) rather than ending at 4.32 as the οὖν at the beginning of 5.1 might suggest. That particle often introduces new paragraphs; 5.1 and 5.2 do not have the same pattern as the earlier injunctions in 4.25–32 since they do not begin with prohibitions (Barth, 555). On the other hand the γίνεσθε of 5.1 picks up the same word in 4.32 and the conclusion of 4.32 leads in suitably to the summons to imitate God (5.1) and the emphasis on Christ's love (5.2), the latter forming here a kind of climax. The content of 5.2b is almost the same as that of 4.32b but gives a more positively shaped Christian ending. Finally 5.3, beginning with an adversative δέ, introduces a new theme, sexual immorality.

4.25–5.2 commences with four brief exhortations on lying (25), anger (26f), theft (28) and impure speech (29). Though lying and anger are associated in T Dan (see on v. 27) there is no reason to suppose that the order in which AE offers these four exhortations was traditional or that he is expanding a brief vice list which contained these four themes. Rather his experience with Gentile converts will have alerted him to the sins into which they were most likely to fall. Lying may come first because of the immediately preceding reference to 'truth' (4.24). The attempt of J. P. Sampley[1]

---

[1] 'Scripture and Tradition in the Community as Seen in Ephesians 4:25ff', ST 26 (1972) 101–9.

to see the injunctions as tied together through an OT background fails for lack of evidence (for another attempt to provide an explanation connecting them to one another, see note at end of 4.32). Their order does not appear to follow any logical development, and this is true of the remaining material in the paragraph. They are not linked together with catchwords as in Mk 9.33–50; catchwords are more characteristic of oral tradition than written. They are held together by their common theme, the treatment of fellow believers. Each of the four exhortations is balanced with a reason for avoiding it, a movement from the negative to the positive as in 4.17–24, from the old person to the new. It perhaps goes too far to describe all the motivations as Christian; some come from Judaism and others could have been found on the lips of any ancient moralist. These four exhortations are followed by a more general warning (v. 30) to readers lest they offend against the Christian position they adopted when they first believed. Two brief associated summaries follow, the first (v. 31), negative, a list of the ways in which anger expresses itself, the second (v. 32a) a brief list of virtues; again a reason is attached in v. 32b, but now one undoubtedly Christian. The paragraph concludes with two positive exhortations (5.1, 2a), the first being closely linked in content to 4.32, and the two are reinforced with a reminder of what Christ has done for the readers (5.32b).

Though the exhortations seem elementary we should not conclude that the readers have only recently become Christians. Some may have been last week's converts and have received as yet very little catechetical instruction but others may have believed for much longer periods. Christians are never free from sin and if they have come from a world as sinful as the one AE depicted in 4.17–19, there is every need to remind them of the elementary rules of behaviour; there has never been a period in the church when 'simple' exhortations have not been necessary. Preachers need to keep repeating the simplest instructions to their congregations. Since AE does not personally know his readers he cannot presume too much on the nature of the instruction they received; contrast 1 Th 4.1 where Paul knows what his readers have already been taught because he taught them. Interestingly almost all these injunctions, though seemingly elementary, continue to form the basis of instruction offered by the Fathers to their flocks; they knew their readers still required them. Indeed no Christian is ever past the need to be told not to be angry or to be honest.

In selecting his exhortations AE has obviously been partly indebted to the normal pattern of catechetical instruction.[2] He commences with a word regularly used in it, ἀποθέμενοι (see on

---

[2] All groups need some regulations, cf Introduction §10.2.3.

4.22), and goes on to introduce essential virtues for the smooth operation of community life. Much of what he writes is similar to what is found in Col 3.8ff and we may assume was common teaching in the Pauline group to which he and A/Col belonged. If he were depending directly on Col 3.8ff it is surprising in the light of his previous discussions on the unity of Jewish and Gentile believers that he does not use Col 3.11. While there may be some reminiscences of Col 3.8f, 12–14, AE's ideas are arranged in a different order and presented in greater detail.

It is worth noting: (i) The exhortations are addressed to Christians in respect of their relationship to one another within the church, implying that AE can assume they are aware of their common membership in the community; 4.25ff reads like a spelling out of 1 Cor 12.26. (ii) Because Ephesians is not written to a single community in which particular failures might be isolated for discussion as in Corinth but to a number of communities, the vices to be avoided and the virtues to be sought may give us a better picture of the general state of the church at this time than letters addressed to specific situations.

25. This first injunction picks up[3] the references to truth and falsehood in vv. 21, 22, 24 and is introduced with the participle of the verb AE used in v. 22. ἀποθέμενοι is not to be taken with the sense 'once for all' as if lying were put off once for all in conversion/baptism, the aorist being taken literally (compare the infinitive in 4.22); the participle is to be understood imperatively (cf 1 Pet 2.1; Heb 12.1; Jas 1.25; on the imperative use of the participle, see on 4.2). It is impossible to speak the truth until lies have been given up; the sense may then be 'once you have put aside the lie, speak the truth'. The verb has an established place in introducing catechetical instruction (1 Pet 2.1f; Jas 1.21; Rom 13.12; Selwyn, *1 Peter*, 394ff). In Col 3.8 the imperative was used in respect of the putting off of a list of vices; 'lying' was not among them but appears in Col 3.9. λαλεῖτε, an imperative, carries the sense that as they give up lying they should continue always to speak the truth.

τὸ ψεῦδος is neither 'the lie' as if implying a false attitude to life (Murray, Rienecker) nor does it imply that AE considered Gentile culture to be a 'lie' or every Gentile statement as false; it refers to the practice or habit of lying and here as in the following verses the reference is to particular sins. Despite this, from the beginning commentators have sought to widen its meaning (e.g. Theod Mops, *omnem simulationem et hypocrisin*) and avoid the simpler and more direct meaning. AE is not writing a dissertation on when truth is necessary (cf Josh 2.4ff; Jas 2.25) but stating a broad principle. The

---

[3] Through a failure to appreciate the continuity of the argument διό is omitted by 𝔓⁴⁶ b m*; Lcf Did.

stress on speaking the truth and the avoidance of falsehood goes back to the Decalogue (cf Mk 10.19; Mt 5.33) and is continually emphasised in later Judaism, Prov 4.24; 6.19; *T Reub* 3.9; *T Issach* 7.4; *T Dan* 1.3; 2.1, 4; 5.1; 6.2; 1QS 10.22; the same stress is of course also found among the pagan moralists, e.g. M. Aurelius 9.1. Despite the way in which he concentrates on sins which would destroy community life, AE does not go as far as Ps 101.7 in suggesting the exclusion from the community of those who lie. Although Paul regularly assures his readers that he is not lying but speaking the truth (Rom 9.1; 2 Cor 1.17–20; 11.31; Gal 1.20; cf 1 Tim 2.7), he does not directly lecture them on the need to be truthful. That the later writings of the NT should stress truthfulness and reject lying is not surprising (1 Tim 1.10; Tit 1.12). The earliest converts came from Judaism and its long-standing stress on truthfulness meant they did not need specific instruction, though that is not to say that they were always truthful. As the number of Gentile converts grew, so did the need to spell out what was implicit from the beginning; it continued to be spelt out in post-apostolic Christianity (1 Clem 35.2; *Did* 5.2; *Barn* 20.2; Hermas, *Mand* 3). Lying should not however be thought of as a particularly Gentile sin since, as we have seen, Jews were continually enjoined to be truthful.

AE reinforces his demand for truthfulness by quoting Zech 8.16, which had been already used for a similar purpose in *T Dan* 5.2 and AE may well then have taken it from traditional catechetical instruction rather than directly from the OT. The only alteration from the LXX is μετά + gen. for πρός + acc., a variation not found in *T Dan* 5.2. While we are aware AE was quoting the OT, were he and his readers? AE does not draw attention to the fact that he is using a quotation. Presumably he knew he was taking the words from some source, either the OT or catechetical instruction. Did his readers? If they did, the quotation will have carried for them an extra motivation beyond its content; if not, the motivation can have come only from the content and the context in which it is set. What did his readers make of the term 'neighbour'? In Zech 8.16 the neighbour is another Israelite; here it appears to be another Christian, for in the final clause of the verse AE employs the conception of the church as a body, and thus gives the injunction a Christian motivation. In Col 3.9 the avoidance of falsehood was simply based on the fact that the readers were new people.

When AE earlier used the conception of the body he had stressed the body as the body of Christ with Christ as its head; he thus laid emphasis on the relationship of believers to their head (1.23; 2.16; 4.7–16) and not as here on their relationship to one another, though 2.16 does relate the group of Jewish to the group of Gentile believers. The relationship of believers to one another within the body had been one of Paul's emphases in his use of the phrase 'body of Christ' (1 Cor 12.12ff; Rom 12.3ff). AE has returned to this original emphasis, an emphasis corresponding with the metaphor's use in the Greco-Roman world (see Detached Note: The Body of Christ). AE does not then introduce the idea here because he has a corporate view of the new person or (*pace* Coune) because he thinks the new person is Christ and the one who puts him on belongs to the church. As members one of another converts stand in a new relationship to each other and must therefore speak the truth to each other. If it is asked whether Christians would lie to one another, the case of Ananias and Sapphira (Acts 5.1–11) and the number of times (see above) Paul needs to assure his readers that he is speaking the truth should be remembered.

If AE has interpreted neighbour in Zech 8.16 as 'fellow believer', has he failed to grasp the Christian meaning of the word? Jesus redefined the Jewish concept of neighbour to mean anyone and everyone (Lk 10.29–37). Jerome (cf Irenaeus, 4.37.4; Mitton; Houlden) is one of the few commentators to note this redefinition but after noting it he makes nothing of it and goes on to take v. 25c as referring to the church. Grotius, followed by Macpherson, takes v. 25c to refer to human society in general and not the church, and so is able to take neighbour in the sense Jesus gave it. Isolated from the letter and taken against the background of the contemporary world this could be the meaning; it would accord with the Stoic idea that all people were members one of another; it is also true that all human society depends on people speaking the truth to one another.[4] If, however, we take v. 25c to refer to the church, as it surely does, does this mean that the speaking of truth by Christians is to be restricted to fellow Christians? If the point had been put directly to AE he would almost certainly have denied any such restriction, yet the restriction is implicitly present. Perhaps AE did not know the parable of the Good Samaritan and Jesus' redefinition of 'neighbour'. Yet what we find here is similar to what can be observed happening in other parts of the NT to the command of Jesus to love all people (Mk 12.31). Fairly rapidly within early Christianity the emphasis was placed on loving fellow Christians (Rom 12.10; 1 Th 4.9; Heb 13.1; 1 Pet 1.22; 2.17; John 13.34f; 15.12, 17; 1 Jn 3.11, 23; 4.11). It is not difficult to see why this change should have taken place.[5] Outside pressures from the wider community, in relation, say, to idolatry, would force Christians in on themselves and they would find themselves upheld in their resistance by their mutual love, and so would stress it. Believing themselves to be a family (Mk 3.31–5; 10.29f) it was natural to emphasise their love to one

---

[4] W. R. Baker, ' "Above all Else": Contexts of the Call for Verbal Integrity in James 5.12', *JSNT* 54 (1994) 57–71; cf P. Minear, 'Yes or No: The Demand for Honesty in the Early Church', *NT* 13 (1971) 1–13.
[5] Cf Best, 'A First Century Sect', *IrishBS* 8 (1986) 115–21.

another. There was also the need to draw a boundary inside which were fellow Christians and outside which were pagans. The stress then on the need to love one another is not surprising; what is, is the gradual forgetfulness of the command to love all, and in our verse the need to be truthful to all. We still find love to all in Paul (Rom 13.8–10; Gal 5.14; 1 Th 3.12; Gal 6.10; in the latter two instances the restricted idea is also present), but it is hard to trace it in the NT after Paul other than in the Synoptic tradition of the teaching of Jesus. The limitation to the community of the exhortation of v. 25 holds true also for the injunctions of the following verses which raise the same difficult question whether Christians should treat non-Christians in a way different from that in which they treat one another. Reciprocal love is also found in *T Sim* 4.7; *T Jos* 17.2–8; *Jub* 20.2; 36.4, 8; *Gos Thom* II, 2 (log 25) 38.10–12; *Treat Seth* VII, 2 62.19–21. It is fair to note that in *T Issach* 7.6; *T Gad* 4.7 love is to be offered to all and that in the case of at least one minor cult in Philadelphia (see Barton and Horsley) members are instructed not to practise deceit against any man or woman; though possibly a higher level of behaviour is expected towards fellow members for they are to be well intentioned (εὐνοεῖν towards their group. *Ps-Phoc* 7 does not restrict those to whom the truth should be spoken.

A second surprising feature about our verse is the motivation for telling the truth. Since Jesus is the truth and God is true in all respects, we might have expected a more theological or christological reason such as Paul introduces in averring his own truthfulness (2 Cor 1.15–22). A quotation from the OT, when no attention is drawn to it as such and it cannot be assumed that the readers realise it comes from an authoritative source, is hardly a theological reason. As for v. 25c it could easily have appeared on Stoic lips since they regarded humanity as a body with members (Seneca *Ep* 95; M. Aurelius 7.13).

26. This forms with v. 27 a unit. The latter by itself, though a true and necessary injunction, requires some context to which it can apply; it is tied in here by μηδέ (Ewald, Abbott). Verse 26a is drawn from Ψ 4.5. The LXX does not render accurately the MT but this would not have concerned AE who may not have known the MT, and who, if he did, for the sake of his readers had to use the LXX. In fact he gives no positive evidence that he is aware that he is using the OT. Ps 4.2 already referred to lying and in *T Dan* 1.3; 2.1; 3.5f; 4.6f; 5.1; 6.8 lying and anger are associated (their association in Col 3.8, 9 is not so close since other vices are listed with them). Probably they were then linked in Jewish ethical tradition and from it entered Christian teaching joined together. If so AE may have used the OT quotation because it also lay in the tradition. When Polycarp, *Phil* 12.1, used Eph 4.26 he described it as scripture and almost certainly did so because he recognised the OT text and not because he regarded Eph 4.26 itself as scripture. Later v. 26b was taken to be a saying of Jesus.[6] Even if AE was aware that he was using the OT we cannot assume his readers were. This is the only place where the Psalm is quoted in the NT; for Christians it was not one of the better-known parts of the OT and it would not have been immediately obvious that AE was making a quotation. Recent converts certainly would not have known from where it came; this is especially so if Ephesians is regarded as a baptismal writing or one directed to recent converts; for them it would then have had no scriptural authority.

At first sight the translation of v. 26a appears to be 'be angry and do not sin'; such a rendering might suggest Christians were required to be angry. This need not however be so if the first imperative is taken as concessive or conditional (see BDR §387 n. 1; Robertson, 949, 1023; Porter, 352f; cf Jn 2.19; 2 Cor 12.16); the meaning is then, 'If you are angry do not sin', 'when angry do not sin'. The grammatical correctness of such a translation has often been disputed.[7] Yet if we take the first imperative in a straightforward way as a command to be angry it would be in conflict with v. 31. It would also spoil the pattern of the passage where each injunction begins with a rejection of certain conduct as unChristian. Finally since not all anger can be right a context is required in which anger may be approved and the present passage does not supply this. 'In Eph 4:26 Paul is placing a moral obligation on believers to be angry as the occasion requires' (Wallace, art.cit., 372). But what is the occasion? Wallace has no answer but to say it must be in relation to a case of church discipline; he provides no evidence however for seeing such a case as under consideration here.

Anger leads easily to the loss of a sense of judgement and so to sin and can appear in different ways, from the passionate outburst to the sullen bearing of grudges; many attempts have been made to describe and define it, especially by secular authors; their descriptions all imply the rejection of unjust anger.[8] Epictetus, 2.12.14f, commends Socrates because he never lost his temper. God is described as angry in both the OT (2 Kgs 17.18; Ps 7.11; 79.5f; 80.4) and the NT, and that not only in relation to a wrath overtaking sinners at the last judgement (cf Rom 1.18ff; 13.4f; cf Mk 3.5; 10.14 and D text of 1.41). If God's anger is presently active, how is it active? In famine, earthquake, natural disaster? This is possible but

---

[6] See A. Resch, *Agrapha. Aussercanonische Schriftfragmente gesammelt und untersucht* (TU 30, 3–4), 1906, 136f, no. 94.

[7] See in particular D. B. Wallace, "Ὀργίζεσθε in Ephesians 4:26: Command or Condition?', *Criswell Theological Journal* 12 (1989) 353–72.

[8] E.g. Aristotle, *Nic Eth* IV 5 (1125B–6B); Seneca, *De ira*; Plutarch, *De cohibenda ira.* Cf S. W. Hinks, 'Anger', *Journal of Christian Education* 86 (1986) 33–9.

Rom 13.4 implies that God has human agents to execute his anger. If they, when they punish wrongdoing, are angry, do they sin? To put this more generally: if God can be legitimately angry, may not his servants be also when dealing with sin? In several instances in the OT human anger appears to be approved (e.g. Num 25.11; 1 Sam 28.18; 1 Kgs 21.22); in these cases the personal element (one person angry with another because their rights or possessions have been attacked) is at a minimum. If believers see a person or a group of people oppressing others, may anger not be their proper response to the situation (Ps 119.53)? The question whether righteous anger is possible goes back as far as Origen (see his discussion of v. 31) and probably led to the variant reading at Mt 5.22, where the accepted text excludes all anger. Rom 12.19 (cf Jas 1.19f) does not necessarily exclude righteous anger; where however people have been personally involved, it is particularly difficult for them to judge whether their anger is justified; private vengeance is wrong and action should be left to God. It is difficult to describe Paul's attitude to those whom he thought were destroying his churches as other than one of anger, though the word itself may not be used. It is unlikely that AE has in mind here anger on behalf of those who are suffering at the hands of others, but the passion aroused in those who believe they themselves have been injured. This is also true of the rejection of anger in the Wisdom literature (e.g. Prov 15.1, 18; 22.24; 29.8, 11, 22; Eccles 7.9; Ecclus 1.22; 27.30; cf 1 Tim 2.8; Tit 1.7). In these cases action should be left to God (Rom 12.19).

Yet since anger does occur in groups of people and destroys their relationship, AE sees the need to put some limitation on it (v. 26b). His approach is thus practical rather than theoretical, and his limitation one of time. It does not mean that a person may be legitimately angry until sunset; were this taken literally it would mean that those who lived in the Arctic or Antarctic would at certain times of the year have no temporal limitation on their anger! If however there is anger[9] it should have vanished after a night's sleep and the morning should bring forgiveness and reconciliation, or, more correctly if we give a Jewish definition to the day, anger should vanish before sunset. 'The day of anger should be the day of reconciliation' (Eadie). Twice in the OT the sunset limitation is introduced as a provision of mercy (Deut 24.15, 23) to prevent hardship. The same provision with a closer relation to anger is also found in CD 9.2–8; 7.2f; 1QS 5.26–6.1. Plutarch, *Mor* 488BC, mentions it in relation to the Pythagoreans. 4.26b may then be a proverbial saying.

[9] παροργισμός (the article is omitted by $\mathfrak{P}^{49}$ $\aleph^*$ A B 1739*) is a rare word, differing little in meaning from ὀργή; only here in the NT but in 3 Kgdms 15.30; 4 Kgdms 19.3; 23.26; Jer 21.5; 2 Esdr 19.18, 26; *Ps Sol* 18.9; it should be understood passively in v. 26.

27. AE now offers an additional reason for the rejection of anger, hence μηδέ and not μήτε (Salmond). Anger gives an opportunity (for διδόναι τόπον cf Wisd 12.10; Ecclus 4.5; 38.12; Rom 12.19; Heb 12.17) for the devil to intervene. A few commentators (e.g. Erasmus, Ewald) have given διάβολος a human reference, 'the slanderer'; while this is a legitimate meaning of the word it is contrary to its normal NT usage, and nothing in the context suggests it. Paul prefers 'Satan' to 'devil' but the other Deutero-Paulines use 'devil' (both terms are found in the Gospels); this may be another minor indication of non-Pauline authorship (but see Introduction §2.7.2); more probably it is a recognition that 'devil' would be more easily understood by Greek readers than Hebrew 'satan'. The understanding of the place and function of the devil gradually changed during the later OT period and continued to change into the beginning of the Christian era. Satan was a late arrival in being regarded as the cause of human sin and evil.[10] Here in v. 27 the sin has already occurred in the anger of the believer before the devil is mentioned. He has not caused the anger, but as God's opponent can be counted on to stir the pot and use it to disturb the relation of believers with those with whom they are angry, who might then themselves respond angrily. Although the devil is associated with lying and anger in *T Dan* 5.1f (cf Hermas, *Mand* 5.1.3), it is not necessary to see this passage, or the tradition which it represents, as directly leading to his introduction here. By the time of Ephesians he is appearing widely in Jewish and Christian thinking. As pointed out in the discussion of 2.1–10, though believers may sit with Christ in the heavenlies they have not escaped his influence (cf 6.11), even though they may think that when they became Christians they left his sphere and entered Christ's. However 'realised' AE's theology may be, he is too wise to ignore the imperfections of believers, and in this he differs in no way from the remainder of the NT despite the peculiarity of his views in 2.5f.

The motivation of v. 27 differs from those offered in vv. 25, 28, 29 since it does not refer directly to the good of the community; it is so general that it would have served as an additional motivation in respect of the injunctions of any of those verses. It is relevant to all behaviour and has an importance of its own (Mussner). It can easily be detached from its context and applied to many situations; preachers have been doing this since at least the time of Cyprian (*Ep* 4.2). Was AE thinking only of anger within the community? There seems no reason to alter the limitation to fellow-believers found in v. 25b. It runs through the passage and when the theme reappears in Polycarp, *Phil* 12.1, the context of 11.1–4 implies the restriction. Moreover the parallel passages in Jewish tradition (see above) imply

[10] See Best, *Temptation*, 44–60.

the same restriction, in their case of course to being angry with other Jews as members of the community. It is also more appropriate to think of the devil as entering the community to disturb it rather than life outside where he would normally be expected to operate.

28.[11] This verse continues the pattern of a negative statement followed by a positive in relation to community conduct.

There are two textual problems (cf Metzger, ad loc.): (i) τὸ ἀγαθόν varies in position and is sometimes omitted. Support for its terminal position is much stronger than any earlier positioning (e.g. K Ψ 88 326; Chr Thret), though the latter may have seemed semantically superior to some copyists. Whatever the position the meaning is hardly affected. (ii) The variations in respect of ταῖς ἰδίαις χερσίν are greater and extend from its total omission to the omission of ἰδίαις alone. Support for total omission is slight (P 33 1739 1881 it^m; Cl Or) and may be the result of the low valuation placed on manual labour in the hellenistic world. ἰδίαις is read by ℵ* A D F G K 81 104 365 1175 1241^s 2464 *pm* it vg^cl; Aug, but omitted by 𝔓^46 𝔓^49vid ℵ² B a Ψ vg^st ww; Ambst. Its presence may have been regarded as superfluous since those described would hardly have been working with hands other than their own, yet in 1 Cor 4.12 where it is equally superfluous there is no evidence for omission. It could have been inserted to emphasise that the thief who stole with his hands must use the same hands to benefit the community. It is difficult to decide whether to read it or not. The uncertainty of copyists is reflected in the occasional substitution of αὐτοῦ. Whatever the reading the meaning is clear.

The area of conduct treated here changes abruptly (there is no connecting particle) and is in the singular unlike the preceding and following injunctions. In the other exhortations the plural could cover both sexes, the singular here would normally not; the masculine is appropriate since women in most parts of the ancient world were not in a position to earn money; if they were in need, they turned to prostitution rather than theft.

While it is probable that lying and anger were connected in some Jewish paraenesis (see on v. 26) theft was not linked with them. Theft was, however, recognised in Judaism from the time of the Decalogue as a major sin (Isa 1.23; Jer 7.9; Lev 19.11; *Ps-Phoc* 153ff; cf SB I, 810–13), and was repudiated in the main streams of Greco-Roman culture; Epictetus, 3.8.10ff, deplores the view he attributes to Epicurus that it is not stealing itself which is wrong but being found out (cf Xenophon, *Anab* 7.6.41; Plato, *Rep* I 344b; Heroditus I 186.3)! There is no reason to see with Agnell, 128, a connection in that the anger of v. 26 was directed against Christian thieves who did not support the community. Theft may be mentioned here because like lying and anger it appears in vice lists

---

[11] I have treated this verse in much greater detail in 'Thieves in the Church. Ephesians 4:28', *IrishBS* 14 (1992) 2–9.

(1 Cor 6.10f; 1 Pet 4.15; cf *Did* 3.5). Thieves fail to play their part in the life of the community, not because they steal from fellow members, but because they make no financial contribution to it; the new conduct demanded of them would positively benefit the community. This corporate aspect ties in our verse with vv. 25ff. All lose their tempers and tell lies but there were probably only a few thieves in each community; there are few cultures from which theft is completely absent. The reference here to thieving indicates something about the kind of people who became Christians in the first century and shows how difficult it was for them when converted to break away from their previous behaviour.

ὁ κλέπτων, present participle, is equivalent to a substantive, 'the thief', the person who steals (contra BDR §339 n. 9; Zerwick §274). The present injunction with μηκέτι would be unnecessary (cf BDR §336 n. 4) if only those who had been thieves in their pre-Christian days were in mind; thieving however still characterises the conduct of some believers. Slaves are hardly in view (*pace* Hendriksen, Masson, Caird) for after giving up theft they were not normally in a position to devote their labour to earning money and to contribute to the welfare of the community; their owners reaped whatever reward lay in their work. The most probable thieves would be day labourers, those with some skill in a trade, or shopkeepers, all of whom could mix stealing with their normal occupation. There were many day labourers in the ancient world[12] who could not depend on regular employment. The work of skilled tradesmen might also have been irregular. There were no funds outside Rome itself to assist the unemployed (Finley, 40). The financially impoverished unemployed may have been forced into occasional stealing to maintain themselves and their families.

Those who have been stealing are bidden to work. Jews valued work highly as a normal human activity (Exod 20.9; Ps 104.23; Prov 6.6; 28.19; Ecclus 7.15; *T Issach* 5.3; Josephus *c. Ap.* 2.291); the idle rich were denounced (cf Amos 6.4–6). Jesus had a trade and teachers of the Law were generally expected to support themselves (*m Abot* 2.2). Work was also highly valued in the Greco-Roman world (Epict 1.16.16f; 3.26.27f; 8.26.2f; Dio *Orat* 7.112f; 123f) though there in contrast to Judaism manual labour was often, but not invariably, regarded as inferior to mental work.[13] AE assumes that those who stole were those who worked with their hands rather than their minds. He neither suggests the thief should restore what he has stolen (contrast Lk 19.1–10; Exod 22.1; 22.6; Lev 6.1–5; Num 5.5f;

[12] Cf M. I. Finley, *The Ancient Economy*, 2nd edn, London, 1985, 73–5, 107, 185f; C. Hezser, *Lohnmetaphorik und Arbeitswelt im Mt 20, 1–16*, Freiburg and Göttingen, 1990, 64–6.
[13] Cf R. F. Hock, *The Social Context of Paul's Ministry*, Philadelphia, 1980, 38ff, 44, 45, 48.

Prov 6.31) nor that he should repent; the former probably because those whose goods have been stolen did not belong to the community; if they had been members harmony in the community would have demanded restitution; as for the latter it is in keeping with AE's failure to ask for repentance in respect of any of the other sins he mentions in 4.25ff. Instead his attention as in the other injunctions of the paragraph is directed to the welfare of the community to which the thief ought to be contributing. Interestingly he does not suggest that the money earned should be given to the poor; his advice contrasts with that of Jesus in Mk 10.21. AE's words in v. 28 are very similar to Paul's in 1 Cor 4.12; he may either have known that passage or, more probably, since the context in 1 Cor 4.12 is different (cf Percy, 209), the words may have been in use in the Pauline school; if Paul is the author then they were probably his customary words.

Our verse provides no 'theology' of work. Its purpose has been viewed in many different ways. Here only the case of reformed thieves is considered: they should work so that they may not be a burden on the community (cf 2 Th 3.6ff). In many ways the connection here is similar to the Jewish link between work and almsgiving (Agnell, 128; cf *T Issach* 5.3; 7 5; *T Zeb* 6.5f; *Ps-Phoc* 22ff). In seeing the purpose of work as for the benefit (χρεία is used of physical need in Mk 2.25; Jn 13.29; Acts 2.45; 4.35; 20.34; Rom 12.13; Phil 2.25; 4.16) of the community AE reflects the emphasis on the sharing of goods among the early Jerusalem Christians (Acts 2.44f; 4.32–5.11; 6.1ff) and in the Qumran community (1QS 1.11ff; Josephus *BJ* 2.122), and the collection made among the Gentile churches for the saints in Jerusalem (Rom 15.26f; Gal 2.10; 2 Cor 8.1ff; 9.1ff). Yet he does not lay the duty of sharing on the community as a whole but only on thieves within it. Sharing is probably the background to his injunction but he only mentions thieves because he has begun each injunction in our passage by mentioning a vice; when he rejects theft as a way of life he has to put something positive in its place.

While the total meaning is clear, the good of the community, τὸ ἀγαθόν, has been understood in different ways (cf Joüon, 460). (a) The phrase may have been deliberately chosen to draw out the difference in moral value between what the thief could do now and what he has been doing, and should be taken adverbially, 'working honestly'. (b) It could be taken as the direct object of ἐργαζόμενος and refer to the product of the work (Agnell, 129); the carpenter, for example, should make a good chair. (c) It could denote the objective of the work (cf Gal 6.10), 'doing what is good with one's own hands'. (d) Since τὰ ἀγαθά can mean 'goods', i.e. material goods, the singular might mean the same. Joüon suggests this but does not provide any evidence for the use of the singular in this way; it is also similar to (b); the latter however reads too much into the word and at the same time is rather narrow (Lincoln); (c) is in the end very little different from (a), but (a) is to be preferred because of the contrast with the person's previous way of life.[14]

Before leaving the verse we should note that AE does not deal with financial theft, that he provides some evidence for the continuance of communal sharing of possessions among the early Christians but none for the sharing of anything else such as wives, that he does not denounce possessions or wealth as wrong in themselves. In the light of the general poverty of the ancient world he does not deal with how believers in general are to be assisted when they fall on evil days, and some on becoming Christians may have been thrown out of their homes and lost their livelihood, and this quite apart from the general poverty of the ancient world; it would have been relevant to the theme of his injunctions to have said something about this. In that light it is not surprising then that he has nothing to say about charity towards non-believers. It might be said that he should have overlooked the sin of theft since those who gained money in this way could still have contributed to the poor but he knows that theft is basically wrong and so cannot encourage a 'Robin Hood' attitude of stealing from the rich for the benefit of the poor.

AE does not discuss the practical question of what was to happen to the thief and his family if he was no longer able to support them through theft and could not obtain work; he and his family instead of contributing to the financial needs of the community would have become a drain on its resources, for there were no general welfare schemes on which victims of poverty could fall back. The situation is thus very different from that of today's Western world where there is some form of welfare relief for those without work. AE restricts what he says to thieves of material goods; theft today cannot be so restricted; financial manipulation or the underpayment of employees can be forms of it. We do not know AE's views on those who having made money in these ways then give vast sums to charitable or religious causes. His simple statement thus gives little guidance for the complex social, financial and industrial set-up of today.

29. While v. 29 is not directly connected to v. 28 it is structurally similar: each begins with a negative statement, moves to a positive and ends with a final clause introduced by ἵνα; they also share two major concepts, ἀγαθός and χρεία. V. 29a contains two probable but not certain Semitisms, πᾶς ... μή (BDR §302 n. 2; MHT, 196;

[14] W. D. Morris, 'Ephesians iv.28', *ExpT* 41 (1929/30) 237, supposes a primitive corruption of the text which originally read τὸν ἄρτον; as with almost all supposed 'primitive corruptions' there is little to be said for this.

Zerwick §447) and ἐκ τοῦ στόματος ... ἐκπορεύεσθαι (cf Deut 8.3; 1 Kgdms 2.3; Jer 17.16; Mt 15.18; BDR §217 n. 8); ἀλλά meaning 'but only' (Beyer, 137) is a possible third. This suggests the origin of v. 29a in Judaism or early Jewish Christianity with v. 29bc as an additional Christian comment. Judaism was certainly aware of the power of speech to do good or evil (Prov 10.31f; 12.17–19; 15.2, 23; Ecclus 5.10–14; 18.15–17; 21.25f; 1QS 7.9; CD 10.17f; *T Issach* 4.14, 17; *b Shab* 30b). The most detailed NT reference to speech is Jas 3.6ff (cf Mt 12.33–7). In v. 29 it is the power of speech to do evil which is introduced first and this with σαπρός, a rather imprecise word.[15] The root presents a contrast with what is good in relation to growth in Mt 7.17, 18; 12.33; Lk 6.43 and to fish in Mt 13.48, but in v. 29a the meaning cannot be directly associated with decaying vegetable matter or rotten fish. It must, given the general sense of 'evil', indicate a sin on the same level as lying and stealing (Robinson); evil speech not only harms the one who utters it, and AE is probably not thinking of this aspect which would be an essentially selfish motive, but harms the community in which it is spoken (Barry); in contrast with what builds up, it destroys (Gnilka) and corrupts its community; it is then a metaphorical parallel to its use in describing decaying vegetable matter and fish. Yet it still leaves open wide possibilities; since v. 25 dealt with lying it may refer to abusive gossip,[16] obscenity, pornography, heresy (cf 2 Tim 2.14), cynicism, sarcasm, or the attribution of evil motives to those who do good; a list open to indefinite expansion.

The mouths of believers should only utter (the main verb must be understood again in v. 29b) good speech which would serve to build up those who hear it. The sentiment of the verse could apply to anyone but the use of two words, οἰκοδομή, χάρις, normally applied to behaviour within the community, together with the general context suggests AE is referring to words spoken within the community (contrast Col 4.6). Though the main sense is clear this is not true of all the details, in particular of χρείας (cf Sellin, 102f). The difficulty of interpreting it led to the variant πίστεως (D* F G *pc* it vg^cl; Tert Cyp Ambst) and to various sophisticated explanations (Findlay, 'a pointed saying', Hofmann, 'commerce'), but in view of its use in v. 28 such explanations should be resisted (Barth), though its meaning in the two verses may not be precisely the same. It should probably, but by no means certainly, be given the sense 'need' or 'opportunity': the building up of another takes place when there is a need for it and/or the opportunity opens for doing so (cf NRSV, REB, NJB). Believers build up one another in worship

---

[15] Cf C. Lindhagen, 'Die Wurzel ΣΑΠ- im NT und AT', *UUA* 40 (1950) 27–69.

[16] Abuse of fellow members was forbidden in some contemporary groupings, e.g. in the Zeus Hypsistos group referred to in Introduction §10.3.2.

through what they say or sing (5.19; 1 Cor 14.3–5, 12, 26) or more generally in day-to-day living (Rom 14.19) where their words may mediate grace (v. 29c). διδόναι χάριν may be used in a general way of doing a good turn to someone (Eadie and Harless give classical references) but in the light of the Christian use of χάρις it is preferable to restrict it to speech conferring spiritual benefit (cf Lk 4.22; Eccles 10.12). The interpretation which sees a reference to the manner of speech as pleasing (Theophylact) is to be rejected, though perhaps Col 4.6 approaches this meaning. Pleasing speech does not appear to have been of great concern to the early Christians, and if AE has known Paul and his manner of speech (cf 2 Cor 10.10; 1 Cor 2.4) he will not be making an aesthetic statement here; this will be even more true if Paul himself is the author. If it refers to spiritual benefit this is not to be taken in any narrow sense of spiritual; it will include words of comfort spoken in a time of sorrow, of encouragement in a time of doubt, of good counsel in a time of uncertainty as to action. In these and other ways the words of any believer can convey grace to hearers. Such helping speech is confined neither to corporate worship nor to the lips of religious officials, though this restriction may be present in 4.12.

30. This verse[17] differs both structurally and in content from the injunctions of vv. 25–9; it contains only a negative (the omission of μή is found in $\mathfrak{P}^{46}$ alone and can be dismissed as probably a simple mistake) injunction with no balancing positive; the motive for action appears in a relative clause and lacks the social aspect. It resembles v. 27 in being a general exhortation and moves the motivation from concern for the good of the community to a deeper level (cf 1 Th 4.8), though of course the Spirit is always the Spirit which is present in the community (1 Cor 3.16) and is generally related to behaviour (e.g. Gal 5.16, 25); at the deeper level it can be applied to all Christian behaviour. Before examining where the verse fits into its context we need to enquire after its content.

Fee, 712–17, sees dependence here on Isa 63.10. At first sight this seems justified but the resemblance relates to content in respect of the MT; verbal agreement with the LXX is much less pronounced; there is as much verbal agreement with 2 Kgdms 13.21, yet this is hardly the source. Generally AE depends on the LXX rather than the MT, though if he regards 4.8 to be based on Ps 68 it shows he could ignore both LXX and MT and makes it possible, though unlikely, that he may have had access to another translation and tradition. While there can be no doubt AE knew Isaiah in its LXX form (see on 2.14, 17; 6.14, 17) there is no evidence that he was familiar with the Hebrew text. Even if he was using it here it is unlikely that his Gentile readers would have realised this.

AE employs an unusually full term for the Spirit; 'Spirit of God'

[17] See Adai, 78ff, and Lemmer, 374ff.

and 'Holy Spirit' are normal; here they are combined (cf 1 Th 4.8). He may have used his elaborate phrase to emphasise the importance of what he was saying[18] or it may simply be another instance of his rotundity. Similar references to the Spirit are found in Judaism (*T Issach* 4.40; *T Dan* 4.5), though we cannot be sure that these references may not have been affected by Christianity, and the idea reappears in Hermas, *Mand* 10.2.1ff; 3.2ff. The two passages CD 5.11f; 7.12 which are sometimes quoted as parallels do not appear to be relevant since they refer to the human spirit. The Spirit is also often related to joy and not grief or pain (Rom 14.17; Gal 5.22; 1 Th 1.6) and to hope (Rom 15.13).

There is a subsidiary issue: is personality ascribed here to the Spirit? There is little else in the letter to help us determine an answer. Towards the end of the first century Christians were increasingly regarding the Holy Spirit as a person, but not with any consistency and unanimity. Probably AE is on the way to accepting his personality and v. 30 reflects this, though the same would not be true of the semi-parallel of 1 Th 5.19. If the Spirit is regarded here as a person, we have an anthropomorphism in the saying about giving pain.[19] Much of what we say about God cannot be expressed other than anthropomorphically, even though it breaks the human categories in which it is expressed. The human sins of our passage do not merely offend fellow believers but the divine Spirit (Theophylact) who dwells in us as well as in those community members against whom we have sinned.

The Holy Spirit sealed and authenticated believers at their conversion/baptism; for ἐσφραγίσθητε see on 1.13; ἐν indicates the Holy Spirit as agent, though it could be instrumental with God as the real subject. Sealing is not exclusively connected with baptism (see on 1.13); it refers to the beginning of the Christian life as 'deliverance' does to its end (Stott). Believers now belong to God and this (πρός), up to the time of, or with a view to, the ἡμέρα ἀπολυτρώσεως (see on 1.7 for the word). The phrase (see Lindemann, *Aufhebung*, 197ff; 230ff; Lona, 423f) is a *hapax legomenon*. The 'day' as indicating a future significant event appears in phrases like 'the day of the Lord' (1 Th 5.2; 2 Th 2.2; 1 Cor 1.8; 5.5; 2 Cor 1.14) which derives from the OT 'day of Yahweh', 'day of Christ' (Phil 1.6, 10; 2.16), and 'day of judgement and wrath' (Rom 2.5). The day of judgement is also a day of salvation (Rom 2.5, 7; 13.11f; Phil 1.6, 10; 2.16) and it is salvation and not judgement which is featured in v. 30. Has the term future significance here? If Paul is the writer there would be no hesitation in accepting the future reference, but if he is not does the lessened eschatological emphasis

---

[18] It was later taken to be an *agraphon*; see Resch, op.cit., 134f no. 92.

[19] The traditional rendering of λυπεῖν as 'grieve' seems rather weak in modern English; the word has a range of meanings; cf R. Bultmann, *TWNT*, IV, 314–25; Spicq, I, 513–19.

of the remainder of the letter (e.g. 2.6) eliminate it? ἀπολύτρωσις itself does not determine the answer for it can be applied to events belonging to the past (Rom 3.24; Eph 1.7; Col 1.14) which affect believers in the present, to present experiences (1 Cor 1.30) and to events affecting believers in the future (Rom 8.23). But even if believers already sit with Christ in the heavenlies (2.6) they are still engaged in a struggle with sin and the powers of evil, or else the injunctions of 4.1–6.18 are irrelevant. Our verse appears in a paraenetic passage counselling future good Christian conduct and containing a reference to the Holy Spirit in regard to whom the future cannot be eliminated (1.13f). A time is coming when believers will enjoy a fuller life. It cannot be denied that the letter contains an unresolved eschatological tension; to insist that the deliverance is fully accomplished is to ignore one side of this tension. By using 'day of deliverance' rather than 'day of the Lord', AE indicates his interest in what happens to believers as distinct from what happens to unbelievers (5.6 may deal with them; see notes there); he has spent considerable time detailing the present position of believers (e.g. 2.1ff; 4.17ff), but he is not interested in doing the same in respect of their future; the term 'deliverance' is imprecise; it implies at least deliverance from those sins and evil powers which have entrapped them in the past and still continue in part to do so.

How does this verse fit into its context? It could be taken in isolation; since at least the time of Tertullian (*Ad martyras* 1.53) preachers and writers have detached it from its context and applied it to whatever sin they were attacking; this seems a weak solution; the καί indicates some connection with the context. There is no precise linkage between v. 30 and v. 31 (for a supposed connection see Pelagius, Schlier) or between v. 30 and vv. 31ff; it would also be unusual to mention the motivation before the vice or virtue to which it referred (Gaugler). It is best then to link it with what precedes (Abbott, Belser, Schnackenburg, Salmond, Lincoln) because of: (i) the introductory καί, (ii) the frequent association of the Spirit with speech (5.18f; 6.17) which was the subject of v. 29, (iii) the sins of vv. 25–9 which are those which frustrate the Spirit in building up the church. (ii) is hardly relevant, for the Holy Spirit is associated as much with action as with speech; περιπατεῖν, a frequent term in Ephesians (4.17; 5.2, 8, 15) is linked with the Spirit in Gal 5.16, 22. As for (iii), the Spirit is the Spirit which operates in the community and therefore whatever corrupts community life frustrates the Spirit. The following two verses also fit in with this stream of thought; the sins of v. 31 hinder the building up of the community by the Spirit while the virtues of v. 32 further that work. Verse 30 then, like v. 27, expresses a different type of motivation to Christian conduct; it does not speak directly of doing harm to the community. It sets the activity of believers in relation to God; if vv. 25–9 run along the lines of the second table of the Decalogue v. 30 corresponds to the first. Pokorný suggests that the same kind of thinking may underlie it as is found in the references to the sin against the Holy Spirit in the Gospels (Mk 3.28f; Lk 12.10). After v. 30 the form of the injunctions in 4.25–9 changes and those that follow are more varied. In that sense v. 30 represents a break in the paraenesis providing a bridge from the one type to the others (Lemmer, 375, calls it a 'hinge' verse) and can refer both backwards and forwards (Zerwick).

31. This verse is negative; v. 32a is positive; v. 32b gives a motivation. The pattern of vv. 25–8 is thus followed (Lincoln), yet vv. 31, 32a differ greatly from the negative and positive portions of the earlier verses in that they do not treat individual vices separately but several vices and virtues at the same time; the resemblance may then be purely chance. AE has been issuing a number of warning exhortations to his readers and it is good psychology to move from negative to positive and add a motivation. Since the positive exhortation of v. 32 relates to behaviour within the community ('one another') the negative exhortation of v. 31 will do the same, and so harmonise with the remainder of the paragraph.

Verse 31 commences with a pentad of substantives, all related to the theme of anger, and ends with a more generalised word for vice. Only the fourth word in the pentad is not necessarily pejorative; κραυγή, the voice raised in shouting, in a cry either for help or of victory or of anger. As a neutral term the context supplies its meaning, and here that is anger. What is the origin of this pentad of vices? A list in Col 3.8 has the second, third and fifth terms together with the sixth (outside the pentad) and final substantive of v. 31. The last vice in the pentad, βλασφημία, corresponds to the αἰσχρολογία of Col 3.8, a word of similar meaning. This may suggest that the impulse to describe anger using a number of terms derives from Col 3.8 or from the Pauline school to which AE and A/Col belonged; however the description of anger using a succession of terms is also found in Stoicism (Chrysippus, *frag* 395, cf 394, 396f, v. Arnim III 96.3ff; Seneca, *De ira* 1.4; cf Philo, *Ebr* 223). For his list AE may then be directly or indirectly indebted to Stoicism; in v. 24 he defined virtue in Hellenistic terms; perhaps he deliberately chose terms known at least to the better educated of his readers.

The first term, πικρία (πᾶσα applies to all five nouns and exercises a generalising function, 'all kinds of'), is not in Col 3.8 but is in the lists of Chrysippus and Philo. An infrequent term in the NT (Acts 8.23; Rom 3.14; Heb 12.15) its use apart from v. 31 derives from the LXX. The root is sometimes used with physical significance (Jas 3.11; Rev 8.11; 10.9, 10) but also in relation to vice (Jas 3.14; Col 3.19) and twice of Peter's repentance after denying

Jesus (Mt 26.75; Lk 22.62). In our verse it indicates that underlying feeling of bitterness and resentment from which anger springs.

The second and third terms are normal words for anger; they were distinguished by some of the moralists in their discussions of anger (Chrysippus, *frag* 395; Diog. Laertes 7.113f; Seneca, *De ira* 2.36) but were often used as synonyms (Rom 2.8; Rev 14.10; Ecclus 48.10; 1 Clem 50.4). Both terms are applied to divine anger (Jn 3.36; Rom 1.18; Eph 5.6; Rev 19.5; Rev 14.10, 19; 15.1, 7) and to human (Mk 3.5; 1 Tim 2.8; Jas 1.19f; Lk 4.28; Acts 19.28; 2 Cor 12.20; Gal 5.20). It is therefore difficult to argue that AE saw them as greatly different; the order is the reverse of that of Col 3.8 but AE has not necessarily brought them into an accepted order; Col 3.8 follows the order of Chrysippus and Philo, Eph 4.31 that of Hermas, *Mand* 5.2.4, though Hermas could have been influenced by Ephesians. The variation in order between Colossians and Ephesians is the kind of variation to be expected between writers who depend on the same pool of material. If the words require to be distinguished in meaning, θυμός indicates the passionate outburst, ὀργή the inward seething. Together they display AE's condemnation of all forms of anger whether smouldering or passionate. For Jewish and Hellenistic teaching on anger see on v. 26.

If the first noun suggested the inner feeling resulting in the anger of the second and third, the fourth and fifth relate to the outward manifestation of anger. Angry people often shout loudly. The fifth term is shared with Col 3.8, and may describe speech directed against God (Mk 14.64; Lk 5.21; Acts 6.11) or against humans (Mk 7.22; 1 Cor 10.30; 1 Tim 6.4; 2 Tim 3.2; Tit 3.2). Though v. 30, linked to the idea of sin against the Holy Spirit and the underlying logic of Mt 25.31–46, might suggest that blasphemy against the Spirit was in view here the general tenor of the paragraph implies AE has primarily a sin against other church members in mind. Angry people shout loudly at and revile the objects of their wrath. There is thus a steady movement from the inner bitter disposition to denunciatory speech.

The interpretation of the five terms as a developing sequence (the same idea is expressed quite differently in *T Dan* 4.2–4) goes back at least to Chrysostom and describes what may happen in a quarrel (Murray). Only the elimination of bitterness can ensure the absence of the other vices. Because of the steady progression and concentration on only one vice it is doubtful if the five nouns can be properly classified as a vice catalogue (see on 5.3 for this 'form') since the catalogues normally list a variety of sins. Anger, then, with all its ramifications is to be put away by readers. AE uses αἰρεῖν here (for the aorist see on 4.22–4; it is probably not a divine passive) whereas Col 3.8 has ἀποτίθεσθαι, the verb with which AE had begun our passage (v. 25); had he been copying Colossians there would have been no need for him to change a verb he uses in both 4.22 and 4.25 in relation to turning away from sin. His variation is probably stylistic; again if he was copying Col 3.8 he did not need to make the nouns into subjects of the verb. The similarity of Ephesians and Colossians arises here from a common fund of material rather than from the use of one by the author of the other.

The final phrase of the verse summarises, broadens (πάσῃ) and concludes the discussion. κακία is a general word for wickedness but there are other such general words; AE has probably selected it because it can also have a more restricted meaning as its use alongside other words shows (Rom 1.29f; 1 Cor 5.8; Col 3.8; Tit 3.3; Jas 1.21; 1 Pet 2.1). In its present context we should take it as continuing the theme of the destructive power originating in bitterness and developing into anger; the linking σύν is probably equivalent to καί, cf Kuhn, *NTS* 7 (1960/1) 337. Probably 'malice' is as good a rendering as any.

AE warned against anger in 4.26f; why has he returned to the theme? He does not return to any of the other sins of vv. 25–9. It may be because anger is more destructive of good community relations than any of those other sins, and he has consistently stressed the need for unity (2.11ff; 4.1ff), or because, since it is treated regularly by the Greek moralists and not ignored by the Jewish moralists, he cannot pass it by, or because, and we know so little about AE's own actual situation, he has just witnessed in his own community an instance of the disruptive power of anger.

32. After v. 31 this verse returns to the pattern of vv. 25–30 with believers as the subjects of the imperatives. Unlike v. 31 it is positive in tone.

Following on the adversatives in vv. 27, 28, 29 δέ (𝔓⁴⁹ ℵ A D² Ψ 33 1739ᵐᵍ 𝔐 lat syʰ; Tert) is probably to be read in preference to οὖν (D* F G 1175 b). 𝔓⁴⁹ B 0278 6 104* 1739* 1881 t vgᵐˢ; Cl lack any particle. δέ may have been considered too adversative and therefore either altered or omitted. The semi-dependence on the clothing metaphor of v. 31 now disappears. If v. 31 dealt with one sin, anger, destructive of Christian community life, v. 32 identifies some of the virtues which make it flourish. Col 3.12f contains a much longer list but there the virtues appear as nouns and not adjectives; there seems no reason why AE should have substituted adjectives if he was copying Colossians. The motivation is also expressed slightly differently. The limitation of the desired virtues to life within the community is made quite explicit through 'one another'. γίνεσθε is to be translated neither as 'show yourselves' nor 'become', though the latter sense in fact governs the paraenetic section of the letter.

χρηστός was in common non-Jewish and non-Christian use to describe a good person.[20] Basically a term of relationship it is used

---

[20] Spicq, II, 971–6; K. Weiss, *TWNT*, IX, 472–81.

in the LXX and the NT to describe: (i) God's goodness to humans (Lk 6.35; Rom 2.4; 1 Pet 2.3; for the noun, see Rom 11.22; Tit 3.4); this use is comparatively infrequent in non-Jewish Greek; (ii), as here, of the goodness of people to one another (2 Cor 6.6; Gal 5.22). Since the verse goes on to relate human to divine conduct its use is appropriate here. It is unlikely that there is any play, as in 1 Pet 2.3 which draws on Ps 34.8, on the similarity of the word to Christ.[21] εὔσπλαγχνος, like many terms relating to the emotions, betrays its physiological origin in its structure. A term used by secular writers, though not in the LXX, it is applied in extra-biblical Jewish texts (*T Sim* 4.4; *T Zeb* 5.1; 8.1; 9.7; *Prayer of Manasseh* 7) to both God and humans. In *T Zeb* 5.1; 8.1; *T Benj* 4.2 it is used of the true attitude to everyone in contrast to that towards neighbours, i.e. other Jews; AE uses it of an attitude to other Christians and not to everyone. It appears in the NT at 1 Pet 3.8 and in later Christian usage (Polyc *Phil* 5.2; 6.1; 1 Clem 14.3). The third element in the sequence is expressed (cf Col 3.13) through a present participle, χαριζόμενοι, suggesting an unlimited succession of acts of forgiveness (cf Mt 18.21f). Good and compassionate people will forgive others and so the vices like anger which would destroy the community (v. 31) are themselves destroyed. The verb, though not originally meaning 'to forgive', gained this sense, presumably through its relation to χάρις; it is not used with this sense in the LXX but is in Josephus *Ant* 6.144; Lk 7.42f; 2 Cor 2.7, 10; 12.13; Col 2.13; 3.13 (it retains its older sense in Lk 7.21; Acts 3.14; 25.11, 16; etc.). χαριζόμενοι enters v. 32 naturally because it has been prepared for with χάρις; there is no similar preparation for its use in Col 3.13; if we had to choose this would favour the priority of Ephesians. Theophylact (cf Origen) rather perversely took ἑαυτοῖς reflexively; it is only a stylistic variation from ἀλλήλους to avoid monotony (the same change is found in Col 3.13; cf Lk 23.12; 1 Pet 4.8–10).

The objects of God's forgiveness are expressed differently in the textual tradition where there is strong support ($\mathfrak{P}^{49}$ B D Ψ 0278 33 1739 1881 𝔐 vg^st ww sy bo^mss; Cass) for ἡμῖν rather than ὑμῖν ($\mathfrak{P}^{46}$ ℵ A F G P 6 81 326 365 614 629 *al* it vg^cl co; Cl Or^lat; MVict Ambst). Since the remainder of 4.25–5.2, with the possible exception of 5.2 (see note there), is in the second plural, if the original reading had been ἡμῖν there would have been great pressure to change it to ὑμῖν. Yet the goodness of God toward humans is regularly expressed with the first plural (e.g. Rom 4.24f; 5.1ff; 8.31–9; Eph 1.7) and if the second plural is the correct reading the customary practice may have enforced a change here. On the whole the textual evidence is stronger for the second plural; either would make good sense; they were often confused in copying since in oral dictation they sounded alike.

[21] On the similarity see M. Karrer, *Der Gesalbte. Die Grundlagen des Christustitels* (FRLANT 151), Göttingen, 1990, 71ff.

A motive is now introduced: God has forgiven believers. The same motive appears in Col 3.13 but there it is 'the Lord' who forgives; though there are textual variants in Col 3.13 the context suggests that 'Lord' indicates Christ and not God (support for the reading 'God' is not strong). The aorist suggests the moment of forgiveness as that of conversion/baptism, though it could possibly have been that of the death of Christ. Christ enters the picture in Ephesians because God has forgiven 'in Christ'. καθὼς καί[22] (cf 1.4; 4.4; 5.2, 25, 29) is certainly causal (forgive because God has forgiven you; God's action in Christ is the basis of Christian behaviour); it may also carry a comparative sense (forgive in the way God forgives; this comparative element comes out more clearly in 5.1) though the 'in Christ' would appear to invalidate the comparison. Christ is introduced here as in 2 Cor 5.19; God's forgiveness is linked to what has happened in Christ (cf 1.7). The two adjectives in v. 32a were qualities which could apply both to God and humans; now human behaviour is directly linked to divine. The parable of the unforgiving servant (Mt 18.23–35) teaches that those who have experienced forgiveness should themselves forgive; equally in Jn 13.34; 1 Jn 4.11, 19 (cf T Zeb 7.2) to be loved by God should lead the one loved to love. The basis of Christian action lies in what God has done for Christians. There is however a distinction here in respect of human and divine forgiveness from that in the Lord's Prayer (Mt 6.12, 14; Lk 11.4; cf Mk 11.25; T Zeb 8.1) where human forgiveness precedes divine forgiveness, even if it is not a prerequisite of the latter. Goodness, compassion and a forgiving spirit are essential for those living in community (cf 1QS 2.24f).

Again we note a limitation (cf v. 25) in that forgiveness is directed only towards other members of the community. Yet Christians belong to other groups and communities and are engaged with their members in commercial, industrial and leisure activities and the qualities that are sought here should be seen as much in those relationships as in the church. Barth defends the present restriction to the church by commenting that it is easier to pardon the far-off villain like Genghis Khan than the brother who lives close at hand. This is true, but the Christian may live as close to pagan neighbours and be involved in dealings of many kinds with them as with other Christians. Our verse spells out Christ's new commandment (Jn 13.34) and not that to love neighbours.

Montagnini, art.cit., noting that the injunctions seem independent of one another and arranged in no logical order, suggests that the background to 4.25–32 is a gathering of the community in worship, probably eucharistic worship. Seen in this light the admonitions hang together. The initial

---

[22] On the various meanings of καθώς in the Pauline corpus see K. Romaniuk, 'De usu particulae ΚΑΘΩΣ in epistulis Paulinis', VD 43 (1965) 71–82.

reference to the members/body image in v. 25 would be appropriate in such a context. Lying or deceit (v. 25) was often associated in Judaism with idolatry (e.g. Jer 3.23; 23.14; 2 Chron 30.40 LXX) and Christian worship ('the truth') is the opposite of idolatry. Yet nothing in the passage suggests that Christian and pagan worship are being contrasted or that there was a danger of actual idolatry being introduced into Christian gatherings. Moreover 'neighbour' is an odd word with which to indicate another worshipper; it is not forced on AE by Zech 8.16 for there was no need for him to use this text. The image of the members of the body certainly applies to the church but was widely known and used in the ancient world. Christians were not only members of one another at worship but continued as such even when not gathered in worship and would not have limited the use of the image to the time of their worship. Montagnini also argues that the function of Christian worship is the upbuilding (v. 29) of the community (see 1 Cor 14); this is so, yet upbuilding goes on outside the context of worship (Rom 15.20; 1 Cor 8.1, 10; 10.23 1 Th 5.11). He further says that λαλεῖν, both here and in v. 25, refers to 'proclamation' rather than simple speech (see again its use in 1 Cor 14) and 'grace' (v. 29) has its appropriate place in worship; the use of the plural 'hearers' in v. 29 suggests the community, yet 'hearing' is a natural word to appear in the context of speech and does not of itself imply communal hearing. βλασφημία (v. 31) may be tied in to 1 Cor 12.3, providing another connection with baptism, but as it appears in the sequence of v. 31 it is directed not against God as in 1 Cor 12.3 but against other believers and therefore to introduce a sin against God is irrelevant. Other verses are even more difficult to fit into a liturgical background, above all v. 28 with its argument to avoid stealing but to work and give to those in need. Here Montagnini falls back on Justin Martyr, *Apol* 1.67, where the wealthy help the poor in the context of worship (cf 1 Cor 11.20f), but the explanation we, and almost all commentators, have offered is much simpler. Why is everyone else except thieves exempt from sharing? (This argument does not apply to the normal interpretation which begins in each case with a negative injunction and moves to a positive; there are liars, thieves and angry people in every community.) It is difficult also to see why warnings about anger (vv. 26f, 31) should predominate in instruction about worship. Were assemblies especially quarrelsome places? Being good to others (v. 32) in the same way as God suits general moral behaviour much better than the situation of worship. Why is not letting the sun go down on wrath appropriate to a service? 'Let not the meeting end while anger persists' would be more apt; the injunction is moreover wholly inappropriate to gatherings for worship which took place in the evening, when those of 1 Cor 11–14, on which Montagnini draws so heavily, seem to have taken place.

Our examination of v. 32 has revealed a number of similarities to and differences from Col 3.12f; the probable reason for these is the membership of both AE and A/Col in the same Pauline school rather than dependence of either on the other (cf Best, 'Who used Whom?'). χαρίζετε ἑαυτοῖς καθὼς καὶ ὁ θεός (χριστὸς) ὑμῖν may have been a saying of that school which each author has modified to suit his own requirements.

5.1. The idea of 4.32b, forgive as God forgives, is now widened here into imitation of God and in v. 2 to 'love'. Naturally a widening to imitation can only be partial for it is impossible to imitate God in everything. Since human beings are part of his creation they can create neither him nor one another. It is only in 5.1 that the NT speaks explicitly of the imitation of God but the theme[23] appears in early post-Ephesian literature (Ign *Eph* 1.1; *Trall* 1.2; *Diogn* 10.4–6; Iren 3.20.2).

μιμεῖσθαι and its cognates are rare in the LXX and where they appear they relate to the making of objects to resemble other objects (Wisd 9.8; 15.9; cf Ezek 23.14Aq) or to one person copying the conduct of another (4 Macc 9.23; 13.9; cf Wisd 4.2; Ezek 16.61Aq; the *v.l.* at Ψ 30.6; cf *T Benj* 3.1; 4.1). It is unnecessary to trace the origin of the concept in the Greek world where it was widespread, being used in philosophy (the material world an imitation of the ideal, man a microcosm of the macrocosm), in art (artistic creation imitates reality), in the Mysteries (the experience of the initiate imitates that of the god). In brief, some kind of model is set up for imitation and this appears in varying forms. Important for v. 1 are those places where one person is regarded as imitating, or exhorted to imitate, another: (1) sons to imitate fathers (Isocrates, *To Demonicus* 4.11); (2) subjects, rulers (Xenophon, *Cyropedeia*, VIII 1.21, 24); (3) pupils, teachers (Dio Chrys, *Discourses* 55.4, 5; Seneca, *Ep* 6.5–6); (4) the good are also to be imitated (Isocrates, *To Nicocles* 22.38; 38.61). Parallels exist to most of these in Judaism: (1) 1 Macc 2.51; Philo, *Sacrif Abel* 64; (3) Philo, *Mosis* 1.158; (4) *T Benj* 3.1; 4.1; 4 Macc 9.23; Philo, *Spec Leg* 4.83. *Ps-Phoc* 77 speaks more abstractly of not imitating evil. Philo provides, if not the bridge from the Hellenistic world to Judaism, an example of how Judaism could adopt the theme.[24] In him we find both the philosophical and cosmological aspects and the personal (in addition to the above references see also *Congressu* 59; cf Jos *Ant* 3.123; *T Asher* 4.3; *Ep Arist* 188, 210, 281).

Certain factors operated against the appearance among Jews of the idea of the imitation of God: the initial sin of Adam and Eve as the desire to be like God, the existence of human sin, the second commandment forbidding the making of any likeness to God, the Hellenistic usage of imitation in relation to sculpture. Indeed the thought of the imitation of the invisible God is paradoxical. As a result it was only towards the end of the first century that the idea began to appear in Palestinian Judaism (Abba Schaul in *Midrash Siphre* on Lev 19.2; *Tg Jer* I, Lev 22.28; see SB I, 472f). None of

---

[23] For the theme and its development see W. Michaelis, *TWNT*, IV, 661–78; H. J. Schoeps, 'Von der Imitatio Dei zur Nachfolge Christi', *Aus Frühchristlicher Zeit*, Tübingen, 1950, 286–301; D. M. Stanley, ' "Become Imitators of Me"': The Pauline Conception of Apostolic Tradition', *Bib* 40 (1959) 859–77; W. P. de Boer, *The Imitation of Paul*, Kampen, 1962, 1–80; A. Schulz, *Nachfolgen und Nachahmen* (SANT 6), Munich, 1962, 199–251; H. Kosmala, 'Nachfolge und Nachahmung Gottes (II Im jüdischen Denken)', *ASTI* 3 (1964) 65–110; H. D. Betz, *Nachfolge und Nachahmung Jesus Christi im Neuen Testament* (BHT 37), Tübingen, 1967, 48–136.

[24] See R. A. Wild, ' "Be Imitators of God"': Discipleship in the Letter to the Ephesians', in *Discipleship in the New Testament* (ed. F. F. Segovia), Philadelphia, 1985, 127–43.

this hindered the acceptance of similarity to God in the age to come (cf 1 Jn 3.2). It is sometimes suggested that equivalent ideas to the imitation of God are to be found in the OT (so Michaelis, art.cit.; contrast De Boer, op.cit., 33ff). e.g. following Yahweh, walking in his ways; these ideas however involve obedience. The very centrality of human obedience in the OT may itself have been another factor hindering the concept of imitation from entering Judaism. Lev 19.2 may seem to provide a parallel to imitation with its implication that Jews should exhibit the same holiness as God, and this is certainly how that passage is understood in 1 Pet 1.15f, but in Leviticus the relation is causal rather than comparative. 1 Pet 1.15f (cf Lk 6.36f; Mt 5.44–8; Jn 17.11, 21; Col 3.13, if Lord means God; 1 Jn 4.11) takes it comparatively, showing the idea had entered early Christianity, though Eph 5.1 is its only explicit statement. Paul writes of imitating Christ (1 Cor 11.1; 1 Th 1.6) and instructs his converts to imitate himself (1 Cor 4.16; 11.1; 1 Th 1.6; 2 Th 3.7, 9; Phil 3.17; cf Gal 4.12) and other Christians (1 Th 1.6; 2.14; 2 Th 3.7–9). We should not then be surprised to find AE speaking of the imitation of God; in doing so he goes beyond Paul, being more open to Hellenistic thought (Ernst). Col 3.10 is not preparation for what AE says for its background is not that of imitation in behaviour but the Genesis creation story; this represents another difference between Ephesians and Colossians (see on 4.23f).

If comparison was absent in 4.32b and perhaps also in 5.2 it is clearly present in 5.1; if so, what features of God's activities are believers to imitate (cf Mackay, 207–11)? The context, 4.32 and 5.2 suggests the readiness to forgive and love, love being a generalisation of forgiveness. Though Philo's statement in *Spec Leg* 4.73 may appear similar, his reason is God's creation of people and not his love for them. In 5.1 believers are described as God's beloved children (cf 1.5); ἀγαπητός is used both of groups of Christians and of individual Christians (Rom 1.7; 11.28; 1 Tim 6.2; Rom 16.5, 8; Eph 6.21), and of Christ (Mk 1.11; 9.7). What is the significance of this address? Are believers to imitate God because they are his children (Bouwman) or in the way children should imitate a parent (Chrysostom) or are both ideas present (Salmond)? As we have seen, the imitation theme was used in the ancient world in respect of fathers and sons (cf 1 Cor 4.14, 16); is this why AE introduces children here? Unlike Mt 5.48 our passage lacks an explicit reference to God as Father. Yet believers as God's children is an important theme of Pauline theology (Rom 8.14–21; Gal 3.26; 4.6f; Phil 2.15) and appears in Eph 1.5. Probably then it was the theme of filial imitation which led to the present description of believers as children, yet it would be hazardous to go further and regard this as implying obedience or any kind of obligation. Action comparable to God's action in forgiving and loving is the primary emphasis.

Imitation of God seems somewhat more arid than imitation of Christ, particularly when the latter is understood as 'living like Jesus'. But imitation of Jesus as seen by Paul is not imitation of the day-to-day life of the historical Jesus; it relates rather to his incarnation and death (Phil 2.5–11; 2 Cor 8.9; Rom 15.3, 7). It may be this which enables AE to move directly from imitation of God to loving like Christ (v. 2), a movement perhaps also inspired in part by the depiction of Jesus as the image of God in the Colossian hymn (1.15), a hymn probably known in the Pauline school. It is through Christ that God's love and forgiveness are known and it is essentially in these that imitation should take place.

2. Since they are children whom God loves (v. 1) love should (καί is almost 'and therefore') characterise the behaviour of believers (for περιπατεῖν see on 2.2; 4.1, 23; the present imperative probably means 'keep on behaving', see MHT, 75). While AE's reference to love might be thought to come from Col 3.14 it is so much the essential characteristic of Christian existence (cf 3.14–19) that its introduction here is perfectly natural and there is no need to identify a precise verse in Colossians from which it may have been drawn. Love builds up the body of Christ (4.15f) and the preceding context suggests AE has the Christian community continually in mind. The nature of love is spelt out as little here as in Mk 12.31 (contrast 1 Cor 13.1ff), though a partial description lies in the positive statements of 4.25ff. No direct connection was made in v. 1 between God's love and that of believers; the latter is now linked to the love of Christ (for the use of the article with Christ see on 1.10). His love is the supreme motivation of human love (cf 1 Jn 3.16).[25] As in 4.32 καθώς καί[26] may be either causal (Christ's love as motivation) or comparative (Christ's love as example) or a mixture of both. As in 4.32 it is difficult to take it as purely comparative for Christ's love, or God's love in Christ, is unique in that Christ gave himself for all. Our love cannot lead us to act soteriologically as he did, though in a willingness to forget ourselves and put others first it can be said to resemble his love.

In the manuscripts the two pronouns in the verse vary between the first and second plurals. In view of their proximity to one another in clauses of similar content it is probable that we should read the same person in both cases. In respect of the first occurrence the evidence is relatively well balanced: ἡμᾶς—𝔓⁴⁶ ℵ² D F G Ψ 0278 33 1739 1881 𝔐 lat sy; Clᵖᵗ Hier; ὑμᾶς—ℵ* A B P 0159 81 326 1175 1241ˢ pc it co; Clᵖᵗ MVict Ambst Spec. This balance is not true in respect of the second occurrence where the evidence for ὑμῶν (B 0278ᶜ 1175 pc b m* co; MVict Ambst Spec) is much weaker than that for ἡμῶν 𝔓⁴⁶˙ ⁴⁹ ℵ A D G K P Ψ 0159 33 81 it vg syrᵖˑʰ; Cl Or Ambst Chrys Hier). We therefore read the first plural throughout. It goes

---

²⁵ Cf Schulz, op.cit., 275–7.
²⁶ Cf Romaniuk, art.cit.; see on 4.32.

better with the similar formula of 5.25 which refers to the church. This reading is supported if either all or part of ὁ χριστὸς ... ἡμῶν is derived from a traditional credal formula, for such formulae are usually in the first plural (1 Pet 3.18 is an exception); the same would be true if, as is most unlikely, part of v. 2 is a quotation from a hymn. The consistent use of the second plural in the surrounding verses could have misled scribes into adopting it in v. 2. The possibility also exists of confusion through oral dictation (see on 4.32). On the readings see Metzger, ad loc. The variant ὑπὲρ ἡμῶν ἐν φθορᾷ for ἡμῶν προσφοράν has very weak support and may be ignored, as can the variation of the order of the words.

In v. 2b action is ascribed to Christ.[27] Normally it is God who is said to love people and either he or a human agent to hand Christ over to death (Rom 8.32). Whenever Christ is the subject of παραδιδόναι (Rom 4.25; 1 Cor 11.23; Mk 9.31; 10.33; 14.41, etc.) the verb is usually passive and the true subject is God or a human. But here, as in 5.25; Gal 2.20, Christ is the real subject, the verbs are active and in each case the aorist tense refers to the historical Christ. Here it is believers whom he loves, in 5.25 the church and in Gal 2.20 Paul. This strongly suggests the use of an accepted form (the idea goes back at least to von Soden). Popkes, 348–41, takes the whole expression as pre-Pauline but it may only be the παραδιδόναι reference which is so (cf Kramer; Perrin; Wengst, 60–77). Within the Pauline school, or at least that part of it to which AE belonged, what Paul said in particular of himself (Gal 2.20) has been generalised so that all believers are set on his level, not that Paul would have wished to imply that he was the unique object of Christ's redemptive activity. If then this is a formula in use within the Pauline school, the acceptance of the first plural reading is made easier. As a formula it may have been originally connected to baptism (cf 5.25; Tit 2.13) with its inspiration coming from Isaiah 53.[28] Christ loved us 'and so', or 'in that he', gave himself up.[29] Christ's love is actualised in his self-surrender (Aquinas, depending on Gregory the Great). Because of the dual usage of παραδιδόναι (God, or Judas and others, gave him up) AE's readers would at once see a reference to Christ's death and this did not need to be explicitly stated. That this death was for the benefit of others was a

---

[27] On v.2b see Romaniuk, L'amour 36–45; E. Lohse, Märtyrer und Gottesknecht (FRLANT 64), 2nd edn, Göttingen, 1963; Kramer, §§25–7; W. Popkes, Christus Traditus (ATANT 49), Zürich, 1967; N. Perrin, 'The Use of (παραδιδόναι in Connection with the Passion of Jesus in the New Testament', Der Ruf Jesu und die Antwort der Gemeinde (FS J. Jeremias, ed. E. Lohse), Göttingen, 1970, 202–12; Wengst, Formeln; N. A. Dahl, Jesus in the Memory of the Early Church, Minneapolis, 1976, 3–9; Schenke, 331–3.

[28] Cf K. Romaniuk, 'L'origine des formules pauliniennes "Le Christ s'est livré pour nous" et "Le Christ nous a aimé et s'est livré pour nous"', NT 5 (1962) 55–76.

[29] Cf A. Urbán, 'La coordinada modal en el Neuvo Testament', Filologia Neotestamentaria 1 (1988) 193–208.

pre-Pauline belief (Rom 3.24f; 4.25a; 5.6–8; 8.32; Gal 1.4; 1 Cor 15.3–5)[30] which Paul continued to hold (e.g. 1 Th 5.10; Rom 14.15; 1 Cor 8.11; 2 Cor 5.14f; and Gal 2.20, if this is not to be placed in the pre-Pauline material); it is also found in Christian literature preceding or contemporary with Ephesians, if Ephesians is non-Pauline (e.g. Mk 10.45; 1 Jn 2.2; 4.10; 1 Pet 3.18). Gentile Christians would have been able to grasp something of the significance of such a death, for dying so that a city or state might benefit and dying as atoning sacrifice were well-known ideas in the ancient world.[31] AE does not provide us here or elsewhere with sufficient information to enable the placing of his view of the benefits of Christ's death in terms of later developed soteriology, e.g. whether Christ died representatively, as a substitute, as liberating ransom, or as atoning sacrifice. Nor can we trace back from his brief reference a clear path to the origin of the idea in Isaiah, in the Maccabean martyrs or in some other source (cf Wengst, 60–77, for discussion). Lacking information about AE's views it is unwise to speculate. It was not his intention here to express a soteriological theory but to remind his readers of Christ's death as one from which they have benefited so that they themselves will live lovingly. The nature of the benefit they receive from Christ's life, death and resurrection is spelt out in other parts of the letter: their sins are forgiven (1.7), they are adopted as God's children (1.5), they have been raised with Christ and sit with him in the heavenlies (2.5f), they belong to his body (4.7ff), they are new people (4.24).

The final words of the verse, which are not part of the formula, are intended to drive home the need to love, but do they not imply an understanding of Christ's death as sacrificial? προσφορά is not a word strongly associated with the sacrificial system; it is not found in the LXX translation of Leviticus (though Aq and Th have it at 1.2); it is frequent only in Ecclesiasticus. θυσία is a very general word. The two words are associated in Ψ 39.7, which is quoted in Ecclus 34.19; Heb 10.5, and with other sacrificial terms in Dan 3.38 (LXX and Th). In view of their linkage in Ψ 39.7 and its Christian usage (Heb 10.5) the Psalm is probably AE's source, though not necessarily directly. Neither noun can be given a precise equivalent in the sacrificial system and they are probably a hendiadys (Lincoln) for the whole system (καί is not explicative as Belser suggests) and illustrate once again AE's use of two words when one would do. Atoning offerings would thus be included but they would not be at

---

[30] See M.-L. Gubler, *Die frühesten Deutungen des Todes Jesu*, Göttingen, 1977, 206ff; G. Delling, *Der Kreuzestod Jesu in der urchristlichen Verkündigung*, Göttingen, 1972, 9–16.
[31] Cf M. Hengel, *The Atonement. The Origin of the Doctrine in the New Testament*, London, 1981, 9ff; S. K. Williams, *Jesus' Death as Saving Event* (Harvard Dissertations in Religion), Missouri, MO, 1975, 153–61; Simpson, 114, n. 2.

the top of AE's mind. When we recollect also the way in which sacrifice is spiritualised in the OT (Hos 6.6; Isa 1.11–15; Mic 6.6–8; Ps 50.13f, 23; 51.17; 141.2; cf 1QS 9.4f; 10.8, 14) and then in the NT (Rom 12.1; 15.17; Phil 2.17; 4.18; Heb 13.15f; προσφορά is used of thanksgiving in Acts 24.17 and θυσία of financial support in Phil 4.18)[32] it seems probable that in our verse it refers only to Christ's self-sacrifice. This should drive AE's readers to love. That this was how the words were understood in the early church can be seen from their application to martyrs in Ign *Rom* 4.2; *Mart Polyc* 14.1, 2. That it is also AE's view is shown by the closing words of the verse which do not stress the benefits of Christ's death for his readers but the acceptability of Christ's action to God.

The final phrase is frequent in the OT (the genitive εὐωδίας is adjectival, a Semitism); though originally understood physically as if God was pleased with the smell rising from sacrifices (Gen 8.21; Exod 29.18; Lev 2.9; etc.) it, like sacrifice, was spiritualised (Ezek 20.41; Dan 4.37a LXX; *T Levi* 3.6; Phil 4.18; cf *Barn* 2.10) and applied to life and action which was pleasing to God. Probably then τῷ θεῷ, though its position suggests it completes the reference to sacrifice (so Abbott), should be taken with εἰς ὀσμήν (there is no reason for taking it with the verb); εἰς ὀσμήν requires something to complete it and is completed regularly in this way in the OT (Exod 29.18, 25, 41; Lev 1.9, 13, 17; 2.9; 3.5; etc.). Alternatively it might be taken as referring to the whole phrase as in many translations, 'a fragrant offering and sacrifice to God'. AE has thus concluded the traditional formula with a great flourish of praise wholly in his manner.

The motivation to conduct provided here and in 4.32 is not just an additional motivation comparable with those in 4.25–31 but is the basic motivation in a Christian ethic in a way those of 4.25–31 are not (cf Halter). They were peripheral; this is central.

---

[32] See Best, 'Spiritual Sacrifice', *Int* 14 (1960) 273–99, and the references given in the note on 2.21.

XII

FROM LUST TO LIGHT
(5.3–14)

P. Dacquino, 'Filii lucis in Eph. 5,8–14', *VD* 36 (1958) 221–4; Roels, 221–6; L. R. Stackowiak, 'Die Antithese Licht-Finsternis—Ein Thema der paulinischen Paränese', *TQ* 143 (1963) 385–421; Kuhn, *NTS*; N. A. Dahl, 'Der Epheserbrief und der verlorene erste Brief des Paulus an die Korinther', *Abraham unser Vater* (FS O. Michel, ed. O. Betz, M. Hengel, P. Schmidt), Leiden/Cologne, 1963, 65–77; Braun, I, 219–22; M. Haug, 'Kinder des Lichts' in Dahl, 149–52; Gnilka, 'Paränetische Traditionem'; Lindemann, *Aufhebung*, 67–71; Halter, 269–81.

3 But sexual misconduct and every kind of impurity or greed
  should not even be named among you,
    as befits those who are holy,
4   and no obscene act and no foolish or smutty talk,
    which are not fitting,
  but rather thanksgiving.
5   For certainly know this,
    that no one who is unchaste or impure or covetous,
    that is an idolator,
    has an inheritance in the kingdom of Christ and of God.
6 Let no one deceive you with specious arguments,
  for because of these (sins) the wrath of God comes upon
    disobedient people.
7   Do not then participate in their sins.
8 For once you were darkness but now light in the Lord;
  behave as children of light
9   (for light's fruit is in all goodness and uprightness and
    truth)
10   finding out what is pleasing to the Lord,
11   and have no share in the unfruitful works of darkness,
    but rather reprove,
12   for it is shameful even to speak of what they have done in
    secret,
13   but all that is reproved by the light is revealed,
14   for everything that is revealed is light;
    therefore it (he) says
      Awake, O sleeper
      and rise up from the dead,
      and Christ shall shine for you.

472

Having dealt with a number of miscellaneous sins in 4.25–5.2, where he ends with a strong Christian motivation, AE now concentrates on two main but related themes: negatively the avoidance of certain sins, predominantly of a sexual nature, and positively the need to live as children of light. Both recall 4.17–24, the first because he mentions in v. 3 two of the sins of 4.19, to which he did not refer in 4.25–5.2, and the second through the contrast he draws between the readers' former condition of darkness ('the old person', cf 4.22) and their present condition of light ('the new person', cf 4.24). Though at first sight a connection may appear to exist between sexual misconduct and physical darkness, this should not be pushed, for prostitutes and mistresses are visited as regularly in daylight as at night; the darkness is moral rather than physical. The two themes however are linked through the idea of participation in vv. 7, 11. This paragraph differs from the preceding in that the sins discussed in it are not criticised because of the harm they may do to other members of the community and are not connected to the pattern of God's love in Christ; instead they are set in the light of the relationship of believers to God. Since neither sexual sin nor greed necessarily involves other members of the community, they need to be given a different setting and motivation.

Verses 3–5 are clearly similar to Col 3.5–7 in thought and language but vv. 8–14 are not linked in any way with Colossians. Since Col 3.5–7 probably depends on a vice catalogue (cf O'Brien, Lohse, Gnilka, etc.) it is impossible to prove AE depends here on Colossians and not directly on that catalogue. In addition to his use of material similar to that in Col 3.5–7, AE employs a number of traditional terms and concepts (kingdom, inheritance, wrath of God, the contrasts of light and darkness, hidden and made known), and concludes in v. 14 with a verse from a hymn or song. Kirby, 148, suggests that 4.25–5.5 is based on the second table of the Decalogue. While many of the sins in these verses can be related to the commandments they do not appear in the same order, and there is no apparent reason why AE should not have retained the order of the Decalogue; the connection moreover is at times tenuous. There is also no abrupt change at v. 6; even if those who speak deceptively do not belong, or claim to belong, to the community we do not move at this point, as Lindemann suggests, to a consideration of the relationship of believers to the world. Nothing in vv. 6ff deals with the attitude believers should take up to the world other than the simple rejection of its ways; they are neither told to evangelise unbelievers nor to treat them kindly or cruelly. This lack of interest in the outside world is confirmed in that vv. 3–5 have no comment to make on the effect of believers on the prostitutes and mistresses to whom they resort and they display no interest in the reaction of the victims of their greed. AE does however take into account the effect of the sins of believers on their relationship to God; they will cease to be thankful to him (v. 4) and lose their position in the church (vv. 5f). What interests AE is the purity of the lives of believers so that nothing is done which by being unfitting might harm the community. The goodness of individual believers and the goodness of the whole community are related. Verses 6ff treat the way God will deal with impure believers and how the community should deal with those believers who sin. In the final issue this is not a matter of formal discipline but of speaking and living in such a way that 'sinners' within the community will be led to reform their ways.

3.[1] Verses 3, 4 are probably to be taken as one sentence with the nouns of v. 4 depending on the verb of v. 3. AE's reference to love in v. 2 may have reminded him of the amount of illicit love in the world which members of the community have left and which may still attract them. He moves also from the theme of self-sacrifice in 5.2 to the danger of self-indulgence (Stott).

The series of three nouns in this verse together with another three in v. 4 and the cognate adjectives of those of v. 3 in v. 5 and the series of three virtues in v. 9 are sometimes said to imply that AE here draws on some of the catalogues of vices and virtues current in the ancient world.[2] Whether the first Christians were more influenced in their use of this form by Judaism or Hellenism is irrelevant since by the time of Ephesians the form was already well established in Christian moral instruction; for lists of vices see Mk 7.21f; Rom 1.29–31; 13.12; 1 Cor 5.10f; 6.9f; 2 Cor 12.20; Gal 5.19–21 and of virtues 2 Cor 6.6f; Gal 5.22f; Phil 4.8. There is no evidence for the existence of basic lists of vices and virtues from which selections were made to create the existing NT lists. It would however appear that the lists of Eph 5.3, 5 may be drawn from the longer list lying behind that of Col 3.5 and not reflect AE's direct knowledge of Colossians; if he has drawn on pre-existing lists AE has made his material look less like a list through the use of connecting particles and the generalising functions of πᾶς. The lists of vv. 4, 9 seem to be his own creation and not in any way to

---

[1] On this verse see E. Peters, ' "Nec Nominatur in Verbis ..." (Ef 5, 3)', *Revista de Cultura Biblica* 3 (1959) 39–43.

[2] On the catalogue form see B. S. Easton, 'New Testament Ethical Lists', *JBL* 51 (1932) 1–12; A. Vögtle, *Die Tugend- und Lasterkataloge im Neuen Testament*, Münster, 1936; S. Wibbing, *Die Tugend- und Lasterkataloge im Neuen Testament* (BZNW 25), Berlin, 1959; G. E. Cannon, *The Use of Traditional Materials in Colossians*, Macon, GA, 1963, 51–94; E. Kamlah, *Die Form der katologischen Paränese im Neuen Testament* (WUNT 7), Tübingen, 1964; J. Thomas 'Formgesetze des Begriffs-Katalogs im N.T.', *TZ* 24 (1968) 15–28; E. Schweizer, 'Gottesgerechtigkeit und Lasterkataloge bei Paulus [inkl. Kol und Eph]', *Rechtfertigung* (FS E. Käsemann, ed. J. Friedrich, W. Pohlmann, P. Stuhlmacher), Göttingen, 1976, 461–77, id. 'Traditional Ethical Patterns in the Pauline and Post-Pauline Letters and Their Development [lists of vices and house-tables]', *Text and Interpretation* (FS M. Black; ed. E. Best, R. McL. Wilson), Cambridge, 1979, 195–209; Berger, *Formgeschichte*, 148–54; id. *ANRW*, 1088–92.

depend on other lists, that of v. 9 not even being three distinct virtues but three ways of describing the Christian ethic as a whole. The use of lists would appear to be more appropriate to a general letter like Ephesians than to a letter addressed to a particular situation. All the Ephesian lists are brief; none exceeds three in number. AE has a love of triads (1.18f; 3.6; 4.2, 4, 5, 6, 13, 17f, 19, 32; 5.3, 4, 5, 9, 19, cf the three sections of the HT); triads are common in the literature of all cultures; they appear regularly in fairy-tales; were the use of lists in ethical instruction not known AE's brief lists would probably have passed unnoticed in respect of their form. The longest list in the letter, 4.31, relates only to one vice, anger, rather than to a variety as found in other lists of vices. We hesitate therefore to class the triads of Ephesians as examples of the catalogue 'form', seeing them rather as a product of the way AE thinks; his use of connecting particles confirms this. It may be that the compilation of lists is a general human phenomenon; we regularly draw up lists of things to buy when going shopping or of things to pack when going on holiday. While it is true that ethical lists appear in Judaism and Hellenism and in the cultures on which they depend, it has never been shown that they do not appear in wholly independent cultures; until this has been done the alternative explanation that this is just one of the ways in which the mind works cannot be refuted. It is interesting that no one seems ever to have classified the triad of virtues of 1 Cor 13.13 as a 'list'.

Two of the three vices named in 4.19 are now repeated and the third replaced with πορνεία, thereby bringing out the sexual connotation of ἀκαθαρσία. A similar triad is found in CD 4.17f with 'defilement of the sanctuary' replacing one of the two references to sexual sin.[3] πορνεία has a wide range of meanings in relation to sexual behaviour including fornication, adultery, homosexuality, prostitution, incest;[4] 'fornication' is therefore too narrow a translation. The context normally indicates its precise significance and since this gives no help here we must take it as referring to all types of sexual misconduct as viewed from a Judaeo-Christian perspective and not a Hellenistic. Jews indeed believed that Gentiles were not pure in relation to sex (m AZ 2.1), but not all Hellenistic counsel in respect of sexual behaviour was libertine. In one Philadelphian cult (see Barton and Horsley) male members of the group are denied sexual relations with married women, both slave and free, other than their own wives; they are also denied sexual relations with boys and virgin girls. Married women were treated more strictly than men and not permitted sexual relations with anyone other than their husbands. Men were not generally forbidden recourse to prostitutes; Musonius Rufus is an exception (Frag 12, Hense, 64.5–12). Even though Jews were scornful of Gentile sexual

[3] See H. Kosmala, 'The Three Nets of Belial', *ASTI* 4 (1965) 91–113.
[4] See B. Malina, 'Does *Porneia* mean fornication?', *NT* 14 (1972) 10–17; J. Jenson, 'Does *Porneia* mean fornication? A Critique of Bruce Malina', *NT* 20 (1978) 161–84; F. Hauck and S. Schulz, *TWNT*, VI, 579–95.

behaviour, their own literature contains so·many rebukes about it in relation to themselves that they could not legitimately adopt a holier-than-thou attitude. Various sexual sins are rejected not only in the OT but in later writing (e.g. Ecclus 23.16–27; T Simeon 5.3; T Levi 14.5; T Jud 14.2ff; CD 4.17, 20; 1QS 4.9ff; Philo, Spec Leg 3.51). πορνεία appears regularly in the NT vice lists (Mk 7.21; Gal 5.19; Col 3.5); Paul continually inveighed against it (Rom 1.26ff; 1 Cor 5.1; 6.13ff; 7.2; 10.8; 2 Cor 12.21; Gal 5.19; 1 Th 4.3).

As in 4.19 πᾶσα is joined to ἀκαθαρσία (see on 4.19 for the term); it and πορνεία are associated in 2 Cor 12.21; Gal 5.19; 1 Th 4.3, 7; Col 3.5. AE has then in mind the broadest possible spectrum of sexual misconduct (Lev 18.6–30 contains a long list of sexual impurities). In view of this sexual 'atmosphere' the introduction (as in 4.19) of the third term, πλεονεξία, seems surprising (for its meaning and associations see 4.19). It is set alongside the other two terms disjunctively (ἤ; cf Meyer, Macpherson), indicating it is not a sin of the same type; in v. 5 it is connected to idolatry. There is no need then to see here a reference to unrestricted sexual greed (Lincoln) or sensual indulgence at the expense of others (Westcott) though greed and sexual misconduct are found together (cf T Levi 14.6; T Jud 18.2; 1QS 4.9–11; CD 4.17f as well as in various vice lists). None of this is enough to prove that πλεονεξία has sexual overtones. The furthest we can go is to say that wealth permits sexual indulgence. Greed is of course regularly condemned by secular moralists, e.g. Dio Chrysostom, Or 17.1–11. The three sins of v. 3 mentioned here as possible sins of believers are the 'grosser' sins and the more subtle like pride are not mentioned; these are even more likely to disrupt a community; perhaps AE feels he has dealt with such sins in 4.2f and is not now discussing what interferes with the harmony of the community. The objection that pride and similar sins are not mentioned may, however, arise out of a theological attitude which places pride among the worst sins and sees it as lying behind and creating others. It may however be precisely because AE regarded avarice as a sin which can be the source of other sins, the love of money being the root of all evil (1 Tim 6.10), that he concentrates on it here. This sentiment was widely accepted in the ancient world (for references see commentaries on 1 Timothy) and entered Judaism and Christianity (Philo, Spec Leg 4.65; Decal 173; Mos 2.186; Ps-Phoc 42; Polycarp, Phil 4.1). In AE's eyes greed may not then have been one of the 'grosser' sins but one out of which others grew.

None of the three sins should be even mentioned (μηδὲ ὀνομαζέσθω, cf Robertson, 1173); with this AE drives home his point even more strongly that they are not to be committed (cf Ps-Isocrates, To Demonicus 15). It is presumably within the community that they are not to be mentioned and this emphasises AE's concern for its spiritual health rather than for its reputation among outsiders. It is however impossible for the community to avoid mentioning the sins. AE has already done so and wherever the letter is read aloud they will again be mentioned. Paul could not have dealt with the sexual offences of the Corinthian church (cf chaps. 5, 6) if he had not been able to name them. The Fathers continually refer to them, as have preachers down the ages. People cannot be warned against them unless they are named. The clause cannot then be taken literally. Perhaps it was caused through a combination of the reference to idolatry and the OT passages which say false gods should not be named (Exod 23.13; Hos 2.17; Zech 13.2) but the approach is an obvious one and is found in secular writers (Herod. II 138.1); it could thus easily have appeared spontaneously. We may regard the sentiment either as an exaggeration or as an indication that unnecessary discussion of these sins concentrates attention on them; 'words are roads to deeds' (Chrysostom); it is often argued today that the showing of sex and violence on TV leads to yet more sex and violence.

AE now supplies a reason for not mentioning or committing these sins, καθὼς πρέπει ἁγίοις, a reason repeated in v. 4 in different words, ἃ οὐκ ἀνῆκεν (for the tense see Burton §32; BDR §388.2; MHT, 90, Robertson, 919f). The sentiment is taken from Stoic thought where it was used of conduct appropriate to various types of people in differing situations.[5] Appearing only in the later parts of the NT (1 Tim 2.10; Tit 2.1; cf Barn 4.9), it would be familiar to Greek readers. Here the type of people who are in mind is specified by ἅγιοι where the absence of the article places the stress not on membership of a group, 'the saints', but on a type of conduct which can be described as 'holy' (Belser, Schnackenburg, Lincoln) and not, as in Stoicism, on conduct which is in accordance with nature. Sexual sin, impurity and greed do not accord with holiness (cf 1 Th 4.3–7).

4. The first three nouns of this verse continue the dependence on the verb of v. 3. It is true that the second and third in referring to forms of speech do not apply to activities in the same way as the nouns of v. 3 but the first noun is similar to those of v. 3 and 'speaking' is not far removed from 'naming'; there is moreover no reason to expect too great exactness in a rather loosely formed argument (cf Lincoln). 5.3 and 5.4 are linked by καί and have a similar motivation, conduct appropriate to a believer, though the repetition of this motivation implies that AE saw them as two triads

[5] Cf M. Pohlenz, 'Τὸ Πρέπον' 'Nachrichten von der Gesellschaft der Wissenschaften in Göttingen, Philol.-Historische Klasse, Berlin, 1933, 53–92. On ἀνῆκεν see K. Weidinger, Die Haustafeln, ein Stück urchristlicher Paränese, Leipzig, 1928, 42ff.

rather than one list of six vices; the first appearance of the motivation at the conclusion of v. 3 also indicates an end to its list by breaking the direct connection. The two triads are to be distinguished further in that that of v. 3, unlike that of v. 4, is taken up again in v. 5 (perhaps the sins of v. 4 are regarded as less heinous, so Rienecker). The two verses are thus parallel rather than continuous.

The three connecting particles in v. 4 vary in the manuscripts between καί and ἤ. The variant καί in respect of the third is the least strongly supported (𝔓⁴⁶ 629 pc; Cyp) and may be ignored. The variant ἤ (A D* F G Ψ 81 104 1241ˢ pc latt sa; Irˡᵃᵗ et) in respect of the first particle though possessing more wide-ranging support is difficult to fit into the context. The variant ἤ (ℵ* A D* F G P 0278 81 104 326 365 1175 1241ˢ 1739 2464 pc latt syʰ sa boᵐˢˢ; Irˡᵃᵗ) in respect of the second καί (𝔓⁴⁶ ℵ¹ B D² 33 𝔐 syᵖ (bo); Cl Hier) is the best supported and textually there is very little to choose between it and καί. Since the second and third substantives refer to speech and the first does not necessarily do so, they are better dissociated from it by καί than by ἤ which would set them all on a level. ἤ may have been produced by a desire to conform the first noun with the other two as indicating shameful speech.

The three vices of v. 4 are *hapax legomena* in the NT and do not occur regularly outside it in vice catalogues. αἰσχρότης strictly refers to shameful behaviour, but in the light of the following two words referring to speech many commentators (e.g. Gnilka, Barth, Lincoln) understand it of shameful speech; the following nouns, with καί understood explicatively, would then be taken as illustrations of such speech. However, there is a word for shameful speech, αἰσχρολογία, which is found in Col 3.8; AE must have known it and, since he has not used it, it seems unlikely that he had intended here a reference to speech. Whether the noun refers to speech or behaviour, it is a general word indicating various forms of obscene action or speech. μωρολογία, strictly 'the language of fools', does not refer to the way those of low intelligence or lack of education speak. Those who describe other members of the community as fools are in danger of hell fire (Mt 5.22); the cross is foolishness to non-Christians (1 Cor 1.18); foolish talk is probably then impious speech. At Qumran it was subject to discipline (1QS 7.9, 14f). In 1QS 10.21–3 it is set in the context of other verbal sins and, as here, contrasted with thankfulness, but there is no reason to see dependence; there are too many other differences. As in Qumran, however, it is the effect of such talk on the community and not on the outside world which is at issue. The first two nouns in v. 4 are thus very general words and commentators and preachers have drawn much from them; AE does not give us enough information to deduce his precise meaning. The final term, εὐτραπελία (the disjunctive ἤ before it marks it off as a distinct vice from the preceding; Ellicott), is unusual in that it was used in various ways.[6] The formation of the word suggests it should have a good sense and it often does; however as Van der Horst has shown it also had from the beginning 'negative overtones nearly as often as positive ones' (173). It has no necessary connection with speech and probably takes on this aspect from its present context and might be translated 'suggestive language' or 'smutty talk', perhaps including humour with *double entendre*; it indicates the type of humour to be found in a pornographic magazine. Its humour 'is often also at someone else's expense'. It could describe 'the way of life of urbane high-society persons, the cultivated, no doubt well-to-do young men, who could afford the life of a gentleman'. It can therefore have a bad sense, probably associated with sex. To some extent the two sins of speech here spell out the more general reference of 4.29. The condemnation of sins of the tongue is a popular ethical theme (e.g. Ecclus 28.13ff; Jas 3.1ff). If it is correct to read ἤ between the second and third nouns, then ἃ οὐκ ἀνῆκεν (for the phrase see on v. 3) probably only refers to these two nouns.

The verse ends positively: if people are to talk in the community then what they say should not be obscene, smutty or impious but full of thankfulness. This provides a good contrast to what has preceded. Origen, followed by Jerome and many others, reads εὐχαριτία for εὐχαριστία, or understands the latter in the former sense, suggesting that the opposite of improper speech was pleasant or gracious talk.[7] There is however no good reason either to emend the word or to understand εὐχαριστία as pleasant speech. 'Thankfulness' provides a much stronger contrast with the earlier words (cf 1QS 10.21–4) and is the word's normal meaning in the NT (cf 5.20; 1 Th 5.18; Col 2.7; 3.15) where Paul's letters usually contain a section of thanksgiving (cf 1.16). There is also probably no word play with εὐτραπελία. Unlike the other nouns in v. 4, it should not be linked to the verb of v. 3 but completed with ἐν ὑμῖν and ἔστω or γινέσθω (Belser). The thanksgiving will be offered to God and this gives a subtle twist to the discussion. Since 4.25 the dangers which might destroy community life have been in the forefront and have provided the motivation away from sin and towards goodness. Now God is introduced and, as we shall see, he becomes increasingly a felt presence in vv. 5ff. The ethic, no longer set solely in relation to the need for good community relations, is given a divine perspective, a return to the thrust of 4.17–24. Thankfulness to God will be expressed within the community in its worship (5.20) and daily life (1.16ff). Just as the recipient of the thanksgiving is not explicitly

[6] See P. W. van der Horst, 'Is Wittiness Unchristian? A note on εὐτραπελία in Eph. v. 4', *Miscellanea Neotestamentica II* (SupNT 48), Leiden, 1978, 163–77, from whom all the quotations in the text are drawn.
[7] Cf O. Casel, 'Εὐχαριστία—εὐχαριτία', *BZ* 18 (1928) 84f.

mentioned, so neither is its content; the remainder of the letter shows it relates to what God has done for the members of the community in choosing them, forgiving their sins, raising them with Christ and making them into new people. Not sexual lust and covetousness, but thanksgiving is the fitting response to God's goodness and is basic to Christian existence.

5. The triad of vices of v. 3 is now repeated by naming the persons who commit or embody them rather than the vices themselves, and a threat is added as motivation. Possibly AE chose to name people rather than sins because he was concerned, not about occasional lapses in conduct, but about those who habitually indulged in illicit sex and greed.

ἴστε can be taken either indicatively or imperatively; in the light of the frequent imperatives from 4.19 onwards and in the verses that follow, the latter sense is better (*pace* Bruce), even though the seeming parallel of 1 Cor 6.9 has the indicative (Gal 5.21 implies an imperative). The imperative has been the normal interpretation since at least Clem Alex, *Paed* 3.4. Coupled with ἴστε is the participle γινώσκοντες; the two are difficult to distinguish in meaning though many have attempted to do so (e.g. Murray, Westcott, Hendriksen); if they are distinguished then τοῦτο becomes difficult (Hugedé). The participle strengthens the imperative (BDR §422 n. 3; MHT, 156f), possibly being used in imitation of Hebraic idiom where the infinitive absolute is used to strengthen the cognate verb; the verbs here, though they have the same meaning, are not cognate and despite the examples of 1 Kgdms 20.3 and Gen 31.15 (cf Ewald; Zerwick §61; MH, 444) this solution is hardly possible. Porter attempts to solve the difficulty by taking vv. 3–5 as a chiasmus.[8] Most of v. 3 and v. 5 could certainly be the balancing initial A and final Aᶜ lines of such a chiasmus but Porter is forced to withdraw part of Aᶜ to form his Bᶜ. τοῦτο ἴστε (C) and γινώσκοντες ὅτι (C´) are his balancing central section. This solution results in the loss of the reference to thanksgiving as the climax to vv. 3–4. The two references to the fitting nature of conduct which should surely balance one another appear in the same section (B). It is not then possible to create a satisfactory chiasmus here. A primitive corruption of the text (Masson) is possible but exceedingly difficult to prove and there is no reason to put a period between the verbs and link the first to v. 4 (so Hofmann; γάρ prohibits this) or to suppose an anacoluthon (Haupt). There must be a simpler solution, and it is probably better to regard the use of the two different verbs as another instance of AE's plerophoric style imparting an impressive emphasis to what is said. The triad of sinners is listed using the idiom πᾶς ... οὐ which while Semitic is also acceptable in Greek (BDR §302 n. 2; MH, 22f, 434; MHT, 196; Robertson, 753) and acts to stress further the importance of what is being said.

A reference to idolatry is added through ὅ ἐστιν[9] (cf BDR §132.2)

---

[8] S. E. Porter, 'ἴστε γινώσκοντες in Ephesians 5, 5. Does Chiasm Solve a Problem?', *ZNW* 81 (1990) 270–5.

[9] The variant ὅς ἐστιν of A D 0278 𝔐; Cl is an obvious correction of the neuter to the masculine in a desire to make the phrase fit its context better. If accepted it would make clear that idolatry referred to covetousness alone.

to the triad of those who act wrongly (for the separate vices see notes on 4.19; 5.3). Does this reference apply only to the final member of the triad or to all of it? πᾶς and ὅ, not ὅς (Moule, 130), might be regarded as holding the three together as a unit; there is much in Jewish tradition which relates sexual lust and idolatry (e.g. Israel going awhoring after other gods, cf Rev 2.20); sexual sin and covetousness are often explicitly connected (Wisd 14.12; T Reub 4.6; T Jud 23.1; T Benj 10.10); sexual sin and idolatry would be linked in the minds of AE's readers through ritual prostitution. There is however also a connection in Jewish tradition between covetousness and idolatry (T Jud 19.1); in Col 3.5, which may represent the thinking of the Pauline school and therefore of AE, idolatry is related only to covetousness. It is also easier to see money and possessions as idols (cf Mt 6.24; Lk 16.13) since these are 'things'; sex or sexual desire is not in itself a 'thing' and cannot be worshipped, though 'sex-idols', who are particular people, may be; but even these are not permanent like money and possessions but constantly change; sexual lust may be continuous but not the person who is desired. It is best then to associate idolatry only with covetousness. In Jewish eyes idolatry was the most deadly divergence from the true way and it is surprising to see it introduced here only in a subordinate clause; it may be AE does not view it as a direct temptation to his readers but uses it rather to stress the seriousness of what they may regard as minor sins, or perhaps he omits direct reference to it because it is not a sin between members of the church but a sin against God. Many commentators speak of sexual sin and covetousness as the chief sins of the pagan world, suggesting this is why AE draws attention to them. But were there not more serious sins? What of pride and the absence of faith, hope and love? Are these not more destructive of community life than sex and greed? AE is perhaps dealing only with the obvious sins, a temptation into which preachers have always fallen. Origen contrasts the threat made against these three types of sinners with the absence of a threat against those who sin along the lines of v. 4; if AE intended a contrast he would have been creating a hierarchy of sins (cf 1 Jn 5.16f). All this raises the question whether he really understood the nature of sin. The absence of love and the presence of pride would surely exclude people from the Kingdom even more quickly.

The three types of sinners mentioned here have and can have (Ellicott) no inheritance (for the word see on 1.11, 14, 18) in the Kingdom, a warning which may have been part of catechetical instruction (so Dahl; cf Gal 5.19–21; 1 Cor 6.9f). The present tense of ἔχει (for the singular see BDR §135.4; Robertson, 405f) coheres with AE's realised eschatology, indicating that believers have already entered upon their inheritance just as they have already risen with Christ and sit with him in the heavenlies (2.6). Yet this cannot be pushed too far for inheritance is something which by its nature can only belong to the future. This may then represent another aspect of the tension between realised and future soteriology we have seen elsewhere in Ephesians (cf Introduction §6.4.4–7). The warning of divine retribution against those who do wrong is not restricted to Christianity, though elsewhere it will be expressed in other religious terms; the members of the Philadelphian cult (see Barton and Horsley) are told that the gods do not tolerate those who transgress.

The Kingdom of God is a frequent NT phrase but the Kingdom of Christ is not, being found only in later writings (2 Tim 4.1, 18; 2 Pet 1.11); Col 1.13 uses an approximately similar phrase 'the kingdom of God's son', and this may suggest that the idea of a kingdom associated with Christ was a concept of the Pauline school. The source of the idea perhaps lay in Paul himself, for in 1 Cor 15.24 he writes of Christ handing over a kingdom to God. Whether that is so or not, the total phrase 'the kingdom of (the) Christ and of God' is unique; its nearest equivalent is Rev 11.15 though, as we have seen, the beginnings of the idea may be present in 1 Cor 15.24. The Kingdom of Christ is not of course the church.

For the presence of the article with Christ see on 1.10; here its presence is not exceptional since the noun governing it has the article. θεοῦ lacks the article but this is normal with the word (MHT, 174; BDR §254.1) and it is regularly omitted in the phrase 'the kingdom of God'. 𝔓⁴⁶ omits the reference to Christ; F G boᵐˢ; Ambst invert the order of Christ and God; these variations were probably theologically inspired arising out of later church discussions on the deity of Christ. Some commentators (e.g. Jerome, Beza, Bengel) have indeed argued that the phrase implies his deity but there is no reason to see here an equation of Christ and God (cf Zerwick §185; Robertson, 786), just as there is none to see a two-stage kingdom, first that of Christ, a present kingdom (cf Rev 11.15; Col 1.13), and then a future, that of God (for the two stages see 1 Cor 15.24–28); what Paul sees as successive kingdoms AE sees as one (Steinmetz, 34).

The idea of a kingdom of Christ, that is, of Christ's active reign and not of a place, fits not inappropriately with AE's conception of Christ as already sitting, that is reigning, in the heavenlies (1.20ff). In the Synoptic Gospels' references to the Kingdom there is a tension between the present and future aspects of God's rule, a tension which is preserved in Paul (present kingdom, Rom 14.17; 1 Cor 4.20; 15.24; cf Col 4.11; future kingdom, 1 Cor 6.9ff; 15.50; Gal 5.21; 1 Th 2.12; 2 Th 2.5). When Paul writes of exclusion from the Kingdom or non-inheritance in it, he always has the future kingdom in mind (1 Cor 6.9ff; 15.50; Gal 5.21; cf 1 Th 2.12; 2 Th 7.5), yet Eph 5.5 seems to refer to the present kingdom. Certainly unbelievers have no inheritance in this kingdom, but are the elect who have been baptised and become members of the community able to lose their inheritance? The problem cannot be solved by saying that for AE the

Kingdom is the church and he is only thinking of exclusion from it (cf 1 Pet 4.15–19); if AE had meant exclusion from the community he would have said so. The problem did not arise in the same way for Paul since for him the inheritance is future, though it cannot be said Paul makes entirely clear in 1 Cor 5.3–5 the ultimate fate of the man who committed incest. The problem appears in other parts of the NT (e.g. Mt 18.15–17; 1 Jn 3.8; 5.16f; 1 Tim 1.20). There would not seem to be much point in AE warning his readers unless the possibility of non-inheritance existed. Since he says that unchastity should not be mentioned among them (v. 3), he must have realised the community had people with unchaste minds in it; the Corinthian church certainly contained unchaste members (the warning of Gal 5.19–21 implies the same for the Galatian churches). It would seem then that some of those who have been chosen in Christ, fore-ordained for adoption and now sit with Christ in the heavenlies may at some point in the future be excluded from the heavenlies and lose their election and adoption. AE's realised eschatology has thus created a real difficulty for him, and thereby caused problems for future systematic theologians and for exegetes who come to him with fixed theological positions into which he must be made to fit.

Before we leave this section of the paragraph, it is important to note that nowhere does AE show any concern for those who suffered through the sexual indulgence and greed of church members. Sexual intercourse involves two people, the church member and another; the covetous person gets more than his or her fair share of money and goods and therefore others get less. AE has no interest in the harm done to others by church members but is only worried about how their sins may harm themselves in depriving them of their place in the Kingdom of Christ and God. This attitude accords with what we found in 4.25–5.2 where his concern lay with the good of the community and he evinced no interest even when its own members were injured by the sins of other members. The purity of the community and of its individual members is the focus of his ethical teaching.

6.[10] The threat of v. 5 is now repeated in a different way; v. 5 suggested possible failure to reach a hoped for goal, v. 6 asserts God's positive reaction to those who have allowed themselves to be deceived into false action or belief. But who are those who might deceive the readers? AE calls them 'disobedient people' ('sons of disobedience'), employing the same phrase as in 2.2 (see there for its form); in 2.2 he applied it to Gentiles who were outside the church and subject to the powers of evil; these would certainly experience the wrath of God. Has AE the same people in mind here? 'Disobedient

[10] For the relation of this verse to Colossians, see the very different views of Coutts, 'Relationship', and Benoit, 'Rapports littéraires'.

people' is a general phrase and not a fixed term for Gentiles; it can therefore be applied in different ways as the occasion demands. Even if AE intended 'Gentiles' in his use of the phrase, believers, when attacking other believers about their beliefs or behaviour, have regularly labelled them with words which they would normally apply to unbelievers in order to emphasise their wickedness. Jews who thought of Gentiles as blind applied the same description to fellow Jews and similarly described both Gentiles and other Jews as hardened or stubborn (for references see on 4.18). 4.25–5.5 showed that AE considered Christians could sin; they did not become perfect at the moment of conversion/baptism. Some of the practices and beliefs of the pagan world will have continued to be present in the church and be the more dangerous if arguments supporting them came from within the community. 5.6–14 contains no clear missionary overtones and v. 6 is as easily explained on the supposition that the community is being perverted by some within it as by those outside. If its background is baptismal catechetical material, as many believe, it is difficult to see how its corrupters would be non-Christians. Above all, the threat of v. 6 would be irrelevant if addressed to outsiders for they would never hear it. So with Gnilka, Barth, Halter, we assume that it is insiders who are disobedient and who endanger the life of the community. In the early second century groups appeared claiming to be Christian but whose claim the contemporary 'orthodox' church denied. Already in the NT we find traces of these groups either within the church or on its fringes; the groups are variously labelled gnostics, semi-gnostics, proto-gnostics, antinomians, libertines, rigorists, ascetics, Judaisers. If then the disobedient people are within or on the fringe of the community, it is a proper and legitimate question to ask which group, or groups, AE had in mind. It is however a question which it is almost impossible to answer because AE provides so few clues to enable an identification of the views he repudiates. The only other point where he may be said to refer to them is 4.14 and, as we have seen, its information is equally inconclusive. It is perhaps then better not to attempt to identify those to whom AE alludes in 5.6 but simply to seek from the context the particular views and practices which are being argued against (cf Ernst). λόγοι might suggest that AE was contending primarily against certain theories, but he is almost certainly concerned with practice rather than belief for the present reference falls in the paraenetic section of the letter and not in the theological. It is true of course that practice and theology are ultimately inseparable, but one may be more directly in mind than the other.

AE has already listed activities which Christians should avoid and, though he sets them out as absolutes, as soon as believers began to think through what they meant they would discover they were not as simple or absolute as they looked. Lying is forbidden, yet are there not times when it may be proper to be economical with the truth and tell white lies? Stealing is wrong, but what of concealing part of the truth in a financial deal? Temper should not be lost, but what of righteous anger? Has anger limits? If one partner in marriage refuses satisfaction or is adulterous, may not the other have some freedom? Greed is wrong, but is wealth creation not a good thing? It is easy to see how specious arguments could soon corrupt a simple set of ethical guidelines. The whole process might be supported by claims that believers live under grace and therefore are free of moral restraint (cf Rom 6.1, 15) or that it is not the purity of the body or outward relationship with others that is important, but the purity of the inner life (1 Cor 6.12ff). We do not have enough information to identify the arguments which were being advanced and which alarmed AE. Necessarily what he writes is very general since he is not addressing a specific situation in one church but is writing to a number of churches. Whatever the arguments being used, AE describes them as κενοί which here does not signify 'meaningless' but 'erroneous' (for the connection with ἀπατάω see T Naph 3.1; Hermas, Mand 11.13). κενοὶ λόγοι may be a biblical phrase (Exod 5.9; Deut 32.47; cf T Naph 3.1; Did 2.5; Josephus c. Ap. 2.225; Diog 8.2) but it would be one easily understood by Gentiles in relation to deceptive arguments which for a time sound good but do not stand up to thorough examination. Those who use them (the neuter ταῦτα probably refers not to the actual arguments but to the deeds or sins which result from them) or accept them when others use them are subject to the wrath of God. The threat of v. 5 which implied exclusion is now expressed positively as implying punishment. That they are subject to God's wrath accords with the application of the same description 'disobedient people' to them as to Gentiles (2.2).

God's wrath (see on 2.3) may be thought of as active either now or in the eschatological future. Both aspects appear elsewhere in the NT and in contemporary and earlier Jewish literature. God's present wrathful activity is seen in Num 12.9; 4 Kgdms 1.18d; 22.13; 2 Chron 19.2; Jn 3.36; Rom 1.18ff; 3.5; 13.4f; 1 Th 2.16; and his future in Lk 21.23; Rom 2.5; 5.9; 9.22; 1 Th 1.10; 5.9; Eph 2.3; 1QS 2.15; 1QM 4.4f; 6.3; context alone can decide which significance is intended. The possibility of a future reference here is not eliminated by the present tense of ἔρχεται for this verb when used in the present often has a future reference (BDR §323; MHT, 63; cf Mt 17.11; Lk 23.29; Jn 5.28; 9.4; 16.2, 4; 1 Th 5.2; Heb 8.8); however when this is so normally something in the context suggests it; here ἐπί may do this as indicating a fate hanging over the disobedient people and impending (Mt 23.35; Lk 14.31; Jn 18.4). It would be wrong to deny that AE sees disobedient people as already suffering God's wrath, for the darkening of their minds and hardening of their hearts (4.17–19) are a present reality. Yet Paul could hold both to the present and future wrath of God and so 4.17–19 does not permit us to deny the same possibility for AE. The future aspect could only be dismissed if it could be shown that AE had eliminated a future beyond this life for believers and unbelievers, and it is impossible to show this. On the whole, however, the thought of God's present wrath suits the letter's realised eschatological position and does not conflict with the context.[11] AE does not specify in what the wrath of God consists but in line with 4.17–19 it might be the hardening of minds and darkening of understanding. Possibly AE has both present and future aspects in mind here (cf Abbott, Schnackenburg).

7. If the readers are not to be deceived by the specious arguments of disobedient people they should not associate with them; συμμέτοχοι forms here with γίνεσθε a periphrastic tense. The word appears only elsewhere in the NT at 3.6 where its meaning is clear: Gentile believers are co-participants with Jewish believers in the promise. There the context shows that the genitive denotes what they share in and the σύν those with whom they share it. αὐτῶν should then denote here what is shared in (so Ewald) rather than those with whom the sharing takes place; if it meant the latter it would have been more appropriately a dative (Ewald, Haupt, Hofmann). Its nearest referent is ταῦτα (v. 6) which, as we saw, refers to the vices already mentioned. The context indicates that those with whom the sharing takes place are the disobedient people. Believers are not to accept their views or participate with them in sexual sin, impurity and greed; it can be assumed that those who offer specious arguments which permit these vices indulge in them. The use of a strong word, συμμέτοχοι, used of fellow believers in 3.6, implies that those who offer the specious arguments and sin are within the community.

AE says nothing as to the nature of non-association with these people apart from saying that his readers should not participate in their vices. If they were not members of the community did that mean that all business and family relationships should be severed? While it might be possible to do this in respect of business dealings should a believer whose spouse was not a member separate from that spouse? If however, as is more likely, those who use the specious arguments are members of the community it may appear surprising that AE says nothing about their exclusion from the community; yet if they held no fixed theological position, as we have suggested, but only offered specious arguments to support sinful activities, it would be difficult to identify them as a group and thus to lay down guidelines by which they might be judged. Would non-association with them mean that there should be no attempt to dissuade them from their beliefs? If attempts were made then it

[11] Cf A. T. Hanson, *The Wrath of the Lamb*, London, 1957, 102f.

would not be possible to do this without naming their sins (cf v. 3). AE in fact offers no guidelines for action to deal with the situation. The problem is one afflicting all groups, whether religious or not, where strong views are held. It is discussed in 2 Cor 6.14ff and at Qumran (1QS 1.4f; 5.10f; CD 6.4f). One difficulty facing AE may have been his ignorance of the precise views of those he opposes; he may never have visited any, let alone all of the communities to which he writes; in such circumstances where dissentient views are not clearly known it is very difficult to propose decisive action. All he can do is to instruct his readers not to share in certain vices; he does not go so far as to forbid sharing in worship (contrast 1QS 6.24ff; Barton and Horsley) with those who may practise these vices nor does he deny them access to the common possessions of the group (4.28).

8. This is one of those verses to which pre-twentieth-century commentators gave relatively little attention but which now receives much more because the religious historical movement brought out the importance of the light–darkness contrast in gnostic and related literature and then the discoveries at Qumran showed that it was also important in contemporary Judaism; it is this latter background which most writers today stress in relation to the verse.

γάρ connects v. 8 to what precedes supplying a reason for the new conduct which should characterise the lives of believers; at the same time it expresses a new approach to that conduct setting it in the perspective of the light–darkness contrast rather than that of new–old persons (4.22–4). As we have already indicated, the contrast of light and darkness was a widespread metaphor and represents two spheres of human existence.[12] It was, as we have seen, present in 4.18; it is frequent in the OT though there as in 4.18 only one side of the metaphor may at times be expressed (Ps 27.1; 49.19; Isa 5.30; 9.2; 42.6, 16; 47.5; 49.6; 51.4; 59.9; 60.1f) and in the NT, which often picks up OT usage (Mt 4.16 = Isa 9.2; Mt 5.14–16; Mk 4.21; Lk 2.32 = Isa 42.6 and 49.6; Lk 11.33; Jn 1.4–9; 3.19–21; 8.12; 9.5; 12.35f, 46; Acts 13.47 = Isa 49.6; Acts 26.23; Rom 13.12f; 2 Cor 4.6; 6.14; Phil 2.15; Col 1.12f; 1 Th 5.5; 1 Pet 2.9; 1 Jn 1.5; 2.8). In addition to the OT the NT writers were influenced by contemporary Judaism (1QS 3.20f, 24f; T Levi 14.4; 19.1; T Gad 5.7); it offered phrases very similar to 'children of light' (1QS 1.9; 2.16; 3.13, 24f; 1QM 1.1, 3) and its opposite 'children, sons of darkness' (1QS 1.10; 1QM 1.7; etc.). Granted the indebtedness of the NT for the light–darkness contrast to Judaism and the OT, the contrast also appeared regularly in Greek literature; it would thus have been easily appreciated by AE's readers. Yet since it is

---

[12] Kuhn, *NTS*; H. Conzelmann, *TWNT*, VII, 424–46; IX, 302–49; W. Harnisch, *Eschatologische Existenz* (FRLANT 110), Göttingen, 1973, 119–21.

found in all strands of early Christianity, there is no reason to seek here a NT source outside Judaism; in any case by the time of Ephesians it was an established Christian contrast in relation to thought and behaviour and may have been used in the catechetical instruction of new believers. It would not then have been unfamiliar to AE's readers.

While 'children of light' can be paralleled, the bald statement 'Once you were darkness; now you are light'[13] apparently can not. For AE to say that his readers were once darkness goes much further than saying that their minds were once darkened (4.18). The clause expresses something other than implying that they once belonged to a 'dark' culture which has been changed to one of light, for it is not culture which has been changed but the individuals who once belonged to it. To say people are light may mean either that they provide light for others as lights shining in a dark world (cf Mt 5.14–16; Rom 2.19) or that they provide light for themselves; it is the latter which is being stressed here, since it is difficult to see how anyone can provide darkness for others and because the whole emphasis of the passage lies on the behaviour of believers (περιπατεῖτε); as light, believers are enlightened people; they have light within themselves to guide them in their conduct. It would be wrong to deny that as enlightened people believers do not provide light to others but this is not what is stressed here. Once, as unbelievers, they had no light and were blind; now they have light and can see. Once darkness characterised their existence, now light does. If they are light from where does that light come? AE says nothing about this explicitly but 'in the Lord' (see Detached Note: In Christ; the phrase is not attached here to the verb) suggests that AE is aware of the early Christian view of the Lord as the light of the world. Through their relationship with the Lord believers have received light, being enlightened in their understanding (1.17f).

The phrase 'children of light' probably entered Christianity from contemporary Judaism[14] but is not unGreek (cf MH, 441; Robertson, 651) and AE's Gentile readers would therefore have understood it. Our discussion at 2.2, 3 showed that 'sons of, children of' was used in two different ways: 'sons of disobedience' (2.2) are disobedient people but 'children of wrath' (2.3) are not angry people but people subject to the wrath of God. In 5.8 'children of light' will follow the pattern of 2.2 and mean 'enlightened people'. Having light within

---

[13] On the once–now contrast see Tachau, 125f; Lindemann, *Aufhebung*, 67–71.

[14] The phrase is found in *Pss Thomas* 1.27f; 8.2; 12.38; *Hyp Arch* II, 4 97.13f; *Apoc Peter* VII, 3 78.25f; *Trim Prot* XIII, 1 37.18–20, 41.16, 42.16, 45.32f. This does not imply it is a gnostic term, for the former of these is probably based on a Semitic *Vorlage* (see A. Adam, *Die Psalmen des Thomas*, BZNW 24, Berlin, 1959, 29f) and the other three writings have all been affected by Christianity, the author of the first being certainly acquainted with Ephesians since he quotes it at 86.23–5.

themselves they are able to behave (for περιπατεῖν see on 2.2) as
enlightened people and discern (v. 10) God's will (for the connection of 'sons of' with behaviour see 1QS 1.8f; 2.16f). Once in
darkness they could only stumble, now they know what God wills
and can and ought to carry it out. Once they were 'old' people, now
they are 'new' people (4.22–4) who have learned Christ (4.20) and
been created anew in righteousness and holiness (4.24). As in
4.22–4 the contrast is absolute; there is no in-between position,
partly old person, partly new, and there is no twilight; it is either
light or darkness. In one respect there is a difference here from the
earlier reference to darkness (4.18); there it was connected with
ignorance, here with immorality. Finally we should note that in v. 8
we move from a statement of the nature of Christian existence (v.
8a) to a call to live in accordance with it (v. 8b), the move common
in NT thought from indicative to imperative.

9. This verse indicates how enlightened people should live and is
parenthetical (the second person plural of v. 8 is continued in v. 10).
The result of their being light will be goodness, uprightness and
truth. Paul had already applied the metaphor of fruitfulness to
conduct (Rom 6.22; Gal 5.22; Phil 1.11; cf Jas 3.18), a connection
also found in the teaching of Jesus (Mt 7.16–20; 12.33–5; Lk 6.43f;
13.7) and before him in that of John the Baptist (Mt 3.10; Lk 3.8f).
The metaphor was in fact used even more widely (*Odes Sol* 8.2;
11.1, 23). In 1QS 10.8, 22; 1QH 1.28 (cf Heb 13.15) it is related to
worship and in Gen 30.2; Lk 1.42 to the children of a marriage. It is
thus very adaptable. If Ephesians is unPauline his influence must be
seen here, not only in the use of the image but in the associated
language. In v. 11 as in Gal 5.19 ἔργα (plural) is used of evil
activity; καρπός here is applied in the singular (cf Gal 5.22) to good
conduct; the singular suggests that the good fruit has a unitary aspect
which unfruitful or evil actions lack. The whole set of ideas may
have been cherished in the Pauline school and AE, if he is not Paul,
now re-expresses it. The contrast between good and bad fruit in
Ephesians is not strictly that between fruit which comes from good
or bad trees, as in the Gospels, but between fruit coming from the
same tree before and after conversion/baptism.

The contrast in the fruit is linked directly to the contrast between
light and darkness. The good fruit comes from the light, φωτός;[15]
the light has produced fruit (φωτός is a subjective genitive). While it
is true that plants die if deprived of light, and this may be the
underlying connection, we should be careful not to introduce
modern botanical theory to explain the text. Light is a good quality

[15] Although the variant πνεύματος has good support ($\mathfrak{P}^{46}$ D² Ψ 𝔐 sy^h) its
appearance was probably influenced by Gal 5.22 rather than 'light' being introduced
because it is the ruling concept of vv. 8–14.

in contrast to darkness and therefore is to be associated with good results.

A triad of nouns, in AE's customary manner (see on 5.3), identifies the fruit and πάση is to be associated with each (cf 1.8, 21; 4.2, 31; 5.5; 6.18) in a generalising fashion (cf 1.3, 8; 3.15; 5.3). ἀγαθωσύνη (see Spicq, I, 11–14) has not been found in non-biblical Greek[16] though its root and cognates are widely used. In scripture it appears in 2 Chron 24.16; Ψ 51.5; 2 Esdras 19.25, 35; Rom 15.14; Gal 5.22 (another connection of this passage with ours); Eph 5.9; 2 Th 1.11. It is difficult to derive from these instances any meaning more precise than 'goodness'. δικαιοσύνη, a favourite Pauline term, is not used here in relation to saving righteousness but with ethical significance.[17] Like ἀγαθωσύνη it is a somewhat general word (see on 4.24), 'uprightness', living in accordance with a divine norm or God's will, seems an appropriate translation. In Rom 5.7 Paul ranks goodness above uprightness but AE sets them on a level; Jerome and others used this equivalence to launch attacks on Marcion; in Phil 1.11 (cf Rom 14.17) Paul rates uprightness more highly. AE has already used ἀλήθεια several times. In 4.25 it is the opposite of what is untrue, but this would impose too narrow a meaning here; 1.13 relates it to the gospel, though it is generally used of human behaviour. In 5.9 it[18] is set in parallel with goodness and uprightness and is not used as in 4.24 to qualify other nouns. The meaning probably lies in the area either of faithfulness, loyalty, sincerity, or of that which exhibits within itself nothing that is false or hypocritical; it does not mean being true to oneself or one's conscience, for both may be false; it might however mean being true to the new person (4.24). The virtues of our verse are sometimes found associated in Qumran (1QS 1.5; 4.2f, 24; 5.4; 8.2) but not in the NT virtue catalogues. As we have explained them, 5.9 does not contain three separate and distinct virtues which might appear in a catalogue, but three different ways of stating the nature of virtuous living. Not a virtue catalogue, they are also not the opposite of the three vices of 5.3, 5, nor can they be differentiated as obligations to self, others, or God (cf Westcott). Each stands for the whole range of Christian virtue revealing different aspects of it. Triads depicting the nature of a life in accordance with God's will are found in Mic 6.8; 2 Chron 31.20 (not in LXX); Jer 4.2; Ψ 44.5. None coincides exactly with that of 5.9 and it would be wrong to think of AE as deliberately copying one of these OT verses or as modelling himself on them. Rather, as we have seen (5.3), he thinks in terms of triads and the three qualities he has chosen would have been easily understood by

[16] Contrast BAGD s.v.
[17] Cf Reumann, §167 = pp. 92f; Ziesler, 154.
[18] Cf. A. C. Thiselton, *NIDNTT*, III, 874ff; J. Murphy-O'Connor, 'Truth: Paul and Qumran' (see on 4.24), 203ff.

Gentile readers. The omission of love is interesting; would readers
have taken this of sexual or other love unless it had been explained
with a reference to Christ?

10. After the parenthesis of v. 9 the main theme is now resumed
with a participle which depends on the imperative of v. 8b. As
enlightened people, believers need to behave in a way which pleases
their Lord so that their lives will bear the fruit of goodness,
uprightness and truth. δοκιμάζειν is a favourite Pauline term which
he applies to God's scrutinising and approving human beings (Rom
16.10; 1 Cor 11.19; 2 Cor 13.5ff; 1 Th 4.4; cf 1 Cor 9.27) and, as
here, to believers determining how they should behave (Rom 2.18;
12.2; Gal 6.4; Phil 1.10; 1 Th 5.21); it was used in this latter way
also by the Stoics (Epictetus 1.20.7; 2.23.6, 8; 4.5.16; 4.6.13;
4.7.40). If AE is not Paul then as a member of a Pauline school he
has picked up the term, yet there is no dependence on any particular
Pauline text; it follows here naturally on the reference to truth in v. 9
(Hugedé). When human beings are the subject more is intended than
the intellectual reasoning out of conduct which pleases the Lord, i.e.
Christ.[19] What is reasoned out needs to be put to the test, and so the
verb carries the sense of testing as well as of discerning (cf Roels);
what pleases the Lord is the practice of what has been determined.

If decisions are to be made about conduct, criteria are needed on
which to base them. Only one is stated here: whatever pleases the
Lord. Paul has the same criterion in Rom 12.2 where he uses the
same verb in relation to God's will (cf Phil 1.10); in 1 Th 5.21 the
sense is more restricted since it relates to discerning truth in
prophetic activity; when AE again introduces a similar criterion in
5.17 he connects it directly to God's will. To set up as the criterion
what pleases the Lord is biblical (Gen 5.22, 24; 6.9; Wisd 4.10;
Ecclus 44.16; Rom 12.1; 14.18; 2 Cor 5.9; Phil 4.18; Col 3.20; Heb
13.21; cf *T Dan* 1.3), but it is vague and affords little help in making
practical decisions. It seems to leave believers on their own. More
help is needed, especially for those moving out of a pagan
environment and even for those who have been converts for some
time but who still live surrounded by a pagan culture, yet the greater
the degree of detailed help in relation to the multitude of different
situations that may arise, the greater the approach to a legalistic
religion. On the criteria provided by AE, by the NT generally and by
the church in succeeding centuries see Essay: Moral Teaching §4.2.

11. From his initial premise that his readers are light in the Lord
(v. 8), AE now draws two conclusions, first a negative (v. 11a) and
then a positive (v. 11b).

[19] D* F G 81* *pc* lat; Ambst read θεῷ for κυρίῳ; it is a natural correction in the
light of passages like Rom 12.2 and clarifies a possible doubt as to the identification
of 'Lord'; here though, as usually in Ephesians, this is Christ.

In v. 11a AE plays on ideas already in the context: darkness, fruitfulness. He might well have omitted τοῖς ἔργοις and used only the simpler τῷ καρπῷ τοῦ σκότους, but in the Pauline vocabulary τὰ ἔργα is pejorative and its presence creates a longer phrase which is both a little 'heavier' in AE's customary style and reflects Pauline usage (Rom 13.12f; Gal 5.19). Interestingly AE does not say that darkness produces bad or rotten fruit (cf Mt 7.17–19; 12.33; Lk 6.43f) or that it fails altogether to produce fruit, either of which might accord better with botanical theory. He also apparently assumes that the fruit is either wholly bad or wholly good, not impaired. In v. 9 he identified the good fruit but does not identify the bad fruit here, perhaps because it would be shameful to do so (v. 12, so Photius and other Fathers). There is no reason to see in these 'works of darkness' a reference to the Mysteries (cf Ambrosiaster ad v. 8). ἄκαρπος is found only in the later parts of the NT (Mk 4.19, assuming the interpretation of the parable of vv. 3–8 was added to the original parable; Tit 3.14; 2 Pet 1.8; Jude 12) and is used in a derogatory sense. Believers are not to take part (συγκοινωνεῖν; for the verb and its cognate adjective see Rom 11.17; 1 Cor 9.23; Phil 1.7; 4.14; Rev 1.9; 18.4) in unfruitful and sinful activities. If they do, they will not be acting alone but taking part with others; this is indicated both by the συν of the verb and by σκότος which was used in v. 8 to describe people. But who are these other people? There is nothing in v. 11a which would enable us to distinguish between believers who had sinned as in vv. 3–5 (other parts of the NT show that believers did sin in the ways described there) and unbelievers, and therefore nothing to suggest that only the latter are intended here.

An emphatic μᾶλλον δὲ καί introducing v. 11b indicates an important new stage in the discussion: not only are believers to avoid wrong conduct; they are to confront it when they see it in others; instead of participating in works of darkness they are to take positive steps against such works or against those who perpetrate them. The object of ἐλέγχετε is undefined; v. 11a would suggest a reference to the works of darkness, v. 12 to those who perform them. ἐλέγχειν has a wide range of meaning as the lexica show.[20] One possible meaning, the disciplining or punishing of those whose works belong to darkness, can hardly be intended since nothing in the context implies this; it is an interpretation automatically excluded if the works are the object of the verb. Many commentators and translations choose the meaning 'expose, reveal'; in this case the object of the verb would be the works of darkness; believers in some way, by word or example, expose to those who perform works of

---

[20] On the word see T. Engberg-Pedersen, 'Ephesians 5, 12–13: ἐλέγχειν and Conversion in the New Testament,' ZNW 80 (1989) 89–110.

darkness the true nature of their actions as works of darkness. If these are believers this disclosure would take place either through word or example, but if they are unbelievers presumably only through example, though 1 Cor 14.24f allows for the 'exposure' of unbelievers through words; 1 Cor 14.24f refers however to a very special situation and not a general one as in our verse. This 'disclosure' interpretation seems to fit the flow of the argument with its emphasis on light yet it would anticipate the later use of φανεροῦν, deprive ἐλέγχειν of its peculiar significance and define the object of the verb as the works of darkness, which, see above, is by no means certain.

Engberg-Pedersen suggests 'confrontation' as offering the true sense of the verb, and the meaning here as 'confronting somebody or something with the sin of showing him or it to be, in some determinate respect, at fault' (art.cit., 97). 'Something' is too vague; the evidence Engberg-Pedersen produces shows that the 'something' is restricted to the deeds or actions of people; we can then modify his interpretation to 'confronting people or their thoughts, words or actions with the aim of showing them to be, in some determinate sense, at fault'. This understanding approximates to two of the meanings often given to the verb, 'convict, convince' and 'reprove, rebuke'; both of these involve confrontation and it is difficult to draw a precise line between them. If the object of the verb is people who do works of darkness, then any of these meanings is possible (cf Jn 8.46; 1 Tim 4.2); if the people are unbelievers this would mean convincing them of their sin and leading them to repentance and conversion along the lines of 1 Cor 14.24f (so Schlier) but, as we have said, the latter passage refers to a very limited situation. Kirby, 142, remarks in respect of a possible reference to conversion that 'a thought that is so obscurely expressed [in vv. 11, 13] can hardly be called a positive approach to the outsider'. If the people targeted are believers, conversion cannot be intended. However, for believers to convince other believers of their wrongdoing could be seen as a Christian duty, and this would emphasise the sense 'rebuke, reprove'. Reproval would not be tactful if unbelievers were its recipients; nothing would be more likely to turn them against Christianity! That church members should rebuke, correct or reprove other members is seen as a Christian duty in a number of passages (1 Tim 5.20; Jas 5.19f; in Tit 1.9, 13 the references relate to the correction of belief rather than behaviour); it is in particular a duty laid on pastors (2 Tim 4.2; Tit 2.15); in Mt 18.15–17 where a more formal procedure for correction is set out it is as in Eph 5.11 a duty laid on all believers. The correction of the faults of one member by others within a closely knit community is a normal communal activity as evidence from Qumran shows (1QS 5.23–6.1; 9.17; CD 7.2f; 9.6–8; 20.4; cf T Gad 6.3, 6; T Jos 6.6); Did 15.3 says such rebuking should not be done angrily but in peace. The idea of reproval within the community runs back into the OT (Lev 19.17; Prov 9.7f; 10.10; Ecclus 19.13ff).

Engberg-Pedersen bypasses the problem whether AE has believers or unbelievers in mind by drawing on 1 Cor 14.24f and Jn 3.20f and arguing that in 5.11ff people are in fact encouraged to confront themselves for they are divided within themselves; 'darkness and light stand for internal attitudes' (art.cit., 104) within them. It is however difficult to read a divided consciousness into either 1 Cor 14.24f or Jn 3.20f. Both can certainly be related to the conversion of unbelievers, but this is a movement from darkness into light, not from 'poor' light into 'good' light. There is moreover nothing in Eph 5.8 to suggest that inner attitudes are a problem for believers, and indeed nothing elsewhere in the paragraph supports such an idea.

We have touched throughout on the manner in which fellow believers should be rebuked and reproved. Since sins are not to be named (5.3), it has been argued that any correction must be non-verbal; 5.3 (see above) however cannot be taken literally, and the same applies to 5.12 (see below). AE continually rebukes and reproves his readers verbally, as does Paul in his letters. In Mt 18.15–17; 2 Tim 4.2; Tit 2.15 the rebukes are verbal; generally in the NT ἐλέγχειν refers to speech rather than action (cf Gnilka). Yet, of course, there is a place also for non-verbal rebuke in so far as good behaviour is itself a criticism of sin (Mt 5.16; Phil 2.15; 1 Th 4.12; 1 Pet 2.12). If reproval is to be verbal, AE does not tell us whether it should be offered privately, or publicly within the community. AE does not seem aware of the danger of appearing censorious in rebuking others, a danger against which Jesus warns (Mt 7.1–5) and which is greatest with verbal rebukes. Finally we should note that whereas in the Pastorals the correction of others is a task for pastors, AE does not restrict confrontation to an 'organised' ministry.

12. While the translation of this verse is apparently straightforward, it is difficult to link it in with what precedes and follows (NA[27] ends v. 11 with a period, UBS[3] a comma). It could be related easily to v. 11 if it could be taken concessively ('rebuke even though it is shameful to speak about ...'), yet γάρ prevents this, or if it is understood parenthetically, 'for it is shameful even to speak about what they have done in secret' (Bratcher and Nida; γάρ introduces a parenthesis in v. 9). On the whole it is probably better to understand it in the latter way and as emphasising ἐλέγχετε. Works of darkness cannot be left unreproved but to rebuke them publicly means admitting their existence within the community, where they ought never to be. It is therefore shameful even (for the climactic use of καί with λέγειν cf Plato, *Rep* 465BC) to have to acknowledge their existence. The idea that some deeds may be too shameful to mention is also found in non-Christian moralists (Philo, *Opif Mundi* 80; Epictetus 4.9.5; 1.6.20; 3.26.8; 4.1.177; cf Demosthenes, *Cononos* 1262.17).

Since v. 8 a contrast has been drawn between light and darkness; now a new but not unrelated contrast is introduced, that between secret and revealed (Bouttier). This contrast appears elsewhere in the NT (Mk 4.22; Lk 12.2; Jn 18.20; Rom 2.16; 1 Cor 4.5; 14.25). There will be a revelation (v. 13) of what has been done secretly (κρυφῇ only here in NT but in LXX at Exod 11.2; Deut 28.57; Judg 4.21B; 9.31B; etc.). Vice fears revelation by light (cf Rom 13.13). The reference to secrecy is not an attack on the Mystery Religions where sexual perversion was commonly believed, at least by later Christians, to be rampant; if that were the case, AE's method of dealing with it is most inadequate (Gnilka). We cannot alternatively suppose the existence of a schismatic group of Christians who met secretly and whose practices were unacceptable (so Knox, *Gentiles*, 199; Beare); the general nature of the letter forbids such a deduction for there would not have been a similar group in every congregation to which AE wrote. AE's attack is on the unfruitful works of darkness (v. 11) which have been committed in secret; those who act secretly in this way (ὑπ' αὐτῶν, constructio ad sensum, BDR §282 n. 3; MHT, 40) are the 'disobedient people' (v. 6). If these are unbelievers, it is difficult to see why AE should refer to what they do as done secretly; elsewhere he suggests Gentile behaviour was unrestricted and blatant in evil (4.17–19, 22). The reference to secrecy is much more easily understood of members of the community, some of whom have indulged themselves covertly in various kinds of sexual sin (there is no suggestion that this would have taken place only in the darkness of night) and in covetousness (5.3–5); covetousness, if it involved financial irregularity, would necessarily have been covert. Loyal members of the community should rebuke those who have gone astray (v. 11b) and drag their sins into the open, sins which it is shameful to mention, especially in a Christian community.

13. This is yet another verse difficult to fit into the flow of the argument, a difficulty realised from the time of the earliest patristic commentators (for their various solutions and all those later ones suggested prior to his time, see Ewald). The verse is linked to v. 11b through the use of ἐλέγχειν and to the idea of secrecy in v. 12 through φανεροῦν. Whatever believers reprove or rebuke is made visible or revealed as wrong because believers are themselves light (v. 8). τὰ πάντα ἐλεγχόμενα and not πάντα τὰ ἐλεγχόμενα suggests v. 13 is a general statement, 'everything which has been reproved (rebuked, corrected) by the light is revealed', but within the argument it must apply to the reproofs administered by believers to other believers in relation to what they have done in secret (v. 12). ὑπὸ τοῦ φωτός, not an emphatic phrase by position, could be taken either with what precedes or follows. Believers are light (v. 8) and if they rebuke then it is light which rebukes, or everything that is rebuked is revealed by the light (= believers). Whichever way it is taken, the revelation does not necessarily refer to a public confession of sin by those who repent. Reproof shows up sin so that it is seen to be what it is; it is no longer left locked in secrecy (v. 12). It is not said to whom the revelation of sin is made. It is presumably to the individual concerned and, if the reproof is in public, to the community as a whole.

14. In some translations and some editions of the Greek text the verses are divided differently and the clause πᾶν γὰρ ... ἐστιν forms the end of v. 13. While the clause itself appears easy to translate ('for everything that is revealed is light'), it is again difficult to understand and fit into the argument. In consequence translations have not been literal as a selection from the most recent will show: 'for everything that is clearly revealed becomes light' (GNB), 'for it is light that makes everything visible' (NIV), 'and anything illuminated is itself a light' (NJB), 'and whatever is exposed to the light itself becomes light' (REB), 'for everything that becomes visible is light' (NRSV). Some earlier translations like the AV solved the difficulty by taking φανερούμενον as a middle with an active sense 'for whatsoever doth make manifest is light'; evidence, however, for the middle with an active sense is missing and in v. 13 the verb is clearly passive. Erasmus (so also Fischer) suggested that the article had been transposed inadvertently from φῶς to the participle, but primitive corruptions are difficult to prove and we must accept the text as it stands. The literal translation seems to be a truism: 'everything that is brought to light is light'; such a truism would not be out of accord with AE's general style; yet in fact it is not a truism; the devil when revealed is not, and does not become, light. As the variety of translations shows, it is necessary in some way to paraphrase the clause to accommodate it to the argument. On our understanding this has run 'Believers are light; some in the community have sinned; believers reprove them and so bring light to bear on their faults; when their faults [note the continual way in which we move in the paragraph between sins and sinners] are reproved they are revealed and every sin that is revealed is no longer sin and the one who has committed it is light, i.e. restored to his proper nature as light.' Beyer, 225, suggests that v. 14a could be understood as a masculine phrase along the lines of Jn 3.6a; 1 Jn 5.4; the acceptance of this would not affect the argument suggested. The purpose of bringing sins or persons to the light is not the negative desire to expose, but the positive wish to reform.

All of this is now confirmed in the second half of the verse with a quotation[21] introduced with the same formula as at 4.8. In Jas 4.6 it introduces scripture. While the possibility cannot be excluded, it is unlikely that AE thought he was citing scripture here; see Introduction §9.1 and §9.2.3. It is, however, certain that he wished his readers to realise he was using a quotation which he and they regarded as in some way authoritative. The use of a quotation is confirmed by the change from the second plural of vv. 3ff to the singular and by the return to the plural in v. 15.

Accepting it as a quotation, from where does it come? Various suggestions have been made: (a) Since it not a direct quotation of any one particular OT text it may be an amalgam of a number, a position often argued in respect of 1 Cor 2.9. Older commentators spent a lot of time and ingenuity attempting to discover suitable passages; Isa 60.1; 26.19; 9.27 are normally suggested[22] but have not been generally acceptable (see Noack for a good discussion); Hendriksen (cf Van Roon) is one of the few recent authors to offer a reasoned, though not wholehearted, defence of this view; (b) A Jewish apocryphal source; it does not however appear in any known to us, yet since much of the relevant material is no longer extant, this possibility cannot be eliminated. (c) A lost saying of Jesus; again this cannot be disproved; however style and content together with the use of the term 'Christ' make this improbable. (d) An early Christian hymn; this seems to have been first suggested by Severian; it becomes probable once we observe that the quotation 'has a certain "lilt" about it, and a parallelism comparable to that of Hebrew poetry' (Moule, 199); if this is correct it may either have formed the whole hymn or, more probably, been part of a hymn (Clem Alex, *Protrepticus* 9.84.2, continues it with a second verse; there is no proof that this belonged to the original[23]). Some justification for the resemblance of the introductory formula to that used in respect of scripture might then exist on the supposition that it was a 'spiritual' hymn (v. 19) spoken by a Spirit-inspired

[21] See Knox, *Gentiles*, 198f; B. Noack, 'Das Zitat in Ephes. 5, 14', *ST* 5 (1951) 52–64; Roels, 224–6; R. Schnackenburg, '"Er hat uns mitauferweckt". Zur Tauflehre des Epheserbriefes', *LJ* 2 (1952) 159–83 at 160–6; P. Siber, *Mit Christus Leben. Eine Studie zur paulinischen Auferstehungshoffnung* (ATANT 61), Zürich, 1971, 200–5; Bankhead, 104–6; Fischer, 140–6; A. J. M. Wedderburn, *Baptism and Resurrection* (WUNT 44), Tübingen, 1987, 52–4, 80–2; Best, 'Use'.

[22] E. W. Jacobus, 'The citation Ephesians 5,14 as affecting the Paulinity of the Epistle', *Theologische Studien* (FS B. Weiss), Göttingen, 1897, 9–29, made the unusual suggestion of a rendering by Paul himself of Jon 1.6. The same suggestion has been made more recently, apparently independently, by R. P. C. Hanson and A. T. Hanson; see A. T. Hanson, *The New Testament Interpretation of Scripture*, London, 1980, 142.

[23] D. M. Stanley, 'The Divinity of Christ in Hymns of the New Testament', *Proceedings of the Fourth Annual Convention of the Society of Catholic Teachers of Sacred Doctrine*, Englewood Cliffs, NJ, 1958, suggests 1 Tim 3.16 as its continuation.

prophet.[24] In form the first two lines are imperatival clauses with their verbs at the beginning in Semitic fashion; the third line is a promise. Those who obey the imperatives will receive the promise. The verse suitably rounds off the discussion which began at v. 8. Though believers are light, some of them seem still to be darkness and Christ needs to shine on them through the words of those believers who have not fallen back into darkness. The concept of light then both begins and ends vv. 8–14.

We turn now to examine the individual lines of the hymn, recognising that their meaning in the present context may not be the same as their original meaning. Sleep is a widely used metaphor,[25] often as a euphemism for death. Paul adopted this usage either from Judaism (e.g. Isa 43.17 LXX; 1 Kgs 2.10; 11.43) or from the ancient world generally and employed it in 1 Th 5.13; 1 Cor 7.39; 11.30; 15.6, 18, 20, 51. Since line ii of the hymn directly refers to death, this may be thought to be the understanding of sleep in line i. Yet can those who are Christians and have therefore risen with Christ (2.6) be envisaged as still dead? Sleep may then be used metaphorically in another way as often in gnosis (e.g. Ap John II, 1 31.5ff) and elsewhere to indicate a lack of alertness, an ignorance of the true nature of a situation, a failure to understand what is going on (cf Rom 12.11–14; 1 Th 5.6f); this would be appropriate here since in v. 11 the readers were warned to avoid the unfruitful works of darkness. They are to arouse themselves from sin, the sin in which they lived before they believed and into which they have fallen back. It is however difficult to see this meaning as continued in line ii which clearly refers to rising from the dead.[26] Believers prior to becoming Christians were dead in sin (2.1, 5). Though they may have reverted to their pre-Christian sinful ways they are hardly regarded as again dead and put back into the category of unbelievers. There are other possibilities: (a) Line i could be taken in the sense of arousal from the sleep of sin (cf v. 11) and so understood might fit into AE's purpose; he then went on to quote the whole verse because line iii also served to round off his argument about light, and because the whole verse was known to his readers he could not omit line ii. This possibility implies AE had deliberately ignored or unconsciously misunderstood the hymn's purport. (b) AE understood line ii metaphorically, 'Arise from your sleep (= death)

[24] Origen, Hom Joshua, GCS 30, 295.14, terms it a 'sermo divinus'.
[25] Cf A. Oepke, TWNT, III, 434ff; H. Balz, TWNT, VIII 545ff; H. Jonas, Gnosis und spätantiker Geist I, 1 (FRLANT 51), Göttingen, 1934, 112–14, 120–2, 126–33; P. Hoffman, Die Toten in Christus (2nd edn), Münster, 1978, 186ff; G. W. MacRae, 'Sleep and Awakening in Gnostic Texts', The Origins of Gnosticism (Messina Colloquium 1966), Studies in the History of Religion, 12, Leiden, 1967, 496–507.
[26] On the form ἀνάστα see BDR §95 n. 7; MH, 210; Robertson, 310, 328. The article with νεκρῶν in this phrase is unusual (BDR §254 n. 8) but not impossible (Mt 14.2; 27.64; 28.7); no significance should be attached to its presence here.

in sin'. As the phrase regularly refers to a physical or spiritual resurrection from death, it is difficult to accept this view, though it must be allowed that in the light of 2.1, 5 death need not be regarded as physical death and could be related to sin. (c) In 4.24 AE told Christians to put on the new person, something they had already done when they first believed but which they needed to continue to do. May he not then be applying here as in 4.24 the language of conversion to believers? If they have failed and have produced the unfruitful works of darkness, they should recover the position from which they began. Whichever solution is accepted, and whatever the original meaning of the verse, the 'coming to life' or 'awakening' should not be interpreted within the context gnostically as the attainment of a true understanding of the self; it has to do with a knowledge of sin.

Line iii firms up the connection of the verse with its context. When the sleeper awakens, when the dead rise, the light who is Christ (for the use of the article see on 1.10) shines (for the form of ἐπιφαύσκω see BDR §101 n. 85) to give them light.[27] Christ as light is an idea found widely in the NT (e.g. Jn 1.4, 9; 8.12; 9.5; 12.46; Lk 1.78f; 2 Cor 4.6). The symbolism of light is even more widespread and its use gives no reason to see the origin of the verse in gnosis. When Christ shines again on the believers they again become light (v. 8).

If that is the interpretation of the hymn in its context, how was it originally understood? If the Semitisms noted above are correct the hymn will be early. In one sense it is difficult to answer the question about original meaning when a context is absent, but in another it may be easier since there is no need to make it fit a context; line ii can then be taken straightforwardly as supplying the meaning for line i so that resurrection is the subject of both. This led Asmussen to make the highly original suggestion that it was the kind of way that Lazarus might have been addressed in the tomb. More probable since resurrection and baptism are closely associated (Rom 6.3ff; Col 2.12) is the suggestion the hymn was addressed to baptismal candidates (so Bankhead, 104–6): let them rise from their past dead and sinful life into a new life where Christ will be the light. The connection of light with baptism appears fairly early (Melito *Frag* 8b; see S. G. Hall, *Melito of Sardis*, Oxford, 1979). Noack suggests that the verse was to be used by a heavenly being to address believers when Christ returns and gives full light to all. While we can understand the singular as addressed to individual believers coming one by one to baptism, surely the plural would be used at the parousia as then believers would be addressed as a group; a parousia context would have been also better suited if the imperatives had been futures, 'you who sleep in death will rise ... and

---

[27] The variant ἐπιψαύσεις τοῦ Χριστοῦ, 'touch Christ (and you will be healed from sin)', lacks strong support (D* b; MVict Ambst Chr^mss); it results probably from the difficulty of interpreting the verse. Jerome mentions yet another reading, 'Christ will touch you' (for discussion of the variants see Robinson, 300).

Christ will be light to you'. Parallels to the hymn have been detected in both
the Mysteries and gnosticism; in respect of the former it has been supposed
that Christians copied a similar cry to initiates at the moment of their
initiation (cf Aristophanes, *Ranae*, 340ff); the evidence for such a cry in the
Mysteries is slender (cf Wedderburn, 52–4, 80–2). In respect of gnosticism,
arguments (e.g. by Dibelius; Schlier; Fischer, 143f; Lindemann; Pokorný,
Gnosis 54, 94f; H. Jonas, *The Gnostic Religion*, Boston, 1963, 68–73,
80–6) have been drawn from the parallels to the idea of enlightenment and
awakening from sleep (e.g. *Acts Thomas* 34; 110, Bonnet, II 2, 151.11ff;
221.21ff; *CH* 1.27f; 7.1; *Odes Sol* 8.3ff; *Ap John* II, 1 31.5f; *Trim Prot* XIII,
1 35.21ff) but a sufficient number of parallels can be found in Judaism and
early Christianity to account for the ideas of the hymn (Gnilka; Schnackenburg, art.cit.; Kuhn, *NTS*; cf Ecclus 24.32f 1QS 2.3; 4.2; 11.3–6; 1QH 4.27;
1 Th 5.3ff; Rom 13.11ff.).

XIII

BE WISE AND FILLED WITH THE SPIRIT
(5.15-21)

Ch. Bigaré, 'L'Épître (Ep 5,14–21): Le Chrétien se conduit comme un sage, il cherche sa plénitude dans l'Esprit', *AsSeign* 75 (1965) 14–25; V. C. Pfitzner, 'Good Songs in Bad Times', *LTR* 12 (1978) 45–53; Adai, 219–31; Lemmer, 403–53.

15 Consider then carefully how you behave,
        not as those who are unwise
        but as those who are wise,
16   making the best use of time
        because the days are evil.
17 So do not be foolish
        but discern what the will of the Lord is.
18   And do not be drunk with wine
        —it brings ruin—
        but be filled by the Spirit
19   addressing one another
            with psalms and hymns and spiritual songs
            singing and praising the Lord from your heart
20   giving thanks at all times for everything
            to him who is God and Father
            in the name of our Lord Jesus Christ,
21   being subject to one another in the fear of Christ.

This further brief paraenetic section turns from exhorting believers to avoid particular sins and follow certain virtues to more general pleas, though these were not entirely missing earlier (4.27, 30; 5.8b, 10). It is impossible for AE to lay down full guidelines for conduct; much must be left to particular communities and the individuals within them to work out. Missing from what he says is any direct reference to many of the reasons commonly offered why believers should be good, e.g. in order to convert unbelievers, present themselves as law-abiding citizens, prove to themselves that they are saved. AE uses one of his favourite terms, περιπατεῖν, to begin the section; it is however wrong with Schnackenburg to see it as necessarily indicating, as in 4.1, 17, a major new step in the argument, for the verb is used also in 5.2, 8 with no such step in mind. If believers have to confront other believers or unbelievers their manner of life is important; important, too, lest they themselves should turn out to be the ones who are confronted. This section thus continues the general direction of the argument. We should not however accept Gnilka's view that AE, because he mentions worship, now imagines himself addressing a community gathered for worship; the whole letter would have been read aloud during a time of worship and worship is therefore the background to all of it. Worship is however the explicit theme of its final verses and should with moral living be the centre of Christian life. In referring to worship AE continues his stress on the mutual responsibility of believers; emphasised in 5.8–14 through the idea of confrontation, it is to be continued through their corporate worship.

The passage is structured around three contrasts expressed through μή and ἀλλά (vv. 15, 17, 18), and, as is normal in paraenesis, participles are extensively used in dependence on imperatives. There are two main themes: 'wisdom' (vv. 15–17) and 'worship' (vv. 19–20), the third contrast (v. 18) forming the transition from the one to the other. There are again similarities with Colossians in the use of the theme of wisdom (Col 4.5a), the unusual phrase of v. 16a and the terms employed in describing worship. Yet there are subtle differences which suggest common membership of a Pauline school (wisdom is a Pauline theme) rather than dependence of one letter on the other (see Best, 'Who used Whom?' and notes on vv. 15, 16, 19, 20); for example, Eph 5.18 introduces worship through a reference to the Spirit but Col 3.16 through a reference to the word of God.

It is difficult to know whether v. 21 is to be associated with vv. 15–20 or vv. 5.22ff; UBS³ makes a break after v. 21, NA²⁷ before it. Its participle is grammatically dependent on the verb of v. 18a but its content appears to make it a suitable introduction to the HT, where we move from mutual responsibility within the community as a whole to that within the individual household. For detailed discussion of the issues involved and reasons for deciding to take it in this section see on v. 21.

15. οὖν indicates a new turn in the argument which yet depends on what has preceded: as those who have learnt Christ (4.20) are new people (4.24) and are light (5.8), it is important that believers should consider their future behaviour carefully (βλέπετε ἀκριβῶς; Van Roon, *Authenticity*, 165 notes the frequency of π and ω sounds throughout the verse). Paul regularly uses βλέπειν in respect of the consideration of conduct (1 Cor 3.10; 8.9; 10.12; 16.10; Gal 5.15; cf Col 2.8; Mk 13.5, 9, 23, 33); other verbs were possible; AE may have chosen βλέπειν not only because of its frequency in Paul but because it follows naturally on a passage (5.8–14) about light.

ἀκριβῶς, a favourite Lukan term (Lk 1.3; Acts 18.25, 26; 23.15, 20; 24.22) but also found in Paul (1 Th 5.2), means here 'carefully, closely' (cf Lk 1.3; Acts 23.15, 20) and is better taken with βλέπετε as in 𝔓⁴⁶ ℵ* B 0278 33 81 104 1175 1241ˢ 1739 pc sa than with περιπατεῖτε as in D F G Ψ 1881 𝔐 b m* sy; MVict which reverse the order of πῶς and ἀκριβῶς and for which the evidence is weaker. The variant may have emerged because πῶς was omitted after ἀκριβῶς through homoeoteleuton and reinserted incorrectly (cf Metzger). The evidence for reading ἀδελφοί is slender: ℵ² A 629 pc a vg (bo); though the word is frequent in the genuine Paulines this would be its only occurrence as an address in Ephesians; had it been present there was no reason to omit it.

In the similar verse, Col 4.5, behaviour is related πρὸς τοὺς ἔξω. The lack of such a reference here does not mean that AE is generalising Colossians (se Beare; Percy, 412); rather its omission is in keeping with the way he discusses conduct only in relation to other believers. He is concerned to formulate an ethic for the internal life of the community and not for the relationship of believers to unbelievers.

Verse 15b contains the first of the three contrasts of vv. 15–18, in this case relating to wisdom; the theme is similar to that of Col 4.5 but is modified by the introduction of the contrast. Two kinds of behaviour ('the two ways'[1]) are possible, expressed here as wise and unwise (cf 1 Cor 1.18–3.23); the pre-Christian life of readers lacked wisdom; its presence should characterise them now. The contrast was already present in Jewish tradition (1QS 3.13ff, especially 4.22, 24); T Levi 13.7 associates lack of wisdom with the blindness and impiety which in Eph 4.17–19 characterise the Gentile world. Wisdom is a wide term needing definition from its context; here it is not primarily insight into God's workings (1.9, 17; 3.10) but the practical wisdom which, depending on such insight, relates to conduct; it is to this aspect of wisdom that a large part of the Jewish Wisdom literature is devoted. Whereas Jewish thought connected it with a life lived in accordance with Torah, Christian thought connects it to Christ who is the wisdom of God.

16. One aspect of practical wisdom is now described in v. 16a; the participle introducing v. 16 depends on περιπατεῖτε (v. 15). The difficulty of the phrase of v. 16a, the same phrase as in Col 4.5, has been recognised since at least the time of Chrysostom; it is perhaps this difficulty that led AE to explain it in v. 16b. In both v. 16a and v. 16b he uses words describing time and these should probably be taken in the same general way. We begin with v. 16b.

The 'day' (singular) in early Christian speech meant the day of the Lord, the parousia (cf 6.13), but v. 16b has the plural. Yet that

---

[1] See the literature on virtue and vice lists given at 5.3 and M. J. Suggs, 'The Christian Two Way Tradition: Its Antiquity, Form and Function', *Studies in New Testament and Early Christian Literature* (ed. D. E. Aune), Leiden, 1972, 60–74.

does not necessarily eliminate the eschatological element, for there are phrases like 'the last days' (2 Tim 3.1; Jas 5.3; 2 Pet 3.3; Mt 24.19ff; cf *T Zeb* 9.5ff; *T Dan* 5.4; *Barn* 4.9) which refer to the End and depict it as one of great evil, the period of the birth pangs of the Messiah (cf Mk 13.9ff). When however the plural 'days' refers to the End, this is made clear either by the addition of 'last' or by the context (Mt 24.19ff). Neither the context nor a qualifying phrase suggests that AE thinks here of the evil days as those of the End. He never argues for an imminent End and does not betray the sense of urgency found in 1 Cor 7.26; Rom 13.11; he does not say the time (days) is short, as did much of early Christianity, but that the time is evil (Knox, *Gentiles*, 199). For him the world is a more permanent place than for Paul (Lindemann, see also his *Aufhebung*, 282–5). Why then are the days evil? Not because they are full of natural disasters, earthquakes, famines, floods; or because Christians are being harassed or persecuted (cf Tertullian, *Fuga* 9.2), of which there is no sign in the letter, though such outside pressure on Christians was then common; or because heretics were giving trouble (cf Bouttier), for the letter contains little trace that AE is contending seriously with heresy and, since his advice to his readers largely relates to their mutual relationships, we should expect such if heresy were present. AE has not however been slow to paint Gentile culture in the darkest of terms (2.12; 4.17–19, 22; 5.8); in that sense for him the days, his own times, were evil, a period of moral decadence. Of course it is not the days themselves which are evil— time is a neutral category—but the people and events which fill them (cf Pelagius; Origen, *Matt Cat* 134, GCS 41, 67.1; *Judges Hom* GCS 30, 467.15ff), and they are not turned into good days (Jerome) by the wise use of time; the people and events of the outside world remain the same. AE may have regarded the days as evil in another way for they are the period when the evil one is active, and which is under the control of the evil powers (6.10ff). That AE could simultaneously hold both these views can be seen from 2.1ff where he switches between personal sin and the control of evil powers. Perhaps then the best adjective to describe these days is 'godless' (cf Roberts). If some days are described as evil this must imply there are 'good' days; since these are not now they must lie in the future (cf Origen); there is then here an implicit reference to a future for believers lying outside and beyond the existing world.

Excluding then any primary eschatological reference in days we turn to v. 16a.[2] It contains an unusual phrase which is found also in Col 4.5; in both places it is associated with περιπατεῖν; the verb is

[2] Cf R. M. Pope, 'Of Redeeming the Time', *ExpT* 22 (1910–11) 552–4; A. Auer, ' "Kaufet die Zeit aus" ', *Die Freude an Gott—unsere Kraft* (FS O. B. Knoch, ed. J. J. Degenhardt), Stuttgart, 1991, 439–44.

common in NT paraenesis and the phrase is used differently in the
two letters; in Col 4.5 it refers to conduct towards those outside the
community and in Eph 5.16 to present evil days without any
reference to behaviour in the outside world. It is the kind of striking
phrase, which once formulated, say in the Pauline school, would be
remembered and used though not always with the same reference.
Here καιρός in accordance with our initial premise must be taken as
a word denoting a period of time like days rather than as indicating a
decisive moment or unique opportunity, though both meanings
might be present. The distinction drawn at times between χρόνος
and καιρός cannot be sustained in respect of the NT[3] for in it the
two words are often synonymous. καιρός is a neutral term taking its
meaning from its context; here it will have something of the flavour
'opportunity'; 'opportunities' to do good exist throughout believers'
lives and are not just rare and occasional moments.

ἐξαγοράζειν (for the word see F. Büchsel, *TWNT*, I, 126–8) is a
commercial term. It is used soteriologically in Gal 3.13; 4.5, but this
meaning would be out of place here and in its only other NT
occurrence at Col 4.5. Out of place here also would be the meaning
'ransom' (cf Robinson), for it is people and not objects or categories
which are ransomed.[4] Dan 2.8 has a similar phrase to that here with
the sense 'gaining time', but this cannot be the meaning here, nor
that of *Mart Polyc* 2.3, 'purchasing eternal life'. It is not clear if in
the compound ἐκ should be given its full meaning 'buy out from'
(so MH, 309) or simply be taken as intensifying the sense of the
stem verb. When people purchase something, and it would strain the
image too much to ask, let alone answer, from whom the purchase is
made, the purchase is normally for themselves (this may be the
significance of the middle). We may then take the phrase in a
general way as indicating that the believers are to employ their time
wisely; it should be used in a disciplined way; opportunities of doing
good are not to be missed (Stott; on the use of time cf Prov. 3.1ff;
M. Aurelius II 4f). Like a housewife setting out to shop with a
limited amount of money, believers have only a limited amount of
time and they must spend it wisely (Asmussen). They are not to
contribute to the evil of the days, but making the best use of time
they will redeem sections of it. In the HT AE goes on to treat three
sections needing to be redeemed.

17. This is the second contrast and it is similar in content to the
first (v. 15b). διὰ τοῦτο probably links it either to v. 16b rather than
v. 16a, since v. 16a is a consequence of being wise (v. 15b) and not
its basis, or to v. 15b since v. 17 re-expresses v. 15b; it might
possibly be linked to v. 15a, though in that case it is not clear why

---

[3] Cf J. Barr, *Biblical Words for Time* (SBT 33), London, 1962, 20ff.
[4] Moule, *Colossians*, ad 4.5, strongly criticises Robinson's views.

διὰ τοῦτο is needed. The readers are not to 'be' or 'become' (either translation of γίνεσθε is possible) foolish; rather they are to continue being what they are already supposed to be, 'wise'. The ἄφρων (for the word see G. Bertram, *TWNT*, IX, 226f) is not someone without a mind but the unthinking person who fails to use the mind he or she already has (for the use of the root in the NT see Lk 11.40; 12.20; Rom 2.20; 1 Cor 15.36; 2 Cor 11.16; 12.6; it is found regularly in the OT Wisdom literature).

Verse 17b has been subject to consideration textual variation. συνιέντες is read by D² (D* F G) Ψ 1881 𝔐 lat syʰ instead of the συνίετε of 𝔓⁴⁶ ℵ A B P 0278 6 33 81 365 1241ˢ 1739 *pc*; Hier Aug. The latter has the stronger support but scribes would be more likely to change a participle into a finite verb than vice versa. The participle, if read, will have imperatival sense. Whichever is read the meaning is unaffected. φρόνημα for θέλημα is poorly supported (only ℵ*), the change probably being made to emphasise the contrast with ἄφρονες. θεοῦ is read by A 81 365 614 629 2464 *pc* a d vgᶜˡ syᵖ boᵖᵗ; Hier Cass, but κυρίου has much the stronger support. The former was probably caused by the frequency with which 'the will of God' appears elsewhere in the NT; in Eph 1.5, 9, 11 it refers to God's plan and intention in the working out of salvation, which is not the reference here. As elsewhere in Ephesians (2.21; 4.1, 5, 17; 5.8, 10, 19, 22; 6.1, 4, 7, 8, 9, 10, 21) and generally in Paul, κύριος refers to Christ; 𝔓⁴⁶ indeed reads χριστοῦ.

The use of συνίημι emphasises the need for intellectual effort (cf 1 Pet 1.13) in discerning the Lord's will. Unlike 3.4 where the noun referred to insight given by God, the verb here refers to human insight, though when set in a Christian context this is never mere human insight but insight guided by the Holy Spirit. True understanding of the Lord's will does not remain theoretical but involves the carrying out of it in practice. AE does not tell how the Lord's will is to be discovered any more than in v. 10 he explained what is pleasing to God. For his possible reasons for not giving detailed instructions here and for the guidelines he does supply, see Essay: Moral Teaching §4. It is sufficient to note that here he stresses the need to use the enlightened mind in seeking out the path of true conduct. Believers have to reason out for themselves what they should do, learning from their personal ongoing experience and the experience of others within their community. This may be why AE moves on in vv. 19f to their common worship, for it gives them the opportunity to learn from one another. The more immediate move is to v. 18, since overindulgence in wine may cloud the mind and render them unable to learn at all.

18. This is the third contrast; it is not made between two entities, wine and the Spirit, but between two conditions, drunkenness and Spirit-possession. In itself the contrast may not be surprising but its introduction at this point is; vv. 15–17 have dealt with generalities of conduct, v. 18a forbids one precise sin, vv. 19–20 again return to generalities. Yet since this is the third of the three contrasts it would be wrong to see here a large jump in the argument. καί indicates an addition leading off into a new area which may be a more restricted one (Abbott, Schnackenburg, cf Mt 1.5; 16.7; 'and in particular', Ellicott, rather than 'and above all'). Because it refers to one particular sin, v. 18 would have been more appropriate to the sequence of 4.25–32; why then does it appear here and what is its significance? Is there anything in the situation of the readers or in the context of the letter which could have led to the reference to the excess use of wine? Wine itself it should be noted is neither condemned nor approved here though scripture has much to say about its use and misuse.

If we seek to explain the reference from the situation of the readers we are in the difficult position of not knowing much about their situation, for the letter is being sent to a number of communities whose actual situations would differ; elsewhere when AE mentions vices he usually does so in very general terms. He does not mention lying, theft, anger, improper talk (4.25–9) because these were particularly rife among his readers but because they were common failings; drunkenness should probably be taken in the same way. Yet it is hardly likely that he thinks of his readers as alcoholics; if he did, he would have been more explicit. Has he then in mind a situation like that of 1 Cor 11.17ff, where some worshippers ate and drank too much at a eucharist or accompanying 'love feast'? Support for such an explanation might come from vv. 19f where the worship of the community is introduced. Alternatively AE may be thinking of the wider situation of the readers as ex-Gentiles; drunkenness was a feature of some of the Mystery Religions, in particular that of Dionysius;[5] AE might then be denying the connection of Christianity with religious drunkenness. Yet if AE had either of these in mind surely he would have made it clearer, for ἀσωτία belongs to the context of daily living rather than of worship and v. 21 which depends on the verb of v. 18b brings us back to the area of moral behaviour. He may however only be continuing in his reference to drunkenness a theme present in Judaism (T Jud 11.2; 12.3; 13.6; 14.1; 16.1; T Issach 7.3; Philo devotes a whole treatise, De Ebrietate, to the drunkenness of Noah, cf Plant 140–7). Drunkenness is always a sin, was common in the ancient world and ought to be condemned. This however does nothing to explain its introduction here. Nor is it explained by noting that AE may be quoting Prov 23.31 (LXX A text; cf T Jud 14.1);

---

[5] Cf Hendriksen; C. L. Rogers, 'The Dionysian Background of Ephesians 5:18', BSac 136 (1979) 249–57; M. Hengel, Between Jesus and Paul, Philadelphia, 1983, 188 n. 7.

this would only account for the form of the reference to drunkenness and not the reason for it.

Can the context then supply a reason? The more general context is the contrast of wise and foolish behaviour (vv. 15–17) and the more immediate that of 'evil days', ἀσωτία (ἐν ᾧ refers to v. 18a and not simply to οἴνῳ within it), and being filled with the Spirit. ἀσωτία is a fairly general term for dissolute and prodigal behaviour (see Spicq, I, 154–6; W. Foerster, *TWNT*, I, 504f; cf Lk 15.13; Tit 1.6; 1 Pet 4.4; Philo, *Spec Leg* 4.91; *Vita Cont* 47; Josephus, *BJ* 4.651). Though it may derive from the same root as σωτηρία it is not used here as the opposite of salvation. Because of the indefiniteness of the word it is best translated with a general term and the context allowed to impart precision, if any is intended. The context of wisdom may suggest drunkenness was introduced because it robs the mind of orderliness and therefore of good behaviour, ordinary moral restraints being loosened; those who are drunk are more likely to imagine they are wise when in fact they are unwise. 'Wine acts like a drug producing folly' (Philo, *Vita Cont* 74, LCL translation). However, had AE intended this he would not have used ἀσωτία but a word like μωρία or ἀφροσύνη. A more remote but still a possible controlling thought arising from v. 8 is that of light, which is associated with sobriety as darkness with drunkenness (1 Th 5.6–8; Rom 13.12f). A much closer contextual reference would be 'evil days' (v. 16); many people resort to alcohol as a way of living through daily harassment. This would imply the evil days were those of the present age and not those of the end period; if the latter, hope would sustain believers without the need for wine. All these attempts to solve the problem look to the preceding context and none is really satisfactory. What then if we look at the context which follows? Can drunkenness and the Spirit be connected?

The Spirit here is not the human but the divine (cf ἐν πνεύματι at 2.22; 3.5; 6.18); the meaning is not 'be filled in your spirits'; if this were so, what is to fill the spirits is left completely undefined. 'Be filled with the Spirit and not spirits' represents what the Greek means but the play on words is not present in the Greek. πληροῦσθε and μεθύσκεσθε are present imperatives (cf Moule, 21; MHT, 76; Robertson, 854, 890); this no more means that they are continually drunk or filled with the Spirit than the present imperatives of 4.25ff imply that believers continually lie, lose their tempers, etc. From time to time these things happen; believers become drunk or the Spirit inspires them (cf Fanning, 336, 'make it your habit not to ... '). πληροῦσθε is the important word in the verse for the four following participles depend on it. The accompanying ἐν could be translated either 'by' or 'with' (cf BDR §172 n. 3; Moule, 76f; MHT, 240; Lemmer, 427–31; cf Ign *Smyrn*, intro.; Col 4.12 *v.l.*)

The Spirit is the real subject of the verb, 'Let the Spirit fill you' when you gather for worship. The filling (cf 3.19) with the Spirit may either precede the time of the participles and lead to worship, or it may depend on them so that worship leads to the coming of the Spirit, but more probably verb and participles are contemporaneous; there is neither worship without the Spirit nor a Spirit which does not lead to worship (for a full discussion see Lemmer, 431–5). What has led to the association of wine and the Spirit? They come together in Lk 1.15 in the angel's message to Zechariah about the future John the Baptist, but there is nothing to suggest AE knew this tradition and in any case it refers to abstention from wine rather than drunkenness. In Acts 2.13 those who speak in tongues are regarded by bystanders as drunk. Whether AE knew this account of Pentecost or not, drink is sometimes associated with spiritual exaltation so that those who desire the latter turn to the former to produce it (the Bacchantes attained ecstasy through wine; see also Isa 28.7; Philo, *Ebr* 147–8; *Vita Cont* 85, 89; Macrob *Sat*. I 18.1; Hipp *Ref* 5.8.6f).[6] Charismatic activity of various kinds might well have been associated with drunkenness so that some believers resorted to wine in order to produce such activity; if, as is probable, a regular meal was associated with the eucharist there would have been an opportunity for some to become drunk and become involved in the wrong way in worship (cf 1 Cor 11.21). Gosnell[7] suggests a background in Greco-Roman mealtime practices where solemn meals were often followed by serious discussion and sometimes singing. Discussion would be hindered if the participants were drunk. Evidence of these meals is drawn from cultured authors (e.g. Dio Chrysostom, II 63; Plutarch, *Mor* I 614D–15C) and the descriptions are of the life of the intellectually inclined. Would AE's readers have been thinking in these ways? Along the same lines, however, but much more likely to have been part of the feature of the lives of AE's readers, were the feasts in trade guilds, burial clubs, and the like (see Intro §10.2.3); drunkenness is a world-wide feature of feasting in meals associated with deaths. Rules are regularly laid down in these guilds and clubs for how discussion should be carried on; permission had to be sought from the presiding officer to speak; the movement from feasting with drunkenness to serious or ribald discussion would have been familiar to many of AE's readers. It was important for them to realise that the love feast before a service should not be marred by drunkenness or else the work of the Spirit in the gathering would be hindered. It may be this as well as the connection between

---

[6] Cf Pokorný, *Gnosis*, 91f; I. M. Lewis, *Ecstatic Religion*, Harmondsworth, 1971, 39; J. T. Bunn, 'Glossolalia in Historical Perspective' in *Speaking in Tongues* (ed. W. E. Mills), Grand Rapids, 1986, 165–78. For the wider idea, common in the ancient world, of divine intoxication see H. Lewy, *Sobria Ebrietas* (BZNW 9), Giessen, 1929.

[7] P. W. Gosnell, 'Ephesians 5:18–20 and Mealtime Propriety', *TynB* 44 (1993) 364–71.

drunkenness and ecstasy that forms the bridge to vv. 19f where we move forward to what may have been regarded as charismatic activity in worship.

19. When Christians are filled with the Spirit they worship together. When this happens they: (i) speak to one another in song (v. 19a), (ii) praise the Lord through song (v. 19b; cf 2 Sam 23.2 for the movement from Spirit to song), (iii) return thanks to Christ and God (v. 20), (iv) submit to one another (v. 21) and this finally leads on directly to the nature of conduct in the home.

ἐν is inserted before the list of songs by $\mathfrak{P}^{46}$ B P 0278 6 33 1739 *pc* lat, but omitted by ℵ A D F G Ψ 1881 𝔐 vg^ms. The evidence is evenly balanced and a decision is difficult; whether read or not the meaning is unaffected; if it was originally present it may have been omitted through harmonisation with Col 3.16. More important is the omission of πνευματικαῖς by $\mathfrak{P}^{46}$ B b d; Ambst; if this represents the true reading, πνευματικαῖς was probably added from Col 3.16; yet since the evidence for its presence is strong ℵ A D F G Ψ 0278 33 1739 1881 𝔐 lat sy co) and omission could have taken place through homoeoteleuton it is probably better to read it (cf Metzger; Zuntz, 94f, is more hesitant). The addition of ἐν χάριτι by A almost certainly comes from Col 3.16. Finally τῇ καρδίᾳ is prefixed by ἐν in Ψ 0278 33 𝔐 and is replaced by the plural, again prefixed by ἐν, in ℵ² A D F G P 365 *pc* latt sy^p hmg co. The plural is probably a grammatical improvement of the singular which is acceptable (cf MHT, 23) and probably original; again whichever is read the meaning is unaffected. As regards the structure of the verse, there is no reason with Hofmann to construe the names of the songs with the subsequent participles which would overload them and leave λαλοῦντες bare.

Apart from what we have just noted, there are other respects in which v. 19 differs from Col 3.16 (see Best, 'Who used Whom?'). καί is used in v. 19 but not in Col 3.16 to link the three names of the songs; this might be a purely cosmetic alteration. More significant is AE's use of the simple λαλοῦντες rather than the διδάσκοντες καὶ νουθετοῦντες of Col 3.16; the fuller phrase of Col 3.16 would have admirably suited both AE's special interest in the life of the community and his love of using two words where one would suffice; if A/Col used Ephesians the double phrase might be his spelling out of AE's simple word in order to identify more clearly the purpose of singing. Von Soden fantasises in suggesting that AE in using Colossians omits the reference to teaching and admonishing because these functions belong only to the ministry and AE has here every believer in mind. AE, if using Colossians, would hardly have omitted ἐν χάριτι for χάρις is one of his favourite theological terms (thirteen times). On the other hand Eph 5.19 has the fuller phrase ἄδοντες καὶ ψάλλοντες (Col 3.16 has only the second participle); this accords with AE's love of synonyms and might represent his enlargement of Col 3.16. Common to both Ephesians and Colossians are the titles for what is sung. These titles may have been those in common use in the Pauline school. On the whole there is slightly more to favour A/Col's use of Ephesians than AE's of Colossians; more probable than either is their joint use of common material belonging to the Pauline school.

As in 4.32, ἑαυτοῖς is not to be taken reflexively ('singing to themselves') as if they sang for their private pleasure but is used as a synonym for ἀλλήλοις (cf MHT, 43; Robertson, 690). It might possibly indicate antiphonal singing, a practice going back into the OT (see Ezra 3.11 and some of the Psalms), and in use among the Therapeutae (Philo, *Vita Cont* 84) and some early Christians (cf Pliny, *Ep X* 96). If this had been what AE wished to say he would have made it clearer; this understanding of the word is not possible in Col 3.16. The use of song in the early church seems to have been extensive; Acts 16.25 provides indirect testimony. Much effort and ingenuity have been devoted to distinguishing and identifying the three names describing what was sung. It is probably better to take them as intended to cover all the singing that went on in worship rather than to differentiate between them.[8] AE never objects to using three words where one would suffice, though, more probably here the three terms come from the usage of the Pauline school. The adjective πνευματικαῖς may apply only to ᾠδαῖς; this, a more general word than either of the others, might need to be identified ('sacred' not 'secular' songs); yet the term is used without such qualification in relation to religious singing in the OT (e.g. Exod 15.1; Deut 32.44; 2 Kgdms 22.1; and the titles of many of the Psalms) and in Rev 5.9; 14.3; 15.3, which gives it a context in the church in Asia Minor. The word did not then need any qualification in Jewish or Christian circles to indicate the singing as religious. The adjective is therefore to be taken with all three nouns, being feminine in agreement with the nearest (BDR §135.3; MHT, 311). In view of the use of πνεῦμα in v. 19 it should be given its full meaning 'spiritual' as in 1.3 (cf Rom 1.11; 1 Cor 2.13; 9.11; 12.1; 14.1; 15.44, 46; Col 1.9); it is singing inspired or controlled by the Holy Spirit.

Is it then spontaneous charismatic singing, or the singing, prompted by the Spirit, of existing songs, or the singing of songs whose origin can be traced to the Spirit? The early Christians both used the OT Psalms and composed hymns of their own. AE has just quoted one in 5.14; part of another appears in 1 Tim 3.16. Luke's infancy narrative contains several (1.46ff; 1.68ff; 2.29ff) as does Revelation (5.9f; 7.15–17; 11.17f; 15.3f); adapted hymns are found in Phil 2.6–11; Col 1.15–20. Christians thus continued the Jewish tradition, which itself was still alive (*Psalms of Solomon*, Qumran

---

[8] For discussions of the individual terms see Gnilka, Schlier, Lincoln, and for the place of singing in worship R. P. Martin *Worship in the Early Church* (2nd edn), Grand Rapids, 1975, 39–52, 136f; M. Hengel, op.cit., 78–96; G. Delling, *Worship in the New Testament*, London, 1962, 82–91; J. M. Robinson as in n. 2 of 1.3–14. On hymns and music in the Greco-Roman world see R. MacMullen, *Paganism in the Roman Empire*, New Haven and London, 1981, 15–24. On the possibility that Ephesians incorporates hymns or fragments of hymns see Best, 'Use'.

hymns); singing was also found in contemporary religious worship. There was thus plenty of traditional material at hand for use. The use of traditional material would of course serve to sustain the community (MacDonald, 141). However, few of these early Christian hymns could be regarded as addressed to other believers; they are almost all in praise of Christ or God. Exceptions are 5.14 and Rev 7.15ff, and Phil 2.6–11, if its main purpose, or that of the underlying hymn, was to inculcate humility. (Any modern hymn-book will have hymns which address God and Christ and those which address other worshippers.) Some songs then existed in which believers addressed one another; in 1 Cor 14.26 Paul writes of believers as each one having a Psalm, a teaching, etc.; in the context of the passage he seems to be referring to spontaneous contributions to worship addressed by believers to one another. Singing to one another is just one of the ways believers exhort one another (Heb 3.13). Paul terms such contributions 'spiritual' (12.1; 14.1) and this may be the significance of 'spiritual' here.[9] This neither excludes the 'spontaneous' use of traditional material nor does it imply it. Philo, *Vita Cont* 80, writes of the introduction of new hymns into the worship of the Therapeutae as well as of their use of existing material. AE has probably both in mind. Although 1 Cor 14.15 allows the possibility there is no reason to think of these hymns as glossolaliac in character; λαλεῖν which introduces the clause would normally indicate intelligible speech and if 'tongues' were intended would require some qualification. Whatever their nature, these songs are a part of communal worship being used either in gatherings of the whole community or individual house churches or within families.

This will also be true of praise offered to the Lord (v. 19b). This clause is not another way of looking at v. 19a, treating inner motivation rather than outer activity (cf Gnilka, Schlier). The praise offered in v. 19b is offered in the course of the same worship as that of v. 19a, but v. 19b speaks of praise directed not to other believers but to the Lord (= Christ, as in v. 17; the reading 'Lord' in Col 3.16 is inferior and was probably influenced by our verse). As we have seen, many Christian hymns already existed, as well as OT Psalms, with Christ or God as object; some may also have been spontaneously created in the course of worship. AE's use of 'Lord' and not 'God' has been held, on the supposition that he used Col 3.15, to be the result of later theological development in elevating Christ; yet this cannot be so, for from the beginning Christ was the subject of creeds and hymns (Phil 2.6–11; Rev 4.11; 5.9, 13). AE, in accordance with his general style, employs here two almost synonymous verbs. Although ᾄδω can be used of instrumental music it does not necessarily carry this idea (cf Rom 15.9; 1 Cor 14.15; Jas

[9] Cf J. D. G. Dunn, *Jesus and the Spirit*, London, 1975, 238f.

5.13) and in the light of the use of the cognate noun in v. 19a it probably does not do so here (*pace* Barth; cf BAGD *s.v.*; Delling, op.cit., 86 n. 4).[10]

This worship is not silent worship in the heart (for 'heart' see on 1.18; cf 3.17; 4.18; 6.5, 22) but worship offered from the heart where the Spirit dwells (Rom 5.5; 2 Cor 1.22; 3.3; Gal 4.6); it comes from the deepest level of existence and is not purely emotional ('hearty') froth but contains considerable intellectual content; the singing was singing with understanding (Theophylact). It is often difficult for us to classify traditional material as hymn or creed, since contemporary hymns were deeply imbued with theology. Inner sentiment (the heart) and outer action (the singing) agree; lips and heart are in harmony; this is important for God listens not to the outward voice but to the heart.

20. This verse forms the third clause dependent on v. 18, and, like those of v. 19, relates to communal worship; believers have spoken to one another in song, praised Christ and now as a kind of climax they are to return thanks to God. Thanksgiving, already seen in 5.4 as the alternative to sinful behaviour, has always formed part of Jewish praise of God as the OT Psalms and the Qumran hymns testify, and quickly became a part of Christian worship (1 Th 5.18; Col 4.2; 1 Tim 2.1). This thanksgiving is to be offered, in a typically plerophoric liturgical expression, at all times (cf Rom 1.9; 1 Cor 1.4; Phil 1.4; 4.4; Col 1.3; 1 Th 1.2; 2 Th 1.3, 11; Philem 4) and for all. 'All times' are all those occasions when worship is offered. The reference in 'for all' is more difficult to determine since πάντων can be either masculine or neuter. Where elsewhere πάντοτε and a part of πᾶς are joined, the latter is masculine but each time the reference is to intercession and not thanksgiving; it is impossible to intercede on behalf of 'things', but it is possible to give thanks for 'things'. It is easy to deduce from his letter some of the things for which AE would wish to thank God: election to be part of God's people, redemption through Christ's blood, enlightenment to understand what God has done, the resurrection and ascension of Christ and of believers with him, the equal status of ex-Jew and ex-Gentile in the church, their relationship to Christ in his body, their new nature, the ability to perform good works. If giving thanks were restricted to giving thanks for people, it would be limited to giving thanks that they believed or that they carried out some Christian duty as prophets or teachers or in the general care of others. In view of this limitation it is then better to take πάντων as neuter and give it a wide sense. If this is so, is the list above exhaustive or should it be extended? Some of the Fathers (e.g. Jerome, Pelagius, Chrysostom),

---

[10] On the use of instrumental music in the early church see J. Foster, 'The Harp at Ephesus', *ExpT* 74 (1962/3) 156.

instancing Job 1.23, suggest that everything that happens, including unfortunate events, should be included. But while it is certainly possible to thank God for the response of people to evil events (famines, earthquakes, etc.), is it possible to thank him for the evil events themselves? Yet it must be recognised as true that some kinds of suffering, principally suffering for the sake of Christ as distinct from the suffering that comes in the normal course of life (e.g. unemployment, sickness), do bring joy. Meyer, followed by Barth, would rightly include such suffering (cf 3.13; Mt 5.11f; Lk 6.22f; Acts 5.41; Phil 4.4ff; Col 1.24; 1 Th 1.6; Jas 1.2f; 1 Pet 1.6; 4.13).

τῷ θεῷ καὶ πατρί is difficult to translate; it probably means something like 'to him who is God and also Father', 'to him who is at once God and Father', God being presented here as Father of believers rather than of Christ. The order of 'God' and 'Father' is also textually uncertain. The sequence translated above is that of א A B D¹ Ψ 0278 33 1739 1881 𝔐 f vg sy⁽ᵖ⁾ boᵖᵗ; Hier; this has a wider spread of reading than the reverse order in 𝔓⁴⁶ D*² F G 1175 2464 pc it; MVict Ambst. The order 'God and Father' is the normal order of the words in the NT and it is unlikely that scribes would alter this unless they wished to associated Father with Christ through proximity; on the other hand given the reverse order scribes might have changed it to the normal.

The 'name'[11] of Christ was used inter alia in baptism (Mt 28.19; Acts 8.16; 10.48), in healing (Acts 3.6; 10.1; Jas 5.14), in relation to the coming together of believers (Mt 18.20; 1 Cor 5.4; cf Mk 9.37) and in intercessionary and petitionary prayer (Jn 14.13, 14; 15.16; 16.26), but only in v. 20 is it used in relation to praise. For AE's use of ἐν cf Col 3.16; AE has however applied it differently. διά is the more usual preposition in relation to praising God through Christ for what he has done in salvation (Rom 1.8; 7.25; 16.27; Col 3.17; Jude 25).

These thanksgivings, whatever their content, are offered to God in the name of our Lord Jesus Christ. The clause forms a fitting climax to this section of the letter (Penna takes it as the climax of the section beginning at 5.3) for it is because of Christ's redeeming life, death and resurrection that God may be approached (2.18; 3.12; cf Rom 5.2; 1 Pet 3.18). After v. 20 we return in vv. 21ff from worship to behaviour. AE slid over easily from behaviour in 4.1–5.18 to worship through the reference to the Spirit; now with a reference to Christ he returns (vv. 21ff) to the way his readers should treat one another in their daily lives. If worship regularly took place in houses then the introduction of the HT in this part of the letter is not unnatural.

Before we leave the subject of worship it is important to ask about its nature. In v. 20 εὐχαριστοῦντες is used; the cognate noun

[11] On ὄνομα see H. Bietenhard, TWNT, V, 242–83; id. NIDNTT, II, 648–56; S. New, 'The Name, Baptism, and the Laying on of Hands' in The Beginnings of Christianity V (ed. F. J. Foakes Jackson and Kirsopp Lake), London, 1933, 121–40.

became a term for the Lord's Supper as early as *Did* 9.1–5; 10.7; 14.1; Ignatius, *Eph* 13.1; *Philad* 4.1; *Smyrn* 7.1; 8.1; Justin, *Apol* I, 66–7. The verb itself was used by Paul in relation to prayer at the Lord's Supper (1 Cor 11.24) and in the Gospel accounts of the Last Supper (Mt 26.27; Mk 14.23; Lk 22.17, 19). In v. 18 there was a reference to wine. Is then the worship described in vv. 19f to be regarded as eucharistic? Adai, 226f, argues that a eucharistic setting is seen even more clearly in Col 3.15–17 on which he believes vv. 19f depend. However, this claim about Colossians is by no means universally supported by those who comment on it (see the commentaries of O'Brien, Moule, Lohse, Pokorný, Schweizer, Gnilka, Bruce, Ernst). Moreover εὐχαριστεῖν is used widely in the NT with its basic meaning of 'giving thanks' without eucharistic implication. It seems simpler then to conclude that while vv. 19f refer to community worship they give no clue as to its nature. It may have been eucharistic, it may not. Finally we should note the coming together in vv. 18–20 of the Spirit, Christ and God the Father. This is not a piece of Trinitarian doctrine but as elsewhere in the letter it provides the rough building blocks from which that doctrine was later forged.

21. That a difficulty exists in relating this verse to the ongoing argument can be seen in the different way it is set out in UBS and NA: the latter makes a major break after v. 20; the former after v. 21. As a general caveat it should be realised that authors do not necessarily think in paragraphs when writing. Most translations split 1.3–14 into two paragraphs though it is one sentence; whether a paragraph division should follow 4.32 or 5.2 is, as we have seen, uncertain; should one be made between 5.5 and 5.6 (so UBS but not NA)? There is at times perhaps a greater flow in the argument than editors care to admit.

In favour of the division after v. 21 are: (1) The participle of v. 21 continues the sequence of participles in vv. 19, 20, all dependent on the imperative of v. 18b. (2) 5.21 deals with the relationship of all believers to one another whereas 5.22–6.9 treats only the relationships to one another of those who live in wholly Christian households. (3) The theme of v. 21 is mutual subordination whereas that of 5.22–6.9 is the subordination of individuals (wives, children, slaves) to other individuals (husbands, fathers, masters). (4) Mutual subordination fits well with 5.19 where all believers mutually address one another and there are no hierarchical distinctions (e.g. 'listen to what the prophets say'). It must be allowed however that between v. 19a and v. 21 the material relates not to speaking to one another but to God. (5) Mutual subordination picks up the theme of the introductory verses to the paraenesis, in particular 4.2, and rounds it off before the move to a new area. (6) Vv. 19–21 may form a chiasmus (cf T. G. Allen, 260); v. 19a and v. 21 treat the

relation of believers to other believers; v. 19b and v. 20 their relation
to God.

In favour of the division before v. 21 are: (1) V. 22 lacks a verb
and since this must be supplied from v. 21, this would link the
verses. (2) 5.22–6.9 deals with a fresh subject, life in the household;
nothing in vv. 18–20 suggests AE had the household in mind when
writing about worship, apart from the fact that worship took place in
houses. (3) The theme of 5.22–6.9 is subordination even though it is
not mutual. (4) The participle of v. 21 could be understood as an
imperative (see on 4.25); yet is it likely that in a sequence of
participles one should suddenly be taken as an imperative? (5) The
references to 'fear' in both v. 21 and v. 33 might be taken to indicate
an *inclusio*, thus joining v. 21 to what follows; but if there is an
inclusio it should connect v. 21 and 6.9; the two references to fear
may then be accidental.

How is this difficulty to be resolved? ἀλλήλοις cannot be deprived
of its sense of equality in mutuality along the lines of Mt 24.10; 25.32;
1 Pet 5.1–5[12] for in these cases an obvious distinction is made; so far
as I can discover no one had thought of solving the difficulty in this
way until the rise of the feminist movement, and it is not therefore
an obvious solution. The word carries the idea of equal mutuality in
Eph 4.2, 25, 32 and in the vast majority of its occurrences in the NT
(e.g. Mk 4.41; 8.16; 9.34; Rom 1.27; 12.5; 13.8; 1 Cor 12.25; 16.20;
Gal 5.13; Col 3.9; 1 Th 5.11). V. 22 is not then a special case of v.
21, 'wives in particular [Barth inserts an "e.g." before v. 22] should
be subordinate' since this would exclude the mutuality which is an
essential part of v. 21.

Clark's solution,[13] 'let then there be subordination among you', excludes
the mutuality and is therefore not possible. Sampley, 117, suggests v. 21
qualifies what would be an absolute submission throughout 5.22–6.9 and
that AE inserted it for this purpose as a criticism of the basic stance of the
HT; this would make v. 21 his correction of the HT; if he had intended it to
be such he would have made this clearer. Roberts solves the difficulty by
treating 5.15–6.9 as the basic unit but 5.15–20 and 5.22–6.9 have little in
common; Roberts may however be correct in regarding v. 21 as a
transitional verse; this seems the best solution.

The concept of mutuality between believers is a regular NT theme
being found in the Johannine form of the love commandment (Jn
13.34f) and appearing in varying ways in the Pauline corpus (Rom
12.10, 16; 15.5, 14; 1 Cor 12.25; Gal 5.13; 6.2; Col 3.13, 16; 1 Th
3.12; 4.18; 5.11, 13; Phil 2.2; cf 1 Pet 5.5); it is present already in
our letter at 4.2. It is the attitude believers as members of the body
should have to one another (1 Cor 12.25f) and is closely related to

---

[12] See H. Maillet, 'ALLA ... PLÉN ...', *ETR* 55 (1980) 566–79.
[13] S. B. Clark, *Man and Woman in Christ*, Ann Arbor, MI, 1980, 74.

the humility to which all are summoned (4.2). Yet at the same time there are those who are teachers and leaders; all are members of the one body but they have different functions. After writing of the way Christians should care for one another in 1 Th 5.11, Paul moves directly to urge (v. 12) respect for their leaders. Paul would have included himself in mutual love with his converts (nothing suggests he could not have penned our verse) yet he continually exercises authority over them (see Best, *Converts*, 139ff); he is one among others in the body of Christ yet superior in authority. Early Christianity contains an unresolved tension between authority and mutuality or, in the terms of our passage (taking in 5.22–6.9), between mutual subordination and the authority of some. If this tension has not been thought through by the time of Ephesians (has it ever been?) then it is not surprising to move from mutual subordination in v. 21 to the subordination of one group to another in 5.22–6.9. It may be necessary to stress mutual subordination because charismatics sometimes tend to override opposition (cf Scott). The possible tension may have been partly veiled from AE because at v. 22 he picks up a block of traditional teaching (cf Col 3.18–4.1) which began with the theme of subordination. Having written 5.21 under the influence of 5.19, AE had the word ὑποτάσσω in his mind; intending to use the HT in some way, this may have seemed to him the appropriate place to introduce it. The verse is then in part transitional in completing vv. 18–20 and in preparing for the HT. It is however better to associate it with what precedes than with what follows.

ὑποτάσσω[14] is a strong word, frequent in the Pauline corpus (Rom 8.7; 10.3; 13.5; Col 3.18; Tit 3.1; Heb 12.9) and used in relation to the position of slaves (Tit 2.9; 1 Pet 2.18; in the latter case the master is assumed to be hostile). There is no reason to accept Lindemann's view that for AE it defines a different attitude from that of 6.1, 5 where ὑπακούω is used; it is however true that the relation of wife to husband is different from that of child to parent or slave to owner, for in the wealthier parts of Roman society the wife will have had some freedom in the choice of husband and her subordination would then in part be voluntary; probably this would be less true away from Rome and in the lower layers of society, though a partial consent may always have been present in the relation. Subordination implies a sense of order in society. Mutual subordination will naturally be voluntary. It is best illustrated by the action of Jesus in washing his disciples' feet (Jn 13.1ff). Jesus associates this type of behaviour, though not using the

[14] Cf G. Delling, *TWNT*, VIII, 40–8; E. Kamlah, 'Υποτάσσεσθαι in den neutestamentlichen "Haustafeln"', *Verborum Veritas* (FS G. Stählin, ed. O. Bocher and K. Haacker), Wuppertal, 1970, 237–43; Barth, 708–15; T. Y. Mullins, 'The Use of ὑποτάσσειν in Ignatius', *Second Century* 2 (1982) 35–9.

word, with the nature of true greatness (Mk 10.43–5) and again his own activity illustrates what he says (Mk 10.45). It is a type of behaviour which tends to disappear when too much wine has been used (v. 18; cf Macpherson). Believers do not fall into mutual subordination easily; the connection of v. 21 with what precedes shows that its attainment is based on the imperative of v. 18b; only when filled with the Spirit do people willingly submit to another and learn not to insist on their own rights. Mutual subordination is of course a necessary basis for democracy.

There are three variants in the final phrase of the verse: D F G add 'Jesus' before or after Christ; K bo^{ms} substitute 'Lord' for Christ'; 6 81 614 630 1881 *pm*; Cl Ambst^{mss} substitute 'God' for 'Christ'. The first is an obvious addition in view of the frequency with which Jesus and Christ appear together, the second has little support and the third probably arises from an attempt to make the motivation stronger since fear is not normally linked to Christ (only at Col 3.22; cf 2 Cor 5.10) but to God, especially in the Wisdom literature where the fear of God is the beginning of wisdom (Prov 1.7; 9.10; Ps 111.10; cf Prov 15.33; Job 28.28).

The connection of fear to Christ follows a trend in which the NT transfers statements made about God in the OT to Christ. It also introduces a new element. φόβος is a word with a wide range of meaning. Here it would be wrong to read into it any idea of 'terror'. It is instead a reverential fear which needs to be balanced by the motivation of love (Rom 12.1; 15.3f; 2 Cor 5.14; Eph 4.32; 5.2). It carries neither a hidden reference to the day of judgement nor even a threat of judgement (*pace* Schlier; Barth, 662f). The attitude Christians should have to their Lord is expressed in many other ways in the NT, above all in the idea of trust. Fear cannot be isolated and discussed on its own but must be regarded as part of a total attitude, and probably not as the most important part.

XIV

BEHAVIOUR IN THE CHRISTIAN HOUSEHOLD
(5.22–6.9)

Up to this point the paraenesis has seemed to jump from subject to subject but now we have a more systematic section centring on the behaviour of those living in Christian households. The style however remains similar to that in 4.17–5.20, the sentences being briefer than in chaps. 1–3, though it must be allowed that they are sometimes longer and more complex than in other parts of the paraenesis since in 5.22–33 theology and paraenesis are intermingled. In large part the style is determined by AE's use of traditional material which in 5.22–33, but not in 6.1–9, he expands to introduce a theological argument. On the traditional material see Detached Note: The *Haustafel*. It contains three sections treating the household groups, husbands and wives (5.22–33), parents and children (6.1–4), masters and slaves (6.5–9).

DETACHED NOTE VI
THE *HAUSTAFEL*

Dibelius, 48–50; K. Weidinger, *Die Haustafeln, ein Stück urchristlichen Paraenese* (UNT 14), Leipzig, 1928; Selwyn, *1 Peter*, 419–39; K. H. Rengstorf, 'Die neutestamentliche Mahnungen an die Frau, sich den Manne unterzuordnen', *Verborum Dei manet in Aeternum* (FS O. Schmitz, ed. W. Foerster), Witten, 1953, 131–45; H. D. Wendland, 'Zur sozialethischen Bedeutung der neutestamentlichen Haustafeln', *Die Leibhaftigkeit des Wortes* (FS A. Koberle, ed. O. Michel and U. Mann), Hamburg, 1958, 34–56; D. Schroeder, 'Die Haustafeln des Neuen Testaments' (unpublished dissertation) Hamburg, 1959; O. Merk, *Handeln aus Glauben*, Marburg, 1968, 214–24; J. P. Sampley, '*And the Two Shall Become One Flesh*' (SNTSMS 16), Cambridge, 1971, 17–30; J. E. Crouch, *The Origin and Intention of the Colossian Haustafel* (FRLANT 109), Göttingen, 1972; W. Schrage, 'Zur Ethik der neutestamentlichen Haustafeln', *NTS* 21 (1974/5) 1–22; D. Lührmann, 'Wo man nicht mehr Sklave oder Freier ist', *WD* 13 (1975) 53–83; E. Schweizer, 'Die Weltlichkeit des Neuen Testaments: die Haustafeln', *Beiträge zur Alttestamentliche Theologie* (FS W. Zimmerli, ed. H. Donner, R. Hanhart, R. Smend), Göttingen, 1977, 396–413; Goppelt, *Petrusbrief*, 163–79; R. P. Martin, *NIDNTT*, III, 928–32; E. Schweizer, 'Traditional ethical patterns in the Pauline and post-

Pauline letters and their development', *Text and Interpretation* (FS M. Black, ed. E. Best and R. McL. Wilson), Cambridge, 1979, 195–209; F. Stagg, 'The Domestic Code and Final Appeal in Ephesians 5:21–6:24', *RevExp* 76 (1979) 541–52; D. L. Balch, *Let Wives Be Submissive: The Domestic Code in 1 Peter* (SBLMS 26), Chico, CA, 1981; id. 'Early Christian Criticism of Patriarchal Authority in 1 Peter 2:11–3:12', *USQR* 39 (1984) 161–74; id. 'Household Codes', *Greco-Roman Literature and the New Testament* (ed. D. E. Aune; SBLSBS 21), Atlanta, GA, 1988, 25–50; id. 'Neopythagorean Moralists and the New Testament Household Codes', *ANRW* II 26.1, 380–411; K. Thaede, 'Zur historischen Hintergrund der "Haustafeln" des NT', *Pietas* (FS B. Kötting, ed. E. Dassmann and K. S. Frank, JAC Ergängzungsband 8), Münster Westfälen, 1980, 259–68; J. Gnilka, *Kolosserbrief*, 205–16; D. Lührmann, 'Neutestamentliche Haustafeln und antike Ökonomie', *NTS* 27 (1980/1) 83–97; J. Gnilka, 'Das Akkulturationsproblem nach dem Epheser- und Kolosserbrief', *Fede e Cultura alla Luce della Bibbia* (Atti della Sessione plenaria 1979 della Pontificia Commissione Biblica, ed. J.-D. Barthelemy), Turin, 1981, 235–47; K. Müller, 'Die Haustafel des Kolosserbriefes und das antike Frauenthema. Eine kritische Rückschau auf alter Ergebnisse', *Die Frau im Urchristentum* (ed. G. Dautzensberg, H. Merklein, K. Müller), Freiburg, Basel, Vienna, 1982, 263–319; J. H. Elliott, *A Home for the Homeless*, London, 1982, 204–20; G. E. Cannon, *The Use of Traditional Materials in Colossians*, Macon, GA, 1983, 95–131; D. C. Verner, *The Household of God: The Social World of the Pastoral Epistles* (SBLDS 71), Chico, CA, 1983; A. S. di Marco, 'Ef 5,21–6,9', *RivBiblt* 31 (1983) 189–207; K. Berger, *Formgeschichte*, 135–41; id. *ANRW* II 25.2, 1078–86; P. Fiedler, *RAC* XIII, 1063–73; L. Hartmann, 'Code and Context: A Few Reflections on the Paraenesis of Col 3:6–4:1', *Tradition and Interpretation of the New Testament* (FS E. E. Ellis, ed. G. F. Hawthorne and O. Betz), Tübingen, 1987, 237–47; id. *Kolosser*, 149–52; B. Witherington, *Women in the Earliest Churches* (SNTSMS 59), Cambridge, 1988, 42–61; E. Lohse, *Theological Ethics of the New Testament*, Philadelphia, 1991, 138–45; MacDonald, 102–22; G. Strecker, 'Die neutestamentlichen Haustafeln (Kol 3,18–4,1 und Eph 5,22–6,9)', *Neues Testament und Ethik* (FS R. Schnackenburg, ed. H. Merklein), Freiburg, 1989, 349–75; S. Motyer, 'The Relationship between Paul's Gospel of "All one in Christ Jesus" (Galatians 3.28) and the "Household Codes"', *VoxEv* 19 (1989) 33–48; Gielen, *passim*; A. Malherbe, 'Hellenistic Moralists and the New Testament', *ANRW* II 26.1, 267–333 at 304–13; A. Weiser, 'Evangelisierung im Haus', *BZ* 34 (1990) 63–86; H. von Lips, 'Die Haustafel als "Topos" im Rahmen der urchristlichen Paränese: Beobachtungen anhand des 1.Petrusbriefes und des Titusbriefes', *NTS* 40 (1994) 261–80; Best, 'Haustafel'. Some of the items in this bibliography restrict themselves to treating only the origin and form of the *Haustafel*, a few deal only with the content of its three sections and others with both areas.

The origin of the HT form has been hotly debated; did it arise within the early Christian church (e.g. Rengstorf, Schroeder), or Hellenistic Judaism (e.g. Crouch), or the Greco-Roman world under the influence of Aristotle (e.g. Balch, Thraede), or Stoicism (e.g. Weidinger) or more widely (e.g. Berger)?

It is now generally agreed that the first theory is incorrect: it was taken over by the church which modified it for Christian usage. We can hazard a guess as to its form prior to its Christian adoption by using the two forms in Ephesians and Colossians:

Wives, be subject to your husbands as is proper [in the Lord];
Husbands, love your wives.
Children, obey your parents;
Fathers, do not annoy your children.
Slaves, obey your [human] masters;
Masters, treat your slaves justly.[1]

The question as to the origin of the form may not be all that important; if people are to live together, there are certain basic areas in which they require moral guidance and Christians must offer them this guidance as much as Jews, Greeks or Romans. One basic area is the household and, though its precise legal definition is unclear,[2] it probably can be taken as including a biological family with their servants and slaves. The household was a social institution in all areas of the Greco-Roman world and especially important for Christians because it was the place where groups met to worship, the base for missionary activity and the place of reception for travelling Christians (Gielen, 68ff). The baptism of households was also a significant feature of early Christianity (Acts 16.14–16, 34–6; 18.8). However, Greek, Roman and Jewish moralists often include another basic area, that of the state. Paul covers this in Rom 13.1–7 and it is the first area in the HT of 1 Pet 2.13–3.7.

It is difficult to know the correct term with which to describe 5.22–6.9. Martin Luther used the word *Haustafel*, yet it fails to cover 1 Pet 2.13–3.7 with its reference outside the household in 2.13–17. 'Code of social duties' or the briefer 'social code' or 'code of stations (in society)' seem more suitable, but since *Haustafel* is the term in general use we shall use it. Apart from Ephesians, Colossians and 1 Peter, we can trace the form, though not always as clearly, in Tit 2.1–10; 1 Clem 1.3; 21.6–9; Ign *Polyc* 4.1–6.1; Polyc *Phil* 4.1–6.3; *Did* 4.9–11; fragments of it also appear in 1 Timothy *passim* and 1 Clem 38.2. The internal arrangement of the form in Ephesians and Colossians, but not in 1 Peter, is often incorrectly described as reciprocal; 'love one another' is a reciprocal relationship as is that of 5.21; 'rule/obey' is not. It is better then to speak of

---

[1] See Best, 'Haustafel', and the exegesis of the individual verses for this basic form.
[2] See F. Laub, *Die Begegnung des frühen Christentums mit der antiken Sklaverei* (SBS 107), Stuttgart, 1982, 19–47; Verner, 27–81; A. Strobel, 'Der Begriff des "Hauses" im griechischen und römischen Privatrecht', *ZNW* 56 (1965) 91–100.

paired relationships in Ephesians and Colossians.[3] Approximately similar forms are found elsewhere, e.g. Philo, *Decal* 165–7; Josephus *c. Ap.* 2.190–219; Seneca, *de Benef* 2.18.1ff, but never as consistently as in Ephesians and Colossians where in each case one member of the pair is superior and the other inferior. The pair governors–governed was impossible in a Christian HT, for Christians did not address 'governors' about their duties though Jews did. In the paired form both the inferior and the superior are addressed; this is natural in respect of slaves and women since they were full members of the community (cf Gal 3.28; 1 Cor 7.21–4; 12.13; Col 3.11); children are also addressed so they were presumably regarded as members (the pairing is parent–child and not young–old); this would be especially true where a whole household had been baptised. The men are addressed as husbands, masters, fathers, thus giving the HT a patriarchal slant with which no one in the ancient world would have quibbled; this however makes difficult the simple transference of the HT to the modern Western world. In the Greco-Roman world it was normally the adult free male who was addressed but from time to time slaves and women were also. In 1 Clem 1.3; 21.6–9; Polyc *Phil* 4.2; *T Reub* 5.5 wives are not addressed directly but husbands are told to instruct them in their duties.

Munro[4] has argued that AE wrote using as basis an earlier and briefer form of Colossians which lacked the HT; he later added it (5.21–6.9); it was then modified and inserted back into Colossians. She believes Eph 5.15–18 is also a later insertion because of its banality following on 5.13f; yet 4.25ff is just as banal. There is no doubt that 6.10 could follow 5.20, but there is no positive reason to suppose it ever did. There is more reason to suppose the HT in Colossians might have been a later insertion since the argument of that letter would be more continuous without it. To return however to Ephesians, the evidence she offers that 5.21–6.9 is later than the remainder of the epistle is: (i) 6.5 is a conflation of 1.18 and Gal 1.10. (ii) 5.25 and 5.2 depend on Gal 2.20 and since 5.2 is simpler than 5.25 the latter is a development of it; this cannot imply its later addition; apart from that, it may be doubted if either 5.2 or 5.25 depends directly on Gal 2.20 and not on a traditional form. (iii) The omission of the article with κεφαλή in 5.23, though present in 4.15, proves that whoever inserted the HT knew 4.15 was already there; but since AE would have known of 4.15 when he wrote 5.23 this does not prove 5.23 was added later. (iv) 5.27f combines 1.4 with Col 1.22; but again it is as simple to suppose AE knew 1.4 and the language of Col 1.22 when he wrote 5.27f. None of this proves that the HT is a later insertion into Ephesians. Finally it should be pointed out that the HT in Ephesians with its teaching on the church fits into the letter's general interest in the nature of the church. The second half of Munro's argument

---

[3] There was a tendency in the ancient world to define by opposites; see W. A. Meeks, 'The Image of the Androgyne: Some Uses of a Symbol in Earliest Christianity', *HR* 13 (1974) 165–208, at 167f.

[4] W. Munro, 'Col. iii.18–iv.1 and Eph. v.21–vi.9: Evidence of a Late Literary Stratum?', *NTS* 18 (1971/2) 434–47.

depends on showing that the HT in Colossians is later than that in Ephesians. Her general position here is that Ephesians depends on all the earlier Pauline letters and is closer to them than is Colossians. It is however very doubtful that AE knew all the Pauline letters (see Introduction §2.6) and if Ephesians and Colossians came out of the same Pauline stable it as easy to suppose they both used Paul's language but used it differently. If Col 3.18f abbreviates Eph 5.22–33 it is surprising in the light of the heresy against which Colossians is directed that its author should omit the reference in Ephesians to Christ as saviour.

Munro, art.cit., is correct in pointing out how easily the HT in Colossians can be detached from its position and leave a continuous argument; this confirms that the HT as used in Colossians and Ephesians was an existing form. This conclusion is supported by the style of the first two areas of the HT in Colossians which is unlike that of the author of the letter, whereas the style of the third (master–slave), where an originally simpler form has been extended, is closer to the style of the remainder of the letter (Gnilka). The HT in Colossians also does not have any direct relation to the anti-heretical christological drive of the letter. The similarity of the form in the two letters has led many to conclude that AE must have drawn it from Colossians, but if it was a piece of tradition no grounds exist for proving this; AE is as likely to have drawn it directly from the tradition as from Colossians; the detailed exegesis will confirm this. In Ephesians the HT extends from 5.22 to 6.9; there are no grounds (*pace* Gielen, 204ff) for including 5.21. None of the other NT parallels have such a verse and its content and form are at variance with the content of the HT (see above on 5.21).

The HT will have been used in the ethical instruction of Christians, but its precise purpose is difficult to determine. In the wider world it was probably originally designed to assist in preserving the good order of society, the family being seen as a microcosm of society and as a basic unit in its structure. This purpose may well underlie its use in 1 Peter where there is an outward look towards society in 2.11f; free men are to honour the forms of society and wives and slaves are not to act beyond their accepted social roles. Adherence to the counsel of the HT would ensure a stabilising influence on the part of the church. In this way the code could also have had an apologetic function. This may also be true in respect of 1 Tim 6.1; Tit 2.10. The form in Ephesians and Colossians has been related to Gal 3.28 as an attempt to damp down expectations of equality (cf Verner, 109), but parents and children are not mentioned in Gal 3.28. A missionary purpose can be seen in 1 Pet 3.1f but this is not the ruling purpose even of that HT, let alone of others, since there is no suggestion slaves should attempt to convert their owners. In common with much other NT ethical instruction, the HT may have been used to guide believers once the expectancy of a speedy parousia had disappeared, but this accounts for neither its precise form nor its content. If used in catechetical instruction it was used after baptism rather than before it. The content of the HT in Ephesians is unrelated to the outside world and its purpose can therefore have been neither apologetic nor missionary. AE may have realised that just as there were always those who told lies or lost their tempers (4.25ff) there would always be households which did not run sweetly, and the HT is an attempt to indicate the kind of behaviour which would remedy that situation. If the form in tradition had a section on relations with the non-Christian world (cf 1 Pet 2.13–17), then AE has omitted this section and this would be in keeping with the way in which his other ethical teaching relates to life within the community and lacks a wider and external reference.

Since the HT was an existing form it does not help us in determining the composition of the communities to which Ephesians was sent, other than that there were some households wealthy enough to have slaves, or the difficulties they were encountering. Its injunctions have an 'absolute' nature like those of the Decalogue and are not contingent. There are two important differences between the codes in Ephesians and Colossians and that of 1 Pet 2.13–3.7; in the latter, unlike the former, advice is given to (i) slaves in respect of angry and abusive masters, and their masters are not addressed, (ii) wives in respect of non-Christian husbands (see 3.1f). It can therefore be assumed that AE and A/Col have in mind wholly Christian households.

There are a number of questions which remain which AE does not address but which would represent problems Christians would have had to face in the ancient world, and that frequently: What was a Christian wife to do if her non-Christian husband ordered her to worship his gods? What was the position of a battered wife? When husbands and wives are addressed are these assumed to be free men and women or are marriages between slaves also in view? Would the marriage pattern have been the same for slaves as for those who were free? Was the primary obedience of the slave's wife, or the women with whom he normally lived, to her husband or her owner? Could the owner split up a married slave couple and sell one off without either his or her agreement or the agreement of the other partner? What was the relation of freed slaves to their patrons or of slaves· to free men or women other than their owners, a situation which might arise when slaves were present at worship in a house other than their owner's? What of the relationships between Christian households? When 'brothers' went to law with one another (1 Cor 6.1ff) what attitude did the other members of their households adopt towards one another? How were households to treat those from other Christian households who might visit them (cf 1 Pet 4.9;

Rom 16.1f)? AE instructs husbands and wives and parents and children how to behave towards one another, but what of the behaviour of siblings to one another? Since the majority of people died before they were forty, the main relationship of people would not be with their parents but with their siblings. Does AE simply ignore this relationship, and others, because they were not mentioned in the traditional HT? Again, did he ignore the position of wives with hostile husbands ands slaves with oppressive non-Christian masters, in contrast to the HT of 1 Peter, simply because these were not mentioned in his traditional HT? What would he have said to the Christian son of slave parents whose master wished to use him homosexually? Does this mean he was to some degree insensitive to the society around him?

AE neither answers these questions nor gives us a clue how he would have answered them, and, more importantly, he accepts a HT which implies that all the members of the community lived in Christian households. If he had not done so he could not have moved so easily between marriage and the relationship of Christ and the church. But the rest of the NT belies the idea that all believers lived in wholly Christian households. Much of the instruction given in the Gospels to disciples is addressed to individuals seen as members of the Christian community but not as members of households. In particular Mk 10.29 envisages disciples who have left, or perhaps been driven out from, their families (cf Mk 3.31–5; Mt 10.34f; Lk 12.51–3). In 1 Cor 7.39f Paul advises widows about marriage, seeming to prefer that they should remain unmarried and therefore outside the scope of those addressed in our HT which gives no consideration to single people. In 1 Cor 7.16 Paul assumes the existence of mixed marriages in the community (cf 1 Pet 3.1f; mixed marriages may also be one of the issues in 2 Cor 6.14–7.1). He may have been thinking of single unmarried men, of whom there were an increasing number in this period,[5] when in 1 Cor 6.13–20 he rebukes those who have illicit sexual relationships and yet does not term them adulterers. It must however be allowed that AE has dealt with illicit sexual relations in a general way in 5.3, 5. Tit 2.6 appears to deal with single unmarried men and 1 Tim 5.2 discusses how to behave towards younger women. Incest existed in households in the church (1 Cor 5.1f) but the HT apparently does not see this as a problem. There were few unmarried women in contemporary society and those that were maintained themselves through prostitution; what advice has AE for a converted prostitute? What of the concubines a pagan husband may have had before conversion? What was he to do with them? If some of the members in a Christian

[5] S. Pomeroy, *Goddesses, Whores, Wives, and Slaves. Women in Classical Antiquity*, London, 1975, 132–3.

community did not belong to Christian households, or indeed to households at all, is not AE's teaching seriously inadequate? The problems for those living in non-Christian households were much greater than those in Christian households as 1 Pet 2.18–3.7 shows; 1 Tim 6.1f in addressing slaves allows for those with either believing or unbelieving owners (cf *Barn* 19.5–7; *Did* 4.9–11; Ign *Polyc* 5.2); Onesimus prior to his conversion served a Christian master, Philemon; Paul's letter shows that such masters needed Christian advice. A young man converted to Christianity could have had very serious problems over food sacrificed to idols for only such food might be on offer in his home; Paul, but not AE, thinks through the problem of food sacrificed to idols in 1 Cor 8–10. Paul also sets celibacy above marriage in 1 Cor 7.8, 25ff, 40 (perhaps AE may be excused for ignoring this; if he dealt with it, he would have ruined his teaching on the church in 5.22ff!). AE's approach to family relationships is thus both limited (*Ps-Phoc* 175–227 shows the wide range of problems requiring treatment) and simplistic, for he has avoided most of the serious problems that would arise within households. It is thus pastorally unrealistic. Would Paul have ever gone about it in this way? By limiting himself to Christian households AE has failed to address many, perhaps the majority, of his readers in respect of their conduct towards their kinsfolk.

How did AE came to incorporate such pastorally defective material in his letter? It is not sufficient to say he took it over from Colossians or from the tradition of the Pauline school to which he and the author of Colossians belonged. To have used it and left untouched so many areas indicates on the part of both AE and A/Col a serious lack of imagination as to the real world, a lack of imagination absent from many of the other Christian HT. Presumably the HT was incorporated into both Ephesians and Colossians simply because it was there. But how did it come to be there? Since Paul shows a much greater realism in his treatment of family ethics he can hardly have composed the HT. It must then have come from outside, and presumably outside the Christian tradition. The origin of many of the difficulties we have seen for the HT derives from its limitation to Christian households; in other households because of their faith individuals would not have been able to participate wholly in the life of the household. Most of these difficulties would have been irrelevant to pagans in a pagan environment; there the obedience of wives and slaves would have been unaffected by a 'faith' difference. Only very rarely would problems arise if a son in a pagan household decided to worship a god other than the principal one worshipped by his parents; normally no exclusive claim would have been made for that god. Husbands would not worry if their wives added another goddess to the number they already worshipped. The HT probably then arose in the pagan, or possibly the Jewish, world where the problems we have discussed would not have been major issues (see Best, 'Haustafel' for a more detailed discussion). The pre-Christian form of the HT was simply transferred to Christian households without a realisation of the changes that needed to be made. The form could possibly have originated in Judaism in so far as mixed marriages are concerned for they were not sufficiently numerous in Judaism for their difficulties to have been explored; for the same reason it could have passed unaltered through Judaism on its way to Christianity.

A

HUSBANDS AND WIVES: CHRIST AND THE CHURCH
5.22–33

C. Chavasse, *The Bride of Christ*, London, 1940; Hanson, 137–41; Thornton, *Common Life*, 221ff; Mussner, *Christus*, 147–60; Best, *One Body*, 169ff; E. Kähler, *Die Frau in den paulinischen Briefen*, Zürich, 1960, 88–140; Roels, 140–5; R. A. Batey, 'Jewish Gnosticism and the "Hieros Gamos" of Eph. v.21–33', *NTS* 10 (1963/4) 121–7; E. Neuhäusler, 'Das Geheimnis ist gross. Einführung in die Grundbegriffe der Eheperikope Eph 5,22–29', *BibLeb* 4 (1964) 155–67; J. Cambier, 'Le grand mystère concernant le Christ et son Église. Éphésiens 5,22–33', *Bib* 47 (1966) 43–90, 223–42; id. 'Doctrine paulinienne du mariage chrétien', *Église et Théologie* 10 (1979) 13–39 at 46–59; R. A. Batey, 'The μία σάρξ Union of Christ and the Church', *NTS* 13 (1966/7) 270–81; H. Baltensweiler, *Die Ehe im Neuen Testament*, Zürich, 1967, 213–35; C. Spicq, *Les Épitres Pastorales*, I, Paris, 1969, 385–425; Steinmetz, 89–94; J. P. Sampley, *'And the Two Shall Become one Flesh': A Study of Traditions in Ephesians 5:21–33* (SNTSMS 16), Cambridge, 1971; R. A. Batey, *New Testament Nuptial Imagery*, Leiden, 1971; D. Fennema, 'Unity in Marriage: Ephesians 5:21–33', *RefR* 25 (1971) 62–71; W. A. Meeks, 'The Image of the Androgyne: Some Uses of a Symbol of Earliest Christianity', *HR* 13 (1974) 165–208; K. Niederwimmer, *Askese und Mysterium* (FRLANT 113), Göttingen, 1975, 124ff; S. Pomeroy, *Goddesses, Whores, Wives, and Slaves. Women in Classical Antiquity*, London, 1975; K. O'B. Wickes, 'First Century Marriage Ethics: A Comparative Study of the Household Codes and Plutarch's *Conjugal Precepts*', *No Famine in the Land* (FS J. L. MacKenzie, ed. J. W. Flanagan and A. W. Robinson), Missoula, MT, 1975, 141–53; A. P. O'Hagan, 'The Wife According to Eph. 5.22–33', *Australian Catholic Record* 1 (1976) 17–26; Halter, 281–6; Meuzelaar, 46–8, 119–25; H. Schürmann, 'Neutestamentliche Marginalien zur Frage nach der Institutionalität, Unauflösbarkeit und Sakramentalität der Ehe', *Kirche und Bibel* (FS E. Schick), Schöningh, 1979, 409–30; S. B. Clark, *Men and Women in Christ*, Ann Arbor, 1980, 72–87; H. Maillet, 'ALLA ... PLÉN ...', *ETR* 55 (1980) 566–74; A. Ammassari, 'Lo statuto matrimoniale del re di Israele (Deut. 17,17)', *Euntes Docete* 34 (1981) 123–7; T. G. Allen, chap. 4; E. Schüssler Fiorenza, *In Memory of Her*, London, 1983, 266–70; G. Dautzenberg, H. Merklein, K. Müller (eds.), *Die Frau im Urchristentum*, Freiburg, Basel, Vienna, 1983; G. Barbaglio, 'L'amore di Christo in Efesini 5,25–27', *PSV* 10 (1984) 175–86; G. Baena, 'La Iglesia Doméstica: Fundamentos de una espiritualidad familiar segun la teologia de Efesios V,21–33', *Theologia Xaveriana* 35 (1985) 29–53; C. Dieterlé, 'Statuts des textes bibligues et théologies du couple', *LV* 34 (1985) 61–72; G. Pella, 'Voile et soumission?', *Hokhma* 30 (1985) 3–20; R. W. Wall, 'Wifely Submission in the Context of Ephesians', *Christian Scholar's Review* 17 (1988) 272–85; S. F. Miletic, *passim*; F. Wessels, 'Exegesis and Proclamation. Ephesians 5:21–33 "Wives, be subject to your husbands ... Husbands, love your wives ..." ', *Journal of Theology for Southern Africa* 67 (1989) 67–76; M. Theobald, 'Heilige Hochzeit. Motive des Mythos im Horizont von Eph 5,21–33', *Metaphorik und Mythos im Neuen Testament* (ed. K. Kertelge, Quastiones Disputatae 126), Freiberg, 1990, 220–54; W. Deming, *Paul on Marriage and Celibacy* (SNTSMS 83), Cambridge, 1995, 50–107; T. K. Seim, 'A Superior Minority? The Problem of Men's Headship in Ephesians 5', *ST* 49 (1995) 167–81.

22   Wives, subordinate yourselves to your husbands,
         as to the Lord,
23   for a husband is head of his wife,
         as even Christ is head of the church,
         he being saviour of the (his) body.
24   Yet as the church is subject to Christ,
         so also wives are subject to their husbands in
            everything.
25   Husbands, love your wives
         as Christ loved the church and gave himself for her
26   that he might sanctify her,
         cleansing her with the washing of water
            with accompanying words,
27   that he might present to himself the church
         glorious, without defect or wrinkle
            or anything similar,
         but that she might be holy and blameless.
28   Consequently husbands should love their wives
         as their own bodies.
      He who loves his own wife loves himself,
29   for no one ever hated his own flesh
         but (everyone) nourishes and takes care of it,
         just as Christ the church,
30   because we are members of his body.
31   For this reason a man will leave father and mother
            and be joined to his wife
         and the two shall become one flesh.
32   This mystery is profound:
         I speak in reference to Christ and the church.
33   To sum up,
         each one of you is to love his wife as he loves himself,
         and as for the wife let her see she respects her husband.

The first main unit of the HT, 5.22–33, treats the relations of wives and husbands. It is much more developed than the similar section in Col 3.18f, especially in relation to husbands. It is sometimes suggested that in 5.22–6.9 AE follows a natural sequence of importance, wife, children, slaves, but though this may appear natural to us, it is neither the sequence of 1 Pet 2.13–3.7 nor necessarily that of the ancient world. 5.22–33 has three main sections: (i) vv. 22–4, where wives, the 'inferior', are the first to be addressed; (ii) vv. 25–32, where husbands are addressed and in which (a) Christ's example is held out to them (vv. 25–8) with a purpose expressed through three ἵνα clauses, and (b) the point is driven home (vv. 28–32) with reasons for the closeness of husband and wife and of Christ and church, with the motivation sealed through a quotation from Gen 2.24 which is applied to both the marital relationship and that of the church and Christ; (iii) a concluding summary (v. 33) bringing us back to the starting-point, the relation of husband and wife. The passage has in effect two conclusions, v. 32 giving that in respect of Christ and the church and v. 33 that in respect of marriage (cf Cambier, 45). The structure is chiasmic for vv. 22–4 and v. 33b deal with wives and vv. 25–9 and v. 33a with husbands (Roberts). Lund[1] works out a much more detailed chiasmic structure (v. 22 and v. 33b refer to wives, etc.) but is forced to eliminate v. 29a to preserve the symmetry. Throughout the passage the thought swings back and forth between human marriage, 22–3a, 24b–5a, 28–9a, (31), 33, and the Christ–church relationship, 23b–4a, 25b–7, 29b–30, (31), 32, and Penna with some justification works out a spiral structure from v. 25 onwards. We should note the use throughout of comparative particles, ὡς (vv. 23, 24, 28), οὕτως (vv. 24, 28, 33), καθώς (vv. 25, 29). The main comparison is between the marital relationship and that of Christ and the church and operates in such a way that the latter is the basis for instruction about the former, and not the reverse. The result is the alteration of what was a straightforward piece of marital instruction in the original HT into a section whose main theme is ecclesiological, emphasising the relation between Christ and the church rather than that between him and the individual believer. We are left with the question whether AE chose to insert the HT which is unrelated to any particular church situation simply because he saw he could develop its first unit in such a way as to give more teaching about his central theme of the church, or, having decided to use it, he then realised it was possible to do this. His comparison was made a lot easier because ἐκκλησία is a feminine and so could be linked to wife; feminine pronouns are normally used in translating this section

---

[1] N. W. Lund, *Chiasmus in the New Testament*, Chapel Hill, NC, 1942, 198–201.

to preserve the comparison; otherwise in non-sexist days there appears no reason why the church should not be regarded as masculine.

Paul discusses marriage in 1 Cor 7 and the relationship of men and women and husbands and wives in 1 Cor 11.2ff; 14.34–6. Nothing here is seriously out of accord with those passages, apart from the absence of the stress on the superiority of celibacy to marriage in 1 Cor 7.8, 25ff. Here, through the comparison made with Christ and the church, marriage is given a more theological basis. The analogy of human marriage and the Christ–church relationship is of course not perfect and must not be overstretched; in the Christ–church relationship Christ is always the giver and the church the recipient; this is not true of husband and wife. Underlying it also is the assumption that both husband and wife are believers; AE has no moral teaching to offer for the difficulties that would arise in mixed marriages, and there must have been many such. The passage also offers no advice where there is a breakdown in the marital relationship. As we go through the passage we shall see that there are other omissions which prevent the passage being accepted as the final word on marriage. While we speak here of the marriage relationship it must be acknowledged that there is some confusion in the passage concerning whether the woman involved is bride or wife, whether it is the wedding ceremony which is in mind or the continuing marriage. In vv. 22–4 and 28ff the latter is the ruling idea but in vv. 26f it is the former. The variation comes about, not because AE wishes to address both brides and wives, but because what he wants to say about the church necessitates the two approaches.

22. This verse lacks a verb and this needs to be supplied from v. 21 (cf v. 24; for its meaning see on v. 21).

Many MSS do in fact have a passive form of ὑποτάσσω, either (1) the second plural of the imperative with position either preceding ὡς (as in K 181 614; Chrysostom) or following γυναῖκες (as in D F G 1985), or (2) the third plural of the imperative whose position again varies either preceding ὡς as in ℵ A I P 0278 6 33 81 104 365 1175 1241⁵ 1505 1739 1881 2464 *pc* lat sy co and the great majority of the Greek Fathers, or following γυναῖκες as in Ψ. No form of the verb is found in 𝔓⁴⁶ B; Cl Hier^mss. Because (i) of the variation in both position and form of the inserted verb, (ii) of the absence of any satisfactory reason for its omission if once present, and (iii) its presence would clarify the connection between v. 22 and v. 21, the absence of any form of the verb is the correct reading. It probably came to be inserted when 5.22–33 was read as a unit in worship; a lectionary reading could hardly begin with a verbless sentence (cf Erasmus).

It is not women in general but wives (for nom. + article in place of the voc. see BDR §147; MHT, 34f; Moule, 31f; Robertson, 465f) who are addressed.[2] We may contrast this direct address with 1 Clem 1.3; 21.6 where husbands are told to instruct their wives in what is proper behaviour, an approach similar to that of 1 Cor 14.34–6. The subordination of women is to their own husbands (for the use of ὑποτάσσω for the relation of wives to husbands see Plutarch, Mor 142D; see also all of 140D–4DE); there is no special stress on ἰδίοις (for its use in place of the possessive pronoun see BDR §286; MHT, 191f; Moule, 121; Robertson, 691f) as if it were only to their own husbands that women needed to subordinate themselves. The manner in which they are addressed throughout vv. 22–33 implies that both wives and husbands are Christians. We do not know enough about the actual situation to find Barth's suggestion (Broken Wall, 223f) convincing that wives were seeking emancipation from rigid marital ties (perhaps incited by Gal 3.28?). Since wives are addressed directly and husbands are not told what to do if the wives do not submit, it is probably right to assume that their subordination will be voluntary; their subordination will of course be to husbands who love them as Christ loved the church (v. 25). However, what we know about the ancient world would lead us to believe that husbands would have the right to enforce submission if it was not voluntarily offered. It is true that the position of wives was not uniform but varied slightly from area to area and from social class to social class; we know most about wives in the educated and upper classes because our information comes from literature emanating from these classes; it may well be that the patriarchal outlook was more firmly held in the lower and uneducated classes, to which probably most of AE's readers belonged. Their position in Asia Minor was probably as favourable as anywhere else (cf Donaldson, 124, 237f; cf Faust, 436f; Trebilco, 104ff), and in the Greco-Roman world generally more favourable (cf Plato, Leg 3.680B; Aristotle, Pol I 1252B, 1256B) than in

---

[2] For the place of wives and women in the ancient world and in early Christianity see J. Donaldson, Woman: Her Position and Influence in Ancient Greece and Rome, and Among Early Christians, London, 1907; J. Leipoldt, Die Frau in der antiken Welt und im Urchristentum, Leipzig, 1962; J. P. V. Balsdon, Roman Women: Their History and Habits, London, 1962; K. Stendahl, The Bible and the Role of Women, Philadelphia, 1966; R. Scroggs, 'Paul and the Eschatological Woman', JAAR 40 (1972) 283–303; id., 'Paul and the Eschatological Woman Revisited', JAAR 42 (1974) 532–7; E. Pagels, 'Paul and Women', JAAR 42 (1974) 538–49; G. Clark, 'Roman Women', Greece and Rome 28 (1981) 193–212; M. R. Lefkowitz and M. B. Fant, Woman's Life in Greece and Rome, London, 1982; J. Peradotto and J. P. Sullivan (ed.), Women in the Ancient World: The Arethusa Papers, Albany, 1984; O. L. Yarbrough, Not like the Gentiles (SBLDS 80), Atlanta, 1985; Ben Witherington, Women in the Ministry of Jesus (SNTSMS 51), Cambridge, 1984, 1–10; id., Women in the Earliest Churches (SNTSMS 59), Cambridge, 1988, 5–23; id., Women and the Genesis of Christianity, Cambridge, 1990, 1–26; A. Standhartinger, Das Frauenbild im Judentum der hellenistischen Zeit, Leiden, 1995. See also from earlier lists in this section, Kähler, Spicq, Schüssler Fiorenza, Pomeroy, Baltensweiler.

Judaism (cf Josephus *c. Ap.* 2.201; Philo *Hyp* 7.3; *Spec Leg* 3.169, 171; *Flaccum* 89); Josephus and Philo were Hellenistic Jews and therefore more likely to be favourable to women than Palestinian Jews. In Judaism their position was traced back to Gen 3.16 and therefore regarded as belonging to God's order of creation rather than of salvation (Cambier, 62).

In the following two units of the HT ὑπακούω replaces ὑποτάσσω. Barth does not regard them as synonyms, seeing the former as the stronger; the latter however is the more inclusive, covering a great many situations in each of which its precise meaning needs to be gathered from the context. Subordination within a chain of command in the army is different from a similar chain in the civil service or an industrial concern. When however both verbs are applied to voluntary conduct it is difficult to distinguish between them (cf Lincoln). In 1 Pet 3.1–6 the husband is 'hostile' towards his wife; in Ephesians he loves her. Relationships can only be defined in terms of the attitudes of all involved in them.

The verse concludes with a motivation, ὡς τῷ κυρίῳ, where the κύριος is not the husband; if a reference to husbands were intended the plural κυρίοις would have been used corresponding to ἀνδράσιν. The husband is not then depicted as 'lord' of his wife (*pace* Aquinas, Mussner, Gaugler); the introduction of 'Lord' however helps to prepare for the following discussion of the relation of Christ to the church. The precise significance of ὡς is difficult to determine. It could mean that wives should submit to their husbands as they would to the Lord, but hardly as implying also 'and not as to men' (Col 3.23 is not a parallel), or, if understood causally, that wives should submit because of the Lord. In either case the wife's relationship to her husband is set within the perspective of her relation to her Lord; the relation of husband and wife is not only 'horizontal'; it contains a 'vertical' component (Miletic, 32f); the wife's subordination is then a religious act and has a wider context than that of the contemporary patriarchal understanding of the family.

The Pauline and deutero-Pauline letters contain contrasting attitudes to women and in particular to wives. That wives are directly addressed here coheres with Gal 3.28, where women are regarded as equal members of the church with men, and with 1 Cor 7.3ff, where husbands and wives have equal sexual rights within marriage and the husband is not depicted as governing his wife in this respect. Another attitude is partly present in 1 Cor 11.2ff; there women are permitted to take part in public worship but are subordinate to their husbands; this attitude is more pronounced in 1 Cor 14.34–6; in 1 Cor 12.13, unlike Gal 3.28, the pairing of men and women is not mentioned. In the Pastorals the less egalitarian attitude predominates and the other is excluded. There is however no reason to see Ephesians as dependent on the attitude depicted in 1 Cor 11.2ff; it was the prevailing cultural attitude.

23. Verse 22 could have appeared in a straightforward Christian HT, as does its parallel in Col 3.18, but for some reason unknown to us, perhaps arising out of the situation which led to the writing of the letter, we have an unlooked-for 'diversion' into teaching about the church. ἐκκλησία is used nine times in Ephesians; six of these occur in 5.22–33; no other paragraph in the NT has such a high density (Bouttier). The relationship of husband and wife to one another is set in parallel with that of Christ and the church. As in the earlier references to the church in Ephesians it is not individual congregations which are in mind but the whole church; if the former had been the case that might have suggested an approval of polygamy!

A variant reading inverts the order of ἐστιν and κεφαλή; support is weak, B 0278 104 365 1175 *pc* lat; Tert; it is probably a case of scribal error. Another variant inserts καί before αὐτός and again the support is weak: ℵ² D¹ Ψ 0278 𝔐 (a b m vg^mss) sy; in this case the variant clarifies the meaning. ἀνήρ has no article indicating it is generic; γυναικός has, indicating that it refers not to women in general but the woman belonging to the 'man', i.e. to wives (cf Henle, Salmond).

Verse 23a supplies the basis for the subordination of wives to husbands (v. 22) by re-expressing the superiority of the husband; while it may be right to speak of this relationship as axiomatic (Ewald) in terms of the contemporary culture, e.g. Aristotle, *Pol* 1253B; Plutarch, *Mor* 142E, yet there is insufficient evidence for the use of κεφαλή to describe the relationship. In the passages from Aristotle and Plutarch the comparison is made to soul and body; this is a dualistic relation, and soul does not occupy the same position as head in relation to the body. AE's use of κεφαλή here however enables him to make his transition to his discussion of the church, for he has already used the term in that connection (4.15f); it was used similarly in Col 1.18; 2.19, implying it was an accepted description in the Pauline churches and therefore known to AE's readers (on the word see Detached Note: The Body of Christ). 1 Cor 11.3 contains a sequence God–Christ–man–woman in which each is successively head of the next. This however is not the source of AE's usage for: (i) 1 Cor 11.3 relates man and woman; AE relates husband and wife; (ii) AE does not depict Christ as head of the husband; (iii) the subordination set out in 1 Cor 11.3 belongs to the order of creation (11.8f; cf 1 Tim 2.11–13) but AE, without denying that, for he later quotes Gen 2.24 which Judaism used to found marriage in the order of creation, views it as belonging to that of salvation as the remainder of the passage reveals. Ephesians may then be said to give a new christological sanction to the order of creation (cf Niederwimmer, 128, n. 19).

Headship (for literature see on 1.22 and Detached Note: The Body of Christ) in the NT embraces a range of ideas including rule, pre-eminence, source, the latter naturally implying priority. All these ideas have been seen in 1 Cor 11.3; while 'pre-eminence' or 'source' are possible in Eph 4.15f, they are unlikely at 1.22 and probably also in 5.23 where the headship of the husband is linked to the wife's subordination. Bedale[3] however takes 'source' to be the meaning in 5.23, yet it could only be so if the husband is regarded as Adam from whom Eve was taken; the wife would then be the second Eve; but if there is any allusion to Adam in our passage it is to Christ as the new Adam. Gielen argues, 250ff, (i) that in the OT a 'head' is always a head over a collective and not an individual, and (ii) that Christ as creator of the church (2.15b) is its source; but as for (i), in the light of the contemporary patriarchal attitude to marriage, had AE wished to suggest the husband was the source of the wife, he would have needed to made this clearer; as for (ii) the material parallel to the Christ–church relationship is not perfect; it is in fact analogical and it is difficult to argue from analogies.

In the second clause of the verse ὡς can be understood either causally (Barth) or comparatively (the majority of commentators): the husband is head of his wife either because Christ is head of the church or in the same way as Christ is head of the church. These are not far apart in meaning; either is in line with what follows; both, each in its own way, make the relationship of husband and wife depend on that of Christ and the church. Since the comparative element predominates in the passage it is better to choose that meaning here. Its choice implies we see the headship of the husband as one of love, not oppression.

ἐκκλησίας introduces the dominating concept of the passage. The relationship of Christ and church is wider than that of headship and a brief parenthetical clause presents another aspect, Christ is saviour of his body, the church; this aspect is developed in what follows. While 23c may fall in the centre of vv. 22–4 and Miletic, 44, may refer to it as its structural and theological centre, it is certainly not the centre of vv. 22–33. It is better understood as a theological 'trailer' for what follows; it may also provide an explanation for Christ's headship (Bratcher and Nida): he is head because he is saviour. The nearest referent for αὐτός is χριστός, not ἀνήρ, though some of the Fathers, e.g. Chrysostom, Oecumenius, and, more recently, Grotius, Robinson, Thornton, *Common Life*, 222, Hugedé have chosen the latter; if both Christ and the husband had been

---

[3] S. Bedale, 'The Meaning of κεφαλή in the Pauline Epistles', *JTS* 5 (1954) 211–15; id. 'The Theology of the Church', in Cross, 64–75.

intended αὐτοί would have been the proper pronoun. Even if this reference were syntactically simpler, it is difficult to see in what way a husband would be the saviour of his body, i.e. his wife. It cannot be that he provides for her daily needs or enables her to fulfil her role of motherhood (Asmussen). Neither fits the passage and it is only later at v. 28 that the wife is described as the husband's body. Tob 6.18 and 1 Cor 7.16 are sometimes suggested as parallels but are irrelevant; the former refers to the driving away of a demon and the latter to a previously unredeemed wife; in Eph 5.23 the wife is Christian.

Christ is not normally described as σωτήρ in the earlier NT writings, in Paul only at Phil 3.20 where the context is future and eschatological (cf 1 Th 1.10), but appears in the later writings (Lk 2.11; Jn 4.42; Acts 5.31; 13.23; 2 Tim 1.10; Tit 1.4; 2.13; 3.6; 2 Pet 1.1, 11; 2.20; 3.2, 18; 1 Jn 4.14); the noun σωτηρία and the cognate verb are used frequently of Christ's redeeming work. σωτήρ has a septuagintal background in the concept of Yahweh as the deliverer of Israel and in Hellenistic Judaism where God is saviour (Philo, *Conf Ling* 93f; *Leg Alleg* 3.27). It was also widely used in the contemporary world being applied to the Roman emperor, the Ptolemies, Asclepius, and the Heavenly Man.[4] At no point does gnosticism connect saviour and body (Mussner, 157). Our verse is indeed the only point where Christ is presented as saviour of the church, though he is said to be saviour of the cosmos in Jn 4.42; 1 Jn 4.14. ' ... its frequent employment in the Septuagint as a predicate of God or of the Messiah seems to supply the most natural antecedent for its Christian usage'.[5] Its meaning varies; for example, it describes day-to-day preservation and care of their subjects by their earthly rulers. However, in the NT it is related normally to the death of Christ (implicit in v. 25), of which the saving significance was set out in 2.14ff. It is thus used both to describe Christ's function and as a title. 'Saviour of the body' is a unique phrase in the NT, but Christ as saving and Christians as saved are common ideas and with this in mind it is easy to see how the phrase could appear in a similar way to that in which 5.25 arose out of 5.2. The combination of saviour and body moves us beyond the simple relationship of husband and wife into a discussion of Christ and the church in vv. 25ff where the idea is further developed. Overlordship of itself does not imply a close relation between the head and those

[4] See W. Bousset, *Kyrios Christos*,[3] Göttingen, 1926, 240ff; M. Dibelius, *Die Pastoralbriefe*,[4] Tubingen, 1966, 74ff; O. Cullmann, *The Christology of the New Testament*, London, 1959, 238–45; Schlier, *Christus*, 72f; W. Foerster, *TWNT*, VII, 1005ff; Fischer, 186–91; J. Schneider and C. Brown, *NIDNTT*, III, 216–21.

[5] A. D. Nock, 'Early Gentile Christianity and its Hellenistic Background' in A. E. J. Rawlinson (ed.), *Essays on the Trinity and the Incarnation*, London, 1928, 51–156 at 92.

he rules but head and body are closely linked; head and body are not however on a par for AE; Christ is the saviour of the body. A clear distinction is thus drawn between Christ and the body (= the church) at the same time as a close relation is created. Saviour and servant (cf Mk 10.42–5) are not far apart; servant and head seem opposed ideas; in a sense also head and saviour indicate very different aspects of the relation of Christ and the church. If he is head the nature of his headship is qualified in that he is also saviour, i.e. he is a saving head (T. G. Allen, 278).

If Christ is saviour of the body, are two existing entities implied, a pre-existent Christ and a pre-existent church, which were brought together in the cross? AE would clearly not have denied the pre-existence of Christ; does this not necessitate the pre-existence of the church? For discussion see Essay: The Church §5.

24. After the parenthesis of v. 23c AE returns to his paraenesis and restates the ideas of v. 23b but in reverse order resulting in a chiastic (abcba) pattern (23a, 23b, 23c, 24a, 24b). The content of the parenthesis of v. 23c does not affect the thought of v. 24 except by contrast but becomes important from v. 25 onwards. As in v. 23 Christ's headship over the church and its subordination to him is taken for granted and used as basis for an argument by analogy for the subordination of wives to husbands.

ἀλλά is difficult as a glance at the translations will show: AV 'therefore'; NEB, REB 'but just as'; RSV 'as'; NRSV 'just as'; NJB 'and as'; GNB 'and so'; NIV 'now as'; Moffatt 'as'. Eadie has a useful note summarising and criticising views prior to his own time. Miletic, 102 n. 6, argues from MHT, 330, that the conjunction can have a consecutive sense and quotes from MHT (giving the wrong reference on two occasions) a number of possible parallels; in each of these it is the clause directly following ἀλλά which is consecutive and here this would be v. 24a, whereas to suit Miletic's argument it should be v. 24b. In any case MHT does not eliminate the adversative sense translating in each case 'well' and not 'and so', thus not making the consecutive sense overwhelming. ἀλλά indicates a movement from v. 23c and must have some element of its adversative sense ('Vir autem non est servator uxoris. In eo Christus excellit. Hinc "sed" sequitur', Bengel); AE has not yet reached the point where he wishes to expand on its significance. 'Yet' or perhaps 'howbeit' (Murray, 'to resume, anyway'; 'the important thing for the moment is') would preserve both the adversative sense and the feeling of movement to a new stage of the argument. B Ψ *pc* b; Ambst omit ὡς; the evidence is not strong and may represent scribal difficulty with the text.

AE discusses neither the nature nor the extent of the church's subordination to Christ (for the article with Christ see on 1.10; there is no reason to suppose he is here emphasising the Jewishness of Jesus). Both nature and extent should be seen in general terms and as similar to that of the subordination of individual believers to

Christ. AE would then be arguing in the same way as he does in 5.25 where he applies to the church a formula which originally related to the individual (cf 5.2; Gal 2.20 and notes on 5.2). Consequently the relationship of Christ and the church will never on the one side be servile nor on the other tyrannical. His rule over the church will accord with Mk 10.44 and her obedience will be offered in joy (Phil 3.1; 4.4). V. 24b which relates husband and wife in a parallel manner to that of Christ and the church lacks a verb and this is to be supplied from v. 24a; as there it will be in the indicative for both clauses of v. 24 are statements of fact, or at least in the contemporary world v. 24b would have been so taken.

The final phrase, ἐν παντί, requires explanation and perhaps qualification. It seems an obvious implication from v. 24a and would appear to put the husband on a level with God who must be obeyed in everything (Fiorenza, *Memory*, 269). Yet husbands are not sinless and perfect as was Christ. In so far as AE treats only Christian households, he is able to eliminate the possibility of the wife's disobedience should the husband order her to sacrifice to the household gods or to perform any other act which would conflict with her faith. AE appears to assume that Christian husbands would never ask their Christian wives to act sinfully. Yet even within a Christian household it would be foolish to say husbands know how everything should be done. When it came to the time to wean a baby probably most wives went their own way, and did not seek guidance from their husbands (what did he know about such things?). Contemporary society may have given a leading role to husbands yet in practice there would always have been areas where they did not interfere, or if they did their advice was not heeded. In much of the Greco-Roman world wives were expected to manage the internal affairs of the household. Our text provides an idealised picture of husbands and wives which only a male author could have depicted, or left unchanged if he drew it from a traditional HT.

Before leaving this verse it is necessary to examine the views of Miletic, 67ff, who sees the discussion in vv. 22–4 as dominated by Adamic speculation (an idea previously suggested by Murray but in a more restrained and less exact manner). Miletic points out that AE never applies ὑποτάσσω directly to the wife; this is true, yet, as in most languages, ellipses are very common in Greek (cf BDR §§479–81; Robertson, 393f, 1201f); the omission of the direct attribution can hardly therefore be regarded as remarkable. Miletic further argues that the presentation of Christ as the new or second Adam is an important feature of Pauline theology (Rom 5.12–19; 1 Cor 15.20–8) and may underlie the argument of other sections of Ephesians (e.g. 1.19–23; 2.15f); there is also in our passage at v. 32 an explicit reference to the story about Adam and Eve and it is possible that in 2 Cor 11.2 the church is viewed as the second Eve (but see Best, *One Body*, 171, 175). Miletic, 86, concludes that AE presents the church in our passage as the new Eve. However if there is Adamic imagery in Ephesians it is the new Adam and not the new Eve who is the object of Christ's sacrificial love (2.15f) whereas it would have to be the new Eve in 5.22–33; thus the Adamic imagery breaks down at a crucial point (cf Lincoln). It also breaks down in the discussion of headship; while κεφαλή may mean 'source', and Adam may have been Eve's 'source', yet as the source of the church Christ (= Adam) was not passive as was Adam but active.

25. Expanding greatly what must have been the pre-existing form of the HT in the Pauline school (cf Col 3.19), AE now switches his attention to husbands; his counsel for them falls into two brief sections, vv. 25–7 and vv. 28–32, and is more extensive than that to wives. While he continues to use the same principal verb as Col 3.19, his advice is very different from that verse for he stresses a positive rather than its negative attitude ('do not be embittered'). His advice also differs from that of 1 Pet 3.7 where what is said to believing husbands had been preceded by lengthy counselling of believing wives married to unbelieving husbands and is indeed part of a joint advice to believing husbands and wives. In vv. 25ff Christ's love is given as an example to husbands and not to wives; are they not to love their husbands? AE does not refer to any reciprocal love on the part of spouses as is found sometimes in non-Christian advice (e.g. Musonius Rufus, *Or* XIIIA, Hense 67f, though male superiority is still asserted; cf Frag XIV, Hense, 73f; Hierocles the Stoic, Stobaeus, IV 502, 503–7). The absence of any instruction to wives to love their husbands was noticed early and Clem Alex widens what is said to include the wife (*Paedagogus* 3.95.1, GCS 12.29). AE's advice to husbands follows a pattern well known in both ancient and modern counselling, the provision of a role model, here Christ. Yet Christ is not presented as a husband but as a saviour who died. An example of course can at times be more than a model and may exercise a transforming influence. So a causal factor may also be present here: the husband should love his wife because Christ loves him. Apart from Christ never having been a husband he cannot be imitated in everything he did, since the husband is not saviour of the wife as Christ is of him, and he cannot sanctify and purify her or ensure that she is without imperfection (vv. 26f). In fact vv. 26f move away from concern with the husband to deal exclusively with Christ's relationship with the church.

The husband is enjoined to love[6] his wife[7] and his behaviour

---

[6] On love see G. Quell and E. Stauffer, *TWNT*, I, 20–55; C. Spicq, *Agapè dans le Nouveau Testament*, Paris, 1957–61; id. *Notes*, I, 15–30; V. P. Furnish, *The Love Commandment in the New Testament*, Nashville, 1972; W. Günther and H.-G. Link, *NIDNTT*, II, 538–47.

[7] F G it vg^cl ww sy add here ὑμῶν; D Ψ 0278 𝔐 (𝔓 629 1739 1881 2464 *pc*); Cl^pt add ἑαυτῶν; neither is necessary; the simple article (ℵ A B 048 33 81 1241^s *pc* vg^st; Cl^pt) is sufficient to denote the wife of the husband and is also the stronger reading.

towards her is not therefore left unrestricted (Grosheide), and, contrasting with the general opinion of the contemporary culture, it is not his 'rights' which are stressed but his obligations.[8] The love referred to here is Christian love and not primarily romantic love; most marriages in the ancient world were arranged and not the result of erotic attraction. The reference to the husband's love follows surprisingly on AE's instruction to the wife to subordinate herself to her husband; in accordance with the contemporary patriarchal nature of society, the husband might have been expected to be told to instruct, advise and control his wife, and if he were told to love her it would be sexual love that would have been in view. Husbands are rarely enjoined in Jewish literature to love their wives (in *Ps-Phoc* 195–7 στέργω is used and not ἀγαπάω; see also *b Yeb* 62b). ἀγάπη is not used in Hellenistic literature in relation to households.[9] If it referred here to erotic love it might also seem to us unnecessary, yet in the days of arranged marriages it would have had its place. Erotic love, for which Greek had a distinctive word, is not then in view here. ἀγαπάω must have the same meaning in both halves of the verse and the love of Christ for the church is certainly not erotic. ἀγαπάω is the word used by Christians to denote Christ's self-sacrificing love and the love they should show one another. The husband's attitude is not then to be one of self-assertion or of ordering his wife about but of self-giving sacrifice (Gnilka), the same as is demanded of all Christians towards one another (1 Jn 3.16); a readiness to surrender life is required of husbands towards wives. This does not of course require the exclusion of sexual love; it is explicitly commended in 1 Cor 7.3–5. While the willingness of the husband to give up life for his wife is implied, it is often more difficult to continue daily to love in little ways when there is irritation, or imagined irritation. There is also a sense in which loving, which requires making decisions, is harder than submitting or obeying where another has made the decision (Grosheide). The solution of marital problems for AE lies in both the subordination of the wife and the love of the husband (Hugedé). AE does not spell out what loving entails; this is done in 1 Cor 13.

Verse 25b introduces either a comparison (the husband's love should be similar to that of Christ for his church, Gnilka) or a reason (the husband should love his wife because Christ loved the church, Zerwick) or both (Schlier). If there is an element of comparison then the *tertium comparationis* is sacrificial love and not the act of

---

[8] That is not to say that husbands were always given unlimited rights over their wives; cf Callicratides, *On the Happiness of the Household*, 106.1–10 (Thesleff), quoted in Balch, *Let Wives be Submissive* 56f; Aristotle, *Nic Eth* VIII 1160B (12.4)–1161A (12.5).

[9] Cf Witherington, *Earliest Churches*, 51 and n. 135; Lohse, *Colossians*, 158 n. 28; Schrage, art.cit.

conception as often in the ἱερὸς γάμος (Mussner, *Christus*, 149); Christ does not impregnate the church. Comparison can hardly be eliminated, but as at 4.32 and 5.2 (see notes) a causal element is probably also present. If this is so, this is yet another point where the parallel in relationships breaks down for it is not suggested that the husband's love is the cause of something else, and if Christ died to love sinners it is not to be supposed that wives are sinners and are redeemed by the love of their husbands. Nothing moreover suggests that husbands should stop loving their wives if they do wrong. Even if the parallel cannot be fully sustained, the husband's love should still be as extensive and intensive as Christ's. At first sight Christ's love appears to be restricted: did he not love the world and not just the church? It is necessary to remember that v. 25b arises out of a confessional formula which necessarily would have been in the first person plural and 'church' is just another way of expressing this. The church here is of course not an earthly denomination but the body of Christ (cf v. 29). The change of tense should be noted: husbands are to continue to love (present) their wives; Christ loved (aorist) the church. The aorist refers to his earthly life, especially his death; the love expressed then has a continuing effect; παρέδωκεν is not an ingressive aorist (Schmid, 268).

Sometimes καθώς may introduce a quotation (so Barth; cf A. Suski, 'Pieśń o miłości do kościoła (Ef 5,25b-27)', *Studia Theologica Varsaviensia* 17 (1979) 3-42) but there are insufficient grounds for seeing vv. 25-7 as part of a hymn or creed. The language of the verses with their synonyms is wholly in AE's style, the third ἵνα clause would provide a line much shorter than the other two, and if the letter is not by Paul the existence in the verses of non-Pauline words is hardly relevant. This is not to deny that v. 25b is a traditional formulation, or contains traditional concepts (see on 5.2). This is the only place in the NT where the church and not individuals is named as the object of Christ's activity (Gielen, 263), though in v. 23 Christ was described as the saviour of his body (= the church).

If Christ loved the church and she is his bride, did she exist prior to his incarnation (so Schlier)? In the light of vv. 26f, was she sinful and imperfect prior to her redemption? For discussion, see Essay: The Church §5. AE may have been led into his present statement by his generalisation of the tradition of 5.2 and Gal 2.20 (in 5.27 he also applies to the church a phrase which he had used of individual believers in 1.4) and by the nature of the parallel he draws between the Christ–church relationship and that between husband–wife in order to instruct husbands.

26.[10] Three final clauses, vv. 26, 27a, 27b, now spell out the purpose of Christ's death for the church; each is introduced by ἵνα.

[10] On the verse see D. Mollatt, 'Symbolismes baptismaux chez saint Paul', *LV* 26 (1956) 61-84 at 69f; R. Schnackenburg, ' "Er hat uns mitauferweckt" ', *LJ* 2 (1952) 159-83 at 178ff.

His death does not leave the church unchánged; though strictly that might suggest the church existed before he died, it would be wrong to push the analogy beyond its limits (see Essay: The Church §5). αὐτήν is emphatic by position, not as if suggesting there was some other body or object which Christ might have cleansed, but as picking up the αὐτῆς of v. 25. An initial act is depicted here in which the church is made holy and cleansed, and the church is now thought of not as wife but as bride at the time of her wedding.

Christ's death has a double effect: it both sanctifies and cleanses. The cleansing, though signified by an aorist participle, does not imply that cleansing precedes sanctification (so many older Protestant commentators on theological grounds); it is an aorist participle of identical action (Burton §§139ff; cf 2.14–16; Mt 27.4; Acts 10.33). The sanctification itself (aor. subj.) is not to be understood as a continuing process (Salmond). The two verbs, ἁγιάζω and καθαρίζω, are difficult to distinguish in meaning. The former (for its root see on 1.1) is used here cultically rather than ethically. Those whom God sanctifies are separated from the secular sphere and brought within that of his holiness (cf Ecclus 33.12; 45.4), and are therefore acceptable to him (Rom 15.16). Sanctification has its basis in Christ's death (1 Cor 1.30, where the context is his death). As soon as the readers began to believe and were baptised they were saints, i.e. sanctified; sanctification and baptism are connected in 1 Cor 6.11, a connection brought out later in our verse. The evidence adduced by Barth, Sampley, 42f, Van Roon[11] that in Judaism taking a wife implied sanctifying her is too late to be relevant and in any case the allusion would hardly have been understood by Gentile readers. καθαρίζω carries on the connection with baptism for water cleanses, though the link may be indirect (Acts 15.9; 2 Pet 1.9; Tit 2.14; in 1QS 3.4, 9; 1QH 11.10–12 water and cleansing are associated, though of course baptism in the Christian sense is not in view).

The aorist verb and participle indicate that readers have already been sanctified and cleansed. When did this take place? Two possibilities exist, either at baptism or at Christ's death.[12] These two are not unrelated in Pauline theology where baptism is explicitly connected to Christ's death (Rom 6.3ff; 1 Cor 1.13; cf Col 2.12; Heb 10.22; 1 Jn 1.7, 9 where the contexts are the death of Christ). Believers and the church, in the sense that word has in Ephesians, were baptised into Christ when he died, but this only became real for

---

[11] For the evidence see M. Jastrow, *A Dictionary of the Targumim etc.*, Berlin, 1926, 1319f; K. G. Kuhn, *TWNT*, I, 97–101; the bride is sanctified to make her unavailable to other men.

[12] A. T. Hanson, *The New Testament Interpretation of Scripture*, London, 1980, 145f, uses some ingenious arguments to see it as taking place during Christ's visit to the underworld.

them at the moment of physical baptism; their sanctification and cleansing were then actualised. The baptismal reference becomes explicit in τῷ λουτρῷ τοῦ ὕδατος; here the articles imply that the readers know what is meant and consequently there is no need of explanation. It is only here in the NT that λουτρόν is used to denote baptism, but see Justin Martyr, *Apol* I, 61.3, 10, 12; *Dial* 13.1; 14.1.[13] Baptism is an individual matter and, though the whole church may have been potentially cleansed in the death of Christ, it is only individuals for whom it becomes real; probably AE is led to speak of a baptism of the church for a similar reason to that which led him to modify the individual nature of 5.2 into the corporate expression of 5.25. The reference to washing may have a secondary meaning. Marriage is part of the context and prior to marriage the bride in Judaism (Ezek 16.9; *Ab R. Nathan* 41; *b Schab* 77b) and in some other cultures (cf A. Oepke, *TWNT*, IV, 299ff) had a 'ceremonial' bath. Macpherson is exceptional in seeing this secondary meaning as the sole meaning. Whether the nuptial bath is alluded to here or not the reference to water excludes any thought of a 'blood' baptism or a Holy Spirit baptism.[14]

ἐν ῥήματι has caused interpreters much difficulty. There are two interrelated problems: (i) To which word or words in the verse does the phrase relate? (ii) To what does it refer? Since readers have been baptised and have seen many baptisms they will know what is meant, and AE has then no need to define the phrase (cf Dibelius). It might refer to: (a) the command of Jesus to baptise (e.g. Mt 28.16–20); (b) the words of the baptismal formula, 'in the name of Christ', spoken over the candidate at the moment of baptism (Chrysostom); (c) the candidate's own baptismal confession, e.g. 'Jesus is Lord' (Mitton); 1 Pet 3.21 suggests the candidate did speak something in the nature of a pledge;[15] (d) a sermon, or proclamation of the word, during the baptismal ceremony, perhaps something as simple as a declaration of forgiveness (Salmond); (e) the gospel through which the candidate began to believe (Jerome, Pelagius, Grotius). (d) and (e) are difficult to distinguish since the preaching of the word at the ceremony would also be a proclamation of the gospel. Of the possibilities (a), (c) and (e) may be eliminated: (a) because this, if it occurred at all, would be prior to baptism ('You must come and be baptised because Jesus has commanded it'); (c) because the emphasis in the passage lies on the action of God or Christ and not on that of believers; (e) because this also would be

---

[13] For the word see A. Oepke, *TWNT*, IV, 308f; E. K. Simpson, *The Pastoral Epistles*, London, 1954, 114f.

[14] E.g. J. D. G. Dunn, *Baptism in the Holy Spirit* (SBT 2nd series, 15), London, 1970, 162ff; for criticism see G. R. Beasley-Murray, *Baptism in the New Testament*, London, 1963, 200–4.

[15] Cf G. C. Richards, '1 Peter iii.21', *JTS* 32 (1931) 77.

preliminary and because where ῥῆμα means the gospel it is always
qualified with Christ or God (6.17; Rom 10.17; Heb 6.5; 1 Pet 1.25).
This leaves (b) and (d). Both imply a relation to God or Christ
through either the use of a given formula or a proclamation in his
name (Cambier, 'Le grand mystère', 75ff). Protestants have traditionally favoured (d) so that the baptism might not appear to be
effective in and of itself without a proclamation of the word to
which faith would respond (the sacraments should always be
accompanied with preaching); (d) can also be supported through 1
Pet 1.23. There is however no reason to suppose that AE is thinking
of the act of baptism as itself, and by itself, effecting redemption; for
him it is always God or Christ who redeems (Calvin); there is also
no actual NT evidence that at the moment of baptism a sermon was
preached. (b) is therefore to be preferred with the great majority of
modern commentators, even though if a formula is in mind we
might have expected an article. The formula in use at that time was
probably not Trinitarian but used only Christ's name (Acts 2.38;
8.16; 10.48; 19.5; 1 Cor 1.13–15; Gal 3.27). Christ's name would
remind candidates that the effect of baptism rested ultimately on
Christ's giving of himself for them. Caird's attempt to evade the
issue by arguing that literal baptism cannot be intended since the
church as such could never be baptised is too subtle; it would also
imply that the church cannot be loved and this would contradict v.
25.

What word or phrase does ἐν ῥήματι then qualify? If it were the
immediately preceding noun phrase we might have expected an
article (Haupt); if this objection is overruled (Ewald) then the
probable meaning is 'the washing of water accompanied by (the)
word' and the 'word' would be (b), though indeed (d) would also be
possible. If the phrase qualified the main verb we would have
expected it to be closer to it and it would need to be understood
instrumentally; but the washing with water is already an instrumental qualification to the verb. It is probably best taken then as
qualifying the noun phrase, or, possibly, the whole clause (Salmond)
and as signifying the baptismal formula 'in the name of Jesus
(Christ)'. Whatever way it is taken it is difficult to translate and so
we have used a fairly general rendering in the plural since ῥῆμα
does not necessarily mean an individual word.

27.[16] The second ἵνα clause begins v. 27; it has been taken as
parallel to v. 26 (Ewald) or as its consequence (Haupt, who gives a
detailed discussion of the various possibilities). The latter possibility
is the better because it makes the presentation of the bride dependent

[16] C. Journet, 'Note sur l'Église sans tache ni ride', *RThom* 49 (1949) 206–21,
provides an account of the way in which the Fathers and early Roman Catholic
scholars interpreted this verse.

on her 'washing'; v. 27 is a further step in the argument and not a repetition of v. 26; had the two clauses been parallel the second might more easily have been introduced with καί. V. 27 is of course indirectly dependent on v. 25.

In 2 Cor 11.2 Paul had already spoken of the presentation to Christ of the church as a bride (on the possible meanings of παρίστημι cf Sampley, 134–7; B. Reicke and G. Bertram, *TWNT*, V, 835–40) yet there are important differences between 2 Cor 11.2 and here: (i) in 2 Cor 11.2 Paul presents the church to Christ; here Christ presents the church to himself; (ii) in 2 Cor 11.2 the bride is an individual congregation; here she is the whole church; (iii) 2 Cor 11.2 depicts a betrothal, the context is eschatological and the marriage is future; elsewhere in our passage the marriage is regarded as already in existence. Some of these points require further elucidation. (i) It is not entirely clear who in ancient usage presented the bride to the groom.[17] At times her father may have done so but normally it was a friend of the groom. Paul looked on himself as the father of his converts (Gal 4.19; Philem 10; 1 Th 2.7, 11), in particular of the Corinthian congregation (1 Cor 4.14f; 2 Cor 6.13; 12.14), and so was a suitable person to present that church. In the OT when the nuptial metaphor is used of the relation of Yahweh and Israel the marriage event is not described and it does not emerge who presents Israel to Yahweh; since no other person is mentioned it is natural to think of Yahweh as the one who presents. It is thus possible to take Christ here as the one (αὐτός ἑαυτῷ emphasises Christ's role) who presents the church to himself. (ii) The move from the individual congregation as bride to the whole church is similar to that from the traditional individualistic formula of 5.2 to 5.25. (iii) Some (e.g. Bruce; Hendriksen; Barth; Muirhead;[18] Gaugler; Houlden; Jeremias, *TWNT*, IV, 1097f), attempting to harmonise 2 Cor 11.2 with Ephesians, argue that in Ephesians the marriage is future, and indeed eschatological; since the church on earth is always imperfect it is only at the End that she could be described as glorious and without fault. But much that AE writes elsewhere suggests he would have had no difficulty in thinking of an existing marriage of Christ and the church as glorious and without fault; already believers sit in the heavenlies with Christ (2.6) and God's glory is seen in them (1.12; cf 1.4; 3.18f). (iv) Nothing indicates when the marriage took place; since the church as bride is described as without fault it may be surmised that it took place at the time of the crucifixion for it is through Christ's death that believers are made free of fault and stain. An alternative, though less likely,

[17] See SB I, 45ff, 500ff; J. Schmid, *RAC* II, 546–8; J. D. M. Derrett, 'Water into Wine', *BZ* 7 (1963) 80–97.
[18] I. A. Muirhead, 'It is only in the End that the Church becomes the Bride', *SJT* 5 (1952) 175–87.

possibility would be the moment of baptism, yet there is no single baptism of the church but a succession of individual baptisms; in any case what happens in baptism happens as a result of the cross.

Christ presents to himself a bride who is ἔνδοξος, a word whose precise meaning needs to be derived from its context (Sampley, 67f). We should not attempt to understand it etymologically as if it referred to divine 'glory', in particular the glory of the End (cf Kähler, art.cit., 115). In v. 27 it probably means 'beautiful'. Brides are supposed to be beautiful, at least in the eyes of their groom, and the bride's beauty is widely celebrated in literature (Ct 4.7; Ps 45.8–11, 13–15; 1QapGen 20.1ff; see Isa 62.1–8 for the glory of Israel). The 'beauty' of a bride is normally her own[19] but here it is the groom who makes her lovely; he, Christ, is the beautician who has prepared the bride, as God beautified Israel in Ezek 16.10–14, for he has sanctified and cleansed her (another point at which the analogy breaks down). Nothing is said about her appearance prior to the marriage and as with all analogies it would be wrong to push the present one too far and think of her as in existence in a defective form prior to Christ's beautifying her (see Essay: The Church §5). He created her, and created her 'glorious'; what Christ creates is good just as what God creates is good (Gen 1.1ff). The beauty of the bride, who is the church, is of course not physical but moral and spiritual. Moral and spiritual purity is a Pauline theme (1 Cor 7.14; 2 Cor 6.14–7.1; 11.2; 1 Th 4.3–8).

The remainder of the verse spells out ἔνδοξος, first negatively and then positively (for the words used see Sampley, 68ff). The negative description uses physical terms: σπίλος, blemish, probably refers to a skin or surface defect (2 Pet 2.13; Jas 3.6; Jude 23; ἄσπιλος is found in 1 Pet 1.19; 2 Pet 3.14); ῥυτίς, unwrinkled, is again a reference to skin condition; for the final generalisation see 1.21; Gal 5.21. The perfect skin condition, suggestive of a young woman, accords with the idea of a bride. But is the church young? In the historical sense and from our point of view it was then in its youth, yet AE could hardly have known it was to continue through two millennia. The church is young since it only came into existence at the cross yet it is also old as the continuation of Israel. Members are youthful in so far as all have recently been converted but old in so far as they have been the elect of God from before the foundation of the world (1.4). Both the age and youth of the church have been emphasised throughout the centuries (cf Hermas, *Vis* 2.4.1 and 3.13.1).

The verse ends with the third ἵνα clause giving the ultimate purpose of Christ's selection of her to be his bride. It provides the positive description of the bride (ἀλλ' ἵνα instead of ἀλλ' οὖσαν)

---

[19] Locke comments that brides take care to spruce themselves!

repeating the description of believers given in 1.4 (see notes there for the words). AE may have used the two words because the use of μῶμος in Ct 4.7 (so Sampley, 68[20]) or because they are linked with παρίστημι in Col 1.22 but more probably because he had already used them in 1.4; it is another instance of the way he transfers descriptions of individual believers to the church.

This brings us to the end of the first admonition to husbands, but the section has been much more concerned with the relationship of Christ and the church than with that of husband and wife. It has however connected the ongoing life of the church to the once-for-all event of the cross (Gielen, 266).

28. The husband–wife theme of the HT is now resumed (vv. 28f) from the same basic position that the husband should love his wife; the Christ–church theme is not however neglected and reappears in v. 29c. Before examining the meaning of v. 28, we need to discuss a variant reading which might affect the sense.

καί is omitted by ℵ Ψ 0278 1739 1881 𝔐 sy^p; Did Epiph, but included as in NA[27] (in brackets) before οἱ ἄνδρες and after ὀφείλουσιν by 𝔓[46] B 33 1175 1505 pc sy^h; it is also included before οἱ ἄνδρες as the first word in the sequence with ὀφείλουσιν as the last by A D F G P 048^vid 0285^vid 629 pc lat; Cl. Taken together the evidence for inclusion is much stronger than for omission but against this must be set the variation in its position when included. It is difficult to see why if it originally preceded or followed οἱ ἄνδρες it was changed to the other position. Moreover without καί there is a certain ambiguity: does οὕτως refer backwards or forwards? Its addition prior to οἱ ἄνδρες would parallel its usage at v. 24 with αἱ γυναῖκες and this may have led to its insertion (Hugedé). Its inclusion at either position resolves the ambiguity in respect of οὕτως in favour of a backward reference: husbands should love their wives even as Christ loved the church. Probably two or more early copyists observing the ambiguity independently inserted καί but at different places and it should not therefore be read.

If καί is omitted (see above) this leaves unresolved the connection of v. 28. Does it (a) continue what precedes with οὕτως picking this up, or (b) does οὕτως indicate a new beginning, it itself being picked up by the following ὡς? In v. 24 the particles move the argument forward but are in reverse order; they also move it forward in v. 33 where they are much closer together. If (b) is accepted, then v. 28 lacks a connection with v. 27 (Meyer). It is thus easier to adopt (a); husbands should love their wives as Christ loved the church, with ἀγαπᾶν picking up ἠγάπησαν in v. 25.[21] ὀφείλω implies a duty or obligation (see Barth for a long discussion of the word). This backward reference should not however be taken with Hendriksen to

[20] Cf M. Cambe, 'L'influence du Cantique des cantiques sur le Nouveau Testament', RThom 62 (1962) 5–25.

[21] So G. Bouwman, 'Eph v 28—Versuch einer Übersetzung', Miscellanea Neotestamentica II (SupNT 48, ed. T: Baarda, A. F. J. Klijn, W. C. van Unnik), Leiden, 1978, 179–90, though he reads καί.

imply that AE is indicating that he expects husbands to assist their wives to grow in sanctification. The church is Christ's body; he loves it. Husbands should then love their wives who are as their own bodies.

σῶμα, previously applied to the relation of Christ and the church, is now used with reference to the action of husbands towards their wives and AE probably chose it because of its earlier reference, for Christ may be said to love his own body when he loves the church. As well as this AE is about to quote Gen 2.24 where σάρξ is used of the relation of husband and wife, and it and σῶμα can be equivalents in depicting the sexual relationship (1 Cor 6.16; cf 15.39f). σῶμα has a wide range of meaning in biblical Greek[22] and does not necessarily carry a strong physical or anatomical connotation. It clearly cannot do this when used of the church and in v. 28 it is interchangeable with the personal pronoun. The parallel between the wife as the husband's body and the church as Christ's is not of course perfect (Bouwman); what we have here is rather a play on words. Sometimes 'body' was used of wives in Hebrew (Sampley quoting b Berak 24a and Jastrow, Dictionary of the Targumim, 225) and in Greek (Plutarch, Mor II 142EF; Aristotle, Pol I 1254AB) but the evidence is weak and, in Hebrew, late; it is then simpler to take it as meaning 'person'. To say that husbands should love their wives as (ὡς is almost certainly used comparatively here and not causally, pace Barth) their own bodies is not as degrading a view of marriage as it appears in English where 'body' is primarily physical, and it is not more egotistical than Lev 19.18 (cf v. 29) to which some commentators (e.g. Bouttier; Sampley, 30–4) see an allusion (see on v. 33). Even if 'body' were understood physically it has to be said that a husband loves his body by feeding and dressing it, and there would be nothing wrong in him doing the same for his wife. But the phrase has here a wider complexion. Whatever a husband would do for himself he must also do for his wife (see v. 29). However, a limitation, absent from v. 25, is now introduced. There because Christ's death indicates the extent of his love for the church it is implied that a man should be ready to surrender his life for his wife; love of oneself can hardly be expressed in willingness to die for oneself! The husband's love in the present context should be viewed more pragmatically as in v. 29. Verse 28b with its change from the plural to the singular has been thought to be a proverb (Ewald) but no such proverb has ever turned up. More probably it is a parenthetical explanation of v. 28a. AE may have realised that the reference to a wife as a body might be misleading and so spells it out through the personal pronoun and uses a singular because he is

---

[22] Cf Best, One Body, 215–21; Stacey, 181–93; Jewett, 201–304; E. Schweizer, TWNT, VI, 1024–91; Gundry, passim. On the plural here see Gundry, 220f.

advancing an argument from observation or experience. Sometimes
(e.g. Abbott) a parallel is seen in Plutarch, *Mor* 142E, where
Plutarch says that a man ought to govern his wife as the soul does
the body; but underlying this is a soul–body dualism and Plutarch
speaks of governing and not of loving (Gnilka).
    29. This verse has been connected both with v. 28a (e.g. Haupt)
and with v. 28b (the vast majority of commentators) yet if v. 28b is
explicative of v. 28a then it is probably better to relate it to the
whole of v. 28 as spelling out the nature of the husband's love
towards his wife. As in v. 28b ἑαυτόν picked up σώματα in v. 28a
so both are now picked up by ἑαυτοῦ σάρκα which itself points
forward to σάρκα in the quotation of Gen 2.24 in v. 31. Another
factor leading to the change from σῶμα to σάρξ may have been the
latter's feminine gender; the same pronoun can therefore refer to it,
the church and the wife, so preserving the underlying continuity of
the argument. σάρξ and σῶμα are different terms but their meanings
overlap and so it is possible to interchange them (1 Cor 6.16; 15.39f;
2 Cor 4.10f). While σάρξ (see on 2.3) in Pauline theology can carry
negative overtones (Gal 3.3; 5.19–21; Rom 8.9) it takes its meaning
from its context and its equivalence here with the personal pronoun
signifies that it is not being used negatively (for similar neutral use
see Rom 3.20; 2 Cor 12.7; Gal 1.16). Verse 29a expresses a fact
drawn from experience, true both negatively, for people do not hate
themselves (ἐμίσεν is a gnomic aorist and may be translated with a
present tense, BDR §333; Burton §43; MHT, 73f; Robertson, 836f;
Porter, 78, 222f), and positively, for they care for themselves. Like
all such generalisations there are exceptions: suicides and maso-
chists may be said to hate themselves and ascetics to neglect care of
themselves; and if 'flesh' means 'wife' there have been husbands
who have hated their wives. AE is however only seeking to say
something with which all reasonable people would agree.
    The positive care that all people have for themselves is expressed
through two verbs in the present tense denoting an ongoing activity.
Their background may be either (a) cosmological, (b) the general
human care of one person for another and in particular that of
parents for children, (c) marital. The origin of the idea of care may
lie in the political sphere. (a) Schlier (260 n. 4 and *Christus*, 70–2)
provides many references where one or other of the words is used of
God caring for and nourishing human beings so that they grow.
While ἐκτρέφω is used in this way there is little evidence of a
similar usage of θάλπω,[23] and the present context is one of human
activity and not divine. Either (b) or (c) is therefore more probable.
(b) The words are used regularly in Jewish Greek of human care in
general (Gen 45.7, 11; 47.17) and in particular of parental care (Eph

---

[23] For this word see Spicq, I, 365–6.

6.4; 1 Th 2.7; *T Naph* 8.5; Hermas, *Vis* 3.9.1; Deut 22.6). While there is no suggestion here of the care of children, the two verbs could appropriately be used of the care of a husband for his wife. (c) That this however is the most likely meaning is confirmed by a marriage contract: θάλπειν καὶ τρέφειν καὶ ἱματίζειν αὐτήν (quoted Preisigke, Wörterbuch, I 665; see also MM on both words). The verbs should not be taken so literally as if suggesting all a husband needs to do is to provide food and clothing for his wife. Their use however eliminates any idea that he has the right to tyrannise her.

In the final clause of the verse AE's central theme returns, the relation of Christ[24] and the church. καθώς is primarily comparative, though it may contain a causal element: husbands should care for their wives because Christ cared for the church. The comparison relates to ἐκτρέφει καὶ θάλπει rather than to the more remote ἠγάπησεν (v. 25) and implies a continual care by Christ of his church. The nature of his care is not explained; 4.16 expresses it differently. Although it has been suggested that his care is seen in the eucharist (cf Warnach, 27; Cambier, 'Mystère', 79; Mussner, *Christus*, 154; the idea goes back as far as Irenaeus, 5.2.2f), this is improbable, for though ἐκτρέφω would fit through its connection with feeding, θάλπω would not be appropriate. Everything which Christ does to build up the life of his church is included in these verbs, baptism, eucharist, preaching, prophecy, social care. The attempt to discover parallels to the two verbs in relation to Christ's care of the church is probably wrong.

30. Many MSS add at the conclusion of this verse a section of Gen 2.23, ἐκ τῆς σαρκὸς αὐτοῦ καὶ ἐκ τῶν ὀστέων αὐτοῦ.[25] This reading is supported by ℵ² D F G (K) Ψ 0278 0285ᵛⁱᵈ 1739ᵐˢ 𝔐 lat syr⁽ᵖ⁾ Ir. (1985 omits ἐκ τῆς σαρκὸς αὐτοῦ, presumably because the scribe's eye inadvertently moved from one αὐτοῦ to the next, and K substitutes στόματος for ὀστέων though why is more difficult to work out.) The addition was certainly present in MSS used by Irenaeus (V 2.2f). That the reading reverses the order of 'flesh' and 'bones' in Gen 2.23 is not an argument for its omission since memory rather than a Genesis scroll may have been its origin (see the variations in Gen 2.24 as quoted in v. 31). The addition may be said to fit the present context since its words are drawn from the verse immediately preceding that quoted in v. 31, v. 30 is difficult to explain without them and they provide a referent for τούτου in v. 31. They could have been omitted by homoeoteleuton αὐτοῦ ... αὐτοῦ. Their inclusion however introduces a new comparison (cf Salmond), and there are already enough of these in the passage. The textual evidence for inclusion is much weaker than for exclusion: 𝔓⁴⁶ ℵ* A B 048 6 33 81 1739* 1881 2464 *pc* vgᵐˢ co; Meth Hier. It is difficult to see why the words if once present were omitted. While

---

[24] The evidence, D² 𝔐 for reading κύριος is weak; Christ has been the term used throughout the passage.
[25] On the reading see P. R. Rodgers, 'The Allusion to Genesis 2:23 at Ephesians 5:30', *JTS* 41 (1990) 92–4.

'members of his body' makes some sense and 'members of his flesh' could be forced into sense, 'members of his bones' is nonsensical, the bones being themselves members of the body. Elsewhere both in Ephesians and generally in Paul where terms are used to describe Christ and the church (body, building, head) they are used analogically; here, if read, flesh and in particular bones appear to be used more literally; at least that is the way the majority of those who accept them understand them. Irenaeus (V 2.2f) used them to refute a gnostic devaluation of the reality of the historical Jesus and to make this passage refer to the eucharist. Others have seen them as teaching the reality of the incarnation or of the church as coming from Christ in a way similar to that in which Eve came from Adam. Views about the genuineness of the words changed with the textual discoveries of the nineteenth century; this has resulted in few commentators today bothering to discuss their meaning; good discussions of their traditional understanding are found in earlier commentaries, e.g. Eadie, Abbott. It is interesting to observe how views originally based on a belief that the words were genuine are still propounded by those who do not read them, e.g. the eucharistic interpretation, the church as the new Eve (see S. F. B. Bedale, 'The Theology of the Church' in Cross, 64–75; Chavasse, 70ff; for discussion see also Best, *One Body*, 178, 180ff).

If the addition of the words from Gen 2.23 are rejected, how then are we to understand v. 30 since at first sight it seems otiose? In v. 29b the argument moved back from husband and wife to Christ and the church. Now it is again people who are at the centre and the first plural replaces impersonal statements. Had the verse read 'because she is his body (flesh)' the sequence of thought would have been explained and the first plural eliminated; but then nothing new would have been said (Gnilka). Masson suggests AE may have written v. 30 to avoid saying 'because she is his flesh' (flesh would be the proper term here) since the church is never termed Christ's flesh. Jerome's solution that individualisation has taken place because believers are the children of the marriage of Christ and the church cannot be sustained. Up to now, apart from 4.25, AE has stressed the relation of the church as a whole to Christ and not the sociological aspect of the 'body' metaphor in which members are individually related to Christ and to one another (cf 1 Cor 12.12–27; Rom 12.4–8). Has he at this point realised the impersonality of his approach and decided to personalise it? 'Lest his readers should think of this as remote from themselves, the author reminds them of their place in this discussion' (Best, *One Body*, 178). It is only because readers are members of Christ's body that they can be addressed as they are in a HT which deals with wholly Christian households. Christ's care of the church is always his care of the individuals composing it. ἐκτρέφω and θάλπω (v. 29) predispose one to think of individuals. If AE is individualising here, it goes too far to say that he is drawing in both husbands and wives to remind them of their mutual duties; the emphasis, 'his body', is on the

Christ–believer relationship and not on that between believers. Yet if both are members of Christ's body this provides an additional reason for the husband to love his wife (Lindemann). **31.** This verse is a quotation of Gen 2.24 from the LXX and follows more closely the B ℵ text than the A. AE's use of the LXX is shown by the appearance of (i) ἄνθρωπος, 'human being', instead of the correct ἀνήρ, 'husband', which AE has been using throughout his discussion of marriage, (ii) οἱ δύο which the LXX added to the MT and (iii) by his preparation for it through his change from σῶμα to σάρξ.

There are several minor variations from the LXX: (a) ἀντί is used instead of ἕνεκεν but without change of meaning (see BDR §208.1; Moule, 71; Robertson, 574; von Soden's rendering 'instead of' referring back to v. 29a is unjustifiable); ἀντί τούτου is thus part of the quotation and τούτου does not have a referent. (b) The twofold αὐτοῦ of Gen 2.24 is omitted; αὐτοῦ is strictly unnecessary in Greek where the article is sufficient to indicate that it is the man's father and mother who are intended. Gen 2.24 is also quoted in Mt 19.5 and Mk 10.7, the personal pronoun being read with both 'father' and 'mother' in the former but probably only with 'father' in the latter. In v. 31 B D* F G omit the articles before 'father' and 'mother' but they are read by 𝔓⁴⁶ ℵ A D² Ψ 048 0278 0285ᵛⁱᵈ 1739 1881 𝔐; Or. It is difficult to see why they should have been omitted if present and easy to see why if not present they were inserted, either through knowledge of Gen 2.24, or its Gospel citations which have them on both occasions, or to make clearer the connection between the man and the father and mother. (c) καί (προσ)κολληθήσεται πρὸς τὴν γυναῖκα αὐτοῦ is omitted by 𝔓⁴⁶ ℵ¹ (*:—αὐτοῦ) A (D* F G: κολλ.) P 0285 31 81 1241ˢ *pc* latt; it is also omitted when Mk 10.7 quotes Gen 2.24 and the better reading of Mt 19.5 has the simple verb κολληθήσεται. As scribes copied Ephesians they would have had in mind not only their knowledge of Gen 2.24, but also its Gospel quotations and in each case might be depending on memory rather than on written texts; harmonisation would thus play an important part in determining what they wrote. All this makes it very difficult to decide what AE actually wrote.

AE introduces a quotation here without saying he is doing so (on AE's use of the OT see Introduction §9.1). At 4.8 and 5.14 he alerted readers to his quotations, but not at 4.25 or 6.2f. In 6.2f which draws on the Decalogue he probably assumed his readers knew it was a quotation; the same probably holds here in view of the widespread use of Gen 2.24 in the Gospels (Mt 19.5; Mk 10.7f) and in Paul (1 Cor 6.16 where he acknowledges it is a quotation).[26] The

---

[26] T. A. Burkill, 'Two into One: The Notion of Carnal Union in Mark 10:8; 1 Kor.[*sic*] 6:16; Eph. 5:13', *ZNW* 62 (1971) 115–20, argues that 1 Cor 6.16 is not a fair parallel since it implies that sexual intercourse within marriage would nullify the presence of Christ. Burkill fails to note that, while in 1 Cor 6.16 the intercourse is with a prostitute, that in Ephesians takes place between believing husbands and wives.

verse was also widely known and used in Judaism for varying
purposes and in varying ways: in CD 4.21 in support of monogamy;
Philo uses it allegorically (*Leg Alleg* 2.49; *Gig* 65) and Pseudo-Philo
(*Bib Ant* 32.15) typologically. Later in gnosticism it was used of the
union of the fallen soul with her brother, the bridegroom (*Exeg Soul*
II, 6 132.21–133.11). It is also used straightforwardly of marriage
and sexual relations in 1 Esdras 4.20–2 and in the rabbinic writings
(cf Sampley, 56f).

How then does AE use it? One theme of vv. 22–33 is marriage
and it must at least apply to this, even though it does not relate
directly to the submission of wives or the love of husbands; it would
serve to strengthen the marriage bond, laying, because of its
immediate context, a greater stress on the duty of the husband; the
discussion had of course been individualised in v. 30. In the Gospels
Gen 2.24 is linked to Gen 1.27 implying that marriage belongs to the
created order; in Ephesians instead it is associated with teaching on
Christ and the church; this results in Christian marriage (both wife
and husband are assumed to be believers) being given a soteriological basis. That does not mean that marriage is no longer a part of
the order of creation for Gen 2.24 lies in the creation narrative. Gen
2.24 is however out of harmony with one feature of our passage; in
v. 27 in accordance with contemporary custom the bride was
presented to the husband; in Gen 2.24 the husband leaves his family
to go to the bride. Again this should be a reminder of the inadequacy
of analogies and preserve us from attempts to argue from them
beyond their original application.

While the connection of v. 31 with human marriage cannot be
ignored there is also, as v. 32 shows, a connection with the marriage
of Christ and the church and this has led many past interpreters,
using the word 'mystery' in v. 32 as a starting-point, to offer various
understandings of v. 31. Such 'religious' understandings can be
supported by the 'religious' use of προσκολλάομαι (cf Deut 11.22;
Josh 23.8; Ψ 72.28). If we abandon such attempts to understand the
text we can still see that AE is using it as a way of unifying what he
wants to say about the relationship both of Christ and church and of
husband and wife. The whole verse applies to the latter relationship
but it is its second half which is particularly relevant to the former.

32. AE now[27] picks up the biblical quotation of v. 31, for τοῦτο
refers back to v. 31 rather than forward to the remainder of v. 32. In
so far as the HT has provided AE with a way into talking about

[27] On v. 32 see O. Skrzypezak, ' "Eu, porém, digo ..." De Gênese 2,24 para
Efésios 5,32', *Revista de cultura Biblica* 6 (1969) 103–14; A. S. di Marco,
' "Misterium hoc magnum est ..." (Ef 5,32),' *Laurentianum* 14 (1973) 43–80; A. J.
Kostenberger, 'The Mystery of Christ and the Church: Head and Body, "One
Flesh" ', *TJ* 12 (1991) 79–94; B. Kaye, ' "One Flesh" and Marriage', *Colloquium* 22
(1990) 46–57.

Christ and the church, we have now reached the apex of his argument and, if Gen 2.24 was his 'text', it comes at the end of the 'sermon' rather than at its beginning. There is here a mystery (see on 1.9 for the word) which is important, significant or profound; μέγα is not used adjectivally to refer to the degree of the mystery (here is something especially mysterious) but predicatively. A disclosure has taken place: something previously unknown, secret or hidden is now revealed. In 3.3, 4, 9 it was disclosed that Jew and Gentile stood on equal terms in relation to Christ; in 1.9f the comprehensiveness of God's will for the salvation of all was made known. 5.32 has nothing to do with the acceptance of the Gentiles or the comprehensiveness of God's will, though the idea of unity may be present in the unity of Christ and the church (Sampley, 95). However 'mystery' can be applied in different ways, in Colossians to 'Christ' and in 1 Cor 15.51f to the events of the End. In v. 32 another aspect appears, a particular secret is revealed; the variation in the application of the word probably comes from the Greek world rather than the Semitic; the latter's influence underlies the other 'mystery' passages in Ephesians.[28] Since outsiders might misunderstand the sexual language, it must be veiled (cf Philo, *Cherub* 42f; *CH* 1.16). It is often argued that because 'mystery' is used in the Semitic way in other parts of the letter it must also be used in the same way here. But if a word can be understood in more than one way it is a mistake to insist that there should be only one understanding of it; context, not the counting of instances, must decide meaning on each occasion.

Not only the word mystery but also the final clause of v. 32 where AE says that he is speaking about Christ and the church encourage us to look for a deeper meaning in Gen 2.24. εἰς[29] is usually given the sense 'about, in relation to' (cf Acts 2.25; Hermas, *Sim* 9.26.6). Di Marco, art.cit., however argues that the preposition is used in Ephesians more dynamically with a sense of purpose; the real purpose of Gen 2.24 relates to the Christ–church relationship and not the human. Yet the human aspect cannot be written out so easily when the total context is taken into account. ἐγώ is emphatic. Elsewhere when AE uses the first person singular he has Paul in mind (3.1; 4.1; 6.21ff; the initial reference to Paul the prisoner in 3.1 serves to identify that it is Paul who is referred to in 4.1; 6.19f); AE is thus probably attributing his present interpretation of Gen 2.24 to Paul and stressing Paul's authority as behind it. Paul addressed his

[28] Cf A. E. Harvey, 'The Use of Mystery Language in the Bible', *JTS* 31 (1980) 320–36.

[29] The second εἰς is omitted by B K *pc*; Ptol[lr] Ir Tert Cyp Epiph; see Zuntz, 221, for discussion. Its omission does not change the meaning; its inclusion accords with AE's plerophoric style. Most of the support for omission comes from the Fathers and may arise from failures in memory when quoting.

readers with apparently varying degrees of authority (e.g. 1 Cor 7.10, 12; see Best, *Converts*, 73–95); the present phrase is too inexact for any deduction to be made as to the degree of authority or whether it differs in any way from that implied in the remainder of the letter. The first person singular may be intended to emphasise that what is being said is one of the more important statements in the letter. When teaching the Christians of his own community AE may have discovered that when he used Gen 2.24 to sustain his argument in respect of the relationship of Christ and the church (there is no logical connection between the marriage relationship and the Christ–church relationship), someone may have pointed out that Gen 2.24 says nothing about the Christ–church relationship; to forestall his readers doing the same, he puts Paul's authority behind what he says and with the word 'mystery' he implies there is something in Gen 2.24 requiring elucidation. If then Paul's authority is put behind AE's interpretation no one should stand against it. δέ is commonly taken here to introduce an element of antithesis (see BDR §277.1; MHT, 37; Robertson, 677f), but it is often used continuatively. If it is used antithetically we do not know with what AE is making the contrast; presumably his readers were aware of its nature. The whole phrase ἐγὼ δὲ λέγω may indicate that AE is opposing an accepted interpretation.[30] Philo and Pseudo-Philo (see above) used Gen 2.24 allegorically and typologically; later Christians whose views AE probably did not know used it speculatively (see below). Certainly the understanding and application of Gen 2.24 in Ephesians differ from those of Mk 10.7f and Mt 19.5f and that underlying 1 Cor 6.16; AE would however hardly have disagreed with what those passages say.

What then is the mystery which AE believes is disclosed in 5.32? Since τοῦτο refers backwards it must lie in v. 31. Is there a new understanding of human marriage disclosed here, or of the words of the text, or of the relationship of Christ and the church? It is unlikely to be the first for ever since Gen 2.24 was written it has been known that husband and wife are one flesh, and it has also been known that wives should obey husbands and husbands love wives as the HT in Colossians shows. Gen 2.24 must then carry an additional meaning to that referring to human marriage.

A previously unknown meaning of Gen 2.24 is then being made known,[31] something other than the surface meaning which relates to human marriage. Some Qumran interpreters believed they could discover new meanings in OT texts (1QpHab 7.1–2, 4–5; CD 1.13–14; cf Bruce). Christians and Jews have drawn meaning from

---

[30] Cf Morton Smith, *Tannaitic Parallels to the Gospels* (SBLMS VI), 1951, 28.
[31] See Lincoln, 'The Use of the OT in Ephesians', *JSNT* 14 (1982) 16–57, and Kostenberger, art.cit.

the OT in various ways. A text may be accepted straightforwardly as when the prophets condemn social injustice and their condemnation is applied to contemporary social injustice; but this is not properly the disclosure of a meaning previously unknown. Some have seen in our verse a prophecy of the incarnation (note the future tenses) or of the parousia (future from the point of view of AE), but for both these interpretations the reference to the mother creates an insuperable difficulty (see below for attempts to get round it); did Christ leave his mother to come to earth or does he return to her? The future tenses in any case belong to the text as AE received it and it would have been difficult for him to alter them; also the passage as a whole teaches a present union of Christ and the church. The future tenses are probably gnomic (Burton §69, BDR §349.1) or categorical imperatives (Zerwick §280; MHT, 96; Robertson, 942f; BDR §362). Jews and Christians have used other ways to find new meanings in texts. In Gal 4.21–31 Paul allegorises the story of Sarah and Hagar and draws new meaning from it; whether allegorisation is a valid hermeneutic is irrelevant; it is present in scripture, and was used by contemporary Christian interpreters. In allegorisation value is accorded to all the details of an event or narrative, but AE does not do this here, and it cannot be done, for if the husband is allegorised into Christ and the wife into the church it is impossible to give any significance to the mother. That is not to say attempts have not been made; Jerome and Augustine (*in Jo Tr* 9.10, re Jn 2.1–11) thought of the mother as the heavenly Jerusalem, but this is no help. Writers who allegorise normally also give some indication that a meaning other than that of the surface is to be drawn from the passage being treated (cf Gal 4.24). Allegorisation is not then the key to unlock v. 31.

A typological interpretation might be possible. In Rom 5.12ff and 1 Cor 15.20ff Adam is a type of Christ; so the husband and wife of Gen 2.24 have been understood as Adam = Christ and Eve = the church. This is worked out in great detail by Miletic. It is true there may be passages in Ephesians where Christ is seen as the Second Adam (e.g. 1.22); Paul knowing Hebrew and Greek would probably see the shadow of Adam when he came on the word ἄνθρωπος,[32] but AE was probably not Paul and even if he was a Jew we cannot assume he had a detailed knowledge of Hebrew; he draws all his OT quotations from the LXX. Gen 2.24 as a general statement rather than one relating specifically to Adam and Eve is unsuitable for typological interpretation. It is also doubtful if 'Adam' is to be found in as many places in Ephesians as Miletic suspects. The presence of the new Adam/new Eve imagery would be seen more easily if the longer text were read in v. 31, and indeed the

---

[32] Cf C. K. Barrett, *From First Adam to Last*, London, 1962, 6.

interpretation originally arose when the longer text was accepted as genuine, and perhaps persists today as an explanation though the main reason for it has disappeared. Jerome drew an entirely different conclusion: as the human race was born from Adam and Eve, so believers are born from Christ and the church (cf Ps–Philo, *Bib Ant* 32.15, where Israel is said to descend from Eve, the rib taken from Adam). It is hard to see this as part of the text. It is probably not the man and wife whom AE says are the mystery but the union of Christ and the church. Gen 2.24 was later widely used by many whom the orthodox denounced as heretical:[33] in *Exeg Soul* II, 6 132.7ff there is a marriage of the soul with her brother who is sent down from heaven; ordinary marriage is a defilement but there is a true undefiled marriage which belongs to the will (*Gos Phil* II, 3 82.4ff). These represent some of the many ways of interpreting the OT and there are many variations of each.

An entirely different approach came through the Vulgate rendering of μυστήριον as *sacramentum*, which led to the view of marriage as a sacrament. Though many continue to look on marriage as a sacrament they no longer use v. 32 as its basis. The rejection of this interpretation of v. 32 goes back at least to Erasmus. Difficulties arise in respect of defining marriage as a sacrament because there is a lack of unanimity on the definition of a sacrament. Most Protestants include in this a requirement that it should have been instituted by Jesus; members of the Society of Friends and some other Protestants regard all life as sacramental. Even the attempt to deduce that marriage is a sacrament from 5.22–33 as a whole encounters the difficulty that the passage does not give a full NT description of marriage; other passages require to be brought into play.

It is probably better then not to attempt to fit what AE is saying into some given hermeneutical method or some predetermined dogmatic pattern, but simply to view him as providing a scriptural basis and theological justification for the drawing together of the husband–wife relation and the Christ–church relation, and at the same time carrying a step further his teaching about the church's close relationship to Christ, a relationship already defined through 'body'. He uses the word 'mystery' with its sense of a secret now revealed because he believes what he says is not something which he has thought up on his own but comes from God.[34]

33. This verse provides a summarising resumption and conclusion (for πλήν in this sense see BDR §449.2; MHT, 338; Robertson,

---

[33] See E. H. Pagels, 'Adam and Eve, Christ and the Church: A Survey of Second Century Controversies concerning Marriage', *The New Testament and Gnosis* (FS R. McL. Wilson, ed. A. H. B. Logan and A. J. M. Wedderburn), Edinburgh, 1983, 146–75.

[34] See Schnackenburg, 331–9, for a *Wirkungsgeschichte* of vv. 31f.

1187; Thrall, 20–5; cf 1 Cor 11.11; Phil· 1.18; 3.16; 4.14) of the original main point of the HT in relation to husband and wife, from which AE moved away to draw in the relation of Christ and church. The form is chiasmic; husband and wife are now treated in the reverse order to that of vv. 22–32. φοβῆται does not pick up the φόβῳ of v. 21 and create an *inclusio* (see on v. 21); the verb, properly understood, fits its context.

In this summary the injunction to husbands is emphatically individualised, 'each one of you', and this individualisation should be understood also as applying to wives. No husband or wife should imagine that what is being said does not apply to them. Though AE has much to say about the church as a whole he is well aware that it consists of individuals who have to relate to one another. This relation in respect of the husband is again defined as love, whose special relevance was spelt out in two different ways in vv. 25–7 and vv. 28–9, but is now varied in one respect; previously his love was to be similar to his love for his body (or flesh) or Christ's love for the church; now it is to be similar to his love for himself (cf v. 28b). Freed from the need to maintain the parallel of the husband–wife and Christ–church relationships, AE drops the word σῶμα to use the simpler reflexive pronoun. As Jerome observed the expression is somewhat similar to Lev 19.18;[35] for Jewish and Christian understanding of neighbour see on 4.25; here in v. 33 the wife as another believer can correctly be described as a neighbour. Textbooks on Christian ethics discuss the relationship of self-love to love of neighbour and we do not need to enter into this general problem. In vv. 28f the neighbour was described as of the same body or flesh as the husband and this, not Lev 19.18, is the basis for the injunction to love. Surely also there must be a distinction between the way a husband loves his wife and the way he loves his neighbour's wife? This may be the reason for ἑαυτοῦ here and in v. 25. 1 Cor 6.16 would in any case imply he should not love his neighbour's wife. His love for his own wife will legitimately have a sexual element (cf 1 Cor 7.3ff) which would, or should, not be present in his relations with other women. Lev 19.18 then needs to be treated with extreme care if taken as a parallel.

Whereas love as the attitude of husband to wife is expressed here in the same way as earlier, a different word is chosen to characterise that of the wife towards her husband. φοβέομαι is substituted for

---

[35] Sampley, 30, incorrectly claims to have been the first to observe this resemblance; unlike Jerome however he provides evidence to support the observation: the one whom the singer woos in the Song of Songs is described as πλησίον (1.9, 15; 2.2, 10, 13; 4.1, 7; 5.2; 6.4). 'Neighbour' was also used in later rabbinic literature in relation to marriage; *b Qid* 41a; *b Nid* 17a; *b Yeb* 37b. Even if this had been contemporary Jewish teaching, the Gentile readers of Ephesians would hardly have been able to see the connection.

ὑποτάσσω; the two were linked in v. 21. The construction is also varied as in v. 27b (cf 2 Cor 8.7; 1 Cor 14.5; Gal 2.10) with ἵνα being used imperatively (cf BDR §387.3; MHT, 94f; Moule, 144f; Robertson, 933, 994).[36] φοβέομαι ranges in meaning from suggesting terror to respect and reverence. As it denotes here the wife's reaction to her husband's love it can hardly lie in the area of terror; yet reverence would not be an exact rendering, for her attitude includes obedience and submission. φόβος is a normal element in all authority structures (cf Rom 13.3, 4, 7; 1 Pet 2.18; Eph 6.5), though if the controlling authority acts unreasonably it may degenerate into terror; in our case the controlling authority is directed by love. As Bouttier points out, all believers are summoned both to fear and love God. Respect is probably the best English rendering. What is surprising is the failure to summon the wife to love her husband.

No logical reason dictates the drawing of a parallel between the relationship of Christ and the church and that of husband and wife; this is evident once marriage is set in a different cultural situation, e.g. matriarchal. AE could only draw the parallel because he lived in a patriarchal culture. Favouring him also was the feminine gender of ἐκκλησία; had ὁ λαός or τὸ ἱερόν been his designation for Christian groups, the parallel would have been impossible. In fact in the parallel he only highlights those factors which suit his purpose; he ignores the dowry which the bride customarily brought to the bridegroom; reference to it would imply a doctrine of works. Indeed AE never argues for the parallel but assumes his readers already know it (through 2 Cor 11.2? Schlier, 264) and uses it, though varying the detail of 2 Cor 11.2.

It is sufficient for our purposes to know that the parallel was present in the Pauline school, but some understanding of its background may help us to see how it would appeal to AE's readers. Do we find elsewhere the relation between a single superhuman person and a group of people expressed in marital terms? The background has been extensively examined and evaluated without a consensus appearing.[37] Since marriage is an experience in the life of most people its metaphorical use should occasion no surprise. Thus it appears in the parables of Jesus (Mt 22.1–14; 25.1–13) and as relating Jesus and John the Baptiser (Mk 2.18–20; Jn 3.23–30). Yet though Jesus is featured in the Gospels as bridegroom or husband the disciples never appear as his wife or bride. The husband–wife analogy however is used in relation to the church in Rev 19.7, 9;

[36] Cf W. G. Morrice, 'The Imperatival ἵνα', *BT* 23 (1972) 326–30.
[37] See Chavasse, *The Bride of Christ*, London, n.d.; Schlier, 264ff; id. *Christus* 60–75; Mussner, *Christus*, 150–60; Cambier, 'Grand mystère'; Batey, *NTS* 10 (1963/4) 121–7; id. 13 (1966/7); Sampley, *passim*; Gnilka, 290ff; Niederwimmer, 134–51; Fischer, 165–200; Ernst, 389ff; Lincoln, 362–5; Gielen, 268ff; Pokorný, 228–32.

21.2, 9; 22.17 (Rom 7.4 is not relevant): In the OT and Judaism Yahweh is depicted as the husband of Israel which more often than not is unfaithful to him (Hos 1–3; Jer 3.8; Isa 54.1–8; Ezek 16, 23). Two writings (Ps 45; Song of Songs), originally composed as poems about human love, came to be applied to the love of God for Israel. 'Bridegroom' however never became a messianic title, yet since statements about Yahweh are often reapplied to Christ in the NT it is not surprising to find the relation of Christ and the church described in marital terms. Philo plays with the image (*Abr* 99ff; *Cherub* 40ff; *Somn* 1.200; see also 1QIs^a 61.10; 2 Esdr 10.25ff, 40ff; *Syb Or* 3.356ff; *Odes Sol* 38.11ff). Non-Jewish sources contain stories of the marriages of gods and goddesses and of divine and human beings, but these are not strictly relevant. However, the second century provides parallels (see Schlier), especially through the *sophia* myth (so Fischer) or Justin's Baruch (so Batey). It is interesting that Ephesians, 2 Corinthians (probably written in Ephesus) and Revelation which use the image all have a connection with Asia Minor where gnostic ideas were later important. Whatever the source of the image we can be sure that it would have been understood by AE's readers in Asia Minor.

We are left with a number of questions; some are unanswerable; the answers to others would take us beyond the legitimate bounds of this commentary series. Did AE use the HT because it provided a useful peg on which to hang a further development of his teaching on the church, or being interested in behaviour did he use it primarily in order to instruct his readers in marriage and then realise its value in relation to the church? While not disputing AE's teaching on the close union of Christ and the church with Christ as ruler of the church, can this relationship be rightly illustrated through marriage and applied to the church? Was it simply an accident of history that contemporary views on marriage fitted AE's teaching on the church? If there is no logical connection between marriage and the Christ–church relationship, can the latter still be used to set the pattern for Christian marriage? Can we evolve a Christian doctrine of marriage from a passage which ignores the sexual and procreative aspects of marriage, has nothing to say on its stabilising influence on society or on divorce, does not suggest that the wife's attitude to her husband should be one of love, treats only the case of believers married to one another, gives no direction as to whom believers should marry (cf 1 Cor 7.39) and does not even imply that there are circumstances in which it is better not to marry because of a commitment to the gospel? The absence of a reference to love on the part of the wife is a surprising omission since v. 21 emphasised a mutual relation; it is even more surprising since she is told to love her neighbour and her husband is her nearest neighbour. If the wife is not called to love her husband does the church not need to love Christ? If, as commentators usually say, husbands should be as ready as Christ to give up their lives for their wives, have there not been wives who have done precisely this for their husbands? We should note that there is no element of polemic in AE's exposition of marriage as if he was refuting false ideas; in particular there is no polemic against gnostic ideas (cf Theobald). The idea that marriage need not be monogamous and permanent is not contested nor is any argument offered that husbands may not keep mistresses; the latter has presumably been already covered by 5.3, 5. The erotic factor in marriage is completely ignored (contrast 1 Cor 7.3–5). AE does not belittle marriage in the way Paul appears to (1 Cor 7.1, 7, 26f, 32ff, 40).

In expounding a theology of the church today is it legitimate to use marriage as a parallel since many modern views of marriage are non-patriarchal? In actual practice also the wife is often the wiser and more sensible person; should she, rather than the husband, not be the controlling person? AE's advice takes no account of the character of particular wives and husbands but makes a blanket judgement. His argument supplies a soteriological, there was already one from creation, basis to the patriarchal view of marriage, and to the behaviour of the husband, yet he supplies no soteriological or theological reason for the behaviour of wives. Is it right that the husband's headship should be theologically justified and the wife's subordination not? Would the Paul who in 1 Cor 7.26f, 32–5, 40 favoured celibacy have been happy with the giving of a soteriological basis to marriage? Yet AE's view provided at the time a bastion against those strains in gnostic thought which may have stressed a spiritual–physical dualism and rejected marriage.

Doubts however about the advisability of tying the Christ–church relationship to marriage should not lead to the rejection of AE's teaching about the church. The relation of wife and husband is the closest of voluntary relationships (parent–child is of course not voluntary); the relation of Christ and church must be as close as that. The non-acceptance of a patriarchal idea of marriage cannot mean that the authority of Christ over the church can be set aside; he is its head.

B

PARENTS AND CHILDREN
(6.1–4)

G. Bertram, *TWNT*, V, 596–624; W. Jentsch, *Urchristliches Erziehungsdenken. Die Paideia Kyriou im Rahmen der hellenistisch-jüdischen Welt*, Gütersloh, 1951; H. I. Marrou, *A History of Education in Antiquity*, London, 1956 (ET of *Histoire de l'education dans l'antiquité*, Paris, 1948); M. P. Nilsson, *Die hellenistische Schule*, Munich, 1955; W. Barclay, *Educational Ideals in the Ancient World*, London, 1959; W. K. Lacey, *The Family in Classical Greece*, London, 1968; P. Gutierrez, *La Paternité spirituelle selon saint Paul*, Paris, 1968; M. L. Clark, *Higher Education in the Ancient World*, London, 1971; S. F. Bonner, *Education in Ancient Rome*, London, 1977; M. Gärtner, *Die Familienerziehung in der alten Kirche*, Cologne, 1985; Gielen, 293–300.

1 Children,
  obey your parents in the Lord
    for this is right.
2 Honour your father and mother,
  for this is a pre-eminent commandment
    carrying with it a promise,
3   so that it may be well with you
  and you will be a long time on the earth.
4 And, fathers,
  do not enrage your children,
  but bring them up in the discipline and instruction of the
    Lord.

The second section of the HT covers the parent–child relationship in a manner similar to Col 4.20f; though longer than Col 4.20f it is much briefer than the section on wives and husbands, for AE has no theology to incorporate here. Parents can choose whether they should have children but children do not have a choice and cannot select their parents. The parent and child relationship is thus of a different nature from that between either husband and wife or owner and slave.

Respect for parents was generally expected of children in the ancient world both among Jews, as shown by the Decalogue (cf Ecclus 3.1–9; Philo, *Decal* 120), and among Greeks and Romans

(Aristotle, *Nic Eth* IX 2 = 1165a; Plutarch, *Mor* 479f). Christians sometimes viewed lack of respect as an indication of depravity (Rom 1.30) or a sign of the nearness of the End (2 Tim 3.1f). The father was the more important parent. In the Greco-Roman world the mother reared the child until he ('he' is used advisedly for the rearing and education of girls was of much less importance than that of boys) was seven, when the father became responsible for his training and education. τέκνα, which denotes children here, though neuter in gender, would have been automatically understood by readers as meaning male children. Children were under the control of their parents, particularly of the father, until either the father died (the normal pattern in Greek society) or was sixty years old (normal in the Roman world). When children are addressed in Judaism they may be adults for no upper limit is put on their age (Ecclus 3.1–9; Philo, *Decal* 120). Indeed in later rabbinic Judaism sermons were delivered to adult children on the theme of obedience to parents.[1] AE offers no clue as to the age of the children he addresses; they must have been old enough to understand what is said, but they could have been small, sub-teenagers, or older teenagers and young adults. When the church met in a house presumably all its children were present (cf 1 Cor 7.14). What information there is, is insufficient to determine if the children had been baptised. Since Christian households are in view the difficult situation of young adult Christians who were members in pagan households is ignored. Were these 'children' to obey their fathers when ordered to worship the household gods or to attend a public ceremony where civic gods were honoured? Such questions would not have arisen in the pagan world which lacked a tight religious bond reinforcing the biological. Jesus was keenly aware of the strains that could arise in a family when one member became a disciple (Mk 13.12; Lk 9.59–62; 14.26). Yet even if believers lost their position in their biological family, they would find new brothers and sisters in the Christian family (Mk 3.31–5; 10.29f). AE says nothing of the actual way in which children are to be reared. In Judaism the real centre of education was the home (Deut 6.7; Prov 13.24; Ecclus 30.1–13; Philo, *Hyp* 7.14; Josephus, *c. Ap.* 1.60),[2] though, as with many Greco-Roman households, children would be sent to outside schools for part of their education. Did this mean children from Christian households would be sent to pagan schools? Probably by this time there would have been no question of them attending synagogue schools. The present section on the relationship of parents and children is a kind of equivalent to the discussion of the relationship

---

[1] S. Safrai in *CRINT* II, 771.
[2] Cf W. Pohlmann, *Die verlorene Sohn und das Haus* (WUNT 68), Tübingen, 1993, 61ff.

of older and younger believers in 1 Pet 5.5; 1 Tim 5.1f; Tit 2.6; there was indeed in ancient society a general respect for age.

V. 1 and v. 2 are similarly structured around imperatives with reasons expressed through ἐστιν clauses. The reason given in v. 1b leads to v. 2 since righteousness and the Law are related. V. 3 supplies a further reason for the injunction of v. 2. V. 4 is differently structured with two imperatives set in contrast with one another.

1. NA²⁷ brackets ἐν κυρίῳ. It is read by 𝔓⁴⁶ ℵ A D¹ Iᵛⁱᵈ Ψ 0278 0285 33 1739 1881 𝔐 a m vg sy co but omitted by B D* F G b; Mcionᵀᵛⁱᵈ Cyp Ambst. Both readings are therefore well supported. If not originally present the phrase is what would be added to 'Christianise' the injunction; if its addition had been influenced by Col 3.20 it would have qualified δίκαιον; if the influence had come from 5.22 or 6.7 ὡς τῷ κυρίῳ would have been expected. The presence of the phrase accords with its general use in the letter (cf 4.17; 6.10) and in Paul. However, if originally present it is difficult to see why it should have been omitted. Marcion provides the earliest evidence for its omission and Masson has suggested that he left it out because he found it difficult to associate κύριος with the Decalogue. This is speculative and does nothing to account for its omission by other church Fathers who did not share Marcion's views on the OT. Had Marcion wished to alter the text it would have been more logical for him to omit the OT quotation. If AE had intended to refer here to the Lord would he not have used ὡς as in 5.22; 6.7? Was there however any need to refer to the Lord? What AE says about obedience is well enough supported by his quotation from the Decalogue which his readers would have seen as a divine instruction. To Jews the commandment would have sounded Jewish but Christians having taken over the OT would have seen it as Christian. With considerable hesitation we prefer therefore to read the shorter text.

If 'in the Lord' is read, it must qualify ὑπακούετε and not τοῖς γονεῦσιν, and would imply children should obey because they are Christians. If the phrase is not read, then the text says nothing more than any Greco-Roman or Jewish moralist would have said. There is a sense in which the divine reference would have been implicit for in Judaism, and even more generally, parents came next below God in the hierarchy of obedience, and obedience to them is closely linked to that to him (Philo, *Decal* 119f; *Mos* 2.198; *Spec Leg* 2.225, 235; Josephus *c. Ap.* 2.206; *Sib Or* 3.593f; *Ps-Phoc* 8; *T Reub* 3.8; Stobaeus, *Anth* 4.25.53 = Hense II 640ff; Cicero, *de Offic* I.58; Diogenes Laertes 7.108, 120; Epictetus 2.17.31; 3.7.26; Musonius Rufus *Or* xvi = Hense 82.3–5). AE then has based his injunction on the general moral connotation of δίκαιον and on the particular connection with the Decalogue; the latter was of course of great importance to his readers and understood by them as a Christian injunction. τέκνα, as its use elsewhere shows, implies a biological relationship and offers no clue as to age. It can imply someone old enough to be a believer (Mt 10.21), to work in the fields (Mt 21.28), or to be held responsible for his or her sins (Mk 2.5; cf Lk 15.31), and it can be used metaphorically of people of all ages (Mt 3.9; 23.37; Mk 7.27; Lk 7.35). The children are therefore full members of the community and it is assumed they are of an age where disagreement between them and their parents (biological parents are meant and not 'fathers in the faith') could occur since, though they had attained their majority, they were still under the control of their parents. ὑπακούω is used here as in 6.5 rather than the ὑποτάσσεσθαι of 5.21. Since a similar change exists at this point in the Colossian HT, it was probably already present in the form of the HT in use in the Pauline school and no significance should be attached to AE's change of verb.

Obedience to parents is said to be δίκαιον; although the root of this word is strongly connected in Pauline teaching to justification, the word is used here in a wider way and in common with its use in the moral teaching of the ancient world (cf Epictetus 1.22.1; 2.17.6), a use already met in 4.24 (cf Phil 1.7; 4.8; 2 Th 1.6; Acts 4.19; 2 Pet 1.13; Col 4.1; Lk 12.57). The parallel passage, Col 3.20, uses εὐάρεστον which AE had already used at 5.10. He had therefore no objection to this word and had he been copying Colossians, there would have been no reason for him to alter it. It is more likely that AE and A/Col independently added to the tradition a qualifying word than that AE deliberately altered Colossians. AE lacks the κατὰ πάντα of Col 3.20; even if he were dependent on Colossians he can hardly have been intending to indicate by its omission that there were occasions when obedience was unnecessary. Jews who kept the Law would certainly have been described as righteous (cf Josephus *Ant* 6.165; 8.208) and presumably the same would be true of Christians. Yet obedience is also 'right' because of the biological relationship of parents and children. It is important to note the absence of the kind of reasons which some parents might give: 'we have lived longer in the world and know better what is good'; 'you owe a lot to us for we brought you into the world'.

2, 3. To drive home his point about obedience AE now quotes the relevant commandment of the Decalogue (see Introduction §9.1 for his use of the OT) and so provides another reason for obedience. τιμάω is a wider and gentler concept than ὑπακούω,[3] involving *inter alia* the care of elderly parents. It may also direct attention to inner attitude rather than actual acts of outward obedience; the latter may come from fear of punishment rather than genuine respect. The change of verb cannot however be attributed to AE (*pace* Grosheide) for it is the verb in the commandment.

The commandment is quoted from Exod 20.12 to which it is

---

[3] On the distinction between the two terms see R. F. Collins, 'Obedience, Children and the Fourth Commandment—A New Testament Note', *LS* 4 (1972) 157–73; on Jewish filial piety see Moore, II 131–4.

closer than Deut 5.16;[4] the one significant change is the omission from Exod 20.12 of the final clause referring to the 'land' as good and given by God. The essential section of the commandment is quoted also in Mk 7.10; 10.19; Mt 15.4; 19.19; Lk 18.20 and may be assumed to have been well known to early Christians, but there is no reason to believe that AE drew it from catechetical instruction and not directly from the OT (*pace* Lindemann, *Aufhebung*, 87). Probably converts quickly learned all the commandments of the Decalogue (cf Mt 5.21, 27; 15.4–6; Mk 10.19; Rom 7.7–11; 13.8–10) and in the light of their knowledge AE did not need to use a formal introductory phrase showing the OT origin of the quotation.

V. 2b speaks of our commandment as the 'first' with a 'promise'.[5] Is πρώτη to be understood numerically (ordinal numbers do not need an article, BDR §256, n. 2; MHT, 178f; Robertson, 793f) or as an indication of significance? The word itself disposes one to the former, an interpretation offered as early as Chrysostom. Yet in the Decalogue the commandment is neither numerically first nor even the first with a promise (see Exod 20.4–6). 'First' also implies a succeeding sequence but there are no other later commandments in the Decalogue with a promise. In an attempt to overcome these difficulties Origen, who appears to have been the first to observe them, followed by Jerome, suggested that 'first' might refer to the whole Decalogue as the first law given after the Exodus or that the promise attaching to the second commandment was not really a promise. Others (e.g. Ambrosiaster, Pelagius) have suggested that the fifth commandment is the first in the second table of the Decalogue. Was it however ever regarded as belonging to the second table? Rom 13.9 does not include it among those generally regarded as belonging to it; in Lev 19.3 it is associated with the first table; Philo, *Decal* 121, regarded it as the conclusion of the first set of commandments which are concerned with the divine. Philo is not however consistent; in *Spec Leg* 2.261 he separates this commandment from those he regards as the chief commandments though in 2.242ff he had associated the fifth with the first four as those for which death is the appropriate punishment and in his general discussion he treats the fifth with the first four. 'First' could also relate to 'promise' and not to the numbering of the commandments in their tables. Thus the evidence is insufficient for taking 'first' as referring to the first commandment of the second table. It has been suggested that since the first thing a child learns is obedience to parents the fifth commandment can be regarded as the first (Abbott);

[4] See A. T. Lincoln, 'The Use of the OT in Ephesians', *JSNT* 14 (1982) 37–40, for details.
[5] The omission by B of ἐστιν is probably a simple mistake; it does not affect the meaning.

but if first relates to 'promise' rather than 'commandment' this idea cannot hold, and there are other commandments dealing with children (cf Gielen, 297). It is not possible to evade the difficulty by arguing that it is the first commandment to deal with children which has a promise attached (Grosheide); this leaves too much to be understood. It is difficult to see how the statement (Exod 20.6) accompanying the second commandment can be regarded as anything other than a promise (Lincoln). Even if we were to disallow this as a promise, there are earlier commandments with promises in 12.13 (ἐντολή is used in connection with this in 12.17); 15.26; 19.5; all these commandments come from the period after the Exodus but prior to the Decalogue. Finally all these interpretations suffer from the weakness that 'first' indicates a following sequence of commandments with promises and it is impossible to discover them in the OT. If we do not restrict 'commandment' to the Decalogue then we have to take into account those that precede it as well as those that follow it. This seems to force us back to accepting 'first' as indicating significance. This has been justified through the use of some rabbinic evidence (*Dt R* 6 on Dt 22.6; SB III, 694ff) which regards the fifth commandment as the 'heaviest' (Dibelius). Deut 22.6f contains a similar phrase to Eph 6.3 and since it is about eggs in a bird's nest it is relatively unimportant and is therefore the 'lightest' of commandments; by contrast the fifth would then be the 'heaviest'. But would AE, let alone his readers, have been aware of such an argument (Gnilka, Schnackenburg, Lincoln)? In the end may it not be simplest to take first as indicating a pre-eminent commandment, one of great importance because it is included in the Decalogue and has a promise?

Whatever the meaning attached to 'first' the nature of the promise is of greater importance; in v. 3 ἵνα governs both verbs (cf BDR §442 n. 8; for the use of the future with it see Burton §198; BDR §369.2; Robertson, 875, 954; for εὖ see BDR §102.3 n. 3; Robertson, 299). The promise originally referred to the dwelling in Canaan of the descendants of those who entered it after the exodus and was appropriately attached to the one commandment which implied a continuing Israel. Once the Jews began to live in other areas this geographical limitation was no longer relevant. γῆ was fortunately ambiguous, deriving its meaning from its context. In later Judaism it was frequently omitted in references to the text (SB I, 705–9; III, 614; it is eliminated in Ecclus 3.1–16; Philo spiritualised it in *Spec Leg* 2.262). AE retains the word but leaves it without a context so that it can be taken as 'earth, world'. In either case it still carries a physical connotation. Since AE has already used 'inheritance' (1.14; 3.6) with a non-physical meaning, does he intend such a significance here (cf Mt 5.5 for a non-physical meaning)? Beginning with Origen (cf Jerome, Thomas) many interpreters have therefore read a deeper non-physical sense into it, usually one relating to eternal life. The first clause of the verse makes this difficult; μακροχρόνιος taken by itself could be interpreted in this way, but it is not unqualified. Moreover when AE reinterprets preformed material (4.7–10; 5.13f) he makes it clear that he is doing so. It is probably best then to take the promise of v. 3 literally. Children who keep the fifth commandment will prosper (εὖ) and live for a long time (Belser, Lincoln). This would accord with much in the OT and with the more prudential ethic of the Pastorals (many have followed Harless in quoting 1 Tim 4.8 to support this interpretation). It is a point of view which contrasts with the immediate eschatological expectation of much of the NT but one into which Christians have regularly declined; it is not surprising to see AE whose ethic rarely touches the deeper levels moving in the same direction. The attempt to justify this 'physical' interpretation by saying that those who live well-ordered family lives enjoy long life while those who do not, do not ('the exception proves the rule') is hardly an argument.

4. AE now addresses the fathers (the καί is almost 'and now as for you fathers') who are as much in need of instruction as the children. In accordance with ancient custom he addresses them alone without mentioning the mothers. It is true that πατέρες can sometimes include mothers (Heb 11.23) but the change from 'parents' of v. 1 is significant; had AE intended to include mothers he would have needed to make this explicit in view of contemporary thought. The admonition to fathers is only about half the length of that to children, but what was said to the latter included a lengthy OT quotation. Like Col 3.21, v. 4 begins negatively but, unlike it, it ends positively. Since in the ancient world fathers had great authority over their children they might tend to hector them, lay down the law and thus enrage them. παροργίζω is found elsewhere in the NT only at Rom 10.19 where Deut 32.21 is quoted, but AE uses the cognate noun at 4.26. Col 3.21 has ἐρεθίζω; it is difficult to see why, if AE used Col 3.21, he should have changed the verb and equally, if A/Col used Eph 6.4, why he should have changed it; the difference in verb, though expressing a similar thought, is a further indication that the writers were independent of one another and of their common membership of the same Pauline school. If fathers enraged their children, this would produce the opposite effect to what they were seeking, for anger is sinful (4.26) and enraged children would then sin. AE's sentiment was not unique in the ancient world (cf Plutarch, *de liberis educandis, Mor* II 8F–9A; Menander in Stobaeus, IV 26.3ff = Hense II, p. 650.1ff; *Ps-Phoc* 207–17). While the age of the children is not indicated, older children are more likely to be enraged by a nagging father, though the later effects on younger children might be more pronounced.

The positive attitude fathers should adopt is expressed first in a general way through ἐκτρέφετε, used here differently from 5.29 in that it relates to the education and upbringing of children, and then through two nouns, παιδεία and νουθεσία, which are difficult to distinguish (so also in Philo who uses them together *Deus Immut* 54; *Spec Leg* 2.239; 4.96); the attempt to distinguish them as referring to instruction through act and word goes back to Grotius but is difficult to sustain. While παιδεία (see G. Bertram, *TWNT*, V, 596–624) is closely related to the educational process, it should not be restricted to academic learning; Greek education involved moral and philosophical training. In the Jewish world, where the word was associated with wisdom, it came to carry the additional idea of the physical discipline accompanying instruction (e.g. Ecclus 42.5; Prov 13.24; 29.19). Even though the use of physical discipline was common in the educational systems of the ancient world, it is unlikely that this Jewish nuance would have been picked up in Asia Minor; it is a nuance not found in Acts 7.22; 22.3; 2 Tim 2.25; 3.16; Tit 2.12, though present in Heb 12.5ff (based on Prov 3.11ff); 1 Cor 11.32; 1 Tim 1.20; Lk 23.16, 22; 2 Cor 6.9. Sometimes it is God and sometimes other humans who exercise discipline; normally the context makes it clear when the physical element enters. The word should be given its wider educational sense in v. 4, while recognising that instruction could involve discipline. νουθεσία is found in the NT only at 1 Cor 10.11; Tit 3.10, though the cognate verb occurs more widely in relation to verbal instruction (Acts 20.31; Rom 15.14; 1 Cor 4.14; Col 1.28; 3.16; 1 Th 5.12, 14; 2 Th 3.15) where obviously the idea of discipline does not enter. The two nouns together denote the process of education though giving no clue as to its content. There is nothing here on which to base an educational theory, except that those theories which permit children to do whatever they like would be excluded. Nothing also here suggests fathers should love their children in the same way as they are told to love their wives; Chrysostom comments that fathers naturally love their children and therefore they do not need to be told to do this. Perhaps the same reason has operated in the omission of any reference to the *patris potestas*; it was so obviously true in that age that it did not need to be mentioned. The intructions of the Philadelphian cult examined by Barton and Horsley go further than what we find here in forbidding to parents both abortion and contraception.

Instruction is to be conducted κυρίου; the genitive cannot mean instruction about the Lord but could mean either 'with the Lord in view', 'in the light of the Lord' (gen. qual. cf MHT, 212–14; BDR §165; so Gnilka, Schlier, Schnackenburg, Lincoln) or with the Lord seen as the ultimate instructor who works through the father (gen. subj.; so Bouttier; Bertram, 623). The former would result in a meaning similar to that of v. 1, yet if ·this was what had been intended, we would have expected the same phrase; the latter understanding is therefore preferable: the father mediates the Lord's instruction. The children whom the father instructs are his own children and presumably also those of his wife; nothing is said about the bringing up of the children of his slaves (concubines?). Slaves are addressed (v. 5) and so apparently treated as human beings but nothing suggests they may have families; this is to dehumanise them. The requirement to rear and educate children suggests that AE does not believe the End is about to arrive.

Nothing is said about the actual detail of the teaching parents should give their children. Presumably they should at least give them the instruction which AE has already supplied earlier in the letter, instruction both about the nature of the church of which they are members, and instruction in morals (speak the truth, don't lose your temper, don't commit fornication, etc.). But this would not be enough; areas omitted by AE would need to be dealt with; children would have to be told how to treat other children and older people who did not belong to the church and the proper attitude to take up to external authority in school, city and state.

There are different strains of thought in the NT with regard to respect for parents. In Mk 7.10–13 Jesus criticises those who put religious obligations of a narrow nature before such respect but in Mk 1.20 he induces James and John to leave their father (cf 10.29f), in 3.34f he sets fellow disciples in the place of physical family and in Lk 9.59f he criticises the man who wishes to bury his father rather than be his disciple. Provided it is understood that AE is writing to sons and daughters in already Christian households there is no difference here between the latter strand in the gospel tradition and what AE writes. If it was a non-Christian household then it might be · proper for new believers to disregard their duties towards their parents.

C

OWNERS AND SLAVES
(6.5–9)

W. L. Westermann, *The Slave Systems of Greece and Roman Antiquity* (ET and updating of his article *Sklaverei* in *RE* VI, 894–1069), Philadelphia, 1955; R. H. Brown, *Slavery in the Roman Empire*, London, 1928; A. M. Duff, *Freedmen in the Early Roman Empire*, Oxford, 1928; M. I. Finley (ed.), *Slavery in Classical Antiquity*, Cambridge, 1960; R. de Vaux, *Ancient Israel*, London, 1961, 80–90; S. Zeitlin, 'Slavery during the Second Commonwealth Period', *JQR* 53 (1962/3) 185–218; E. E. Urbach, 'The Laws Regarding Slavery as a Source for Social History of the Period of the Second Temple, the Mishnah and Talmud', *Papers of the Institute of Jewish Studies London*, I (ed. J. G. Weiss), Jerusalem, 1964, 1–94; S. Treggiari, *Roman Freedmen during the Late Republic*, Oxford, 1969; S. S. Bartchy, ΜΑΛΛΟΝ ΧΡΗΣΑΙ: *First Century Slavery and the Interpretation of 1 Corinthians 7.21*, Missoula, MT, 1973; J. Vogt, *Ancient Slavery and the Ideal of Man* (ET of *Sklaverei und Humanität*), Oxford, 1974; D. Lührmann, 'Wo man nicht mehr Sklave oder Freie ist', *WD* 13 (1975) 53–83; R. Gayer, *Die Stellung des Sklaven in den paulinische–Gemeinde–und bei Paulus*, Frankfurt am Main, 1976; T. Wiedemann, *Greek and Roman Slavery*, London, 1981; P. Stuhlmacher, *Der Brief an Philemon* (EKK XVIII), Benziger and Neukirchener, 1981, 42–9; J. Gnilka, *Der Philemonbrief* (HTK 10/4), Freiburg, 1982, 54–81; F. Laub, *Die Begegnung des frühen Christentums mit der antiken Sklaverei* (SBS 107), Stuttgart, 1982; Y. Garlan, *Slavery in Ancient Greece* (ET of *Les esclaves en Grèce ancienne*, 1982), Ithica and London, 1988; D. C. Verner, *The Social World of the Pastoral Epistles* (SBLDS 71), Chico, CA, 1983; M. I. Finley (ed.), *Classical Slavery*, London, 1987; K. R. Bradley, *Slaves and Masters in the Roman Empire. A Study of Social Context*, Oxford, 1987; C. Hezser, *Lohnmetaphorik und Arbeitswelt in Mt 20,1–16* Fribourg, Switzerland, and Göttingen, 1990, 91ff.

5 Slaves, obey your human lords
    with fear and trembling,
    in singleness of heart,
        as (if) to the Lord,
6   not with superficial care,
    like those who seek to please others,
    but as Christ's slaves
        who do God's will from the heart,
7   serving with cheerfulness,

> as to the Lord and not human masters,
> 8   knowing that everyone,
>   whether slave or free,
>   who does something good
>   will be recompensed by the Lord.
> 9   And as for you, masters,
>   treat them similarly
>   without threats,
>   knowing that both their and your Lord is in heaven,
>   and that he draws no distinctions between people.

This final section of the HT deals with a third important relationship in many ancient households, slaves and their owners. As in the other sections it commences with the inferior group, slaves, and moves to the superior, masters or owners. Both slaves and owners are addressed initially with an imperative which is expanded with participial clauses, those of v. 6b and v. 7 being parallel, and the final participial clause in each case is introduced with εἰδότες; these two final clauses set both slaves and owners together on a plane of equality before God. The two subsections are linked by καί as in vv. 1– 4. The whole paragraph is Christ-centred (Stott); it refers to him five times. It was easier to introduce him into this section than the preceding since the term 'slave' could be used to describe his earthly life whereas he was neither husband, wife, nor father.

Several other NT passages deal with slaves (Col 3.22–4; 1 Cor 7.21–4; Philemon; 1 Pet 2.18–25; 1 Tim 6.1f; Tit 2.9f); the frequency of reference raises the question whether there were slaves in the church who were proving unruly in their new-found Christian freedom; more probably the prominence given them in the NT is a result of their numbers coupled with the need to work out a satisfactory relation between them and others in the church. When slaves and masters lived together over a period of time, personal relations might either grow or deteriorate; AE takes no account of this but discusses only their 'formal' relationship (Ernst). Since the slaves are directly addressed we may assume that at least some were present when the letter was read out in the house where the church was meeting, but would these have been only those belonging to that household? Slaves were of course accustomed to being addressed by their master and given orders, but probably not to being addressed on an equality with their masters.

In approaching the nature of slavery in the ancient world we should remember that almost all our knowledge comes from writers who lived in large households with many slaves and this should be taken into account in any discussion; very much less is known about small households with one or two slaves or small businesses employing a few slaves. We should also forget what we know of the treatment of slaves in the plantations of the southern United States and also any idea that colour differentiation was important in the first century in the way it became connected with slavery in the USA. AE does not question the existence of slavery nor discuss its origin (Augustine, *Civ Dei*, 19.15, attributes it to human sin). It was an essential part of the economic and social fabric of the ancient world[1] and was rejected only by Essenes and similar groups (Philo, *Quod Omnis* 79; *Vita Cont* 70; Josephus *Ant* 18.22), perhaps because members surrendered all possessions on entering the community; members of associated communities living in normal society may however have owned slaves (CD 11.12; 12.11); Jews generally did not object to slavery (de Vaux, 80–90; *Ep Arist* 15, 12.27; *Ps-Phoc* 223–7; SB IV, 728ff). It has been estimated that more than a third of the population of the early Roman Empire were slaves. The great farms and estates of rural areas depended on slave labour and at times slaves on them were regarded as little better than animals, but in the urban areas, to which our letter was addressed, they were often important members of households. Their permanency within the household however was much less than that of wives and children, once the wife had entered the household, apart from divorce, she would always be there; children born in the household continued there until after marriage they created their own households. Slaves for their part were purchased and brought into the household and could be sold off at any time; children born to slave parents in the household could still be sold off and their relationship to their parents severed. They were the property of their owners; this was at least part of the reason why Paul returned Onesimus to Philemon; he could not then be accused of theft. Aristotle, *Nic Eth* VIII 11 (1161A–B) allots them a very low position but later they were treated more humanely as Stoic teaching shows (Seneca, *de Benef* 3.18–28; Pliny, *Ep* 5.29; cf Westermann, 107–9); yet earlier and cruder views probably prevailed in popular thought (cf Juvenal, *Satires* 6.219–23; Seneca, *de Ira* III 40.2–3). The basic insecurity of slaves is illustrated from the case of Pedanius Secundus, a senator, who was murdered by one of his slaves; after discussion the Senate upheld an ancient law that all the slaves, some 400, in the household should be executed even though only one was the murderer (Tacitus, *Ann* 14–43.5).

In earlier centuries people were enslaved through being taken captive in war or through piracy; however in the more peaceful first century AD most were slaves because they had been born to slave parents (the children of slaves belonged to the owner of the parents),

---

[1] According to D. L. Balch, *Let Wives Be Submissive* (SBLMS 26), Chico, CA, 1981, 34, there are only 'three or four criticisms of slavery in all extant Greek literature'.

could not pay their debts, were sold by their parents, or exposed as children; a few even became slaves through marrying a slave or sold themselves into slavery because slavery provided some economic security when as day labourers they found difficulty in obtaining constant employment (see on 4.28). This meant that many slaves had talents and skills useful to their owners; they might work at some craft in a business; while in larger households some did the 'dirty' work, others found openings as musicians, medical advisers, educators, stewards, mistresses, companions of the elderly. Sometimes owners hired them out to work for others and were paid for their work. Slaves who held responsible positions would be well treated; though owners had total power over them, valuable assets were not to be wasted. There was little teaching in the ancient world about improving their lot though Seneca, *Ep* 47, does argue in this way. In Judaism masters and slaves were taught how to live together (Ecclus 4.30; 7.20f; 33.31; Philo, *Spec Leg* 2.66–9, 89–91; 3.137–43; *Ps-Phoc* 223ff), though the attitude of owners was not always expected to be humane (Prov 29.19, 21). In society generally if they occupied responsible positions they were often rewarded with their freedom or found themselves able to buy it. If freed they still owed some duties to their owners as patrons. AE, or the HT before him, does not consider the position of freed slaves; perhaps they were few in the churches; Paul did not encourage manumission (1 Cor 7.20–4); he sent back Onesimus to his owner (cf Ign *Polyc* 4.3). Even the Stoics, whose ethical teaching approached most closely to Christian teaching, did not regard freedom from slavery as important; what was important was inner freedom from the chances and tragedies of life (Epict 4.1; 2.1.27; on Stoic views of freedom cf Gayer, 38ff; M. Pohlenz, *Stoa* (2nd edn), Göttingen, 1948, I 135f; Westermann, 39f). It is not then surprising that the NT does not condemn the institution of slavery.

Slaves were accepted as full members of the church and included among those termed 'brothers' (Philem 16). Christians were not however unique in according slaves an equal position in religion with free men and women, for they were fully accepted as members of some of the pagan Mysteries and other religious and semi-religious groups.[2] There is no reason to suppose slaves were refused 'ministerial' positions in the church; the Pastorals do not list freedom among the qualifications for those eligible as bishops and deacons. Pliny says he examined under torture two maid servants who held some kind of official position in the church (*Ep* X 16).

6.5–9 would provide a test case for the examination of the relation of

---

[2] See R. L. Fox, *Pagans and Christians*, London, 1986, 84; Laub, 56ff; Gayer, 54ff.

Ephesians to Colossians,[3] if we could be sure that AE and A/Col were not independently using a traditional HT. More than in the two other parts of the HT the sections on slaves and owners are of similar length in the letters. Many words and phrases appear in both, sometimes these occur at the same relative position in the argument, e.g. ὑπακούετε; sometimes they appear to have moved their position in a purely random manner, e.g. προσωπολημψία is in the section referring to slaves in Col 3.25 but in that to masters in Eph 6.9, κομίσεται is applied to punishment in Col 3.25 but to reward in Eph 6.8, the owner is to be feared in Eph 6.5 but Christ in Col 3.22, the negative emphasis on wrongdoing in Col 3.25 is a positive emphasis on doing good in Eph 5.8. It is difficult to give reasons for these variations and few commentators do. It AE was using a copy of Colossians then the nature of the alterations suggests that he did not have it in front of him as he wrote but was remembering it (cf Percy, 400). More probable than the use of Ephesians by A/Col or of Colossians by AE is the use by both of the same piece of tradition, the traditional HT. Many of the variations represent the kind of way which phrases once heard or read would remain in the mind and eventually emerge differently. Of course this does not foreclose the argument that AE was Paul who remembered phrases he had used and used them again differently in slightly different contexts.

Merklein offers a more general argument saying that the position of the *Haustafel* in Ephesians reveals AE's dependence on Colossians and not on the tradition itself.[4] For detailed criticism of this and of Merklein's view that Eph 4.1–5.20 is a transformation of Col 3.1–17 see Best, 'Who used Whom'.

5. In vv. 5–8 slaves are addressed and it is assumed they are morally responsible; though the masculine is used it may be held in accordance with normal custom to cover also the feminine; whether female slaves however were ultimately accountable to their husbands (5.22ff) or to their owners is not made clear. Slaves are commanded to obey (ὑπακούω as in 6.1 and Col 3.22) their owners with a willing and wholehearted obedience. This obedience is developed in vv. 6–8. Tit 2.9f indicates the kind of temptations to which slaves might succumb and so become disobedient. The obedience of slaves to owners was the general expectation of society and AE does nothing to suggest any alteration within Christian households. In these it would be unlikely that slaves would be called on to perform religious duties to which as Christians they objected. By the very fact that he addresses slaves, AE implies that their obedience should flow willingly out of Christian faith and not be forced from them by their master (cf Calvin; Calvin goes beyond the

---

[3] For detailed study of the relationship of the two letters here see Best, 'Who used Whom'.

[4] H. Merklein, 'Eph 4, 1–5, 20 als Rezeption von Kol 3. 1–17 (zugleich ein Beitrag zur Problematik des Epheserbriefes)', *Kontinuität und Einheit* (FS F. Mussner, ed. P.-G. Müller and W. Stenger), Freiburg, 1981, 194–210.

text, however, when he suggests that it was God who imposed on slaves their position as slaves).

Slaves are to obey their κύριοι; this is an ambiguous term, used extensively in scripture for Yahweh and Christ; at the end of v. 4 it referred to Christ but this is not its meaning here; to ensure its correct understanding, even though the plural ought automatically to exclude error, AE qualifies it with κατὰ σάρκα.[5] Although σάρξ can have negative overtones it is used here merely to distinguish earthly masters from the heavenly Lord (for the use of the phrase in this sense see Rom 1.3; 4.1; 9.3, 5; 1 Cor 10.18; 2 Cor 5.16, and for the literature see on 2.3) But why did AE use the ambiguous term 'lord' since the unambiguous δεσπότης was available and in the ancient world was used more frequently in this connection (Laub, 3ff); it is what is used in similar contexts in 1 Tim 6.1; Tit 2.9; 1 Pet 2.18? If it is answered that AE took it from Col 3.22, then the same question must be directed to its author who uses lord and adds the same defining phrase to avoid ambiguity. The most probable answer is that the pre-Christian form of the HT contained κύριος which in a non-Christian, non-Jewish context would have been at once understood as referring to owners; when Christians, or Jews, took over the HT they had to define the word more precisely (see Best, 'Haustafel'). In most other forms of the HT the offending word is not used (1 Pet 2.18; 1 Tim 6.1; Tit 2.9); Did 4.10f is an exception. If κύριοι was then forced on AE by the tradition, it is wrong to think of him as playing on the word throughout vv. 5–9 (pace Lincoln). There would of course be female owners and mistresses of slaves; the lady of the house in larger households had her own slaves. To avoid sexual distinction 'owner' is a preferable term to 'master', though the latter would be the more accurate translation.

Obedience is to be offered in 'fear and trembling'.[6] Here AE varies (if he knew it) the expression of Col 3.22 in respect of both wording and direction. His phrase is frequent in the LXX (Gen 9.2; Exod 15.16; Deut 2.25; 11.25; Isa 19.16; Ψ 2.11; 54.6; Jth 2.20; 15.2) though the MT has no exact equivalent. Paul uses it at 1 Cor 2.3; 2 Cor 7.15; Phil 2.12. The pre-Christian form of the HT may have had a reference to fear; if so, it was probably in the form found in Col 3.22 which has no scriptural orientation and where lord can be understood as owner; the κατὰ πάντα of Col 3.22 would also be not inappropriate in a non-Christian HT. For AE the object of fear is the owner (cf 5.33) and not God as it appears to be in Pauline usage. Since owners are Christian fear is not to be understood in the sense of terror but rather of deference and respect. The attitude of slaves is further described as

---

[5] The position of the phrase varies; 𝔓⁴⁶ D F G Ψ 𝔐 place it after κυρίοις; this is only a stylistic variation not affecting the meaning. If it was the original position the text may have been produced under the influence of Col 3.22.

[6] Cf K. Romaniuk, 'Μετὰ φόβου καὶ τρόμου', RivBibl 13 (1965) 145–59.

one of ἁπλότης.[7] The word signifies both an inner attitude and the corresponding behaviour; it involves purity of intention and dedication to whatever task is being undertaken; it should be practised and exhibited by those who serve God (Wisd 1.1; 1 Chron 29.17; 1 Macc 2.37, 60, *T Reub* 4.1; *T Sim* 4.5; *T Levi* 13.1; Rom 12.8; 2 Cor 11.3; Philo, *Opif Mundi* 156, 170). It is regularly associated as here with a word like 'heart' (for 'heart' see on 1.18) thereby indicating its inner nature in relation to the task in hand:[8] slaves should dedicate themselves wholeheartedly to whatever task their owners set them; vv. 6f develop the idea implicit in the word (Haupt).

A christological orientation, made necessary to show the Christian nature of the HT, concludes the verse. The master does not replace Christ (contrast *Did* 4.11; *Barn* 19.7) nor does he represent Christ to the slave, and Christ is not the pattern for the slave's behaviour as in 1 Pet 2.18–25. Slaves are to serve their owners with the same devotion they serve Christ; when they do so they will in fact be serving him. AE might have gone on to say, but does not, that thereby others would be drawn to Christ.

6. The nature of the service slaves should offer is now expressed first negatively and then positively (v. 6a); the positive side is then expanded in a participial clause (v. 6b); v. 7 follows in parallel with v. 6b.

Slaves though constrained to do what they are told should not do it simply to get by or satisfy the eye of supervisors; they should perform their tasks conscientiously and thoroughly even though their owner's back is turned.[9] Necessarily, of course, owners must be satisfied (ἀνθρωπάρεσκοι; for the word see Ψ 52.6; *Ps Sol* 4.7, 8, 19; cf 2 Clem 13.1; Ign *Rom* 2.1), otherwise punishment follows; but work is not to be done in a fawning manner merely to gain approval or curry favour (Erdman) but should be sincere. Slaves should display the same attitude in their work as Paul in his missionary activity (Gal 1.10; 1 Th 2.4) for slaves are slaves of Christ just as much as was Paul (Rom 1.1; Gal 1.10) or were Paul and Timothy (Phil 1.1; cf Acts 20.19). Yet there is an essential difference: Paul chose to call himself a slave of Christ, and his use of δοῦλος of himself does not indicate social status; this however is the significance of the word in vv. 5–9, and it is a status which slaves had probably not chosen voluntarily. Slaves have both human owners and a divine Lord. No contrast is intended here between their present position and their pre-Christian when they were slaves to sin, the Law and the powers.

---

[7] Cf Spicq, I, 125–9; H. Bacht, *RAC* IV, 824; J. Amstutz, ΑΠΛΟΤΗΣ: *Eine begriffsgeschichtliche Studie zum Jüdisch–Christlichen Griechisch*, Bonn, 1965, esp. 114–16.

[8] ℵ 323 945 1739 1881 *al* omit the article with καρδίας.

[9] Cf C. F. D. Moule, 'A Note on ὀφθαλμοδουλία', *ExpT* 59 (1947/8) 250.

If their true allegiance is to Christ, they will express this by doing (pres. part. indicating a continuing activity) the will of God; AE uses here a traditional phrase (cf Mk 3.35; Mt 7.21; 12.50) which qualifies not only the reference to eye-service but the whole life of the slave. All Christians are expected to do God's will, so in effect what slaves are summoned to do is the same as is asked of other believers. Since it is Christian households which are being treated it can be assumed that the will of owners and the will of God coincide (Gielen, 305); slaves should serve their owners with the same readiness as they serve God. Doing the will of God must of course be inwardly motivated, ἐκ ψυχῆς. With most editors (apart from WH) this phrase is to be associated with what precedes rather than what follows, for δουλεύοντες already has a qualification expressing an inner attitude. Alford's objections that if this connection is correct the phrase should have preceded ποιοῦντες or τήν have preceded it are without real foundation. ψυχή ('heart' is a better English translation than 'soul') implies here an inner attitude as did καρδία in v. 6; functioning in this way the two terms are almost equivalent (cf Deut 6.5; Mk 12.30). While a set of laws can be obeyed without inner involvement the whole person comes into play in doing God's will.[10]

7. This verse parallels the participial clause of v. 6b and summarises the previous positive statements about the way slaves should serve; οὐκ ἀνθρώποις also take up ἀνθρωπάρεσκοι (v. 6a). The ellipsis of the participle after ὡς[11] is frequest (MHT, 158; BDR §425 n. 6). εὐνοία, though regular in Greek from classical times, is a *hapax legomenon* in the NT (for the cognate verb see Mt 5.25); it appears in the later parts of the LXX (e.g. 1 Macc 11.33, 53; 2 Macc 9.21, 26; 11.19; 12.30) and in the papyri (cf MM *s.v.*). It was sometimes used to describe the attitude of people to their rulers and so could be applied to the manner in which slaves should carry out their tasks (Lucian, *Bis Accusatur* 16; P.Oxy 494.6: cf Xenophon, *Oec.* 12.5.7; see Spicq, III, 316–22). These should be done, not grudgingly, but cheerfully, willingly and sincerely; in the Christian household especially, a ready goodwill (cf Robinson) is required rather than cold loveless service.

8. The final participial clause introduces a motivation for the faithful work of slaves which should strengthen their willingness to serve and thus this clause supports the preceding clauses. Owners might at times forget (since they are Christian owners we ought not to attribute worse failings) to reward the faithfulness of slaves. εἰδότες (cf Rom 6.3, 6; 1 Cor 15.58; Eph 5.5) is spoken to the

---

[10] On the later interpretation of this phrase by Ambrose, Jerome and Augustine see J. Doigon, 'Servi facientes voluntatem Dei ex animo (Eph. 6.6)', *RSPT* 68 (1984) 201–11.

[11] ὡς is omitted by D² K L Ψ 326 614 629 1241¹* 2495 *al*; Ambst.

slaves as Christians and implies they are being reminded of something of which they are already aware. We cannot tie down the occasion(s) when they were so instructed; it could possibly have been at baptism (Bouttier) but how much instruction they received then is doubtful; it if better to assume that as they (and their owners) met for worship their attitude to their work would be brought up in periods of instruction or during the preaching of the word; the two cannot be easily distinguished for good preaching is always instructive.

There are at least five different versions of the words following ὅτι:
(i) ἕκαστος ὁ (—ℵ*) (ἐ)άν (ˢℵ) A D* F G P 0278 33 81 104 326 365 1175 1241ˢ 2464 pc
(ii) ὁ ἕκαστος K vgᵐˢˢ; Hier
(iii) ὁ ἐάν τι ἕκαστος (ˢD²) Lᶜ (Ψ) ℵ
(iv) ἐάν τι ἕκαστος L* 630 1739 1881 2495 al
(v) ἕκαστος ἐάν τι B d
(ii), (iii) and (iv) lack sufficient support to be given serious consideration. Both (i) and (v) place ἕκαστος first and since this is later developed into 'slave or free' it is the leading idea of the verse and appropriately comes first. There is little to choose between the two; probably (v) should be preferred.

The need to practise active goodness, expressed in different ways, is regularly emphasised in the Pauline corpus (2 Cor 9.8; Gal 6.10: Eph 2.10; Col 1.10; 1 Th 5.15; 1 Th 2.17). The nature of the goodness is determined by the context; here it is willing and faithful service at set tasks which the Lord will reward (τοῦτο refers back to ἀγαθόν; for the use of κομίζω in this connection see 2 Cor 5.10; 1 Pet 5.4); the Lord is of course not the owner here for he is the ἐλεύθερος and cannot be thought to reward himself. Nothing is said about what the reward will be, least of all that it will be the granting of freedom or some other earthly recompense e.g. leisure time or money. The context suggests a non-earthly or eschatological recompense, a spiritual reward for spiritual faithfulness (cf Gal 6.8; Col 3.24 however has a negative outlook), and this fits with the idea of God as the one who recompenses; this also gives another indication that AE's eschatology is not entirely realised. For the proportionality of reward to activity see Mt 16.27; 25.31ff; Rom 2.6; 1 Cor 3.12–14; 1 Pet 1.17; Rev 22.12. The problem of the relation of reward to justification by faith is already present in Paul and AE does nothing to solve it (e.g. is it ethical to persuade people to do what is right so that they may be rewarded?). We note however that AE does not encourage slaves to be obedient and faithful in order to be manumitted.[12] Faithful slaves were often rewarded in this way, but sometimes slaves who already lived in good households rejected

---

[12] On manumission see Treggiari; Duff; Bartchy, 78ff.

manumission, and Christian households ought to be good. Perhaps AE does not refer to manumission because it would be expected anyway from Christian owners, or perhaps he does not wish to motivate slaves to good behaviour to obtain some personal advantage for themselves. By the end of the NT period the manumission of slaves was being advocated (1 Clem 55.2; Ign *Polyc* 4.3; Hermas, *Sim* 1.8). Yet there is also a danger of owners saying to themselves, 'I needn't reward him/her now; there is a reward waiting for them in heaven', and so going on to exploit their slaves. It is perhaps to avoid such a conclusion that AE moves on at once to advise owners how they should behave.

The final phrase of the section on slaves, 'slave or free', brings slaves and owners together and is suggestive of some kind of equality; AE thereby prepares the way for a transfer of attention to owners. Where the phrase occurs elsewhere it is one of a series of alternative (1 Cor 12.13; Gal 3.28; Col 3.28) and possibly connected to baptism, though it is not clear how such a phrase would fit into a baptismal ceremony. It occurs naturally in the present context, giving no reason to think AE derived it from a sequence of alternatives and even less to see a baptismal reference.

9. And now for owners (καί as in v. 4); the conclusion of v. 8 provided the transition and the first clause of v. 9 continues the linking of slaves and owners in some kind of equality. The second half of the verse recalls owners to previous instruction in the same way as slaves were recalled in v. 8.

In some respects owners faced greater problems than slaves: could an owner whip, or have whipped, a slave with whom he had shared the bread and wine of the eucharist? Apart from one piece of concrete advice, that owners should abstain from a threatening attitude, the remainder of the advice to them is vague: τὰ αὐτὰ ποιεῖτε, act towards them, i.e. slaves, in the same way. But what is the same behaviour which is required from owners as from slaves? It certainly cannot imply a reversal of roles and be equivalent to 5.21 (Ernst) with owners serving slaves; slaves remain slaves and owners owners (Masson). The phrase can hardly be linked to εὐνοία (v. 7; so Jerome, Chrysostom, Bengel, Ewald) for it is too remote and indicates a manner in which behaviour should be offered, whereas our phrase indicates actual activity. τι ... ἀγαθόν is closer and is also linked to ποιέω (Haupt) yet it describes behaviour towards owners, and the behaviour of owners towards slaves will be different unless both are incorporated under some general rubric like 'doing God's will'. Perhaps it is best to take the phrase in some such general way with *mutatis mutandis* understood (Alford).

What then is God's will for the way owners should treat their slaves? Only one example is given, the non-use of threats, though εἰδότες suggests there has been earlier and wider instruction.

Threats, and the resulting punishment if the threat went unheeded, were the normal way of controlling slaves (Tacitus, *Annal* 14.44); Jewish owners are warned against unnecessary severity (Ecclus 4.30; 7.20; 33.31) and also occasionally pagan owners (Plutarch, *Mor* 7E). Threats would be the natural product of the owner's anger at slaves' behaviour (Seneca, *De ira*, 3.24.1; 3.32.1). If Christian owners are to lay aside threats, they must also lay aside the punishments which would follow (cf Joüon, 462). Are they then left with no means of controlling slaves? AE does not consider this for he writes for the ideal situation where Christian slaves will always obey, but that does not help owners to know what to do when Christian slaves fail in their duty. If threats are set aside that does not mean rewards will be also (cf Philo, *Decal* 167); this leaves one means of control. What about slaves holding positions of authority within households? AE offers no advice to them on how they should exercise their authority (and discipline their fellow slaves?).

AE envisages a solidarity as existing between slaves and owners, not because of their common humanity, as some Stoics might have allowed, but because both have the same heavenly master (the reference to heaven is a necessary qualification of the secular κύριος in a Christian context; cf v. 5). Perhaps Seneca approaches most closely to what is said here when he places both owners and slaves as humans under the same *fortuna*. AE does not consider the more difficult case where the Christian slave is owned by a pagan. In the case of husband and wife and of parents and children there was no need to stress solidarity; the former are 'one flesh' (5.31); the latter are biologically related. Normally owners and slaves are related only because one has purchased the other. The relevant attribute of God in respect of those in solidarity is προσωπολημψία, a LXX word (in Col 3.25 the word was used in relation only to slaves and not owners and slaves). At times when the actual word is not used in the OT, the concept still appears, the most famous instance being that of David, 1 Sam 16.1–13 (cf Deut 10.17; Mal 1.9; Ecclus 35.12f; *Ps Sol* 2.16; *Jub* 5.16, and in the NT Gal 2.6; cf *Did* 4.10). The quality is transferred in v. 9 from God (Rom 2.11; 1 Pet 1.17) to Christ. It is also applied to human behaviour (Lev 19.15; Mal 1.8; Ecclus 4.22, 27; Lk 20.21). It means no account is taken of the rank, status, wealth, race, colour, sex, or position, within church or state, of believers. Divine impartiality in respect of owners and slaves differs from that in respect of Jews and Gentiles, for in the latter case the actual distinction is abolished and one new group, the Christian, appears alongside the other two. For AE religious distinctions founded on race are of a different quality from social distinctions and he does not envision the disappearance of that between owners and slaves. We note with Erasmus that though AE quotes the OT in respect of both marital and parental relationships he does not do so in relation to slaves and owners; had he wished to bring in the OT he could have used texts about the release of slaves in the seventh year (Exod 21.2–11; Lev 25.39–46; Deut 15.12–18). The OT attitude to slaves is not wholly consistent for in several passages (Lev 25.44–6; 2 Chron 28.8–15) it is implied that Israelites should not enslave fellow Israelites but treat them as paid workers (Lev 25.39–43). If it is said that AE does not introduce the OT because the relevant Jewish law relates only to fellow Hebrew slaves and is not applicable in Christian households, then it should be remembered that in 4.25 AE paralleled neighbour, which equalled fellow Israelite in the original, with believer, thus applying to believers what had related to Jews. Perhaps for AE the OT is only a guide in ethical matters where it suits him! Should not Christian owners offer freedom to Christian slaves after six years of enslavement?

The relative proportion of material devoted to slaves and owners is a little surprising. It may be there was some restlessness among Christian slaves who had begun to view themselves as religiously equal to their owners (Gal 3.28; 1 Cor 12.13; Col 3.11) and they may have flaunted that equality (1 Tim 6.2), or AE may have belonged to the 'owner' category and assumed that owners would require less teaching because they would naturally behave in a Christian manner, or perhaps the temptations to slaves were greater (Schnackenburg) yet this in itself is a bourgeois point of view (i.e. one taken by a middle-class owner), or the difference may simply reflect the social make-up of the church (there were more slaves than owners). The relationship of slaves and owners would have been especially difficult if in worship the slaves were more gifted charismatically, or if a slave held an 'official' position in the church. Probably AE hopes that friendship will develop between owners and slaves as indeed often happened in the ancient world.[13] They worked alongside one another in small businesses and at times sat at the same table.[14] AE gives no teaching on the way slaves should treat one another as he gave none on how siblings should live together; there must have been times when they were at odds with one another; AE probably supposes the injunctions of 4.25ff would govern their behaviour towards one another. He gives no advice on the relation of the owner to freed slaves; manumitted slaves were still tied in some respects to their previous owners. More surprisingly he does not suggest that all are slaves of Christ, though this would be as relevant as his final remarks in v. 9. He has nothing to say about how day labourers should do their work or how employers should treat such employees.

---

[13] Cf Vogt, 103–21, 129–45.
[14] Cf Finley, *Slavery in Classical Antiquity*, 57.

Before we leave the HT we should recall:

1. Only Christian households are in view; the NT does not provide a blueprint for all situations and it should not be read as if we lived in the first century, or the sixteenth, and the HT govern our conduct today.

2. The established order in respect of households is accepted, though its normal harshness is ameliorated; many of the exhortations are similar to those of the better contemporary moralists.

3. AE does not suggest social change within the household let alone in society as whole. He does not provide a substantially new basis for the ethic of the Christian household.

4. AE presents an individualistic ethic rather than a social. Quite apart from discussions about society or even the place of believers in the wider world, the interrelationship of households is not discussed. The obedience of slaves, wives and children is not set in the context of the need for a stable society.

5. Even if 5.21 is a heading for the HT, AE never works out how mutual subordination should affect household relations; the nearest he comes to this is in 6.8f whose ideas if accepted would eliminate a tyrannical attitude on the part of superiors.

6. There is nothing basically revolutionary in AE's ethics of the household. In Mk 10.42–5 Jesus set out the relation of superior and inferior and despite the use of δοῦλος none of what he said appears to have affected AE's injunctions. It is true that there have been changes in social relationships since AE's time but the impulse towards change has come from other parts of the NT and not from Ephesians. The absence of the revolutionary ethic of Jesus makes it unlikely that the HT had its origin in his teaching.

7. The position of the single person, whether male or female, and of the widow is ignored.

XV

CONFLICT
(6.10–20)

A. Harnack, *Militia Christi*, Tübingen, 1905 (ET by D. McI. Gracie, Philadelphia, 1981); R. Leivestad, *Christ the Conqueror*, London, 1954, 160–3; A. E. Travis, 'The Christian's Warfare: An Exegetical Study of Ephesians Six', *SWJT* 6 (1963) 71–80; J. P. Lafuente, 'El christiano en la metafora castrense de san Paulo', *Studiorum Paulinorum Congressus 1961* (AnBib 17–18), Rome, 1963, II, 89–100; J. Pierron, 'L'Épître (Ep 6,10–17). Être armés pour le combat chrétien', *AsSeign* 76 (1964) 14–28; Kamlah, *Paränese*, 189–96; Roels, 215–21; V. C. Pfitzner, *Paul and the Agon Motif* (SupNT 16), Leiden, 1967; P. F. Beatrice, 'Il combattimento spirituale secondo san Paolo: interpretazione di Ef 6,10–17,' *Studia Patavina* 19 (1972) 359–422; Fischer, 165–71; A. Lindemann, *Aufhebung*, 63–6, 235f; id., 'Bemerkungen zu den Adressaten und zum Anlass des Epheserbriefs', *ZNW* 67 (1976) 235–51; R. A. Wild, 'The Warrior and the Prisoner: Some Reflections on Ephesians 6:10–20', *CBQ* 46 (1984) 284–96; E. Lohse, *Militia Christi* (Bursefelder Universitätsreden), Göttingen, 1990; Faust, 447ff; Kitchen, 112–28.

10 Finally, be strengthened in the Lord,
      that is, with the vigour of his might.
11 Put on the armour of God
      so that you may be able to stand firm
      against the stratagems of the devil.
12 For our struggle
      is not against anything human
      but against the rulers,
        against the authorities,
        against the cosmic masters of this darkness,
        against the spiritual powers of evil in the heavenlies.
13 Therefore buckle on the armour of God
      that you may be able to offer resistance
        in the evil day
      and be prepared in every respect to stand firm.
14 Stand then,
      girt round your loins with truth,
      and clothed with the breastplate of righteousness,
15 and your feet shod

584

                    with the stability of the gospel of peace,
16   in all circumstances taking the shield of faith
                    with which you will be able to quench all the devil's
                                    fiery darts,
17   and receive the helmet of salvation.
            and the sword of the Spirit which is a word of God,
18   praying with every kind of prayer and intercession
            at every opportunity in the Spirit,
            and for this purpose being vigilant
             . with all perseverance
            and intercession on behalf of all the saints,
19   and on my behalf
                that words may be given to me
                when I open my mouth with frankness
                to make known the mystery of the gospel,
20   on behalf of which I am a chained ambassador,
                so that I may be frank and bold
                in the way I am compelled to speak

With v. 10 the subject changes abruptly and one of the most original
sections of the letter begins. No clear connection exists between the
behaviour of members of a household, all of whom are believers and
who are not depicted as in conflict with one another, and a struggle
between every believer and the superhuman powers (cf Leivestad,
162). It is true that by instructing his readers from 4.1 onwards in the
nature of conduct befitting Christians AE implies that their behaviour leaves something to be desired, yet what he writes now goes far
beyond what is to be expected either in a summing up of what has
preceded or in a concluding peroration. It is also true that the
metaphor of battle was present in 4.8, yet there it was Christ and not
Christians who were involved in conflict. An exhortation to readers
to pray and be watchful (cf 1 Cor 16.13; 1 Th 5.6–8) would not have
been out of place; these ideas do appear in vv. 8–20 but that in no
way accounts for the picture of the warrior in vv. 11–17. Likewise a
call to stand firm against temptation or against those who might lead
them astray would not have been out of place. But the passage does
not deal with human failure in human terms but in supernatural. It is
not a question of a conflict within a divided self (Rom 7.7ff) or a
battle for the moral life, but a battle for the spiritual. If this is the
letter's *peroratio* we should see it then in the light of 1.3–3.21 rather
than of 4.1–6.9, for it does not exhort readers to fight against
dishonesty or sexual indulgence but returns to the supernatural
nature of Christian existence as set out in 1.3–3.21. A failure to
stand against the powers would entail for believers their loss of
salvation and would not simply be another sin from which they
would need to repent. The devil does not set out to lure believers

into telling another lie or committing an act of fornication but to shatter their Christian existence. The paragraph may indeed function as a *peroratio*, but it also resembles the kind of speech with which a general would hearten his troops before they go into battle (e.g. 1QM 15).

The paragraph moves from the earlier depiction of the Christian life as one of steady movement (περιπατέω, 4.1, 17; 5.2, 8, 15) towards a goal to one of it as struggle, supernatural struggle. AE might have chosen for his purposes the 'athletic' metaphor with its emphasis on a goal to be attained (1 Cor 9.24–7; Gal 2.2; Phil 2.16; 3.12–14); he ignores this because he wishes to stress the need to stand firm, and finds this in the military image. It is an image found widely in the ancient world:[1] Yahweh as Lord of hosts, the stories of war among the gods in Greek and oriental legend, initiation in the Mystery Religions (Tertullian, *de Corona* 15; Apuleius *Metam* 1.13); and it reappears in some Greek moralists (Epict 3.22.69, 24.34; Seneca *Ep* 107.9), though in the moralists the opposition is not necessarily supernatural. Paul depicts the Christian as a warrior (1 Th 5.8; 2 Cor 6.7; 10.3–5; Phil 2.25; Philem 2; Rom 6.13; 13.12), a theme which has continued in Christian use from the Apostolic Fathers onwards (1 Pet 4.1; 2 Tim 2.3–5; Polyc *Phil* 4.1; Ign *Polyc* 6.2; Hermas, *Mand* 12.2.4), and has been expressed especially in the hymns of the church. The immediate background to the Christian usage lies in the OT and in Qumran, for example in the *War Scroll*,[2] though the tracing of a precise relation with the latter is difficult for it does not spiritualise the items of armour nor is the war one directly between human and supernatural beings; it is also conceived in a more physical manner than in the OT and Paul. The image of course came to AE through Paul, if AE is not Paul.

Kitchen understands the passage in terms of the church rather than of the individual believer; the church is to stand firm and put on armour. Kitchen however does not make clear what he understands by the church; if the church is the body of Christ, his bride or his fullness, it is difficult to see why it needs to put on armour; it is already secure. If however the church is the local community, then it is composed of individuals who must wear the armour together and not independently. Kitchen correctly criticises an over-individualistic Christianity but goes too far in doing so. All the earlier injunctions about conduct were addressed to individuals (could the church commit fornication?) and AE gives no indication in 6.10ff that he has anything other than individual believers in mind; see also below on v. 12.

Once the believer has been depicted as a soldier his (since the image is masculine it is impossible to avoid the use of the masculine

---

[1] Cf Knox, *Gentiles*, 201–3.
[2] Cf O. Bauernfeind, *TWNT*, VII, 701ff; Pfitzner, op.cit., 157ff; Schlier, 298–300.

pronoun) equipment needs to be detailed.[3] The individual items are conventional and would have been known to anyone in the ancient world; there is no need then to imagine Paul, if he is the writer, drawing the imagery from the Roman soldier guarding him; a soldier guarding an individual would not in any case have needed the large shield of v. 16. The equipment may be conventional but its metaphorical explanation probably derives from Isa 59.17, a passage which had already been developed in Wisd 5.17–20.[4] Isaiah 59 is one of those passages which are referred, or alluded, to fairly frequently in the NT (see Rom 3.15–17; Lk 1.79; 1 Pet 1.17; Rev 20.12f; 22.12; Lk 13.29; Rom 11.26f). In Isa 59.17 the armour is spiritualised and God is the warrior who wears it; he is described as a warrior in many other places, e.g. Ps 35.1–3 (see also notes on the individual verses of our passage); sometimes he is even described as the armour of his people (e.g. Gen 15.1; Ps 3.3; 18.2; 2 Sam 22.3, 31; cf Murray). In 1 Th 5.8 Paul transferred the imagery from God to the believer while continuing to spiritualise the armour. AE has drawn two elements of his description from Isa 59.17, introduced others not all of which would have fitted an OT context, omitted some (javelin, greaves) and dropped those which were spiritualised into anger and vengeance; these could not be part of the Christian's weaponry; their exercise must be left to God. The items AE has selected would all have formed part of the equipment of the heavily armed Roman infantryman.

None of this accounts for the introduction of the supernatural powers as opponents of the Christian warrior. 6.10 is couched in non-mythological language as is most of the rest of the letter. There is a change at v. 11. In 2.1–3 the pre-Christian predicament was described in both human and supernatural terms; the supernatural reappeared, though in different ways, at 3.10 and 4.27. AE's readers would then have been ready to see opposition as coming not only from other people who might tempt them into greed or lust, or might persecute them, but from supernatural powers. The struggle depicted here is not one with persecutors, least of all with Judaisers, as supposed by Beatrice for whom the powers are the powers of the Law which create discordance between Jews and/or Jewish Christians and Gentile Christians. Beatrice also understands the struggle as part of the messianic conflict when Christians would fight the powers of evil; but after v. 10 Christ disappears from the passage and God occupies the central place. The paragraph has in the strict sense a *theo*logical and not a *christo*logical orientation.

When we ask why at this point AE starts to use mythological

---

[3] On the details of the weapons and armour of the ancient world see A. Oepke and K. G. Kuhn, *TWNT*, V, 292–315.
[4] On the influence of this passage on the NT imagery see C. Romaniuk, 'Le Livre de la Sagesse dans le Nouveau Testament', *NTS* 14 (1967/8) 498–514.

language we may be creating a problem for ourselves by the way we phrase the question. Any answer depends on the understanding of 'myth'. If it means the expression of the supernatural in natural terms, the letter is in fact full of this type of language for throughout it behaviour is set in relation to Christ and God. To many Christians today this seems ordinary language while to speak of the tricks of the devil is not. However for AE and his readers the devil and his/her sub-devils belonged as much to ordinary language as did God. They envisaged conduct on the one hand as entirely on the human plane of the interrelationship of people and on the other as a part of the struggle between God and Satan. Theological problems concerning the existence of Satan were as unreal to them as those concerning the existence of God. This may help to explain the position of this paragraph in the letter; summoned to behave as Christians they know that they may be frustrated by others, but they also know there are factors other than people which may frustrate them. So AE tells them how to counter these other factors by wearing God's armour which will be no encumbrance (contrast 1 Sam 17.38f); they do not need to go and look for armour; God will provide it (Hendriksen). But were not these other factors overcome when Christ triumphed over the powers (1.21) and raised believers to sit, presumably in triumph, with him in the heavenlies (2.6)? We have probably here another example (Christians are light, 5.8, yet they continue to do some of the deeds of darkness) of the tension between AE's theology and his common sense; his theology sees victory as already complete in Christ, his common sense knows the fight is not yet over. We do not then need (*pace* Fischer, 165f) to solve the inconsistency by assuming AE adopted here a piece of tradition which had originally an eschatological orientation.

Christ has attacked and defeated the powers and yet, inconsistently, they are still active. Believers however are not summoned to attack the powers but instead to defend themselves. Thus the equipment God supplies for the struggle is essentially defensive. In keeping with this believers are not ordered to advance but to stand firm, that is, they are to hold the position which had been won for them. While they live there is no end to the need to hold their position; the struggle to do so began the moment they believed and were baptised; yet the language used is not baptismal language, nor is the paragraph part of a baptismal address. The need to hold their position will go on as long as the church exists. It is impossible then to deduce from the paragraph that the communities were facing a crisis of confidence (Lincoln, 440). A crisis of confidence, and in a church context it must surely be one of spiritual confidence, is the position, or should be the position of every congregation at all times; a real crisis of spiritual confidence only exists for a congregation when it is unaware that it is in one.

After the introduction of v. 10 the passage divides into three units: (a) vv. 11f identify the true foes of believers and indicate God is on their side against their foes and will assist them; (b) vv. 13–17 describe how God equips them so that they can defend themselves; it is not the individual items of the armour which are important but what they represent; (c) vv. 18–20 deal with something believers must do on their own, pray and keep alert. The relation of this last section to the first two is not immediately obvious. While the subject-matter changes, the participles of v. 18 depend grammatically on what has preceded (cf the difficulties of relating grammar and content at 5.21–2). It is possible, but unlikely, that prayer is set out as another piece of armour. The mood of the paragraph is exhortatory as evidenced by the imperatives running through it; these are developed with participial and final clauses and phrases of one kind and another. This passage has then a similarity with the style of the first half of the letter and is a move away from the simpler and more direct address of the paraenesis.

Finally it needs to be emphasised that the language used here to describe the Christian life is entirely masculine. If supernatural foes exist women have also to contend with them as much as men, yet women may not think in warlike categories in the same way as men.

10. There are three separate variant readings in this verse of which two are found in respect of the first three words and of which only one, the second, may affect the meaning; whatever the readings, the introductory phrase indicates that a new stage in the argument has been reached.

(i) ἀδελφοί or ἀδελφοί μου is inserted by ℵ² A F G Ψ 0278 𝔐 lat sy bo; this support is poor and the reading should be rejected. As a form of address it is not found elsewhere in the letter; it is absent perhaps because Paul, assuming he is the author, does not personally know the readers; yet he uses the term regularly in writing to the Romans though he did not know them. Zuntz, 175f, suggests it was added for liturgical reasons at what was the beginning of a new lectionary section. Since each section of the HT begins with a direct address it may have been thought that an address drawing all the readers together was again necessary.

(ii) τὸ λοιπόν is read by ℵ² D F G Ψ 𝔐 and τοῦ λοιποῦ by 𝔓⁴⁶ ℵ* A B I 0278 33 81 1175 1241ˢ 1739 1881 2464 pc. The latter support is stronger. The former is the more regular term in the Pauline corpus (1 Cor 7.29; Phil 3.1; 4.8; 2 Th 3.1) and this may have occasioned the alteration if the other was original. It is interesting that τὸ λοιπόν is read in quite a number of the manuscripts which also read 'brothers'; possibly the acceptance of one variant led to the other under the influence of Phil 3.1; 4.8; 2 Th 3.1 (cf Belser). Difficulty also exists over the meaning to be given τοῦ λοιποῦ (cf BDR §186.4; Moule, 161f; MHT, 235, 336; Thrall, 25ff). In Gal 6.17 it has a future sense, but it can hardly have that here for the struggle of 6.10ff is one in which believers are already engaged, not one which commences when its recipients read the letter, nor is it an apocalyptic struggle belonging to the period of the parousia. In a sense all advice about conduct relates to the future (there is not much use in saying, 'that is how you ought to have behaved'); what v. 10 says has already been prayed for in 3.16; v. 10 then refers to the present. We therefore take the phrase to mean 'finally' in line with the view that 6.10ff is AE's concluding appeal to his readers.

(iii) the simple verb δυναμοῦσθε and not the compound is read by 𝔓⁴⁶ B 33; if this was the original reading it may have been altered to agree with the use of the compound in v. 11.

In v. 10 AE returns to the 'power' language he has already used in 1.19; 3.16, 20; it is appropriate here where a struggle with the 'powers' is envisaged. ἐδυναμοῦσθε could be either middle, 'draw on your inner reserves of strength' (cf 1 Cor 16.13), these reserves having been already built up through faith in Christ, or passive, 'let God make you strong'. The verb is employed of divine empowerment in the Pauline corpus at Rom 4.20; Phil 4.13; 2 Tim 2.1 (cf 1 Clem 55.3; Hermas, Vis 3.12.3) and elsewhere in our letter words denoting power are used to indicate divine strengthening (cf Col 1.11; 1 QH 7.6f). In this light there is no need to think of AE accepting the idea of divine empowering from the example of generals empowering their troops (Faust, 447). The verb is then to be taken passively with the Lord as its real subject. ἐν κυρίῳ gives the source of strengthening and is probably to be understood here as referring to Christ (cf 2.21; 4.1, 17; 5.8; 6.1, 21), even though in other passages relating to power in Ephesians God is the source, e.g. in 1.19f it is God who raises Christ. The verse is completed with an explanatory phrase (καί epexegetical, so Henle, Masson, Schlier; the phrase adds nothing fresh to the argument pace Salmond) where as often in the letter a noun is following by a synonym in the genitive (for the words see on 1.19; the δύναμις of 1.19 is echoed here by the verb). If 1.19 supplies the words relating them to God's mighty act in Christ, 3.16 parallels the idea in relating Christ's power to believers and shows that their strengthening is an act of grace (cf 3.20). Christ has power, for God in raising him from the dead gave him the power; just as the power of God and Christ is seen in the weakness of the cross, so his power is seen again in the weakness of believers (2 Cor 12.9).

11. Why AE summoned his readers to be strong is now made clear: they are involved in a struggle with the devil. For this they need both strength and protective armour; God provides both (Masson). They need not then go to the fight unequipped. For the aor. imperat. ἐνδύσασθε see 4.22–4; there is however a difference in use, for while here it is possible to think of ill-equipped Christians who need better equipment, it was impossible in 4.22–4 to think of Christians who were not new people. Believers are not automatically equipped with armour; indeed at the beginning when they became

Christians they will not have realised the true nature of the struggle in which they were involved. ἐνδύω is regularly used of the putting on of armour (cf Rom 13.12; 1 Th 5.8) and there is no reason to see a connection with baptism, irrespective of what is decided as to its use in 4.24. The aorist may imply a definite step but once donned the armour will continue to be worn; it is presumably put on top of the new person! In saying that it is God's armour this means neither that there is alternative armour supplied by someone else (*pace* Harless) nor that believers can supply their own armour through asceticism, ritual, good works or any other way. Although in the OT the items of armour are worn by God, AE can hardly be thinking of that here, for God cannot be said to wear the qualities into which the items are spiritualised. There is then no idea of mystical unity with God here (*pace* Dibelius, Kamlah); in any case if there is mystical unity in Ephesians, it is that of believers with Christ and not with God. Parallels have been drawn (e.g. by Origen, Jerome) between the putting on of armour and the putting on of Christ (Rom 13.14); these have been worked out in detail by Beatrice, art.cit., and refuted in detail by Barth, 789ff; while the believer wears the same armour as God (Isa 59.17), Christ is nowhere depicted as wearing the armour of our passage.

The equipment is detailed in vv. 14–17; here a general word, πανοπλία,[5] is used which does not necessarily, but may, carry the sense of 'whole' or 'complete'. This flavour is present in v. 11 and the word means, as often, a set of armour (2 Kgdms 2.21; 2 Macc 3.25; 4 Macc 3.12A; Herod 1.60.4; 4.180; Polyb 3.62.5; 4.56.3; Thucyd 3.114.1; Josephus *BJ* 2.649; *Ant* 7.104; 20.110; Lk 11.22). The actual details of vv. 14–17 do not correspond exactly with the equipment of any particular known soldier in the Roman or any other army, but approach most closely to the heavily armed Roman infantryman. Although Barth, 793f, argues that the splendour or beauty of the equipment is intended in the description, most of his arguments are irrelevant. The purpose (πρὸς τό + infin. indicates purpose, cf BDR §402.4; MHT, 144; Robertson, 1003, 1075) of the armour is to enable believers to stand firm against the stratagems of the devil.[6] δύναμαι is only an auxiliary verb and it is wrong to understand it etymologically as another word for power and so overstress it (*pace* Arnold, 107). AE's emphasis lies on the need of holding on to a position and not of advancing or attacking. It is probably more difficult to stand and await attack, perhaps made with unknown weapons, than with the adrenalin flowing to rush forward

---

[5] See A. Oepke and K. G. Kuhn, *TWNT*, V, 295–302.

[6] Kitchen, 126, sees the reference to standing as one to the position adopted in public worship, especially in prayer; the context is not one of prayer but of conflict and ἀνθίστημι in v. 13 cannot ·be taken in the simple sense of standing upright. In 3.14 AE indicates kneeling as the position for prayer.

592 COMMENTARY ON EPHESIANS

in attack. Believers occupy advanced outposts which are always in danger of being overrun by the forces of the devil; they must stand firm as opposed to running away (for ἵστημι in this sense see Xenophon, *Anab* 1.10.1; 4.8.19; Thucyd 5.101–4; Exod 14.13; Nah 2.9)[7]. The need for Christians to stand firm is seen also in Rom 11.20; 1 Cor 10.12; 15.1; 16.13; 2 Cor 1.24; Gal 5.1; Phil 1.27f; 4.1; Col 4.12; 1 Th 3.8; 2 Th 2.15, though in relation to different contexts and situations.

Believers are opposed by the devil (see on 4.27) who has at his disposal a vast array of deceptive ploys (for μεθοδεία see on 4.14; 'stratagems' is the best translation here in keeping with the military metaphor). We are not told what the devil's tricks are; suggestions have been made: persecution (*Mart Polyc* 2.4; Cyprian, *Ep, passim*) but there are no signs of this in the letter; idolatry (Chrysostom); false doctrine (Ambrosiaster; cf 2 Tim 2.25f); Eve's temptation of Adam (Gen 3.12); David's numbering the people (1 Chron 21.1, but not 2 Sam 14.1); Paul's thorn in the flesh (2 Cor 12.7) or his inability to visit the Thessalonians caused, maybe, by bad weather (1 Th 2.18); lust; greed; the general way in which unbelievers live, of which AE has a low opinion (4.18f). Before conversion believers belonged to the sphere of the devil and he ruled their lives (2.2f); their conversation and baptism did not shatter his power and he now seeks to get them back into his grip, continually patrolling their positions (1 Pet 5.8) and endeavouring to catch them off guard (4.27). For AE and his readers, whatever modern readers may think, the devil was a personal being, an external centre of evil, who is not to be demythologised or explained away psychologically.

12. The supernatural nature of the struggle with the devil is now underlined and his agents in enticing believers from their faith identified, thus justifying the need for supernatural armour.[8] There is no reason to accept the view of Carr, 104–10, that this verse is an interpolation (see Detached Note: The Powers).

The reading ὑμῖν is strongly supported: 𝔓[46] B D* F G Ψ 81 1175 *pc* it vg^ms sy^p; Lcf Ambst Spec; it is however difficult to see how, if original, it was altered to the weaker ἡμῖν of ℵ A D² I 0278 33 1739 1881 𝔐 a g* vg sy^h co; Cl Or. The first plural goes against the run of the text which both preceding and following v. 12 is in the second plural. The variants could be attempts either to correct a perceived error or a simple mistake as the scribe

---

[7] Cf A. von Dobbeler, *Glaube als Teilhabe* (WUNT 2.22), Tübingen, 1987, 176–9.

[8] On the verse see Everling, *Angelologie*, 109–12; M. Dibelius, *Die Geisterwelt im Glauben des Paulus*, Göttingen, 1909; Percy, 255–61; D. E. H. Whiteley, 'Ephesians vi.12—Evil Powers', *ExpT* 68 (1956/7) 100–3; A. M. La Bonnardière, 'Le combat chrétien', *Rev Etud Aug* 11 (1965) 234–8; K. Romaniuk, 'Le Livre de la Sagesse dans le Nouveau Testament', *NTS* 14 (1967/8) 498–514; C. J. A. Lash, 'Where do Devils Live?', *VC* 30 (1976) 161–74; Adai, 260–72; C. E. Arnold, 'The "Exorcism" of Ephesians 6.12 in Recent Research', *JSNT* 30 (1987) 71–87.

is carried along by the argument. If the first plural is correct then AE has deliberately chosen to associate himself with his readers at this point; their struggle is also his (i.e. Paul's) struggle.

πάλη[9] originally referred to the hand-to-hand encounter of wrestling but in time was applied more widely to other types of fighting, including battles and war; this means there is no need to envisage here, where the word is negatived, an encounter with the contestants a distance apart and not meeting hand to hand (*pace* Pfitzner, 159); yet it may suggest an individualising of the struggle (Ellicott): the church will not fail (Mt 16.18) but individuals may. Philo used the term metaphorically of the struggle against temptation (*Mut Nom* 14; *Leg Alleg* 3.190; *Sobr* 65). AE's use is also non-literal and too much should not therefore be read into the literal meaning of the word. αἷμα καὶ σάρκα is a Semitic phrase (cf SB I, 730f), though the nouns are usually in the reverse order (Mt 16.17; 1 Cor 15.50; Gal 1.16; Eccles 14.18; *1 En* 15.4; the order of Ephesians appears only elsewhere at Heb 2.14). It denotes humanity primarily as transitory and weak, though here it is not the quality of humanity that is the issue (an easy battle because only humans are involved) but the nature of the battle as one not with human foes but with those from outside the human sphere. The struggle is not against what may come from human foes: persecution, harassment, temptation, poverty, injustice, or the temptations that may arise out of the self (cf Rom 7.7ff). It is instead against eternal evil beings. Four titles identify these. AE has already used the first two[10] together at 1.21; 3.10; see also Rom 8.38; Eph 2.2; 1 Pet 3.22; 1 Cor 15.24; Col 1.16; 2.10, 15; such terms do not always have a supernatural reference (cf Rom 13.1–3; Tit 3.1) but there is no reason to doubt that reference here. It is unlikely that the third and fourth are intended as descriptions to help identify the first two (*pace* von Soden). These beings are presumably the agents of the devil (v. 11) and AE probably spells them out because they are names known to his readers.

κοσμοκράτωρ,[11] only here in the NT, came to be used in astronomy and astrology and was applied to various gods (the names of the planets show their association with deities). The word is found also in *T Sol* 8.2; 18.2, in both cases qualified by a reference to darkness as in Ephesians; it is not clear whether the *Testament of Solomon* predates Ephesians, depends on it, or uses the word independently; if the last were the case it would indicate the probable existence of the word prior to Ephesians; alternatively it

---

[9] See H. Greeven, *TWNT*, V, 717f; Arnold, 115–17; Schmid, 146.
[10] 𝔓[46] substitutes μεθοδίας derived from v. 11 for the first two terms; it is not clear why.
[11] Cf W. Michaelis, *TWNT*,.III, 913; Arnold, 65–8; J. Y. Lee, 'Interpreting the Demonic Powers in Pauline Thought', *NT* 12 (1970) 54–69; Schmid, 145.

may have been AE's own creation. It would be a suitable term to apply to God as ruler of the cosmos; in 6.12 however it obviously has an evil connotation as its qualification with darkness[12] implies; the qualification may have been necessary if the word was already in use in some circles, perhaps with reference to earthly rulers, without an 'evil' connotation. 'Darkness' itself carried the idea of evil (e.g. in 5.8) and, in a sense, is also linked to astronomy for it is only in darkness that the planets are visible. The world rulers belong to the sphere of darkness rather than the time of darkness (cf Gnilka). The term then indicates in 6.12 a group or class of supernatural evil beings and since these belong to the darkness they will attempt to lure believers away from the light, i.e. from redemption (Schlatter).

The final term in AE's sequence appears to be comprehensive as if he were seeking to avoid omitting any evil supernatural power (cf 1.21; 5.27). GNB therefore wrongly makes the first three terms explanatory of this fourth. πνευματικός is normally used in the NT in relation to the Holy Spirit (e.g. Rom 1.11; 1 Cor 2.13; 3.1; 9.11; 12.1; 14.1), and was used in this way earlier in the letter (1.3; 5.19). But there are of course evil spirits (cf *T Sim* 3.5; 4.9; *T Levi* 18.12; *1 En* 15.8–12; 99.7; 1QM 13.2, 4; CD 12.2; Lk 7.21; 8.2; Acts 19.12f) and the qualification here with πονηρίας ensures that the reference is to these and not good spirits. Evil spirits are regularly associated with the devil (cf v. 11). Here they are not of course the demons which may inhabit humans and require to be exorcised; exorcism is not mentioned in respect of the defeat of any of those named here. These evil spirits dwell in the heavenlies (cf 2.2; *T Benj* 3.4; *2 En* 29.4f; *Asc Isaiah* 7.9; 11.23), and this accords with the association of the powers with astrology. Contemporary Judaism thought of a multiplicity of heavens; do the powers then live in the same heaven as Christ and God (the last phrase of the verse referring to the heavenlies covers all four named categories and not just the fourth)? Since AE uses the same plural phrase here as in 1.20, this suggests he thought they did. Such a possibility gave patristic commentators difficulty.[13] Chrysostom, Theod Mops, Theodoret all understood ἐν as if it were περί or ὑπέρ implying that the struggle was not about earthly but heavenly matters. 𝔓[46] *Did* avoid the difficulty by omitting the phrase. Some Fathers read ὑπουρανίοις, 'under heaven'; Theod Mops is aware of this reading though he does not accept it. Jerome believed that the powers were in the heavenlies and this also seems to have been the opinion of Tertullian, *adv. Marc* 5.18. The conclusion cannot be evaded that AE presents the powers as heavenly inhabitants and the war between

---

[12] After σκότους ℵ[2] D[2] Ψ 1739[mg] 1881 𝔐 sy[h**]; Tert insert τοῦ αἰῶνος identifying the darkness as this world's; support however is weak.
[13] For full discussion see Lash, art.cit.

them and humans as taking place there where believers already are (2.6); yet it should also be recognised that heaven is a fluid concept. But, despite Rev 12.7; 13.1ff, can there be war in heaven? To avoid this implication Chrysostom and Theod Mops spoke of a war waged on behalf of the Kingdom (i.e. heaven). From Origen onwards many have connected 6.11 to 2.2 and sought a distinction between an upper and a lower heaven; Pelagius identified the latter with the sphere of birds. Whatever the precise resolution of this problem, it is important to realise that AE wishes to drive home to his readers that as believers their struggle is of a superhuman nature. The repeated πρός stresses both the fact of the struggle and its many aspects. AE's emphasis obviously impressed the early church; the first two volumes of *Biblia Patristica* contain forty-three references to quotations of it or allusions to it. It also attracted the attention of gnostics (in NHC *Hyp Arch* II, 4 86.23–35; *Exeg Soul* II, 6 130.35–131.13; *Teach Silv* VII, 4 117.14–18; *Ep Pet Phil* VIII, 2 137.10–30; *Testim Truth* IX, 3 32.28; cf *Exc Theod* 48.2). The concept of battle with the powers is also found in *Melch* IX, 1 20.22–3.

In what follows the defensive armour of believers is listed but the weapons with which they are attacked are not enumerated. Other contemporary Jewish and Christian references do however suggest their nature: deception, strife, fate, distress, error, alcoholic intemperance, sexual promiscuity, flattery, injustice, lying, arrogance, idolatry, heresy, false prophets, pretended signs and wonders (see *T Sol* 8.2; *T Jud* 16.1; *T Reub* 8.3–6; *T Dan* 5.6; *T Naph* 3.3; *1 En* 19.1; 99.7; *Jub* 10.3–5; 1QS 2.11–19; 2 Cor 4.4; 11.11–13; 1 Jn 4.1f; 1 Tim 4.1f; 2 Th 2.9). The devil has then a wide range of stratagems at his disposal; has AE any or all of them in mind? He can hardly have been thinking of the ordinary run of temptations like evil thoughts, greed, lust for, if so, he would have counselled repentance and he does not do this. To accord with the supernatural aspect of the passage the devil's weapons must rather be those threatening to destroy the hope of salvation; AE may have in mind despair, heresy, doubt of God, doubts about the resurrection and the fact of eternal judgement (cf Theophylact), belief that one can save oneself without God's help. Using such devices the powers would seek to win away believers from their faith. It cannot be denied that the identification of the powers has been a happy speculative hunting ground going back as far as Origen who included Barabbas among them (*Lk Cat* GCS 49.2, 332.6f; *Mt Comm* 16.23 GCS 40, 556.17).

13. V. 12 was almost parenthetical in expanding on the nature of the enemy with whom Christians contend; v. 13 returns to the themes of v. 11: the need to sustain the fight and the promise of armour. Many of the terms of v. 11 reappear so that v. 13 is in part parallel to v. 11 (Bouttier) but in addition it reveals the time of the conflict, the evil day. Everything needs to be ready before combat is entered into. Because of the nature of the enemy (τοῦτο refers back to v. 12) believers cannot depend on their own resources but require to be divinely equipped[14] if they are to stand their ground and withstand the enemy (ἀνθίστημι replaces the simple ἵστημι though the latter reappears at the end of the verse; there is little difference in meaning here). The emphasis is on the need to resist the enemy and this readers can do by holding their position.

This however will not be easy in 'the evil day' (v. 13b gives the purpose for the armour). What and when is the evil day? The same words, but in the plural, were interpreted in 5.16 to refer to the moral decadence Christians believed lay around them outside the church. However, the singular, and often the plural when qualified, normally refer to the parousia, the day of judgement or the end of the world, times which though good for some would be evil for others (Amos 5.18–20; Joel 1.15; 2.32; Zech 14; Dan 12.1; *T Levi* 5.5; *1 En* 55.3; 96.2; *T Moses* 1.18; *Apoc Abr* 19.8f; 1QM 1.10–13; 1 Cor 1.8; 1 Th 5.2–4).[15] If the singular is stressed what particular day would be in mind? Suggestions include the day of death (Erasmus) or, what is almost the same, the time of the passage of the soul to heaven; in neither case is there evidence elsewhere for the need of weapons on that day. If the reference to standing implies standing before God, or Christ, on the day of judgement (Jerome), this would normally have been made explicit through the introduction of the name of God or Christ (cf Schnackenburg), and it would also entail an unusual change in the meaning of the verb from v. 11 (and v. 14). It is much more probable that the singular, if stressed, should be taken apocalyptically and refer to the End. Yet Ephesians says relatively little about the End and the conflict is one already in process; the weapons are needed now. Jewish apocalyptic however sometimes envisaged a period of severe oppression leading up to, and immediately prior to, the End, the birth pangs of the Messiah (Dan 7.21ff; 12.1; Joel 2; 4 Ezra 13.16–19; *2 Bar* 25; 68; *Jub* 23.13ff; Mk 13; Rev 7.14; 12.3, 7, 13; cf H. Schlier, *TWNT*, III, 139–48; Russell, op.cit., 272ff). In 1 Th 5.8 Paul counsels believers to put on armour in a context relating to the final days, and though in Rom 13.12 the armour is not particularised the context is again eschatological. Perhaps then AE sees the present struggle of believers as part of, or as leading to, the final eschatological conflict (Hugedé); as Schnackenburg notes, AE's eschatology is somewhat

---

[14] For the use of ἀναλαμβάνω in regard to the putting on of armour see Herod 3.78.2; Deut 1.41; Jth 6.12; 2 Macc 10.27; Josephus *Ant* 4.88; 20.110.

[15] Cf G. von Rad, *Old Testament Theology* II, Edinburgh, 1965, 119–25; E. Jacob, *Theology of the Old Testament*, London, 1958, 317ff; D. S. Russell, *The Meaning and Message of Jewish Apocalyptic*, London, 1964, 92–6, 264ff.

hazy. There may be a parallel with his conception of redemption (so Lincoln) where he both envisages believers as already sitting in heaven (2.6) and also, as his exhortations to good behaviour show, engaged at the same time in a perpetual struggle against evil. Fischer, 166, offers no real evidence other than the difficulty of the expression for his supposition that AE used here a piece of tradition which was apocalyptically oriented, presumably without realising what he was doing. If however the apocalyptic colouring of the phrase needs to be entirely eliminated and the present nature of the struggle emphasised, then it should probably be taken as referring to moments of particular danger or crisis (NEB 'when things are at their worst'; Beare suggests the time of a bad horoscope); yet since such days would recur this interpretation would properly require the elimination of the article and we should have 'an evil day' and not 'the evil day'. Probably the best solution is to see believers as already within the period leading up to the End, even though AE never suggests that it is close.

Some uncertainty also surrounds κατεργασάμενοι; the verb can signify either 'prepare' (so the vast majority of commentators) or 'overcome' (Chrysostom, Scott, Schlier). The latter interpretation would render unnecessary the instructions which follow to put on armour (why prepare for battle if the foe is already overcome?) and leaves ἅπαντα without a referent, for if it means 'in every respect' it only serves to reinforce the totality of the victory. The first interpretation of the verb should then be accepted as it both fits the context and is the overwhelming meaning in its use elsewhere in the NT where it occurs twenty-one times, nineteen of them in the Pauline corpus and invariably carrying the sense of preparation. Believers are to be prepared in every respect for the present and future struggle so that equipped with supernatural weapons they may stand firm against all the assaults of their supernatural foes.

14. Verses 14–17 list some of the individual items of a soldier's equipment. In part the items are derived from the OT and in part from observation of soldiers. It is not however the weapons themselves which are important, for this is not a physical war, but the explanations AE gives to them; these explanations have no logical connection with the individual items. The weapons are primarily defensive since a position has to be held; any direct attack on the powers is left to Christ and is conceived as already having taken place (1.20–3). The armour is assumed to be even now ready for believers to don (note the aorist participles); yet only if it is worn can Christian warriors stand against their foes; its putting on is a necessary preliminary to standing firm. The aorist imperative of the main verb is to be distinguished from that of the participles; the equipment is received once for all; it is necessary to stand firm as long as the conflict lasts (see on 4.22–4 for the use of the aorist).

Unlike the putting on of the new self, the donning of the armour can be seen as a fresh step taking place at a time later than conversion.

The first item is the 'girdle'; it is by no means clear what is meant; the normal English translation 'belt' gives too precise a connotation and is probably wrong. The origin of the associated metaphor goes back, at least in the Near East, to the 'wrestling belt',[16] yet when AE used the metaphor the thought of its origin probably entered neither his mind nor those of his readers. The metaphor was understood in a wide variety of ways in both the Greco-Roman and Jewish worlds.[17] As to its physical nature 'girdle' could be: (a) the leather apron which was put on under the breastplate and offered some protection to the lower part of the abdomen while leaving freedom of movement and readiness for action; (b) the belt from which the sword hung; (c) the sash over the armour denoting the wearer as someone in authority; (d) the purse fastened round the body; this however is not an item of military equipment. (b) and (c) were put on after and not before the breastplate, which is the next item, and as for (c) nothing suggests AE is attempting to give a distinguished position to believers (*pace* Barth). (a) is then the most probable meaning. Some of the Fathers (e.g. Origen, Jerome) thought of the girdle as intended to control the 'loins' of the wearer so that lust should not overcome him! Apart from what soldiers actually wore, AE was subject to another influence in his description, the OT. Here Isa 11.5 is significant for in depicting the Messiah qualities of faithfulness and righteousness similar to those of our verse are instanced. However, it is not the identification of the article of military equipment which is important, but the quality 'truth' which is linked to it and this link with truth is probably derived from Isa 11.5. We leave what is meant by truth until we have dealt with the breastplate.

This protected its wearer from shoulder to upper thigh level.[18] It is interpreted here as righteousness following Isa 59.17; Wisd 5.18; in 1 Th 5.8 it is faith and love. While armour for the back was sometimes provided, none is mentioned here suggesting that if the Christian warrior does not stand firm but turns and runs he is completely vulnerable. The same would be true of the shield (v. 16) which was held in front of, or over the top of, the body. ἐνδύω, used here of armour, was used in 4.24 of the putting on of the new person and there, as here, δικαιοσύνη is in the context suggesting that we should give the same significance to the word here as there; there it denoted a human quality. However, δικαιοσύνη in 4.24 (see references there) is not linked to ἐνδύω but to κτισθέντα and its

[16] Cf E. Levine, 'The Wrestling Belt Legacy in the New Testament', *NTS* 28 (1982) 560–4.

[17] See A. Oepke, *TWNT*, V, 302–8.

[18] See Oepke, art.cit., 308–10.

prevailing meaning in the Pauline corpus sees it as a gift of God rather than a human quality. Here in v. 14 it is again God's gift and, though righteousness of behaviour in Christians may be said to derive ultimately from him, the gift of the breastplate is given more directly. It is difficult to see the gospel of peace (v. 15), salvation (v. 17) and the word of God (v. 17) as human activities. Thus it is better to take righteousness here as that justifying righteousness which is the foundation of Christian existence (so Barth, Zerwick). It is this, and not simply moral failure, which is under attack from the devil and his powers.

What then is the significance of 'truth'? Most commentators take it as indicating something like sincerity, faithfulness, loyalty, integrity, which keeps it in the area of human activity yet leaves open a wide range of meaning. It could however be God's truth, doctrinal truth, the gospel. Ephesians uses ἀλήθεια both of the human virtue (4.24, 25; 5.9) and of God's truth (1.13; 4.21); the context alone can determine which meaning is intended and the general run of vv. 14–17 suggests that it is God's truth which is in mind (cf Gaugler). God's truth provides a defence against heresy, false philosophies, pagan religions, all possible weapons used by the devil to lure believers away from their belief.

15. The text does not identify the third item of equipment other than to say that it relates to the feet.[19] Lightly armed soldiers who needed to move quickly wore sandals; the heavily armed Roman legionaries wore heavy boots (the *caliga*). Since the other items of armour are those used by the latter probably heavy boots are intended here. These were necessary for long marches and, what is more important in the present context, ensured a firm grip on the ground enabling their wearers to stand firm. Some scholars detect in v. 15 the influence of Isa 52.7 because of its reference to feet in association with the gospel of peace; Isa 52.7 may also have influenced 2.17; Nah 2.1 provides a similar possible influence. Those who discern the influence of these passages have to insert in their translations a word suggestive of movement; the Greek has no such word, but has instead ἑτοιμασία, found only here in the NT, though appearing fairly regularly in the LXX. It has three possible relevant meanings: readiness, preparation, firmness. The majority of commentators accept one or other of the first two and take it to refer to the readiness or preparation for the outward-going movement required for the proclamation of the good news of peace. If proclamation of the gospel is in mind, to whom is it to be made? There is nothing elsewhere in the letter advocating the involvement of readers in missionary expansion; this was only explicit at 3.10 and there it is to the powers that the gospel is proclaimed. This could

---

[19] On possible footwear see Oepke, art.cit., 312–14.

be said to fit the present context where the powers are the foes; peace needs to be brought to them. Yet the struggle is about neither the spread of the gospel (*pace* Conzelmann), though presumably the powers would wish to hinder any spread, nor the salvation of the powers, but about the continued salvation of those who are already believers. It may be better then to accept the third sense, firmness. Buscault[20] worked this out in detail quoting 2 Ezra 3.3 and Ψ 88.15 for the meaning 'foundation, basis' (see also Bengel, Lock, Barth). It is noticeable that Roels, 217f, who in the light of his main theme might be expected to see missionary activity here, also chooses this meaning; Westcott combines this sense with that of preparation. The soldier's heavy boots give him the necessary firm foundation to stand firm. This interpretation accords with the major stress of vv. 11–17 on the need to stand firm and on the defensive nature of the armour, though heavy boots might be used offensively in close combat. If this solution is accepted it implies Isa 52.7 does not lie behind the verse.

The introduction of peace may seem paradoxical since the context is that of warfare but most of the readers were Gentiles; the gospel through which they became Christians was a gospel which made peace between them and God and between them and Jewish believers; hence the appropriateness of the reference. It was believers' knowledge of, and belief in, this gospel which would repel supernatural foes. The gospel of peace would neutralise the enmity of the hostile powers (cf Ign *Eph* 13.2). The gospel of peace falls into the same semantic field as truth, righteousness (v. 14), faith (v. 16), salvation and word of God (v. 17).

16. The fourth piece of armour is the shield, spiritualised as faith; the importance of taking it (for ἀναλαμβάνω see on v. 13) is stressed by the initial ἐν πᾶσιν, whatever meaning is given to it.

ἐν πᾶσιν is difficult both in respect of text and meaning; the latter difficulty is probably the cause of the former. It would be possible to link the phrase to the conclusion of v. 15 but that attachment would hardly be relevant to v. 15. A D F G Ψ 𝔐; Ambst, Hier read ἐπί in place of ἐν; the latter however has strong support through 𝔓46 ℵ B P 0278 33 104 1175 1739 1881 2464 *pc* latt; Meth and is to be preferred. It has been variously understood as 'in addition to' (i.e. to all the other pieces of equipment) or 'in all circumstances' (cf Joüon; Moule, 78, apparently takes this to mean 'above all').

In v. 16 as in v. 15 the OT is not explicitly referred to even though the shield[21] is a frequent OT metaphor; God is the shield of faithful Israelites (e.g. Gen 15.1; Ps 18.3; 33.20). Normally when the OT

---

[20] A. F. Buscault, 'The "Preparation" of the Gospel of Peace', *ExpT* 9 (1897) 38–40.

[21] On shields see Oepke, art.cit., 312–14.

uses 'shield' metaphorically ('the Lord is my shield') the LXX term is ὑπερασπιστής; in Wisd 5.19 it is ἀσπίς; θυρεός is only used metaphorically in Ψ 34.2 (cf also Aq, Sm Job 41.7; Aq Ψ 21.7; 83.12). Its use here is then not derived from the OT but from observation of the actual armour of soldiers. It is the long shield of the Roman legionary protecting most of the front of the body against missiles (for its description and use see Polyb 6.23.2; Herod 7.91). If its use here comes from observation it would be wrong however to think of Paul as seeing it as part of the equipment of the soldier guarding him; it would not have been part of the equipment of a soldier guarding a single prisoner.

The shield which enables (δυνήσεσθε; the future does not have an eschatological significance but refers to what follows after the picking up of the shield) believers to hold their ground is faith (πίστεως, gen. of apposition). This could mean either 'trust' or 'the faith'. If it is trust its object is unstated but is presumably God or Christ (cf 1.13, 15; 3.12; 4.13; 6.23); it is not self-confidence. Trust in God or Christ was operative in the salvation of believers (2.8) and it is through it that Christ dwells in their hearts (3.17). As with the other items of equipment it is given by God. When believers trust God it is as if they had a shield around them. Just as Jesus in the temptation narratives turned away the attacks of the devil (for ὁ πονηρός = the devil see Mt 6.13; 13.19, 38; Jn 17.15; 2 Th 3.3; 1 Jn 2.13f; 5.18) through the use of God's word, that is, of God himself, so believers depend on God to withstand the devil's fiery missiles. However, since πίστεως is governed by the article, faith here could be 'the faith', what is believed; however, it depends on a noun which already has an article, so this need not be the case. But given this interpretation 'faith' lies in the same semantic field as truth, righteousness, gospel and it is best to understand it in this way.

The devil's missiles are described as fiery.[22] Sometimes in ancient warfare arrows, spears, and other missiles were coated in pitch and set alight before being thrown. If they hit home they inflicted deadly wounds; the long shield offered good protection against them, but only while the soldier stood firm; if he began to retreat it was no help. When attacks with fiery missiles were expected, the leather portions of shields were soaked in water since a dry shield would not extinguish a burning missile, only divert it; even a wet shield would not necessarily extinguish one. If the missile did not penetrate the shield it would fall to the ground and be relatively harmless; if it penetrated, the moisture would do something to counteract the burning pitch; a damp shield would certainly not be set on fire. The image is not wholly satisfactory (Conzelmann). (On the use of

----

[22] Though good Greek requires the reading of the article here it is omitted in 𝔓46 B D* F G; its reading may be a correction.

burning missiles and on defence against them see Josephus *Ant*
1.203; Herod 8.52; 1QH 2.26; CD 5.13; Sallust, *Bellum Jug* 57.5, 6;
Livy 21.8.10–12; Prov 26.18; in Ps 7.13 God is said to use them.)
We are not told the nature of the devil's fiery darts which could
destroy believers; they are presumably the same as his stratagems (v.
11).

17. The final two items of military equipment are now listed. The
first, the helmet, returns us to the OT and Isa 59.17 (Wisd 5.18 both
uses a different word for helmet and understands it differently, as
does Ign *Polyc* 6.2).[23] In Isa 59.17 God as victorious warrior wears
the helmet of salvation; now he gives it to believers for their
protection. At least here, if not elsewhere, we can see that AE
depends on the OT for the significance he imparts to this item of
equipment. Previously he had used a sequence of participles
depending on στῆτε to itemise the equipment; now he introduces
a new finite verb, δέξασθε.[24] The soldier, already partially equipped, receives from his armour bearer his helmet[25] and sword; the
Christian receives from his God salvation and the word of God; this
is not to suggest he collected the other items of equipment for
himself; all his military hardware comes from God (cf Gnilka,
Schnackenburg, etc.). The helmet is depicted as salvation;
σωτήριον, an adjective used as a noun (Moule, 96; MHT, 13f), is
rare in the NT appearing only in Lk 2.30; 3.6; Acts 28.28, all
passages heavily dependent on the OT; it is found more frequently
in the LXX, and is used in Isa 59.17. However, when Paul used Isa
59.17 in 1 Th 5.8 he substituted for it the normal NT noun σωτηρία;
AE's retention of the LXX word confirms his dependence here on
Isa 59.17. Paul had also varied the LXX in another way by speaking
of the helmet as the *hope* of salvation, thus imparting an eschatological flavour. Since AE retains the original LXX noun he cannot
be regarded as correcting 1 Th 5.8, which he probably did not know
(see Introduction §2.6.5), and he is not then deliberately reducing
the eschatological element (Paul in any case quotes Isa 49.8 which
speaks of the present nature of salvation approvingly in 2 Cor 6.2).
It would however be wrong to conclude from these variations from
Paul in the use of Isa 59.17 here and in v. 14 that Paul did not write
Ephesians; authors have the right to modify their metaphors if it is
necessary to express what they wish to say in a different situation;
the change is only another minor count against Pauline authorship. If
the attacks of the powers (see for these on vv. 11f) are on the

---

[23] *Pace* Barth, no light is thrown on our passage by later rabbinic use, cf SB III,
618.

[24] The verb is omitted by D* F G b m*; Tert Cyp Amst Spec; this is not strong
evidence and the absence of the verb would do nothing to lessen the idea that the
helmet and the sword come from God.

[25] On the helmet see Oepke, art.cit., 314f.

Christian existence of believers, that is, on their salvation, believers can only survive if their salvation does not depend on their own efforts but is a 'given', and this it has been since they began to believe (cf 2.5, 8). AE's stress here on the present nature of salvation is in line with his normal understanding of it (see Introduction §6.4).

The final piece of armour is the short-handled sword.[26] There is no OT passage from which this could have been directly derived (it is difficult to see why UBS[1], but not UBS[3], should have set the words in the type reserved for OT quotations), though all its nouns are found in the OT, with two of them sometimes linked together in the same context, but never closely. Isa 11.4 links 'word', though not ῥῆμα, and Spirit and is adjacent to 11.5 which probably influenced v. 14. Isa 49.2 associates the sword and the mouth (words issue from mouths), an association found in Heb 4.12; Rev 1.16; 2.12, 16, 19; 15.21 (though a different word for sword is used in Revelation). It is also true that God's words can slay (Hos 6.5; cf Wisd 18.16; *Odes Sol* 29.9–11; in these references however the sword is not mentioned). Wisd 5.20 uses a different word for sword but relates it to God's wrath and not directly to his speech. What we then have is a play on concepts from the OT and later Judaism, rather than direct dependence on any actual OT passage. The sword is a normal part of a soldier's armour and had to be included; a bare mention was not sufficient; it must also as with the other pieces of armour be related to something which comes from God, and his word meets this requirement.[27] Isa 11.2, 4 may have led to the introduction of the Spirit; there it is a destructive power and that would be appropriate to a conflict with the powers. The sword is not itself the Spirit, for believers do not wield the Spirit; it is the sword which the Spirit either supplies or empowers; strength is necessary for fighting and power is one of the characteristic gifts of the Spirit; in either case a spiritual sword is intended but not in the weakened sense of a sword which belongs to the sphere of religion (*pace* Haupt).

The sword of the Spirit requires further identification and the final words of the verse supply this (ὅ refers to the previous phrase as a whole rather than to its one neuter word; cf Burton §295; BDR §132.2; Robertson, 411f, 712f). What is the ῥῆμα θεοῦ? Here it must be a word which protects the user from destruction by the powers. It is not then God's energetic and creative word (Theod Mops), or his prophetic word (though it might on occasion be a word from the prophets), or the OT as a whole (Hodge), though it could be a saying drawn from the OT (1 Pet 1.25; Rom 10.8). It

[26] See W. Michaelis, *TWNT*, IV, 530–3.
[27] Knox, *Gentiles*, 203n, says that sword and word are frequently conjoined in Judaism.

could also be the gospel (Barry; Adai, 140) as preached (Thomas) or summarised in a confession or creed. In 5.26 the determination of the meaning of ῥῆμα offered some difficulty; there as here it lacks the article. In 5.26 it probably indicated the baptismal formula 'in the name of Jesus'. Here it probably means a saying or formula behind which God stands (Haupt), drawn from the OT and with whose use the devil may be withstood. It could also be a word uttered by a NT prophet fitted to the occasion. All such words of God are powerful for they have been inspired by the Spirit. It was with such words that Jesus repelled the devil in the temptation stories. The Roman short sword was very necessary in close combat; it kept foes at bay. It, or any of the other pieces of equipment, will not kill the·devil or any of his powers; only Christ can do that (1.20f), but through the use of a word of God his followers can live through the attacks that they launch on them.

18.[28] This verse with its fourfold use of πᾶς and alliterative play on π consists of two parallel participial clauses each carrying imperatival value. But do the participles depend on δέξασθε (v. 17, e.g. Gnilka) or στῆτε (v. 14, e.g. Lincoln, Bruce)? They are hardly wholly independent of what has preceded; if they were, then vv. 18–20 would have to be taken as a separate paragraph (so Adai, 234; Pokorný). The verbs of both v. 14 and v. 17 are aorist imperatives appropriate to the once-for-all donning of armour while the participles of v. 18 are present tenses appropriate to continuing prayer but lacking a reference to its beginning; it is not a case of 'each piece put on with prayer' as in George Duffield's hymn, and certainly not of prayer only in relation to the helmet and the sword. στῆτε is probably still the controlling verb. Standing firm and praying should go on without ceasing. Prayer is not itself another weapon; Bengel takes it to be the spear which is not otherwise mentioned (cf Fee, 729–32, who thinks the praying may have been in tongues); if either it or vigilance were a weapon, they would have a spiritual activity attached to them as do the other pieces of armour (see Barth, 785f, for fuller discussion) or be themselves qualifications of pieces of physical armour. Yet prayer has its place in struggle (Rienecker) as the prayer of Jesus in Gethsemane shows. It denotes the attitude in which the weapons are to be used, and presupposes the wearing of the armour (Jones, art.cit.). If believers are to stand firm against the powers they need both to pray and to be alert.

At the conclusion of his HT A/Col moved directly to prayer (4.2); AE has separated the two with his account of the struggle with the powers. The two letters however exhibit both similarities in wording

[28] Cf P. Jones, 'La prière par l'Espirit: Ephésiens 6:18', *Revue Réformée* 27 (1976) 128–39.

and content (in each case prayer is requested for Paul) and dissimilarities (different verbs are used in relation to vigilance). The content of the prayers moreover differs; in Col 4.3 prayer is to be offered not only for Paul but also for his companions and thanksgiving is mentioned; Ephesians refers neither to companions nor to thanksgiving. Prayer is appropriate to the conclusion of a letter and in Ephesians it flows naturally out of the preceding discussion; indeed most commentators regard vv. 10–20 as the complete paragraph and not vv. 10–17; in Colossians however there is a sharp break in the argument. Probably members of the Pauline school believed that it was appropriate for a call to prayer and vigilance to come near the end of a letter and each has finished his letter in this way. Nothing suggests that AE had Colossians before him as he wrote or that A/Col had Ephesians.

In the first participial clause readers are exhorted to pray with (διά of accompanying circumstances, Moule, 57; MHT, 267: BDR §223.4) every kind of prayer and request. προσευχή is a general word covering all kinds of prayer; δέησις is usually limited to prayers involving requests.[29] The words are found together elsewhere (3 Kgdms 8.45; 2 Chron 6.19; Acts 1.14 (v.l.); Phil 4.6; 1 Tim 2.1; 5.5; Ign *Magn* 7.1) and may form a hendiadys. AE probably intends them to be taken as a comprehensive expression for all kinds of prayer, though he only expands the second noun in what follows. Prayer is to be offered at every possible opportunity (καιρός; for the phrase see Lk 21.36; cf Ψ 33.1; 105.3; Prov 6.14; Eccles 9.8; Ecclus 29.3); this was Paul's practice and one he enjoined on believers (e.g. Lk 18.1; 24.53; Rom 9.1; 12.12; 1 Cor 1.4; 1 Th 1.2f; 2.13; 3.10; cf 1 Tim 5.5). Believers need to pray continually because their struggle with the powers is never ending. The injunction is not however to be taken so literally as to imply believers should spend all their time in prayer; what is required is a constant attitude of dependence on God. Prayer is to be offered ἐν πνεύματι;[30] this is not intended to contrast prayer freely offered from the heart with formal set prayers, but to indicate a relation to God's Spirit. AE had previously used the phrase at 2.18, 22; 3.5; 5.18. Though the Spirit and prayer are related, we are not to think of praying in tongues but of prayer which is Spirit-led or directed (cf Rom 8.15f; Gal 4.6; Jude 20; 1QH 16.11; 17.17). Prayer is not to be given up lightly but persisted in (for προσκαρτέρησις see Spicq, II, 758–61; the noun only here in the NT; the verb appears more regularly and is often connected to prayer, Acts 1.14; 2.42; 6.4; Rom 12.12; Col 4.2).

Prayer in the Spirit is to be accompanied by vigilance, watchfulness

---

[29] On the words see H. Greeven, *TWNT*, II, 39–42, 806–8; H. Schönweiss, *NIDNTT*, II, 860–4.

[30] For the relation of the Spirit to prayer see O. Cullmann, *Prayer in the New Testament*, London, 1995, 72–80.

and wakefulness;[31] this could be a continuance of the military metaphor (watchfulness and standing firm are linked in 1 Cor 16.13; 1 Pet 5.8f) but is probably not since prayer and watchfulness are frequently associated; ἀγρυπνέω however is less usual in this respect than γρηγορέω (Mk 13.33, 38; Lk 21.36; Mt 26.41; Col 4.2; *Barn* 20.2; 1 Esdras 8.58; 2 Esdras 8.29) and it might be thought to suggest 'sleepless' prayer or night vigils (cf Schlier); vigils became a regular feature in a later period of church life; the first certain reference, and it is to an Easter vigil and not to vigils in general, is in the second-century *Ep Apostolorum* 15. Our passage in conjunction with Ps 119.62; Lk 6.12; Acts 12.12; 16.25; 1 Th 3.10 may have led to the practice.

Prayer can never be aimless but must be directed; here its object is not only that those who pray should stand firm against the devil but it looks outward in stressing intercession for the saints (believers and not angels) and Paul (v. 19). AE had already prayed for the saints (1.16ff; 3.14–19), though not specifically for Paul. The saints, Paul and those who are bidden pray for them are involved in the same conflict with the powers; they must stand together and pray together or they will fall together. When they stand together the church is sustained. Calvin raised the point whether believers were to pray only for the saints; this is probably what AE had in mind; indeed such a restricted sphere of prayer fits in both with the general objective of the letter and the immediate context; there is no prayer here for those outside the church (contrast 1 Tim 2.1–3).

περί is used in relation to those who will benefit from it but in v. 19 in relation to Paul the more normal ὑπέρ (Rom 10.1; 2 Cor 1.11; 9.14; Phil 1.4). The two prepositions are often synonymous (MHT, 269–71; BDR 229, 231; Zerwick §96; Moule, 63; Robertson, 681). περί is used of intercessory prayer in 1 Th 5.25; Lk 22.32; cf Ecclus 21.1. The change of preposition probably indicates that Paul is thought of as a special person.

19. The struggle against the powers now appears to slip into the background but it is still present in that Paul's preaching, for which intercession is made, relates to the mystery of the gospel which has to be brought to the knowledge of the powers (3.9, 10). AE, if he is Paul, requests his readers to pray for him, and, if he is not Paul, then to pray for Paul; yet if AE is not Paul, Paul is dead and why pray for one who is dead? The request must then be understood as part of the pseudepigraphical framework. In the similar passage in Col 4.3 it is not Paul alone but Paul and his co-workers for whom prayer is to be made; a reference to co-workers is normal in Pauline letters and its absence may be because AE nowhere else refers to other workers or because he sees Paul as occupying a unique position in the economy

---

[31] Cf E. Lövestamm, *Spiritual Wakefulness in the New Testament*, Acta Universitatis Lundensis, vol. 55, 1962–3, Lund, 1964.

of salvation (3.3, 8ff). Elsewhere Paul desires his churches to pray
on behalf of him and his co-workers (Rom 15.30; 2 Cor 1.9–11; Col
4.3; 1 Th 5.25; 2 Th 3.1). Assuming AE is using Col 4.3 his
omission of a reference to others is surprising.

While believers are to intercede for Paul it is not suggested that
they pray for his release from prison; AE, if he is not Paul, may have
realised that his readers knew Paul had died during, or at the end of,
his imprisonment, and he did not wish to include a prayer which his
readers would know had never been granted. Instead what he seeks
for Paul, or what Paul seeks for himself, is God's gift (δοθῇ is a
divine passive) of speech in relation to the mystery of the gospel.
Although λόγος can refer to glossolaliac speech (1 Cor 14.9, 19) it
need not necessarily do so; speech can be divinely inspired without
being in tongues (e.g. 1 Cor 1.5; 12.8; Phil 1.14; 1 Th 2.13). The
'opening of the mouth' was a biblical phrase (Ψ 50.17; 77.2; Ezek
3.27; 29.21; 33.22; Dan 3.25; 10.16; Wisd 10.21; Ecclus 5.15;
51.25) which was taken up into the NT (Mt 5.2; Acts 8.35; 10.34;
18.14; 2 Cor 6.11). There is a significant difference from Col 4.3
which referred to the opening of a door. God could be the real
subject of this solemn phrase, 'when God opens my mouth' (so
Westcott), but if this were so it could be assumed that God would
supply the words and δοθῇ λόγος would then be superfluous. The
prayer is that whenever Paul speaks God should fill his mouth, as
once he filled that of Jeremiah (Jer 1.9), and as it is promised that he
will do in times of trial (Mt 10.19f; Mk 13.11). Lemmer, 470f,
suggests an underlying connection with v. 17; Paul needs the sword
of the Spirit, a timely word of God. The prayer is not for eloquent
utterance or the ability to express the inexpressible (Caragounis, 28),
but for inspiration; inspired words may be eloquent but eloquence is
not essential to them.

Paul's mouth is to be opened to make known the mystery of the
gospel ἐν παρρησίᾳ (for the word see on 3.12 and the literature
cited there). It is not clear whether the phrase qualifies what
precedes or what follows (Salmond has a good discussion of the
possibilities); whichever way we take it the meaning of the sentence
is hardly affected. The wider context of v. 20 which draws attention
to Paul as a prisoner might suggest a connotation for the word in the
area of courage (cf Wisd 5.1) but the immediate reference to
mystery implies the idea of clarity, that Paul should make clear the
mystery of the gospel when he speaks. Wild, art.cit., stresses the
'freedom' aspect: the oppressed prisoner is actually within himself
the freest of all, yet the cognate verb in v. 20 implies an activity on
Paul's part rather than a state of existence. It is difficult to tie the
word down to one narrow meaning and it perhaps should be
understood as indicating a courageous openness and clarity (cf Van
Unnik, art.cit., 277).

What Paul is to make known (γνωρίζω is a favourite word of AE; 1.9; 3.3, 5, 10; 6.21) is the 'mystery' (see on 1.9); the total phrase is almost the same as in 1.9 and 3.3. In those passages the mystery was made known by God to believers in general (1.9) or to Paul in particular (3.3; cf 3.4); here Paul makes the mystery known. Of course he could not do this unless the mystery had not first been made known to him. Mysteries remain mysteries unless they are communicated, so there may be in vv. 19f as allusion to missionary endeavour (Penna, *Mysterion*, 39). What is it then that is made known here? In 1.9 the mystery relates to the consummation of all but in 3.3f, 9 to the knowledge that God accepts Gentiles. The latter more restricted meaning seems appropriate here (cf Caragounis, 59) since to readers of Ephesians Paul is especially associated with the preaching of the gospel to Gentiles; the gospel however is more than the equality of Jew and Gentile in God's eyes, though Ephesians stresses this aspect. There is no need (*pace* R. P. Martin, Lindemann) to see a veiled reference to the desire of AE and his readers that the gospel should spread in Asia Minor; the letter refers nowhere else to its physical spread and for AE and his readers Paul was in prison in Rome. What we have is just another detail reinforcing Paul's authorship if he did not write it himself. The problem is eased if τοῦ εὐαγγελίου is not read.

א A D I Ψ 0278 33 1739 1881 𝔐 lat sy co read τοῦ εὐαγγελίου but B F G b m*; MVict Ambst Spec omit it. 𝔓⁴⁶ is uncertain (cf Zuntz, 95). Without some word to define it 'mystery' seems indeterminate; it may have been this that led to the addition of 'gospel', but if this were so we might have expected there would have been a number of alternative additions (e.g. 'of Christ'). On the other hand its presence would accord with AE's love of lengthy phrases and it may have been omitted in order to leave μυστήριον unqualified in view of its different connotations. Since the evidence is slightly stronger for inclusion it is better to read it. It may be said that gospel itself is indeterminate without an explanatory addition but unlike mystery it was a word in regular use among believers and so would not require definition.

20. The argument now appears to be slipping further away from the struggle of believers with the supernatural powers of evil, yet in so far as Paul was preaching to liberate believers from their grip he was involved in that struggle. The strength to defeat supernatural power is called into being through prayer, so the prayer is not one for the loosing of Paul from his chains or for the opening of a door before him so that he can continue his mission work (cf Col 4.3). It is instead a prayer that though imprisoned he may still continue the struggle. Paul, or AE writing in his name, does not bemoan his fate in being a prisoner but seeks to continue his preaching.

The antecedent of οὗ is not certain; if εὐαγγελίου is not read in v. 19 it will naturally be μυστήριον; if it is read it could be either noun, but since the former defines the latter there will not be much difference in meaning. It is unlikely that οὖ refers to the whole preceding clause but, again, if it did, it would not greatly affect the meaning. αὐτῷ has the same general reference. The variant αὐτό read by 𝔓⁴⁶ B 1739 1881 is probably due to the influence of Col 4.4.

The metaphor of the ambassador which in 2 Cor 5.20 Paul applied either to himself and his co-workers or to all believers is now restricted to Paul alone. This restriction may also be true of Philem 9, though there more probably the cognate noun depicts Paul not as an ambassador but as an old man. We cannot be certain AE knew 2 Corinthians (see Introduction §2.6.3), but even if he did not the image may have been part of the Pauline school's inheritance; it reappears in Ign *Philad* 10.1. The term was used of imperial legates and clearly represents someone of importance (cf LSJ). In 2 Cor 5.20 Paul, and at least his fellow helpers, were Christ's ambassadors; here they are the gospel's; it is however difficult to distinguish between gospel and Christ. Ambassadors are important officials and it is paradoxical for them to be in chains; the singular ἁλύσει (Col 4.18 has the same idea but uses a different Greek word) is used probably to emphasise the condition of restraint rather than its actual physical means; in any case it is impossible to work out what historical situation is in mind other than that of the imprisonment of 3.1; 4.1. Wild, art.cit., views Paul here as an example for believers, yet this would lose the paradox between prisoner and ambassador. It is however quite true that suffering and working for the gospel are not disparate ideas but go together; in 2 Cor 11.23ff Paul lists his sufferings to prove he is a faithful servant of the gospel (cf 2 Cor 4.7ff).

Is the second ἵνα clause coordinate with the first (Schlier), subordinate to it, or wholly independent of it but dependent on the preceding relative clause (Haupt)? The first position is favoured by the similar content of the two clauses; the second by the introduction of the new element of compulsion. As for the third it is difficult to think of Paul as imprisoned in order that he might proclaim the gospel; he did this whether a prisoner or not; it is also difficult to see the second ἵνα as adding a sufficiently new element to the first so as to be dependent on it. Probably the two are coordinate. παρρησιάσωμαι will carry the same meaning here as the cognate noun did in v. 19. Examples of Paul's bold and frank activity are recorded in Acts (9.27; 13.46; 14.3; 19.8) and can be deduced from his letters (2 Cor 3.12; Phil 1.20; 1 Th 2.2). Such bold and frank speaking cannot be restricted to Christians (Dio Chrys *Or* 32.11; Epict 3.22.26f; 4.13.1ff; Lucian, *Demonax* 3). It is however not only in prison but at all times that Paul was compelled to courageous proclamation (λαλέω carries this sense here; it is associated with παρρησία in this sense also at Mk 8.32). Stress on divine necessity has not been prominent in Ephesians since the initial eulogy which implied the existence of a divine plan where believers were allotted a position even before the foundation of the world. Paul elsewhere affirmed that a divine necessity was laid on him to proclaim the gospel (1 Cor 9.16f; cf Acts 9.6, 16; 19.21; 23.11; 27.24; cf Bouttier). In Ephesians his unique position in carrying out God's purpose in relation to the Gentiles meant that the divine revelation given to him (3.3) also laid on him the necessity of making it known (3.7ff). His life is wholly under God's direction and control, even to the extent that he is a prisoner. It is of the very nature of the gospel that to know it means to proclaim it; good news must be told.

In this passage the Christian life has been presented not as a steady progress towards a heavenly inheritance or as a sweeping missionary endeavour to bring all the world to Christ but as a struggle, and this not against conflicting internal psychological impulses or the obstacles and temptations placed in its way by other human beings, but as a struggle against supernatural forces. Though Christ has already defeated these (1.20–3), they are still active in attempting to detach his followers from him. They surround believers in the guise of pagan gods or magical practices, or of unChristian and heretical beliefs cutting away at the core of faith. It is not for believers to attack them in an attempt to inflict another defeat, for believers have not been equipped with the javelins necessary for attack; instead they need to stand where they are; if they hold their line, that itself will be another defeat for the powers. The background to the life of believers is thus expressed in cosmic terms, terms almost wholly absent from the presentation of 4.25–6.9. Just as in 2.1, 2 the pre-conversion life of believers was presented under a double aspect, as sin for which they themselves were responsible and as subject to the power of the devil, so the same double aspect is present in 4.1–6.20, though now in relation to post-conversion life. In order that they should be able to resist, believers have been supplied with super-natural armour which is to be worn with prayer and alertness. It is not for believers to build a protective wall around themselves which will preserve them but to accept, as it were, the wall which God builds for them.

As was pointed out at the beginning of the discussion of this passage, this is essentially a male presentation of the nature of the Christian life. Is there an equivalent female presentation? Origen was at least aware of the problem, even if he offers no solution, for he says that women should imitate men in standing firm (*Josh Hom* GCS 30, 385, 8). Is there an imagery which is suitable to cover both sexes? Or is it necessary to construct an exclusive imagery for women just as we have here an exclusive one for men? Can struggle be depicted in female terms? Would women wish to present the

Christian life as one of struggle? May not the idea of struggle as a
way of life be also essentially male? If we criticise AE for not
thinking this through, we should remember that he lived in a period
when women were relatively unimportant and that his depiction of
the Christian life as struggle is balanced by his presentation of it as
one of steady progress (περιπατέω is the key word) throughout
4.1–6.9, and this is applicable as much to women as to men. More
importantly it should be noted that while the imagery is masculine
the spiritualisation of each piece of armour is not in any way
masculine. The question goes however beyond the possibility of
separate presentations of struggle for men and women to whether it
is correct to express the Christian life in terms of martial imagery at
all. While AE's is somewhat remote from daily life for us, it was not
so for believers in the ancient world. The difficulty for us appears
once we substitute modern weapons of war for ancient ones. Should
preachers encourage hearers by referring to the gas canister of the
Holy Spirit or the riot shield of righteousness?

Today some do not believe in the existence of the powers but
recognise that there are non-supernatural economic, political, cultural and personal forces which affect their lives (see Detached
Note: The Powers). Individuals, and often groups of individuals, are
powerless to change these. It may be the loss of a job, some tragic
happening to a loved one, a natural disaster; these cannot be
eliminated, let alone defeated. They require to be lived through; the
only attitude then can be one of defence; no attack is possible.
The spiritualisation of the armour that AE suggests should provide the means to live through tragedy which cannot be changed.[32]

[32] For a *Wirkungsgeschichte* in respect of this passage see Schnackenburg,
337–42.

XVI

INFORMATION AND FINAL GREETINGS
(6.21–4)

W. G. Doty, *Letters in Primitive Christianity*, Philadelphia, 1973; K. Berger, 'Hellenistische Gattungen im Neuen Testament', *ANRW* II 25.2, 1330–2, 1348–50; J. L. White, *ibid.*, 1740f, 1752; Schnider and Stenger, op.cit. (see on 1.1–2), 131ff.

21 So that you may know my situation,
    how I fare,
    Tychicus, beloved brother and faithful minister in the Lord,
    will make known everything to you,
22   whom I am sending to you
      with the very purpose
      that you may know about us
      and that he may strengthen your hearts.
23 Peace and love to the brothers
   from a faithful God the Father and Lord Jesus Christ.
24 Grace be with all
    who love our Lord Jesus Christ
    with incorruptibility.

AE has just requested prayer for Paul; good prayer is always informed prayer, so he moves to ensure his readers do not lack information about Paul. Not that he himself is going to provide the information; Tychicus will supply it when he takes the letter around. This allows AE to avoid any pitfall that might result from the provision of wrong information and protects the pseudonymity. The greetings from and to individuals which are customary at this point in the genuine Pauline letters are missing; Tychicus can be presumed to give and receive greetings in each church. AE may not have known enough about Paul in prison to create a true scenario. If Paul is the author then it may be that he has been held for so long as a prisoner in close confinement that he has lost touch with his local Christian community and so has no greetings to send from them. It can hardly be that he did not wish to betray to the Roman authorities the names of associates for he has no hesitation in supplying names in Colossians. He had no greetings for members in the churches to which the letter will go because he has never visited them and does not know whom to greet; yet if Romans 16 is a part of that letter,

Paul greeted Christians in Rome though he had never been there. It may then be that the greeting of individuals would not be appropriate in a circular letter.

6.21–2 forms the greatest difficulty in framing any theory about the relation of Ephesians and Colossians: if the writers of the two letters were wholly independent of one another why should 6.21f and Col 4.7f have so many words in common and in the same order (for precise details see Best, 'Who used Whom?')? If AE had access to Colossians and reveals by his use of it that he knew its content, but he has not used it in such a way as to suggest that he was copying from it, why would he at this point turn to it and copy it? The same question arises if A/Col used Ephesians. It is important to note also that though AE commences in the first person singular he moves into the first plural in the final long section which is common to this passage and that in Colossians; in the latter the first plural is used. There is no means of identifying whom AE has in mind as associated with Paul when he moves to the first plural. It looks then as if AE had Col 4.7f before him as he wrote, or that A/Col had Eph 6.21f before him. Yet there are difficulties in such a view. The five words with which AE begins have no parallel in Colossians and form a ἵνα clause which does not add anything to the information given in the second ἵνα clause; they only serve to make the sentence clumsy and while AE writes at times in a complex way he does not write clumsily. Ephesians and Colossians share the phrase τὰ κατ' ἐμέ; this is somewhat indefinite and AE's τί πράσσω clarifies it and looks as if it had been added to do so. In the description of Tychicus both letters describe him as beloved brother and faithful minister but A/Col also describes him as a σύνδουλος; it is not clear why but it may be because it places him on the same level as Paul; δοῦλος was probably not a negative term among believers (cf Phil 1.1 and see notes on 6.6). Col 4.9, unlike Eph 6.21f, refers to Onesimus and Col 4.10ff contains a number of personal greetings none of which are found in Ephesians; indeed Ephesians does not contain greetings to or from anyone.

To some extent the additions and omissions cancel one another out and make it as likely that if the author of one letter used the actual text of the other, it is as probable that A/Col used Ephesians as the reverse. In fact a slightly better case can be made for A/Col's use of Ephesians than for the latter. A/Col can then be seen to have removed the first five clumsy words of Eph 6.21, the very awkward καί (see below) and the redundant τί πράσσω; he would have added σύνδουλος to the description of Tychicus, so raising him to the level of Paul, and added the reference to Onesimus and the personal greetings of vv. 10ff, perhaps realising as AE had not done that this was the way in which Paul concluded all his letters. Yet more probable than the use of one letter by the author of the other is their common membership in the same Pauline school; they may have discussed together how they should end their letters and decided to introduce the name of Tychicus as messenger who would provide further information about Paul, thus creating a standard way of expressing such sentiments.

It is also possible that the two letters had a common author who simply repeated in the second more or less what he had written in the first; this would necessarily imply that the letters were written about the same time and that their common author had a good memory. The hypothesis of a secretary is however of no real help in reconciling the similarities and dissimilarities between the letters (see Introduction §2.5.9.1); instructions to a secretary would have had to have been quite complex. If there was a common author it is probably better to assume that Ephesians was the first to be written and that when the author came to write Colossians he realised the complexity of his conclusion in Ephesians and simplified it.

For a more detailed discussion of the relationship of 6.21f and Col 4.7f see my 'Who used Whom?'

21. δέ is non-adversative here and indicates a new section in the argument (cf 3.20; 4.7; 5.3); this begins with the first of the ἵνα clauses; while unusual such clauses can take the leading position (Mt 9.6 and par.; 17.27; Jn 19.28, 31; Acts 24.4; cf MHT, 344). AE writes in a more complex way here than he needed to do; all he required to say was 'that you may know my situation, I have sent Tychicus to you ...'. Perhaps he did not himself know in any detail who Tychicus was or felt his readers might be in the same position and so he supplies enough information to identify him. Yet it is unlikely that he would have used the name of Tychicus, a real person, if he believed his readers were ignorant of it; its use serves to authentic the letter.

There are two inversions of order in the manuscripts of this verse; neither affects the meaning. (i) B Ψ 0278 1739 1881 𝔐 vg^ms; Ambst Hier read εἰδῆτε καὶ ὑμεῖς but εἰδῆτε is the final word of the phrase in ℵ A D F G I P 81 326 630 1241ˢ 2464 2495 *al* lat and 𝔓⁴⁶ 33 vg^mss have this word alone; as we shall see the phrase is difficult to interpret and this probably caused the variant readings; the reading of Vaticanus is to be preferred. (ii) A 𝔐 vg^cl reverse the order of γνωρίσει ὑμῖν; however the evidence for the text is overwhelming.

The assumption that καί means 'also' in the phrase καὶ ὑμεῖς has led to a number of different interpretations: (a) 'That you, my readers, as well as the Colossians may know ...' (Haupt). This interpretation presupposes that his readers know Colossians which is unlikely, though it could have resulted from a careless slip on the author's part if he had just written Colossians. This interpretation implies the same person wrote both letters (Paul?) and that Ephesians was written after Colossians. (b) 'That you may know about me just as I already know about you' (Gaugler); this presupposes knowledge on the part of AE about his readers, a knowledge which has not been very prominent elsewhere in the letter. (c) 'That you also as well as the other groups to which Tychicus takes the letter may know ...' (Bouttier); there is however no suggestion at this point of a number of groups and the interpretation implies a very precise scenario in respect of the despatch of the letter. (d) 'That you, like the other churches I (Paul) founded, may know ...' (Belser); this is too vague. (e) More probable than any of these is the view that AE's use of καί here is lax as in 1.15; 2.1 (Gnilka; Percy, 390; see notes on the two passages) and that it has no particular significance. τὰ κατ᾽ ἐμέ is imprecise and relates generally to the situation of the author or whoever is the subject of attention (cf Acts 24.22; 25.14; Phil 1.12; Col 4.7; see BAGD *s.v.* κατά 6; Schlier, 306 n. 2, says it is a customary epistolary phrase). If AE used Colossians he may have drawn it directly from Col 4.7, but its use at Phil 1.12 suggests it may have been a Pauline expression picked up, perhaps independently, by AE and A/Col. The next phrase, τί πράσσω, to which there is no parallel in Colossians, carries almost the same significance; AE says the same things twice. It can hardly be taken literally; Paul is in prison and cannot be expected to be preaching, travelling or visiting friends; it must refer to what is happening to him, how he is faring in prison (for the meaning see LSJ *s.v.* II).

Tychicus is to inform the readers how Paul is getting on. According to Acts 20.4 Tychicus was an Asian; Paul is said to have sent him once to Ephesus (2 Tim 4.12) and again to Crete (Tit 3.12). All this is late tradition but there is no need to doubt that at some stage he had been associated with Paul who had used him as a messenger. As an Asian he may have been the preserver of the Pauline tradition in Asia (Lindemann); in any case he is a further witness to that tradition. If Ephesians is non-Pauline we do not know whether he was still alive and in Asia at the time either of its writing or of Colossians (see Col 4.7). He was however probably dead, for if he had been alive in the area he could too easily have said he never carried the letter. He is described here as beloved, a term of affection used by Paul of others (Rom 16.5, 8, 9, 12; 1 Cor 4.17; Philem 1, 16; cf Col 1.7; 4.7, 9, 14; 2 Tim 1.2); AE has already used it in a more general way in 5.1. It could mean either that those so described were loved by the writer or speaker or that he regarded them as loved by God; the former is probably the case here since the word qualifies 'brother' which ties Tychicus to the author; the latter sense would seem more appropriate in 5.1. Believers called one another 'brother'[1] (we do not know what they called female believers), so emphasising their consciousness of being a group. Paul regularly addresses the members of the communities to which he wrote as brothers, but AE has not used the word earlier (if we reject the reading at 6.10) though he does so at v. 23 with this significance. 'Faithful' is another term Paul applied to his associates (1 Cor 4.17; cf Col 1.7; 4.7, 9). Here it qualifies διάκονος (for the word see on 3.7; 4.12), a difficult word to render into English here. It carries the general sense of the service of others (e.g. Mk 10.43, 45) but later came to denote 'officials' or 'ministers' (1 Tim 3.8); we

---

[1] For the word see especially K. Schäfer, *Gemeinde als 'Bruderschaft'. Ein Beitrag zum Kirchenverständnis des Paulus*, Frankfurt am Main, 1989.

see the beginning of this in Phil 1.1. Alongside 'brother' it can hardly have this significance here.[2] With his use of 'brother' AE set up a relationship between Tychicus and Paul, and with 'minister' he does the same. Since Tychicus ministers to Paul, Paul can despatch him with the letter. As the varying text of the *subscriptio* shows, Tychicus was eventually assumed by some to have been also its scribe. What is the significance of ἐν κυρίῳ? In accordance with its normal paraenetic usage we might have expected the phrase to come at the end of v. 22; in its present position it is perhaps used to link Tychicus to those to whom he is going or, more probably, to tighten the bond between him and Paul (see Detached Note: In Christ; GNB wrongly translates it 'in the Lord's work'). It probably qualifies both 'brother' and 'minister' (Westcott). AE does not describe Tychicus as σύνδουλος (cf Col 4.7), perhaps because the term would place Paul and Tychicus on the same level (for Paul as δοῦλος see Rom 1.1; Gal 1.10; Phil 1.1). If a letter is a substitute for the personal presence of the writer[3] then both the letter and Tychicus are substitutes for Paul's presence.

22. Paul is sending (ἔπεμψα, epistolary aorist, Burton §44; BDR §334; Moule, 12; MHT, 72f; Robertson, 845f) Tychicus both to inform readers about how he, Paul, is and to strengthen their Christian resolve; the second ἵνα clause repeats the subject-matter of the first and extends it; εἰς αὐτὸ τοῦτο is yet another vague phrase. Tychicus will have carried the letter; there was no postal service then for letters apart from government correspondence; they had either to be taken by a friend or entrusted to a complete stranger who happened to be travelling to the area of the addressees.[4] Paul normally sent one of his assistants with his letters. In v. 22, unlike v. 21, Tychicus is to inform readers about *us*, a surprising plural since no one has been associated with Paul previously in the letter. The plural can be explained on the assumption AE is borrowing from Col 4.8 yet why did AE as he used it not spot and correct the error? Probably he retained it as covering both Paul and Tychicus, or if he did not borrow from Col 4.8 he intended it to cover both. Paul is in prison but Tychicus is free and able to move around and so would have news of the churches in the area, probably Rome, where the letter was written (see Introduction §5 and notes on 3.1; 4.1). What Tychicus was doing would thus also interest the addressees. The purpose of the sending of Tychicus is not restricted to conveying the letter and probably not also merely to giving information; when he

---

[2] *Pace* E. E. Ellis, 'Paul and His Co-Workers', *NTS* 17 (1971) 437–52.

[3] Cf R. W. Funk, 'The Apostolic *Parousia*: Form and Significance', *Christian History and Interpretation* (FS John Knox, ed. W. R. Farmer, C. F. D. Moule, R. R. Niebuhr), Cambridge, 1967, 249–68; Schnider and Stenger, op.cit., 92–107.

[4] J. L. White, 'New Testament Epistolary Literature in the Framework of Ancient Epistolography', *ANRW* II 25.2, 1732f.

arrives in a church he will be received as a distinguished visitor, as one beloved to Paul and his faithful servant; he will then be expected to address the community; this will enable him to inspire, comfort and strengthen its members (for παρακαλέω see on 4.1, though the technical sense used there is not the meaning here; for καρδία see on 1.18). He will in effect continue what the letter itself is intended to achieve, and apply it more directly to their condition, in solving their local problems, in building up their faith and in encouraging them in all their activities. He will also be an example to them of the Christian life (Origen, Jerome).

23–4. Writers in the ancient world usually concluded their letters with a wish for the welfare of their addressees. Paul turned this wish into a benediction-type prayer and AE follows him in this, except that he supplies not one but two benedictions (yet see 2 Th 3.16, 18). Paul's benedictions vary in length, the shortest being 1 Cor 16.23 (or Col 4.18b if by Paul) and the longest 2 Cor 13.13. The double benediction of 6.23f is much longer than any of these, indeed each of its two benedictions is individually longer than any other Pauline benediction except 2 Cor 13.13. Apart from length it differs from them in one more essential feature, for it is not expressed in the second person plural but in the third (Rev 22.21 is the only NT parallel); this gives it a certain aloofness (Barth), solemnity (Ernst) and impersonality; the use of the third person may arise either from the author's ignorance (or supposed ignorance if he is not Paul) of the addressees or from the letter's nature as directed to a wider circle than one Christian community. It also accords with the way the letter never comes to grips with any actual situation in the life of its readers. The length and style of the benedictions bear the marks of AE's hand though it may be that they had these aspects because he drew them from their existing use in some community with which he was associated. Most Pauline benedictions are built around the term 'grace' (so v. 24 here) but can also feature 'peace' (Rom 15.33; 2 Th 3.16), grace, love and fellowship (2 Cor 13.13). AE used peace and grace together in 1.2.

23. 'Peace' (see on 1.2; 2.14 for the concept) is the first term in the first benediction.[5] Has AE deliberately given it this prominent position because it is one of his leading themes (cf 2.14–18; 6.15; so Gnilka and most commentators), or because it is one of the leading terms used in benedictions (Rom 15.33; 2 Th 3.16) and is a frequent term near the end of letters (Gal 6.16; 1 Pet 5.14; 3 Jn 15)? Or does chance alone account for its prominent position? At 1.2 grace precedes peace; here it heads the second benediction. It is impossible to answer these questions but at least it can be said that its

[5] On the form see T. Y. Mullins, 'Benediction as a New Testament Form', *Andrews University Seminary Studies* 18 (1977) 59–64.

present emphatic position is not out of accord with AE's theology. Since it appears in a prayer it must be understood as a peace coming from God. God's peace is his salvation (Haupt). AE is primarily praying that the brotherhood should be favoured with God's peace rather than that there should be peace among its members (between Jewish and Gentile Christians? *pace* Calvin, Henle), though the latter would follow naturally from the former (2.14–18); again AE is not praying directly for peace in individual hearts (so Origen, Jerome), though this would be a further consequence of God's salvation. God's peace is directed towards the brothers,[6] i.e. the believers (for 'brother' see on v. 21). The term, unlike 'believer', 'Christian' or 'those who love the Lord' (v. 24), sets up a relationship between those addressed and the writer; they are seen, not as individuals, but as a group, as members one of another (4.25), as belonging to the same household (2.19), as within the one church which has been the subject of so much of the letter.

AE's readers are also to be the recipients of God's love.[7] Love is another basic concept of his theology (1.4; 2.4; 3.17–19; 5.2, 25), as it was of all early Christianity. The emphasis lies not on the love of believers for one another but on God's love for them which pre-existed their existence and elected them to be believers (1.4f); God's love should lead those who are brothers to love one another.

Though the precise relationship of peace and love is never defined in the letter, they belong as terms to the same semantic field denoting God's beneficent attitude towards people; the same cannot be said, at least at first sight, of the third term in the benediction, πίστεως; it instead normally denotes the attitude of believers towards God. In addition it is not introduced with a simple καί which would set it in parallel with peace and love but with μετά. Yet to translate, 'together with trust in God', moves it away from their area as gifts of God. However, as we saw at 4.2 the conjunction and the preposition can be equivalent, with μετά representing the Hebrew עִם (cf BAGD *s.v.* II 6). As far as the meaning goes it is possible to understand πίστις as a quality of God (cf Bouttier), for in the OT God is depicted as faithful to his covenant. God's believers are then assured that he will remain faithful to them in peace and love. This interpretation also allows μετά a more normal sense, since πίστεως need not then be taken as parallel with peace and love but as qualifying them as to the manner in which the peace and love are given. The movement is from God to believers. For the terms used here to identify God see on 1.2, 3; 5.20. In v. 23 God is defined as Father and presumably as Father of believers and neither simply as

---

[6] 𝔓⁴⁶ reads ἁγίοις, perhaps because of the general absence from the letter of other references to 'brothers'. 𝔓⁴⁶ was not among the mss reading it at 6.10.

[7] Ἔλεος is read here by A, probably under the influence of 1 Tim 1.2; 2 Tim 1.2; Jude 2.

Father of Jesus Christ as in 1.3, nor as Father of all men and women.

24. Χάρις begins the second benediction; it is the most common word in the terminal benedictions of the NT (Rom 16.20, 24; 1 Cor 16.23; 2 Cor 13.13; Gal 6.18; Phil 4.23; Col 4.18; 1 Th 5.28; 2 Th 3.18; 1 Tim 6.21; 2 Tim 4.22; Tit 3.15; Philem 25; Heb 13.25); it is followed with the usual μετά relating it to the recipients. However these are not addressed with the normal second person plural but identified with a phrase in the third person, 'all who love our Lord Jesus Christ'. The idea that people love, or should love, God (the Lord) is common in the OT and Judaism (Exod 20.6; Deut 5.10; 7.9; Judg 5.31; Ψ 96.10; 121.6; 144.20; 2 Esdr 11.5; Tob 13.14; 14.7; Ecclus 1.10; 2.15, 16; *Ps Sol* 4.25; 6.6; *T Sim* 3.6; *Test Abr* 3.3 (Rec A); *1 En* 105.8) and may almost be termed a formula (Gnilka, Schlier); it reappears in the NT, yet in the light of the latter's much greater general emphasis on love comparatively rarely (Rom 8.28; 1 Cor 2.9; 8.3; Jas 1.12; 2.5; 1 Jn 4.10, 20f; 5.1). Perhaps more surprising is the scarcity of references to loving Christ, in view of the fact that to Christ are attributed many of the functions exercised by God in the OT. Our passage aside, there is only 1 Cor 16.22, but there φιλέω is used and not ἀγαπάω and the idea is negative, and 1 Pet 1.8 (2 Tim 4.8 is not a proper parallel); outside the NT there are instances in Ign *Eph* 15.3; *Philad* 1.1; *Polyc* 5.1; Polyc *Phil* 3.3. The idea of loving Christ is then a late development in early Christianity; Paul prefers to speak of a faith relationship with Christ. The love of God for Christians is of course a frequent idea (in Ephesians at 1.4; 2.4; 3.18f; 5.2, 25; 6.23). Our verse provides one of the few places where AE might be thought to define who Christians are, those who love the Lord Jesus Christ; in 1 Cor 16.22, which may be part of a liturgical formula, lack of such love in people prevents them being regarded as Christians. As a definition of being Christian (an alternative and more frequent definition sets Christians out as those who call on the Lord, 1 Cor 1.2; Rom 10.12–14; Acts 9.14, 21; 2 Tim 2.22), these two ideas emphasise the attitude of the persons concerned rather than their election by God as in 1.4. Often 1 Pet 1.8 is quoted here in extenuation; those who have not seen Christ can hardly be expected to love him; yet they are expected to trust him though they have not seen him. 5.1 moreover requires the imitation of God who has not been seen. Thus the fact that Christ is not seen can hardly be relevant.

The final phrase ἐν ἀφθαρσίᾳ is troublesome. There are three related questions: (1) What is the significance of ἐν? (2) What is the meaning of the noun? (3) With what in the preceding statement should the phrase be connected? (1) In 6.2; 4.19 ἐν has the sense 'and', probably showing Semitic influence (Kuhn, 337); if that is its sense here it would link up with χάρις, 'grace and incorruptibility be to all . . .' (cf Bengel, Abbott, Bouwman). If however it has one of its more normal senses (Chrysostom takes it as equivalent to διά but this is highly unlikely) the phrase could be linked in at several points in the verse. (2) The noun is found only in the later portions of the LXX and appears to lack a Hebrew equivalent (Wisd 2.23; 6.18f; 4 Macc 9.22; 17.12; cf Wisd 12.1; 18.4). In the NT it is found at 1 Cor 15.42, 50, 53f; 1 Tim 1.10 (cf Rom 1.23; 1 Cor 9.25; 15.52; 1 Tim 1.17) and in the Apostolic Fathers at 2 Clem 14.5; 20.5; Ign *Philad* 9.2; *Eph* 17.1; *Magn* 6.2; *Mart Polyc* 14.2; 19.2 (Robinson has an extensive discussion of its meaning; see also G. Harder, *TWNT*, IX, 94–106). Its use probably represents a Hellenistic touch on AE's part in an attempt to accommodate his readers. It describes a condition rather than a temporal or infinite continuity and moves in the area of indestructibility and immortality; it is not an ethical term (*pace* Origen, Chrysostom, Theod Mops, Erasmus, etc.) and contains no idea of Christians being freed from moral incorruption, though this itself may be true. (3) If ἐν is not the equivalent of καί, the phrase must be linked to: (a) 'our lord Jesus Christ' (Dibelius), (b) χάρις (Pokorný), (c) ἀγαπώντων, or (d) the whole of v. 24a; it is in fact difficult to distinguish between (c) and (d) since ἀγαπώντων is the main word in the verse. (a) While God is eternal (cf 1 Tim 1.17) nowhere else is this predicated of Christ and there is nothing in the letter to suggest AE would wish to make this connection. Prete,[8] accepting this linkage, sees it in a different way as referring to the raised Christ and thus connects the meaning of the word to its use in 1 Cor 15.42, 50, 53f in relation to the resurrection. However, if this is the connection we should expect the article with the phrase and there are easier ways of expressing this interpretation. It is also relevant to ask why love of Christ should only relate to his risen state. (b) is difficult because the words are so far apart. (c) or (d) is the solution accepted by many translations (RSV, NRSV, REB, GNB, NIV, Moffatt; cf Belser), 'love with an undying love'; this is awkward. The connection could however be made in a different way and refer to those whose love is not transitory but persists. This interpretation gives a more suitable close to the letter. The promises of the gospel which it contains are for those whose Christian faith is not a passing whim but stands the test of time. There is a sense then in which this picks up and concludes the conflict of 6.10–17 in which those conquer who stand firm for ever.

א² D Ψ 𝔐 a b sy bo^pt add ἀμήν as a final conclusion; this word terminates the preferred text of Romans, Galatians and is a variant but inferior reading at the conclusion of the remaining letters of the Pauline

---

[8] B. Prete, 'Il senso dell'espressione ἐν ἀφθαρσίᾳ in Efes. 6,24', *Studi sull'Oriente e la Bibbia* (FS G. Rinaldi), Genoa, 1967, 361–77.

corpus. The evidence is insufficient to compel its acceptance here; it is an obvious addition.

Now at the end of our letter we need to look back along the way we have come and summarise our understanding of it. It was probably written not by Paul but by someone strongly under his influence who had also been associated with the author of Colossians. Probably they both belonged to a continuing group of Paul's disciples.

The author's aim was limited. He was not concerned with the wider issues of the life of the church or its members in the secular world but with the internal harmony of individual Christian communities. He thus leaves unexamined vast areas of ecclesiology and his decision not to discuss these areas must have been deliberate; he is not to be blamed for omitting them; they are covered in other parts of the New Testament.

The letter is carefully planned and the author does not wander at random from topic to topic. Its theology and paraenesis serve the same purpose, the maintenance of the unity of Christian communities. The consistency of his thinking displayed in this appears in lesser areas: his christology makes no reference to Christ as the servant of God or humanity, and accordingly the life of believers is not stressed as one of service; Christ's ascension is emphasised and with it the exalted position of believers. Since his main theme is the inner unity of Christian communities, he has no need to refer to the future in terms of the parousia, yet he has an interest in the ultimate unity of all things (1.10). God has given the church its unity yet believers must strive to preserve it or it will be lost. Since the two halves of his letter relate to this unity it is wrong to suggest that one or other is the more important. His moral teaching may lack profoundness, but the causes of division in congregations are rarely great issues but come from the little ways in which people do not get on with one another. He uses one section of a traditional *Haustafel* to explore the relation of Christ and the church which he parallels to marriage, making here an important new contribution to the doctrine of the church. While generally his theology lies within the ambit of Pauline teaching, there is a certain broadening or rephrasing of ideas to meet Hellenistic thinking.

It goes too far to describe the letter as the crown of Paulinism; while it treats the formal nature of the church in greater detail and with deeper understanding than Paul, many areas of Pauline thought lie untouched and the level of moral teaching falls below his. Because of its very general nature the main message of the letter can be easily transferred to the situation of local congregations, for in these there are always factors which would destroy fellowship and break up unity.

ESSAY I

THE CHURCH

A. Wikenhauser, *Die Kirche als der mystische Leib Christi nach dem Apostel Paulus*, Münster, 1937; G. Eichholz, 'Der Ursprung der Kirche', *EvT* (1937) 255–75; Thornton, *Common Life*; N. A. Dahl, *Das Volk Gottes*, Oslo, 1941; G. Johnston, *The Doctrine of the Church in the New Testament*, Cambridge, 1943; L. Malevez, 'L'Église, corps du Christ: sens et provenance de l'expression chez Saint Paul', *RSR* 32 (1944) 27–94; J. Bover, ' "In aedificationem corporis Christi": Eph 4.12', *Estudios Biblicos* 3 (1944) 313–42; Hanson; L. Cerfaux, *La Théologie de l'Église suivant saint Paul*, Paris, 1948; Schlier and Warnach; O. Perels, 'Kirche und Welt nach dem Epheser- und Kolosserbrief', *TLZ* 76 (1951) 391–400; Best, *One Body*; H. Schlier, 'Die Kirche nach dem Brief an die Epheser' and 'Die Einheit der Kirche im Denken des Apostels Paulus' in Schlier, *Die Zeit der Kirche*, Freiburg i. Br., 1956, 159–86, 287–99; P. Benoît, 'Corps, tête et plérôme dans les Épîtres de la captivité, *RB* 63 (1956) 5–44; S. F. B. Bedale, 'The Theology of the Church' in Cross, *Studies*, 64–75; K. Barth, *Church Dogmatics* IV.2, Edinburgh, 1958, 614–41; C. Kearns, 'The Church the Body of Christ according to St Paul' (Part 3), *Irish Ecclesiastical Record* 91 (1959) 1–15, 313–27; M. Barth, *Israel und die Kirche im Brief des Paulus an die Epheser*, Munich, 1959; R. Schnackenburg, 'Gestalt und Wesen der Kirche nach dem Epheserbrief', *Catholica* 15 (1961) 104–20 (= *Schriften zum Neuen Testament*, Munich, 1971, 268–87); P. S. Minear, *Images of the Church in the New Testament*, London, 1961; B. M. Ahern, 'The Christian's Union with the Body of Christ in Cor, Gal, and Rom', *CBQ* 23 (1961) 199–209; E. Schweizer, 'The Church as the Missionary Body of Christ', *NTS* 8 (1961/2) 1–11; M. Barth, 'The Church according to the Epistle to the Ephesians', *The Ecumenical Dialogue at Cornell, Sept 60–Sept 62*, 7–49; id. 'Conversion and Conversation. Israel and the Church in Paul's Epistle to the Ephesians', *Int* 17 (1963) 3–24; C. F. Mooney, 'Paul's Vision of the Church in "Ephesians" ', *Scr* 15 (1963) 33–43; Roels, L. Benoit, 'L'unité de l'Église selon l'épître aux Éphésiens', *AnBib* 17–18, Rome, 1963, I, 57–77; P.-A. Harlé, 'Le Saint-Esprit et l'Eglise chez saint Paul', *VCaro*, 19 (1965) 13–29; Löwe; R. Schnackenburg, *The Church in the New Testament*, New York, 1965; H. Ridderbos, *Paul: An Outline of His Theology* (ET), Grand Rapids, 1975 (originally 1966), 327–95, 429–86; P. Benoît, 'L'Église corps du Christ', *Populus Dei. II Ecclesia* (FS A. Ottaviani), Rome, 1969, 971–1028; N. Koulomzine, 'Images of the Church in Saint Paul's Epistles', *St Vladimir's Theological Quarterly* 14 (1970) 5–27; J. Gnilka, 'Das Kirchenmodell des Epheserbriefes', *BZ* 15 (1971) 161–84; I. H. Marshall, 'The Biblical Use of the Word "Ekklesia" ', *ExpT* 84 (1972–3) 359–64; J. L. Houlden, 'Christ and Church in Ephesians', *SE* 6 (=*TU* 112) 267–73; J. Ernst, 'From the Local Community to the Great

Church', *BTB* 6 (1976) 237-57; K. Berger, 'Volkversammlung und Gemeinde Gottes', *ZTK* 73 (1976) 167-207; C. F. D. Moule, *The Origin of Christology*, Cambridge, 1977, 69-89; K. Kertelge, 'Offene Fragen zum Thema "Geistliches Amt" und das neutestamentliche Verständnis von der "Repraesentatio Christi" ', *Die Kirche des Anfangs* (FS H. Schürmann, ed. R. Schnackenburg, J. Ernst, J. Wanke), Leipzig, 1978, 583-605; R. Schnackenburg, 'L'idée de "Corps du Christ" dans la lettre aux Ephésiens; perspective pour notre temps', *Paul de Tarse. Apôtre du notre temps* (ed. L. De Lorenzi), Rome, 1979, 665-85; R. Banks, *Paul's Idea of Community*, Exeter, 1980; J. Gnilka, 'Das Akkulturationsproblem nach dem Epheser- und Kolosserbrief', *Fede e cultura alla luce della Bibbia* (ed. J. D. Barthelemy), Turin, 1981, 235-47; R. Y. K. Fung, 'Some Pauline Pictures of the Church', *EvQ* 53 (1981) 89-107; D. Guthrie, *New Testament Theology*, Leicester, 1981, 742ff; T. G. Allen; Schnackenburg, 293-310, 321-31; F. Grob, 'L'image du corps et de la tête dans l'Épître aux Éphésiens', *ETR* 58 (1983) 491-500; C. van Engen, 'The Holy Catholic Church – on the Road through Ephesians', *RefR* 37 (1984) 187-201; E. P. Clowney, 'Interpreting the Biblical Models of the Church', *Biblical Interpretation of the Church* (ed. D. A. Carson), Exeter, 1984, 64-109; F. Mussner, 'Was ist die Kirche?', and F. Schröger, 'Zur kosmischen Ekklesiologie des Epheserbriefes', both in *Diener in Eurer Mitte* (FS Antonius Hofmann), Passau, 1984, 82-90 and 110-23; J. L. Breed, 'The Church as the "Body of Christ": A Pauline Analogy', *Theology Review* (NEST) 6 (1985) 9-32; F.-J. Steinmetz, 'Jenseits der Mauern und Zäune', *GuL* 59 (1986) 202-14; Reynier, 112-24, 173-94; G. L. O. R. Yorke, *The Church as the Body of Christ in the Pauline Corpus – A Re-examination*, Lanhan, 1991; B. Prete, 'L'ecclesiologia della Lettera agli Efesini', *Saccra Doctrina* 37 (1992) 133-95; J. Roloff, *Die Kirche im Neuen Testament*, Göttingen, 1993, 222-49; Schmithals, 155-81; A. Lindemann, 'Die Kirche als Leib', *ZTK* 92 (1995) 140ff.

1.1. The rise of the ecumenical movement has led in recent years to a deeper study of the teaching on the church in Ephesians. It is not inappropriate then to summarise that teaching. Many commentators indeed hold this to be the central theme of the letter. The word ἐκκλησία is used more regularly in it (nine times) in proportion to its size than in any of the other Paulines, with the possible exception of 1 Corinthians (twenty-two times). In secular Greek the word indicates an assembly and in the LXX it is applied to Israel as the people of God. Judaism used two words, ἐκκλησία and συναγωγή, either of which the Christians might have applied to their groups; they chose the former, perhaps because the Jews already used the latter of their gatherings. The Christians used their word in three ways referring to (a) the local Christian community in a town, (b) Christian gatherings in a house, (c) the whole group of Christians in all parts of the world.

1.2. The discussion of the nature of the church may be approached from either the sociological angle or the theological. To adopt the former would lead to an examination *inter alia* of the church in terms of its position among the other social entities of its culture, its relationship to the state, its internal structure, the selection and appointment of its office-bearers, the type of people who belonged to it and the sociological factors which led to its formation. Ephesians is, at least on the surface, not interested in these matters but instead in the relation of the church to God, to Christ and to the Holy Spirit; in so far as it is defined it is defined in respect of God, Christ and the Spirit, and in terms of its membership, not in relation to other bodies of people. For AE the church is neither the result of the determination of a number of people with similar interests to associate with one another to further a common goal, nor an inevitable development of the historical process; its existence was determined by God prior to the historical process (1.4f, 9–11). The earlier Paulines contain no specific teaching on the nature of the church; what Paul writes on it in each letter is incidental to his main concerns in that letter; in responding to other issues he occasionally finds it necessary to say something about the church; for example, the image of the diversity of members within the one body of Christ (1 Cor 12.12ff) is evoked by the overemphasis on the part of the Corinthian community on glossolalia. In contrast to this incidental treatment, what AE has to say on the church is not related to any particular church problem. This of course does not of itself imply that Paul did not write Ephesians, for behind the occasional references to the church in his other letters there is a consistent and developed view of the church which only surfaces as need requires. Modern ecumenical theologians may make extensive use of Ephesians when discussing church unity, yet this does not itself imply that AE's main stress is on the church's unity. Though he may not have some particular congregation or problem in mind as he writes, what he says about the church is neither theoretical nor speculative. The attention he gives to it is linked to the total purpose of his writing.

   1.3. Even if intending to write theologically about the church AE cannot avoid statements which have sociological significance. Theological theories about social entities must relate in some way to society. If AE has nothing to say about the place of the church in relation to the state yet he sees it as a place of light in a culture of darkness (4.17–19), though of course he expresses what he has to say in theological rather than sociological terms; the result is an almost sectarian outlook, yet there is no sense of a ghetto mentality (see Best, 'Types of Existence'). He does not lay down limiting barriers by which the church may be distinguished from what lies outside it; baptism is the only such marker; yet he is clearly aware that there is a distinction between the church and the world; in the church is light but in the world darkness (5.8); if he does draw a distinction it is rather between the life of believers before and after conversion (2.1–3; 5.8). AE is also aware of the relation of the

church to the supernatural world, for the culture of darkness outside
the church is controlled by evil supernatural forces (2.2; 6.10–17).
In so far as he writes about the behaviour of members he is making
sociological statements. They are not to lie to one another, be
abusive, thieve from non-Christians (4.25ff), or sin sexually with
one another or with outsiders (5.3ff). In indicating these as sins into
which his readers might fall he only does so because he is aware that
sometimes they did; in this way he provides a picture of his readers.
Yet we must be careful here for when he dealt with household
relationships (5.22–6.9) he writes as if all his readers belonged to
households in which everyone was a Christian; it is difficult to
believe that churches ever existed which consisted only of totally
Christian households; AE may not then be very much aware of the
actual way in which his readers lived and his depiction of the sins
into which they were most likely to fall may be completely
erroneous. Yet nothing we know about the early church suggests he
was ignorant in this way. Other things he says tell us something
about the lives of his readers. They have been baptised (4.5; 5.26),
worship together (5.19f) and have some form of ministry (4.11).
They also accept the ideas of their surrounding culture on slavery
and the relationship of husbands and wives. On the whole however
he provides little information about his readers and their manner of
life; this is probably a result of the nature of his letter. We learn
most about Paul's readers in those letters where he writes to an
individual community which he knows; AE is however writing a
letter either to a number of communities or more generally to
Christians as a whole and he will have had no individual knowledge
of the majority of their communities. If however it is impossible to
deduce from his letter the proportions of rich and poor in the
communities, we can be certain that they contained some wealthy
enough to be slave owners and some poor enough to be slaves.
Surprisingly however we learn that he did not see membership of the
church as restricted to humans on earth for it also includes heavenly
inhabitants (see on 1.18; 2.19).

   2.1. Since he is writing with either a general Christian audience
or a number of congregations in mind, it is not unnatural that he
should discuss the nature of the whole church rather than that of
local congregations.[1] In doing this he might have conceived of the
whole church as the sum total of a number of local communities;
instead he thinks of it as the sum total of believers. He has no need
then to lay down a set of rules for individual congregations or to
instruct them in the steps to take if problems should arise within

---

[1] For the political models on which AE may have drawn see E. A. Judge,
'Contemporary Political Models for the Inter-Relation of the New Testament
Churches', *RefTR* 22 (1963) 65–76.

them; he does not tell them when facing a difficulty in the congregation to summon a church meeting (cf 1 Cor 5.1ff) or to pray for God's help. Sometimes it is suggested that Paul, assuming he did not write Ephesians, lacked a concept of the church as a whole. Yet there is evidence that he did not wholly lack this: he does not write to the church *of* Corinth but to the church *in* Corinth; he has a common policy for all the churches (1 Cor 4.17; 14.33); if Christ is the foundation of the church in Corinth (1 Cor 3.11) he is that for every other local church; if the church in Corinth is God's field and building (1 Cor 3.9) so will every other congregation be; it is not only the church in Corinth that is Christ's body, every community is, and Christ does not have a number of bodies. The rock of the whole church is present as an outcrop in every local congregation. In writing to individual congregations Paul had no need to discuss the nature of the church as a whole and so he did not do so. Colossians is a kind of stepping-stone between the earlier letters and Ephesians, for it contains explicit references both to the local community (Col 1.2; 4.15) and to the whole church (1.18, 24); its author was dealing with one community with a specific christological problem which also had a more general reference. AE, by concentrating on the whole church and on it alone, is able to set ecclesiology more firmly within the divine economy (Schnackenburg, 294). At the same time, though writing of the whole church, he avoids idealising or spiritualising it for in his paraenesis (4.1ff) he has the needs of actual members in mind.

2.2. A number of different influences affected AE as he formulated his church teaching. While these can be listed individually they cannot be rigidly separated from one another. They include: (a) the cultural and intellectual world of his time, gnosis, Philo, Hellenistic Judaism, and funeral, trade and minor religious associations; (b) the OT and post-biblical Jewish thought; (c) Paul; (d) the Pauline school of which he and A/Col were members; (e) his own experience of living within a Christian community. The nature of the last of these is the most difficult to determine, yet it may have been the most important.

3. There are at least three major theological ways of describing the church: (i) as God's people; (ii) as related to Christ (e.g. as his body), the corporate aspect; (iii) as the realm of the Holy Spirit's activity. The first is rooted in the OT in a way in which the second and third are not. The second is the area in which AE makes his main contribution, though naturally he has much to say in respect of the other two. For him the church is something essentially new which did not exist prior to Christ's incarnation. Judaism thought of Israel as the body neither of God nor of the Messiah, though it did think of God and Israel in a marital relationship and used the image of building in relation to Israel; yet even where continuity of image exists there is also profound variation brought about by the new factor of the incarnation. Images are always flexible and open to modification when new factors and situations arise.

We go on now to outline briefly AE's various descriptions of the church, making use of the results of our earlier discussions of the relevant Ephesian passages. It is true of course that the various aspects (people of God, Spirit, body of Christ, etc.) cannot be wholly distinguished from one another, yet for purposes of discussion they require separate treatment.

3.1. The Church as People of God
This idea is less explicit in Ephesians than in other parts of the NT (e.g. Rom 9–11; 1 Pet 2.9f). Its implicit presence however underlies much of the letter and is seen in the adoption of concepts and images already applied to Israel. Thus AE describes the church as ἐκκλησία and believers as οἱ ἅγιοι, terms common in the LXX and later Judaism to describe the people of God. Christians are the chosen of God, his elect (1.4), as were the OT people of God. AE draws the images of building and wife from the OT though reinterpreting them in relation to the church. 2.11–22 is the passage where the 'people' idea becomes explicit; Gentiles inherit the promises originally made to Israel (2.12) and though once excluded are now within the people of God. Yet there is a profound change for the people is no longer a continued Israel but a new people, a 'third people', comprising both believing Jews (the first people) and Gentiles (the second people). 2.11–22, though centring on the idea of the people of God, also provides a link to another leading idea: Jews and Gentiles are reconciled in Christ's body, not his physical body but the body which is the church; the two bodies are of course related since were it not for the dying body on the cross there would be no church (2.16). Paul had already expressed the union of Jews and Gentiles in one body (1 Cor 12.13). The corporate aspect of the one people of God is seen also in the harmonious fitting together of the stones, that is, the people, in the temple (2.21). Other links between the two aspects appear in that holiness, a characteristic of the people of God (they are saints), is attributed to the church as wife or bride of Christ (5.27), and that Gentiles are both fellow heirs (a people of God term) with Jews and within the same body (3.6).

The church as the people of God raises in an acute way its relationship to Israel, God's 'old' people. Clearly there is some degree of continuity, otherwise OT terms used of Israel would not be applied to the church and the church would not have looked on the OT as an authoritative book. Yet nothing is said of a continuing physical Israel after the cross. AE evinces no interest in such an Israel but then he is only interested in the unity of the church. In a sense a continuing Israel would be no different from a continuing non-Israel, the Gentiles; both are sources for converts and members of both need the same salvation that comes through the cross and resurrection of Christ. Ephesians differs at this point from Colossians in that the latter (3.11) sees the abolition within the church of the distinction between slave and free, barbarian and Scythian, as well as of that between Jew and Greek. In Ephesians social distinctions are not abolished, only the religious distinction between Jew and Gentile.

3.2. *The Church of the Spirit*
For Ephesians, as for the certainly genuine Paulines, the Spirit's realm of activity is the church. Neither Paul nor AE had occasion to discuss the nature of inspiration in the arts or in philosophical and scientific thought and thus develop a theology of the role of the Spirit in society as a whole. In fact AE's picture of the world outside the church (4.17–19) leaves no place for that activity except in so far as the Spirit can be conceived as leading unbelievers to see the truth of the Gospel. If any spirit is at work in society it is an evil spirit, or evil spirits (2.2; 6.10ff). Within the church the Spirit is one (4.4) and gives unity to the church (4.3). Believers are sealed with the Spirit (1.13; 4.30) and given access to God (2.18); it (we do not know enough to decide whether AE ascribed personality to the Spirit; hence the use of 'it' rather than 'he/she') strengthens (3.16) and fills them (5.18); it controls and inspires their worship (5.19); it leads their prayers (6.18). Believers are equipped in their fight against the powers of evil with a sword empowered by the Spirit (6.17). If they sin against the life of the community (4.25–9) the Spirit grieves (4.30). While in 1 Corinthians and Romans God or Christ may be the ultimate source of charismata, these in fact are depicted more directly as endowments of the Spirit (1 Cor 12–14); in Ephesians, though the charismata are not particularised, they are regarded as the gift of Christ (4.7f); office-bearers are also his gift (4.11). If in that way the Spirit's role may seem to be diminished, it must be recollected that in 1.3 the blessings which God gives to the church, though they are not spelt out, are associated with the Spirit. The Spirit again is a source of revelation (1.17) to the church guiding it through its original leaders into the acceptance of the Gentiles (3.5). God dwells in the church in his Spirit (2.22); this varies in a minor way from 1 Cor 3.16 where it says the church is indwelt by the Spirit of God.

Body (=the church) and Spirit are linked together in the theme of unity in 4.4; this linking provides a suitable passage to the discussion of the more corporate aspects of the church.

4.1. *The Church as Building*
This image, drawn ultimately by Paul from Judaism, came to AE via Paul; despite its Jewishness it was also to some extent present in Greco-Roman culture and so could be readily appreciated by

Gentiles. In distinction from Jews, Christians understood it as tied
specifically to the Christ-event. He is its angle-stone (see on 2.20 for
the word) and his apostles and prophets its foundation. The church
has then a foundation different from any that Judaism believed to
exist. Consequently it is essentially a new building, and as such can
be built with Gentile 'stones' as well as Jewish. That it should be
constructed with these two types of stones was not an afterthought
when Judaism rejected Christ, but was intended from the beginning,
even though Gentiles were not immediately admitted. On the
foundation of apostles and prophets with Christ as the angle-stone
believers are fitted together so that there results, as we might say, a
building secure against rain and storm. It is not however any
building but a particular building, a temple in which God dwells.
Though this building may have begun in the Christ-event and be
envisaged as growing, there is also a certain sense of completeness;
if it were not complete God would not dwell in it. This is the tension
we have observed as running all through Ephesians; what is to
happen is conceived as having already taken place. The building is
not then thought of simply as a future heavenly Jerusalem; it exists
now. Its growth is moreover one not in numbers but in maturity.
Linked with this building image, which is not restricted to that of the
temple, is that of the family home; believers are the family
inhabiting it (2.19) and the family is God's family.

This raises the question regarding the membership of the family
of God and of the church. Certainly AE accepts as members those
who have faith and have been baptised. He does not provide enough
information for us to know if he would have made any other
requirement, such as regular participation in the eucharist. The
absence of a reference to the eucharist is itself surprising since in 1
Cor 10.16f Paul related it to the unity of believers, a central theme of
AE; yet it was probably only because of local difficulties in Corinth
that Paul made this link; similar difficulties did not necessarily exist
among the Christians to whom AE was writing. Granted his readers
meet all of AE's requirements, are they the only members of the
church? In 2.19 Gentile believers are described as fellow citizens
with the saints. Who are the saints? Here and in 1.18 they are
probably good supernatural beings, possibly including the believing
dead (see on 1.18; 2.19). In 2.6 believers are said to be already in the
heavenlies and the church has a cosmic dimension (3.10, 21). Thus
the church may have members other than believers on earth but AE
is not primarily interested in them; he advises only on the behaviour
of those on earth.

4.2. *The Church as Body of Christ*
(See also Detached Note: The Body of Christ.)
In the two major passages in which Paul teaches about the church as

the body of Christ (1 Cor 12.12ff; Rom 12.3ff) he discusses the varying functions of believers, which he relates to their gifts of grace, and their interrelationship. In these two passages the image functions paraenetically. In Ephesians the variety of the charismata of believers is not spelt out though it is said that they have gifts to exercise (4.7); some indeed have special gifts, or are rather themselves special and diverse gifts to the church (4.11f). The paraenetic emphasis is less prominent in Ephesians, being only explicit at 4.25. However, believers continue to be seen as related to one another (4.16, 25), though this is not stressed as much or in the same way as in earlier letters; the emphasis is not on the general togetherness of believers but of Jews and Gentiles within the one body (3.6) through the cross (2.13–16). While in the earlier epistles the image was specifically related to particular congregations, though that is not to say that a wider sweep might not have lain in the background, in Ephesians the image is used in relation to the whole church. In the earlier use of the image Paul considered only the relationship of the church to Christ and not its relationship to the world; Ephesians, in agreement with Colossians, continues this way of thinking. Three new aspects of the image however appear in Ephesians: the body is said to grow (4.12, 16; cf Col 2.19), is depicted as Christ's wife or bride (5.22ff), and Christ is set out as its head; this latest aspect is present also in Colossians. It is natural to think of growth in relation to organisms; the human physical body as organism is complete in the sense that every part of it is there from birth and yet it grows from infancy to adulthood; its growth is a maturing of capabilities already present from the beginning; it is not a growth out of chaos into unity. In a somewhat similar way the church is one from the begining but matures and in that way grows. Christ is the source of all its growth (4.15f; for the idea of growth see 2.21). The idea of the church as mature person, if this is taken to be the meaning of 4.13, accords with this kind of thinking. An immature church could easily be led into error (4.14).

4.2.1. It was inevitable that once the church was likened to the body of Christ there would be questions about his relationship to his body. If Paul, or his school, did not raise the issue themselves others may have faced them with it. The phrase 'body of Christ' was not an easy one for those reared in Hellenism to understand because of their dualistic approach; the body was material but soul or spirit were non-material; the person was linked to the body yet superior to it. Apart from its normal physical meaning as the uppermost part of the body κεφαλή was used metaphorically in many ways of which two are significant for biblical thought, 'origin, source' and 'over-lord, ruler'. In theory it would be possible to apply either sense to Christ as head of the cosmos or head of the church. Both the thematic and cultural context of 5.23 imply overlordship as the meaning in 5.22–33; the thematic context of 1.22 requires the same connotation; incidentally we should note that in the latter text head is used without any direct reference to a body, though in some contemporary non-Christian thought the cosmos was regarded as a body. However, the meaning 'source' is possible in 4.15f, though not necessarily so if we take the source of the growth to be Christ rather than the head. There is however no reason why we should not find both understandings of the word within a single writing provided both are possible; where words have more than one meaning the context must decide which meaning is meant. We do not need then to force a consistent significance on AE though in fact he may have been consistent; if so the meaning will be 'overlord'. However, if Christ is ruler this does not mean he holds his position like either an elected president whom voters choose from a slate of candidates or a monarch who becomes ruler through the sheer chance of birth within a royal family.

Yorke evades the difficult problem of the precise relationship of Christ to his body by denying that in the Pauline corpus the church is the body of Christ; it is simply the body which Christ possesses or which belongs to him; χριστοῦ in the phrase is a possessive genitive. However: (i) He does not explore what 'possessing' or 'belonging to' means; in 'I possess my hand' and 'I possess my pen', 'possess' has two different senses; similarly with respect to 'my hand belongs to me' and 'my pen belongs to me'. (ii) He fails to make clear why Christ is so regularly mentioned in passages which present the body as the church; if Yorke's view were correct the reference to Christ in many passages where it occurs in relation to the body would be unnecessary. (iii) In his discussion he isolates the phrase 'body of Christ' and does not examine the other ways in which Christ and the church or Christ and believers are related; these other ways include phrases like 'in Christ', 'into Christ', 'members of Christ', 'dying with Christ', and the parallel of Adam and Christ. (iv) Yorke does not adequately explore the meaning of σῶμα itself.

4.2.2. If Christ is head both of the cosmos (1.22) and of the church, does this imply a relation between cosmos and church? There are other signs that a relationship may exist: Christ fills both (1.23; 4.10); believers already sit in the heavenlies (2.6); the families, or social groupings, of humans and angels have been brought together (3.15); believers are engaged in a continual contest with the powers that are in the heavenlies (6.12ff). All this is surprising since AE does not set church and society in relation and since the cosmos, the totality of existence, includes society within itself, though it is not identical with it. The church is not commanded to evangelise society yet in 3.10 the church is summoned to make known to all supernatural sentient beings in the cosmos God's wisdom and is at the same time engaged in a continual warfare with these, or with some of these beings (6.10ff). A significant difference however exists between the relation of Christ to the cosmos and to the church in that while he is the saviour of the church (5.25) he is the conqueror of the powers in the cosmos (1.21). Despite this difference all things, and this must include the powers as well as all human beings, are summarised or brought to a conclusion in him (1.10).

4.2.3. A further aspect of the relation of Christ to the church, which is not unrelated to the image of the body, is revealed by the terms 'fullness' and 'filling'; these are not used in the earlier Paulines in the same way as in Ephesians; they were however probably terms with a special significance for the Pauline school as their use in Ephesians shows. Whether the Colossian heretics introduced the terms into the discussion or not is irrelevant for our purposes. God fills Christ and Christ fills the church (1.23). Christ is the means whereby God works in the church; Ephesians however tends to stress what Christ does rather than what God does, though God is always in the background. It is not made clear with what Christ fills the church, but it is at least his presence. There is a parallel here to the relationship of believers and Christ, in that Christ fills the church and the church is in him just as believers are in him and he dwells in them (3.17).

The church is Christ's body; he fills the church; he is its head; all this implies a very close association between Christ and church; it is not surprising then that in 3.21 Christ and the church are apparently given equal status in respect of the glory of God. Lest this should appear too high a status for the church in relation to Christ, in the marital image, to which we now turn, she is called to offer to him her obedience.

4.3. *The Church as Wife (or Bride)*
This image brings out further important aspects of the relation of Christ and the church. Though in the later church the image was transferred to the individual believer, usually a female religious as a bride of Christ, in Ephesians it is always the whole church which is seen as in a marital relation to Christ. The church is never actually termed 'bride' or 'wife' in Ephesians; it is the marital relationship which carries the significance. In using the marital metaphor Ephesians follows an OT train of thought where Israel is presented as bride or wife of Yahweh. There are however significant differences: the church is the wife of Christ and not of Yahweh or God; the unfaithfulness of the church as wife to Christ is not discussed as was the unfaithfulness of Israel to Yahweh. Indeed the church is already beautiful (5.27), this presumably in Christ's eyes and not just her own, and there is no paraenetic stress on the church to work to gain its faithfulness to Christ. As noted in the exegesis of 5.22–33, AE's presentation of the image contains an inconsistency; in most of the passage the church is the wife of Christ, but occasionally she appears

as his bride, as if the marriage is taking place or is just about to do so
(5.26f). As Christ's bride or wife the church is the object of his love;
he is her saviour and devotes all his attention to her (5.23, 25); as
bride he prepares her for the marriage ceremony (5.26f); as wife he
cares for her and provides for all her needs (5.25, 28f). As either
bride or wife she is subordinate to him and should obey him (5.24,
33). The distinction between Christ and the church is thus made clear
through her subordination in a way which does not always appear in
the other images where church and Christ may seem at times to
merge into, or interpenetrate, one another.

4.4. These then, the body of Christ, the building, the fullness, the
wife, are in Ephesians the main images of the church in relation to
Christ. Minor images also exist of which the most important is that of
the family or household (2.19; 3.14f). The Jews had belonged to the
family of God but now both Jewish and Gentile believers belong to a
reconstituted family whose father is God (3.14f; cf 2.18); within the
family all are brothers, though AE does not stress this horizontal
relationship in the way Paul or Jesus does. The relationship is of
course also seen in phrases like 'in Christ' and 'with Christ' (2.6).

Each image presents a different aspect of the relationship. How
are they to be reconciled to one another? The image of the body has
often been taken as the most important. Can this be sustained? For
AE Christ's relationship to the church is real, yet as each image
presents it, it to some extent distorts it, for each image brings out
important factors not contained in all of the others. When map
makers have to depict the globe of the earth on a two-dimensional
surface they inevitably distort part of the earth's geography, as can
be seen when we examine those atlases which display different
projections. When we encounter these differences we are not led to
doubt the reality of the earth's existence or its spherical nature. In a
similar manner each image relating Christ and church shows one or
more aspects of that relationship yet at the same time distorts or
obliterates other aspects. That should not lead to doubts of the
reality of the relationship. To ask which is the most important image
is then to ask a foolish question. Importance relates to situations; the
polar explorer needs a different projection of the globe of the earth
from those who live on the equator. So each image of the church has
its own importance and this importance relates in a special way to
the situation in, or the purpose for, which it is being used. The very
nature of variety in the use of the images implies that they can never
be fully reconciled to one another. It should be noted also that there
may be helpful images, not presented in scripture, which can be
envisioned and these may be useful in today's situations.[2] Images
excite the imagination and it is open to us to vary and adapt them to

[2] For a fuller discussion see Best, *One Body*, 98–100.

our own special purposes; this was already happening in scripture, for the body image is altered between the earlier and the later epistles in that in the latter Christ is seen as head, and in the building image he is changed from foundation to angle-stone. But if we make such variations we cannot claim that they posses scriptural authority. Many theologians and preachers have found it useful to develop from the body image the idea of the church as the extension of the incarnation, but if they do so they should not claim Paul's authority, or AE's, for this development.

5. The marital image raises acutely a problem which exists to a lesser degree elsewhere. If Christ washed and cleansed the church before he married her did she exist prior to the wedding (5.26)? Did she already exist when he gave himself up for her (5.25)? If the church is given a cosmic role does this entail her eternal existence as part of God's eternal economy (3.11)? If believers are elect in Christ and he was pre-existent did they then also pre-exist with him? In Greek thought souls were often regarded as pre-existing and sent at the moment of birth into bodies, and this teaching had begun to penetrate Hellenistic Judaism (SB II, 340ff; Josephus *BJ* 2.154f; Philo, *Gigant* 12f) but was not accepted everywhere in the Judaism of the first century (cf *m Aboth* 3.1). Ephesians contains no trace of the idea of souls existing apart from, or in distinction from, bodies. The problem does not of course relate to the historical existence of the church; believers are baptised into an existing body. Did that body however only begin to exist when the first disciples were called, or when Christ died and rose, or when Abraham was called, if the church is taken as continuous with Israel? Could the church have existed from all eternity if its foundation is the historical apostles and prophets (2.20)? It might be argued that the church only began when Gentiles as well as Jews were seen as proper members of God's people and admitted into it and their admission depends on the historical event of the cross (2.14–18). An equivalent question to the one raised here arises in respect of Abraham and was noted by Jewish thinkers: did Israel pre-exist Abraham (cf 2 Esdr 6.55, 59; *Test Moses* 1.12f; Sifrè Deut §47)?[3] More generally, did Judaism envisage an actual, as distinct from an ideal, pre-existence of Israel (SB III, 579; Schliêr, 49 n. 4; Hofius, see on 1.4)? If it did, this could have lead to Christian Jews accepting the pre-existence of the church. In later orthodox and heretical Christian thought the idea of the pre-existence of the church is found regularly, e.g. Hermas, *Vis* 2.4.1; 2 Clem 14; Justin, *Apol* I, 46; *Tri Trac* I, 5 57.33–59.1; *Treat Seth* VII, 2 60.25; 65.33–66.11.[4] The problem, as we have seen, is

[3] On the whole question of pre-existence see R. Schnackenburg, *The Gospel according to St John*, London, 1968, Excursus II, 494ff.
[4] On the appearance of the idea in the Fathers see Warnach in Schlier and Warnach, 75, n. 118.

created by the use of the image of the church as bride and perhaps should not be taken over-seriously for metaphors and images should never be driven too far. But the problem also appears when Ephesians speaks of the election of believers in Christ and of their foreordination to salvation (1.4f). Did they pre-exist their birth? As we have seen, Christ is said to have loved the church (5.25) but this is only a widening of 5.2 where his love is directed at individuals; did then individual believers who were not physically alive at the time of the cross exist in some way? Is anything more intended than that the church and individuals existed from the beginning in the mind of God?

Another approach can be made to the question of the pre-existence of the church. Christ is elect; the church is elect in Christ; Christ pre-existed; therefore the church pre-existed. This line of argument would be similar to that underlying the death of believers with Christ. This does not mean they imitate his death on being initiated in baptism or that they die at the moment of conversion, but that they died with Christ when he died (cf Best, *One Body*, 44–64). Later AE argues that Christians have not only died with Christ but that they have already risen with him and sit with him in the heavenlies (2.5f). If he can think of this as having already taken place, he may well equally have thought of the church as coming into existence before creation through its election in Christ. Behind all of this would lie the idea of Christ as a representative or inclusive figure (see Detached Note: In Christ). Is there a parallel with the choice of Israel in Abraham (*Gen R* 44 (27a), see SB III, 579)? If so, that choice was not pre-temporal but took place in history through physical descent from Abraham.

We are involved here in the philosophical problem of the relationship of time and eternity and can only recognise the existence of the problem and that it is inherent in much Christian thought. We have to leave its consideration to the systematic theologians. On the whole the grounds for believing that AE thought of a pre-existent church are not sufficiently strong to convince, yet they cannot be wished away.

6. *The Unity and Role of the Church*
6.1. Ephesians is the NT writing which is often held to express most firmly and clearly the unity of the church. It is true that Paul, facing those who would disrupt his converts, regularly argues for the importance of their unity (e.g. Rom 12.3ff; 1 Cor 12.12ff; Gal 3.28), yet the unity of the readers of Ephesians does not seem to be under threat from within their own communities or from outside. The only division to which AE refers is that between Jewish and Gentile believers, and this has already been healed and so belongs to the past. He makes no reference to those other unities between men and

women, slaves and free, to which Gal 3.28 and Col 3.11 refer. The diversity in worship which is a prominent feature of the Corinthian church (1 Cor 12.12ff) hardly appears in Ephesians; 4.7 only reflects it in a pale way. There is no trace of parties within the church (cf 1 Cor 1.11ff). Unity on the one hand is an existing fact (4.4–6), on the other there is a need to maintain it (4.2f). In contrast with Colossians which is interested in the unity of the cosmos, Ephesians is interested in that of the church. Although the unity portrayed by AE already exists, it is not a static but a dynamic unity, dynamic not in the sense that it keeps on including more and more previously divided groups but in the sense that it matures. A 'body' is always one, but it can develop through maturing. In his concern for unity AE does not argue for organisational unity (he has no interest in organisation) or remind readers of the leaders to whom they should give their loyalty. No emphasis is placed on a need to search for unity so that the secular world may be impressed by the church's harmony in comparison with the world's disorder and so turn to Christ. AE relates unity strongly to Christ, but this is not because discordant elements have argued for a unity based on some other centre (Pokorný, 228f) for there are few signs of discordant elements and the long paraenesis with its emphasis on the need to avoid sins which would disrupt unity does not stress Christ at all. Unity is not given a focus in the bishop or any other minister as in the Ignatian letters, or, as is so common today, in the eucharist. 4.4–6 might seem to be a focus but contains no single unifying factor. The need for a focus usually derives from external pressures. Perhaps AE is led to stress unity by no deeper cause than the minor frictions which every pastor observes in the way members of his flock drift apart. That minor factors are the cause is confirmed when we notice that AE does not set down boundaries in faith or conduct by which believers might be condemned or even excluded.

6.2. The emphasis on unity in Ephesians might lead us to expect that the church would take the lead in reconciling existing divisions in the world, but AE is only interested in the division between Jewish and Gentile believers, and, since the steps for its elimination lay in the cross and resurrection of Christ, it has been already accomplished (2.14ff). The church itself is the result of the removal of that division and so in the strict sense cannot be an intermediary to it. For AE Christ's death and resurrection also healed the division between God and humanity, heaven and earth, yet the church continues to have a cosmic role in making known God's wisdom to the powers (3.10). AE has an interest in cosmic affairs (cf §4.2.2 and Introduction §6.2): believers already sit in the heavenlies (2.6); the families or social groupings of humans and angels have been brought together (3.15); believers are 'saints', a term also used of heavenly beings (1.18; 2.19); they are at war with the heavenly powers (6.10ff). Thus AE is quite explicit about the cosmic position and role of the church. That makes it all the more surprising that the church is not given a similar role in evangelising secular society. That AE is not unaware that this needs to be done is seen in the role he allotted to Paul as evangelist to the Gentiles (3.8f), and in the instruction given to the apostles and prophets that the Gospel applies to Gentiles as much as to Jews (3.5f; this goes back to such passages as Mt 28.16–20; an instruction which believers may know, see on 3.5). In another way the need to evangelise is implied both in the very existence of the communities to which AE writes, for the Gospel must have been made known to them, and in the comparison of the church as the sphere of light and the world as the sphere of darkness. If unbelievers live in darkness (4.17–19) and are subject to the control of evil powers (2.1–3) then surely those who are in the light should bring light to them (cf Mt 5.14–16)? Has then AE simply assumed that evangelism is going on? He acknowledges the existence of evangelists (4.11), yet as we saw at 4.11 these were not evangelists in our sense.

6.3. The failure of AE to instruct his readers to evangelise may not seem so strange when we compare Ephesians with the certainly genuine letters of Paul; in them Paul never directly summons his converts to evangelise their cities. Certainly the church grew as members made the Gospel more widely known (1 Th 1.8), yet little can be learned from the NT about how this actually took place. There are vague glimpses as when Paul instructs Christians in mixed marriages to maintain the marriage in the hope of gaining the unbelieving partner (1 Cor 7.12–16; cf 1 Pet 3.1–6). In Phil 1.14–18 he recognises that others preach the Gospel, even if he does not fully approve of their methods. 1 Cor 14.22ff implies that unbelievers stumbling into a service in a house might be converted. If these examples represent what might be termed positive evangelism, there is also a negative evangelism which comes about through the effect of believers' actions on others; they should take care not to offend unbelievers through their conduct (1 Th 4.10–12; Col 4.5; 1 Pet 2.12; 1 Tim 3.7; 1 Cor 10.32f; cf Mt 5.16; Acts 2.47). Ephesians however does not refer even to such negative evangelism. This absence is the more striking when we examine in the paraenesis the behaviour AE wishes from his readers. In a sense the whole paraenesis lies under the rubric of 4.25 about speaking the truth to fellow believers without any reference to speaking the truth to unbelievers. Thieving should cease not because it harms unbelievers but that the thief may contribute to church funds (4.28). Believers are to be kind to one another, but nothing is said about kindness to those outside their community (4.32). AE's HT contains no section on duty towards the state (cf 1 Pet 2.13–17), though the Pauline legacy of Rom 13.1–7 must have been known in the Pauline school of which AE was a member, and was of course certainly known to Paul if he is the author. AE might defend himself by saying that, since he was writing to several churches or to Christians in general and not to a single local situation, he did not need to refer to duty towards the state, yet 1 Peter is also directed to several churches and it sees the need to deal with this area of life. It is probably best to assume that the duty of evangelising was so well known that it did not need to be stated; it is in fact implicit in much that AE says. Rather surprisingly Roels entitles his book on Ephesians *God's Mission*; to justify this he has to look to indirect evidence as he depicts a missionary role for the church.[5]

There are of course some who argue from AE's presentation of the nature of the church that this nature can only be truly fulfilled if the church is a missionary community.[6] It is probably true that the missionary nature of the church is implicit in AE's teaching on it, but that is not to say that AE drew missionary consequences from his teaching; he does not appear to have done so; in writing he did not have in mind the evangelistic task of the church. Caird, 76, is correct when he says 'The *building up of the body of Christ* [his italics] is not achieved by pastoral concentration on the interior life of the church, but by training every member for his part in the church's mission to the world.' AE has however concentrated on the interior life of the church; it is to this his paraenesis is directed and not to training for mission. We should permit authors to settle their own priorities and not force ours on them.

7. The Church's Inner Life

7.1. AE's paraenesis shows that he is very interested in the inner life of the communities who will read his letter (4.25–6.9). Despite this he evinces little interest in their organisation, though he allows that there are those who hold office within them and serve them (4.11ff). The lack of interest in organisation is surprising since believers who were or had previously been members in trade guilds, funeral associations and minor religious cults would have been used to work within organisational frameworks. As for a ministry within the communities two of the five groups he names (4.11), the apostles and prophets, have already fulfilled their function (2.19); the remaining three, evangelists, shepherds, teachers, are still active and

---

[5] Cf also H. H. Culpepper, 'One Mission–Missions and Evangelism', *RevExp* 60 (1963) 388–98; S. Basevi, 'La missione di Cristo e dei Cristiani nella lettera agli Efesini', *RivBiblt* 38 (1990) 27–55. If Paul did not write Ephesians it is useless to quote passages from other letters in respect of missionary work, and if he did, then in Ephesians he confined his interest to the internal life of the church and not its outreach.

[6] Roels, *passim*; R. P. Meyer, *Kirche und Mission im Epheserbrief*, Stuttgart, 1977; D. Senior and C. Stuhlmueller, *The Biblical Foundations for Mission*, London, 1983, 199–210.

will continue to be active. AE sees these latter ministries as
christological in origin though it may well have been sociological
pressure which first led to their creation. Their actual functions as he
presents them arise out of the nature of the gospel. AE tells us
nothing directly about what they do, except what can be deduced
from their titles; probably he did not need to spell out their functions
because his communities knew what they were. Special duties, e.g.
presiding at the eucharist, are not ascribed to any of them. As a
group they are to serve the remainder of their community. We can
discern here, more than in the earlier Paulines, the beginning of the
clerical–lay division which later came to dominate the internal life
of the church. Like the 'officials', the ministry of the 'laity' is
directed towards the inner life of the community and none are
exempt from this ministry. Directed towards one another it includes
both worship (5.19f) and loving service (4.32).

7.2. Though sections of Ephesians are couched in the language of
worship (1.3–14; 3.14–21) little is said about its nature. Believers
sing and pray (5.19; 6.19ff). Baptism is clearly important for it is
mentioned in the piece of tradition quoted in 4.5 (cf 5.26), but there
is no reference to the eucharist, which of course does not mean it
went unobserved. Baptism is the rite of initiation (cf 1 Cor 12.13),
but that does not mean that immersion in water using a defined
formula made a non-believer into a believer. Those who come
forward for baptism will be those who have faith (1.1, 13, 15, 19;
2.8; 3.17), and prior both to faith and baptism is election by God
(1.4).

8. Conclusion

8.1. The church might have been described as the community of
the elect, the saved, the baptised, for it certainly consists of these,
but it is instead described in corporate terms, body of Christ,
building, wife. Yet if it is described in this way it is as the union of
believers and not of a number of congregations. Though the church
is part of God's plan for the redemption of the universe, it is not
presented as the soul or conscience of society. Very little sets it in
relation to society, to the nation or to the governing authorities.
Instead it is set in relation to Christ as his body and his wife or bride;
it is also God's people and the place where the Spirit dwells. It is at
all times subject to Christ its Lord and husband. A tension exists
between its heavenly and its earthly settings: members already sit in
the heavenlies (2.6) and make known the wisdom of God to the
powers; glory is given to the church (3.21); yet members have to be
instructed how to live with one another (4.25ff). The heavenly
nature of the church does not then lead to its removal from history.
AE depicts a church which, as we might say, has its eyes directed
both upwards and inwards but not outwards. The inward look of

course coheres with the ethical teaching of the letter. Despite the emphasis on the behaviour of members towards one another there is no suggestion of a ghetto mentality.

Ephesians is one of the most useful of the writings in the New Testament for those concerned with ecumenics and all who wish to discuss the nature of the church; it is one of the least useful for those who wish to outline the way Christians and the church should live in their culture. In this respect its picture of the world is too extreme; it sees secular society as dominated by hostile spiritual powers and as a place of darkness; it is difficult to move from such a presentation to a post-Christian society which Christianity has already entered and modified, or indeed into any society in which there is some goodness.

8.2. Traditionally four marks have been ascribed to the church: one, holy, catholic and apostolic.[7] Taking these words at their simplest it is not difficult to see that the first three can be applied without hesitation to the church as depicted in Ephesians. The church is one (4.4) and holy (5.27) as are its members (1.1); both its unity and its holiness have been given to it by God. It is catholic for it embraces all within itself, Jews and Gentiles (2.11–22), men and women (5.22–33), slaves and free (6.5–9). The fourth mark, apostolicity, is more difficult to apply. The church is certainly apostolic since apostles are part of its foundation (2.20) and the full glory of the gospel was revealed to them (3.5). Yet in these two texts, the only ones setting out a theology of apostolicity, prophets are linked to apostles and that with a common article which ties them very closely together. If then we wish to use these texts to confirm the apostolicity of the church we are forced at the same time to ascribe to it a prophetic nature (cf 4.11), and there is no reason for regarding the prophetic nature of the church as less important than its apostolic nature. This suggests that proper to the nature of the church is an element of unpredictability, yet an unpredictability guided not by tradition but by the Holy Spirit, an element which in proclaiming God's will may continually disturb the church's accepted order. Indeed if we examine the history of the church we see that it has been frequently subject to prophetic disturbance and that this disturbance has been for its good. Prophets preserve the church from being at ease with itself and settling down contentedly into a routine and conservative way of life; they come from within it and stir it up, directing it into new paths.

Christians have regularly been perplexed by the contrast between what the church is supposed to be and what it actually is, and have attempted to solve this by contrasting the visible and invisible

---

[7] Barth, *Israel*, 6, says Ephesians displays these four marks of the church more clearly than any other Pauline letter; cf Penna, 66f.

churches. AE seems quite unaware of this problem. What he writes in 3.1–4, 16 might suggest he had the invisible church in mind yet he makes no distinction when he goes on to describe the activities of its members. Believers who are capable of telling lies to one another are members of the one body of Christ (4.25), who can commit fornication (5.3, 5) belong to the bride of Christ who is without spot or wrinkle (5.27), who can steal (4.28) are members of the people of God, who can be drunk (5.18) are in the building of God where God dwells (2.22). AE is unaware of the visible–invisible distinction.

ESSAY II

MORAL TEACHING

L. H. Marshall, *The Challenge of New Testament Ethics*, London, 1947, 217ff; M. S. Enslin, *The Ethics of Paul*, Nashville, 1957; W. Lillie, *Studies in New Testament Ethics*, Edinburgh, 1961; V. P. Furnish, *Theology and Ethics in Paul*, Nashville, 1968; J. L. Houlden, *Ethics and the New Testament*, Harmondsworth, 1973, 231–44; Fischer, 147–72; J. T. Sanders, *Ethics in the New Testament*, London, 1975, 68–81; Halter, 227–86, 384–409; G. Strecker, 'Strukturen einer neutestamentlichen Ethik', *ZTK* 75 (1978), 117–46; J. Gnilka, 'Das Akkulturationsproblem nach dem Epheser- und Kolosserbrief', *Fede e cultura alla luce della Bibbia* (ed. J. D. Barthelemy), Turin, 1981, 235–47; W. Schrage, *Ethik des Neuen Testaments*, Göttingen, 1982; K. Müller, 'Die Haustafel des Kolosserbriefes und das antike Frauenthema. Eine kritische Rückschau auf alte Ergebnisse', *Die Frau im Urchristentum* (ed. G. Dautzenberg, H. Merklein, K. Müller), Freiburg, Basel, Vienna, 1983; R. N. Longenecker, *New Testament Social Ethics for Today*, Grand Rapids, 1984; R. Schnackenburg, *Die sittliche Botschaft des Neuen Testaments*, Freiburg, Basel, Vienna (2nd edn), 1986, vol. 2, 84–95; S. Schulz, *Neutestamentliche Ethik*, Zürich, 1987, 571–88; MacDonald, 86ff; U. Luz, 'Überlegungen zum Epheserbrief und seiner Paränese', *Neues Testament und Ethik* (FS R. Schnackenburg, ed. H. Merklein), Freiburg, Basel, Vienna, 1989, 376–96; E. Lohse, *Theological Ethics of the New Testament*, Minneapolis, 1991, 146ff; Best, 'Types of Existence'.

1. AE sets out his moral teaching no more systematically than any other NT writer. While the ethical teaching of many sections of other letters is generally, but not always, clearly determined by the situation of their readers as a response to their particular problems, it is difficult to discern the particular situation, if any, to which AE was responding. Yet, while the sequences of injunctions in Rom 12.9ff and 1 Th 5.14ff are difficult to tie in with the main themes of those letters, the apparently similarly haphazard sequence of Eph 4.25–5.2 does go along with the letter's central theological message concerning the nature and unity of the church, and the same is true of almost all the remaining moral teaching in the letter. The sequence of Mk 9.33–50 is held together by catchwords because it was originally oral teaching; Eph 4.25–5.2 is held together by its content relating to life within the church. If the paraenesis of Ephesians cannot easily be related to the particular situations of its intended readers, this accords with the general nature of the letter.

Implicit in the way AE outlines his paraenesis is a contrast between the conduct of believers before their conversion/baptism and what it should be afterwards; 4.17–19 (cf 2.1–3) depicts the life of the Gentile world outside the church and fittingly precedes the actual detailing of the new behaviour which AE desires for his readers. None of this means that the ethical instruction of Ephesians is vague or imprecise; it always treats areas of conduct which are the concern of many believers.

2. It may however justifiably be asked whether an ethic is necessary for believers who sit in the heavenlies (2.6). Does this not imply that their behaviour is already perfect? That despite this AE provides moral teaching is part of the tension which runs throughout the letter, exemplified in that Christ has overcome the powers (1.20–3) and yet they are still active in misleading believers (6.10ff). Even though readers are appointed to preordained 'good works' (2.10), it is necessary to spell out what those works are. While they could be defined in general terms as activities which are in accordance with God's will (5.10, 17) this is vague and needs filling out.

2.1. Paul's letters do not follow a single pattern. In the Corinthian correspondence and Philippians ethical teaching is mingled with other material (cf Hebrews). In Romans the ethical teaching follows (at 12.1) a long theological disquisition. In 1 Thessalonians it comes at 4.1 after Paul's discussions in the first three chapters of his movements and personal behaviour. In Galatians it follows at 5.1 his defence of his conduct and theology. Each of these three letters has a precise turning-point where the paraenesis commences. So has Ephesians and its turning-point is 4.1. Preceding it are sections of prayer and devotion and of theology. After it ethical teaching dominates the material, though it contains two theological sections (4.7–16; 5.23–32), but these are integral to that teaching in developing the basis for Christian communal living.

3. *Areas of Ethical Concern*

Roughly speaking the paraenesis of Ephesians covers three main areas: 4.25–5.2, 6–14 treats the conduct of believers towards one another, 5.3–5, 15–18 the personal conduct of believers which may affect themselves but not others within the community, and 5.22–6.9 the conduct of believers within their own homes. Believers are always envisaged as members of groups and not simply as individuals. For the most part it is all believers who are being instructed though at times smaller groups are addressed. So in the HT men who are husbands, fathers and owners of slaves, and wives, children and slaves are picked out for individual attention. The group of 'ministers' is also singled out in 4.11 and given duties in 4.12. It is not clear why these groups are selected and others omitted such as widows who come in for considerable attention elsewhere in the NT (Acts 6.1–6; 1 Cor 7.39f; 1 Tim 5.3ff). It can be assumed that those specifically mentioned in the HT are also addressed in the more general injunctions of the paraenesis.

3.1. The areas of life in which AE instructs his readers are roughly those of personal behaviour in which individuals relate to one another within the community and by their conduct may ensure or disrupt its smooth running. AE is much more concerned with this than with personal piety. 4.2f are key verses, 4.2 (and 5.21) setting out the essential virtues in this respect and 4.3 indicating their purpose. 4.2f is followed directly with theological teaching about the community whose unity and peace are to be maintained. The theme is then developed in greater detail: truthfulness and good temper towards fellow members are commended (4.25–7); thieving is condemned but only because no good accrues to the community through it (4.28); careful attention to what believers say to one another is important (4.29; 5.4) for bawdy talk would corrupt the community; love towards other community members is stressed (4.32); the examples of God and Christ are set before members (4.32–5.2); those who would upset the community with false teaching are to be avoided (5.6f); in times of common worship inspiration with the Spirit is preferable to drunkenness.

3.1.1. There are also sins to be avoided which may affect people outside the community but not fellow members, fornication, lust and greed (5.3, 5); however no thought is given to the effect of these on those outside the community; the sins are presumably to be avoided only because of the harm they do to the members themselves and through them to the community. In addition the HT lays down positive lines for the mutual behaviour of husbands and wives, parents and children, masters and slaves; curiously fornication is not mentioned as destructive of family life; perhaps AE thinks it inconceivable within a Christian household, though Paul did not (1 Cor 6.12ff). In all this the stress is mainly negative relating to sins to be avoided rather than positive in encouraging the cultivation of particular virtues, though these are mentioned in respect of those which promote unity (4.2), and include love and forgiveness (4.32; 5.2) in imitation of Christ and God. Positive action is however often left very general (4.24; 5.8b, 9, 10, 15, 17); time is to be used in a disciplined way (5.16). This enumeration of virtues and vices may appear to make them unrelated but they are held together through a continued stress on community life.

3.1.2. If the ethical teaching has a main thrust, it is love. It was his love which moved God to act. His election of believers was not arbitrary but came from his love (1.4f) as did their redemption (2.4; 5.2, 25). His love is immeasurable (3.18f). The main agent in his work is Christ, his 'beloved' (1.6), and believers are in their turn termed 'beloved' (5.1). They are rooted and grounded in love (3.17); love builds them up into maturity (4.16). Yet it is strictly the church as a whole which is the object of God's love (5.25); within it believers as individuals are loved (5.2). Though AE refers only to God's love towards believers it may be that had he been asked he would have said God loved all people. Since, as AE presents it, it is his love which has led him to elect those he loves, it is better to assume that AE had never thought out the problem of the relation of love and election. Given his emphasis on God's love it is not surprising that when he turns to the way believers should live almost his first thought is of love (4.2). If the church is to grow it must grow in love (4.15f). 4.32 may not name love but it forms its basis. When AE wishes to describe the behaviour of husbands towards their wives, love is the word he uses (5.25, 28, 33) and this cannot be erotic love because it is identical with the love with which Christ loves the church. Love then for AE is more than one virtue among others; it is the virtue which sustains the others. As far as its content goes love should be understood in terms of self-sacrifice, for it is in that way that Christ's love is described (5.2).

Love was central to the ethic of Jesus as a love which his disciples should show to all people (Lk 10.25–37); love remains the keystone of Paul's ethic. But, beginning with Paul though only partially with him, we find love towards all (Rom 13.10; Gal 5.14) being restricted to love towards other believers (1 Th 3.12; 4.9). This restriction became normal in many of the later NT writings (Jn 13.34ff; 1 Pet 2.17; 1 Jn 3.11, 23); in Ephesians it coheres with the way God's love is expressed in election. However, in writing only of love towards other believers AE does not go as far as 1 Pet 2.17 which distinguishes between the attitude of believers to one another and to non-believers. Love, for AE, binds the community together (4.2) and is expressed through the various virtues expounded in 4.25ff. If περιπατέω is the dominant general word in Ephesians to describe conduct (2.10; 4.1, 17; 5.2, 8, 15), it is appropriate that it is associated with love in 5.2 for love underlies and sustains all true behaviour.

3.2. AE's stress on behaviour within the community can be seen even more clearly when we recollect what is omitted in the actual virtues which he emphasises: truthfulness is stressed as important when exercised towards others in the community, but it goes unmentioned in relation to those outside; theft is criticised only because it deprives the community of money, not because of the loss sustained by the person whose property has been stolen; no thought is given to the harm done to the other person who is used in fornication; the HT only sets out duties towards fellow Christians. It is true that most of the other NT letters give greater attention to behaviour within the community than to behaviour towards the outside world, but this largely arises because their writers are dealing with specific problems that have arisen within the community; at the same time the effect of believers' conduct on those outside is never entirely ignored.

To see the narrowness of AE's ethical concern it is necessary to look not only at the areas which he has covered but also at those to which he has given no consideration. Obviously he cannot be expected to cover areas arising out of the complexity of modern civilisation, e.g. trade-union legislation, green issues, social reform. We should not view what he says from the perspective of our times and expect condemnations of slavery or male domination. But there are areas of concern relating to his own time on which he does not touch. The household is clearly important in AE's eyes yet he only considers households all of whose members are Christian, and even then he says nothing about the relation of siblings to one another or the position of widows[1] and grandparents; he does nothing to resolve obvious points of tension (does the slave wife owe primary obedience to her husband or to her owner?). Divorce was frequent in the ancient world; perhaps AE's failure to refer to it may be excused because it would not be expected to occur in unmixed households. He might however have paid some attention to the victims of wrongful activity on the part of believers, e.g. the prostitute whom the believer has used (5.3, 5, contrast Epict 2.4.1ff, 10.17; 3.24.23), the person whose wealth the thief has taken (4.28, contrast Lk 19.8). When he discusses whether the Christian should eat food which has been sacrificed to idols, Paul takes into account possible occasions of the effect on unbelievers (1 Cor 10.27–9). Interestingly Epictetus comments that adultery has a wide effect on society (2.4.1ff) and renders the victim less than human (2.10.17).

In fairness it is important to remember that Ephesians is so brief that it would have been impossible for AE to treat every problem, yet there are areas of which it is difficult to see how they could have escaped his notice. These relate largely to the interaction between believers and the world outside their community. Every day believers must have been reminded of the dangers of idolatrous worship, yet idolatry is only mentioned in passing in 5.5 and in such a way as if it could be assumed everyone would reject it. If Arnold's claim, *passim*, that magic formed an important element in the background to the letter is correct, and it certainly was a major feature of the ancient world, it is surprising to find it is not condemned (cf Acts 19.19; 8.19–24; 13.4–12; Gal 5.20; 2 Tim 3.8; 3.13; Rev 9.21; 18.23). Christians would have encountered the outside world through the people who lived next door, as shopkeepers who sold

---

[1] The treatment of widows occupies a large place in the Pastorals, cf. Y. Redalié, *Paul après Paul*, Geneva, 1994, 438.

goods to all and sundry, as those who bought goods wherever they were on sale. The fornicator met the unbelieving prostitute and the thief the unbeliever with possessions. In mixed households the believer could not avoid daily encounters with unbelievers; AE does not consider even the possibility of broken homes as a result of one member becoming a Christian (Mk 3.31–5; 10.29; Mt 10.34f; Lk 12.51–3).

3.2.1. Quite apart from such limited and individual areas there were, as we learn from other NT writings, major areas where the outside world impinged on believers and some mention might have been expected:

(a) Christians were continually put under pressure, if not actively persecuted, to conform to secular culture. The Gospels prophesy that persecution will come on Christ's followers (Mk 13.9–13; Mt 5.10–12); even if these prophecies are *post-factum* creations and not actual sayings of Jesus, they represent the experience of early believers. Acts recounts many occasions of persecution coming from both Jews (5.17f; 8.3; 12.1–5) and non-Jewish civic authorities and mobs (13.50; 14.19; 16.19–24; etc.). The epistles and Revelation give evidence of the same pressure (1 Th 2.14f; 2 Cor 11.23–7; Phil 1.27–30; 1 Pet 3.14; 4.12–14; Heb 10.32–4; 13.13; Rev 2.10, 13; 3.10; 6.9; 20.4). The absence then of any reference to external pressure is surprising, for AE has depicted Paul as a prisoner and Ephesians belongs to a region adjacent to, if not the same as, that to which 1 Peter and Revelation were addressed.

(b) Ephesians contains no injunctions on the need to evangelise the pagans among whom believers live. It is true that one theme in the letter is Paul's evangelisation of the Gentiles and 3.10 refers to the effect of the church on the powers, but why does AE not refer to its effect on the surrounding pagan world? While there are few explicit injunctions to evangelism elsewhere in the NT except in the final paragraphs of the Gospels (Mt 28.16–20; Lk 24.45f; Acts 1.8; cf Mk 6.7ff) and while Paul rarely exhorts his readers to evangelise, though he does emphasise his own missionary activity (e.g. Gal 2.1–10), his letters provide ample evidence that evangelisation was taking place (1 Cor 14.22ff; Phil 1.14f, 27–30; Col 1.23).

(c) Apart from evidence in the NT of active evangelism there are many references to the quiet effect of the lives of believers on others (Mt 5.14–16; 1 Th 4.10–12; Col 4.5; 1 Tim 3.7; 1 Pet 2.12; Tit 3.2; Jn 17.20f; cf Acts 2.47; 1 Cor 10.32f; 1 Pet 3.15f). Ephesians contains no reference to this negative evangelisation; when believers are encouraged to act it is always towards other believers.

(d) Elsewhere in the NT we find varying attitudes advocated in relation to the world: Mk 12.13–17; Rom 13.1–7; 1 Pet 2.13–17; Tit 3.1; 1 Tim 2.1f imply in different ways a positive relation to civil authority; Ephesians does not suggest any such attitude, not even a

negative one. Everyone was taxed, but Ephesians offers no advice
on this though the questions arising from it were in no way local but
universal and therefore not necessarily to be omitted from a general
letter. The same applies to the issue of Christians holding public
office.

(e) Problems are created for believers because they have to be
careful in their relation with the outside world, e.g. 1 Cor 5.9–13;
6.1–8; 7.31; 10.27–9; 2 Cor 6.14–7.1; 1 Jn 2.15–17; Tit 3.2; Jn
17.15f. We find no suggestion that this might be so for readers of
Ephesians. 4.17–19 provides the one point where the existence of
the non-Christian, non-Jewish world is acknowledged and there it is
characterised in the darkest of colours. The context of this passage
in no way suggests a positive relation to the outside world; it could
be read as implying a complete avoidance of it.

3.3. The total impression created by the areas of life for which
AE provides guidance suggests that his ethic might be defined as a
'church ethic', that is, one applying to life within the church but not
dealing with the relationship of either the church or its members to
what takes place in the world outside the church. This description of
the moral teaching of AE as a church ethic is not out of accord with
the way in which when he depicts the church (see Essay: The
Church) he stresses its inner life rather than its relation to the world.
This does not mean that if AE had been asked he would not have
been willing to outline an ethic designed to govern the attitude of
Christian communities and individual Christians to the world
outside the church. For some reason he decided that he did not need
to do this. If he had done it something of the way he presents the
church and its life shows that his approach would not have been
sectarian. He does not provide a list of rules as some Christian
groups do today, e.g. do not smoke or dance, attend the eucharist at
least once a month, believe Jesus is God; rules like these serve to
mark off believers from their surrounding culture and offer opportunities for discipline if they are not kept. AE in his situation might
have said members should not eat food that had been sacrificed to
idols, attend temple worship or join with non-Christians in business
ventures. His failure to provide a set of church rules saves him then
from the charge of sectarianism.

4. Guidelines

4.1. Neither AE nor any other NT writer is able to provide a
sufficient number of injunctions to cover all the situations in which
moral decisions require to be made. Those who entered Christianity
from Judaism already had guidelines covering a great many possible
situations, but most of AE's readers came from the Gentile world
with its very varied religious and philosophical backgrounds ranging
from those where behaviour was not regarded as important to

Stoicism where great stress was laid on it. Gentiles entering Christianity would bring with them the ethic of their previous religious and philosophical culture. In many cases (e.g. truthfulness, kindness) these coincided with what was taught in their new faith, but in other cases there would be slight or wide divergence. It is impossible to deny that AE has taken over a large part of contemporary ethical culture; he retains broadly speaking the patriarchal structure of society and he accepts without query the existence of slavery.

4.2.1. What assistance by way of criteria of conduct does AE offer his readers as they endeavour to live in their new Christian communities? Wide and imprecise statements about doing God's will (5.17; 6.6), pleasing the Lord (5.10; cf Rom 12.2), behaving wisely (5.15), doing what would serve to build up the church (4.2, 3, 15f) or what is fitting (5.3, 4; unlike Paul he only thinks of what is fitting to the church and not what is fitting to external society, 1 Cor 11.2ff, 14ff; 14.40) are of no real help even though they may be drawn from the OT and are found in other parts of the NT (Gen 5.22, 24; 6.9; Wisd 4.10; Ecclus 44.16; Rom 12.1; 14.18; 2 Cor 5.9; Phil 4.18; Col 3.20; Heb 13.21; cf *T Dan* 1.3). How are his readers to move from these to their actual situations?

4.2.2. More practical criteria are needed, not only for those who as new converts have very recently moved out of pagan culture, but also for those who have been converts for some time yet who continue to live surrounded by that culture. Through the centuries the church realising this has attempted to express what pleases the Lord by stressing variously or together the Decalogue, Jesus as example, traditional Christian behaviour in either its puritanical or catholic forms. Alternatively an appeal is sometimes made to conscience (cf Rom 9.1; 13.5). AE however adopts none of these approaches. Yet he has certainly not left his readers to determine for themselves on every occasion what pleases the Lord. The paraenetic half of his letter is a setting out of the kind of conduct he understands as pleasing the Lord. Since behaviour has always to be linked to the actual situation in which it is lived, and he is writing a general letter, he is able to paint only with broad brush strokes. We never find him arguing a case in detail as Paul does in 1 Corinthians in respect of food sacrificed to idols; he leaves his readers to carry out such detailed arguing for themselves. Broad brush strokes entail his seeing everything in black and white; actual decisions are much more complex and often lead only to the choice between two imperfect solutions.

4.2.2.1. As a help to his readers AE offers first of all the precise injunctions given in his paraenesis, but these fail to cover many situations where decisions need to be made. An examination of these injunctions shows that he sometimes bases his counsel on the OT.

As a Jew this was the natural place to look for guidance. He brings in Zech 8.16 at 4.25, Ps 4.4 at 4.26 and the Decalogue underlies 4.28 and is explicitly quoted at 6.2f. (Gen 2.24 is not used directly in relation to behaviour when quoted at 5.31.) Interestingly, pagan moralists would not have rejected the content of what he says in any of these instances. His use of the OT is probably intended to enforce the authority of what he says, though at 6.3 he modifies his OT quotation to remove from it a limitation which he would not wish to enforce. If he introduces the OT he has no general advice to give on where its teaching should be followed and where ignored. He never discusses the relation of God's will to the Law of Moses (cf Schulz, 575–8). In 4.24 he gives a general principle for behaviour which could have come from pagan moralists, though he probably draws it from Hellenistic Judaism which had accepted it (see on 4.24). Why did he not use here an OT passage like Hos 6.6 or Mic 6.8?

4.2.2.2. To help his readers he also draws on accepted Christian tradition like the HT and he selects what he wishes from traditional vice and virtue lists. Again in this material there is little with which many pagan moralists would have disagreed. They might not have accepted his development of the marriage metaphor in 5.22ff, but he develops it for theological rather than ethical purposes. Accepted tradition can also change; whereas Paul believed that this world was passing away and the End coming soon and allowed this to shape some of his judgements (e.g. 1 Cor 7.25ff), for AE the world is a more stable place and so judgements on conduct are not made in the belief that all would soon be changed.

4.2.2.3. Role models are a help in ethical instruction, but for Christians they need to be drawn from Christian and not pagan sources. Paul uses himself as a model (1 Th 1.5–7; 1 Cor 4.17; 11.1; Phil 3.17), but only does so to churches where he has ministered; if he wrote Ephesians it would not have been possible for him to present himself as a model since he was unknown in person to its readers; if AE was not Paul he would have been aware not to use Paul as model. In addition to himself, Paul used Christ as role model and this AE could do and did (5.2, 25); he uses God in the same way (5.1). But his use of Christ and God is in very general terms and would not have given much assistance in actual decision making. It would have been helpful if he had referred to incidents in Jesus' life or to some of his sayings (cf §6.3.1). The former of these only appears in relation to Christ's sacrificial death. None of Jesus' sayings are referred to explicitly in Ephesians. Indeed they feature only rarely in Paul. Yet if Ephesians is later than Paul, would the tradition about Jesus not have been more widely known? 4.20f may possibly indicate knowledge by readers of this tradition. If AE knew the tradition he may not have been able to use his knowledge, since in writing to a wide area he would not have been aware what parts of the tradition were known in each particular Christian community. A Christian guideline is perhaps supplied implicitly in 4.7–16 in that within the community conduct which would help the community to mature should be followed.

4.2.2.4. Generally speaking, readers are largely left to make up their own minds and for this, as 5.17 suggests (cf 1 Pet 1.13), some intellectual effort is necessary; the use of συνίημι in 5.17 emphasises the need for such effort. While in 3.4 the cognate noun referred to insight given by God, the verb in 5.17 refers to human insight, though when set in a Christian context this is never mere human insight but always insight guided by the Holy Spirit. True understanding of the Lord's will does not remain theoretical but involves it being carried out in practice. This means AE cannot cover every situation, for he does not know the precise circumstances of his readers and does not have enough space to cover everything. He does not even list a set of guiding axioms which believers might apply to their individual situations. They will have to reason out for themselves what they should do, learning from their ongoing experience and from the experience of others within their community. This may be why AE moves on after 5.17 to refer in vv. 19f to their common worship. The immediate move is to 5.18; overindulgence in wine may cloud his mind!

If AE has not been able to give guidelines to meet all the situations of his readers, still less has he been able to do it for us. He may have, and indeed has, much to say to us on many topics of personal conduct but he supplies no assistance on wider issues, for example the environment or social policy. Even if we accepted his advice on personal matters we would be left continuing a patriarchal attitude and accepting slavery.

5. Motivation

It is one thing to know what to do; it is another to do it. AE therefore not only indicates the nature of proper Christian activity but also attempts to persuade his readers to behave in the way he proposes. How does he do this? There are many different factors which lead people to act in the way they do: to maintain the integrity of their own lives (I could never look myself in the face again if I did that), the need (hunger, poverty, sickness) of others tore at their hearts so they had to help. It is also possible to ignore such claims. An initial impulse from outside may be necessary. It need not always be Christian (4.25, 26, 28); it could be a negative motivation arising out of not wishing to appear selfish in the eyes of others or out of the fear of punishment.

5.1. Traditionally for many Christians one outside impulse has been the fear of eternal punishment (whether action through fear is morally good or not is another matter), but this is not a significant factor in Ephesians; it appears only at 5.5f, 14; 6.9, and its reverse, a reward for good behaviour, at 6.8. It is noticeable that only 5.5f clearly indicates possible punishing action by God; this action is his response to sexual sin and greed, the former presumably and the latter possibly involving other people outside the community. No divine sanctions are attached to the sins against the community of 4.25–5.2. It is not said that the community does or should act in respect of such sins. Since fornication takes place outside the community its members may have been unaware it was happening. 6.9 reminds slave owners of their responsibility before God; was that because the community itself was powerless in the face of the sin of wealthier members or because slaves would be slow to denounce their owners? That God punishes wickedness and rewards goodness is an almost universal idea; Paul probably derived it from Judaism (cf 1 Cor 3.13–15; 4.5; 2 Cor 5.10; cf 1 Cor 7.29). For slaves fear, not of God, but of their owner, appears in 6.5. Public shame can also affect conduct; for believers this would not be shame in the sight of all but shame before other believers; this idea may underly AE's suggestion that certain conduct is not fitting (5.3f) among the saints. Associated with this may be his stress on the new position of believers; they must not fall back into the old ways of their previous pagan life (2.3ff; 4.17ff); a sharp line is drawn between Christian existence and that of the pagan world (4.17; 2.1ff; cf 1 Th 4.12; 1 Cor 5.1; Gal 2.15).

5.2. Basically the essential motivation for behaviour arises out of believers' own existence, an existence based on, and inspired by, what Christ and God have done for them. It is better to speak here in general terms of Christian existence rather than of some special element within it. Baptism will always have remained a significant event for them, as would also the words of the preacher from whom they first heard the gospel. AE however does not make much of either of these; he prefers a more rounded appeal: they have been called, forgiven, raised to the heavenlies, and are members of the church; the last of these is perhaps the most important in AE's eyes. Significant here is the separation of the earlier theological discussion from the ethical. The transition from the one to the other takes place at 4.1 and contains a plea to believers to live a life worthy of the call they have received. The transition is signalled by οὖν, as in other letters where we have the separation of the paraenetic element from the preceding discussion on which it depends (Rom 12.1; 1 Th 4.1; Gal 5.1; Col 3.1). The particle throws us back to the theology of the earlier chapters; of these it is only necessary to pick out the highlights of the blessings they have received from God (1.3). He chose them (1.4, 12) to receive redemption through Christ's sacrifice (1.7; cf 5.2, 25) and certified it to them through his exaltation of him (1.19ff). For their part they had not rejected what God had done but believed (1.13, 18), received the Holy Spirit and were given a future hope (1.13f). Once they had been dead in sin and under the devil's control but now they have been made alive (2.1, 5), raised with Christ and exalted with him to the heavenlies (2.6). Nothing in themselves could have brought this about, only God's grace (2.8–10). Indeed, as Gentiles, they could not even have expected this, for God appeared to be interested only in the Jews; now they stand on the same plane with the Jews before him (2.11–22). Their new position was no afterthought on God's part but belonged to his eternal plan (3.2–13). As they understand all this they will be moved to worship (3.14–21) and then to live in the way God wants them to. In theoretical terms the first three chapters set out the indicative of God's action, the second three the imperative in detailing the conduct that should ensue (for the idea see also Gal 5.1, 13; Rom 6.2f, 11ff; 12.1ff; 13.11–14). Yet as we move through the 'imperative' the indicative continually reappears, for believers do not stand alone but have been joined together in one body with one head and are the recipients of the ministry of apostles, prophets, evangelists, pastors and teachers (4.11). Immediately prior to the detailing of their new way of life they are reminded that they are new people (4.24). It is only as they grow into being new people that they will be able to fulfil the demands of their new life. The indicative/ imperative concept is repeated throughout the paraenetic section in various ways. They are to forgive and be kind to one another because Christ has forgiven them (4.32) and to live lovingly because Christ has loved them (5.2; note the use of καθώς in both these verses and in 5.25, 29). For people to know they are loved helps them to love.

5.3. If there is a specifically Christian motivation, does AE suggest any resources to support his readers in following it up, for it is not easy to walk lovingly and do God's will? The first half of the letter sets out their Christian position; it is one that lifts them out of and beyond normal human inner resources; support comes because their salvation and election have been gifts and they have risen with Christ and sit with him in the heavenlies. They can forgive because they have been forgiven (4.32); they can love because they have experienced love (5.2, 25). God has equipped them with armour so that they can stand firm (6.10ff); they have been given his truth and righteousness, and are at peace with him; they have faith, salvation and his word. They may have to struggle but they do not do this alone, for they are members of the church which is Christ's body and of which he is head; this truth has been the main burden of the letter; thus they are in a network of corporate salvation. It should not then be surprising that AE does not at the outset of his paraenesis encourage them to pray to God for help; they already know that because of their position his help is always present. Only at the end, though not as an afterthought, is prayer mentioned (6.18). Their prayers should not be selfishly directed to their own spiritual needs but should be for all their fellow believers, among whom Paul is special (6.19f). With prayer comes the need to be watchful and alert.

6. *Continuity and Discontinuity*

6.1. Any profound moral teaching not only continues what it finds good in existing teaching but also innovates new teaching; it commences with an existing understanding and modifies it. The teaching of Jesus began with the Jewish tradition in which he had been reared, but he went on to criticise and radicalise it (e.g. Mt 5.21ff). That AE continues what he has received (see Introduction §9.2) can be seen in a number of ways: (i) He incorporates Jewish material into his teaching (e.g. 4.25). (ii) He uses pieces of Christian tradition e.g. the HT, selections from vice and virtue lists, the hymn of 5.14; there is however no reason to suppose he took over an existing baptismal catechism. (iii) While he may have used sections of tradition from his Christian culture, the origin of some of it lay outside both Christianity and Judaism in Greco-Roman ethical teaching. Apart from particular pieces of tradition, in any culture there is also unexpressed material accepted by everyone, and any group with distinctive views within that culture will also draw on what is common in it but modify it for its own special needs. Despite AE's criticisms of his culture in 4.17–19, he draws on it regularly, or at least on its more developed aspects. It is only necessary to note the number of times in the exegesis in which attention is drawn to parallels to Stoic teaching (see index re Epictetus, Seneca, etc.). (iv) At the same time AE gave a new perspective to the teaching which he adopted; thus though the attitude he argues should exist between husband and wife differs little from that of much contemporary ethical teaching, it is seen in a new way through the parallel of Christ and the church. The main difference here between his teaching and traditional ethics lies in the motivation (see §5) arising out of the parallel, and in some areas of his teaching it is the difference in motivation which basically distinguishes his ethic from that of the contemporary pagan world.

6.2. When AE's Gentile readers became Christians they already possessed ideas from their culture of what was good and bad, but they were now brought into the stream of tradition which flowed through Judaism into Christianity. Jewish teaching itself was critical of aspects of pagan teaching, e.g. it rejected idolatry, emphasised humility (ταπεινοφροσύνη, see on 4.2) and made a strong and essential connection between religion and morality. The extent of the Jewish element in AE's teaching can be seen in the number of parallels to be found to it in the Wisdom literature, Philo, Pseudo-

Phocylides, *Testaments of the Twelve Patriarchs*, etc. With the
exception of the ἐν κυρίῳ of 6.1, and its reading is not certain, all of
6.1–4 might have been written by a Jew; the sentiment, if not its
precise expression, would also have been acceptable to most pagan
moralists.

6.3.1. If AE's teaching is in many ways continuous with both
pagan and Jewish teaching, it displays discontinuity when he draws
on the streams of tradition which took their origin in Jesus and Paul,
though of course what they taught depended in part on teaching that
existed before them. The streams of tradition flowing from Jesus and
Paul were not independent of one another; Paul was, for instance,
influenced by Jesus in the primary place he gave to love; Paul,
however, rarely acknowledges his dependence by explicitly quoting
the teaching of Jesus. In this he is followed by AE (perhaps an
argument favouring Pauline authorship?), though AE's letter is so
brief that it would be unwise to conclude he did not know any of the
sayings of Jesus. There are however places where their use would
have been appropriate if he had known them. Mt 5.33–7 could have
been quoted at 4.25; Mt 5.21f at 4.26f; Mk 7.15 at 4.29; Mk 10.21 at
4.28. Mk 3.31–5 and 10.28f would have strengthened his teaching
on the togetherness of believers in the church. To have missed one
of these would not be surprising but to miss so many is, and the later
the date of the letter the more surprising it is. The restriction of the
love commandment to fellow believers is the most striking divergence from Jesus, but it is a divergence in which AE is at one with
almost all late-first-century Christianity. AE also seems unaware
that Jesus recognised that when he called people to follow him this
would result in the breaking up of homes, for he provides no
teaching for single believers. Rather than suggesting, as AE does,
that believers should not associate with those who did not think in
the same way as himself (cf Eph 5.6f), Jesus went out of his way to
associate with tax-collectors and immoral women (Mk 2.16; cf
9.38f). AE does not challenge his readers to give up all for Christ
(Mk 8.34–6; 10.21, 29), to live in faith as children (Mk 10.15), to
think of themselves as last and servants of all (Mk 9.35; 10.43–5), to
give sacrificially (Mk 12.42–4), or to go out on mission with little or
nothing to support them (Mk 6.8).

6.3.2. AE was influenced also by the stream of ethical teaching
originating in Paul, especially in his basic approach through indicative and imperative and in his rejection of behaviour as a path to
salvation. The details of his teaching also show many resemblances
to Paul, as can be seen from our exegesis of his paraenesis where
there are continual references to his letters, though this can hardly
surprise if AE was Paul. However, if a rounded picture is to be
provided it is important also to approach the problem the other way
round. If we begin with the list of vices in Gal 5.19–21 we find

many of them reappearing in Ephesians but we note the absence of φαρμακεία, which we would expect to find if magic is part of the background of the letter as Arnold alleges, and of ζῆλος and φθόνος, which are more destructive of community spirit than any of the vices AE mentions since they represent deeper elements in human sin; AE in his desire to emphasise Christian unity might have been expected to introduce them; more surprising perhaps is his failure to refer to pride and self-confidence (1 Cor 13.5; Phil 2.3; Gal 6.3; Rom 12.16) and to boasting (1 Cor 13.4; 5.6; 2 Cor 10.13–18; 11.16f), all of which are very corrosive to good community relations.

Over and above this we miss the type of thinking found in many of Paul's striking verses; there is nothing in AE similar to the penetrating insights of Rom 12.1f; 15.1f; 1 Cor 10.24; 9.22; 2 Cor 12.9; Gal 6.2; Phil 4.11f and of the hymn to love of 1 Cor 13 (whether Paul wrote it or not he included it). If AE appears as patriarchal in his views on women as Paul, yet he lacks passages like those in Paul which show an approach to equality between man and wife (1 Cor 7.2–5; Gal 3.28). There are also significant differences from Paul; the latter values celibacy over marriage (1 Cor 7.7, 26, 28, 32ff); for AE marriage is the normal and approved condition.

6.4. Granted that AE lies within the stream of ethical tradition emanating from Jesus and Paul, we cannot ignore the lack of their penetration and bite in his teaching. We have already mentioned how he falls below Paul; the same is true when we compare him with Jesus. The pungency of the beatitudes is missing, as is the penetration of sayings like Mk 8.35; 10.42–5; 12.41–4; there is no concern for the victims of believers' sins (cf Lk 19.8f).

7. Conclusion

7.1. AE's moral teaching does not begin from an initial axiom or proposition like 'Love your neighbour', from which it would be possible to deduce proper conduct in particular situations. This is not to imply AE lacks an overall point of view. Whatever believers do should be pleasing to God (5.10), in accordance with his will (5.17), appropriate to a church context and fitting therefore among holy people (5.3). It is this final statement which is distinctive of his approach. He does not discuss how believers should behave in relation to life outside the church; he looks at the non-Christian world only to depict its darkness and depravity. Elsewhere the NT discusses the attitude of believers to the secular authorities (Mk 12.13–17; Rom 13.1–7; 1 Pet 2.13–17). AE's lack of teaching here might be defended on the ground that Christians could do nothing in those days to affect secular authority, yet such authority must have impinged on the lives of believers and Paul and Peter did not ignore the need to say something about it. But if the relation of Christian behaviour to secular authority might be played down, that to individual non-believers could not. They were encountered every day as the people who lived next door or the people from whom believers bought and to whom they sold. AE's approach has a certain consistency here in that in the HT he deals only with Christian households and not with those in which believers lived alongside non-believers. His moral teaching is then, as we have said (§3.3), properly termed a 'church ethic'.

7.2. AE displays his consistency in another way in that his teaching on the church dealt with its inner nature and not its relation to the world. This twofold consistency cannot be a matter of chance, but must have been the result of deliberate decision. He cannot have failed to realise the difficult position of believers in the world, but in this letter he has not chosen to enlighten them on what that position should be. It would be wrong to say that he has no views on this, but correct to say that he has consciously chosen not to express them. His letter is so coherent in its major lines of approach to his readers that we must conclude that his decision not to treat the area of the relation of the church and believers to the world was conscious. If he had wished to treat that area he could have written another letter, and perhaps he did and it is not extant. It is impossible to say why he restricted himself to the internal life of the church. It cannot have been because, writing a general letter to a number of communities whose situation in relation to the secular authorities would have varied from city to city, he could not have given universal advice, for, whatever attitude civic authorities took up to Christianity, the attitude of the imperial authority would have been everywhere more or less the same. More importantly, the personal relationship between believers and unbelievers would have had constant elements. 1 Peter is also written to a wide area and not to a single community and it has something to say on the way believers should regard those outside their communities; it in fact distinguishes behaviour towards other believers which should be governed by love from that to non-Christians who should be honoured (τιμάω, 2.17). AE makes no such distinction; we do not know if he would have done so if he had been pressed to it, nor do we know if he would have resisted the pressure. It is also not possible to excuse him ignoring this area because no one writer can cover everything, for the area he ignored was a major area. Other NT writings may concentrate on life within the community but that is because they are directed to particular situations within a community, yet even then they always exhibit some concern about the world outside their community. Certainly nothing can be said to excuse the way he ignores behaviour within mixed households. It might be said that his moral teaching is not situationally directed; but a situation may be that of a culture rather than of an individual community. He does

direct his attention to untruthfulness (4.25), anger (4.26f), unwillingness to forgive (4.32), pride or self-importance (4.2), sexual lust
(5.3, 5), all of which were widespread in the pagan world and in
danger of entering the community, or, perhaps more accurately, of
not being left behind by those who had been converted. He does not
then omit to deal with some areas of general behaviour.

7.3. The content of AE's moral teaching for believers within their
communities has turned out on examination to be a little humdrum
and conventional, reflecting perhaps a period when the initial flush
of enthusiasm has died down. It is an ethic for neither ascetics nor
an elite of moral athletes. There is no call to leave all and follow
Christ as is found in Mk 1.16–20; 2.14; 10.21; it is true that these
passages may have originally been summonses to disciples to leave
the world, yet Mark has left them in his Gospel which is directed
towards those who are already believers; there is no stage at which
believers can ignore such demands. There is also no challenge in
Ephesians to sacrificial generosity (cf Mk 12.41–4), though the
recollection of Christ's own sacrificial giving (5.2) may go some
way to balance this. Certainly the sins that are repudiated, untruthfulness, anger, gossip, greed, sexual lust, are those which have
always plagued the church; sexual lust may seem unduly emphasised being with greed the only sin which is threatened directly with
divine judgement, but, if so, the stress probably reflects the desire to
avoid the sexual behaviour common in parts of the ancient world,
but which was sometimes spoken against (cf Barton and Horsley,
and Stoic teaching). Even if the ethic is a little conventional, and
would have appeared so to Jews and Stoics, it may not have seemed
like that to many Gentile converts, not all of whom would have been
affected by the Stoic ethic; certainly, if 4.17–19 represents AE's real
belief about the outside world, he would not have thought of them as
previously influenced by that ethic. Yet the moral teaching of AE
may have been what was needed at the time. The one point where it
is undoubtedly unrealistic and deficient is in the HT where he deals
only with unmixed households; it is an evasion to say that in it he is
setting out the idea for Christian households; people live in real and
not ideal situations and need guidance for their real situations, which
in many cases may be in non-Christian households.

7.4. To summarise, the main criticism of AE's moral teaching is
its lack of depth and penetration when compared with the teaching
both of Jesus and the genuine Paulines. Their most profound insights
are absent. On the other hand while Paul envisages only a brief
period before the parousia and allows his ethic at times to be shaped
by this, AE's teaching is for a continuing situation; it is an ethic
which can guide for ever; marriage, for example, is recognised as a
permanent institution.

7.4.1. Yet if AE assumes that his ethical teaching is a guide for all time, is it really that? Is it not tied too much to his own cultural situation to be of any help when culture changes? Today in few countries where there is a Christian church is slavery also found, and AE's injunctions to owners and slaves cannot be transferred to employers and employees, least of all where the employers are anonymous financial institutions. The relation of men and women in the culture of most countries of the Western world is profoundly different from AE's time and AE gives no clue as to how believers are to adapt to this, or how to criticise it when they regard it as wrong. Individuals today cannot avoid decisions in political matters; they may have to choose between candidates in elections; they certainly have to decide whether to vote at all; AE offers no guidance for these decisions. While the household is still a basic unit in society its membership has altered; there are no slaves; one-parent families are widespread; grandparents are sent off to old people's homes. New areas in leisure, sport and work exist and may be as influential and important in formulating behaviour as traditional family relationships. AE says nothing which would help us to know whether believers should work primarily to change individuals or to change society; indeed he has nothing to say about changing society, though perhaps he may be excused since in his time believers were so tiny a group that they could not influence society. All this might not matter so much if AE had provided a basis from which an altering social and cultural situation might be viewed and evaluated. He does not seem to see that cultural situations might differ, yet he must have been aware that Jewish and pagan culture differed widely. Though Paul may have accepted the social culture of his time, Gal 3.28 leaves open an approach for judgements in different cultural situations. That AE was writing a general letter and not just responding to particular problems should have made him more aware of the existence of general problems.

7.5. There is however a final and necessary comment to be made in AE's favour. He treats all, women, children and slaves, as well as men, as morally responsible; he addresses them directly and does not tell husbands to instruct their wives in their duties, as very shortly after his time Clement was doing (1 Clem 21.6; it is possible also to read the same limitation into 1 Cor 14.35). Moreover he also sets the same standards of conduct before all; in that way he helped both to increase the sense of togetherness of believers and eventually to prepare the way for greater equality.

INDEX OF AUTHORS, ANCIENT AND MODERN, AND OF ANCIENT WRITINGS

661

672 INDEX OF AUTHORS